PEOPLE AND NATIONS

REVISED EDITION

A World History

GENERAL EDITOR

Dr. Theodore K. Rabb
Department of History
Princeton University

CONTRIBUTING EDITORS

Dr. Thomas Africa
Department of History
State University of New York
at Binghamton

Dr. L. Carl Brown
Department of Near Eastern
Studies
Princeton University

Thomas J. Butler
Ph.D. Candidate,
Research Assistant
in African Studies
Department of History,
Graduate School
Columbia University

Dr. Warren Dean
Department of History
New York University

Dr. Barbara Jean Horan
Social Studies Department
Valhalla High School
Valhalla, New York

Dr. Joan W. Scott
School of Social Science
Institute for Advanced Study
Princeton, New Jersey

Dr. Ann Waswo
Nissan Institute of
Japanese Studies
Oxford, England

READER CONSULTANTS

Marjorie Irwin
Formerly Chairperson, Social
Studies Department
Lanier High School
Austin, Texas

Rose Marie R. Armetta
Social Studies Teacher/
Coordinator
Herbert Lehman High School
Bronx, New York

Michael Clancy
Social Studies Chairman
Scituate High School
Scituate, Massachusetts

Elizabeth A. Kelly
Social Studies Department
Bloom High School
Chicago Heights, Illinois

Robert J. Rock
Social Studies Coordinator
NE Independent School District
San Antonio, Texas

Richard Sachen
Social Studies Department
Mountain View High School
Mountain View, California

Frank Mosher
Social Studies Department
Mountain View High School
El Monte, California

PEOPLE AND NATIONS

A World History

REVISED EDITION

Anatole G. Mazour
John M. Peoples
Theodore K. Rabb

HBJ **Harcourt Brace Jovanovich, Publishers**

Orlando   San Diego   Chicago   Dallas

The cover illustration is a detail from one of the main rooms of the palace of Darius at Persepolis in Persia (now Iran). The title page illustration is an impression of Venice from a 16th-century manuscript.

AUTHORS

Anatole G. Mazour was Professor of History at Stanford University for 25 years. He received an M.A. from Yale University and a Ph.D. from the University of California. His other books include *Russia: Past and Present; Finland Between East and West; The Rise and Fall of the Romanovs;* and *Russia: Tsarist and Communist.*

John M. Peoples taught world history and other social studies courses at Alameda High School in California for 35 years. Dr. Peoples received both an M.A. and a Ph.D. from the University of California.

Theodore K. Rabb is a distinguished historian and Professor of History at Princeton University. He received a B.A. from Oxford University and an M.A. and a Ph.D. from Princeton University. Professor Rabb has also taught at Stanford University, Northwestern University, and Harvard University. He has written extensively on European history and is coeditor of *The Journal of Interdisciplinary History.*

Requests for permission to make copies of any part of the work should be mailed to: Permissions, Harcourt Brace Jovanovich, Publishers, Orlando, Florida 32887

For permission to reprint copyrighted material, grateful acknowledgment is made to Abingdon Press for the passage by Martin Luther adapted from *Here I Stand: A Life of Martin Luther* by Roland Bainton, 1955; Basic Books for a letter to Sigmund Freud from Albert Einstein in *The Life and Work of Sigmund Freud* by Ernest Jones; Doubleday and Company and the National Trust for "The White Man's Burden" from *Rudyard Kipling's Verse: Definitive Edition*; Harper & Row, Publishers, Inc., for the adapted excerpt from *Sources of English Constitutional History: A Selection of Documents from A.D. 600 to the Interregnum* by Carl Stephenson and Frederick George Marcham; Indiana University Press for "Dawn in the Heart of Africa" by Patrice Lumumba from *Poems from Black Africa*, ed. by Langston Hughes; Random House, Inc., for an excerpt from *Future Shock* by Alvin Toffler, copyright © 1970 by Alvin Toffler; the U.S. Army Department for "Trials of the Major War Criminals Before the International Military Tribunal," Volume XXII; and Elmer Davis for "We Lose the Next War" by Elmer Davis, in *Harper's Magazine*, March 1938; Harcourt Brace Jovanovich, Inc., for the illustrations by Enrico Arno reproduced from *The Tiger's Whisker and Other Tales and Legends from Asia and the Pacific*, © 1959 by Harold Courlander.

Printed in the United States of America
ISBN 0-15-373465-5

CONTENTS

MAPS

CHARTS

FEATURES

HISTORY AND YOU

Why does anyone bother to study history? Asking that question may seem a strange way to start a book about the history of the world, but you ought to have some idea about possible answers before you begin. Otherwise, you will have no idea what to look for, or why history has seemed important to all peoples.

There are many answers to the question. They may differ for each person. It is useful, though, to see what others have thought about the value of history—why so many writers, politicians, teachers, and artists have believed that it is important to understand the past.

The earliest audience for history consisted simply of people who liked a good story. The two words, *story* and *history*, are essentially the same, and the appeal of history for many was that it brought to life real people and events, rather than invented ones. Before long, though, these real-life stories came to have a moral purpose—they taught lessons about how one should behave. The brave and the good usually succeeded; the cowardly or evil did not.

History was also considered important because it could explain—even without moral teachings—how or why things turned out as they did. It could show how a war happened, why one side won, and what the results were. By studying the past, people could thus learn what mistakes to avoid and what good examples to follow.

Finally, history came to be seen as a way of understanding ourselves and our own world. We cannot understand why Americans place such faith in their Constitution, why Islam is so important to Iranians, or why the Chinese think their revolution is still continuing, if we do not understand their history.

These different reasons for studying the past can be contradictory. Someone who looks for the moral lessons of history may not reach the same conclusions as someone who wants to explain the success of certain policies. Sometimes, for example, immoral behavior has proved successful. The historian has to assess these matters, try to reach conclusions about them, and thus determine their significance for our times.

As you read this book, think of yourself as a historian. Try to figure out why some people or events of the past seem more interesting to you than others. What do they tell you about yourself and your times? By keeping such questions in mind, you will be able to form your own answer about the reasons for studying history.

It may also help you to realize that a number of powerful forces have helped shape history in all periods. If you read thoughtfully and critically, you can learn what these forces are by asking yourself questions like these:

1. How has geography influenced the course of history? Have people simply adjusted to their environment, or have they tried to modify it?

2. How have people worked and earned their living? In other words, how have they organized their economy? What roles have farming, trade, and manufacturing played? How has income been distributed?

3. How have people been governed? Has politi-

cal power been held by a few, or by many? Have individuals had rights and liberties? How have rights and liberties been gained, protected, or lost? In what way were laws made and enforced? How have they worked in practice, and for whose benefit? Why and how have people changed their form of government?

4. How have people gained knowledge, and how have they passed it on to their descendants? Have they had a formal system of education? Who has been educated? Have societies learned from one another? Have science and invention played an important part in people's lives?

5. How have different religions arisen, and how have they influenced people's lives? You will read, for example, that the original religious beliefs of the Romans were influenced first by the Etruscans, then by the Greeks, then by various other peoples. Finally Roman religion was replaced by Christianity. Why did these changes take place, and how did they affect Roman life?

6. How have the arts—literature, painting, sculpture, architecture, and music—reflected the people who created them and the times in which they were produced? What arts have flourished and why?

7. How have nations settled their conflicts? Have they tried to reach peaceful solutions, or have they gone to war? Did the wars settle the issues that caused them? Did they create other problems?

8. Throughout history, many civilizations, national states, and political regimes have risen and fallen. What forces led to their rise, decline, or fall? Did people learn from the experiences of the past, or did they seem to repeat earlier mistakes?

If you try to find answers to such questions, you will be learning about the many forces that have worked together to make the world what it was and what it is. You will learn about the power of ideas, such as the belief that every human being has worth and dignity that must be respected. You can watch ideas like this appear, develop gradually, become strong, and finally be accepted by enough people to be put into practice. You will see other ideas decline and die out.

People have been pondering questions and ideas like these since earliest times. As you seek your own answers, you will be discovering what kind of person you are and want to be; you will be shaping your own role in the world of the future.

A.G.M., J.P., and T.K.R.

xviii

USING THIS BOOK

People and Nations has been created to present the basic facts and ideas of world history as clearly as possible. This is how the book has been organized:

Units

There are seven units, which group the chapters into broad historical periods. Each unit opens with a large illustration, symbolizing its contents, and with a list of the chapters it contains. Each chapter title is accompanied by the dates covered in the chapter. (See, for example, page 3.)

Chapters

The 32 chapters of *People and Nations* are organized around definite periods or topics. Like the units, each begins with a single illustration symbolic of its contents. Above the illustration is a schematic map of the world that locates the area or areas discussed in the chapter. (See page 4.)

Chapter Sections

After an introduction there is a list of the sections into which the chapter is divided. (See page 5.) A chapter may contain from two to six sections, each numbered. At the end of each section is a Checkup to help you review and check your understanding of the material you have just read. (See page 9.)

Chapter Reviews

Every chapter ends with a two-page review. First there is a *Time Line,* which presents in graphic form the most important events—with their dates—discussed in the chapter. It is followed by a *Chapter Summary,* which traces the main ideas of the chapter. The questions, activities, and research projects that complete the Chapter Review are divided into four parts: *Checking What You Know, Practicing Your Skills, Relating Past to Present,* and *Investigating Further.* (See pages 14 and 15.)

Unit Reviews

Each of the seven units ends with a one-page Unit Review. Here you will find a number of questions that will help you review what you learned in the unit. (See page 63.)

Maps and Charts

The 103 maps will give you the location of every place mentioned in the text as well as show you topography, the size of empires, the thrust of invasions, and the extent of alliances. Each map is placed as close as possible to the relevant text. (See page 10.) Important sequences of events or ideas are summarized in chart form. (See page 38.)

Illustrations

The hundreds of illustrations show you how people and places looked throughout the history of the world. The illustrations are grouped together in one- or two-page essays and are described by informative captions.

Features

You will find three kinds of special features running throughout the book. Combining text and illustrations, they will give you additional insights into world history:

HOW DO WE KNOW? The 14 essays describe the methods by which historians reconstruct the past, using archeological finds, documents, photography, journalism, and other "tools." (See page 40.)

CONNECTIONS A series of 20 illustrated features shows how familiar customs and traditions such as money, music, theater, games, and others have been common experiences in all times. (See page 19.)

HISTORY THROUGH ART Some works of art are especially illuminating as historical witnesses. Nearly 50 such works, from the earliest known portrait to contemporary architecture, are given special attention in these features. (See page 25.)

Chronology of Historical Events

A series of integrated time charts at the back of the book shows you what was happening in widely separated areas of the world at the same time.

Atlas

At the back of the book, a series of maps presents all the countries of the contemporary world.

Glossary

Important historical terms are defined in the Glossary that appears at the back of the book.

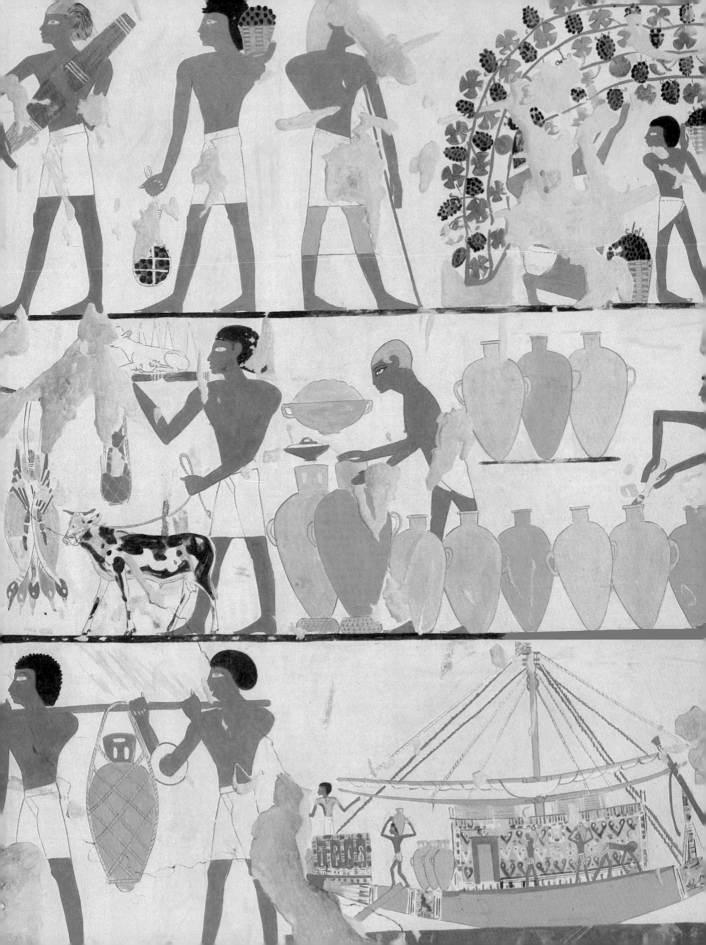

THE BEGINNINGS OF CIVILIZATION

Egyptian servants and slaves with crops and livestock, from a wall painting in an ancient tomb in Thebes

(4,000,000–2000 B.C.)

1

Cultures and Civilizations Began in Prehistoric Times

This is a book about history, but it begins long before human beings really had a history. We know where they lived, and we can examine the thousands of objects they left behind. However, what we can say about how they lived is very limited, because they did not leave us any comments of their own about their times.

We can study their pots, their knives, their bones, and even some of their pictures that have survived. But we have to figure out for ourselves what all of these things mean. We can never be too sure, because the people of these times did not tell us directly what we want to know. The problem is that they did not write anything down.

As long as we do not have written records from a period, we do not consider it to have a history. That is, we do not know the names of any of the people, what events they lived through, or even the language they spoke. They thus seem to have lived before history began, in a **prehistoric** age.

Nevertheless, we do know that many of the features of life that are still familiar to us appeared in prehistoric times. As you will see in this chapter, the earliest people did much that we still do. For example, they invented tools, they created beautiful art, and they buried their dead. Their concern about getting enough food has remained important throughout history. So has their tendency to live in families.

It was in the prehistoric period, too, that cities and forms of government were first established.

A prehistoric cave painting found in Africa

The earliest people gradually settled down and created what we call **civilizations**—highly organized societies, with complex institutions and attitudes that link a large number of people together.

With civilizations came the first forms of writing and thus the end of the prehistoric period. Our main story, the story of history, could begin.

THE CHAPTER SECTIONS

1. Prehistoric people made important discoveries

2. The first civilizations began in four great river valleys

1

Prehistoric people made important discoveries

How can we learn anything about the people who lived before there was writing? Surprisingly enough, we can find out a great deal. There are researchers called anthropologists who have been able to discover many things about prehistoric times, often by using scientific methods. They do have to rely on guesses, but usually they are quite confident about the conclusions they reach. They have been able to tell us when important changes took place thousands of years ago. They have also been able to describe some of the ways the first human beings spent their lives.

Anthropologists obtain information by looking at three kinds of remains from prehistoric times: (1) the bones of early people, which they use to reconstruct the size and appearance of the first men and women; (2) the bones of animals that were found near the human bones, which indicate what was being killed, eaten, or tamed; and (3) the weapons, tools, and other utensils that were near the bones. By looking at these items anthropologists can see how people hunted, made things, or ate.

These tools and weapons are called **artifacts**—that is, things made by human skill. Because the greatest number of artifacts that have survived from the earliest times are made of stone, the period of human development from which they come is called the **Stone Age**.

Early humans

Anthropologists now know that humanlike creatures appeared on the earth millions of years ago. For a long time, human progress was slow. This earliest period of human development is called the Old Stone Age, or **Paleolithic** (pay·lee·oh·LITH·ik) **Age**. The word *paleolithic* comes from the Greek words *palaios,* meaning "old," and *lithos,* meaning "stone."

In the eastern part of Africa, anthropologists discovered parts of a humanlike skeleton that may be four million years old. By examining the bones found at the excavation site, they were able to guess what this creature may have looked like. It appears to have walked on two legs, but to have had a brain that was only the size of that of a modern chimpanzee.

Creatures similar in appearance lived in eastern Africa two million years ago, but they had slightly larger brains. Tools made of chipped stone were found with the bones of these creatures. Anthropologists are still not certain what relation—if any—there is between these early discoveries and present humans. But many believe that upright posture and the ability to make tools were very early developments in human progress.

Early people were probably fruit eaters. People of later generations ate seeds and nuts and eventually became hunters of large animals. In order to hunt successfully, humans had to work together, communicate with one another, and make tools. For all of this, an inquiring mind and hands freed by an upright posture were necessary.

As humans became successful hunters, they wandered over great distances in search of food. From Africa they spread to Asia, where they settled some 750,000 years ago.

The knowledge we have of early humans and of humanlike creatures that were on earth millions of years ago is theoretical. Scientists often disagree on the interpretation of the bones and other materials found at excavation sites. Future discoveries may lead to theories that are different from those commonly held today.

The Ice Age

Human history and that of the earth itself have been greatly influenced by extremes of climate.

Four times within the last 1.5 million years, the earth has had periods of extremely cold weather. Four times the northern polar icecap (a permanent ice sheet near the North Pole) moved south and was joined by glaciers—large, slowly moving masses of snow and ice—that formed in the mountain ranges. Each of these four cold-weather periods lasted from 10,000 to 50,000 years. Together they are known as the **Ice Age.**

It is difficult to imagine the extent of these great ice sheets. Today, ice covers about one-twelfth of the earth's land surface. During the third and longest period of the Ice Age, ice covered about one-third of the earth's surface. In some places the ice sheet was several miles thick. Large areas of northern North America, Europe, and Asia were under ice.

The Ice Age affected the earth in various ways. Some humans and animals migrated to warmer, ice-free areas. Many kinds of animals and plants disappeared entirely. The grinding, chiseling effect of the moving ice made great changes on the surface of the earth. While much of the northern half of the earth was covered with ice, the rest of the earth received unusually large amounts of rainfall. Rivers and lakes rose. Inland seas formed. Regions that had been deserts began to produce vegetation and support animal life.

On the other hand, the sea level dropped because so much water was frozen in the icecaps. As the sea level fell, underwater ridges became uncovered and formed "land bridges." These linked some of the continents and islands that are today separated by water. Over some of these land bridges moved many humans and animals trying to escape the ice.

In the times between the four periods of the Ice Age, the icecap and glaciers gradually melted. Humans and animals moved back toward the north. We are now living in a warm era after the fourth period of the Ice Age, which ended between 10,000 and 25,000 years ago.

Java and Peking people

Anthropologists are just beginning to learn about the humanlike creatures whose remains have been found in eastern Africa. They have slightly more information about two forms of prehistoric people who lived in the early part of the Ice Age, from 1 million to 1.5 million years ago. Their remains have been found at two widely separated places in Asia—on the island of Java, in Indonesia, and in a cave near Peking, China (see map, page 10). These two discoveries are frequently called Java "man" and Peking "man." However, anthropologists are not certain whether these and other bones are those of men or of women.

Complete skeletons of these early people have not yet been found. But anthropologists have made guesses about their appearance on the basis of the bones that have been excavated. They were short, squat, and powerfully built people. They had powerful jaws with sharply receding chins. Their low foreheads had heavy eyebrow ridges. They sometimes used caves as shelters. They also made stone tools and probably knew how to use fire for cooking and keeping warm.

Neanderthal people

Further evidence of human development belongs to a much more recent period of the Old Stone Age. In caves located in the Neanderthal (nee·AN·dur·thal), a valley in Germany, anthropologists have found the remains of Neanderthal "man" (see map, page 10). These humans probably lived some 40,000 to 70,000 years ago. They were short and powerfully built, with heavy jaws, thick eyebrow ridges, and large noses.

Neanderthal people made more efficient tools than the humans who preceded them. They lived in caves, wore clothes made of animal skins, and knew the use of fire.

Neanderthal people differed from earlier humans in another way. They buried their dead. What is more, they buried with them tools, weapons, and even food. They must have expected these items to be of use to the dead person after his or her death. Clearly, this practice shows a belief in some sort of life after death. Such a belief is basic and common to most religions. We do not know exactly what Neanderthal people believed, but know they had some kind of religion.

Like earlier forms of humans, Neanderthal people disappeared. We do not know why. Glaciers had again advanced southward and covered much of Europe and North America, and Neanderthal people may have died out because of the cold. They may have been overcome by people who

Prehistoric peoples

Prehistoric peoples left no written records about how they lived, but we can find out much about them from their remains. The sharpened stones (above) from the Stone Age show the kinds of tools and weapons early peoples needed and learned to make. Even more interesting is the evidence, this early in human history, of a desire for things that were not only useful but also beautiful. The cave painting (right) and the delicately carved bison (above right), fashioned from a reindeer antler, reveal a fascination with nature and with beauty. Such works of art may have had a religious significance for these early humans. So, too, the great stones they erected in circular patterns may well have marked sacred places. The majestic stone circle (below), in the Orkney Islands in northern Scotland, is a silent monument to prehistoric people.

were stronger physically and more alert mentally. It is also possible that they were absorbed by more advanced types of people.

Cro-Magnon people

Some 40,000 years ago—just about the time Neanderthal people disappeared—a new kind of people moved into Europe, perhaps from Africa or Asia. They were better equipped to survive than were Neanderthal people, for they were stronger and more intelligent and made better tools and weapons.

This new kind of human is called Cro-Magnon "man," from the name of a cave in southern France where remains were found (see map, page 10). But the France of 40,000 years ago was very different from the France of today. It was quite cold. The polar icecap of the fourth period of the Ice Age extended far south into Europe. We know Europe was cold because with the Cro-Magnon bones were found the remains of plants and animals that live only in a cold climate.

We know much more about Cro-Magnon people than we do about any of the other early humans. For one thing, more of their remains have been found. Then, too, these people themselves "told" us more. They could not write, but they could draw and paint. Cro-Magnon people were probably the first real artists. In the caves of southern France and Spain where Cro-Magnon people lived, the walls are covered with their paintings of the animals they hunted. Among the animals they painted were the woolly mammoth and the reindeer. These paintings are full of life and movement. The Cro-Magnons also made small clay and limestone statues of animals and carved figures on bones and antlers.

Cro-Magnon people looked almost the same as modern men and women. They lived on earth for many thousands of years. By the end of the Old Stone Age, however, the Cro-Magnon as a distinct type no longer existed. In appearance, people had become as they are today.

The Middle Stone Age

The period from about 10,000 to about 8,000 years ago is called the Middle Stone Age. It is also called the **Mesolithic Age,** from the Greek words *mesos,* meaning "middle," and *lithos,* meaning "stone." After the end of the fourth period of the Ice Age, extensive forests appeared in many parts of the world. Larger animals died out and smaller ones became the basis of the human food supply. Stone tools of this period are much smaller than those made during the Old Stone Age.

People made much progress during the short Mesolithic period. They **domesticated,** or tamed, the goat. They also domesticated the dog, which proved valuable in hunting smaller animals. They invented the bow and arrow, as well as fishhooks, fish spears, and harpoons made from bones and antlers. Mesolithic people also learned to fit a handle to the hand ax. By hollowing out logs, they made dugout canoes so that they could fish in deep water and cross rivers.

The New Stone Age

About 8,000 years ago, in certain parts of the world, basic changes occurred in the way people lived. The period that began then is called the New Stone Age, or **Neolithic Age.** Its scientific name comes from the Greek words *neos,* "new," and *lithos,* "stone."

In the Old Stone Age and Middle Stone Age, stone was chipped to produce an edge or a point. In the New Stone Age, people discovered a better way. They learned that stone could be polished to a fine edge and a sharp point on a flat piece of sandstone. They learned to use many kinds of stone, as well as wood. With the new methods and materials, they could make special tools—awls, wedges, saws, drills, chisels, and needles.

But other changes during the New Stone Age were far more important. Earlier people had been **nomads,** or wanderers, who followed animals from place to place. Neolithic people, however, settled down in villages. They could do so because of two important developments: (1) the taming of several additional kinds of animals, and (2) the development of agriculture.

Paleolithic and Mesolithic hunters never knew if enough food would be available. They might have bad luck in hunting, or animals might starve or migrate. The food supply became much more certain once animals were domesticated. Mesolithic people had tamed dogs and goats, but Neolithic people learned also to raise cattle, horses, sheep, and pigs. Some of these animals were used for food, and their hides for clothing.

The greatest discovery made by Neolithic people was **agriculture**—raising crops for food. It is not quite clear how people learned that seeds could be planted and made to grow year after year. In any case, they somehow learned to plant wheat, barley, rice, and millet. They also learned to use fertilizer and invented the plow.

The shift from food hunting to food producing was so important that it has often been called the **Neolithic Revolution.** (Although the word "revolution" is most often used to mean the overthrow of a government, it may also mean a very important change in people's lives.)

The new sources of food permitted Neolithic people to settle permanently in one region and to build homes. There was more time to work on tools, more time for art and other activities. Neolithic people built furniture, made pottery, and wove cloth. More people could live together in communities. They developed rules to regulate their living. In other words, they created the first organized governments.

CHECKUP

1. IDENTIFY: prehistoric age, artifacts, Stone Age, Ice Age, Java people, Peking people, Neanderthal people, Cro-Magnon people, nomads.

2. What evidence of prehistoric people tells us about their daily life?

3. What were some of the effects of the Ice Age? What happened during the periods when the ice melted?

4. List the accomplishments of the following periods: (a) Paleolithic, (b) Mesolithic, (c) Neolithic.

5. Why was the discovery of how to raise crops considered a "revolution"?

2

The first civilizations began in four great river valleys

People had made much progress by the end of the Stone Age. They had learned to make tools and weapons, use fire, create works of art, tame animals, and grow their own food.

HISTORY THROUGH ART
Prehistoric Ivory Head

A Cro-Magnon artist carved this ivory head of a woman about 40,000 years ago, during the Old Stone Age. It was found in France and can be held in the palm of the hand. From works like this, we learn that some prehistoric peoples had a sense of beauty similar to our own. Such artifacts also tell us that some prehistoric groups had time for other activities besides looking for food and making tools. This carving is one of the earliest known attempts to create a portrait. As its small size suggests, it may have been an object of worship that the owner could easily carry from place to place.

We use the word **culture** to describe the total of these basic human activities. We also use the word "culture" when speaking of the way of life of a specific group of people, for example, an Indian tribe or an ethnic group in a modern city.

Using the word "culture" in the second sense, we can speak of Neolithic culture, meaning a Stone Age culture based on farming. However, it should be remembered that not everyone developed this way of life during the Neolithic Age. Not all areas of the world had soil and climate suitable for farming. In some regions, where there were pasture lands covered with grass, people maintained a herding culture. That is, they moved their flocks from one place to another to graze.

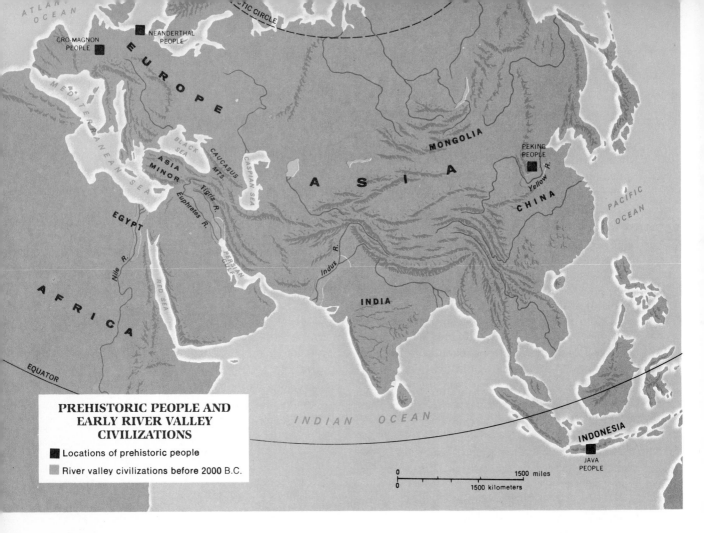

PREHISTORIC PEOPLE AND EARLY RIVER VALLEY CIVILIZATIONS

■ Locations of prehistoric people

▨ River valley civilizations before 2000 B.C.

0 — 1500 miles
0 — 1500 kilometers

They continued to be nomads, wandering about in small groups or tribes and never settling down.

Moving into the river valleys

During Paleolithic times people lived in small groups wherever there was food and shelter. But in Neolithic times farmers gathered in larger settlements with fertile soil and adequate water.

There were many small areas on earth where people settled together. But the settlements in four great regions were to have particular importance in later human development. These four regions were: (1) the Nile River Valley in Egypt; (2) the valley of the Tigris and Euphrates (yoo·FRAY·teez) rivers in southwestern Asia; (3) the Indus River Valley in southern Asia; and (4) the Yellow River Valley in northern China (see map, this page).

In these four river valleys, people first developed the advanced form of culture known as civilization. All people belong to some sort of culture. Only when a culture becomes highly developed is it called a civilization.

Most civilizations have at least four characteristics: (1) The people have advanced technical skills, such as the ability to use metals. (2) A civilization will often have cities, with some sort of government. (3) There is a division of labor. That is, different people perform different jobs, instead of one person having to do all kinds of work. (4) A civilization will also have a form of writing and a calendar.

Learning to use metals

The discovery of metals was probably accidental. It may have happened, for example, when someone built a fire over an area that contained the metal copper. Afterward, some bright, shining lumps of this metal could have been noticed in the ashes. People may then have learned how to shape the heated metal.

About 6,000 years ago people in both the Nile Valley and the Tigris-Euphrates Valley were making copper weapons, tools, utensils, and jewelry. Copper tools and weapons were used for several thousand years. They were not entirely satisfactory, mainly because copper was too soft to keep the sharp edge that is necessary for heavy work. In time, a better metal came into use. This was bronze, an alloy—or mixture—of copper and tin. This alloy is harder than copper. Bronze was made into jewelry and weapons in Egypt and the Tigris-Euphrates Valley 5,000 years ago. It was also used at an early date in India and China.

Iron is a stronger material than either copper or bronze. Iron ore—that is, the iron as it exists in the earth mixed with other minerals—is found in more places and in larger amounts than either copper or tin. Yet its use came much later, because it was extremely difficult to separate the iron from the ore. One important step was the invention of the forge. This is a kind of furnace where great heat is produced by forcing air through fire.

After the ore had been softened by the extreme heat of the forge, the hot metal had to be hammered. The hammering eliminated the impurities. If left in, impurities would weaken the iron and make it useless. We do not know when the process of making iron was invented or who invented it. It may have originated separately in several different areas.

Irrigation, government, and cities

The valleys of the Nile, Tigris-Euphrates, Indus, and Yellow rivers have a feature in common that greatly influenced their early histories. Once a year their rivers rise and flood the valleys. Except during these periods, however, there is little, if any, rain. The rest of the year is hot and dry.

This problem of climate meant that the farmers of the valleys somehow had to get water to their crops during the dry season. They could do so by building systems of **irrigation**—that is, creating artificial means such as ditches and canals to bring

in the water. Violent floods occurred in three of these river valleys—the Tigris-Euphrates, the Indus, and the Yellow. Therefore, farmers in these valleys also had to build dikes to control high water during the rainy season.

Farming in these river valleys, then, depended on irrigation and the ability to control floods. Large irrigation and flood-control projects could not be built by individuals working alone. People had to learn to work together in groups. It took teamwork to build ditches and canals for irrigation and dikes to control floods.

Governments may have originated through such cooperation. In other words, as people worked together, they developed governments through their efforts to plan, direct, and regulate their work.

The first valley dwellers had moved into their valleys in tribes. Each tribe settled in a village along the river. People lived together in the village and went out to work the surrounding land. In time, more and more people banded together to work on group projects and for common defense. Some of these village communities grew to become cities.

Another reason for the growth of cities was an increase in population, made possible by improved farming methods. Improved farming meant more and better food and, therefore, a healthier and more comfortable life for each person. The large number of people living in cities also had the resources to create great palaces, temples, and other kinds of public buildings.

Division of labor

As methods of farming improved, fewer people had to work in the fields in order to produce enough food for all. Some people were able to specialize in work other than farming. Experts at tool and weapon making could devote all their time to this type of work. Then they would trade their products for food. Thus a class of skilled workers, called **artisans,** appeared.

Other people became merchants and traders. They made their living by buying goods from farmers or artisans and then selling the goods to anyone who needed them, especially people in cities. Traders not only transported goods to be sold, but they also passed along ideas. For example, they were responsible for spreading systems of counting that showed how many articles were bought and sold.

Developing a calendar

The people in the great river valleys developed calendars early in their history. Because these people were farmers, the changes of the seasons were important to them. They had to know, for example, when the yearly floods would start and stop. One way was to regard the time from flood to flood as a year and to divide the interval according to the phases of the moon. These changes in the moon's appearance were the most regular repetitions that early people could see in the sky.

The time from one new moon to the next new moon would be a month. Twelve of these lunar months would equal a year. But there is a difficulty. A month based on the movement of the moon—that is, on the time it takes the moon to revolve once completely around the earth—is only about 29½ days long. Twelve "moon" months thus equal 354 days. But we know that there are approximately 365¼ days in a year when it is measured by the time it takes the earth to revolve once completely around the sun. A calendar based on the moon was therefore about 11 days short. As a result, the months came earlier each year and twelve months did not fill the time until the next flood. As you read more about river-valley civilizations, you will see how early people coped with this problem.

In this book we will be using a system of dating with letters B.C. and A.D. The letters B.C. are an abbreviation of "*Before the birth of Christ.*" Thus, the date 2000 B.C. means 2,000 years before Christ's birth. The letters A.D. with a date stand for the Latin phrase *Anno Domini,* which means "in the year of our Lord," or "since the birth of Christ." The year 1900 A.D. thus stands for 1,900 years after Christ's birth.

This method of dating is only one of several ways of figuring time. Muslims, Chinese, Jews, and Hindus have other ways of counting the years.

Inventing writing

With the many changes of late Neolithic times, life became increasingly complex. People in settled communities developed rules for living together and for protecting property. They developed agreements as to how they should work together. Governments were established, and with them taxes to pay the costs of government. Trade also developed between communities.

Speech was now no longer sufficient as the only means of communication. What was needed was written language, as a means of preserving and passing on ideas and information. Although its development was a long and complex process, it may be summarized in four chief steps:

(1) *A picture represents a thing.* Thus a picture of a tree stands for the word "tree." Picture signs of this sort are called pictograms. You can see that pictograms have disadvantages. It is easy to show a tree or a man. But how would you represent an idea, such as truth or life after death?

(2) *A picture stands for an idea.* As time went on, people began using symbols to stand for ideas. Suppose a farmer had orchards. In this case the farmer might use the drawing of a tree to represent the idea of "wealth." Picture signs of this sort are called ideograms.

(3) *A picture stands for a sound, usually a syllable.* In using pictograms and ideograms, a great many pictures are needed. Fewer are required if a certain symbol can represent a sound, not just one meaning. Thus the tree symbol could stand not only for "tree' but also for the syllable "trea" in the word "treason." Signs of this sort are called phonograms.

(4) *A sign represents a single consonant or vowel.* These signs, or letters, form an alphabet. An alphabet is the final stage in the development of writing. Over the years, two things happened to the tree symbol. It became simplified so that it was easier to draw. And it came to stand for the beginning sound of the phonogram, not the whole sound. Thus a simplified version of the picture—the letter *T*—came to represent just the first sound of "tree." This story of the development of the letter *T* is an imaginary and simplified one, but it illustrates how people invented alphabets.

The family in early civilizations

In prehistoric times, as you have read, people found food through hunting and gathering. While men went out in search of animals, women

SCIENTIFIC DATING Because prehistoric peoples left no written records, other kinds of information are needed to understand their societies. This information is found in human bones and tools, weapons, and other objects that have been unearthed. It is essential to put a date on these objects, so that historians can know when they were made and what other objects people had at the time.

In recent years the dating of such objects has been greatly helped by a scientific discovery. In 1907 a chemist found that radioactive minerals decay at a regular, fixed rate. This discovery has helped scientists calculate the age of rocks and of the earth itself. A basic concept in this analysis is the notion of the half-life, the amount of time it takes a radioactive substance to lose half its original form.

The most useful application of this discovery has been with radiocarbon, contained in small amounts in all living things. When a living thing dies, its supply of radiocarbon begins to decay. Since scientists know the rate of this decay, they can tell the age of the remains within a thousand years or so. This technique, known as **radiocarbon dating,** can be applied to plant and animal remains, as well as to any artifact made of organic material. Thus, it has been vital to the study of the early periods of human history.

---

remained near the campsite to care for the children. Women also trained the children in the culture of the group. Women and children would gather plants and fruit from nearby areas for food. Because they gathered plants for food, women probably first noticed that seeds could be planted and grown. This discovery made agriculture—and thus civilization—possible.

When civilization developed, men gave up hunting and became farmers, but women continued some of the farming, such as planting and harvesting crops. In the early river-valley civilizations that you will read about in greater detail in Chapter 2, men were responsible for farming and for making metal products, such as weapons. Women were responsible for managing the family and for making in the home items necessary for survival, for example, food and clothing. Women also probably invented pottery and weaving.

Religion was important in the lives of early families. Early people believed in many gods and in the unseen forces in nature. They believed that all aspects of their lives were controlled by the gods and these forces. People feared that their crops would not grow. Crop failure would mean starvation. Thus, they begged their gods to provide water and to make seeds grow.

The families in early civilizations were large. In addition to mothers, fathers, and children, they consisted of grandparents, aunts and uncles, and cousins. Medical knowledge was limited, and most children died as infants. When people grew old, they expected to be taken care of by their children. People looked to their relatives for help in everyday affairs.

In most early civilizations the father was considered the head of the family. But because women were responsible for managing the family, they also had great authority. However, this authority did not often extend into other areas of social activity, such as politics or religion.

CHECKUP

1. IDENTIFY: culture, civilization, alloy, forge, artisans, lunar month, B.C., A.D.

2. LOCATE: Nile River, Tigris River, Euphrates River, Indus River, Yellow River.

3. How did the need for irrigation and flood control lead to the development of governments?

4. Why was a calendar necessary?

5. Why was written language needed? What were the four chief steps in developing a written language?

CHAPTER REVIEW

4,000,000	10,000	8000	6000	4000	2000	B.C.	A.D.	2000

4,000,000 years ago	Earliest humanlike creatures in Africa	40,000 years ago	Cro-Magnon people
2,000,000 years ago	Humanlike creatures using tools	8,000–10,000 years ago	Middle Stone Age
1,500,000 years ago	Beginning of Ice Age	6000 B.C.	Beginning of New Stone Age
1,000,000–1,500,000 years ago	Java and Peking people	3000 B.C.	Use of bronze
40,000–70,000 years ago	Neanderthal people		

CHAPTER SUMMARY

The first human beings left behind bones, artifacts, and pictures. From these, anthropologists have been able to figure out what the first human beings looked like, what they ate, where they lived, and what some of their customs were, such as burying the dead.

We can also tell that during prehistoric times people gradually developed greater skills. As one moves from the Old Stone Age to the Middle Stone Age and the New Stone Age, one finds that people produced more effective tools. They learned to hunt more efficiently. They created the earliest works of art. And eventually they stopped roaming around as hunters. They settled down in villages, because they learned to tame animals and to raise crops through agriculture.

These changes brought on one of the most important turning points in human history—the development of civilization. The first major areas of settlement, in the four great river valleys of Africa and Asia, developed the first civilizations. Their people learned how to use metals. They built cities, promoted economic activity, and established governments. Their societies became quite complicated, dividing labor among different groups. Religion was very important to them. And they made considerable intellectual progress—for example, they developed workable calendars, most of them based on the phases of the moon.

One of their most significant discoveries was writing. The ability to keep records gave civilizations continuity. It also allows us, for the first time, to find out what people thought about their own times. With the discovery of writing, prehistory ends and history begins.

CHECKING WHAT YOU KNOW

1. Match each term at the left with its definition at the right:

   a. prehistoric age
   b. civilization
   c. artifacts
   d. Paleolithic Age

   1. tools and weapons of a specific civilization or time period
   2. a highly advanced culture that has government and cities
   3. earliest period of human development
   4. period before written records were kept

2. Place the items in each of the following three lists in chronological order from most ancient to most recent:

   a. plow, upright posture, meat eaters, use of fire
   b. Peking people, East African people, Cro-Magnon people, Neanderthal people
   c. farming, hunting, herding of animals, gathering of fruits and seeds

3. How did the lives of early people change after they learned to domesticate animals and to raise food crops?

PRACTICING YOUR SKILLS

1. **Using maps.** Using the map on page 10, list the large bodies of water that are closest to the four major river-valley civilizations. Which of these civilizations was most likely, because of its location, to have some trading contact? Which one seems the most isolated from the others?

2. **Using pictures**. From the pictures in this chapter, what can you tell about the cultures of prehistoric people? What seem to be their most important concerns? Using books in your school or local library, examine prehistoric cave paintings from two of the following places:

a. the Sahara region of North Africa
b. South Africa
c. southern France and Spain
d. the American Southwest

What are the similarities and differences in subject matter? What can you tell about these cultures by looking at these paintings?

3. **Making charts.** Make a chart comparing the achievements of Paleolithic people and Neolithic people. You may use the following topics as headings:

a. method of obtaining food
b. tools
c. government
d. important discoveries

RELATING PAST TO PRESENT

1. What was the role of women in Neolithic society? On what can we base this view? How have the roles of women changed in the past 25 years? What new tools and attitudes have brought about these changes?

2. What would a civilization from outer space learn of our culture from investigating the contents of our garbage dumps, cemeteries, and junkyards?

3. Over a period of thousands of years, prehistoric people discovered new skills and inventions that greatly changed their lives. Among these were methods of agriculture, the use of metals, and the calendar. Choose a modern skill or invention and explain how it has changed our lives today. Why do you think it took prehistoric people thousands of years to make a few important discoveries? Why are we able to absorb many discoveries and methods in such a short time today?

INVESTIGATING FURTHER

1. In your school or local library, read about primitive societies in the world today. For example, you might read Elizabeth M. Thomas's *The Harmless People* (Random House), which is about the Bush people of southern Africa. Or you might choose the Pygmies of central Africa, who are described in Colin M. Turnbull's *The Forest People* (Simon and Schuster). Other groups that might be used are New Guinea tribes, Amazon tribes, or Philippine tribes. Periodicals such as *National Geographic* would be good sources for your research. Then write a report describing:

a. how the group is organized and governed
b. the roles of men and women
c. how food is obtained and distributed within the group
d. the group's religious practices
e. the physical environment and how it affects the way the people live
f. the types of tools made and used

2. Use encyclopedias to locate information about the calendars of other peoples, for example the Chinese, Hebrew, Muslim, or Hindu calendars. How do each of these calendars figure a one-month period compared to the calendar we use? Why does each of these calendars have a different beginning of the year?

3. Excavations leading to the discovery of bones and artifacts in East Africa that are many millions of years old have been made by the Leakeys, a family of anthropologists. Both the story of the discoveries and the methods of anthropologists are vividly portrayed in *Origins* by Richard E. Leakey and Roger Lewin (E. P. Dutton). Give an oral or written report based on this book.

4. Use the book *Gods, Graves, and Scholars* by C. W. Ceram (Bantam) to find out more about expeditions that recovered the remains of early societies. Choose one of the expeditions and write a report about the discoveries that were made.

2

Great Civilizations Developed in the Middle East

Two of the four great river valleys in which civilizations first appeared were in the area of the eastern Mediterranean that we call the Middle East. In both of these valleys—along the Nile River and along the Tigris and Euphrates rivers—complex societies and strong governments developed.

The two civilizations were not very far apart. It is about 600 miles (960 kilometers) from the Nile to the Euphrates. There was some contact between them, but their societies turned out to be very different. We shall see throughout history that even people who are next-door neighbors can develop entirely separate cultures. The kind of society that develops is determined by immediate circumstances—for example, geography.

The Nile River is fairly well protected from invasion. Along its banks the Egyptians created a very stable society. Over the centuries they developed long-lasting traditions in the arts, government, religion, and thought. The achievements of Egyptian civilization can be seen to this day.

The valley along the Tigris and Euphrates, on the other hand, was more easily invaded, and here less stable societies developed. A succession of peoples conquered and settled the Tigris-Euphrates region. Each created its own institutions and culture. Many of these peoples spread beyond the valley, creating a series of powerful empires throughout the Middle East.

Among the many peoples who lived in the Middle East in these years, two deserve special men-

Statue of the Egyptian pharaoh Rameses II

tion, even though they did not set up strong governments or great empires. The first were the Phoenicians (fuh·NEE·shunz), traders who spread their influence by sea. Second were the Hebrews, the creators of a remarkable religion called Judaism, which defined new ideals in law and faith.

We will see in this chapter how diverse these various peoples were. It is important to understand why such differences developed. It is also necessary to recognize that each of these peoples, in their own way, had something special to contribute to the shaping of human history.

THE CHAPTER SECTIONS

1. The Egyptians built a civilization along the Nile River

2. The culture of ancient Egypt reached impressive heights

3. Sumerian civilization arose along the Tigris and Euphrates rivers

4. Several empires were established in the Fertile Crescent

5. The Phoenicians and the Hebrews made lasting contributions

1

The Egyptians built a civilization along the Nile River

Of all the ancient river-valley civilizations, that of Egypt is probably the best known today. Its ancient landmarks, such as the pyramids and the Sphinx, are familiar to almost everyone in the world.

The Egypt of ancient times probably looked very much like the Egypt of today. Egypt is a large country, but most of it is a sandy desert. Here and there is an oasis—a place in the desert where there is irrigation or an underground spring. But in this vast country, crops can be grown only in one long, narrow strip of land–the valley of the Nile River. The Nile flows north from the mountains of east-central Africa to the Mediterranean Sea (see map, page 18).

"The gift of the Nile"

Many centuries after the early period of Egyptian history, a Greek historian named Herodotus (hih·RAHD·uh·tus) wrote of his travels in Egypt. "All Egypt," he said, "is the gift of the Nile." Herodotus wrote accurately, for he was describing a remarkable feature of Egyptian geography. Each year, from June to October, rain and melting snow from the mountains at the source of the Nile cause the river to overflow and spread out over the flatland of the southern Nile Valley. The flood reaches its highest level at the beginning of September. As the flood recedes, the gentle slope of the land allows the water to drain off gradually. A layer of silt, or fertile soil, which the river has carried along in its flood, is left behind.

From earliest times Egyptian farmers have planned their work according to the flood. They know when it will come every year. They harvest their crops before it begins, then wait for the water to soak the hard, dry earth before it drains off and leaves its new, fertile soil. There is little or no rainfall in Egypt, so the flood moisture is sufficient for only one planting. Early in their history, however, the Egyptians learned to irrigate the land by using water from the Nile and carrying it to the fields in short canals. Then they could plant and harvest two or even three crops a year.

You can easily see the importance of this regular flooding of the Nile. Each year the valley receives a fresh layer of soil. Because of this, the land of the Nile Valley has been farmed continuously for more than 6,000 years. And it is still farmed today.

Other natural advantages

The Nile Valley had other natural resources besides the amazingly fertile soil. There was the climate, for example—a sunny climate that is free of frost all year and well suited to farming.

The Nile Valley also has deposits of clay, granite, sandstone, and limestone. These minerals are used for building. The ancient Egyptians needed these materials, for there were few forests to furnish lumber. Egypt is primarily an agricultural society. It has remained chiefly a farming country to the present day.

Finally, there was one other natural advan-

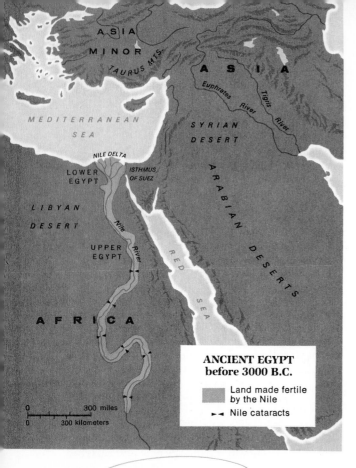

**ANCIENT EGYPT
before 3000 B.C.**

Land made fertile
by the Nile

◄ Nile cataracts

0   300 miles
0   300 kilometers

Egyptian writing. Along with the other major developments of Egyptian civilization came writing. By about 3000 B.C. the Egyptians had worked out a system of writing called **hieroglyphics** (hy·ur·uh·GLIF·iks). The word comes from the Greek *hieros*, "sacred," and *glyphe*, "carving." Hieroglyphic writing uses pictures or symbols to indicate words or sounds.

At first, Egyptians carved hieroglyphics on rock, but this was a long and difficult process. Searching for a better writing material, they used what they found near them. A plant called papyrus grew in the marshes near the Nile. The Egyptians cut papyrus into long, thin slices. They then placed the slices together and moistened and pounded them to form a mat with a smooth surface. This product was also called papyrus, from which we get our word "paper."

A united kingdom

Over the centuries early Egyptian settlements were united to form the two kingdoms of Upper Egypt and Lower Egypt. (A **kingdom,** one of the earliest forms of government, is headed by a king or a queen. Another name for a kingdom is a **monarchy.**) Upper Egypt lay farthest south from the Mediterranean Sea, along the upper Nile River. Lower Egypt lay to the north, nearest the sea (see map, this page).

Then, about 3100 B.C., a ruler known as Menes (MEE·neez) united all Egypt into one kingdom. Menes and his successors put down rebellions, gained new territory, regulated irrigation, and encouraged trade and prosperity.

Much of the power of these rulers came from the fact that they were religious leaders as well as political leaders. They were regarded as gods. In later years they took the title **pharaoh,** which means "great house," after the palace in which they lived.

The pharaoh's position as god placed him far above ordinary people. He was the leader of the government, as well as a judge, a high priest, and a general of the armies. Although the pharaoh had absolute, or unlimited, power, it was his duty to protect and care for his people.

Menes founded a **dynasty,** or family of rulers. In a dynasty the right to rule is hereditary—that is, it is passed on within the family, usually from

tage—the valley's location. The Nile Valley is surrounded by deserts and seas. These provided a natural protection against invaders. The natural barriers were broken in only one place—at the Isthmus of Suez (see map, this page). The isthmus was a link—a land bridge—between Asia and Africa. Throughout history it has been the route for traders, for the exchange of ideas, and for invading armies.

Early steps toward civilization

The long valley of the Nile has been inhabited since earliest times. Paleolithic remains have been found there, and a Neolithic culture developed sometime around 6000 B.C.

The people of the Nile Valley soon began to take other steps along the road to civilization. They learned to use copper to make needles, chisels, and jewelry. They discovered how to make bronze, the alloy of copper and tin. They may have invented the potter's wheel, a rotating disk that made it easier to make round vessels.

father to son or daughter. This hereditary rule ends only when a family is overthrown or dies out, so that there is no one left to become ruler. In more than 2,500 years, beginning with the time of Menes and continuing to about 300 B.C., there were about 30 Egyptian dynasties. This span of time is divided into four periods—the Old Kingdom, the Middle Kingdom, the New Kingdom, and the Decline.

The Old Kingdom

The Old Kingdom existed from about 2700 B.C. to 2181 B.C. It was probably the greatest period of all Egyptian history. Many important discoveries in science and the arts took place then. During this period the largest pyramids, which are regarded as symbols of Egyptian civilization, were built. For this reason the period of the Old Kingdom is sometimes called the Pyramid Age.

In the early dynasties there were only two main groups of people in society: (1) an upper class, consisting of the pharaoh, the royal family, and the priests and officials who helped govern the country, and (2) a lower class, consisting of everyone else. The majority of this lower class consisted of peasants, or farmers. They owed the pharaoh services, such as a period of duty in the army or work on the irrigation system or on the pyramids and other public buildings.

As time passed, officials in the upper class gradually became a hereditary group of nobles. Toward the end of the Old Kingdom, the pharaohs grew weaker and the nobles grew stronger. For 250 years after the end of this period, the country was torn by civil wars as rivals claimed the throne.

The Middle Kingdom

In about 2000 B.C. a strong new line of pharaohs united Egypt again, beginning a period known as the Middle Kingdom. The pharaohs restored order and prosperity for a while. However, the problems of making and carrying out all decisions by themselves were too great for all but the strongest and best rulers. Other officials—for example, priests and governors of regions—became more and more powerful in the government. They also became wealthy. Thus the power of the pharaoh again was weakened by the rise of a hereditary class of nobles and priests.

connections

Cotton

The painted figures on ancient Egyptian temple walls and mummy cases wear draped garments of woven cotton cloth. Egypt has long been a major source of cotton (right), the most important agricultural product besides food in the world today. Egypt's warm climate and the irrigation provided by the Nile combine to produce a highly desirable type of cotton. Because of its high quality, Egyptian cotton is exported to lands throughout the world.

Cotton probably appeared first in India around 3000 B.C. There is also evidence that it existed long ago in Peru and in what is now Arizona. Some kinds of cotton are named after the places from which they originally came. For example, the cotton we

know as madras is named after the port of Madras in India.

The fabric woven from the fluffy blossoms of the cotton plant absorbs moisture and remains cool even in hot weather. It is so comfortable that manufacturers today use it in clothing of all kinds, from pajamas to jeans. Cotton is used in many other products, too, such as bandages, life vests, and the stuffing for sofas. Its popularity spans thousands of years, and the demand for cotton is now greater than it has ever been.

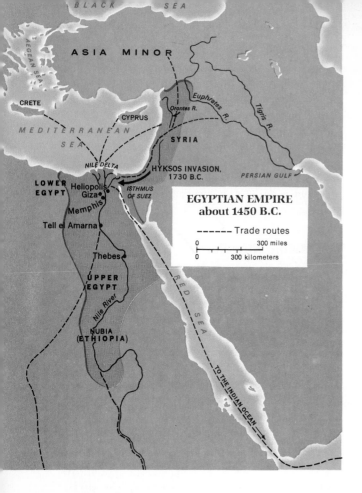

EGYPTIAN EMPIRE
about 1450 B.C.

- - - - - Trade routes

0   300 miles

0   300 kilometers

The Middle Kingdom ended in disorder around 1780 B.C. The country was weakened by rivalries, conflicts, and the division of power. Then, about 1730 B.C., Egypt was invaded for the first time in many centuries. A people from Asia called the Hyksos crossed the Isthmus of Suez and conquered part of the Nile Valley. The Hyksos army had horses and chariots and was far better equipped than that of the Egyptians. The Hyksos ruled parts of Egypt for about 150 years.

The New Kingdom

Eventually, the nobles of Upper Egypt rebelled against the Hyksos and drove them from the country. Egypt was again united under a number of strong pharaohs who ruled from the city of Thebes far up the Nile. The period in which they ruled—from about 1550 B.C. to about 1085 B.C.—is called the New Kingdom.

The new line of pharaohs regained much of the authority held by earlier pharaohs. For a time, at least, the pharaohs once more had absolute power. They kept strict control over the government and created a strong army. They adopted the horse-drawn chariots of the Hyksos and began to use iron weapons.

The Hyksos invasion had terrified the Egyptian pharaohs, who realized that their homeland could be invaded. They were determined that it would not happen again. Since a defense line at the Isthmus of Suez had not stopped the Hyksos, the Egyptians had to find a better line farther to the east. As a result, they conquered territory along the eastern end of the Mediterranean Sea (see map, this page). To strengthen their defenses in the south, they also conquered Nubia. In doing so, they were creating an empire. (An **empire** is a form of government that unites different territories and peoples under one ruler, usually an emperor or empress.)

Like many other peoples, however, the Egyptians found it easier to conquer territory than to keep and govern it. Usually they allowed the local prince of a conquered region to act as governor. To be sure of his loyalty and obedience, they took his son back to Egypt as a hostage to be trained at the palace of Thebes.

Only the strongest pharaohs, however, were able to hold the empire together. Whenever the government of Egypt became weak, some part of the empire revolted and tried to break away.

Amenhotep's religious revolution. One famous pharaoh was Amenhotep IV (ah·mun·HOH·tep), who ruled from about 1379 to 1362 B.C. He was not a famous conqueror, nor even a very good ruler. But Amenhotep is remembered because he brought about a social and religious revolution.

Before Amenhotep became pharaoh, Egyptians believed in the existence of many gods. Belief in many gods is called **polytheism** (PAHL·ee·thee·iz·um), from the Greek word *polys*, meaning "many," and *theos*, meaning "god." The greatest of the gods was Amon, whose center of worship was at Thebes.

Amenhotep tried to change Egyptian religion. He believed that the only god was the sun, Aton, and that the pharaoh was Aton's earthly son. This belief in only one god is known as **monotheism** (MAHN·uh·thee·iz·um), from the Greek *monos*, meaning "one," plus *theos*. To honor the god Aton, Amenhotep changed his own name to

20

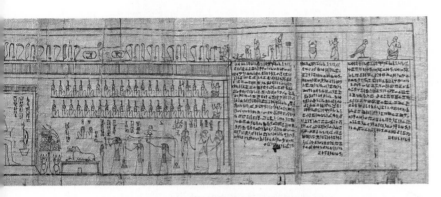

Pharaohs and the afterlife

The tombs of the Egyptians tell us much about their religion, including their deep concern with life after death. They believed that their rulers were divine beings who rejoined the gods when they died, especially if their bodies were preserved by embalming. In a tomb painting (top left) the queen Nefertiti is being guided by Isis, the goddess who brought the dead back to life. A statue of the pharaoh Tutankhamen (above), with royal headdress and whip, accompanied his body into the tomb. So did the holy fan (left), decorated with a scene of the pharaoh hunting. The Book of the Dead (center left), on papyrus, was also placed in a tomb. Its magical texts helped the soul on its journey after death.

Akhenaton (ahk·uh·NAH·tun), which means "he who is beneficial to Aton."

The priests of Amon had become so powerful that they interfered in all affairs. To help break their power, Akhenaton moved his capital from Thebes, where the great temple of Amon was located, to a new city, Tell el Amarna. At Tell el Amarna, he devoted his time to religion and neglected the ruling of the empire. The pharaoh also tried to force his new religion on the Egyptian people. He took over the temples and insisted that only Aton be worshiped.

Reaction to Akhenaton's religion. The priests of Amon were furious. The wealth that formerly came to them at their great temple of Thebes now went to the temple of the new god in the new capital. Their easy life was being disturbed. Appointments to high positions, which formerly went to the priests of Amon, now went to believers in Aton.

The priests of Amon and of the other gods began to cause trouble for Akhenaton. Because they had a strong hold on the people, they were able to stir up opposition to the pharaoh. Akhenaton soon learned that he could not change people's religious beliefs by command. The bitter struggle between pharaoh and priests caused much conflict in Egypt. When Akhenaton died, the priests of Amon reestablished their power. They forced his successor, Tutankhamen (toot·ahnk·AH·min), to move the capital back to Thebes.

After the death of Akhenaton, there were few strong rulers in Egypt. Rameses II, however, was powerful. He ruled from about 1304 to 1237 B.C. and held Egypt and the empire together. His successors could not maintain the empire or prevent corruption in the government. Slowly Egypt sank into chaos.

The Decline

Beginning about 1100 B.C., Egypt grew steadily weaker. The empire was lost, and foreign invaders—including the Nubians, the Assyrians, and the Persians—conquered Egypt. Even during these times dynasties of Egyptian pharaohs continued to reign. As you will read, it was not until the 300's B.C. that native rule in Egypt finally came to an end.

CHECKUP

1. IDENTIFY: hieroglyphics, monarchy, Menes, dynasty, Hyksos, empire, polytheism, monotheism, Rameses II.

2. LOCATE: Nile River, Upper Egypt, Lower Egypt, Nubia, Thebes, Tell el Amarna.

3. Explain this statement: "All Egypt is the gift of the Nile."

4. How did the ruler of Egypt get his title? What does it mean?

5. What were the new ideas taught by Akhenaton? Why was there opposition to Akhenaton's religious reforms?

The culture of ancient Egypt reached impressive heights

The culture of a group of people, as you have read, refers to their way of life. The culture of the Egyptian people extended over many centuries. However, it was a remarkably stable culture. Change did occur, of course, but it came about very gradually. This stability resulted partly from favorable conditions, particularly the regular Nile floods and Egypt's protected geographic location.

Farming and trade

Farm land in Egypt was divided into large estates. Farming was done by peasants, who used crude hoes or wooden plows. Even these simple tools produced good crops because of the rich soil, warm climate, and irrigation. The peasants kept only part of the crop. The rest went to the pharaoh for rents and taxes, which were paid by giving grain, cattle, and wine.

Wheat and barley were the chief grain crops. Flax was grown to be spun and woven into linen. Cotton was an important Egyptian crop, just as it is today, and was woven into cloth.

Ancient Egypt produced more food than its people required. The surplus was traded with other peoples for products that Egypt needed. Egyptians were among the first to build seagoing

22

Daily life in ancient Egypt

As Egyptian civilization advanced, certain occupations became important in the daily life of the people. For example, the belief in an afterlife gave rise to the complex craft of embalming the dead. A painting from the side of a coffin (left) shows the jackal-headed god of funerals binding a body with strips of cloth. The hieroglyphic carving from the base of a statue (below) announces a funeral offering and bears the name of a pharaoh's son. The scribe (center left) probably knew more than 600 hieroglyphic signs. Responsible for keeping the tax rolls, scribes were among the most respected members of Egyptian society.

Making and sailing boats were also essential occupations in ancient Egypt. On the Nile River, winds from the desert swept sailboats upstream, while currents pushed them down. The magnificent model of a boat (bottom) was found in the tomb of a pharaoh.

ships. These ships sailed into the Mediterranean and Aegean seas, the Red Sea, and along the African coast. Merchants riding donkeys and camels traveled overland into western Asia and deep into Africa (see map, page 20). They traveled in **caravans**—groups of people traveling together for safety over long distances.

Social classes

Egyptian society, as you have read, was divided into two classes—an upper class consisting of the royal family, nobles, and priests, and a lower class including everyone else. Within the lower class it was possible for people to improve their status. But, for the most part, Egyptian social classes were rigid.

Women were the equals of their husbands in social and business affairs. An Egyptian woman could own property in her own right and could leave it to her daughter. In many ways, Egyptian women at that time were better off than women in other cultures of the Middle East.

Architecture and the arts

When you think of Egypt, it is likely that the first things that come to your mind are the pyramids and the huge stone figure of the Sphinx. They still stand after nearly 5,000 years. Pyramids were built as tombs for the pharaohs. During the period of the Old Kingdom, Egyptians believed that only the pharaohs, who were considered gods, were sure to have life after death. Therefore, it was important that the pharaohs' burial places reflect their splendid position. It was important also that their remains and the objects provided for their well-being in the next world be protected and preserved.

There are about 80 pyramids still standing. Most of them are in groups along the west bank of the Nile. The best known are at Giza, including the Great Pyramid, which was built about 2600 B.C. This gigantic structure is more than half a mile (800 meters) around at the base and is 450 feet (137 meters) high. It consists of over two million blocks of stone, each of which weighs 2.5 tons (2.3 metric tons).

The building of these pyramids obviously required skillful engineering. Egyptian architects and engineers were among the best in the ancient world. They built ramps—sloping walkways along which enormous stones were pushed or pulled to raise them above the ground. Levers were also used for moving heavy objects.

Like their architecture, other arts of the Egyptians were of high quality. In addition to large-scale works, sculptors also made small, lifelike statues of kings and sacred animals from copper, bronze, stone, or wood.

Egyptians decorated many of their buildings with paintings showing everyday life. Scenes might include artisans at work, farmers harvesting grain, and people enjoying banquets. Egyptians developed a distinctive way of drawing the human figure. The head was shown in profile, the shoulders facing forward, and the feet in profile. In spite of a certain stiffness, the paintings are colorful examples of the Egyptian enjoyment of life.

Science and mathematics

At an early date the Egyptians invented a lunar calendar, that is, one based on the moon's movements. As you have read, such a calendar caused difficulties because it did not fill the entire year. Then, somewhere in the Nile Valley, someone noticed that a very bright star began to appear above the horizon just before the floods came. This was the star we now call Sirius, the Dog Star. The time between one rising of Sirius to the next was 365 days, almost exactly a full year. The ancient Egyptians based their year on this cycle, dividing it into 12 months of 30 days each. This system left them with five extra days, which they used for holidays and feasting.

Numbering the years was no great problem. At first, years were known by an outstanding event— the year of the great flood or the year the locusts swarmed over the fields. Later, people used the reigns of pharaohs—the first, second, or twentieth year of the reign of a certain pharaoh. Using this method, we can trace back the yearly record in Egypt to about 2780 B.C. Some historians believe that this is the earliest recorded date in history that can be firmly established in terms of our own system of dating.

Early in their history the Egyptians recognized the need for exact measurements and for a system of mathematics. They developed a number system

Funeral Mask of a Pharaoh

One of the most beautiful treasures in the world is this life-size funeral mask of the pharaoh Tutankhamen. The discovery of his tomb in 1922 captured the imagination of people around the world. What was extraordinary about the find was that the tomb had not been robbed of its treasures. It contained over 5,000 works of art, which revealed to scholars many aspects of Egyptian life.

The mask is made of beaten gold, inlaid with jewels and colored glass. It shows Tutankhamen as the handsome youth he was when he died, more than 3,200 years ago, at the age of 18. The decorative beard on the mask is a symbol of Osiris, the god of the dead. On the headdress are symbols of the vulture and cobra goddesses. They represent Upper and Lower Egypt.

based on 10, similar to the decimal system we use today. In arithmetic they used fractions as well as whole numbers. They used geometry to fix the boundaries of fields after the flood waters went down and to lay out canals and irrigation ditches.

The Egyptians also made discoveries in medicine. They knew a great deal about the human body and used this knowledge in treating illness and in preserving bodies. *The Book of Healing Diseases,* written during the period of the Old Kingdom, classified diseases according to symptoms and prescribed treatments. Some of the treatments were only magic spells, but many others were more scientific, specifying herbs and drugs.

Education and religion

It would have been impossible for the Egyptians to gather and pass on all their knowledge without a system of education. Egyptian education was partly religious, and schools were usually in temples. Most education, however, was aimed at training clerks, or scribes, for the government. For a fee clerks would read or write for those who could not. Clerks might also be employed by the wealthy to keep accounts. They might even rise high in government service.

Religion was extremely important in Egyptian life. The Egyptians worshiped the sun and moon. In early days each village and district had its local god or gods. In time some of these were accepted and worshiped throughout the country. Each god had an animal symbol, and it was considered sacred. Among the sacred animals were the cat, the bull, the crocodile, and the scarab (a beetle).

The afterlife. At first, Egyptians believed that only the pharaohs and a few others chosen by the pharaohs had an afterlife, or a life after death. Later, Egyptians believed that everyone, including animals, had a life after death. They thought

25

that the spirit would be happier if the body were preserved. Therefore, they worked out a way of preserving the body by mummification—that is, treating it with chemicals so that it would dry and keep for centuries.

The mummy was placed in a tomb and provided with clothing, food, jewelry, tools, weapons, and even servants in the form of sculptured or painted figures. These were considered necessary for the long journey to a place called the Realm of the Dead. The number and richness of the articles in the tomb depended on the importance of the dead person. On this final journey it was thought that the soul would be attacked by serpents and demons. To guard against these dangers, the Egyptians put in the tomb *The Book of the Dead.* This was a collection of hymns, prayers, and magic chants that formed a kind of guide to the afterlife.

When the soul reached the Realm of the Dead, it entered the Hall of Truth, where the beloved god Osiris sat in judgment. Here the soul had to testify to the kind of life it had lived on earth. It had to take an oath that it had not lied or murdered or been proud.

When the soul had testified and taken the oath, it was weighed on a great scale against a feather, the symbol of truth. If the scales balanced, the soul had spoken the truth. It could then enter into the presence of the sun god and enjoy eternal happiness. But if its sins outweighed the feather, the soul was thrown to a horrible monster called the Eater of the Dead. Thus, good character and a good life were very important because they were believed to be rewarded in the afterlife.

Egyptian tombs. Because of the precious articles buried with the dead, Egyptian graves were constantly being robbed. The pyramids built during the Old Kingdom were opened and their contents stolen. During the Middle Kingdom and New Kingdom, the Egyptians cut elaborate secret tombs into cliff walls. But thieves robbed most of these tombs, too. In 1922 A.D., however, archeologists discovered the previously unopened grave of Tutankhamen. This tomb, cut into rock, dated from the 1300's B.C. It contained gold, objects decorated with jewels, furniture, and household items that have taught us much about life in ancient Egypt. The possessions from Tutankhamen's tomb may be seen in museums today.

1. IDENTIFY: pyramids, Sphinx, *The Book of Healing Diseases, The Book of the Dead,* sacred animals.

2. What were four important agricultural products of the ancient Egyptians?

3. Why did the Egyptians build the pyramids? What did Egyptians believe about life after death?

4. How did Egyptians apply their understanding of mathematics to both agriculture and construction?

3

Sumerian civilization arose along the Tigris and Euphrates rivers

While one great civilization—the Egyptian—dominated the Nile Valley for thousands of years, a number of civilizations rose and fell in an area of western Asia called the Fertile Crescent.

The Fertile Crescent

How did the Fertile Crescent get its name? Look at the map on page 27. Note the light green strip of land that begins at the Isthmus of Suez. It extends north along the eastern end of the Mediterranean Sea and swings over in a half-circle south of Asia Minor and Armenia. Then it curves southeast, following the valley of the Tigris and Euphrates rivers, and ends at the Persian Gulf. Because of its shape it is called a crescent—a word that describes the first-quarter moon. Parts of this crescent of land were fertile.

Like Egypt, the Fertile Crescent was surrounded by deserts and mountains. One great difference in geography, however, made the history of the two areas quite different. The deserts and hills around the Fertile Crescent were not as barren as those around Egypt. Thus there was enough grass and other plant life there to feed tribes of wandering herders. These people were wild, fierce, and toughened by their way of life. They envied the richer, easier life of the people who lived in the valley. At various times the people of the Fertile Crescent grew weak. Then the herders conquered them and settled down.

The story of ancient Egypt was the story of one people living in one place. Sometimes they expanded their territory, and at other times they were conquered by enemies from outside. But throughout ancient times, Egypt was the home of people living in essentially the same land as their ancestors.

The situation was quite different in the Fertile Crescent. Here people were on the move. They came into the region from outside, conquered it and extended their empires, and then in turn were overthrown by new invaders.

Migration—that is, the movement of groups of people from place to place—is one of the most important factors in history. Sometimes people are forced to migrate when their crops fail or when they fear attack by an enemy. You have already read about how people migrated to warmer climates during the Ice Age. Sometimes people migrate to conquer new land, seize wealth, or overthrow their hostile neighbors. The history of the Fertile Crescent is the story of a succession of migrating peoples.

The Tigris-Euphrates Valley

The Tigris and Euphrates rivers both begin in the hills of Armenia. The Tigris flows about 1,100 miles (1,770 kilometers) to the Persian Gulf. The Euphrates, to the west, flows about 1,700 miles (2,740 kilometers) before reaching the Persian Gulf. At one point the two rivers come within 20 miles (30 kilometers) of each other, then spread apart until the valley between them is more than 150 miles (240 kilometers) wide. They then flow together at the Persian Gulf.

The Tigris has the greater amount of water. It cuts a deep path in the earth, lowering the water level below that of the land and making irrigation difficult. The Euphrates, too, creates problems for those who live along its banks. Its current is fast and violent, carrying five times the amount of silt, or soil, the Nile does. Because this silt builds up at the bottom of the river, the Euphrates often overflows and floods the surrounding land. Canals and dikes have to be dug, to bring water to the fields and also to carry away excess water.

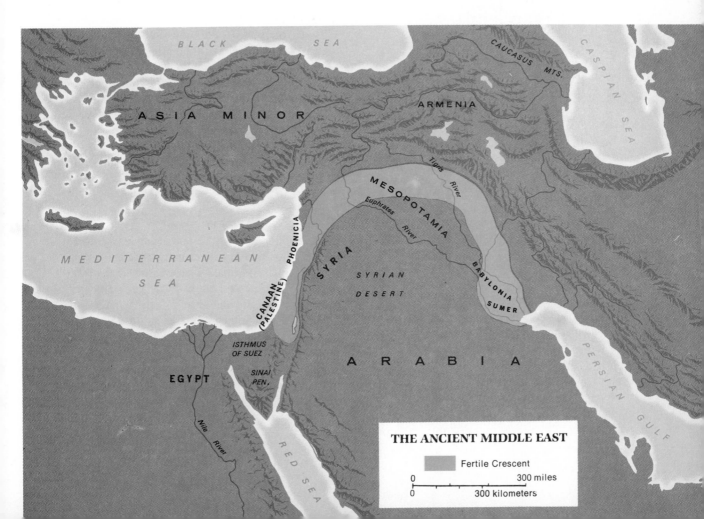

THE ANCIENT MIDDLE EAST

Fertile Crescent

0 — 300 miles
0 — 300 kilometers

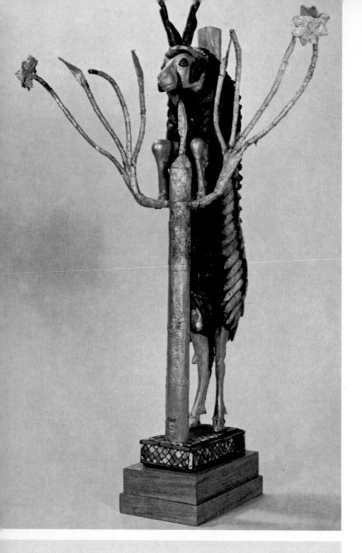

Sacred Sumerian Animal

This beautiful statue of an animal peering through the branches of a flowering tree was crafted in Sumer about 4,500 years ago. It is made of wood decorated with gold, lapis lazuli, silver, and mother-of-pearl. Scholars think the animal may be a goat or a ram. The combination of the flowering tree and the animal leads some to think that the statue had an agricultural meaning. Sumer was in an area with little rain and depended on water from the unpredictable flooding of the Tigris and Euphrates rivers. Each spring farmers worried whether the floods would come on time and bring enough water for the year. The animal may have been used in ceremonies to ensure the fertility of the fields.

The flood of the Tigris and the Euphrates, unlike that of the Nile, is unpredictable. It may come anytime between the beginning of April and the early part of June. Not only is the time unpredictable, but the extent of the flood cannot be guessed. It is no wonder that the people of the valley thought of nature and the gods as being angry and unreasonable. Their world was quite different from that of the Egyptians, who generally saw only goodness in nature.

Various names have been given to certain regions of the Tigris-Euphrates Valley. Mesopotamia (meaning "between rivers") is the name the Greeks gave to the northern part. The southern part has usually been known as Babylonia. The entire valley is today part of the nation of Iraq.

Sumer and its people

The lowest part of the Tigris-Euphrates Valley—that is, the southern portion of Babylonia—contains the rich soil carried by the rivers as they pour into the Persian Gulf. This area, called Sumer, was especially fertile. Here Neolithic people settled and grew crops.

Two groups of people moved into Sumer from the east and mingled with the original inhabitants. They created a culture known as Sumerian. By 3000 B.C. these people were using metal and had developed a kind of writing.

The Sumerian culture was at least as rich and as advanced as that of Egypt. In many ways the Sumerians were even more original than the Egyptians. In fact, some historians believe that civilization began in Sumer.

City-states

Early in their history the Sumerians developed a kind of government called the **city-state.** This was a town or city and the surrounding land it controlled. The people believed that each city-state belonged to a god or gods. Priests managed the god's land and interpreted the god's will to the people. They also directed worship and governed the city.

The many Sumerian city-states were seldom united under a single government. There was much rivalry among them, particularly over land boundaries and water rights. This inability to unite weakened the Sumerians. They were finally conquered by a people who were warriors, as you will read later in this chapter.

The Sumerians had three distinct social classes. At the top was a privileged class of nobles, including priests and government officials. Next came a group of merchants and artisans. At the bottom were peasants and slaves.

Sumerian writing

Sumerian writing looked quite different from Egyptian writing. While Egyptian hieroglyphics were carved on stone, Sumerian writing began as marks pressed into clay tablets. Because the writers used a pointed stick, called a stylus, most of the signs were combinations of wedge shapes. The Latin word for "wedge" is *cuneus,* so we call this writing **cuneiform** (kyoo·NEE·uh·form) writing. There were about 600 cuneiform signs.

The papyrus reed, which the Egyptians used to make paper, did not grow in Sumer. So the Sumerians did not learn to make paper. Instead, throughout their history, they wrote on clay. They rolled out a lump of soft clay, made their wedge-shaped marks on it, and then allowed the clay tablet to dry until it was hard. Hardened clay would last for many years. It might shatter, but the pieces could always be fitted together.

Farming and trade

Most of the Sumerian people were farmers who grew grain, vegetables, and dates. Their domestic animals included cows, sheep, and goats, as well as oxen to pull plows and donkeys to pull carts and chariots. Sumerians developed a dairy industry very early. They wove fine woolen goods and raised flax for linen.

All the land, as you have read, belonged to the god of the city-state. Most of it was farmed in his behalf—that is, to support his temples and priests. Some of the land, however, was given to wealthy persons, and other parts were rented.

Enough food was produced to allow many people to work as traders and as artisans. Sumerians were trading with other peoples of the ancient Middle East before 3000 B.C. Merchants had agents in far places. Others traveled from city to city to sell Sumerian products.

Architecture, engineering, and science

The Sumerians used sun-dried clay bricks to build houses. Their brick structures did not last as long as the stone buildings of the Egyptians, but they were well planned and well built. The Sumerians may have invented several important architectural designs. One was the arch, a curved structure over an opening. The arch is one of the strongest forms in building. By combining several arches, the Sumerians built rounded roofs in the shape of domes or vaults. They also knew how to use the ramp and even built sewers beneath their buildings. Over the sewers were arches made of brick.

The most striking Sumerian buildings were the temples known as **ziggurats.** They were built on hills that were specially constructed on the flat land of the valley. A Sumerian temple was built in layers, each one smaller than the one below, so that it looked somewhat like a wedding cake. On some ziggurats each story was painted a different color. Usually there were seven stories, with the top one serving as the shrine of the god.

Sumerian engineers and scientists made many important discoveries. Some scholars think that Sumerians were the first Neolithic people to develop and use the wheel. Later the Sumerians developed some of the principles of algebra. In mathematics they used a system of numbers based on 60. Large numbers were stated in 60's—for example, 120 was expressed as two 60's and 180 as three 60's. They divided a circle into 360 degrees (six 60's), each degree into 60 minutes, each minute into 60 seconds. When you look at a compass or a watch, you are seeing a principle developed by the Sumerians thousands of years ago.

The Sumerians developed a calendar with 12 months based on the movement of the moon. When the passage of years made their calendar inaccurate, they added a thirteenth month to bring it back into line with the seasons.

Education and religion

The Sumerians considered education very important, although only upper-class boys were educated. Schools were usually in the temples and were run by priests. Writing and spelling were the chief subjects. Students learned to write by copying religious books and songs. They also studied reading, history, mathematics, foreign languages, and map making. There was advanced education in law, medicine, and surgery. Much time was spent learning divination, that is, the attempt to predict the future from various signs and omens.

The Sumerians were polytheistic—they believed in many gods. Their gods were identified with the forces of nature, such as the sun and moon. The people believed the gods had the same habits and feelings as ordinary humans but were much more powerful.

Sumerians did not have a firm set of beliefs about a future life. They did not believe in reward in heaven or punishment in hell, but they did believe that there was some sort of life after death. They were afraid of ghosts. They thought, for instance, that if they did not bury with the dead such personal objects as jewelry, their spirits would be displeased and would return to haunt their homes and families.

CHECKUP

1. IDENTIFY: city-state, stylus, cuneiform writing, ziggurat, divination.

2. LOCATE: Fertile Crescent, Babylonia, Mesopotamia, Persian Gulf, Sumer.

3. Where do the Tigris and Euphrates rivers rise? Where do they empty? Why did the inhabitants of the Tigris-Euphrates Valley regard nature as a hostile force?

4. Describe the Sumerian contributions to architecture.

5. Explain the mathematical ideas that originated in the Sumerian culture.

Several empires were established in the Fertile Crescent

Sumerian city-states, as you have read, were not united under one government. This lack of unity was a fatal weakness.

After 2400 B.C. the Sumerians were conquered by a people who also lived in the region of Meso-

potamia. Unlike the Sumerians, these people spoke a Semitic language, that is, a language closely related to the modern Hebrew and Arabic. The most powerful of the Semitic kings was Sargon of Akkad, who established a great empire that united Mesopotamia and extended as far west as Syria. This empire—the Sargonid Empire—lasted about 150 years. When it ended, Sumerian city-states once again became prosperous.

However, new waves of invaders soon entered Mesopotamia. A new and powerful Semitic state arose, this time centered at the large new city of Babylon.

Hammurabi and his laws

About 1792 B.C. a strong ruler named Hammurabi came to power in Babylon and conquered the upper Tigris-Euphrates Valley (see map, page 31). Hammurabi was more than a great military leader. He turned out to be a wise and just political leader as well. He is best known for the Code of Hammurabi, a collection of laws passed under his direction.

Hammurabi's code had 282 laws. These laws controlled all aspects of life in Babylon. Agriculture was carefully regulated. For example, people who failed to cultivate their fields or to keep the irrigation canals and ditches in good condition were punished. Some laws concerned commerce and industry, with provisions regarding wages, hours, and working conditions. There were laws dealing with property rights, contracts, and bankruptcy. Others dealt with marriage and divorce. The laws were enforced by judges, under the supervision of the king's advisers and officials.

The laws of Hammurabi gave some degree of justice to everyone. In that sense, they were a real advance over the political and social customs of the rest of the ancient world. The laws regarding punishment, however, were harsh. The idea of punishment was "an eye for an eye, a tooth for a tooth." If a man caused another to lose an eye, then his own eye was put out.

Justice was not equal for all people, however. If a wealthy man destroyed the eye of a poor man, he did not lose his eye but merely paid a fine. A thief who could not repay what he had stolen was killed. If he had money, he had only to repay more than he had stolen.

Babylonian culture

Like the Sumerians, the people of Babylon—the Babylonians—were primarily farmers. They raised domesticated animals and grew large amounts of food. They also wove textiles that were not quite as fine as those of the Sumerians. However, as traders the Babylonians were even more successful than the Sumerians. They traded with other parts of the Fertile Crescent, with Egypt, and even with India.

The social organization of the Babylonians was also like that of the Sumerians. There was a nobility made up of priests and government officials, a middle class of artisans and merchants, and peasants and slaves on the lowest level.

Babylonian women seem to have had slightly fewer privileges than Egyptian women. However, their position was higher than that of most women of the time. Some ancient peoples considered women as property to be owned, to be treated as slaves. Babylonian women had legal and economic rights, and their property was protected. However, a man might sell his wife and children to pay his debts.

Babylonian women could be traders and merchants and could work in other professions. They could even become priests. There is some evidence that they were paid as much as men doing the same work.

Babylonian religion

The Babylonians took over many Sumerian religious ideas. Marduk, god of the city of Babylon, became the principal god. However, the old Sumerian gods remained. The Babylonians made many sacrifices to their gods for such things as good harvests or success in business. They believed that life after death was gloomy and hopeless.

Babylonian priests were as powerful as Sumerian priests. They had much influence because of the spells they used against evil spirits. They also claimed to have the power to predict the future.

The rise and fall of the Hittites

Many times in history, you will read of conquerors who adopted the culture of the people they con-

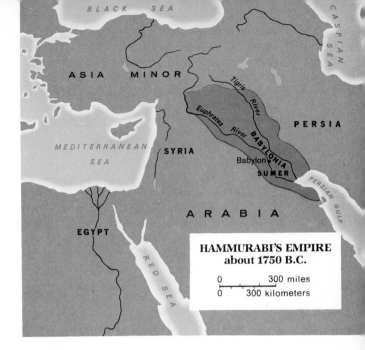

HAMMURABI'S EMPIRE
about 1750 B.C.

0   300 miles

0   300 kilometers

quered. This was certainly true of the Babylonians after they conquered the Sumerians. However, it was definitely not true of the Hittites. This warlike people invaded the Tigris-Euphrates Valley about 1600 B.C.

Originally, the Hittites were herders from the region north of the Black and Caspian seas. Like other peoples from this area about whom you will read later, they spoke an Indo-European language. About 2300 B.C. they migrated south and west to Asia Minor.

The Hittites were the first people to make extensive use of iron for weapons. Their most important achievement, however, was their laws, which were less brutal than the Code of Hammurabi. The punishment of death was given only for major crimes, such as rebellion. Hittite law called for a person to pay for any damage or injury that may have been done. For example, if a man broke the arm of someone else, he paid 20 pieces of silver rather than have his own arm broken. In determining the punishment, the law also took account of premeditation—that is, whether a person intended beforehand to commit the crime.

When the Hittites invaded the Tigris-Euphrates Valley, they conquered and looted Babylon itself. But the Hittites were too far from their homeland to control Babylonia permanently. They soon withdrew. However, they remained powerful in the western part of the Fertile Crescent, where

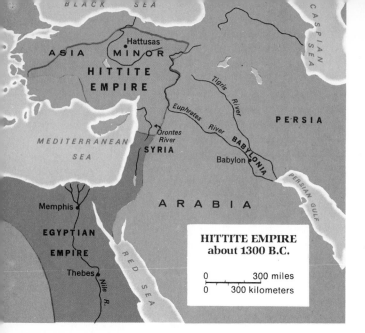

HITTITE EMPIRE
about 1300 B.C.

0   300 miles
0   300 kilometers

the mountains. They were overwhelmed in turn by the Assyrians, one of the most warlike of all ancient peoples.

The Assyrians first settled along the Tigris River, northwest of Babylonia. There they built the city-state Assur, named for their chief god. It was from the word *Assur* that both the region, Assyria, and the people took their name.

Assyrians were specialists in warfare. Instead of chariots they used cavalry—riders on horses. They used many iron weapons and invented the battering ram to break through the brick walls of cities they attacked. The Assyrians believed in frightening their enemies as much as possible. Captured enemy leaders were often skinned alive. The Assyrians frequently sent conquered peoples to other areas, replacing them with Assyrian colonists. In this way they controlled conquered lands more easily and gained many slaves. By 730 B.C. the Assyrians controlled Syria and Babylonia. Later, Egypt fell to them (see map, this page).

they came into conflict with the Egyptians. When the pharaoh Akhenaton neglected Egypt's role as a conqueror of neighboring regions, the Hittites were able to dominate Syria. They maintained their position against later pharaohs. About 1200 B.C. the Hittites were overwhelmed by the Sea Peoples, invaders from the Balkans, in southeastern Europe. You will read about the Sea Peoples later in this chapter.

The conquering Assyrians

The Hittite invasion of Babylon was followed by the conquest of the Kassites, another people from

Assyrian government

The Assyrian king had total power. Every priest and government official took orders from him and had to answer to him. He himself was responsible only to the god Assur, whose representative on earth he claimed to be.

The government of the Assyrian Empire was cruel and harsh, but it was also very efficient. Roads were built so that troops could move about quickly. The kings established a postal service to help the army receive information about rebellions. Governors ruled conquered lands, collected high taxes, and had to make regular and frequent reports to the king. Inspectors checked on their activities. An army was always stationed in a conquered area to keep the native people under control. This army usually consisted of **mercenaries**—professional soldiers who are paid to serve in a foreign army.

The Assyrians were the first people to work out an effective method of governing an empire. All other empires of the ancient Middle East were modeled on it. In other fields, however, the Assyrians contributed little to civilization. Their religion contained no new ideas. In literature, art, and sculpture they imitated other people, rather than creating their own styles.

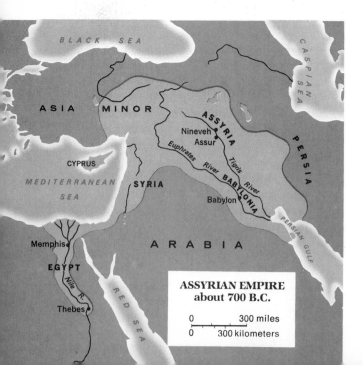

ASSYRIAN EMPIRE
about 700 B.C.

0   300 miles
0   300 kilometers

32

Assyrian greatness and decline

After the Assyrians became powerful, they made the city of Nineveh (NIN·uh·vuh) their capital. Here they displayed all the wealth taken from conquered countries and from the labor of slaves. Nineveh was the symbol of the pride and cruelty of the Assyrians. They tried to make it the strongest fortified city in the world. A huge double wall, 50 feet (15 meters) thick and 100 feet (30 meters) high, stretched around the city. There were 15 gates, each beautifully decorated and strongly defended. There was a large library in which scholars collected clay tablets from all over Assyria and Babylonia.

Powerful Nineveh was not powerful enough. As so often happens with a bully, Assyria had many enemies. Finally, in 612 B.C., three of them—the Chaldeans (kal·DEE·unz), Medes, and Persians—united their forces. Together they captured and destroyed Nineveh and later divided up the Assyrian Empire.

The Chaldeans

The people who organized and led the combination of armies that overthrew the Assyrians, and who took the largest part of the Assyrian Empire, were the Chaldeans. Under a wise ruler named Nebuchadnezzar (neb·uh·kud·NEZ·ur), who ruled from the capital city of Babylon between 605 and 562 B.C., they conquered most of the Fertile Crescent (see map, this page).

The Chaldeans of Babylon enjoyed a high standard of living and surrounded themselves with beautiful buildings. Perhaps the most impressive building of all was the palace of Nebuchadnezzar, which had an enormous courtyard and huge rooms. Its most unusual feature was the Hanging Gardens. There is a legend that Nebuchadnezzar's wife had lived in the mountains and was homesick on the flat plains of Babylonia. To please her, the king planted tropical plants and flowers on the roof of the palace. The Greeks regarded the Hanging Gardens of Babylon as one of the Seven Wonders of the World.

All the strength of the Chaldeans seemed to lie in the ability of Nebuchadnezzar. His successor was a religious fanatic like the Egyptian pharaoh Akhenaton. He opposed the priests, who then betrayed the city to the Persians. Thus the Chaldean Empire ended.

Like the Assyrians, the Chaldeans contributed little to civilization. They were deeply interested in astronomy, however, and correctly calculated the length of the year within 26 minutes. The Chaldeans also believed in astrology—the supposed influence of the positions of the stars on human affairs.

The mighty Persians

You have read of herders who lived north of the Caucasus Mountains, between the Black Sea and the Caspian Sea. Some of these peoples spoke Indo-European languages. About 1800 B.C. two such tribes, the Medes and the Persians, moved southeast to the area that is now Iran. This region has also been known as Persia, from which the people take their name. In time, both tribes became united under the Medes and joined the alliance that overthrew the cruel Assyrian Empire. After the Assyrian downfall in 612 B.C., the Medes and Persians occupied all of Iran and part of the northern Tigris-Euphrates Valley.

Cyrus, Darius, and Xerxes

About 550 B.C. Cyrus, a Persian and one of the greatest leaders in all history, led a revolt against the Medes. He defeated their king and became ruler of the two tribes. The Persians were fierce

(continued on page 36)

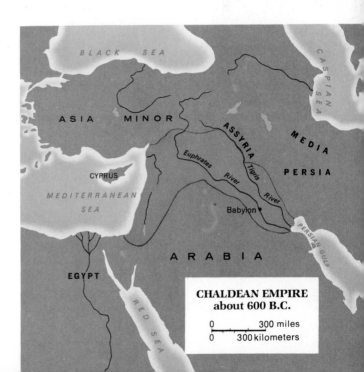

CHALDEAN EMPIRE about 600 B.C.

0   300 miles

0   300 kilometers

33

Peoples of the Fertile Crescent

Many peoples inhabited the Fertile Crescent, each possessing unique skills. The Assyrians were great warriors, who rode their horses into battle (near right), killing their enemies with arrows. Archers were paid from the plunder found in the captured cities. In contrast, the social qualities of the Sumerians are apparent in the sculpture of a courting couple (right).

The Hittites left many examples of hieroglyphics (far right) and an impressive legal system. Their laws were more lenient than the earlier Code of Hammurabi, the ruler of the Babylonians. Hammurabi brought order and unity to the many laws of the independent towns. His code is inscribed in cuneiform on the stele (below right), beneath a relief of him receiving inspiration from the sun god, Shamash.

Like other early peoples, the Babylonians were intrigued by the lion. They built a majestic approach to one of their temples and lined each wall with 60 glazed tile lions (opposite page). Sacred to the goddess Ishtar, the lion also figured prominently in Persia (below left). Here on a wall outside a palace at Persepolis, the lion of summer bites the bull of winter.

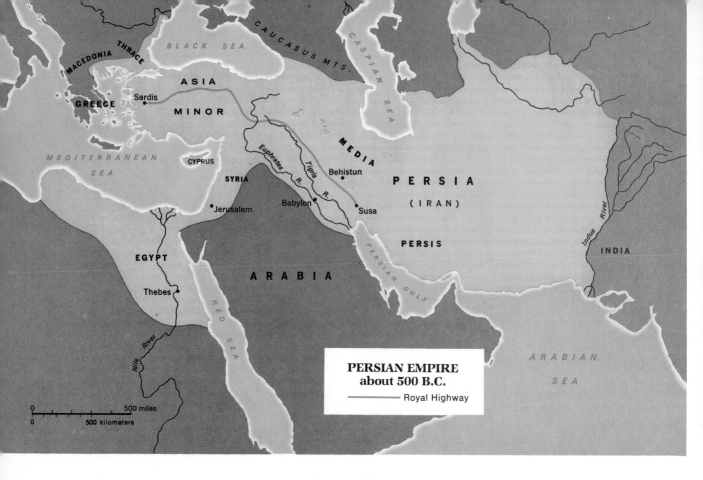

PERSIAN EMPIRE
about 500 B.C.
——— Royal Highway

fighters who made extensive use of soldiers on horseback and of archers using bows and arrows.

After defeating the king of the Medes, Cyrus began a series of conquests. He defeated the Chaldeans, captured Babylon, and took over the rest of the Fertile Crescent and Asia Minor. His son conquered Egypt.

A later Persian ruler, Darius the Great, added regions south and east of Iran as far as the Indus River in India, as well as parts of southeastern Europe (see map, this page). Both Darius and his son Xerxes (ZURK·seez) invaded Greece in the 400's B.C. As you will read in Chapter 5, they were unable to conquer it. Nevertheless, the Persians ruled the mightiest empire known up to that time.

Persian government

The early Persian kings were not only great generals but were also wise rulers. They were all-powerful in government, but they showed great concern for justice. Tax collection and the administration of justice were fair.

In governing their large empire, Persian rulers chose the best officials they could find, often from among the conquered peoples. They paid close attention to local customs and allowed the people they conquered to keep their own religion and laws. This tolerant practice won the favor of the priests and the loyalty of the people.

The Persians copied some things from the Assyrians, especially the kinds of officials that were used to govern the empire. They also extended the Assyrian road system. The most famous road, the Royal Highway, extended from Sardis in Asia Minor to Susa, one of the capitals of the empire. The roads were built mainly for the army and postal riders, but they were also used by merchants. There was a lively exchange of customs and ideas in the empire.

Persian religion

The greatest cultural contribution of the Persians was in religion. At first, like other early peoples, they worshiped many gods. Then, about 600 B.C., a great prophet and religious reformer completely changed their religious ideas. His name was Zoroaster (zoh·roh·AS·tur).

Zoroaster taught that the world was a place where human beings were trained for a future life. In the world there was a great struggle between the forces of good and evil. Human beings could choose sides and help in this struggle. Those who chose the good would be rewarded with eternal life. Those who chose evil would face darkness and misery after death. In the far, far distant future, the forces of good would finally triumph. Then the earth would disappear, for it would have served its purpose as the stage on which the great conflict had taken place.

Zoroaster's ideas, called Zoroastrianism, strongly influenced the lives of the Persians. According to him, nothing was so shameful as lying. Persian children were taught that they must always tell the truth. Getting into debt was considered a form of lying and therefore disgraceful.

The thinking of the Hebrews and, later, of the Christians seems to have been affected by Zoroaster's idea of a struggle between good and evil and a final judgment in which reward or punishment depended on human choice.

The decline of the Persians

The Persian kings who followed Darius and Xerxes were not as strong or as wise. As time went on, both the government and the army grew weak. In 331 B.C., as you will see, Alexander the Great conquered the Persian Empire.

CHECKUP

1. IDENTIFY: Nebuchadnezzar, Hanging Gardens, astrology, Cyrus, Darius, Zoroastrianism.

2. LOCATE: Babylon, Nineveh, Caucasus Mountains, Persia, Indus River.

3. (a) List five of the main ideas of the Code of Hammurabi. (b) How did the Hittite laws vary from Hammurabi's code?

4. Describe the privileges that women had in Babylonian society.

5. List briefly the accomplishments of: (a) the Babylonians, (b) the Hittites, (c) the Assyrians, (d) the Chaldeans, (e) the Persians. Which do you believe to be the most important? Why?

The Phoenicians and the Hebrews made lasting contributions

In this section you will read about the peoples who lived in the western end of the Fertile Crescent. This narrow strip of land along the Mediterranean Sea today forms portions of the modern nations of Egypt, Israel, Jordan, Lebanon, and Syria. The historic name of the northern part, however, is Phoenicia. The southern section had several names at different times in history, including Canaan, Israel, and Palestine.

The Sea Peoples and the Philistines

Around 1200 B.C. this western portion of the Fertile Crescent was disturbed by tribes of warlike invaders from southeast Europe and from areas around the Aegean Sea. Some of the invaders came in ships, while others moved over land. Together these tribes are known as the Sea Peoples.

The Sea Peoples destroyed the Hittites. One group sacked the city of Troy in Asia Minor. Some of the Sea Peoples even wandered as far as the island of Sardinia, in the western Mediterranean. Not long after 1200 B.C., the pharaoh Ramses III defeated an attack by the Sea Peoples on Egypt. But some of the invaders remained on the coast and set up city-states. These people were known as Philistines. The Philistines became the rivals of another group of people who lived there—the Hebrews.

To the north lived the Phoenicians, after whom the region is named. Of all the peoples who lived in the western part of the Fertile Crescent, the Hebrews and the Phoenicians had the greatest impact on civilization. Their influence came about not because of wars they fought or empires they built. It came, instead, from their culture and their ideas.

The Phoenicians

Phoenicia was a loose union of city-states, each with a king. On the map on page 39, notice the cities of Tyre and Sidon. Both of these seaports

Peoples of the Fertile Crescent

3000–2000 B.C.	Sumerians
2300–1200 B.C.	Hittites
1800–1600 B.C.	Babylonians
1200–586 B.C.	Hebrews
1000–700 B.C.	Phoenicians
900–612 B.C.	Assyrians
612–539 B.C.	Chaldeans
550–331 B.C.	Persians

became world famous. The Phoenician city-states were rarely independent. Throughout their history they were either conquered by or under the influence of the Egyptians, Hittites, Assyrians, Chaldeans, Persians, and Greeks.

Phoenicia had hills and mountains, and there was little fertile land. No large-scale farming was possible, and because of the high Lebanon Mountains, the people did not migrate eastward. From very early times the people of Phoenicia turned to the sea and to commerce for their living. They became the greatest traders of the ancient world.

The Phoenicians built seagoing ships very early in their history. To us these ships seem small and frail, but the Phoenicians were skillful and fearless sailors. Propelled by sails and oars, Phoenician ships traveled all over the Mediterranean Sea. Some historians believe that the Phoenicians sailed as far as Britain for tin. They also sailed around Africa. In those days, it took great courage to make such long voyages.

Articles of trade

Phoenicia did not have minerals. The only important natural resource was lumber—the beautiful cedar trees of the Lebanon Mountains that many ancient peoples used in their building. Despite the lack of minerals, the Phoenicians were skilled artisans. They bought the metals of other lands and created beautiful objects of gold, silver, copper, and bronze. From the Egyptians they learned how to make exquisite glass.

Along their seacoast the Phoenicians found a shellfish called murex, which they used to make purple dye. Phoenician woolen cloth, dyed purple, was a valuable possession in the ancient world. It was so expensive that only the wealthy could afford it. That is why purple became the color worn by kings—the royal purple.

The Phoenicians sold their own fabrics, metal goods, and glassware. But they also traded goods manufactured by other peoples and were shrewd in business.

Phoenician colonies

Between 1000 and 700 B.C., Phoenician trade increased throughout the Middle East. The Hittite and Egyptian empires had disintegrated. The Phoenician city-states were united under Tyre, the center for trade. Phoenician colonies were established throughout the Mediterranean region.

The Phoenicians set up colonies as centers for trade on the islands of Sicily, Sardinia, and Malta. Farther west, beyond the Mediterranean Sea, they established a colony on the site of the modern city of Cádiz, Spain.

The Phoenicians boasted that they had founded almost 300 cities on the northern coast of Africa. The greatest of these was Carthage.

Phoenician culture

The Phoenicians imitated the culture of other peoples. They copied their government and most of their culture from the Egyptians and Babylonians. Through trading they indirectly spread the knowledge of what they had learned throughout the Mediterranean area.

The religion of the Phoenicians was harsh. They worshiped many gods and sometimes sacrificed their own children to win favor from the gods. The Phoenicians did not believe in an afterlife.

The most important contribution of the Phoenicians was the alphabet. Earlier there had been similar alphabets in Canaan and in the Sinai Peninsula, but the Phoenicians developed the alphabet that became the model for later Western alphabets.

The spread of the alphabet is a good example of how ideas can be spread by commerce. To the practical Phoenicians, writing was useful in their business for recording contracts and drawing up bills. Phoenician commerce spread the knowledge of alphabetical writing throughout the Mediterranean world.

The Greeks adopted and improved the Phoenician alphabet by adding signs for vowel sounds. Later the Romans copied this alphabet from the Greeks. It is the Roman alphabet that you are now reading and that is used today in the Western world. Thus the letter symbols of our alphabet trace back through the Romans and Greeks to the improvements that were made long ago by the Phoenicians.

Canaan

To the south of Phoenicia was a small strip of land known as Canaan. (In later times this region was called Palestine.) Canaan had no forests and there were few minerals or other natural resources. As you can see on the map on this page, the land consists of two regions. The northern part is watered by the Jordan River. There the soil is fertile enough to grow grain, olives, figs, and grapes. The southern region, around and south of the Dead Sea, is mostly desert. The soil there is poor and rocky.

Because of its location Canaan was involved in the history of all the ancient Middle Eastern civilizations. In one way, its location was an advantage because it lay along the great land bridge between Asia and Africa. Through Canaan ran the route from Egypt to the Tigris-Euphrates Valley. The merchants who carried the goods, and also the ideas, of these two great civilized regions traveled this route.

In another way, however, the location was not an advantage, for armies also passed along the route. The peoples of Canaan had to fight for their freedom against Egyptians, Hittites, Assyrians, Chaldeans, and Persians. They were conquered often, for they were not powerful.

The early Hebrews

Like the eastern part of the Fertile Crescent, Canaan was inhabited by a series of peoples. The people who had the greatest influence on their own times and on all later history were the Hebrews, or Jews. They did not always live in

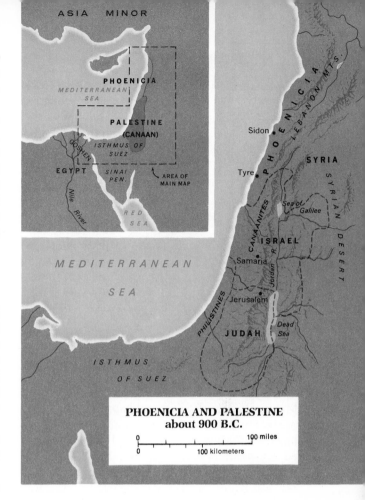

PHOENICIA AND PALESTINE
about 900 B.C.

0   100 miles
0   100 kilometers

Canaan. Abraham, according to the Bible the founder of the Hebrew people, once lived in Sumer. He left there and led his people across the Syrian Desert to the borders of northern Palestine. They went farther south and crossed the Isthmus of Suez into Egypt. They settled in the "Land of Goshen," east of the region where the Nile flows into the Mediterranean Sea.

These Hebrews lived peacefully in Egypt for some time, but eventually they fell from favor. Some scholars believe that one group of Hebrews entered Egypt along with the Hyksos in the 1700's B.C. When the Hyksos were expelled in the 1500's, the Hebrews in Egypt were forced to work as slaves.

Then a great leader, Moses, arose among the Hebrews and led his people out of slavery and into the deserts of the Sinai Peninsula. The traditions about Moses and the escape from Egypt are described in the Bible in the books of Exodus, Numbers, and Deuteronomy.

How do we know?

SACRED BOOKS Most of the world's religions regard a special set of writings as holy. In both Judaism and Christianity, the holy books are referred to as the Bible, although Christians include the New Testament and Jews do not. The five books of Moses have special significance for Jews and are called the Torah.

By reading scriptures, one gains an understanding of the faith that is founded on them, and the attitudes and assumptions of each faith. For example, an important reason for the strength of family life and respect for elders that has been traditional with Jews is the Torah's clear position on this subject. The central laws of the Torah, the Ten Commandments, make the first rule of behavior toward other people, "Honor thy father and mother."

The Torah also tells us a great deal about the life of the Jews at the time that their faith was established. The slavery they endured in Egypt, their escape, and the sufferings of 40 years in the wilderness are all described with vivid details that we could not otherwise know. For similar reasons the New Testament is a unique source of information about the Holy Land in the time of Christ.

Establishing a homeland

Many of the Hebrews were unhappy in the deserts of the Sinai Peninsula. They and their ancestors had lived in Egypt for centuries. They had accepted Egyptian customs and worshiped Egyptian gods. They thought that life in Egypt, even in slavery, was better than life in the harsh desert. It was then, according to the Bible, that Moses went up Mount Sinai and came back to the Hebrews with the Ten Commandments—the moral laws revealed to him by the Hebrew God Yahweh, or Jehovah. Moses claimed that Canaan was a Promised Land. Inspired by his words, the Hebrews eventually traveled to Canaan.

The Hebrews who had come from Egypt joined those who had lived for so long on the borders of northern Canaan. By this time they were all desert tribes again, hardened by the harsh desert life. But establishing a homeland in Canaan was not easy. The good land in the northern part was held by a people known as the Canaanites. The Philistines were settled along the coast. Both groups fought hard to hold on to their land. The struggle lasted for more than 100 years. The Canaanites were the first to be conquered, so that some of the Hebrews were able to settle down in the Jordan Valley. The Philistines were fiercer. The Hebrews drove them closer to the seacoast but never conquered them completely.

A new government and new customs

As nomads the Hebrews had been divided into twelve tribes. Some tribes had religious and military leaders called judges. The long years of fighting, however, made it desirable for the tribes to unite under one king. The first king of the united kingdom called Israel was Saul. He was succeeded by David, then Solomon.

The Hebrews did not remain united. Those in the north settled down in towns, making their living by farming. They adopted the customs of the conquered Canaanites, and many worshiped the Canaanite gods instead of Yahweh, the Hebrew God. Southern Palestine remained a rural region of herders, where people clung to their old ideas, ways of living, and religion.

In southern Palestine, David occupied the city of Jerusalem and made it a royal city. His son, Solomon, built palaces there and a great temple for Yahweh. The cost was enormous for a poor country. Taxes were heavy, and many were forced to work on the great buildings without pay.

At the end of Solomon's reign, in 922 B.C., there was a revolution and the kingdom split into two parts. The northern area became the kingdom of Israel, with its capital at Samaria. The southern part, situated around the Dead Sea, became the kingdom of Judah, with Jerusalem as the capital (see map, page 39).

The Hebrew kingdoms were not strong enough to withstand invasions from the east. The Assyrians captured Samaria and conquered Israel about 722 B.C. They captured many Jews and made them slaves. Later, in 586 B.C., the Chaldeans captured Judah and its capital, Jerusalem. They destroyed Solomon's temple and took the southern Hebrews into captivity. But after Cyrus, the Persian king, conquered the Chaldeans, he allowed the Hebrews to return to Palestine and to rebuild the temple at Jerusalem. Thereafter, however, the Jews were conquered by one people after another.

Jewish law and the Old Testament

The Jewish code of laws included the Ten Commandments as well as laws developed during later periods. It is called Mosaic law, after Moses. Mosaic law, like the Code of Hammurabi, demanded "an eye for an eye," but it set a much higher value on human life. Although Jewish law accepted slavery, for it was the custom of the ancient world, the law demanded kindness for slaves. Hammurabi's code punished a slave more severely than a free person for the same crime. Jewish laws also required kindness to the poor and to strangers, as did Babylonian laws. Mosaic law was most severe against witchcraft and sacrifices to idols. These were crimes punished by death. In Hebrew thinking, people needed only to trust in Yahweh and the religious leaders.

The great Hebrew work of literature is the Old Testament of the Bible. Its 39 books tell the story of the creation of the world, the special mission of the Hebrews, their escape from slavery in Egypt, and the progress of their history and beliefs over a thousand years. The history is told in about one third of the books. The rest is poetry, laws, religious instruction, and prophecy.

Prophets were not necessarily thought of as people who could predict the future, though some said they could. Rather, they were considered great religious and moral thinkers. The message they conveyed—in such phrases as "a soft answer turneth away wrath," "there is no peace unto the wicked," and "thou shalt love thy neighbor as thyself"—has remained the foundation for moral and ethical behavior ever since. And the stirring language in which the Old Testament was written has inspired every generation of writers and poets.

Judaism

The religion of the Hebrews, called Judaism, was great partly because it was able to change throughout history. The early Hebrews worshiped Yahweh as a God who belonged to them alone. He was what might be called a tribal war god. According to the Ten Commandments, Yahweh was a jealous God. If people sinned against God, not only would they be punished, but also their children and generations to follow. This was a God to fear, not to love.

The Hebrews changed their idea of Yahweh partly because of their many sufferings and partly because of the teachings and writings of their prophets. In general, the prophets insisted that Yahweh was more concerned with a person's moral behavior than with religious rituals.

The Jews came to think of Yahweh as a loving father, a God who lived in the hearts of his worshipers. They began to think of Yahweh as the God of all peoples. Other ancient peoples thought of their gods as having human qualities, but as more powerful. To the Jews, Yahweh was not like a human being but was a spiritual force. The kings of other ancient peoples claimed to be gods or the representatives of gods in order to gain power. Jewish kings were not gods. Only Yahweh was divine.

Belief in one God, as you have read earlier, is called monotheism. Because of its emphasis on ethics, or proper conduct, the Jewish form of monotheism is often called **ethical monotheism.** It is the most important contribution of the Jews to Western civilization.

CHECKUP

1. IDENTIFY: Abraham, Moses, Canaanites, Philistines, Saul, David, Solomon, prophets, ethical monotheism.

2. LOCATE: Tyre, Sidon, Jordan River, Dead Sea, Syrian Desert, Goshen, Jerusalem, Samaria.

3. How did the Phoenician sea trade benefit the peoples of the Mediterranean?

4. Why did the Hebrews leave Egypt? Why was it hard for the Hebrews to conquer Canaan?

5. What were three of the most important contributions of the Jews to our civilization?

CHAPTER REVIEW

6000	3000	2500	2000	1500	1000	500	B.C.	A.D.	500	2000

6000 B.C.	Beginning of Nile Valley Neolithic culture	**1792 B.C.**	Code of Hammurabi	
		1720 B.C.	Hyksos invasion of Egypt	
3100 B.C.	Unification of Upper and Lower Egypt by Menes	**1600 B.C.**	Hittite invasion of Tigris-Euphrates Valley	
3000 B.C.	Flourishing civilization in Sumer	**1550–1085 B.C.**	New Kingdom in Egypt	
2700–2181 B.C.	Old Kingdom in Egypt	**1379–1362 B.C.**	Akhenaton's religious revolution	
2000–1780 B.C.	Middle Kingdom in Egypt			

1000–700 B.C.	Height of Phoenician trade and colonization
922 B.C.	Division of Hebrew kingdom
612 B.C.	Downfall of Assyrians
605–562 B.C.	Rule of Nebuchadnezzar in Babylon

CHAPTER SUMMARY

Because of its geography and climate, Egypt was able to create a long-lasting and distinctive civilization. Around 3100 B.C. the country's two halves, Upper and Lower Egypt, were united into a single kingdom, ruled by pharaohs. The successive dynasties of pharaohs made Egypt a considerable power for some 2,000 years. But after the 1300's B.C., when there was a religious revolution under the pharaoh Akhenaton, the strength of the Egyptians steadily declined.

Under this long stable rule, the Egyptians developed a remarkable society and culture. The arts, literature, science, and religion became highly sophisticated. A complex and effective agricultural system was worked out. At the same time, strict divisions were maintained between social classes. It was a rigid, but also inventive, society.

In the Fertile Crescent a succession of conquests and empires led to a greater variety in societies and cultures. The Sumerians organized city-states, invented a new form of writing, and made many discoveries in architecture and engineering. The Babylonians were famous for their laws, written down in the Code of Hammurabi. The Assyrians were warriors and extended their conquests farther than any previous empire. They were succeeded eventually by the Persians, who established an even larger empire. The Persians developed a complex and effective government for their enormous territory. They also adopted an influential new religion, Zoroastrianism.

The Phoenicians never were as powerful as these other peoples, but they were the world's first great sea traders. They organized themselves in a confederation of cities and colonies around the Mediterranean that were linked by the sea. The alphabet that the Phoenicians developed and spread became the model for later Western alphabets.

The Hebrews were fewer in number than any of these peoples. However, they produced a system of law and a religious faith, Judaism, that has had a major influence on Western civilization. The great work of Judaism, the Old Testament, introduced the concept of ethical monotheism, which has shaped Western history ever since.

CHECKING WHAT YOU KNOW

1. Match each ruler at the left with an accomplishment at the right:

   a. Akhenaton
   b. Menes
   c. Hammurabi
   d. Nebuchadnezzar
   e. Cyrus

   1. Created a code of law in Babylon.
   2. Built the Hanging Gardens of Babylon.
   3. United Medes and Persians.
   4. United all Egypt into one kingdom.
   5. Founded a religion with Aton, the sun, as the only god.

2. Match each culture at the left with a location at the right:

   a. Persian
   b. Sumerian
   c. Hittite
   d. Hebrew
   e. Egyptian
   f. Phoenician

   1. Asia Minor
   2. all of western Asia
   3. Nile Valley
   4. Tyre and Sidon
   5. Palestine
   6. Tigris-Euphrates Valley

3. Describe the two different forms of writing in the Nile and Tigris-Euphrates valleys.

4. Compare the government of Egypt with that of the Persians as to:
   a. the role of the pharaoh or king
   b. the way the empire was organized and maintained
   c. the use of the army

PRACTICING YOUR SKILLS

1. **Making charts.** List the peoples of the Fertile Crescent. Next to each group, write down their most important achievements.

2. **Using maps.** Using the maps in Chapter 2, name the geographic barriers between civilizations. How do you think the peoples of early civilizations overcame these barriers?

3. **Making comparisons.** Using the information in the text, compare the legal systems of the Babylonians, the Hittites, and Hebrews. How are they similar? How do they differ? Under which system would you have preferred to live? Explain your choice.

4. **Analyzing information.** The environment has an enormous impact on how a group of people live and on the ideas and attitudes they hold. Choose two groups of people in this chapter and show how the environment affected:
   a. their way of life
   b. their way of making a living
   c. their ideas and attitudes

RELATING PAST TO PRESENT

1. Look up the word *justice* in a dictionary. How would you define it in your own words? How does our concept of justice today compare with the concept of justice in Hammurabi's code?

2. Throughout history, trade has been an important source for the spread of ideas from one culture to another. How does trade in the world today aid the spread of ideas from one culture to another? What effects do you think American movies and records might have on other cultures? Can you give other examples?

3. In this chapter you read about the pharaoh Akhenaton's conflict with the priests of the god Amon. This was an early example in history of a conflict between governmental authority and religion. Review how the relationship between church and state in the United States is dealt with in the First Amendment to the Constitution.

4. Economic power is an important part of being a major empire.
   a. Explain the economic power of ancient Egypt.
   b. What was the basis of the economic power of the Fertile Crescent?
   c. Explain the economic power of oil-producing countries today. How does this affect the political and military power of the United States and the Soviet Union?

INVESTIGATING FURTHER

1. Cotton continues to be an important crop in Egypt and many other parts of the world, including the southeastern United States. Using encyclopedias and statistical abstracts, find out about the size and nature of the American cotton industry. What are some of the items produced from the American cotton crop?

2. Use encyclopedias to find out more about the religions of Judaism, Christianity, Zoroastrianism, and the religion of ancient Egypt. What beliefs does each religion have about the struggle between good and evil? Why do you think that the conflict between good and evil is a persistent theme in most religions?

3. The pyramids are among the most impressive structures left by any civilization. Research and write a report on the techniques of Egyptian building. You might use the following books as sources: Ahmed Fakhry, *The Pyramids* (University of Chicago Press), and James Finch, *The Story of Engineering* (Doubleday), which has a chapter on "The Chief Works of Ancient Egypt."

(2500–1028 B.C.)

3

Early People Created Civilizations in Asia

From your earlier reading you know that civilizations developed in the valleys of the Indus River in ancient India and the Yellow River in China. This chapter will describe these civilizations in the period from about 2500 B.C. to 1000 B.C.

In Egypt during this time hieroglyphic writing was being developed, the pyramids were being built, and a remarkably stable society was developing along the banks of the Nile. In the Fertile Crescent, city-states and empires were rising and falling as one people conquered another. By the year 1000 B.C. adventurous Phoenician merchants were starting to build their far-flung commercial empire. And in Palestine, David, the successor to Saul and father of Solomon, was reigning over the twelve tribes of the Hebrews from the beautiful capital city of Jerusalem.

The civilizations of China and India were similar in some ways to these early civilizations of the Nile and Tigris-Euphrates valleys. In this chapter, for example, you will see the early peoples of India and China learning to farm, discovering writing and calendars, and developing a complex civilization that included trade, cities, and a sophisticated government. Through philosophy and religion they tried to understand the mysterious forces of nature, the mind, and the soul.

There were, however, important differences between Eastern, or Oriental, civilizations and those of the West. Unlike Western civilizations, those of India and China have been nearly contin-

A priest-king or god from Mohenjo-Daro

uous from earliest times to the present day. Such a long and continuous history gives rise to deep-seated customs and traditions. The people of these civilizations today are using many of the ideas and customs of their ancestors. For example, in India the Hindu priest still recites ancient prayers. The bull is still an object of worship. The same specialized crafts are still practiced. It could be said that, while the problems of East and West have often been the same, the solutions reached by the people of the two regions have frequently been different.

THE CHAPTER SECTIONS

1. The first Indian civilization arose in the Indus Valley

2. Aryan invaders ruled India's northern plain during the Vedic Age

3. Geographic and cultural features helped shape Chinese history

4. The first Chinese civilization flourished under the Shang dynasty

1

The first Indian civilization arose in the Indus Valley

The earliest civilization of ancient India developed in the Indus Valley. In time, people settled all over the territory of ancient India, until now there are nearly 850 million people living in India and in neighboring countries. As you read about the Indus Valley civilization, you will see that it is referred to as "Indian" civilization. Remember that ancient India included what are the modern countries of India, Pakistan, and Bangladesh.

The four regions of Indian geography

India is shaped like two triangles joined base to base. The point of the smaller triangle lies in the mountains to the north. The point of the larger triangle lies nearly 2,000 miles (3,200 kilometers) to the south, in the Indian Ocean. At its widest point, where the bases of the triangles join, India stretches nearly 1,400 miles (2,250 kilometers)

from the Arabian Sea to the Bay of Bengal (see map, page 46).

India is often called a subcontinent of Asia, which is to the north. It is nearly half as large as the United States. However, the contrasts of India's geography and climate are greater than those of the United States. There are dense rain forests, great fertile plains, high plateaus, and dry deserts. There are also narrow coastal plains, vast rivers, and the highest mountains in the world.

Geographically, India can be divided roughly into four main regions. Each region has its own geographic features, climate, and natural resources. As you read about each region, look carefully at the map of India on page 46.

(1) *The northern mountains.* Two mighty mountain ranges, the Himalayas (hih·MAHL·yuz) and the Hindu Kush, meet in the north. The Himalayas are a series of parallel mountain ranges that stretch east and southeast for more than 1,500 miles (2,400 kilometers). In all this distance there are few usable mountain passes.

The Hindu Kush are not quite so rugged as the Himalayas. There are some usable passes. The Khyber Pass is the most famous. Through these passes, migrating and invading tribes have been able to enter India. As a result of immigration and invasion, the population of India became as varied as the geography and climate.

(2) *The Indus-Ganges plain.* Two great rivers lie south of the mountains. The Ganges (GAN·jeez) is the more important. It flows to the southeast, through an immensely fertile valley. The Indus flows southwest through drier lands. The northern ends of their two valleys are separated only by a low divide, or ridge. It is helpful to think of the two valleys as one broad plain stretching more than 1,500 miles (2,400 kilometers) from west to east. After immigrants and invaders made their way through the narrow mountain passes, they spread out along the plain and made contact with the people already there.

(3) *The Deccan.* South of the Indus-Ganges plain is the interior region of the Indian peninsula. This area is a high plateau called the Deccan, which means "southland." A range of hills—the Vindhya (VIND·yah) mountains—separates the Deccan from the Indus-Ganges plain. The Vindhyas have formed a cultural barrier between northern and southern India. At the western edge

of the Deccan are the Western Ghats, a low mountain range that slopes gradually eastward to the inland plateau. The eastern edge of the Deccan is marked by a lower mountain range called the Eastern Ghats. The Deccan is a varied region, with agricultural, grazing, forest, and mining lands.

(4) *The coastal rim.* The coastal rim of flatlands extends around the lower triangle of India, facing the Arabian Sea on the west and the Bay of Bengal on the east. The western rim is narrow and is hemmed in not far from the sea by the abrupt rise of the Western Ghats. The eastern rim is broader, sloping gradually upward toward the Eastern Ghats.

The people of the coastal rim turned to the sea very early. Those in the west traded with the people of the Fertile Crescent, Egypt, and the Mediterranean region. Those in the east traded with what is now Sri Lanka (Ceylon) and Southeast Asia. The coastal people had more contacts with people overseas than with the people of the Indus-Ganges plain.

The climate of India

Two features dominate the climate of India: the monsoon and the heat.

The **monsoon** is a wind that changes direction as the seasons change. From late September until the

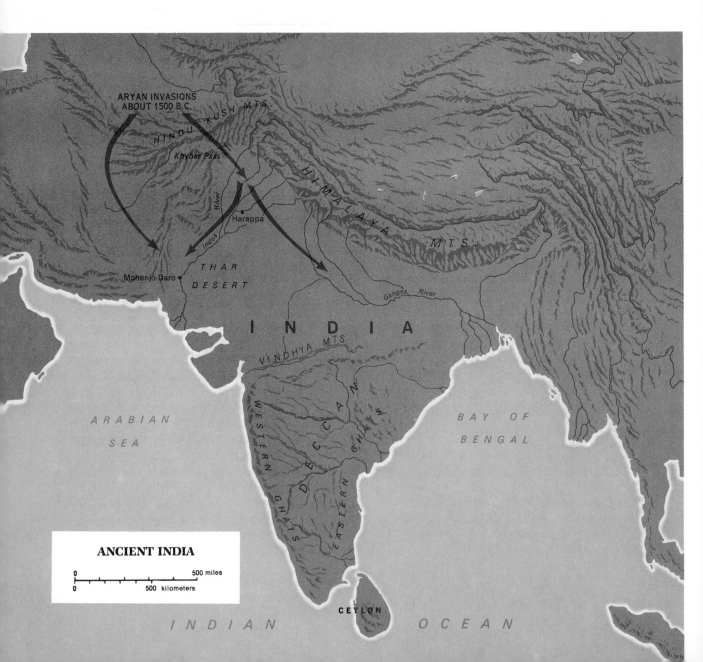

ANCIENT INDIA

0   500 miles

0   500 kilometers

end of the following March, the monsoon blows from the north and northeast. Any moisture it carries falls on the northern slopes of the Himalayas before reaching the rest of India. Then the monsoon swings around and, beginning in late May or early June, comes out of the southwest. As it crosses the Indian Ocean, it picks up moisture, which falls unevenly throughout India. Rainfall is heavy along the coastal rim but light behind the Western Ghats. However, the rain is heavy in the lower Ganges Valley and heaviest of all in the eastern Himalayas.

Thus, in most of India, the rainfall for the entire year comes during the four months when the monsoon comes out of the southwest. This is the critical time. If the monsoon is late or if the rainfall is light, crops are lost and there is starvation. If there is too much rain, destructive floods result. Two or more crops can be grown in a year if enough moisture is available.

The second important feature of India's climate is the heat. The heat in the entire coastal rim and on the Deccan is not excessive. But heat as a cruel force of nature—oppressive, crushing, furnace-like—is common on the Indus-Ganges plain. The winter months of December, January, and February are cool, but most of the rest of the year is hot. There may be many days in a row in May and early June with temperatures of 120°F (49°C).

Early civilization in the Indus Valley

An impressive civilization appeared in India around 2500 B.C., not long after Egypt and Sumer developed civilizations. Like the others, it started in a river valley—the valley of the Indus River.

Our knowledge of this early civilization is incomplete. We know about it from numerous archeological findings since its rediscovery more than a hundred years ago. The use of radiocarbon dating of some of the remains provides the most accurate means of dating the time span of this civilization. It may have existed between 2500 B.C. and 1700 B.C.

Harappa and Mohenjo-Daro. This early Indus Valley civilization is best seen in the remains of two cities—Harappa and Mohenjo-Daro (see map, opposite). Both were built on the remains of earlier villages, carefully laid out according to the same systematic plan.

For their day, Harappa and Mohenjo-Daro were miracles of city planning and convenience. The cities were alike in plan. Streets were laid out in a regular pattern, intersecting at right angles. Main streets were wide. Each city had a water system, with public baths (possibly associated with temple worship), and a covered brick sewer system for private homes, which connected with a central system in the streets.

The two cities were built of bricks superior to those used in Sumer. The bricks were baked in kilns, or ovens, instead of being sun-dried. They have not crumbled over the centuries. All the bricks were the same size. Thus, some archeologists believe that a strong, centralized government must have existed in order to impose this uniformity of city planning and brick construction. The buildings of Harappa and Mohenjo-Daro were designed for use, not beauty.

The two cities seem to have been twin capitals and not rivals. Each had a strong central fortress built on a platform of bricks. At Harappa there were large storehouses for grain. These granaries were large enough to store the wheat and barley needed to feed the 35,000 people who lived in the city. The excess food was shipped to the cities of the Tigris-Euphrates Valley.

Indus Valley culture. The areas surrounding Harappa and Mohenjo-Daro were agricultural regions. Because the Indus River has a swift current with heavy silt, irrigation problems must have been difficult. Archeologists do not know how the Indus Valley people solved these problems, because since then the level of the plain around the two cities has been raised by silt deposits.

City dwellers earned their livings by industry and trade. There is evidence that they traded with people of the Tigris-Euphrates Valley as early as 2300 B.C. Their industries produced fine articles for trade. They made excellent cotton cloth and painted pottery. Articles were made with both copper and bronze. Bronze sculpture of the Indus Valley shows a fine artistic ability. Excavated articles include weapons and implements of copper and bronze, and a copper model of a two-wheeled cart. Gold and silver jewelry were of fine quality.

These early Indus Valley people had a written language. Examples have been found dating back to about 2300 B.C. The system of writing used mainly pictograms. We cannot yet read the language, partly because most of the examples found are short inscriptions on personal seals, probably the names of individuals. Additional writing has also been found on clay pots and fragments. No connection with any other language has been established. One theory is that the people of Harappa and Mohenjo-Daro took the idea of writing from the Sumerians but did not use Sumerian characters.

The little we know of Indus Valley religion indicates that it was a form of **animism.** This means that the people believed that spirits inhabited everything—animals, trees, and other natural objects, as well as people. These spirits could influence a person's life, so it was necessary to try to control them and to please them. No temples, shrines, or religious writings have been found. The people seem to have worshiped animals associated with physical power and fertility, such as bulls, elephants, rhinoceroses, tigers, crocodiles, and snakes. One of the most important of these symbols was the unicorn, a fabled animal with one long horn jutting from its forehead.

Fertility was also symbolized through pictures of a sacred tree and a mother goddess. These customs did not die out with the early Indus Valley civilization, but were handed down through generations of peasants to become part of Indian religious tradition.

The people of Harappa and Mohenjo-Daro ruled the valley for about a thousand years. But sometime after 2000 B.C. the civilization seemed to decline. This decline can be seen in the objects uncovered and tested for age by radiocarbon procedures. Many reasons have been given for the decline of the Indus Valley civilization. At first the simplest explanation seemed to be that the valley was conquered by tribes who came from outside.

However, more recent evidence shows the destructive power of the mineral salts of underground water upon the baked bricks of Mohenjo-Daro. A change in the salt content of underground water could have made agricultural production impossible. It would also have disintegrated the bricks of the buildings of the cities.

There is evidence, too, of major earthquakes and flooding of the region around 1700 B.C. The discovery of several unburied skeletons, together with homes and personal belongings hastily abandoned, seems to indicate some disastrous event at Mohenjo-Daro. But the evidence is incomplete. Therefore, final conclusions regarding the decline of this civilization cannot be made.

CHECKUP

1. IDENTIFY: monsoon, animism.

2. LOCATE: Arabian Sea, Bay of Bengal, Himalayas, Hindu Kush, Indus-Ganges plain, Deccan, Harappa, Mohenjo-Daro.

3. Name and briefly describe the four main geographical regions of India.

4. Based on archeological findings in the Indus Valley, describe the political, economic, and social aspects of city life. What evidence has been found that would give clues about the religious ideas and practices in the Indus Valley?

Aryan invaders ruled India's northern plain during the Vedic Age

About 1500 B.C. a new group of people began working their way through the northwestern mountain passes into the Indus Valley. Like the Hittites, Medes, and Persians, they came from the region north of the Black and Caspian seas and spoke an Indo-European language.

The conquering Aryans

The Indo-European tribes that forced their way into northwestern India, one after another, are called Indo-Aryans, or Aryans (see map, page 46). They spoke a language known as Sanskrit and were a simple people who herded sheep and cows. (Their word for "war" meant "a desire for more cows.") Strong, brave, and skillful fighters, they conquered the Indus Valley and then spread eastward along the Ganges until they controlled the entire northern plain.

The Aryans had no use for cities and trading. They also were not builders. Their language had no word for "brick." They left the ruins of the cities to decay. They had no written language, and their history for several centuries after their ar-

48

Indus Valley civilization

About 2500 B.C., shortly after Egyptian civilization developed, a similar civilization appeared in the Indus Valley of India. Organizational skills and a highly developed sense of beauty are apparent in the buildings and objects that have survived. The fortified city (above) had straight streets, large buildings, sewers, and waterworks, indicating careful planning and skillful engineering. The brick homes of the wealthy appear to have been two stories tall, equipped with bathrooms and garbage chutes.

The oil lamp (left), made in the shape of a woman, reveals expert craftsmanship and a sense of artistry. We also learn something about the means of transportation from the small two-wheeled clay cart (below). Drawn by two animals, it was probably a child's toy.

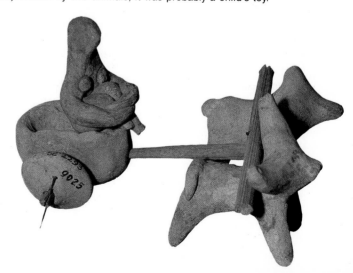

HISTORY THROUGH ART
Seals from the Indus Valley

Much of our knowledge of the Indus Valley civilization comes from tantalizing bits and pieces. Seals like the ones shown here are the most puzzling of the remains that have been unearthed. Such objects have on them the only known examples of the pictographic, or picture, writing of the Indus Valley people. Scholars have been unable to translate this writing, but a widely held opinion is that the seals were used to stamp property or to identify their owners.

Many of the pictures on the seals seem to have a religious meaning. The most common carving is that of a bull, an object of worship throughout the ancient world. The seated figure may represent a god. Because Indus Valley seals have been found in the Tigris-Euphrates region, scholars think the people of the Indus Valley traded with the Middle East.

rival is only vaguely known. What we do know comes from the Vedas, the great literature of the Aryan religion. The period from 1500 to 1000 B.C. is known as the **Vedic Age** in Indian history.

The Vedas

The word *veda* means "knowledge." The Vedas are books of sacred knowledge—collections of religious rituals and hymns to the gods. Only four major ones have survived: (1) the *Rig-Veda,* hymns of praise; (2) the *Sama-Veda,* melodies or chants; (3) the *Yajur-Veda,* rituals of sacrifice; and (4) the *Atharva-Veda,* magic spells.

Since the Aryans had no system of writing, the Vedas were memorized and handed down by word of mouth. They were not written down until long after the Vedic Age.

The Vedas contain an amazing variety of subjects. The *Atharva-Veda* has chants for many purposes—to obtain children, to ward off evil, to prolong life, or to destroy enemies. The *Rig-Veda,* the greatest of the Vedas as literature, has more than a thousand hymns of praise to all the objects of Aryan worship.

Aryan religion

The earliest gods mentioned in the Vedas were forces of nature, such as the sky, sun, earth, light, fire, wind, storm, water, and rain. These natural objects and forces were personified—that is, they were regarded or represented as persons. Thus, the sky became a father, the earth a mother.

The Vedic religion of the Aryan people was not fixed, but changing and developing. The development of the god Varuna best shows how Aryan religion changed. He began as the heaven. His garment was the sky, his breath the storm. As the spiritual understanding of his worshipers matured, so did he. He became the guardian of ideas of right and wrong. He watched over the world through his eye, the sun. He rewarded good and punished evil. Thus he became the enforcer of an eternal law of morality—of right and wrong.

Although the Vedic religion is full of references to many gods, there is also a very important hymn to celebrate the creation of the universe. This suggests a more sophisticated concept of God (who is called "That One") as the creator of order out of the original chaos in the universe.

Like the Persians, the early Aryans believed in personal immortality. After death the soul was either thrust by Varuna into a dark pit of eternal punishment or raised into a heaven where every earthly joy was endless. Through repeated ritual sacrifices and correct ritual action (karma), a person would reach this heaven free of his or her earthly body. Later in Indian history (as you will read in Chapter 7), these rather simple ideas of a future life became much more complex.

There were apparently no temples or images in the early Vedic religion. Rituals consisted of burnt offerings. New altars were built after each sacrifice. The usual offering was a libation, or pouring out, of the juice of the sacred soma plant, along with the pouring of liquid butter into the fire. The important point was to perform the ceremony properly. The good qualities of the person performing it did not matter.

As time passed, the rituals of sacrifice became more complicated. The spoken language of the Indian people also changed, until it became quite different from the Sanskrit of the first Aryan invaders. Since proper observance was so important, priests who knew the proper forms and were learned in Sanskrit also became more important. These priests were called **Brahmans.** They fixed the proper ceremony for almost every occasion of life and charged heavily for their services.

Early Aryan society

The Aryans had been nomads, with the habits and customs of wanderers. In the Indus-Ganges plain, however, they found one of the richest and most fertile areas in the world. Here they settled down. With farming and settled living, they also developed simple forms of government.

Aryan tribes joined to form small states. Each tribe was led by a chief and a tribal council. Each state was ruled by a king and a council of warriors, but each state was made up of nearly independent villages. Each village was governed by an assembly of heads of families.

There were physical and social differences between conquerors and conquered. Aryans were light-skinned. The original Indus Valley people were dark-skinned. Aryans had been nomads. The Indus Valley people had been city dwellers. The conquerors looked down on the people they had conquered. Although they were outnumbered by the original Indus Valley people, the Aryans believed they had to maintain their identity. Therefore they passed laws prohibiting marriages between Aryans and the valley dwellers.

Class divisions began to form during the Vedic Age, but it was not until later that fixed hereditary classes appeared. The early Aryans considered warriors to be the most admirable members of society. But when peace came, and farmers needed the help of religion against the forces of nature, the Brahman priests became important. However, many centuries passed before they were considered more important than warriors.

The Vedas provide a great deal of information about family life in the Vedic Age. Marriages took place by kidnapping, by purchase, or by mutual consent. It was considered a great compliment for a woman to be stolen. To be bought and paid for was more flattering than to be married by consent. Men were permitted to have more than one wife. They were considered to own their wives and children. In certain circumstances, a man might sell his wives and children.

One of the primary duties of the wife was to produce sons who would help the father in caring for the herds of cattle and other animals. Sons were also expected to go to battle to bring honor to the family and to perform the correct rituals at the funeral of the father.

The Aryan economy

When the Aryans took up farming in the Indus-Ganges plain, they raised barley as the principal crop. Rice, the most important food in India today, was apparently unknown in Vedic times. Each village divided its land among its families, but irrigation was the responsibility of the village as a whole. Land could not be sold to outsiders. It could be willed only to male heirs. Most Aryans owned their land. To work for someone else was considered a disgrace.

Handicrafts gradually appeared in the villages. There was not much trade because transportation and trading methods were poor. Early trade was by **barter,** the exchange of one item for another without the use of money. Later, cattle were used as money.

Thus we see that the Aryan invaders made significant contributions to the civilization of the Indian subcontinent. Among these contributions were a new social order of classes, a new language, and new religious interpretations of how the world works. Aryan contributions began to blend with the previous civilization of Indus Valley people. Herding was gradually displaced by farming. Religious values began to change, and classes in society became more distinct and separate. In other words, society became more rigid and closely identified with ritual purity.

CHECKUP

1. IDENTIFY: Sanskrit, Vedic Age, *Rig-Veda,* libation, Varuna, karma, Brahman, barter.

2. What were the contributions of the Aryans to Indian civilization?

3. What are the Vedas? How were they used in Aryan society?

4. Summarize the most important beliefs and rituals of the Aryan religion.

5. Describe the class divisions that began in the Aryan society.

3

Geographic and cultural features helped shape Chinese history

China's story begins, as you read in Chapter 1, with the Paleolithic remains found at Peking. Later Neolithic developments along the Yellow River were similar to those elsewhere. The people domesticated animals, improved their tools and weapons, and developed permanent communities. All this occurred as agriculture became the main way of life.

Before picking up the story of China at this point, however, it is helpful to do two things. First, we must examine the geography of China. Second, we must learn about the basic patterns of Chinese history.

The geography of China

The geography of China is less unified than that of the other early centers of civilization. The land area is separated into many distinct regions by intersecting chains of mountains. Travel from one region to another has never been easy.

On the map on page 53, notice how much of China is mountainous. The great mountain ranges of the west, northwest, and southwest slope down to high plateaus, which are either deserts or semi-deserts. In the south the plateaus give way to a region of many low hills and valleys. In the north the plateaus slope gradually down to a coastal plain along the Pacific Ocean. This is the North China Plain. Much smaller than the plain that stretches across northern India, the North China Plain was the center of early civilization in China.

Notice also the range of mountains that cuts from west to east across the center of China. This range separates the valleys of the two greatest rivers of China—the Yellow and the Yangtze. Known as the Tsinling Range, it marks the boundary between North and South China. The range also forms the boundary between the two major agricultural areas of China. In the north, where relatively little rain falls, wheat is the principal crop. In the center and south, where there is more rainfall, rice is the leading farm product.

Throughout its history China has also been divided politically into two main parts. The smaller and more important part lies along the seacoast and stretches inland up the valleys of the Yellow and Yangtze rivers. This is the heart of China, which may be called China Proper or often just China.

The second part surrounds China Proper with a great semicircle of regions, including Tibet, Sinkiang, Mongolia, Manchuria, and Korea. At various times throughout its history, China Proper has conquered and ruled these regions, usually to protect itself from attack by their nomad populations. On a few occasions one or another of these outlying regions has conquered and ruled China Proper.

The rivers of China Proper. China Proper has many rivers, but the Yellow, the Yangtze, and the Si (SHEE) have played especially important parts in its history. The Yellow River, called the Hwang Ho by the Chinese, is 2,900 miles (4,600 kilometers) long. Yet it is so shallow that most of it is useless for navigation except by small boats. However, the Yellow River is vital for irrigation, and

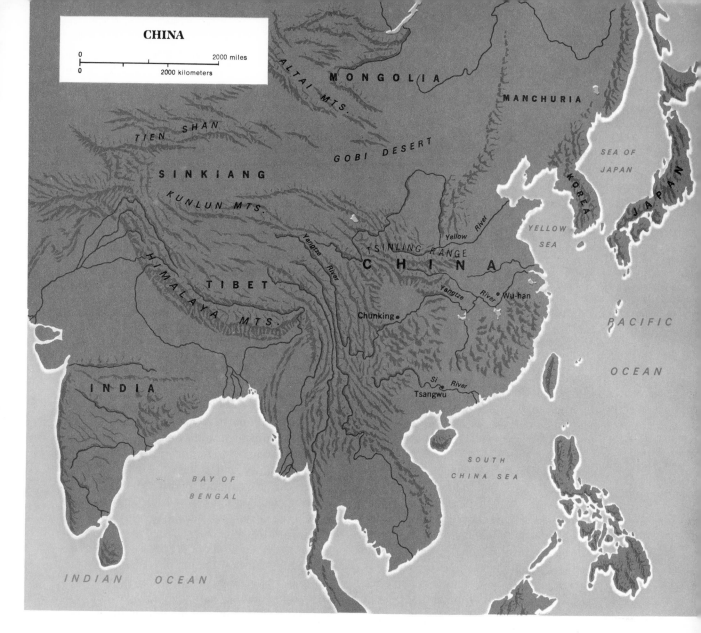

CHINA

0   2000 miles
0   2000 kilometers

controlling its water has always been a problem. The river carries a large amount of silt that is yellowish in color and gives the river its name. When silt settles rapidly to the bottom of the river, the water level is raised higher than the surrounding land.

The Chinese have built dikes to keep the Yellow River within its banks. If the dikes break in flood time, however, the river runs wild. Sometimes it cuts a completely new channel to the sea. The river has changed its course often during China's long history. In ancient times it flowed into the sea far to the north of its present mouth.

Because of its destructiveness and the difficulty of controlling it, the Chinese called the Yellow River "China's Sorrow."

The Yangtze River in central China is 3,400 miles (5,400 kilometers) long and cuts a deep channel. In modern times, large ocean-going ships have been able to go 600 miles (960 kilometers) upstream to the great city of Wu-han. Smaller ships can go as far as Chungking, about 1,300 miles (2,000 kilometers) from the sea.

The Si River in southern China is more than 1,200 miles (1,900 kilometers) long. Like the Yangtze, it is important as a commercial water-

53

way. Large ships can navigate the Si River as far as Tsangwu, about 220 miles (350 kilometers) inland.

China's isolation. Civilization in China developed in relative isolation from the civilizations of India and the West. China was separated from them by great distances, by the towering mountains of central Asia, and by such formidable deserts as the Gobi. As a result, China developed and retained its own distinctive culture. Although the Chinese did adopt ideas as well as skills from other peoples, they probably owed less to outside influence than any other people you have read about.

There was some Chinese trade over the mountains with India. There was also a long overland caravan route from northwestern China over deserts and through mountains to the Black Sea and the Middle East. Some ideas and merchandise passed back and forth over this route. However, the trip was long and hard, and as a result trading was infrequent and irregular.

Until modern times China's only fairly regular contact with foreigners was with the nomads from the dry lands to the north and northwest of China Proper. These peoples did not have agriculture but instead raised sheep and horses. They spoke their own languages and had their own tribal religions. Usually they traded peacefully with the Chinese, exchanging livestock for grain and other agricultural products. Sometimes, however, they organized bands of mounted warriors and attacked Chinese settlements. To the Chinese, these nomadic peoples were known as "barbarians," in other words, inferior in culture to themselves.

The lack of contact with other peoples whom they considered civilized helped give the Chinese a strong sense of identity and superiority. They regarded their land as the only civilized land and called it *Chung-kuo,* or the Middle Kingdom. To them it was the center of the world. Only by learning the Chinese language and adopting Chinese customs could other people become equally civilized in their eyes. Even when outsiders overran the Middle Kingdom, as sometimes happened, the Chinese believed that the strangers would in time lose their identity and be absorbed into China's vast population. "China," they said, "is a sea which salts all rivers that run into it."

Patterns of Chinese history

China has a long and interesting history. In reading about it you will encounter many ideas and customs that differ from the ideas and customs of your own civilization. As you learn about China's past, keep in mind two basic patterns of its history. One is the dynastic cycle. The other is cultural evolution.

The dynastic cycle. From the beginning of its recorded history until the early 1900's China was ruled by a succession of dynasties. The first was the Shang dynasty, which was established around 1500 B.C. The last was the Ching dynasty, which ruled China from 1644 to 1912 A.D. Some of these ruling dynasties lasted only a short time. Others, like the Ching, held power for centuries. All of these dynasties went through similar stages, however. In other words, all of them went through a similar dynastic cycle.

First came the founding of the dynasty. An individual leader gained the right to rule the country by defeating his rivals in war. That right then became hereditary in his family, and a new dynasty was born. Next came a period of great power. The new dynasty appointed officials throughout the country and collected taxes and labor services from the people. The dynasty used its wealth to build grand palaces, to improve roads and irrigation systems, and to support education and the arts.

Then came a period of decline. The ruling family and high officials thought only of living in luxury. They raised taxes wherever they could, creating hardship among the people. Because they also acquired tax-free lands for themselves in the countryside, their government ran short of money. It neglected dikes and irrigation systems, making floods more likely. It became unable to defend the northern frontier of China, and invasions by nomads began to increase. When the decline reached a low point, with disorder and rebellion in many parts of the land, the dynasty was overthrown. A new leader emerged, and the dynastic cycle would start again.

Cultural evolution. The dynastic cycle is a useful way of describing the political history of China, but it does not explain everything about China's past. Beneath the recurring pattern of events in politics was a continuous evolution, or develop-

Ancient Chinese Elephant

This small, boldly decorated elephant made of bronze is a container that probably once held food. It was buried as an offering to the spirit of a river or mountain near where it was found in Hunan Province in China.

Containers such as this give us an idea of the importance of nature to the early Chinese. The elephant is covered with spiral designs that stand for clouds and rain. The use of these symbols was widespread during the Shang dynasty, when the container was made. It is also decorated with real and imaginary animals—tigers, birds, snakes, and dragons. The animals stood for the spirits of nature or for particular families. These ceremonial containers are extraordinary examples of bronze casting, a craft the Chinese developed into a great art.

ment, of culture over the centuries. During some stages of the dynastic cycle the pace of cultural evolution quickened. During others it slowed down. Over the centuries, however, civilization in China maintained a steady development.

In later chapters you will read about the many economic, social, artistic, and intellectual achievements of the Chinese people during their long history. You will learn about the emergence of a large, powerful empire and a rich cultural tradition. Your knowledge of China's past will help you understand more recent events in China.

CHECKUP

1. IDENTIFY: China Proper, cultural evolution.

2. LOCATE: Yangtze River, Tibet, Sinkiang, Mongolia, Manchuria, Si River, Gobi Desert, Yellow River.

3. List three geographical features that made travel in ancient China difficult.

4. Explain why the Yellow River has been called "China's Sorrow."

5. Why did the Chinese consider all other people to be "barbarian"?

6. What was meant by the statement, "China is a sea which salts all rivers that run into it"?

7. Describe the stages of China's dynastic cycle.

The first Chinese civilization flourished under the Shang dynasty

To the Chinese, it was important that the distant past be explained and connected with historic times. The Chinese have many legends about the beginnings of the world and about early China and its people. The legends tell of P'an Ku, the first man, who worked for 18,000 years to create the universe. They tell of hero-kings who ruled for more than a century each and personally created such institutions and inventions as marriage, music, painting, and the wheel. The legends also tell of the Hsia (SHYAH) dynasty, which ruled the Yellow River region from about 2000 B.C. to about 1500 B.C.

The Shang dynasty

As soon as Neolithic people learned to shape clay and metal, they made jars and containers to hold liquids. Without such vessels it was impossible to store liquids or to drink easily. From the earliest times, too, people decorated their jars, so that they would be pleasing to the eye as well as practical. The Chinese earthenware jar (above), from the Neolithic period, has a dramatic swirling pattern and two elegant handles. Made on a potter's wheel, it was probably used in a funeral.

During the Shang dynasty (1500–1028 B.C.), rapid technological advances were made in casting bronze. The bronze, probably made from imported copper and tin ores, was also used to make containers for liquids. The intricately carved cup (right) was very likely designed to hold wine. The bronze ceremonial vessel, shaped like an animal (below), may have been intended to be amusing as well as useful.

Unfortunately, the Chinese legends contain more charm than proven facts. Whether or not the Hsia dynasty existed, however, there is no doubt that the people of the Yellow River Valley made great advances during these five centuries. They improved their agriculture. There is some evidence that they began to use written symbols. With the appearance of writing, China was prepared for its first historic dynasty, the Shang.

We know that the Shang dynasty began about 1500 B.C. along the Yellow River. But we do not know how the Shang rulers established themselves there. We can make some informed guesses, however, based on the geography of the region.

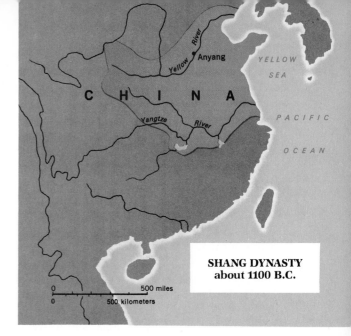

SHANG DYNASTY
about 1100 B.C.

500 miles
500 kilometers

Irrigation systems

Prosperity in the valley of the Yellow River has always depended upon irrigation and flood control. Dikes along the banks of the river must be kept in repair because of the high level of the water, especially at flood time. Irrigation is easy because of the high water level. But excess water must be carried away in long drainage canals to a point far downstream, where it can flow back into the river.

Throughout China's history, any break in the dikes along the river has brought disaster to crops, animals, and people. Also, as you have read, the flooding Yellow River may cut a new channel, leaving irrigation and drainage systems useless. An organized, centralized government is needed to build and maintain such systems and to guard against floods. Prior to the coming of the Shang, the people of the valley did not have a government to provide for irrigation, drainage, or flood control. They lived well in good years but starved when the area was stricken by drought or flood.

Beginning with the Shang dynasty, this situation changed. Legend tells us that the Shang were immigrants, not natives. It seems likely that they introduced simple irrigation and flood control systems. Control of these systems meant control of the country.

Government under the Shang

The first Shang rulers are said to have conquered 1,800 city-states. Apparently the Shang moved their capital city a number of times, either because it was hard to defend or because of floods. During the last centuries of Shang rule, the capital was situated near the modern city of Anyang.

Shang government was relatively simple. There was a hereditary king, who granted land to his principal followers. In return they pledged loyalty, performed certain services for the king, and paid dues. The valley of the kingdom was surrounded by less advanced peoples. The Shang maintained their power against these peoples by using war chariots and superior weapons made of bronze. Their military force enabled them to gain territory and to spread the knowledge of their more advanced civilization. At one time or another, they ruled most of northern and central China (see map, this page).

The position of king was a demanding one. He was the leader in battle, in hunting, and in certain sacrifices and religious ceremonies. People believed that the spirits helped him in war and in planning for good crops. However, the king had to produce results. Poor crops or defeat in battle meant that he had lost favor with the spirits and was likely to lose favor with the people.

Civilization under the Shang

The years of the Shang dynasty, from about 1500 to 1028 B.C., were a significant period of development for Chinese culture and civilization. Under

57

the Shang, Chinese people improved upon the discoveries and skills of earlier periods and developed new ones. Later dynasties built upon the basic advances that were made during the time of the Shang.

Economy and handicrafts. The Shang economy was mainly agricultural. Farmers grew a grain called millet as their main crop, along with some barley. They also grew some rice, but more was imported from the south. Compared with millet, rice was regarded as a luxury. Wheat was not grown until late in the dynasty.

Domesticated animals included cattle, horses, sheep, pigs, chickens, and dogs. The Shang used elephants from southern Asia in war and for some other kinds of work. Sometime during the Shang dynasty, the Chinese learned to raise silkworms, to spin thread from their cocoons, and to weave silk cloth from the thread.

Not all the Chinese were farmers, however. In the cities lived merchants and artisans. Some made clothing from silk, and others made cord from hemp. Artisans carved jade to make jewelry. They also carved ivory and bone to make various objects inlaid with turquoise.

Shang artisans of the cities laid the foundations for all later Chinese ceramic art. They learned to use kaolin (KAY·uh·lin), a fine white clay, and to shape items on the potter's wheel. They glazed some of their pottery. Shang potters developed every form and shape that was used later in Chinese ceremonial vases.

The bronze castings of Shang artisans are still regarded as outstanding works of art. The Chinese may have learned the technique of casting from the Middle East, possibly Sumer. However, the forms of the vessels and the designs of the decorations were essentially Chinese. Chinese artisans probably imported copper and tin ores and mixed the bronze themselves. They cast small figures as well as large ceremonial vessels whose surfaces were covered with delicate relief work.

Astronomy and the calendar. An accurate calendar was as important to Shang farmers and their rulers as it was to the peoples of Egypt and the Fertile Crescent.

The Chinese had a calendar based on the movement of the moon. The shortest period of the calendar was ten days. Three such periods, sometimes shortened by a day, made a month. Six ten-day periods made a "cycle." Six cycles made a year of up to 360 days. To provide enough days for a full 365-day year, those in charge of the calendar added days as needed.

Adjustment of the calendar was the work of priest-astronomers employed by the government. They had to be responsible and skillful. The king's popularity depended upon the success of the harvest, which in part depended upon the time of planting as determined by the calendar.

The Shang calendar may seem confusing to us, but apparently the astronomers were skillful enough to make it work. We know that they could calculate eclipses of the moon in advance so accurately that an error of 24 hours alarmed the authorities. Because of their skill with the calendar, the astronomers were given the duty of keeping other records. Thus, the Chinese had very early what might be called official historians.

Language and writing

The Chinese are one of the few peoples known to have developed an original written language. To understand the Chinese writing system one must first understand some characteristics of spoken Chinese.

Almost all of the basic Chinese words are of one syllable. To express a new or more complicated meaning, the Chinese put together two or more simple words. Thus the word for "magnet" is made up of three one-syllable words meaning "pull-iron-stone." Each word-syllable keeps just as much of its original meaning as is needed to give the meaning of the compound word. This compound meaning is something new, not just a collection of the three things named.

A second characteristic of Chinese is its lack of inflection—that is, a word does not change its form according to number, tense, or person. The same noun can be either singular or plural. For example, the Chinese word *kuo* can mean "countries" as well as "country." Verbs, too, are not inflected. They do not have tenses, as in English and many other languages. The Chinese verb *kau* can mean "see" or "saw." In English we must also inflect, or change, a verb to correspond to the person who is the subject of the sentence. We say "I go" and "she goes," "I sleep" and "he sleeps." In the Chinese language, the verbs meaning "go" and "sleep" remain the same no matter what the subject of the sentence is.

Because of these characteristics of their language, the Chinese did not need a phonetic system of writing. Instead they assigned each and every word in their language its own special symbol, or character. At first these characters were pictograms, that is, drawings of objects. Later, as their culture and therefore their language became more complex, the Chinese developed ideograms and phonograms. Many written characters came to consist of two parts. One was a signific, or "idea sign." It gave a clue to the meaning of the charac-

ter. The other was a phonetic, or "sound sign." It told how the character was pronounced.

The Chinese developed their system of writing in an effective way. By combining signs, they were able to invent new characters freely. The system spread throughout most of eastern Asia. The traditional written language is difficult to learn, since each character must be memorized. For centuries, a well-educated Chinese had to know more than 10,000 characters. Thus, until a simplified version of the language was developed in recent times, the ability to read and write was limited to a fairly small percentage of the Chinese people.

connections

Harvest Festivals

When Americans sit down for Thanksgiving dinner each year, they are repeating a celebration found in almost every society in the world. All peoples find a way to give thanks when they have finished gathering the harvest. The summer is over, and the food has been grown. There is a feeling of gratitude that the earth has

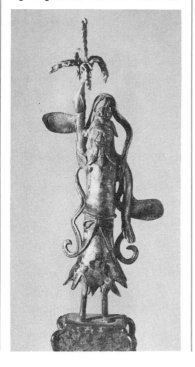

once again provided grain, vegetables, and fruits.

Long ago the ancient Hebrews celebrated a fall thanksgiving, a holiday called Succoth that Jews today still celebrate.

As early as the Shang dynasty, there were harvest gods in China (left). Later Chinese celebrated the Harvest Moon Festival, and they saw a rabbit's form in the moon. They ate cakes in the shape of rabbits and moons, and gave thanks at altars adorned with wheat. In Japan today

the harvest is honored by placing the produce of the earth on altars. The Japanese also hold large parades and carry giant fish to thank the ocean for the food it provides.

Among the early American Indians there were many rituals of planting and harvest (above). The ancient wish to give thanks when the farmer's work is done, and when the earth gives up its harvest, continues. The forms differ from place to place, but the importance of the land is the same for people all over the world.

Unlike the Aryans of India, the Chinese from early days used writing to compose and preserve literary works. Characters were written with a brush on silk, bamboo strips, or paper, which the Chinese invented in 105 A.D. The lines ran from top to bottom, beginning on the right side. Writing itself became an art, called **calligraphy** (kuh·LIG·ruh·fee). It became a challenge to form the characters beautifully. The Chinese admire beautiful calligraphy as much as they admire beautiful painting.

Religion in the Shang period

The religion that developed during the Shang dynasty was a combination of animism and ancestor worship. In animism many things in nature are personified. People believed in a dragon that lived in the seas and rivers and was all-powerful and kindly. He could rise into the clouds. Summer thunderstorms that brought rain were thought to be caused by dragons fighting in the heavens. In time the good dragon became the symbol of Chinese rulers.

The Chinese held great religious festivals in spring and autumn. In spring, the planting time, there were ceremonies to bring good crops, when the ruler plowed the earth for the first time. In autumn there were ceremonies of thanksgiving for the harvest.

Along with these animistic beliefs, the idea developed that reverence had to be given to the elders and ancestors of the family. The family was regarded as both earth dwelling and spirit dwelling. That is, all members of the family—the living as well as the dead—were united forever through their religion. The duty of the child toward the parent was most important. In Chinese writing the character that indicates the honor and reverence that was owed to parents shows a son supporting his aged father as he walks.

There were priests in Chinese religion. Some were priest-astronomers. Others foretold the future in order to tell the wishes of the spirits, especially of the spirits of ancestors. The priests wrote questions on bone or tortoise shell, into which they thrust a heated metal rod. They interpreted the answers of the spirits from the pattern of cracks that appeared, and wrote the answers on the bone or shell. Scholars have learned much about Shang culture from these questions and answers.

The Chinese were not greatly interested in such otherworldly problems as the existence of a life after death. Thus, Chinese priests never became as important as the Indian Brahmans. In fact, their power declined as time passed. The Chinese were more concerned with ethical problems—with proper behavior in this life. They believed that their ruler received his power through communication with the spirits and orders from them. Such orders were called the **Mandate of Heaven.** There could be rebellion against the ruler, however. If it succeeded, it proved that he had lost divine favor. It is significant that the legendary ruler P'an Ku was considered a man, not a god.

Fall of the Shang dynasty

Documents of a later period tell of the overthrow of the last Shang king in 1028 B.C. The Shang rulers probably lost their original vigor, becoming less able to carry on the constant hard fighting that was necessary. Legends say that the last king and his wife were monsters of corrupt wickedness and cruelty. We must remember, however, that these are legends about a defeated ruler, possibly invented by his successors.

Earlier the Shang had conquered a western people, the Chou (JOH). The Chou were less advanced than the Shang, but their leaders learned to appreciate Shang culture. As the Shang became weaker, the Chou joined with other western tribes to overthrow them, much as hill and desert people overthrew weakening valley peoples in the region of the Fertile Crescent.

CHECKUP

1. IDENTIFY: Hsia dynasty, kaolin, calligraphy, ancestor worship, Mandate of Heaven.

2. What was the relationship between flood control of the Yellow River and the establishment of the Shang dynasty?

3. List the duties of the king under the Shang dynasty.

4. Why was the calendar important to the development of Chinese civilization?

5. What were the religious beliefs of the Chinese during the Shang dynasty?

CHAPTER REVIEW

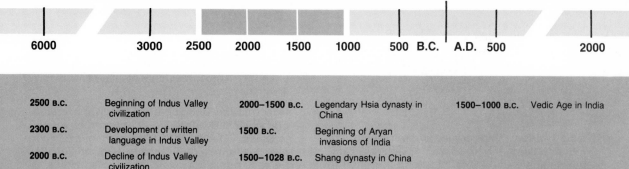

| 6000 | 3000 | 2500 | 2000 | 1500 | 1000 | 500 B.C. | A.D. 500 | 2000 |

2500 B.C. Beginning of Indus Valley civilization	**2000–1500 B.C.** Legendary Hsia dynasty in China	**1500–1000 B.C.** Vedic Age in India	
2300 B.C. Development of written language in Indus Valley	**1500 B.C.** Beginning of Aryan invasions of India		
2000 B.C. Decline of Indus Valley civilization	**1500–1028 B.C.** Shang dynasty in China		

CHAPTER SUMMARY

The subcontinent of India is divided roughly into four geographical regions: the northern mountains, the Indus-Ganges plain, the Deccan, and a coastal rim of flatlands. Monsoons and oppressive heat are the dominant features of India's climate.

About 2500 B.C. an impressive civilization appeared in the Indus Valley. Industry and trade centered on such cities as Harappa and Mohenjo-Daro. Indus Valley people had a written language and a form of animistic religion.

About 1500 B.C. the Aryans began to enter the Indus Valley civilization from the northwest. Because the Aryans lacked a written language, knowledge of their early history comes mainly from the Vedas, their sacred books. Originally herders and nomads, the Aryans became farmers and founded small tribal states. Intermarriage with the original Indus Valley people was prohibited, and class divisions began to form during the Vedic Age. At first warriors were the most admired members of Aryan society, but gradually Brahman priests became more important.

Like India, China was influenced by its geography. China is divided into two main parts, China Proper and the vast semicircle of regions that surrounds it.

Chinese political history is the story of many ruling dynasties, which rose and fell in a recognizable pattern or cycle. Chinese cultural history tells of the gradual evolution of civilization over the centuries.

According to legend, the Hsia dynasty ruled China in ancient times. The first historic dynasty was the Shang, which began along the Yellow River. The Shang introduced simple irrigation and flood control systems that were essential to the prosperity of the valley. Shang artisans produced excellent work. A calendar based on the moon's movement was developed, as was an original written language. Shang religion combined animism and ancestor worship.

CHECKING WHAT YOU KNOW

1. Match each dynasty or civilization at the left with its description at the right:

   a. Hsia dynasty
   b. Indus Valley
   c. Aryan society
   d. Shang dynasty
   e. Sumerian culture

   1. Used writing on tortoise bones to tell wishes of the spirits.
   2. Possible source of Indus Valley written language.
   3. Used *Rig-Veda* as source of hymns for worship.
   4. Ruled the Yellow River region from about 2000 B.C. to 1500 B.C.
   5. Had sewer system and used standard-sized bricks in their city planning.

2. What changes did the Aryans bring to Indus Valley civilization?

3. Describe the geographical features in both India and China that were barriers to the spread of their cultures.

4. Explain how the climate influences agricultural production in the four geographical regions of India and in North and South China.

PRACTICING YOUR SKILLS

1. Using maps. Trace a map of both China and India. Indicate the areas that have heavy rainfall. Indicate the areas that need irrigation in order to grow crops. Show the desert areas (Thar Desert and the Gobi Desert) that might be used for grazing. Indicate the wind direction for summer and fall monsoons and for winter winds.

2. Making charts. Make a chart listing the accomplishments of the Indus Valley civilization, the Aryans, and the Shang dynasty.

3. Analyzing information. What differences and similarities can you find between the civilizations of the Indus Valley and the civilizations that you read about in Chapter 2? How would you account for them?

RELATING PAST TO PRESENT

1. Animism is the term used to describe the ancient religious beliefs of both the Indus and the Shang civilizations. List some of their ideas and practices and compare them with what people today call "superstitions." What are some of the symbols considered "lucky" and "unlucky" today?

2. What problems of city planning did the people of Harappa and Mohenjo-Daro solve? What are some city-planning problems today that were unknown to the inhabitants of these ancient civilizations?

3. How was the Chinese attitude toward foreigners, whom they regarded as barbarians, related to Chinese geography? What evidence can you give that other people have had similar attitudes to outsiders? Can we find the same situation in the United States or in other countries? Give examples, if possible.

INVESTIGATING FURTHER

1. Present an oral report to the class on the achievements, mysterious beginnings, and sudden end of the Indus Valley civilization. Good sources for your report are "The Valley of the Indus" in *The Horizon Book of Lost Worlds* by Leonard Cottrell (American Heritage) and "India's Forgotten Civilization" in *Readings in World History* by Leften S. Stavrianos et al. (Allyn and Bacon).

2. Learn to write about 10 characters of the Chinese language as an art form. You may use *Chinese Calligraphy* by Chiang Yee (Harvard University Press) as a source. Report to the class the skills learned in the use of the brush.

3. Look at the pictures in this chapter of different types of bronze items from the Shang dynasty. Study the pictures to discover the religious functions as well as the aesthetic value of the bronzes. Present a report to the class.

UNIT REVIEW

1. Match each term at the left with its definition at the right.

   a. artisans
   b. hieroglyphs
   c. polytheism
   d. Vedas
   e. dynasty
   f. animism
   g. city-state

   1. belief in many gods
   2. books of sacred knowledge
   3. belief that spirits inhabit everything
   4. class of skilled workers
   5. town or city and surounding land it controlled
   6. form of writing
   7. family of rulers

2. Identify the specific society or culture with which each of the following ideas or facts is associated:

   a. Constructed pyramids as royal tombs.
   b. Built large granaries to store food for city-state.
   c. Worshiped in seven-storied temples called ziggurats.
   d. Permitted women to own property in their own right.
   e. Lacked direct contact with other great civilizations and believed peoples of other cultures were barbarians.
   f. Had a religion that placed emphasis on earthly struggle between good and evil.
   g. Gradually changed class status, making priests more important than warriors.
   h. Conquered territories and replaced original inhabitants with own colonists.
   i. Developed the alphabet that became the model for later Western alphabets.
   j. Believed that Canaan was their Promised Land.
   k. Correctly calculated the length of the year within 26 minutes.

3. Explain the beliefs about God (or gods) and an afterlife in three of the following civilizations:

   a. Egyptian
   b. Sumerian
   c. Hebrew
   d. Aryan
   e. Shang
   f. Persian

4. Almost all civilizations originally developed around rivers. What advantages did rivers provide to early civilizations?

5. Describe some of the laws included in the Code of Hammurabi and in Mosaic law. Explain why such codes of law became important as people lived together in groups.

6. Identify the ancient societies in which women had the following rights:

   a. control over their own money
   b. opportunity for higher education
   c. the right to participate in decisions such as marriage

7. A variety of goods, ideas, inventions, and cultural activities can be produced easily in cultures that have cities. Demonstrate the proof of this statement in the following civilizations:

   a. Egyptian
   b. Sumerian-Babylonian
   c. Indus
   d. Shang

8. Using evidence from the civilizations listed above, discuss the following statement: "Cultures obtain more ideas and ways of doing things from other cultures, rather than creating ideas and methods that are unique to themselves." Among the topics that should be considered are:

   a. agricultural methods
   b. written language
   c. forms of government

9. Develop a dialogue between:

   a. the pharaoh of Egypt and his advisers in which they decide what countries to be friendly with and what countries to attack. The dialogue should be taking place in the year 1000 B.C.
   b. the pharaoh of Egypt and the emperor of China in which they debate who has the superior civilization.
   c. a Hebrew prophet, a follower of Zoroastrianism, and a Brahman in which they argue about the role of religion in shaping the values of their particular societies.

CIVILIZATIONS OF THE ANCIENT WORLD

A stone carving of Roman soldiers carrying treasures from the ruined temple in Jerusalem after their victory in 70 A.D.

(3000–338 B.C.)

4

Greek City-States Once Dominated the Mediterranean

So far in this book, the spotlight of history has shifted from Egypt to the Fertile Crescent to India and China. Now it swings back from China to the eastern end of the Mediterranean Sea. There, in Greece and Asia Minor and on the nearby islands, developed one of the greatest civilizations the world has ever known—Greek civilization.

The ancient Greeks were quarrelsome and could never agree among themselves for very long at a time. They were not particularly efficient empire builders. However, we take a special interest in them because they were the first people in history to think and act in ways clearly similar to our own.

For example, in government the Greeks were the first people to experiment successfully with the idea that citizens might govern themselves. In science the Greeks were curious about everything, and what they observed and wrote down may be regarded as the beginning of modern scientific thought. Many of our other ideas and traditions have their roots in ancient Greece.

Greek civilization, like the others you have read about, developed gradually. By the 500's B.C. it was about to enter one of its greatest periods—the Golden Age. The Golden Age of Greece has been given that name because it was one of the most creative periods in human history. During a hundred years or so after 500 B.C., the Greeks produced some of the most influential works of art, philosophy, and literature that the world has ever

Ruins of a Greek temple in the hills at Delphi

known. Much of **Western civilization**—the civilization that in later centuries evolved in Europe and spread to the Americas—had its foundations in early Greece.

The ideals of beauty that the Greeks established have influenced Western artists ever since. Many of our buildings have adopted the forms they developed. Our notion of the perfect, beautiful human shape is derived from Greek sculpture. Greek influence has been just as strong in philosophy and drama. For hundreds of years all Western philosophers have started with Plato and Aristotle when working out their own ideas. All of our playwrights owe something to the theater that flourished in Greece.

We continue to marvel at the lasting contributions made by the ancient Greeks to our Western heritage.

THE CHAPTER SECTIONS

1. Early Greeks settled in city-states

2. Greek government and society became more varied

3. Sparta and Athens developed different ways of life

4. Daily life in Athens combined recreation and public duties

5. Greek art represented the ideals of Greek civilization

6. Philosophers and writers added to the heritage of Greece

1

Early Greeks settled in city-states

History is always influenced by geography. In Greece, for instance, the location of cities and areas around them influenced the way they grew and what happened to them. The history of Greece as a whole was affected by a special and powerful geographic influence—the Mediterranean Sea (see map, page 68).

The land and the sea

The Mediterranean is the world's largest inland sea. It borders the shores of three continents—Europe, Asia, and Africa—and has many good harbors. Early in history the Mediterranean Sea became a busy pathway for trade and ideas. As a result, the Mediterranean area was the center of Western civilization for many centuries.

At the extreme eastern end of the Mediterranean is the great Balkan peninsula, which is separated from Asia Minor by the Aegean (ih·JEE·un) Sea. The southern tip of the Balkan peninsula consists of many small peninsulas that form the mainland of Greece.

Look at the many islands of the Aegean Sea, and note how close together they are. It was not difficult to sail from one to another, even in small boats. From Egypt and the Fertile Crescent, people brought knowledge and ideas to these islands, to the mainland of Greece, and to the Aegean shores of Asia Minor.

It may seem surprising that Greece became the home of such an important civilization. Nature was unkind in some ways. Look at the map of Greece on page 77. Notice how the mainland is cut up and divided by short mountain ranges. These mountains separated communities and prevented them from developing a sense of unity.

Greek civilization was not a river-valley civilization, for Greece has no rivers worth mentioning. But there was enough good soil, a mild climate, and sufficient rain to grow grain, grapes, and olives in the small valleys and on the lower slopes of the mountains. The foothills of the mountains also provided pasture land for sheep and goats. Greece itself, however, could never produce enough food for its population. The Greeks had to become traders to live. For this purpose Greek geography was ideal. There were many good harbors on both the mainland and the islands. The long, irregular coastline brought every part of the mainland close to the sea. Thus the Greeks learned to fish and became sailors, traders, and eventually the colonizers of new lands.

Minoan civilization

Look again at the islands of the Aegean and at the long island of Crete to the south. The earliest civilization of the region began on these islands.

People on Crete and the Aegean Islands developed a Neolithic culture before 3000 B.C. In time they learned to use copper and bronze and to make beautiful pottery. Distinctive ways of life grew up. The culture of the Aegean Islands is usually called Aegean civilization. Traces of this civilization have also been found in Asia Minor.

The culture of Crete was related to the Aegean but was more highly developed. According to legend, an early king of Crete was named Minos (MY·nus), so Cretan civilization is called Minoan (mih·NOH·un). Minoan civilization was at its height between 2000 B.C. and 1400 B.C. The Minoans were influenced by the great civilizations of nearby Egypt and the Fertile Crescent, but they also added ideas of their own. The royal palace and the homes of the nobles were equipped with running water. They were decorated with colorful **frescoes**—paintings made on wet plaster walls. Artisans made beautiful carved figures of ivory, stone, gold, silver, and bronze.

The Minoans controlled the Aegean Islands and probably founded some colonies there and in Asia Minor. They were excellent sailors and built ships that were powered by both oars and sails. They traded widely, bringing much of the art and civilization of Egypt and the Fertile Crescent to Crete. The kings of Crete were so confident that

their navy was strong enough to protect them that they did not fortify their cities.

About 1500 B.C. a volcanic explosion on a nearby island caused great damage on Crete. Not long after, warriors from Greece occupied Crete. The glories of the Minoans were soon forgotten, but through trade and religious ideas they had influenced the peoples of mainland Greece.

Early migrations into Greece

During the period when Aegean and Minoan civilizations were developing, important changes were taking place on the Greek mainland. Beginning about 2000 B.C. new people came into Greece from the north. They spoke an Indo-European language that was an early form of Greek.

The invaders were organized into clans and tribes. Several related families formed a clan, headed by a chief. A number of clans made up a tribe, with a tribal chief. The clan chiefs formed a council to help in governing. In Greece these wandering people learned how to grow grain, grapes, and olives. They also learned how to sail and often became pirates.

THE MEDITERRANEAN REGION about 550 B.C.

Greece and Greek settlements

Phoenicia and Phoenician settlements

0   500 miles

0   500 kilometers

One group, the Ionians, settled in central Greece and on the islands of the Aegean. The other group, the Mycenaeans (my·suh·NEE·unz), swept through the entire Greek mainland.

The Mycenaeans were the dominant power on the Greek mainland in the period from about 1600 B.C. to 1100 B.C. They built fortified cities in the Peloponnesus (pel·uh·puh·NEE·sus), the southern part of Greece. These included Mycenae (my·SEE·nee), Tiryns, and Pylos (see map, this page). Mycenae was the first of these settlements to be excavated in modern times. The Mycenaeans were a warlike people who carried on raids throughout the eastern Mediterranean area. They conquered Crete and were influenced by Minoan civilization.

Like the Minoans, the Mycenaeans were literate—they knew how to read and write. However, only a few of their economic and religious documents have survived. They probably weakened themselves through constant warfare. By 1200 B.C. the major Mycenaean cities, such as Mycenae, were looted. According to tradition, the city of Troy in Asia Minor was destroyed about this time. Perhaps these centers perished in the general upheaval of migrating tribes, the movement of the Sea Peoples. After the collapse of Mycenaean society, more barbaric Greeks—the Dorians—moved into the peninsula and occupied the Peloponnesus and Crete about 1100 B.C. The newcomers were illiterate, and knowledge of writing was thus lost when the Mycenaeans fell. A dark age descended on Greece until Phoenician traders introduced the alphabet about 750 B.C.

Between the fall of the Mycenaeans and 750 B.C. there is no detailed history of the Greeks. There were no records in the dark age in Greece. Later Greeks preserved oral traditions of this period, and a good deal can be guessed from the poems of Homer, one of the great Greek poets.

The city-states of Greece

Because of the geography of Greece and their own tribal organization, the early Greeks settled down in city-states. The Greek word for city-state was *polis*. Originally the word meant a fort, a refuge in time of danger. As a village or city grew up around the fort, *polis* came to mean not only the fort, but also the city and the surrounding region,

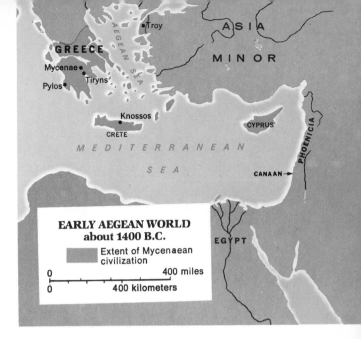

EARLY AEGEAN WORLD about 1400 B.C.

Extent of Mycenaean civilization

0   400 miles

0   400 kilometers

and the government as well. Our words *police*, *politics*, and *policy* all come from the Greek word *polis*.

Greek city-states differed in many ways, but they all had certain physical features in common: (1) *Small size.* Athens at its greatest extent was not even 1,000 square miles (2,590 square kilometers). Sparta, the largest city-state, was approximately 4,000 square miles (10,360 square kilometers). Contrast this with the entire area of modern Greece, which is more than 50,000 square miles (129,500 square kilometers). (2) *Small population.* The Greeks considered the ideal city-state population to be 5,000 to 10,000 citizens (plus slaves and other noncitizens). In such figures the number of citizens is limited to adult males, because the Greeks did not count women or children. Some city-states had a population of more than 10,000 citizens, but most of them had fewer. Athens at its height had approximately 40,000 citizens. (3) *The original polis.* In most city-states the fort stood on an *acropolis* (uh·CROP·uh·lis), a hill or mountain, together with temples and other public buildings. (4) *A public meeting place,* where all citizens could gather. Sometimes it was the city marketplace.

In the following section you will learn how Greek ideas about government changed between the years 1000 B.C. and 500 B.C. Greek city-states contributed in different ways to the development of these ideas.

Crete and Mycenae

The islanders of Crete and the Mycenaeans of the Greek mainland developed different but related cultures. The works of art they created reflected their customs and beliefs. The magnificent death mask (above), found at Mycenae, was formed from a thin sheet of gold pressed to the face of the dead man. It reminded those who saw it of his likeness and served as a costly and dramatic memorial. The skills of the Mycenaeans are also visible in the enormous structure (right). Two lions are carved at the top of the gateway. Holes near the top of the animals suggest that their heads, now lost, were attached separately.

To the people of Crete the bull was sacred, figuring in activities of religious significance. It was also used in sport (below). Here men and women are somersaulting over the back of a charging bull.

1. IDENTIFY: Ionians, Mycenaeans, Dorians, polis, acropolis.

2. LOCATE: Balkan peninsula, Aegean Sea, Crete, Mycenae, Troy, Athens, Sparta.

3. Name the favorable geographic conditions that led to the development of Greek civilization.

4. What were the accomplishments of Minoan civilization?

5. What were the four things that all Greek city-states had in common?

2

Greek government and society became more varied

Once the Greeks had settled their land and established their city-states, they began to develop their distinctive culture. For about 500 years they lived under kings, nobles, and tyrants. Toward the end of that period, however, different forms of government began to emerge. The city-states never united, and thus a variety of governments could be found throughout Greece.

The Age of Kings

Little is known about the period in Greece between 1000 B.C. and 700 B.C. We do know that the city-states had similar forms of government that were based on the tribal systems introduced during the early migrations. These tribal systems gradually developed into small kingdoms, or monarchies. The period is often known as the Age of Kings. There was constant warfare among the city-states, and as a result there was little trade.

Greek culture at this time was not very advanced. Few people knew how to write, and poets wandered from village to village and sang or recited folk songs, ballads, and epics. Epics were long poems describing heroes and great events.

Sometime during the 700's B.C. much of this oral poetry was gathered together and woven into two great epics—the *Iliad* and the *Odyssey*. According to tradition, they were composed by the blind poet Homer. In fact, the period is often also referred to as the Homeric Age because of Homer's magnificent description of it.

The Homeric epics were composed against the background of the Trojan war. Legends told how a Trojan prince, Paris, stole Helen, the beautiful wife of a Greek king. The Greeks then sent a great sea expedition against Troy. After years of fighting, Troy was captured by a trick and looted. The *Iliad* describes incidents in the tenth year of the war centering on the Greek hero Achilles and the death of the Trojan prince Hector. The *Odyssey* tells the story of the many adventures of the Greek hero Odysseus on his long journey home from the Trojan war.

Although the *Iliad* and the *Odyssey* supposedly describe the Mycenaeans of the 1200's B.C., they actually provide the best and richest source of information about the life, customs, and ideals of the Greeks during the period from 1000 B.C. to 700 B.C.

Religious and moral beliefs. The religion that developed among the Greeks during the Homeric Age was quite different from the religions of the Egyptians, Persians, and Hebrews. The Greeks asked three things of their religion: (1) an explanation for such mysteries of the physical world as thunder, lightning, and the change of the seasons; (2) an explanation of the passions that could make people lose the self-control that the Greeks considered necessary; and (3) a way to gain such benefits as long life, good fortune, and abundant harvests.

The Greeks' ideas of morality were only vaguely connected with their ideas about religion. They did not expect their religion to save them from sin, to bring them spiritual blessings, or to ensure a life after death. There were no commandments.

Greeks of the Homeric Age were not as concerned as some other peoples—for example, the Egyptians—about what happened to them after death. Often they cremated, or burned, the dead with only a simple ritual. They thought that with a few exceptions the spirits of all people went to a gray and gloomy place called Hades (HAY·deez). It was not a place of punishment except for extremely evil people.

The Greek gods. In their beliefs about the gods the Greeks were practical people. They thought of gods as having human weaknesses and wants

connections

Stadiums

Millions of sports fans jam stadiums each year to watch their favorite teams compete. The idea of a big "bowl," with terraced steps on which people can sit, goes back nearly 3,000 years, to the ancient Greeks. When the first Olympic Games were held in 776 B.C., the events took place in a magnificent stadium built for the occasion in the city of Olympia. Ancient stadiums still stand, such as the one at Pergamum, in Turkey (top).

The Greeks, and later the Romans, erected many of these arenas, which often were used for entertainments other than sports. Circuses were held there, and plays were performed on a stage at one end.

Today, stadiums continue to have various uses. Yankee Stadium in New York City, for example, is mainly a place to play baseball. Yet it has also held huge crowds who have wanted to attend a concert or to hear the pope during his visit to the United States.

Ancient stadiums were smaller than those we know. One of the largest, the Colosseum in Rome, could hold perhaps 40,000 people. Modern stadiums have room for many more people. The soccer stadium in Rio de Janeiro, Brazil, can hold 200,000, and one in Prague, Czechoslovakia, has a capacity of 240,000.

In the United States, the football stadium in Los Angeles, California, has room for 100,000 (center), and the Astrodome, the indoor stadium in Houston, Texas, can house 60,000 (below). Putting a roof over a stadium is a modern innovation. It solves the one problem that makes scheduling events in the open air so difficult: bad weather.

The appeal of sports thus goes back many years. So, too, does the need to create a place where a large number of people can watch an event at the same time. The stadium remains the best way of meeting that need.

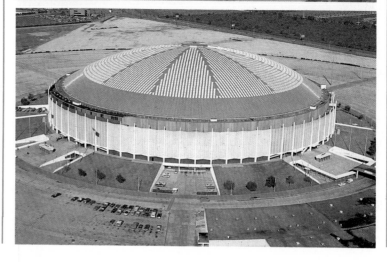

much like their own, only on a larger scale. Greek gods lived not in some remote heaven but on the top of Mount Olympus, a peak in northern Greece (see map, page 77).

To explain their world, the Greeks developed **myths**—traditional stories about the deeds and misdeeds of gods, goddesses, and heroes. The Greeks believed that there were many gods and goddesses, and no one of them was considered much higher than the others. Zeus (ZOOS), god of the sky, was the king of the gods and the father of some humans. Hera was his sister and wife, the protector of women and marriage. Poseidon (poh·SY·dun), brother of Zeus, was god of the sea—a very important god to the seafaring Greeks. Pluto, another brother of Zeus, was lord of Hades, the underworld.

Athena, daughter of Zeus, was the goddess of wisdom and womanly virtue, the special protector of the great city-state of Athens, which was named in her honor. Aphrodite (af·ruh·DY·tee), another daughter, was goddess of love and beauty. Apollo was god of light, music, and poetry, as well as the symbol of manly beauty. Dionysus (dy·uh·NY·sus) was the god of fertility and wine.

Religious practices. At certain sanctuaries called oracles, the gods were believed to speak through priests or priestesses, usually in answer to questions about the future. The most famous oracle was that of Apollo at Delphi.

Because the gods were thought to be pleased by displays of strength and courage, the Greeks held athletic contests in their honor. Most famous were the games at Olympia, held every fourth year in honor of Zeus.

At first the Olympic games consisted only of foot races. Later, jumping, javelin and discus throwing, boxing, wrestling, and horse and chariot racing were added. At the games winners received only wreaths of wild olive branches, but when they returned home they received many honors and rich gifts. The games were so important that the Greeks used them for dating events. Beginning in 776 B.C. they figured time in four-year periods called Olympiads.

Rise of the nobles

Around 700 B.C. the nobles—the chief landowners—began taking power from the kings. One reason for the nobles' importance was the fact that they supplied cavalry to the military forces. Another reason was that population was increasing, but the amount of land that could be farmed was not. Small farmers had trouble providing for their families. When a crop failed, small farmers frequently had to mortgage their land to a noble.

Another development affecting farmers was the increasing number of slaves. People who could not pay their debts were sold into slavery. Some slaves were imported from Asia Minor. Prisoners of war were enslaved, and the children of slaves were slaves from birth. Free workers found it difficult to compete with slave labor.

Some unemployed peasants and workers moved to the cities, where a commercial class of merchants developed. The merchants could become wealthy but always remained beneath the nobles in social position.

The nobles encouraged discontented peasants and laborers to leave Greece and go out to establish colonies. Colonization was often well planned, with leaders, laws, and forms of government chosen in advance. Greek settlements, established as city-states like those on the mainland, were planted on islands and shorelines throughout the Black, Aegean, and Mediterranean seas (see map, page 68). Greek colonies spread Greek culture throughout the Mediterranean. Soon Sicily and much of southern Italy were Greek areas.

The nobles controlled many Greek city-states until about 650 B.C. The city-states governed by nobles were called **aristocracies.** (Today the word *aristocracy* is often used to mean a privileged ruling class.) During this time there were many changes that eventually weakened the nobles' power. Foot soldiers became more important in war so that the nobles' cavalry was not needed. Nobles fought among themselves. Great numbers of people became discontented with the rule of the nobles and looked for leaders who could promise better things.

The Age of Tyrants

The leaders who appeared with the promises were called **tyrants.** To the Greeks, a tyrant was some-

(continued on page 76)

Gods and myths

Gods and myths were favorite topics for Greek writers, artists, and builders. The most impressive buildings were temples honoring the gods, such as the early temple (above) on the island of Aegina. Temples were often decorated with friezes, or stone carvings, that pictured the gods. The gods were also frequent subjects of sculpture. Here we see Athena (right), the goddess of wisdom, wearing her traditional helmet. A charioteer (far left) takes on godlike stature in this powerful piece.

The favorite Greek myths were also retold through art. On a decorative plate (lower left), the great hero Hercules battles the half-man, half-fish Triton, surrounded by dancers. Hercules, the son of Zeus, possessed massive and unmatched strength. This made it possible for him to complete the 12 labors he had to undertake for killing his family in a fit of madness. The carving (upper left) celebrates Hera, the queen of the Greek gods and the wife of Zeus. Because Hera was believed to protect married women, brides brought her gifts in the hope that she would bless and preserve their marriages.

one who seized power by force rather than inheriting it. Tyrants always promised to bring peace and prosperity and to defend the poor against the nobles and officials. Many of the tyrants were excellent rulers. Their interest in commerce made them want peace. They therefore put an end to the nobles' struggles for political power, encouraged trade, and passed just laws.

Tyrants ruled many of the Greek city-states during the period from 650 B.C. to 500 B.C. As time went on, some of them became harsh and unjust, giving the word *tyrant* its present meaning of a ruler who exercises absolute power brutally and oppressively.

Popular government

During the period from 1000 B.C. to 500 B.C., Greek ideas about government changed. At various times power was held by kings, or by nobles or tyrants. However, there was also constant development of the idea of **popular government**—the idea that people could and should rule themselves and not be ruled by others. By the time the Age of Tyrants was ending, this idea had taken root in many city-states.

When cities ousted their tyrants, some restored the old monarchies or aristocracies. Others developed the form of government called **democracy**— a government in which all citizens took part. Even in monarchies and aristocracies a council of citizens limited the power of the rulers.

At this time, there were many influences that might have led the Greeks to unite. All spoke the same language, which they regarded as a common tie. They referred to peoples who did not speak Greek as "barbarians." The ancient Greeks also believed that they were descended from the same ancestor, the hero Hellen. Thus, they called themselves Hellenes and their country Hellas. They had a common religion, and great festivals such as the Olympic games brought them together. They joined in common management of certain temples, such as those of Zeus at Olympia and Apollo at Delphi.

However, other factors kept the Greeks apart. One was geography. The rugged mountains separated the small valleys and their populations from each other. Another was the fierce spirit of independence that made Greeks proud of their individual city-states and distrustful of each other. Each city-state had its own laws, calendar, money, and system of weights and measures. Citizens loved their city and were willing to give their lives for it.

CHECKUP

1. IDENTIFY: Age of Kings, Homer, *Iliad, Odyssey,* Zeus, Athena, aristocracies, tyrant, popular government, democracy.

2. List three religious beliefs of the Greeks.

3. How did the nobles win power in Greece? Why did they lose power? What part did tyrants play in the process?

4. There were many factors that might have led the Greeks to unite. Name them and discuss why the Greek city-states did not unite.

Sparta and Athens developed different ways of life

There were both similarities and differences among Greek city-states. The wide range of differences that existed is clearly shown by comparing the two city-states that became the most important, Sparta and Athens.

Totalitarian Sparta

You have read about the different groups of people who invaded the mainland of Greece from the north starting about 2000 B.C. The Dorians, the last of these groups, moved south to the Peloponnesus about 1100 B.C. They conquered and settled the region of Laconia and made the city of Sparta their capital (see map, opposite). The conquerors maintained their separate societies but forced the natives to work for them as serfs. **Serfs** were rural laborers, or peasants, who were not allowed to move away from the land on which they worked. The serfs outnumbered the Spartans about five to one, but the Spartans controlled them by force. The serfs were always hostile.

In spite of this danger, Sparta was built in a valley, and no wall surrounded it. Spartans were boastful people, and one of their leaders said, "A city is well fortified which has a wall of men instead of brick." Nearly everything in Spartan culture was devoted to this militaristic idea—this "wall of men."

Social groups

The population of Sparta was divided into three groups. Most important were the citizens, the descendants of the Dorian invaders. They controlled the government. To support the citizens and their families, the government divided all its land equally among citizens. With each allotment of land went serfs to work it.

The Spartans called the second group of people by the Greek word that meant "neighbors." They were free, but were not citizens. They lived in the towns, and most of them worked in commerce and industry. Some "neighbors" became rich, but they could never be citizens.

The lowest group were the serfs, who were called **helots** (HEL·uts). Because the Spartans lived in constant fear of a helot revolt, they tried to prevent the helots from developing any leaders. Sometimes, the Spartans killed helots who were defiant. The brutal system worked, but as you will see, it had its price.

Government in Sparta

An Assembly of all citizens over thirty years of age elected the officials and voted on major policies. A Council of Elders consisting of two kings and twenty-eight members, all over sixty years of age, proposed the laws and policies on which the Assembly voted. The two kings were hereditary and served as high priests, judges, and army commanders.

The Council of Elders could overrule any act of the Assembly, but the authority of the kings was often challenged by five ephors (meaning "overseers") elected by the Assembly. These five men had power to act as guardians of the state, but they served for only one year.

Sparta's rulers used their unlimited powers harshly. For example, because the ephors feared that the people would come to love money and luxuries, they prohibited the use of gold and silver. Money was made of iron bars, which were too

ANCIENT GREECE

Major Greek settlements in Asia Minor underlined

heavy to carry around and would not buy much. The ephors also feared that contact with outside peoples and ideas would weaken discipline and obedience. Therefore, they did not permit citizens to travel, and foreign visitors were made to feel unwelcome.

The military machine

The lives of the citizens of Sparta were regulated from birth to death. All the rules had a single basic aim—to make every adult male citizen part of an efficient military machine. This army was needed to control the conquered people and to extend Spartan power.

The development of Spartan fighting men, and of women fit to marry them, began at birth. New-born babies were examined by a group of officials. Any child who seemed weak, unhealthy, or deformed in any way was left by the roadside to die. At the age of seven, boys were taken to live in barracks, in military groups. They were taught to read and write, but the greater part of their education was military. They were trained in the use of weapons and in the "Spartan virtues"—courage, strength, endurance, cunning, and devotion to Sparta.

It was a harsh education. To learn endurance, boys wore only a single garment, summer and winter. They never wore shoes. Often they were beaten publicly so that they would learn to bear pain without crying out. To teach them to search for food for themselves in wartime, the authorities provided food that was coarse and scanty. The boys had to steal food to keep from starving.

The citizen began his military service at the age of 20. He remained in the army until he was 60. At 30 a Spartan was expected to marry, but he had little family life. He spent most of his time in military training. He ate his meals and spent his leisure time in a military club. He was not allowed to engage in any trade or business, because business activities and love of money were considered bad for military discipline.

Spartan girls, as the future mothers of soldiers, had to be healthy, too. They received strict physical training for strength and endurance. They were also trained in patriotic devotion.

Today there is a name for the Spartan kind of civilization. A system in which the government controls every aspect of the individual's life is called a **totalitarian** system. Totalitarian societies often glorify war, as did Sparta. The strict discipline of Sparta did lead to efficient government and an almost unconquerable army. However, the Spartans produced nothing in the fields of art, literature, philosophy, or science.

Democratic Athens

The early history of Athens was quite different from that of Sparta. In Athens there was no military class of conquering invaders imposing its rule upon a conquered people, as in Sparta.

Much of the soil around Athens was rocky and unproductive. The Athenians were compelled to become sea traders to make a living. They built Athens inland to protect it against pirates and constructed Piraeus (py·REE·us) as a special port city for Athens (see map, page 77). Athens itself was a typical polis. The city was built around the rocky, fortified hill of the Acropolis. The entire city was surrounded by a strong wall. It was a place of defense for all of the surrounding region in time of war.

Social groups

As in Sparta, the population of Athens was divided into three groups. First were the citizens. In Athens, as a rule, one could be a citizen only if both one's father and mother were citizens. If only one parent had been a citizen, a person might become one by decree. Although women were citizens, they could not vote or hold office and were regarded legally as minors.

Next came the aliens—those who were not Athenians—who were called **metics.** Most metics were merchants or skilled workers. They were free but could not own land or take part in government. Metics, however, paid the same taxes as citizens and moved about freely.

Lowest of all were the slaves. At the time of Athens' greatest glory, more than half the population consisted of metics and slaves. In Athens, as in all of Greece, slaves were considered property, dependent on their master's will. An Athenian master could not treat his slaves brutally, nor did he have the power of life and death over them. However, if a slave complained or was killed, the word of the master was accepted by the court. If the master permitted it, the slave might acquire property and even become wealthy. A slave who was freed became a metic.

To the Greeks, slavery was a necessity and part of the natural order of things. The philosopher Aristotle believed that the other people of Europe were so stupid and those of Asia so cowardly that nature intended them to be slaves—for Greeks.

Early government in Athens

After the Age of Kings, there was an aristocratic government in Athens. Citizens were divided into four classes according to the amount of land they owned. Only the three highest classes voted.

The voters met in an Assembly and elected nine **archons,** or rulers, from the two highest classes. The archons served terms of one year each. They appointed all officials and made all the laws, but these laws were not written down. The judges, who were always nobles (the first of the four classes), interpreted the laws and applied them in each case. Needless to say, the laws always seemed to favor the noble class.

Four reformers

Four rulers—Draco, Solon, Pisistratus (py·SIS·truh·tus), and Cleisthenes (KLYS·thuh·neez)—influenced the political development of Athens.

Athenian Democratic Reformers

621 B.C.   Draco drew up code of laws

594 B.C.   Solon abolished enslavement for debt, set up Council of Four Hundred, permitted fourth class of citizens to vote, established court of appeals

560–527 B.C.   Pisistratus abolished landowning requirement for citizenship, divided estates among landless peasants

510–? B.C.   Cleisthenes abolished class divisions based on wealth, broadened Assembly membership, increased Council to 500 members

Draco, who was archon in 621 B.C., is known for the code of laws he drew up. The laws were harsh and severe, but they were written down so that everyone could know them.

Conditions in Athens remained unsatisfactory under Draco. Nobles and metics became wealthy from trade, but small farmers grew poorer. More and more citizens were being sold into slavery for debt. The poor began to demand that their debts be canceled and that the land be divided equally. Creditors and landowners opposed both of these demands.

In this emergency, Athens came under the control of Solon, a trusted business leader, who served as archon about 594 B.C. He took a moderate position between debtors and creditors. He canceled the debts of the poor and made laws providing that there should be no more enslavement for debt. He freed those who had been enslaved for nonpayment.

To check the power of the archons, Solon set up a Council of Four Hundred, with members chosen from the three upper classes. The Council proposed the laws voted on by the Assembly. Solon also permitted the fourth class of citizens to vote. To check the power of the judges, he set up a court, composed of large numbers of citizens, to which a citizen could appeal.

Athens still suffered much unrest. The nobles formed rival political groups and struggled for control of the government. Then Pisistratus, a wealthy aristocrat and a relative of Solon, created a following among the lower classes. About 560 B.C. he became a tyrant and remained one off and on until 527 B.C. Pisistratus lessened opposition by exiling nobles who disagreed with his policies. Their estates were seized and divided among landless peasants. He also encouraged farmers to grow grapes for wine. Grapes were better suited than wheat to the soil of Attica, the peninsula on which Athens lies. Grain was imported from abroad.

About 510 B.C. Cleisthenes came to power in Athens. He seized power in a brief civil war and imposed a democratic system of government. Although a man of wealth and high social position, Cleisthenes was interested in the welfare of the common people. He opposed class divisions based on wealth and instead divided citizens into ten tribes based on geographic location. All male citizens over 20 years of age became members of the Assembly. The Council was increased to 500 members, 50 from each tribe, who were selected from all male citizens over 30 years of age. The Council took over many of the powers and duties formerly held by the archons.

A democratic state

Cleisthenes' reforms made Athens an almost complete democracy. The Assembly of all citizens had full and final power. It chose archons and generals and could punish them for wrongdoing. The Council of Five Hundred proposed laws to the Assembly.

Even the courts were completely democratic. Jurors and some officials were chosen by lot, in keeping with the Athenian belief in the equality and fitness of all citizens for government service. Each man could plead his own case. There was no judge. The jury of citizens was the entire court, and juries were very large—501 was a common number. Each juror voted by secret ballot.

For those who were allowed to participate, it was probably the most completely democratic government in history. However, more than half of the residents were not citizens. Many an Athenian was able to give so much of his time and service to his government because he was supported by slaves.

1. IDENTIFY: helots, Council of Elders, ephors, totalitarian, metics, archon, Solon.

2. LOCATE: Laconia, Piraeus, Attica.

3. How was Sparta governed? How did Spartans try to prevent helot revolts? How did they discourage love of luxury?

4. What was the aim of the regulations under which Spartans lived? How were Spartans educated to fulfill this aim?

5. How did the system of slavery aid both the economic and political development of Athens?

6. Describe the different features of Athens' early government. What reforms occurred to transform this government into more of a democracy?

Daily life in Athens combined recreation and public duties

The citizens of Athens and the other Greek city-states lived in much the same way. Their lives consisted of work, recreation, and the fulfillment of their responsibilities to the city-state.

Farming

Farming was the most honored occupation for an Athenian citizen. More than half of all citizens were farmers, including many farmers who usually owned the small plots of land that they worked. Unlike small farmers and peasants in most other societies, they could vote and hold public office.

Because the soil around Athens was poor, fields had to lie unplanted every second year to regain fertility. To make matters worse, there was little level land for raising grain. Thus farmers concentrated instead on growing olives, grapes, and figs on terraced hillsides. Athens exported olive oil and wine and, as you have read, imported much of the grain that was necessary to feed its people.

The principal domestic animals were sheep and goats. Goats furnished milk for making cheese. In addition, sheep were valued for their wool and meat. However, Athenians did not eat much meat. Fish and cheese were more common in their diet.

Manufacturing and trade

Athenian manufacturing was carried on in small shops. The largest business establishment was a shield factory owned by a metic, which employed 120 workers. However, a shop with 20 workers was considered large. Many artisans worked in their own homes. Members of the family labored side by side with slaves and free employees. The quality of the work was extraordinarily high. Today, Athenian vases and household utensils are highly valued for their simple grace and beauty. Yet most of them were made not by famous artists but by ordinary artisans.

Foreign trade formed an extremely important part of the Athenian economy. The need to increase the food supply influenced all government policy. It made foreign trade a necessity and led to the building of the Athenian fleet and the establishment of colonies. Athenian ships went everywhere in the Mediterranean world, from the Black Sea in the east to Spain in the west. The ships sailed out with olive oil, wine, and manufactured goods. They brought back the all-important grain and raw materials that could not be provided at home.

Homes and streets

The Athenians built beautiful temples and other public buildings. There was a remarkable contrast between these structures and private homes. The Athenian ideal was to spend money on buildings to beautify and benefit the whole community, not on private homes.

Houses were simple and plain, built close to the street, and usually one story high. The walls were made of sun-dried brick. The street wall was plain except for a door that led into an open court. From the court, doors opened into the living room, dining room, bedrooms, storerooms, and kitchen. Little attention was given to the appearance of the house itself, and its contents were usually simple. The only heat came from open pans that held burning coals. Light was furnished by

Daily life in ancient Greece

The ancient Greeks proudly re-created scenes of everyday life in their art. The scene on a vase (above left) shows students being instructed in two of Greece's most honored fields of study—music and writing. The vase (left) shows a more commonplace occupation—that of a fishmonger preparing a customer's order.

Every four years, one day was lifted out of the ordinary. On that day, the citizens of Athens gathered at their marketplace. They formed a long procession that wound its way to the Parthenon, a temple built to honor the goddess Athena. The horsemen (below) appear on a frieze on the Parthenon depicting that procession. Horses were prized possessions for the ancient Greeks, who sometimes chose them to decorate their personal seals (above right).

dim lamps that burned olive oil. There was no plumbing and no running water. Water was carried from wells or springs in large jars.

Most streets were narrow and crooked. They were usually dirty, too, because people threw rubbish and garbage into them. There were no sidewalks, no sewage system, no garbage collection, no street cleaning, and no paving.

Family life

Athenians considered marriage a major institution. Its main purpose was the bearing and rearing of children. Marriages were always arranged by the parents. A girl married early, at 13 or 14. Usually her husband was at least twice her age.

A married woman had few legal rights. She could not make a contract or bring a suit in court. When a man died, his wife did not inherit his property. Because of poor medical knowledge, many women died in childbirth. If a family could not afford to raise a baby, it was "exposed," that is, abandoned by the side of the road. More female babies were exposed than male babies.

In social life, too, women were considered inferior to men. Their duty was to manage the household and the slaves and see to the upbringing of the children. They rarely appeared in public, and then only by permission of their husbands. If there was a banquet or entertainment in the home, the wife withdrew to another part of the house.

In the well-to-do household, the Athenian mother, aided by a woman slave, took care of both boys and girls until they were six. At the age of six a boy was placed in the care of a male slave. The slave taught the boy manners and went everywhere with him, including school. Girls stayed in the home, rarely going outside, and then only when accompanied by their parents. They learned how to run a household but received no other schooling.

Education and recreation

Most Greeks were poor and worked hard. They toiled long hours at monotonous work, with little time off. The rich despised working hard with their hands and had slaves to do it. Intellectual and physical excellence were important to them. They spent most of their time engaging in politics, gossip in the marketplace, conversations with friends, and athletic activities.

The Athenians realized that if their democracy was to be successful, its leaders had to be educated. Boys attended elementary schools, which charged fees.

Three main subjects were taught in these elementary schools—grammar, music, and gymnastics. Grammar included reading, writing, and arithmetic. Boys learned to write on a wooden tablet covered with wax. Much of their reading consisted of traditional Greek literature, such as Homer's *Iliad* and *Odyssey*. Boys were taught to sing and to play musical instruments.

The Athenian ideal was a sound mind in a healthy body. Grammar and music developed the mind and the emotions. Gymnastics developed the body. In open fields at the edge of the city, boys practiced running, jumping, boxing, and throwing the discus and the javelin.

Schools for older boys were conducted by men who called themselves Sophists, from the Greek word *sophos,* meaning "wise." Here the boys studied poetry, government, ethics, geometry, astronomy, and rhetoric (RET·uh·rik). **Rhetoric** was the study of oratory, or public speaking, and debating, which were so important in Greek life.

When a boy was 18, he received a year of military training. At 19, in an impressive public ceremony, he became a full citizen. After becoming a citizen, a young man served in the army for a year. This system was for those who could afford to pay for weapons and armor. The poor served the city by rowing warships.

CHECKUP

1. IDENTIFY: grammar, Sophists, rhetoric.

2. Why was Athens so dependent upon trade for its economy?

3. What did homes in Athens look like? Why were they not more elaborate?

4. Describe Greek attitudes toward women as shown in marriage customs, the rights of citizenship, and social life.

5. List three ways in which the lives of the poor in Athens differed from those of the upper classes.

5

Greek art represented the ideals of Greek civilization

Because Athens was wealthy and powerful, artists and teachers were attracted to the city. Athenians were active in the arts, and some were leaders in their fields. The cultural activity at Athens during the 400's B.C. has led to this period being called a Golden Age.

Architecture

The Athenians showed their love of Athens, and their pride in it, by erecting many beautiful public buildings—temples, gymnasiums, and theaters. They decorated buildings and all public places with their finest works of art, especially sculpture. The Athenians made beautiful art a part of their daily life.

The Acropolis, the hill where the original polis was located, was the scene of special artistic creations. A magnificent gate stood at the entrance to the path up the hill. Inside the gate towered a huge bronze statue of the goddess Athena, 70 feet (21 meters) high. As the special protectress of the city of Athens, she was armed with shield and spear.

On top of the Acropolis stood the Parthenon, a temple in honor of the goddess Athena. Begun in 447 B.C., it is considered the finest example of Greek architecture. The beauty of the Parthenon lay not in its great size but in its pleasing proportions—the relation of length to width, and of both to height. A Greek ideal was the Golden Mean: "Nothing in excess, and everything in proportion."

Each end of the Parthenon was adorned with sculptured figures. Like much Greek sculpture, these figures were painted in various bright colors. A series of columns, the colonnade, encircled the building. Many works of sculpture stood outside the columns. The temple itself had doors but no windows. Greek temples were shrines rather than meeting places for worshipers. Within the Parthenon stood another large statue of Athena. Its surface was of carved ivory, and there were draperies of gold decorated with jewels.

Painting

The best-preserved Greek paintings are those that were used to decorate vases. Vase painters illustrated everyday life as well as myths. They delighted in showing graceful and natural movements. The best of them could depict light and shade on the pottery and could show contours and depth in figures and draperies.

Other Greek painters decorated public buildings with murals, or wall paintings. Few of these have survived. Our knowledge of Greek painting comes mainly from literary descriptions and from Roman copies. The mural painters often chose to illustrate scenes from the *Iliad* or *Odyssey*. On one of the public buildings of Athens, for example, an artist painted "The Sack of Troy." With a true sense of tragedy, he did not depict the massacre at the moment of victory, but the silence of the following day, with the defeated lying in death amid the ruins of the city.

Sculpture

Probably the greatest Greek art was sculpture. Not many original works of Greek sculpture are still in existence. What we know about Greek sculpture has also come to us chiefly through copies made during Roman times.

Two of the greatest sculptors of all time lived during the Golden Age. The first was Myron, whose most famous figure is the Discus Thrower. The second was Phidias, who created the two wonderful statues of Athena—one at the entrance to the Acropolis and one in the Parthenon. His greatest work was the statue of Zeus at the Temple of Olympia. Greeks who attended the Olympic games looked at it with awe. In ancient times this statue was considered one of the Seven Wonders of the World.

Praxiteles (prak·SIT·uh·leez), who lived about a hundred years after Phidias, made quite different sculpture. Phidias' works were large, formal, and dignified, as was appropriate for the gods. Praxiteles made his figures more human and lifelike. Often they were life-sized. They were more graceful than those of Phidias, but they did not inspire awe and reverence as had the works of the earlier master. Above all, Praxiteles expressed the Greek admiration for the beauty of the human body.

The nature of Greek art

All that you have learned about Greek architecture, painting, and sculpture will help you to understand the Golden Age, for the art of the Greeks reflected their culture.

What were the most important characteristics of this great art? First and foremost, it glorified humans as the most important creatures in the universe. It is true that much of the painting and sculpture portrayed gods and goddesses, but you will recall that the Greeks thought the gods existed for the benefit of people. When humans glorified the gods, they glorified themselves. To gain this effect, the Greek painter or sculptor idealized the subject, omitting any blemishes. The faces and figures of men and women represented the Greek ideal of beauty. The statues suggested ideal traits admired by the Greeks—strength, intelligence, pride, grace, and courage.

Second, Greek art symbolized the pride of the people in their city-states. At the same time, it honored the gods, thanked them for life and fortune, and tried to win their favor. Thus, in giving Athena a beautiful shrine in the Parthenon, the Athenians showed their love for their city and their hope for its continuing good fortune.

Third, all Greek art expressed Greek ideals of harmony, balance, order, and moderation—the qualities of simplicity and restraint.

Finally, the Greeks believed in combining beauty and usefulness. To them, the useful, the beautiful, and the good were closely bound together. They wanted their art, and even their furniture and kitchen utensils, to be both serviceable and beautiful.

CHECKUP

1. IDENTIFY: Golden Age, Parthenon, colonnade, murals, "The Sack of Troy," Myron.

2. Briefly explain the meaning of the following quotation: "Nothing in excess, and everything in proportion."

3. What do the paintings on Greek vases depict? How is the subject matter different from that of sculpture?

4. What was the difference between the sculpture of Phidias and that of Praxiteles?

5. List four main characteristics of Greek art.

HISTORY THROUGH ART

Greek Funeral Stele

By the time of the sculptor Phidias, in the 400's B.C., the Greek attitude about death was not a very religious one. Funerals were held without priests, hymns, or prayers. Emphasis was on the human element, on preserving the memory of the deceased. The Greeks erected steles (STEE·lees), or slabs of stone, to commemorate their dead permanently and publicly. The earliest steles were rough pillars used only to mark gravesites. In time, steles became more elaborate, with stylized figures symbolizing how the dead had lived, for example, as soldiers, farmers, or politicians. By 400 B.C., steles consisted of simple scenes showing the deceased with their families, in courageous feats, or preparing for death.

This grave stele of Hegeso was done in the late 400's B.C. It captures the lovely Athenian woman as she carefully selects a precious jewel from a jewelry box held by her servant. Perhaps Hegeso is planning to wear the jewel on her journey to the next world. The stele is set inside an architectural frame, typical of the classic style. Symmetry and balance, so important in Greek art, are evident in this stele. Hegeso's right hand is located precisely in the center of the relief. In keeping with the Greek idealization of human beings, the unknown sculptor suggests that Hegeso was beautiful, in life as well as in death.

6

Philosophers and writers added to the heritage of Greece

The Greeks have been honored through the ages for their artistic and intellectual achievements. No people before them—and few since—demonstrated so clearly the greatness of which the human hand and mind are capable. The Greeks were eager to learn all they could and to think through everything that the human mind is capable of understanding. These characteristics are clearly shown in the record of the Greek thinkers and writers.

Socrates

One of the greatest thinkers and teachers of all time was Socrates (SAHK·ruh·teez), who lived in Athens from 469 B.C. to 399 B.C. Trained as a sculptor, he gave up that profession to be a teacher. He would not take pay for teaching and lived in poverty. Most people loved him because he was wise, honest, and kindly.

Socrates was a critic of Athenian education, especially of the Sophists. He said they boasted too much of their wisdom and made their pupils conceited. He would not allow himself to be called a Sophist, preferring the term *philosopher*—a word which in Greek means "lover of wisdom." From this term comes our word **philosophy,** which may be defined as inquiry into the most fundamental questions of reality and human existence. The Greeks were the first people to reason about the entire range of human experience in a systematic way.

Socrates wanted people to learn to think for themselves and not imitate their elders. Only then could they learn wisdom, which would lead to right living. Only evil could result from ignorance. People must depend on their reason to guide their lives, to show them what was truly important.

Socrates himself did not teach as the Sophists did, which was by memorizing. Instead he asked questions of anyone he met, anywhere. The purpose of his questions was not to get information, but to make people think in order to answer the questions themselves. "Know thyself" was his

motto. He wanted people to understand what such ideas as love, friendship, duty, patriotism, honor, and justice really meant to them. Each person must find his or her own answers to these problems. This way of teaching is known as the "Socratic method."

Socrates inspired great love among his followers, but he also made enemies. His questions often made public officials look foolish. He was very critical of democracy. He felt that it was unwise to elect unskilled people to positions of power, and he did not trust the wisdom of the Assembly. After all, he said, we do not elect doctors or ship pilots—so why should we elect rulers? Young aristocrats flocked to hear Socrates mock democracy and its leaders, who did not find him so amusing.

Even though Socrates honored the gods of the city, his enemies accused him of denying the existence of the many Greek gods. He was brought to trial on charges of teaching false religion and corrupting the minds of Athenian youth.

At the trial Socrates said that his conscience made him teach. If he were allowed to live, he would continue to teach, because his conscience would compel him to. He was found guilty and condemned to die by drinking a poison made from the hemlock plant. He died in 399 B.C.

Plato

Socrates had always been too busy teaching to write down his ideas. Later generations learned about them from the writings of Plato, the greatest of his students. Plato was a wealthy young aristocrat. After Socrates' death, he began to teach in the grounds of the Academy, a public park and athletic field.

Plato's writing is in the form of dialogues, that is, imaginary conversations among several people. There are dialogues on government, education, justice, virtue, and religion. In each dialogue, Socrates usually asks questions of the others. The dialogues, however, express many of Plato's own theories.

To answer the question "What is justice?" Plato wrote a long dialogue called the *Republic*. This dialogue described Plato's concept of the ideal form of government. People, he said, should do

HISTORIANS   From the earliest days, people have wanted to keep some record of their achievements. Thus they build monuments, or they tell stories from parents to children, or they write things down. To give shape to their stories, to show how events related to one another, ancient people began to write what we call histories. In both Greek and Latin, the word *historia* means a story or a narrative. Historians were regarded as those who told the story of the past.

Because of the investigations of historians, who try to find out exactly what happened at important moments, we have learned many things about the past. One of the earliest historians, a Greek named Herodotus, always tried to make sure that information was as accurate as possible. Herodotus lived in the 400's B.C. He wrote a detailed account of the Persian Wars, the great struggle between the Greeks and the Persians that had taken place in the years before he was born. (You will read more about the Persian Wars in the next chapter.)

A great deal of our information about these wars exists only because Herodotus found it out and wrote it down. Here, to give one example, is his account of how the battle of Salamis began. This was a naval battle at which the Athenian ships defeated the Persian fleet in the year 480 B.C. It was one of the turning points of the war, and the question was how the Greeks, badly outnumbered, dared to fight. Here is how Herodotus explained it:

> Themistocles (the Athenian leader) . . . told them to board their ships. . . . Whereupon the Greeks put to sea. The fleet had hardly left shore when they were attacked by the Persians. At once most of the Greeks began to retreat, and were about to touch land again when one of the Athenian captains shot forward and charged one of the enemy. The two ships became entangled, and could not be separated. At this the rest of the Greek fleet came up to help, and engaged with the Persians. Such is the account which the Athenians give of the way the battle began.

Herodotus, *Persian Wars,* Book VIII, Chapters 83–84.

Ever since Herodotus, historians have recovered and preserved information about past events that otherwise would have been lost. Thus they have been able to tell us things that we would not have known and to explain seemingly mysterious developments. Modern historians have continued to look for new information which, just like the stories recorded by Herodotus, helps us understand the past more clearly and more accurately. The usefulness of historians and their works has been recognized by a number of American Presidents, who have made professional historians part of their White House staffs.

the work for which they are best fitted. Those noted for bravery should be in the army. People interested in material things like food, clothing, and luxuries should conduct the business and do the labor. Plato's ideal government was to be operated and controlled by a few individuals. They were the philosophers, who were to be chosen for their wisdom, ability, and correct ideas about justice.

You will recognize that Plato's ideal government was an aristocracy—a government ruled by an upper class. However, it was not an aristocracy of birth or of wealth but one based on intelligence, ability, and high ideals.

Aristotle

Among Plato's students in the Academy was a young man named Aristotle, who founded his own school at Athens in 335 B.C.

Aristotle was an accomplished scientist as well as a great philosopher. He set himself the task of investigating every kind of knowledge. He collected as many facts as possible. Then he arranged and organized them into systems, comparing one fact with another to try to find out what they meant or showed. He was especially skillful at definitions and grouping similar or related facts. This process is an important part of modern scientific thinking.

Aristotle almost accomplished his purpose of searching out every field of knowledge in his time. He collected, described, and classified plants and animals. In order to describe the principles of government, Aristotle studied the political organization of 150 city-states and put down his conclusions in a book called *Politics*. For his book *Ethics*, he examined the acts and beliefs of individuals so as to learn what brought the greatest virtue and happiness. In his *Poetics*, he made a study of Greek drama to show the differences between a good and a bad play. His *Logic* is an attempt to show the principles of correct reasoning.

Mathematics and science

In the 500's B.C., before the Golden Age, Pythagoras (pih·THAG·ur·us), a philosopher and mathematician, wrote that everything could be explained or expressed with numbers. He is proba-

bly best known for the Pythagorean theorem, the geometric theory which states that the square of the hypotenuse of a right triangle is equal to the sum of the squares of the other two sides.

The Greeks of the Golden Age made some advances in science. However, Greek scientific achievements did not reach their fullest development until a later period. Aristotle laid the foundations of botany, zoology, and anatomy. The Greek philosopher Democritus (dih·MAHK·ruh·tus) believed that all matter is composed of moving atoms—small particles that he thought could not be divided. Science has since proved that the atom can be divided, but the theory that all matter is made of atoms is still an accepted idea.

One of the greatest scientists of the Golden Age was Hippocrates (hih·PAHK·ruh·teez), who is considered the founder of medicine. He taught that all disease comes from natural causes, not as punishment from the gods. The best cures, he said, were rest, fresh air, and a proper diet. Hippocrates had high ideals for physicians. The Hippocratic Oath—a pledge based on his teachings—is still used and may be seen in many physicians' offices.

History

The Greeks were the first people to take the writing of history seriously. Herodotus was the first great historian of the Western world. An enthusiastic traveler, he visited Babylonia, Phoenicia, and Egypt. His impressions of these countries and their people are included in his histories.

Herodotus was a fascinating writer and a wonderful storyteller. Sometimes he exaggerated, but he was always careful to distinguish between the things he had personally seen or investigated and those he had been told. He often expressed doubt about legends but reported them for whatever they were worth. Historians still consult his writings for information about the world of his time.

Another Greek historian was Thucydides (thoo·SID·uh·deez), famous for his *History of the Peloponnesian War*. (You will read about this war in Chapter 5.) Thucydides wanted his history to be a guide for future leaders, so he emphasized the importance of power politics. His work, also, is still read today.

Greek drama

A surprising proportion of the world's greatest literature was written by Greeks who lived in Athens during the Golden Age. That brief period saw a tremendous flood of creative writing. Greek literature was great because of its simplicity, beauty, and realism. Greek literature shows truthfulness in portraying how people live and act.

The Greeks were the first people to write dramas. It is in this form of literature—the play—that they excelled. Greek plays were almost always written in poetic form. They were spoken or sung by two or three actors and a chorus. Plays were performed in outdoor theaters, often on the slopes of hills. The audience sat on seats built into the hillside. The actors performed on a stage at the bottom of the hill. There was almost no scenery. Instead, the chorus—a group of singers and dancers—described the scene.

The actors were always men, each with a voice trained to play several parts, including women's parts. They wore elaborate padded costumes and thick-soled boots to make them look larger than human beings. Actors used masks to indicate the characters and emotions they were portraying.

The plays often had a religious theme and were almost always given in connection with religious festivals. For three successive days at the Festival of Dionysus, three tragedies were given each day. Each day the audience selected the best one, judging it by the beauty of the language and the wisdom of its ideas. The winning author was awarded a crown of ivy. One Athenian leader considered these plays so important in educating citizens that he provided free admission for all citizens who could not afford to pay for admission to the great festivals.

Tragedies. A Greek tragedy showed the central character struggling against fate. Usually the character was overcome by a combination of powerful outside forces and a weakness of personality. This weakness was often what the Greeks called **hubris** (HYOO·bris), that is, an arrogant disregard for moral laws. The outcome was inevitable and could not be escaped.

Three great writers of tragedy lived during the 400's B.C. Aeschylus (ES·kuh·lus) was considered the founder of Greek tragedy. He wrote of the old religious beliefs about the relationship between gods and humans. Most famous of his plays to survive today are three that center on the murder of Agamemnon, the king who led the Greeks against Troy, and the revenge that followed it.

Another writer of tragedies, Sophocles (SAHF·uh·kleez), defended the traditional values. His most famous play was *Oedipus the Tyrant,* which Aristotle called a perfect example of tragedy.

Euripides (yoo·RIP·uh·deez), the third playwright, was more of a realist than Aeschylus or Sophocles. Like Socrates, he questioned many old beliefs and ideas. Earlier writers often glorified war for its deeds of courage and heroism. In *The Trojan Women,* Euripides showed war as it really was, with all its miseries.

Comedies. Greek comedies were what we would call **satires**—works that made fun of ideas and people. The Athenians were accustomed to criticism of government leaders. Their satires often ridiculed politicians who tried to fool the people. Sometimes they praised leaders or their ideas by making fun of people who opposed them.

Aristophanes (ar·iss·TAHF·uh·neez) was the greatest writer of comedies. No person or institution was safe from his wit. In *The Clouds* he poked fun at Socrates for his theories about education. Some plays showed women taking over the government. This amused the Athenians greatly because of their low opinion of women. Aristophanes also used satire to make Athenians think about war and its causes.

CHECKUP

1. IDENTIFY: philosophy, Pythagoras, Democritus, Hippocrates, Herodotus, Thucydides, hubris, Aeschylus, Sophocles, Euripides, Aristophanes.

2. Why did Socrates criticize the Sophists? What method of teaching did Socrates use? What was its purpose?

3. What were the chief characteristics of good government described in Plato's *Republic?*

4. Why is Aristotle considered a scientist as well as a philosopher? List the major ideas of *Politics, Ethics, Poetics,* and *Logic.*

5. Describe at least three basic features of Greek drama.

CHAPTER REVIEW

3000	2500	2000	1500	1000	500	B.C.	A.D.	500	1000	1500	2000

3000 B.C.	Neolithic culture on Crete and Aegean Islands		
2000 B.C.	Beginning of Ionian and Mycenaean invasions of Greek mainland		
2000–1400 B.C.	Height of Minoan civilization		
1600–1100 B.C.	Height of Mycenaean civilization		
1100 B.C.	Dorian invasions	469–399 B.C.	Socrates
1000–700 B.C.	Age of Kings	447 B.C.	Building of Parthenon begun
700–650 B.C.	Control of Greek city-states by nobles	335 B.C.	School founded by Aristotle in Athens
650–500 B.C.	Age of Tyrants		
400's B.C.	Golden Age of Greece		

CHAPTER SUMMARY

The geography of Greece was not as favorable to settlement as that of the great river valleys. The Greeks could never grow enough food for themselves. Therefore they became traders. Their culture developed first on the islands in the Aegean Sea and on the large Mediterranean island of Crete. The Minoan culture of Crete was an important early influence on the Greeks.

Around 2000 B.C. various invaders entered Greece. They dominated the country for more than a thousand years. The most important invaders were the Mycenaeans. The period when they dominated Greece is called the Mycenaean Age.

The great achievement of this early period of Greek history was the creation of many city-states, each one independent and enjoying its own form of government. They fought one another constantly. Yet a distinct Greek culture united the cities.

After being ruled by kings, nobles, and tyrants for hundreds of years, many cities adopted popular governments, or democracies. But the contrast among the various systems of government that the Greeks followed still remained. It is best seen in the very different cities of Sparta and Athens.

Sparta was a powerful totalitarian state. A small group of its inhabitants were considered citizens, and they ran the government. Sparta was known for its discipline and its military skill.

Athens gradually became a democratic system, although more than half of its population, and particularly women, could not participate in government. Even at its most democratic, Athenian society depended on slaves. Nevertheless, those who did participate in government enjoyed one of the most complete democracies the world has ever seen.

Athenian society depended on farming, manufacturing, and trade. Public buildings were the pride of Athens. Large sums of money were spent to make them as beautiful as possible. The temples on the Acropolis, especially the Parthenon, were the highest expression of the Greek ideal of beauty. The same ideal can be seen in their sculpture, which demonstrated the Greek admiration for the beauty of the human body.

The philosophers of Athens were as original as the artists. Socrates wanted the citizens to think for themselves. Plato asked them to try to define, then pursue, justice. Aristotle wrote about many subjects, observing the world around him and reaching new conclusions about science, politics, poetry, and logic.

Greek scientists also began some of the earliest work in mathematics, botany, and medicine. Greek playwrights created the forms of tragedy and comedy that we know today. And Greek historians were the first writers to study the past seriously. In every one of these areas, we still look to the Greeks as models.

CHECKING WHAT YOU KNOW

1. Place the following in chronological order:
   a. Mycenaean civilization
   b. early aristocratic city-states
   c. Minoan civilization
   d. early age of democracy
   e. Age of Tyrants

2. In each of the following sets of three statements, one may be considered the cause and the other two the results. List the cause first and then the results:

   a. The Mediterranean became the center of early Western civilization.

   The Mediterranean borders on Asia, Africa, and Europe.

   The Mediterranean was a pathway of trade and ideas.

   b. Tyrants promised to bring peace and prosperity.

   Nobles proved to be poor leaders.

   People became discontented with the rule of the nobles.

   c. Athens exported olive oil and wine.

   Poor soil made the growing of grain difficult in Athens.

   Athens built a large navy and established colonies throughout the Mediterranean.

3. Compare the form of government in Sparta with the form of government in Athens in the fifth century B.C.

4. How did democracy develop in Athens? How did slavery fit into Athenian democracy?

PRACTICING YOUR SKILLS

1. **Using photographs.** Many of the public buildings in our national capital, Washington, D.C., were influenced by the architecture of ancient Greece. Using your school or local library, find a picture book with photographs of buildings in Washington, D.C., and another with photographs of ancient buildings still standing in Greece today. Compare the buildings shown in each book. List the ways in which they are similar and the ways in which they differ. What were the ancient Greek buildings used for? What functions do the buildings in Washington, D.C., serve?

2. **Using readings.** Read selections from Plato's *Republic*. Then choose one idea from this work on each of the following subjects:

   a. education
   b. the role of women
   c. the organization of society
   d. the definition of a state

   Discuss the ways in which these ideas were reflected in the city-state governments of ancient Greece.

3. **Making comparisons.** Compare Greek religion with the religions of the Egyptians, Persians, and Hebrews. What are the differences and similarities?

RELATING PAST TO PRESENT

1. Sports were important in the culture of ancient Greece, which was the home of the Olympic games.

   a. How does the importance of sports and physical fitness in our society compare with that of ancient Greece?

   b. In what ways do the modern Olympics differ from the ancient Greek Olympics?

   c. The ancient Olympics had only individual competition. The modern Olympics has both individual and team competition. In what ways does this reflect the values of the respective cultures?

2. Compare the ideas and practices of Greek democracy with the democratic ideals of American government in the following areas:

   a. right of citizenship
   b. right to hold public office
   c. right to vote
   d. passage and review of laws

INVESTIGATING FURTHER

1. In your school library, use the card catalogue or the *Readers' Guide to Periodical Literature* to find books or magazine articles about the excavations at Mycenae. Then write a report on this important archeological site.

2. Read Sophocles' *Oedipus the Tyrant* (sometimes translated as *Oedipus Rex* or *Oedipus the King*) and Shakespeare's *King Lear*. Describe the character of each of the kings. Why are each of these plays classified as tragedies? How is the human flaw of hubris developed in each of these plays?

3. During the period of Athen's Golden Age, women were subordinate to men in matters of education, legal rights, and participation in government or business affairs. Yet during this same period great plays about strong women were composed by Euripides (for example, *Medea*) and Sophocles *(Antigone).* What role in Greek tradition did these women play?

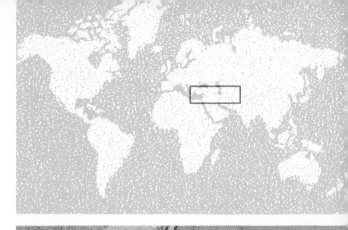

CHAPTER

(546–146 B.C.)

5

Greek Civilization Triumphed During the Hellenistic Age

As you have read, Greek culture reached high levels during the Golden Age in the 400's B.C. It may seem astonishing that one group of people could have created, in a short period of time, enduring contributions in politics, thought, and art. Their achievement appears even more astonishing if we consider that it took place at a time of fierce military struggle. As you will read in this chapter, the Greek city-states were fighting among themselves during much of this period. They also faced serious danger from enemies outside Greece.

In the 300's B.C. the Greek city-states were conquered by an outside power, Macedonia. An extraordinary commander, Alexander the Great, created a vast empire and carried Greek culture throughout the eastern Mediterranean region and the Middle East.

By creating a much larger area within which Greek ideas and art could thrive, Alexander made possible the development of a new culture. The new culture was basically Greek, but much was added from other cultures of the Mediterranean region. This mingled culture, known as **Hellenistic** culture, established the influence of the Greeks for centuries.

Remarkable advances were made in philosophy, and long-lasting discoveries were made in science. Hellenistic mathematics, physics, medicine, and astronomy were the basis of Western beliefs about the physical universe until the 1600's.

Alexander the Great battles the Persians

Greek civilization defended itself and expanded

Sparta, Athens, and other Greek city-states established many colonies around the shores of the Aegean, Black, and Mediterranean seas. These colonies, and Greece itself, developed for a long time without interference from the powerful empires of the Middle East. Finally, however, this freedom from interference came to an end.

The Persian Wars

In 546 B.C. the Greek city-states on the western shores of Asia Minor were conquered by the Persians. The conquered Greeks always resented Persian rule, and in 499 B.C. revolts broke out in several city-states of Asia Minor (see map, opposite). These rebellions, which were aided by Athens, began a series of conflicts that lasted until 479 B.C. Together these conflicts are known as the Persian Wars.

The revolts were easily crushed by the Persian emperor, Darius I. He was more determined than ever to control the city-states on the Greek mainland as well as those of Asia Minor.

With this goal in mind, Darius sent a Persian army and a fleet toward Greece in 492 B.C. (see map, opposite). The fleet was wrecked in a storm off the coast of Macedonia, but the army was able to cross into Thrace and other parts of the mainland. However, this attempt to conquer Greece failed.

Darius' next plan was to gain dominance through peaceful means, but this too failed. He then gathered a great army and fleet and again set sail for Greece in 490 B.C. The army landed on the coast of Attica and set up camp on the plain of Marathon, some 20 miles (32 kilometers) from Athens.

According to the Greek historian Herodotus, the Athenian army was outnumbered by the Persians ten to one. Although he may have exaggerated, it is certain that the smaller Athenian army attacked bravely and drove out the Persians.

After their defeat at Marathon, the Persians went home, threatening to return with a larger army that would conquer all of Greece. Darius did not live to see that day.

In 480 B.C. the dreaded news spread throughout Greece—Darius' son Xerxes was coming with a vast army and fleet from every part of the Persian Empire. Herodotus, who loved a good story, wrote that the Persian army was so large that when it drank water, whole rivers ran dry. The exaggeration pointed to the truth—Xerxes was marching with little opposition through Thrace and Macedonia toward northern Greece.

To advance from northern Greece into central Greece, the Persians had to march through the narrow mountain pass of Thermopylae (thur·MAHP·ih·lee). There they were met by King Leonidas of Sparta and a force of 300 soldiers. For three days the Spartans held the narrow pass against the entire Persian army. Finally a Greek traitor showed the Persians a secret pass through the mountains. Surrounded, the Spartans refused to surrender and fought until every one of their soldiers was killed.

With the pass cleared, the Persians had an unobstructed route to Athens. Athens itself was in turmoil. The able Greek general Themistocles (thuh·MIST·uh·kleez) persuaded the Athenians to abandon their city and sail to the island of Salamis. With Athens evacuated, Xerxes' army entered the city and destroyed it.

Themistocles' next step was to trick Xerxes into attacking the Athenian fleet. From his throne high atop the coastal plain, Xerxes watched in horror as the Athenian ships rammed and sank many of the Persian ships.

After abandoning the naval attack, Xerxes withdrew most of his army and returned home to put down revolts that had broken out in the Persian Empire during his absence. The portion of the army left behind in Greece was defeated by a combined Greek army the next year, 479 B.C., at

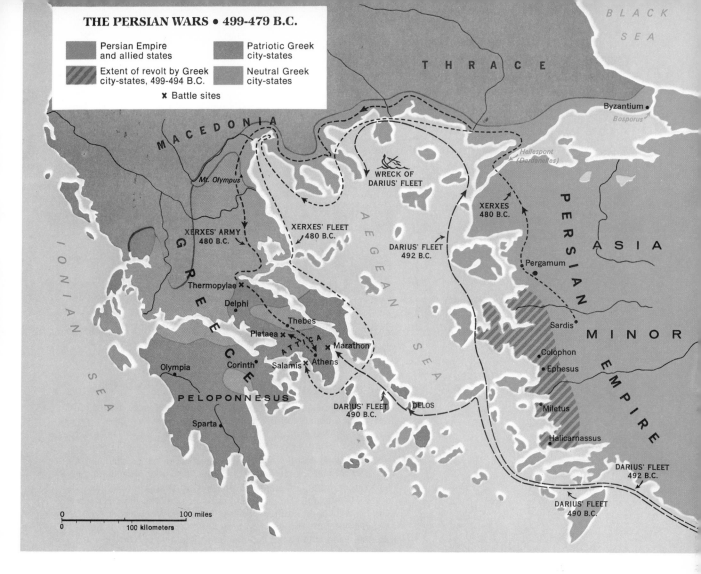

Plataea (pluh·TEE·uh). With this battle the military phase of the Persian Wars ended.

Importance of the Greek victories

The immediate results of the Persian Wars do not seem like a great victory for Greece. The Persian Empire remained powerful, and its rulers continued to meddle in Greek affairs. It became a fixed Persian policy to try to prevent any unity in Greece. The Greek city-states regarded the Persians as their traditional enemies.

From a long-range viewpoint, however, the battles of Marathon, Salamis, and Plataea are considered important and decisive in history. Athens took credit for the defeat of Persia and conducted a naval war to free the Greek cities in Asia Minor.

Athens soon used this policy to create an empire in the Aegean area. The wealth of this empire paid for the great achievements of the Golden Age of Athens. Success against the Persians had made the Greeks arrogant toward other peoples and encouraged them to extend their power throughout the Middle East.

Athens as leader

After these destructive wars, Athens was completely rebuilt. Its temples, public buildings, and walls were more magnificent than before. Although the remnants of Xerxes' army had been defeated, threat of invasion from the Persian Empire continued as long as Xerxes lived. Unity among the Greek city-states seemed necessary.

93

The Persian Wars

The Greeks treasured their political freedom and were determined to resist being dominated by other powerful empires. In 499 B.C. their resistance against Persian rule started the Persian Wars. These battles were the first in Western history about which there are detailed records. Surviving pictures and objects, moreover, give a vivid sense of this combat and the participants. Darius, the great Persian king who failed to conquer Greece, is shown (left) wearing the royal head-dress. His servant, holding a fan, protects him from the blazing sun. The breastplate and other pieces of armor (above) were discovered in a soldier's tomb. The painting from a pottery vase (below) shows a warship filled with soldiers clinging to their shields. The master oarsman, standing, encourages his men to push onward to win the battle.

Sparta wanted unity under its own leadership. The Spartans tried conquest, but fear of helot revolt kept them from sending expeditions far from home. Even their army could not extend Spartan power much beyond the Peloponnesus.

As the leading city-state, Athens led the way in the formation of a system of alliances among some 140 other city-states—the **Delian League.** Each contributed either ships or money to the alliance. No city-state could withdraw from the league without unanimous consent. The league's funds were deposited on the island of Delos (from which the name Delian is derived). Athens was given the power to decide how many ships and how much money other city-states would contribute.

With the death of Xerxes in 465 B.C., the threat of Persian invasion ended. The Delian League, however, continued under Athens' domination. By the 450's B.C. it had, in effect, become an Athenian empire.

Pericles, Athenian leader

During this time Pericles (PER·uh·kleez) rose to power in Athens. He was the greatest of Athenian leaders. His ability and reputation for honesty were so great that he was chosen general for 16 successive years. Even when he did not hold this official position, he was the most influential speaker in the Assembly.

Pericles was the real leader of Athens for more than 30 years—from 461 to 429 B.C.—the time of its greatest power and prosperity. This period of Athenian history is called the **Age of Pericles.**

Pericles continued Athenian control of the Delian League and increased the empire by forcing more city-states to join. He moved the league treasury from Delos to Athens. He also used the money openly to benefit Athens. Revolts by other city-states against these policies were crushed.

Athens wanted to weaken its commercial rival, Corinth. In order to do so it made alliances with several nearby city-states. To defend itself against Athenian ambition, Corinth became an ally of Sparta, which feared that Athens planned to seize the northern Peloponnesus. The long rivalry between Athens and Sparta increased. Athens' policies could end in only one of two ways—either Athens would control all of Greece, or there would be a great war.

CHECKUP

1. IDENTIFY: Darius, Xerxes, Themistocles, Age of Pericles.
2. LOCATE: Macedonia, Thrace, Thermopylae, Salamis, Delos, Corinth.
3. Why are the battles of Marathon, Salamis, and Plataea considered decisive in the history of the world?
4. What was the Delian League? How did Athens use it? Why did other Greek city-states have reason to fear Athens?
5. What qualities gave Pericles his great hold over the people of Athens?
6. How did the Persian Wars show both the strength and the weakness of Greece?

Macedonia became powerful after the Peloponnesian War

Athens and all of Greece were politically unsettled during the Age of Pericles. Athens had turned the Delian League into an Athenian empire. It had then quarreled with Corinth and Sparta. Rivalries among city-states led to a devastating war, which lasted from 431 to 404 B.C. This involved the whole Greek world as well as Persia. Greece was left in ruins. The war is called the Peloponnesian War because much of the fighting took place in the Peloponnesus, where Sparta and Corinth are located.

The Peloponnesian War

The responsibility for the Peloponnesian War was shared mainly by Athens and Sparta. There was, of course, economic and commercial rivalry among a number of city-states. But there was also a long-standing social and cultural rivalry between Athens and Sparta. Athens was progressive, commercial, and culturally advanced. Sparta was conservative, agricultural, and culturally backward. Athenians regarded Spartans as rude and ill-mannered. Spartans thought Athenians were money-mad.

Actual fighting was started by the Spartans, but they had been provoked into action by the Athenians. Neither side made much effort to avoid war. Thucydides, the great Greek historian of the Peloponnesian War, wrote: "The Peloponnesus and Athens were both full of young men whose inexperience made them eager to take up arms."

The Spartans invaded Attica, destroying fields and villages. The Athenian army and the entire population withdrew behind the walls and the fortifications of Athens. The Spartans and their allies could not starve them out because Athens controlled the sea. However, a great plague broke out among the Athenians. Many people died, including Pericles himself.

The war went on for a generation, with great loss of life. Even during a period of peace, Athens could not resist the temptation to attack the great city of Syracuse in Sicily. In Sicily, however, Athens suffered a great defeat. After the failure in Sicily, some Athenians lost faith in democracy and allowed aristocrats to seize power in the city. They were soon overthrown and democracy was restored, but its prestige was shaken. Since the war was largely a naval war, Sparta asked Persia for money to equip its fleet. In return, the Spartans handed over the Greek cities of Asia Minor to Persian rule. Finally Athens surrendered to the Spartans in 404 B.C.

Greek disunity

Much of Greece lived under the control of Sparta between 404 and 371 B.C. The Spartans proved even more harsh and selfish than the Athenians had been with the Delian League. Furthermore, Sparta lacked the people, money, and sea power to rule effectively. Conditions were ripe for another power struggle. The city-state of Thebes formed a league against Sparta. Aided by Athens and other city-states, and by Persia, Thebes defeated Sparta and dominated Greece from 371 to 362 B.C. Leadership by Thebes was not successful, however, and the ruinous wars continued.

All the city-states realized that unity was necessary, but each wanted to dominate any union that was formed. Some promised democratic rule, others aristocracy, but all practiced tyranny. Some Greeks believed that union could come only

under a foreign power. Persia seemed the logical choice. However, the Persians had interfered in Greek affairs again and again to prevent unity, and most Greeks still distrusted them.

Philip of Macedon

The power that finally unified Greece came from an unexpected direction. Look again at the map on page 77. North of Greece is a mountainous land called Macedonia. In the 300's B.C. it was inhabited by a hardy, warlike people who were closely related to the Greeks. The Macedonians lived in small villages, each ruled by a powerful noble. Macedonia had a king, but his power depended on his own ability and the help of the nobles.

In 359 B.C. a remarkable young man known as Philip of Macedon became king. In his youth he had been taken as a captive hostage to Thebes, where he spent three years. During that time, Philip came to admire Greek ways of living.

Philip was determined to be a strong king and to control the unruly Macedonian nobles and people. Instead of depending on the nobles to supply troops for an army, Philip built up the first regular, paid army in Macedonian history.

After unifying his own kingdom, Philip extended his power by conquering surrounding peoples. He increased his control of the northern Aegean coast by taking some Greek towns that Athens claimed as colonies. Then he turned south and began the task of unifying the Greek city-states under his rule.

Opinion about Philip was divided in Greece. In every city-state some people looked upon him as a savior who could bring unity to Greece. Others opposed him as a menace to liberty. In Athens the opposition was led by Demosthenes (dih·MAHS·thuh·neez), one of the greatest **orators,** or speakers, of all Athenian history.

Demosthenes used all his great powers to arouse the Athenians to the danger posed by Philip of Macedon. He attacked Philip bitterly in a series of speeches to the Assembly and tried to get Athens to lead the Greeks once more in a fight for liberty. In spite of his great oratory, Demosthenes failed to arouse the Athenians. There was no united opposition to Philip of Macedon.

Philip marched south with his army, conquering

the Greek cities one by one. Some resisted and were defeated. Others were turned over to him by traitors. As he said: "No fortress is inaccessible if one can only introduce within it a mule laden with gold." When the Athenians did decide to fight, it was too late. Philip defeated them at the battle of Chaeronea (ker·uh·NEE·uh) in 338 B.C. (see map, this page) and became master of Greece.

Finally the Greeks were united, but they were no longer free. Philip organized the cities into a league to support his plans for an invasion of Persia. In 336 B.C., however, before Philip could carry out his ideas, he was assassinated.

CHECKUP

1. What were the causes of the rivalry between Athens and Sparta?

2. How was Athens finally defeated in the Peloponnesian War?

3. Why did Demosthenes and other Athenians oppose Philip of Macedon?

4. What factors contributed to Philip's success in conquering the Greek city-states?

3

Alexander the Great created a huge empire

Philip was succeeded in 336 B.C. by his 20-year-old son, Alexander. History knows him as Alexander the Great. The period from the beginning of his reign until the Roman conquest of Greece in 146 B.C. is called the Age of Alexander, or the Hellenistic Age. As you will see, the civilization of this period is different from that of early Greece. The Macedonians conquered far-off lands in Asia and the Middle East and brought Greek culture to these areas.

Alexander the Great

Alexander proved to be even more remarkable than his father. Although they were very much alike, the two could never agree and often quarreled bitterly. However, Philip did everything to give his son the best training and education possible. Alexander received his military training in the

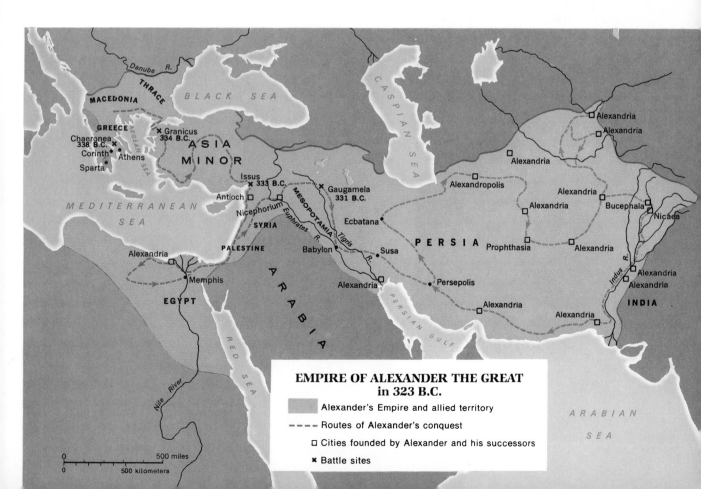

**EMPIRE OF ALEXANDER THE GREAT
in 323 B.C.**

    Alexander's Empire and allied territory

- - - Routes of Alexander's conquest

  □ Cities founded by Alexander and his successors

  ✕ Battle sites

Alexander the Great

In 13 years Alexander the Great conquered nearly all of the world known to him. The greatest hero of ancient times, he inspired artists both during and after his lifetime. Later rulers often had themselves portrayed as Alexander because he represented bravery and power.

Alexander was only 20 when he came to the throne, and his youthful spirit is captured in the carved head (left). The ornate crown (below left) symbolizes royal power, as does the scepter Alexander is shown holding on the coin (above). The bow in his hand represents his military superiority. The mosaic (below) commemorates the Battle of Issus in 333 B.C., one of Alexander's major victories. In this portion of the mosaic, the defeated Darius turns back to take a last look at his conqueror before fleeing in his chariot.

Macedonian army. To train Alexander's mind, Philip sent for Aristotle, the greatest living Greek philosopher, to be his tutor. The fine education Alexander received made him a lifelong admirer of Greek culture.

When the time came for Alexander to command the army, he proved to be an even better general than his father. His campaigns are considered among the greatest in history. He was strong and brave to the point of rashness. His dramatic arts in battle so captured the imagination of his troops that they were willing to follow him anywhere.

Alexander began his military career by crushing rebellions in the Greek city-states and making himself master of Greece. Then he marched into Asia Minor and defeated the Persians, first at the battle of Granicus and a year later at Issus. Having conquered all of Asia Minor, Alexander then took Syria. Next he invaded Egypt, meeting almost no resistance. From Egypt he moved into Mesopotamia, defeating another Persian army at Gaugamela, and in 331 B.C. captured Babylon. Farther east he took control of the entire Persian Empire (see map, page 97).

Alexander now ruled a huge territory, but he was still not satisfied. Beyond Persia lay India, the end of the world as it was then known to the people around the Mediterranean Sea. For four years he led his army eastward. He met little resistance in going as far as the Indus River. From there he wanted to march on to the Ganges River and so control the whole of the vast plain of northern India. But his long-suffering army had finally had enough fighting and forced him to turn around and go back.

At Babylon, in 323 B.C., Alexander became ill. In a few days he was dead of a fever at the age of 33. In 13 years he had conquered almost all of the world known to him.

Alexander's plan. Alexander the Great wanted to create a world empire with himself at the head. Even in his short lifetime he was able to change the world. It is difficult to imagine what he might have done had he lived to old age.

Alexander planned to create his united world empire in three ways. First, he wanted to found new cities and rebuild old ones as cultural centers of his empire. He actually established more than 70 such cities, many of them named Alexandria in

his honor. Groups of Greeks and Macedonians settled in each one. Alexandria, in Egypt, was founded by Alexander 2,300 years ago.

Alexander's second aim was to merge the Macedonians and the Persians into one ruling group to run his empire more efficiently. He married a Persian princess and made his generals do the same. But the Macedonians saw themselves as superior to all other Asians, and this aim of Alexander was frustrated.

Alexander's third goal was to be considered by his subjects a divine monarch—a god-king. By the end of his life, he was convinced that his real father was not Philip but the god Zeus-Ammon. He insisted that all of his subjects honor him as being part human and part divine. The Persians did not believe in god-kings, but the Egyptians did; and the Greeks thought that some heroes became gods.

Alexander's death in 323 B.C., however, brought his ambitious plans to an end. His mighty empire soon broke apart.

The break-up of Alexander's empire

After Alexander's death, his generals murdered his family and divided his empire. A fierce power struggle went on until 301 B.C., when the last attempt to hold the empire together under one ambitious general failed. The three surviving generals divided the empire and were honored as god-kings.

Alexander's empire was divided into three main kingdoms—Macedonia, Egypt, and Syria. The dynasty of Antigonus (an·TIH·go·nus) ruled Macedonia and dominated Greece. The dynasty of Ptolemy (TAHL·uh·me) ruled Egypt with great efficiency, gaining total control over the people and growing rich from taxes. Their capital was Alexandria, with a population of many different peoples. Alexandria was the largest city in the Hellenistic world—that is, the area ruled by Alexander and his successors. The dynasty of Seleucus (sih·LOO·kus) ruled the possessions in Asia Minor from the capital city of Antioch in Syria. The empire of Seleucus, or the Seleucid (sih·LOO·sid) Empire, was the largest in size, but it was difficult to control so many different people.

The three kingdoms were often at war with one another. The cities of Greece were pawns in their struggles, and much wealth and energy were wasted on war. After 200 B.C. a new people, the Romans (see Chapter 6), interfered in the Greek area, and over the years they conquered the three kingdoms.

The Hellenistic Age and the Jews

The Hellenistic world followed the models set by Alexander. Divine monarchy was the major form of government, and new cities prospered throughout the Middle East. Through these cities Greek culture spread rapidly, and the upper classes in the Middle East adopted Greek customs, that is, they became Hellenized. Greek was the language of government, commerce, and culture, and ambitious natives took Greek names.

Many Macedonians and Greeks moved to the new cities and married natives. But the city people who had adopted Greek culture did not respect the old native cultures. They looked down on peasants and their "old-fashioned" ways. Thus the usual tension between people in the cities and in the countryside was increased by differences in culture.

A dramatic clash between cultures took place in Palestine, when the Seleucid king, Antiochus IV, tried to introduce Greek culture in Jerusalem. In the Hellenistic period, many Jews in Palestine were attracted to Greek culture. Antiochus mistakenly thought that all Jews wanted to become Hellenized. In the 160's B.C. he tried to impose Greek religious rituals in the Temple at Jerusalem. However, the Jews rebelled under Judah Maccabee, and the Seleucids then lost control of Palestine.

CHECKUP

1. IDENTIFY: Zeus-Ammon, Antigonus, Ptolemy, Seleucus, Antiochus IV, Judah Maccabee.

2. LOCATE: Granicus, Issus, Gaugamela, Alexandria (Egypt), Antioch.

3. How did Greek culture influence Alexander?

4. What were Alexander's three goals for an empire?

5. How did Alexander's generals divide his empire?

6. How did Macedonians and Greeks attempt to Hellenize the Middle East? Why did this policy fail in Jerusalem?

Hellenistic culture spread throughout the Mediterranean region

The conquests of Alexander the Great carried Greek culture to Egypt and other lands of the Middle East, right up to the border of India. Greek ideas continued to influence these areas long after Alexander's death in 323 B.C. At the same time, Greek culture at home was modified by ideas brought from the other lands by Alexander's followers. New advances in philosophy and science were the greatest achievements of Hellenistic culture. The writers of the Hellenistic Age influenced Western thought for centuries.

The economy

Throughout the Hellenistic world much land was owned by the ruler or the government. The land that was owned privately was usually held in large estates by wealthy aristocrats. Slaves or poorly paid free laborers did the work. There was a small class of very wealthy people and a large class of miserably poor people. However, the middle class increased because of the many opportunities for wealth.

Trade was the most profitable activity. The main trading centers were the cities of Alexandria, in Egypt; Rhodes, on the island of Rhodes off the coast of Asia Minor; and Antioch, in Syria. Trade routes now connected the whole Mediterranean world and even reached as far east as India. Ships were bigger and better than they had been in earlier times.

The new cities built or rebuilt by Alexander were the wonders of the Hellenistic world. They were carefully planned and laid out with straight streets. They had market squares and large public buildings, including indoor theaters, schools, and public baths. Homes of the wealthy were improved to include elaborate furniture, running water, and drain pipes. Alexandria, in Egypt, was the greatest city, with a population perhaps as large as one million. Its museum and library made Alexandria a great center of learning as well as of commerce. The library there contained 750,000 papyrus rolls.

Changing attitudes

As the middle class expanded, education became more widespread. Novels and digests were popular. The old values of Greece were less respected, and the condition of women improved. Hellenistic women circulated more in public, and they had more rights regarding property and divorce. Another major change was a new definition of what it was to be a Greek. A Hellenized Egyptian or Syrian was considered a "Greek." There were still the pressures and stresses that resulted when Greeks, Hellenized Greeks, and non-Greeks lived side by side. But the old Greek bias against "barbarians" gradually disappeared as contact with non-Greeks increased.

Philosophy

The philosophers of the Hellenistic Age were more concerned with ethics than with fundamental questions of reality and human existence. There were three chief schools, or groups, of Hellenistic philosophers—the Cynics, the Stoics, and the Epicureans.

The **Cynics** taught that people should seek virtue only. They scorned pleasure, wealth, and social position. The most famous Cynic was Diogenes (dy·AHJ·uh·neez), about whom there are many stories. One concerns the meeting of Diogenes and Alexander the Great. "If I were not Alexander, I would prefer to be Diogenes," the conqueror said. But Diogenes growled in reply, "If I were not Diogenes, I would prefer to be any man except Alexander." Today the word *cynic* means a person who is sarcastic and believes that the motives for people's actions are always selfish and insincere.

The philosopher Zeno, born on the island of Cyprus, established the **Stoic** philosophy in Athens in the late 300's B.C. He and his followers believed that the world was directed by divine reason. That is, whatever was, was right. People should not complain. They should learn to accept whatever the laws of nature might bring and to be indifferent to grief, fear, pain, and pleasure.

The Stoic philosophy had great influence later on the thinking of the Romans and the Christians. The word *stoic* means much the same now as it did in Hellenistic times—a person who remains outwardly unaffected by either pain or pleasure.

Epicurus, founder of the **Epicurean** philosophy,

connections

Memorials

What is the name of your school? Many schools, libraries, colleges, and towns are named after famous people. In this way we remember them and honor their contributions long after they have died. In the United States our two most famous leaders are honored in the Washington and Lincoln Memorials in Washington, D.C., in the state and cities called Washington, and in the 19 cities and towns named after Lincoln.

Probably the person who has left his name over a wider area, and in more places, than anyone else is Alexander the Great. As he conquered cities and towns, he gave them his name (right). Beginning in Alexandria, Egypt, one can trace Alexander's route eastward by following the towns having his name or that of Iksander, his name in Arabic.

Sometimes names change with history. For example, Idlewild Airport in New York was renamed in honor of John F. Kennedy following his death.

Look around your town at the names of parks, roads, playgrounds, athletic fields, or even cars parked on the streets. Perhaps you will think of other people who have been memorialized in this way.

Hellenistic art

Alexander the Great spread Greek ideals and the Greeks' sense of beauty to new territories. Most of the Greek art that has survived comes from the period of Alexander's empire, the Hellenistic period. For almost 300 years after his death in 323 B.C., Hellenistic artists produced copies of Greek masterpieces and created superb works of their own. The richly ornamented gold earrings (below right) reveal the wealth of the empire.

One of the empire's artistic centers was the kingdom of Pergamum, in modern Turkey. The ruins of its buildings testify to its glories (below). Perhaps the most famous Hellenistic sculpture came from this kingdom. Completed around 200 B.C., it shows the goddess Victory descending from the skies onto a ship's prow (right).

taught that the aim of life was to seek pleasure and avoid pain. Pleasure to him was intellectual, not physical. After his death, however, his followers sought the pleasures of the senses and appetites as well. Their motto was "Eat, drink, and be merry, for tomorrow we die." Today the word *epicure* means a person who enjoys the pleasures of the senses, particularly someone who enjoys fine food.

Mathematics and physics

Greeks of the Hellenistic Age were outstanding scientists. Extremely important work in mathematics was done by Euclid. He developed geometry into a system by showing how geometric statements of truth, or theorems, develop logically from one another. His textbook, *Elements,* was used for over a thousand years and is the basis for many of today's geometry books.

Archimedes (ar·kuh·MEE·deez) was the greatest all-round scientist of the Hellenistic period. He used geometry to measure spheres, cones, and cylinders. He calculated the value of π (pi), the relation between the diameter and circumference of a circle. He also used mathematics to explain the principle of the lever and built many machines in which levers were used. His inventions included the compound pulley (or block and tackle) and cogged wheels used as gears.

Medicine

Hellenistic scientists added greatly to the medical knowledge of the Greeks. Alexandria became the center for the study of medicine and surgery. The knowledge of human anatomy was greatly advanced by dissection of the bodies of executed criminals. Alexandrian physicians studied the nervous system and learned that the brain is its center. They performed delicate surgery, using anesthetics (pain killers) to deaden pain.

Astronomy and geography

In astronomy, Hellenistic scientists added to the knowledge of the Middle East and the Golden Age of Greece. They used mathematics to calculate the position of stars and planets from day to day. Aristarchus of Samos believed that the earth

and other planets move around the sun, but he was unable to convince other scientists of his day. Hipparchus of Rhodes calculated the times of eclipses of the sun and the moon, and the length of the year according to both the sun and the moon. He was the first scientist to make systematic use of trigonometry.

Hellenistic geographers knew that the earth was round. At Alexandria, Eratosthenes (er·uh·TAHS·thuh·neez) calculated the diameter of the earth with an error of less than 1 percent. He also claimed that people could reach India by sailing westward around the world. But no ship built then could risk so long an ocean voyage.

Characteristics of Hellenistic science

Two features of Hellenistic science are remarkable. One is that scientists learned so much with such simple instruments for observing and measuring. They had no microscopes or telescopes. They did not know of the compass. They lacked delicate balances for weighing small quantities.

A second striking fact is that the Hellenistic Greeks made little effort to apply their scientific knowledge in practical ways, except perhaps in the field of geography. They valued knowledge for its own sake and on the whole were not interested in inventions or mechanical progress. For example, an Alexandrian scientist named Hero invented a steam engine, but it was regarded only as an interesting toy. One explanation for this attitude was the fact that Hellenistic civilization was based on slavery. These labor-saving inventions would have aided only the slaves, and it was not thought necessary or fitting to improve the slaves' situation.

CHECKUP

1. IDENTIFY: Diogenes, Zeno, Epicurus, Euclid, Archimedes, Aristarchus, Hipparchus, Eratosthenes, Hero.

2. LOCATE: Rhodes, Antioch, Samos.

3. What people were considered to be Greek during the Hellenistic Age?

4. List the main ideas of each of the three major Hellenistic philosophies.

5. Why was there relatively little interest in applied science in the Hellenistic Age?

CHAPTER REVIEW

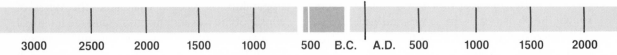

| 3000 | 2500 | 2000 | 1500 | 1000 | 500 | B.C. | A.D. | 500 | 1000 | 1500 | 2000 |

546 B.C. Persian conquest of Greek city-states in Asia Minor	**404–371 B.C.** Spartan rule of Greece	**301 B.C.** Division of Alexander's empire
	371–362 B.C. Theban rule of Greece	
499–479 B.C. Persian Wars	**338 B.C.** Defeat of Greeks by Phillip of Macedon at Chaeronea	**160's B.C.** Revolt of Judah Maccabee in Palestine
479 B.C. Defeat of Persians at Plataea by Greeks		
461–429 B.C. Age of Pericles	**336–323 B.C.** Conquest of vast empire by Alexander the Great	
431–404 B.C. Peloponnesian War	**336–146 B.C.** Hellenistic Age	

CHAPTER SUMMARY

In the 500's B.C. the Persians began to conquer some of the territory controlled by the Greeks. Eventually they threatened to invade Greece itself. The country's defense was organized by Athens, which won a series of great victories. Greek independence was thus preserved.

This was a prosperous time for Athens. Its government flourished under its ablest leader, Pericles. And many other city-states acknowledged Athens' supremacy in much of Greece. But the most powerful city-state, Sparta, challenged Athens' control over its neighbors. The result was the Peloponnesian War, which Sparta won.

From 404 to 371 B.C., Sparta dominated Greece. But then further wars broke out, and the country became completely disunited. This provided an opportunity for an outsider, Philip of Macedon. He invaded Greece, conquered all the city-states, and united them under his rule.

Philip's son, Alexander the Great, went on to conquer the whole of the former Persian Empire and more. He hoped to rule the world, but when he died his empire broke up into three separate kingdoms. Eventually, large parts of them were conquered by the Romans.

As a result of Alexander's conquests, Greek culture, known as Hellenistic culture, spread throughout the Mediterranean area. Philosophers made contributions to our understanding of ethics. Mathematicians and scientists made many advances, especially in geometry, physics, medicine, and astronomy. Their ideas remained influential for more than a thousand years.

CHECKING WHAT YOU KNOW

1. Match each philosopher or scientist at the left with his contribution at the right:

   a. Diogenes
   b. Zeno
   c. Epicurus
   d. Euclid
   e. Archimedes
   f. Aristarchus
   g. Eratosthenes
   h. Hipparchus
   i. Aristotle
   j. Hero

   1. Calculated the diameter of the earth.
   2. Calculated the times of eclipses and length of a year according to the movement of the sun and the moon.
   3. Theorized that earth and planets move around the sun.
   4. Founded the Cynic philosophy that people should seek virtue only.
   5. Founded modern geometry.
   6. Invented a steam engine.
   7. Founded Stoic philosophy that the world was directed by divine reason.
   8. Was the teacher of Alexander the Great.
   9. Created Epicurean philosophy of seeking pleasure and avoiding pain.
   10. Used geometry to measure spheres, cylinders, and cones.

2. Match each leader at the left with his accomplishment at the right:

   a. Xerxes
   b. Pericles
   c. Darius
   d. Themistocles
   e. Philip of Macedon
   f. Alexander
   g. Demosthenes

   1. Conquered Greek colonies in Asia Minor.
   2. Conquered Egypt, Syria, Mesopotamia, and Persia.
   3. United all Greek city-states under his rule.
   4. Opposed the rule of Philip of Macedon.
   5. Led Athens during the period of its greatest power.
   6. Tried to conquer Greece and spread his empire westward.
   7. Defeated Xerxes at Salamis.

3. How did the Persian Wars contribute to the Golden Age of Greece?

4. Compare the Delian League as a unifying force with the unification of Greece under Philip of Macedon. Which of these two plans of unification for Greece was more successful? Why?

PRACTICING YOUR SKILLS

1. **Using maps.** Look at the maps on pages 68, 69, and 97 and compare the extent of the following civilizations:

   a. Phoenician
   b. Mycenaean
   c. Greece in 550 B.C.
   d. Empire of Alexander the Great

   Which of these civilizations extended the farthest? Which was smallest in size?

2. **Using the library.** Use the card catalogue in your library to find books about Alexander the Great. Prepare a report on one of the following aspects of Alexander's life:

   a. his early life and education
   b. his military leadership
   c. his march to India
   d. his empire and how it was ruled

RELATING PAST TO PRESENT

1. Athens formed a system of alliances because it felt that unity was necessary for the protection of the Greek city-states. Why do countries form alliances today? How do these alliances compare with the Athenian system?

2. In this chapter you read how Alexander the Great's name was given to many of the places he conquered. Explore your town or city to find streets, parks, or buildings that have been named after people. Which of these people have been memorialized in other parts of the United States?

3. Give examples of how Hellenistic culture influenced the forms of government and economics of the regions it came in contact with. What aspects of American culture have spread to other countries today? Consider forms of government, music, styles of dress, foods, language, and manufactured products.

INVESTIGATING FURTHER

1. Choose one of the mathematicians or scientists, such as Pythagoras or Hippocrates, mentioned in Chapters 4 and 5. Discuss with a math or science teacher how their ideas were developed and are used today. Investigate other mathematicians or scientists who may have tried to prove them wrong or who have greatly modified the original ideas.

2. Report to the class on the speeches of Demosthenes and discuss the arguments that he advanced against Philip of Macedon. You can locate the appropriate speeches in Lewis Copeland and Lawrence Lamm, *The World's Great Speeches* (Dover), and in Houston Peterson, *Treasury of the World's Great Speeches* (Simon and Schuster).

3. In your library find the magazine article "In the Footsteps of Alexander the Great" (*National Geographic*, January 1968). Prepare a list of the locations shown in the pictures. What evidence is given of the influence of Alexander today on the lands he conquered?

6

Rome Ruled the Western World for Centuries

The date 146 B.C. is often given as the end of the Hellenistic Age because by that year Romans from Italy had extended their power over large parts of the eastern Mediterranean. Who were the Romans? How did they become powerful enough to gain control of the Mediterranean area and, eventually, of much of Europe as well? The geography of Italy and the location of the city of Rome itself had a great deal to do with this rise to power.

Italy is the central peninsula of the three great peninsulas in the Mediterranean region. The Iberian peninsula is to the west of it and the Balkan peninsula to the east. On the map on page 108, note that Italy resembles a boot, with its top in the Alps to the north and its toe and heel in the Mediterranean Sea to the south. Italy juts into the Mediterranean so far that it cuts the sea nearly in half. The toe of Italy is only about 2 miles (3 kilometers) from Sicily, which is only 80 miles (128 kilometers) from Africa. Italy is the heart of the Mediterranean region. It is also the obvious base from which to control both the eastern and the western halves of this region.

The people of Italy have often had to fight to protect their territory. The high Alps that separate Italy from the rest of Europe may seem to be good protection against land invasion, but the protection is not perfect. The mountains have a gentle slope to the north and a sharp drop to the south. There are several passes in the Alps

A statue beside a pool at Hadrian's palace

through which invaders can enter the peninsula. Invaders can also enter anywhere along Italy's long seacoast. Italy has often been overrun by hostile peoples.

Geographical factors made unity possible in Italy, whereas in Greece the geography prevented it. Notice on the map that the peninsula is divided by the Apennine Mountains, which run the full length of the "boot." The Apennines of Italy are less rugged than the mountains of Greece, and they did not prevent trade and travel. In addition, although Italy has a long coastline, there are fewer good harbors than in Greece. For these reasons, the people living in the early coastal settlements turned inland for trade and growth rather than toward the sea, as the Greeks had done.

Except for the long coastal plain to the west and the great valley of the Po River to the north, where grain is grown, most of Italy is foothill and mountain country. The soil is sandy and easily washed away and is useful mainly for pasture. Nevertheless, Italy's mild climate and plentiful winter rains enable farmers to raise vegetables, olives, grapes, and citrus fruits.

Italy's rivers are short and shallow. Most of them are partially blocked at their mouths by soil washed down from the higher land, making the surrounding region swampy. Throughout history the peninsula has had epidemics of malaria and other fevers carried by mosquitoes that thrive in these marshes.

The Italian peninsula, well situated at the center of the Mediterranean area, became in time the heart of a vast empire. Like most empires, it took shape gradually.

THE CHAPTER SECTIONS

1. The Romans founded a republic on the Italian peninsula

2. The Roman republic expanded into the entire Mediterranean region

3. The Roman republic was transformed into an empire

4. The Romans developed a distinctive society and culture

5. Christianity took root in Palestine and spread widely

6. A weakened Roman Empire declined and fell

1

The Romans founded a republic on the Italian peninsula

There were people living in Italy as early as the Old Stone Age. They had developed a Neolithic culture there before 3000 B.C. After 2000 B.C. the peninsula was invaded from the north many times. As in Greece, these early invaders were peoples from north of the Black and Caspian seas.

Early peoples in Italy

About 1000 B.C. the invasions increased in number. Many peoples entered and settled in various parts of the peninsula. The most important were the Latins, who settled in the west-central plains region called Latium (LAY·shee·um). Some of the Latin settlers built villages along the Tiber River. In time these villages were united into the city of Rome (see map, page 108), one of many cities on the plains of Latium.

The Etruscans, a people believed to have come from Asia Minor, entered Italy sometime after 900 B.C. They first conquered and held the coastal plains of Etruria to the north of the Tiber. In the late 600's B.C. they captured the plains of Latium, including the city of Rome, and held the area for about a century. In Rome an Etruscan family called the Tarquins ruled as kings for a time. The Etruscans lost control of Rome in 509 B.C., and they were later absorbed into the mixture of peoples who came to be known as Romans.

Although the Etruscans as a people disappeared, their culture lived on through its influence on the Latins. The Etruscans had a written language with an alphabet based on Greek characters. Scholars have not yet deciphered it. They made fine clothing and jewelry and were skilled workers in metal, pottery, and wood. From the Etruscans the early farmers of Latium learned how to pave roads, drain unhealthy marshes, and build sewers.

There were also Greeks in early Italy. Greek colonies in Sicily and southern Italy became city-states, as disunited and quarrelsome as those of the homeland. The Greek culture of these colonies had a strong influence on the Romans.

Rome and the Romans

Latins, Etruscans, and other peoples living in and around Rome gradually began to think of themselves as Romans. At first, Rome was only one of many city-states on the plains of Latium. It later became the most powerful city-state for several reasons.

Look again at the map of Italy and find the city of Rome in the west-central part. It is built on seven hills along the Tiber River. Rome is not at the mouth of the Tiber, but some 15 miles (24 kilometers) inland. The city was built where the waters of the Tiber are especially shallow and where there is a small island in the river. Thus it was located at the easiest river crossing for many miles.

Rome was the center of land trade routes that spread out in all directions. Early Romans were not much interested in shipping. Later, when foreign commerce became important, a port city named Ostia was built on the coast.

Roman expansion

For more than two centuries after the expulsion of the last Etruscan king in 509 B.C., the Romans fought many wars against neighboring peoples in Italy. These wars usually were fought to remove some threat to Roman frontiers.

In the south, for example, the Greek city-states began quarreling among themselves. One side in the dispute begged for help from Rome. The other side looked to the Greek kingdom of Epirus for aid. Rome, entering the dispute, conquered and then annexed the Greek colonies. When the Romans defeated a neighbor, they retained control of its territory so that they would not be disturbed again. The defeated peoples were usually made allies of Rome, but the Romans decided all important matters for their allies.

By 265 B.C. Roman territory included all of Italy south of the Rubicon River on the northeast coast. The Po Valley and all Italy north of the Rubicon were held by a people known as the Gauls. This region was called Cisalpine Gaul, meaning "Gaul on this side (the Roman side) of the Alps" (see map, page 113). The rest of Gaul was called Transalpine Gaul—"Gaul on the far side of the Alps"—or simply Gaul.

The early Roman republic

When the Romans drove out the last Etruscan king, they set up a republic. A **republic** is a form of government in which those who are entitled to vote choose people to run the government. In the early Roman republic, only adult male citizens were entitled to vote. Most men at this time were farmers, and even the wealthiest men worked in the fields. No one was very rich and no one was miserably poor.

As time went by, distinctions among classes became greater. A powerful aristocratic class, the **patricians,** gained control of the government. All other citizens were **plebeians** (pluh·BEE·uhns).

Plebeians were at a great disadvantage for many years. They could not hold public office and were forbidden to marry patricians. They could not even know what the laws were because the laws were not written down. In court, the laws were stated and applied by a judge—and all the judges were patricians.

Gradually the plebeians increased their power by making demands and by strikes. They gained the right to marry patricians and to hold office in the government. One of the greatest victories of the plebeians was to have the laws written down.

ANCIENT ITALY
about 325 B.C.

200 miles
200 kilometers

ALPS

CISALPINE GAUL

Po R.

GAULS

Rubicon R.

ETRURIA
ETRUSCANS

Tiber R.

CORSICA

Rome

Ostia

LATIUM
LATINS

Mt. Vesuvius

GREEKS

ILLYRIA

ADRIATIC SEA

APENNINES

SARDINIA

MEDITERRANEAN SEA

SICILY
GREEKS

Strait of Messina

Carthage

AFRICA

Etruscan Archers and Discus Thrower

The Etruscans were a powerful people of ancient Italy. They were skilled fighters and merchants, whose wealth came from shipping. The Etruscans traded widely across the Mediterranean, especially with the Greeks and Egyptians.

Wealthy Etruscans built magnificent tombs for their dead. They filled the tombs with items they thought the dead might need in their future life. Much of our knowledge of Etruscan customs comes from objects found in these tombs. They tell us that Etruscans loved music, games, wrestling, horseback riding, and chariot races.

Sometimes the Etruscans cremated, or burned, their dead. The bronze funeral urn shown here was used to hold ashes. Etruscan funeral urns were decorated with scenes of real life. The discus thrower and four mounted archers may have been placed on the lid to represent pleasures the dead person had once enjoyed.

They were engraved on tablets known as the Twelve Tables and were placed in the Forum—the chief public square—for all to see.

Government

Three groups of citizens helped govern Rome:

(1) The Senate was composed of 300 men. It controlled public funds and political appointments. It also determined foreign policy and sometimes acted as a court. The Senate was the most important and powerful of the three governing bodies.

(2) The Assembly of Centuries took its name from a military formation of a hundred men. The formation was called a "century" after the Latin word *centum,* meaning "hundred." There were 193 centuries in the Assembly, and each voted as a unit—170 centuries of foot soldiers, 18 centuries of cavalry, and 5 centuries of noncombatants. The majority of centuries were made up of rich men and well-to-do farmers. The Assembly elected the people to serve in the government and declared war and peace.

(3) The Assembly of Tribes was made up of citizens grouped into 35 tribes according to where they lived. Plebeians controlled this Assembly. It elected officials called tribunes (see next page) and was democratic by Roman standards. In 287 B.C. a law was passed making the Assembly of Tribes the legislative body of Rome.

The officials who ran the government day by day were called magistrates. All magistrates were elected by the Assembly of Centuries. The most important were the major magistrates who had the authority to interpret and carry out laws. At first only patricians could become major magistrates, but by 339 B.C. these positions were open to plebeians as well. All members of the Senate were former major magistrates.

There were four kinds of major magistrates in the early Roman republic.

(1) Consuls were two officials elected for one-year terms. They were the chief executives who ran the government and were also the army commanders. Each could **veto**—refuse to approve—acts of the other. (The Latin word *veto* means "I forbid.")

(2) Praetors (PREE·tors) were below the consuls as military commanders, but they were also

109

judges. They were very important because they actually created most of the laws of Rome by their decisions in court cases.

(3) Censors registered people according to their wealth for taxes and membership in the Assembly of Centuries.

(4) A dictator had absolute power for a term limited to six months. He could be nominated by the consuls and elected by the Assembly of Centuries. A dictator was chosen only when Rome was in great danger.

The tribunes did not take part in day-to-day government, but they were the most important officials without administrative authority in Rome. There were ten tribunes. They were elected each year by the Assembly of Tribes, over which they presided. They had to be plebeians and represented only the plebeians. Their importance rested on the fact that they could veto any act of any magistrate. This veto power protected the interests of the plebeians somewhat against abuses of power by patricians.

The Romans of the republic feared monarchy and were suspicious of Greek-style democracy. Their system of government worked well because it gave the common people the right to elect officials and make laws. However, since no official received a salary, only patricians and rich plebeians could afford to hold office. The rich controlled the Assembly of Centuries, and aristocrats from powerful families ran the Senate. Magistrates were overshadowed by the Senate. And ambitious tribunes, hoping for higher offices, sometimes cooperated with the Senate in using their veto power. Through skillful political maneuvering, therefore, the rich and the aristocrats were able to dominate the republic.

The army

Every adult male citizen was obliged to serve in the army when needed. In the early days men fought without pay and had to supply their own weapons. The most important military unit was the legion, consisting of 4,500 to 6,000 men, called legionaries. Because of excellent organization and training and the high morale of individual soldiers, the Roman legions were able in time to defeat even the great Macedonian army.

The Roman army was a citizen army. No man could be a candidate for high office until he had served at least ten years in the army. Only citizens could serve in the legions. Discipline was strict and was enforced by harsh punishments.

The people of some conquered areas were given Roman citizenship. However, citizens had to come to Rome to vote. Great numbers of them could not make this trip and therefore were not represented in the government. Other conquered peoples became allies. Allies kept much of their self-government. However, Rome required them to furnish troops for war and controlled their relations with other cities and countries.

The family

The family was the most important unit in Roman society during the days of the republic. It was the center of religion, morals, and education. A Roman family included all unmarried children, married sons and their families, all dependent relatives, and the family slaves.

The father had absolute authority. He conducted religious ceremonies, made all important decisions, and looked after the education of his sons. Roman women were more honored than Greek women. The mother managed the household, did the buying, and shared with her husband the entertainment of guests.

Education and religion

Roman education aimed more at good habits than at knowledge. Children were trained to be loyal citizens and above all obedient to their elders and superiors. They received their early education at home. The Roman father taught the sons farming and the duties of citizenship. The mother instructed the children in reading, writing, and arithmetic. Children also memorized the Twelve Tables.

The religion of the early Romans was a form of animism. The Romans believed that the spirits inhabiting everything had neither form nor sex. They had to be made friendly by rituals and sacrifices because people depended on them.

To the Romans the spirits of the home were the most important. These included the lares (LAIR·eez), who were ancestral spirits, and penates (puh·NAY·teez), guardians of the storeroom. Fam-

Daily life among the Romans

As a center of the powerful Roman Empire, the city of Rome was a busy and exciting place to live. The streets were noisy with the sounds of people, chariots, and animals being herded to market. Outdoor markets thrived under the warm Mediterranean sun. They drew people in search of all manner of goods, from food to imported glassware to pillows (above).

Goods were not the only thing traded in Rome—trade in ideas and learning was also highly important there. Philosophers and poets (left) gathered under trees to discuss the teachings of great thinkers of earlier times, like Plato. Fortunately for later students of philosophy, their thoughts were often recorded and passed along, perhaps by a scribe (above left). Scribes were highly valued in Rome, where many people could not write.

ily worship centered on Vesta, guardian of fire and hearth. Other spirits governed every aspect of farm life.

Contacts with other peoples changed Roman beliefs. Under Etruscan influence, Romans came to think of their spirits as having human forms and qualities. Thus Jupiter was thought of as the father of the gods and Juno as his wife. From the Etruscans the Romans also adopted the practice of trying to learn a god's will by observing the entrails of animals or the flight of birds. The Romans also adopted much of Greek religion and mythology. For example, the Greek supreme god, Zeus, became identified with Jupiter, and Zeus's wife Hera with Juno.

In time, the old family religion became a state religion with temples, priests, ceremonies, and processions. The high priest, elected for life by the Assembly of Tribes, was called the Pontifex Maximus.

CHECKUP

1. IDENTIFY: Gauls, patricians, plebeians, Twelve Tables, consuls, veto, praetors, censors, tribunes, legion, Pontifex Maximus.

2. LOCATE: Alps, Apennine Mountains, Po River, Latium, Tiber River, Rome, Ostia, Rubicon River, Cisalpine Gaul.

3. What did the Latins learn from the Etruscans?

4. How was Rome ideally located for trade?

5. What was the difference between a patrician and a plebeian? Why were the Twelve Tables so significant for the plebeians?

6. Name the three groups of citizens that helped govern the Roman republic. Which group was the most powerful? Why?

2

The Roman republic expanded into the entire Mediterranean region

By the middle 200's B.C. the Roman republic was well established and had extended its power over all of the Italian peninsula south of the Rubicon River. The addition of so much territory and so many new people to the republic increased its power and strength, but the burden of defending the republic was also increased.

Rome versus Carthage

Rome soon came into contact with Carthage, a large and powerful city on the coast of North Africa, directly across the Mediterranean Sea from the western tip of Sicily. Carthage had been founded as a colony by the Phoenicians. It became a great commercial power, with territory in North Africa and Spain and colonies scattered about the central and western Mediterranean areas (see map, opposite page).

Carthage had no colonies on the Italian peninsula. However, there were Carthaginian settlements on the nearby islands of Sicily, Sardinia, and Corsica. By 265 B.C. Carthage was a great sea power, with many merchant ships and a large navy.

After the Romans occupied southern Italy, Carthage feared that they would also try to take Sicily. The Romans in turn were afraid that the Carthaginian navy would close the Adriatic Sea and the narrow Strait of Messina between Italy and Sicily. War probably could have been avoided, but neither side tried very hard to do so. Rome and Carthage fought three wars which, with intervals of peace, lasted from 264 to 146 B.C. These are called the Punic Wars, because the Latin adjective for "Phoenician" was *punicus*.

The opponents were well matched. Rome had the better army, Carthage the better navy. Carthage had more wealth. Roman lands were more compact and more easily defended. At first, Carthaginian military commanders were more skillful, but Rome finally found generals who could win.

The first Punic War. The first war began in 264 B.C., and after five years Carthage asked for peace. It had to pay a large **indemnity**—money for the damages it had caused—and give up its control of Sicily. Within a few years, the Romans expanded their control to all of Italy and had major overseas holdings. But the Carthaginians wanted revenge.

The second Punic War. The second Punic War began in 218 B.C. The Carthaginian forces were led by Hannibal, one of the great generals of all

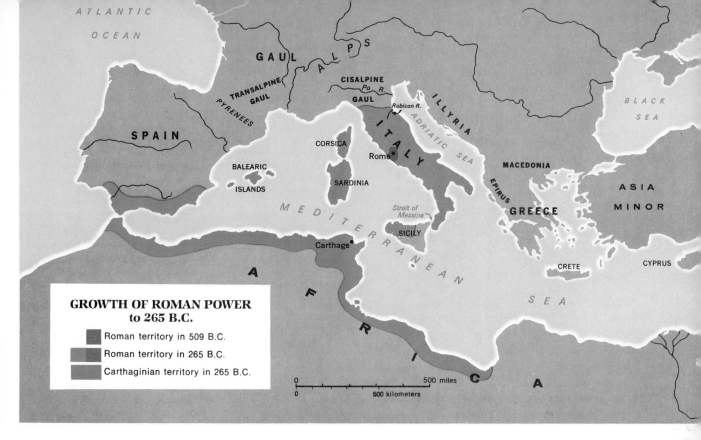

time. Hannibal assembled an army of infantry, cavalry, and armored elephants in Spain. They marched across what is now southern France and began the difficult job of crossing the Alps into Italy. Hannibal lost nearly half his army there, but he did reach the Po Valley (see map, page 117). The Roman armies were no match for him. He defeated several of them and for 15 years ranged up and down Italy, rarely provoking the Romans into battle.

Then a Roman army invaded Africa and threatened Carthage. Hannibal's government ordered him home to defend the city. In Africa he finally met his match—the Roman general Scipio. Hannibal and his army were defeated in 202 B.C. at the battle of Zama, near Carthage (see map, page 117). Once more Carthage asked for peace and had to pay a huge indemnity. It also gave up its Spanish colonies. The city of Carthage remained independent, but its power was broken.

The third Punic War. As a result of Hannibal's defeat, Rome had gained the rich prize of Spain, where there were gold and silver mines. The natives of this region did not welcome Roman occupation, and it took the Romans many years to subdue them. In Rome there were some veterans of the war against Hannibal who passionately hated Carthage. Though the city was no threat, the Senate finally decided to crush it. On a flimsy excuse, Rome declared war against Carthage in 149 B.C. After a bitter siege, the city fell in 146 B.C. and was totally destroyed. The wars in Spain wore on, but Rome was supreme in the West.

Conquest of the Hellenistic East

During the second Punic War, Macedonia had been allied with Carthage. Out of revenge Rome started a war against Macedonia and defeated it in 197 B.C. The Greek cities now came under Roman "protection." The Romans soon defeated the Seleucid king and gave parts of his territory in Asia to their allies. By 146 B.C., after more conquests, Rome's supremacy in the East was total.

In many situations the Romans had used the jealousies and fears of their neighbors to Rome's advantage. They did not keep faith with their allies, and they played one city or king against another. The basic principle of Roman foreign policy was "divide and conquer."

The Roman army

The army was the basis of the Roman Empire's remarkable expansion. Without its successes on the battlefield, Rome could not have come to dominate the Mediterranean so rapidly. Every adult male was required to serve in the army if called upon. It was also necessary to serve at least ten years to be eligible to run for public office. As the empire expanded, however, it became necessary to have a professional army.

The soldier's main defensive equipment was his helmet, shield, and armored tunic (left). Much of his body, especially the arms and legs, was left exposed. In the carved column (below) commemorating Roman victories, soldiers are shown helping their wounded comrades. Visible among the soldiers are the military insignia they carried into battle. These long poles (below left) were decorated with the symbols of Rome and of the particular legions carrying them.

Problems of Roman expansion

By 133 B.C. the Roman state had grown from a federation of Italian cities into a great Mediterranean power.

Government. Rome itself retained a republican form of government. But the operation of the government changed in certain ways to meet the problems of ruling the greatly increased territory. The Senate had control of the army, finances, and foreign affairs, and of the new territories. The power of the aristocrats was greater than ever.

The provinces. Government in the recently organized territories, called provinces, was poor. The people were not given citizenship, nor were they made allies like the people of conquered Italian cities. Instead, the people of the provinces were taxed without mercy.

Provincial cities became centers of local government and new cities were built in rural regions. The provinces became a collection of city-states, each one subject to Rome.

Each province had a Roman governor called a proconsul. He was appointed by the Senate and backed by a Roman army of occupation. Because his term was for one year only and he received no salary, he was under strong temptation to accept bribes and to neglect the needs of the people.

The proconsuls were not the only Romans who became wealthy by stealing from the provinces. The system of collecting taxes was called tax farming. In Rome the censors made contracts with officials called publicans. The publicans agreed to collect the taxes and pay a fixed amount to the Roman treasury. They were then allowed to keep whatever they collected in excess of this fixed sum. Tax farming was another example of the widespread corruption in the provinces.

Changes in agriculture. Rome's annexation of distant territories lessened the role of the small citizen-farmer in Roman life. The Roman government owned much land in the new provinces and leased it in large estates to anyone who could pay the price. Only wealthy people could afford to rent the land and buy the slaves who did the work. As time passed, Rome came to depend on the provinces for most of its grain, which was the chief item of food.

Small farmers in Italy could not compete with the cheaper grain grown by farmers in the provinces. Nor could they compete with the cheap slave labor increasingly used by owners of large estates. Thus, much Italian land was turned into pasture for cattle or used to grow grapes and olives. Many small farmers gave up their land and moved to the cities. Not all of them could find jobs there, and they depended upon the government for food.

The movement of small farmers to the cities was only one trend that made wealthy Romans wealthier and poor ones poorer. Manufacturing was done by small businesses. The Romans saw little reason to invent labor-saving devices or to increase production because most small businesses used the labor of slaves or freed slaves.

Growth of commerce. While farming and manufacturing declined in Italy, trade within Rome's vast empire increased. The business people formed a class called equites (EK·wih-teez). They had great wealth but little political power. In addition to wealth from trade, they made money from contracts for public works, tax farming, and the loot of war.

Social change. The increase of slavery, the decline of the small independent farmer, and the growth of jobless masses in the cities weakened the old-fashioned ideals of discipline and devotion to the state. People were judged by their wealth rather than by their character.

Other changes had taken place. Roman citizens were no longer exclusively Italian. Some were former slaves from other regions. By Roman law a freed slave became a citizen. Skilled slaves were a good investment, and owners let them keep part of what they earned to buy their freedom later. A Roman freed slave had more rights than free people who were not citizens.

CHECKUP

1. IDENTIFY: *punicus,* Hannibal, Scipio, proconsuls, tax farming, publicans, equites.

2. LOCATE: Carthage, Sicily, Sardinia, Corsica, Adriatic Sea, Strait of Messina, Zama.

3. How were Rome and Carthage in competition with each other?

4. What were the final results of the Punic Wars?

5. How did the government of Rome change as a result of the conquest of new territories?

3

The Roman republic was transformed into an empire

By 133 B.C. many problems had arisen. The increasing number of slaves made life difficult for free farmers and workers. The provinces were governed badly. In addition, the strain of so many wars made military service a burden. Only land-owners served in the legions, and this was very hard on small farmers.

Reformers and problems

Two brothers, Tiberius and Gaius Gracchus (GRAK·us), who came from a noble family, were among the first to attempt reforms. Tiberius was elected tribune in 133 B.C. He saw that some senators were using public land for their own benefit. He therefore limited the amount of public land they could use and settled many poor people from the cities on the land to work as farmers. This policy made them eligible for military service, but it also saved them from poverty. Some senators opposed Tiberius, and he was eventually murdered by them.

His brother Gaius, elected tribune in 123 B.C., tried to increase the power of the Assembly of Tribes. Gaius used public funds to purchase grain to be sold at low prices to the poor. Other measures improved the political status of the equites. Gaius was killed in 121 B.C. in a riot.

The land reforms worked for a time. However, the sale of grain at low prices set the example that private citizens should be supported at public expense. This practice eventually became a drain on the treasury.

The next leader to appear was Gaius Marius, a plebeian and a military hero. In 105 B.C. Cisalpine Gaul was invaded by Germanic tribes from the north. (You will read more about these tribes later in this chapter.) Marius defeated these invaders and changed the course of Roman history. To fill his legions, he signed up any citizen, regardless of whether he had land or not. The soldiers served for pay and for booty—whatever they could steal from the enemy. When they were discharged, the soldiers expected their general to

get public land for them. In other words, Marius had substituted a professional army for an army of draftees. Armies became loyal to their leaders instead of to the Roman government.

Military rule

In 88 B.C. Lucius Cornelius Sulla was elected consul to repel an invasion in Asia Minor. Marius wanted to take over his command. Sulla turned to his army and led them into Rome—the first revolution in Roman history. He drove out Marius and put his own supporters in power. Sulla had shown what an ambitious general could do with a professional army. When he left for Asia Minor, civil war broke out in Rome. Marius returned to power and executed his enemies. Seven years later, Sulla returned to Rome with his army and defeated the followers of Marius. With terrible brutality, Sulla executed thousands of citizens.

Sulla then ruled as a military dictator. He placed all the powers of government in the hands of the Senate. Increasingly, however, army commanders who had the loyalty of their troops could force the Senate to do what they wanted.

When Sulla retired in 79 B.C., there was a struggle for power among a new group of leaders. Two generals, Gnaeus Pompey and Marcus Licinius Crassus, had become famous. When the Senate refused to elect them consuls in 70 B.C., they threatened to use force, and the Senate gave in.

The First Triumvirate

A rising politician of this time was Julius Caesar, a nephew of Marius. Caesar was a spellbinding orator and a great spender of money. With fine speeches and gifts of grain, he built up a huge following among the poor citizens of Rome.

Caesar, Pompey, and Crassus each had many enemies in the Senate, so they decided to join forces. In 60 B.C. they formed an alliance that became known as the First Triumvirate. The word *triumvirate* means "rule of three."

Caesar in power

Caesar realized that he could not win power without an army loyal to him, so he made himself proconsul of Gaul. At this time Rome controlled only

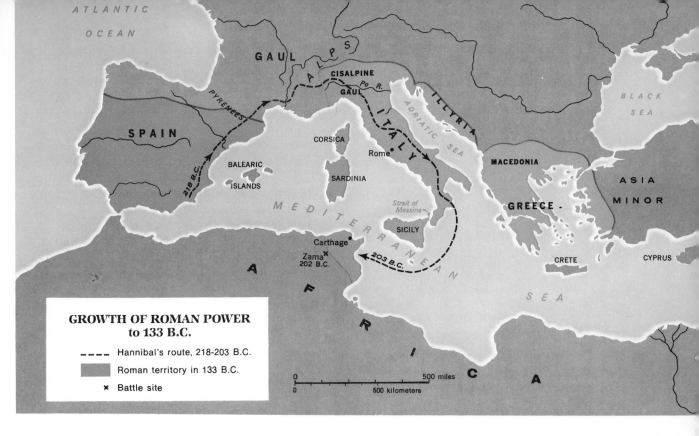

GROWTH OF ROMAN POWER
to 133 B.C.

- - - - Hannibal's route, 218-203 B.C.

▨ Roman territory in 133 B.C.

× Battle site

Cisalpine Gaul and the southernmost part of Transalpine Gaul. In his ten years as proconsul, Caesar brought all Gaul under Roman rule. He was a superb military leader and organizer.

Crassus was killed in battle in 53 B.C. Pompey meanwhile was growing jealous of Caesar's rising fame. To head off his rival, Pompey had himself made sole consul. Then he persuaded the Senate to order Caesar to return home without his army. Caesar refused to give up his military command and take second place to Pompey. Instead he led his army toward Rome in 49 B.C.

Pompey and his followers fled to Greece, and the way was open for Caesar to assume sole power. He first made himself secure in Italy and Spain and defeated Pompey in Greece. He then went to Egypt, which had come increasingly under Roman domination. There Caesar put Cleopatra, a daughter of the ruling Ptolemy family, on the throne as an ally of Rome.

In 46 B.C. Caesar returned to Rome and took control of the government. He had become so powerful that in 45 B.C. he was appointed dictator for life. The form of the republican government was kept, but Caesar was king in everything but

name. Caesar showed himself to be an able politician as well as general. He granted citizenship to many people in the provinces. Under his rule the government gave public land to the poor.

Caesar also reduced the Senate to the position of an advisory council and raised its membership to 900 senators. Among them were Roman equites, leading citizens of Italian and provincial cities, chieftains of conquered Gaul, and even sons of slaves. Caesar also ordered the establishment of a calendar of 365¼ days. It was used in Europe until relatively modern times.

The conservative families of Rome did not welcome Caesar's new status. Some 60 men, who envied his great power, formed a conspiracy against him. Two of these were men Caesar considered his friends: Gaius Cassius and Marcus Brutus. In 44 B.C. the conspirators stabbed Caesar to death.

The Second Triumvirate

Although Caesar had named his grandnephew Octavian as his heir, there was a scramble for power after Caesar's death.

Roman Emperors
27 B.C.–180 A.D.

27 B.C.–14 A.D.	Augustus
14–68 A.D.	Julian Emperors
	Tiberius (14–37 A.D.)
	Caligula (37–41 A.D.)
	Claudius (41–54 A.D.)
	Nero (54–68 A.D.)
68–96 A.D.	Emperors controlled by the army
96–180 A.D.	The Good Emperors
	Nerva (96–98 A.D.)
	Trajan (98–117 A.D.)
	Hadrian (117–138 A.D.)
	Antoninus Pius (138– 161 A.D.)
	Marcus Aurelius (161– 180 A.D.)

(Dates in parentheses are those of reigns)

Octavian was only 18 and was away in Greece when Caesar was murdered. In Rome, Marc Antony, a general and an ally of Caesar, and Caesar's second-in-command, Lepidus (LEP·uh·dus), drove out the conspirators and took control. The three men—Octavian, Marc Antony, and Lepidus—formed the Second Triumvirate in 43 B.C.

Antony took an army east and reconquered Syria and Asia Minor from the armies of Brutus and Cassius. Then he fell in love with Cleopatra and joined her in Egypt. Meanwhile Octavian forced Lepidus to retire from political life and built up his own power in Italy.

Octavian, the Emperor Augustus

Antony and Octavian divided the Roman world between themselves. Antony took the east and Octavian the west. Within a few years, however, Octavian persuaded the Senate to declare war on Antony and Cleopatra. In 31 B.C., in a great naval battle at Actium in Greece, Octavian defeated their fleet. Both Antony and Cleopatra committed suicide a year later. Octavian then took Egypt as his own personal province. The wars were finished, but the republic was also finished, for Octavian made himself supreme ruler.

Although there was no opposition to Octavian, he proceeded cautiously. Julius Caesar had been assassinated because many people feared his power. Octavian was determined to avoid his granduncle's fate. In 27 B.C. Octavian resigned his offices and announced that the republic was restored. But this was only a political maneuver. The Senate thanked him and then granted him a number of new offices and titles. In fact, they made him sole ruler, but he was careful to preserve the outward form of the republic.

The Senate gave Octavian the title *Augustus,* which means "exalted" or "majestic." He has been known ever since as Augustus Caesar, or simply Augustus. Many later Roman rulers used the word *Caesar* as part of their title.

Augustus was made proconsul of all the provinces. He commanded all the armies and had power to declare war, make peace, and propose or veto laws.

Although Augustus himself did not use the title, he is generally called the first Roman emperor. The Roman state beginning with his rule is called the Roman Empire. Under Augustus, Rome's territory stretched from Spain in the west to Syria in the east, from the Rhine and Danube rivers in the north to Egypt and the Sahara in the south.

The Julian Emperors

Augustus died in 14 A.D. For the next 54 years the Roman Empire was ruled by men who were related in some way to Julius Caesar. Thus they are called the Julian Emperors. Tiberius (14–37 A.D.), the adopted son of Augustus, was an adequate ruler. His successor Caligula was insane and was murdered.

Caligula was followed by Claudius, an intelligent and scholarly man who administered the empire wisely. It was during his rule that Britain was added to the Roman Empire. During the reign of Nero, which began in 54 A.D., Rome was swept by a disastrous fire. Nero was widely hated and was forced to commit suicide in 68 A.D.

The Good Emperors

After Nero, Rome was ruled by a number of emperors who were supported by the army. Then, in 96 A.D., the Emperor Nerva came to the

The Roman emperors

The Roman emperors knew the power of propaganda and used it effectively. They had many portraits of themselves made, and as a result we have a good idea of what they looked like. Among their proudest accomplishments were their military victories, and so they often had themselves portrayed as soldiers, wearing armor. Thus the statue of Augustus (above) shows him wearing a superbly decorated breastplate, depicting the mythical figure of a centaur. Half man, half horse, the centaurs were famous for their fighting ability. The Emperor Hadrian (below) is also in armor. The decoration on his armor is the sun, a symbol of great power that has been used by rulers throughout history. The victory column (right) was erected by Marcus Aurelius to commemorate his victories in battle.

ROMAN EMPIRE AT ITS HEIGHT
117-180 A.D.

Greatest extent of the Roman Empire, 117 A.D.
⌐⌐ Roman walls
✕ Battle site

throne. He was the first of a group of five, known as the Good Emperors, who ruled Rome for almost a hundred years. Trajan, who ruled from 98 to 117 A.D., was a Spanish general. He added new areas that brought the empire to its greatest size (see map, this page).

Hadrian. Hadrian, Trajan's successor, was a supporter of art and an able ruler. Born in Spain, he understood the provinces and spent much time organizing and Romanizing them. To help protect the boundaries of the empire, Hadrian built fortifications along the frontiers and encouraged frontier peoples to enter the army. He disapproved of wars to conquer neighboring regions and gave up the areas that Trajan had acquired in Asia.

Marcus Aurelius. Hadrian died in 138 A.D. and was succeeded by Antoninus Pius, whose long reign was uneventful. In 161 A.D. Marcus Aurelius became the next emperor. Marcus Aurelius was the last of the Good Emperors. He had to give much attention to the defense of the empire, which was threatened by attacks from the north and east. The troops returning from the east brought with them a great plague, which lasted several years and caused many deaths.

After the death of Marcus Aurelius in 180 A.D., Rome underwent a long period of confusion and decline.

CHECKUP

1. IDENTIFY: Marius, Sulla, Pompey, Cleopatra, Cassius, Marc Antony, Lepidus, Nero, Hadrian, Marcus Aurelius.

2. What was the First Triumvirate?

3. Why was Julius Caesar so popular with the people? Why was he killed by a conspiracy?

4. Why was the Second Triumvirate formed? What caused it to break apart?

5. What powers did Augustus hold as ruler of the Roman Empire? What was his strategy for gaining these powers?

4

The Romans developed a distinctive society and culture

You have read how Rome grew to be an empire and about the kinds of people who ruled it in the period up to 180 A.D. There were several essential features that helped the Romans build their empire and maintain it in peace.

The Romans had a talent for ruling others and maintained their authority through an efficient government both at home and abroad. Law, military organization, and widespread trade and transportation held the empire together and brought peace for over 200 years.

The period from 27 B.C. to 180 A.D.—from the beginning of Augustus' reign until the death of Marcus Aurelius—is known as the time of the **Pax Romana,** the "Roman Peace."

Government

Government was the strongest tie uniting the empire. It maintained order, enforced the laws, defended the frontiers, and provided relief when areas were damaged by fire or earthquake.

The position of the emperor was a demanding one. He had to make all policy decisions. He appointed the officials who controlled the provinces and ran the entire government. The responsibilities of the emperor's job were too much for one person, however. If the emperor was weak, incompetent, or selfish, good government depended on the other officials of government.

From the time of Augustus on, government officials were appointed and promoted on the basis of their ability alone. The positions were highly desired not only for the salary but also for the honor.

The provinces

The provinces were much better governed during the time of the Pax Romana than they had been under the republic. A closer check was kept on provincial governors. Any citizen in the provinces could appeal directly to the emperor over a governor's decision.

The western provinces, especially Gaul and Spain, benefited greatly from their closeness to Roman civilization. Each of the new cities built there was a small copy of Rome, with a senate building, theaters, and public baths. Most of the cities brought in water by aqueducts, and most had paved streets and sewer systems. Usually there were no direct taxes because government income was received from publicly owned land, mines, and quarries. Wealthy citizens of the provinces took great pride in their cities. They gave large gifts of money to be used for public buildings, streets, schools, and entertainment.

Law

Roman law was another important tie binding the empire together. The code of the Twelve Tables had grown out of a small agricultural society. These laws had to be developed to fit a huge empire with its varied conditions.

The Twelve Tables were modified and expanded in two ways. First, new laws were passed as they were needed. Second, judges interpreted the old laws to fit new circumstances. Roman law was adapted to fit the customs of all peoples throughout the provinces.

Roman judges helped develop the belief that certain basic legal principles are common to all humans. For example, Roman law established an idea we believe in today—that an accused person is considered innocent unless proven guilty.

In later years the Roman system of law became the foundation of the laws of all the European countries that had been part of the Roman Empire. Roman law also had a strong influence on the laws of the Christian Church.

The army

The Roman Empire was held together mainly by military force. Augustus had reorganized the army. The Praetorian Guard—first organized by Augustus to guard the *praetorium,* or headquarters of the commander in chief—was a small, elite force stationed in Rome to protect the emperor. The bulk of the army was the Roman legions, made up of citizens who served 20 years. The legions were stationed in great fortified camps along the frontiers. People often settled around these camps, and these settlements eventually grew into towns and cities.

The Roman army was aided by forces made up of people from the provinces or the border tribes. They enlisted for 25 years. When they completed their service, they were promised Roman citizenship.

Thus there was a population of trained soldiers to help guard the frontiers. There may have been between 250,000 and 300,000 soldiers under arms at the time of Augustus' death. Although this number increased under later emperors, probably there were never more than 500,000 troops in the army.

In some regions the Romans built great lines of fortifications for protection. In Britain, for example, Hadrian's Wall stretched entirely across the island in the north. There was also a line of forts between the Rhine and Danube rivers. Between the great camps of the legions were protective ditches, fortresses, and walls. Many portions of these walls still stand. Paved highways joined military outposts with cities in the interior, and all provincial cities were linked to Rome by highways—the origin of the saying, "All roads lead to Rome."

Trade and transportation

Throughout the time of the Pax Romana, agriculture remained the basic occupation of most people in the empire. In Italy itself most farming was done on large estates devoted to vineyards or livestock. In the provinces there were more small farms. However, much grain land had become worn out, and farming districts in Greece and southern Italy were abandoned. Even though new farms were established in Gaul and North Africa, the grain supply throughout the Roman Empire was always uncertain.

A new type of agricultural worker—a tenant farmer known as a **colonus**—began to replace slaves on the large estates. Each of these farmers received a small plot of land from the owner. The colonus had to remain on the land for a certain period and pay the owner of the land with crops. A colonus worked long and hard and had little to show for it.

Such a vast empire, with so many different lands and peoples, provided great opportunities for commerce. Taxes on trade were low, and the same currency was used everywhere. Therefore, the exchange of goods was easy. Rome and Alexandria, in Egypt, were the empire's great commercial centers.

From the provinces Italy imported grain and raw materials such as meat, wool, and hides. From Asia came silks, linens, glassware, jewelry, and furniture to satisfy the tastes of the wealthy. During Roman times and on through later centuries, India was the source of many products that Europe had never known before. Demand for Indian spices, cotton, and other luxury products was great.

Manufacturing also increased throughout the empire. Italy, Gaul, and Spain made cheap pottery and textiles. As in Greece, shops were small and most work was done by hand.

Transportation was greatly improved during the period of the early empire. Travel by sea was cheaper and faster than travel by land. Roads and bridges for land travel were well built, and there was postal service from all parts of the empire to Rome. However, even with improved transportation and communications, it took a Roman messenger at least ten weeks to cross the empire, traveling at top speed and using every known means of transportation.

Living conditions

The time of the Pax Romana was prosperous for many people, but wealth was not evenly shared. The rich citizen usually had both a city home and a country home. Each residence was furnished with many conveniences, such as running water and baths.

The lives of the wealthy included much time for leisure—rest, exercise, public baths, and banquets. Many wealthy Romans ate and drank enormous quantities at banquets, and drunkenness was common.

The contrast between the lives of the wealthy and the poor was extreme. In Rome the poor lived in three- or four-story wooden apartment houses. There was always danger from fire or from the collapse of these cheaply constructed buildings.

Most Romans were poor and hardworking. Some were artisans or agricultural workers, but they had little security because of frequent unemployment and low wages. In Rome rents were high, but grain was given free of charge to residents of the capital. This helped, but no one could survive on free grain alone.

Both the government and candidates for public office provided the people with amusements and public baths either free or quite cheaply. Small farmers who lost their land drifted to the towns to find work.

Many slaves, especially agricultural slaves, led miserable and hopeless lives. However, the number of slaves declined greatly during the early days of the empire. A slave was expensive to feed, clothe, and care for. An owner of a large estate might find it more profitable to free a slave and make that slave a colonus.

Amusements

Romans enjoyed the theater, especially light comedies and satires. Performers such as jugglers, dancers, acrobats, and clowns were quite popular.

Romans also enjoyed savage and brutal sports. Greek games like boxing were made more bloody with the use of brass knuckles. Large crowds watched chariot racing in the huge Circus Maximus of Rome, a kind of racetrack. There were organized "fan clubs" for the popular chariot racers.

Spectacles in the Colosseum, the great amphitheater in Rome, were also popular. Wild beasts, made more savage by hunger, were let into the arena to fight one another. Sometimes humans fought against animals. Often condemned criminals or slaves were thrown into the arena to be killed by the beasts.

Most popular were combats between gladiators—trained fighters who were usually slaves. They sometimes fought animals, but they often fought one another, either singly or in groups. The fights usually ended in death for one or both fighters. When a gladiator was wounded, he appealed for mercy to the crowd, which signaled whether he should be killed or spared.

connections

Baths

Ancient peoples were just as fond of taking a plunge into water as we are. The Romans were particularly fond of bathing and built many large public pools and baths. There were often pools of different temperatures, heated either by natural hot springs or by underground furnaces. The Roman bather would go from one pool to the other, combining dips with exercises followed by massages with fine oils.

Some of the Roman bath houses also contained libraries, sports facilities, gymnasiums, and shops. The public bath was a social gathering place, where people could meet, gossip, and even do business. The largest public bath in Rome is remembered as the main achievement of its builder, the Emperor Caracalla, who ruled in the 200's A.D.

The Romans built baths wherever they settled. One place in England,

which had natural hot springs, became known as the city of Bath (above). People enjoyed its refreshing waters long after the Romans left England.

Today public baths, which are used as neighborhood gathering places,

are popular all over Japan. There is also a very ornate public bath in Moscow, the capital of the Soviet Union. In the United States, outdoor and indoor public swimming pools provide the same enjoyment and recreation the ancient Romans knew.

Accomplishments of Rome

The Roman Empire is noted for many accomplishments, in addition to its military successes. The Romans were the greatest engineers of the ancient world. Not until very recent times has their ingenuity and ability been surpassed. Among the enormous projects they completed was a system of aqueducts, which carried water for towns across long distances. Portions of the Roman aqueduct system still stand, their tiers of arches intact. The aqueduct in Segovia, Spain (above), was built during the reign of the Emperor Trajan.

Sculptors and stone workers (left) were constantly at their task, decorating buildings and other public works. These and other artisans belonged to guilds. At the height of Rome's glory, there were 125 guilds. They included goldsmiths, ropemakers, tanners, and ironsmiths. For recreation, Roman citizens gathered in gigantic stadiums built for public entertainments. There they watched gladiators, warriors who fought wild animals and each other for sport (below left).

Science, engineering, and architecture

The Romans were less interested in scientific research to increase knowledge than in collecting and organizing information. Galen, a physician who lived in Rome during the 100's A.D., wrote several volumes that summarized all the medical knowledge of his day. He was long regarded as the greatest authority on medicine. Ptolemy's theories in astronomy were also widely accepted. A scientist from Alexandria, Ptolemy believed that the earth was the center of the universe. Most people accepted this theory until the 1600's.

The practical Romans applied the scientific knowledge they gained from the Greeks in planning cities, building water and sewage systems, and improving farming and livestock breeding. Roman engineers surpassed all ancient peoples in constructing roads, bridges, aqueducts, amphitheaters, and public buildings. They were probably the first to use cement.

Architecture was the greatest contribution of the Romans in the field of art. Great public buildings—law courts, palaces, temples, amphitheaters, and triumphal arches—were erected for the emperor and the government. Roman buildings were based on Greek models to some extent. However, the Romans used the arch and vaulted dome, which the Greeks had not known how to build, and emphasized size rather than pleasing proportion.

Education

Every important town or city throughout the Roman Empire had elementary, secondary, and higher schools. A boy or girl of the free classes entered elementary school at the age of seven and was taught reading, writing, arithmetic, and music. At about the age of 13, students entered a secondary school, where they studied grammar, Greek, literature, good writing, and expressive speech. The teachers were often Greeks who had been slaves.

The equivalent of our college education was given in rhetoric schools, where the chief subjects were oratory, geometry, astronomy, and philosophy. Students entered a school of rhetoric at the age of 16 and stayed as long as they liked. For further education there were schools at Athens for philosophy, at Alexandria for medicine, at Rhodes for rhetoric, and a school called the Athenaeum at Rome for law, mathematics, and engineering. Students in all schools paid fees for their education.

Literature

Augustus and several of the Good Emperors encouraged art and literature, often supporting artists and writers. Greek influence was strong, but a number of Romans produced works of distinction, particularly in the field of literature.

One of the most important writers of the late republic was Cicero, a great orator noted for his works on politics. The greatest Roman poet was Vergil, who lived during the reign of Augustus. His *Aeneid* is an epic, a sort of sequel to Homer's *Iliad*. It tells the story of Aeneas, prince of Troy and supposed ancestor of the Latins. When the Greeks captured Troy, Aeneas fled and, after many adventures, came to Italy. His descendants, Romulus and Remus, founded Rome. Another Roman poet, Horace, wrote odes, satires, and epistles (letters), all in poetry. He had great knowledge of human emotions. Ovid wrote love lyrics and the *Metamorphoses,* a collection of legends written in verse.

Tacitus was one of the greatest Roman historians. His *Annals* is a history of Rome under the Julian Emperors. He was pessimistic about the luxurious living of the wealthy and the lack of public virtue. Another of his works, *Germania*, is an account of the Germanic tribes along the borders. Tacitus may have exaggerated the virtues of the Germanic peoples because he wrote the book to shame the Romans for their decadence. But it is almost the only, and certainly the best, account of the early Germans.

Plutarch, a Greek who lived in Rome, wrote *Parallel Lives.* These are a series of biographical sketches, one of a famous Greek followed by one of a Roman whose life in some way resembled that of the Greek.

Language

The Romans learned the Greek alphabet from the Etruscans and changed some of the letters. The Roman, or Latin, alphabet of 23 letters—plus the

J, U, and W, which were added after Roman times—is the alphabet we use today.

Long after the end of the Roman Empire, the Latin language continued to be used, with some changes, in most of Europe. It was the language of most medieval European universities. It became the official language of the Christian Church and was the sole official language of the Roman Catholic Church until the 1960's. For centuries all government laws and decrees in Western Europe were written in Latin. Latin was the parent of the modern Romance (a word derived from Roman) languages—Italian, French, Spanish, Portuguese, and Rumanian.

Today many scientific terms have either Latin or Greek origins. Although the English language developed mainly from the language of the early Germanic peoples, more than one third of all English words are of Latin origin.

CHECKUP

1. IDENTIFY: Pax Romana, Praetorian Guard, Circus Maximus, Colosseum, Galen, Ptolemy, Athenaeum, Romance languages.

2. How did the army aid in the protection and expansion of the Roman Empire?

3. Explain how farming changed during the period of the Roman Empire.

4. Why did trade expand so rapidly throughout the empire? What products were traded and where did they come from?

5. Describe briefly the Roman accomplishments in applied science.

6. Name three important Roman writers, and describe the writings of each.

Christianity took root in Palestine and spread widely

It was the policy of the Romans to respect the various religions in the provinces, if only to keep the people peaceful. However, as Roman power expanded throughout the Mediterranean region, the Roman emperor was more and more regarded as a divine monarch. Every resident of the empire was expected to honor the gods of Rome and the "divine spirit" of the emperor. Through such a ritual act, people demonstrated their loyalty to the state.

Jews and the Roman Empire

In Roman times most Jews lived in Palestine, but there was a large Jewish population in Alexandria, Egypt, and a Jewish community in the city of Rome. As monotheists believing in a single God, Jews could not honor the Roman gods or the "divine spirit" of the emperor, and they were excused from doing so. Caesar, Augustus, and Claudius were known for their friendly attitudes toward the Jews. Prayers for the reigning emperor were offered by the Jews in the Jerusalem Temple.

By the 60's B.C. Palestine had become a Roman province. It was ruled by Jewish kings who reigned with the consent of the Romans. These kings were not popular among Jews, and for much of the time after the death of Herod the Great in 4 B.C., Palestine was ruled directly by a Roman governor.

Many Jews in Palestine hoped they could again be independent and be ruled by a king in the tradition of David. During the Hellenistic and Roman periods the Jews of Palestine were extremely dissatisfied with their leaders, especially with Herod's dynasty. They yearned for a king like David—for a Messiah. (Jewish kings were anointed with oil, and the word *Messiah* means "the Anointed One.")

As the years of rule by the Romans continued and independence became increasingly unlikely, the Jews' dream of a Messiah became more miraculous. He was seen as a magical liberator who would be aided by angels. Various individuals claiming to be Messiahs appeared from time to time in Palestine, but they were usually executed as rebels by the Romans. Occasionally the Jews would turn to more practical measures and would revolt against the Romans. After the great revolt of 66–70 A.D., however, the Romans sacked Jerusalem and destroyed the Second Temple.

The destruction of the Second Temple was a major turning point in Jewish history. With the Temple gone, priests ceased to be the religious leaders of Judaism. Their role was filled by rabbis—scholars learned in the scriptures and commentaries on religious law.

Under the emperors Trajan and Hadrian there were more Jewish revolts in Palestine. The last one, under Simon bar Kokba, was a fierce struggle against the Emperor Hadrian. After Simon's defeat in 135 A.D., there were no more Jewish revolts in Palestine.

Christianity—the religion founded by Jesus Christ—arose out of this setting. It drew on the expectations for a Messiah that were so common in Palestine during these centuries.

The life and teachings of Jesus

Jesus was born in the town of Bethlehem, near Jerusalem, in southern Palestine. Roman histories written during his lifetime do not refer to him at all. Our knowledge comes mainly from the Gospels—the first four books of the New Testament of the Bible.

Very little is known about the early life of Jesus. He grew up in the town of Nazareth and was said to have been a carpenter and a student of the writings of the Jewish prophets. In time he began preaching. As he traveled through the villages of Palestine, he gathered a small group of disciples, or followers. From these he chose twelve, the Apostles, to help him preach.

Jesus spoke of "my Father in heaven," and his followers believed that he was the Messiah, the Son of God. He traveled about with his disciples as a wandering rabbi, depending for his needs on the charity of the people. According to the Gospels, he created great excitement among the people, performing miracles of healing and defending the poor and the oppressed.

The teachings of Jesus have become one of the greatest influences on the Western world. He accepted the Hebrew Ten Commandments as guides to right living but gave them further meaning. He summarized the ten rules in two great commandments: People must love God above all else, and they must love others as they love themselves. Here are more of his important teachings:

(1) God cares more for people than for laws. He desires a new relationship between God and humans based on His love, to which people respond in faith.

(2) Jesus saw himself as the link that would reestablish the loving relationship that God desires. Jesus called this new relationship the "Kingdom of God." The "Kingdom of God" would be both here on earth and in an eternal life beyond this world.

(3) God will forgive people their sins if they will admit the wrong and ask to be forgiven. People must also forgive one another in recognition of what God has already done for them.

The death of Jesus

Jesus claimed that he was the Son of God. When he traveled to Jerusalem in about 30 A.D., many Jews there hailed him as the Messiah and as "King of the Jews." Others, however—especially the conservative priestly class of Jews—denied that he was the Messiah and, in addition, regarded him as a revolutionary.

Also, the Romans feared that Jesus wanted to lead an uprising and regarded him as an enemy of the state. Jesus was tried before Pilate, the Roman governor. Pilate was reluctant to act—apparently because he was concerned about maintaining the peace in Palestine. But eventually he agreed to Jesus' execution. Jesus was finally put to death by crucifixion—a common Roman punishment at that time.

The spread of Christianity

According to the Gospels, Jesus arose from the dead, remained on earth for 40 more days, and then ascended into heaven. His resurrection became the central message of Christianity—through the death of Christ, the Son of God, who had died for the sins of the human race, all people could achieve redemption. Jesus' disciples set out to convert everyone to his teachings through this message. At first the disciples worked mainly in the Jewish communities of the Middle East.

Some years after the crucifixion of Jesus, there occurred an event that was to spread the Christian religion far and wide. A Jew named Saul from the town of Tarsus in southern Asia Minor was converted to Christianity. He then took the name Paul and became a great Christian missionary, carrying on his work not only among Jews, but among all peoples. Between about 45 and 65 A.D.

he made several long journeys and spread the teachings of Jesus throughout the eastern Mediterranean region (see map, opposite page).

Paul's missionary work spread the religion rapidly. His Epistles, or letters, to Christian congregations in Greece and Asia Minor form an important part of the New Testament. Paul visited Rome, where, according to tradition, he was put to death by the Emperor Nero.

Paul is a key figure in the development and spread of Christianity. He insisted that Jesus was not just the Jewish Messiah, but a divine universal savior who would soon return to judge the entire human race. By following Jesus' teachings, all people could be saved from the consequences of their sins. They could avoid damnation and instead enjoy the bliss of salvation in paradise after death.

Christianity and its rivals

Christianity spread slowly, but its appeal increased as life within the Roman Empire became more difficult. The worship of the emperor and the many old religions within the empire offered no comfort for unhappy people. The Persian cult of Mithras did promise happiness after death, but it excluded women. The cult of Cybele (SIB·uh·lee) in Asia Minor and the Egyptian cult of Isis worshiped goddesses, but it was expensive to belong to these cults.

Christianity was open to everyone and charged nothing. It welcomed the poor and rich alike and promised salvation after death. In this world Christians were expected to be good citizens and to obey the laws. They were encouraged to practice charity and care for the poor and outcast.

Persecution of the Christians

The Romans were tolerant of the various religions of the empire. As long as a person performed the rituals that honored the emperor, he or she was free to believe or practice any religion. Only Jews, as you have read, were exempt from this obligation to the emperor. At first the Roman government thought Christians were a Jewish sect. However, by the 100's A.D. they recognized the difference, and Christians had to make a difficult choice.

The early Christians were good citizens. Their religion taught them to respect government, but they refused to worship the emperor as a god.

To the emperors this refusal was a defiance of Roman religion and law. Therefore, it soon became a crime to be a Christian. The property of Christians was seized and some Christians were executed. Even the Good Emperors followed this policy, although not every emperor tried equally hard to enforce the laws. Some tried to stamp out Christianity entirely. Others thought that the government should act only when Christians were accused and found guilty of breaking the law.

Execution of Christians and seizure of their property did not stop the spread of Christianity. It has been said that "the blood of the martyrs is the seed of the Church."

In the 200's A.D., as you will read later, the Roman Empire was shaken by civil wars. Many people turned to Christianity during these terrible years. City dwellers of the middle and upper classes suffered greatly, and many of them were converted to this new religion, which gave them hope. By the end of the 200's A.D., the Christian Church had become too big for the government to try to punish all its members. By 260 A.D. Christianity was accepted by law as a religion. There was a final attempt at persecution from 303 to 311 A.D., but it failed. With one exception, the emperors during the 300's A.D. were Christians.

The success of Christianity

The position of the Christians was vastly improved early in the 300's A.D., when the Emperor Constantine became a supporter of Christianity. According to one story, in 312 A.D. Constantine was leading his army into battle when he saw a blazing cross in the sky. Beneath it were the words *In Hoc Signo Vinces,* Latin words meaning, "By this sign you will conquer." He is said to have placed himself and his army under the protection of the Christian God. Although this story is probably a legend, Constantine did win the battle, and he became devoted to the Church.

Finally, in 380 A.D., Emperor Theodosius made Christianity the official religion of the Roman Empire. Within 400 years, Christianity had spread from its birthplace in Palestine to become the religion of a huge empire (see map, opposite).

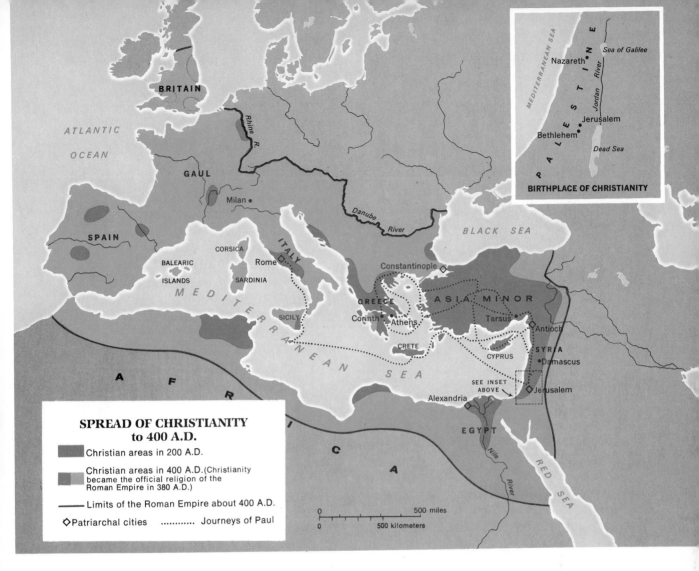

**SPREAD OF CHRISTIANITY
to 400 A.D.**

- Christian areas in 200 A.D.
- Christian areas in 400 A.D. (Christianity became the official religion of the Roman Empire in 380 A.D.)
- —— Limits of the Roman Empire about 400 A.D.
- ◇ Patriarchal cities   .... Journeys of Paul

BIRTHPLACE OF CHRISTIANITY

Organization of the Church

During the first few years after the crucifixion of Jesus, there was little need for Church organization. Christians lived together in groups, sharing their possessions and holding all property in common. Members were selected to hold church services, preach, and help the sick and needy.

By the last years of the Roman Empire, a more definite church organization developed. Under this organization, a priest served the people within the smallest division, a parish. A number of parishes made up a diocese (DY·uh·seese), which was administered by a bishop. The cathedral church—the official church—of the bishop was located in the most important city of the diocese. (*Cathedra* is the Latin word for the bishop's throne, or chair.) Several dioceses were combined into a province, which was ruled by an archbishop. Five of the empire's cities—Rome, Constantinople, Alexandria, Antioch, and Jerusalem—gained special importance as administrative centers for the Church. The bishops of these cities were called **patriarchs.**

The services of the new Church centered on rites called **sacraments.** These were special ceremonies at which the participants received the direct favor, or grace, of God to help them ward off the consequences of sin. By the 1100's leaders of the Church recognized seven ceremonies as sacraments—baptism, Holy Eucharist (or Communion), confirmation, penance, ordination (or holy orders), matrimony, and extreme unction (the anointing of the dying). The parish priest admin-

129

Beginnings of Christianity

Early Christians used works of art to remind them of Biblical stories and to strengthen their faith. Instead of seeing pictures and sculptures as idols, they thought of them as means to encourage devoutness. In a carving on a stone coffin, the three Wise Men of the East bring gifts to the infant Jesus (center).

Churches were decorated with splendid mosaics and paintings, usually scenes from the life of Christ. The fresco of the Last Supper (below) is from a church in Turkey. Christ is seated at the head of the table, with eleven apostles on one side. The twelfth apostle, Judas, the betrayer of Jesus, sits alone on the other side. A very early Christian building still standing in Ravenna, Italy, contains a tomb and a chapel (above right). Although the building is a plain brick structure on the outside, the walls inside are a dazzling display of mosaics on Christian themes.

istered all but two of these sacraments. Only a bishop could confirm a person in the Christian Church or ordain a member of the clergy. A bishop supervised the priests, managed Church property, and directed relief for the poor and needy.

CHECKUP

1. IDENTIFY: Messiah, Gospels, disciples, Constantine, Theodosius, bishops, sacraments.

2. LOCATE: Bethlehem, Jerusalem, Nazareth, Tarsus.

3. What did Jesus believe his mission to be? State three teachings of Jesus.

4. Why was the work of Paul important to the spread of Christianity?

5. What conditions in the Roman Empire favored the spread of Christianity?

6. Why were the Christians persecuted by the Romans?

7. How was the early Christian Church organized?

6

A weakened Roman Empire declined and fell

The Roman Empire grew constantly weaker until it broke up in the 400's A.D. To understand this long decline, it is necessary to turn back to the time of the Good Emperors.

When Marcus Aurelius, the last of the Good Emperors, picked his successor in 180 A.D., he failed to show his usual wisdom. Instead of choosing an able person, he appointed his son Commodus, who was weak and spoiled. His reign ended the great period of the empire.

Civil wars

After a reign of 13 years, during which the strength of the empire declined, Commodus was assassinated. Three candidates for emperor, each backed by a different group in the empire, struggled for power in a civil war. The winner was Septimius Severus, a general from the African provinces. Severus used his power to strengthen the military dictatorship. The dynasty founded by Severus held power from 193 to 235 A.D., but its members were weak or incompetent and in 235 A.D. it collapsed in a military mutiny.

During most of the 200's A.D., the empire experienced dreadful confusion and civil war. There were 20 emperors in the period from 235 to 284 A.D. All but one died violently. The legions, moreover, did not perform their job of defending the frontiers. Every frontier of the empire was invaded by barbarian tribes.

Problems of the empire

Many aspects of Roman life were affected by the political disorder. Travel became unsafe, and merchants hesitated to send goods by land or sea. The rural population grew even poorer than before. Population decreased throughout the empire, partly because of a great plague that spread through the provinces and caused several million deaths.

It became very difficult to collect taxes. Money was so scarce that taxes were often paid in grain. In 212 A.D. the government granted citizenship to all the peoples of the empire in order to collect from everyone the inheritance tax that citizens had to pay.

The only relatively prosperous people in the empire were the large landowners. As small farmers were forced to sell their land, large estates grew even larger. Many landowners left the cities and moved to their country estates. They organized and paid private armies and defied the government officials who came to collect taxes. With the decline in population, there was danger that there might not be enough farmers. The emperor refused to permit farmers who inherited their land to leave it.

The people in the cities were no better off. Many artisans tried to leave the cities and find work in the country. To prevent this, the government made use of the workers' trade associations, called **collegia** (kuh·LEE·jih·uh). A law made workers' membership in the collegia compulsory. The government required members of the collegia to stay at their jobs and to perform certain public services. When some people tried to resign from the collegia, another law made membership not only compulsory but also hereditary.

131

Diocletian

The Roman Empire would probably have collapsed in the late 200's except for two able emperors, Diocletian (dy·uh·KLEE·shun) and Constantine. Their reforms and reorganizations postponed the collapse for nearly 200 years.

Diocletian, the son of a peasant, had risen through the ranks of the army to become a general. The army made him emperor in 284, and he proved to be an able administrator.

Diocletian's greatest work was the reorganization of the administration of the empire. The empire was too much for one person to manage, so Diocletian appointed a co-emperor. Each was known as an augustus. Each augustus chose an assistant, called a caesar, to help him rule and to be his successor.

Although the empire was not officially divided, each augustus administered approximately half of its territory. Diocletian ruled in the east. He established his headquarters at Nicomedia, a town in northern Asia Minor. His fellow augustus, Maximian, ruled the western half of the empire from his headquarters at Milan in northern Italy. Rome was no longer the capital of the empire.

Although Diocletian shared his power with others, he himself held supreme authority. He ended lawlessness within the empire, and he drove out the invading barbarian tribes. He also tried to improve commerce and manufacturing and to increase the wealth of the empire. But his achievements were not long-lasting.

Constantine

The system of divided rule set up by Diocletian did not work well after he retired in 305. Rivalry between the co-emperors and their caesars was intense. Constantine, who came to power as a caesar in 306, became sole emperor in 324. His reign is known for two great events. The first was his conversion to the Christian religion. The second was his creation in 330 of a new capital at Byzantium. It was renamed Constantinople in his honor. (Today it is the Turkish city of Istanbul.)

Constantinople controlled navigation through the narrow passage from the Black Sea to the Aegean Sea (see map, opposite page). The city was difficult to attack from both land and sea, and thus it had tremendous military and commercial advantages.

After Constantine's death in 337, there were some 50 years of stability. However, the government was inefficient and corrupt, and the poor suffered greatly. The Spanish emperor Theodosius was the last ruler to control a unified empire. On his death in 395, authority was divided between his two weak sons. By the year 400, there were in effect two empires, one in the west and one in the east. The one in the west grew constantly weaker. Power had shifted to the east, where the wealth was.

The Germans

It might seem that the western Roman Empire would have fallen apart from inner weaknesses alone. However, there were also pressures from the outside. During the 200's, while the government was weakened by civil wars, enemy peoples attacked every frontier of the empire. The most important of these peoples were the Germans, who lived beyond the Rhine and north of the Danube rivers. One Germanic tribe, the Ostrogoths, eventually migrated southeastward to settle north of the Black Sea. Another tribe, the Visigoths, occupied land north of the Danube River (see map, opposite page).

The Germans were a warlike people who had no written language. We know about them mostly through Roman writings. The Germans did some simple farming, but most of the men were warriors rather than farmers. Some of their tribes had kings with considerable powers, but most of the important decisions were made by assemblies of all warriors.

Germans in the empire

The northern frontier of the Roman Empire along the Rhine and Danube rivers was strongly fortified against the Germans. As early as the reign of Augustus, however, many Germans began crossing the frontier peacefully. Some enlisted in the Roman army.

Beginning about 375 the movement of Germans into the Roman Empire increased greatly. At this time, the Huns, an Asiatic tribe, were moving into the region north of the Black Sea. The Huns were

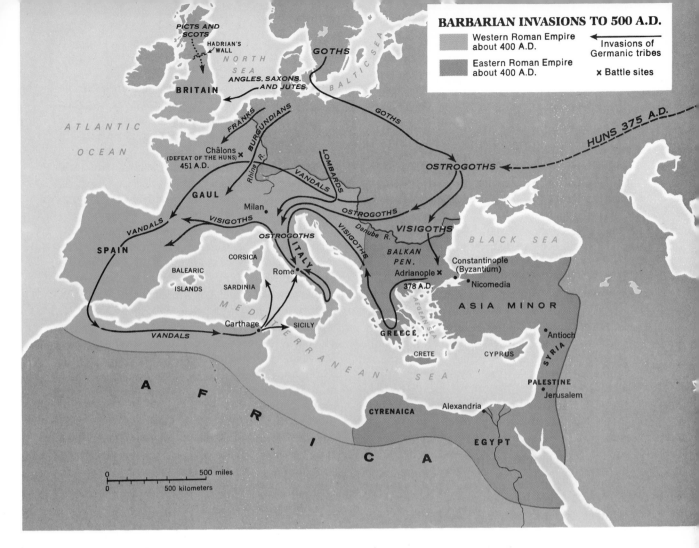

BARBARIAN INVASIONS TO 500 A.D.

Western Roman Empire
about 400 A.D.

Eastern Roman Empire
about 400 A.D.

Invasions of
Germanic tribes

x Battle sites

nomads who lived by raiding and plundering and whose fierceness terrified the people of Europe.

Among those menaced by the Huns were the Ostrogoths of the Black Sea area. These Ostrogoths moved westward into land held by the Visigoths, who were still living north of the Danube River on the Roman frontier. Many Visigoths were Christians and some were literate, but all were warlike.

The Visigoths begged the eastern emperor, Valens, for permission to cross the Danube. They were allowed to cross the river and settle on Roman land. However, Roman officials soon began mistreating the new settlers. In 378 the Visigoths revolted. In a battle at Adrianople they destroyed a Roman army and killed Valens, who led it.

An ambitious leader named Alaric now became king of the Visigoths. In 401 he led the Visigoths westward into Italy (see map, this page). The western emperor ordered many Roman troops from the northern frontiers to return and defend Italy, but they could not defeat the Visigoths. Alaric captured Rome in 410 and plundered the city.

Final invasions of the west

The two parts of the empire drifted farther and farther apart. The east revived and gained strength, while the west sank into ruin. In the west, the northern frontiers had been stripped of troops. Barbarians poured in everywhere. Britain was overrun by Picts and Scots from the north and by the Germanic Angles, Saxons, and Jutes from the continent.

A number of Germanic tribes overran Europe. Northern Gaul was taken by the Franks, eastern Gaul by the Burgundians. Southwestern Gaul and Spain fell to the Visigoths. The Vandals set up a kingdom in North Africa. (They were so destructive that the word *vandal* has come into our language meaning one who causes senseless destruction.) Italy was overrun by the Ostrogoths (see map, page 133).

In the mid-400's a strong leader named Attila came to power among the Huns. Attila led his Huns in an attack on Gaul. An army of Romans and Visigoths defeated the Huns in a great battle at Châlons in 451. Attila himself died two years later. His army quickly broke up, and the Huns were no longer a threat. But it was now far too late to save the western Roman Empire, which was weakened and shattered beyond repair.

The last Roman emperor in the west, Romulus Augustulus, was overthrown in 476 by a barbarian commander. Because of this event, people sometimes refer to the "fall" of the Roman Empire in 476. Actually, there was no such thing as a single "fall," but instead a gradual disintegration.

Results of Rome's decline

European civilization suffered a grave setback when the western Roman Empire broke up. The Germans who invaded the west established tribal kingdoms, but they were not capable of ruling an empire. The result was **anarchy**—the absence of any government at all.

Roads and bridges fell into disrepair, for there was no one to see that they were kept up. Trade and manufacturing almost disappeared, for few people had money to buy goods. It was not even safe to move goods from place to place, for there was no protection against bandits.

Towns and cities were regularly attacked by wandering bands of barbarians. Most people left the cities, both for greater safety and to find food. In the country, however, crops were often destroyed in the fighting, and fields were overgrown with weeds. Learning declined, for there was no government to set up and maintain schools. Libraries, with their great stores of knowledge, were destroyed. Western Europe was to suffer anarchy and disorder for hundreds of years after the breakup of the empire.

Why Rome declined

Historians have offered many explanations for the collapse of the Roman Empire. Slavery has been stressed by some historians as the cause of Roman decline. It produced a class of people who were always discontented and often in revolt. It tended to make slave owners brutal, selfish, and lazy. However, the number of slaves decreased greatly during the period of the empire. In fact, the number was lowest when Rome was weakest.

The army also has been blamed as a weakening factor. After the time of the Good Emperors, leadership was poor and discipline could not be enforced. Military interference in the choice of an emperor made the government unstable. The army was also very expensive to maintain.

It is undoubtedly true that barbarian invasions played an important role in Roman collapse. However, barbarian tribes lived on the frontiers throughout the time of both the Roman republic and the Roman Empire. Their numbers were small compared to the millions of people who lived within the empire. Not until the empire had declined were the barbarians able to break through the frontiers.

The important point to remember is that no one cause was responsible for Roman decline. Like many other complex movements and events in history, it resulted from a combination of different forces. Between the years 200 and 400, no aspect of Roman life—political, economic, or social— was free from decay. Each aspect influenced and acted upon the others.

Political weakness. Rome tried to control the entire Mediterranean world with a government originally designed for a small city-state. The miracle is that it worked for 600 years. In an age of slow transportation, the empire grew too fast and became too large for the kind of governmental organization the Romans could set up.

Another political weakness was the lack of civilian control of the military. Many dynasties did win the loyalty of the army, but the emperor had to be strong to keep the legions loyal. Dynastic succession was orderly, but prolonged weakness in a ruling family prompted ambitious generals to try their luck in seizing control. The common soldiers lost a sense of loyalty to Rome and instead served anyone who could pay them better.

Economic decline. Even more important than political breakdown was economic decline. Government expenses were heavy. Taxes had to finance the construction of public buildings, the maintenance of the army, and, in the later empire, the cost of two capitals—one in the west and one in the east. Even unbearably heavy taxes could not produce enough money to run the government. For centuries the Roman government maintained itself on rich plunder from foreign wars. After Trajan, however, this source of revenue was exhausted.

Some emperors tried to fix prices and regulate business activity, but they failed. Decreased revenue for the government resulted in unrepaired roads and bridges and increased banditry. The greater danger in travel, in turn, led to a decrease in trade. When trade declined, manufacturing suffered. Eventually, nearly all trade and manufacturing disappeared, and people began to leave the towns. Agriculture suffered the same fate as trade and commerce. Small farmers—once the strength of the empire—gradually lost their lands to a few great landowners.

Basically, the Roman economy did not produce enough wealth to support a great civilization permanently. What wealth was produced went into too few hands. One historian, writing about Rome in the 400's A.D., has pointed out that, in a world where poverty was a disgrace, poverty steadily increased.

When the barbarians invaded the empire, Roman armies fought heroically, but when they lost, the empire lacked the leadership to recover. Moreover, there was a loss of morale because of the grinding oppression of the government. The urban middle class was crushed by taxes and public service. The farmers were now coloni (plural of colonus) and were taxed heavily. The great landowners did not pay their share of taxes. The courts were corrupt and did not serve justice. Yet the government seemed to be locked into this system and unable to change it.

The Roman heritage and Christianity

The fall of the western Roman Empire is one of the major turning points in history. However, important changes had taken place even before the barbarian invasions. The east had grown in importance, and the peoples of the empire had converted to Christianity. The barbarians never overwhelmed the east, and the rulers at Constantinople claimed that they were continuing the Roman Empire. But their language was Greek and their focus was on eastern affairs and not on the west.

In the west, the provinces and even Italy were rapidly taken over by barbarians. Except in Italy and a few other areas, the network of cities had not been established long enough to survive. The number of literate and learned people grew smaller and smaller. Knowledge of the world and the past declined and was replaced by ignorance and fantasy. Without cities, trade, communications, and literacy of some kind, civilization could not survive. It had taken centuries to build a civilization in the west, but it was lost in a few generations.

In the wreck of the Roman world, two key ideas did survive in the west—the Roman heritage and the presence of Christianity. The barbarians whose kingdoms had once been part of the Roman Empire were influenced by its customs and civilizations. The leaders of the barbarian peoples remembered that unity under an emperor had once existed. Ambitious rulers in later centuries tried to regain this unity.

At the same time, Christianity became the official Church, that is, the one religion recognized by the state. Its leaders would play key roles in the post-Roman world. In addition, the Christian Church became the main preserver of Roman ideas and civilization.

CHECKUP

1. IDENTIFY: Commodus, Septimius Severus, collegia, Ostrogoths, Visigoths, Huns, Alaric, Attila, Romulus Augustulus.

2. LOCATE: Nicomedia, Milan, Constantinople, Black Sea, Aegean Sea, Rhine River, Danube River, Adrianople, Châlons.

3. Describe the economic problems of the Roman Empire under Diocletian and Constantine.

4. What was the system of divided rule? What were the problems caused by this organization?

5. How did the German tribes contribute to the decline of the Roman Empire?

CHAPTER REVIEW

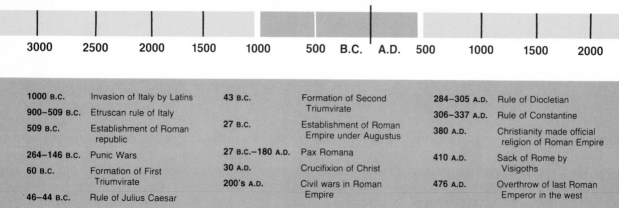

| 3000 | 2500 | 2000 | 1500 | 1000 | 500 | B.C. | A.D. | 500 | 1000 | 1500 | 2000 |

1000 B.C. Invasion of Italy by Latins	**43 B.C.** Formation of Second Triumvirate	**284–305 A.D.** Rule of Diocletian
900–509 B.C. Etruscan rule of Italy		**306–337 A.D.** Rule of Constantine
509 B.C. Establishment of Roman republic	**27 B.C.** Establishment of Roman Empire under Augustus	**380 A.D.** Christianity made official religion of Roman Empire
264–146 B.C. Punic Wars	**27 B.C.–180 A.D.** Pax Romana	**410 A.D.** Sack of Rome by Visigoths
60 B.C. Formation of First Triumvirate	**30 A.D.** Crucifixion of Christ	
46–44 B.C. Rule of Julius Caesar	**200's A.D.** Civil wars in Roman Empire	**476 A.D.** Overthrow of last Roman Emperor in the west

CHAPTER SUMMARY

Helped by the strategic location of Italy, the Romans created one of the largest empires the world has ever seen. Starting with early victories around the city of Rome in the 400's B.C., the conquests of the Romans continued until they dominated the entire Mediterranean area in the 100's B.C. For the next 500 years, Rome was the most powerful force in Europe, and eventually also in western Asia.

During the centuries of its rise, Rome was a republic. Although some attention was given to the lower classes, known as plebeians, most of the power was in the hands of aristocrats, known as patricians. They controlled the Senate, the most important governing body in Rome. They also provided the consuls, the chief executive officers of the republic, who were appointed for one year. Both law and public building projects were developed to highly sophisticated levels. Great emphasis was placed on citizens serving in the army, which became the most efficient fighting force of the age.

The growing importance of the army brought the republic to an end as military commanders repeatedly gained control of Rome's government. The last and most successful of these military leaders was Julius Caesar. His greatnephew, who succeeded him, became the first emperor—Augustus. From the 20's B.C. onward, Rome was an empire, not a republic.

The abilities of the emperors varied greatly, but they maintained internal stability and a continued expansion of Roman territory until the late 100's A.D. The empire was held together by an army of half a million men and by splendid communications.

Education and literature flourished, as did engineering and architecture. However, corruption and political disorder gradually increased. The empire was getting too large to be run from Rome. Around 300 A.D. two reforming emperors, Diocletian and Constantine, divided the empire into eastern and western halves.

By this time a new force had arisen in the Mediterranean area—Christianity. Emerging from the hopes of the Jews in Palestine for a Messiah, this new religion was at first persecuted by the Romans. It spread so rapidly, however, that in the 300's it became the official religion of the empire. The Church it created preserved Roman civilization after the western half of the empire lost its old strength and was overrun by invaders in the 400's. Only in the east did the descendants of the Romans preserve their independence in an empire centered on the city of Constantinople.

CHECKING WHAT YOU KNOW

1. Match each Roman leader at the left with his accomplishment at the right:

   a. Julius Caesar
   b. Diocletian
   c. Constantine
   d. Augustus
   e. Marcus Aurelius
   f. Hadrian

   1. Organized and brought Roman rule to the provinces.
   2. Created a new capital in the east.
   3. Reformed the calendar to 365 1/4 days.
   4. Considered the last Good Emperor.
   5. Defeated Antony and Cleopatra.
   6. Reorganized the administration of the empire.

2. Place the three items in each of the following lists in chronological order:
   a. the First Triumvirate, the Third Punic War, the Julian Emperors
   b. the German invasions, the life of Jesus, Julius Caesar in power
   c. Reforms under Tiberius and Gaius Gracchus, creation of new capital at Byzantium, Latin settlers along the Tiber River
   d. the Hun invasions, the Carthaginian invasions, the Etruscan invasions
   e. the letters of Paul, Vergil's *Aeneid*, the battle of Adrianople

3. Compare the government of the Roman republic with the government of the Roman Empire.

4. How did the use of written law help to strengthen the Roman government?

5. Describe three contributions of Roman culture to Western civilization.

6. Discuss three of the most significant causes of the decline of the Roman Empire.

PRACTICING YOUR SKILLS

1. **Making comparisons.** Compare the role of citizens in Athenian democracy with that of citizens in the Roman republic. What are the similarities and differences? You may wish to refer back to Chapters 4 and 5 for information on Athenian democracy.

2. **Using art.** Study the pictures in this chapter and give examples from both sculpture and architecture to show how Roman art glorified the state.

3. **Comparing maps.** Compare the extent of Roman territory shown on the maps on pages 113, 117, and 120. What was the farthest extent of Roman territory to the east? When was it accomplished? What was the farthest extent to the south?

RELATING PAST TO PRESENT

1. The Roman republic had a citizen army instead of a professional army. What kind of army do we have in the United States today? What are the advantages and disadvantages of each type of army? What kind of army provides the better defense system?

2. Discuss how the persecution of the Christians in Rome affected the spread of Christianity. Choose a country where religious persecution exists today. What effect does this have on the members of the religious group being persecuted? on the religion worldwide?

3. The Roman historian Tacitus used his treatise *Germania,* which is about the Germanic tribes, as a means of criticizing the corruption and immorality of Roman society of the times. Choose a book, play, or movie today that comments on contemporary events or people, and describe the "message" that is being put forward.

INVESTIGATING FURTHER

1. Read Shakespeare's play *Julius Caesar.* How did Shakespeare depict Caesar? Based on what you have read about Caesar in this chapter, is the character in the play historically accurate? Was Caesar really trying to become a dictator?

2. In 79 A.D. the city of Pompeii in southern Italy was destroyed by an eruption of Mount Vesuvius. The volcanic ash that buried Pompeii preserved the ruins, and from them we can learn much about daily life of the time. Prepare a report on the destruction of Pompeii. Two useful sources are the article "Last Moments of the Pompeians" (*National Geographic,* November 1961) and Moses Hadas, *Imperial Rome* (Time-Life Books).

(1000 B.C.–589 A.D.)

7

Ancient Asian Civilizations Developed Lasting Traditions

Our spotlight now turns back from the West to Asia. This chapter tells the stories of India and China from about 1000 B.C. to about 600 A.D.

In Asia as in the West, you will read of wars and rulers and of empires that rose and fell. Of greater importance, you will read about one of history's most momentous coincidences—the simultaneous lives in India and China of two great leaders whose influence upon Asian life has remained strong for almost 2,500 years. The Indian was Gautama Buddha, a religious leader who was born about 563 B.C. The Chinese leader was the philosopher Confucius, born about 551 B.C.

When historians say that Indian and Chinese civilizations have been more nearly continuous than Western civilization, they have in mind, among other things, the enduring influence of these great leaders on Asian life. Both of them shaped the existence of millions of people, not only in India and China, but also in the Middle East and other parts of Asia.

The lives of Buddha and Confucius represent heights of achievement in human history. As you read about them, remember that the Persian philosopher Zoroaster had only recently presented the ideas about the struggle between good and evil that greatly altered Persian religious thinking. In Palestine, prophets like Ezekiel were refining the ethical monotheism that would become the most important contribution of the Jews to Western civilization.

A gilded Buddha from China

In Athens, Pisistratus and Cleisthenes were bringing about reforms that paved the way for Greece's Golden Age. At the same time, the first great Athenian dramatist, Aeschylus, was writing heroic tragedies about Greek gods and humans on earth. And, little noticed by anyone, Romans were establishing a republic in their small city on the banks of the Tiber River.

Thus, across much of the world in the 500's B.C., the foundations of many great civilizations were in the first stages of development. Some would survive and some would not. In all of them people were working out ideas and creating traditions that are still shared by most of the nations of the world.

THE CHAPTER SECTIONS

1. The caste system and Hinduism took hold in India

2. Buddhism began in India and spread throughout Asia

3. Civilization in India flourished under the Guptas

4. Chinese civilization evolved through changing dynasties

5. Ancient China produced distinctive philosophy and culture

1

The caste system and Hinduism took hold in India

The earliest known civilization of India, you recall, developed in the valley of the Indus River. Beginning about 1500 B.C. the subcontinent was overrun by the Aryans, Indo-European invaders from the north. During the Vedic Age, from about 1500 to 1000 B.C., they pushed eastward until they controlled the valley of the Ganges River as well. In the period from 1000 to 500 B.C. they formed numerous city-states.

The Aryan city-states resembled each other in many ways. A **rajah,** or minor king, ruled each city-state. He acted as military leader, chief priest, lawmaker, and judge. A royal council of friends and relatives assisted the rajah. For hundreds of years, the city-states enjoyed peace and independence.

The great epics

You will recall that the Vedic Age was named after the Vedas, collections of religious rituals and hymns to the gods. The **Epic Age,** the period from 1000 to 500 B.C., also takes its name from religious literature.

As you have read, interpretation of the rituals and hymns of the Vedas was left to priests called Brahmans, who became increasingly important in Aryan society. During the Epic Age the Brahmans gained even more importance when they composed the *Upanishads* (oo·PAN·uh·shadz). The *Upanishads* were complex philosophical explanations of the Vedic religion.

Ordinary people were no more able to understand the *Upanishads* than they could the Vedas themselves. But they could understand stories in which many ideas about Vedic religion were made clearer. These stories were told from generation to generation. Finally they were combined by unknown geniuses in two epics, the *Mahabharata* (muh·HAH·BAH·ruh·tuh) and the *Ramayana* (rah·MAH·yuh·nuh).

The *Mahabharata* is the longest epic poem in world literature and is considered a part of sacred Hindu scripture. It primarily tells the story of a great civil war in a kingdom near Delhi, in what is northern India today. The last 18 chapters of this epic are known as the *Bhagavad-Gita.* Their theme is religious. They stress that doing one's moral duty (called dharma) according to one's responsibilities is the highest fulfillment in life. Krishna, a human incarnation of the god Vishnu, also explains in the *Bhagavad-Gita* how love and devotion to Vishnu can be another way to reach salvation.

The *Ramayana* is the story of two royal heroic figures—Rama (another human incarnation of the god Vishnu) and his devoted wife Sita. By their faithfulness to duty and their devotion to each other as well as to people of their kingdom, Rama and Sita are the ideals of Indian manhood and womanhood.

From the *Mahabharata* and the *Ramayana,* and from the *Upanishads* and the Vedas themselves, scholars have been able to piece together the ori-

The God Siva

Along with Brahma and Vishnu, Siva is one of the three great gods of Hinduism. Siva had many roles but is best known as the destroyer whose actions bring forth new life. The god is also worshiped as time, justice, and the sun. In this bronze statue the role of destroyer is emphasized. Around the edge of the circular frame and in one left hand are the flames of destruction. The other left hand points to a dwarf, an enemy overcome by Siva as the lord of death.

Another of Siva's roles is shown by a hand raised in a gesture that means "do not fear." It represents the god's kindliness. A fourth hand holds a drum, the instrument that made the first sound in the universe. The power of meditation is symbolized by a third eye, engraved on the forehead. Siva is often shown dancing and is worshiped as the god of dancers.

gins of the two most important influences in Indian history—the caste system and Hinduism.

The caste system

The **caste system** was a form of social organization. It began in northern India when the invading Aryans laid down rules to prevent intermarriage between themselves and the peoples they had conquered. By the beginning of the Epic Age, four distinct classes had emerged in Indian society: (1) At the top were the rulers and warriors, called Kshatriyas (KSHAHT·rih·yuz). (2) Next came the priests, scholars, and wise men, called Brahmans. During the Epic Age, the Brahmans and the Kshatriyas changed positions, with the Brahmans becoming first. (3) Next came the merchants, traders, and owners of small farms, called Vaisyas (VY·syuz). (4) At the foot of the social ladder were the Sudras, who were peasants bound to work the fields of large landowners.

A fifth group of people in Indian society were not even on the ladder. These people were the pariahs (puh·RY·uz). They were also called untouchables, because it was thought that merely to touch them would make one impure. Indeed, it was believed that even a pariah's shadow would contaminate a Brahman. Many of the conquered peoples were included among the pariahs.

As time passed, the original four groups were subdivided many times into smaller groups called castes, and the caste system emerged. As society became more complex and new occupations were created, castes themselves were subdivided and new castes appeared.

Eventually some 3,000 hereditary castes developed. Each had its own fixed social position and rules about eating, marriage, labor, and worship. For example, people could not eat or drink with someone of a lower caste, but they could perform services that were consistent with the duties of their caste toward other people. They could work only at those occupations recognized for their caste. They could not marry outside their caste.

Hinduism

The major religion of India, Hinduism, developed through interpretations of the Vedas by Brahman scholars. According to the *Upanishads,* everything in the world is filled with a basic divine essence known as Brahman. Atman—or self—refers to the essence of an individual person. When Hindus—followers of Hinduism—say that

Brahman and Atman are one and indivisible, they mean that God and human beings are one. This idea is called **monism.**

The world known to our senses is merely an illusion called Maya, which betrays people, giving them sorrow and pain. People can be delivered from their suffering if they identify what Maya is. However, this requires lifetimes of experience. This experience, according to a major belief of Hinduism, is provided by **reincarnation,** or the transmigration of souls. According to this belief, the soul does not die with the body but enters the body of another being and thus lives second, third, and more lives.

The progress of the soul toward deliverance from suffering depends upon the life each person lives as a fulfillment of moral duty—dharma. The present condition of one's life is wholly the result of what was done or not done during the previous life of one's soul. Ultimately each person hopes to be the one who ends the repeated transmigrations and enables the soul to be reunited with the soul of Brahman.

Hindu religious practices

Good persons are rewarded, evil ones are punished. Reward means that the soul enters the body of someone of a higher caste. Evil people are punished when their souls are reborn in the bodies of people of lower castes. Since all souls are part of the Universal Soul, or Brahman, Hindus respect the sanctity of all life in all forms. Brahmans have to be particularly careful not to bring injury or violence to any living thing. One religious practice for some people is **yoga,** a physical and mental discipline harmonizing body with soul. A Hindu practicing one form of yoga might, for example, sit for many hours in a certain position in order to free the mind of bodily concerns.

The Brahmans taught that salvation could be achieved by fulfillment of one's dharma and by worship of any aspect of Brahman. Brahman's aspects included a basic trinity of god composed of (1) Brahma the Creator, (2) Vishnu the Preserver, and (3) Siva the Destroyer. Below these came many other gods, represented in the spirits of trees, animals, and persons.

Some Hindus pay special reverence to certain animals. Cows are especially sacred. They provide the power for the plow and the cart. They produce food (milk and butter) and fuel (dung) for the family. For these reasons most Hindus will not eat the meat of the cow.

To Westerners, this religion of many gods sounds polytheistic. Hindus insist that it is monistic—that the basic trinity and all of the other gods are merely different representations of the oneness of the universe.

Establishment of the caste system and of Hinduism were the most important developments of Indian history in the Epic Age—or, indeed, of any age in Indian history. These two ideas became interwoven in the fabric of Indian society.

CHECKUP

1. IDENTIFY: *Upanishads, Mahabharata, Bhagavad-Gita,* dharma, Krishna, *Ramayana,* Rama and Sita, reincarnation, Universal Soul, yoga.

2. What was the origin of the caste system? List the five distinct groups that had emerged in India by the beginning of the Epic Age.

3. What do Hindus believe are the ways for a soul to reach salvation?

4. Why do Hindus consider their religion monistic?

Buddhism began in India and spread throughout Asia

During the Epic Age a great religious leader emerged in India—Gautama Buddha. His family name was actually Gautama. The word *Buddha* was given to him later as a title meaning "the Enlightened One."

The early life of Buddha

Gautama was born about 563 B.C. and died about 483 B.C. The son of an Indian prince, he was himself a prince. He lived in luxury, shielded from the ordinary people of his native city. At the age of 29, he ventured into the city streets. He was very disturbed by what he saw—an old, decrepit man, a very sick man covered with boils, and a corpse about to be cremated. He wondered about the great problems of life: Why is there suffering? Of what value is life and death?

Gautama decided to spend the rest of his life seeking answers to these questions. In what is called the Great Renunciation, he put aside all his possessions, left his wife and infant son, and set out to search for the truth.

Gautama followed all the practices that were recommended as leading to wisdom. He lived as a hermit and a scholar. He practiced the mental and physical discipline of yoga so strictly that he almost died. He tried fasting and self-torture. None of these things gave him the answers he wanted so much to find.

Then one day, after six years of searching, as Gautama sat meditating under a fig tree, he felt that he understood the truth on which life is based. In that moment, according to his followers, he became Buddha, the Enlightened One. He spent the remainder of his life teaching the Enlightenment, the Way of Life.

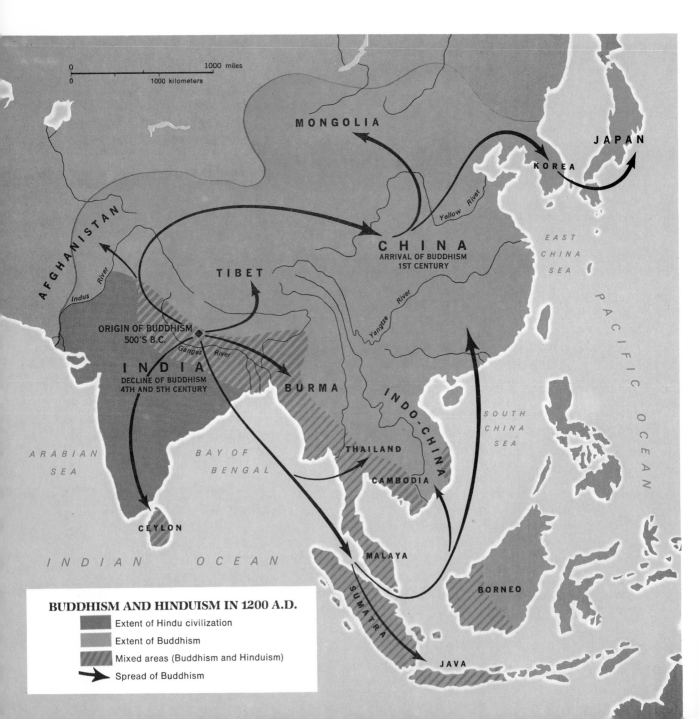

BUDDHISM AND HINDUISM IN 1200 A.D.

- Extent of Hindu civilization
- Extent of Buddhism
- Mixed areas (Buddhism and Hinduism)
- → Spread of Buddhism

Buddha's teachings

Buddha accepted the Hindu belief that the progress of the soul depends on the life a person leads and that good is rewarded and evil punished. People must seek good and avoid evil. However, Buddha said that since only deeds, good or bad, are important, salvation cannot come through self-torture or from the sacrifice of animals. This belief was a departure from Hindu belief. Salvation, according to Buddha, comes from knowing the Four Noble Truths and following the Middle Way.

The Four Noble Truths are these: (1) All human life is full of suffering and sorrow. (2) Suffering and sorrow are caused by a greedy desire for pleasure and material things. (3) By renouncing desire, people are freed from suffering and their souls attain nirvana. Nirvana is the perfect peace, in which the soul is freed from having to be born again. (4) Renunciation of desire and attainment of nirvana may be gained by following the Middle Way.

The Middle Way may be pursued by following the Eightfold Path, eight guides to thought and conduct. These are right views, right intentions, right speech, right action, right living, right effort, right mindfulness, and right concentration.

Buddha stressed ethics—a code of morals and conduct—rather than ceremonies. Unselfishness was the key to his ethics, and he gave definite rules for unselfish behavior. A person was not to kill, steal, lie, gossip, find fault with others, use profanity, or be greedy.

Buddha did not accept the Hindu gods as sacred. According to Buddha, people alone could do the supreme thing—change good to evil and evil to good. They did not need the help of gods or priests or temples or idols. Buddha taught that there are only two kinds of people—the good and the bad. Thus, although he did not attack the Hindu caste system openly, he did not accept it.

The spread of Buddhism

Buddha gained some followers in his lifetime, but not many. Over several centuries, however, his teachings—called Buddhism—won wide acceptance (see map, opposite page).

By the 100's B.C. Buddhism had split into two branches—Hinayana, or the Lesser Vehicle, and Mahayana, or the Greater Vehicle. Hinayana kept the traditional beliefs of Buddhism and regarded Buddha simply as a teacher. This form of Buddhism in time spread to countries other than India, among them Burma, Thailand, and Cambodia.

Believers in the Mahayana form of Buddhism regarded Buddha as a god and the savior of humanity. They made Buddhism into a religion with priests, temples, creeds, and rituals. Mahayana Buddhism spread over a wide area, including Afghanistan, central Asia, China, Korea, and Japan.

In India itself Buddhism was opposed by the priestly Brahmans. Their high position depended on people's acceptance of the idea of reincarnation. The Brahmans were bound to oppose any religion which taught that people, regardless of caste, could reach nirvana without help if only they were good.

Despite the opposition of the Brahmans, Buddhism gained many followers in India over several centuries and then declined. Buddhism had greater success in the areas to which it spread.

Rule of the Nine Nandas

Darius, as you have read, sent a Persian army to invade the Indus Valley in the 500's B.C. and organized the area as a part of the Persian Empire. Herodotus, the Greek historian, says that the area was prosperous, for it was rich in gold and supplied numerous well-trained archers to the Persians in their attacks upon Greece. Some of these archers were among the Persian forces that were defeated by the Greeks at the battle of Plataea in 479 B.C.

Indian kingdoms slowly reduced Persian control of northwestern India. This region was finally absorbed by the kingdom of Magadha, in northeastern India. Magadha was ruled from 413 to 322 B.C. by a dynasty called the Nine Nandas. It was a Nanda ruler and his army that were defeated by Alexander the Great at the Indus River in 326 B.C. Alexander wanted to go on but, as you recall, his army mutinied and he was forced to turn back. He stayed long enough, however, to see the great Indian city of Taxila, which was a bustling center of learning.

The Maurya Empire

A new kingdom arose in the area in 322 B.C. as a result of the conquests of a powerful young adventurer named Chandragupta. He established what is called the Maurya dynasty.

Chandragupta Maurya. We know a good deal about Chandragupta because a Greek ambassador to his court wrote a fascinating book about him. According to this account, Chandragupta was an able administrator. He took over Pataliputra on the Ganges and made it a magnificent city. He learned the science of government and methods of warfare from the Macedonians. His army of 700,000 soldiers was equipped with 10,000 chariots and 9,000 elephants. He maintained an efficient postal service that moved swiftly over excellent roads. He united northern India from the delta of the Ganges to the region west of the Indus. Eventually he took over all of northwestern India up to the Hindu Kush.

Chandragupta was an able ruler but he was also highly autocratic, that is, he ruled with absolute power. Enemies dug tunnels under the palace in attempts to kill him. To avoid assassination, he changed his bedroom each night and employed food tasters as protection against being poisoned at meals. Finally, according to tradition, he abdicated the throne in favor of his son.

Asoka. One of India's greatest rulers was Asoka, Chandragupta's grandson, who came to the throne about 270 B.C. By this time the Maurya Empire had been extended far to the south. Asoka enlarged the empire by conquest until it included all of India except the southern tip (see map, this page). Asoka's campaign became a war of annihilation in which 100,000 people were killed, and 150,000 taken captive. Many more people died in the aftermath of the war.

Asoka became so sickened by this slaughter that he renounced war and became a devout Buddhist. He did not force the Indian people to accept Buddhism, but during his rule many did. He sent his brother as a missionary to what is now Sri Lanka (Ceylon), and sent other missionaries to Tibet, China, Burma, Java, and even to Egypt, Syria, and Macedonia.

After his conversion to Buddhism, Asoka thought constantly of piety and duty. He urged religious toleration and relaxed the harsh laws that had supported the autocratic rule of his father and grandfather. He pardoned prisoners and forbade animal sacrifices.

When Asoka died about 230 B.C., the Maurya Empire began to fall apart. The last Maurya ruler was assassinated in 184 B.C. A series of foreign rulers controlled northern India after the Maurya dynasty collapsed. A Greek kingdom called Bactria, a remnant of Alexander's empire, was established in the northwest. Bactria was conquered by a nomadic tribe, the Kushans, who had been driven from their home in central Asia by the Huns.

When the last known Kushan king died in 220 A.D., there followed a period of 100 years in which Indian civilization was chaotic and about which little is known.

CHECKUP

1. IDENTIFY: Enlightened One, Great Renunciation, Nine Nandas, Hinayana, Mahayana, Kushan.

2. LOCATE: Magadha, Taxila, Pataliputra, Bactria.

3. What ideas from Hinduism did Buddha accept? What Hindu ideas did he reject?

4. Explain the Four Noble Truths and the principles of the Eightfold Path.

5. What did Chandragupta Maurya and Asoka accomplish as rulers?

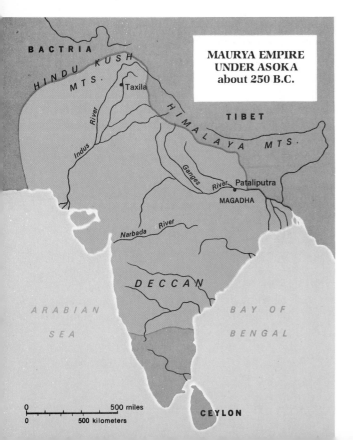

MAURYA EMPIRE
UNDER ASOKA
about 250 B.C.

3

Civilization in India flourished under the Guptas

The period of disorder in India, after the death of the last Kushan king, ended when a new line of kings, the Guptas, began ruling in 320 A.D.

The Gupta rulers

The Guptas first came to power in the Ganges Valley, but through intermarriage and conquest they extended their power over a wide area of India (see map, page 146).

The Gupta rulers were autocratic. However, the best of them—the first three, who ruled from 320 to about 412 A.D.—used their great powers benevolently. The first Gupta king was Chandragupta I, the warrior king (who was not related to the earlier Chandragupta of the Maurya line). He was followed by Samudragupta, the poet king. The third king was Chandragupta II, under whom the empire reached its greatest extent. He established the Gupta capital at Ayodhya (uh·YOHD·hyah), in the northeast.

The Guptas claimed that they had been appointed to rule by the gods. They favored Hinduism over Buddhism, since Hinduism stressed the gods and Buddhism did not. The Guptas were tolerant of Buddhism, but they favored the Brahmans, who wanted to restore Hinduism to its former strength. By the end of the Gupta period, Buddhism had declined in India itself, while gaining strength in other parts of Asia. Hinduism, somewhat influenced by Buddhism, again became the dominant religion of India.

Economy and social life

From ancient times the land had provided a living for nearly all the people of northern India. For a limited few at the top of the caste system, the land provided great luxury, but most people were poor. During the Epic Age the rajahs in theory owned all the land and took what they wanted from those who farmed it. By the time of the Guptas, the rulers were taking one-sixth of the agricultural produce as their share.

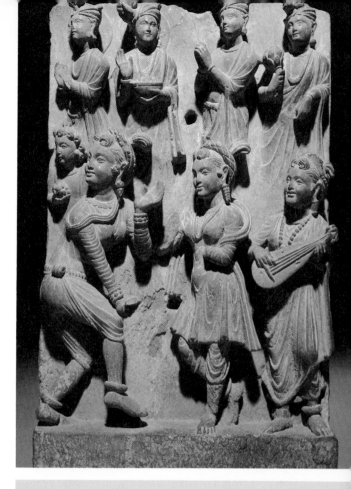

Relief Sculpture from Gandhara

One of the earliest meetings between East and West took place in Gandhara, in what is now northern Pakistan. Gandhara was under Persian rule when it was conquered by Alexander the Great in 327–325 B.C. Later, while under Indian control, the people of Gandhara were converted to Buddhism. Some of the earliest Buddhist sculptures appeared in Gandhara.

The relief above dates from the 100's and 200's A.D. It shows the influences of several civilizations. The dancers, musicians, and other people are honoring and making offerings to Buddha. The offerings are probably fruit, rice, and flowers—items commonly presented to him. The jewelry is Indian, as is the stringed instrument. The costume of the dancer in the center is Persian, while the dancer on the right wears a Roman toga. The way in which the figures and clothing are modeled, however, is Hellenistic in style. The artists of Gandhara blended different cultural elements but in doing so created a distinct style of their own.

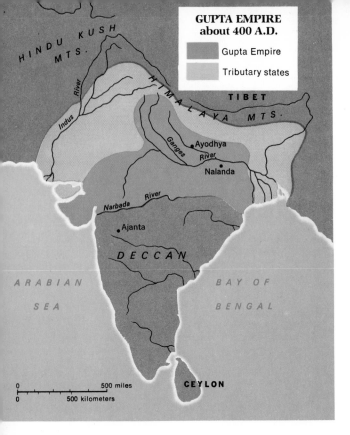

GUPTA EMPIRE
about 400 A.D.

- Gupta Empire
- Tributary states

HINDU KUSH MTS.

Indus River

HIMALAYA MTS.

TIBET

Ganges River

Ayodhya

Nalanda

Narbada River

Ajanta

DECCAN

ARABIAN SEA

BAY OF BENGAL

0 500 miles
0 500 kilometers

CEYLON

In Gupta India a woman's status was lower than a man's. The *Mahabharata* called a man's wife his "truest friend," but a Gupta legal treatise recommended that the wife worship her husband as a god. **Polygamy,** or marriage to more than one wife, was common in the Epic Age and became widespread under the Guptas. Another practice that became common during the Gupta period, especially among the upper castes, was **suttee.** In this practice, a widow would commit suicide by throwing herself on top of her husband's flaming funeral pyre.

Literature

Throughout Indian history the most popular writings were the two great epics, the *Mahabharata* and *Ramayana*. People also enjoyed the stories in the *Panchatantra,* a series of fables from the Gupta period. Among its stories were those about Sinbad the Sailor, Jack the Giant Killer, the Magic Mirror, and the Seven League Boots—stories that are known all over the world. Next to the Bible, the *Panchatantra* is the most widely translated book in the world today.

Indian drama developed greatly under the Guptas. Unlike Greek plays, those of India always had a happy ending. They offered little action and used different dialects for different characters. Indian plays were performed in a courtyard, using only simple scenery. Actors formed a distinct caste.

Kalidasa, who lived in the 400's A.D., was one of India's greatest dramatists and poets. He wrote three plays, the most famous of which is *Sakuntala*. The story, a romantic one, concerns a king and the daughter of a wise man, who fall in love and marry. A curse causes the king to lose his memory of the marriage, and the pair are separated. A boy child is born. The king, returning from battle, recognizes his son and the lovers are reunited.

Art and architecture

Not much is known about Indian art before the reign of Asoka in the 200's B.C. because earlier Indian artists used wood and other perishable materials. Throughout his empire Asoka set up pillars with his laws carved on them. A common building during Asoka's time was the **stupa,** in the shape of a hemisphere. In the stupa were artifacts and objects associated with Buddha. Asoka is said to have built 84,000 stupas.

By the time of the Kushan kings, images of Buddha showed Greek influence. Many resembled Greek statues of the god Apollo. During the rule of the Guptas, however, Indian sculptors developed their own style, more formal and less realistic. This style has been followed down to the present day. It was also in this period, as Hinduism increased in importance, that Indians created a special style of Hindu temple. This distinctive style—a square building with heavy walls that enclosed a god's statue—remained basically the same for centuries.

Mural paintings in caves tell us something about the artistic style of early Indian painters. However, we know most about mural painting in the time of the Guptas. Today thousands of people visit the caves at Ajanta in central India every year to admire paintings of Buddha and his followers. These paintings are a valuable source of information about the daily life of Indian people under the Gupta rulers.

The Maurya and Gupta empires

Indian art was often inspired, as was Christian art, by religious themes. The powerful ruler Asoka, who reigned in the 200's B.C., built many special shrines to hold relics of Buddha. Known as stupas, these huge hemispheres were made of solid stone. Asoka is said to have built 84,000 such stupas. The most famous to have survived (below) is in central India and was probably built after Asoka's death. It is about 100 feet (30 meters) in diameter and about 40 feet (12 meters) high. The elaborately carved gateway to the stupa (left) shows scenes from the life of Buddha. He is represented by his symbols—his tree, his footprints, an empty throne. Indian art also depicted scenes from the everyday life of the times. The beautifully designed piece of terra cotta (above) is of a musician, reflecting the importance of music and dance in this culture.

Education

Although the children of the poor learned only crafts or trades, upper-class Indian children had formal lessons. Just as Greek children learned to read Homer's *Iliad* and *Odyssey,* Indian children learned to read the *Upanishads* and the great Indian epics, the *Mahabharata* and the *Ramayana.* Formal schooling began at the age of nine.

By the time of the Guptas, the city of Nalanda had replaced Taxila as the chief center of Indian scholarship. Nalanda, located in the lower Ganges Valley, attracted students from as far away as Tibet, China, and Korea. It had more than a hundred lecture halls, three large library buildings, dormitories, a model dairy, and an observatory to study the skies. The curriculum included religion, philosophy, medicine, art, architecture, and agriculture.

One Gupta ruler supported Nalanda with the income from 100 large villages. Some students received financial help from the government.

Mathematics and astronomy

Indian mathematicians had greater ability at dealing with abstract numbers than did the mathematicians of Greece and Rome. Indians actually invented the numeral system that we call Arabic—1 through 9 and the zero. It was brought to the West from India by Arab traders. These so-called Arabic numerals are known to have been in use in India by 595 A.D. and were probably used before the end of Gupta rule in 535 A.D.

Indians also had a concept of negative numbers (numbers preceded by a minus sign), without which algebra could not exist. They calculated the square root of 2 and prepared a table of sines, used extensively in trigonometry. Aryabhata (AHR·yuh·BUT·uh), who lived in the 400's A.D., computed the value of π (pi) more exactly than the Greek mathematician Archimedes had. He also solved algebraic equations.

Indian astronomers identified the seven planets that can be seen without the aid of a telescope. They knew that the planets and the moon reflected the sun's light. They understood the daily rotation of the earth on its axis. They also predicted eclipses, calculated the diameter of the earth, and developed a theory of gravity.

Medicine

The earliest Indian medical writings appeared soon after the birth of Christ. They resemble the studies of the Greek physicians Hippocrates and Galen. Indian physicians understood the importance of the spinal cord. Their surgery included bone setting and plastic surgery on ears, noses, and lips. They perfected the technique of inoculation—communicating a mild form of a disease to a person so that the person will not fall ill with the more serious form. They used the less harmful cowpox to inoculate against smallpox, a method unknown in the countries of the Western world until the end of the 1700's.

Free hospitals were built in India in the early 400's. Susruta, a great Indian doctor, practiced strict cleanliness before an operation and sterilized wounds—another procedure that Western surgeons did not use until modern times. Susruta urged that dissection be permitted to aid medical education. Like Hippocrates, he insisted on the highest moral standards among physicians.

The end of the Guptas

Civilization in India had reached a high peak during the rule of the Guptas. Their rule has been called a golden age because of the brilliant civilization that flourished then. Gupta rule ended in 535 A.D., when Hun invaders pushed into northwestern India. These Huns were related to those that invaded Europe under Attila in the 400's A.D. Although a league of Indian princes succeeded in preventing the Huns from expanding into the Deccan, the Huns ravaged northern India and destroyed Taxila.

Southern India

Few of the Indian empires you have read about controlled southern India. That of Asoka extended farthest south, but it did not last long. Neither the Kushans nor the Guptas ruled south of the Narbada River.

As you read in Chapter 3, a range of hills separates the Indus-Ganges plain from the Deccan, the southern plateau. Because of these hills, southern India was isolated from the north and thus developed differently.

connections

Fairy Tales

"Once upon a time . . ." is a phrase we all recognize from fairy tales we heard as children. These stories occur in every culture, and a number of themes are familiar to us all.

The Jataka Tales, ancient Indian stories taken from Buddhist writings, tell of animal and human kindness (right). Their theme is goodness contrasted with evil. The same theme underlies the story of Cinderella. Her fairy godmother represents good, and evil is personified in the wicked step-mother and stepsisters. In the Chinese version of this tale, the fairy god-mother's role is played by a talking fish, but the slipper, the prince, and the wedding are all there. In the Algonquin Indian version, the gods, rather than the prince, search for the true Cinderella. One collector of fairy tales estimates that there may be almost 300 different versions of the Cinderella story.

Another worldwide theme is that of the sleeper and the awakening. A wicked witch or fairy gives a curse, and the sleeper sleeps until awakened by a person of good will. We know this theme in Sleeping Beauty. In an Indian story, the Hindu king Muchukunda is awakened by the Lord Krishna. In an ancient Roman legend, the beautiful maiden Psyche sleeps her magic sleep, in which she is married to Cupid.

A third universal theme is that of magical transformation, usually brought about by love. Pinocchio (below right) turns from a wooden puppet into a donkey, and finally into a real boy. In a Chinese fairy tale, Mrs. Number Three is turned into a donkey and back again.

Psychologists see fairy tales as a way in which societies pass their values along to their young. Such tales also provide vivid examples of different kinds of human character. And they communicate eternal human concerns, dreams, and fears—the triumph of good, the power of nature, and the chance of success even for the most unlikely people.

Two influences played a major role in the history of southern India: location and natural resources. The peninsula of India is located midway between Africa and southwest Asia, with the Arabian Sea on the west and the Bay of Bengal on the east. The land produced cotton, pepper, and other spices, and also had large amounts of ivory and gold. Thus southern Indians, particularly those along the coast, turned to the seas and to commerce, both because of their geographical location and because they had products that other peoples were eager to obtain.

Southern Indians became successful merchants and business people. Special organizations regulated crafts and trade. Commercial ties, especially with Arabia and the Roman Empire, made the region wealthy. Indian poets wrote of the magic of this foreign commerce, and the Roman writer Pliny the Elder described trade with India in the 70's A.D.

Although southern India was isolated from the north, Hinduism penetrated the region sometime after the 600's B.C. The first recorded date in the history of southern India is 250 B.C., when Asoka sent Buddhist missionaries to the Deccan. During the period of Maurya decline, beginning around 230 B.C., the Andhra dynasty arose in the south. The Andhras created an empire that eventually included a large part of southern India. When the empire declined, about 225 A.D., the south broke up into a number of small states that were constantly at war with one another.

CHECKUP

1. IDENTIFY: Guptas, Chandragupta I, suttee, *Panchatantra*, Kalidasa, *Sakuntala*, stupa, Aryabhata, Susruta, Andhra.

2. LOCATE: Ayodha, Ajanta, Nalanda, Narbada River.

3. Why did the Guptas favor the religion of Hinduism over that of Buddhism?

4. Explain how Indian drama differed from Greek drama.

5. From what books did Indian children learn to read? What subjects were studied at Nalanda?

6. What contributions were made in the fields of mathematics, astronomy, and medicine during the rule of the Guptas?

Chinese civilization evolved through changing dynasties

Around 1000 B.C. important changes were taking place in the Western world. It was at this time that the Dorians were settling down in Greece and the Latins were moving into Italy. In China, too, a new people, the Chou, appeared on the scene. As you read in Chapter 3, the Chou overthrew the Shang dynasty in 1028 B.C. That year marked the beginning of a dynamic era in Chinese history.

Under three successive dynasties—the Chou, the Ch'in, and the Han—China eventually became a large and powerful empire. As in ancient Greece and Rome, great technological and economic growth occurred in China during this first imperial age—that is, the age of an empire. It was also a time of tremendous philosophical activity, when ideas and theories of lasting importance to Chinese civilization were established. As in the West, this imperial age was brought to an end by internal weaknesses and foreign invasions.

In this section you will read about the rise and fall of the first Chinese empire. In the next section you will read about its lasting philosophical and cultural achievments.

The Chou dynasty

The Chou were a people from the Wei River Valley in north-central China. Their culture was not advanced, but they were better warriors than the Shang. Among other things, they used chariots in battle. With these, and with the help of a number of allies, they toppled the Shang forces and established their own dynasty (see map, opposite page). It was the longest dynasty in China's history. It lasted from 1028 to 256 B.C., nearly 800 years.

During these centuries significant changes took place in China's technology and economy. Probably the most important development was the introduction of iron into China in the early years of the dynasty. This helped to bring about a great expansion in agriculture. By using iron farm tools and plows pulled by oxen, Chinese peasants were able to bring new lands under cultivation and produce more grain than ever before. As a result,

China's population grew steadily. By the 700's B.C. China probably was the most densely populated land in the world. Internal trade expanded, and copper coins came into use as money.

Under the Chou dynasty China was not yet a unified empire. There was a central government in the capital city, but there were also many independent local governments. The Chou had conquered the Shang with the help of allies. These allies were given lands as a reward for their help. As a result, hundreds of small city-states developed. Although they owed certain obligations to the Chou, they could also act on their own.

After 700 B.C. many of these city-states began to assert their independence. They began to fight among themselves and expand their territories. By the 400's B.C. the Chou had no real power outside their own city-state. They continued to reign as kings for some time, until finally they were replaced by a new dynasty, the Ch'in.

The Ch'in dynasty

The Ch'in dynasty was founded by a young man named Cheng. He came to power in 221 B.C. by using cavalry armed with bows and arrows, a military technique new to the Chinese. Once in power, he called himself Shih Huang Ti (SHIR HWAHNG DEE), which means "first emperor"—the first, that is, of many Chinese emperors.

From its capital at Hsien-Yang, the Ch'in dynasty ruled a larger area than either of the preceding dynasties and controlled it more firmly. Although it lasted only a short time, until 207 B.C., the Ch'in dynasty succeeded in unifying China under a strong central government for the very first time. This dynasty, from whose name the Western name for China comes, created the first Chinese empire.

Shih Huang Ti is sometimes called the Chinese Caesar, partly because of his conquests and partly because of far-reaching changes he made in China's government. Not satisfied with ruling northern China and parts of the Yangtze Valley, Shih Huang Ti sent his armies far to the south. In a brilliant campaign, he conquered the central part of southern China as far as the delta of the Si River (see map, page 152). He also tore down the walls of the many city-states, disarmed their rulers, and ended their independence. China was divided into military districts under governors who used stern military and civilian authority. Conflicting local laws were made uniform in the code of Ch'in, and a single tax system was put into effect throughout the country.

The Ch'in as builders. To guard against invasion, particularly invasion from the north and west, the Chinese over the years had built several walls. The Ch'in completed and connected these walls to form the Great Wall of China. This massive structure, 25 feet (7.5 meters) high, ran 1,400 miles (2,250 kilometers) from Kansu province to the sea (see map, page 152). It was 15 feet (4.5 meters) wide, and a road along the top enabled soldiers to travel quickly to any area of the frontier that was threatened. Much of this Great Wall still remains standing today.

Understanding the importance of transportation and communications, Shih Huang Ti built

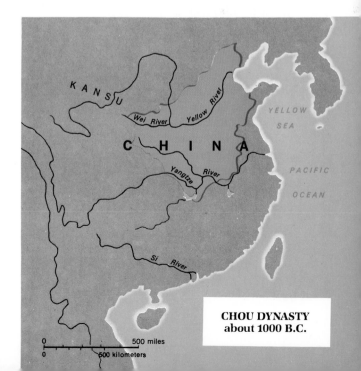

CHOU DYNASTY about 1000 B.C.

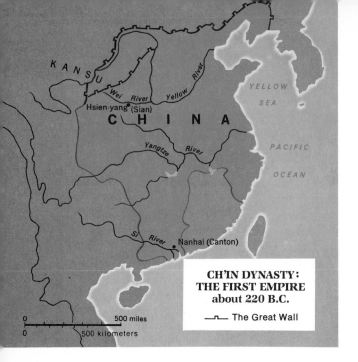

CH'IN DYNASTY:
THE FIRST EMPIRE
about 220 B.C.

—ᴖ— The Great Wall

0   500 miles
0   500 kilometers

broad, tree-lined highways. He set a standard width for the axles of carts and other vehicles so that they could pass each other easily on roads and bridges. He also standardized the currency system and weights and measures.

Harshness of the Ch'in. Ch'in rule was orderly, but it was also autocratic. Like autocrats ever since, Shih Huang Ti saw the danger of allowing scholars to investigate and discuss problems freely. He began his attack on the scholars by burning the important books called the *Classic of Songs* and the *Classic of Documents*. When scholars did not heed this warning, Shih Huang Ti had 460 of them executed.

Discontent became widespread under the Ch'in in a very short time. There was a great gap between the ruler, supported by his warriors, and the mass of people. Many workers had suffered building the Great Wall—it is said that each of its stones cost a life—and peasants resented the heavy taxes they had to pay. In 207 B.C. a general of peasant background, Liu Pang, led a revolt against the Ch'in. He overthrew them and in 202 B.C. founded the Han dynasty.

The Han dynasty

The new dynasty took its name from the Han River, where Liu Pang had been stationed as a general for several years. Like the Ch'in, the Han dynasty ruled over a centralized and expanding empire. Unlike the Ch'in, however, it succeeded in maintaining its power for a long time, roughly four centuries. So great was the impact of the Han dynasty on Chinese history and culture that even today many Chinese still refer to themselves as "Sons of Han."

The most famous Han emperor was Wu Ti, who ruled from 140 to 87 B.C. He established his capital at Changan (now Sian) and extended Chinese territory northward into Manchuria and Korea, southward to Indochina, and westward to central Asia (see map, page 154). Wu Ti's government was strong, but he was less autocratic than the Ch'in rulers had been.

It was during the Han dynasty that the Chinese **civil service** system was established. (A civil service administers the government on a day-to-day basis, and its members are usually appointed on the basis of competitive examinations.) Candidates for civil service positions were examined on the great classics of Chinese literature and law, so that they had to be scholars as well as administrators. In 124 B.C. Wu Ti established a national school to help prepare candidates for the civil service examinations.

For a long time the Chinese people had suffered hardships because of the rise and fall of prices for farm products. To prevent this, Wu Ti instituted an economic policy called **leveling.** In years of good crops, government agents bought and stored surpluses to keep prices from falling. Then, in years when there were few crops, the agents sold the food that was stored to prevent scarcity and high prices.

The Pax Sinica. Wu Ti fought vigorous battles with the nomadic people of central and eastern Asia who might have threatened the frontiers of his empire. About a hundred years before the Pax Romana began in the West, Wu Ti established what historians call the Pax Sinica, or Chinese Peace, throughout much of the continent of Asia.

During this period of peace, merchants were able to open the famous Silk Route from China across central Asia to the Mediterranean area (see map, page 154). Long camel caravans carried silk, jade, and other valuable Chinese goods to be sold to the wealthy people of Greece and Rome. They returned with glass, amber, asbestos, and wool

ARCHEOLOGY Archeology is the study of physical, material remains of past cultures in order to find out more about ancient peoples. Archeologists look at buildings, at fossils, at pieces of stone, clothing, pots, at anything they can recover. They dig these items up out of the ground or from the bed of the sea. Some archeologists do their research in scuba diving gear; others use delicate sieves so that they can sift through their finds.

From the objects they discover, archeologists try to understand how people lived or what beliefs they had. When they unearth fragments, they try to reconstruct what the complete object looked like. From the foundation of a house they try to visualize what the whole house looked like—and what type of people lived in it. If various objects are found near one another, they try to relate them. Seeds, shells, animal bones, and ashes are all important finds at an excavation site. The level in the ground of a discovery is also important, because evidence from ancient civilizations is sometimes covered over by later ones. With the help of scientific dating (see page 13), archeologists can reconstruct some of the practices and customs of a particular period.

One of the most fascinating archeological discoveries of recent times occurred in 1974 in China. Some farmers were digging wells near the ancient capital city of Sian. They came upon an underground vault filled with lifesize clay figures of warriors and horses. Archeologists were called in to supervise further digging. Carefully the workers removed layer after layer of dirt, revealing thousands of sculptures, in fact an entire army of soldiers and horses.

The archeologists studied these magnificent treasures, wondering who created them and why. Nearby was the large tomb of China's first emperor, Shih Huang Ti. From the location of the statues and from other evidence, the archeologists concluded that the clay figures were related to the tomb. From their knowledge of other ancient rituals and customs, they concluded that the statues had been placed outside the tomb to help protect the body of the emperor from his enemies, a common practice in the ancient world.

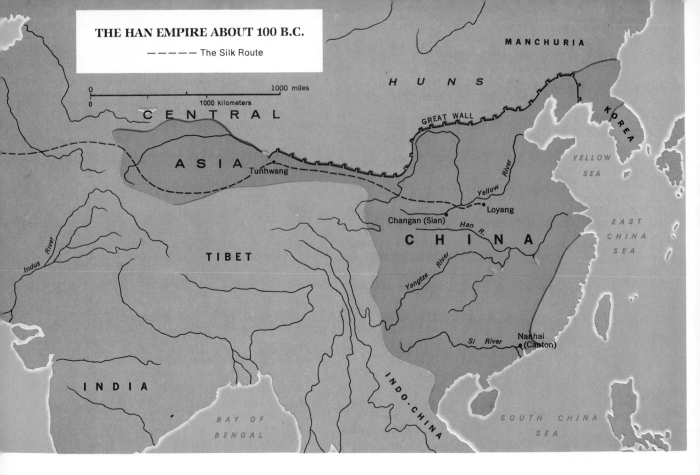

and linen textiles, which were purchased by the Chinese.

Wu Ti's successors were not so capable as he, and there was an interruption in the Han dynasty when a rival took over the throne in 9 A.D. He was ousted in 25 A.D., however, and the Han dynasty then returned to power until 220 A.D. At that time a revolt overthrew the last Han emperors.

The Six Dynasties

For more than 350 years after the end of the Han dynasty, China was plagued by wars from within and without. A succession of six different dynasties tried to restore order, but none was successful in setting up a strong central government. The empire of the Ch'in and Han had collapsed.

One of the most important events of this period occurred in 316 A.D., when Huns from central Asia successfully invaded northern China. These invaders were related to the people who brought on the end of the Roman Empire in the 400's and invaded India in the 500's. Invaders from Tibet

and Mongolia followed the Huns, each establishing rival kingdoms in the north.

Many Chinese fled before the invaders to southern China, which at that time was still a relatively thinly settled region. Chinese leaders in the south tried frequently to recapture the north, but their efforts were unsuccessful. As you will learn in Chapter 8, the goal of reunifying China was finally achieved in 589 A.D. by a general from the north.

CHECKUP

1. IDENTIFY: Great Wall, Liu Pang, "Sons of Han," civil service, leveling, Pax Sinica, Silk Route.

2. LOCATE: Wei River, Hsien-Yang, Yangtze Valley, Si River, Changan.

3. Describe the government under the Ch'in dynasty.

4. Two emperors, Shih Huang Ti and Wu Ti, are considered among China's greatest. What did each do to earn his reputation?

5. How were Chinese government officials chosen during the Han dynasty?

154

5

Ancient China produced distinctive philosophy and culture

During the centuries of China's early history, important developments took place in Chinese ways of thinking and living. These developments had a lasting impact on China and the Chinese people.

As you read earlier, the Chou rulers began to lose control over the many city-states of China as early as 700 B.C. From then until the end of the dynasty, there was growing political disunity and almost constant warfare. Nevertheless, these centuries marked one of the most creative periods in the history of Chinese thought. As in other ancient civilizations at roughly the same time, new political, economic, and social problems gave rise to many new ideas and theories. Here you will read about four important branches, or schools, of philosophy that developed in China during this turbulent era.

Naturalism

Like all other Chinese philosophers at the time, the Naturalists were far more interested in human beings and the real world than in divine or otherworldly matters. They attempted to explain the workings of nature by certain cosmic principles—that is, principles that applied to the whole universe. One of their basic ideas was the dualism, or two-sidedness, of nature. The Naturalists defined this dualism of nature as its *yin* and *yang*. *Yin* was female, dark, cold, and passive. *Yang* was male, light, hot, and active.

Yin and *yang* were not in conflict, however, as were the concepts of good and evil in Western civilization. Rather they were dependent on one another, and a balance between them was constantly achieved. Day, which was *yang*, gave way to night, which was *yin*. Summer gave way to winter.

The Naturalists believed that balance was inevitable in human affairs also. Extremes—for example, harsh government on the one hand, or anarchy (that is, no government) on the other—could not exist for long.

Confucianism

K'ung Fu-tse (meaning Kung the Philosopher, or Reverend Master Kung) is known to Westerners as Confucius. He lived from about 551 to about 478 B.C. His father died when he was only three years old, and the family was left in poverty. In spite of this, Confucius managed to get a good education. At the age of 22 he set himself up as a teacher and soon gained a great following. His ideas and teachings became known as Confucianism and exerted a more powerful influence on later Chinese life and thought than any other philosophy.

Confucius was primarily interested in politics and wanted to put an end to the disorder of the times in which he lived. He believed there were two ways to accomplish this. First, every person should accept his or her assigned role in society and perform the duties of that role. Second, government should be virtuous. That is, instead of relying on military power, rulers should be honest and have concern for others. Only educated and virtuous officials should be appointed to run the government.

Confucius hoped to put his ideas into practice by becoming adviser to a local ruler. The story is that he was given a high post, minister of crime, in his native province of Shantung. Within a year, according to the story, crime had almost disappeared. Neighboring rulers, however, became jealous and in time Confucius had to retire. He spent the rest of his life teaching. Eventually, the teachings of Confucius took on religious significance. In 195 B.C., for example, Liu Pang (founder of the Han dynasty) visited the tomb of Confucius and offered a sacrifice to his spirit. In 58 A.D. the emperor decreed that schools were to make sacrifices to Confucius.

Legalism

Like Confucianism, the school of philosophy known as Legalism was concerned with politics. Its teachings, however, were very different from the teachings of Confucianism. The Legalists believed in power, not virtue. They also believed in harsh laws. In their view, people were by nature selfish and untrustworthy. Only by threatening them with severe punishment if they failed to do what was expected of them could peace and prosperity be achieved.

The ideas of Legalism developed in the 200's B.C. in the city-state of Ch'in. When the Ch'in dynasty was established in 221 B.C., these ideas were put into practice by the first emperor, Shih Huang Ti. He succeeded in creating a powerful empire, but, as you recall, his dynasty was brief. Later Chinese thinkers believed that the Ch'in dynasty failed because its methods were too extreme. There was not a proper balance between *yin* and *yang.*

The Han dynasty succeeded in creating a lasting empire because it did achieve a balance. The government of the Han dynasty was Legalist in structure—that is, it was highly centralized and had great power. But it was Confucian in operation, since it was run by educated officials who believed in the ethical principles of righteousness and compassion.

Taoism

Lao-tzu (LOW·DZU), who is thought to have lived in the 500's B.C., was the founder of a philosophy called Taoism (DOW·iz·um). Taoism got its name from its central idea, Tao, which can be defined as the Way of Nature. Lao-tzu said that Tao is an indescribable force that governs the universe and all nature. Only by withdrawing from the world and contemplating nature can people understand Tao and bring themselves into harmony with it.

According to Lao-tzu, people should not strive for learning, riches, or power. They should try, rather, to bring themselves into harmony with Tao by being quiet, thoughtful, and humble. As Lao-tzu said, "He who overcomes others is strong; he who overcomes himself is mighty." Unlike Confucius or the Legalists, Lao-tzu was not interested in politics. He advised people to withdraw from public affairs and not to participate in them.

In time Taoism became the second most important philosophy in China, ranking after Confucianism. Taoism appealed to the masses of peasants because of its concern with nature and natural forces, which reminded them of their traditional religions. It also appealed to artists and poets because it encouraged artistic expression as a means of understanding Tao. Indeed, Taoism appealed to many Confucianists as well, because it

added balance to their lives. Being concerned only with politics and social problems was too restrictive. Even officials and the emperor needed a temporary escape from governing the country. They found that escape in the Taoist contemplation of nature.

Thus, like *yin* and *yang,* Taoism and Confucianism came to be complementary parts in Chinese culture. Each supplied what the other lacked.

Society and culture under the Han

During the Han dynasty China's population grew to more than 60 million people. The imperial capital at Changan became a huge city, with imposing palaces and broad avenues. On its many side streets were the shops of merchants and artisans. There one could find luxury goods from distant lands and many products that were made in China. Among the latter were two of the greatest of all Chinese inventions, paper and porcelain. Both spread from China to the Western world in later centuries and had a profound impact on Western life. Porcelain—that is, highly glazed ceramic ware—is still known today as china.

Farming. Despite the growth of cities and towns, the vast majority of Chinese people continued to live as farmers in small villages. Their lives were hard. On the one hand, they had to contend with nature. If too much or too little rain fell, their crops might be ruined and starvation would result. On the other hand, they had to contend with government. In addition to paying taxes, peasants were also expected to perform labor services. For a month or so every year they had to leave their farms and work on roads, canals, or other local construction projects.

Some of these projects were useful to them. For example, many large-scale irrigation and flood control systems were built in northern China during the Han dynasty. These lessened the danger of disastrous floods or droughts. Some of these systems were so well constructed that they are still in use today, more than 2,000 years later. Other projects benefited the ruling class only. If peasants felt oppressed by high taxes or labor services, they might flee to the tax-free estates of high officials. Or they might revolt or become bandits. Peasant uprisings were one of the clearest signs of the decline of a dynasty in Chinese history.

The early Chinese dynasties

The brilliant craftsmanship of the Chinese was already apparent during the first dynasties. Artists worked in a wide variety of materials, and the surviving objects display remarkable skills. The elaborate jade carving (left), with its ornate design, is one of the oldest and finest examples of an art form that continued for centuries. Like most art from the late Chou dynasty, it was made to please lords who tried to outdo one another by owning expensive objects of art.

During the Ch'in dynasty, massive public projects were built, rivaling those of Rome. The Great Wall of China (below), extending 1,500 miles (2,400 kilometers) across China, protected the country from fierce invaders along its northern borders. Under the Han dynasty, China grew and prospered. The serene figure of a woman (below left) is probably from the tomb of a noble. Like the ancient Egyptians, the Han rulers constructed elaborate burial vaults in which they placed various articles to amuse the dead person.

Family and social life. The family, not the individual, was the most important unit in Chinese society. Each family consisted of the father, his wife, the sons with their wives and children, and the unmarried daughters. The Chinese father, like the Roman father, was the source of all family authority. The older he was the more authority he had, for age was respected as a source of wisdom. As you read earlier, respect for one's aged parents and especially for one's father was an important virtue. Each family kept a careful genealogy, or record of the family tree, even including third cousins. When family members died, they became honored ancestors and were worshiped as links between the family's past, present, and future.

The Chinese father arranged his children's and his grandchildren's marriages, decided how much education, if any, his sons would receive, and chose their careers. Women were subordinate to men and had no property rights of their own. Upon marriage a young wife became almost a servant in the household of her husband's family. Before her wedding she often cried, not because she did not yet know her husband, but because she might not like her mother-in-law. But with motherhood and age the wife became an important figure in the family.

According to Confucian teachings, the family was of key importance to the state. If every family were properly run, political affairs were bound to be healthy. The government was a sort of guardian of the relationships among families. The same values that governed family life—respect for age and acceptance of the decisions made by one's superiors—governed national life as well. The emperor was portrayed as the father of all the people.

Scholar-officials. Next to the imperial family itself, government officials enjoyed the highest status in Chinese society. As you recall, Confucius believed that only educated and virtuous people should enter government service. This idea became the basis for China's system of civil service examinations. Individuals did not inherit high rank and government office from their fathers, as was the case in other traditional societies. They had to study the classics of Chinese literature and the writings of Confucius. Those who passed these examinations were eligible for government posts.

As a result, the best scholars in the country became its officials.

In theory, the examinations were open to anyone, and cases in which a poor boy rose to great heights in the civil service were not unknown. Since education was expensive, however, few peasant families could afford it for their sons. Generally, only the sons of wealthy landowning families had a chance to become scholar-officials.

Still, there was probably a greater opportunity to move upward in ancient Chinese society than anywhere else in the world until modern times. Families in ancient China continually rose and fell in status, depending on whether or not they produced successful candidates for the civil service examinations.

Science

Chinese astronomers had computed the year at 365¼ days as early as 444 B.C. During the Han dynasty these calculations were refined even further. In 28 B.C. astronomers in China observed sunspots, which were not known about in Europe until the 1600's A.D.

Sometime before 100 A.D., Chinese astronomers built special instruments with which they observed the orbit that the sun apparently follows. Using these instruments, an early astronomer estimated the number of stars at 11,520. Other scientists invented a primitive seismograph that registered earthquakes so faint they were unnoticed by the royal court.

CHECKUP

1. Explain the concept of *yin* and *yang*.

2. What are the basic teachings of Confucianism? How did the ideas of Taoism complement the ideas of Confucianism?

3. List the ideas of Legalism.

4. What were the problems of farmers during the Han dynasty?

5. Explain the importance of the family in Chinese government and social life.

6. How were scholar-officials chosen in Chinese society? Do you think this was a fair system? Why or why not?

CHAPTER REVIEW

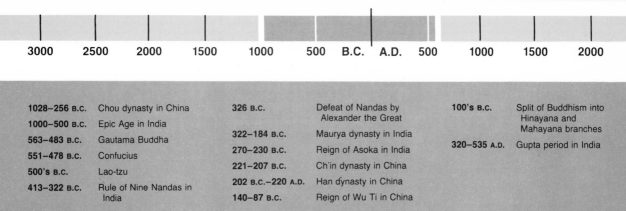

3000	2500	2000	1500	1000	500	B.C.	A.D.	500	1000	1500	2000

1028–256 B.C. Chou dynasty in China
1000–500 B.C. Epic Age in India
563–483 B.C. Gautama Buddha
551–478 B.C. Confucius
500's B.C. Lao-tzu
413–322 B.C. Rule of Nine Nandas in India

326 B.C. Defeat of Nandas by Alexander the Great
322–184 B.C. Maurya dynasty in India
270–230 B.C. Reign of Asoka in India
221–207 B.C. Ch'in dynasty in China
202 B.C.–220 A.D. Han dynasty in China
140–87 B.C. Reign of Wu Ti in China

100's B.C. Split of Buddhism into Hinayana and Mahayana branches
320–535 A.D. Gupta period in India

CHAPTER SUMMARY

In the centuries between 1000 B.C. and 600 A.D. powerful empires rose and fell in both India and China. Of greater and more lasting importance were certain ideas and institutions that developed during this period. These ideas and institutions continued to influence Asian civilization for centuries.

The Aryan invaders of India developed a class system which led in time to the formation of some 3,000 hereditary castes. Each caste had its own fixed position in society and its own rules about eating, marriage, labor, and worship. Caste is still an important part of social organization in India today.

Brahman scholars composed the *Upanishads* to explain the Vedic religion. Out of these explanations grew a complex set of ideas known as Hinduism, which remains the major religion of India. Hinduism teaches that the world of the senses is an illusion. Only by means of reincarnation can a person gain the experience to escape from suffering and be reunited with the Universal Soul.

Gautama was an Indian prince who became known as Buddha. He taught that people could attain salvation by accepting the Four Noble Truths and following the Middle Way. These teachings, which became known as Buddhism, exerted an even more powerful influence on the rest of Asia than on India itself.

During the Chou, Ch'in, and Han dynasties developments of lasting importance also took place in Chinese thought. China's most influential philosopher was Confucius. He taught that good government depended on virtuous rulers and officials. That idea became the basis for China's civil service examination system.

Lao-tzu, the founder of Taoism, taught that people should withdraw from the world and try to achieve harmony with nature. In time Taoism became the second most important set of beliefs in China.

Two other significant schools of Chinese philosophy were Naturalism and Legalism. Naturalism explained nature through the principles of *yin* and *yang*. Legalism stressed political power and harsh laws.

The main unit in Chinese society was the family. Age was highly respected, and fathers had great authority. Government officials had high status in China. Usually only those from wealthy families could afford the education necessary for the civil service.

CHECKING WHAT YOU KNOW

1. Match each religion or philosophy at the left with an idea at the right:

   a. Hinduism
   b. Buddhism
   c. Confucianism
   d. Taoism
   e. Legalism

   1. Suffering and sorrow are caused by selfish desire for pleasure and material things.
   2. Belief in power not virtue.
   3. Progress toward salvation depends upon fulfilling your dharma.
   4. Government and people should emphasize virtue and education.
   5. Bring yourself into harmony with the universe by being quiet, thoughtful, and humble.

2. Match each leader at the left with a dynasty at the right. You may use a dynasty more than once.

   a. Shih Huang Ti   1. Han
   b. Asoka   2. Ch'in
   c. Chandragupta I   3. Maurya
   d. Wu Ti   4. Gupta
   e. Chandragupta Maurya
   f. Liu Pang

3. How did location and natural resources affect the development of southern India?

4. Compare the ideas of Buddhism and Confucianism on how best to establish goodness in this life.

5. How was the Ch'in dynasty both good because of its accomplishments and bad because of its repression?

PRACTICING YOUR SKILLS

1. **Making categories.** Put each of the following names or ideals in one of these six categories: literature, mathematics, science, philosophy, religion, government.

   a. Ajanta caves
   b. Susruta
   c. *Bhagavad-Gita*
   d. *Panchatantra*
   e. inscriptions on pillars
   f. monism
   g. leveling
   h. Rama and Sita
   i. Pax Sinica
   j. civil service examinations
   k. *Sakuntala*
   l. *yin* and *yang*
   m. the Middle Way
   n. Four Noble Truths
   o. standard width of axle for carts
   p. Great Wall
   q. uniform law code
   r. teachings of Confucius
   s. large-scale irrigation and flood control
   t. *Classic of Songs* and *Classic of Documents*

2. **Making comparisons.** Compare the role of women in China during the Han dynasty with that of women in India during the reign of the Guptas.

3. **Using maps.** Use tracing paper on text maps of India and China (page 144 and 154). Show the extent of territory for each of the following dynasties:

   a. Maurya
   b. Gupta
   c. Chou
   d. Ch'in
   e. Han

RELATING PAST TO PRESENT

1. It is sometimes said that a culture can be judged by the people to whom the greatest honor is paid. Which people were most honored in India? in China? Which people do you think Americans today respect or honor most? What makes these people so highly regarded?

2. Compare the ideas of Confucianism and Legalism as to how society should be changed. Are any ideas or values from these two different systems used in our society today? Give examples from newspapers to back up your opinion.

INVESTIGATING FURTHER

1. In your school or local library, find a book on the paintings in the Ajanta caves. One possible source is Benjamin Rowland, *The Ajanta Caves: Early Buddhist Paintings from India* (New American Library). What can you tell from these pictures about the lives of the Indian people during the Gupta period?

2. Using encyclopedias, find out more about Chandragupta Maurya and Asoka. Prepare an oral or written report on the life and accomplishments of one of these Indian rulers.

3. In your school or local library read the *National Geographic* articles, "China Unveils Her Newest Treasures" (December 1974) and "A Lady from China's Past" (May 1974). Describe what items have been uncovered in the tombs of the Han dynasty. What can we conclude about medicine, silk weaving, art forms, and entertainment interests from the tomb of the Han noblewoman? Describe the methods used to preserve the items found.

UNIT REVIEW

1. Name the individuals who might have made the following statements. Explain why each statement is significant.

   a. "King Philip of Macedon should not be allowed to rule over the Greeks."
   b. "If I succeed at Salamis I will have victory over all the Greeks."
   c. "I will unite all of India and teach the people the Way of the Buddha."
   d. "Barbarians must be kept out of our culture, so I will build a Great Wall."
   e. "All the world should enjoy the benefits of Hellenistic culture under my rule."
   f. "We must make Athens a center of culture, beauty, and good government."
   g. "Life is full of pain and suffering caused by people's selfish desire."
   h. "Whoever would find harmony with the Tao in the universe must cultivate a condition of no action."
   i. "You must love God first and then love your neighbor as yourself."
   j. "People must cultivate both virtue and education."
   k. "I wish to extend the *Pax Romana* to all the world and eliminate all possible rivals to my position as first consul."
   l. "I will write of the great legends of the ancient Greeks and how they conquered Troy."
   m. "I believe that all information should be classified so that study will be rational and knowledge will advance."

2. Match each item at the left with the item at the right that happened at approximately the same time in history.

   a. the life of Buddha
   b. the Etruscan invasion of Italy
   c. the life of Jesus
   d. the beginning of the Gupta dynasty
   e. the Hellenistic period after Alexander the Great

   1. Julian Emperors
   2. the rule of Constantine
   3. Ch'in Empire
   4. the life of Confucius
   5. Greek Age of Kings

3. How did the concept of Greek democracy differ from the Roman concept of a republic?

4. Trace the development of written law from Draco to Pericles to the Twelve Tables to Roman imperial law. Consider the individual rights of citizens, women, and slaves. Why was Roman law considered superior to Greek law?

5. List the scientific accomplishments of each of the cultures that you read about in this Unit.

6. Compare and contrast family life in ancient Rome and in China under the Han.

7. Choose one of the current issues listed below and discuss it from the point of view of one or more of the philosophies described in this Unit:

   a. the necessity to build up military armaments in order to ensure world peace.
   b. the need for society as a whole to accept responsibility for those who cannot take care of themselves.
   c. the need to maintain the family as a support of our civilization.
   d. the rights of the individual versus the rights of the government.

   Suggested religions or philosophies could be: Christianity, Buddhism, Confucianism, Legalism, Stoicism, Hinduism, and Taoism.

8. Choose two of the four cultures studied in this Unit (Greece, Rome, India, China). Explain how the religion or philosophy of each culture is reflected in its arts. The art forms may include sculpture, architecture, painting, mosaics, drama, and poetry.

9. What do these two periods in history have in common: Athens under Pericles and India under the Guptas?

10. Describe the lasting contributions made by each of the four cultures you read about in this Unit. Which culture was the most innovative? Which borrowed the most from other cultures?

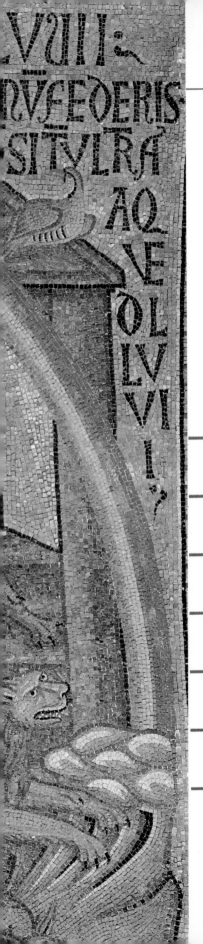

CIVILIZATIONS OF THE MEDIEVAL WORLD

Noah and his family escorting pairs of animals from the ark, in a mosaic from St. Mark's Cathedral in Venice

163

8

(100–1644)

Civilization in East Asia Reached New Heights

During the thousand years following the 400's A.D., as the West struggled to reorganize after the collapse of the Roman Empire, great civilizations flourished in East Asia. Both the Chinese and Japanese established complex patterns of government, society, and culture. The attitudes and institutions they developed then were to last until modern times.

The achievements were particularly noticeable in China. This was a remarkably inventive civilization, whether in finding new ways to make books or new ways to cook. Its writers, artists, and artisans created works of great beauty. What is noteworthy is that all of these accomplishments were possible even though there was considerable political unrest. Chinese society, despite these upheavals, remained basically stable.

During this thousand-year period, the Chinese were repeatedly troubled by invasions and wars. The most famous of the intruders were the Mongols. These fierce warriors from central Asia conquered China along with other vast territories. Like most invaders they left their mark on the areas they invaded. Yet, in spite of this foreign domination, two elements of Chinese society continued over the centuries—the government, which was run by a carefully selected civil service, and the system of domination by landlords. The religion of the people, a mixture of Buddhism and Taoism, also took a form in this period that was to last for centuries.

Chinese women tending children

Across the sea, on the islands of Japan, a different civilization emerged. Although China's influence on Japan was enormous, a distinct culture emerged. The Japanese created their own blend of religious beliefs, their own form of writing, and their own literature and art. In political and social organization, their combination of central and local concentrations of power was more like the European than the Chinese systems. Despite the country's safety from invasion, there was also less political stability in Japan. Yet its civilization developed traditions as long-lasting as those of China.

These two countries thus advanced over the course of more than a thousand years to a level of social and intellectual achievement that the West could well envy.

THE CHAPTER SECTIONS

1. China flourished under a restored empire

2. Central Asian nomads invaded China and the West

3. Japan gradually developed its own politics, society, and culture

1

China flourished under a restored empire

In the West the Roman Empire never revived after its collapse in the late 400's A.D. In China, however, Huns and other invaders from Tibet and Mongolia were finally defeated and a unified empire was reestablished.

By the 600's A.D. the Chinese empire was stronger, wealthier, and grander than the empire of the Han dynasty had ever been.

The Sui dynasty

The work of reuniting China was accomplished by the short-lived Sui (SWEE) dynasty. Yang Chien, a general, took over the throne of the largest kingdom in North China. He then reunited North and South China. Yang Chien founded the Sui dynasty in 589, but it lasted less than 30 years.

During this period the Grand Canal was formed from existing waterways between the Yellow and Yangtze rivers and was extended to link North and South China. However, the Sui dynasty was overambitious and unskilled in administration. The Sui rulers tried unsuccessfully to conquer southern Manchuria and northern Korea. Yang Chien's successor wasted much government money and was defeated by invading Turks in 615. He then fled to southern China, where he was assassinated.

The T'ang dynasty

The uprising against the Sui dynasty was led by Li Yuan, who established the T'ang (TAHNG) dynasty in 618. The early T'ang rulers defeated the invading Turks to the north and west and extended the frontiers of China farther west than ever before (see map, page 166). T'ang rulers made contact with India and the Muslim Empire (see Chapter 10), and Chinese ideas greatly influenced China's eastern neighbors, Korea and Japan.

The T'ang capital was established at Changan (see map, page 166). The city was not only the center of government but also a center of culture. People from many parts of the world lived side by side in Changan.

Like the Han dynasty centuries earlier, the T'ang gave China a golden age. The T'ang dynasty itself lasted only until 906. However, it began a thousand-year period during which China was the most powerful, most sophisticated, and wealthiest country in the world.

The T'ang dynasty was known for its poetry. Later Chinese anthologies itemize more than 2,300 T'ang poets and 48,900 poems. Two men of the 700's, Li Po and Tu Fu, symbolize the best of T'ang poetry. They were opposites in personality.

Li Po was a Taoist, a pleasure lover, and a favorite of the royal court. His writings happily, lightly, and often elegantly described the delights of life. According to Chinese legend, Li Po became tipsy and drowned while reaching from a boat for his reflection in the moonlit waters.

Tu Fu, on the other hand, was a serious, even solemn, man and a devout follower of the teachings of Confucius. His carefully written lyrics showed his deep interest in the suffering and tragedy of human life.

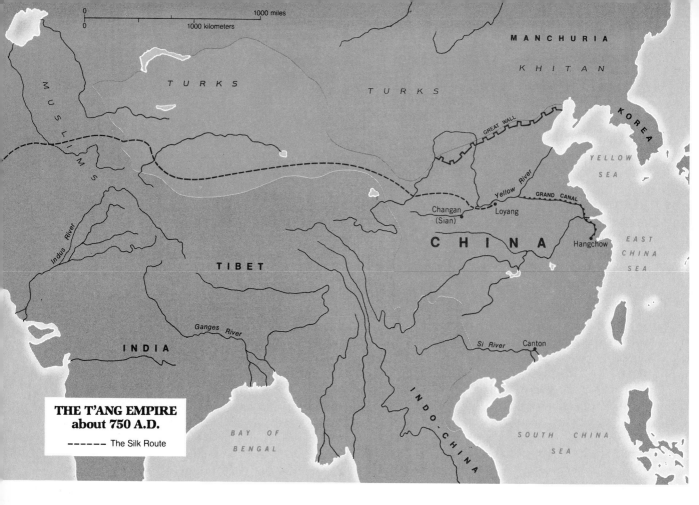

**THE T'ANG EMPIRE
about 750 A.D.**

- - - - - The Silk Route

Buddhism in T'ang China

Indian Buddhism had been introduced into China by missionaries during the Han dynasty. Unlike Christianity in the Roman Empire, which first appealed to poor people, Buddhism first appealed to wealthy and educated Chinese. They were attracted by its elaborate ceremonies, beautiful art, and rich literature.

When the Han dynasty was breaking up and Huns from the north were raiding China, many more people, especially peasants, converted to Buddhism. People were looking for comfort in this time of crisis. Mahayana Buddhism, with its worship of Buddha as a savior, offered an escape from the miseries of the present.

Buddhism reached its highest point in China around 700. Monasteries had been built throughout the country and had received gifts of tax-free land from wealthy believers. Many different sects developed. The most famous sect is known by

its later Japanese name, Zen. Zen Buddhism stressed meditation and enlightenment and was similar to Taoism. Indeed, to many Chinese peasants, Buddhism and Taoism were closely related. Inspired by the example of Buddhism, they had organized Taoist sects and parishes—that is, they had made Taoism a religion. In later centuries the religion of the common people in China became a complicated blend of both Buddhist and Taoist teachings.

The growing wealth of Buddhist monasteries began to alarm government officials. They tried to tax the monastery lands and sometimes seized the monasteries' precious art objects for the emperor's treasury. In the middle of the 800's, a fanatically anti-Buddhist emperor, who is said to have been insane, began to persecute Buddhists. He destroyed 40,000 shrines and 4,600 monasteries and forced 260,000 monks and nuns to give up their religious practices and return to ordinary life. Buddhism continued to exist as a religion in

China, but it never again became as important a force in Chinese life.

The T'ang dynasty reached its height about 750 and then gradually declined under weak emperors. By 900, T'ang rulers had lost their power. Tax revenues had diminished, nomadic peoples were invading, and governors in the provinces were challenging the emperor's power. Finally, in 906, the last T'ang emperor, a child, was overthrown and murdered.

The Sung dynasty

T'ang rule was followed by more than 50 years of disunity and civil war. Order was finally restored in 960, when Chao K'uang-yin (JOW KWAHNG-YIN) established the Sung (SOONG) dynasty. It inherited the same difficulties that the T'ang had faced, including foreign invasion and civil wars.

By the mid-900's, the principal foreign pressure came from the north, from a Mongolian people called the Khitan. They had occupied Chinese territory in southern Manchuria and in time invaded as far south as the Yellow River. When they threatened the Sung capital at Kaifeng (KY-FUNG), the Sung emperors decided to make peace. They did so by paying the Khitan a huge **tribute**—a sum of money paid each year.

Another menace to the Sung appeared in the 1100's. A new central Asian people, the Jurchen, moved into Manchuria behind the Khitan and took over northern China. China was again divided. The Jurchen established the Chin dynasty in the north, with its capital at Peking, while the Sung dynasty ruled in the south from Hangchow (see map, this page).

Sung civilization

Despite the problems of the Sung emperors, Chinese civilization remained at a high level under the Sung. Foreign trade expanded, aiding the hard-pressed economy. Overseas commerce centered on Hangchow and Canton. A thriving caravan trade also brought goods in from central Asia and India.

A Chinese customs list of the year 999 shows exports of gold, silver, and copper "cash" (a small coin). It also lists porcelain, which, from this period on, was one of China's most valued exports.

Sung artisans perfected the art of making porcelain, creating delicate vases as thin as an eggshell.

Another art perfected during the Sung dynasty was that of landscape painting. Inspired partly by the Taoist love of nature, Sung artists painted scenes of majestic grandeur, with jagged mountain peaks rising over misty hills and rushing water. Many of these landscapes were painted on silk.

Under the Sung the Chinese also perfected their civil service system. Examinations were held in the capital every three years on such subjects as literature, law, and history. To qualify for the examination, an individual first had to pass an examination at the local level. Fewer than 10 percent of those who tried succeeded, and fewer than 10 percent of those who took the national examination passed.

Because of the intense competition for civil service employment, steps had to be taken to prevent cheating or favoritism—that is, jobs being given to those who were friendly with government officials. Candidates were watched by guards while taking the examination. Each candidate was identified by number, not name. The candidate's paper was recopied by clerks so that no one's

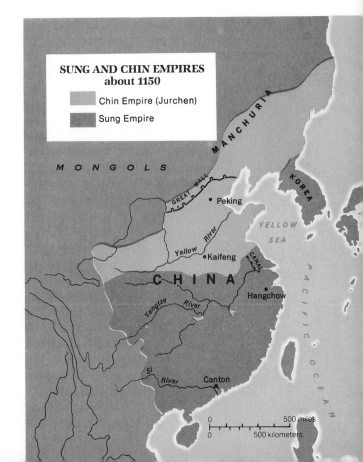

SUNG AND CHIN EMPIRES
about 1150

Chin Empire (Jurchen)

Sung Empire

Achievements of Chinese art

Since early history, people of many different cultures have regarded the horse as a symbol of military strength. The Chinese were no exception. A bronze sculpture of a war chariot proclaims its purpose as much through the fierceness of the horse as through its battle ax (bottom). And yet the horse also represented other aspects of Chinese life, as shown in a painting on silk (right). Here horses symbolize the peace and calm of the countryside. This painting was completed hundreds of years after the bronze chariot, during the Yüan dynasty.

The next dynasty, the Ming, is renowned for its distinctive porcelain. This superbly decorated bowl (below) is an example of an art form much imitated in other areas of the world.

handwriting would be recognized. Finally, three judges read each paper.

Great inventions. The Chinese invented gunpowder during the T'ang dynasty but used it at that time only for firecrackers. They first used it in warfare (as an explosive, not in guns) around the year 1100.

An even greater invention of the Chinese was printing. They had learned very early how to make ink and paper. The first step toward printing probably came in the year 175 A.D., during the Han dynasty, when the Chinese classics were carved in stone. Artisans could copy these writings by carefully fitting damp paper over the stone inscription and patting the flat surface with soot. The result was a white-on-black picture of the original.

The next step probably came with seals of metal or wood on which an inscription was carved in reverse. By the 600's such seals had become quite large and were similar to today's block prints.

The oldest printed book is the *Diamond Sutra,* a Buddhist religious text. It was printed in China in 868, during the T'ang dynasty. It was made in the form of a roll of six sheets of paper pasted together. Carved blocks were used to print the words on the roll.

Movable type, by which separate characters can be rearranged freely to form words and sentences, apparently came into China from Korea about 1030. The characters were made of wood, porcelain, or copper. This technique did not become common in China, however. Since there are so many characters in the Chinese language, printers would have had to make about 40,000 separate movable blocks to represent them all. For this reason the Chinese preferred blocks carved with an entire page of text.

Life in Sung China

By the middle of the 1000's, China's population may have been more than 100 million people. Most of these people were peasants, who lived and worked in the countryside. But two important changes had taken place in peasant life during the T'ang and Sung dynasties.

One change stemmed from technological improvements in agriculture. Many extensive water-control projects had been built in South China. As a result, there was an increase in the number of irrigated fields where rice could be grown. The planting of a new kind of quick-ripening rice from Southeast Asia made it possible to grow two crops of rice each year instead of only one. Also from Southeast Asia came an entirely new crop, tea, which soon became a popular drink throughout China.

Thus, agricultural productivity increased greatly, especially in South China. Peasants had more work to do than ever before, but they also had a greater chance to produce surplus food. That surplus could be sold in the many local market towns found in rural areas.

The second important change in the life of the peasants was the result of a change in the agricultural tax system during the T'ang dynasty. In the past, individuals had been taxed. Every peasant owed the government a certain amount of agricultural produce and labor service each year. Peasants living on the tax-free estates of high officials, however, were exempt from these obligations. After the 700's land itself was taxed. Labor services were gradually reduced, and taxes had to be paid in produce according to the area of land a person owned. There were no more tax-free estates.

This change was good for the government, but it was very hard on peasants. They could no longer escape to tax-free estates when they produced too little to pay taxes. Instead, they had to sell their land to others and become tenant farmers. As tenant farmers they paid the landlords high rents, which might be as much as half of the crops they raised. From Sung times on, the power of landlords became a serious problem in China. It was not solved until the 1900's.

As a result of the new tax system, life for many Chinese peasants became a struggle for survival. To avoid losing their land, they had to stay out of debt. If they lost their land and became tenant farmers, they worried about not having enough food to eat after paying their rents. During the growing season they worked in the fields from early morning until sundown. During the winter they repaired their simple tools and wove cloth. Young children were kept busy collecting firewood, bringing in water for the home, and seeing that no harm came to the family's chickens or pigs. Only for a short time each winter could they go to

T'ang Camel

This lively ceramic figure of a two-humped camel, approximately 2.5 feet (.75 meters) tall, was used as a tomb figure during the T'ang dynasty (618–906 A.D.). The practice of burying pottery replicas of servants and favorite animals was widespread in ancient times. It replaced the older, more primitive custom of killing slaves and cattle in order to provide the dead person with company and food in the afterworld.

In addition to servants and animals, the Chinese also buried figures of musicians, dancers, bodyguards, and grooms. Although tomb figures were made long before the Han dynasty (202 B.C.–220 A.D.), the realistic horses and camels of the T'ang period are regarded as the finest.

The brilliant colors, the sense of drama, and the joyous pose of this camel are typical of the rebirth in art that took place under T'ai Tsung, the second T'ang emperor. During his reign China experienced great prosperity and expanded its borders. Ceramists began to borrow colors and motifs from Persia, India, and Syria, becoming more international in style.

school—if there was a school in their village—to learn a little writing and arithmetic.

Two or three times a year, peasant families had a chance to relax. That was when festivals were held in the villages. Everyone would gather together to watch jugglers or acrobats. There would be feasting and music. Then the daily routine of hard work would begin again.

City life. During Sung times a larger share of China's population than ever before came to live in cities and towns. Hangchow, the capital of the dynasty after 1127, had a population of almost one million. Marco Polo, a merchant and explorer from Venice, visited the city in the 1200's and was amazed by its size and its beauty. In addition to Hangchow, there were several smaller cities and many towns. Although outnumbered by peasants, the city dwellers came to dominate Chinese society and culture.

The cities of Sung China bustled with activity. Huge shipments of rice, fish, and vegetables arrived daily, to be sold in the marketplaces. Streets were jammed with traffic—carts for transporting goods, sedan chairs in which wealthy people were carried along by servants, peddlers with their goods on bamboo poles, and large numbers of pedestrians. The canals that crisscrossed many cities in South China were jammed with boats and barges. Shops specializing in luxury goods—embroidered silks, pearl necklaces, chess sets, and printed books—lined the main streets. Shops selling noodles, candles, and other articles of everyday use lined the narrow side streets and alleyways. There were amusement quarters where people went to see puppet shows, plays, and performances of dancers or acrobats.

Officials and wealthy merchants lived in fine houses that were surrounded by gardens and artificial lakes. Ordinary people lived in crowded apartments, with only one or two rooms for an entire family. Some people had no homes at all. They begged for food and slept wherever they could find shelter. The government set up hospitals and orphanages to help the poor. It also gave food and money to the needy after fires or other disasters. However, poverty remained a serious problem in China's cities. In times of great floods or famines, peasants would crowd into the cities and increase the numbers of poor.

Chinese food. Chopsticks, which the Chinese use instead of knives and forks, came into use during the Chou dynasty. Many of the foods that are served in Chinese homes and restaurants today were also served during the Sung dynasty. The development of agriculture in South China made rice the basic food of the Chinese diet. Ordinary people ate rice three times a day, with small portions of dried fish or pork on the side. Wealthy people enjoyed a healthier diet. They could afford fresh fruits and vegetables and greater quantities of fish and meat.

Whether rich or poor, the Chinese prepared their food in the same way. Because firewood was scarce, food had to be cooked as quickly as possible. It was cut up into tiny pieces first and then stir-fried for just a few minutes. To add flavor, various spices and seasonings were used. For centuries the Chinese had believed in the concept of "the five flavors"—bitter, salty, sour, hot, and sweet. They tried to achieve a mixture of these flavors in the meals they cooked, which made even simple peasant food varied and interesting in taste.

CHECKUP

1. IDENTIFY: Li Po, Tu Fu, Zen, Khitan, tribute, Jurchen, *Diamond Sutra.*

2. LOCATE: Grand Canal, Changan, Kaifeng, Peking, Hangchow.

3. What dynasty was established by each of the following and when: (a) Yang Chien, (b) Li Yuan, (c) Chao K'uang-yin?

4. What subjects were tested in the civil service examination? How were the civil service examinations administered?

5. Describe the invention and development of printing in China.

6. What two important changes in the lives of Chinese peasants took place during the T'ang and Sung dynasties?

Central Asian nomads invaded China and the West

You read in Chapter 3 about the nomadic peoples who lived in central Asia, to the north and northwest of China Proper. The lands they inhabited were not well suited to agriculture, so they raised horses and sheep instead. They spent their lives moving their herds from one area of pasture to another, sometimes covering vast distances in a year. They were sturdy, self-reliant, and used to the hardships of outdoor life. They were also fierce warriors. All that was required was a strong leader, who could organize these rival clans of nomads into a disciplined fighting force.

Such leaders emerged among the Huns in the 300's A.D. and among the Khitan and Jurchen during the time of the Sung dynasty. You have read how the Huns invaded China and the outskirts of the Roman Empire. You have also read about the Khitan and Jurchen conquests of North China. Here you will learn about the greatest nomadic fighting force of all time—the Mongols under Genghis Khan (JEN·giz KAHN) and his successors. In the 1200's they created the largest empire the world has ever known (see map, page 172).

The Mongol Empire

The Mongols inhabited the area to the northwest of China Proper, in what is now known as Mongolia. At most, they numbered two million people. Their army at its height amounted to only about 130,000 cavalry troops. Usually no more than 30,000 of these troops were involved in any one campaign. What enabled them to conquer vast and heavily populated territories was their superior military technology and battle tactics.

Until the invention of firearms, warriors on horseback had a great advantage over soldiers on foot. Mongol troops, who took extra horses with them on campaigns, could cover up to 90 miles (145 kilometers) in one day. Specially designed saddles and iron stirrups enabled them to fire arrows with deadly accuracy while moving at full speed. On the open plains of central Asia they learned to make good use of their speed and

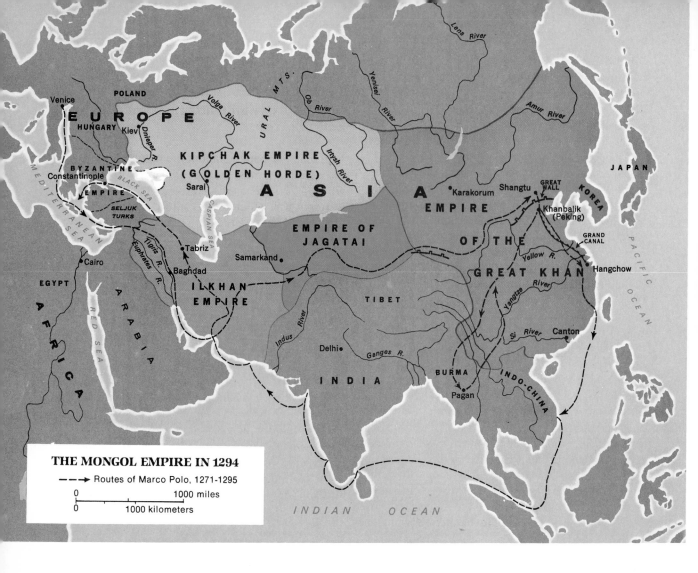

THE MONGOL EMPIRE IN 1294

- - -> Routes of Marco Polo, 1271-1295

0 _____ 1000 miles

0 _____ 1000 kilometers

mobility on horseback. In battle they would send numerous columns of riders against their enemies, surrounding them just as they surrounded wild game. Equally important, they enjoyed combat. It was a test of their abilities, and a way to acquire riches, honor, and personal power.

In the early 1200's Mongols under Genghis Khan swept down from Karakorum, their headquarters. They captured Peking and renamed it Khanbalik. Then they turned westward, conquering central Asia and most of Persia. Under Kublai Khan, a grandson of Genghis Khan, the Mongols completed the conquest of China, defeating the remaining Chin forces in the north and the Sung dynasty in the south. The Mongols also conquered Korea and tried unsuccessfully to conquer Japan.

Another grandson of Genghis Khan, Batu, invaded Europe, sweeping with his troops across Russia, Poland, and Hungary to the outskirts of Vienna. City after city was attacked and plundered and the inhabitants killed or taken as slaves. To terrified Europeans, the Mongolian forces became known as the Golden Horde—"golden" for all the riches they acquired, and "horde" after the Mongolian word *ordo,* which means "elite cavalry force." The Mongols eventually left Poland and Hungary, but they kept control over Russia for almost 200 years.

In 1260 Kublai Khan was named Great Khan and was recognized as the head of the whole Mongol Empire. Actually, however, the empire was divided into four parts—(1) the Empire of the Great Khan, which included China; (2) the

Empire of Jagatai in Turkestan; (3) the Ilkhan Empire in Persia; and (4) the Empire of Kipchak, or the Golden Horde, in Russia (see map, opposite). These four parts remained united for about a century and then slowly began to drift apart.

China under Mongol rule

In 1271 Kublai Khan established the Yüan dynasty in North China. As first emperor of the dynasty, he made Peking his capital. Yüan forces defeated the Sung dynasty in South China in 1279 and ruled all of China until 1368.

Under Mongol rule China made notable economic progress. During more than a century of invasion and warfare its population had declined from 100 million to only 59 million. Once peace was restored the population began to increase.

Kublai extended the Grand Canal from the Yellow River to Peking in order to ship rice from South China to his new and expanding capital city. Next to the canal he built a stone-surfaced highway that stretched for 1,100 miles (1,770 kilometers) between Hangchow and Peking. A messenger could cover this distance in 40 days. Kublai also linked China to India and Persia by post roads, which greatly improved trade.

Contacts with Europeans. During Mongol rule, Europeans and Chinese came to know one another a little better than before. Among Europeans living in China were Russian artisans and soldiers captured by the Golden Horde, a Parisian goldsmith kidnapped in what is now Yugoslavia, and the nephew of a French bishop.

King Louis IX of France and the pope in Rome sent ambassadors to China during the 1200's. Christian missionaries also made the trip. Marco Polo, the Venetian merchant of whom you read earlier, became the most famous of all European travelers in China. He had a counterpart in Rabban Sauma of Peking. In the 1280's Rabban Sauma traveled across Asia to Persia, then to Constantinople, and eventually to Italy, where he talked with the pope. He also went to France, where he met King Philip IV and visited the University of Paris.

Chinese-Mongol differences. The Yüan dynasty had brought certain benefits to China. But there was a natural antagonism between the conquerors and the conquered that was increased by

Chinese Dynasties 589–1644	
589–618	Sui dynasty
618–906	T'ang dynasty
906–960	Disunity and civil war
960–1279	Sung dynasty (after 1127, in southern China only)
1127–1234	Chin dynasty (northern China)
1271–1368	Yüan dynasty
1368–1644	Ming dynasty

striking differences between Mongol and Chinese ways of living. Their languages differed. As warriors, the Mongols valued action. The Chinese, on the other hand, valued accomplishment in literature and the arts. The Chinese disliked the smell and appearance of the invaders, who did not often wash. They also objected to the freedom Mongol women were allowed.

When Kublai Khan died in 1294, he left China to weak successors. Seven Mongol emperors ruled China over the following 26 years. During this period the country experienced many problems. The Yellow River flooded, destroying crops, and famine spread over the land. Many secret organizations were formed calling for revolution. Among them was the White Lotus Society, which later became an important force in China's history. Finally, in 1368, the last Mongol emperor was overthrown and the Yüan dynasty came to an end.

Later Chinese historians denounced the Mongols as savages. They claimed that the Yüan dynasty had no lasting effect on China. The Mongols influenced China in important ways, however. Among other things, they improved communications and made local governments directly responsible to the central government in Peking. The last two Chinese dynasties, the Ming and the Ch'ing, built upon the Mongols' political reforms to concentrate greater power than ever before in the hands of the emperor.

Founding of the Ming dynasty

The rebellion against the Yüan dynasty was led by Chu Yüan-chang, who founded the Ming dynasty

The Mongols in China

The Mongols, fierce nomadic tribes from the plains of Asia, swept into China with their swift cavalry forces. The Chinese, even with their splendid four-horse war chariots (below), were no match for the invaders, who specialized in surprise attack. Therefore the Chinese accepted the Yüan dynasty that the Mongols established. Kublai Khan, the first and most famous Yüan emperor, and his wife are shown (right) in portraits painted on silk. Kublai Khan had a magnificent summer palace north of Peking. Many centuries later it was described by the English poet Samuel Taylor Coleridge:

> In Xanadu did Kubla Khan
> A stately pleasure-dome decree,
> Where Alph, the sacred river, ran
> Through caverns measureless to man
> Down to a sunless sea.

(see map, this page). Like Liu Pang, founder of the Han dynasty, Chu Yüan-chang was of ordinary birth. He was orphaned as a child and became a Buddhist monk. Later he joined a band of rebels. Because of his skill as a leader, he was able to gain control of the entire Yangtze Valley. Then he captured Peking and became emperor. From Nanking, which he made his capital, the new emperor reestablished order in China and suppressed all secret organizations. He restored scholar-officials—whom the Mongols had not used—to the civil service and issued a new code of law called the Code of Great Ming.

The Ming dynasty lasted for almost 300 years, until 1644. During the early Ming period, China gained influence in foreign areas. You will recall that Indian traders had been traveling to Southeast Asia and to islands in the Pacific Ocean for a long time. Now China sent naval expeditions to some of these same places, including what are now Vietnam, Cambodia, Thailand, and Indonesia. In these areas China's influence was second only to India's.

In the mid-1400's these foreign expeditions, some of which had gone as far as Africa, ended as suddenly as they had begun. China withdrew from the affairs of the world. Historians are not entirely sure why this great change took place, but some possible reasons have been suggested. The Chinese may have felt that they had achieved the good life and did not need to seek elsewhere for it. Also, since the Ming dynasty was not as eager to encourage commerce as earlier dynasties had been, overseas ventures may have had less support. Merchants in China were not as important as merchants were in the West, and this may have reduced the drive for expansion. These conditions help account for the sudden end of the foreign expeditions, but they do not seem to be a complete explanation. It is a subject on which historians are still seeking answers.

China was able to maintain a stable and self-sufficient society until the mid-1800's. The Chinese took no part in the great intellectual, scientific, and technological revolutions that swept over Europe in these centuries. As a result, the Chinese found themselves at a great disadvantage when they were forced to open their country to economic, political, and cultural contact with Westerners in the 1800's.

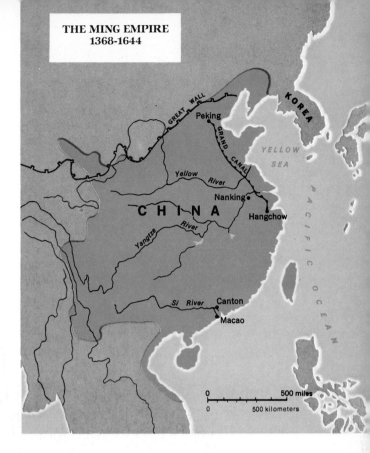

THE MING EMPIRE
1368-1644

CHECKUP

1. IDENTIFY: Genghis Khan, Kublai Khan, Batu, Golden Horde, Rabban Sauma, White Lotus Society, Chu Yüan-Chang.

2. How were the Mongols able to conquer so much land in Asia so quickly?

3. Why did the Chinese despise the Mongols? What were some of the good features of Mongol rule?

4. List the accomplishments of the Ming period.

3

Japan gradually developed its own politics, society, and culture

Japan is a chain of islands in the Pacific Ocean off the northeast coast of Asia. Most of the country's large population lives on the four main islands of Honshu, Kyushu, Shikoku, and Hokkaido (see map, page 176).

JAPAN ABOUT 1600

| 0 | | 300 miles |
| 0 | | 300 kilometers |

Climate and location

All of Japan is mountainous, and only about one-sixth of the land can be used for farming. The farmland, however, is among the most productive in the world. There is much rainfall in Japan, which means abundant water for irrigation and a large supply of timber. But nature is not wholly kind to Japan. Earthquakes, tidal waves, and typhoons often strike the islands, causing extensive damage.

Until modern times, the seas surrounding Japan shielded the islands from unwanted foreign influences. The Japanese were able to choose for themselves whether or not to have contact with other peoples. At times in their history they have been very interested in the outside world, especially China. At other times, they have preferred to live in isolation.

Even the Mongols under Kublai Khan were unable to conquer Japan, although they tried several times. Once, in 1281, a Mongol fleet of 3,500 ships carrying more than 100,000 soldiers assembled to invade Japan. However, the fleet was dispersed by the "Divine Wind" which the Japanese call the Kamikaze. It was a typhoon of extraordinary power.

Japan's beginnings

The people of Japan migrated to the islands long ago from the Asian mainland. The two oldest and most basic characteristics of their society have been the Shinto religion and a deep reverence for their emperor.

Shinto, an ancient religion, is similar to the religion practiced by certain nomadic tribes in eastern Russia today. Shinto means "the way of the gods." It is animistic, teaching that spirits are present in such objects as sand, waterfalls, and great trees. It is also a polytheistic religion. Shinto has a number of gods called Kami, which means "superior." The Kami are generally helpful, especially in promoting fertility in families and crops. From one viewpoint, Shinto is not so much a religion as a set of prayers and rituals to satisfy the Kami.

Reverence and respect for the emperor is also a foundation of Japanese life. According to tradition, Jimmu, the first emperor, was crowned in 660 B.C. This date was chosen in 601 A.D. by counting back 1,260 years, a period of time that the Japanese borrowed from the Chinese as representing a major historical cycle.

Jimmu probably was a mythical figure. The first real, or historic, emperor was Sujin, who reigned in the 300's A.D. Japanese emperors claimed divine descent from the sun goddess. This belief was not officially denied until 1945, after the Japanese were defeated in World War II. The Japanese have had only one imperial family in their entire history, making it the longest unbroken dynasty in the history of the world.

Early history of Japan

Early records of Japanese history are scanty. It is known that the Chinese knew about Japan before 100 A.D. Chinese writing was introduced into Japan about 405 and was adapted by the Japanese to write their own language. Another Chinese influence came in about 550, when a Buddhist monk brought Buddhism to Japan. At first the new religion was opposed by conservative advisers to the emperor. One of them threw a statue of Buddha into a canal. Soon after, an epidemic broke out. The epidemic was taken as a sign of the power of the new religion, and the emperor

connections

Parks and Gardens

There are times when you just want to "get away from it all." When this happens to people in Japan, many seek a garden such as this one (right) to refresh their spirits. Gardens in Asia are designed to imitate nature. They are miniature representations of the world, where rocks stand for mountains, ponds represent oceans, and sand and gravel are rivers. Frequently the gardens are open and in harmony with the hills around them.

In contrast, some gardens, particularly in China, are completely walled. Inside, visitors enjoy special views that change with the time of day or the seasons. Sometimes there are platforms where one can sit and look at the moon.

Some private homes and many public parks in Japan have tea gardens with paths leading to small houses. There tea is served with great ceremony. In the public parks are rows of cherry trees, and in springtime families have picnics under the blossoms. The Japanese government sent similar cherry trees, now planted around the Tidal Basin in Washington, D.C., so that Americans could enjoy them too.

You may have picnicked or camped out in one of the many national or state parks in the United States. Peo-

ple who live in or near cities visit Central Park in New York, the Public Gardens in Boston, Grant Park in Chicago, or Golden Gate Park in San Francisco. The people of Paris enjoy walking and sitting in the Tuileries (below), near the Louvre Museum.

The Tivoli Gardens in Copenhagen, Denmark, and the Prater in Vienna, Austria, have giant ferris wheels and other entertainments. A number of parks in the United States have special themes. Sometimes they contain animals and are game preserves.

allowed several Buddhist monasteries to be built. Buddhism then won many converts among nobles at the emperor's court.

In later centuries Buddhism spread among the common people and became an important part of Japanese life. It did not replace Shinto, however. For most of Japanese history the two religions coexisted peacefully, and people believed in both religions at the same time. Important events, such as births and marriages, were celebrated according to Shinto rituals. Funerals were held according to Buddhist rituals.

Japanese adoption of Chinese writing and Buddhism led to the introduction of other Chinese ideas and ways of life. Artistic designs, road engineering, medical knowledge, weights and measures, and styles of clothing were also adopted by the Japanese.

The Japanese sent their first ambassadors to China in 607. Japanese students returning from China in the 640's thought that Japan was inferior in various ways and worked to have other aspects of Chinese culture adopted in Japan.

In 702 a law code modeled on one from the T'ang dynasty in China was issued by the Japanese emperor. The code regulated all aspects of life in Japan and established a highly centralized government under the emperor.

During this period the Japanese built two capital cities. The first, at Nara, was an almost exact duplicate of the T'ang Chinese capital at Changan. Later, in 794, the Japanese built a new capital named Heian (HAY·AHN), which became the modern city of Kyoto.

At Heian, members of the ruling class began to modify some of the practices that had been adopted from China and created their own distinctive culture. For example, earlier poetry had been written in Chinese. Now many poems were written in Japanese.

Women enjoyed a high position in upper-class society at Heian. They could own property, and they played an important role in the literary life of the capital. Several women wrote diaries. Around the year 1000, Lady Murasaki Shikubu wrote *The Tale of Genji,* the world's first novel. It tells the story of Prince Genji, the perfect courtier. Written in a quiet, sensitive style, and filled with poems about the beauties of nature, it is one of the masterpieces of Japanese literature.

Feudal Japan

Although emperors continued to reign at Heian, the centralized political system adopted from China gradually fell into decline after the early 800's. In its place Japan developed a system of local power that in many ways resembled the system at work in Europe at this time. This system is known as **feudalism.** You will read about how it worked in Europe in Chapter 12.

In Japan the feudal system had two conflicting sources of power. One was an indirect form of central government under which an important family held power in the name of the emperor. The other source of power was outside the control of the central government. It consisted of military units that had authority in the territories they occupied.

Central government. The first family to gain control over the emperor and to use his power to their advantage were the Fujiwara. By holding important government offices and by marrying into the emperor's family, the Fujiwara controlled the central government from the early 800's to the mid-1100's.

After a power struggle the Minamoto family finally won control in 1185 and held power until 1338. In 1192 the Minamoto introduced a new kind of official called the **shogun.** He appeared to be the chief officer of the emperor and was always careful to be dutiful to him. In fact, however, he was the agent of the Minamoto and of the powerful families that succeeded them. From this time on, the major aim of an ambitious family was to gain control of the shogunate, that is, the office of shogun.

The shogun was the chief military officer of the central government. He also controlled finance, law, the courts, and appointments to office. He often governed from his military headquarters at Kamakura. In 1338 the Ashikaga family took over the shogunate from the Minamoto. They controlled the office for more than 200 years.

Local military rule. The leading families and their shoguns were powerful, but they were not strong enough to extend their power to local levels. There, military units were led by warrior-landlords called **samurai** (SAM·oo·ry). The power of a samurai rested on his control of land, on descent from earlier local leaders, and on his abil-

Feudal Japan

The feudal period of Japanese history was dominated by powerful warrior families. The men liked to be painted in their military splendor. Richly clothed and ferocious looking, they were most forbidding astride their horses (right). Japanese women, by contrast, were kept within the home (below). Their function was to offer comfort and support, and they were carefully sheltered.

Out of this feudal society, two great art forms were born: painting and drama. There were very few characters in Japanese theater, and they were symbolized by masks (top). The masks represented animals, gods, and people. Through dignified performances the dramas conveyed self-control and discipline. These were the very qualities that soldiers, too, cherished.

ity with the sword. The samurai had a code called bushido (BOO·she·doh) that stressed bravery, loyalty, and honor. Samurai were expected to endure great physical hardship without complaint and to have no fear of death. A form of ceremonial suicide called seppuku (also known as hara-kiri, or "belly slitting") was regarded as the honorable way for them to avoid torture, execution, or defeat in battle.

In time the samurai developed an order of preference among themselves. At the top were the **daimyo** (DY·myoh), who gained the loyalty of the lesser samurai. As the power of the daimyo increased and they became like petty kings, the samurai lost power and prestige.

Life in feudal Japan

There was frequent warfare in feudal Japan. Rival military units competed for power at the local level, and leading families competed for the shogunate. Nevertheless, the feudal period was a time of considerable economic and cultural growth.

Instead of weakening the country, warfare seems to have enriched it. The daimyo encouraged peasants to grow larger crops, since larger crops meant more taxes for the daimyo. They also promoted and taxed trade, using the money they received to finance their military campaigns.

For ordinary people, the frequent warfare offered a chance to rise in the world. Any man who could use a sword or a lance could join a daimyo's army. If he proved himself a good fighter and leader, he might be promoted to a higher rank. Or he might even lead a revolt against his daimyo and become daimyo himself.

The spread of Buddhism. The feudal period in Japan was a time of religious awakening. Many new Buddhist sects were established, including several that taught that salvation was possible through faith alone. According to the older Buddhist sects, a person had to make contributions to monasteries and study Buddhist scriptures to achieve salvation. Only wealthy people could afford that. The new sects appealed to ordinary people.

Warriors were particularly interested in Zen Buddhism, a sect that was introduced from China in the late 1100's. Zen stressed salvation through enlightenment, not faith. To achieve enlighten-

ment, a person had to engage in long hours of meditation and rigorous self-discipline. Warriors found that practicing Zen gave them the courage and determination they needed for fighting.

Zen and Japanese culture. The Ashikaga shoguns were great supporters of Zen Buddhism. They built Zen monasteries throughout the country and encouraged the artistic efforts of Zen monks. Several new art forms inspired by Zen developed during the late 1300's and early 1400's, when Ashikaga power was at its height. One was landscape architecture, that is, the art of designing gardens. By the careful arrangement of rocks, trees, and water, Zen believers tried to represent the essential beauty of nature.

Another new art form was the tea ceremony, a ritual designed to produce spiritual calm. A few people gathered in a small, simply furnished room that overlooked a garden. They sat quietly while one of them slowly and deliberately made tea. Then they drank the tea, admired the pottery bowls in which it was served, and enjoyed the beauties of nature in the garden outside.

Another artistic expression of Zen was the *no* play. *No* plays were highly stylized dance dramas, first performed in the 1300's. The subjects were usually religious. Like Greek plays, *no* plays were performed on a bare stage by male actors wearing masks. A chorus chanted the story.

The Ashikaga retained control of the shogunate until 1573, but after about 1460 they had no political influence in the country as a whole. Real power was in the hands of the many daimyo, who now began to fight among themselves for supremacy. For about a century there was no central government in Japan. You will read about this period and the shogunate that followed it in Chapter 18.

CHECKUP

1. IDENTIFY: Shinto, *The Tale of Genji*, shogun, Ashikaga, samurai, bushido, seppuku, daimyo.

2. Describe the favorable and unfavorable features of Japanese geography.

3. What were the major contributions and influences of China upon Japan?

4. Name the two centers of power in Japanese feudalism. How did they complement each other? How did they conflict with each other?

5. How did Zen influence Japanese culture?

CHAPTER REVIEW

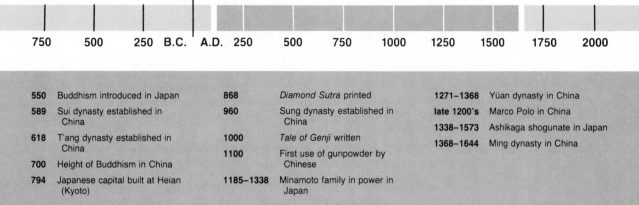

750	500	250	B.C.	A.D.	250	500	750	1000	1250	1500	1750	2000

550	Buddhism introduced in Japan	868	*Diamond Sutra* printed	1271–1368	Yüan dynasty in China
589	Sui dynasty established in China	960	Sung dynasty established in China	late 1200's	Marco Polo in China
618	T'ang dynasty established in China	1000	*Tale of Genji* written	1338–1573	Ashikaga shogunate in Japan
700	Height of Buddhism in China	1100	First use of gunpowder by Chinese	1368–1644	Ming dynasty in China
794	Japanese capital built at Heian (Kyoto)	1185–1338	Minamoto family in power in Japan		

CHAPTER SUMMARY

A unified empire was reestablished in China in 589 A.D. by the Sui dynasty. Soon China was stronger and wealthier than ever before.

During the T'ang and Sung dynasties, the Chinese civil service system was perfected. Important inventions, such as gunpowder and printing, were made. Poetry and the art of painting flourished. Cities grew in number and in size, but the majority of Chinese remained peasants. Many peasants fell into debt and had to sell their fields and become tenants. This remained a serious problem in China until the 1900's.

In the 1200's the nomadic Mongols of central Asia were united into a powerful fighting force under Genghis Khan and, later, his grandson Kublai Khan. They conquered China, Persia, and much of eastern Europe. Mongol rule brought economic growth to China, with an increased population, internal improvements such as roads and canals, and trade with other peoples. However, the Mongols were resented by the Chinese. After a rebellion against the Yüan dynasty, the Ming dynasty reestablished China's independence.

Japan was influenced by China but created its own distinct culture. Its island location made it safe from foreign invasion. The difficult terrain encouraged a political system in which there was both central and local power.

Japan developed a feudal political system. The central government was controlled by the shogun, who held power in the name of the emperor. At the local level, power was in the hands of the samurai, warrior-landlords. The most powerful samurai were the daimyo. The religion of the Japanese was also distinct, a combination of Zen Buddhism and Shinto-ism. Buddhism was especially influential in Japanese art, the tea ceremony, and drama.

CHECKING WHAT YOU KNOW

1. Match each Chinese dynasty at the left with an accomplishment at the right.

   a. Sui
   b. T'ang
   c. Sung
   d. Yüan
   e. Ming

   1. Perfected landscape painting.
   2. Built stone-surfaced highways.
   3. Sent naval expedition to Southeast Asia.
   4. Built the Grand Canal.
   5. Wrote beautiful poetry.

2. Match each Japanese historical period at the left with specific features of its time.

   a. Early history before Heian (court) period
   b. Heian (court) period
   c. Feudal period

   1. One imperial family established as emperor.
   2. Military rulers held real government power.
   3. Upper-class women enjoyed much independence.
   4. Buddhism introduced from China.
   5. Zen Buddhism became popular.
   6. *Tale of Genji* written.
   7. Chinese writing introduced and adapted by Japanese.

181

3. What agricultural improvements took place in China during the T'ang and Sung dynasties? What area of China was most affected by these changes? How did these changes influence city life in China?

4. Explain the tax reforms introduced during the T'ang dynasty. Why was this change good for the government and bad for the peasants?

5. Summarize your knowledge of Japanese history by answering the following questions:

   a. Why was the position of shogun established in Japan?
   b. Did the emperors of Japan have absolute power over their subjects?
   c. How was the role of emperor in Japan different from the role of emperor in China?

PRACTICING YOUR SKILLS

1. **Using maps.** (a) Using the map of China on page 53 and the map of the T'ang Empire on page 166, list the physical obstacles a merchant would have to overcome in his travels along the Silk Route.

   (b) Using the maps of the T'ang Empire (page 166), Sung Empire (page 167), Mongol Empire (page 172), and Ming Empire (page 175):
   1. Compare the size of each empire.
   2. Describe the importance of the Great Wall and the Grand Canal.
   3. Retrace Marco Polo's journeys from his starting place in Europe.

2. **Using art.** From the pictures of China on page 168 and those of Japan on page 179:

   a. Describe the activities and place in society of the people shown.
   b. Look back at the art of the Roman Empire (page 124). What activities of the people are similar? What activities are different?

RELATING PAST TO PRESENT

1. Consult an American history textbook to learn how and why the United States government introduced civil service examinations in the late 1800's. Compare the beginnings of the American civil service examinations to the beginnings of the civil service examinations in China.

2. In this chapter you read of the invention of gunpowder in China. What were its first uses in China? How has the use of gunpowder evolved from the T'ang dynasty?

3. Describe the development of printing in early China. How are the copy machines of today similar to the block prints of early China? What impact have mass-produced paperback books had on our society today?

INVESTIGATING FURTHER

1. Read poems written by the Chinese poets Li Po and Tu Fu. One possible source is Cyril Birch, *Anthology of Chinese Literature* (Grove Press). What do these poems tell you about life in China during the T'ang dynasty?

2. Find out more about Marco Polo's description of the Mongol capital of China and his impressions of the Chinese people. You might want to read selections from Ronald Latham, *The Travels of Marco Polo* (Penguin) to learn about court life, city life, and social customs. Report to the class on your findings.

3. Study Zen Buddhist painting to appreciate the emphasis on simplicity, meditation, and the close relationship to nature. You may use Sherman Lee, *A History of Far Eastern Art* (Prentice-Hall) as a source. What religious ideas can be found in the paintings?

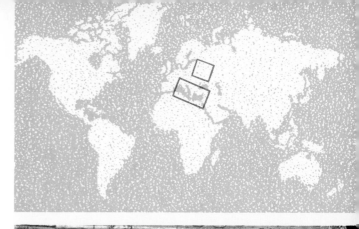

9

(500–1589)

The Byzantine Empire Preserved the Heritage of Rome

The collapse of the Roman Empire brought to an end the unity of the area around the Mediterranean Sea that had lasted for hundreds of years. In the west, as we will see, the result was fragmentation—the disappearance of strong governments and a return to isolated regions that were cut off from one another. However, in the east there was a very different heritage from Rome.

The last Roman emperors had moved east and established their capital at Constantinople. Thus, this half of the empire maintained its traditions and was not abandoned to barbarian invaders. In the east the Church strengthened the central position it had achieved under Constantine in the early 300's. Here, too, the great legal achievements of the Romans were preserved.

This new eastern empire took its name—the Byzantine Empire—from Byzantium, the ancient name for Constantinople. The Byzantine Empire lasted a thousand years. It created a distinct culture and a distinct branch of Christianity—the Byzantine, later the Eastern Orthodox, Church.

The most important area influenced by the Byzantines was a territory that eventually became known as Russia, a place-name derived from a people called the Rus. As the Rus and other peoples of the territory struggled for political identity, they looked to the Byzantine Empire for their religious and cultural inspiration.

The people of the territory created a sturdy agricultural society. In the 1200's the Slavic ter-

A wooden carving of a Byzantine empress

ritories were overrun by the Mongols, who created the largest empire the world has ever seen. The Mongol influence on the people they conquered was more political than cultural. As a result, the people of the area continued their Byzantine traditions.

THE CHAPTER SECTIONS

1. The Byzantine Empire helped preserve Western civilization
2. The Kievan states had strong ties with the Byzantine Empire
3. The Mongols established a vast empire in Eurasia

1

The Byzantine Empire helped preserve Western civilization

While barbarians overran the western part of the Roman Empire in the 400's and 500's, the Byzantine Empire in the east lived on. Throughout its long history the Byzantine Empire was surrounded by enemies. Nevertheless, it maintained itself for a thousand years.

Territory of the empire

In the year 500 the Roman Empire in the east included Greece and the northern Balkan penin-

sula, Asia Minor, Syria, Palestine, Egypt, and Cyrenaica. Although the eastern empire was invaded by Germanic tribes earlier than the western empire, it had internal strengths that enabled it to survive the attacks. By the early 500's the empire in the west had broken down into a group of Germanic tribal kingdoms (see map, this page). The eastern empire, on the other hand, had rid itself of barbarians and was ready for a great political, economic, intellectual, and artistic revival.

The leader of this revival was the emperor Justinian, who ruled from 527 to 565. While the new Germanic kingdoms in the west quarreled among themselves, Justinian's armies regained many territories in the Mediterranean region. With these conquests the territory of the eastern empire reached its greatest extent (see map, opposite). However, the eastern empire was unable to hold the regained territory for long. By the early 600's Germanic tribes had won most of it back.

After Justinian's death the weakened eastern empire suffered half a century of civil wars, made worse by attacks from the outside. From the east came the Persians. The Balkan peninsula was invaded by an Asiatic group, the Avars, and by a European people called the Slavs. Italy was overrun by the Lombards.

Justinian's successors defeated the Persians in the late 500's. During the 600's they faced a new and highly energetic force—the armies of the Muslim Empire, which you will read about shortly. The Muslims soon conquered Armenia, Syria, Palestine, and much of North Africa, including Egypt. After 650 the eastern empire consisted of little more than Asia Minor, the southern Balkan peninsula, parts of Italy, and the nearby islands (see map, page 202). However, the empire survived 800 more years.

Strengths of the empire

The Byzantine Empire survived for a long time because its people were skilled at adapting to change. It also had other strengths.

Political strength. The government of the Byzantine Empire was highly centralized and autocratic. The emperor was all-powerful. His commands and policies were carried out by well-paid officials who were efficient, skillful, and usually loyal. They were also strong enough to survive

GERMANIC KINGDOMS
in 526 A.D.

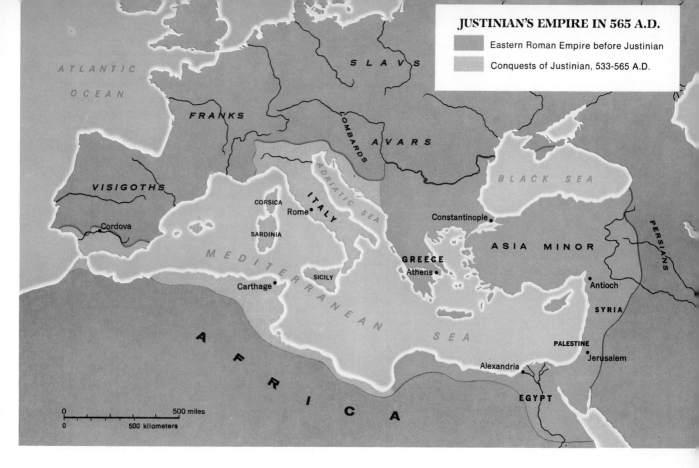

during bad times of weak emperors or civil war.

The Byzantines were especially skillful diplomats. They often used gifts and bribery, and their excellent intelligence service kept the emperor well informed of important foreign developments. Byzantine princesses were often married to foreign princes to help prevent attacks on the empire. It was also Byzantine practice to provoke one neighbor to attack another in order to prevent either one from attacking the empire.

Military strength. Part of the military strength of the Byzantine Empire lay in its good defenses. Despite the large size of the empire, it could be defended with a fairly small army. Regiments were assigned to the various districts of the empire, where they kept watch and defended the frontiers.

After the Muslims became a threat in the 600's, the Byzantines developed a good navy. Byzantine ships used battering rams, but the sailors' chief weapon—a "secret weapon"—was a flammable liquid called Greek fire which they hurled at enemy ships to set them on fire.

Economic strength. The east had always been the wealthy part of the Roman Empire. The wealth of the region was based on agriculture, manufacturing, and trade. Constantinople was the heart of the empire. Its advantage lay in its location. Situated on the border of Asia and Europe, it was at the entrance to the Black and Mediterranean seas (see map, this page).

Merchandise from all parts of Europe as far away as Sweden and overland from China and India poured into the markets of Constantinople. There and throughout the empire, the government regulated trade and manufacturing to produce large tax revenues. The taxes were used to pay government officials and the army and to build great public buildings.

The Christian Church

As you have read, the patriarchs of Rome, Constantinople, Alexandria, Antioch, and Jerusalem were important figures in the early Christian Church. In time, Rome and the pope came to

185

Egyptian Christian Cloth

The power of the Byzantine Empire helped Christianity to spread throughout the lands around the Mediterranean Sea. There were even Christian converts in Egypt. Copts, as Egyptian Christians were called, adopted aspects of Christian art that had developed in Italy and Byzantium. These they combined with traditional Egyptian style, which resulted in a unique art of their own.

In this ancient woven fabric we see an excellent example of Coptic art. Gazing out from the cloth is an elegant Byzantine lady. She is surrounded by a series of waves. This spiral design is one of the oldest in Mediterranean culture. It was in use as a decorative form long before the time of Jesus. In the circles on the four sides are ducks. This was typical of the decoration used by early Egyptian artists, who portrayed all kinds of animal and plant life.

The face of the lady, stylized and two-dimensional, is similar to the early portraits on Egyptian coffins and mummy cases. However, the lady's headdress, jewels, and robe look very much like the mosaic picture of a Byzantine empress in an early Christian church in Ravenna, Italy.

have supreme authority in the west. However, this authority was not recognized in the Byzantine Empire. There the patriarch of Constantinople came to be the most important Church leader.

As time went by, two branches of the Church developed. They drifted apart partly because of doctrine and partly for political reasons. The split became final in 1054, when the pope and the patriarch at Constantinople excommunicated each other. The Church in the west eventually became known as the Roman Catholic Church. The Byzantine Church eventually became known as the Eastern Orthodox Church.

The Christian faith was of overwhelming importance to the Byzantines. They were keenly interested in matters of dogma, that is, the major beliefs of the faith. The Byzantine faith was a source of both weakness and strength for the Byzantine Empire. Conflicts over dogma tended to divide and weaken the empire. One such conflict helped to make possible the easy Muslim conquest of Egypt and Syria. (You will read more about the Muslims in the next chapter.)

In the heart of the empire—the region around Constantinople—the Byzantine Church provided the basis for a kind of patriotism that strengthened the government. The people accepted the emperor as head of the Church with little question. The emperor insisted upon religious unity, a policy that meant all opposition to Byzantine dogma was strictly forbidden. Christian groups who disagreed with the emperor were later willing to accept rule by the Muslim Arabs.

Byzantine culture

The Byzantine Empire performed a great service for civilization. Its scholars did not produce much that was original, but they did preserve and pass on classical learning—the learning of ancient Greece and Rome. For a thousand years, while Western Europe was struggling to develop a new way of life, Constantinople was the center of a brilliant civilization.

The Byzantines not only preserved the culture of the Mediterranean world but also carried it beyond the borders of their empire. An example of Byzantine cultural influence was the work of two brothers, Cyril and Methodius, who lived in the 800's. As missionaries they worked to convert to Christianity the Slavs of central and eastern Europe, including the Balkan region. The Slavs had no written language, and Cyril wanted them to be able to read the Bible. He created an alphabet which later became the Cyrillic (sih·RIL·ik) alphabet after further changes were made. The Slavic peoples of central and eastern Europe still use the Cyrillic alphabet or one derived from it.

The missionary work begun by Cyril and his brother Methodius was successful, and the Church later elevated them to sainthood. The Balkan Slavs were converted to Byzantine Christianity in the 800's. The Eastern Slavs converted in the 900's. Great numbers of these people still follow the Byzantine faith.

Art. Byzantine art is noted for its use of color and ornamentation. In the markets of Constantinople, artists and traders sold tapestries that were luxuriously embroidered in gold. There were also enamels framed in gold, delicately carved ivory, and jewelry made of bronze inlaid with silver.

Byzantine art primarily glorified religion. The walls and ceilings of churches were covered with murals. Floors, walls, and arches were bright with colored **mosaics**—pictures or designs formed by inlaid pieces of stone, glass, or enamel. Both painting and mosaics were used in **icons**—small religious pictures set up in churches or homes, or carried on journeys as aids to devotion.

The subjects of this art, whether angels, saints, or martyrs, were quite formal and displayed an otherworldly appearance. This formal style was designed to inspire reverence and to emphasize the importance of renouncing the pleasures of this life to prepare for the life hereafter. The calm, meditative faces were similar to Buddhist art in their purpose. The placing of a particular image, fresco, or mosaic in certain locations in the church indicated how important the person shown in the work of art was in Church doctrine. For example, some image of Christ was always placed in the dome of the church.

Architecture. Architecture, especially religious architecture, was the greatest of Byzantine arts. The finest Byzantine building—indeed, one of the architectural masterpieces of the world—is the church of Santa Sophia (meaning "holy wisdom") in Constantinople.

Santa Sophia, begun in 532, was built by order of Justinian. It is a huge building. The ground plan, in the form of a cross, measures 240 by 270 feet (73 by 82 meters). The interior, lighted by windows in domes and side walls, was marvelously decorated. Every available surface was covered with murals, mosaics, stone carvings, and metal work. The pulpit was inset with ivory, silver, and jewels. The patriarch's throne was solid silver.

The central feature of Santa Sophia is a huge dome, 165 feet (50 meters) high. It rests on massive columns instead of walls and has a half-dome at either end. Byzantine architects were the first to solve the difficult problem of placing a round dome over a rectangular building.

When Santa Sophia was completed in 537, one Byzantine writer said that it was a church "the like of which had never been since Adam, nor ever will be." The church was solemnly consecrated by Justinian himself. As he first entered Santa Sophia, he exclaimed, "O Solomon, I have outdone thee!" He was referring to the famous temple of King Solomon described in the Bible.

The preservation of Roman law

Of all the Byzantine contributions to civilization, the greatest was probably the preservation of Roman law. Early in his reign the Emperor Justinian ordered his scholars to collect and organize all Roman law. The entire collection is known as the *Corpus Juris Civilis* (Latin for "Body of Civil Law"). It is also called Justinian's Code. It is in four parts called the *Code,* the *Digest,* the *Institutes,* and the *Novels.*

The *Code* was a collection of Roman laws, omitting repetitions, inconsistencies, and statutes dealing with Roman religion. The *Digest* was a summary of the writings of the great Roman legal experts, organized alphabetically by ideas. The *Institutes* was a textbook on the basic principles of Roman law. Justinian's own laws were published in the *Novels.* In Western Europe, Roman law was studied chiefly from the *Digest* and *Institutes.* Justinian's Code forms the basis of many modern European legal systems.

Decline of the empire

In the 1000's the Seljuk Turks, originally a nomadic people from central Asia, captured most

(continued on page 190)

The Byzantine Empire

The Byzantine Empire lasted more than 1,000 years after the Roman emperor Constantine moved his capital to Constantinople in 330 A.D. It reached its greatest glory under Emperor Justinian in the early 500's. Constantinople (above) grew into one of the world's most splendid cities. Its population exceeded one million when this picture was painted in the 1400's.

Constantinople reflected the great importance of religion in Byzantine life. Nowhere in the city was this importance more evident than in the church of Santa Sophia (above right). Its graceful domes and towers seemed to dominate the city, reminding its citizens of their religious beliefs and of their duty to pray. The wealthy among the faithful used beautiful prayer books like the one shown here (right). Its gold and jewels depict the archangel Michael.

Santa Sophia was built on the orders of Emperor Justinian (left) and his wife, Empress Theodora (above left). When Justinian became emperor in 527, he named Theodora his joint ruler and shared authority with her. Theodora's influence helped Justinian to retain his throne when revolution threatened during his reign.

of Asia Minor. This area was a vital part of the Byzantine Empire. When the Turks prepared to attack Constantinople, the Byzantine emperor appealed to the west for help. As you will read in Chapter 13, help came in 1096 and 1097 with the First Crusade. Europeans recaptured western Asia for the Byzantines. The Fourth Crusade, however, became an attack on the Byzantine Empire, and Constantinople fell to the invading crusaders in 1204.

After half a century of Western rule, the Byzantines recaptured the city. The empire was reorganized and continued to exist for nearly two centuries, but it was never able to regain its strength. A new Asiatic people, the Ottoman Turks, rose to power. In 1453 they captured Constantinople, and the Byzantine Empire at last came to an end.

CHECKUP

1. IDENTIFY: Justinian, Greek fire, patriarch of Constantinople, Slavs, mosaics, icons, Santa Sophia.

2. Using the maps on pages 184 and 185, describe the area of the Roman Empire in the west that Justinian had conquered by 565 A.D. Name the peoples that were affected by these conquests.

3. What sources of strength enabled the Byzantine Empire to survive as long as it did?

4. What did Cyril and Methodius contribute to the civilization of central and eastern Europe?

5. Name and explain the four parts of Justinian's Code.

2

The Kievan states had strong ties with the Byzantine Empire

A vast plains region stretches across eastern Europe and central Asia. It extends southward from the Arctic Ocean and the Baltic Sea to the Black and Caspian seas, and eastward from the Carpathian Mountains in Europe to Manchuria in eastern Asia. It is divided north to south by the long range of the Ural Mountains. These mountains separate the continents of Europe and Asia. Because the two continents actually form one great land mass, they are sometimes referred to as Eurasia.

The European part of the vast plains region is generally known as eastern Europe. It is geographically defined by three mountain ranges—the Urals in the east, the Carpathians in the west, and the Caucasus in the south (see map, opposite). Much of eastern Europe consists of grassy plains called **steppes.** These grassy plains roll on for miles without trees. The soil of the grassy steppes is very black, very fertile, and very good for farming, especially in the area now known as the Ukraine.

The steppes are crisscrossed by a number of rivers that provide good transportation within the region. The Dvina River and the Vistula River flow directly into the Baltic Sea. The Dniester (DNYES·tur), the Dnieper (DNYEH·pur), and the Don flow into the Black Sea. The Volga and Ural rivers flow into the Caspian Sea.

Slavic and Viking influences

The southern part of eastern Europe has been inhabited since Neolithic times. Greek merchants traded with the peoples north of the Black Sea. Later the area was the scene of many migrations, often caused by barbarian invasions from Asia. Beginning in the 200's, much of eastern Europe was settled by Slavs. Because they were peaceful and had only a loose political organization, they were often ruled by invaders, including the Huns, the Avars, and the Magyars.

During the 800's new invaders came into eastern Europe. They were Vikings from Scandinavia, and they came more as traders than as conquerors. In the fall of the year they would sail up the rivers from the Baltic Sea and from Lake Ladoga (see map, opposite). When winter came, they would put their ships on large sleds and haul them overland to one of the rivers that flowed into the Black Sea. In the spring, when the ice melted, they would sail southward to trade in the Black Sea region. They would return to their homeland by retracing their route.

The Kievan states

Several cities grew up along the Viking trade routes. One of them was Novgorod (Russian for "new fort"), south of Lake Ladoga. Another was

Kiev (kee·EV), on the Dnieper River. Kiev prospered. With its strategic location, it controlled the rich trade route that extended from Constantinople and the Black Sea to the Baltic Sea and northern Europe (see map, this page).

In the 860's the people of Novgorod were threatened with conflict. According to legend, they asked Rurik, a Viking, to restore order. Soon Rurik, his princes, and their successors became rulers of a large region around Novgorod. Kiev grew to be the most important of several principalities in the region. For this reason historians group the principalities together as the Kievan states.

The Kievan states developed links with Constantinople and the Byzantine Empire. The people of the area were converted to Byzantine Christianity beginning in the 900's, and they gradually adopted Byzantine traditions and cultural links. Many historians trace the roots of modern Russia to the Kievan states.

In the early 1000's Kiev was as strong and as wealthy as any Western European capital of the time. Its greatest period came under Yaroslav I, called Yaroslav the Wise, who ruled from 1019 to 1054. During his reign the first law code in the area was compiled. It remained in force in parts of the region until 1550.

KIEVAN STATES TO ABOUT 1200

Kievan States about 1200

Viking Trade Routes

0   500 miles
0   500 kilometers

The Kievan economy

The most important economic activities in Kievan society were agriculture and trade. The majority of the people were farmers. Trade, mainly with Constantinople, was controlled by the upper classes. The fact that the bulk of the people lived by agriculture is indicated by the names this society chose for the months of the year. Each month is named for the main task that is performed at that time—for example, the month when trees are cut down, the month when trees are dried, and so forth.

Agriculture. The Kievan states were divided into various agricultural regions. In the north was the forest zone known as the **taiga** (TY·gah). Here rainfall was abundant, but the cold temperatures meant that the growing season was rather short. Only about four months of the year were suitable for growing crops, and the need for speed encouraged the use of cooperative labor. Everybody in the family had to work day and night to complete the required tasks. Yet the taiga region was also rich in natural resources. The forests, for example, offered wood for building and for trade. The taiga was also a source of iron and salt.

Farther south and east, in the steppes region, rainfall was more limited and vegetation was more sparse. But here the climate permitted a growing season of six months, giving the people

connections

Spices

When you have a bowl of chili, do you realize you are eating food seasoned with the same spices that the Incas in Peru used 2,000 years ago? At almost every meal you are enjoying the taste of a spice—ginger in ginger ale or gingerbread, oregano in tomato sauce, anise in licorice, mint in peppermints, and cinnamon on toast.

Over 800 years ago the Aztecs in Mexico ground and mixed hot chili peppers with other spices and made chili powder. Today hot peppers are used throughout the world. In tropical countries legend says that hot food stimulates the liver and brings good

health. Chili peppers are often used in Southeast Asia, especially in the Chinese provinces of Szechuan and Hunan.

We get almost the same zing found in chilis from pepper. The black peppercorn is the whole berry, picked while it is green and spread out to dry. White pepper is made from the core of the ripe berry. This spice was originally grown on the western coast of India and was brought to Europe by traders.

When Rome was sacked by barbarians in 410 A.D., the ransom they demanded included pepper as well as gold and silver. Pepper was later used as money, and longshoremen had to have their pockets sewn up so they would not steal it from the ships they were unloading.

In the 1400's spices from the East were in great demand in Europe. As a result, explorers began to search for new and faster routes to bring pepper and other spices from India to Europe. Columbus was looking for such a route to India when he sailed west and landed on Santo Domingo.

As trade has become international, so has the taste for foreign dishes and flavors. Today, spices are sold all over the world, as in this market in the Middle East (left).

enough time to sow, cultivate, and harvest their crops of grain. In this area, farms were run by hardy, independent individuals who did not depend on cooperative labor for their success.

Trade. Agricultural goods and wood, iron, and salt from the taiga were traded, along with various items that were highly valued in Constantinople. The most important of these products were fur, wax, honey, animal hides, flax, hemp, burlap, and hops. In return, the people of the Kievan states obtained wine, silk, religious art objects, spices, precious stones, steel blades, and horses from the Byzantines. From Western Europe they received textiles, glassware, and metals.

Agricultural and trade regulations were part of the first law code, called *Pravda Russkaia*. It established penalties for moving land boundaries. It also used a farming unit as the basis for taxation. A single agricultural unit worked by a family was called a "plough," which became the basic unit on which taxes were imposed.

Kievan social classes

In the varied economy of the Kievan states, different social classes emerged. The highest ranks included the local prince and his family. Below this level was the local nobility, which usually had at one time been related to the ruling family. These nobles became a distinct group known as the **boyars.** The boyars became involved in trade, and as trade grew, towns became an important part of the society. In the towns lived both artisans and merchants who devoted themselves entirely to trade.

Another important group in Kievan society was the Byzantine clergy, who not only performed religious rituals but also ran schools, hospitals, and other charities.

The largest portion of the population, however, consisted of peasants. These were the people who lived in small villages and provided the agricultural output of the Kievan states. The people were divided into two categories—the free, who could move wherever they wanted, and the bonded, who had to remain in a particular place with a particular boyar.

In the Kievan states the majority of the peasants were free. Only later were they all to be tied to the land—that is, they all became serfs. Nevertheless, even in this period no peasant had any influence or position in society as an individual. Each one was considered only a part of the extended family, which was the basic unit in agricultural society.

Government and religion

In the Kievan states, government was in the hands of a ruling prince. Sometimes the prince was advised by a council of boyars. An important institution was the *veche,* or town meeting. Here all heads of households would meet in the public marketplace at the request of the prince. They would consider such matters as a call to war, a dispute between princes, or a special emergency law proposed by the prince. The *veche* was widely used in both Kiev and Novgorod in the period of the Kievan states.

In 988 Vladimir, then the ruler of the Kievan states, converted to Byzantine Christianity and imposed baptism on all his subjects. Many people continued to recognize ancient gods of nature and the spirits of their ancestors as objects of worship. The Byzantine Church, however, became increasingly important as a spiritual force. Many new saints were canonized by the patriarch of Constantinople, resulting in a stronger attachment to the Byzantine Church.

The Church was further strengthened by the founding of new monasteries, which soon became centers of social services, education, and artistic expression. The best indication of the growing popularity of the Church—and its more permanent place in the cultural lives of the people—was the shift from wood to stone in the construction of churches and monasteries.

Religious feelings and subjects dominated Kievan culture in this period. Epic poetry and historical chronicles were written. They dealt with wars and the personal tragedies associated with war. The major outpouring of literature, however, was in religious hymns and sermons. Icon painting, which began in the Kievan period, became the most distinctive Byzantine art form, and it is exclusively religious. There was no attempt to create perspective or a three-dimensional quality. In this practice the Kievan people followed the Byzantine tradition, which interpreted the second of the Ten Commandments.

This Commandment read: "Thou shalt not make unto thee any graven image." The Commandment was interpreted to mean that any art resembling sculpture was forbidden. Thus mosaics, frescoes, and icons—which were two-dimensional—were the only correct representations of religious subjects.

1. IDENTIFY: Eurasia, steppes, Vikings, Rurik, Yaroslav the Wise, taiga, *Pravda Russkaia*, plough, boyars, *veche*.

2. LOCATE: Arctic Ocean, Baltic Sea, Black Sea, Caspian Sea, Carpathian Mountains, Ural Mountains, Caucasus Mountains, Dvina River, Vistula River, Volga River, Novgorod, Kiev.

3. What were the differences between the northern and southern agricultural regions in the Kievan lands?

3. Describe the social classes in the Kievan states.

4. What ties did the Kievan states have with the Byzantine Empire?

3

The Mongols established a vast empire in Eurasia

After the rule of Yaroslav I, Kiev declined in power and wealth. The rulers of Kiev gave their younger sons outlying towns to rule as independent princes. These princes and their descendants fought among themselves and with the ruler of Kiev itself. Kiev's trade fell off because of raids by the Pechenegs, Asiatic peoples who controlled the region to the south of Kiev. Trade also fell off because the Italians were developing new trade routes in the Mediterranean Sea.

A group of princes eventually united in 1203 to capture and loot Kiev, ending its prosperity. As these princes fought among themselves, new invaders appeared. These new invaders were the Mongols from Asia.

The Mongols came from the Asian part of the vast plains region west of the Urals. You have already read in Chapter 8 about the huge Mongol Empire established in China. You will now read about the conquests of the Mongols in Eastern Europe and of their impact on Kievan society.

The Mongols in Eastern Europe

The Mongols first attacked Eastern Europe in force in 1237. Kievan resistance was not strong enough to hold back the fierce attack. By 1240 all of the Kievan states had fallen to the Mongols. The Mongols who overran Eurasia belonged to the Empire of Kipchak—the Golden Horde. They pushed on across the Carpathian Mountains into Hungary and across the plains into Poland, defeating the Hungarian and Polish armies. Then the Mongol leader learned of the death of the ruler who had succeeded Genghis Khan. He rushed back to the Mongol capital in central Asia to use his influence in the choice of a successor. Although terribly damaged by war and savage plundering, Hungary and Poland were spared continuing Mongol rule. The Kievan region, however, remained under the Mongols until the late 1400's.

The Mongols who had conquered the Kievan Rus were interested only in collecting tribute from the people. As long as the tribute was paid, the Mongols allowed the people to live under their own princes and keep their own religion and customs. The Mongols themselves grazed their flocks on the steppes north of the Caspian Sea and the Sea of Azov, where they had little contact with the Slavs. The Mongols established their capital at Sarai on the lower Volga River, far from Kiev and the area's other cities.

During the time of Mongol rule the Slavs of Eastern Europe were out of touch with Western Europe. Lithuania and Poland took territory from the northern part of the Kievan states in the late 1300's, forming a kingdom that was unfriendly to the Rus. Religious conflict also was present. The Poles had been converted to Western Christianity. The Eastern Slavs clung to their Byzantine faith, which set them apart from both the Poles and the Mongols. The Eastern Slavs, including the Rus, grew suspicious of Europeans and their influence.

While the Mongol Empire remained united, the Eastern Slavs traveled overland to China and brought back goods and ideas.

Eastern Slavs

In the Middle Ages, the civilization of the Eastern Slavs centered around a dominant church and strong religious traditions. The eastern, or Byzantine, form of Christianity swept through the Kievan states. The Eastern Slavs, including the Rus, saw themselves as the true heirs of early Christianity.

Consequently, all great events that took place in the medieval Kievan states were seen in a religious framework. When the city of Novgorod, for example, maintained its independence in the 1000's against the powerful princes of rival cities, the events were portrayed in religious terms (right). An awesome army approaches. It is beaten back, however, with the help of a sword-yielding angel.

Even the Mongol conquest in the 1200's, led by Genghis Khan (below right), did not alter the people's religious zeal. The monastery (below), with its onion-shaped domes, was built in the 1300's. It remains in active use to this day.

Sacred Icons

As Christianity spread into the Kievan states region in the 900's, the people were baptized and told to destroy their pagan idols. Holy pictures, or icons (from *eikon,* the Greek word for portrait), were hung in their lavish new churches. Gold- or silver-painted backgrounds made the icons easier to see in dimly lit interiors. Icons were also carried by troops marching into battle. In this icon from Kiev we see three popular Byzantine saints: St. Vassilios; the eloquent St. John Chrysostomas; and St. Grigorios Theologos, who was often shown shedding blood into the sacrificial chalice or cup.

Despite their flat, two-dimensional style, icons conveyed both individuality and a sense of godliness. Byzantine artists were expected to lead pure lives to demonstrate this feeling of holiness. Only then were they worthy enough to transfer God's goodness to men and women.

Later, when the empire broke up into independent parts, trade with East Asia declined.

Society and culture under the Mongols

The Mongol rule in Eastern Europe displaced Kiev's dominance in the region. Small new city-states and principalities emerged. The government of each had to obtain the approval of the Mongol overlord of the entire region. Taxes in the form of forest products were paid to the Mongols. In return, the prince of each new state was guaranteed peace and the right to rule.

Some foreign trade continued, but under the Mongols there was more internal trade. Agriculture once again provided only for subsistence, with output entirely for local or family consumption. The northern city-states of Novgorod and Moscow enjoyed a kind of semi-independence because they were farther away from the Mongol capital at Sarai.

The local landlord had the authority to collect taxes and to administer justice. Peasants had two primary obligations to their landlords—labor at specified times and a payment either in money or in goods. The second obligation was considered the more important of the two. Since peasants in the north often received their land directly from the government, their taxes were paid directly to the government. Those who had been enslaved by the Mongols performed personal services for their lords. Generally they did not work the land.

Although the Mongols were only a small ruling class, they did influence Kievan society in a number of ways. They built some important roads and improved methods of taxation and communication. They left some of their words in the language that came to be called Russian. The most important cultural development—the growth of the Church—took place despite the Mongol presence, not because of it.

The rise of Moscow

Mongol rule grew weaker in time and the princes of the area became more independent. They made themselves absolute rulers in their own regions. As trade declined, farmers and peasants became the only productive group in the region, supporting everyone else. The princes bound these workers to the land as serfs.

During the 1300's the city-state of Moscow, or Muscovy, became the strongest in the territory, partly because of its cooperation with the Mongols. Prince Ivan I, who ruled from 1325 to 1341, was rewarded with the title of Grand Prince. His power was increased further when the chief patriarch of the Orthodox Church moved from Kiev to Moscow.

By the time of Ivan III, Grand Prince from 1462 to 1505, Moscow was powerful enough to refuse to pay tribute to the Mongols. Mongol rule was thrown off in 1480. Ivan III united many other states in the area and emerged as an autocratic ruler—the first ruler of an independent state that was now called Russia.

The growth of the Church

As in Western Europe, the Church in Russia continued to expand its landholdings, primarily through gifts from people who saw these donations to the Church as a guarantee of spiritual salvation. By 1500 as much as one fourth of all cultivated land in Russia was in the hands of the Church.

During the Mongol period the Orthodox Church became increasingly independent of the patriarch of Constantinople. In 1448 the metropolitan of the Orthodox Church in Moscow was confirmed without the authority of Constantinople. The final break with Constantinople occurred in 1589, when Moscow's metropolitan was crowned patriarch and given equal rank with those of other Eastern Orthodox Churches.

Important theological support for the independence of the Russian Church was gained through a revision of the history of how Russia had been Christianized. St. Andrew, one of the original twelve disciples of Jesus, was now said to have brought the religion to Russia directly from Jerusalem. Moscow was now looked upon as the "third Rome." In 1510 a Russian abbot wrote that the first Rome had fallen becaue of heresy and the second Rome (Constantinople) because of infidels. The third Rome (Moscow), he said, was destined to be the final one that would bring light to the whole world.

This new confidence affected Russian art. Magnificent stone churches with ornate decorations were built. The Cathedral of the Assumption in Moscow exemplifies the artistry and religious fervor of the period. The church has the domed-roof style so popular in both the Byzantine and Russian cultures. Every inch of the interior walls was covered with some form of art work. There were sparkling chandeliers and candles in every alcove. The highest central dome was covered with the face of Christ. The cathedral's overall beauty and magnificence was designed to produce a strong mystical response from the people.

Some leaders of the Church objected to religious experiences that involved all of the senses. Instead they wished to emphasize contemplation and a search for inner spirituality. This group of Church leaders objected to the worldly possessions of the Church, whether they were icons, landholdings, or comfortable monasteries. They believed monks should be poor, work hard, and reject the pleasures of this world. They were called "nonpossessors," and they wanted the Church to be independent of the government.

A Church council in 1503 declared that the beliefs of the "nonpossessors" were in error. As a result of this decision the Church was preserved, and added support was given to those leaders who opposed any reforming tendencies. In the future any attempt to reform or change the Church in Russia could be interpreted as the work of the devil.

CHECKUP

1. IDENTIFY: Pechenegs, subsistence agriculture, third Rome, nonpossessors, Ivan III.

2. LOCATE: Sea of Azov, Lithuania, Poland, Moscow.

3. What were some of the reasons for the area's isolation from, and suspicion toward, Western Europe?

4. How did the Mongol rulers maintain control over the Kievan territories?

5. What were the two obligations of the peasants to their landlords?

6. How did Muscovy become independent from Mongol rule?

CHAPTER REVIEW

| 750 | 500 | 250 | B.C. | A.D. | 250 | 500 | 750 | 1000 | 1250 | 1500 | 1750 | 2000 |

527–565	Rule of Byzantine Emperor Justinian
532–537	Building of Santa Sophia
800's	Viking invasion of Eastern Europe Creation of Cyrillic alphabet
1000's	Invasion of Asia Minor by Seljuk Turks

1019–1054	Rule of Yaroslav I
1054	Christianity splits into Roman and Eastern Churches
1204	Fall of Constantinople to crusaders
1240–1480	Mongol rule in Eurasia

1325–1341	Rule of Ivan I
1453	Fall of Byzantine Empire
1462–1505	Rule of Ivan III in Russia

CHAPTER SUMMARY

During the thousand years following the fall of the Roman Empire, three great empires went through rather different developments in the border area of eastern Europe and western Asia.

The Byzantine Empire's entire history took place during these years. A brilliant and sophisticated civilization, it was the chief preserver of the heritage of the ancient world in the West. It kept alive the traditions of Roman law and Greek and Roman literature. It also developed its own distinctive Christian Church and its own cultural forms. Although the empire was under constant pressure from its Muslim neighbors, it survived until the 1400's, and its cultural influence has continued in eastern Europe to this day.

The main inheritors of Byzantine traditions were the Kievan states. This region stretched across thousands of miles and created a flourishing society based on agriculture and trade. It adopted the Orthodox Church, which became essential to its educational, charitable, spiritual, and cultural life.

The Kievan states were easily overrun by the Mongols, who had already conquered China and who established in the 1200's the largest empire the world has ever seen. Despite some influence from the Mongols, on the whole, local institutions and culture continued in the same directions as before. As Mongol control weakened, the beginnings of a strong state, centered on Moscow, started to emerge in the 1500's.

CHECKING WHAT YOU KNOW

1. Match each government listed at the left with the appropriate descriptions at the right. Use each government as often as necessary.

   a. Byzantine Empire
   b. Kievan states
   c. Mongol Empire
   d. Muscovite Russia

   1. Justinian Law Code established.
   2. Princesses married to foreign princes to help prevent attacks on the government.
   3. Mongols established control.
   4. The *veche* used to settle disputes.
   5. First Russian law code compiled.
   6. Ivan III united territories into Russia.
   7. Semi-independent city-states developed.
   8. Rulers gave younger sons outlying towns to rule independently.
   9. Government regulated trade and manufacturing to produce large tax revenues.

2. Describe Byzantine art, architecture, and law. What features of Byzantine culture were adopted by the people who eventually formed Russia?

3. In eastern Europe, how did the Viking trade routes affect the growth of cities such as Kiev?

4. What effects did the Mongol invasion have on the Kievan states?

5. How did the Russian Orthodox Church branch out from the Eastern Orthodox Church? Explain how the Eastern Orthodox Church in the Kievan-states region was strengthened during Mongol rule.

PRACTICING YOUR SKILLS

1. **Understanding chronology.** Indicate the correct time period for each of the following events.

300–600	900–1200
600–900	1200–1500

   a. Mongols capture Kiev.
   b. Justinian rules the Byzantine Empire.
   c. Yaroslav I rules.
   c. Eastern church splits from the Roman Catholic Church.

2. **Making categories.** Place the following items into one or more of these four categories: cultural achievement, economic system, political institution, religious contribution.

   a. Justinian's Code
   b. mosaics and icons
   c. nonpossessors
   d. *veche*
   e. plough
   f. names for the months of the year
   g. subsistence agriculture
   h. Santa Sophia
   i. third Rome
   j. *Pravda Russkaia*

3. **Using maps.** (a) On an outline map of the present-day Soviet Union, trace the rivers mentioned in this chapter. Check the body of water into which each river flows. Note whether it might freeze in the winter and what access to the rest of Europe is provided by that body of water. Which rivers might be most important for transportation?

(b) Using the maps on pages 191 and 172, compare the territories of the Kievan states with the Kipchak Empire (Golden Horde).

   1. What areas overlap?
   2. What territory of the Kievan states is not included in the Kipchak Empire?

RELATING PAST TO PRESENT

1. Use either *The Statesman's Year-Book* or a world almanac from your library to obtain a list of products that the Soviet Union and Turkey import and export today. Compare these lists with what was traded by the Byzantine Empire and the Kievan states.

2. Visit a Greek or Russian Orthodox Church and a Roman Catholic Church. Write a report on the types of art, architecture, and decorative pieces you were able to observe. Try to explain any similarities or differences you observe between these modern churches and the description of the churches in this chapter.

INVESTIGATING FURTHER

1. Using encyclopedias or books on the Byzantine Empire, prepare a report on the emperor Justinian. Include in your report a description of his life and his accomplishments.

2. The building of Santa Sophia was begun over 1,400 years ago during the reign of Justinian. Look at the pictures of Santa Sophia in this chapter. Using encyclopedias, prepare a report on the construction of this massive and beautiful structure.

3. Interview people from Eastern Europe (Greek, Russian, Turkish, Ukrainian) for information on the celebrations of special religious occasions—Christmas, Easter, weddings, birth of a child, funerals. Report your findings to the class. Compare this information to your own experiences on similar occasions.

CHAPTER

(570–1707)

10

Islam Became a Powerful Force from Spain to India

The next of the major religions of the modern world to appear was Islam. Founded by the prophet Muhammad in the 600's A.D., it spread from his homeland of Arabia with extraordinary speed. Sweeping around the Mediterranean in one direction, and into India in the other direction, it captured the fervent support of millions of people in just a few decades.

The success of Islam was due partly to military conquest. Indeed, Muhammad preached at the founding of the new faith that the followers of Islam—known as Muslims—must fight for their beliefs. "The sword is the key of heaven and hell," he said. However, he also offered simple spiritual teachings, encouraging people to lead humble, generous, and tolerant lives. This was a powerful message for many who were seeking religious faith to guide their lives.

As Islam spread, it encouraged the establishment of well-organized and vigorous states. Economic and cultural life flourished. Islamic philosophers, scientists, and artists created works that were to have considerable influence on Western as well as Muslim culture.

After the first wave of expansion in the 600's and 700's, Islam settled into more stable patterns, holding on to its gains. In the 1300's the Turks appeared. These were an aggressive people who were to create a powerful Islamic empire in the 1400's and 1500's.

Farther east, the advance of Islam had pro-

A Muslim praying at an ancient mosque

found effects on Indian society and culture. Muslims first entered India in the 700's, but it was not until the 1100's that they attempted a major conquest. By the 1230's they controlled all of northern India. They dominated the area and persecuted the Hindus until the 1500's, when a new empire—the Mogul Empire—was founded.

THE CHAPTER SECTIONS

1. Islam and the Muslim Empire spread outward from Arabia

2. Muslims created an advanced civilization

3. Muslim and Mogul rulers brought important changes to India

1

Islam and the Muslim Empire spread outward from Arabia

While the Byzantines were ruling Asia Minor and the Balkan region, a new empire—the Muslim Empire—was taking shape to the south and east. The Muslims, like the Byzantines, developed a civilization that far surpassed that of Western Europe for centuries. It began in Arabia.

Arabia and the Arabs

South of the Fertile Crescent lay the great peninsula of Arabia (see map, page 202). Most of it was a desert plateau whose scanty vegetation could support only herders and their flocks of sheep. These Arabs, who lived as nomads, were called **Bedouin** (BED·oo·in). They were organized into tribes, each under the absolute rule of a sheik, or chief.

Some coastal regions of Arabia, with greater rainfall, could support more people. Here towns grew up. The Arabs who lived in these centers were traders. Goods from Asia and Africa were brought to the port of Jidda, then taken overland to Mecca, the starting point of a caravan route running north to Syria. The Arabs who lived in towns had a higher level of culture than the nomadic Bedouin.

The life of Muhammad

Muhammad, the founder of Islam, was born in Mecca around 570. He was orphaned at an early age and spent his youth in poverty. Having little formal education, Muhammad probably never learned to write. He became a camel driver and a caravan trader.

While still a young man, Muhammad began to think seriously about religious and ethical problems. At that time the Arabs worshiped many gods. Through meditation and prayer, Muhammad became convinced that there was but one Supreme Being, one God, whom he called Allah.

When he was about 40 years old, Muhammad had a great religious experience. He believed that the archangel Gabriel ordered him to preach to the Arabs to bring them religious purity. Muhammad did not claim to have any supernatural powers. He considered himself a prophet and teacher, like Moses.

Muhammad's preaching was bitterly opposed by the rulers of Mecca. Fearing for his life, he took his little band of followers to the nearby town of Medina. The event is known as the **hegira** (hih·JY·ruh), meaning "flight." It was such an important event in Muhammad's life that the date, 622, became the first year of the Muslim calendar.

In Medina, Muhammad made many converts and became the leader of the community. In a few years he returned to Mecca at the head of an army and captured the city. By a combination of wise policies, toleration, and force he converted many of the Bedouin tribes to his new religion. By 632, when Muhammad died, almost all Arabia had accepted Islam (see map, page 202).

The faith of Islam

The central belief of Islam is simple: "There is no God but Allah, and Muhammad is his prophet." Like most religions, Islam has a holy book and definite rules for its believers and emphasizes certain moral teachings.

The holy book of Islam is the **Koran** (meaning "recital"). It is a presentation of Muhammad's most important teachings and contains much that is also found in the Bible. All Muslims recognize the Koran as their sacred book. Because it was

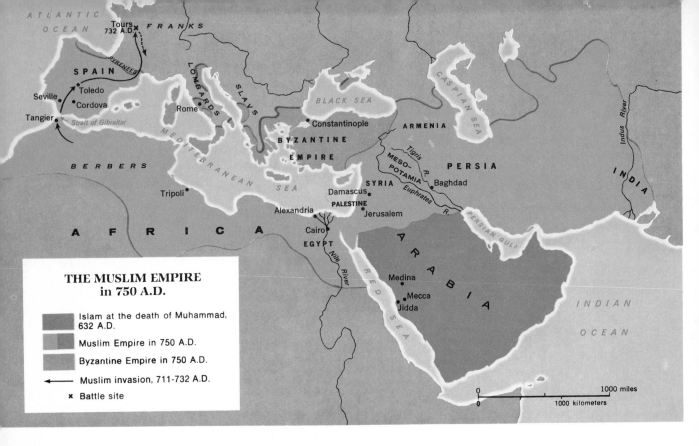

THE MUSLIM EMPIRE in 750 A.D.

- Islam at the death of Muhammad, 632 A.D.
- Muslim Empire in 750 A.D.
- Byzantine Empire in 750 A.D.
- ← Muslim invasion, 711-732 A.D.
- × Battle site

written in Arabic, and because its translation into other languages was discouraged, Arabic became a common language among Muslims.

A Muslim must meet five chief obligations—(1) Recite the words of witness: "There is no God but Allah, and Muhammad is his prophet." (2) Pray five times a day facing Mecca, the holy city of Islam. (3) If possible, make a pilgrimage to Mecca at least once. (4) Give alms—assistance—to the needy. (5) Fast from sunrise to sunset during the month of Ramadan—the ninth month of the Muslim year. The month is considered sacred because it was the month in which Muhammad had his vision of the archangel Gabriel and received Allah's instructions, which were later written in the Koran.

Muhammad required and emphasized the virtues of temperance, humility, justice, generosity, tolerance, obedience to authority, and courage. A Muslim man was allowed to have as many as four wives, but only if he treated them all with equal kindness. Slavery was permitted, but slaves had to be treated humanely. Muslims were forbidden to drink alcoholic beverages or to eat pig's meat.

In contrast to the teachings of Jesus, Muham-mad praised what he called the Holy War—fighting to defend or spread the faith of Islam. A fallen warrior was promised rewards in heaven.

Islam has no religious images because Muhammad forbade his followers to make representations of human or animal forms. The faith has no elaborate ceremonies. There is no formal priesthood, but there are men called **mullahs,** learned in Islamic faith and law. At a service in a Muslim temple, or **mosque,** the people pray together under the guidance of a leader. Friday is the holy day in the week when all male worshipers must gather at noon for sermon and prayer.

The spread of Islam

When Muhammad died in 632, an informal assembly of Muslims chose as his successor Abu Bakr (AH·boo BAHK·ur), who was his father-in-law and probably his first convert. He was called **caliph,** a word meaning "successor to the prophet." When Abu Bakr died, an assembly chose his friend and counselor Umar as caliph. To avoid civil wars over the succession, both Abu Bakr and Umar followed a policy aimed at conquering neighboring territory of non-Muslims. This policy diverted attention from the selection of the new caliph.

Fortunately for the caliphs, the Arabs had many opportunities for conquest in the 600's. Both the Byzantine and Persian empires were weak and unstable, partly because they had been fighting each other for years.

Arab conquests were made easier by the Arab policy toward conquered peoples. The Arabs were fierce and fearless in battle but generous in victory. Non-Muslims who surrendered could choose either to accept Islam or pay an annual tribute. However, anyone who refused was killed. Those who paid the tribute could keep their religion and customs.

In less than a century after the death of Muhammad, his followers had overrun Arabia, Palestine, Syria, Armenia, Mesopotamia, Persia, part of India, Egypt, and the rest of North Africa (see map, opposite). Then they took to the sea and eventually conquered the islands of the Mediterranean. They controlled the southern part of that sea for trade. They attacked Constantinople, but were turned back.

At the other end of the Mediterranean Sea, Muslims had more success in entering Europe. A people of North Africa called the Berbers were recent converts to Islam and eager for conquest. In 711 a general named Tarik led an expedition against the Visigoths in Spain, past the great rock that guards the strait between Africa and Spain. The rock was named Jabal-al-Tarik, the "Mountain of Tarik." Europeans have altered the name to Gibraltar.

Spain was an easy conquest. In seven years the Moors—the Muslims of Spain—had passed beyond the Pyrenees to raid the plains of what is now central France. In 732, near Tours, as you will read in Chapter 12, they were defeated by the Franks and driven back into Spain (see map, opposite). They ruled there for over 700 years.

Islam divides

Early in the history of Islam, rival groups began to emerge. Disputes arose over Muhammad's successors and over interpretations of the Koran. These divisions persisted into modern times.

One group, the Sunnis (SOO·nees), claimed that the only mediator between believers and Allah

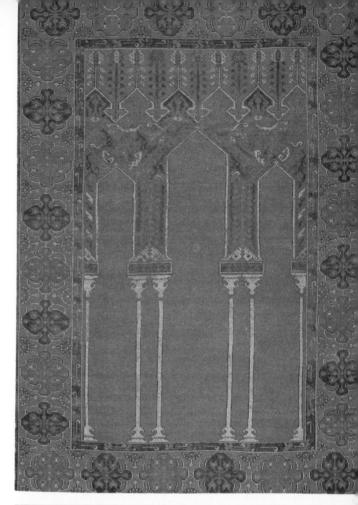

HISTORY THROUGH ART

Oriental Carpets

People have been weaving rugs for at least 3,000 years. Used at first as protections against cold, carpets soon had other purposes as well. They became symbols of wealth and popular items of trade. In Turkey, Persia, and central Asia, the making of rugs became a great art. Many Oriental carpets remain unsurpassed for their texture, richness of color, and beauty of design.

Through the centuries, Muslims who could afford them have knelt and prayed on beautiful rugs. During prayer, the rug must be placed on the floor so that the arch in the design points toward Mecca, Muhammad's birthplace. The prayer rug shown here was woven in Turkey during the late 1600's or early 1700's. Typical of almost all Oriental carpets, it has a border of wide and narrow strips and different geometric and stylized designs. The parts of the carpet have specific meanings. The color red, for example, stands for happiness and wealth. The trees above the arches are probably symbols of the tree of life.

203

was the Koran. Another group, the Shiites (SHE· ites), believed that a person, rather than the Koran itself, was the proper intermediary between Allah and believers. This person had to be a direct descendant of Muhammad and was called the **imam.** Shiites looked to the imam as having spiritual and secular authority. In countries where the Shiite sect took root, the supreme religious authority was also the leader of the government.

Basic to both Islamic groups was the interpretation of the Koran by the faithful. Since the Koran was regarded as having been directly dictated by Allah to Muhammad, it could not contain errors. One had to decide which verses or ideas took precedence over others in order to establish the authority needed for the particular community.

As Islam spread beyond Arabia, there were numerous opportunities for direct contact with Christian and Jewish concepts and practices. By the 700's Muslim mystics had adopted some Christian values—for example, voluntary poverty and the idea that one must have complete faith in God.

CHECKUP

1. IDENTIFY: Bedouin, Muhammad, Allah, hegira, Koran, Holy War, mullahs, Abu Bakr, caliph, Berbers, Jabal-al-Tarik, Moors, imam.

2. LOCATE: Arabia, Jidda, Mecca, Medina, Pyrenees, Tours.

3. List the major beliefs of Islam. Describe the five chief obligations or duties of a Muslim.

4. How did Muslims treat the non-Muslim peoples they conquered?

5. Explain the differences in beliefs and practices between Sunni Muslims and Shiite Muslims.

Muslims created an advanced civilization

Islamic government was tightly organized. Great authority was given to its rulers. Within the stable society that was created, both economic and cultural activity were encouraged and flourished.

Government and economy

At the head of the government was the caliph. He was the supreme civil, military, and religious leader of the whole vast empire. Although at first the caliph was elected, the position later became hereditary. The territory of the empire was organized into provinces, with Arabs in all the high positions.

Later the empire was divided into three parts. These were called caliphates, since each was ruled by a caliph. Headquarters for these were at Baghdad, in Persia; Cairo, in Egypt; and Cordova, in Spain.

The Arabs had long been traders, and Muhammad had praised and encouraged commerce. Goods from India and China were brought across the Indian Ocean to the Persian Gulf and the Red Sea, then overland to the ports of Syria and to Cairo and Alexandria in Egypt (see map, pages 272–73).

Manufacturing increased because of the demands of trade. The empire produced silk, cotton, and linen textiles, as well as tapestries and carpets. There were luxuries such as jewelry, perfumes, and spices. Metal products included objects made of gold, silver, steel, brass, and copper. Steel swords from Damascus in Syria and Toledo in Spain became world-famous. There was a great variety of pottery and glassware. Tangier in North Africa and Cordova in Spain made fine leather goods.

The Arabs encouraged the development of agriculture everywhere. Fruits, vegetables, and other products native to any part of the empire were introduced in other areas where they might grow.

Society and art

In Islamic families the father was the absolute head of the household. The family provided the individual with both economic security and physical protection. Age was respected, and there was a constant concern for the needs of the family as a whole. Islamic families were large and included parents, children, and grandparents, as well as aunts, uncles, and cousins.

The position of women in Islamic society was clearly defined. In the Koran is the pronounce-

Muhammad and Islam

Muslim civilization was initially inspired by Islam, the faith spread by the revered prophet Muhammad in the years before his death. One night, according to biographers of Muhammad, a host of angels, including the archangel Gabriel, appeared before the prophet (below). Gabriel washed the heart of Muhammad, whose face is traditionally shown with a veil. Muslim culture encouraged bravery, reverence for the faith, and creativity in the arts. The engraved silver inkwell (above) typifies the intricate style of Muslim decorations. The Muslims were also keen observers of the heavens (left). Muslim writings preserved many discoveries from the Hellenistic era that might otherwise have been lost.

ment, "Good women are obedient." A father or husband was responsible for a woman's behavior. Parents arranged marriages for their children, and a purchase price was paid by a groom to his bride. This money was kept by the bride in the unlikely event of a divorce. However, if either husband or wife had a complaint against the other, it would be heard before a religious court. If the problem could not be resolved there, a husband simply had to say "I divorce thee" three times. After a waiting period of three months, the divorce would become final.

Education in Islamic society was the responsibility of the family and the mosque. Subjects of required study were based on the Koran. The ability to speak well and to write were considered the standards for an educated person. A person with a superior intellect might memorize as many as 300,000 religious quotations.

Because Islamic law prohibited the use of the human form to depict God, the decorative arts and calligraphy assumed a special importance.

Islamic art often used geometric and floral designs. Pictures of people were used only to show daily activities such as hunting or fighting.

Advances in science

Though divided politically, the Muslim world remained united in one great civilization. The Arabs were willing to adopt the best ideas, customs, and institutions they found. They took the science and philosophy of Greece, Rome, and Asia and tried to combine them.

Muslim scientists wrote handbooks and encyclopedias on many subjects. Their geographers and navigators were the finest in the world. They perfected the astrolabe, an instrument used in navigation to determine the altitudes of planets and stars. From the Chinese, Muslims learned paper making.

Muslims added much medical knowledge to that of Hippocrates and Galen. At Baghdad in the early 900's, Rhazes (RAY·zeez), a Muslim physi-

connections

Medicine

Who was the first person in your life to set eyes on you? Most likely it was a doctor. Doctors and medicine have existed since ancient times. Early Egyptian books contain directions for setting fractures, and X-rays of mummies reveal healed bones.

The Greeks were the first people we know of who recorded their research so that it could be used by others. They had medical centers where people could go, first to be cured, and then to sacrifice to the gods in thanks. The Romans established a medical school in Egypt. There Galen, a famous Greek physician, made studies that were used in Europe for the next 1,300 years.

In the Middle East the Arabs developed their own interests in medicine. Legend says that in 765 A.D. the founder of Baghdad had an indigestion his doctors could not cure, so help was sought from a Persian med-

ical school. From then on, Persian doctors practiced in Baghdad and taught the Muslims about surgery performed with anesthesia. They started traveling clinics whose doctors went from place to place by camel, caring for the sick (above).

When the Muslims invaded Spain, they brought their medical knowledge to the Spanish universities. From

there it soon spread to other centers of learning. Monks in Italy had preserved the old medical knowledge, and now, combined with the new learning, medicine was taught at Italian universities. Farther north, young men studied medicine at the universities of Paris, Oxford, and Cambridge. These colleges are still well known for medical studies.

cian, wrote about surgery, diseases of the eye, smallpox, and measles. He compiled a huge medical encyclopedia which, translated into Latin, was used in Europe for centuries.

Muslims were excellent mathematicians. They perfected algebra as a science. Our word *algebra* comes from the Arabic words *al-jabr,* meaning "the reunion of broken parts." Another Muslim contribution to mathematics was the introduction of Arabic numerals to the Western world. As you have read, mathematicians of India developed this system, but the Arabs learned it from them and transmitted it to the West.

Arab scholars were particularly influential in the development of geography as a science. Map making was perfected not only from the observations of travelers but also from astronomical calculations. Arab geographical studies adapted a Hindu idea that each hemisphere of the world had a center, or summit, that was equally distant from the four cardinal points of north, south, east, and west. This theory was known by Christopher Columbus and was the basis of his conclusion that the earth was not flat.

Arab astronomers also studied astrology—the influence of the stars upon the lives of people. Many thinkers in Asia and Europe had studied astrology in the past and were to continue to do so for centuries, often influenced by Arab writings. Latin translations of Arab astrological studies were available by the 1100's.

Europeans came into contact with Muslim culture in two ways. One was through Spain. The cities of Cordova and Toledo were famous for learning, and Seville was a center of art and luxury. Christian and Jewish scholars brought Muslim learning from Spain into Western Europe. The other point of contact was the Crusades—the efforts by Europeans to recapture the Holy Land from the Muslims. You will read more about the Crusades in Chapter 13. In Palestine and other Muslim regions, the crusaders learned of the Muslim achievements. They took back ideas that greatly influenced European culture.

The great era of Muslim culture lasted from about 700 to 1000. After that, those who believed in "following the letter of the Koran" became powerful in the Muslim world. These people opposed free thought and foreign ideas. Invasions by Turks and Mongols also lowered the cultural level by disrupting trade and destroying cities. Muslim culture flourished longer in Spain because this region was more independent.

The Turks

The Seljuk Turks, as you have read, seized much of Asia Minor from the Byzantines during the 1000's. They also extended their rule into the Muslim territories of Syria and Mesopotamia. For the next 200 years there was a great deal of confusion in the eastern Mediterranean area. There were conflicts not only among Arabs, Turks, and Byzantines, but also between these peoples and Europeans in the Crusades.

Then, at the beginning of the 1300's, a new group of Turks appeared. They were called Ottomans after their first ruler, Osman. The Ottomans fought as well as the Seljuks and were much better at administering a government.

Ottoman success in battle and in government was due, in part, to a group of slaves called **Janissaries.** Most of the Janissaries were taken as children from conquered Christians. All of them were carefully instructed in Islamic beliefs and laws.

The Janissaries were a standing army of disciplined, trained infantry. As bodyguards to the Turkish rulers, the **sultans,** they became influential in the government. Encouraged by promotions for merit and by a system of rewards and punishments, they were at first a source of great strength. Later they gained much power and became a danger to the government.

During the first half of the 1300's, the Ottomans conquered most of northwestern Asia Minor. Then they invaded Europe and established their capital at Adrianople, northwest of Constantinople. By the late 1300's the way was open for them to move against Constantinople itself. Although they were halted temporarily by a new force, the Mongols, they eventually captured the city in 1453 and made it the capital of the Ottoman Empire.

The Ottoman rulers allowed non-Muslims to practice their own religion. Religious minorities were grouped into communities—called millets— and were allowed some self-government. They could establish their own schools, administer a civil government with its own courts, and collect taxes. However, any Muslim involved in a crime was not subject to the millet's authority.

As other national groups established trade contact with the Ottomans, they were also granted special privileges. In Constantinople, for example, Greeks and Armenians held a privileged position and were influential in politics and trade. You will read more about the Ottoman Empire in later chapters.

CHECKUP

1. IDENTIFY: caliphate, Rhazes, algebra, astrology, Seljuk Turks, Ottomans, Janissaries, millets.

2. LOCATE: Baghdad, Cairo, Cordova, Damascus, Toledo, Tangier, Seville.

3. What items were manufactured in various locations throughout the Islamic Empire?

4. Describe the organization of an Islamic family.

5. List what you consider to be the three most important scientific contributions of Islamic culture.

6. How did the Ottoman Turks use the millet system and the Janissaries in the organization of their government?

3

Muslim and Mogul rulers brought important changes to India

Islam also had profound effects far to the east. As you read in Chapter 7, Gupta rule in India came to an end in the 500's A.D. At that time the Huns invaded through the northwestern mountain passes and conquered all of northern India. Disorder and confusion followed, until the reign of a ruler named Harsha.

Harsha's rule

By the early 600's, when the Huns had been overcome, three warring states controlled the Ganges Valley. In one of them a leader named Harsha rose to power and built an effective army. When it was on the move, cavalry rode ahead of the infantry, which advanced with spears and large shields. Elephants wore armor plates.

Harsha came to power in 606 A.D. and in six years conquered what had been the Gupta Empire

(see map, page 146). He failed when he tried to push through the hill country south of the Narbada River to conquer the Deccan. He then settled down to govern his empire in northern India, which for a long time he did wisely and well.

A Chinese Buddhist pilgrim to India, Hsüan-tsang (SHU·AHN DZAHNG), wrote of the excellence of Harsha's early reign. The people were law-abiding, taxes were low, and living standards were high.

In the later years of his reign, Harsha had poor advisers and became cruel and suspicious. By 647 A.D. his rule had become so oppressive that his army assassinated him.

The Rajputs

After Harsha's death northern India split into numerous small states, ruled over by the Rajputs (RAHJ·poots). *Rajput* means "son of a king." The Rajputs were descended from tribes that had migrated from central Asia into northern India during the 400's and 500's. Claiming divine origins, the Rajputs intermarried with Hindus, adopted the Hindu religion with its caste system, and took control of the small states.

Rajput rule was generally stable. Literature of the time included codes of chivalry stressing respect for women, fair play in combat, and mercy for fallen warriors. There were also advanced law codes. Civil cases were decided on the evidence of sworn witnesses or written statements. A man's children inherited his property. His widow was entitled to support by her husband's family and was further protected by a dowry from her husband. The caste system was strictly enforced. Among ordinary villagers, marriages could be arranged only for people of similar caste status.

Northern Indians under the Rajputs took great pride in their land. One visitor wrote that Indians "believe that there is no country but theirs, no nation like theirs, no kings like theirs, no religions like theirs, no science like theirs."

The economy of northern India was based, as it had long been and would long remain, on agriculture. Goods were traded and services were offered both within the village and between villages. Overseas trade also flourished. All villagers had to give free labor to the government once a month.

Southern India

Southern India developed independently of northern India except for a short period in the 200's B.C., when most of it was part of Asoka's empire.

In the 600's A.D. a dynasty called the Chalukya (CHAH·look·yuh) held power in the Deccan. It was a Chalukya ruler whose army bravely defeated Harsha in 620 when Harsha tried to invade the Deccan.

Other dynasties ruled elsewhere in southern India along the east coast and in the southernmost region. All of these states of southern India were wealthy, mainly from trade. An Arab traveler of the 800's ranked a Deccan king with the caliph of Baghdad, the Byzantine emperor, and the emperor of China.

Muslims in India

Beginning in the 600's, you will recall, the Muslim followers of Muhammad began spreading out in several directions, inspired by zeal for the Islamic Holy War. In the early 700's Indian pirates from the Indus Valley began attacking Muslim ships. About 712 the Muslims struck back by conquering the Indus Valley (see map, this page). They organized the valley as a Muslim province but gave the Indians considerable freedom. Muslim criminal law applied to everyone, but Indian civil cases were tried according to Indian law.

The Muslims made no further conquests in India for about 300 years. Meanwhile Turkish Muslims had occupied the area now called Afghanistan, northwest of the Indus River. About the year 1000 they began invading India through the northwest mountain passes. One by one they conquered the small states of the Rajput princes. In battle the Indians always outnumbered the Muslims and made use of war elephants. However, the Muslims, adopting tactics originally worked out by Alexander the Great, used riders on horseback to turn the elephants back upon their own troops. In 1193 the Muslims occupied Delhi, and by 1236 they controlled all of northern India (see map, this page).

The Delhi sultans. One Muslim leader, Muhammad of Ghor, conquered a large area of northern India. When he died in 1206, one of his lieuten-

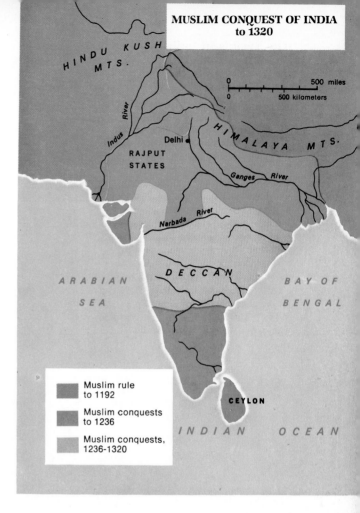

MUSLIM CONQUEST OF INDIA to 1320

- Muslim rule to 1192
- Muslim conquests to 1236
- Muslim conquests, 1236-1320

ants, formerly a slave, took over and founded a new line of rulers. Because they used Delhi as their capital, they are called the Delhi sultans. This dynasty lasted about 300 years. Many of its rulers were fanatical and cruel, but they did provide unity for northern India. Early in the 1300's, one of the Delhi sultans conquered the Deccan. By 1320, Indian resistance to the Muslims had collapsed throughout most of the subcontinent of India.

Tamerlane. The rule of the Delhi sultans was interrupted, first by civil wars and then by the devastating onslaught of the Mongol leader Tamerlane.

Tamerlane (Timur the Lame) claimed to be descended from Genghis Khan and was as ferocious as his supposed ancestor. Following the usual pattern of Asiatic nomad fighters, he created an army and established his power in central Asia, with his capital at Samarkand. Then, about 1380,

209

The Moguls in India

The most dramatic event in Indian history during the centuries of Muslim rule was the conquest of Delhi by Tamerlane. This ferocious warrior virtually destroyed Delhi. Yet he was represented in paintings as a sedate overlord, seated amid flowers (below right). His descendant, Babur the Tiger, captured Delhi again just over a hundred years later, in the 1500's, and founded a new dynasty of Mogul emperors. Babur sought to establish a reputation for justice. He is shown here receiving petitions (top right).

Perhaps the most famous creation of the Mogul period was the work of the emperor Shah Jahan. In the mid-1600's he built the Taj Mahal (below), a magnificent tomb for himself and his wife. Built of marble and studded with gems, it is one of the architectural wonders of the world.

he began a career of conquest. After defeating the Golden Horde north of the Caspian Sea, he led his army into India (see map, this page).

Tamerlane captured Delhi in 1398 and is said to have slaughtered 100,000 of its inhabitants. When his campaign was over, he returned to Samarkand, taking with him all of the surviving artisans of Delhi. The city was left to die. Tamerlane reportedly said of the deserted capital, "For two whole months, not a bird moved in the city." After returning to Samarkand, Tamerlane moved westward again. He captured and looted Baghdad and Damascus and massacred their inhabitants. His forces defeated the Ottoman Turks in a great battle at Angora (modern Ankara) in Asia Minor, capturing the sultan.

The Turks at the time were menacing what was left of the Byzantine Empire, and their defeat at the hands of the Mongols saved Constantinople for another 50 years. Tamerlane was planning a campaign against China when he died in 1405.

Tamerlane's successors in India ruled until 1450. At that time the Delhi sultans again gained power and maintained their rule until 1526.

Results of Muslim rule

Despite the interruption of Tamerlane and his Mongol successors, the long period of Muslim rule in India had important and lasting consequences. Most northern Indians and nearly all southern Indians were Hindus. At first the Muslims carried out ruthless, wholesale slaughter of Hindus. Later they were content to confiscate land, leaving village life to go on as it had for so long. Even so, many Hindus were converted to Islam, either to gain favor with the conquerors or to escape from the Hindu caste system.

Muslim and Hindu religious differences were profound. Hindu worship of many gods and of idols repelled the Muslims. The Hindu caste system contradicted Muslim belief in the equality of all people before God. Muslims introduced the seclusion of women—called *purdah*—into India. They also introduced the harem of several wives, which Hindus disliked. The cows so sacred to the Hindus were eaten by the Muslims, while Hindu fermented beverages were rejected by Muslims. Hindus used music in their religious ceremonies; Muslims did not.

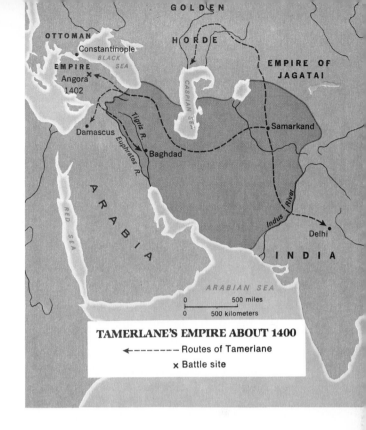

TAMERLANE'S EMPIRE ABOUT 1400
← - - - - - - - Routes of Tamerlane
✗ Battle site

The Muslims made several positive contributions to Indian life. They introduced a new and important language—Urdu. This language combines Persian and Arabic words with Hindu grammar. Indian architects learned from the Muslims how to build the dome and the arch. From China the Muslims imported paper, gunpowder, and the art of making porcelain.

The Mogul Empire

As the Delhi sultanate drew to a close, Rajput princes began struggling for control of India. Thus, as in the time of Tamerlane, India lay open to Mongol attack. It came under the leadership of the youthful and talented "Babur the Tiger," a descendant of Tamerlane. He captured Delhi with a small force in 1526 and brought the Rajputs under his control. He then set up the Mogul Empire (see map, page 212), which lasted until 1761. "Mogul" is a form of the word *Mongol*.

Babur died in 1530 but was succeeded by a series of energetic and talented rulers. They finally brought most of southern India, as well as northern India, under their control. After Tamerlane, Indians had reason to fear Mongol rulers. But instead the Moguls encouraged unity, orderly government, and the arts.

Babur's grandson, Akbar, was considered the greatest of the Mogul emperors. He reigned from 1556 to 1605. After conquering neighboring kingdoms in northern India, he gained more effective control of the region than did the Mauryas or the British in later centuries. One of his greatest contributions to Indian civilization was the fostering of toleration for all religions. Akbar repealed the special tax that non-Muslims had been forced to pay. He took a Hindu wife and encouraged Hindu as well as Muslim artists. These artists, supported by the royal household, developed delicate and colorful miniature paintings based on the styles of Persia.

The rule of the Mogul emperor Shah Jahan, from 1628 to 1658, was outstanding. He is best remembered for two famous buildings that he ordered built—the magnificent Taj Mahal at Agra and the Hall of Private Audience in the Red Fort at Delhi. The Taj Mahal was built as a tomb for Shah Jahan's favorite wife. In the cornices of the Hall of Private Audience are carved these famous lines:

> If on earth be an Eden of Bliss,
> It is this, it is this, it is this.

These great buildings of marble, inlaid with semi-precious stones, were enormously expensive. Their cost was a grinding tax burden on Shah Jahan's subjects. It took 22,000 workers 22 years to finish the Taj Mahal.

The Moguls attempted a grand synthesis of both Hindu and Muslim cultures. A mystic prophet, Nanak, attempted in the late 1400's to bring about a total union of these two faiths. Out of his teachings was born a new religion—the Sikh (SEEK) faith. This faith stressed loving devotion to one God and the brotherhood of all, an idea in conflict with the Hindu notion of caste. Nanak was the first guru (leader) of the Sikh faith. By the late 1600's the Sikhs had developed military power and became fierce enemies of the Mogul Empire and Muslims.

In 1658 Shah Jahan, who was ailing, was imprisoned by his son Aurangzeb (OR·ung·zeb), who then became Mogul emperor. A fanatical Muslim, Aurangzeb began a campaign of persecution against Hindus. He also executed the guru of the Sikhs when he refused to convert to Islam.

Aurangzeb's persecution led to revolts throughout his empire—by Sikhs and Rajputs in the north and among peoples in the Deccan. Thus, although the Mogul Empire reached its greatest territorial extent under Aurangzeb, it was seriously weakened by his policies of persecution. After his death in 1707, the empire began to disintegrate.

THE MOGUL EMPIRE
1526-1690

0   500 miles
0   500 kilometers

HINDU KUSH MTS.

Indus River

Delhi

RAJPUT STATES

Agra

HIMALAYA MTS.

Ganges River

Narbada River

DECCAN

ARABIAN SEA

BAY OF BENGAL

CEYLON

INDIAN OCEAN

Mogul Empire under Babur, 1526

Expansion of the empire to 1690

CHECKUP

1. IDENTIFY: Harsha, Hsüan-tsang, Rajputs, Chalukya, Tamerlane, Urdu, Babur, Akbar, Mogul, Shah Jahan, Nanak, Aurangzeb.

2. LOCATE: Delhi, Samarkand, Angora, Agra.

3. Why were Turkish Muslims and the Mongols able to conquer northern India?

4. What were the differences between Muslims and Hindus that led to antagonisms?

5. Why was Akbar considered the greatest of the Mogul emperors?

CHAPTER REVIEW

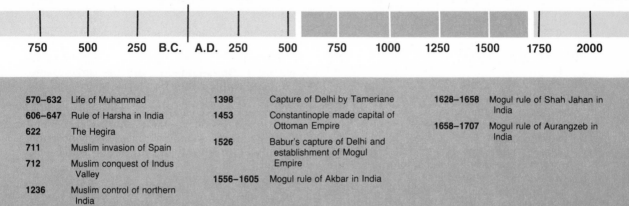

750	500	250	B.C.	A.D.	250	500	750	1000	1250	1500	1750 2000

570–632	Life of Muhammad	
606–647	Rule of Harsha in India	
622	The Hegira	
711	Muslim invasion of Spain	
712	Muslim conquest of Indus Valley	
1236	Muslim control of northern India	

1398	Capture of Delhi by Tamerlane
1453	Constantinople made capital of Ottoman Empire
1526	Babur's capture of Delhi and establishment of Mogul Empire
1556–1605	Mogul rule of Akbar in India

1628–1658	Mogul rule of Shah Jahan in India
1658–1707	Mogul rule of Aurangzeb in India

CHAPTER SUMMARY

The rise of Islam transformed much of Asia and parts of Africa and Europe. Its early believers spread the faith of Islam aggressively—the most rapid spread of a new religion the world has ever seen. Although the wave of conquests died down in the 700's, the Muslims made further advances in India 400 years later. A new expansionist force, the Ottoman Turks, rose to prominence in the 1300's and 1400's.

The faith of Islam emphasized humility and obedience. The result was the creation of stable states throughout the Muslim world. Economic activity was encouraged, and the Muslims became great traders, linking east and west. Their stable societies also promoted notable advances in science, philosophy, and art. Muslim contributions to medicine, mathematics, and geography, in particular, were to have considerable influence on later scientific work.

In India the Muslim presence was felt at first in the 700's. It became of major significance only in the 1100's, when the Muslims conquered northern India. Muslim rule brought new ideas, and even a new language, Urdu, to India. It also brought unrest and upheaval. The Muslims came as conquerors, and they persecuted the Hindus whom they found. The Mogul Empire that replaced the Muslims in the 1500's was much more peaceful. The Moguls encouraged a remarkable flowering of the arts, most notably represented in the building of the Taj Mahal.

CHECKING WHAT YOU KNOW

1. Match each individual listed at the left with a specific accomplishment at the right.

   a. Shah Jahan
   b. Tamerlane
   c. Abu Bakr
   d. Akbar
   e. Muhammad
   f. Tarik
   g. Rhazes

   1. Physician who wrote about surgery, smallpox, and measles.
   2. Founder of the religion of Islam.
   3. General who led an expedition against the Visigoths in Spain.
   4. Built the Taj Mahal.
   5. First convert to Islam; later became caliph.
   6. Mongol leader who captured Delhi.
   7. Mogul ruler who fostered toleration of all religions.

2. Discuss the effects of the Muslim conquest on Indian culture. Which effects do you think were positive? Which were negative?

3. Although the Muslim world was politically divided, it developed a high civilization. Using evidence from the textbook, explain how Muslims made progress in trade, art, math, science, and education.

4. Compare the treatment of non-Muslims under the Ottoman Turks to the treatment of non-Muslims under the Mogul Empire in India.

PRACTICING YOUR SKILLS

1. **Understanding chronology.** In each of the groups below, place the three events in chronological order.

   a. Battle of Tours.
      Hegira of Muhammad.
      Spain conquered by Muslims.
   b. Taj Mahal built.
      Delhi sultanate established.
      Harsha conquered Gupta Empire.
   c. Tamerlane conquered Delhi.
      Aurangzeb persecuted Hindus and Sikhs.
      Babur established the Mogul Empire.
   d. Muslim mystics adopted Christian values.
      Abu Bakr became first caliph.
      Ottoman Turks captured Constantinople.
   e. Use of Janissaries by Ottoman Turks.
      Translation of Arab astrology into Latin.
      Medical encyclopedia written in Baghdad.

2. **Using maps.** Describe in general the territorial changes that occurred in North Africa, southern and eastern Europe, and western Asia from about 550 to 1450 A.D. Use the following maps for comparison: (a) Justinian's Empire in 565 A.D. (page 185); (b) Muslim Empire in 750 A.D. (page 202); and (c) Tamerlane's Empire about 1400 (page 211).

3. **Using art.** Analyze the subject matter and style of the paintings of the Mogul Empire found on page 210. What do these paintings tell us of court life or of the political rulers? What glimpses of the daily lives of people do we have? What is the influence, if any, of religion upon this art form?

RELATING PAST TO PRESENT

1. In early Islamic culture women were expected to be obedient and were kept in seclusion. Discuss the roles of women today in Muslim countries such as Egypt and Turkey. Compare and contrast these roles with the more traditional roles of women in such countries as Saudi Arabia and Iran. Use current newspaper or magazine sources to obtain information.

2. Many words of the English language have been borrowed from other languages. The coffee tree was introduced in Arabia in the fifteenth century. Coffee made from the ground and roasted coffee beans became a favorite beverage of the Arabs. From Arabia, coffee spread to Egypt and Turkey and then to Europe and North America. Look up the word *coffee* in your dictionary. Where does it come from? What conclusion can you make about borrowed words and trade?

INVESTIGATING FURTHER

1. An important event in a Muslim's life is a pilgrimage to Mecca, the birthplace of Muhammad. In some years more than 400,000 Muslims visit the city. Using encyclopedias or magazine articles, prepare a report on the holy places in Mecca and the religious ceremonies that take place during the pilgrimage.

2. Use encyclopedias or biographies of Muhammad to prepare a report on his life and teachings. You may want to read portions of the Koran to learn about Muhammad's ideas on Allah, the duties of individuals, Paradise, and the Last Judgment.

3. Oriental carpets made in Persia (Iran) have long been popular in the United States. Research and report to the class on the history and background of these rugs. Include the following information in your report:

   a. how the rugs are made
   b. the importance of rugs in the Persian home
   c. how the subject matter and design are consistent with Islamic teaching

Among the books you might use are Walter Hawley, *Oriental Rugs: Antique and Modern* (Dover) and Murray L. Eiland, ed., *Oriental Rugs: A Comprehensive Guide* (N.Y. Graphic Society).

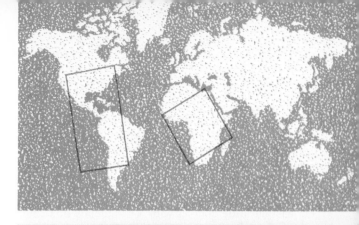

11

(1800 B.C.–1500 A.D.)

Africa and the Americas Produced Complex Civilizations

The northern strip of Africa, stretching along the Mediterranean from the Red Sea to the Atlantic, has already been seen as a place of some significance in the ancient world. Here the great civilization of Egypt and the rival to the young Roman republic, Carthage, created powerful states. Later the entire northern strip of the continent was conquered by Muslims. But the remainder of this enormous continent, the home of millions of people, emerged more slowly onto the stage of world history. The same is true of the varied lands and peoples of North and South America.

Before the 1500's there was almost no interaction between the peoples of Africa and the Americas and the peoples of Europe and Asia. As a result, we know much less about events before 1500 in Africa and North and South America than we do about events in Europe and Asia. The peoples of Africa and the Americas left few written records of their civilizations. Nor did they produce the extensive literatures that have come down to us from Greece, Rome, China, India, and Islam. We have had to reconstruct their history from physical remains—bits of pottery, bronze statues, pieces of cloth—and from ancient folk traditions. As a result, our knowledge of Africa and the Americas remains fragmentary and often uncertain. We cannot recover the full, detailed understanding of social, political, eco-

Early North American Indian cliff dwellings

nomic, and cultural activities that is possible in Europe and Asia.

That is not to say that Africa and the Americas had no history before the 1500's. Complex and active societies developed, remarkable for their political forms and their cultural achievements. Archeologists have uncovered the walls of elaborate cities and fortresses and the foundations of huge temples.

Although the peoples of Africa and the Americas had little contact with, or influence on, other parts of the world, they are essential to an understanding of human history. Their societies reveal both contrasts and similarities with European and Asian societies.

THE CHAPTER SECTIONS

1. Many methods uncovered Africa's early history

2. City-states and kingdoms arose throughout Africa

3. People migrated from Asia to the Americas

4. Empires rose and flourished in Mexico and Peru

Many methods uncovered Africa's early history

You have read about North Africa at several points in this book. Written records and surviving monuments and ruins provide evidence of the great civilizations that thrived in this region.

Less well known but equally important developments were taking place in the rest of Africa—the vast portion of the continent south of the Sahara Desert. This is a region beset with numerous obstacles of geography and climate. Disease-carrying insects and parasites abound. The natural features of the land, the vegetation, and climate vary greatly from one area to another. As a result, it is almost impossible for a people to migrate to unsettled lands and survive.

Yet, in the 2,000 or so years before 1500 A.D., much of sub-Saharan Africa—that is, the portion of Africa south of the Sahara—was settled. During this time the peoples of Africa made cultural and political advances that are all the more remarkable in light of the harsh environment.

The African land

The continent of Africa sits over the equator like a giant inverted bowl, uplifted in the middle and then dropping sharply to the ocean shore. The steep shoreline has few harbors. Most rivers, including the important Niger, Zaïre (zah·EER) or Congo, and the Zambezi, are navigable only for relatively short distances into the interior because of numerous rapids. The pattern of rainfall is irregular throughout much of Africa. In the north is the enormous Sahara Desert, and in the south the Kalahari Desert (see map, opposite). A vast area of relatively dry grasslands called **savannas** and an area of tropical rain forest are in the central and south-central areas of the continent. Mountain ridges, high plateaus, and immense lakes produced by ancient volcanoes are found in eastern and southern Africa.

The absence of harbors and navigable rivers and the diversity of climate and geography have made communication and contact among the peoples of Africa extremely difficult.

Rediscovering the African past

Writing was either unknown or at least not practiced in most of Africa. Lacking written documents, many scholars have concluded that Africa had no history. However, in the past several decades new methods have been developed to interpret unwritten evidence. Many important questions about early Africa remain to be answered. Nevertheless, it is now clear that Africa's past is as varied and rich as that of any land.

The spread of languages

Bantu is a family, or group, of closely related languages spoken in many parts of Africa. The question of where Bantu originated—and how and when it spread throughout Africa—has long puzzled people who studied Africa. New methods used by scholars have helped solve this puzzle. **Linguists**—scholars who study languages—have used computers and mathematics to compare the roots of words and common vocabulary. This technique is known as lexico-statistics, and it has helped solve the mystery of how Bantu spread throughout Africa. The spread of Bantu lan-

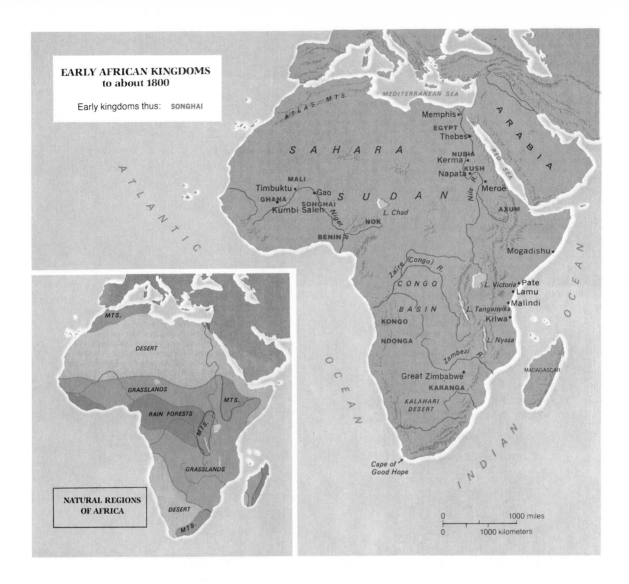

EARLY AFRICAN KINGDOMS
to about 1800

Early kingdoms thus: SONGHAI

NATURAL REGIONS
OF AFRICA

guages suggests that what occurred was one of the great population movements of human history.

An original "cradle land" of the Bantu language was in the southeastern region of the modern country of Nigeria. From there, beginning perhaps 2,000 years ago, Bantu-speaking people who were fishers and hunters began to migrate southward into what are the modern countries of Cameroon and Gabon.

From there they spread eastward. Moving into the forest, they settled in the vicinity of the Kasai River in modern Zaïre. And from there Bantu spread through central, southern, and eastern Africa. By the 700's A.D. Bantu was in use on the island of Zanzibar, in the Indian Ocean off the east coast of Africa.

Between the 1100's and 1400's, Bantu-speaking people in the vicinity of modern Uganda and western Kenya encountered peoples of another language family—the Nilotes (ny·LOH·tees), who spoke Nilotic languages. These Nilotic peoples were themselves migrating from a homeland on the upper reaches of the Nile River. In the period before 1500, the movements of people speaking Bantu and Nilotic languages established the patterns of settlement in sub-Saharan Africa. The great Bantu expansion took place over hundreds of years. It consisted of the gradual movement of

217

connections

Trumpets

As the music from the band drifts across the football field, the sound of the trumpets carries clearly into the stands (below right). This sound has been echoing around the world for a long time.

The first trumpets were made from hollow branches or reeds. They were used to frighten away evil spirits, to make mournful sounds at burials, and in the evening to appeal to the sun to return the next day. In some parts of Switzerland, the alphorn still sounds the evening prayer. In Rumania and Tibet men play long wooden trumpets at funerals.

In early Africa horns were used to send messages over long distances (below). In present-day Nigeria, horns are still sounded at celebrations (right). The Aztecs used trumpets to call the rain gods, and horns of silver, copper, and wood were used by the

Incas in Peru. They also had clay trumpets with bells shaped like jaguar heads.

Both the Egyptians and the Hebrews used metal trumpets to attract the attention of the gods. The Bible says that when Joshua fought the battle of Jericho, the blast of seven trumpets made the walls fall down. Today, at the ceremony to celebrate the Jewish New Year, the *shofar* is sounded. Carved from a ram's horn, it is a reminder of ancient days in the desert.

Trumpets as we know them are shaped like those used in Europe in 1500. Many musicians feel that the peak of trumpet performance has come only recently, with the great playing of America's jazz musicians.

individuals, families, and villages. Peoples settled for a period of time and then moved and resettled. It was a slow filtering of people throughout the African continent.

Oral traditions

The study of **oral traditions**—poems, songs, or stories passed by word of mouth from one generation to another—has been another source of information about specific African clans, villages, and dynasties.

Africans have always had a strong sense of their own history. Individual families or villages preserved the memory of important events by incorporating them into poetry or song. These were then passed on from one generation to another, with each generation adding to the tradition. In a similar way, in the royal households of African kingdoms, professional reciters were retained to record in song the important events of a dynasty. Much of this oral tradition has now been written down by anthropologists and historians.

Music and archeology

Other fields of scholarship have also helped to unlock the secrets of Africa's past. For example, scholars who study music have noted similarities in the design and tuning of xylophones in East Africa and Indonesia, in Southeast Asia. Thus, they have suggested that people migrated at some early date from Asia to Africa. Similarly, scientists have studied the spread to Africa of the banana, a plant that grows in Southeast Asia. And linguists have studied the Malagasy language, which is spoken on the island of Madagascar, in the Indian Ocean off the east coast of Africa. Malagasy has many words in common with languages spoken on the islands of Indonesia. From these fields of scholarship—the study of music, plants, and language—scholars have confirmed that people from Indonesia migrated to East Africa about 300 A.D.

Archeology has also added much to our understanding of African history. Excavation sites throughout the continent have shed light on daily life in early Africa. Much of this work has helped to support or disprove what has been learned from oral traditions and other sources.

The efforts to discover Africa's unwritten history have contributed to a new understanding of the complexity and achievements of the African past.

CHECKUP

1. IDENTIFY: savanna, Bantu, Nilotes.

2. LOCATE: Niger River, Zaïre (Congo) River, Zambezi River, Sahara, Kalahari Desert.

3. What geographic factors made contact difficult among peoples in the interior of Africa?

4. How do scholars determine the origin of a language like Bantu?

5. What is meant by the term "oral tradition"?

6. What nonwritten evidence can be used to identify migrations of people?

City-states and kingdoms arose throughout Africa

A remarkable variety of kingdoms, empires, and small city-states arose in the different areas of Africa before 1500.

The kingdoms of Kush and Axum

Although Egypt was the major ancient kingdom of the Nile, another African kingdom grew and flourished in its shadow. Along the Nile River, south of the major centers of ancient Egypt, lies an area known as southern Nubia. A source of gold, granite, and timber, it was also an important trade center. Here goods were taken by caravan from the Red Sea to barges on the Nile. And here arose a powerful kingdom, known as Kush (see map, page 217).

The kingdom of Kush traces its roots to the city of Kerma. Kerma was a trading center of southern Nubia that was developed by the Egyptians around 1800 B.C. Egyptian influence was very strong in this region. Nevertheless, the pottery, jewelry, and other ornaments uncovered in this region show that a distinctly local Nubian culture was emerging despite Egyptian influence.

Over the next centuries Kush emerged as a distinct kingdom. It had its own dynasty and a capital at Napata, a city upstream from Kerma. It was closely linked culturally and economically with Egypt. By the 1100's B.C. Kush had become virtually independent of Egypt, and about 750 B.C. it conquered Upper Egypt. For about 100 years—until the Assyrian invasion in 671 B.C.—a Kush dynasty ruled a unified Egypt.

With the Assyrian invasion, the Kush kingdom was briefly weakened. Following the Assyrian plunder of Napata in 591 B.C., the kingdom reorganized itself around a new capital at Meroë (MER·oh·ee). A new period of growth and cultural achievements began. Meroë was one of the earliest centers of iron working in Africa. Today, the remains of huge heaps of slag, the waste from smelting, rise out of the desert. These indicate the importance of this ancient activity. The Kush kingdom also controlled trade routes from the Red Sea to the Nile.

Kush civilization reached its height in the period from 250 B.C. to 150 A.D. Impressive pyramids and temples were built, and exquisite pottery and ornaments were crafted. A Kush language developed, but it remains undeciphered. The reasons for Kush's fall are not known. However, its decline seems to be connected to the rise of a rival state—Axum.

Situated in the Ethiopian Highlands south of Kush, Axum was strategically located to dominate the Red Sea trade routes into the interior of Africa (see map, page 217). As Kush declined, Axum became a major competitor for control of this trade.

Finally, in 325 A.D., King Ezana of Axum inflicted a crushing defeat on Kush. For the next 400 years Axum was able to control the African side of the Red Sea trade. The influence of Axum beyond this region, however, ended with the rise of Islam. By the early 700's A.D. Muslim forces were in control of both the Arabian and the African sides of the Red Sea.

East Africa and trade

Throughout history, communities along the East African coast participated in the trade of the Indian Ocean. The seasonal monsoon winds provided a reliable means of travel. Sailing vessels were developed, and trade routes that linked all shores of the Indian Ocean were discovered.

The earliest evidence of this trade comes from a Greek sailor's handbook in the years immediately after the birth of Christ. The handbook refers to the ancient port of Rhapta, which is believed to have been on the coast of modern Tanzania (tan·zah·NEE·ah). The sailor also writes of the various goods traded, such as hides, tortoise shells, ivory, and slaves. However, little more is known of this early period in Africa.

The spread of Islam to northeastern Africa also created favorable conditions for trade. Along the East African coast a golden age began, lasting from the 700's through the 1300's A.D. The opportunity to make money in Africa attracted merchant families, adventurers, and refugees from Arabia and Persia. They settled on islands and easily defensible spits of land, where they soon established trading centers.

The trade that flourished was widespread. African slaves were sent as far as China, and Chinese porcelain was sent to Africa. Over several generations, a unique African culture—Swahili—developed on the East African coast. The Swahili language was basically a Bantu language, but it was greatly influenced by Arabic and Persian. The Swahili were not a unified ethnic group, but were bound by their common pursuits—especially trade—and by the Swahili language.

Coastal city-states

No large kingdoms like Kush and Axum emerged on the coast. Instead, there arose a series of city-states that dominated coastal trade. The earliest of these were in the north—Mogadishu (mug·ah·DEE·shoo), Lamu, Pate (PAH·TAY), and Malindi. Gradually, commercial activity shifted southward. By the 1100's Kilwa, the most famous city-state, was the leading port along the African coast.

Under Kilwa's leadership, coastal culture flourished. Ibn Battuta (IB'n bah·TOO·tah), a famous Muslim traveler of the 1300's, described Kilwa as one of the most beautiful and well-constructed towns in the world. Recent archeological excavations have revealed the wealth and achievements of Kilwa. A massive trade center and a large mosque have been uncovered. The golden age of the coast lasted until the 1400's when the arrival of the Portuguese inaugurated a new age in Africa. You will read about this phase of African history in Chapter 16.

Central Africa and Great Zimbabwe

Kilwa grew as a port for the shipment of gold mined in central Africa along the Zambezi River. For centuries, gold and other goods had reached the coast from there, passing eastward through several small-scale trade networks that were based on the exchange of essential goods such as salt, tools, or cloth.

The growth of Indian Ocean trade after the 900's A.D. dramatically increased the demand for gold. With this increased demand came a consolidation of control over the mining and shipment of gold to the coast. The people who achieved this control were the Karanga. They first emigrated onto the plateau land of modern Zimbabwe (zim·BOB·way), in central Africa, about 850 A.D. Gradually the Karanga asserted control over local peoples and mining activities. Archeologists have located over 7,000 mine shafts, an indication of the importance of mining to the local economy.

There is little definite information about the Karanga people. They built fortified enclosures and were probably very wealthy and powerful. Great Zimbabwe, the largest and most famous of these fortresses, was the administrative and religious center of the Karanga state. It had walls 32 feet (10 meters) high and 17 feet (5 meters) thick, with some 900,000 large granite blocks.

Excavation of the site has revealed a rapid and seemingly mysterious decline in the 1400's. Scientists now believe that the area may have experienced an ecological disaster. One theory is that the population grew so quickly that local water and food resources were not enough, leading to starvation and decline. The kingdoms that succeeded the Karanga—the Mwene Mutapa (MWEH·nay moo·TAH·pah) and the Changamire (chahn·gah·MEE·ray), or Urozvi—survived into the era of European exploration.

Kingdoms and cultures of West Africa

In West Africa, between Lake Chad and the Atlantic Ocean, several important African societies developed. One of the earliest of these was

HISTORY THROUGH ART

Royal Figure from West Africa

The people of Ife, in what is now southwestern Nigeria, began making lifesize bronze heads over 600 years ago. The sculptures are magnificent examples of bronze casting. The beaded crown tells us that the head is of a king. The vertical lines represent ritual scarring—a practice still followed by some Africans. A beard and a moustache were attached to the holes around the mouth. After a king died, the bronze head was attached to a wooden body and carried about the city. The ceremony indicated that although the king was dead, the power of the office remained.

that of the Nok, a people who thrived between about 700 B.C. and 200 A.D. in what is now northern Nigeria. What little we know of Nok culture comes from the work of archeologists. Living in semi-independent villages, the Nok people were among the first to master the art of iron working. Fine examples of jewelry and distinctive terracotta sculptures have been found in excavated Nok ruins. This creative culture declined and disappeared after 200 A.D.

221

Africa's past in art

The products of African crafts workers and artists present a varied record of the continent's long past. The broken granite wall (below) is at Axum, in eastern Africa. The people of Axum, who were at the height of their power in the 300's and 400's, were fine builders. They perfected the art of dry-stone construction—that is, building without mortar. Axumite stone remains include irrigation systems and hillside terraces.

Benin, a kingdom in western Africa, flourished in the 1600's. The brass plaque (right) from Benin shows military leaders wearing helmets and decorated robes. From central Africa come the coiled basket (above) and the carved wooden mask (below right). Most masks of this sort were worn by dancers in religious rituals. For this reason, hundreds of them were seized or destroyed by early Christian missionaries.

The Nok artistic tradition reappeared in the bronze sculptures of Benin, a kingdom that prospered in the 1400's in what is now southern Nigeria. Possibly after the collapse of Nok, refugees made their way to this region, where the Nok heritage was preserved.

To the north and west of the Nok region, in an area between desert and savanna, three of the most famous African kingdoms emerged. These were the kingdoms of Ghana, Mali, and Songhai (see map, page 217). Knowledge of these kingdoms comes largely from oral tradition and from the writings of Muslim scholars. The wealth and strength of these kingdoms depended on control of the trade routes across the Sahara Desert. Salt, mined in the desert, and gold, extracted from the forest zone, were exchanged at the desert's edge. There, important commercial cities grew up and flourished.

Ghana was the earliest of these kingdoms. It traces its origin to the founding in the 200's A.D. of Kumbi Saleh, a trading village situated in the southeast of modern Mauritania. Ghana was at its peak in the 900's, but its period of prosperity was short-lived. In the 1000's Berber tribes, who had themselves once controlled trade in the Sahara, were stirred up by a Muslim religious revival and the preaching of a Holy War. They invaded Ghana. The kingdom never recovered from this attack and in 1203 ceased to exist.

The fall of Ghana was followed by the rise of a successor kingdom—Mali. This new kingdom came to power in the region that had been Ghana, as well as in vast areas to the north and west and along the upper Niger River. Under its ruler, Mansa Musa, who was in power from 1307 to 1322, Mali's power reached its peak. Musa supported education, the arts, and building. His capital, Timbuktu, was an important center of Muslim learning, visited by scholars from Egypt and Arabia.

Mali was weakened by disputes over dynastic succession. Nonetheless, it managed to maintain control over the desert trade routes until the 1400's. Then in 1468, Sunni Ali, leader of an area that had broken away from Mali's authority, captured Timbuktu. This began the age of the third kingdom—Songhai.

The kingdom of Songhai was centered on the important trading city of Gao (GOH). From there it controlled a kingdom even larger than that of Mali. Sunni Ali, its most important ruler, hoped to avoid a succession crisis after his death. Therefore, he established a government designed to ensure tighter control over his subjects. He also built a fleet of warships to enforce peace along the Niger River, which had become a major route of commerce. His policies made Songhai a powerful and efficient kingdom that continued to thrive until the late 1500's.

African societies

Despite the difficulties imposed by geography and climate, Africans succeeded in creating a high level of culture. They established powerful kingdoms and participated actively in local and international trade.

Most Africans lived in small, independent villages and were farmers or herders. Relationships of kinship, age, and sex provided the ties that bound the different societies together. Within this system women played a crucial role. As childbearers they assured the continuation of the clan. As laborers they performed much of the agricultural work. In Great Zimbabwe women worked in the mines.

Chiefs or elders usually exercised authority over the village. However, since land was plentiful and migration a real choice for those who were unhappy, a chief's rule had to be fair. The villages of Africa were closely bound to the agricultural cycles of planting and harvesting. Through the rise and fall of numerous kingdoms, the village survived as the basic unit of society and the economy. Its persistence makes it a vital part of the African heritage.

CHECKUP

1. IDENTIFY: Kush, Swahili, Karanga, Great Zimbabwe, Nok, Benin, Mansa Musa, Sunni Ali.

2. LOCATE: Kerma, Napata, Meroë, Axum, Kilwa, Lake Chad, Ghana, Kumbi Saleh, Mali, Timbuktu, Songhai, Gao.

3. What metals were mined in the ancient kingdoms of Africa?

4. Give evidence to support the idea that Ghana, Mali, and Songhai were powerful, wealthy kingdoms.

5. Briefly describe African village society.

3

People migrated from Asia to the Americas

From the beginning of history until about 500 years ago, the peoples of the Eastern Hemisphere and Western Hemisphere had almost no contact with each other.

Some Chinese missionaries may have reached Central America in the 400's A.D. Daring Viking explorers landed at several places on the coast of North America around the year 1000. However, accounts of their voyages were not well known, so the journeys were not followed up by others. Old European maps showed a vast blank space or fanciful islands where the Western Hemisphere lay. In fact that vast region of the world was already densely populated.

The great migrations

While the Ice Age still gripped the earth, people migrated from Asia to the Americas across what is now the Bering Strait, off the coast of Alaska (see map, page 812). This strait is the narrowest point between the continents of Asia and North America. At several periods in the past, there was a "bridge" of land there. Even when there was a water barrier, the strait was only a few miles across and could easily have been crossed by small boats.

There was neither a single large migration nor a continuous flow of people from Asia. Rather, there was a series of waves of different peoples on the move. Changes in the climate in Asia may, from time to time, have forced people northeastward and across the strait. From there they would move southward toward warmer climates. Finding some areas already inhabited by those who had come earlier, they would move on, looking for a favorable place to settle.

These migrations took thousands of years. The remains of some of the early people have been found and studied. Archeologists have found remains in western North America that may date back almost 30,000 years. The people were hunters who lived in caves and hunted the giant bison, or buffalo.

Some people moved into the eastern and central areas of North America. Others drifted farther south, through Mexico and Central America and across the narrow Isthmus of Panama. From there all South America was spread out before them.

About 14,000 years ago, some groups moved eastward into what is now Venezuela. However, the rain forests of the Amazon River basin made it difficult for people to penetrate farther into the eastern bulge of South America. Instead they kept to the western shoreline, pushing ever southward. Some groups settled in the Andes Mountains. Others kept moving until they could go no farther eastward into what are now Brazil and Argentina, or southward into what is now Chile.

The development of agriculture

The earliest traces of farming in the Western Hemisphere have been found in south-central and northeastern Mexico, along the coast of Peru, and in the southwestern United States. The first farmers planted sunflowers (for seeds), corn, beans, squash, and a variety of other crops. In the highlands of Peru the potato was the most important food. In South America and on the islands of the Caribbean, various root crops were planted, mainly manioc and other crops that were similar to sweet potatoes.

Farming began at about the same time in both hemispheres but was adopted more gradually in the Americas. The plow was not invented in the Americas partly because animals large enough to pull it did not exist there. For the same reason the wheel was not invented either. Without the plow it was not possible to plant crops on grasslands. As a result, farming had to be done on forested land that was first burned to clear off the trees. Fertilizers were also not known in this early period.

Nevertheless, agriculture was productive enough to support village life and the beginnings of towns. By the time of the arrival of Columbus in 1492, tribes as far north as the northeastern United States and Canada and as far south as Argentina were largely dependent on farming for their food supply. In Mexico and in the Andes Mountains, agriculture and food storage formed the basis of civilizations almost as advanced as those of Egypt and Sumer.

None of the inhabitants of the Americas learned to make iron. Copper was used only rarely to make tools. In a few places it was used for ornamental purposes. Gold and silver were widely known. Jewelry from the Americas amazed European artists and artisans when they saw it for the first time. Even though the higher civilizations of the Americas were limited to tools of stone and wood, they managed to build immense temples, palaces, and fortresses.

Earliest cultures

By about 1500 B.C. the peoples along the coast of Peru and in central Mexico were beginning to live in villages. In another 500 years ceremonial and trading centers began to appear. These centers were supported by the food surplus of many villages. The remains left at these sites are still largely mysterious because no written records accompany them.

The earliest of these cultures, in Mexico, is called the Olmec (OHL·meck). These people left giant stone heads and many objects made of jade. There are also signs that the Olmecs had developed a priestly class and worshiped a god who was represented by the image of a jaguar. In the highlands and the coast of Peru, a culture called Chavin (shuh·VEEN) developed about the same time. The Chavin also worshiped the jaguar.

Near the modern city of Oaxaca (wah·HAH·kah) in Mexico is Monte Alban, a high hill topped by ceremonial structures that may be as ancient as those of the Olmecs. Signs can be found there that human sacrifice was practiced. Both the Olmec culture and Monte Alban seem to have been devastated by war, possibly civil war, and the Chavin culture also abruptly disappeared.

In the first century A.D. the villages of the valley of Teotihuacán (tay·oh·tee·wah·KAN), a few miles north of Mexico City, joined together to form a large city. At its peak it had a population of almost 100,000. The center of the valley is dominated by two immense pyramids, the larger one 215 feet (66 meters) high. Like other pyramids in Mexico and South America, they were intended as altars.

At about the same time, another city, or perhaps a ceremonial center, was built in the highlands of Bolivia. This was Tiahuanaco (tee·ah·wah·NAH·koh), near the shores of a large lake.

INDIAN CULTURES OF THE AMERICAS

The temples at this site are astonishing for the size of the stones used, some weighing 100 tons (91 metric tons). Teotihuacán was destroyed by warfare sometime between 650 and 750 A.D. Tiahuanaco fell into a gradual decline during the same period.

The Maya

The most advanced culture of the Americas was that of the Maya. They occupied the tropical lowlands of southern Mexico and nearby areas of Central America considerably before 1000 B.C. (see map, this page). Their history for many centuries can only be guessed at. Possibly they had strong early connections with the Olmecs. Some time before 300 B.C. they began to build ceremo-

Early American cultures

Long before Europeans came to America, its people had
created works of lasting beauty. The ear ornaments (below)
were made by the Mochica people, who lived in what is
now Peru centuries before the Incas. Made of gold and turquoise and depicting bird-headed messengers, the earrings
probably belonged to someone of wealth and high rank. An
ordinary citizen—possibly a farmer—is represented by the
ancient clay figure (right) found in present-day Colombia.

The ruins (bottom) are at Chichén Itzá, a Maya center in
the Yucatán. In the foreground is a carving of a priest,
topped by a feathered serpent. This deity, Quetzalcoatl to
other Mexican Indians, was known to the Mayas as Ku-
kulcán. The temple in the background is dedicated to this
god. Like other Maya sites, Chichén Itzá was a ceremonial
center, peopled only during religious festivals.

nial centers with many small, steep pyramids. They were built with the most advanced architectural techniques found in the Americas at that time.

The Maya were advanced in the study of astronomy. They learned to predict solar eclipses and had devised a calendar more accurate than the one used in Europe at the time. The Maya developed a counting system that was based on the number 20 and included the zero. They invented a writing system that seems to include pictograms, ideograms, and phonograms. Much of the Maya script is still undeciphered, and nearly all of their manuscripts were destroyed by the Spaniards in later years. In fact the writing and arithmetic skill of the Maya seems never to have been put to practical use, but was used only for religious and commemorative purposes.

Although the farming techniques of the Maya were very simple, they produced a great deal of food with less effort than was needed by European farmers of the time. The Maya continued to live in villages and enjoyed a high standard of living. They supported noble and priestly classes. The religion of the Maya was complex, involving astrology and the worship of various and constantly changing gods.

In contrast to some of their neighbors, the Maya were a peaceful people who worshiped peaceful gods. Sometimes in periods of crisis, such as droughts, they would make human sacrifices to the gods, hoping for rain. However, this was not an important part of their religion.

Maya decline

About 800 A.D. the Maya civilization was suddenly stricken by some catastrophe. The population declined sharply and the ceremonial centers were abandoned. The agricultural methods used by the Maya may have worn out the soil. A foreign invasion may have overwhelmed them, or a peasant revolt may have overthrown the nobles and priests.

In fact all of the higher civilizations of North and South America declined at about the same time. In both regions there were migrations from north and south by groups with lower cultural achievements. For several centuries there was a decline in knowledge and invention. Warfare was intense and widespread, trade diminished, and people returned to living in villages.

CHECKUP

1. IDENTIFY: Olmecs, Chavin, Monte Alban, Maya.

2. LOCATE: Isthmus of Panama, Amazon River, Andes Mountains, Teotihuacán.

3. List the important crops grown in the Americas. What were three difficulties in farming that would limit productivity?

4. What minerals were extracted in the Americas? What mineral was lacking?

5. List three contributions of the Maya that prove they had an advanced civilization.

Empires rose and flourished in Mexico and Peru

The decline of the Chavin in Peru and the Olmecs and Maya in Mexico was followed by the rise of civilizations that were more elaborate than before. These civilizations developed systems of irrigation that were very extensive and effective. The availability of water for agriculture made possible the growth of very large populations in the highlands of Mexico and Peru. Cities grew to greater size. Gods of war came to be worshiped. Great empires were formed that brought thousands of villages and millions of people under the influence of a single ruler.

Early kingdoms

Central Mexico was invaded from the north by a people called the Toltecs (TAHL·tecks). They built a capital city at Tula (see map, page 225) and spread their influence as far south as the Yucatán peninsula by about 1100 A.D. In the Yucatán they encountered the Maya, who were rebuilding their culture. The influence of Toltec religion and designs is noticeable in the ruins of the chief Maya city of Chichén Itzá (chee·CHEN eet·ZAH).

Like the Maya, the Toltecs built pyramids. However, their art was not as advanced as the ear-

Later Indians of Latin America

"They will not let the work out of their hands until it is absolutely perfect." So said a Spaniard of the Aztec crafts workers he saw in Tenochtitlán in the 1500's. Much earlier, such a painstaking worker made the mosaic mask (right), thought to represent Quetzalcoatl. Equal care was taken by Indian weavers. The pouch (above), made by the Nazca people of Peru, displays rows of llamas. These animals, related to the camel, were among the few beasts of burden available to the Indians before the coming of Europeans. They may have helped carry goods to and from Machu Picchu (above right). High in the Andes near Cuzco, this Inca stronghold was never found by European explorers. Thus many of its sturdy houses and public buildings still stand, tributes to Inca skills in construction.

lier Maya art. The Toltecs extended trade much farther than had the Maya. They introduced the working of gold and silver, which they may have learned from people in the Andes Mountains. The Toltecs also spread the worship of their god, Quetzalcoatl (ket·sahl·koh·AT'l), the feathered serpent. The ruling class was the military, and Toltecs practiced human sacrifice in connection with their warfare.

In South America, along the northern coast of Peru, another important culture arose in the 1300's. This culture was known as the Chimu (chee·MOO). The Chimu irrigated an area that was, like Egypt, a desert. The greatest of their cities was Chan-Chan. The ruler of the Chimu kingdom was worshiped as a god.

Two other important cultures of South America at about the same time were the Chucuito (choo·KWEE·toh), in Bolivia, and the Chibcha, in Colombia. The Chibcha are most famous for the many beautiful objects of gold they produced.

The Aztecs

Around 1200 A.D. there were further invasions of central Mexico by peoples from the north. Unlike the Toltecs, these peoples were probably still hunters and seed gatherers at the time of their arrival. A number of these groups fought one another in central Mexico. Out of these struggles emerged the strongest group—the Aztecs.

The Aztecs had been wandering warriors, fighting for whoever would pay them. According to legend, their priests finally instructed them to settle where they should see a sign—an eagle sitting on a cactus and devouring a serpent. They finally saw the sign on one of a pair of islands in Lake Texcoco, in Mexico. There they built their city of Tenochtitlán (tay·noch·tee·TLAHN).

From about 1325 on, their power grew until the Aztecs were the dominant people in central Mexico. Conquered tribes paid them tribute in gold, turquoise, corn, animals, and slaves.

By building causeways and stone foundations, the Aztecs expanded Tenochtitlán to make room for great pyramid-temples, marketplaces, and palaces for the nobles and wealthy families. The city of Tenochtitlán may have had more than 100,000 inhabitants at its period of greatest power and prestige.

The Aztecs took over the inventions of tribes they conquered or traded with. They soon learned the use of metals, weaving, pottery making, the calendar, and mathematics. Their artisans produced very finely finished pieces of art.

The Aztecs perfected farming on **chinampas**— floating artificial islands in their many lakes. This was the most productive form of agriculture in the world.

Aztec society was dominated by the military. Warfare carried the most prestige and led to wealth and power. The Aztecs believed that the sun would not move in the sky unless human sacrifices were made to it. The god of war also demanded human offerings. The victims were captives from defeated tribes, and hundreds might be put to death each year. In 1478, the period when Aztec power was at its height, 20,000 victims were sacrificed.

Just as the great Aztec civilization had grown rapidly, so it was to fall in a very short time. In summary, the Aztecs built a major empire which exhibited outstanding accomplishments in the development of architecture, agriculture, education, and the arts.

The Incas

At about the same period that the Aztecs were building their civilization in Mexico, another group was creating a civilization in the Andes Mountains of South America. The religion of these tribes was based on sun worship. Their name—Incas—meant "children of the sun."

The Inca empire expanded steadily. By the late 1400's it extended along most of the west coast of South America and far into the Andes, covering much of the present-day nations of Peru, Ecuador, Bolivia, and Chile (see map, page 225). Like ancient Egypt, it was a state in which everything belonged to the Inca ruler, and everyone owed absolute obedience to him. Although he was an autocrat, his power was directed toward improving the empire.

The Inca capital was Cuzco (KOOS·koh), known as the "City of the Sun." The Incas built fortresses and irrigation systems and laid paved roads from one end of their realm to the other. Pack animals carried goods and swift runners brought news to the Inca capital. The rulers of the empire maintained storehouses and moved food supplies to vil-

North Americans before Columbus

America north of the Rio Grande was a sparsely populated region, most of whose people depended on hunting and fishing. The lively animals on the rock wall (above) were drawn hundreds of years ago in what is now Washington state. They may have been scratched in hopes of good luck on the hunt or in thanks after a successful kill. Eskimos of Alaska, who hunted such sea mammals as whales and seals, carved the wooden mask (below). Also of wood are the large carvings (left) made by the Tlinglit Indians of the northwest coast. The tall pillar, a totem pole, is a sort of family history. Legendary birds and other creatures represent spirit forces, important in the tribal past. Southwestern Indians were among the few in North America to lead the settled lives of farmers. A Pueblo potter shaped the fine vase shown here (above left).

lages when crops failed. Thus they were able to prevent local famines.

The rulers sought to eliminate tribal diversity in their empire. In order to pacify and colonize newly conquered lands, they transferred entire villages. They established a public school system that taught the Inca religion and history. The result was that the Inca language—Quechua (KECH·wah)—is still spoken today by millions of native people in five South American countries.

The Incas did not have a system of writing. They did keep records by means of the **quipu**—a kind of knotted string that was used to assist the memory. They were quite advanced in the practice of medicine, including the use of anesthetics and even brain surgery.

Both the Inca and the Aztec empires were brought to a sudden and disastrous end by the Spanish conquest, about which you will read in Chapter 16.

North Americans

In other areas of North America—that is, the United States and Canada—there were no major civilizations like those of the Maya, Aztecs, or Incas. There were many different cultures, however, and some were highly organized societies (see map, page 225).

A well-developed culture in what is now the United States was that of the Pueblo tribe of the Rio Grande Valley. These people were farmers who lived in permanent settlements. They used **adobe**—a sun-dried brick—to build communal houses for all the members of a community. Some of these houses were several stories high, and others were clustered together beneath overhanging cliffs so that they could be better defended.

On the northwest coast of North America lived several tribes whose economies were based largely on fishing. These peoples were also expert woodworkers and weavers. They were famous for their totem poles—great wooden carvings of people and beasts that symbolized tribal history.

An entirely different culture flourished in the vast plains region between the Rocky Mountains and the Mississippi River. Here tribal peoples lived by hunting the huge herds of wild buffalo that roamed over the land. The Plains tribes ate the meat of the buffalo, made clothing of its skin,

and used its hide to build their cone-shaped tents, called **tepees.** They were skilled fighters and placed a high value on deeds of bravery.

One of the highest cultures of North America flourished in the midwestern and southern regions of the United States. The peoples who lived there are sometimes called the Mound Builders because of the large number of earthen mounds they constructed throughout the area.

Most of the mounds were built as burial places. The tools, jewelry, and weapons found in them reveal that these peoples had highly developed artistic skill. Some of the mounds are in the shapes of animals. One in Ohio, the Great Serpent Mound, is more than 1,300 feet (400 meters) long. Building the mounds obviously took cooperative effort. Much mystery still surrounds them. Archeologists do not know what happened to the builders or why such building ceased.

On the eastern seaboard of North America were a number of related tribes. They had a farming and hunting economy, but also showed great skill and organization when they made war. They lived in walled towns and had a high level of political organization. Their common language was Iroquois (EER·uh·kwoy).

In the 1400's and 1500's, five of these tribes—the Cayugas, Mohawks, Oneidas, Onondagas, and Senecas—formed the League of the Iroquois. The League was established in an attempt to stop warfare among the tribes, and it lasted several hundred years. Its influence expanded to several other tribes. Some historians believe that if it had been allowed to develop unhindered, its peaceful influence might eventually have extended to all the North American tribes.

CHECKUP

1. IDENTIFY: Toltecs, Quetzalcoatl, Chimu, Chibcha, Aztecs, chinampas, Incas, Quechua, quipu, adobe, tepees, Mound Builders.

2. LOCATE: Tula, Yucatán peninsula, Chichén Itzá, Tenochtitlán, Cuzco.

3. What factors contributed to the growth of large populations in Mexico and Peru?

4. What were the methods of farming and distribution of food supply of the Incas?

5. What was the Iroquois League? How did its goals differ from those of the Plains people?

CHAPTER REVIEW

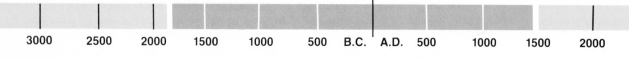

| 3000 | 2500 | 2000 | 1500 | 1000 | 500 B.C. | A.D. 500 | 1000 | 1500 | 2000 |

700 B.C.–200 A.D.	Nok people in western Africa	1300's A.D.	Beginning of Chimu culture in South America
250 B.C.–150 A.D.	Height of Kush civilization in Africa	1307–1322 A.D.	Rule of Mansa Musa in Mali kingdom in Africa
325 A.D.	Defeat of Kush by Axum		
800 A.D.	Decline of Maya civilization in Central America	1400's A.D.	Benin kingdom in Africa Inca empire in South America
850–1400's A.D.	Karanga state in central Africa	late 1400's A.D.	Height of Aztec power in central Mexico
900's A.D.	Height of Ghana kingdom in Africa	1400's–1500's A.D.	Iroquois League in North America
1100's A.D.	Toltec civilization in central Mexico	1468–late 1500's A.D.	Songhai kingdom in Africa

CHAPTER SUMMARY

A remarkable variety of societies arose on the African continent from ancient times through the 1500's. The great kingdoms of Kush and Axum dominated the interior of eastern Africa. On the coast, independent city-states, notable for trading, were established. And in central Africa, Zimbabwe controlled a large area. To the west, large kingdoms, such as Mali, were created. Within these large political structures, Africans lived primarily in small villages, though major cities and trading centers did appear. Some of these, such as Timbuktu, also became centers of great cultural creativity.

The Americas were settled by successive waves of migration from Asia. As agriculture and small towns developed, the first of a series of great cultures arose—the Olmecs of Mexico. The most advanced of these cultures was the Maya, occupying the area from southern Mexico downward. The Maya were building remarkable ceremonial pyramids by 300 B.C. and were notable for their knowledge of astronomy.

A great disaster struck the Maya around 800 A.D. They were later conquered by a new, though similar, people—the Toltecs. Finally, in the 1200's, two new powers arose—the Aztecs in Central America and the Incas in South America. They created brilliant civilizations that dominated the Americas until the 1500's.

To the north very different cultures existed in the various regions. North American tribes included the fishers of the northwest, the hunters of the plains region, the Pueblo farmers of the southwest, and the Mound Builders of the midwest and south. In the 1400's and 1500's, five eastern tribes formed the League of the Iroquois to reduce wars.

CHECKING WHAT YOU KNOW

1. Match each African area or culture at the left with a description at the right.

    a. Meroë
    b. Nok
    c. Karanga
    d. Ghana
    e. Mali
    f. Kilwa

    1. Built Great Zimbabwe.
    2. Terra-cotta sculptures led to later bronze sculpture of Benin.
    3. Early East African center of iron working.
    4. First West African kingdom to build up salt-gold trade.
    5. Timbuktu, the capital, was a center of Muslim learning.
    6. The most famous city-state for East African trade.

2. Match each American culture at the left with an accomplishment at the right.

    a. Maya
    b. Aztec
    c. Inca
    d. Olmec
    e. Toltec
    f. Chimu

    1. Developed a counting system based on 20.
    2. Irrigated desert along coast of Peru.
    3. Made giant stone heads and jade objects.
    4. Expanded trade and made objects of gold and silver.
    5. Were advanced in medical practices.
    6. Farmed on floating artificial islands.

3. What evidence supports the claim that the Maya were the most advanced culture of the Americas?

4. How does the use of metals and type of buildings reflect the accomplishments of a civilization? Give an example from one African and one American civilization.

5. What types of trade developed across the Sahara and along the eastern coast of Africa? What items were traded in the American civilizations? Who traded with whom? What similarities or differences in trade do you notice in all of these civilizations?

6. List the evidence of cross-cultural contact in ancient times between Asia and East Africa in the following areas:

   a. plants
   b. languages
   c. music

PRACTICING YOUR SKILLS

1. **Using maps.** Using information in this chapter, trace on the maps of Africa and the Americas the migration routes of the peoples who later established the great civilizations. What were the climatic and geographical obstacles that they had to overcome? What approximate dates are given for these migrations?

2. **Analyzing information.** Review the functions of the pyramid structures of the Maya, Toltecs, and Aztecs and the purposes of the large stone structures of the Karanga. What do these structures tell us about the cultures they represent?

3. **Making charts.** List the great kingdoms of Africa and the Americas. What reasons are given for their decline? Prepare a chart, listing the reasons in three categories: political, economic, and social. Which category has the most reasons?

RELATING PAST TO PRESENT

1. The Bush people of the Kalahari Desert and the Bantu-speaking peoples of East and South Africa live much the same way as their ancestors did hundreds of years ago. Use encyclopedias or history books on Africa to find out more about the culture of one of these groups.

2. Many English words have roots in Latin American cultures. Use your dictionary to find the origin of these words: chocolate, hammock, potato, quinine, tapioca, tobacco, tomato, avocado.

INVESTIGATING FURTHER

1. Basil Davidson has written several books describing ancient African kingdoms. Among them are *A History of West Africa* (Longman), *African Kingdoms* (Time-Life), and *The Lost Cities of Africa* (Little, Brown). Using these books as sources, prepare a report on one of the African kingdoms mentioned in this chapter. Discuss the following in your report:

   a. its form of government
   b. features of its economy
   c. religious beliefs

2. In 1911 Hiram Bingham discovered the lost city of Machu Picchu, part of the Inca Empire in the wilderness of the Andes Mountains. Read his account in *Lost City of the Incas* (Atheneum). Check other sources to determine if additional research has discovered new information about the purpose of this city, the organization of its society, the uniqueness of its buildings, or its methods of farming.

3. Form study groups to prepare reports on the Indians of North America. Each group can choose one Indian culture to research. Assign each member of the group a particular area of study, such as clothing, shelter, transportation, or religious beliefs. One source for your research is Alvin Josephy, *The Indian Heritage of America* (Knopf).

12

Feudal Lords and the Church Dominated Medieval Europe

As we look back from the present day to the collapse of the Roman Empire in the west, we can view it as a continuous process. The Roman Empire did not end with a sudden crash. Rather it fell apart a little at a time so that few people realized what was happening. A border fort would be abandoned. A legion would be withdrawn. Mail and news no longer came to a city. The aqueducts were not kept in repair and water was hard to get. Slowly, ever so slowly, what had been an empire lay in splintered ruins.

Gradually Roman culture died out. For example, people forgot how to construct buildings as the Romans had done. For those people who remained in the cities, temples and stadiums were often nothing more than a source of stones to patch up a house when it was near collapse. In Rome itself the beautiful buildings of the Forum and even the Colosseum were partly wrecked. Portions of them have been found in all parts of the city, where they were used to make repairs for a thousand years after the last emperor died.

The period following the collapse of the Roman Empire—between ancient times and the modern period—is called the **Middle Ages,** or the **medieval** period. (The word *medieval* comes from the Latin word *medius*, meaning "middle," and *aevum*, meaning "age.") This period is generally considered to have lasted from about the year 500 to about 1500 A.D.

The idea of calling this period the Middle Ages

St. Edmund, an Anglo-Saxon king

is a fairly recent one. The people of that time never thought of themselves as living in a "middle age," or indeed in any kind of age at all. They thought of human history as a chain of events from the Biblical era to their own time. In general, they did not feel that they were very different from their ancestors. They might wonder about some of the remnants of past glory that they saw here and there, but they had little understanding of the past. Yet they did develop new customs and distinctive institutions to suit the particular conditions under which they lived.

THE CHAPTER SECTIONS

1. Frankish rulers governed much of Western Europe for centuries

2. Germanic peoples from northern Europe conquered Britain

3. Medieval life was organized around feudalism and the manor

4. The Church had many roles during the Middle Ages

5. Kings and nobles struggled for power in France and England

6. Popes and emperors clashed over Germany and Italy

1

Frankish rulers governed much of Western Europe for centuries

When the Roman Empire fell apart in the 400's, Western Europe descended into anarchy and confusion. Government nearly ceased to exist, and invaders roamed about almost at will.

You have read how Germanic tribes, including Visigoths, Vandals, Burgundians, and Ostrogoths, overran Europe. These tribes set up kingdoms, but they did not create strong governments. The invaders were usually a small group ruling a much larger population by military force. Many groups were defeated, and others were absorbed into the native population without leaving much trace.

Some Germanic tribes, however, were destined to play greater roles in history. Of all these, the Franks were the most important. They first entered the Roman Empire in the 300's, near the mouth of the Rhine River. One source of their strength was that they spread slowly and permanently, never losing touch with their homeland in the Rhine Valley. They settled in the area of northern Gaul corresponding roughly to present-day Belgium and the Netherlands.

Clovis and the Merovingians

In 481 a ruler of great ability, Clovis, became king of one of the Frankish tribes. He and his successors were called Merovingians because Clovis traced his family back to an ancestor named Meroveg. Clovis was brutal, but an excellent military leader. Under his command his people conquered the other Frankish tribes and soon controlled all northern Gaul.

A few years after Clovis became king, an important event took place. Influenced by his Christian wife, he made a vow to accept her religion if he won a certain battle. He did win, and not only kept his vow but forced 3,000 of his warriors to be baptized. Clovis became a strong supporter of Christianity, and he and his Franks gained the support of the Church.

Later, Clovis conquered southwestern Gaul from the Visigoths. He thus ruled most of present-day France (which took its name from the Franks). Unfortunately for the Franks, however, Clovis was unable to pass on to his successors either his strong qualities of leadership or his united kingdom. In accordance with Frankish custom, the kingdom was divided among Clovis' sons.

The later Merovingian kings thought only of the pleasures and luxuries of palace life. One writer of the period tells of a Merovingian king who spent his time combing his long yellow curls with a jeweled comb. These kings left the business of governing to palace officials.

Although in theory there was only one Frankish kingdom, there were actually several because of the custom of dividing the kingdom among a monarch's heirs. In these Merovingian kingdoms, the chief of the royal household was called the Mayor of the Palace. These Mayors of the Palace often became the real rulers of the various Frankish kingdoms. In about the year 700, Pepin II, the

Reliquary of St. Faith

This golden image of St. Faith illustrates an important feature of medieval religion. It shows the devotion Christians had for the relics, or remains, of saints. St. Faith was a French girl who was killed during the last Roman persecution of Christians in the early 300's A.D. Five hundred years later, tales of miracles she had performed began circulating. People flocked to the church in France where some of her remains had been taken. Christians hoped to see more miracles. As time passed, the church gathered a large collection of gold, jewels, and other valuables that pilgrims had donated as offerings. In about 985, they were used to make this reliquary—a container for relics. The little saint's skull is in a cavity in the back, wrapped in a covering of silver.

Mayor of the Palace of one kingdom, succeeded in making the office hereditary. His successors were Frankish kings in everything but name.

Charles Martel and Pepin the Short

The able son of Pepin, Charles Martel (meaning "Charles the Hammer"), succeeded his father as Mayor of the Palace. In 732 Muslims invaded France from Spain, as you read in Chapter 10. Charles Martel fought them with his cavalry near Tours, in central France. They were driven southward, back toward Spain. The Frankish victory stopped the Muslim advance in Western Europe, removing an immediate danger and a constant menace.

When Charles Martel died in 741, he left his son Pepin III, or Pepin the Short, a large and strong kingdom to rule. Pepin's title, however, was still only Mayor of the Palace. He wished to be king in name as well as in fact. He wrote to the pope in Rome, asking his opinion. The pope, bishop of Rome, was recognized as the spiritual head of the Church in the west.

The pope replied that the man who held the real power should also have the title. In 751 an assembly of Franks took the throne from the Merovingian king and elected Pepin king of the Franks.

Three years later, in 754, the pope traveled to France and personally crowned Pepin "king by the grace of God." His action was regarded as a precedent (a standard for future actions) by later popes, who claimed that they had the authority to install and overthrow kings.

The pope also asked for Pepin's help against the Lombards. They were a Germanic tribe who had conquered and settled in the valley of the Po River—a region in northern Italy that is still called Lombardy. In the 740's they had begun to raid and conquer central Italy and to threaten the city of Rome.

Pepin led an army of Franks into Italy and defeated the Lombards. He took territory around Rome from the Lombard king and gave it to the pope. This gift of land, called the Donation of Pepin, created the Papal States, a region ruled by the pope for centuries afterward and in time greatly expanded.

It is not known whether the pope and Pepin actually made an agreement—Pepin's defense of

Rome in exchange for his coronation by the pope. It is certain, however, that these events began an alliance between the Franks and the pope that greatly strengthened both sides. The way was prepared for the greatest of all Frankish kings, Charlemagne (SHAR·luh·mane).

The empire of Charlemagne

Charlemagne was the son of Pepin. His Latin name was Carolus Magnus, from which comes the name of his dynasty, Carolingian. Charlemagne was king of the Franks from 768 until 814 and is considered one of the outstanding rulers of history. He was deeply religious and highly intelligent, although he had little formal education.

Charlemagne spent much of his life at war. He defeated the Lombards in Italy and the Saxons in northern Germany. In a single battle in the central Danube region, he defeated the invading Avars, a nomadic people much like the Huns. He drove Muslim invaders back across the Pyrenees into Spain and was thus able to gain a small strip of Spanish territory. However, he failed in his attempt to conquer all of Muslim Spain. By the end of his reign, Charlemagne controlled Western Europe from just south of the Pyrenees to the North Sea and from the Atlantic Ocean to the Elbe and Danube rivers and south beyond the city of Rome (see map, this page).

On Christmas Day in the year 800, Charlemagne knelt at worship in St. Peter's Church in Rome. The pope placed a crown on Charlemagne's head and declared him "Emperor of the Romans." The title had almost nothing to do with the Frankish Empire. The peoples that Charlemagne ruled represented a mixture of Roman, Germanic, and other cultures. Charlemagne himself was a Frank, speaking the language and maintaining the customs of his people.

The new title was important, however. It showed that Charlemagne, who had united much of Europe for the first time in 400 years, was regarded as a successor to the emperors of Rome. His coronation by the pope also dramatized the close ties between the Frankish people and the Church.

Government. Charlemagne's empire was divided into several hundred regions, each ruled by one of his representatives who was called a count.

Each count formed armies and administered the laws within his own lands. Charlemagne established his capital at Aix-la-Chapelle (now Aachen, West Germany), but he traveled through his empire a great deal.

There were no direct taxes on land or people. Government expenses were not great, and they were paid for by the wealth produced on the vast estates owned by the emperor. Each person who lived in the empire contributed in some way to the army. Wealthy lords provided the cavalry. Free peasants usually served three months of every year. Thus the emperor had an army at no expense to himself or the government.

Education and learning. Charlemagne was greatly interested in education. To teach his own children and the other young nobles, he founded a school at the palace. Learned scholars from England, Ireland, Germany, and Italy were invited to teach at the school, along with Frankish scholars.

Bishops were ordered to create libraries by copying ancient Latin manuscripts and to organize schools. Intelligent children from the lower classes were admitted to these schools along with the children of nobles.

CHARLEMAGNE'S EMPIRE IN 814 A.D.

Frankish territory before Charlemagne

Charlemagne's conquests, 768–814 A.D.

Charlemagne

Charlemagne came to be regarded as the "Emperor of the West" because he united most of Europe. The lavish jeweled bust (left) shows a dazzling, imperial Charlemagne, in magnificent armor and glittering crown. Actually, he dressed very simply in ordinary Frankish clothes.

Two of Charlemagne's major accomplishments reflect his religious nature. One involves his coronation by Pope Leo III (top left). This coronation resulted from the pope's gratitude to Charlemagne, who had defended Leo from Romans who wanted to remove him from the papacy. The other involves Charlemagne's desire to produce a readable and authentic Bible. He assembled scholars from all over Europe to complete this task. His own copy of the Bible is shown here (top right). Charlemagne is shown in another mood (above) with his daughters and his chief aide, the legendary hero Roland.

The decline of the Frankish Empire

Charlemagne's empire was united by the power of his own energy, ability, and personality. The local counts had to be watched constantly to make certain that they were serving the emperor, not themselves.

The empire began to fall apart during the lifetime of Charlemagne's only surviving son, Louis the Pious. At Louis' death the Frankish lands were divided among his three sons. After some quarreling they agreed, in 843, to a settlement called the Treaty of Verdun. The treaty divided the empire into three parts. Each brother took a part as his own kingdom. Charles the Bald took the western part of the empire, roughly the area of present-day France. Louis the German received the eastern region, which included much of present-day Germany. In between was a long narrow strip of territory extending from the North Sea through northern Italy. Lothair received this middle kingdom (see map, this page), as well as the title of emperor.

Charlemagne's descendants were incompetent rulers. They fought among themselves instead of uniting against powerful and ambitious local rulers. By 870 Lothair's middle kingdom was broken up and divided between his brothers Charles the Bald and Louis the German. Fifty years after the Treaty of Verdun, the great lords of both the east and west Frankish kingdoms no longer obeyed the Carolingian monarchs. Instead they were electing kings of their own choice.

The empire of Charlemagne was torn apart not only by internal feuds, but also by invaders who swarmed into it from every direction. During this period Europe suffered from invasions more terrible than the invasions of the 400's (see map, page 240).

From North Africa came Muslims, who conquered and occupied Sicily, Sardinia, and Corsica and terrorized the whole Mediterranean coast. From the east came the Slavs, pressing from eastern into central Europe. From Asia came a new group of nomads, the Magyars. They were so much like the earlier Huns that Europeans called them Hungarians. After a century of terrifying raids, the Magyars settled down and established a kingdom in what is now the modern country of Hungary.

TREATY OF VERDUN • 843 A.D.

0   500 miles
0   500 kilometers

The Vikings

The most feared of all invaders were those from Scandinavia, in the north. The Germanic peoples of what are now the countries of Norway, Sweden, and Denmark called themselves Vikings. The English called them Danes, while other Europeans called them Northmen, or the Norse. Although there were kings and nobles among the Vikings, their government was remarkably democratic. The Vikings honored work, and all classes worked. Land was widely distributed, and there were few large estates. Assemblies of landowners made the laws.

Vikings had been hardened by a bitter struggle for existence and were very courageous. They enjoyed battle. A Viking once complained that "peace lasted so long that I was afraid I might come to die of old age, within doors, on a bed."

During the 800's many Vikings sailed from their homeland in search of food, treasure, wives, and slaves. Viking ships were sturdy and were propelled partly by sail but mostly by oars. The

Vikings sailed along the coasts of Europe and up the rivers of Germany, France, and the eastern Baltic area. They also sailed across the Atlantic Ocean to Iceland, then went on to Greenland and the northeast coast of North America.

The Vikings sometimes captured strongly fortified towns. Their savage fighting and cruelty caused people everywhere to fear them. The Vikings settled in England, Ireland, France, and Eastern Europe. A large settlement of Vikings in northwestern France gave the region its name. The French word for "Northmen" was Normans. Thus this area became known as Normandy. As you will read, the Normans later carried out raids and settled elsewhere in Europe.

CHECKUP

1. IDENTIFY: Middle Ages, Franks, Merovingian, Mayor of the Palace, Donation of Pepin, Emperor of the Romans, Louis the Pious, Treaty of Verdun, Magyars, Vikings.

2. LOCATE: Papal States, Danube River, Aix-la-Chapelle, Normandy.

3. What were the accomplishments of Clovis? of Charles Martel?

4. How did Pepin the Short become king of the Franks? What precedent was established with the crowning of Pepin?

5. Discuss the contributions of Charlemagne in terms of government and education.

6. Give two reasons for the breakup of Charlemagne's empire.

Germanic peoples from northern Europe conquered Britain

The early inhabitants of Britain, like the Gauls of continental Europe, were Celts. The Celts had a fairly high culture and were good soldiers, but they were no match for the Romans. Most of Britain fell to the Romans in the 40's A.D. and was a Roman province for nearly 400 years.

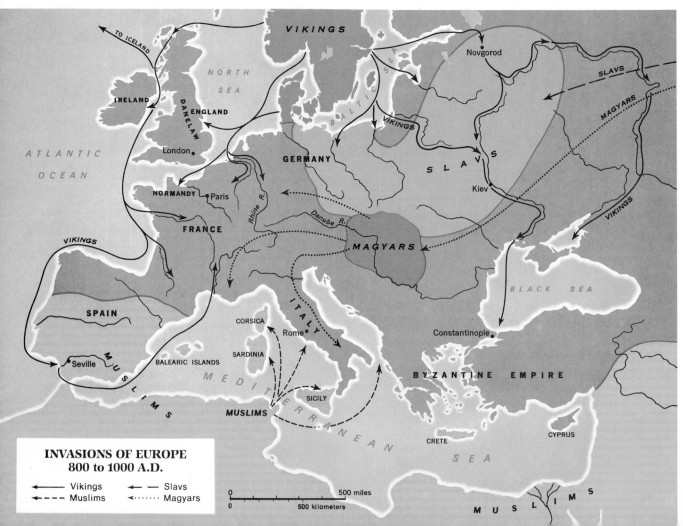

**INVASIONS OF EUROPE
800 to 1000 A.D.**

— Vikings   ◄— Slavs
◄---- Muslims   ◄······ Magyars

0   500 miles

0   500 kilometers

Roman legions controlled the province from their fortified camps. Latin and some Roman customs were introduced. Britain, however, did not adopt Roman culture as completely as did many other regions of the empire. Neither the Latin language nor Roman traditions became thoroughly rooted there.

Saxon invasions

Roman legions remained in Britain until about 410, when they were called back to guard frontiers in central Europe. Around 450 the island was raided by Germanic tribes who came from northern Europe. They came first as raiders, but many of them stayed as settlers. Although there were three different Germanic tribes—Angles, Saxons, and Jutes—the Saxons eventually dominated the others. The term *Saxons* is often applied to the descendants of all three groups. The Angles, however, gave their name to the new land; the word *England* comes from *Engla-land,* meaning "land of the Angles." Thus the English are often referred to as the Anglo-Saxons.

Historians use the name *Britain* to refer to the eastern island of the British Isles during pre-Roman and Roman times. The word comes from the Latin *Britannia,* meaning "land of the Britons." The name England refers to the island—except for Scotland in the north and Wales in the west—after the Germanic invasions.

During the invasions some native Celts were killed and some were enslaved. Others retreated to Ireland and into the highlands of Wales and Scotland. Roman culture, Latin, and Christianity disappeared. They were replaced by Germanic customs, the Anglo-Saxon language, and the animistic religion of the Saxons.

The Saxons in England formed several small independent kingdoms. Later these kingdoms combined into three important ones: (1) Northumbria, in what is now southern Scotland and northern England; (2) Mercia, in central England; and (3) Wessex, in southern England (see map, this page). In time each kingdom was divided into districts called shires. These were governed by officials known as shire-reeves (which became the word *sheriffs*).

The government of each kingdom was simple. The king had a great deal of power. A council of

ANGLO-SAXON KINGDOMS OF ENGLAND
about 800 A.D.

nobles, called the Witan, advised him. Together, the king and the Witan made laws and levied taxes. Below the king and the nobility were the free people, who were nearly all warriors. There were many slaves.

Christianity in Ireland and England

Christian missionaries first arrived in Ireland in the 400's. St. Patrick, the best known, began his work there in 432. Several monastic schools were founded. These were the basis of an advanced culture that lasted from about 500 to about 800. Missionaries and teachers from Irish schools went out to all parts of the British Isles and to the royal families on the continent of Europe. Ireland in these years was the greatest center and preserver of ancient and Christian culture in western Europe.

About the year 600, missionaries were sent to England by Pope Gregory I. Pope Gregory's missionaries, led by a monk named Augustine, were successful in England. Eventually, all England

241

The invasions of England

Wave after wave of invaders swept into early England—Celts, Romans, Saxons, Danes, and Normans. The beautifully worked golden belt buckle (bottom) is one of the treasures found in a Saxon burial ship, the gift of a chieftain who died around 660. From then until the 1000's, the Saxons fought to maintain their power in England, although the Danes, or Vikings, mounted many attacks on them.

Edward the Confessor (right) was the next to last Saxon king. He was succeeded by Harold, the youth he is here shown instructing. Harold's reign was cut short, however, when William, the Duke of Normandy, invaded England with the best-trained army in Europe (below).

accepted Christianity. Augustine was made the first archbishop of Canterbury and eventually came to be called St. Augustine of Canterbury. Canterbury became the center of the Christian Church in England.

The Danes and Alfred the Great

By the year 800 the kingdom of Wessex controlled almost all of England. Then came new Germanic invasions, by the Vikings from Scandinavia.

The Vikings—known to the English as Danes—attacked England in the early 800's. At first, like the Saxons before them, they came as raiders for plunder. Then they began to take over land and settle permanently. Saxon resistance was ineffective until the time of Alfred, who became king of Wessex in 871.

Alfred, known as Alfred the Great, led Saxon armies to their first real victory over the Danes. Although he was unable to drive them out of the island entirely, he forced them to remain in northeastern England. There they lived under their own laws and governed themselves.

Alfred the Great is best known for his peaceful accomplishments. He was an educated and scholarly man who wanted his people to be educated too. He established schools and invited scholars from Ireland and the European continent to teach. He himself translated books from Latin into Anglo-Saxon. At his command scholars began a history of England from the earliest times. This *Anglo-Saxon Chronicle,* written in Anglo-Saxon, was continued for 250 years after Alfred's death.

Alfred and his successors won back much land from the Danes. England was united for the first time. The government was strengthened, and the Christian Church was firmly established. Then in the late 900's a series of weak rulers came to power. The Danes again attacked from Scandinavia and conquered the whole country by 1013.

In 1019, under the Danish ruler Canute, England became part of a large kingdom that included most of Scandinavia. Canute lived in England most of the time and ruled wisely. His sons and successors, however, were not strong rulers. By 1042 the Danes were driven out of England, and a Saxon, Edward the Confessor, ruled again.

The Norman Conquest

Edward the Confessor was Saxon only on his father's side. He had been brought up in Normandy by his Norman mother. One of his relatives was William, Duke of Normandy. When Edward died in 1066, William claimed that the childless Saxon king had promised him the throne of England. The Saxon nobles refused to give the throne to William and elected Harold of Wessex. The Norman duke appealed to the pope, who upheld his claim, William gathered a fleet and an army of nobles, promising them plunder if his invasion succeeded.

William and his invading Normans landed at Hastings, on the southeastern coast of England, in 1066. They defeated the Saxon forces and killed Harold. William was crowned in London as King William I of England. He is usually called William the Conqueror.

It took William several years to overcome Saxon resistance in other parts of the island. It took many more years for the Norman conquerors to overcome the hatred of the defeated Saxons. The Saxons did not adopt Norman ideas, customs, or language willingly. Anglo-Saxon, a Germanic language, remained the language of the people. Norman French, a Romance language based on Latin, was the language of the nobles.

As time went on, however, the culture of England became as much Norman as Saxon. Even the language became a mixture. Eventually, Anglo-Saxon and Norman French blended to form the English language of today. About half of the words in English are of Anglo-Saxon, Germanic origin. A little more than a third are of Latin origin through both Roman and Norman-French influence. The remainder come from Greek, Arabic, and other sources.

CHECKUP

1. IDENTIFY: Celts, Britannia, shire-reeves, Witan, St. Patrick, St. Augustine, *Anglo-Saxon Chronicle,* Canute, William the Conqueror, Harold.

2. LOCATE: Northumbria, Mercia, Wessex.

3. What three waves of invasion did England undergo between 400 and 1066?

4. What did Alfred of Wessex do to earn his title "the Great"?

3

Medieval life was organized around feudalism and the manor

On the continent of Europe, organized government again disappeared within a century after Charlemagne's death in 814. Local lords had to protect and govern their own territories because weak kings were unable to do so. Europe entered upon a time of small, independent local governments. The political system that grew up is called **feudalism,** and the time during which it flourished is known as the **feudal period.** By the end of the 900's, feudalism was firmly established in northern France. By the middle 1000's, it was the way of life throughout most of Western Europe.

Feudalism

Feudalism began when local lords had to govern their own lands because there was no strong central government. To get needed military help, weak kings granted powerful lords the use of land from the royal estates. The strong lords, with more land than they needed, granted the use of part of it to less powerful lords in return for military aid and other services. Many small landholders who needed protection gave their land to more powerful lords. In return, they were granted the right to occupy and use the lands but had to provide military service to the lord.

The person who granted land was a lord. The one who held land in return for services was a **vassal.** The grant of land was called a **fief.** The Latin word for fief is *feudum,* from which comes the word *feudal.* In time the fief became hereditary. Legal ownership of the land passed from the lord to his son, while legal possession and use passed from the vassal to his son. Only the oldest son inherited, for a fief was never divided. Many lords held more than one fief.

A woman could obtain fiefs as her dowry—the gift she received from her father when she got married. But her husband would take over the dowry, and she exercised direct control only if he died. That is not to say that women could not be influential in society and politics. However, their legal property rights were limited.

Many of the powers of government were held by local noble landholders. The king himself had become just another feudal lord. In theory every holder of land was a vassal to the king, but in practice the king had power only over those who lived on his own feudal lands.

The Church, too, eventually became part of the feudal system. By the 900's it owned vast amounts of land. Some of this land was granted as fiefs to laymen in return for military protection.

The feudal relationship. In order to understand the relationship between lord and vassal, it is helpful to remember three things:

(1) It was an honorable relationship between legal equals. Only nobles could be vassals. The greater lords were vassals and tenants of the king. The less powerful lords were vassals and tenants of the greater lords, and so on down.

(2) The same man might be both vassal and lord—vassal to a more powerful lord above him and lord to a less powerful vassal below him.

(3) It was a very personal relationship. Each man's loyalties and obligations were owed only to the lord immediately above him or to the vassal below him.

The obligations of feudalism. The granting and holding of a fief was really a contract between lord and vassal. The lord granted the use of the land. He also guaranteed the vassal protection.

The vassal had more obligations than did the lord. He promised to provide the lord a certain number of fully equipped cavalry riders and foot soldiers and agreed to pay their expenses while at war. Military service was usually limited to 40 days a year.

Another obligation of a vassal consisted of feudal aids—special payments to help cover extraordinary expenses of the lord, such as ransom if the lord were captured in war. The vassal was also expected to house and feed the lord and his companions for a certain number of days a year, to attend such ceremonies as the marriage of the lord's daughter, and to serve on the lord's court to administer justice.

Feudal justice

Feudal justice was quite different from Roman ideas of law. Decisions at trials were made in any one of three ways:

(1) *Trial by battle.* The accused and the accuser, or men representing them, fought a duel. The outcome determined guilt or innocence.

(2) *Compurgation,* or oath taking. The accused and the accuser each gathered a group of people who swore that "their" man was telling the truth. Compurgators, the oath takers, were similar to the character witnesses in today's trials.

(3) *Ordeal.* The accused carried a piece of hot iron in his hand, or walked through fire, or plunged his arm into a pot of boiling water to pick up a hot stone. If his wounds healed rapidly, he was judged innocent. If not, he was found guilty.

Warfare. War was frequent during feudal times. Sometimes two kingdoms fought, or a king tried to subdue a powerful, rebellious vassal. Most wars, however, were private fights between feudal lords or between lords and vassals.

In the early Middle Ages, the armor of the fighting man was simple. He wore an iron helmet and a shirt of chain mail—small metal links hooked together to form a flexible protection. He carried a sword, a large shield, and a lance. Armor became complicated in later medieval times, with metal plates replacing chain mail. Because this armor was so heavy, a knight often had to be hauled or boosted onto his horse.

For nobles, wars were opportunities for glory and wealth, but they brought suffering and famine to the rest of society. The Church tried to improve conditions by limiting private wars. It issued decrees, known together as the Peace of God, that set aside certain places, such as churches, where fighting was not permitted. The Church tried to get all lords to accept another decree, known as the Truce of God, that forbade fighting on weekends and holy days. Gradually more days were added to the Truce of God, until there were only 80 days a year during which fighting was legal. These restrictions, however, could not be strictly enforced. Private wars continued until kings were strong enough to stop them.

The manor

Feudalism, as you have read, was essentially a governmental and military system. The economic basis of early medieval life was a large estate that included a village. Such an estate was called a **manor.** The manor was the economic unit of the early Middle Ages, just as the fief was the governmental unit. While a small fief had only one manor, large fiefs had several.

Because of the breakdown of central authority and trade, each manor tried to be self-sufficient— that is, to produce everything it needed. Most manors produced their own food, clothing, and leather goods. Only a few items, such as iron, salt, and tar, were imported.

The land of a manor (see below) was divided among the lord and a number of peasants. The lord kept about a third of the manor land, called the domain, for himself. It was often divided into several plots, although it might form one large block near the lord's house. The peasants paid for the use of the remaining land by giving the lord part of their crops and by working on his land. They also performed other services on the manor and paid many kinds of taxes.

A typical manor village had houses along a single street. The manor house or castle of the lord stood a short distance away. The village was usu-

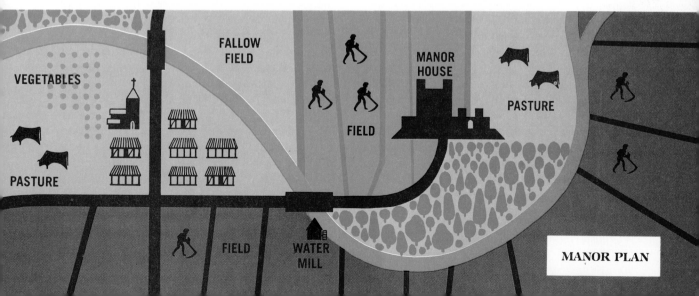

MANOR PLAN

ally located on a stream that furnished water power for its mill. The land of the manor extended out from the village. This land included vegetable plots, cultivated fields, pastures, and forests.

The cultivated land of the manor was often divided into three large fields for growing grain. Only two fields were planted each year. Each field had to lie fallow, or unplanted, every third year to regain its fertility. The large fields in turn were divided into small strips. Peasants held their own strips in each field. If the lord's domain was divided, he too had strips in each field.

Peasant life

Most of the peasants on a manor were serfs, whose legal status was less than free but higher than slave. They were bound to the land. That is, they could not leave it without the lord's permission, and the price of his permission was usually a sum of money they could not afford. Serfs were not slaves, for they could not be sold away from the land. If the land were granted to a new lord, the serfs became his tenants.

There were some free people on the manor who rented land from the lord. This group included the skilled workers necessary to the village economy, such as millers, blacksmiths, and carpenters. Most villages also had a priest to provide for the spiritual needs of the villagers.

Daily life was hard, with long hours spent working the fields. Food was poor, consisting mainly of coarse black bread, cabbage and a few other vegetables, cheese, and eggs. Beer was plentiful in northern Europe, and wine in the grape-growing regions farther south. Meat was rarely eaten.

We know very little about the life of ordinary people in these times. We can assume that they did not live long, and that they married late and had few children because they could not support a large family. The average life expectancy was probably less than 40 years. There was no protection against disease, and no alternative except starvation when harvests were poor. Because people in their forties were regarded as old, this was a much younger society than our own. Important people could become prominent by their twenties, and a bright child would be encouraged at an early age. When a village priest did spot a particularly intelligent boy, he could arrange to have him edu-

cated for a career in the Church, and thus a life in the wider world.

Such opportunities to escape the village were very rare. For the most part, people died where they had been born. If there was a terrible disaster, such as a famine that lasted many years, they might leave. Usually, however, they stayed on, struggling to keep small families alive.

One of the few things about family life that we do know is that, during these early years of the Middle Ages, a child's status was sometimes determined by its mother, not its father. If a serf married a woman from a free family, for example, their children might in some cases be considered free, not serfs. This did not happen often, and even free people hardly ever left their villages.

The life of the nobility

When people today think of the Middle Ages, they sometimes picture luxurious castles and knights in shining armor. However, the life of the nobility was not necessarily luxurious or even easy.

A castle was a fortified home for a lord, serving as a base for protecting the surrounding countryside and enforcing his authority. Most people picture a castle as a great stone structure. Actually castles of this type were not built until the later Middle Ages. Throughout the early medieval period, castles were relatively simple structures built of earth and wood.

Castles were built for defense, not for pleasant living. They were located on hills or in other places that were easy to defend. If a castle had to be built in flat country, a moat—a ditch often filled with water—surrounded the outer walls. The gate to the courtyard inside the walls was reached by a drawbridge across the moat. In case of an attack the drawbridge was raised.

The main part of the castle was called the keep—a strong tower that contained storerooms, barracks, and workshops, as well as the lord's living quarters. In the great hall the lord received visitors. Here the family also lived during the day. The lord and his family usually had a separate bedroom, but everyone else slept in the great hall with little privacy. There was not much furniture. The thick walls with their small, usually glassless windows made the rooms dark, damp, and chilly.

Medieval life

Daily life in Europe during the Middle Ages was filled with agricultural pursuits. The farming tasks of early spring are shown (left) in a French book of the 1400's. One peasant is plowing, while another is seeding. Others prepare an orchard, and a shepherd looks after the sheep and newborn lambs. Dominating the countryside are the great castle of the lord, God in heaven, and the stars in their astrological constellations. Pisces and Aries, the fish and the ram, are the signs for March.

The daily lives of the nobles differed greatly from those of the peasants. The nobles developed elaborate courtship rituals in which proper behavior led to the uniting of a family tree (above). In special tournaments known as jousts (below left), knights demonstrated their qualities of horsemanship and bravery.

Fowl, dogs, and other small animals ran everywhere. The floors were covered with straw that was usually filthy.

Most of a lord's day was spent looking after his estate and making sure that the area around his castle was under control. He might have to spend some time each year fighting, for one of three reasons: (1) because his own lord was at war and asked for his help; (2) because he himself had a quarrel with another lord; or (3) because he had to quiet troubles in his own area. But the lord's main activities involved looking after his lands and giving justice to his vassals.

A lord depended a great deal on help from his wife and children, as did peasants at this time. Marriage was a way to advance one's fortunes, and perhaps a way to inherit new lands. It also produced children who had to be taken care of. A lord had to provide a dowry for a daughter. For a son he would have to provide land or a job in the Church or serving the king.

The greatest sport of the feudal lord was the tournament—a mock battle. In early medieval times these were real fights, but later they were more like pageants.

Chivalry

During the 1100's feudal society was changed by the development of **chivalry**—a code of conduct for knights. The word comes from the French word *cheval,* meaning "horse." A knight was usually mounted on horseback when performing deeds demanded by the code of chivalry.

In the early days becoming a knight was quite simple. Any noble, by proving himself in battle, could be knighted by any other knight. As time passed, chivalry became much more complex.

To become a knight, a boy had to pass through two preliminary stages of training supervised by a knight. At the age of seven a boy became a page, learning knightly manners and beginning his training in the use of weapons. In his early teens he became a squire, a knight's assistant. He continued his training in both manners and weapons. He took care of the knight's horses, armor, weapons, and clothing. When he was considered ready, he accompanied the knight in battle to prove himself worthy. Then he was initiated into knighthood in an elaborate religious ceremony.

Chivalry required a knight to be brave—even foolishly brave. He had to fight fairly, according to the rules. Tricks and strategy were considered cowardly. He had to be loyal to his friends, keep his word, and treat conquered foes gallantly. He had to be especially courteous to women.

Chivalry made a great improvement in the rough and crude manners of early feudal lords. Behavior, however, did not become perfect by any standards. The courtesy of the knight was extended only to people of his own class. Toward all others his attitude and actions were likely to be coarse and arrogant.

CHECKUP

1. IDENTIFY: vassal, fief, Peace of God, Truce of God, manor, domain, serfs.

2. What was feudalism? Why did it develop?

3. What were the obligations of vassals and lords under the feudal relationship?

4. Explain the three methods of feudal justice.

5. Describe the different ways in which land on a manor was divided and used.

6. Under the rules of chivalry, what were the steps leading to knighthood?

The Church had many roles during the Middle Ages

You have seen that central government in medieval Europe was weak and often did not exist at all. Many of the responsibilities of modern governments were performed by the Church. In one way or another, the Church touched the lives of medieval people at almost every point.

The Church hierarchy

All members of the clergy occupied a place in the hierarchy (HY·uh·rahr·kee)—that is, they were organized in ranks according to their powers and responsibilities. The levels of the hierarchy, starting at the bottom, were as follows:

(1) *The parish priest.* The parish priest was usu-

ally of peasant origin, with little formal education. He was the hardest working and poorest clergy member and could hardly be distinguished from the peasants among whom he lived.

Though he was at the bottom of the hierarchy, the priest was, in one sense, the Church's most important officer. He conducted the church services in his parish and administered all the sacraments except confirmation and ordination. He supervised the moral and religious instruction of his people and the moral life of the community. Often, however, the beliefs of villagers were as much pagan and superstitious as Christian. They relied on local "wise women" and "cunning men" for spiritual help, sometimes more often than on the priest.

(2) *The bishop.* The bishop managed a diocese consisting of several parishes. He administered the sacraments of confirmation and ordination. He also appointed and removed parish priests and managed Church property in his diocese.

The choice of a bishop was usually controlled by the king or great nobles. Bishops were often feudal lords or vassals and had vassals themselves. They were frequently chosen for their family connections and political power.

(3) *The archbishop.* The archbishop had a diocese himself and all the powers of a bishop. In addition, he exercised some authority over the other dioceses and bishops in his province. He could summon provincial councils of the clergy to decide questions of Church belief and policy.

SPREAD OF CHRISTIANITY 600 to 1300 A.D.

Christian areas in 600 A.D.
Areas Christianized 600-800 A.D.
Areas Christianized 800-1100 A.D.
Areas Christianized 1100-1300 A.D.

SCOTLAND
NORTH SEA
ST. PATRICK 432-461 A.D.
IRELAND
ENGLAND
ST. AUGUSTINE 597-604 A.D.
Canterbury
GERMANY
Paris
Chartres
Worms
ST. BONIFACE 722-754 A.D.
Prague
FRANCE
STS. CYRIL AND METHODIUS 863-885 A.D.
Constance
RUSSIA
RUSSIANS 988-1015 A.D.
ROMAN CATHOLIC CHURCH
EASTERN ORTHODOX CHURCH
BALTIC SEA
Avignon
Canossa
SERBS 900'S A.D.
BULGARIANS 800'S A.D.
BLACK SEA
SPAIN
CORSICA
Rome
ITALY
Constantinople
BALEARIC ISLANDS
SARDINIA
Monte Cassino
ASIA MINOR
MEDITERRANEAN
SICILY
CRETE
CYPRUS
SYRIA
Antioch
SEA
Jerusalem
Alexandria
AFRICA
EGYPT

0 500 miles
0 500 kilometers

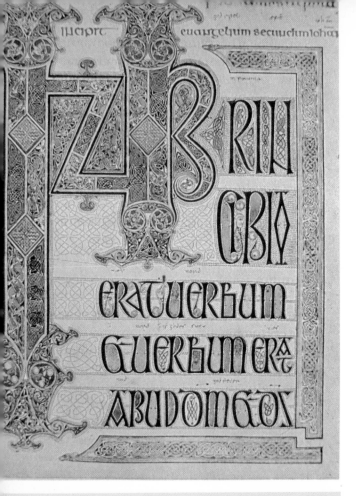

Lindisfarne Gospel

During the early Middle Ages, monks were among the few people in Europe who could read and write. Almost all books dating from this period were written out by hand in monastery workshops. In this age of great faith, the work that was copied most often was the Bible. The monks were painstakingly careful, for a manuscript containing the word of God was considered to be a sacred object whose visual beauty should reflect the importance of its contents. To glorify God, the monks illuminated, or illustrated, the pages with gold leaf and intricate designs.

The Lindisfarne Gospels are among the most beautiful of the early illuminated books. They were produced around 700 A.D. in the monastery of Lindisfarne. Now called Holy Island, Lindisfarne is off the northeastern coast of England. It was one of England's early centers of learning.

The page shown here is the beginning of the Gospel According to St. John, part of the New Testament. Interlaced ribbons, circles, and other designs decorate the border of the page and the words. The Latin words mean, "In the beginning was the Word, and the Word was with God."

(4) *The pope and his curia.* As you have read, the organization of the early Church included patriarchs in various cities. The bishop of Rome was the only patriarch in Western Europe. According to Church doctrine, Jesus had appointed as head of the Church the Apostle Peter, who was believed to have traveled to Rome and served as its first bishop. Because of this tradition, and because Rome had been the capital of the Roman imperial government, the bishop of Rome gradually gained recognition as the head of all the bishops in Western Europe. He came to be called pope, from the Latin word *papa,* meaning "father." By 400 A.D. the pope was the spiritual leader of the Church in Western Europe.

Gregory I, called Gregory the Great, was the first pope to hold great power. He became pope in 590, during the occupation of northern and central Italy by the Lombards. Gregory became the real ruler of Rome and successfully led its defense against Lombard attack. It was Gregory the Great who sent out the missionaries that converted Anglo-Saxon England, Lombard Italy, and Visigothic Spain to the Christian faith (see map, page 249). At the end of his reign, the pope's authority was recognized in Italy, Spain, France, North Africa, and most of England.

To advise him, the pope had a group of counselors called the curia. It was made up of officials appointed by the pope. The most important members were the cardinals, who advised the pope on legal and spiritual matters. After 1059 the cardinals elected the new pope.

Only in the Church hierarchy could the son of a commoner rise in the world. It did not happen often, but a man of great ability, regardless of birth, might rise to great heights in the Church.

The Church as a state

The medieval Church was much like a present-day government. Everyone became a member, just as we become citizens. The Church had its own laws and courts. It could enforce these laws, even upon kings and emperors, by such means as excommunication and interdict.

Excommunication meant that an individual was cut off completely from the Church. He or she could not receive the sacraments or be buried in sacred ground. All Christians were obliged to avoid the excommunicated person, and the state treated that person like an outlaw. After death, an excommunicated person was thought to be surely damned.

Interdict was the punishment of an entire region. No religious services could be held, no sacraments administered except baptism and extreme unction. Everyone who lived in the region was in danger of eternal damnation.

Like a national government, the Church had the power of taxation. Through the parish priest it collected from all Christians the **tithe**—that is, a tenth of their income. In England and Scandinavia there was also "Peter's Pence," a tax of one penny per year on every household. The Church received fines from its courts and fees for the performance of ceremonies such as baptism and marriage. Finally there was also vast income from Church-owned lands. In the early 1200's, when the Church was at the peak of its power, its income was greater than that of all the kings of Europe combined.

Monasticism

Priests, bishops, and the pope belonged to what was called the secular clergy. They lived, according to the Latin phrase, *in saeculo*, meaning "in the world," or among ordinary people. They administered the sacraments and preached the gospel. A second group of church people were called regular clergy because they lived according to a strict rule, or *regula*. These were the monastics—monks and nuns.

Monks and nuns believed that one of the best ways to live a perfect Christian life was to withdraw from the world and its temptations and to serve God by prayer, fasting, and self-denial. At first each monk lived alone. Later monks gathered in religious communities and lived in monasteries. Nuns lived in nunneries or convents.

Monasticism—the monastery system and way of life—in Western Europe lacked organization and direction until the early 500's. At about that time Benedict, a young Roman noble, became disgusted with worldly corruption and left Rome to become a hermit. In time his reputation for holiness attracted so many followers that he established a monastery at Monte Cassino in central Italy (see map, page 249).

Benedict drew up a set of standards—the Benedictine Rule—to regulate the lives of the monks. It was adopted by monasteries throughout Europe.

A monk could own absolutely nothing. Everything he used or wore belonged to the community of monks. Property was controlled and distributed by the abbot, who was the elected head of the community. The monk promised to obey the abbot in all things.

Monks spent several hours every day in prayer. Work was a second obligation. All the necessary tasks in and about the monastery were assigned by the abbot to groups of monks.

Monasteries filled two especially important needs—intellectual and charitable—for the surrounding society. The most learned scholars of the time were often monks. The libraries of the monasteries were the main preservers of ancient and Christian literature. A number of monasteries also ran schools where the clergy could be trained. It was to such a school that a particularly bright village boy might be sent by his local priest.

Over the years monasteries became very rich. As an act of piety, for example, a noble might leave his land to a monastery. Or a monastery might receive a large gift in return for accepting a young man as a monk. There were fewer convents than there were monasteries, and they were not as rich as monasteries. But like the monasteries, convents usually gave some of their wealth to charity in nearby communities. They often cared for the sick and gave food to the hungry and clothing to the poor.

Some monks, at the command of their superiors, left the monasteries to become missionaries. St. Patrick in Ireland, St. Augustine in England, and St. Boniface in Germany were among those who did important missionary work.

The Church and medieval life

Both the secular and the regular clergy played a leading part in medieval institutions and medieval life. The Church sought out the best minds among all classes to become members of the clergy. During the early Middle Ages, Church leaders were almost the only educated people in Europe.

Since printing was unknown in the early Middle Ages, all books had to be copied by hand. Monks did most of this work. To relieve the tedious work of straight copying and to beautify the texts, the monks often added small paintings at the beginning of a page or along the side margins. The gold leaf and brilliant colors they used brightened the pages so much that such works are called illuminated manuscripts. They were the finest artistic works produced during the period of the early Middle Ages.

Political role. The Church entered into the political life of the Middle Ages in many ways. In the Papal States the pope was the political as well as the spiritual ruler. In addition, many popes claimed that the Church was politically supreme and that all monarchs had to obey them. Church leaders also held positions of power as feudal lords and as advisers to emperors, kings, and nobles.

The Church preached that people should obey the laws of kings unless these laws conflicted with Church laws. The Church had its own code of law, called canon law, and courts where members of the clergy were tried.

Economic life. The moral ideas of the Church affected all economic life. The Church was opposed to people gaining wealth by exploiting others. It insisted that labor was in keeping with the dignity of free people.

Monks were leaders in agriculture. They developed new ways of raising crops, breeding cattle, and cultivating fruit. Monks greatly increased the amount of land that could be farmed by clearing forests, draining swamps, and building dikes and roads.

Monasteries carried on widespread trading activities. They owned their own pack animals, ships, markets, and warehouses. Their routes were carefully mapped. Often, monks built roads themselves.

Social work. The family was of great social importance to the Church. Divorce was forbidden. The Church took responsibility for all widows and orphans. It also took complete charge of all social work, such as aid to the poor.

To help the sick and distressed, it established hospitals, orphanages, and poorhouses. Special religious orders provided hospital care and burial for the poor. Monasteries gave gifts of food and clothing to the poor and provided the best inns for travelers.

Problems of the Church

At the very peak of its power, the Church faced certain difficulties and problems.

(1) *Lay investiture.* The tremendous wealth of the Church created problems, especially after Church leaders became feudal lords and vassals. Appointments to high Church positions were made for political reasons.

The appointment of Church officials led to the problem of lay investiture—that is, the investing of, or granting authority to, a member of the clergy by a king or noble. Church leaders believed that only a Church member could grant spiritual authority to another member of the Church. However, in medieval times a king or lord would often grant a new bishop his fiefs. Often they gave these rich offices as rewards to friends, or as gifts to relatives, not for spiritual reasons.

(2) *Worldly lives of the clergy.* Some members of the clergy were criticized because they lived in luxury and seemed to be more interested in wealth than in holy living.

(3) *Simony.* In feudal times, positions in the Church were often purchased and sold. The buying and selling of Church positions is called simony (SY·muh·nee). The purchaser expected to get money back on his investment from Church income or by charging high fees for performing religious services.

(4) *Heresy.* The Church did not permit anyone to question the basic principles—the doctrines—that were the foundation of the Christian religion. People who denied these truths or preached unauthorized doctrines were considered heretics, or unbelievers, guilty of the sin of heresy. Heresy threatened the Church itself, as treason does a modern government.

Attempts at Church reform. Many Church leaders and secular rulers tried to solve Church problems by various reforms. Two religious groups, or orders, established in the 1200's were dedicated to reform. They were the Franciscans, founded by St. Francis of Assisi, and the Dominicans, founded by St. Dominic. Members of both orders lived and preached among the people instead of secluding themselves in monasteries.

In the mid-1200's the pope ordered the Dominicans to seek out heretics and to eliminate heresy. This search came to be known as the **Inquisition.**

Those suspected of heresy could be tried in secret and tortured in order to force confessions. Heretics who confessed that they had been wrong had to perform heavy penance. Heretics who did not reform were condemned and turned over to the civil government to be punished, usually by burning at the stake. These severe penalties were thought necessary to save the souls of heretics and to prevent heresy from spreading.

CHECKUP

1. IDENTIFY: Gregory I, curia, cardinals, excommunication, interdict, tithe, Peter's Pence, Benedictine Rule, canon law, St. Francis of Assisi, Inquisition.

2. Name the ranks of the Church hierarchy and describe briefly the duties of each.

3. What were three ways in which the medieval Church resembled a state?

4. Explain three contributions made to medieval life by the Church.

5. Describe three major problems facing the Church during the medieval period.

5

Kings and nobles struggled for power in France and England

Kings had little power during the 800's and 900's. Some great lords were as powerful as the kings themselves and served them only when it was convenient. Therefore, kings and lords often struggled for power. From this struggle gradually emerged such kingdoms as France and England, where the king's authority grew stronger than that of the lords.

Rise of the Capetian kings in France

In 987 the last Carolingian king of France died without an heir. An assembly of nobles chose Hugh Capet, a French noble, as king. The line of kings he founded, called the Capetians, ruled France for over 300 years.

As king, Hugh Capet ruled only a small region around the city of Paris called the Île-de-France.

Île is the French word for "island," and this region was indeed a small island of royal authority in the midst of feudal lands. Even there the king's vassals resisted him.

The rest of what we know today as France was divided into provinces ruled by powerful feudal lords (see map, page 254). The Capetian kings set out to unite these provinces and to develop a strong central government.

The Capetians had one great advantage. They did not divide their kingdom among their sons. Only the eldest son could inherit. And for over 300 years they always had a son to inherit the throne. Thus the Capetians were able to outlast many other noble families.

The history of the Capetian kings is a good example of the feudal struggle for power. Strong kings increased royal lands and authority. Weak kings allowed nobles to regain power and privileges. Fortunately for the Capetians, able kings came often enough to outweigh the losses.

The strong Capetian kings added to their power in three ways: (1) by adding to the royal lands; (2) by developing a strong central government; and (3) by increasing the revenue from taxes.

The growth of royal territory. Kings added to the royal lands by various means. They married the daughters of great feudal lords and thus gained fiefs that were often included in dowries. Some noble families died out and the kings took over the nobles' lands.

After 1066, when William of Normandy conquered England and became its king, the territorial problems of the Capetians became even more complicated. For centuries the English kings owned vast territories in France. Strong Capetians were always alert to regain these lands. The shrewd Philip Augustus, king of France from 1180 to 1223, seized much English-owned land in France. By 1328, when the last Capetian king died, the only large land areas that the English had in France were parts of the provinces of Aquitaine and Gascony (see map, page 254).

Central government. For a strong central government, the Capetians needed loyal, trained officials. They could not rely on undependable feudal lords. Philip Augustus sent out inspectors loyal only to him to make investigations, hear complaints, and report to the King's Council. It was this body that conducted government affairs.

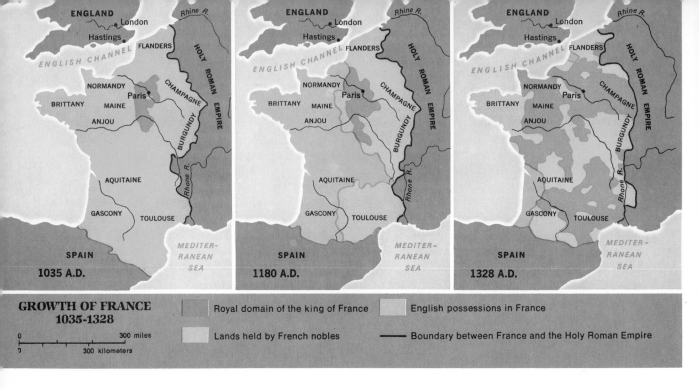

ENGLAND	ENGLAND	ENGLAND
1035 A.D.	1180 A.D.	1328 A.D.

**GROWTH OF FRANCE
1035-1328**

0 ___ 300 miles
0 ___ 300 kilometers

- Royal domain of the king of France
- Lands held by French nobles
- English possessions in France
- Boundary between France and the Holy Roman Empire

During the 1200's and early 1300's, two new government departments were set up. A Chamber of Accounts collected and looked after the taxes, and a supreme court, called the Parlement of Paris, heard appeals from all parts of the kingdom. These departments, and the King's Council as well, were staffed and run by trained officials.

Revenues. A strong central government needed money for a paid army because feudal armies were unreliable. Money was also needed to pay officials and for other expenses. The growing royal territory produced more wealth, as did fees and fines from royal courts. Because a wealthier country would produce more revenue from taxes, the Capetians encouraged the growth of towns, trade, and manufacturing (see Chapter 13). This policy also gained kings the support of townspeople against the feudal lords. By the early 1300's France was a strong, well-organized country, and the power of the king was supreme. The three sons of Philip IV, however, each died without a male heir, and in 1328 the long line of the Capetians came to an end.

Feudalism in England

William the Conqueror, who reigned from 1066 to 1087, imported feudalism from France to England. It was a form of feudalism in which the king, rather than the nobles, held the authority. William kept much English land as his own. The fiefs he gave his followers were scattered throughout England, to weaken the lords and prevent them from uniting.

Each feudal lord had to swear allegiance directly to William rather than to the lord immediately above him. Thus all the feudal lords became vassals of the king. In this way William laid the foundation for a centralized government. Nevertheless, England, like France, underwent a feudal struggle for power.

In order to determine the population and wealth of England, William sent out commissions to gather information on everyone in the country. This information was then used to determine taxes. Since it was said that it would be easier to escape doomsday—God's final judgment—than to avoid the royal commissioners, the survey became known as the *Domesday (Doomsday) Book.*

Reforms under William's successors

William was succeeded by his sons William Rufus and, later, Henry I. Henry I, who ruled from 1100 to 1135, made the central government more efficient. He set up a new department, the Exchequer (eks·CHEK·ur), to handle finances. His other contribution was in the legal system. He wanted to weaken the feudal lords by having as many cases as possible tried in the king's courts rather than in feudal courts. He sent judges out to travel through the country and hold court sessions at many different places.

Under Henry II, who reigned from 1154 to 1189, royal authority increased greatly. To get a dependable army, he required every free man to obtain arms and to serve in the king's army. He allowed nobles to pay him instead of doing military service and used the money to hire a professional army. He also required that careful accounts be kept of the government's finances. To do this, he reorganized the Exchequer.

Henry II made greater use of the traveling judges than earlier rulers had done. He also established definite circuits, or routes, on which they were to travel. Thus they became known as circuit judges.

To let the judge know what cases should be tried, the king appointed groups of men called juries in each district. A grand jury of 25 or more submitted the names of suspected criminals. Later, in the 1200's, there developed the petit (PET· ee) jury of 12. (*Grand* is the French word for "large," and *petit* the French word for "small.") At first petit juries decided only civil cases, such as disputes over land. Criminal cases were still tried by the feudal procedures of ordeal or combat. In time, however, petit juries came to decide criminal cases too. Thus the king's law replaced feudal law.

In his efforts to increase his authority, Henry II tried to transfer trials of certain members of the clergy from Church to royal courts. The Archbishop of Canterbury, Thomas à Becket, refused to allow this, and the two men became bitter enemies. The quarrel was finally settled when a group of the king's knights, thinking they would be doing the king a great favor, murdered the archbishop in his cathedral.

Henry II denied any part in the assassination. However, it forced him to abandon further attempts to reduce the power of the Church. Thomas à Becket at once became a saint. His shrine in Canterbury became the most popular holy place for pilgrims to visit in England.

Political problems

Henry II had inherited the provinces of Normandy, Maine, and Anjou in northwestern France. To these lands he added Gascony and Aquitaine by marrying Eleanor, daughter of the Duke of Aquitaine. Before the end of his reign, he also acquired Brittany. These English territories on the continent (see map, opposite) influenced both English and French history. For centuries English kings divided their interests instead of concentrating on England.

The last years of Henry II were troubled. His sons often plotted against each other because of their jealousy and hatred. When they did unite, it was to plot against their own father. Just before his death Henry learned that Philip Augustus of France had gained the support of two of his sons in a rebellion against him.

At Henry II's death in 1189, his son Richard (known as the Lion-Hearted) became King Richard I of England. He is famous for deeds during the wars against the Muslims in the Holy Land, but he was a poor king. He disliked England and was bored by the problems of governing the country. During his ten-year reign, he spent only six months in England. The English were heavily taxed to pay for Richard's heroic adventures in the Holy Land and for his ransom when he was captured. Many people in England were relieved when Richard was killed in 1199 while fighting in France.

King John and the Magna Carta

Another son of Henry II, John, succeeded Richard as king. He lost much of the land and power his father had gained. Philip Augustus defeated him in France and took Normandy, Brittany, Maine, and Anjou. In England, John brought on a revolt among the nobles by forcing them to pay taxes they considered unjust.

In 1215 the English nobles forced John to accept a document known as the **Magna Carta** (Latin for "great charter"). It was intended mainly to protect the lords' liberties. Some provisions, however, dealt with rights of ordinary people, and it is these parts that have come to be considered the most important provisions in the document.

How do we know?

COURT RECORDS Every society has some kind of legal system and procedures for determining if someone has violated a law. These proceedings are usually known as trials.

Since earliest times the courts that administered justice have kept records of what happened in each case they tried. The records serve as guides for similar cases that occur at a later time. For historians, court records often provide the most detailed descriptions of how people dealt with one another in a particular period. Court records tell a great deal about such topics as social attitudes, the importance of law, family relations, and the nature of crime.

Here is part of an account of a trial in a royal court in England in the 1220's. It shows how a criminal was brought to justice. It also reveals that in this period a priest could not be tried by a royal court, even if he was a criminal.

> Hugh Hop-over-Humber accused Thomas of Dean for this offense. On St. Giles's day he and his cousin William of Leigh were guarding the park of Cuckfield for the Earl de Barenne. The same Thomas came with many men armed with bows and arrows and attacked them. Thomas aimed an arrow at the said William and hit him in the leg. William died of the wound in nine days. Hugh was present, saw it, and asserts that Thomas did this in violation of the king's peace. He says pursuit was made and a hue and cry was raised to find Thomas. Twelve jurors then indicted Thomas for the killing. William, while he was still alive after being wounded, blamed Thomas for shooting him and for his death.
>
> Thomas appeared and rejected the charge because he is a priest. Robert of Dean, his brother, produced letters from the Bishop of Chichester to prove this. The Bishop says justice will have to be done in the Church court. Thomas is therefore handed over to the Bishop, who is to bring him to justice as a priest.

Adapted from Carl Stephenson and Frederick George Marcham, *Sources of English Constitutional History* (New York, Harper, 1937).

A court record can thus bring to life incidents that otherwise would be unknown and can convey the flavor of a period, its attitudes, and its social relations. Historians consider records of trials a unique source for understanding the feelings and outlook of a specific time in the past.

The king made several promises. He agreed not to collect any new or special tax without the consent of the Great Council—a body of important nobles and church leaders who advised the king. He promised not to take property without paying for it, and he agreed not to sell, refuse, or delay justice. The king also promised to grant any accused person a trial by a jury of peers, or equals.

Basically, the Magna Carta meant that the king was not above the law—the king had to obey the law just as his subjects did.

Although the charter was not considered unusually significant at the time, later political thinkers regarded many of its clauses as important precedents. The Magna Carta provided guidelines to be followed in the future.

Parliament and the common law

In the century that followed the Magna Carta, the two most important trends in English history were the development of Parliament and the growth of the common law.

Parliament grew out of the Great Council. In the 1260's there was a nobles' revolt against King Henry III. The leader of the nobles, Simon de Montfort, ruled England for several months. He hoped to get greater support for the nobles' cause by broadening the representation in the Great Council.

In 1265 de Montfort summoned representatives from the middle class to meet with the higher nobles and clergy in the Great Council. They came from all areas of England. There were two knights from each shire and two burgesses, or citizens, from each of several towns.

De Montfort's revolt was crushed, but a precedent had been set—that of including knights and burgesses in the meeting of the Council. At first all groups sat together. In time this representative body came to be called Parliament. It was eventually divided into two parts, or houses. The upper house consisted of nobles and clergy and was called the House of Lords. The lower house was made up of knights and burgesses and was called the House of Commons.

The early Parliament did not have the power to pass laws, but it did have the important right of refusing to agree to new and special taxes. As the cost of running the central government increased, new taxes were necessary, and Parliament's approval became vital. Over the years Parliament used this power to its advantage.

You have read about developments in English law courts under Henry I and his successors. Edward I, who ruled from 1272 to 1307, divided the king's court into three branches. The Court of the Exchequer kept financial accounts and tried tax cases. The Court of Common Pleas tried cases between private citizens. The Court of the King's Bench heard cases that concerned the king or the government.

Each of the three royal courts handed down many verdicts, or decisions. Each year the most important verdicts were collected and written down. These written decisions became the basis for future decisions made in the king's courts and in the circuit courts. This type of law, which is based on judge's decisions rather than on a code of statutes like that of the Romans, is known as **common law.** It received this name because it was common to all of England. It forms the basis for the present-day legal systems in the United States as well as in England.

CHECKUP

1. IDENTIFY: Hugh Capet, Philip Augustus, Parlement of Paris, Henry I, Henry II, grand jury, petit jury, Thomas à Becket, Eleanor of Aquitaine, Richard I, Simon de Montfort.

2. LOCATE: Aquitaine, Gascony, Brittany, Maine, Anjou.

3. What problems did the Capetian kings of France face? What advantage did they have?

4. Explain how the strong Capetian kings added to their power.

5. Name four of the main provisions of the Magna Carta. What was its basic importance?

6. How did each of the following develop in England: Parliament? common law?

Popes and emperors clashed over Germany and Italy

You have read how important the Church was in the medieval period. Its spiritual authority was recognized throughout Europe. However, many conflicts arose over the temporal authority of the Church—that is, its role in affairs of the world.

After the time of Pope Gregory the Great in the late 500's and early 600's, the papacy grew weaker. Charlemagne used the Church almost as a branch of his government. Later the Church became feudalized. Bishops and abbots became feudal lords or vassals. The pope himself was a feudal lord. For a time the nobles of Rome controlled the papacy, and it lost much of its spiritual influence. The greatest threat to the power of the medieval popes came from the rulers of Germany.

Kings and the Church

Kings and popes clashed frequently during the Middle Ages as each sought to define and consolidate his own area of rule. Emperor Otto I, whose crown is shown here (top left), gained for his successors the power to name the popes for nearly a century following 961. Then Pope Gregory VII, later proclaimed a saint (top right), helped to break this hold and establish Church power over the naming of Church officials.

Conflicts continued, however, most notably in England between Henry II and the Church courts. After this struggle led to the murder of Thomas à Becket, Henry submitted to humiliating punishment at the hands of bishops, priests, and monks (right). Henry's son, King John (above), was also forced to bow to Church power after a quarrel with Pope Innocent III.

The Holy Roman Empire

After the breakup of Charlemagne's empire in the late 800's, Germany was little more than a group of practically independent states. There was an elected king, but he was merely a feudal lord among other feudal lords.

Italy, part of which had belonged to Charlemagne's empire, was in a state of feudal anarchy. Several of Charlemagne's descendants held the title of Emperor of the Romans without really ruling. Later no one had even the title. The pope ruled the Papal States. Some parts of Italy were held by the eastern Roman Empire. Muslims held the island of Sicily and often invaded the Italian mainland.

In 936 Otto I, known as Otto the Great, was elected king of Germany by the great feudal lords. He was a powerful ruler and might have developed a strong kingdom in Germany, like that of the Capetians in France. However, he was more interested in Italy, and he took over some of its territory in the north. Then Pope John XII begged Otto's help in his struggle with the Roman nobles. Otto supported the pope, who crowned him Emperor of the Romans in 962. Otto later made his own secretary pope, and for the next 40 years, German kings chose the popes.

Although Otto's title was the same as that given Charlemagne 162 years earlier, he ruled a different territory—Germany and northern Italy. This territory was called the Holy Roman Empire (see map, page 286). It was a vaguely defined empire, but it lasted, in name at least, for centuries.

The power of the Holy Roman Emperors reached a high point under Henry III, who reigned from 1039 to 1056. Like Charlemagne, Henry regarded the Church as a branch of the royal government. At one time during Henry's reign, three different men claimed to be pope. Henry III deposed all three claimants and had a German elected. He also chose the next three popes.

Struggle with the papacy

Henry III's son, Emperor Henry IV, was only a child when his father died. For this reason and because there was civil war in Germany at this time, the Church had a chance to increase its power. Shortly after Henry IV became old enough to rule, Gregory VII became pope.

The new pope was determined to restore the papacy to power. He believed that as representative of God he had supreme power not only over the Church but also over all worldly rulers and their subjects. As pope he controlled the most terrible punishments of the Church—excommunication and interdict. Gregory used these weapons in his conflicts with emperors, kings, and nobles. His greatest struggle was with Henry IV.

The struggle between Gregory VII and Henry IV was long and complex. It concerned chiefly the issue of lay investiture. Henry IV insisted that he had the right to appoint bishops within the Holy Roman Empire. Gregory disagreed and finally excommunicated the emperor, releasing all his subjects from their oaths of allegiance and urging them to elect another emperor. Soon afterward Henry gave in to the pope on this issue. He journeyed to Italy, to the castle at Canossa where Gregory was staying. Barefoot and dressed as a pilgrim, he received the pope's forgiveness.

The struggle over lay investiture continued during the reign of Henry's son. Finally, in 1122 at the German city of Worms (VORMS), there was a great Diet, or assembly. Church leaders, nobles, and representatives of the Holy Roman Emperor reached an agreement known as the Concordat of Worms. The emperor agreed that Church officials should elect bishops and grant them their spiritual powers. The emperor promised not to try to influence the elections. He was allowed to grant only lands and secular powers to Church officials.

The struggle between popes and emperors was by no means ended, however. Later conflicts involved not only the powers of the Church and temporal rulers, but also the territories each claimed to rule. German rule in Italy continued to threaten the pope's rule in the Papal States. The pope therefore opposed all attempts of the Holy Roman Emperors to rule any part of Italy.

Frederick Barbarossa

The greatest medieval German ruler was Frederick I, called Frederick Barbarossa (meaning "Frederick of the Red Beard"). He ruled from 1152 to 1190. Like the emperors who preceded him, Frederick could have been a real ruler in

Germany, but he too was more interested in Italy.

The rich city-states of Lombardy in northern Italy—Milan, Parma, Padua, Verona, and Bologna—had become wealthy trade centers. They had also become increasingly independent. Each city-state had a wealthy merchant class, and the governments were partly democratic. Frederick sent representatives to take over the government in the cities. When Milan refused to receive his representative, Frederick captured the city, destroyed it, and drove out the population.

The other Lombard cities, aided by the pope, united to form the Lombard League. They formed an army and defeated Frederick in 1176. The peace settlement was a victory for the league and the pope. The cities recognized Frederick as overlord, but he had to agree that they could govern themselves.

Papal power under Innocent III

Innocent III, who was pope from 1198 to 1216, led the papacy to the height of its prestige and power. A learned and intelligent man, Innocent wrote books on law, theology, and Christian discipline. He was also a skillful diplomat and one of the greatest political leaders in all history.

Innocent III made even more sweeping claims to power than had Gregory VII and was more successful in enforcing them. He believed himself supreme over both the clergy and all temporal rulers. He believed, in fact, that emperors and kings were merely servants of the Church. Thus Pope Innocent III claimed the right to settle all political and religious problems. No person or group could do more than advise him. All final decisions were his alone.

Innocent took part in disputes throughout Europe and made free use of his powers of excommunication and interdict. In a quarrel with King John he placed England under interdict. To have the interdict lifted, John had to become the pope's vassal and pay money each year to Rome.

Innocent dominated all of Italy. In Germany he overthrew two kings and put his own choices on the throne.

Under Innocent III almost all of Europe was dominated by the pope, but it did not remain so. To maintain such power, a pope of almost super-human ability and energy was needed. Innocent III was such a man. Even so, his success came partly because conditions in Europe were favorable to his claims and activities. Later popes were less skillful, and circumstances were less favorable. Thus they did not have the power or influence that Innocent had possessed.

Frederick II

The last German who tried to rule Italy was Frederick II, who reigned from 1215 to 1250. Besides his lands in Germany, he was heir to the powerful Kingdom of the Two Sicilies, which included southern Italy as well as Sicily.

Frederick II was more interested in Sicily than he was in Germany. In Germany he kept the rivalries of the great families stirred up so that powerful lords would not unite against him. On the other hand, he granted various privileges to the German nobles in order to have his infant son accepted as his heir. Frederick tried, but failed, to unite Italy into a single kingdom. At his death his son ruled briefly as emperor. There followed a long period of civil war in Germany. Later German rulers kept the title of Holy Roman Emperor, but they did not try to rule Italy.

You can see that the attempts to unite Germany and Italy not only failed, but also prevented either one from being united. Germany remained a jumble of independent cities and feudal states, over which the emperor had little authority. Italy was disunited too, with the Lombard cities in the north, the Papal States in the central region, and the Kingdom of the Two Sicilies to the south. Neither Germany nor Italy became a unified nation until the 1800's.

CHECKUP

1. IDENTIFY: Otto I, Pope John XII, Holy Roman Empire, Henry III, Frederick Barbarossa, Lombard League, Frederick II.

2. LOCATE: Canossa, Worms.

3. What major problem was involved in the conflict between Gregory VII and Henry IV? How was the issue resolved?

4. What were the provisions of the Concordat of Worms?

5. Why was the papacy of Innocent III so important?

CHAPTER REVIEW

432	St. Patrick in Ireland	
450	Britain raided by Angles, Saxons, and Jutes	
732	Muslims defeated at Tours by Charles Martel	
754	Crowning of Pepin by pope	
768–814	Rule of Charlemagne	
843	Treaty of Verdun	
871	Beginning of rule by Alfred the Great	
962	Otto the Great crowned emperor	
987–1328	Rule of Capetian kings in France	
1066	Norman Conquest of England	
1100–1135	Rule of Henry I in England	
1122	Concordat of Worms	
1152–1190	Rule of Frederick Barbarossa	
1154–1189	Rule of Henry II in England	
1198–1216	Height of papal authority under Innocent III	
1215	Magna Carta	

CHAPTER SUMMARY

After the Roman Empire declined, Germanic tribes overran Europe. Clovis, king of one of the Frankish tribes, and the Merovingians who succeeded him created a large kingdom in France. It was later controlled by Charles Martel and Pepin the Short. The greatest Frankish king, Charlemagne, created an empire that included much of Western Europe.

Britain too was ruled by Germanic tribes, the Saxons. During their rule the people were converted to Christianity, and England was invaded by the Danes. Although they were driven out of England, the country was soon overwhelmed by the Normans.

Two important medieval institutions were feudalism and the manorial system. Feudalism was basically a political system, with lords granting fiefs to vassals in return for military duty and other services. The manorial system was an economic system based on the self-sufficient manor worked mainly by serfs.

During the Middle Ages the Church performed many functions. All the clergy occupied a place in the hierarchy. The Church had its own laws and the power of taxation. Monasticism attracted many people. Both secular and regular clergy played important roles in education and in political, economic, and social life. However, the Church was troubled by lay investiture, the worldly lives of the clergy, simony, and heresy. Attempts at reform included the founding of the Franciscan and Dominican orders and the establishment of the Inquisition.

Kings gradually extended their authority. The Capetians in France added territory, developed a strong central government, and increased tax revenues. In England the Exchequer was set up, royal courts were strengthened, and the jury system was developed. The ruler himself was made subject to the law when King John was forced to accept the Magna Carta. The 1200's were also the time of the development of Parliament and the common law in England.

Germany and northern Italy were ruled by the Holy Roman Emperors, who struggled for power with the papacy. Popes such as Gregory VII and Innocent III made sweeping claims to power. Strong emperors, including Henry IV, Frederick Barbarossa, and Frederick II, tried but failed to make the Holy Roman Empire a meaningful political force.

CHECKING WHAT YOU KNOW

1. Match each document at the left with its description at the right.

   a. Treaty of Verdun
   b. Concordat of Worms
   c. *Domesday Book*
   d. Magna Carta
   e. *Anglo-Saxon Chronicle*

   1. Required the English king to consult the Great Council regarding taxes.
   2. Divided the empire of Charlemagne among his three sons.
   3. Tried to settle the issue of lay investiture.
   4. History of England from earliest times to the 1100's.
   5. Census of people to determine taxes.

2. Match each leader at the left with a specific accomplishment at the right.

a. John (England)
b. Henry II (England)
c. Holy Roman Emperor Frederick II
d. Philip Augustus
e. Alfred the Great
f. Charlemagne
g. William the Conqueror
h. Pepin the Short
i. Simon de Montfort

1. Tried to unite Italy into a single kingdom.
2. Was forced to sign the Magna Carta.
3. Unified Western Europe; crowned Emperor of the Romans.
4. Ordered scholars to begin writing the *Anglo-Saxon Chronicle*.
5. Gave territory around Rome to the pope.
6. Broadened representation in the Great Council.
7. Seized much English-owned land in France.
8. Defeated Harold to establish rule over England.
9. Established the jury system in England.

3. How did the Church become part of the feudal system in Europe? In what ways was the Church independent of the feudal system?

4. Discuss the conflicts between Church and state that were shown in the disputes between:

a. Henry II and Thomas à Becket
b. Henry IV and Gregory VII

PRACTICING YOUR SKILLS

1. Understanding chronology. Give the correct date for each of the following events and arrange them in chronological order.

a. Concordat of Worms.
b. Clovis became king of Frankish tribe.
c. Invasion of England by William the Conqueror.
d. Invasion of Spain by Muslims.
e. Charlemagne crowned Emperor of the Romans.
f. Capetian line of kings founded.
g. Signing of Magna Carta.

2. Analyzing information. In both England and France, kings increased their power at the expense of the nobility. List the ways by which William the Conqueror and his successors and the French Capetian kings added to their power and developed central governments. Explain how these measures increased royal authority and decreased the nobles' power.

RELATING PAST TO PRESENT

1. Compare life on a medieval manor with life on a modern American farm. In which would you find greater self-sufficiency? You may want to refer to books or magazines in your library for information on life on American farms.

2. Use a book on American civics or government to find the following information:

a. What are the kinds of cases that go before a grand jury today?
b. Why do some cases use a petit jury and others use just a judge?
c. What is the role of the judge?
d. What are the different types of courts in your state?

Now compare your findings to the information you have read about the beginnings of the court system in England.

INVESTIGATING FURTHER

1. Read the medieval play *Everyman* (Dutton).

a. Describe five of the main characters.
b. What are the values that the Church wants people to cherish the most?
c. What is the importance of Good Deeds?

2. Read *Medieval People* by Eileen Power (Harper & Row), which tells the story of a peasant's life during the reign of Charlemagne. In the selection "Madame Eglentyne," the author describes life in a nunnery.

a. What religious duties were performed by the nuns?
b. What evidence of "worldliness" is given?

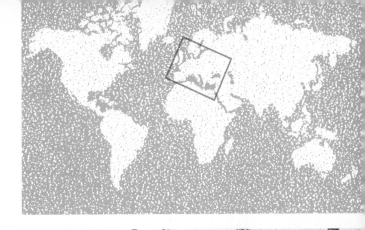

(1000—1500)

13

Trade Revived and Nations Developed in Europe

If you had lived during the Middle Ages, you would probably have grown old without being aware of any changes in the world around you. Few people journeyed very far. There were no newspapers. News traveled by word of mouth, carried from place to place by wandering peddlers, monks, and performers. There were few books, and most people could not read. The average person, and even many nobles and clergy, knew almost nothing about the world beyond the local village.

During the Middle Ages there was no unified state like the Roman Empire to give a sense of political unity to the people of Europe. There was unity of a different kind under the Church, which influenced almost every aspect of people's lives. The Catholic Church was the only church of Western Europe. (The term *catholic* comes from the Latin word *catholicus,* meaning "universal.") The Church taught everyone basically the same traditional beliefs and the same truths.

Most Europeans could not understand all the teachings of the Church, because ideas like "grace" and the "sacraments" were too complicated for them. They held on to many ancient pagan and magical beliefs about demons, witches, and spirits. Nevertheless, the priest was an important figure in their lives, and his actions and attitudes were roughly the same wherever he was located. There were differences of opinion within the Church about true Christian doctrine. Never-

A knight and escort entering a medieval town

theless, the Church was basically a force for unity in European society. Most of the literature, learning, and art of the period was devoted to the glory of God and the Church. Thus, the period of the Middle Ages in Europe has been described as the Age of Faith.

In spite of the unity provided by the Church, Europe in the Middle Ages was not a land where everything was the same. There were great contrasts. On the one hand were faith and chivalry, on the other hand, drudgery, violence, and old pagan and magical beliefs. A majestic cathedral might be surrounded by dark, filthy streets where no one dared walk after nightfall. Beneath the castle on the hill huddled the miserable huts of the serfs.

Changes were occurring, too. After centuries during which European life was based almost entirely on farming, cities began to grow. Cities were large towns, often the home of a bishop and his cathedral. Sometimes the city had special privileges of self-government.

Trade also increased, as people wanted more and better goods. Merchants began to look outward, away from Europe, seeking new products and new ways of making money.

Another influence was also at work. For years the Christian world had maintained an armed truce with the Muslims, who followed the religion of Islam. In the later Middle Ages the two groups came into conflict. Christian armies went to foreign lands to conquer the Muslims by force of arms. They returned, little realizing that they themselves had been conquered—by new and remarkable ideas.

THE CHAPTER SECTIONS

1. The Crusades changed the lives of the people of Europe

2. After a period of decline, trade began to increase

3. The growth of towns brought great social and political change

4. The culture of the Middle Ages flourished in towns and cities

5. Feelings of patriotism spread throughout Western Europe

6. The temporal power of the Church was challenged and weakened

1

The Crusades changed the lives of the people of Europe

The Arabs, as you have read in Chapter 10, conquered Palestine, the Holy Land of Jesus' birth, in the 600's. Although the Arabs were Muslims, they were usually tolerant of other religions. If Christians or Jews paid their taxes and observed other regulations, they could live in Palestine and keep their religion. For centuries, Christian pilgrims visiting Palestine met with little interference. European traders generally were able to do business there.

During the 1000's, however, the Arabs lost Muslim leadership to the Seljuk Turks. The Turks were a warlike people, originally from central Asia, who had adopted the Muslim faith. They won control of Palestine and attacked Asia Minor, which was part of the Byzantine Empire (the successor to the Roman Empire in the east). When they threatened the city of Constantinople, the Byzantine emperor appealed to the popes at Rome several times. He asked for soldiers to help defend his city and regain the territories he had lost to the Seljuk Turks.

In Palestine the Turks proved much less tolerant than the Arabs had been. Reports of persecutions of Christian pilgrims began to come back to Europe. The Byzantine emperor's appeal for help now found a warm reception.

The pope's call for a crusade

Pope Urban II was eager to regain the Holy Land from the Muslims. In 1095 he called a great meeting of Church leaders and French nobles at Clermont, France. He urged the powerful feudal nobles to stop warring among themselves and asked Christians to join in one great war against the "unbelievers."

Urban's plea fired his listeners with enthusiasm, and they joined in one mighty cry, "God wills it!" From Clermont, people traveled through France preaching the cause. Those who joined the expeditions sewed a cross of cloth on their garments. They were called **crusaders,** from the Latin word *cruciata* meaning "marked with a cross."

People joined the **Crusades,** the expeditions to regain the Holy Land, for many different reasons. The pope promised both heavenly and earthly rewards. All the sins of a crusader were forgiven. If he died on a crusade, he went straight to heaven. His property and family were guaranteed protection by the Church during his absence. A debtor who joined a crusade had his debts canceled. A criminal was relieved of punishment.

Knights were dazzled by the lure of lands and plunder in the rich Middle East. Merchants saw a chance to make money. The Crusades were partly religious expeditions, but they also appealed to a love of adventure, the hope of gain, and the desire to escape debts or punishment.

The First Crusade

The First Crusade, which lasted from 1096 to 1099, was led by French and Norman nobles. In three organized armies they moved across Europe to Constantinople (see map, this page).

It is not surprising that the crusaders were not welcomed in Constantinople. The Byzantine emperor had asked for some fighters, but now he saw three armies approaching the city. He was afraid that they might capture and plunder Constantinople. After much discussion the Byzantines allowed the crusaders to pass through Constantinople to begin their long, hot march across Asia Minor toward Palestine.

With their garments of wool and leather and their heavy armor, the crusaders suffered severely from the heat. Because of a shortage of pack animals, supplies of food and water were inadequate. The leaders quarreled over fiefs in the lands they captured. If the Turks had not also been quarreling and disunited, the expedition would have failed. The crusaders captured the city of Antioch and marched on toward Jerusalem.

Conditions improved as the crusaders marched down the seacoast toward Palestine. Fleets of ships from the Italian cities of Genoa and Pisa brought them reinforcements and supplies. The crusaders captured Jerusalem after a short battle and slaughtered the Muslim inhabitants in a terrible massacre.

In the Middle East the crusaders set up four small states: (1) the County of Edessa, (2) the Principality of Antioch, (3) the County of Tripoli,

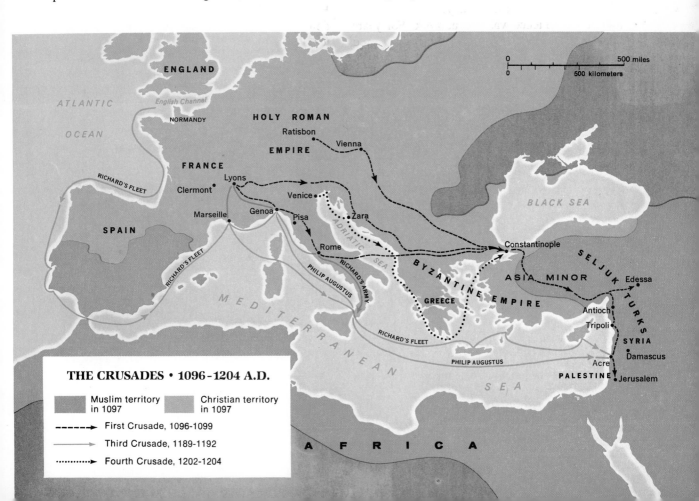

THE CRUSADES • 1096–1204 A.D.

- Muslim territory in 1097
- Christian territory in 1097
- ----→ First Crusade, 1096–1099
- ——→ Third Crusade, 1189–1192
- ·········→ Fourth Crusade, 1202–1204

The Crusades

The purpose of the Crusades was not only to reconquer the Holy Land from the Muslims but also to protect pilgrims traveling there. When the crusaders set out, they did so under the banner of the pope—a pair of crossed keys (top). The crusaders were usually rowed across the Mediterranean in galleys, ships that were powered by banks of oars rowed by slaves or prisoners.

After the crusaders scored their initial successes, they built powerful castles to keep control of the Holy Land. Many of the ruins have survived and are vivid reminders —for example, Belvoir, built high on a cliff overlooking the Sea of Galilee (center). Pilgrims then streamed to the Holy Land (right), bringing back stories of the Muslims that helped end Europe's many centuries of isolation.

and (4) the Kingdom of Jerusalem (see map, this page). European feudalism was introduced, and the land was subdivided into fiefs, with vassals and lords. For almost a century the Europeans occupied these lands. There was brisk trade with Europe, carried mostly in Italian ships. Christians and Muslims lived in close relations and grew to respect each other. Many Christians adopted eastern customs and came to prefer eastern food and clothing.

The Second Crusade

The Second Crusade began in 1147, after the Turks recaptured the important city of Edessa and threatened the Kingdom of Jerusalem. In this crusade King Louis VII of France and the Holy Roman Emperor Conrad III led armies to the Holy Land.

The Second Crusade was a failure. The armies of the two monarchs met many misfortunes on the march to the Holy Land. They fought separately and did not join forces until they reached Damascus, which was held by the Turks. Even then the large combined forces of Louis and Conrad failed to capture the city. After only two years the defeated armies returned to Europe.

The Third Crusade

In 1187 the news reached Europe that Jerusalem had been recaptured by the Muslim leader Saladin. Europe's response was the Third Crusade, from 1189 to 1192, called the "Crusade of the Three Kings." King Richard the Lion-Hearted of England, King Philip Augustus of France, and Emperor Frederick Barbarossa of the Holy Roman Empire each started out at the head of a great army to regain the Holy Land.

Again there was failure. Frederick Barbarossa drowned on the way to the Holy Land, and most of his army turned back. Philip and Richard quarreled, and Philip took his army home to seize English lands in France. Several times Richard might have gained the whole Kingdom of Jerusalem by diplomacy, but he preferred military adventure. In the end he made no gains worth mentioning. In this Crusade, which accomplished so little, an estimated 300,000 Christians and Muslims lost their lives.

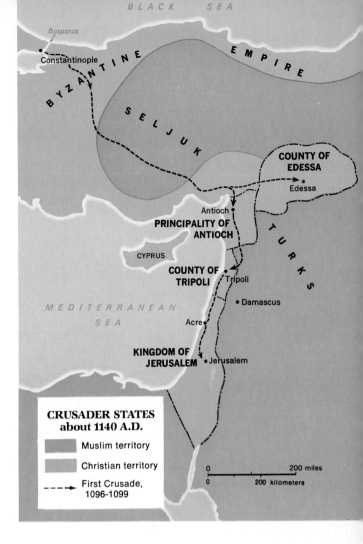

CRUSADER STATES about 1140 A.D.

Muslim territory

Christian territory

- - -> First Crusade, 1096-1099

Later crusades

Pope Innocent III persuaded a group of French knights to go on the Fourth Crusade in 1202. The city-state of Venice agreed to provide transportation, but the cost was too high for the crusaders to pay. Venice then offered to lower the cost of transporting the crusaders if they would attack Zara, a city on the Adriatic coast. Zara was a Christian city, but it was also a commercial rival of Venice. The crusaders captured Zara, and Pope Innocent excommunicated the entire army of crusaders for attacking a Christian city.

Soon after the capture of Zara, the leaders of Venice and the crusaders planned an attack on Constantinople. It, too, was a Christian city, but its capture offered loot to the crusaders and commercial advantages to Venice.

In 1204 the crusaders seized Constantinople

The Crusades

1095	Pope Urban II called a meeting at Clermont, France
1096–1099	First Crusade took Antioch and Jerusalem
1147–1149	Second Crusade, led by King Louis VII and Emperor Conrad III
1189–1192	Third Crusade, "Crusade of the Three Kings"
1202–1204	Fourth Crusade, ending in seizure of Constantinople
1212	Children's Crusade
1291	Acre taken by Muslims

and set up a feudal kingdom there, with feudal states scattered throughout Greece. The loss of Constantinople was a terrible blow to the Byzantine Empire. Since the reign of the Roman Emperor Constantine, it had been a thriving, prosperous, and brilliant Christian society. Constantinople had not acknowledged the authority of the pope in Rome, and it had developed its own traditions. These traditions influenced all of eastern Europe.

After 50 years the Byzantines regained Constantinople and a part of their lands from the crusaders, but their great city and empire were both permanently weakened. They were finally to fall to the Turks 200 years later, in 1453.

There were additional crusades after 1204, although historians differ on the correct numbering of them. Crusading was, in fact, a continuous process that lasted from 1096 to 1291, when the last Christian stronghold, in Acre, was captured by the Muslims. For two centuries scarcely a year went by in which new groups did not go to the Holy Land. There was a constant flow of people from west to east and back again. The religious zeal of the crusaders, however, steadily dwindled. None of the later crusades was as large as the Third Crusade.

Results of the Crusades

From a military standpoint all the Crusades except the first were failures. Jerusalem and the rest of Palestine were taken from the Turks by the Christians in the First Crusade and held for nearly a century, but the Muslims recaptured them.

However, Europeans learned about many things of military importance, including the crossbow and the use of carrier pigeons to transmit messages. From the Byzantines they learned such new siege tactics as the undermining of walls and the use of catapults to hurl stones. In addition, they may have learned about gunpowder from the Muslims, who probably acquired knowledge of this explosive from the Chinese.

The effect of the Crusades in Europe was to increase the power of kings and decrease the power of feudal lords. Kings were able to raise new taxes and to lead armies drawn from their entire countries. At the same time, many nobles died in the Crusades.

Others, as you will read later, sold political privileges to towns in order to raise money to go on a crusade. The political role of the Church was also strengthened for a while in Europe.

There were other important results of the Crusades. The status of women changed. With their husbands absent, many wives took over the management of feudal estates. Europeans were influenced, too, by the ideas that were exchanged, both among the crusaders of different countries and between the crusaders and the other peoples they met.

Commercial changes also occurred. Italian cities benefited from their role in transporting crusading armies. Europeans learned about products from the Middle East—rice, sugar, lemons, apricots, and melons, among other things—which stimulated trade in such goods. Cotton was also introduced into Europe in the form of muslin (cloth of Mosul, a city in Persia) and damask (cloth of Damascus).

CHECKUP

1. IDENTIFY: Urban II, Louis VII, Conrad III, Saladin, muslin, damask.

2. LOCATE: Clermont, Genoa, Pisa, County of Edessa, Principality of Antioch, County of Tripoli, Kingdom of Jerusalem, Damascus, Venice, Zara, Acre.

3. What motives led people to go on the Crusades?

4. The Crusades are sometimes called successful failures. What is meant by this statement?

2

After a period of decline, trade began to increase

Trade nearly died out in Western Europe after the 400's. Manors became almost entirely self-sufficient, growing or making nearly everything they used. Towns and cities, which depended on trade and manufacturing, decreased in population and size. Some towns disappeared completely.

Those who wanted to trade faced many obstacles. There was a shortage of money. Roads were poor and there were few bridges. Robbers on land and pirates at sea made travel dangerous. There were many tolls. Each feudal lord charged tolls for the use of roads and bridges in his territory.

Church laws also made trade difficult. The Church insisted on a "just price." This price did not permit the seller to make a large profit. The Church prohibited the purchase of articles for resale at a higher price. It also prohibited **usury,** which at that time meant the charging of interest for the loan of money. Various ways were invented to evade these prohibitions, but they did hamper the growth of trade.

Trade routes

Trade first began to revive in Italy. Neither trade nor towns had declined as much there as elsewhere. Also, the Italian peninsula was in a favorable geographic location. It lay between northern Europe, where people were becoming interested in goods from Asia, and the Middle East, where such goods could be bought.

Goods from Asia were brought westward by Chinese and Muslim traders along three main routes: (1) overland to ports on the Black Sea and then by ship to Constantinople; (2) by water through the Indian Ocean and the Red Sea and then by land to ports in Egypt; and (3) by water through the Indian Ocean and the Persian Gulf and then by land to ports on the eastern Mediterranean (see map, pages 272–73). The Italians became the great European distributors in this trade—distributors for traders from Asia, on the one hand, and traders from central and northern Europe, on the other.

During the late 900's and early 1000's, Italian traders began to make contacts with the Middle East. By a combination of force and negotiation, the Italian city-states of Venice, Genoa, and Pisa won trading rights in Constantinople, Syria and Palestine, and in North Africa. Trade, however, did not flow freely in every nation or region. Trading rights were a privilege to be bought or won.

By the time of the Crusades, Italian city-states were eager to carry crusaders to the Holy Land and bring back rich cargoes of goods from the East. From Italian seaports these goods were carried by pack train through northern Italy and across the Alps into central and northern Europe. This overland trade route led to the growth and increasing wealth of cities in Lombardy, southern France, and Germany.

There was also a revival of trade in northern Europe. Before the year 1000, Viking traders from Kiev, in what is now the Soviet Union, traveled regularly to the Black Sea and on to Constantinople to collect goods from the East. They brought these items northward and then traded them in the cities of northern Europe.

Old Viking routes also linked the Baltic Sea and the North Sea with England, the Atlantic coast of Europe, and the Mediterranean Sea. By the 1100's German merchants carried on a busy trade along the Baltic and Atlantic coasts. Beginning in the 1200's Italian merchants, too, traded along the Atlantic coast. Ships from Genoa and Venice sailed through the Strait of Gibraltar and northward to England and Flanders.

The region of Flanders, which is now part of Belgium and northern France, gained importance. It was the meeting point of trade routes that led across France, down the Rhine River from Germany, across the English Channel from England, and down from the coasts of the Baltic Sea. Moreover, the chief product of Flanders—fine woolen cloth—was eagerly sought by people throughout Europe. During the 1200's Flanders became the textile headquarters of Europe. Such cities as Ghent and Bruges became thriving centers of population and wealth in Flanders.

The Hanseatic League. Hamburg, Lübeck, and Bremen were the most important commercial cities on the coasts of the North and Baltic seas. Because there was no strong central government in Germany, these trading cities formed a league

Commerce and trade

During the late Middle Ages the commercial and trading activities of Europe grew rapidly. One of the chief economic centers was the city of Venice (top right). In the foreground is the many-domed cathedral of St. Mark's, which reflects the strong ties that Venice had to far-off Byzantium. In Venice, gondolas, or boats, were the main form of transportation because the city was built on dozens of islands.

The Italians were among the first to have banks (above), which issued letters of credit that could be cashed in other cities. Entire families staffed the early banks. As trade increased, a greater variety of goods became available in stores. Apothecary shops, for example, became well stocked with exotic spices, as in the Spanish shop (right) of the 1300's.

called the Hanse for protection (see inset map, page 273). The Hanseatic League, as it is usually called, eventually had over 70 member cities and became a powerful influence upon the commerce of northwestern Europe during the 1300's and 1400's. It was not a political organization but existed only for trading purposes.

The Hanseatic cities had permanent trading posts in Flanders, Scandinavia, England, and Russia. Any member that failed to abide by League agreements lost its trading privileges. If the privileges of Hanseatic traders were taken away by a nation, the League stopped all shipments of goods to that country. Sometimes League members even carried on a small-scale war in order to regain trading rights.

Articles of trade

By far the most profitable trade for medieval merchants was in luxury products and goods from Asia and the Middle East. These were articles that had a high value but were available only in small quantities. Trading these items brought enormous profits. Because of the Crusades, there was a great demand for spices, drugs, perfumes, dyes, and precious gems from Asia. Manufactured goods included silks, cotton, linen, and art products in gold, silver, and ivory. The Middle East also supplied textiles, rugs, grain, and fruit.

Europe offered various products in exchange for Asian goods. The Baltic region supplied fur, timber, fish, and grain. From Spain came wine, oil, leather, and arms and armor. Other European products included metal goods and glassware from Venice, fine woolen cloth from England and Flanders, and wine from France.

Markets and fairs

As trade grew, merchants needed places where they could exchange goods. Many villages had weekly market days, but such markets did not attract large crowds. Some merchants began to sell goods during religious festivals. Then some feudal lords established fairs for the sale of imported goods. They realized that they could make themselves wealthy by charging fees on the merchandise sold. The feudal lords guaranteed special protection to merchants for the holding of a fair. Fairs were held for several days or weeks each year.

The most important and best-known fairs were those of Champagne, a region in northeastern France (see inset map, page 272). Champagne was ideally situated for trade. It lay directly along the route used by traders traveling between Italy and northern Europe. In Champagne the textiles, wool, and wines of Europe were exchanged for Asian luxury goods brought overland from the south. Six fairs, each lasting four to seven weeks, were held at four towns in Champagne. The fairs were scheduled to come one after another. Thus they provided a central marketplace for all of Europe during most of the year.

A simple **barter economy**—that is, one in which goods are exchanged for goods without the use of money—could not meet the needs of fairs as large and elaborate as those of Champagne. Even though little money might actually change hands at a fair, the value of goods had to be fixed in terms of a definite medium of exchange. Since there were many different kinds of coins, a special class of moneychangers became important at the fairs. One of their jobs was to estimate the value of the currency of one region in relation to the currency of another. In that way the moneychangers helped in the exchange of goods.

Fairs helped to break down the separateness of each region and the narrow outlook of the people. Travelers came from great distances to attend large fairs, which offered more than just buying and selling. They were festive occasions. Jugglers, clowns, and musicians entertained crowds as at county fairs today.

Capitalism and banking

Two important aspects of the revival of European trade were capitalism and banking.

Capital is wealth earned, saved, and invested in order to produce profits. **Capitalism** is the economic system in which private individuals use wealth in this way. Capitalism did not suddenly appear during the Middle Ages. It dates back to the earliest business activities and certainly existed during Greek and Roman times. However, it became more important in the later Middle Ages than it had been before.

(continued on page 274)

CHIEF TRADE ROUTES
OF THE LATER MIDDLE AGES

——————— Routes of Italian traders

- - - - - - - Routes of German and Flemish traders

——————— Routes of Chinese and Muslim traders

·············· Old Viking trade route

ATLANTIC OCEAN

NORWAY

SWEDEN

Stockholm

NORTH SEA

BALTIC SEA

LITHUANIA

RUSSIAN

Novgorod

STATES

ENGLAND

London

Hamburg

Danzig

POLAND

Kiev

Bruges

HOLY

Ghent

ROMAN

Paris

Nuremberg

FRANCE

EMPIRE

EUROPE

Rhine R.

Lyons

ALPS

HUNGARY

Danube River

Dnieper River

Azov

Genoa

Venice

Pisa

Marseille

ITALY

Rome

BLACK SEA

Constantinople

CASPIAN SEA

A

Trebizond

SPAIN

BYZANTINE

PORTUGAL

EMPIRE

ASIA

MINOR

Lisbon

Toledo

Mosul

Cordova

MEDITERRANEAN SEA

Antioch

Seville

Tunis

SYRIA

Baghdad

Strait of Gibraltar

Tyre

Damascus

PERSIA

Tangier

PALESTINE

Tripoli

Alexandria

Cairo

AFRICA

EGYPT

Nile River

ARABIA

Jidda

RED SEA

Mecca

PERSIAN GULF

ATLAS MTS.

SI

INDI

PRINCIPAL MARKET TOWNS AND FAIRS

ENGLAND

NORTH SEA

Danzig

Stourbridge

Hamburg

London

Magdeburg

HOLY

Antwerp

Cologne

Leipzig

Ypres

Bruges

ROMAN

Aachen

Frankfurt

Paris

Nuremberg

EMPIRE

Lagny ∧ ∧ Provins

Troyes ∧ ∧ Bar

Augsburg

FRANCE

ATLANTIC OCEAN

Venice

Genoa

Florence

Pisa

Marseille

ITALY

PORTUGAL

Medina del Campo

SPAIN

Seville

∧ Fairs of Champagne

PAGE 272

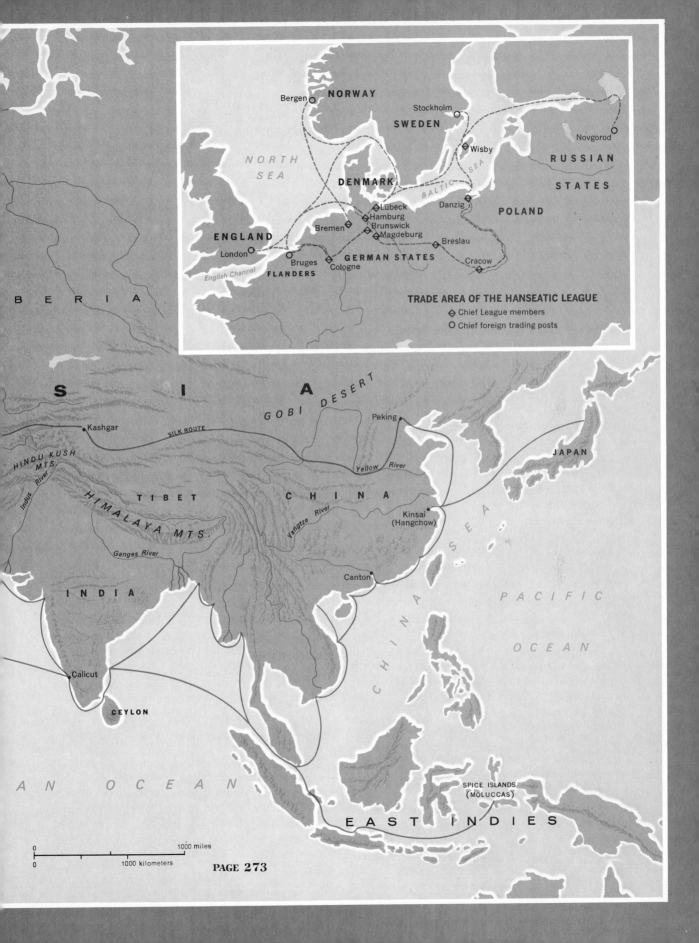

TRADE AREA OF THE HANSEATIC LEAGUE
◇ Chief League members
○ Chief foreign trading posts

NORTH SEA

NORWAY
Bergen○

SWEDEN
Stockholm○
Wisby◇

BALTIC SEA

RUSSIAN STATES
Novgorod○

DENMARK

POLAND
Danzig◇
Breslau◇
Cracow◇

ENGLAND
London○

FLANDERS
Bruges○

GERMAN STATES
Lübeck◇
Hamburg◇
Brunswick◇
Magdeburg◇
Bremen◇
Cologne◇

English Channel

SIBERIA

A S I A

GOBI DESERT

Kashgar
SILK ROUTE

HINDU KUSH MTS.
Indus River

TIBET

HIMALAYA MTS.

Ganges River

CHINA

Yellow River

Yangtze River

Peking

Kinsai (Hangchow)

JAPAN

Canton

CHINA SEA

PACIFIC OCEAN

INDIA

Calicut

CEYLON

INDIAN OCEAN

EAST INDIES

SPICE ISLANDS (MOLUCCAS)

0 _____ 1000 miles
0 _____ 1000 kilometers

PAGE 273

As trade increased, shipbuilding and the financing of voyages became good investments. People with capital formed shipping companies. Each contributed part of the cost and received a share of the profits.

Another capitalist activity was manufacturing. A new method of production, used in many industries but seen best in the woolen industry, was the **domestic system.** The system was so named because the work was done in workers' homes rather than in a shop or factory. The capitalist bought wool and distributed it to different workers. For an agreed price, each of them did a particular job, such as spinning, weaving, or dyeing. The capitalist then collected the finished cloth and sold it for the highest price he could get, certainly for more than his expenses. This system began in towns, but by the end of the Middle Ages it had spread to the countryside.

Banking was still another capitalist activity that developed in the later Middle Ages. In addition to evaluating and exchanging various currencies, moneychangers now began to provide other services. Thus banking gradually developed. The word *bank* comes from the Italian word *banca,* meaning the moneychanger's table.

The most important service performed by early bankers was lending money. Rulers, nobles, and merchants often needed to borrow funds to finance their activities. During the early Middle Ages, Jews had done much of the moneylending because the Christian Church did not allow interest to be charged on loans. By the 1200's, however, Christians became involved in moneylending.

Officially moneylenders did not charge interest but paid themselves by rents and charges for services and damages. They also made the transfer of funds from one place to another easier by developing special notes, called letters of credit, which were used as money. A person could take a letter of credit made out by a banker in Ghent and cash it with another banker in Venice.

CHECKUP

1. IDENTIFY: just price, usury, Hanseatic League, barter economy, domestic system.

2. LOCATE: Baltic Sea, North Sea, Strait of Gibraltar, Flanders, English Channel, Ghent, Bruges, Hamburg, Lübeck, Bremen.

3. Why did trade decline during the early Middle Ages?

4. Why were fairs important in medieval society?

5. What is capitalism? In what capitalist activities did medieval businesses engage?

The growth of towns brought great social and political change

The revival of trade in the Middle Ages was accompanied by the growth of towns and cities. In fact, trade and cities always grow together. The two kinds of growth are related to each other, and there is an interaction between them.

Trade is essentially an exchange of goods. The goods must, of course, be produced by someone. To carry on trade, the producer must have a surplus—that is, more than the amount needed for one's own family. This surplus is exchanged for the surplus merchandise of some other producer so that both parties receive something each wants. In a town or city, we find all the conditions needed for exchanging surpluses of goods.

Towns did not disappear completely during the period from 400 to 1000, although they grew smaller in population and size. Many Roman towns survived, especially those that were easy to defend. During those years some new towns even grew up around castles, shrines, cathedrals, or mines.

Beginning in the late 900's, however, old towns began to grow larger and new ones came into being. These new towns grew up at locations important for trade—natural harbors, the mouths of rivers, and transfer points where goods were shifted from ocean-going ships to river barges.

The rights of townspeople

As towns increased and their populations grew, it became clear that the town dweller did not fit into the feudal system. Townspeople were neither lords nor vassals nor serfs. Manufacturing and trade, at which they made their livings, played little part in the village agricultural economy.

Townspeople wanted to control their own governments. Under feudalism, however, each town was subject to some lord. Naturally, the lords were unwilling to give up their control without receiving something in return. Sometimes townspeople won rights of self-government by peaceful means. In some cases, however, they resorted to violence and even war.

Some lords granted political liberties to towns in order to encourage their development, for a lord could get a rich income from a town on his lands. Sometimes towns bought charters of liberties—written statements of their rights—from their lords.

Town and city charters differed widely from place to place. In time, though, everyone who lived in a town in Europe was assured of at least four principal rights:

(1) *Freedom.* No matter what their birth or origin, people who lived in a town unchallenged for a year and a day became free. All ties to a manor or manor lord were broken. A serf who escaped to a town could thus become free.

(2) *Exempt status.* Inhabitants of towns were exempt, or free, from having to perform any services on the manor. Services owed to the lord were owed by the entire community, not by an individual. The services were always carefully defined and written down.

(3) *Town justice.* Towns had their own courts, made up of prominent citizens familiar with local customs. Townspeople and their cases were tried in town courts, not in feudal courts.

(4) *Commercial privileges.* Townspeople had the right to sell freely in the town market and to charge tolls to all outsiders trading there. Some towns, especially the Lombard cities in northern Italy, gained the right of complete self-government. Their officials were elected by the leading citizens.

Guilds

As trade increased and towns grew larger and wealthier, medieval merchants began to unite in associations. The dangers of travel were great, and it was safer to travel in convoys—groups with armed escorts. Arranging such convoys took much planning and money. Gradually merchants founded associations called guilds.

Merchant guilds became powerful and exclusive. In each town a merchant guild gained a monopoly, that is, the sole right to trade there. Merchants from other towns or foreign nations could not trade in that town unless they paid a fee. The guilds also fixed standards of quality for manufactured goods. In addition, guilds acted as welfare and charitable organizations. They made

connections

Tolls

Toll roads are not modern inventions. If you had been in a camel caravan arriving in the Middle Eastern city of Petra, over 2,000 years ago, you would have paid a stiff toll before leaving the city.

About this time the Romans built a network of highways extending from the Wall of Hadrian in northern England to the Persian Gulf. Roads were kept in repair by the collection of tolls at the city gates. Many of the roads were still in use in the Middle Ages (right).

In medieval times some tolls were collected by barring the road with a pike, or pole, and then turning the pike to allow the traveler to pass. Early in the development of the North American colonies, private companies built "turnpikes" and charged travelers tolls to use them. Now the government gives money to the states for road construction, and each state collects the tolls.

Rivers and canals have also provided natural opportunities for toll stations. By the year 1300, there were more than 35 places along the Rhine River, in Germany, where fees were collected. In England there was a charge for passage both over and under London Bridge. Today, ships pay tolls to go through the Welland Canal in Canada, as well as through the Suez and Panama canals.

Medieval Tapestry

The large stone castles of the Middle Ages were dark and damp. To make their homes warmer and more cheerful, nobles often hung tapestries on the walls. These skillfully woven fabrics were both decorative and practical. They not only gave protection against the cold but also could easily be packed up and moved. The hangings were woven so that they could be cut into smaller pieces and resewn to fit rooms of various sizes.

The weavers of France and Flanders were especially skilled. They made tapestries with complicated pictures—usually with religious, historical, or mythological themes. The tapestry shown here, "A Walk on the Bank of the Loire," was woven in France around 1500. Flowers form the background for scenes illustrating the daily life of the nobles. Tapestries such as this one are highly valued for the skill with which even the smallest details are woven.

loans to members and looked after those who were in any kind of trouble. They supported the widows and children of former members.

In time the skilled workers who were engaged in manufacturing also formed guilds. Each of these guilds included all the people engaged in one particular craft, such as shoemaking or weaving. Thus they were called **craft guilds.** A craft guild regulated wages and set hours and conditions of labor. It also set prices and conditions for selling the goods. It disciplined workers and looked after those who were ill or disabled.

The apprentice system. Craft guilds supervised the training of skilled workers through the apprentice system. To become a master worker— that is, a fully accepted member of the guild, a position reserved for men—a candidate went through two preliminary stages of training.

In the first stage he served as an apprentice. When he was still a boy, his parents apprenticed him—bound him by legal agreement and often after paying a hefty fee—to a master worker to learn a trade. He lived at the home of the master. The master gave the apprentice food, clothing, training, and moral guidance. The apprentice promised to obey his master, to keep the secrets of his craft, and to behave properly. The period of apprenticeship varied from 3 to 12 years.

When he completed his apprenticeship, a young man went on to the second stage, that of journeyman. A journeyman was a skilled worker who worked for a master for daily wages. After working for wages for some time, he could become a master by submitting proof of his skill—a "masterpiece," or piece of work judged worthy of a master. If this were approved by the guild masters, he could open a shop of his own.

Toward the end of the Middle Ages, the line between masters and journeymen became much more distinct and much harder to cross. The journeyman usually remained a wage earner all his life. Increased prosperity turned masters into a sort of industrial aristocracy. Often the master's son inherited the business and position without the required apprenticeship.

The rise of townspeople

You can see that medieval society was changing. Between nobles at the top and peasants at the bottom, there was now a new class of merchants, master workers, and skilled workers. The members of this class were called burgesses in England, *bourgeois* (BOOR·zhwah) in France, and *bürger* in Germany—all from the word *burg,* or *borough,* meaning town.

The rise to prominence of this class was one of the most important developments in European society during the later Middle Ages. Townspeople tended to want stable and uniform governments to protect trade and property, so they usually favored kings against nobles. To gain their support, kings began to consult them and to employ them in government positions.

Along with the rise of townspeople went a decline in the number of serfs. The growing towns offered serfs a chance to improve their hard lives. They might escape to the town and become free. Even if they did not, the town changed their way of living. Because the town needed food, serfs could sell their produce for money. Thus they could pay for the use of their lands in money rather than in work.

As the number of serfs declined, changes also occurred in agricultural methods and production. In England, for example, some landowners fenced off part of the farm land for use as sheep pastures. This action left some serfs without work. Another reason there were fewer serfs was a devastating epidemic of disease that began in 1348. In that year the bubonic plague, which Europeans called the Black Death, swept out of Asia into Europe. In England alone, a third of all the people died. Farm labor became scarce, and, as a result, those who farmed could expect high wages.

Life in medieval towns

Medieval towns and cities were small by modern standards. According to some estimates, Paris in the 1300's had a population of about 60,000. Ghent and Bruges, with about 50,000 inhabitants each, were considered huge. London, with about 35,000, was far above average. The usual city had from 5,000 to 10,000 people.

Physically, the medieval city was compact. It was often built on top of a hill or at the bend of a river so that it could easily be defended. Because city land was scarce and valuable, houses were

built five or six stories high. To increase the space inside a building, each story projected out a little farther than the one below. Thus, at the top the houses almost met in the middle of the street. Each city had some outstandingly fine buildings such as a cathedral, a town hall, and the guild halls.

The streets of medieval cities were dark and filthy. The only way of disposing of sewage was in open gutters that were cleared only when it rained. Epidemics were frequent. There was no street lighting. Honest people who went out at night were accompanied by servants who protected them from robbers, for there were no police. Despite the uncomfortable conditions, medieval town life was not completely disagreeable. The medieval city was a busy place, alive with people—peddlers, lawyers, merchants, strolling actors, musicians, and jugglers.

CHECKUP

1. IDENTIFY: charters of liberties, monopoly, apprentice, journeyman, masterpiece, bourgeois, Black Death.

2. Why are towns and cities essential to trade?

3. How did townspeople gain rights of self-government? What were their most important liberties?

4. What were the differences between merchant guilds and craft guilds?

5. How did the rise of towns contribute to the decline in the number of serfs?

The culture of the Middle Ages flourished in towns and cities

You will recall that civilization itself developed only after early humans settled in towns and cities. In a similar way the culture of the Middle Ages did not flourish until city life had revived.

Language and literature

Latin was the written language of Western Europe for centuries after the Roman Empire ceased to exist. In a form called Medieval Latin, it was spoken by most educated people. During the Middle Ages, however, the common people began to speak **vernacular languages**—that is, "everyday" speech that varied in different places. These languages included English, Italian, French, German, and Spanish.

In time, writers also began to use vernacular languages. The first vernacular literature consisted of troubadour songs. Troubadours were minstrels, or traveling singers, who wrote lyrical poems of love and chivalry and sang them in the castles and courts of feudal lords.

Another form of vernacular literature was the national epic. In England there were stories about King Arthur and his knights of the Round Table, which became popular all over Europe. France had its *Song of Roland*. Roland was a brave knight who lost his life in Spain while guarding the retreat of Charlemagne's army northward after an unsuccessful campaign against the Muslims. Germans had the *Nibelungenlied*, a legend of how the hero Siegfried gained a magic treasure guarded by a dragon.

The growth of towns created an audience for a new kind of literature which the French called *fabliaux* (FAB·lee·oh). The *fabliaux* were short comic stories in rhymed verse. They made fun of chivalry and ridiculed the foolishness of all human beings. They were especially critical of the clergy. Similar to the *fabliaux* were animal stories or fables. Those about Reynard the Fox were especially popular among the more worldly and cynical people who lived in towns.

Another form of vernacular literature that developed during the Middle Ages was the mystery play, or miracle play. Originally these plays were short religious dramas on Biblical subjects. They were written in Latin and were added to the church services at Easter and Christmas. Later, as towns grew, miracle plays were written in vernacular languages, lengthened, and presented in town marketplaces to large audiences. One very popular miracle play was *Noye's Fludde (Noah's Flood)*. It told how Noah built his ark, collected pairs of all creatures, and kept them and his family safe during the flood.

Dante and Chaucer. Two great writers, Dante and Chaucer, represented the flowering of medieval vernacular literature. Dante Alighieri (DAHN·tay ah·lee·GYAI·ree) was born in Florence, Italy, in 1265. He used Latin for his scholarly works. When writing poetry, however, he preferred the Italian dialect of his native region of Tuscany. Because Dante used the Tuscan dialect in his most famous works, which were widely read throughout Italy, it became the written language of all Italy. Thus Dante is considered the father of modern Italian.

Dante's greatest work is *The Divine Comedy*. It tells of a pilgrimage in which Dante is guided by the Roman poet Vergil. Together, the two men pass through hell, purgatory, and heaven. They meet the souls of famous people, good and evil. A work of this sort gave Dante the opportunity to criticize the society of his own time, and he used it fully. *The Divine Comedy* is like a mirror that reflects the period in which Dante lived.

Geoffrey Chaucer was born in England in 1340. His *Canterbury Tales* is a series of stories told by a group of pilgrims on their way to Thomas à Becket's shrine in Canterbury. Chaucer poked good-natured fun at the English and, like many other writers of the time, satirized the clergy. Chaucer used the Midland dialect of English. Because of the popularity of his writings, this dialect became the forerunner of modern English.

Universities

During the early Middle Ages, only a few nobles and some clergy were educated, mainly at monasteries or by teachers in the Church. Gradually, however, schools developed in which anyone could study. These new schools were located in prosperous towns. They had simple beginnings. Anyone who had something to teach could set up in a town and try to attract students. Anyone who wanted to study with the teacher could do so by paying a fee. This educational system was very much like that of Athens when Plato and Aristotle taught.

As the number of teachers and students increased, they united to form guilds for protection and privileges. Such a guild was called a *universitas,* a Latin word that meant any association of people. Gradually the word *university* came to mean an association of people for the purpose of teaching and learning.

Four great universities developed between 1000

and 1200. Those at Paris and Oxford specialized in theology and the liberal arts. In the Middle Ages the liberal arts was a definite course of study including Latin grammar, logic, rhetoric, arithmetic, geometry, astronomy, and music. The University of Bologna, in Italy, taught Roman and canon law. The University at Salerno, also in Italy, specialized in medicine. During the 1200's and 1300's, universities were founded throughout Western Europe.

In time, medieval universities established standard courses of study, with uniform requirements for the various stages of progress. These stages were shown by academic degrees. The degree of Bachelor of Arts showed that a student had finished the apprenticeship.

After further study and examination, the student qualified for the degree of Master of Arts and was then ready to teach the liberal arts. The student was admitted to the guild of teachers at a ceremony called a commencement because it signified the beginning of work as a teacher. Only then was it possible to take up one of the specialties offered at medieval universities—theology, law, or medicine.

Philosophy

During the Middle Ages, scholars spent much time trying to reconcile Aristotle's ideas with those of the early Church writers. Aristotle emphasized human reason. The early Church writers, however, emphasized faith. The attempt of medieval philosophers to reconcile faith and reason is often called **scholasticism.** The aim of the scholastic philosophers was to discover how people could improve themselves in this life by reason and ensure salvation in the life to come.

Peter Abelard, who taught at the University of Paris in the 1100's, was an important scholastic philosopher. In his book *Sic et Non (Yes and No),* he raised many questions about Church doctrine. After each question he placed opinions gathered from the Bible, decrees of the popes, and the writings of Church philosophers. Many of these opinions conflicted with one another. Abelard made his students work out the problems for themselves. He wanted them to think and to inquire. His motto was: "By doubting we come to inquiry, and by inquiring we perceive the truth."

Probably the greatest of all medieval philosophers was Thomas Aquinas, a Dominican monk. His principal work, written in the late 1200's, is a summary of Christian thought called *Summa Theologica.* In it Aquinas took up each point of Church doctrine, examined it, and tried to show that it could be arrived at by logic or reason as well as faith. Today the *Summa* is the basis for all teaching of theology in Roman Catholic schools.

Science

There was little scientific progress during the Middle Ages. Medieval thinking was deductive. That is, an idea was taken from an authority, usually the Bible, accepted as true, and used as a basis for reasoning. Classical writings, like those of Galen and Ptolemy, formed the basis of much medieval science.

There were some important technological advances, notably the invention of the plow, the windmill, the clock, and eyeglasses. However, there were no attempts to increase knowledge by observing nature more closely, and there were few significant advances in scientific theory. It was left to the Arabs to preserve the great accomplishments of Hellenistic science. Only two subjects received serious attention in the West: mathematics, which was abstract, and optics (the study of light), because God's influence was thought to be carried by light. In these subjects some important work was done, especially in the 1200's, 1300's, and 1400's. However, it was not until the following century that a major interest in science reappeared and led to vast changes in the understanding of the physical world.

Art and architecture

During the Middle Ages, architecture, painting, and sculpture were used almost entirely in the service of the Church. Church architecture was the central art of the period, and the other arts were used to embellish, or beautify, it. The building and beautifying of a church was considered a community project during the Middle Ages. In their churches, medieval people expressed both religious feeling and local pride.

During the period from 1000 to 1200, most

(continued on page 282)

Cultural life in the Middle Ages

The cultural life of the Middle Ages was deeply marked by the Christian faith. The centers of cultural life were the cities, and their focal points were their cathedrals, like the one at Reims in France (right) and Notre Dame at Paris (lower far right). Their soaring arches were intended to lift one's thoughts and aspirations heavenward. Stained-glass windows seen from within and statuary carved on their walls and doors told stories from the Old and New Testaments. Such pictorial representations of familiar stories could be understood by the faithful, who generally could not read.

For those who could read, there were exciting new works of literature, written in the vernacular. In English, there was Chaucer's *Canterbury Tales* (below). In Italian, there was Dante's *Divine Comedy*. Its last section, *Paradise*, tells of Dante's journey and that of his beloved Beatrice through heaven. (They are the D and B of the illustration, right top center.) For those seeking higher learning, there were great centers like the medieval University of Paris (top far right), run for young scholars under the direction of the Church.

280

medieval church builders used the round arches, domes, and low horizontal lines of Roman architecture. This style later came to be called Romanesque (meaning "similar to the Roman"). The enormous weight of the domed stone roof of a Romanesque church made it necessary to have thick walls and only a few small windows. For this reason the interior was dark, but the simple style of the columns and arches lent the building dignity and serenity. There was little sculpture inside Romanesque churches, but many were adorned with frescoes—paintings done on wet plaster.

During the mid-1100's, master builders in Western Europe began to develop a new style of church architecture. This style was so different from the Romanesque that critics in the 1500's ridiculed it because it did not conform to the standards of classical architecture. They called it Gothic, after the barbarian Goths. The name stuck, but Gothic has come to be considered one of the most beautiful styles of architecture ever developed. France has many of the finest examples of Gothic architecture, among them the cathedral of Notre Dame in Paris and the cathedrals at Chartres (SHAR·tr') and Reims (REEMZ).

Gothic churches, in contrast to the low, heavy Romanesque churches, were tall and delicate in appearance. Builders used rows of supporting ribs, called flying buttresses, outside the walls, connecting them to the church with arches. Thus part of the outward push of the roof was carried away from the walls and onto the buttresses. The walls could be high and thin, with large windows. Arches were pointed. Tall spires replaced low, flat towers. It has been said that everything in Gothic churches pointed toward heaven.

The inside of the Gothic church was also very different from that of the Romanesque church. Statues of saints and rulers lined the interiors, sculpture in relief adorned the walls, and stained-glass windows let in shafts of sunlight.

In many ways the Gothic church exemplified the changing world of the late Middle Ages. The tall structure rose above the growing town around and below it. Traders with goods from the Middle East and Asia were active in marketplaces in the shadows of its spires. Religious pageants and miracle plays were given within the church and outside its carved doors. All the skills of the medieval

world went into the building of these beautiful monuments to God.

CHECKUP

1. IDENTIFY: vernacular language, troubadours, miracle play, Dante, Chaucer, liberal arts, scholasticism, Abelard, Aquinas.

2. Name some medieval epic poems. How did the *fabliaux* differ from the epics?

3. How did the Church teach the Bible stories to those who could not read?

4. How did medieval universities originate?

5. What were some characteristics of Romanesque churches? of Gothic churches?

Feelings of patriotism spread throughout Western Europe

During the 1100's many of the nations of Western Europe—nations that are still in existence today—developed out of the small fiefs and states of feudal days.

Under feudalism in the early Middle Ages, the power to rule was divided among feudal lords. The king himself was little more than a feudal lord. The people of a country did not look to a central government for defense or help, nor did they feel any loyalty toward the country as a whole. Instead, they were loyal to a local feudal lord, or to a manor village, or to a town.

The development of a nation usually started with the growth of patriotism among its people. Patriotism is a feeling of loyalty to the country as a whole. It is the feeling of belonging to a large society rather than to only a small locality. Patriotism, which was almost entirely lacking during the early Middle Ages, began to appear after 1100.

England

The authority of the English king, although partially checked by Parliament, was strengthened by various means. These included the development of a single system of law and courts, and increased revenue as the country grew more prosperous. Also important were the military strength of a professional army and the support of the townspeople, who sided with the king against the feudal lords.

The power of feudal lords decreased as that of the English king increased. Manors began to disappear as the number of serfs declined. By the end of the 1400's, there were no serfs in England. The villages and farms of free peasants dotted the English countryside.

The Hundred Years' War. English prosperity and the development of a strong national government received a setback during a long war with France. The Hundred Years' War, which began in 1337, had three basic causes. The first was the rivalry over the provinces of Aquitaine and Gascony in France, which were claimed by the English king. Second was the English king's attempt to take the French throne when the male Capetian line died out. Third was rivalry over the commercially rich territory of Flanders. The war brought two important developments.

(1) Feudalism was weakened by the use of two new weapons—the longbow and the cannon. Important battles took place in France, at Crécy (kray·SEE) in 1346, Poitiers (pwah·TYAY) in 1356, and Agincourt (AJ·in·kort) in 1415. There the French feudal cavalry was completely defeated by English foot soldiers armed with longbows. Soldiers using the English longbow could shoot so fast and accurately that mounted opponents could not get near them. Longbows helped put an end to knights on horseback.

Cannons were used during the attack on the town of Calais (kal·AY), France, in 1346. Europeans may have learned the use of gunpowder from the Muslims during the Crusades. To this knowledge they added the use of the gun. At first the gun was only a crude tube of wood and metal from which the explosion of gunpowder hurled stones or chunks of metal. Cannons were developed from these rather simple weapons.

The powerful blast of a cannon could break through the thick walls of castles. Castles, which had been very important as protection for the feudal lord and his soldiers, were no longer such a strong defense. Armies made up of ordinary people, armed with longbows and cannons, could defeat powerful lords. These two weapons helped

to weaken feudalism and thereby increase the power of a strong king.

(2) The English Parliament temporarily gained more power over the king. Through its right to grant or withhold taxes, Parliament forced some weak English kings during times of war to recognize a number of important principles: (a) Parliament, as well as the king, had to approve any changes in laws. (b) Parliament gained the right to impose all taxes. Any new tax had to be proposed first by the House of Commons rather than by the House of Lords. (c) The king could spend money only for the purpose for which Parliament had appropriated it.

Despite the English victories mentioned above, when the Hundred Years' War ended in 1453, England had lost all its lands in France except Calais (see map, page 284). Actually, these losses helped England in the long run. Now the English king could pay attention to governing his own country.

The Wars of the Roses. The strengthening of centralized government in England was delayed for 30 more years by civil war—the Wars of the Roses. This conflict, which began in 1455, was a struggle for the throne between the York and Lancaster families. The Yorkists used a white rose as their badge, the Lancastrians a red rose—thus the name Wars of the Roses. Most of the fighting was done by small bands of nobles and their vassals. The monarchy profited because the great nobles were discredited as a power in England by the chaos their fighting caused.

In 1485, Henry Tudor, a member of the House of Lancaster, ended the wars by defeating the Yorkist king. He seized the throne of England and, by marrying the daughter of one of the Yorkist claimants, gained the support of both families. He became Henry VII, founder of the Tudor dynasty. The English people, tired of war and disorder, were willing to accept the strong government that Henry VII established.

France

The history of France during the 1300's and 1400's resembled that of England. Capetian kings had developed a strong monarchy, although the Hundred Years' War with England caused French kings to lose some of their power.

France suffered much more than England during the Hundred Years' War because the war was fought on French soil. Even during the periods of relative peace, the countryside was ravaged by bands of robbers. Rivalry broke out between two branches of the royal family—Burgundy and Orléans—when one king became insane. This rivalry made it difficult for the French to unite in fighting England. Defeat followed defeat.

Joan of Arc. French fortunes in the war were revived by Joan of Arc, an uneducated peasant girl in her teens. Joan said she heard voices telling her to leave her small village and help the French defend the city of Orléans, which the English were attacking. She persuaded the French authorities of her sincerity and made her way to the city. In 1429, inspired to greater efforts by Joan's presence, the weary French troops saved the city. That same year Joan helped the heir to the French throne take the crown as Charles VII.

Eventually Joan was captured by enemy forces and turned over to English authorities. A Church council tried her for witchcraft and convicted her.

She was burned at the stake by the English in 1431. As the sentence was being carried out, an English leader cried, "We are lost! We have burned a saint!"

Joan's fate created strong patriotic feeling among the French. Her example helped to bring about the successful conclusion of the war in 1453. The English were driven out and a strong monarchy was reestablished.

The Estates-General. For a time during the Hundred Years' War, it looked as if the Estates-General of France might become the real ruler of the nation. The Estates-General, a representative assembly resembling the English Parliament, was established by Philip IV. It took its name from the groups that attended the meetings—members of the clergy (First Estate, or class); nobles (Second Estate); and townspeople (Third Estate). During the war, when no strong king was on the French throne, the Estates-General controlled finances and passed laws. When the war ended, however, Charles VII was strong enough to rule without the Estates-General, which seldom met thereafter. It never gained the right to approve taxes, which was so important for the English Parliament. In France the king could raise taxes on his own authority.

Louis XI. The French monarchy was further strengthened by Louis XI, one of the most remarkable French kings. He became king in 1461 and ruled until 1483.

Louis avoided war except as a last resort, although he kept soldiers in readiness at all times. He preferred to use diplomacy, at which he was a master. His opponents called him "The Spider." He used any methods to get what he wanted. His administration was harsh and taxes were heavy, but he used the money from taxes to strengthen the kingdom.

Louis' great problem was the increasing power of the dukes of Burgundy. Charles the Bold, duke of Burgundy, ruled over a large area along France's eastern borders (see map, this page), including the prosperous region of the Netherlands. He was fearless and eager for war. His great ambition was to revive the middle kingdom of Charlemagne's successor Lothair (see page 239) as an independent state.

Louis XI used diplomacy to build an alliance against the duke. He frightened the Holy Roman

FRANCE AFTER 1453

■ English possessions in France

Burgundian possessions until 1477

— Boundary between France and the Holy Roman Empire

× Battle sites (Hundred Years' War)

NORTH SEA

London
ENGLAND
Calais
FLANDERS
NETHERLANDS
HOLY
Agincourt ×
1415 × Crécy
1346
ENGLISH CHANNEL
Paris
ROMAN
BRITTANY MAINE
F R A N C E
ANJOU
× Orléans
1428-1429
BURGUNDY
SWISS
CONFED.
Poitiers
1356 ×
EMPIRE
AQUITAINE
GASCONY
PROVENCE
MEDITERRANEAN SEA
S P A I N

0   200 miles
0   200 kilometers

Emperor into opposing the idea of a kingdom of Burgundy. Louis also persuaded the leaders of Switzerland, which was independent, that such a kingdom would threaten Swiss freedom.

The Swiss did Louis' fighting for him. They were armed with pikes—long poles with metal spearheads. These Swiss pikes were so effective against cavalry charges that, like the English longbows, they helped end the military supremacy of feudal knights. Twice in 1476 the Swiss foot soldiers defeated the cavalry of Burgundy. In another battle in the following year, the duke of Burgundy was killed. Since the duke had no son, Louis XI was able to seize much of the territory of Burgundy.

The French king soon met with more good luck. Various provinces that had once been part of the royal territory were now ruled by French nobles. In 1480 the Anjous, one of the great French families of nobles, died out. Louis regained the province of Anjou for France. At the death of the count of Maine, Louis also gained the provinces of Maine and Provence. The only great province outside royal control was Brittany, and Louis' son gained it by marriage. Thus all of France was unified under the monarchy.

Because of the increased authority of the French kings, the power of French feudal lords declined, but not as much as that of the English nobility. French nobles remained rich and influential until the middle of the 1700's. They had many privileges, including exemption from taxes.

French peasants did not gain as much personal freedom as the English did. Unlike the English, they still had to pay many dues and give services to the manor and its lord.

Spain

By 1400 there were four chief Christian kingdoms on the Iberian peninsula—Portugal, Castile-León, Navarre, and Aragón (see map, this page). They shared the peninsula with the Moorish kingdom of Granada. (Muslims in Spain were called Moors.) Over the years the Christians had captured Moorish territory in Spain until Granada was the only stronghold left.

The first real step toward unification of the peninsula came in 1469. In that year Isabella of Castile-León married Ferdinand of Aragón. The

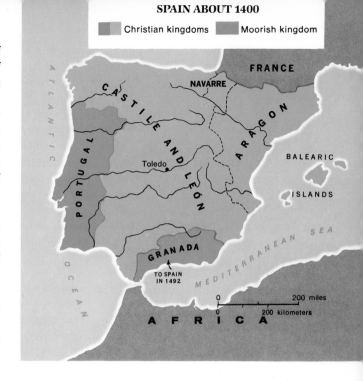

SPAIN ABOUT 1400

Christian kingdoms   Moorish kingdom

two kingdoms remained separate, but the rulers joined forces in a war against the Moors. In 1492 the state of Granada was captured. In the 1500's Castile-León and Aragón were united to form the new nation of Spain, and the kingdom of Navarre was added to its territories.

Ferdinand and Isabella made Spain a powerful monarchy. They took powers away from the Church courts and the nobles. Ardent Catholics, they looked with displeasure at the many Moors and Jews in Spain. Even after the fall of Granada, Moors had continued to live peacefully in Spain. Jews had been in Spain ever since it was a part of the Roman Empire.

In 1492 Ferdinand and Isabella ordered that all Jews within their two kingdoms must either become Christians or leave Spain. Several years later they offered the Moors the same choice. Most people of both groups chose to leave rather than accept Christianity. In the long run this policy weakened Spain because Moors and Jews were leaders of industrial and commercial activity.

The Holy Roman Empire

Strong nations were formed in England, France, and Spain after 1100. However, Germany and Italy—the regions that made up the Holy Roman

Empire—did not become unified nations until the 1800's. In theory the empire was ruled by the Holy Roman Emperor, but few of the emperors were powerful enough to have complete control.

In the early days of the Holy Roman Empire, the emperor was elected by the rulers of many German states. Gradually the number who could vote for emperor grew smaller. Finally, by a decree in 1356, Emperor Charles IV ruled that there were to be seven electors. These electors were the archbishops of Cologne, Mainz, and Trier, and the rulers of Bohemia, Saxony, Bradenburg, and the Palatinate, a region along the Rhine (see map, this page).

The electors were afraid to give too much power to one of their own group or to any other

powerful prince. For many years they elected as emperors only princes who had little land or power. The Holy Roman Emperor had no real authority, but he did have prestige. For this reason the election was always an occasion for bribery and the demanding of political favors. Many powerful princes promised to give up certain of their powers if they were chosen emperor. By doing so, they prevented the emperors from increasing their power or building a strong central government for the empire.

Around 1300 a member of the Hapsburg family, which ruled a small state in what is now Switzerland, was elected emperor. The first Hapsburg emperors were only weak princes with little land. However, the family used the prestige of the title

EUROPE ABOUT 1500

—— Boundary of the
Holy Roman Empire

of Holy Roman Emperor to arrange marriages with powerful families. Through marriage the Hapsburg family gained control of the duchy of Austria and nearby lands. Through many such well-planned marriages, they eventually controlled vast amounts of territory in the empire.

After 1437 the Hapsburgs were always able to maneuver cleverly enough to ensure that the election went to a member of their family. However, even the most powerful Hapsburg emperor did not rule Germany, but only the family lands. Germany remained a nation in name only, made up of more than 300 separate and independent governments.

Italy, too, suffered from being a part of the Holy Roman Empire. Another problem that delayed the unification of Italy was that it was divided, as by a belt across the middle, by the Papal States, ruled by the pope.

CHECKUP

1. IDENTIFY: Joan of Arc, Charles VII, Estates-General, Charles the Bold, Ferdinand and Isabella, Hapsburgs.

2. LOCATE: Crécy, Agincourt, Calais, Orléans, Portugal, Castile-Léon, Navarre, Aragón, Granada.

3. What were two important results in England of the Hundred Years' War? What ruler ended the Wars of the Roses and established a strong monarchy in England?

4. Why was the reign of Louis XI important to France? What territory did he gain?

5. Explain why Italy and Germany failed to become nations during the later Middle Ages.

6

The temporal power of the Church was challenged and weakened

As you read in Chapter 12, Innocent III, most powerful of all the popes, made himself both the supreme ruler of the Church and the judge of political questions throughout Europe. After his time, however, the temporal, or worldly, power of the Church began to weaken. There were several reasons for this weakening.

Europe was changing. Kings were developing strong national governments with rich revenues from the commerce and industry of the growing cities. Their officials were trained for professional service and were often students of Roman law. Townspeople were growing in importance, and they often felt that trade and industry were hurt by the restrictions of Church laws.

A new learning began to appear—the wisdom of the Muslims and the pagan Greeks. Much of it did not agree with the teachings of the Church. As a result a spirit of skepticism, or questioning, began to develop. The Church was increasingly criticized because of its great wealth, its methods of raising money, and the worldly lives of some members of the clergy.

Boniface VIII versus Philip IV

As patriotic feelings increased, the authority of the papacy was challenged. The popes claimed they alone had the right to make all appointments to Church positions. They also demanded that the clergy not have to obey national laws or pay taxes. This question led to a serious clash between the Church and secular authority.

In 1294 Philip IV of France (called Philip the Fair) demanded that the clergy pay taxes to the national treasury. His demand angered Pope Boniface VIII, a man of learning and culture, but proud, tactless, and eager for power. The pope created much antagonism in Italy by interfering in the affairs of Italian cities, and by wars to extend the territory of the Papal States. Boniface did not wish to anger France, which had long supported the popes against the German emperors. Still, he feared that taxation of the clergy by national governments would weaken the independence and the great economic power of the Church.

In 1296 Boniface moved against royal taxation of the clergy by issuing a papal bull—an official order—which said that the clergy did not have to pay taxes without the consent of the pope. Philip struck back by forbidding the export of gold and silver from France, thus cutting off payments to the pope. Boniface had to modify his order. He permitted the clergy to make voluntary contributions for the necessary defense of a kingdom, but the necessity would be determined by the king.

Boniface resumed his struggle with the French

Turmoil in Europe

Europe in the later Middle Ages was beset by unrest. Both the Church and the kings battled among themselves. For a 70-year period in the 1300's, Rome ceased to be the center of the western Church as the popes moved to Avignon in France. Rome was pictured (top far right) as an abandoned widow.

Among the European states, the two main antagonists were England and France, locked in conflict in the Hundred Years' War. The English king ruled territories in France, and for these he had to pay homage to the king of France. Thus Edward II had to pay homage to Philip the Fair of France (above).

In 1428 the English besieged the French city of Orléans. When a convoy bringing fish to the troops was ambushed by the French, the English attacked and won the Battle of the Herrings (below right). But that same year, 1429, the French heroine Joan of Arc (above center) broke the siege of Orléans. Dressed in armor, she became an inspiration to the French troops who eventually forced the English from most of France.

king later. Another order issued in 1302 stated that the pope was supreme on earth in both spiritual and temporal matters. He was judge of all others, but he was responsible only to God.

To block the pope, Philip the Fair summoned a meeting of the Estates-General in 1302. (This was actually the first meeting of the Estates-General.) On this occasion Philip protested against Boniface's demands, accused Boniface of simony and heresy, and demanded that a general council of the Church bring him to trial. The French king then had his envoy in Italy seize the pope and hold him prisoner. Although he was quickly released, Boniface died soon afterward. After his death the political power of the papacy lessened.

The Babylonian Captivity

Shortly after Boniface's death, Philip IV managed to have one of his French advisers elected pope. The new pope moved the seat, or headquarters, of the papacy from Rome to Avignon (ah·vee·NYAWN), in southern France. The next six popes were also French, and Avignon was the papal capital for nearly 70 years.

This period of papal history—from 1309 to 1377—is known as the Babylonian Captivity, named after the time when the Hebrews were prisoners in Babylonia. It was an unfortunate time for the papacy. For a thousand years, Rome had been the center of the western Church. With the pope living in France, peoples in other countries became suspicious. The French popes seemed more interested in their luxurious households than in the spiritual welfare of Christians. Rome fell into lawlessness in the pope's absence.

The Great Schism

The 1370's were an especially difficult time for the papacy. A French pope was persuaded to leave Avignon and return to Rome, where he died. The threats of a Roman mob forced the College of Cardinals to elect an Italian pope. In 1378 the French cardinals elected a French pope, who remained at Avignon. The Italian pope excommunicated the French pope and cardinals, replacing the French cardinals with Italians. The French pope in turn excommunicated the Italian pope and cardinals.

289

The period from 1378 to 1417 is known as the Great Schism (SIZ·um), meaning a division into hostile groups. For political reasons each of the two popes was supported by certain national rulers. Generally the people and clergy of a country followed the choice of their ruler.

In 1414 a Church council met at Constance in Germany. It remained in session for four years. Among its tasks were to heal the schism and to consider reforms of all the weaknesses of the Church. The schism was quickly dealt with. The council got rid of both the Italian and French popes. It agreed that a new pope should be elected, but not until reforms were adopted.

The Council of Constance had more difficulty agreeing on reforms. Everyone agreed that corruption in the Church and immorality among the clergy must be ended. However, there was such great disagreement about the details of a definite plan that no conclusion could be reached.

After long and bitter debate, the council compromised. It decided that Church councils should be called regularly to deal with problems, including needed reforms. The cardinals were then allowed to elect a new pope, and the council drew up a statement of reforms to be made.

Continued criticism of the Church

The Babylonian Captivity and the Great Schism weakened the authority and prestige of the papacy and increased criticism of the Church. Some of this criticism came from inside the Church itself.

In 1324 two members of the Franciscan order, Marsilius of Padua and John of Jandun, wrote an influential work called *Defender of the Peace*. It expressed original ideas about the Church. The Church, it said, was made up of the entire group of believers. The only duty of the clergy was to save souls by preaching and administering the sacraments. The clergy could decide purely religious questions, but they could not fix worldly penalties for sins because God alone could punish.

According to the writers, the pope was only the elected head of the Church and had no other power. All power belonged to the members of the Church. They could delegate power only to a general Church council. A council had authority to make wide-scale reforms in the entire Church, including the papacy.

John Wycliffe. In England these beliefs were adopted and spread in the late 1300's by John Wycliffe, a member of the clergy and teacher at Oxford University. He attacked the wealth of the Church and immorality among the clergy. Wycliffe wrote that the pope's claim to absolute authority in the Church was unjustified. He also said that Jesus could save one's soul without the aid of a priest. The authority of salvation was in the Bible, not in the clergy. About 1382 Wycliffe translated the Bible from Latin into English so that people could read it and learn what to believe and how to act.

John Huss. Wycliffe's books were widely read both in England and elsewhere in Europe. John Huss of Bohemia, a teacher at the University of Prague, was influenced by Wycliffe's writings. Huss became popular with the people of Bohemia by denouncing abuses in the Church, but he angered the clergy and was excommunicated in 1410. He was told to appear before the Council of Constance to answer charges of heresy. Huss was tried by the council and condemned as a heretic. In 1415 he was burned at the stake.

By the end of the 1400's, the Church was still criticized throughout Europe, but it seemed to have weathered the worst of its troubles. The demand for councils had died away, and the popes, wealthier than ever before, held unchallenged authority over the Church. The accusations of Wycliffe and Huss that spiritual needs were being ignored had made little impact. Yet those spiritual needs were to cause far greater problems for the popes than had the Babylonian Captivity and the Great Schism.

CHECKUP

1. LOCATE: Avignon, Constance, Prague.

2. Why did the temporal power of the Church decline after the reign of Innocent III?

3. What was the dispute between Boniface VIII and Philip IV? How was it resolved?

4. What were the Babylonian Captivity and the Great Schism? Why did they weaken the Church?

5. Explain the importance of the ideas of *Defender of the Peace*. How were these ideas further developed by both Wycliffe and Huss?

CHAPTER REVIEW

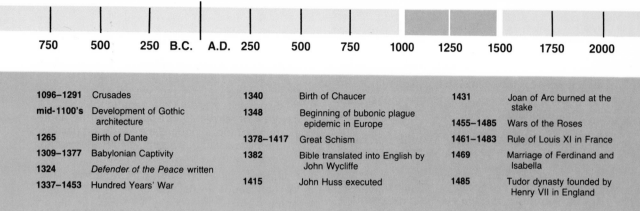

| 750 | 500 | 250 B.C. | A.D. | 250 | 500 | 750 | 1000 | 1250 | 1500 | 1750 | 2000 |

1096–1291 Crusades	**1340** Birth of Chaucer	**1431** Joan of Arc burned at the stake	
mid-1100's Development of Gothic architecture	**1348** Beginning of bubonic plague epidemic in Europe	**1455–1485** Wars of the Roses	
1265 Birth of Dante	**1378–1417** Great Schism	**1461–1483** Rule of Louis XI in France	
1309–1377 Babylonian Captivity	**1382** Bible translated into English by John Wycliffe	**1469** Marriage of Ferdinand and Isabella	
1324 *Defender of the Peace* written	**1415** John Huss executed	**1485** Tudor dynasty founded by Henry VII in England	
1337–1453 Hundred Years' War			

CHAPTER SUMMARY

The Crusades were organized chiefly to regain the Holy Land from the Muslims. Although these expeditions were military failures, they had several important effects on Europe—the introduction of new weapons, increased royal power, the weakening of feudal lords, and intellectual and commercial stimulation.

Even before the Crusades, trade had begun to revive in Europe. Italians acted as distributors for traders from Asia and for those from central and northern Europe, where the Vikings and German merchants played vital roles. Flanders had great commercial importance, as did the Hanseatic League. Trade was aided by fairs and led to the development of capitalism and banking.

Towns grew as trade revived. Townspeople gained important rights—freedom from services on the manor, town justice, and commercial rights. Merchants and artisans organized guilds. As time went on, townspeople became increasingly important in European society.

Medieval culture flourished with the revival of towns. Vernacular languages developed and were used by such writers as Dante and Chaucer. At great universities, scholastic philosophers, including Abelard and Aquinas, sought to reconcile faith and reason. Outstanding medieval monuments were the Romanesque and Gothic churches.

National governments continued to grow stronger. Although the Hundred Years' War and the Wars of the Roses helped slow centralization in England, the process was greatly aided by Henry VII, founder of the Tudor dynasty. In France, patriotism was spurred by Joan of Arc and the French victory over the English in the Hundred Years' War. Louis XI added much land to the royal territory and helped France become unified. In Spain, Ferdinand and Isabella created a strong monarchy but weakened the country by driving out Moors and Jews. Germany and Italy remained disunited until the 1800's.

The papacy's temporal power declined as patriotic feelings increased. A quarrel between Philip IV of France and Pope Boniface VIII weakened papal authority, which was further diminished by the Babylonian Captivity and the Great Schism. The Church was criticized by such reformers as Wycliffe and Huss.

CHECKING WHAT YOU KNOW

1. Match each literary work with its place of origin. You may use a country more than once.

   a. *Canterbury Tales*
   b. *Song of Roland*
   c. *Divine Comedy*
   d. *fabliaux*
   e. *Nibelungenlied*
   f. stories of King Arthur and the knights of the Round Table

   1. France
   2. Germany
   3. Italy
   4. England

2. What were the effects of the Crusades on Europe?

3. Summarize the teachings of Peter Abelard and Thomas Aquinas. How did they build upon the teachings of Plato and Aristotle?

4. Describe the Romanesque and Gothic styles of church architecture. Why was the name Gothic used for the newer styles?

291

PRACTICING YOUR SKILLS

1. **Using maps.** Use the map of the Crusades on page 265 and the map of Europe today on page 810 to answer the following questions.

   a. List the bodies of water, cities, and islands that Richard's fleet passed through or stopped at.

   b. List the cities and bodies of water that were passed through by crusaders in the First and Fourth Crusades.

2. **Understanding chronology.** In each of the following groups, place the events in chronological order.

   a. End of the Hundred Years' War.
   Beginning of Black Death in Europe.
   End of the Crusades.

   b. Babylonian Captivity.
   Pope's call for the First Crusade.
   Fall of Constantinople to Seljuk Turks.

   c. Influence of Hanseatic League.
   Beginning of growth of towns.
   France unified under monarchy.

   d. Expulsion of Jews and Moors from Spain.
   Joan of Arc burned at the stake.
   Summa Theologica written by Aquinas.

3. **Making comparisons.** Compare life in the early Middle Ages with life in the later Middle Ages. You may include the following categories in your comparison: the economy; organization and role of government; living conditions; cultural achievements; role of the Church. You may wish to refer to Chapter 12 for information on the early Middle Ages.

RELATING PAST TO PRESENT

1. In the late Middle Ages the longbow, cannon, and pike changed the nature of warfare and contributed to the decline of feudalism. Read Chapter 3 in James Burke, *Connections* (Little, Brown) to find out more about medieval weapons. Then name some of the weapons developed in the 1900's. What effects have these weapons had on the modern world?

2. Consult your village, town, or city planning agency. Obtain the following information:

   a. What are some of the major building code regulations for housing?

   b. How is sewage, clean water, and garbage disposal provided for or regulated?

   c. Was the street layout planned by the community before people moved in or did the area grow without planning? What was the result of this kind of development?

   Compare your information with what you have learned about towns and cities in the Middle Ages.

INVESTIGATING FURTHER

1. Using encyclopedias or books on the Middle Ages, collect additional information about one of the Crusades. You might find "Triumph of the First Crusade to the Holy Land," *National Geographic* (December 1963), helpful in your research. Then pretend you are a crusader and write an imaginary diary of your experiences on your journey to the Holy Land.

2. The development of the wool trade between England and Flanders is shown in greater detail in "Thomas Betsen, A Merchant of the Staple in the Fifteenth Century," in *Medieval People* by Eileen Power (Harper & Row). After reading this selection describe:

   a. the importance of the wool trade to England's economy

   b. the marriage customs of the day

   c. the business of the stapler

   d. the advantages of the fairs for the stapler

   e. the handling of business accounts

3. Read *Song of Roland* in *Barbarian Europe* by Gerald Simons (Time-Life), which depicts the values of chivalry and the love of battle.

   a. What does the poem describe?

   b. Why is Roland considered a hero?

   c. Why is the poem illustrated in stained glass in a church?

UNIT REVIEW

1. Match each of the following cultures with the appropriate description from the list below:

   a. Byzantine   g. Japanese
   b. Islamic   h. Franks
   c. Ottoman Turks   i. English
   d. Kievan Russia   j. Maya
   e. Mogul   k. Inca
   f. Chinese   l. Ghana

   1. Used Janissaries as both soldiers and administrators.
   2. Artistic expression represented by the tea ceremony and *no* plays.
   3. Unified territory in Europe, including Roman, Celtic, and Germanic peoples.
   4. Conquered most of India; known for the building of the Taj Mahal.
   5. Spread from Arabia with a new religion believing in one God for all peoples.
   6. Carried on a gold-salt trade across the Sahara.
   7. Continued the Roman Empire in the east and helped Christianity spread into Russia.
   8. Erected fortresses, built irrigation systems, and laid paved roads to all parts of the empire.
   9. Decided at the *veche,* or town meeting, issues of peace or war.
   10. Built steep pyramids as ceremonial centers, had a counting system based on 20, and had a calendar that could predict solar eclipses.
   11. Perfected civil service examinations.
   12. Established a representative body that had the right to grant or withhold taxes.

2. Identify the person who might have said each of the following:

   a. I used my native Italian language to describe a spiritual pilgrimage through hell, purgatory, and heaven.
   b. I was branded a heretic by the Council of Constance.
   c. I brought the papacy to the height of its power and influence.
   d. I was crowned Emperor of the Romans in 800 A.D.
   e. I traveled extensively over most of the Mongol Empire as a trader, keeping a record of my experiences.
   f. As a Taoist and a pleasure lover, I wrote poetry that pleased the T'ang court.
   g. In the early 1200's my forces swept across Asia; my successors created the largest empire the world has ever known.
   h. I asked my followers to believe in one God, Allah, and accept me as his prophet.
   i. I established circuit judges and grand juries to expand the judicial system of England.
   j. I tried to merge Hinduism and Islam but ended by establishing a new religion.
   k. I conquered England in 1066 A.D. but also retained control over large territories of France.
   l. I called for all good Christians to join me in one great war against the "unbelievers."
   m. I was forced by my nobles to sign a charter protecting their rights and limiting my power.
   n. I set an example of religious tolerance by marrying a Hindu princess and repealing the special tax on non-Muslims.

3. Explain why the Christian Church split. Identify the two branches. What factors contributed to the split in Islam? What two sects emerged?

4. Trade and city life are considered essential to the strength of a civilization. Defend or attack this idea as it would apply to three of the following:

   a. Western Europe
   b. China
   c. Russia
   d. Western Africa

5. Compare the Western European culture of the Middle Ages to Islamic culture of the same period with regard to:

   a. scientific accomplishments
   b. language and literature
   c. concepts of law and justice

THE EMERGENCE OF MODERN NATIONS

A view of London from Blackfriars Bridge, spanning the Thames River, from a print made in 1802

(1350–1700's)

14

The Renaissance and the Reformation Brought Great Changes to Europe

When you think of the differences between medieval and modern times, you probably think first of the great difference in material objects. Modern people have machines, tools, and weapons that medieval people never dreamed of. There is, however, another and perhaps even greater difference, a difference in attitudes when thinking about life.

The heart of the change from medieval times was people's willingness to look in new ways at what happened in the world around them. One of the main features of modern times is the interest in explaining events and natural developments in their own terms.

Religious belief remained strong, but it ceased to be the only means of describing how events occurred. Politics, for example, was no longer explained in spiritual terms, but was seen as a form of human behavior. In studying the physical world, people no longer felt the need to blame supernatural forces for such events as floods or volcanic eruptions. Finally, people gradually came to believe that what one achieves on earth can be worthwhile in itself.

Of course, these changes in attitude did not occur overnight, nor did they affect all of Europe. Like many other changes, they cannot be traced to exact periods of time or definite places. Many historians believe that they grew out of a philo-

The English humanist Sir Thomas More

sophical and artistic movement that began in Italy around 1350, spread into northern Europe, and had effects well beyond 1700. Because this movement centered on a revival of interest in the classical learning of Greece and Rome, it is known as the **Renaissance** (REN·uh·sahns), a French word meaning "rebirth." Some scholars think of the Renaissance as merely a continuation and development of the Middle Ages. Others think of it as a break with medieval life and thought, the beginning of modern times.

The term *Renaissance* is applied not only to a philosophical and artistic movement but also to the period during which it flourished. This period saw many important developments—the invention of the printing press, advances in science, and a new emphasis on reason. It also was a period in which criticism of the medieval Church led to a movement in Christianity that was known as the **Reformation.**

We will look at the political changes of these centuries in the next chapter. Here we will examine the remarkable achievements in intellectual and cultural life.

THE CHAPTER SECTIONS

1. Renaissance writers and artists created outstanding works

2. The Protestant Reformation changed religious attitudes

3. Calvinism and the Counter-Reformation brought further changes

4. Popular culture took new forms and influenced daily life

5. A scientific revolution swept Europe and spurred many changes

Renaissance writers and artists created outstanding works

The Renaissance began in Italy. One of its characteristics was a renewed interest in Roman literature and life. Thus it was natural that this interest would be reawakened in Italy, which contained numerous remains from Roman times. Also, trade with the Middle East had brought Italians into contact with Byzantine civilization, whose scholars had preserved much classical learning.

The most important cities of the Renaissance were Florence, Rome, and Venice. In these cities, especially Florence, an intellectual movement called **humanism** developed. Humanism was the basis of the Renaissance.

Humanism

Beginning about the middle 1300's, a number of Italian scholars developed a lively interest in classical literature, particularly that of the Romans. Medieval scholars had also studied ancient times, but they had tried to make everything they learned harmonize with Christian doctrine. The Italian scholars of the 1300's studied the ancient world to try to understand it on its own terms so they could imitate its greatness. They believed, for example, that people of their times could learn from the Greeks and Romans much of value about human virtue and moral conduct.

These Italian scholars stressed the study of grammar, rhetoric, history, and poetry, using classical texts. These studies were called the humanities, and those who pursued them were called humanists. Humanists searched out Greek and Roman manuscripts that had been neglected during many centuries of the Middle Ages. The humanists were interested not only in the meaning of a manuscript, but also in its style. They thought that, if one imitated the way Greeks or Romans wrote, one could teach people to be as virtuous as the ancient people were thought to have been. In this analysis of form as well as content, the humanists developed a critical attitude that had been lacking in much medieval scholarship. The revived interest in classical texts and critical study of them formed the basis of humanism.

As time went on, humanism became more than a certain type of scholarship. It also came to mean a new outlook on life. One characteristic of this outlook was the belief that knowing how things were done, how things worked, was very important. This led humanists to place great emphasis on education. They also wondered whether a life that consisted only of contemplation gave a person enough opportunities to be moral. Therefore, humanists felt more and more that one had to become involved actively in practical affairs—for example, in politics.

The result was a new enthusiasm for life in this world. Humanists looked on existence not only as a preparation for the life to come but also as a joy in itself. They thought that men and women, with all their faults, were intelligent beings who could make their own decisions. Along with this belief in individual dignity went an admiration for individual achievement. Many individuals of this period were remarkable for the variety of their talents. One might be not only a poet and musician but also a scientist and painter.

Italian Renaissance writers

The first humanists were grouped around Francesco Petrarch (PEE·trark), who lived in Florence in the 1300's. He is often called the founder of humanism. Many of the humanists were known mostly for their scholarship and teaching, but Petrarch was also a great poet.

Petrarch's main influence, however, came from his ideas about the Romans and about virtue. He believed that the Romans were the best examples of ethical behavior and that they could best be imitated if one studied their writings. This study of the ancients came to be called classical education. It was based on the reading of great Roman authors. Mastery of Latin, the language of the ancient writers, was thought of as the mark of an educated person.

Petrarch and his followers felt superior to earlier Europeans who had ignored Roman teachings, and who therefore had lived in the "middle ages" between ancient times and the new classical times. The humanists were also deeply committed to Christian teachings. Sometimes, however, they felt a tension between their commitment to the Romans and to Christianity. Petrarch, for instance, agonized over his lust for fame (a well-known Roman ambition), which he feared would hurt his chances for salvation. Usually the Italian humanists thought it important to lead a full and active life here on earth, even if that meant less time was devoted to purely spiritual concerns. Their ideas were so admired that by 1500 humanists were leading figures in all the noble households and cities of Italy.

Probably the most famous of Italian Renaissance writers is Niccolò Machiavelli (mahk·ee·uh·VEL·ee) of Florence, a diplomat and historian. In 1513 he wrote a famous essay, *The Prince,* which described government, not in terms of lofty ideals, but as it actually worked. In the real world, he said, power counts more than ideals. In his words, "It is safer to be feared than loved."

The Prince advised rulers to maintain the safety of their states by whatever means they thought necessary, and not to be hampered by considerations of honesty, justice, or honor. Today we use the word *Machiavellian* to describe people who use deceit and are unconcerned with morality in getting what they want.

Machiavelli can be considered a humanist because he looked to the Romans for models and because he was always interested in how things, such as politics, worked. However, his lack of concern for morality in *The Prince* set him apart from the other humanists, who considered virtue their main aim.

The Northern Renaissance

Humanist thought was not confined to Italy. The new ideas soon traveled northward to Germany, the Netherlands, France, and England. They were often transmitted by students from northern Europe who studied at Italian universities and took the new ideas back with them.

New ideas were also passed along by means of a remarkable new invention—printing. Hundreds of years before, the Chinese had learned how to create a wooden block that could have writing or pictures cut into it. When the block was inked, it could be pressed onto paper, which absorbed the ink. Thus the writing or pictures could be reproduced many times. The Chinese had also learned how to assemble the block from separate pieces, or type, that could be used again and again.

The Arabs had also learned these techniques. In the 1400's printing began to appear in Europe, where it had its first major impact on intellectual life.

The earliest books produced from movable type are thought to have been made around 1450 by Johann Gutenberg of Mainz, Germany. Many publishers followed his lead, and books soon helped spread new ideas to a large audience.

Perhaps the first person to take full advantage of printing was Desiderius Erasmus (ih·RAZ·mus), the greatest of the humanists of northern Europe. Erasmus had learned about the ideas of the Italians from books. Born in the Netherlands around 1466, he entered a monastery as a young man but soon decided to spend his life in the study of the ancient Greeks and Romans.

What set Erasmus and the other northern humanists apart from the Italian humanists was that they were interested in the early Christian period as well as in early Roman and Greek culture. Erasmus applied humanist analyses to the Bible, arguing for a return to the original, simple message of Jesus. Erasmus was unhappy that the medieval scholars had made Christian faith less spiritual and more complicated and ceremonial. His beliefs led him to publish stinging criticisms of the Church's lack of spirituality. This was the subject of much Northern Renaissance writing, and Erasmus was its leading champion. Moreover, he deliberately wrote popular books so that printing could bring his ideas to a wide audience.

The most famous book by Erasmus, *In Praise of Folly*, is a satire ridiculing ignorance, superstition, and vice among the clergy and ordinary Christians. He criticized fasting, pilgrimages to religious shrines, and even the Church's interpretation of some parts of the Bible. Erasmus felt, however, that the Church could be reformed from within.

A similar view was taken by his friend, the English humanist Thomas More. In 1516 he published *Utopia*, a book that was as popular as *In Praise of Folly*. In *Utopia*, More criticized the society of his day by describing an imaginary ideal society. According to More, the ideal society was to be made up entirely of free citizens who would elect their own governing officials. Laws would be enforced not by police but by conscientious citizens themselves. Money and greed would vanish, and everyone would practice a simple, ethical religion. More's *Utopia* became so popular that today the word *utopia* means an ideal place or society.

Renaissance literature in England reached its peak in the late 1500's and early 1600's in the plays of William Shakespeare. Like other playwrights Shakespeare often used familiar plots, but around them he built masterpieces of poetic drama that have few equals in any language.

Shakespeare had learned from humanism. He was fascinated by the heroes of ancient Rome, and his characters grapple with the questions of virtue and morality that humanists addressed. Shakespeare went far beyond his own times and background in his portrayal of personality and human emotions. The jovial Falstaff, the moody Hamlet, the young lovers Romeo and Juliet, and the tragic Macbeth seem as real today as when they were first created.

The Italian Renaissance in art

Great literature was only one aspect of the Renaissance. Another was art. The Renaissance in art was one of the greatest creative outbursts the world has ever known.

Like humanism, these innovations in painting and sculpture began in Italy. The most noticeable characteristic of Renaissance painting is its realism in representing natural life and forms. Renaissance painters admired Roman culture, and Roman art had been intensely realistic. In the paintings of the Renaissance, the human figure became ever more lifelike, and landscapes in the background showed the countryside that the artists knew.

Renaissance painters could make their works lifelike because they had learned a very important technique of painting called **perspective.** By making distant objects smaller than those in the foreground, and by arranging them in certain ways, they could create the illusion of depth on a flat canvas.

The early realists. The earliest pioneers of the new interest in portraying reality were Giotto (JAH·toh), around 1300, and Masaccio (mah·ZAHT·choh), in the early 1400's. Both worked in Florence and created human figures that had a much more solid quality than those in medieval art. Masaccio was especially fascinated by Roman painting.

The interest in reality and the ancients developed throughout the 1400's in Florence. It influenced such paintings of scenes from classical mythology as the famous "Birth of Venus" by Sandro Botticelli (baht·ih·CHEL·ee).

The High Renaissance. Italian painters of the late 1400's and early 1500's displayed such genius that this period is often called the High Renais-

The changes in painting from medieval to modern times can be seen in the work of the great early Renaissance artist Giotto. In this painting the angel of God tells St. Anne that she will have a child, Mary, who will be the mother of Jesus. There is a three-dimensional quality in the lighted room, in the rooftops that recede into the dark, and in the faces of the women and the angel. Thus Giotto makes us feel the scene is an actual event rather than a symbolic one.

Giotto was an architect as well as an artist. His interest in architectural detail and perspective heighten the realism of his work. Like other Renaissance artists, he was interested in showing a building or a landscape as it appeared through a person's own eyes. Later Renaissance painters developed perspective mathematically and were able to portray distances with great accuracy.

sance. Among the many great painters, four were particularly outstanding.

Leonardo da Vinci (duh·VIN·chee) was a versatile man—artist, musician, architect, mathematician, and scientist. As a painter, he made use of his experiments in science. Studies of anatomy helped him in drawing the human figure, and he used mathematics to organize the space in his paintings. His mural of "The Last Supper" is widely known. Probably his most famous painting is the portrait called "Mona Lisa."

Another master of Renaissance art was Michelangelo Buonarroti (my·kul·AN·juh·loh bwaw·nar·RAW·tee). He preferred sculpture to painting, and his stone carvings of such Biblical figures as David and Moses have a massive dignity. His paintings reflect this quality, too. Thousands of persons have visited the Sistine Chapel of the Vatican, the residence of the pope in Rome, and looked with wonder at the murals he painted on the ceiling. Almost as versatile as Leonardo, Michelangelo was also a poet and an outstanding architect. He was one of the people who designed St. Peter's Church in Rome.

Raphael did much of his work in Rome. Like Michelangelo, he was hired by the pope to beautify the Vatican. His frescoes in the papal library include "School of Athens," which depicts the great philosophers of classical Greece. Raphael was also noted for his madonnas (representations of the Virgin Mary).

Titian (TISH·un) spent most of his life in Venice. His works are noted for their rich colors. A vivid sense of drama characterized his paintings of religious subjects, such as his "Assumption of the Virgin." He was supported by the Holy Roman Emperor and the king of France. And he was one of the few painters of the period to acquire a fortune through his work.

These, however, are only a few of the dozens of artists who were active in Italy in the 1400's. That there could be so many was the result of another aspect of the Renaissance. Like Petrarch, many leading figures of the time took from the Romans a burning desire for fame. Princes thought that their names would live forever if they supported humanists and that they would be remembered if great artists painted their portraits. Thus they provided jobs for many painters and made possible the enormous creativity of the period.

Northern Renaissance artists

The new ways of painting were too forceful and their appeal too widespread to remain only in Italy. Countries that traded with Italian cities were the first to be influenced. Merchants carried Italian paintings home, and painters from northern Europe went to study with Italian masters.

The artists of Flanders were especially creative. It was they who perfected the technique of painting in oils on canvas. Among the first Flemish painters (the word "Flemish" means "from Flanders") were the brothers Hubert and Jan van Eyck, who lived in the 1400's. Their interest in detail is evident in such works as the altarpiece at Ghent, called "Adoration of the Lamb."

One of the greatest Flemish artists was Pieter Bruegel (BROY·gul), who painted in the mid-1500's. Bruegel loved the countryside and the peasants of his native land and painted lively scenes of village dances, wedding feasts, and skating parties. He used his paintings to criticize the intolerance and cruelty he saw around him.

The German artist Albrecht Dürer was most famous for his copper engravings and woodcuts. During his lifetime, in the late 1400's and early 1500's, the printing press was beginning to make books available. Dürer was one of the first to see the possibilities of printed illustrations in books.

Hans Holbein the Younger was a German, too, but he did most of his work in other countries. During the 1500's Holbein traveled throughout Europe to paint portraits of such famous people as Erasmus, Thomas More, and King Henry VIII of England. This emphasis on portrait painting reflects the Renaissance interest in the individual and in fame among the leaders of the time.

CHECKUP

1. IDENTIFY: Petrarch, Machiavelli, Shakespeare, Giotto, Leonardo da Vinci, Michelangelo, Raphael, Titian, Bruegel, Dürer.

2. Explain the meaning of the term *Renaissance*. Why did the movement begin in Italy?

3. Define humanism, giving both its early and later meanings.

4. Explain how humanism moved northward.

5. What was the most notable characteristic of Renaissance painting? How was it achieved?

The Protestant Reformation changed religious attitudes

Around 1500 a number of northern humanists were suggesting that the Church had lost sight of the spiritual mission proclaimed by Jesus himself. Instead of setting an example of moral leadership, they said, popes were becoming political leaders and warriors. Instead of encouraging inner piety, priests were concerned about the details of ceremonies. And the Church as a whole, they said, seemed more interested in its income than in salvation. What the northern humanists were seeking was a new emphasis on personal faith and spirituality. When their message went unheard in the Church, a new generation of reformers urged believers who were unhappy with official religion to join a new church. This religious revolution, which split the Church in Western Europe, is called the Reformation.

The origins of the Reformation

The first outright break with the Church of Rome came in Germany. Unlike some nations at the time, Germany was a country without a strong central government. Because it did not have a powerful monarch, Germany could not easily resist demands for money that came from the pope. At the same time, the ruler of Germany, the Holy Roman Emperor, was also too weak to control independent ideas about religion that were expressed in local areas within Germany. For both these reasons—the weakness against the pope and the inability to stop new ideas—the political situation of the time helped give the Reformation its start.

In 1514 Pope Leo X started a campaign to rebuild St. Peter's Church in Rome. He thought of Germany as the best place to raise the money. One of his representatives, a monk named Johann Tetzel, was in charge of finding funds in northern Germany. Using a technique that had become accepted in the Church, Tetzel asked people to buy **indulgences.** An indulgence was a pardon given in return for repentance. It was supposed to

(continued on page 304)

Renaissance art

Renaissance art truly reflected the humanism that gave rise to the period and the reverence for earlier Greek and Roman art. For example, the Italian architect who designed the baptistery in Florence (left center) imitated the symmetry and rounded arches of Roman architecture.

Italian artists grew increasingly more accomplished in imitating the realism of the ancients. Leonardo da Vinci's great talent drove him to create works that sometimes disregarded beauty entirely in pursuit of realism (right). Michelangelo's work seems to come to life. His painting of the brooding Biblical prophet Jeremiah in the Sistine Chapel (top left) and his statue of the determined young David (far left) convey the personalities of both men. Della Robbia also achieved new heights of realism, as in the ceramic portrait of a saint (upper right).

Artists of the Northern Renaissance adopted the techniques the Italians had mastered. One of the greatest, the German Albrecht Dürer, produced works that combined realism with a deep spiritual sense (above).

303

guarantee sinners that they could reduce the time their souls spent in punishment in purgatory.

Indulgences had originally been a reward for exceptionally pious deeds, such as helping a poor person to go on a crusade. By 1500 they were simply being sold and had often become a means to raise money. This misuse of indulgences appalled people like the northern humanists, who wanted the Church to become more spiritual.

The concern was especially strong in Germany, where the sellers of indulgences were given great freedom of movement by the political authorities. One unhappy observer, Martin Luther, protested Tetzel's behavior in 1517. The lack of a strong central government in Germany, so beneficial to the popes, also helped Luther. He remained free to develop his protest into a major movement of religious change, with little interference from political authorities.

Martin Luther's protest

Martin Luther was born in 1483, the son of a miner. As a young man he considered himself a terrible sinner and was desperately worried about the salvation of his soul. He was so distressed that he gave up studying to become a lawyer in order to enter a monastery and spend his whole life in search of salvation.

The trouble, he found, was that he gained no comfort from the Church's methods for overcoming sin. He did all the things he was required to do, including making a trip to holy places in Rome. However, nothing relieved his feeling that his soul was damned. The ceremonies and the good deeds simply did not help.

One evening while Luther was studying the Bible, a flash of understanding came to him that he later described as the opening of the "doors into paradise." What he suddenly understood was that all the ceremonies and deeds made no difference in saving a sinner. The only thing that counted, Luther believed, was an inner faith in God. There was no reason God should allow sinful people into heaven. Nothing they did helped their cause. In some mysterious way God decided that some people, after all, would be forgiven. As long as you did not rely on your own actions, but believed God would save you, then you could be one of those to whom salvation was granted.

This insight was the heart of the new beliefs Luther developed, beliefs that were later known as Lutheranism. Such a simple path to salvation was available to all, Luther felt. Thus it was a crime for poor people to be asked by Tetzel to give up their precious money for false promises of forgiveness. In 1517 Luther denounced Tetzel, and sales of indulgences began to drop off. Soon the news was all over Europe that a monk had challenged the sale of indulgences.

Luther had no wish to break with the Church. He had criticized Tetzel by posting on the local church door 95 theses, or statements, about indulgences. He thought religious scholars would debate and probably accept them. However, because his ideas challenged Church practices, its leaders denounced him. As he found his ideas being rejected, Luther developed new positions that further challenged Church authority.

Luther's break with the Church

By 1520 Luther had worked out his ideas to the point that he could say that many Church doctrines were wrong. The sole authority, he said, was the Bible. Popes and bishops could not tell a person what to believe. Ceremonies did not counteract sins. Therefore, the priest had no special role in helping people to salvation, and all people with faith were equal. Luther considered his Church a "priesthood of all believers."

Taking advantage of the power of print to spread ideas, Luther published three books in 1520 that put forward his position. In these books he outlined his doctrines, attacked the pope, and called on all Germans to support his views. The same year he was declared a heretic—an unbeliever—by the pope and was expelled from the Church.

To put this decision into effect, the Holy Roman Emperor summoned Luther in 1521 to a special meeting of the rulers of the empire, called a Diet, at the city of Worms. The emperor asked Luther to withdraw his ideas. When Luther refused, the Diet prohibited the sale or printing of his works. However, because Germany lacked a strong central government, Luther was protected by local princes and was not harmed.

A few years later, the princes who supported Luther protested the emperor's treatment of

AUTOBIOGRAPHIES One way to learn about the past is through written accounts of events and personal experiences. For example, Julius Caesar wrote a book describing the wars he fought. St. Augustine recounted his spiritual struggles in a series of *Confessions.* Such self-analyses became more common from the Renaissance onward. The following quotation by Martin Luther describes his discovery that salvation was possible through faith alone. This passage tells us something about his personal development that we could not otherwise have known. It also conveys, in his own words, the intensity of the experience.

> I greatly longed to understand Paul's letter to the Romans. Nothing stood in my way except one expression, "the justice of God." I understood this to mean the justice that God uses to punish those who have sinned. Although a virtuous monk, I stood before God as a sinner. I had no confidence that my goodness would satisfy him. Therefore I could not love such a just and angry God. Yet I desperately tried to understand what Paul meant in his letter. Night and day I thought about it until I saw the connection between the *justice* of God and the statement in *Romans* that *"the just shall live by faith."* Then I understood what is meant by the justice of God. It means that God saves us through *faith* alone. Before, the words "justice of God" had filled me with hate. Now they became to me inexpressibly sweet in great love.

Lutheranism. Because of the protest, the followers of Luther, and of the other reformers who appeared, came to be called "Protestants."

Luther's works continued to circulate and his movement kept spreading. During the remaining 25 years of his life he was able to establish a new church. He translated the Bible from Latin into German so that all Christians could learn God's word for themselves. And he kept the organization of the new church, which came to be called the Lutheran Church, as simple as possible. All ceremonies except regular church services were abolished. Ministers were allowed no special powers, but served merely to guide their congregations to the true faith. Ministers also lost importance because Luther permitted only the two sacraments that were mentioned in the Bible— baptism and the taking of communion. The traditional Church had seven sacraments. At its ceremonies involving sacraments the actions of the priest, rather than the faith of the members of the congregation, were considered crucial.

Lutheranism in Germany. In the 1530's wars broke out between the Lutheran princes in Germany and the Holy Roman Emperor. Many princes and their subjects joined Luther because they were genuinely moved by the simple faith he offered. Others were attracted by material rewards. When a prince joined the new movement, he usually seized the rich property that the Church owned in his territories. Luther also placed his church under the authority of the local prince. This made a change of loyalty appealing to some princes. A number of them saw Lutheranism as a way of becoming more independent of the Holy Roman Emperor's authority. This was another reason the emperor fought the princes in the 1530's and 1540's.

The emperor won most of the battles with the princes, but in the end he could not defeat them or the new Lutheran Church. He therefore had to compromise at the Peace of Augsburg, which was signed in 1555.

Among its provisions was the right of each German ruler to decide for himself and his subjects which religion would be followed in his state. The people had to accept the ruler's decision or move away.

The spread of Protestantism

Luther touched a very deep desire for a simpler, more direct faith among the people of Europe. Within a short time after he took his stand, dozens of other reformers appeared who were dissatisfied with the Roman Church. Many found enthusiastic followers. In these other movements ordinary believers often had a far greater say than they did in the prince-controlled Lutheran Church.

The sects. The growth of numerous new religious groups took place in much of Germany and Switzerland in the 1520's and 1530's. There may have been hundreds of these separate groups. They were called **sects** because they did not form organized churches with clear-cut rules, authority, discipline, and membership. Instead, a sect consisted of a few people who gathered together, usually around a preacher, and allowed believers to join or leave whenever they wished.

Most of the sects hoped to withdraw from worldly affairs to seek God. Most rejected violence and were among the first advocates of religious toleration. However, some sects did not pursue peaceful means. A few wanted to speed up the coming of God's day of judgment, even by violence. The leaders of organized churches were frightened by this. They also feared that the sects' lack of organization and their willingness to let believers decide their faith without guidance would undermine law and order.

The members of the sects were therefore terribly persecuted, by Lutherans as well as by the Roman Church. The survivors fled to the few tolerant areas in Europe—first to Poland and then to the Netherlands and to England. Eventually some settled in America, where they became the ancestors of many modern denominations.

The Anglican Church. If Protestantism was to resist the traditional Church, it had to create strong churches of its own. (The traditional Church had come to be known as the Catholic, or universal, Church because it claimed to be worldwide, or universal.) The sects were too weak, and Lutheranism was taking hold only in northern Europe. A new church—the Church of England, or the Anglican Church—was founded in England in the 1530's. However, it had little influence outside that nation.

Some Protestant ideas had filtered into England by the 1530's. The English also had a tradition of resistance to the popes that went back to John Wycliffe in the 1300's. The final break with the papacy was the work of the English ruler, King Henry VIII. Henry thought that strong royal power depended on his having a son to succeed him. He and his wife had not produced a male heir, so he wanted a divorce in order to remarry.

Divorce was forbidden by the Catholic Church, but exceptions could be made by the pope. When the pope refused in this case, Henry took England out of the Church in the 1530's and decreed his own divorce. He eventually married six times and did produce a male heir. More important, by creating the Anglican Church and making England Protestant, he created a refuge for the new religious ideas. This was so even though the organization of the Anglican Church was not much different from that of the Catholic Church. It retained the role of bishops, but, instead of the pope, the king of England was the head of the Anglican Church. England returned briefly to Catholicism under Henry's oldest daughter, Mary I. However, under Mary's sister, Elizabeth I, the Anglican Church was firmly established and became England's official church.

CHECKUP

1. IDENTIFY: Reformation, Tetzel, indulgences, 95 theses, Protestants, Peace of Augsburg, Anglican Church.

2. What specific issue caused the Reformation?

3. Why did princes in Germany support Luther?

4. What were the main differences between Luther's ideas and those of the Roman Catholic Church?

5. How were the sects different from the organized churches? Why were the sects persecuted?

6. Why did Henry VIII break away from the Roman Catholic Church?

3

Calvinism and the Counter-Reformation brought further changes

The Anglican Church, like Lutheranism and the sects, did not pose a major problem to the Catholics except in a few areas of northern Europe. However, another reformer, John Calvin, and his followers challenged the Catholic Church even in countries, such as France, where it was strong. Up to about 1550, the dynamic forces in religion were the Lutherans, the Anglicans, and the sects. After 1550 the religious conflict was dominated by the followers of Calvin and by a remarkable Catholic revival known as the Counter-Reformation.

Calvin and Calvinism

The main Protestant church that had a powerful popular following and did not rely on the support of princes was founded by John Calvin, a French theologian. Calvin's great achievement was to work out a complete and clear set of beliefs. His main work, *Institutes of the Christian Religion,* was first published in 1536 and was continually expanded until his death in 1564. This work laid down exactly what the faithful ought to believe on every major question of religion. Calvin thus provided his followers—known as Calvinists—with a code that united them and gave them strength in the face of opposition and persecution.

Calvinism became the official religion of the Swiss city of Geneva, where Calvin settled in the 1540's. From there, missionaries traveled through Europe bringing the faith to ordinary people.

Calvin kept the reliance on faith and the Bible preached by Luther, but he also placed a new emphasis on the community of believers. He said that God had decided at the beginning of time who was to be saved and who was to be damned. The lucky ones, called the "elect," were predestined (or chosen before) for salvation. They formed a special community and were expected to live up to their position by following the highest moral standards. These included devoutness, dislike of frivolity, self-discipline, attendance at sermons where one's sins were denounced, and complete dedication to God's wishes.

Those who joined Calvinism felt a tremendous sense of dedication. They took strength from the common purpose they shared with other Calvinists—to be an example to the rest of the world. Calvinists were carefully organized from Geneva, often in secret groups or "cells." Their energy and determination in winning converts made them a powerful and widely supported movement.

They were particularly successful in resisting the persecutions they soon faced, notably in France, where they were known as Huguenots (HYOO·guh·nots). Although France remained mostly Catholic, by the mid-1550's Huguenots made up about one-fifteenth of the French population. For the next 40 years they were forced to defend themselves in a series of bloody civil wars with the Catholics. Eventually, in 1598, the king of France issued a decree called the Edict of Nantes (NAHNT), which gave the Huguenots freedom of worship and some political rights.

Calvinist minorities were also found in Poland and Hungary in eastern Europe. The Calvinists were most successful, however, in Scotland, in the northern Netherlands, and in certain parts of Germany. In these countries the strength of the Calvinists among ordinary people persuaded rulers to come over to their side. Thus, by 1600, various Protestant churches in Europe were established and strong, but none more so than that founded by the Calvinists, with its forceful backing from ordinary people.

The Counter-Reformation

The Catholic Church took a long time to realize how much of a threat Protestantism was. The pope at first dismissed Luther's criticisms as "a monk's quarrel." However, there were a number of people within the Catholic Church, such as Erasmus, who had called for internal reforms even before Luther appeared. Gradually, as the threat became more obvious, these reformers convinced the pope that drastic changes were needed.

In the 1530's a major effort of revival began that is known as the **Counter-Reformation.** It is also called the Catholic Reformation. One of its first aims was the creation of a new, more spiritual outlook in the Catholic Church. A second aim was to define the doctrines of the Church more clearly.

The influence of printing

Printing was of enormous importance to the religious upheavals of the 1500's. The first great achievement of this new invention was, in fact, a Bible. It was printed in the German city of Mainz between 1453 and 1456 by Johann Gutenberg. Like manuscripts, early Bibles were still decorated by hand (right). Such decoration was frowned upon by the stern reformer John Calvin (above), shown here in a characteristic pose holding a book. The speed with which books spread the Reformation forced the Catholics, in response, to deal with a number of issues of textual interpretation at the Council of Trent (top).

Finally, an aggressive campaign against Protestants had to be pursued.

Revival in Rome. The revival of a more spiritual outlook in the Church was the deliberate policy of Pope Paul III (1534–1549). He made bishops stay and work in their home dioceses, or districts. He also appointed learned and pious cardinals as leaders of the Church. Cardinals were especially important because they elected each new pope. Pope Paul also supported the establishment of an Inquisition and an Index in Rome. The Inquisition was a special court that tried heretics. The Index listed books that Catholics were forbidden to read—a recognition of the important part printing had played in spreading the Reformation.

The Council of Trent. Pope Paul also realized that new attitudes were not enough. He knew no counterattack against Protestantism would be possible if Catholic doctrines were not clearly defined. One reason heresy had been hard to oppose was that Church authorities often disagreed about complicated doctrines, such as the position of the priest. Paul therefore summoned a Council of Church leaders, even though many of his advisers feared that such a Council might become a threat to the pope's authority. The Council, which met at the Italian city of Trent from 1545 to 1563, defined official Church doctrine with the same precision Calvin had used to define his faith.

The Council tried to correct some abuses that Protestants had criticized. It banned the sale of indulgences and tightened discipline for the clergy, who had often been the target of Protestant attacks. In most cases, however, the Council reaffirmed the importance of those doctrines that the Protestants rejected. It emphasized the need for magnificent ceremonies, arguing that God ought to be worshiped with pomp and splendor. Grace, it noted, was obtained only through the Church, not on one's own. Therefore the priest's help was essential. The Council stressed that everyone enjoyed free will. Whether a person went to heaven depended not only on faith, as Luther claimed, but on actions as well. In other words, rituals and ceremonies, the special role of the priest, and good deeds to promote salvation were all strongly endorsed by the Council—in direct opposition to Protestant teaching.

This was a very effective position to take. There may have been thousands of people who found Protestantism's simplicity and austerity appealing. But there were many more thousands who took comfort from gorgeous ceremonies, beautifully decorated churches, the authority of the priest, and the idea that one could do things to gain salvation. The Counter-Reformation thus had its effect. By the time the Reformation had stopped spreading in the 1600's, Catholics were more numerous than Protestants in Europe.

New religious orders

A major reason for the success of the Counter-Reformation was a new aggressiveness on the part of the Catholic Church. This took many forms, including tighter discipline over priests. Now they had to be much better educated and had to work more forcefully for the Church. At the same time, new religious orders, or groups, were founded to promote the Church's aims. The most famous and effective was the Society of Jesus, whose members were known as Jesuits.

The founder of the Jesuits was Ignatius Loyola, a Spaniard. Born in 1491, he was in many ways as remarkable a reformer as were Luther and Calvin. Loyola, too, wondered how he could be saved despite his sins. The answer came to him in a vision that he recorded in his book, *Spiritual Exercises*, published in 1548. According to Loyola, salvation could be achieved by self-discipline and a tremendous effort of will to do good deeds—in other words, one's own actions. He soon convinced a small group of disciples to follow him. In 1540 Pope Paul III recognized them as an official order of the Church.

From then on, the Jesuits became the most disciplined and effective agents in spreading Catholicism. Their missions took them as far away as Japan. In Europe, their preaching and hearing of confessions were crucial to Catholic successes in opposing Protestantism in Poland, Germany, and France. The colleges they founded became the best in Europe, teaching the latest ideas but also turning out fervent supporters of the Church.

The Jesuits were vital to the Catholic revival, though they always opposed killing a heretic. They were confident that, if given a chance to discuss religion, they could convert a Protestant and thus gain a soul.

Unfortunately, few other religious groups took such a nonviolent view in the 1500's. They preferred to kill heretics. The period from the 1530's onward was a time of devastating religious wars in Germany, Switzerland, France, and the Netherlands. These wars did not end until the 1600's. Only then could the results of the Reformation and Counter-Reformation be fully seen.

Results of the religious upheaval

The most striking result of the great religious struggle of the 1500's was that there was no longer only one Christian Church. Religion divided Europe. While southern and eastern Europe and the population of Ireland remained firmly Catholic, France and the Netherlands were split. Switzerland, northern Germany, England, Scotland, Norway, Denmark, and Sweden became Protestant (see map, below).

Another far-reaching result of the Reformation and Counter-Reformation was a new interest in education. This had begun earlier, because of the humanists' concern for teaching. Many new universities appeared in the 1400's and 1500's, and after the mid-1500's enrollments increased dramatically. The religious reformers gave this trend major new support.

Protestants believed that people could find their way to Christian faith by studying the Bible. As a result, training in reading became important. The Jesuits and other new religious orders set up dozens of schools to strengthen the faith of the Catholics. Education did not mean tolerance of new ideas, however. Luther, Calvin, and their followers felt obliged to set up standards of faith and practice. They did not permit views that differed from their own, nor did Catholic authorities.

The Reformation also led to an increase in the power of national governments and a decrease in

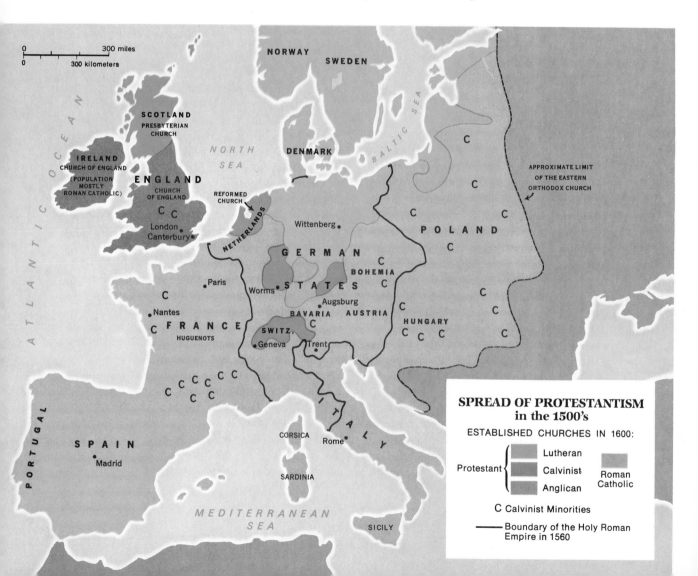

SPREAD OF PROTESTANTISM in the 1500's

ESTABLISHED CHURCHES IN 1600:

Protestant:
- Lutheran
- Calvinist
- Anglican

Roman Catholic

C Calvinist Minorities

— Boundary of the Holy Roman Empire in 1560

the power of the pope. In Protestant regions, each government took responsibility for the leadership of the established Church. In Catholic areas, rulers often obtained considerable control over their churches in return for remaining loyal to the pope. These developments reflected the growth of the power of governments that will be discussed more fully in the next chapter.

CHECKUP

1. IDENTIFY: Huguenots, Edict of Nantes, Counter-Reformation, Pope Paul III, Ignatius Loyola.

2. What were the ideas of John Calvin? Why did Calvinism spread so rapidly throughout Europe?

3. Why was the Council of Trent summoned? What actions did it take?

4. What role did the Jesuits play in the Counter-Reformation?

Popular culture took new forms and influenced daily life

The ideas that shaped the Renaissance, the Reformation, and the Counter-Reformation were the work of a handful of people. What we must see now is how ordinary men and women viewed themselves and the world around them. We will see how those views also changed between the 1300's and 1600's.

Magic in everyday life

Most Europeans lived in small villages. They spent their entire lives raising food and combating nature to survive. For people close to the land, life was never predictable. One could never know when a cow might suddenly fall ill, when lightning might burn down a cottage, or when butter would fail to form out of the milk. Nothing was sure, from the weather to personal behavior.

If they turned to the local priest for answers, the villagers were likely to hear that misfortune was God's will or the punishment for sin. Good luck was, again, a matter of chance or of God's wishes.

God was a distant, unknowable force. In order to explain directly what was happening in their lives, people thought of the world as populated by spirits. There were good spirits, of course, but more often there were demons, or devils, making life difficult.

Because of the belief in spirits, nothing that happened was considered an accident. If lightning struck a house, it was because a demon had made it do so. If the butter would not form, a demon was preventing it. If a pitcher of milk spilled or a woman could not have a baby, the cause was the same—the evil work of a demon.

Before the Counter-Reformation, priests were often not much better educated than their parishioners. They usually accepted these beliefs or at least pretended to ignore them. Priests certainly offered the ordinary villager no better explanations of the way the world worked. Yet villagers often believed that certain actions of the priest were helpful. For example, every spring, in a special ceremony, the priest would go out to the fields to bless the earth and pray for good crops. His blessing of a couple at a wedding was supposed to give them a good start in life. Baptism was a safeguard for a newborn child.

Nevertheless, the priest was not the only person to whom the villagers turned at times of trouble. There was usually also a so-called "wise" or "cunning" man or woman. This person, who was generally fairly old, was thought to have a special understanding of the way the world operated. To these "wise" folk the ordinary people would take their problems—a lost ring, a cruel husband, a sick pig, or even an ominous sign. Since nothing was believed to happen by accident, something unusual, such as a frog jumping into a fishing boat, was at once taken to be a warning. One went immediately to the "wise" man or woman to find out what it meant, or, if misfortune then took place, to obtain a remedy.

The remedies were what gave the "wise" folk their reputation. They did not have to succeed at all times. When the suggestion of a "wise" person did not work, the villager with the problem would assume it was because he or she had not applied the remedy properly. As long as there were times when the advice seemed to succeed, perhaps for a neighbor, villagers continued to believe in the "wise" person. That was so even if the recommen-

311

dations were unusual—a strange spell to be chanted, a potion to be drunk, or a good luck charm to be hung on one's walls.

The belief in witchcraft

When misfortunes became too great to bear, or when a "wise" person was suspected of helping the demons instead of soothing them, the villagers' anxieties could often lead to violence. "Wise" people were often called "good" witches. However, if their relationship with their neighbors turned sour, "wise" people might be accused of being "bad" witches. In many cases, the accused would be an old widow. Perhaps too weak to work, and without a husband or family to support her, she would be the most defenseless person in the community and an easy target for attack.

Stories about witches spread easily. Once an accusation against a person was made, the stories would become more and more sensational. The witch was said to fly on a broomstick and to stick pins in dolls. Or she and other witches were accused of dancing with the devil in the woods at night. As soon as an accusation was believed, a "wise" person would be unable to convince a mob it was wrong. In some cases, the priest might be asked to hold a ceremony to exorcise, or drive out, the demon that was thought to have taken over the witch's body. In other cases, she might be dragged to a bonfire, tied to a stake, and burned, perhaps with the approval of the local lord.

In any event, an episode of witch hunting was a sign that the normal harmony and cooperation of village life had broken down. Witch hunting was a dark side of the ordinary person's view of the way the world worked.

Forms of recreation

For most people, daylight meant work and night meant sleep. Because it was a time of simple farming methods, one needed as many hours as possible to raise food. In the evening villagers were tired. In any case, they could not afford the candles needed to light nighttime activities. Still, life was not without relaxation.

Every village had its gathering place, where people came together to drink, to sew, to do simple chores, or to tell stories. They might also play games, such as skittles (a form of bowling) and dice. Occasionally, traveling companies of players would pass through a village and put on a simple show. There were frequent holidays. Some of them were decreed by the Church, while others were in honor of some local saint or in observance of a local tradition. At these times, the villagers might dress up and would often put on their own ceremonies.

The favorite ceremony was one that poked fun at the familiar sights and scenes of village life. In different parts of Europe it had different names— "rough music," "charivari," "abbeys of misrule." The basic ceremony was always much the same. The young men of the village would form a procession and march along ridiculing the accepted customs or the foolish people of the village. Two of them might dress up like a couple known to everyone because the wife beat the husband. They would be pulled along in a cart and, as they passed by, the other villagers would jeer and hoot at them. The same sort of ridicule might be directed at an old man who had a young wife.

Sometimes the marchers had more serious targets. Their aim was often to show how things would look if the poor or the weak had power. They would dress a fool like a bishop, or they would put the poorest man on a throne. These were no longer lighthearted jokes. They indicated some of the resentments the villagers felt about the hard lives they led and the privileges of those who ruled them.

Violence and protest in the village

Villagers lived in close-knit communities. They could turn angrily on neighbors or on outsiders who seemed to upset their traditions or their sense of proper behavior. Accusations of witchcraft often led to violence. The same could happen during "rough music" ceremonies. Favorite targets in the procession might be a cruel lord, a greedy tax collector, or some official who was taking away food or supplies for a nearby army. At times of hardship or famine, these outsiders would be the targets of more than jokes.

The authorities sometimes tried to ban "rough music" processions, because they feared violence would result. An official's house might be burned, the official might be caught and beaten, or even

Games

People throughout the ages have played games for amusement and diversion. In some cultures, games gave children an opportunity to learn skills that would be useful to them in later life. In addition, games provided relief and relaxation from the routine of hard work in the home or the fields.

In ancient Greece, a favorite game of children was played with knuckle-bones of sheep. They used these pieces in a way similar to the way that we use dice today.

More than 400 years ago, the Flemish artist Pieter Bruegel painted the large picture shown here (above). It is almost an encyclopedia of the games played by children of that time. Bruegel, who loved to show the activities of peasants and working people, depicted at least 80 games in this paint-

ing. They include everything from marbles to hockey to ring-around-the-rosy and hoop rolling. How many of the games can you identify?

Many of the same games are played by adults as well as by children. Hockey, for example, can be a pickup game in a neighborhood park or a schoolyard, or a competition among professional athletes. In recent years, people of all ages have been equally fascinated by the new games and twists on old games that electronics and the computer have made possible.

This wide appeal of games as recreation may account for a feature of Bruegel's painting that has never been explained. Some people think that all those playing games look like adults. Bruegel may have wanted to suggest that adult activities are no different from children's games. However, we cannot know for sure. What we do know is that many of these games and activities are common amusements today (left), for children as well as grownups.

313

killed, or a baker's shop might be ransacked. Often it was the women of the village who led these attacks. Responsible for feeding their families, they felt at firsthand the impact of taxes or food shortages. Women were the ones who dealt with bakers and other suppliers of food. It was they who were the first to suspect that precious bread was being hoarded or being sent elsewhere for higher profits. If troops were sent to quiet a disturbance, the women would stand in the front line, because it was widely understood that soldiers would be more reluctant to shoot at women than at men.

Printing and the Reformation

In the 1500's these violent episodes became more common, largely because of changes in the world beyond the village. The first outside impact the villagers felt was from the Reformation. It came in two forms—in some areas from traveling preachers, and everywhere from books.

Very few ordinary villagers could read. In some cases even the village priest was unable to read. Very soon after the invention of printing, however, cheap books and single printed sheets known as broadsides began to appear. They arrived in the village in the packs of the peddlers who were the main sources of goods from the outside world. Books and broadsides became popular items. When the villagers gathered around a fire in the evening, they enjoyed listening to someone reading the latest book. Or they would chuckle over a new broadside, which usually had a picture and some verses making fun of a favorite object of humor, such as monks.

Publishers quickly became aware of this new market and produced cheap books that would appeal to country folk. The most common were almanacs, the ancestors of *The Farmer's Almanac* of today. These were lists of predictions about the weather and about the prospects for growing crops, arranged like a calendar. They also contained traditional advice about daily living, such as the warning that someone who put on the left shoe before the right shoe in the morning would have bad luck all week. Almanacs became best sellers, because they reflected the beliefs about nature and life that made up the ordinary person's view of the world.

Soon after Luther's break with the Church, new religious ideas began to reach the villages. Either preachers came to visit or, more often, different kinds of books came out of the peddlers' packs. Some writings by Erasmus attacking the Church took the form of simple stories. They may well have been read to the villagers at their evening get-togethers. Certainly the messages of Luther and Calvin traveled in this way, as did translations of the Bible.

As Protestants and Catholics battled for the loyalties of ordinary people, they did not hesitate to encourage their followers to use force against their enemies. It was better, many said, to kill a heretic than to allow a soul that was damned to live. The result was the appearance of a major new source of violence in the village. "Rough music" processions came to be directed at religious opponents, ending up with the ransacking of a church or the beating up of a preacher. In extreme cases, members of whichever group was the minority might even be killed.

The decline of traditional culture

The entry into village life of powerful outside forces like the Reformation and the Counter-Reformation drastically changed popular culture. The increasing violence of the 1500's was a sure sign that the traditional harmony was breaking down and that tensions and divisions were splitting village communities apart. Not only religious groups but also government authorities were trying to extend their control over ordinary people, with far-reaching results.

The most striking evidence of the changed atmosphere was a gigantic outburst of witch hunting that exploded throughout Europe in the mid-1500's and lasted for over 100 years. Religious leaders were ready to pounce on "witches," whom they regarded as rivals to their own position as advisers in times of trouble.

Political authorities were also eager to use law courts to prosecute witches. By doing so, they could gain greater control over village life, establishing orderly proceedings instead of mob rule. The changed atmosphere actually encouraged accusations of witchcraft, because they were taken seriously by local authorities.

Eventually, however, the hysteria began to get

Ordinary people

During the 1400's and 1500's the various social classes had different ways of entertaining themselves. For the wealthy, the banquet was a favorite occasion (below). At courts, such as this one in Renaissance Italy, the stress was on elegant clothing, refined manners, and graceful conversation. For the villager, the great occasion was the public procession, known as a charivari. Here a procession is led by a "knight" dressed in barrels, accompanied by his "bride" wearing a necklace of eggshells (above).

As a comfortable merchant class became more important, a new living style appeared. There was a growing concern for privacy. The feeling of the small family wanting to be by itself is captured in paintings showing Dutch middle-class life in the 1600's (left).

out of control. For example, accusations would feed on one another until half a village, or even a local lord, might be brought to trial. In the late 1600's, therefore, a deliberate effort was made by religious and political authorities to slow down the prosecution of witches. Only a handful of cases came to trial after 1700, and hardly anyone was executed. The witch craze and its ending were clear indications of the influence of outside forces on the village.

Changes in everyday life. It was not only religious and political changes that altered the traditional ways people thought and acted. Within the village, differences in wealth were becoming greater during the 1500's and 1600's because the population was growing. Some families had too many mouths to feed. Other families, however, had good agricultural land that produced more food than was needed. These families could make more money by selling the extra food. Villagers therefore had less of a common concern for one another. As it became too difficult for some villagers to support a family, they left to go to a city in hopes of a better livelihood.

Because of all these changes, the traditional close-knit community of the village began to break down. Hostilities intensified, outsiders appeared more often, and long-time inhabitants began to leave. For centuries most villages had had their own small councils to run common affairs. By the 1700's, as the feeling of shared interests within the village declined, these councils gradually vanished.

Many old-fashioned practices, of course, continued. Many people still observed what we consider "superstitions," such as avoiding walking under ladders because they might bring bad luck. However, acceptable behavior was more and more being determined by religious or political authorities beyond the village. These authorities wanted uniformity throughout their countries instead of lots of local traditions that differed from village to village.

As people left the countryside and traveled to cities, traditional popular culture was further altered. In the city one was not so close to nature. Food came from a shop, not the fields. There were still fires and illnesses, but now local governments were more likely to help out when disaster struck. If there was a food shortage, they distrib-

uted bread. If there was a plague, they set up hospitals and quarantines. If crime was a problem (as it was in all cities), there was a small force of law officers to deal with it. And by the late 1600's, if there was a fire, many cities had firefighters. In other words, there now seemed less need for magic and "wise" folk.

Gradually, more sophisticated attitudes began to take hold among the residents of towns and cities, especially as the ability to read spread. The result was the destruction of traditional culture. In particular, people's understanding of how things happened in the world began to change. Demons and spirits were erased from daily life. In their place people attempted to understand day-to-day events in their own terms. This development has been called the "disenchantment" of the world—the removal of "enchantment," or magic, from nature. One of the most important influences on the growth of this new attitude was the creation of modern science.

CHECKUP

1. IDENTIFY: "wise" folk, "rough music," broadsides.

2. What was the relationship between the invention of printing and the spread of the Reformation?

3. Why were almanacs such popular books for country people?

4. What were the reasons for the decline of traditional culture?

A scientific revolution swept Europe and spurred many changes

Unlikely though it may seem, one of the origins of the revolution in thinking that created modern science was the belief in magic. In the 1500's it was not only ordinary people who thought the world was controlled by hidden forces. The early scientists were also hoping to discover what they called the secrets of nature. That is why many of them were also alchemists and astrologers. Alchemists used spells and magic formulas to try to change one substance into another—for example, lead into gold. Astrologers believed that the position of the stars affected human life.

What made the early scientists more than just alchemists, astrologers, or "wise" folk was that they had very general interests. They wanted to find out why stones fall, why the stars seem to move, or what function the heart serves. They also attempted to uncover the invisible structure of the universe by performing experiments and using mathematics—two methods that were more effective than chants or spells.

In the end, the success these investigators had in solving ancient problems in astronomy, physics, and anatomy created a new way of thinking that no longer relied on magic. This new way of pursuing knowledge we call science.

Experiments and mathematics

The Europeans' main ideas about the universe had come to them from the ancient Greeks and Romans. People like Aristotle and Galen were considered absolute authorities who knew the truth. However, as the humanists unearthed more classical manuscripts, they found that even the respected writers of the ancient period held different opinions. And as people began to examine the world around them—for example, the movement of stars in the sky—they made observations that did not fit very well into ancient beliefs.

As a result, people in the 1500's began to question traditional opinions. They began to experiment for themselves. Above all, they were willing to describe nature without any reference to previous beliefs. This approach was based on the principle of doubt—that nothing was to be believed unless it could be proved by experiment or mathematics. It was this approach that became the new way of studying the world. The transformation in thinking that was caused by the development of this new system of investigation is known as the **Scientific Revolution.**

The reliance on experiments was essential to the new approach. In the 1500's and 1600's new instruments were invented that improved the ability to observe and measure. Among these were the barometer, the microscope, and the thermometer. At the same time, mathematical calculations were improved and became essential to investigations of nature.

Astronomy, physics, and anatomy

The use of experiments was important in the development of science. Even more significant was the new willingness to reject ancient theories and to rely instead on observations and mathematics to understand the universe. This readiness to start from doubt and to create one's own answers was characteristic of the pioneers of modern astronomy, physics, and anatomy—Copernicus, Kepler, Galileo, Vesalius, and Harvey.

Copernicus. For centuries astronomers had believed in the theory stated by Ptolemy in the 100's A.D. This was the belief that the earth was the center of the universe and that the other planets and the sun moved around it. This theory is called the geocentric ("earth-centered") theory, from the Greek words *ge,* meaning "earth," and *kentron,* meaning "center."

In the 1500's a Pole named Nicholas Copernicus came across ancient writings arguing that the sun was the center of the universe. This was the heliocentric theory, from the Greek word *helios,* meaning "sun." The ancient theory interested and excited Copernicus, and he began a long period of study and observation. He became convinced that all the known facts of astronomy of his time were best explained by the heliocentric theory. His conclusions were published in 1543 in a book that was entitled *On the Revolutions of the Heavenly Spheres.*

The book caused little excitement at the time. Few people believed in the heliocentric theory. It seemed to contradict the evidence of the senses. Anyone could "see" that the sun and planets moved around the earth. Anyone could "feel" that the earth was solid and not moving.

Copernicus could not test and prove the heliocentric theory with the instruments or the mathematics available to him. Proof of the heliocentric theory had to wait for the work of two later scientists, a German named Kepler and an Italian named Galileo.

Kepler and Galileo. Johann Kepler did his great work in astronomy in the early 1600's. He was a brilliant mathematician. Using mathematics as a tool, he tried to test the heliocentric theory of Copernicus. At first Kepler could not make it fit the observed facts. It is said that he calculated the problem 70 times before he discovered the error.

Renaissance science and technology

The interest in observation and measurement took many forms during the Renaissance. Sailors had long been concerned about their exact location at sea. They used the stars to determine where they were (below). Their skills improved enormously with the invention of the compass. Perhaps the most detailed observations of the 1500's were of the human body. In 1543 the anatomist Andreas Vesalius produced a magnificently illustrated book containing the latest observations (below right).

Observation also led to inventions. A fertile inventor was Leonardo da Vinci, who made suggestions ranging from improved machines, with ratchets and gears (above left), to possible ways of flying. Engineering skills were also required to build and maintain a press like the one in this printing shop (above right).

Copernicus had written that the earth and other planets went around the sun in orbits, or paths in space, which are exact circles. Kepler found that the orbits are not exact circles, but ovals called ellipses. Now everything fitted together. The theory could be proved mathematically.

Kepler's proof, however, could be understood only by mathematicians. It could not be seen or observed. This additional kind of proof was given by an Italian professor of mathematics, Galileo Galilei.

Galileo had read of a Dutch spectacle-maker who put two glass lenses together in a tube to make a telescope. With this instrument he could see distant objects more clearly. Galileo made such a telescope for himself. By modern standards it was only a small one. However, it allowed him to see more of the heavens than anyone had ever seen before. He could see the mountains and valleys of the moon, and the rings around the planet Saturn. He observed sunspots and proved that the sun rotated on its axis. His discovery that the moons of Jupiter revolve around the planet helped disprove the geocentric theory of Ptolemy. It showed that not every heavenly body revolves around the earth.

Galileo published his findings in 1632 in a work called *Dialogue on the Two Great Systems of the World.* His work caused much more of an uproar than the work of Copernicus had. Many people now wanted telescopes. Many others believed them to be the devil's work and refused to have anything to do with them. Scholars who accepted the authority of Ptolemy refused to believe this new theory. The Church also disapproved because the theory seemed to contradict the Bible. Galileo was summoned to appear before the Inquisition at Rome. He was ordered to renounce his theories publicly, which he did, but the new ideas continued to advance.

Galileo was interested in physics as well as astronomy. Perhaps the most remarkable of his discoveries was one that disproved a belief common in his time—that heavier bodies fall faster than lighter ones. He was able to prove mathematically that all objects fall at the same speed in the absence of air friction, regardless of their weight. This discovery laid the foundation for the modern science of mechanics, the study of matter in motion. Above all, Galileo showed that the same laws of physics that worked on earth also operated in the heavens.

Vesalius and Harvey. Progress was also made in the field of anatomy. Andreas Vesalius, born in Brussels, was a pioneer in the study of anatomy. Vesalius refused to accept without question what Galen had written hundreds of years earlier. Instead he conducted investigations of his own to see how the human body was constructed. In 1543–the same year that Copernicus published his book—Vesalius published a work called *On the Fabric of the Human Body.* This book, with its beautiful illustrations, is a landmark in the history of medicine.

Equally important was the work of William Harvey, an English physician. He was the first person to understand and describe the circulation of the blood, the working of the heart, and the function of the blood vessels.

The triumph of science

The effects of these discoveries were felt throughout Europe. So much had been accomplished. Knowledge had advanced so far that the scientists' methods became the examples for everyone.

One of the most influential advocates of science was René Descartes (day·KART), a French philosopher and scientist. His *Discourse on Method* (1637) argued that all thought had to follow the clear, orderly progression of scientific reasoning. Everything had to be proved—even one's own existence. According to Descartes, he knew he was alive only because he was thinking: "I think, therefore I am."

His contemporary, the English philosopher Francis Bacon, put the case even more strongly. Science, he thought, would help humanity conquer nature and would end all the suffering in the world. For one observer, the French philosopher Blaise Pascal, such ideas seemed dangerous because they ignored the power of faith and the need to rely on God. Few people took notice of Pascal. Instead they made a hero of the man who was taken to be the supreme example of the new reasoning powers of science, the English mathematician and philosopher Isaac Newton.

Newton and other scientists. In 1687 Newton, one of the greatest scientists of all time, published his *Mathematical Principles of Natural Philoso-*

Lady with a Unicorn

The work of the great Italian artist Raphael reflected the intellectual and artistic ideals of the Renaissance. His paintings combined spiritualism and artistry with the search for realism and truth that characterized his age. Raphael studied and worked in Florence, in the schools of Michelangelo and Leonardo. There he became so accomplished that he was called to Rome to help decorate the Vatican. Some of his most famous works are marveled at each year by millions of visitors to Rome.

In his paintings Raphael conveyed a feeling of balanced space, giving the viewer a sensation of both tranquility and joy. In this painting we see a Renaissance lady holding a baby unicorn. The unicorn is snugly enclosed in the lady's arms, yet relaxed in the spaciousness of her lap. The main figure takes up almost the entire canvas and the landscape stretches back into the distance, yet there is no sense of crowding. The glowing fabric of the lady's dress and the beauty of her pendant reveal the splendor of Renaissance taste.

Raphael's respect for antiquity and his knowledge of the classical world are demonstrated in the little unicorn. This fabled animal appeared in the art of ancient civilizations (see page 48). In Christian art of the Middle Ages it was often used as a symbol for the purity of Christ and the Virgin Mary.

phy. In it he combined and related the contributions of Copernicus, Kepler, and Galileo.

These scientists had shown that the planets, including the earth, revolve around the sun. Newton explained the laws of force and motion that control these motions of the planets. His law of universal gravitation stated that the force of gravity prevents objects from flying off the earth. Gravity also holds the whole system of sun and planets together by keeping them in their orbits.

Newton's work had an immense influence on the thinking of his own age and on all later scientific thought. The English poet Alexander Pope described Newton's great impact:

"Nature and nature's laws lay hid in night;
God said, 'Let Newton be,' and all was light."

New discoveries were made elsewhere in Europe. Newton and a German philosopher and mathematician, Gottfried Wilhelm von Leibniz, independently developed calculus. This is a branch of mathematics that studies continuously changing quantities. A Dutch scientist, Anton van Leeuwenhoek (LAY·vun·hook), used the microscope—an invention of the late 1500's—to discover bacteria. It also enabled him to observe a whole new world of life that could not normally be seen by the eye.

Robert Hooke of England was another scientist who worked with the microscope. He was the first person to identify cells in living matter. Hooke examined a thin slice of cork and noticed that it was made up of small rectangular "rooms." He called them "cells" because they looked like the cells in which bees store honey.

An English scientist of the late 1600's, Robert Boyle, is known as the founder of modern chemistry. Chemistry is the science of the composition of materials and the changes they undergo. Boyle conducted many experiments with air pressure and worked out a basic principle describing gases that is known as Boyle's Law. Another English chemist, Joseph Priestley, discovered the element later called oxygen. (Elements are the fundamental substances that make up matter.)

It was a French chemist and physicist, Antoine Lavoisier (lah·vwah·ZYAY), who named oxygen. He showed that fire was not an element, as many had believed. Instead, he proved that it was the result of the rapid combination of oxygen with another substance. Lavoisier also demonstrated that matter is indestructible. It can be neither created nor destroyed but only changed from one form into another. For example, when water boils down, it does not disappear but forms steam, which combines with the air. Its substance has changed but it has not disappeared. Lavoisier's discovery is known as the law of the conservation of matter.

The Enlightenment

Priestley and Lavoisier both worked in the 1700's. By this time the scientific point of view dominated European thought. The people of the 1700's spoke of their times as an "Age of Enlightenment." They felt they were the first to have discovered the "light" of logical thinking revealed by science.

People were expressing their admiration for the scientific attitude of mind even before Newton. However, during the 1700's the idea that science does not accept anything as true that cannot be proved by mathematics and experiment became widely accepted. Every natural phenomenon was believed to have a cause, and every cause an effect. The thinkers of the Enlightenment attempted to test everything by observation and to determine the cause-effect relationship of natural events.

Another characteristic of the Enlightenment was **rationalism.** This is the belief that truth can be arrived at solely by reason—by rational, logical thinking. Because of this characteristic, the period is also often called the Age of Reason.

The thinkers of the Enlightenment tried to apply scientific methods to all human ideas and customs. They examined critically the political and social institutions under which they lived. They tried to learn how institutions had developed. They analyzed the power of kings, the special position of churches, the privileges of clergy and nobles. Several thinkers of the Enlightenment attacked the idea of privileged classes. They thought that political and social institutions should be changed to benefit everyone instead of just certain groups. Scientists met in special societies and published journals to exchange ideas. Similar organizations were also created to discuss politics, art, and other subjects.

The Enlightenment was characterized not only by the scientific attitude and by rationalism but also by belief in natural law. The discoveries of Newton and other scientists seemed to point to an orderly universe. Many individuals came to feel that there was a natural law that governed the universe and all of its creatures.

God, they believed, had created the world and made rules for all living things. Just as the law of gravitation governed the physical movement of planets, so other laws governed human behavior. In order to live in harmony, people had to discover natural law by using their reason. If they lived according to natural law and made their institutions and government conform to it, the world would become a perfect place.

A new view of the world

The outlook of Enlightenment writers was very different from the accepted views of medieval times. Since the Renaissance, a major shift had taken place in European culture. It might be said that the new attitudes represented a "disenchantment" of the world.

What had developed was a new willingness to accept nature and humanity for their own sakes. They were no longer explained solely by means of preconceived ideas or by a belief in supernatural causes. Religious faith was still profoundly felt, but it did not restrict the new interest in practical matters. This separation of the material from the spiritual, and the consequent readiness to try to change and improve the conditions of daily life, set Europe apart by the 1700's from the rest of the world.

CHECKUP

1. IDENTIFY: Scientific Revolution, Copernicus, Kepler, Galileo, Vesalius, Harvey, law of the conservation of matter.

2. How did Descartes and Bacon adapt the ideas of science to their writings?

3. What were Newton's scientific contributions?

4. Describe the contributions of three other scientists of this period.

5. How did the belief in natural law differ from the medieval attitude toward life?

CHAPTER REVIEW

mid–1300's	Beginnings of humanism and the Renaissance	**1530's**	Anglican Church created Beginning of Counter-Reformation	**1545–1563**	Council of Trent
1450	Gutenberg's printing press	**1536**	Calvin's *Institutes of the Christian Religion*	**1555**	Peace of Augsburg
1513	Machiavelli's *The Prince*			**1598**	Edict of Nantes
1516	More's *Utopia*	**1540**	Founding of Jesuit order	**1632**	Galileo's *Dialogue*
1517	Luther's 95 theses	**1543**	Copernicus's *On the Revolutions of the Heavenly Spheres*	**1687**	Newton's *Mathematical Principles of Natural Philosophy*
1521	Diet of Worms				

CHAPTER SUMMARY

In the late 1300's a literary and artistic movement known as the Renaissance swept Italy and then the rest of western Europe. It grew out of humanism, an intellectual movement characterized by a renewed interest in classical learning, a critical spirit, and enthusiasm for life in this world. These ideas were reflected in the work of such writers as Petrarch, Erasmus, and More. The Renaissance also inspired masterpieces in painting, sculpture, and architecture.

Around the year 1500, many humanists in northern Europe began to apply their ideas to religious matters. Their criticisms developed into a religious revolution that split the Church in western Europe.

In Germany, Martin Luther broke away from the Roman Catholic Church and began the Protestant Reformation. The doctrines he developed, known as Lutheranism, spread throughout northern Europe. In England, a new church, the Anglican Church, was founded. John Calvin's teachings spread from Switzerland to France, the Netherlands, Scotland, and parts of Germany.

In the 1530's the Roman Catholic Church began a major revival effort known as the Counter-Reformation. At the Council of Trent, Church leaders defined official doctrines. New religious orders, such as the Jesuits, were founded to halt the spread of Protestantism.

During this period, the development of the printing press and the religious changes of the Reformation brought new ideas to the lives of ordinary people. New attitudes toward nature and toward the community took hold.

The Scientific Revolution of the 1500's and 1600's transformed the methods and understanding of astronomy, physics, and anatomy. Important technological and scientific achievements were made. The scientific attitude dominated European thought during the Enlightenment of the 1700's. The writings of this period were characterized by a belief in rationalism and natural law.

CHECKING WHAT YOU KNOW

1. Match each artist at the left with a work at the right:

   a. Holbein
   b. Leonardo
   c. Michelangelo
   d. Bruegel
   e. Dürer
   f. Titian

   1. Sistine Chapel
   2. "Henry VIII"
   3. "Mona Lisa"
   4. scenes of peasant life
   5. "Assumption of the Virgin"
   6. copper engravings and woodcuts

2. Match each author at the left with an idea at the right:

   a. Luther
   b. Copernicus
   c. Descartes
   d. Newton
   e. Loyola
   f. Erasmus

   1. "I think, therefore I am."
   2. Explained the law of universal gravitation.
   3. Salvation is possible through faith alone.
   4. Earth revolves around the sun.
   5. Individual actions can bring salvation.
   6. Ridiculed ignorance and vice among Christians.

3. What did each of the following people contribute to the development of humanism:

   a. Petrarch
   b. Machiavelli
   c. Erasmus
   d. Shakespeare

4. What were Martin Luther's ideas on each of the following:

   a. salvation
   b. the sacraments
   c. the clergy

5. What was the Counter-Reformation? What did it try to accomplish?

6. During the time of the Reformation, most people in Europe lived in small villages. Describe how villagers explained the different natural events that occurred in their lives.

PRACTICING YOUR SKILLS

1. **Using pictures.** Select a work of art of the Renaissance and compare it with one from the medieval period (see Chapter 13). What are the differences in subject matter and style? How do these differences reflect the changing outlook on life?

2. **Using readings.** Read "The Doctrines of Calvin" in Sydney Eisen and Maurice Filler, eds., *The Human Adventure* (Harcourt Brace Jovanovich). What does Calvin mean by predestination? Who are the members of the "elect"? What does Calvin mean by the "calling" of an individual?

3. **Making comparisons.** Compare Europe during the Middle Ages with Europe at the end of the 1600's. (You may wish to refer back to Chapters 12 and 13 for information on the Middle Ages.) Use the following categories in your comparison:

   a. scientific knowledge
   b. literature
   c. religion

RELATING PAST TO PRESENT

1. A Renaissance person is defined as one who is knowledgeable in both science and art. Give an example of someone in today's world who might be called a Renaissance person. What are the advantages and disadvantages of this combination of knowledge for an educated person?

2. In this chapter you read Luther's description of how he came to understand the nature of God. Why do you think people write autobiographies? Select an event in recent history and find out if any of the participants have written accounts of it. What might you learn from their own stories?

3. How did the invention of printing revolutionize the spread of knowledge and ideas in Europe during the time of the Reformation? Describe how radio and television have changed our understanding of the world today.

INVESTIGATING FURTHER

1. Leonardo da Vinci was one of the greatest geniuses of the Renaissance. Prepare a report on Leonardo's many talents and achievements. You may use the following sources: "The Scope of Genius" in John Hale, *The Renaissance* (Time-Life Books) and "Leonardo da Vinci" in *Horizon Book of the Renaissance* (American Heritage).

2. In encyclopedias or biographies, read more about one of the Renaissance artists or writers that you read about in this chapter. Prepare a short report on that person's life and major achievements.

3. The invention of the printing press caused a revolution in communication. Find out more about Gutenberg's invention and its development. Sources include: Douglas McMurtie, *The Book: The Story of Printing and Bookmaking* (Oxford University Press) and "The Birth of Printing" in Edith Simon, *The Reformation* (Time-Life Books). Present your findings to the class.

(1480–1800)

15

Central Governments Throughout Europe Increased Their Powers

By the early 1500's there were important differences between the way England, France, and Spain were governed and the way other European countries were governed. In the three western countries, central governments headed by strong rulers began to establish their authority. In the 1600's well-organized governments were also formed in the Netherlands, Sweden, and Russia. In the rest of Europe, especially in Germany and Italy, local rulers held on to political power, and central governments remained weak.

In every country there was tension until the mid-1600's between those who wanted to enlarge the authority of central governments and those who hoped to retain local independence. Not until a series of revolts in the 1640's and 1650's ended was it clear how this conflict would be resolved. So many upheavals took place at this time that the resulting turmoil has been called the "crisis" of the 1600's. After the period of crisis was over, the way in which the various countries were to be ruled was settled for the next hundred years.

On the whole, the countries that had developed strong governments before 1640 continued in this direction, while weak governments remained weak. However, there was now a significant difference among the countries that established strong governments. Some—notably England and the Netherlands—established a constitutional system. In their governments a king or queen and

Elizabeth I, a shrewd and powerful monarch

ministers held power, but representatives of the people also had a say in the country's policies. Other countries—especially Spain and France—created governments in which the central authority, usually a king, controlled all policy and did not consult the people or their representatives.

These trends in government were influenced by two major factors. The first was religion. The governments wanted all their subjects united by one faith. However, the people often held different religious beliefs and were willing to fight their rulers to protect these beliefs. This struggle over religion intensified the struggle over authority.

The second influence was warfare. War became increasingly complicated and expensive in the 1500's and 1600's. Only central governments had the resources to support large armies. They needed full-time professional soldiers, officials who supplied the troops, and taxes to pay for their services. To meet these needs the central governments made more and more demands on their citizens and thus strengthened the governments' powers. The demands, however, often made the subjects angry and ready to resist their governments. This tension was one of the main causes of the "crisis" of the mid-1600's.

THE CHAPTER SECTIONS

1. Spain and then France dominated Europe in the 1500's and 1600's

2. English monarchs clashed with Parliament

3. England established a constitutional monarchy

4. After years of unrest, France dominated Europe

5. Russia became a major power in the 1700's

6. Austria and Prussia competed for power in central Europe

Spain and then France dominated Europe in the 1500's and 1600's

Throughout the 1500's Spain was the most powerful nation in Europe. During the 1600's Spain's power declined, and France took over the dominant position in Europe.

Charles V

You have read that the Hapsburgs of Austria were highly successful in arranging marriages that increased their lands and power. Through a series of such marriages, a Hapsburg came to the throne of Spain as Charles I in 1516. Three years later he was elected emperor of the Holy Roman Empire, having influenced the election with money borrowed from the Fuggers (FOOG·urz) of Augsburg, a powerful banking family. He received the title of Emperor Charles V. As king of Spain and as the Holy Roman Emperor, Charles ruled huge areas of Europe, as well as vast territories in the Americas. (You will read about overseas exploration by European nations in Chapter 16.)

Charles found that his titles and power brought with them problems and responsibilities. First there was the problem of his own nationality. He was born in Flanders and spoke French. However, as king of Spain, he had to have a Spanish outlook. At the same time, as emperor of the Holy Roman Empire, he had to be sympathetic to German aims.

As emperor, Charles was responsible for defending Europe against the Turks of the Ottoman Empire, who invaded central Europe and attacked European ships on the Mediterranean. In Germany, Charles was also responsible for upholding the Roman Catholic states against the Protestant princes. As ruler of so many lands, Charles was faced with the fear and jealousy of other European countries, especially France. All these problems had to be handled at the same time.

The wars of Charles V. Charles had several advantages on his side. The Spanish army at that time was the strongest and best organized in Europe. The Spanish fleet was powerful. Great wealth from the Americas made it possible to buy supplies and weapons and to hire mercenary soldiers. On the other hand, Spain's government, though tightly controlled by the king, could not operate efficiently over such a large area. Also, Spain did not have many industries and had difficulty feeding its people because so much land was devoted to the raising of sheep.

In 1529 Charles halted Turkish penetration of central Europe by driving the Turks back from Vienna. In Germany he made strong but unsuccessful efforts to bring Lutherans and Roman Catholics into agreement. As you have read, a religious war broke out there in the 1540's and was settled with the Peace of Augsburg in 1555.

Even before the Peace of Augsburg, Charles had decided to give up his throne. In 1555 he divided his vast territory (see map, opposite page). His son Philip received Spain and its possessions and ascended the Spanish throne as Philip II. His branch of the family became known as the Spanish Hapsburgs. Charles' brother Ferdinand, king of Hungary and Bohemia, became emperor of the Holy Roman Empire. He and his successors are called the Austrian Hapsburgs.

Philip II's rule

Philip II was born and educated in Spain and proudly considered himself a Spaniard. He wanted Spain to continue as the leading power in Europe and the world, and he worked to make the nation stronger at home so that it might be stronger abroad.

Philip strengthened the central government, made it responsible only to the king, and established his capital at Madrid. To unite his subjects in religious faith, Philip ordered the Spanish Inquisition to redouble its efforts to find and stamp out heresy. To protect Catholicism and advance Spain's glory, Philip also became involved in foreign wars. Even the great treasure from the Americas was not enough to pay the costs. The Spanish government imposed heavy taxes, which hurt Spanish trade and industries. Financial problems only grew worse in Philip's reign, and he had to declare himself bankrupt four times.

Philip centralized all power so tightly that an efficient government became impossible. He had to approve every important decision. His communication with the enormous empire was so slow that there was a saying: "If Death had to come from Spain, we would all live forever."

Philip did capture Portugal and gained its empire when the Portuguese king died without an heir in 1580. However, this only added huge new territories for him to have to defend, which he could not do. During the time of Spanish rule (1580–1640), the Portuguese Empire lost much of its importance.

Trying to subdue the enemies who feared Spanish power and Catholicism turned out to be impossible. Fights with the Turks in the Mediterranean ended in stalemate, despite a great Spanish victory at Lepanto in 1571. An attempt to attack England in 1588 with an Armada, or huge fleet of ships, ended in disaster (see Chapter 16). And an attempt to invade France to prevent a Protestant from becoming king was an expensive failure. The most costly disaster, however, was Philip's policy in the Netherlands.

The rise of the Dutch nation

The 17 provinces of the Netherlands that Philip inherited had been a great trading center since the Middle Ages—one of the richest areas of Europe. Their people had a proud tradition of independence. By the 1550's Calvinism was already making headway in the area. The way Philip handled his subjects in the Netherlands—their wealth, their independence, and their religion—led to catastrophe for Spain.

From the start Philip was distrusted by his subjects in the Netherlands. He seemed to be a foreigner, a Spaniard, unlike his father Charles V, who had been born in the Netherlands. He turned this distrust into rebellion by making three fundamental errors. First, he ignored the long tradition of self-rule of the Netherlands and insisted that he, not the local nobles, had to have all authority. Second, he taxed the trade of the Netherlands heavily to finance Spanish wars. Third, he persecuted Calvinists viciously.

When revolt broke out in 1568, Philip was unable to stop it, despite his powerful army. The people of the northern provinces lived on land that was below sea level, protected by large dikes. They simply opened the dikes, flooded the country, and thus left Philip's army helpless. Also, the Calvinists were more numerous in the north and made the resistance more determined.

The revolt of the northern provinces was commanded by William the Silent, Prince of Orange. He held their small army together and relied on raids by bands of soldiers to keep the Spaniards off balance. This military technique is now known as **guerrilla warfare.**

Under William's leadership the northern provinces declared their independence from Spain in

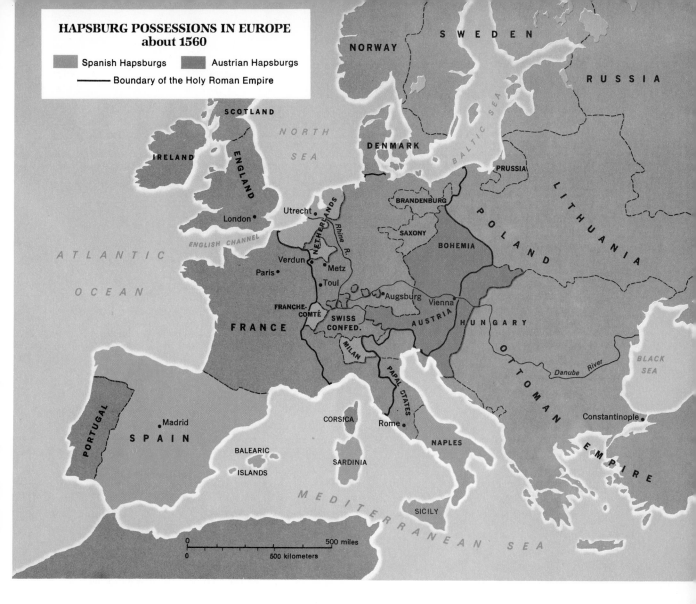

HAPSBURG POSSESSIONS IN EUROPE
about 1560

- Spanish Hapsburgs
- Austrian Hapsburgs
- —— Boundary of the Holy Roman Empire

1581 and became the United Provinces, or the Dutch Netherlands. (Today they are called simply the Netherlands or Holland, after their most important province.)

William was assassinated in 1584, but his sons continued the struggle of the Dutch against Spain. Eventually, in 1609, the Spaniards agreed to a truce.

By this time the Spaniards had won back the loyalty of the southern provinces of the Netherlands. They were able to do this partly because the southern provinces were more heavily Catholic and partly because Spain promised them greater independence. This area remained for some time under the rule of Spain and was known as the Spanish Netherlands (see map, page 343). It later became the Austrian Netherlands and, eventually, the country of Belgium.

Dutch society. The people of the Dutch Netherlands created one of the most remarkable societies in Europe. They were primarily traders and throughout the 1600's dominated European commerce. Their ships carried most of the world's trade. The city of Amsterdam was the financial capital of Europe. Dutch banks, trading companies, manufacturing enterprises (especially shipbuilding), and overseas colonies were models of efficiency.

The Dutch people had an extraordinarily open society. Although only Calvinists could hold polit-

327

Spanish power

The Hapsburgs dominated the politics of Europe in the 1500's. They were also great patrons of the arts, hiring the finest artists and craftsmen of the time to portray them. One of their favorite activities was hunting, which was widely regarded as a properly vigorous and athletic activity for a monarch. Charles V (above) always found time for the hunt, even though he constantly traveled among his domains, scattered across half of Europe. His son, Philip II of Spain, was married briefly to Mary I of England, a union commemorated in portraits on gold coins (above left). Yet the first major defeat for the Hapsburgs was in fact to come from the English—not on land, but with the defeat of the great Spanish fleet, or Armada, in 1588 (left).

ical offices, all inhabitants were free to hold whatever religious opinions they wished. Amsterdam became the liveliest cultural center in Europe, a home to philosophers like René Descartes and to painters like the great Dutch master Rembrandt van Rijn.

This society seems especially vivid to us because its people were painted by Rembrandt. No one in the history of art has undertaken a more profound exploration of human character through painting. His canvases show us all individual types, from stiffly formal officials to ordinary men and women at everyday tasks.

The Dutch were ruled by a representative assembly called the Estates General. The Estates had some conflicts with the House of Orange—the descendants of William the Silent. The House of Orange headed the army and wanted to centralize power for themselves. The Dutch went through a crisis in the 1640's over whether local or central authority was supreme. The House of Orange later became a hereditary monarchy. However, the Dutch remained more willing than any other country in Europe to give a voice in government to a broad section of the people.

Spain's power declined

Spain's loss of the Netherlands in 1581 was the worst but only one of many shocks that undermined Spain's power. There was also a revolt in the old kingdom of Aragón in the 1590's. It was put down, but it revived in 1640 and lasted over ten years. By then the Spaniards had ended the truce with the Dutch and had been trying to reconquer them since the 1620's. The silver supply from the Americas was dwindling, and all these conflicts were destroying Spain's wealth. To add to the troubles, Portugal revolted in 1640. A few years later the Spanish territories in Italy also revolted. Since Spain had also been at war with France since 1635, the burden now became too great to bear.

Spain lost Portugal in 1640 and finally recognized Dutch independence in 1648. Peace was made with France in 1660. By this time it was clear that Spain was no longer Europe's dominant power. The Spanish monarchy survived with its absolute powers intact. However, the country never regained its prominence in international affairs.

France emerged as a great power

The new power in Europe was France. It had recovered rapidly from the religious wars of the 1500's because of the policies of King Henry IV (1589–1610). He was the first of the Bourbon family to be king of France. Though he had been a Huguenot, he realized he could not rule the country as a member of a religious minority. He therefore converted to Catholicism but issued a special order, the Edict of Nantes (see page 307). The Edict guaranteed freedom of worship and political rights to the Huguenots. This defused the religious conflict and ended the civil wars.

Henry also attempted to resolve two other major problems. Powerful nobles had undermined royal authority in the 1500's. Henry either got them to join the central government or quieted them with large bribes, thus regaining real control throughout the country. France's financial difficulties were not so easy to solve, despite the best efforts of the Duke of Sully, the talented chief minister in charge of finances.

The French system of taxation was inefficient, corrupt, and unjust. As in the Roman Empire, the taxes were farmed—that is, the right to collect them was sold to private individuals who paid the government a fixed sum and then collected all they could. It has been estimated that less than half of the money collected reached the treasury. Nobles and clergy did not have to pay taxes, so the burden fell heavily on the peasants.

Sully could not make the system just. Nobles and clergy continued to be free from taxation for centuries. However, he limited the expenditures of the royal household, discharged dishonest tax collectors, and supervised the tax farming more carefully. Finances improved until there was even a sizable surplus in the treasury. Sully used the money to build up both trade and industry.

Louis XIII and Richelieu

Henry's son and successor, Louis XIII, was only eight years old when his father was assassinated in 1610. The boy's mother, Marie de Medici, became regent—that is, she took over the actual rule of the country. At the age of sixteen, Louis XIII took control of the government. Louis was not a strong ruler, but he selected good advisers and

Rembrandt Self-portrait

The successful Dutch revolt against the Spanish monarch created a new society, one that was dominated by Protestants rather than by Catholics. It was one in which the middle class rose to power. This new society also made way for a new art, concerned more with daily life than with religion.

Dutch artists were no longer dependent upon the Church or the aristocracy for patrons. They now were free to paint what they liked. Their new subjects were the wealthy merchants who, proud of their success, clamored to have their portraits painted.

In the mid-1600's, the Dutch Netherlands probably had more painters than any other country. About this time, in 1633, the 27-year-old Rembrandt van Rijn settled in Amsterdam. No painter has ever captured the human spirit so completely. His psychological interpretation of character is evident in this deeply moving self-portrait. It is one of 60 self-portraits that Rembrandt did during his lifetime. Here the artist, an aging and financially troubled man, lets us see inside his soul.

supported them against all opposition. Louis XIII chose as his chief minister Cardinal Richelieu (ree·shuh·LOO), who was the actual ruler of France from 1624 until his death in 1642.

Richelieu was one of the ablest political leaders of his time. He had a keen understanding of what was possible, politically and diplomatically. Although he wore a cardinal's robes, he was a shrewd politician.

Richelieu wanted to make the king supreme in France, and France supreme in Europe. To accomplish the first aim, he set out to destroy the political independence of the Huguenots and the power of the nobles. He also wanted to strengthen France economically by continuing Sully's policy of encouraging trade and industry. To make France supreme in Europe, Richelieu planned to reduce the power of the Hapsburgs as rulers both of Spain and of the Holy Roman Empire.

Richelieu's program for France

Richelieu believed that the provisions of the Edict of Nantes that allowed the Huguenots to govern fortified cities were politically dangerous. These cities were like states within a state. They made strongly centralized government impossible. In 1627 Richelieu moved against them and attacked the Huguenot seaport of La Rochelle and other fortified towns. After stubborn but futile resistance, the Huguenots asked for peace. Richelieu took away their right to self-government in towns, but he allowed them to worship freely, hold public office, and attend schools and colleges.

The cardinal next turned to the problem of the nobles. Here he had to finish the work that Henry IV had begun. Moving first to crush the military power of the nobles, he ordered that all fortified castles not necessary for the defense of France be torn down. The nobles complained, but in vain.

Richelieu's next step was to reduce the nobles' political power. With the king's consent, he appointed as governors of provinces only those who favored a strong monarchy. He also strengthened the local administrators known as *intendants*. For these positions he chose middle-class people who welcomed the chance to reduce the authority of the nobles. The *intendants* were given strong military, political, and administrative powers. They were responsible directly to the king.

The final part of Richelieu's program involved foreign policy. After unsuccessful attacks on the Hapsburgs during the first ten years of his rule, he finally entered the Thirty Years' War in 1635 against both Spain and the Holy Roman Emperor. You will read more about this war in Section 4 of this chapter. Although Richelieu died in 1642, before the end of the war, he had launched France toward a dominant position in Europe.

His successor, Cardinal Mazarin, brought the war to a triumphantly successful conclusion. By the time he made peace with the Holy Roman Emperor in 1648 and with Spain in 1660, the French were the most powerful force on the continent of Europe. By then, too, as you will see later in this chapter, France had survived its own political crisis, and the authority of its king was no longer challenged.

CHECKUP

1. IDENTIFY: Philip II, Ferdinand, William the Silent, United Provinces, Henry IV, Marie de Medici, Louis XIII, Cardinal Mazarin.

2. LOCATE: Vienna, Madrid.

3. What were the different territories under the control of Charles V? Why were his two titles a problem?

4. Why did the people in the Netherlands revolt against Philip II? What was the outcome of this revolt?

5. How did both the Duke of Sully and Cardinal Richelieu strengthen the power of the central government of France?

6. What was the Edict of Nantes? Why did Richelieu attempt to modify this Edict?

2

English monarchs clashed with Parliament

Of all the revolts in the mid-1600's, the most severe was in England. The clash there led to civil war and a **revolution.** A revolution is a violent attempt to change the very structure of a country's government and society—the way it is ruled and the way different groups relate to one another. Such an attempt was made in England in the 1640's and 1650's. Although it did not succeed, it influenced both English history and political ideas throughout Europe.

The rule of the Tudors

During the 1500's England's rulers, the Tudor family, made the same efforts as the rulers of France and Spain to strengthen their powers. The most successful were Henry VIII (1509–1547) and his daughter Elizabeth I (1558–1603). During their reigns the official religion of the country became Protestantism. Thus the monarchy obtained new resources by taking over land that had belonged to the Catholic Church. The government gained new powers, and trade and commerce advanced rapidly. Moreover, the Spanish Armada was defeated, and a beginning was made in founding an overseas empire. However, this strong central government faced two major problems, which eventually caused a civil war.

The religious problem. The first problem was religious. The government had led the break with the pope and the establishment of Protestantism in England, but there were many who felt that the change had not gone far enough. They wanted to "purify" the English church even further, and thus they were called Puritans. What they objected to was the continuation of many practices from Catholicism. For example, the Anglican Church still had bishops. Priests still dressed in elaborate robes for services. The congregation knelt during communion, and there was an altar in every church. The Puritans thought that customs like these were too Catholic, and they wanted to abolish them.

Like many monarchs at the time, the Tudors thought that religious disunity was a threat to stability. They wanted all their subjects to be united in their faith. Therefore they persecuted both those who remained Catholics and the Puritans. They did not stamp out either group, but in the Puritans they created a dangerous enemy. Puritans were very sure of their own righteousness. They set very high moral standards and became increasingly unhappy about the English church. Eventually that unhappiness was to make them willing to revolt against their king.

The Tudors and Parliament. The Tudors' second major problem was with Parliament. As we saw in Chapter 12, this body of representatives from the whole country had the right to approve all taxes and pass laws. It had gained power and prestige in the 1530's, when it was used by Henry VIII to pass the laws that made England a Protestant nation. Moreover, Parliament was looked to as a restraint on the monarchy because it represented the wishes of people outside the central government.

The House of Lords was made up of nobles and higher clergy. The House of Commons represented two classes—gentry and burgesses. The gentry were landowning people of good family and social position. Some of the gentry were the younger sons of nobles, who could not inherit their fathers' titles or positions. Burgesses were merchants and professional people from the towns and cities.

Actually, the gentry and burgesses mingled to a surprising extent. Class lines were not so sharply drawn in England as in continental Europe. Rich merchants might buy land and be considered gentry. Younger sons of nobles might go into the professions and come to be regarded as burgesses. Together the two groups had considerable power, which the monarch had to handle carefully.

Elizabeth managed Parliament very cleverly. She got all the taxes she needed without letting the members influence her policy too directly. The Puritans in Parliament did criticize her sharply, and she sent some of them to prison. Despite her skill, Elizabeth found it increasingly difficult to prevent the members of Parliament from attacking government policies. Under her less clever successors, Parliament gained a more important role in the nation's political life. Eventually, a revolution was begun by Parliament when its views were rejected.

The causes of the English Revolution

Between 1603, when Elizabeth died, and 1640, the relations between the monarchy and its subjects deteriorated. The main stages in that deterioration suggest how and why it happened.

James I. The first problem arose almost immediately. Elizabeth's successor was James I, a member of the Stuart family who had long ruled Scotland. His English subjects suspected that, as a foreigner, he did not really understand how their parliamentary system worked. At his very first Parliament, some of the members drew up an "Apology"—a document that explained rather haughtily the way England ought to be ruled. They objected also to James' plan to unite England and Scotland, and blocked his attempt to create a union between them.

During the remainder of James' reign (until 1625), the difficulties he faced had to do mainly with finance and foreign policy. The Puritans were left largely alone. James ordered a new translation of the Bible into English—known as the Authorized Version, or King James Version. It is one of the most famous English translations. This version of the Bible was welcomed by the Puritans.

Trouble came not from the Puritans, but rather from Parliament. The 1600's were a time of inflation. Government activities were growing, and James never had enough money to pay for his policies. When the taxes passed by Parliament proved insufficient, he used other means—such as increased customs duties—to add to government income. Parliament objected to these methods. It was also unhappy when, toward the end of his reign, James tried to make an alliance with England's old enemy, Spain.

Charles I. When James died, relations between king and subjects were uneasy. They became far worse under his son, Charles I (1625–1649). Charles was an arrogant and tactless man, who had a very high opinion of royal power. When he could not get his way with Parliament, he tried to force people to loan him the funds he needed. Those who refused were sent to prison.

The result was a terrible confrontation in a Parliament that met in 1628 and 1629. The members presented Charles with a document known as the **Petition of Right.** Among other things, it demanded that no taxes be imposed without consent of Parliament and that nobody be imprisoned without legal cause. Charles agreed, but then went on raising taxes. When the members of the House of Commons tried to object, Charles dissolved Parliament. The members nonetheless passed several resolutions denouncing government policies.

For the next 11 years Charles refused to call Parliament into session again. He used drastic methods to collect taxes and long-ignored dues and fees. The antagonisms only increased. Charles liked a very formal and ritualistic Protes-

London of the Tudors

London grew rapidly under the Tudors. Its chief building was still, as it had been for centuries, the Tower of London (left). It served many functions—as a storehouse for weapons and as a jail for important prisoners, for example.

Henry VIII (above left) was the most powerful of the Tudor kings. He was a patron of the arts. This portrait was painted by the German artist Hans Holbein, who served at the English court. But Henry was also a stern leader, who imprisoned his friend Thomas More in the Tower and then had him executed. Henry's daughter, Queen Elizabeth, was a shrewd manipulator of her subjects and particularly clever at getting her way with Parliament. At its opening session at Westminster, near London, she appeared, in all her finery, in the House of Lords (above right).

tantism, the very sort that the Puritans most hated. They also despised the way he lived, which they thought frivolous and wasteful. Charles in turn increased the restrictions on Puritans. During the 1630's many thousands of Puritans left the country for New England in America. However, many stayed behind, determined to resist the king's policies.

They were joined by members of Parliament who thought Charles' rule tyrannical, and also by many lawyers. The king was avoiding the system of common law by offering cheap and rapid justice in the royal courts. Decisions in these courts were made in secret by judges, not juries. The common lawyers resented these rivals to the circuit-court system, especially because they were sure the judges were controlled by the king. One of the royal courts was particularly effective at prosecuting Puritans and critics of government policy. It was known as the Court of Star Chamber and was bitterly disliked.

It seemed increasingly that the king was imposing his own absolute rule. He used his own legal system, ignoring the country's representatives in Parliament. And he crushed the Puritans who did not accept religious uniformity. Those who opposed the growing power of the central government were waiting only for their opportunity to reverse these trends.

The opportunity came when Charles tried to impose a standard prayer book on his Scottish subjects. The Scots had accepted a branch of Puritanism known as Presbyterianism. The Presbyterian Church was ruled by elders known as presbyters instead of by bishops. The Presbyterians had their own prayer book. Their response to Charles' order to use the standard prayer book was to raise an army and declare war to preserve their independence.

Charles had no army to meet them. To assemble one he needed money, and thus new taxes. For this he needed Parliament. He called elections, and in 1640 a Parliament assembled once again. Although it quickly quarreled with the king and was dissolved, Charles had to summon a new one within a few weeks. This Parliament was dominated by Puritans, who had the opportunity at last to change the government's policies. The actions of this Parliament were to lead to civil war and revolution in England.

The English Revolution

The second Parliament that Charles summoned in 1640 remained in session off and on for 20 years. It is known as the Long Parliament. The Puritans who controlled the House of Commons took a number of actions that limited absolute monarchy in England. They abolished the king's power to dissolve Parliament and passed a law requiring a meeting of Parliament at least once every three years. They put an end to all forms of illegal taxation. They also abolished the Court of Star Chamber. Two of the king's most hated advisers were executed.

While the Long Parliament was reducing the king's authority, Charles also faced trouble in Ireland. England had ruled Ireland since the late 1100's, but it had never brought the Irish completely under control. Relations between the two countries had grown worse since the time of Henry VIII. The Irish remained Roman Catholic and refused to accept Protestantism. The Tudors followed a policy, which the Stuarts continued, of seizing land from Irish owners and giving it to English and Scottish settlers. In 1641 the Irish rebelled.

Because of the rebellion in Ireland and the need to deal with the Scottish invasion, Charles at first gave in to Parliament and accepted the changes it made. Then, however, the most radical Puritan group tried to pass an act doing away with bishops in the Anglican Church. At that point, Charles led troops into the House of Commons and tried to arrest the leaders of the opposition. This hostile act led in 1642 to the outbreak of a civil war between supporters of the king and supporters of Parliament.

Civil war and the Rump Parliament

The king's supporters were called royalists or Cavaliers. They included Anglicans, Roman Catholics, nobles, and all who disagreed with the Puritans on political or religious grounds. Supporting Parliament were the Puritans and all who felt that the powers of the king had to be severely curbed.

Oliver Cromwell, leader of the Puritans, organized his forces into an army that the Cavaliers could not match. It was a strong army of well-

connections

Theaters

People have enjoyed going to see plays and entertainment since the earliest times. In ancient Greece and Rome, performances were given in great open-air arenas (right). In ancient Japan the *no* plays were popular entertainment.

During the Middle Ages, sacred stories and plays with Christian themes—called morality plays—were performed in or near churches. By the time of the Renaissance, special houses were built for the performances, and these buildings came to be known as theaters.

Perhaps the most famous theater in history was the one built in the late 1500's on the south bank of the Thames River, across from London. This octagon-shaped theater was called the Globe (below). Here most of William Shakespeare's plays had their earliest performances.

Londoners flocked to see the latest comedies and tragedies of writers like Shakespeare, Christopher Marlowe, and Ben Jonson. These writers no

longer wrote morality plays. Imitating the models of classical Greece and Rome, they created dramas that were full of romance, humor, violence, and despair.

Plays had to be seen in the daytime, when there was enough natural light to illuminate the stage. The center of the theater was open to the sky, and that was where the ordinary tradespeople sat or stood, ready to be rained upon if the weather turned bad. Nobles and rich merchants sat in boxes round the side. The stage itself, where the actors performed, was covered by an overhanging roof.

The human emotions explored by the plays of this period are so profound and universal that many of the plays continue to be performed. Love, ambition, madness, revenge—these were the themes of ancient Greek dramas as well as the works of modern playwrights. Our enjoyment of the theater is one way in which we are closely linked with our ancestors.

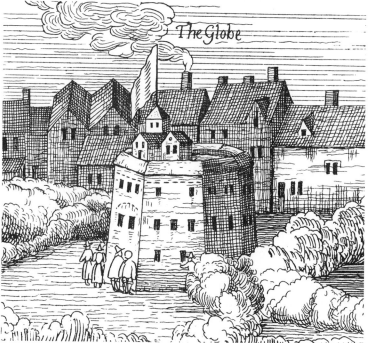

The Globe

drilled, disciplined, zealous soldiers, who were fined if they swore, and who charged into battle singing hymns. They were pious, prayerful, and highly efficient. After two defeats in battle, Charles I surrendered in 1646.

Now began a great maneuvering among various groups to see who would control the government. Chief among them were Presbyterians, like the Scots, and those who followed Cromwell, who were called Independents. Cromwell's army, made up of Independents, won the struggle. Troops were used to keep all Anglican and Presbyterian members from entering the House of Commons. They left only 60 members, all Independents, sitting in Parliament. This remnant became known as the Rump Parliament, since it was the only part of the parliamentary body still sitting.

The Rump Parliament abolished both the monarchy and the House of Lords. It proclaimed England a Commonwealth, a word used at that time to mean a republic. The Rump Parliament appointed a special court to try Charles I for treason. He was condemned and beheaded early in 1649. Cromwell took over the reins of power and became essentially a military dictator.

Cromwell's Commonwealth

The Commonwealth might have been overthrown except for three factors. (1) It had enough money from taxes and the sale of confiscated royalist lands to support the government and army. (2) Its enemies, the Irish and the royalists, had no organized army. (3) Its own army was disciplined and powerful.

Cromwell suppressed the Irish so mercilessly that his name is still hated by them. The royalists never posed a serious threat.

The domestic policy of Cromwell's government was designed to develop manufacturing and trade. Dutch merchants and ships had built up a profitable trade with England and its colonies during the troubled times of the civil war. Cromwell had Parliament pass the Navigation Act of 1651 to restore this trade to English merchants and shipowners.

He also carried on a commercial war with the Dutch from 1652 to 1654. The war ended indecisively, but the English navy gained prestige.

Oliver Cromwell was an unusual man. A devout Puritan, he closed all the theaters and limited many other forms of popular entertainment. He was honest and upright, a powerful orator, and a skilled leader. He was convinced, however, that his ways were the only correct ones, and he suppressed political and religious opposition with great severity.

Despite the power he held, Cromwell was a reluctant dictator. He preferred parliamentary government and made several attempts to create one. He tried twice to establish a **constitution**—a document outlining the fundamental laws and principles that govern a nation. One of them, known as the Instrument of Government, was the first written constitution of a major European nation. It gave Cromwell the title of Lord Protector and provided that Parliament would be elected by the landowners.

Cromwell held the title of Lord Protector from 1653 until 1658. This period of the Commonwealth is often called the Protectorate. Cromwell's experiment was not successful. There was almost as much friction between him and Parliament as there had been between the Stuart kings and Parliament. The old resentment of central power reappeared and Cromwell was forced to dissolve Parliament. He ruled alone during most of the Commonwealth period.

The end of the revolution

Cromwell died in 1658. His son Richard tried to rule as Lord Protector but was unable to win the necessary support of the army.

By then, too, there had been a change in the feelings of the English people. Some had favored the execution of Charles I, but the period of the Commonwealth had brought only confusion and resentment of Cromwell's rule.

In 1660, after some hesitation, Parliament invited Charles II, the son of Charles I, to return to England from his exile on the Continent. The revolution was over, and it was time now to see what long-term effects it would have on England. The country seemed to have weathered its troubles. However, another 30 years had to pass before anyone could be certain that the lessons—especially the need to give Parliament an important role in government—had been learned.

1. IDENTIFY: Puritans, James I, Presbyterians, Cavaliers, Rump Parliament, Commonwealth, Instrument of Government, Protectorate.

2. What actions of Charles I angered his subjects?

3. In what ways did the Long Parliament limit absolute monarchy in England? How did the revolution begin?

4. Oliver Cromwell is said to have been a reluctant dictator. Explain this statement.

3

England established a constitutional monarchy

The struggles between king and Parliament were not over in 1660. There was to be an echo of the crisis in the 1680's. After that uncertainty passed, however, the English created a stable government that linked monarch and Parliament in a close partnership.

Charles II and the Restoration

The revolution had ended in 1660, when Charles II regained the throne. The period of his rule is called the **Restoration,** because monarchy had been restored in England.

Charles II had learned much from his years in exile. As he said, he had no desire "to go on his travels again." When his policies met determined opposition, he gave in, although he often tried to gain his ends by roundabout methods. He loved entertainment and good times and was called the "Merry Monarch." Restrictions on the theater were removed in a reaction against the stern Puritanism of the Commonwealth.

Charles II continued and extended the commercial policy favored by Cromwell. His actions brought wars with the Dutch. During these wars England took the Dutch settlement of New Amsterdam in North America and renamed it New York. Charles II wanted an alliance with France, but English protests forced him to oppose France. This shift marked the beginning of 150 years of rivalry between England and France.

Charles II was tolerant of Roman Catholics and hoped to lift some of the legal restrictions on them in England. However, his attempt to do so met with such strong parliamentary opposition that he gave up the effort. Parliament had become overwhelmingly Anglican in its make-up.

As time went on, it seemed certain that Charles would be succeeded on the throne by his younger brother James, who had converted to Roman Catholicism. This situation led to the development of England's first political parties.

Parliament was divided into two groups of almost equal strength. One group, the Tories, wanted a strong hereditary monarch, though not an autocratic one. To keep the monarchy hereditary, they were willing to accept a Roman Catholic as ruler, provided the heirs were Protestant. Opposing the Tories were the Whigs, who favored a weak monarch and a strong Parliament. They were vigorously opposed to the idea of a Roman Catholic ruler.

In 1679 Parliament passed an important measure, the Habeas Corpus Act. It provided that anyone who was arrested could obtain a writ, or order, demanding to be brought before a judge within a certain period. The judge would decide whether the prisoner should be released or charged and tried for a crime. The writ itself was called *habeas corpus*, Latin for "you shall have the body." The Habeas Corpus Act protected individuals against illegal arrest and unlawful imprisonment.

James II and the Glorious Revolution

Charles II died in 1685 and his brother came to the throne as James II. James, like his brother, had lived in exile for many years but had learned less from the experience. As a Roman Catholic and an ardent believer in royal power, he antagonized both Whigs and Tories by his arrogance.

One of the chief problems during the reign of James II involved the succession to the throne. James' daughters Mary and Anne were both raised as Protestants by order of Charles II. They had married Protestant princes. Mary was the wife of William of Orange, ruler of the Dutch Netherlands. Anne had married a Danish prince. However, James' first wife had died, and he had married again, this time a Roman Catholic princess.

In 1688 she gave birth to a son, who would by law succeed his father. Since the boy's father and mother were both Catholics, it was certain that he would be raised in the Catholic faith.

Now all the groups in opposition to James combined to bring about the event known as the **Glorious Revolution.** Both Whigs and Tories agreed that James must abdicate. They invited Mary and her husband William of Orange to rule England. In 1688 William landed in England with a Dutch army, but armed force was hardly necessary. Unable to rally anyone to his support, James fled to France. Parliament gave the crown to William and Mary as joint rulers.

New ideas about government

The English civil war and the events that followed had led not only to changes in government but also to new ideas about government. One of the most influential writers to analyze government was an English philosopher, Thomas Hobbes. Hobbes lived through the English civil war and was disturbed by the chaos of the time. He set forth his political philosophy in a book called *Leviathan,* published in 1651.

Hobbes explained that, in the past, people had lived in anarchy, or what he called a "state of nature." Life was violent and dangerous under these circumstances, so people chose a leader to rule them. In order to maintain a stable society, they had made an unwritten "social contract." Hobbes argued that under this contract they had to give the monarch absolute power, or anarchy would again result. The people retained only the right to protect their own lives.

John Locke, another English philosopher, adopted many of Hobbes' ideas but interpreted them differently. Locke had supported those who overthrew James II in the Glorious Revolution. He established the principles on which they acted in a book called *The Second Treatise of Civil Government,* published in 1690.

Like Hobbes, Locke believed that people had first lived in a state of anarchy and then made a social contract. However, he believed that people had given up only some of their individual rights and had kept others. These rights, called natural rights, included the right to live, the right to enjoy liberty, and the right to own property.

According to Locke, a ruler who violated these rights violated natural law and broke the unwritten social contract. The people then had the right to overthrow him and replace him with another ruler who would pledge to observe and protect their rights. Locke thus gave grounds for the forced abdication of James II and the offer of the crown to William and Mary. Locke's ideas were influential in later revolutions in France and America, as you will read in Chapter 17.

Safeguards against absolute rule

Parliament set up safeguards even before granting the throne to William and Mary. In a famous document it fixed conditions to which the new rulers agreed in advance. This document, known as the **Bill of Rights,** became a law in 1689.

First and foremost, the Bill of Rights declared that the ruler was merely an official chosen by Parliament and subject to its laws. The ruler could not proclaim or suspend any law, impose any tax, or maintain an army in peacetime without Parliament's consent. Parliament was to meet frequently. Its members were to be elected without interference from the ruler and were guaranteed the right to express themselves freely.

The Bill of Rights also protected private citizens. All citizens had the right to petition the government for relief of any injustice. No one could be required to pay excessive bail or be subjected to cruel and unusual punishment.

In 1689 Parliament also passed the Act of Toleration. This act granted freedom of conscience and the right of public worship to non-Anglican Protestants. It did not, however, bring complete religious freedom. Roman Catholics, for example, still lived under heavy restrictions, and non-Anglican Protestants could not hold public office.

In 1701 Parliament passed the Act of Settlement. It provided that if William should die without children to succeed him (Mary had already died), Mary's sister Anne should inherit the throne. If there were no children to succeed her either, the throne should go to a Protestant granddaughter of James I, the German princess Sophia of Hanover. Thus, great care was taken to keep the Roman Catholic descendants of James II from gaining the English throne.

The English civil war

The English civil war matched a king with a very high regard for his own powers, Charles I, against a blunt and down-to-earth soldier, Oliver Cromwell. Charles was a great patron of the arts. Not surprisingly, a royal decree, written in Latin, that he issued in 1627 was a beautiful document (below). It is decorated with the lion of England, the royal symbol, and with Charles himself, in all his robes, sitting on his throne. Cromwell, by contrast, liked to be shown as an ordinary soldier in his armor (above). He is said to have told one artist not to make him look handsome, but to paint him warts and all. The confrontation between the two men reached its climax at a trial in the House of Commons (left) at which Charles was condemned to death. He is shown seated in the center, alone, with his back to us.

Parliament rules England

The Bill of Rights and the Act of Settlement marked the end of the long struggle between monarch and Parliament to see who would rule the country. By 1700 it was clear that, although England remained a monarchy, Parliament was the real ruler. However, it did not by any means represent all the people. The House of Lords was made up of hereditary nobles and higher clergy. Even the House of Commons, which was gradually becoming the more powerful of the two houses, represented only about 15 percent of the male population—the gentry landowners and the middle-class businessmen. The right to elect members to the House of Commons was limited. Workers could not vote and therefore were not represented at all.

In the 50 years after 1689, Parliament continued to gain importance as the real power in the government of England. The organization and institutions characteristic of English government today gradually emerged.

William of Orange, who became King William III of England, knew little and cared less about the domestic problems of England. His interests lay in checking the vast ambitions of Louis XIV of France on the continent of Europe. As long as he was free to handle foreign affairs, William was quite willing to allow others to deal with domestic issues. He could do so because a new system of governing the nation had developed.

For centuries, a group of advisers had met with the English monarch to discuss government problems and ways of solving them. In time this council became too large to be efficient. Beginning with the reign of Charles II, a smaller group of advisers began to meet separately. Most of them were ministers, or heads of government departments. They were able to make policy and deal with issues effectively because they were leaders in the House of Commons. They became known as the **Cabinet.**

At first the Cabinet included members of both parties. However, during William's reign it became clear that the government ran more smoothly when all the ministers of the Cabinet belonged to the majority party in the House of Commons. Thus the monarch chose his or her ministers accordingly.

Several other steps increasing parliamentary control of the English government came during the reign of William III and shortly thereafter. Parliament gained the right to declare war. The monarch ceased to veto acts of Parliament. Queen Mary's sister Anne, who reigned as queen from 1702 to 1714, was the last monarch to veto an act of Parliament.

In 1707 the Act of Union merged the separate governments of England and Scotland into one kingdom known as Great Britain. The Scottish Parliament was abolished. Scots were given seats in the House of Lords and the House of Commons. There was opposition at first, particularly in Scotland, but the union proved to be beneficial. By removing trade barriers, it encouraged commerce and brought greater prosperity to both England and Scotland.

Parliamentary control increased under the successors to Queen Anne. When Anne died in 1714 without children to succeed her, the throne went to the Elector of Hanover—the son of Sophia of Hanover, who had been designated in the 1701 Act of Settlement. He became George I, the first of the Hanoverian dynasty of Great Britain. Both he and his son George II were German born. George I, who ruled until 1727, spoke no English. George II, king until 1760, spoke English, but is said to have mispronounced both English and German. Although both kings were interested in the details of British government, neither understood the larger issues. As a result, the Cabinet became increasingly important in the British system of government.

A constitutional monarchy

For over twenty years—from 1721 to 1742—the Whig party controlled the House of Commons. The recognized leader of the Whigs, Sir Robert Walpole, was always chosen as a minister. He was a strong leader and came to be recognized as the prime minister—that is, first minister. Actually, the prime minister was not known officially as such throughout most of the 1700's. Instead, he usually had the title of First Lord of the Treasury. In time the prime minister became the real head of the government of Great Britain.

By the 1700's Great Britain had become a **limited constitutional monarchy.** It was a monarchy, of course, because there was a king or queen. It was a limited monarchy because the powers of the ruler were less than absolute. It was a constitutional monarchy because the monarch's powers were limited by a constitution.

The British constitution is not a single written document like that of the United States. It consists partly of great documents such as the Magna Carta, the Petition of Right, and the Bill of Rights. It also includes acts of Parliament, which any succeeding Parliament may change. Several features of the system are not written down anywhere—for example, the powers of the prime minister and the functions of the Cabinet.

Great Britain is one of the oldest constitutional governments in the world today. Its limited monarchy furnished a model for many other nations. The British experience from 1603 to 1760 became a guide to those who wanted to abolish absolute monarchy elsewhere.

CHECKUP

1. IDENTIFY: Restoration, Tories, Whigs, Act of Toleration, Act of Settlement, Act of Union, Walpole, limited constitutional monarchy.

2. What role did the issue of Roman Catholicism play in the Glorious Revolution?

3. Compare and contrast the political philosophies of Hobbes and Locke.

4. How did the English Bill of Rights limit the powers of the monarch? How did it protect private citizens?

5. Why did the Cabinet gain importance during the reigns of William III, George I, and George II?

After years of unrest, France dominated Europe

In most countries of Europe, the crisis over the powers of central governments was settled by the 1660's. The form of government, especially its responsiveness to the people, varied from country to country. Everywhere, however, local areas lost much of the independence they had had since the Middle Ages. After the 1660's, the central government was to control each nation.

In international affairs, as you will read, many years of war ended with new order in relations between countries. The country that would benefit most from this new stability was France. Having withstood its own internal conflicts, France would become the dominant power in Europe.

The power of central governments

Throughout Europe in the mid-1600's local authorities were making a last effort to hold back the spreading power of central governments. Their resistance caused a crisis, and when they failed this crisis ended. The result was that central governments had a greater influence on ordinary people's lives than they had had before.

From the mid-1600's, governments increasingly came to control the local areas throughout their countries. They were always worried about unrest, and therefore they took measures to ease discontent. To relieve the worst hardships of the poor, they set up charitable institutions. To lessen famines, they distributed food to the hungry. And they helped traders with laws that reduced competition from foreigners. Gradually, people began to realize that they could turn to the central government for help in times of difficulty.

To maintain all these activities, governments needed many more officials, who now became familiar figures even in distant villages. These government officials were called **bureaucrats,** from the French word *bureau,* or desk, at which they worked. Official justice and tax collecting became a part of ordinary life everywhere. No area, however remote, avoided being drawn into the control of the central government. This was one of the great changes of political and social history, and its results have remained essential to modern countries. Even the revolutions of the 1700's and 1800's did not reduce this new presence of the government in the lives of all its citizens. The settlement of the crisis of the mid-1600's thus had permanent effects within countries.

The Thirty Years' War

In the early 1600's the relations between the countries of Europe deteriorated sharply. For a time it seemed that Europe might descend into total chaos. A war began in 1618 that lasted, with intervals of peace, for 30 years. The fighting became completely uncontrolled, with armies supporting themselves by looting the countryside. Most of the battles took place in Germany, which lost about a third of its population to casualties, famines, and disease. About a dozen different states became involved in the war at one time or another, and there seemed to be no way to restore order or to end the fighting.

The Thirty Years' War began because the religious struggles between Protestants and Catholics in Germany had never completely died down. There had been conflicts ever since the Peace of Augsburg in 1555, with both sides always ready to take up arms again. Other conditions also led to war. There was constant rivalry among the German princes, rulers of some 300 independent states. Many of them wanted to be independent of the Holy Roman Emperor. In addition, France, Denmark, and Sweden looked for opportunities to diminish the power of the Hapsburgs and the Holy Roman Empire.

The Thirty Years' War was really a series of wars. It began as a Protestant revolt in Bohemia, part of the Holy Roman Empire. The Holy Roman Emperor was able to suppress this rebellion in 1620, but in doing so he gained the ill will of Protestant German princes and Protestant Denmark and Sweden. Denmark entered the war, but after several defeats its king had to promise not to interfere in German affairs. Sweden then took up arms in the struggle, leading an alliance against the Hapsburgs.

France, headed by Cardinal Richelieu, threw its support behind the Swedes, rather than helping the Catholic Hapsburg emperor. At first, Richelieu did everything possible to prolong the war without involving France directly. Thus the other nations were weakened while France remained strong. But in 1635, as you recall, France declared war. Although Richelieu died a few years later, his successor, Cardinal Mazarin, carried on his policies.

By 1648 the French and their allies were victorious after a series of successful military campaigns. Most of the warring nations were exhausted after decades of fighting.

The Peace of Westphalia

The Peace of Westphalia, which ended the Thirty Years' War, was signed in 1648. It was a landmark in the history of Western Europe because it made changes that were to affect Europe for centuries. Some of the principal consequences are listed here.

(1) Territorial changes were made that greatly strengthened France and Sweden. France received Alsace, a valuable territory along the Rhine River. Sweden received German lands along the Baltic Sea and the North Sea. The north German state of Brandenburg, which was ruled by the Hohenzollern family, was also strengthened by the addition of lands along the Baltic and several areas in Germany. (For a map of these territorial changes, see opposite page.)

(2) The Dutch Netherlands and Switzerland were recognized as independent nations, which weakened the Hapsburgs.

(3) The Hapsburgs were further weakened because the princes in Germany were made virtually independent of the Holy Roman Emperor. Their freedom from interference, even to the extent of controlling their own foreign policies, was confirmed when the next Hapsburg emperor, Leopold I, came to the throne in 1658. Acceptance of the princes' independence meant that the German crisis was settled. A major issue in the Thirty Years' War had been whether the Holy Roman Emperor or the princes would have real power in Germany.

(4) Because the Hapsburgs no longer exercised real authority in Germany, they began, in the late 1600's, to look eastward rather than westward. Out of that change in direction was to come a long struggle with the Turks and eventually the cre-

EUROPE IN 1648
after the Peace of Westphalia

- Spanish Hapsburgs
- Austrian Hapsburgs
- Sweden
- Brandenburg-Prussia
- —— Boundary of the Holy Roman Empire

ation of a new empire along the Danube River. It was to be centered in the countries of Austria and Hungary, and was thus to be known as the Austro-Hungarian Empire.

(5) Because the Peace of Westphalia brought so many states together and solved so many different problems, it was seen as the answer to the chaos in international relations of the previous years. Disputes and wars continued, but after 1648 governments and diplomats felt that they were operating within a clear, orderly system. The whole of the map of Europe had been drawn. Further adjustments now would be made within that framework. Order, it seemed, had once again been restored in Europe.

France under Louis XIV

France gained the most from the Peace of Westphalia and from the order in Western Europe that followed. This country, too, had its troubles in the mid-1600's. Between 1648 and 1652 a series of revolts threatened the central power that had been built up by Richelieu and Mazarin. The rebellions were led by nobles but supported by peasants in many areas and by the citizens of Paris. The rebels wanted to revive the independence of local regions and of the nobility. When their revolts were crushed, the issue was settled. No major attempts to hold back central power were made for more than a hundred years.

343

The king who benefited from this strengthening of central authority was Louis XIV (1643–1715). When Mazarin died in 1661 Louis began to run the government himself. He considered his power to be absolute and allowed no opposition. To emphasize the glory of his country and his own power, he had an enormous palace built at Versailles (vur·SY), a few miles outside of Paris. He moved the government and the most important nobles of France to Versailles. The nobles had to serve the king at all times, whether by helping him dress in the morning, joining him in a hunt, listening to a concert or play, or doing government business. In this way Louis could keep an eye on the nobles and also involve them in the splendor of Versailles and the work of the government. Instead of trying to gain power by fighting the monarchy, the nobility could now advance by getting royal favors and offices.

Versailles became the ideal of European royalty. Its architecture was copied in many countries, as were French clothing, manners, and cooking. French became the language spoken by much of the nobility throughout Europe.

Louis XIV took himself and his work as king seriously. To help him, he chose competent advisers, although he alone made the decisions. One of the most outstanding of his advisers was Jean Baptiste Colbert (kawl·BAIR), an expert in the field of finance.

Colbert, a member of the middle class, followed the ideas of Sully in promoting the economic development of France. He tried to build up French industry at home and French trade abroad. Private companies received government subsidies to build new industries or strengthen existing ones. High tariffs were placed on foreign imports, transportation was improved, and forests were replanted.

Like Sully, Colbert tried to improve the tax-collecting system by eliminating corruption and waste. For some years there was enough money to finance all the improvements in France, maintain a large army, and support exploration abroad. Colbert encouraged French companies to establish colonies and carry on trade in Canada, the West Indies, and East Asia.

Louis believed that all direction of the country's affairs should come from a central authority. He was therefore concerned that the French were still not unified in their religious beliefs. The Huguenots, he believed, disturbed the unity of the country. Consequently, in 1685 Louis revoked the Edict of Nantes, ending toleration for Protestants, and forced more than 100,000 productive citizens to leave France. This hurt the French economy, but Louis considered unity and obedience to be more important.

Military policy

Louis chose as his minister of war François Louvois (loo·VWAH), a military genius. Under his direction the army was completely reorganized. Soldiers were promoted on the basis of merit, rather than by buying commissions. Louvois also created a quartermaster's department to furnish supplies to his troops so that they did not always have to live off the land. By the early 1700's the French had 400,000 soldiers under arms. No such army had ever been seen in Europe. Officers and soldiers were highly trained and equipped with splendid uniforms and improved weapons.

Louis XIV needed this large an army because of his territorial ambitions. He was convinced that the security of France depended on having natural frontiers. The Alps, the Mediterranean Sea, the Pyrenees, the Atlantic Ocean, and the English Channel protected France on the southeast, south, west, and northwest. To make France even safer, Louis wanted to reach the Rhine River in the northeast and east. Here his ambition came into conflict with other powers. The Netherlands barred his way to the northern Rhine, and the Holy Roman Empire prevented him from expanding eastward.

Military campaigns

To gain his ends, Louis XIV fought four wars between 1667 and 1713. France could easily have defeated each of its opponents singly. Every victory would have gained some territory that France wanted and would have made it that much harder for the next country to resist France.

This prospect alarmed many of the other countries of Europe, even those whose lands were not threatened. To counteract the great power of France, other nations united. At various times the Dutch Netherlands, England, Sweden, Spain, and

France dominates Europe

Absolutism in France was the work of a series of strong-willed rulers in the 1600's. A major step toward absolutism was taken during the reign of Louis XIII, when the government was run by Cardinal Richelieu (above). A brilliant politician, Richelieu acted to crush all rivals to royal power.

The reign of Louis XIII's son, Louis XIV, witnessed the height of absolutism. Louis deliberately cultivated an image of great magnificence. His portrait (left) shows him in splendid robes, covered with lilies, the symbol of the French royal family. It is apparent at once how powerful and wealthy he is. Louis built the largest palace in Europe at Versailles (below). It was set in the countryside not far from Paris. Here all the nobles who sought favor came to serve the king's every need.

Denmark, as well as Austria, Brandenburg, and other German states formed alliances to create enough power to equal or surpass that of France. The principle of maintaining a kind of equilibrium in international politics is known as the **balance of power.**

By the end of Louis' third war in 1697, Louvois and other French military leaders were dead. So was Colbert. The treasury was empty. Taxes were heavy, and trade and industry suffered.

The last war of Louis XIV centered on the question of who should succeed to the throne of Spain. The last Spanish Hapsburg king died in 1700 and left the throne to a grandson of Louis XIV, who was indirectly related to the Spanish Hapsburgs. Many European nations feared the prospect of Bourbon rulers in both Spain and France. If Louis had been willing to agree that the two thrones would never be joined under one monarch, he could probably have won recognition for his grandson. However, he would not agree to this, so England, the Dutch Netherlands, and the Austrian Hapsburgs allied against him.

The resulting War of the Spanish Succession began in 1701. It was fought throughout Europe, on the seas, and in America. French armies and fleets were defeated everywhere, and Louis was forced to agree to a peace in 1713.

The Treaty of Utrecht. The Treaty of Utrecht, which ended the War of the Spanish Succession, was important in the history of both Europe and America. It recognized Louis' grandson as King Philip V of Spain, but provided that the French and Spanish crowns were never to be united. Great Britain had become the chief enemy of France and made the largest gains. From France, Great Britain obtained several possessions in North America—the Hudson Bay territory, Newfoundland, and Nova Scotia. From Spain, Great Britain gained the fortress of Gibraltar at the southern tip of Spain, the island of Minorca in the western Mediterranean, a monopoly on the slave trade to America, and the right to send one shipload of goods each year to the Spanish colonies.

The Austrian Hapsburgs were given the Spanish Netherlands, which then became known as the Austrian Netherlands. The Hapsburgs also received the island of Sardinia, the Kingdom of Naples, and the Duchy of Milan in Italy (see map, opposite page).

Two minor provisions of the treaty had great importance for the future. The ruler of Brandenburg, a member of the Hohenzollern family, was recognized as king of Prussia, a state along the southeastern shore of the Baltic Sea. The island of Sicily was given to the Italian Duchy of Savoy. (In 1720 Savoy and the Austrian Hapsburgs exchanged Sicily and Sardinia. The territories of Savoy and Sardinia together were known as the kingdom of Sardinia.) Both Prussia and Savoy were to play vital roles in the next century.

Louis XIV's heritage. Despite defeats, Louis had made France the most powerful nation in Europe. Overseas, Great Britain became the strongest European nation in the 1700's. But within Europe, France remained the largest, the richest, and the most influential. Moreover, for more than 50 years after Louis died, the French government was remarkably stable. His successor, Louis XV (1715–1774), held unquestioned authority, though in fact the country was run by a succession of ministers.

The Enlightenment in France

You have read in Chapter 14 how thinkers of the Enlightenment tried to apply scientific ideas to all human ideas and institutions. France during the time of Louis XV was home to a number of political philosophers. The writings of these philosophers were to have a strong impact on future political and social developments in France and in other countries.

John Locke's ideas, about which you read in the previous section, were adopted by a group of French writers in the 1700's. In a book called *The Spirit of the Laws,* published in 1748, the Baron de Montesquieu (mahn·tus·KYOO) tried to describe a perfect government. After studying all existing governments, Montesquieu concluded that the English form was the one most nearly perfect. He wrote that its greatest strength lay in the fact that power was equally divided among the three branches of government—the **legislative** (which made the laws), the **executive** (which administered them), and the **judicial** (which interpreted and applied them). Each branch balanced and checked the others.

Actually, Montesquieu's praise of the English government was based on a misunderstanding of it. Even when he wrote, the legislative and exec-

EUROPE IN 1721
after the Treaty of Utrecht and related treaties

■ Austrian Hapsburgs   **■** Prussia
— Boundary of the Holy Roman Empire

utive powers were not divided between the two branches of government, but were largely combined in the House of Commons. Nevertheless, his ideas had great influence on the formation of limited monarchies in Europe. And the idea of checks and balances provided by a separation of powers was to be embodied in the Constitution of the United States.

Another influential writer in France was Jean Jacques Rousseau (roo·SOH). His most famous book was *The Social Contract,* published in 1762. In it he wrote that people are born good but become bad because of their environment, education, and laws. The free and good state to which people are born can be preserved only if they live under a government of their own choice and control. In other words, just laws and wise government must be based upon what Rousseau called **popular sovereignty**—the free choice of the people. This idea had enormous influence.

Voltaire. As famous and influential as Rousseau was the French writer François Marie Arouet, known as Voltaire. In one of his pamphlets he attempted to select the greatest man in history. He considered such men as Alexander the Great and Julius Caesar, but passed them over and named as his choice Isaac Newton.

Voltaire savagely attacked all things he considered sham or superstition. He advocated religious toleration and freedom of speech. He is credited

347

with a famous statement on free speech: "I do not agree with a word you say, but I will defend to the death your right to say it."

Diderot and the *Encyclopedia*. The leaders of the French Enlightenment left a monumental summary of their views on all subjects in a 28-volume *Encyclopedia* edited by Denis Diderot (DEE·duh·roh). It was compiled between 1751 and 1772 and typifies the time in which it was written. It was one of the first attempts to encompass all human knowledge, including new ideas in science and government.

The most brilliant writers of the period, including Rousseau and Voltaire, contributed articles to the *Encyclopedia*. These articles contained much thinly disguised criticism of the Church, the government, and the special privileges of nobles and clergy. For their critical writings, Diderot and several others were imprisoned. However, the *Encyclopedia* was widely read, and its ideas were enthusiastically adopted.

CHECKUP

1. IDENTIFY: Versailles, Colbert, Louvois, balance of power, War of the Spanish Succession, Treaty of Utrecht, Louis XV.

2. What were the causes of the Thirty Years' War?

3. List some provisions of the Peace of Westphalia.

4. How did the construction of Versailles contribute to the absolute power of Louis XIV?

5. Why did Louis XIV revoke the Edict of Nantes?

6. Name the major French political philosophers of the 1700's. What were their contributions to political thought?

Russia became a major power in the 1700's

After more than two centuries of Mongol rule, Russia became independent in 1480, as you read in Chapter 9. By this time the rulers of Moscow had become the most important in Russia, and they continued to expand their territory by conquests, marriages, and alliances.

Early Russian isolation

At the time Russia became independent, several factors tended to separate it from Western Europe. First, of course, there had been many years of Asian influence under Mongol domination. Second, there was the fact that, even as a Christian nation, Russia was different from the nations of Western Europe. Western civilization had reached Russia from Constantinople and the Byzantine Empire, not from the West. The Russians had been converted to Christianity by missionaries from Constantinople, and Russia's religion was Eastern Orthodox rather than Roman Catholic or Protestant. Russia's use of the Cyrillic alphabet proved to be a barrier to communication with the rest of Europe, which used the Roman alphabet.

It was geography that did most to isolate Russia in the late Middle Ages and early modern times. In a period when people and goods moved mostly by sea, Russia was almost entirely landlocked— that is, without a seacoast. It was blocked from the Baltic Sea by the stronger kingdoms of Sweden and Poland. To the south the Ottoman Turks held the Crimean peninsula, the north shore of the Black Sea, and the city of Constantinople.

The wide plains of Poland and eastern Europe lay to the west of Russia. However, these vast expanses of land gave little opportunity for commercial contacts. Russia had many navigable rivers, but they did not flow toward the great oceans and seas of commerce—the Mediterranean, Atlantic, and Pacific. Some ran south into the Caspian Sea, which had no outlet. Others flowed into the Black Sea, which was closed to Russia by the Turks. Still others ran north into the frozen, ice-choked Arctic Ocean and were no help to overseas trade.

Starting in the late 1400's and continuing through the 1500's, the rulers of Moscow gained power. Although there was a kind of feudalism, nobles were completely dominated by the princes of Moscow. These princes constantly added new territories to their realm (see map, page 350).

Ivan III, who reigned from 1462 to 1505, had extended his control over most of what is now northwestern Russia. Ivan IV, also known as Ivan the Terrible (1533–1584), added much territory to the south and east. He was the first Russian ruler

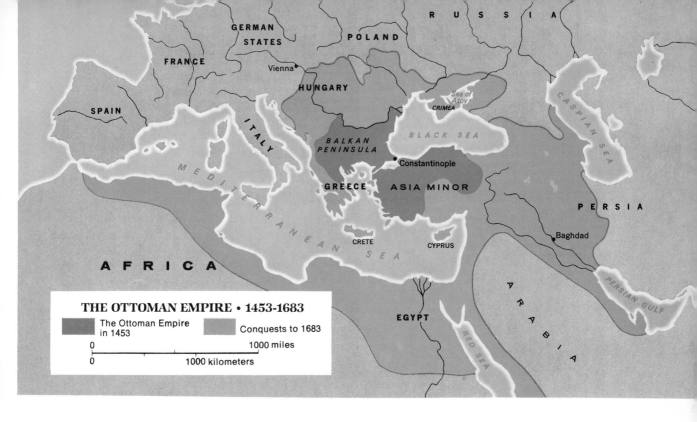

THE OTTOMAN EMPIRE • 1453-1683

The Ottoman Empire in 1453

Conquests to 1683

0   1000 miles

0   1000 kilometers

to be known as **czar**—the Russian form of Caesar. During his reign Russia also began its expansion eastward into Siberia. In order to consolidate his power, Ivan created a new class of landlords, who were given land in return for services to the czar. To maintain the loyalty of these new landlords, Ivan prohibited the free movement of peasants. In a census taken by the government, peasants were registered with the land that they worked for the landlord. Thus, they became serfs.

After the death of Ivan IV, there was a period of unrest lasting until 1613. In that year, Michael Romanov became czar. He was the first of the Romanov dynasty that was to rule Russia for 300 years. In the mid-1600's the Romanovs' government also went through a crisis. First there was a revolt by the Cossacks, a people of southern Russia. Then a group of religious dissenters known as the "Old Believers" tried to break away from the official church. Both attempts were suppressed by the czars, who also put serfdom into its final form in the mid-1600's. The power of the central government was thus firmly established in this period in Russia. Then, in 1682, a ruler came to the throne who was to use this power to influence both Russia and Europe.

Peter the Great

Czar Peter I, or Peter the Great, was a remarkable leader of great vision. He decided that Russia's future lay toward the west, in contacts with European nations. One of his major goals was sought also by later Russian governments—the acquisition of warm-water seaports that were not dominated by other nations.

To the south of Russia lay the Ottoman Empire, which controlled all the land between the Black Sea and the Mediterranean Sea. Under a succession of powerful rulers, this Muslim state had expanded into the Balkan and Crimean peninsulas and had taken North Africa and much of the Middle East. Sulayman I, also known as Sulayman the Magnificent, was sultan from 1520 to 1566. He was the greatest Ottoman ruler. During his reign the Turks invaded Hungary and almost captured Vienna. When Peter the Great became czar in the late 1600's, the Ottoman Empire presented a formidable barrier (see map, this page).

Peter sought to extend Russian territory southward, toward warm-water ports, but he was blocked by the Ottoman Empire. At first, Peter tried to gain the Sea of Azov. After two wars his troops took the city of Azov but failed to obtain control of the sea itself. Peter then realized that in order to defeat the Turks permanently, he needed two things—help from Western Europe and a stronger, more efficient Russia.

Peter's mission and its results. In 1697 a Russian delegation was sent to Western Europe to negoti- ate an alliance against the Turks. The mission failed in this purpose, but even so it was of great importance.

Peter, who went along with the delegation, often disguised himself as a private citizen. He vis- ited England, the Dutch Netherlands, Prussia, and Austria. There he met scientists, artisans, and leaders in many fields. He persuaded many of

GROWTH OF EUROPEAN RUSSIA
1462-1796

- Russia in 1462
- Acquisitions to 1682
- Acquisitions to 1725 (during the reign of Peter the Great)
- Acquisitions to 1796 (at the death of Catherine the Great)

0   500 miles
0   500 kilometers

them to take their skills to Russia. In the Netherlands he worked as a carpenter in a shipyard so that he could learn how ships were made. He visited schools, factories, hospitals, and arsenals to learn Western techniques.

When Peter returned to Russia, he reorganized his army along French lines and equipped it with the best European weapons. He then decided to try to gain warm-water ports in the Baltic Sea. At this time Sweden ruled Finland and parts of the Baltic region and northern Germany. In a war that lasted from 1700 to 1721, Russia gained important territory and ended Sweden's role as one of the great powers of Europe.

Russia's new territory was at the northeastern end of the Baltic Sea, at the Gulf of Finland (see map, opposite). There Peter decided to build a "window to Europe," a completely new city that would be his capital. The city, built only after many hardships, was named St. Petersburg. On the map opposite, you can see how Peter's new capital brought the center of Russian government closer to the nations of Western Europe. St. Petersburg was symbolic of the new Russian policy of facing toward Western Europe. With this port, Peter was able to establish a shipbuilding industry and build up a navy.

Domestic policy. Peter's mission to Western Europe had made him determined that Russia should be Westernized. He made several minor reforms. He insisted that women should abandon their isolation and take part in the life of the community. He himself taught some of his advisers to dance and to smoke tobacco. He forced the nobles to wear European-style clothing. He issued a decree ordering them to cut off their long beards. When the nobles were reluctant, Peter himself cut off some beards.

But these changes were minor. Much more important were the changes Peter made in Russian trade, finances, industry, and government. Armies and navies cost money, and to get it, Peter taxed nearly everything—from long beards to the birth of babies. He encouraged the development of trade with the West as well as with Asia. He also made great efforts to develop manufacturing industries.

In government, Peter followed the ideas of Louis XIV of France. The Russian czar had complete control of a highly centralized administration. Nobles were entirely under the influence of the monarch. The Church became a branch of the government, under control of the czar. As in France, the central government controlled local governments completely.

Peter found the hereditary nobles too set in their ways. He ordered many young nobles to study abroad and then serve the government.

By granting titles, Peter created a new nobility, one of service rather than of hereditary rank and privilege. The title and privileges depended on the amount of service a person gave the central government. To the members of this new nobility, Peter granted large estates with thousands of serfs. Many of these serfs had formerly been free farmers.

Peter's changes not only increased the number of serfs but worsened their condition. A Russian serf was almost entirely at the mercy of his or her master. At a time when serfdom was rapidly declining throughout Western Europe, the serfs of Russia were more completely bound to the land than ever before.

Catherine the Great

After the death of Peter the Great in 1725, a number of relatively weak monarchs ruled Russia. Peter's work was not carried forward until the reign of a remarkable woman, Catherine II, known as Catherine the Great. A princess from a small German state, Catherine had married the heir to the Russian throne. Her husband ruled for only six months in 1762 and then died mysteriously. As czarina, Catherine took over the throne and ruled until 1796.

Catherine the Great did not earn her title "the Great" from her domestic policy. She extended serfdom and made the conditions of the serfs even worse. It is true that she supported the arts, science, literature, and the theater. However, these changes meant little to most Russians, who lived in deep ignorance and poverty.

Foreign policy. Catherine's foreign policy continued the policies of Peter the Great, and it was in this field that she earned her fame. Russia still sought to control the Sea of Azov and the Black Sea. Another goal was expansion westward across the Polish plains. In each of these undertakings, Catherine was successful.

Russia became a major power

The increasing influence of Russia in European affairs went hand in hand with the growing power of the czars. Remarkable advances took place during the reign of Peter the Great. He built for himself an entirely new capital city, St. Petersburg (now Leningrad), and nearby started construction of a magnificent summer palace. Known as Peterhof, it became famous for its fountains, which to this day are kept going by gravity (above). It was a favorite home of Catherine the Great (right). Both rulers tried to westernize their people, an idea captured in a cartoon in which Peter is snipping off the beard of an unhappy Russian noble (below).

Catherine's first move was to fight a successful war in the south against the Turks. Russia gained control of the Sea of Azov, most of the northern shore of the Black Sea, and won a protectorate over the Crimean peninsula. Russia also became the protector of Eastern Orthodox Christians in the Ottoman Empire and gained the right to send ships from the Black Sea through the Bosporus and the Dardanelles to the Mediterranean Sea.

In the west, Catherine also made great gains. She took advantage of the fact that Poland was declining in strength. Poland was large but had many weaknesses. The kings were elected by the nobles. Until late in the 1500's, the nobles had usually elected the legal heir of the king. After this time, however, they chose anyone they thought they could control. This development brought both domestic and international troubles. Prussia, Austria, France, and Russia each plotted to put its favorite on the Polish throne.

Poland had a legislature, the Diet, in which only nobles were represented. This body rarely accomplished anything because any one member could veto whatever legislation was being considered. Furthermore, any member could dissolve the Diet and thus veto everything that had been done until then.

Poland contained large minority groups of different nationalities and religions. In western Poland there were large numbers of German Lutherans. Ukrainians of the Orthodox religion lived in the eastern part. The Polish government showed little wisdom in handling these groups. Most Poles were Roman Catholics. They often discriminated against and oppressed the minority groups including the Jews. From time to time, the minorities appealed to Prussia, Austria, or Russia for help.

In 1772, according to a previously made agreement, Russia, Prussia, and Austria each took a slice of Polish territory in what is known as the First Partition of Poland (see map, this page). The land seized by the three powers amounted to a fourth of all Poland. It was occupied by a third of the Polish population.

The Polish government was shocked into trying to reform and strengthen the nation. In 1791 Poland adopted a new constitution and abolished the veto privileges of members of the Diet. However, in 1793, before reforms could be carried out,

PARTITIONS OF POLAND

1772	Russia, Prussia, and Austria
1793	Russia and Prussia
1795	Russia, Prussia, and Austria

Russia and Prussia took a second helping of Polish lands. This Second Partition led to a Polish rebellion that threatened to spread throughout eastern Europe. To prevent the Polish revolt from spreading, Russia, Prussia, and Austria met in 1795 and agreed on a Third Partition. This operation was final, and Poland disappeared from the map of Europe.

CHECKUP

1. IDENTIFY: Romanov dynasty, "window to Europe," Diet.

2. LOCATE: Black Sea, Caspian Sea, Sea of Azov, Gulf of Finland, St. Petersburg.

3. What factors separated Russia from Western Europe?

4. Describe how Peter the Great tried to Westernize Russia both culturally and politically.

5. How did Catherine the Great continue Peter's foreign policy?

6. What conditions in Poland made it easy for foreign powers to divide the country?

6

Austria and Prussia competed for power in central Europe

Although the Holy Roman Emperor lost his authority over German princes in the mid-1600's, the Hapsburgs still hoped to dominate the German states. Germany was split among many small territories and therefore was vulnerable to the ambitions of various powers. Eventually the struggle for dominance came to be between Austria and Brandenburg-Prussia.

Austrian expansion

Austria had been weakened by loss of territory in the Thirty Years' War. It had also lost authority because of the increased independence granted other German states by the Peace of Westphalia in 1648. However, Austria remained by far the most powerful and important of the German states in the Holy Roman Empire. The Hapsburg rulers of Austria could almost always be sure of election as Holy Roman Emperors, although the elections were still occasions for bargaining and political maneuvering.

Austria's territorial losses as a result of the Thirty Years' War were more than made up during the next century by gains of territory elsewhere. These gains came from two main sources:

(1) *Wars against the Turks in central Europe and the Balkan peninsula.* From the time of Emperor Charles V in the 1500's, Holy Roman Emperors had fought many wars to drive back the Ottoman Turks. Eventually the Turks were forced to give up some of their holdings in the Balkan peninsula. By 1700 the Hapsburgs had completely regained Hungary, and Hapsburg emperors were recognized as kings there.

(2) *The War of the Spanish Succession.* By the Treaty of Utrecht, as you have read, the Hapsburgs received the Mediterranean island of Sardinia, the Kingdom of Naples, and the Duchy of Milan. They also received the Spanish Netherlands, which then became the Austrian Netherlands. Notice the territorial gains of the Hapsburgs on the map on page 347.

Maria Theresa

In 1740 Maria Theresa of the House of Hapsburg became ruler of Austria and the other Hapsburg lands. Her father, who had been Holy Roman Emperor, had tried to make it safe for her to rule. At great expense he had persuaded European rulers to sign an agreement called the **Pragmatic Sanction.** By this agreement, the rulers of Europe promised not to take Maria Theresa's territory.

The laws of the Holy Roman Empire prevented Maria Theresa from being elected empress, but in 1745 she gained the title of Holy Roman Empress by having her husband elected emperor—the only non-Hapsburg elected in 300 years.

The Austria that Maria Theresa inherited was a strange territory. Although it was a large area with tremendous resources, it was a patchwork of territories and peoples. In addition to the ruling group of Germans, Austria contained Hungarians, Italians, Belgians, Rumanians, and various Slavic peoples such as Poles, Bohemians, Serbs, Croatians, and Slovenes. As a result, there were many conflicts of language, religion, and national interest.

Austria was surrounded by envious rulers. Several German states were rivals of Hapsburg power. Bavaria, in southern Germany, jealously guarded its lands and independence, sometimes by forming alliances with France against the Hapsburgs. The German states of Saxony and Hanover also preferred to act independently.

The Hapsburgs had several advantages. They could count on the strong support of the papacy. As Holy Roman Emperors, they had derived their power from the Roman Catholic Church. They were also the defenders of Christian Europe against the Turks. Moreover, the Hapsburgs were related to most European royal families.

The Hohenzollerns of Brandenburg-Prussia

As you have read, the Treaty of Utrecht in 1713 recognized the Elector of Brandenburg as king of Prussia. The Elector was a member of the Hohenzollern family. This recognition was an important step in that family's rise to power.

During the Middle Ages the Hohenzollerns had ruled only a small territory in southern Germany.

Rivalry between Austria and Prussia

The rivalry between Austria and Prussia intensified after 1740, when Maria Theresa became the empress of Austria and Frederick the Great became the king of Prussia. Despite being a woman and thus not regarded as having military skills, Maria Theresa proved to be a formidable opponent for Frederick. She reviewed her troops (right) and held her own against most of Frederick's territorial ambitions. Prussia's invasion of Bohemia in 1757 began the main phase of the Seven Years' War in Europe. The attempt failed, and Frederick's forces were beaten back. This was a low moment in his fortunes, as shown in a portrait after his defeat (below). Later the same year Frederick won a great victory against Austria in Silesia, his only military success. When Maria Theresa died, Frederick paid her a well-deserved compliment: "She was an honor to her sex and to her throne."

Hohenzollern rulers were ambitious and eager to get more land. They were willing to use any methods as long as they increased the power, influence, and the landholdings of the family. Toward the end of the Middle Ages, one branch of the family settled in Brandenburg, in northern Germany. The ruler of Brandenburg eventually became an elector of the Holy Roman Emperor.

During the Reformation the Hohenzollern rulers of Brandenburg became Lutherans and seized all the Catholic Church lands in their territories. At the beginning of the Thirty Years' War, they gained control of Prussia, on the Baltic Sea. By the end of the war, they ruled several widely scattered territories in Germany.

In the mid-1600's, Brandenburg-Prussia was ruled by one of the greatest of the Hohenzollerns, Frederick William, called the Great Elector. He guided his state through the difficult last years of the Thirty Years' War. Then he turned to the rebuilding and further strengthening of Brandenburg-Prussia.

The Great Elector first reorganized the armies of all his lands into one strong force. Then he improved the system of tax collecting and encouraged agriculture, industry, and transportation.

The Great Elector's successor, Frederick, was ambitious to have the title of king. To gain the necessary consent of the Holy Roman Emperor, Frederick supported the Hapsburgs in the War of the Spanish Succession. It was as a reward for this support that he was granted the title Frederick I, King of Prussia. From this time on, all the Hohenzollern possessions in northern Germany were usually referred to as Prussia. The state originally known by that name became known as East Prussia (see map, page 347).

Frederick William I, King of Prussia

Frederick I did not live long to enjoy the title of King of Prussia. His successor, Frederick William I, came to the throne in 1713. He disliked French ways intensely. His father had tried to copy the Versailles of Louis XIV and had furnished his palace lavishly. Frederick William got rid of much of this luxury.

He used the money he saved to strengthen Prussia. The army was doubled in size and was so well organized and drilled that it became the best and most efficient fighting force in Europe. Frederick William was so strict in his discipline that it was said he ran all of Prussia, including his palace, like a military barracks.

Frederick William I strengthened his country in many ways. He reorganized the civil service, hiring and promoting efficient people, regardless of their birth. He also encouraged trade and built up industries, spending government money where necessary. The collection of taxes and the spending of money were carefully planned so that the treasury had a surplus for emergencies. Frederick William I was convinced that all children should have a primary education. He issued a decree requiring all Prussian parents to send their children to school.

Frederick the Great

Frederick William I had a real worry as he neared the end of his life. His son had little interest in either military life or government service. Instead, he spent his time writing poetry, playing the flute, and reading philosophy. The king used the harshest methods, even imprisonment, to force his heir to be more nearly the son he desired.

As it turned out, Frederick William's son proved to be an even stronger ruler than his father. He turned out to be one of Prussia's greatest military and political leaders and is known as Frederick the Great.

Frederick William's son took the throne of Prussia as Frederick II in 1740, the same year in which Maria Theresa became ruler of Austria. He was a skilled administrator, who instituted social reforms and began work on a Prussian law code. Like his grandfather, he admired French culture. He also wrote several books, including a history of Brandenburg and a book on the duties of rulers.

Conflict between Prussia and Austria. The year 1740 was one of decision in Germany and in all of Europe. Each of the two strongest states of the Holy Roman Empire had a new ruler. Prussia was emerging as a challenger to the dominance of Austria in the German part of the empire. The clash between the two states came soon.

Austria and Prussia each had strengths and weaknesses. Maria Theresa ruled the vast Hapsburg territories and had some claim on the loyalty of all the German states. Her position was aided by the pledges of European rulers in the Pragmatic Sanction, by her relationship to many rulers, and by the support of the pope.

There were also many Austrian weaknesses, including discontented nationalities under Hapsburg rule and inefficient administration of the government. Maria Theresa's father had almost emptied the treasury to get signers for the Pragmatic Sanction. Despite their pledges, few countries were willing to help Austria if that involved any risk to themselves. However, if France opposed Austria, as it usually did, Austria might get help from Great Britain and the Dutch Netherlands, traditional enemies of France.

Prussia had a smaller territory and population than did Austria. Its lands were widely scattered and therefore hard to defend. However, unlike Austria, the population was solidly German. Prussia also had a healthy economic system, a well-organized and efficient government, and a strong army. In a conflict with Austria, Prussia could count on help or at least friendly neutrality from Bavaria, Saxony, and Sardinia.

In 1740 Frederick the Great seized the Austrian province of Silesia, which lay close to his own lands (see map, page 347). Silesia was a valuable region with rich farm lands and iron deposits. Its population was largely German. Frederick argued that his father's promise in agreeing to the Pragmatic Sanction was not binding on him.

The seizure of Silesia began a series of campaigns, known as the War of the Austrian Succession, which lasted until 1748. Other countries were involved, too. In general, France, Bavaria, and Saxony fought on the side of Prussia, while Great Britain, Russia, and the Dutch Netherlands sided with Austria. Prussia lost almost 10 percent of its population, mostly young men. The Prussian countryside was devastated. The city of Berlin, capital of Prussia, was invaded three times.

After the war there was a diplomatic shift, with both Great Britain and France changing sides. This only intensified the rivalries, and in 1756 a major conflict erupted—the Seven Years' War, which involved almost every European country. Great Britain and France, rivals for lands overseas, battled for colonies in India and in North America. In America the war was generally known as the French and Indian War.

At one point Prussia was surrounded by enemies in Europe, with only financial help from Great Britain. Fighting against great odds, Frederick dashed from one front to another to hold off his enemies. For all his great skill, he was saved only because Russia switched sides and came to his assistance. Finally, however, his enemies agreed to the Peace of Hubertusburg in 1763. By the terms of this treaty, Prussia was allowed to keep Silesia.

Prussia's peacetime gains

In the years of peace that followed 1763, Frederick the Great showed that he had genius for organization and administration as well as for war. He expanded and further improved public education and the already excellent civil service system. He allowed religious freedom, made legal and court reforms, and encouraged trade and manufacturing. Through hard work and wise direction, the expanded state of Prussia recovered its prosperity.

Prussia's territorial gains continued. Frederick the Great helped to bring about the First Partition of Poland in 1772. By taking Polish territory along the Baltic coast, Frederick was able to join together Prussia and East Prussia. Thus, at his death in 1786, Frederick the Great left behind him a solidly formed, greatly enlarged, and prosperous nation. By 1800 Prussia had become a formidable rival of Austria for control of the German states, and a first-class power in Europe.

CHECKUP

1. IDENTIFY: Maria Theresa, Pragmatic Sanction, the Great Elector, Frederick William I, Seven Years' War, Peace of Hubertusburg.

2. LOCATE: Bavaria, Saxony, Hanover, Silesia, Berlin.

3. What were the strengths and weaknesses of Austria during the 1700's?

4. List the accomplishments of the reign of Frederick William I.

5. What were the reasons for the War of the Austrian Succession? What were its results?

6. What were the major achievements of Frederick the Great?

CHAPTER REVIEW

1568–1648	Revolt against Spain in the Netherlands	1660	Restoration of English monarchy	1740	Beginning of Maria Theresa's rule of Hapsburg possessions
1589–1610	Rule of Henry IV in France	1682–1725	Rule of Peter the Great in Russia	1740–1786	Rule of Frederick the Great in Prussia
1618–1648	Thirty Years' War				
1624–1642	Richelieu in power in France	1688	Glorious Revolution in England	1756–1763	Seven Years' War
1625–1649	Rule of Charles I in England			1762	Rousseau's *Social Contract*
1642–1660	English Revolution	1690	Locke's *Second Treatise of Civil Government*	1762–1796	Rule of Catherine the Great in Russia
1643–1715	Rule of Louis XIV in France	1713	Treaty of Utrecht	1772–1795	Partitioning of Poland

CHAPTER SUMMARY

Spain dominated Europe in the 1500's. Charles V, a Hapsburg, ruled a vast empire. His son, Philip II, strengthened the central government, intensified the Spanish Inquisition, and tried to conquer England. He ruled the Netherlands as a Spanish colony, but the Dutch finally achieved independence in 1648.

In the 1600's, France became the dominant power in Europe. Henry IV improved the country's finances. Richelieu, chief minister under Louis XIII, destroyed the political independence of the Huguenots and the power of the nobles.

In England, the strong central government of the Tudors faced religious strife and troubles with Parliament. Economic difficulties under the Stuarts intensified these troubles, and clashes between Charles I and Parliament led to civil war. The king's supporters were defeated by the Puritans, led by Oliver Cromwell. After the execution of Charles I, Cromwell governed England. However, two years after Cromwell's death, the monarchy was restored.

In the Glorious Revolution, Parliament deposed James II and declared William and Mary joint rulers. The new monarchs accepted the Bill of Rights, which limited royal authority and safeguarded the rights of Parliament.

After the chaotic period of the Thirty Years' War, new international relationships were established. The Peace of Westphalia, signed in 1648, strengthened France at the expense of the Hapsburgs. Under Louis XIV, France enjoyed enormous power and prestige. Louis fought four wars to gain territory, but ruined France economically.

In Russia, Peter the Great made far-reaching changes. He built a new capital, stressed Westernization, and centralized the government. Catherine the Great continued Peter's policy of securing warm-water ports, gaining important territory. With Prussia and Austria, Russia divided Poland until it no longer existed.

Austria and Prussia were rivals for control of the German states. Maria Theresa, the Austrian ruler, inherited a vast realm that was a patchwork of territories and peoples. Prussia was strengthened by the Hohenzollern family. Frederick William I doubled the size of the army, reorganized the civil service, and promoted trade and industry. His son, Frederick the Great, carried on a series of European wars, gaining the Austrian province of Silesia, and made numerous internal reforms.

After this long period of crisis in Europe, the dominance of central governments over local authorities was established. This was a decisive period in creating the political forms we still see in the modern world.

CHECKING WHAT YOU KNOW

1. Match the rulers at the left with their contemporaries at the right:

   a. Philip II
   b. Maria Theresa
   c. Oliver Cromwell
   d. William III of England
   e. Sulayman the Magnificent

   1. Charles I
   2. Elizabeth I
   3. Peter the Great
   4. Charles V
   5. Frederick the Great

2. Match each document at the left with the ruler during whose reign it was put into effect:

a. Petition of Right
b. Instrument of Government
c. Edict of Nantes
d. Act of Toleration

1. Henry IV
2. William and Mary
3. Charles I
4. Cromwell

3. Which of the provisions of the Peace of Westphalia weakened the Austrian Hapsburgs?

4. What were the views of each of the following writers on the relationship between the government and the people being governed:

a. Thomas Hobbes
b. John Locke
c. Baron de Montesquieu
d. Jean Jacques Rousseau

5. Compare the reigns of Peter the Great and Catherine the Great. How were they similar? What were the important accomplishments of each?

PRACTICING YOUR SKILLS

1. **Using maps.** Make an outline map of France around 1721 by tracing the map on page 347. In a second color, add the boundaries that Louis XIV wanted for France. Compare Louis XIV's ideal France with the boundaries of present-day France (see map, page 810). What are the similarities and differences?

2. **Making charts.** Make a chart summarizing the accomplishments of the following Prussian rulers: Frederick William, Frederick I, Frederick William I, and Frederick II.

3. **Analyzing information.** Between 1500 and 1750, some traditional ruling families firmly established their power while other empires began to weaken. Explain why France and Prussia emerged as strong powers while the empires of Austria and Spain declined.

4. **Interpreting paintings.** As you have read, the 1500's and 1600's saw the rise of central governments throughout Europe. Select two paintings from this chapter that portray rulers who headed these new governments. What adjectives would you use to describe how each king or queen wished to be seen? What evidence in the portraits supports your answer?

RELATING PAST TO PRESENT

1. The Petition of Right, the Habeas Corpus Act, the English Bill of Rights, and the Act of Toleration covered many important rights of individual citizens. List the rights protected by these measures. Use American civics or government books to find out how many of these rights are protected today by the United States Constitution.

2. Reread the following sentence from page 335: "Love, ambition, madness, revenge—these were the themes of ancient Greek dramas as well as the works of modern playwrights." What Shakespearean play have you read that developed one of these dramatic themes? What current plays or movies prove that such themes are indeed timeless?

3. It has been said that Louis XIV's control of a large and fine army gave him the desire to use it. Does the existence of great armies today lead to the same result? Explain your answer.

4. The 1600's are often called the French century. What nation will the 1900's be named after? Give reasons for your answer.

INVESTIGATING FURTHER

1. Mary Stuart, the Queen of Scotland, competed with Elizabeth I for the throne of England. Use encyclopedias or biographies of these women to find answers to the following questions: What were the religious problems of Mary's rule? of Elizabeth's? What special problems did these rulers face because they were women? Why do you think one monarch succeeded and the other failed?

2. The novels of Alexandre Dumas deal with France during the reign of Louis XIV. You might find it interesting to read one of these novels to discover more about life in France during this period. *The Three Musketeers* would be especially appropriate.

3. St. Petersburg, founded by Peter the Great, became a symbol of the the new Russian policy of facing toward Western Europe. Using books in your library, prepare a short report on this city, concentrating mainly on its founding.

(1400–1800)

16

Europeans Explored, Traded, and Settled in Distant Lands

If you had looked around the world in the year 1400, you would probably have considered Europe one of the weakest and least important areas. The rich and powerful rulers of China, India, Africa, the Americas, and even Europe's neighbor Turkey would have outshone the greatest of Europe's monarchs. Unless you had been an inspired prophet, you would not have predicted that the situation would change very much over the next few centuries. Europe seemed concerned with its own problems, such as the troubles of the papacy. It hardly seemed to have the interest, let alone the energy and the resources, to influence the rest of the world.

By about 1750, less than 400 years later, Europe had become the dominant civilization on earth. European rulers had conquered and toppled ancient empires. Europeans had taken over the richest part of the world's trade. On every continent colonists and merchants from Europe were important and influential. Their success brought European ideas and attitudes to every part of the globe. This remarkable transformation of the relations among the world's people was one of the most significant developments in history. Its results are still felt today.

The expansion of European civilization marked the end of the separate, unconnected histories of the different parts of the world. By the 1800's, and in many cases before then, countries that had been going their own ways, with little outside con-

A Mediterranean seaport of the 1600's

tacts except with neighbors, were no longer isolated. Interaction between distant areas became common. By the 1900's no place on earth could consider itself unaffected by major events, however far away. In this book up to this point we have treated the history of each large region mostly by itself. From now on, we can speak more and more of a single history that covers the entire world.

THE CHAPTER SECTIONS

1. Europeans had new reasons for exploring overseas

2. Portugal and Spain took the lead in exploration

3. Portugal and Spain acquired many foreign colonies

4. England, the Netherlands, France, and Russia expanded

1

Europeans had new reasons for exploring overseas

Europeans had not been totally isolated during the late Middle Ages. You have read about Marco Polo, the Italian merchant who traveled to China in the 1200's. Other Europeans traded with Arabs in order to buy valuable spices and silks and with Asians to buy jewels. The Crusaders had marched to the Holy Land to try to reclaim it for Christianity. The stories told by these travelers helped create an interest in the world beyond Europe.

Most Europeans in the early 1400's did not have the ability or the interest to explore foreign lands. By the late 1400's, however, many had developed this ability and interest because of major changes in four areas—technology, politics, economics, and society.

Technological advances

One of the main goals of the first European explorers was to get to Asia in order to acquire spices, silks, and jewels. These were very valuable trading items. Even small amounts had high value. A ship filled with spices—which were used for preserving as well as flavoring food—had a cargo worth more than a hundred times that of the same ship filled with timber or grain.

Spices, silks, and jewels were produced mainly in India, China, and the islands of East and Southeast Asia. There, Europeans had to compete with powerful Arab traders as well as with local traders. If the Europeans were to compete successfully, they had to have more advanced equipment to defeat their rivals. They needed better instruments of navigation, better ships, and better guns. In other words, what they needed was more advanced technology.

Map making. Map making had improved during the Renaissance because of the growing interest in pictorial accuracy and in the writings of ancient geographers. One ancient writer whose works attracted the attention of Renaissance scholars was Ptolemy. His maps showed that the world was round, as most scholars knew. Renaissance maps also gave information about Africa and Asia. Italian sailors were soon preparing even more accurate charts of coastlines. These charts were essential for explorers, who recorded their routes for others to follow.

Navigation instruments. Equally important were new navigation instruments. These helped make it possible for ships to sail far out to sea instead of having to stay close to the coastlines for fear of losing their bearings. The development of the compass made long sea voyages possible. As early as the 1100's, Europeans knew that an iron needle rubbed against a piece of lodestone—a kind of magnetic rock—would be magnetized and turn toward the north. They may have learned this from the Arabs, who in turn learned it from the Chinese. At first the magnetized needle was floated on a piece of cork in water. In the 1300's it was fixed to a card marked with directions to create a true compass.

Another important instrument was the astrolabe, which had been perfected by the Muslims. Sailors used it to determine the relative height of stars and planets. From this information they could calculate a ship's latitude—that is, its distance north or south of the equator.

New ships. Improvements in ships were also essential for long-range exploration. In 1400 European ships were inferior to those of the Arabs, Indians, and Chinese, but by 1600 they were the best in the world.

Before and even during the 1400's, most European coastal trade was carried on by long ships called galleys. They were propelled by oars—25 or 30 on each side—and were rowed by slaves or prisoners of war. In deeper waters, particularly on the oceans, traders used sailing ships. Before the late 1400's, however, most sailing ships were small and clumsy. Some could only sail in the direction in which the wind was blowing.

In the late 1400's ship designers in Portugal and Spain made important improvements in the shape of sails and in the rudder, the ship's steering device. These improvements allowed ships to sail against the wind, to travel quickly, and to be steered with reasonable accuracy.

The cannon. The invention of the cannon was another major technological advance. Although the Chinese had discovered gunpowder hundreds of years earlier, Europeans first applied it to warfare in the 1400's and 1500's. Shipboard cannons, and the handguns sailors carried, helped Europeans defeat the vastly larger navies of their enemies. The capture of Arab coastal forts and victories over Arab navies were decisive in overcoming these trading rivals in Asia. Weapons were also crucial in the Spaniards' easy conquest of the natives of Mexico and Peru. Without guns, Europeans could never have established themselves so quickly, both in Asia and in the Americas.

Political change

Technical advances alone could not have made successful explorations possible. Money was also needed for such exploration. This was provided, first of all, by the stronger and more ambitious governments that emerged in Europe in the 1400's and 1500's. In Portugal, Spain, and France, monarchs and their advisers led the way. They not only financed voyages but also controlled exploration and the building of overseas empires. In England and the Netherlands, governments played lesser roles, but they still gave some support for exploration.

In the 1200's European rulers had not been powerful or wealthy enough to support overseas explorations. By the late 1400's and early 1500's they not only had the power and the wealth, but they also had the will. They saw that overseas possessions could bring their countries great riches.

They also realized that ordinary people were excited about and proud of their country's empire. One envious Englishman complained that Spain's rulers had "extended their dominions, increased their trade, enriched their subjects and their overflowing treasure, and given strength and reputation to their kingdom." England's kings had not, and these were reasons enough to fight for their own empire.

The rivalry between different countries kept new waves of explorers and colonists coming out of Europe. As the Portuguese, and then the Spaniards, lost the energy to explore, the Dutch, the English, and the French took their place. The ambitions of these nations were often fed by their hatred of one another. Governments used appeals to patriotism to help build their empires. The change in both political power and in relations among nations was thus essential to Europe's overseas expansion.

Economic change

The development of new economic policies and methods was important for explorations to be possible. In some cases developments that had already begun, such as the use of money and the services provided by banks, simply speeded up. In other cases, the old methods of doing business became inadequate, and Europeans worked out new ones. The European economy changed so much from about 1500 to about 1750 that some historians refer to the economic developments of this time as the **Commercial Revolution.**

Europeans had had different kinds of money since the early Middle Ages. However, several handicaps had prevented its widespread use. One was the scarcity of precious metals. Europe produced almost no gold and very little silver. A second hindrance was the great variety of money in use. In England and France the national governments minted coins. Elsewhere individual cities and even nobles and bishops made their own coins. A third difficulty was the lack of a fixed standard for money. That is, the value of certain coins might change depending on the amount of precious metal used to make them. In other words, money did not have a fixed value. It took an alert expert to tell how much a coin was really worth.

A Mariner's Astrolabe

The explorers of the 1500's sailed the oceans with only a few simple instruments to guide them. But with these, along with the stars and sun, they were able to navigate the world. They could plot and hold a course, measure their progress, and estimate their position in relation to land.

The bronze astrolabe shown at the left was an instrument used to measure latitude. It has an outer edge divided into degrees, and a movable center bar with pointers on each end. Grasping the astrolabe by the ring at the top, the viewer sighted along the bar, rotating it until one of the pointers aimed at the sun. The figure at the other end indicated the correct latitude. This is the origin of the expression "shooting the sun."

In the 1400's, however, Europeans began to develop standard systems of money. Italian cities, deeply involved in trade, led the way in producing coins that had a fixed value. As a result, the gold florin of Florence and the ducat (DUK·ut) of Venice became very dependable. Then, as the Spanish colonies in the Americas sent home tons of silver and gold, the king of Spain used it to pay the debts he owed to German and Italian bankers. These payments helped relieve the shortage of precious metals in Europe and made standard systems of money possible.

The standardization of money made economic transactions much more stable and reliable. This, in turn, encouraged the growth of international commerce and the rise of banks. Large sums of money were accumulated in banks. The banks made loans to monarchs as well as to major trading companies. Some bankers, such as the Medici (MED·ih·chee) of Florence and the Fuggers of Augsburg, became extremely powerful throughout Europe. The lending by banks and the availability of money made the financing of huge overseas explorations possible.

When governments did not put up the money themselves, individual merchants often combined their resources in a new type of business organization called a **joint-stock company.** Such a company raised money by selling stock, or shares, in the company to investors. These shareholders became joint owners. Profits were divided among shareholders according to the number of shares of stock they owned. The part of the profit paid out for each share of stock was called a dividend.

By getting many people to invest their savings in this way, joint-stock companies were able to raise large amounts of money for all kinds of ventures. Both the English East India Company and the Dutch East India Company, which controlled trade with Asia in the 1600's, were joint-stock companies.

Mercantilism

The political and economic changes that led to overseas expansion also contributed to a new economic theory called **mercantilism.** According to this theory, there was a fixed amount of wealth in the world. In order to get a larger share, one country had to take some wealth away from another country. The richer a nation was, the more powerful it was. Therefore, a nation's government had to do everything it could to increase the nation's wealth.

Obtaining gold and silver from mines at home or in colonies overseas was one way to become rich. Another was to get these precious metals through trade. In trading, a nation tried to sell

How do we know?

CARTOGRAPHY Whenever a place, a direction, or a route cannot be described clearly in words, people resort to drawings. Historians can learn a great deal about a society from the way it chooses to produce such drawings, which we usually call maps.

The oldest surviving maps are clay tablets and papyrus remnants from Babylonia and Egypt. Called cadastres (kah-DAS-ters), they are sketches of property lines, showing where one person's property ended and another's began. The survival of these maps from 4,000 or more years ago indicates how important it was in ancient societies to define exactly the property that a person held.

Cadastres were based on careful observation and some mathematical skill. The same was true of another kind of drawing, the chart. Charts were often produced by travelers, either to show the route from one place to the next or, more commonly, to guide sailors at sea. A chart would show the shoreline, indicate the location of dangerous rocks, and help a ship's captain navigate along a coast. Charts became especially useful during the 1400's, 1500's, and 1600's, when overseas exploration became important.

When people could not observe directly, they had to estimate and use mathematical projections to create what we now recognize as maps. Mapmakers used such estimates to create maps of their countries and of the world. What they showed tells historians a great deal about their attitudes and beliefs. Christian mapmakers, for instance, often showed the holy city of Jerusalem as the center of the world. The Dutch, on the other hand, liked to make maps with the west, instead of the north, at the top. In this way the seacoast of the Netherlands was at the top of the map. Distortions sometimes revealed the hopes of explorers who thought, for example, that it would be easy to sail around the northern part of America. Maps were also made of mythical places like Thomas More's Utopia.

Only in modern times has accuracy in map making improved greatly, as a result of surveying techniques and aerial photography. The very accuracy of our maps also tells something about us—that we live in a scientific age.

more goods in foreign countries than it bought, thus creating a favorable **balance of trade.** In doing so, more money came into the nation, and its foreign rivals, who had to pay for the goods with gold and silver, were weakened. In order to have more money flow into the country than left it, governments put tariffs, or import taxes, on foreign goods. They also increased production at home and expanded any overseas business that produced new wealth.

Colonies played an important part in mercantilism. Those that produced gold and silver were most desirable. Next best were those producing raw materials that could not be produced at home. By buying these materials in its colonies, a nation could avoid buying from a foreign rival. Thus money did not go out of the nation or empire.

For example, the mainland of North America was rich in valuable products. The pine forests were among the most valuable because they were sources of pitch, tar, rosin, and turpentine—naval stores (supplies) that were used to build and maintain ships. England itself did not produce naval stores and had to buy them from Sweden or Russia. Therefore, the English government encouraged their production in North America by giving money to colonists who produced them.

Besides their value as sources of raw materials, colonies were important as markets for the manufactured products of the home country. Governments passed laws to prevent colonists from buying foreign manufactured goods or selling their raw materials to anyone but the home country.

Social change

Government policies, though important, could not alone have created a willingness to explore and settle overseas. Because of changes in society, exploration and resettlement abroad became attractive to some people.

The most important social change was the increase in the population of Europe during the late 1400's and 1500's. Farmlands became overcrowded and peasants left their villages in search of better opportunities. One good prospect for work seemed to be a life at sea. Sailors were paid, fed, and given a place to stay. The more adventurous hoped that traveling overseas would give them a fresh start and a better life.

Colonies offered settlers various attractions. Although living conditions in the colonies were harsh, the promise of a new life and the hope of obtaining some land drew thousands of people overseas.

Many more people went to the colonies in the hope of quick profits. Tales of gold and jewels, of fabulous cities like El Dorado in South America, were enough to persuade thousands that easy wealth lay overseas.

Others went overseas because of persecution or political problems at home—for example, Protestants in France, and Puritans in England. Like the poor peasants or the unsuccessful nobles, they helped found colonies because they were escaping difficulties at home. Those who went overseas for more positive reasons, such as converting natives to Christianity or expanding Europe's trade, were a small minority. On the whole, it was the hardship caused by social change that prompted people to participate in Europe's expansion.

CHECKUP

1. IDENTIFY: astrolabe, latitude, galleys, ducat, Medici, Fuggers, joint-stock company.

2. How was a compass constructed? What civilization is believed to have invented the compass first?

3. Describe the improvements in navigational aids and ship construction that made long-range explorations possible.

4. Why was the standardization of money important?

5. Explain the term mercantilism. What role did colonies play in mercantilism?

6. What were some of the reasons people left Europe to settle in the colonies?

Portugal and Spain took the lead in exploration

Explorers sailing for Portugal and Spain made the first voyages into unknown waters. Driven by curiosity and by religious and economic aims, and supported by their governments, they made discoveries throughout the world. The ventures of these early pioneers formed the basis for the empires their countries later founded.

Portugal and Prince Henry

The small nation of Portugal was one of the first to become seriously interested in exploration. This interest was due largely to a member of the royal family, Prince Henry, often called Henry the Navigator. He had four main aims for Portugal. (1) He wished to acquire new lands and peoples for Christianity by a crusade in Africa. (2) He sought to encircle and outflank the Muslims by finding and joining forces with Prester John, a legendary Christian king who Prince Henry thought lived somewhere in Africa. (3) He wanted to acquire a share of the African slave trade that the Muslims then controlled. (4) He wanted to start trading with Asia.

Early in the 1400's Prince Henry founded a school in Portugal in which navigators were trained. Soon his sea captains began a series of explorations westward into the Atlantic and southward along the western coast of Africa. They slowly worked their way south, each captain going a little farther than the one before him. As they explored, they claimed for Portugal a number of islands, such as the Azores in the Atlantic. Far to the south, below the desert region of the Sahara, the Portuguese began to trade in black slaves, gold, and ivory.

Further explorations brought even greater gains to the Portuguese. In 1488 Bartholomeu Dias (DEE·ahsh) sailed around the Cape of Good Hope, at the southern tip of Africa. Finally, in 1498, Vasco da Gama sailed around Africa and across the Indian Ocean to India (see map, pages 370–71). He came home with a fabulous cargo of spices and jewels.

The voyage of da Gama was a tremendous stroke of good fortune for Portugal. Portuguese ships could sail to India and the East Indies and bring back rich cargoes of Asian goods. It was now cheaper for the Portuguese to bring goods directly to Europe from Asia than it was for the Arab traders and the Italian merchants they dealt with. Ships could carry cargoes more cheaply than could animals traveling over land. Ships also did not have to pay tolls that merchants traveling on land often had to pay. However, the Portuguese

did not sell their goods at prices lower than their competitors in order to get control of the market. Instead, they kept their prices at the same level and simply took a larger profit. This allowed the Italians to continue their eastern trade and maintain their wealth for over a hundred years.

Christopher Columbus

Even before Vasco da Gama brought wealth to Portugal, Spain also had become interested in the search for new trade routes. Its rulers, Ferdinand and Isabella, decided to finance a voyage by Christopher Columbus, an Italian navigator. Thinking that the world was much smaller than it actually is, Columbus believed he could reach India quickly and easily by sailing westward.

In August 1492 Columbus set sail with three small ships from Spain and crossed the Atlantic. His small fleet landed in October on a tiny island in the Caribbean Sea. He named the island San Salvador (see map, pages 370–71). After visiting several other islands, Columbus returned triumphantly to Spain in the spring of 1493 to report his discoveries. He believed the islands to be off the coast of India and therefore called their inhabitants "Indians." Actually, he had discovered the islands later known as the West Indies. Although Columbus made three more voyages between 1493 and 1504, he believed until his death that the lands he had found were part of Asia.

Dividing the new lands

Spain and Portugal often claimed the same newly discovered lands. Their dispute was referred to the pope for arbitration. In 1493 he resolved the conflict by drawing the so-called papal line of demarcation—an imaginary line down the middle of the Atlantic Ocean, from the North Pole to the South Pole. Spain was granted rights to all newly discovered lands west of the line. Portugal could claim all those to the east. A year later, the Treaty of Tordesillas between Spain and Portugal moved the line farther west (see map, pages 370–71).

As you can see by looking at a globe, if either of these nations kept on exploring in the direction they were permitted, their claims would eventually conflict on the other side of the world. For practical purposes, however, the line worked. A

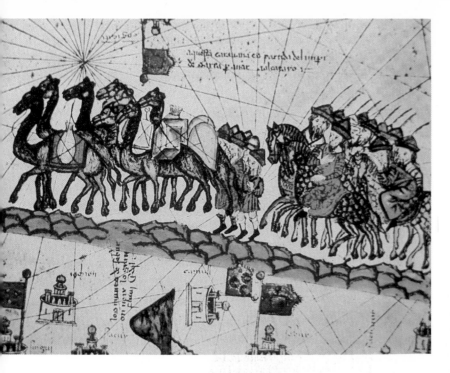

Early explorers

Europe's interest in other areas of the world is usually dated from the Crusades and the travels of the family of Marco Polo of Venice. A manuscript of the 1200's showed Marco Polo's father and uncle setting out in a caravan for Asia (above left). Marco joined them on their second trip when he was 17 and wrote an account of his travels. One hundred and fifty years later, the Portuguese began to seek a sea route to the East. Their chief patron from 1415 until his death in 1460 was Prince Henry the Navigator (above). The next breakthrough came in 1492, when Columbus reached America. The very next year a letter in which he described his discoveries was published. It was illustrated with a picture of the "new world," filled with imaginary but splendid cities, and showed Columbus aboard his ship (left).

Portuguese captain, Pedro Alvares Cabral, reached the east coast of South America by accident in 1500. He was sailing for India along da Gama's route, but strong winds blew him off course and forced him westward. When he claimed what is now Brazil for Portugal, his claim was honored because he had landed east of the line fixed by the pope.

In 1529 the line was extended completely around the globe. Thus, most of Central and South America was claimed by Spain. Portugal claimed regions in Asia.

Other explorers

Columbus was followed westward by other explorers. Between 1497 and 1503, another Italian, Amerigo Vespucci (ves·POO·chee), took part in several Portuguese expeditions across the Atlantic. Vespucci became convinced that the land he saw was not part of Asia. He described what he had seen as a "New World." After reading his writings, a German geographer named the new land America after Vespucci's first name ("Americus" in Latin).

In 1513 a Spaniard named Vasco Núñez de Balboa crossed the Isthmus of Panama and looked out on a great ocean. He called it the South Sea and took possession of it for Spain. Now it seemed clear that the New World was really a distinct land mass, separate from Asia. It was Ferdinand Magellan, a Portuguese navigator sailing for Spain, who proved it to be so.

Magellan and his crew succeeded in doing what in that day seemed nearly impossible—they sailed westward until they reached home again. In 1519, with five ships, Magellan set out from Spain, crossed the Atlantic to South America, and sailed along its eastern shore until he reached the southernmost tip. After passing through the strait that is now named after him, he found himself in a great ocean. Magellan first sailed on the ocean when it was very calm. He therefore named it the Pacific Ocean, from the Latin word *pacificus,* meaning "peaceful." This was, of course, the same ocean Balboa had named the South Sea.

Magellan sailed westward across the Pacific and reached the Philippine Islands, which he claimed for Spain. There, in 1521, he was killed in a fight with the natives. The surviving members of the crew sailed on. Only one ship, the *Victoria,* and 18 crew members survived to finish the voyage and return to Spain in 1522. For the first time, humans had sailed completely around the earth.

CHECKUP

1. IDENTIFY: Prince Henry, Prester John, Dias, da Gama, Treaty of Tordesillas, Cabral, Vespucci, Balboa.

2. LOCATE: Azores, Cape of Good Hope, San Salvador, Brazil, Isthmus of Panama, Strait of Magellan, Philippine Islands.

3. What were Prince Henry's four main aims for Portuguese exploration?

4. What was the objective of Christopher Columbus? What was the result of his exploration?

5. What did Magellan and his crew accomplish?

3

Portugal and Spain acquired many foreign colonies

With the great geographical discoveries of the 1400's and early 1500's, the small world of medieval Europe suddenly expanded. New lands were waiting to be settled, new peoples were found who had never heard of Christianity, and new possibilities for trade opened up. Almost anyone willing to cross the sea could own land—a dream come true, because in medieval Europe owning land was the mark of social position and wealth.

In addition to the wish to escape problems at home, two powerful positive motives lay behind much European exploration and colonization— the desire to gain wealth and the wish to spread Christianity. Gradually, however, the wish to gain wealth became more important than the missionary purpose.

Portuguese expansion

The Portuguese were the first Europeans to establish an overseas empire (see map, pages 370–71). First, as you have read, they acquired the Azores in the Atlantic. Next they took parts of the western coast of Africa, setting up a colony in what is today Angola. Portuguese trading posts on the eastern coast of Africa included Mozambique and Zanzibar. You will read more about the Portuguese in Africa in Chapter 18.

About the year 1510, the Portuguese conquered part of the southwest coast of India and began to use its port of Goa as a trading and administrative center. Next they attacked and conquered Malacca on the southwest coast of Malaya in Southeast Asia. From Malacca they moved eastward to take the fabled Moluccas, a group of islands in the East Indies. Europeans called them the Spice Islands because they were rich in cloves, nutmeg, and other spices.

Trade with China. Malacca gave the Portuguese a base from which to push on to China. The first Portuguese sailors and traders landed in China in 1514. They quickly aroused the antagonism of the Chinese, who called them "ocean devils." The Ming dynasty, then ruling in China, was following a policy of isolation. The Chinese expelled the Portuguese several times, but each time they returned. Finally, under a special treaty, a Ming emperor allowed the Portuguese to establish a trading post on an island in the Si River delta. However, they were not permitted to move inland. Here the Portuguese built the city of Macao (muh·KOW) as a center for their dealings with Chinese traders.

The Chinese did allow Christian missionaries into the country. The missionaries brought with them some of the best thinking of Renaissance Europe, including the idea of scientific inquiry and their knowledge of mathematics, astronomy, physics, and geography.

The Portuguese in Japan. The Portuguese may have reached Japan as early as 1542. According to tradition, some Portuguese sailors, lost at sea, landed in that year at a small island off the southern tip of Japan. The Portuguese eventually came to the city of Kyoto. Although they disliked most Asians, Portuguese merchants respected the Japanese and got along well with them.

Portuguese merchants brought raw silk and silk textiles and traded them for Japanese silver. This silver was then reinvested in Portugal's Asian trade and brought in good profits. The merchants also traded goods for copper mined in Japan.

Christian missionaries followed the Portuguese merchant sailors. A Jesuit, Francis Xavier (ZAY·vee·ur), arrived in Japan in 1549 after preaching in Goa and the Spice Islands. He preached in Japan

(continued on page 372)

connections

Money

In early times any object that everyone accepted as valuable could serve as money. The Romans, for example, paid their soldiers with what was then a prized commodity, salt. From this custom we get the phrase, "worth one's salt." Other items that have been used as money include shells, tobacco, feathers, and whale teeth.

Probably the first money made specifically as a medium of exchange appeared in China during the Shang dynasty. Because farmers often had traded spades and knives for other goods, this ancient money was shaped like spades.

Increasingly, rare metals, espe-

cially gold and silver, came to be used as money. They were fashioned into coins, which could be carried easily.

Governments jealously guarded the right to make coins and to estab-

lish their value. Often, however, government officials would clip pieces off coins. Then they would melt these down to make more coins so that they could buy more. During the 1500's this process brought on inflation and was stopped only when milled, or grooved, edges were put on coins (left). This enabled people to see at once if the coins had been clipped.

About this time, too, paper money became more common. The Chinese, the first to use both paper and movable type, were also the first to use paper money, about the year 1060 A.D. Paper money was even more convenient than coins and became especially useful as long-distance trade grew increasingly important.

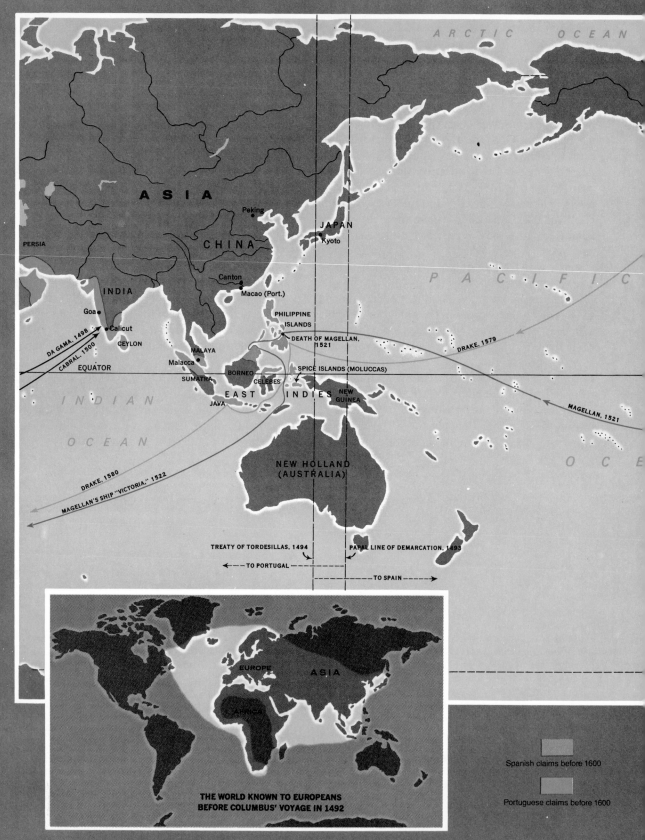

ARCTIC OCEAN

A S I A

Peking

JAPAN
Kyoto

PERSIA

CHINA

PACIFIC

INDIA

Goa

Canton

Macao (Port.)

DA GAMA, 1498

Calicut

CEYLON

CABRAL, 1500

PHILIPPINE
ISLANDS

DEATH OF MAGELLAN,
1521

DRAKE, 1579

EQUATOR

MALAYA

Malacca

SPICE ISLANDS (MOLUCCAS)

BORNEO

SUMATRA

CELEBES

I N D I A N

EAST   INDIES

NEW
GUINEA

MAGELLAN, 1521

JAVA

O C E A N

NEW HOLLAND
(AUSTRALIA)

O C E

DRAKE, 1580

MAGELLAN'S SHIP "VICTORIA," 1522

TREATY OF TORDESILLAS, 1494

PAPAL LINE OF DEMARCATION, 1493

← — TO PORTUGAL — →

— TO SPAIN — →

EUROPE

ASIA

AFRICA

**THE WORLD KNOWN TO EUROPEANS
BEFORE COLUMBUS' VOYAGE IN 1492**

Spanish claims before 1600

Portuguese claims before 1600

THE AGE OF EXPLORATION AND DISCOVERY

EXPLORERS FOR PORTUGAL
Dias, 1487-1488
da Gama, 1497-1498
Cabral, 1500

EXPLORERS FOR ENGLAND
Cabot, 1497-1498
Drake, 1577-1580
Hudson, 1610

EXPLORERS FOR SPAIN
Columbus, 1492-1493
Balboa, 1513
Ponce de León, 1513
Cortés, 1519
Magellan, 1519-1522
Pizarro, 1531-1533
De Soto, 1539-1542
Coronado, 1540-1542

EXPLORERS FOR FRANCE
Cartier, 1535-1536
La Salle, 1681-1682
EXPLORER FOR THE NETHERLANDS
Hudson, 1609

for three years and converted about 2,000 Japanese to Christianity.

During this time Japan was undergoing important changes, about which you will read in Chapter 18. The idea of isolation from the rest of the world was becoming more popular in Japan. In the early 1600's all missionaries were deported and Japanese converts were ordered to give up their Christianity or suffer severe penalties.

Although trade and missionary activity declined, some Portuguese influence remained in Japan. Portuguese words entered the Japanese language—for example, *kappa* (from the Portuguese word *capa,* meaning "cape"). European castle architecture, with its moats and stone walls, influenced Japanese building.

The Portuguese in Ceylon. When the Portuguese had gained footholds in China and Japan, they turned back to add another link to their chain of bases for trade and empire. This new link was the island of Ceylon, off the southeast coast of India. Ceylon was important as a stopping point between Goa and Malacca and as a source of tea and spices. With Ceylon and Malacca as bases, the Portuguese for a time dominated the entire trade with the East Indies.

The Portuguese in Brazil. Portuguese colonies in Asia were small, consisting of little more than trading bases. In Brazil, however, the Portuguese founded a much larger colony. This huge country in South America was divided by the Portuguese into enormous agricultural estates to grow sugar for export. The labor force on these farms consisted almost entirely of slaves.

Weaknesses of the Portuguese Empire

Portugal's rise to wealth and empire was rapid. Its decline was almost as fast for a number of reasons. First, the Portuguese government was neither strong nor well organized. It had difficulties controlling its officials at home and found it impossible to control those in its colonies.

Second, the empire was a drain on Portugal's small population. Portuguese ships made enormous profits in trade, but they were extremely dangerous. They were built to carry so much cargo that they were top-heavy and thus dangerous to sail. The voyage from Portugal to India took six to eight months. It was a miserable journey. The ships, often run by inexperienced sailors and usually in need of repair, were almost helpless in storms. Disease among the crew was common. Each year Portugal sent out its strongest, most daring young men as sailors or traders. Only half, and sometimes fewer, returned. The situation in Portugal became so desperate that criminals and other unwanted persons were sent on the voyages, with ill effects on the colonial settlements.

A third reason for the decline of Portugal was its annexation by Spain in 1580. The Spaniards limited Portuguese trade and neglected the colonies that Portugal had established.

As a result of these weaknesses, the Dutch and English were able to capture much of the Asian trade from the Portuguese in the 1600's. Small Portuguese colonies survived in Africa, India, and China, but they were no longer sources of great wealth. Only Brazil remained a major Portuguese colony.

The Spanish Empire

As you have seen, the main interests of the Portuguese, with the exception of Brazil, lay in Africa and Asia. The Spaniards, on the other hand, turned most of their energies to the Americas. In Asia, only the Philippine Islands were of any great interest to them as a colony.

After the time of Columbus and Balboa, Spaniards explored the West Indies, Central America, and parts of the mainland of North and South America (see map, pages 370–71). They found out, as you know, that America was not Asia and that the lands they explored were not the East Indies. They did not find the spices they wanted. However, the soil was fertile, there were numerous minerals, and the climate was good. Unfortunately, they were able to control and eventually destroy the native population and the remarkable civilizations that had developed there.

Spanish colonization began in the West Indies. From Santo Domingo, in what is today the Dominican Republic, Spanish explorers went forward to conquer Puerto Rico, Cuba, and parts of the South American coast. From Puerto Rico, Juan Ponce de Léon (PON·say day lay·ON) sailed northward in 1513 and explored Florida.

Other explorers went to Yucatán in Mexico and learned of the great Maya civilization that had

The Portuguese abroad

As the Portuguese made contact with new areas of the world, the strangeness of the encounter was apparent to both sides. The Portuguese remarked about the differences in appearance, clothing, housing, and habits of the peoples of Africa and Asia. The inhabitants of these continents were equally amazed. When the Portuguese merchants arrived in Japan, accompanied by Jesuit missionaries, the Japanese were struck by their strange clothes and their extraordinary ship. The Japanese portrayed the Europeans on a beautifully decorated folding screen (left). For the Africans, other aspects of the Portuguese were noteworthy. In addition to strange clothes, they wore armor and crosses around their necks and had strange and powerful weapons. In saltcellars carved from ivory tusks, the Africans left their impressions of the Portuguese (above).

flourished there. With 10 ships and 600 men, Hernando Cortés invaded Mexico in 1519. He defeated the Aztec ruler Moctezuma (mahk·tuh·ZOO·muh), captured Tenochtitlán with its vast wealth in gold, and eventually conquered the entire Aztec Empire. Horses and guns, unknown in the Americas, helped the small Spanish force overcome the much larger Aztec armies.

The Spaniards also heard of a great and rich civilization in South America. Francisco Pizarro led an expedition of 180 men and 27 horses from the Isthmus of Panama to the Inca Empire in present-day Peru and seized it for Spain.

Other explorers were less successful in their fervent search for wealth. Hernando De Soto, exploring westward from Florida, discovered the Mississippi River, but no gold. Francisco Vásquez de Coronado led an army from Mexico into southwestern North America in search of the fabled "Seven Cities of Cíbola." He saw many small Indian villages, and one of his lieutenants discovered the Grand Canyon of the Colorado River, but again there was no gold.

Developing the colonies. In time, Spain controlled a vast empire in the Americas, consisting of the West Indies, Central America, southern North America, and a large part of South America. The Spaniards became colonizers in the true sense of the word. Unlike the Europeans in Africa and Asia, who were mainly traders, the Spaniards in the Americas established settlements.

Very early in their settlement of the Americas, the Spanish developed a centralized form of government for their colonies. The colonies were ruled by **viceroys,** who were representatives of the monarch. These officials were responsible to a council in Spain, which in turn was responsible to the ruler. Thus, the development of the Spanish colonies was planned and directed.

Spain grew enormously rich from its colonies. The basis of Spanish wealth was the discovery of valuable silver mines in what is now Bolivia and northern Mexico. Agricultural and mercantile development was of some importance, but the main asset of the Spanish Empire was its mineral resources. The Spaniards' desire for cheap labor, both to farm the land and to work the mines, led them to force the native Americans to work for them. The results were disastrous.

The Spaniards brought with them diseases that were new to the Americas. Wherever the Europeans went in the Americas, they passed on germs—especially smallpox—against which the native inhabitants had no resistance. The massive epidemics that followed killed millions of native Americans. These devastating epidemics were probably the greatest population disaster the world has ever seen, greater than any wars or famines. In Mexico alone, the native population had been around 10 million when the Spaniards arrived in 1519. By the 1600's only 1.5 million were left.

Raids on Spain's treasure ships

The Spanish government made every effort to keep the wealth of the Americas for Spain alone. Foreigners were kept out of the Spanish colonies. Silver and gold from the Americas could be carried only in Spanish ships and only to the Spanish port of Seville.

It was one thing, though, to make rules, and quite another to enforce them. Spanish treasure ships became rich prizes. They were attacked by pirates who prowled the seas, and also by the ships of European nations who envied the Spanish wealth. Late in the 1500's the Spaniards developed a convoy system, with warships escorting the treasure vessels on the homeland voyage across the Atlantic. For a time, most of the treasure reached Spain safely.

First the Netherlands, and later England and France, used various means to get a share of the wealth from the Americas. They sent ships to American ports, carrying manufactured goods that Spain itself was unable to supply. They made secret deals with individual Spaniards to sail the treasure ships to European ports outside of Spain. Instead of trying to suppress the pirates, they encouraged them to attack Spanish ships.

Decline of the Spanish Empire

The mighty Spanish Empire declined in the 1600's. The chief reason for this decline was the importation of huge amounts of gold and silver from the Americas, which drove up prices in Spain. As the supply of precious metals increased, they became less precious, and people demanded more of them in exchange for goods and services.

High prices prevented the growth of Spanish industry. It already lagged behind that of other European nations for two chief reasons: (1) Spanish nobles thought work was degrading, and (2) the Moors and Jews, who had once formed an enterprising middle class, were expelled from Spain in the late 1400's.

Because France, England, and the Netherlands did develop industries, much Spanish wealth simply passed through Spain on its way to buy goods from these other nations. The gold and silver enabled Spain's enemies to develop their industries and grow strong at Spain's expense.

Another reason for the decline of the Spanish colonial empire was the kind of administration Spain provided. Although the government of Spain and its colonies was highly centralized, it was inefficient. In the colonies the attempt to maintain a strict monopoly by shutting out all foreign trade brought attacks by England, the Netherlands, and France. With all of these weaknesses, the Spanish Empire could not survive.

CHECKUP

1. IDENTIFY: "ocean devils," Francis Xavier, Cortés, Moctezuma, Pizarro, De Soto, Coronado, viceroys.

2. LOCATE: Angola, Mozambique, Zanzibar, Goa, Malacca, Moluccas, Macao, Ceylon.

3. How were the Portuguese received by the Chinese and Japanese? What examples of Portuguese influence in Japan can you give?

4. Explain the weaknesses that led to the decline of the Portuguese Empire.

5. In what way were the Spaniards true colonizers? How did they affect the native population?

6. What factors contributed to the decline of the Spanish Empire?

England, the Netherlands, France, and Russia expanded

The nations of northern Europe were latecomers in the race for empires. England and France were occupied with internal problems during most of the 1500's. The Netherlands was under Spanish rule until the early 1600's. Russia was just beginning to emerge from Mongol control.

By the late 1500's, when northern European nations were ready to acquire colonies of their own, the Spanish Empire was at its height. The Portuguese Empire, although beginning to decline, was still powerful. Just as the Spaniards and Portuguese had tried to break the monopoly of the Italian cities a century earlier, now the English, Dutch, and French challenged the Spanish and Portuguese monopolies.

English sea power

Because of England's location, its people had always been interested in the sea. Over the centuries they had developed a rich overseas trade. Shortly after Columbus reached America, an Italian captain named John Cabot was commissioned by the king of England to voyage to North America. In 1497 and 1498 he explored the coasts of Newfoundland, Nova Scotia, and New England (see map, pages 370–71). His voyages gave the English a claim in the New World. (Northern European nations did not recognize the line drawn by the pope dividing the world in two.) However, it was almost a century before the English took steps to develop this territory.

In the second half of the 1500's, during the reign of Queen Elizabeth I, there appeared in England a hardy breed of sea captains. They were both traders and pirates, and the English called them **sea dogs.** These men—John Hawkins, Francis Drake, and Walter Raleigh, among others—challenged Portuguese and Spanish monopolies of overseas trade.

Hawkins and Drake seized slaves from the Portuguese and sold them in Spanish colonies. Drake, seeking to steal from Spanish ships where they were not protected by convoys, sailed through the Strait of Magellan into the Pacific Ocean, which the Spaniards considered to be their private sea. His takings were so great that the gold and jewels stowed below deck served to steady the ship in the waters. From the Pacific coast of North America, Drake sailed westward and returned home as the first English sea captain to sail around the globe (see map, pages 370–71).

King Philip II of Spain protested to Queen Elizabeth about the attacks of the English sea dogs, but she claimed that she was helpless to control them. Secretly she supported the sea dogs and shared what they had stolen. For his achievements, she knighted Drake on board his ship.

King Philip was greatly angered by the English attacks. He also wanted to wipe out what he considered "Protestant heresy" in England. He therefore decided to invade England. In 1588, as you have read, he sent a fleet of 130 ships—which he called the "Invincible Armada"—northward toward the English Channel.

The English gathered all their ships to meet the Spanish Armada. The English ships were smaller than those of the Spanish fleet, but they were easier to handle. Also, their guns fired faster and had a longer range. They damaged and sank a number of the great Spanish vessels. The Spaniards ran low on ammunition and tried to escape. A terrible storm added to the destruction, and only half of the Spanish ships returned to Spain.

The English in India

The defeat of the Spanish Armada marked the beginning of the decline of Spanish sea power. It also encouraged the English to establish colonies overseas. In 1600 Queen Elizabeth granted a charter to a trading company called the English East India Company.

This company set up trading posts at Bombay, on the northwest coast of India; at Calcutta, to the northeast in the delta of the Ganges River; and at Madras, on the southeast coast. The company dealt mainly with local rulers, for India had become divided into many little states as the Mogul Empire declined in power. Where a ruler was weak and submissive, the company gave aid. Where force was needed to overcome opposition, it was used without hesitation. If bribery was a better means, a generous "gift" was extended. The English were so successful with these methods in India that they remained there as rulers for 350 years.

The East India Company eventually set up a few trading posts in Malaya and the East Indies, but India remained the main source of English trade and wealth. Within a short time the East India Company became extremely wealthy and powerful, with a vast fleet of merchant ships and warships to protect its interests.

The English in the Americas

England was slow to establish colonies in North America because of its great interest in Asia. In fact, the first English explorations into North America were made in search of a Northwest Passage to India—that is, a water route around the Americas to the north and west. The route south and west, around Cape Horn in South America, was dominated by Spain.

One of those who searched unsuccessfully for such a route was Henry Hudson. In 1609, on a voyage for the Dutch, he explored much of the coast of eastern North America and discovered the river that is named for him. On a voyage for the English in 1610, he discovered Hudson Bay in northern Canada (see map, pages 370–71).

While the search for a Northwest Passage to India went on, the English became interested in North America and began to establish colonies there. The colonies were founded by private companies or individuals. During the 1600's several English colonies were set up along the east coast of North America (see map, pages 378–79). The first permanent settlement was Jamestown, established in 1607 in what is now Virginia. The second, Plymouth, was set up in 1620 in what is now Massachusetts.

These settlements were founded primarily for commercial purposes. The people who supported them hoped that the settlers would raise the products that England had to import from Asia and thus make the home country more self-sufficient. However, the North American colonies proved to be a disappointment. Few of the original investors got their money back or made profits. Many individual colonists, however, had other reasons for settling in North America. They hoped to find greater political and religious freedom and to make better lives for their families.

The emphasis on self-government set England's empire apart from the other colonial empires. Most English colonies had some form of representative assembly, or governing body, and control by the home country was loose. The one area in which the home government did intervene was the economy. Following mercantilist principles, the English government tried to make sure that the Americans' growing trade—especially with the West Indies and Africa—benefited England by

Explorers in the Americas

Explorers from many European nations came to the Americas during the 1500's. The potential wealth whetted many appetites, and Europeans were eager to learn about the lands and their inhabitants. Artists carefully recorded both—whether they had actually seen them or not.

Ponce de León found Indians in Florida whose swamp dwellings and dugout canoes (left) must have seemed exotic indeed to European eyes. Europeans, with their armor, swords, and horses, must have seemed just as exotic to the Indians, as shown by the Indian drawing of Hernando Cortés in Mexico (below left). Jacques Cartier's arrival in North America (below right) was fancifully re-created by a European artist who had not been there at the time.

means of customs duties. Until the mid-1700's, however, trade restrictions were often ignored by the colonists, and smuggling in order to avoid paying the English duties became quite accepted.

What made the English Empire like the others was its use of slavery in the colonies, especially from Maryland southward and in the West Indies. The settlements in Caribbean islands, such as Barbados, were a commercial success in large part because of slave labor. Also, some of the islands produced sugar, a valuable product.

The Dutch colonial empire

Because the Netherlands was situated on the North Sea, the Dutch became a seafaring people. In the age of exploration, Dutch merchants set up a number of companies to trade in various parts of

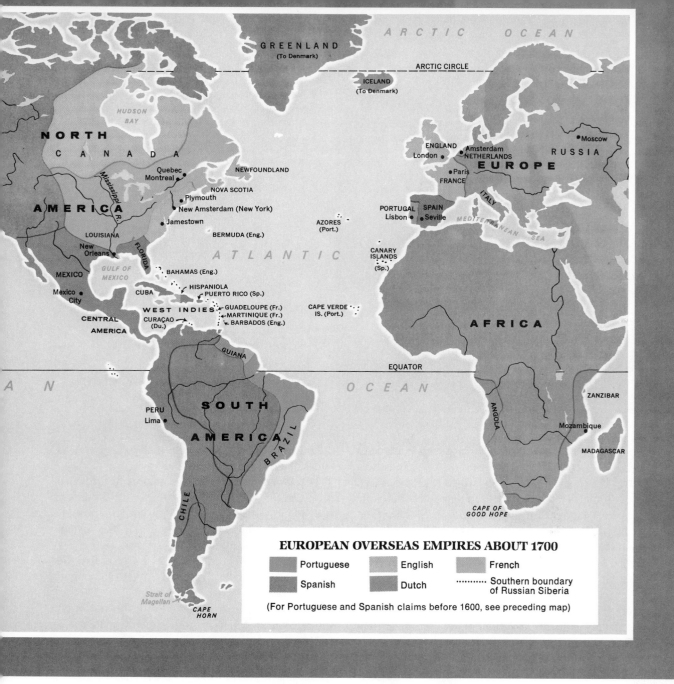

EUROPEAN OVERSEAS EMPIRES ABOUT 1700

Portuguese   English   French

Spanish   Dutch   ······· Southern boundary of Russian Siberia

(For Portuguese and Spanish claims before 1600, see preceding map)

the world. The Dutch were excellent sailors, and they built very efficient ships.

You have read in Chapter 15 of the long struggle begun in the 1500's by the northern Netherlands to gain its freedom from Spain. After Spain annexed Portugal in 1580, Portuguese ships and possessions became fair game to the Dutch. They first attacked ships carrying goods from Portugal to northern Europe. Then they assaulted ships

bringing treasure from Asia to Portugal. These attacks were the beginning of the attempts by the Dutch to take over the Portuguese Empire.

In 1602 the Dutch combined several of their trading companies into one powerful organization—the Dutch East India Company. The Dutch government gave this company the sole right to carry on trade between the northern Netherlands and Africa and the East Indies.

"Young Woman with a Water Jug"

What does this lady see as she gazes through the window? The map on the wall behind her is of the Dutch provinces, and perhaps it has led her thoughts to faraway places.

The window lets light in on her starched linen headdress, while the sun sparkles on the metal pitcher and tray and defines the pattern on the oriental rug. The rug is an example of the varied goods that overseas trade brought to the Dutch people after they had won their independence from Spain.

In the 1600's Dutch merchants grew rich enough to buy handsome silks and linens for their wives and to commission artists to paint for them. Artists flourished in the prosperous economy of the Netherlands, and Jan Vermeer, who painted this picture, was one of the finest. His painting gives us an accurate look at daily Dutch life, as well as a highly satisfying artistic experience.

The first Dutch settlement in Asia was made at Batavia, on the island of Java, in 1619. From Java the Dutch expanded westward to take the island of Sumatra and eastward to seize the valuable Spice Islands from the Portuguese. Malacca and the island of Ceylon came next, as well as Cochin on the southwest coast of India. In 1652 the Dutch also founded a colony at the southern tip of Africa, at the Cape of Good Hope. This helped them protect their trade along the African coast (see map, pages 378–79).

Dutch colonial government was stronger than that of Portugal. The colonies were administered by a governor general, assisted by a council. The governor general had a great deal of authority over local officials, but he was closely controlled by the home government.

The Dutch tried to avoid a mistake that the Portuguese had made. The Portuguese had held only strategic points along coasts in order to control the sea lanes. The Dutch realized that a successful empire required much wider control over the land and the people. For example, they did not stop with establishing a trading post at Batavia. Instead, they reached out and gained control of the entire island of Java, with its large population and its sugar, tea, coffee, and spices.

The Dutch gained some commercial influence in Japan. Since they did not come as missionaries, the shogun—the Japanese military ruler—accepted them, although reluctantly. In 1638 a Dutch ship with its big guns helped overthrow the last Portuguese stronghold in Japan. As a reward, the Japanese allowed the Dutch to trade in Japan and to have a trading post at Nagasaki.

The Dutch also founded colonies in the West Indies, South America, and North America. In 1626 they purchased Manhattan Island from the Indians. There they founded New Amsterdam, which later became New York City.

The French in North America and Asia

Among the first French explorers of North America was Jacques Cartier (kahr·TYAY), who made several voyages between 1534 and 1541. On a voyage in 1535 and 1536, he sailed up the St. Lawrence River as far as the present city of Montreal. This voyage gave the French a claim to much of eastern Canada. However, no permanent French settlements were made until the 1600's. In 1608 Samuel de Champlain established the first permanent French settlement at Quebec. France then set up several other settlements in the St. Lawrence Valley and in the Great Lakes region. The French developed a profitable fur trade with the Indians. Fishing off Newfoundland and Nova Scotia also became important.

The French colonies in North America developed slowly until the reign of King Louis XIV in the latter half of the 1600's. Then settlement and colonization were encouraged by the government, and the entire Great Lakes region was explored. Robert de La Salle sailed down the Mississippi River to the Gulf of Mexico and claimed the entire inland region of North America for France. He named the region Louisiana in honor of Louis XIV (see map, pages 378–79).

The French set up profitable sugar-producing colonies in the West Indies, including the islands of Guadeloupe and Martinique.

In Asia, French efforts were directed by the French East India Company, formed in 1664. The company established a trading post at Pondicherry, on the southeast coast of India. During the 1700's an extremely able colonial administrator, Joseph François Dupleix (du·PLEKS), set up a smoothly working administration. French trade increased rapidly, and the French expanded into other regions of India. In many places they became rivals of the English.

Russian expansion

During the 1500's Russia lacked seaports. Thus it was barred from the kind of overseas expansion carried on by Western European countries.

To the east, however, lay the vast region of central Asia, with its small population of nomadic tribes. It was in this direction that Russia grew.

Russia's eastward expansion was carried on mostly by a nomadic, freedom-loving people called Cossacks. Like frontier people everywhere, they loved open spaces. What drew them east was trade, especially the fur trade. Central Asia was a perfect place for trappers and fur traders, for there were many animals and they were easy to trap. Most important was the sable, whose fur was very valuable. In 1581 a group of Cossacks conquered the remnants of the Mongol Golden Horde. They captured the small city of Sibir, east of the Ural Mountains, that was then the Mongols' capital. With its capture, the way lay open to the entire region east of the Urals. This region was known as Siberia (see map, pages 378–79).

Russian pioneers gradually forced their way eastward. To protect themselves from attack, the early Russian settlers built blockhouses much like American frontier forts. As centers for trade and defense, these posts became the towns and cities of Siberia. By the 1640's the Russians had reached the Pacific Ocean.

Russian pioneers moved eastward in two streams—one to the north and one to the south. Neither was stopped by any strong native people until the southern group reached the Amur River. Here they came in contact with the Chinese. Fifty years of skirmishes and warfare failed to overcome the resistance of the Chinese. In 1689 the Russians and Chinese signed a treaty that fixed a boundary between them north of the Amur River and provided for Chinese-Russian trade. Russia traded furs and raw materials with the Chinese in exchange for such items as silk and tea.

Like the nations of Western Europe, Russia was changing the map of the world. All these nations used force to expand their territory and trade. However, their main assets were determination, economic and technological skill, and a restless sense of adventure.

CHECKUP

1. IDENTIFY: Cabot, sea dogs, Hawkins, Drake, Raleigh, Northwest Passage, Hudson, Cartier, Champlain, La Salle, Cossacks.

2. LOCATE: Newfoundland, Nova Scotia, Bombay, Calcutta, Madras, Jamestown, Plymouth, Barbados, Java, Sumatra, Nagasaki, Quebec, Mississippi River, Siberia, Amur River.

3. Why was the Spanish Armada sent against England? What were the results of its defeat?

4. How was the English Empire like the other colonial empires? How was it different?

5. List the colonial acquisitions of the Dutch and the French during the age of exploration.

6. Unlike the Western European countries, Russia had no seaports to use as starting points for overseas exploration. How did Russia manage to expand its territory to China?

CHAPTER REVIEW

B.C.	A.D.		1300	1400	1500	1600	1700	1800	1900	2000

early 1400's	Prince Henry's school for navigators	**1519–1522**	Circumnavigation of the earth	**1600**	English East India Company chartered
1492	Discovery of West Indies by Columbus	**1549**	Francis Xavier's arrival in Japan	**1602**	Dutch East India Company established
1497–1503	Explorations by Vespucci	**1580**	Portugal annexed by Spain	**1607**	English settlement of Jamestown
1498	Da Gama's voyage to India	**1581**	Conquest of Sibir by Cossacks	**1608**	Founding of Quebec by French
1513	Discovery of "South Sea" by Balboa			**1619**	Dutch settlement at Batavia
1519	Invasion of Mexico by Cortés	**1588**	English defeat of Spanish Armada	**1664**	French East India Company formed

CHAPTER SUMMARY

An era of European exploration began in the 1400's. Improved maps, advances in navigation instruments, and better ships made successful exploration possible. At the same time, political and social developments in Europe stimulated overseas expansion.

The European economy changed greatly. Money became standardized, encouraging the growth of banking. Joint-stock companies were formed to produce capital for expansion. A new economic theory, mercantilism, took hold. It stressed tariffs, exports, and self-sufficiency. Colonies were especially valued as sources of raw materials and markets for manufactured goods.

Portugal and Spain were the first nations to become involved in exploration. Portuguese explorers sailed progressively farther along the coast of Africa. In 1498 Vasco da Gama sailed around Africa and reached India. Columbus, sailing for Spain, looked for a route westward to India. He landed at islands in the Atlantic that he thought were part of Asia.

The Portuguese set up trading posts in Africa, India, Malaya, the Spice Islands, and Ceylon, and gained trading rights in China and Japan. However, Portugal was not able to control these possessions for long. Portugal's power declined after it was annexed by Spain in 1580. Spain created a more stable empire. Its colonies in the Americas were ruled by viceroys, who were responsible to the Spanish government.

Northern European nations began to acquire colonies in the 1600's. The English established trading posts in India and settlements in North America. The Dutch conquered many former Portuguese possessions and founded colonies in the Americas. The French made claims in North America and became rivals of the English in India.

Russia, too, was expanding—not across the sea, but across the vast lands of Siberia. In the 1600's Russian expansion reached the Pacific and the borders of China. By 1700 Russia, like the Western European nations, had helped change the map of the world.

CHECKING WHAT YOU KNOW

1. Match each colony at the left with the European country that had acquired it by 1700. You may use a country more than once.

   a. Peru
   b. Brazil
   c. Philippine Islands
   d. Mozambique
   e. Louisiana
   f. Jamestown
   g. Newfoundland
   h. Java

   1. England
   2. France
   3. Netherlands
   4. Spain
   5. Portugal

2. Match each explorer at the left with the area he explored (use the map on pages 370–71):

   a. Cortés
   b. Balboa
   c. Dias
   d. Columbus
   e. Cabot
   f. Cabral

   1. northern coast of North America
   2. west coast of Africa
   3. east coast of South America and east coast of southern Africa
   4. Mexico
   5. San Salvador
   6. Isthmus of Panama

3. What changes in technology made it possible for Europeans to explore foreign lands?

4. Describe some of the motives for exploration and colonization.

5. How was Spanish colonization different from Portuguese colonization?

6. Name the areas acquired by the following countries and the trade goods derived from them:
   a. Portugal
   b. Spain
   c. England
   d. the Netherlands
   e. France
   f. Russia

PRACTICING YOUR SKILLS

1. **Using maps.** During the age of exploration, certain geographical areas were important to navigation, exploration, and trading routes. Using the map on pages 378–79 and information in your textbook, explain the geographical importance of the following:
   a. Cape of Good Hope
   b. Strait of Magellan
   c. African coast
   d. Isthmus of Panama
   e. Mississippi River

2. **Making charts.** Make a chart of the European explorers that you read about in this chapter. Use the following headings: name of explorer, country sailed for, date of voyage, discovery or accomplishment.

3. **Using pictures.** Review the illustrations on pages 373 and 377. Based on these pictures, describe how the Aztecs, the Africans, and the Japanese viewed the Europeans who visited their lands.

RELATING PAST TO PRESENT

1. Study a present-day world map and locate the Suez and Panama canals. What kind of shortcuts would they have provided to early European explorers? Why are they of such political and strategic importance today?

2. Write a brief account of what Columbus or Vespucci might have experienced during their voyages with respect to the following categories:
   a. navigation and technology
   b. food supplies
   c. transportation
   d. impressions of the places explored
   e. dangers anticipated or encountered

   Then write the same sort of account of an astronaut traveling to the moon. Use the five categories above to describe the voyage. What are the major similarities and differences you notice in your two accounts?

3. During the age of exploration and colonization, European countries strived to claim areas with the most potential for valuable products. In this way they could become rich and powerful. What were considered valuable products during that period of time? Today nations work through trade or commercial alliances to obtain what they need. What items are valued today and where may they be found?

INVESTIGATING FURTHER

1. Using an encyclopedia, investigate the banking organization of the Medicis of Florence. How did they rise to power? How did the Medicis help in empire building?

2. Prepare a report on the Spanish Armada. Discuss the following in your report: What was the background of the Spanish-English conflict? Why did Philip II want to conquer England? How was religion a factor in this incident? How was Elizabeth I regarded by other European monarchs? How was the Spanish fleet defeated? What was the significance of the English victory? You could use encyclopedias or Garrett Mattingly, *Armada* (Houghton Mifflin) as sources for your research.

3. Rulers such as Queen Isabella of Spain and Queen Elizabeth of England supported voyages of exploration. Using books in your library, find out more about these rulers and why they supported these adventures.

17

Revolutions Changed the Course of Western Civilization

This chapter deals with an extraordinary series of changes that occurred in Western civilization in the late 1700's and early 1800's. During this period new attitudes developed about the way nations ought to be governed and about how people ought to relate to one another. The movements that put these new ideas into practice are known as revolutions. We will be looking at two of the most important—the American Revolution and the French Revolution.

Revolutions had occurred before. As you have read in Chapter 15, there was a revolution in England in the mid-1600's. However, this and other previous revolutions had been local and short-lived. Each had affected just one country, and its influence had been limited to that particular country.

The events of the late 1700's were different. The impact of the American and French revolutions was so great that they continued to inspire people in later generations, even to our own time. The American and French revolutions were the beginning of a revolutionary tradition. The American experience, in particular, gave encouragement to people in other countries who opposed oppressive governments. The ideas of the revolution—that all people have rights that no one can take from them and that the powers of government belong to the people—swept the Western world. These ideas are still at work in many parts of the world today.

Signing the Declaration of Independence

The creation of this revolutionary tradition was an important development in the emergence of the modern world. Our ancestors in the 1700's thought that all change was dangerous and to be avoided. A major reason our times are so different is that many have come to believe that change can be useful. Some people disagree strongly. Nevertheless, the fact that totally new ideas about change became prominent in the West in the late 1700's marks this as one of the decisive, transforming periods in modern history.

THE CHAPTER SECTIONS

1. The American Revolution created a new nation in North America

2. The French Revolution affected all of Europe

3. After a period of turmoil, the French monarchy was overthrown

4. The French Republic faced disorder at home and war abroad

5. Napoleon built an empire that spread across Europe

6. European nations united to defeat Napoleon

1

The American Revolution created a new nation in North America

The first of the influential revolutions of the late 1700's took place in North America. You will recall from Chapter 16 that the English had established colonies along the eastern seaboard of North America by the mid-1600's. Although the colonies were governed from Great Britain, each colony had considerable control over its own affairs.

The revolution that began in the 1700's differed from the English Revolution of the 1600's because it involved only part of the people ruled by the British government—the colonists. Thus, the fighting between the two sides was a war of independence—the colonies in North America struggling to free themselves from British rule. It was also a revolutionary conflict—the colonists rebelling against the British government.

Mercantilism and the English colonies

As you read in Chapter 16, mercantilism was an economic theory maintaining that colonies existed for the benefit of the home country. Colonies were to supply needed raw materials and furnish a market for the manufactured products of the home country.

In line with mercantilist policies, the English government passed a number of regulations that affected its North American colonies, beginning with the Navigation Act of 1651. One regulation listed, or "enumerated," colonial products to be sold only in England. These goods could not be sold to any other country, where the colonists might have received higher prices for them.

Other regulations discouraged Americans from manufacturing. For example, they were forbidden to ship woolen cloth that they had manufactured to places outside of the colony in which it was made. They could carry on only the first stage of iron manufacturing—the making of pig iron. The pig iron had to be shipped to England, where English manufacturers produced iron tools and utensils from it.

The trade regulations aroused resentment, and colonists found many ways to evade them. They avoided paying taxes whenever and however they could. Smuggling became a respectable occupation, difficult to prevent because of the long American coastline with its many harbors and inlets.

British-French rivalry

While the British were establishing colonies along the Atlantic coast, the French had been developing settlements to the north and west—a vast region they called New France. In the 1700's American settlers began to go westward across the Appalachian Mountains in search of new land. As you can see on the map on page 386, conflict with the French was inevitable if this westward movement continued. You have read how, beginning with the reign of Charles II, Great Britain opposed France in Europe. Such conflicts as the War of the Spanish Succession had counterparts in North America in small frontier skirmishes. The colonies counted on British aid for defense against the French and their Indian allies.

Finally there came a decisive conflict that settled British-French rivalry in North America. This was the French and Indian War. It began in 1754 with clashes between British and French troops west of the Appalachian Mountains. It ended nine years later with British victories not only in North America but all over the world. The resulting Treaty of Paris in 1763 confirmed the sweeping British victory in the Western Hemisphere. The British now dominated the region from the Atlantic Ocean to the Mississippi River, and from the Gulf of Mexico almost to the Arctic Ocean (see map, opposite page).

The French and Indian War put an end to France as a strong power in North America. It also reduced colonial dependence on Great Britain because the colonies no longer needed British help against the French.

Increased control over the colonies

The French and Indian War and the other worldwide conflicts between 1754 and 1763 had left the British with a large debt and heavy taxes. The American phase of this warfare had been fought for the protection of the colonists. The British felt that the colonists should help pay for it and thus relieve British taxpayers of some of their heavy burden.

As part of this policy, after 1763 Great Britain attempted to bring its North American colonies under closer economic control. It decided to

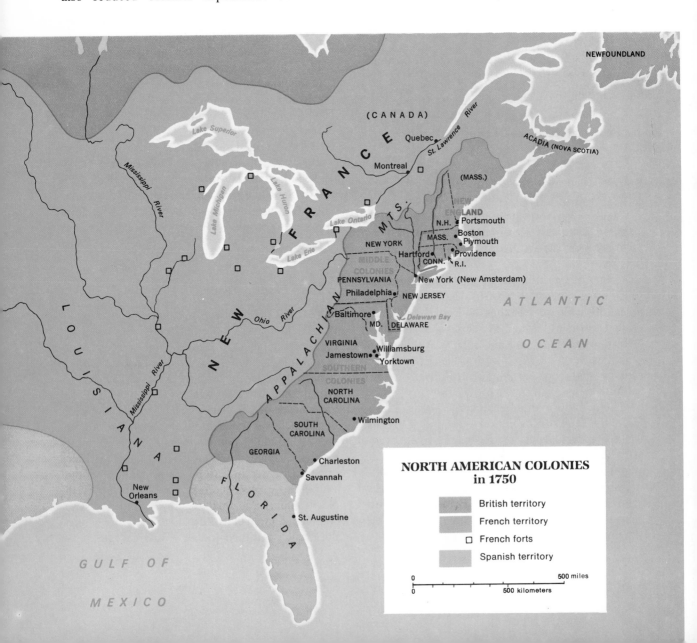

NORTH AMERICAN COLONIES
in 1750

British territory
French territory
□ French forts
Spanish territory

0   500 miles
0   500 kilometers

enforce its mercantilist trade regulations, which it had not done consistently before. The Sugar Act of 1764 set new taxes on sugar and many other items imported into North America from non-British colonies. The British were determined to collect these taxes. They also imposed other regulations, such as a new law forbidding the colonies to issue their own paper money.

In 1765 Parliament passed the Stamp Act. This law required that special stamps, for which the colonists were taxed, be used on wills, mortgages, contracts, newspapers, pamphlets, calendars, playing cards, and almanacs. The opposition of the colonists to the Stamp Act was so strong that it was repealed in 1766.

The enforcement of the trade laws led to conflicts between the colonists and the British government and to an increase in smuggling by the colonists. The government considered searches and prosecution of merchants necessary to stop the smuggling. The colonists, however, considered these actions by the British government a denial of their rights.

In the years from 1763 to 1775, relations between the British government and the American colonies grew steadily worse. The British insisted that laws should be enforced, that taxes should be paid, and that colonists should be obedient. The colonists argued that they should not have to pay British taxes because they were not represented in the British Parliament. "Taxation without representation," they said, was tyranny.

Tensions rose as many colonists refused to buy British goods. In doing so, they brought economic pressure on British merchants. The merchants, in turn, complained to Parliament. Other colonists committed acts of violence, such as tarring and feathering tax collectors. British attempts to punish such illegal acts enraged the colonists.

As time went on, many colonists believed that their rights could be guaranteed only if the colonies became completely independent. However, the people of the colonies were by no means united in wanting independence.

Possibly a third of the colonists were strongly opposed to the idea. They were called **Loyalists.** Among them were many of the wealthiest and most powerful people in the colonies. Another third of the people did not take sides. Only about a third of the colonists actively favored indepen-

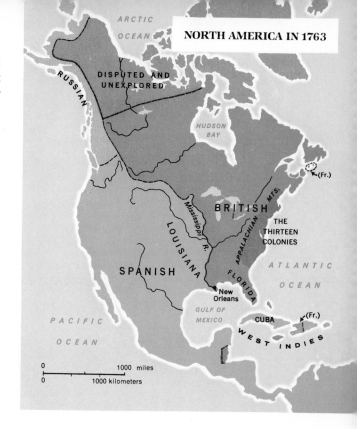

NORTH AMERICA IN 1763

dence. They were called Patriots. Some of them, like George Washington and John Hancock, were wealthy, but most were not.

The conflict intensified

In 1774 Great Britain passed a series of laws so hated by the colonists that they were called the Intolerable Acts. One of the acts, for example, closed the port of Boston to all shipping. The Patriots now decided to take action. In the fall of 1774, delegates from all the colonies except Georgia met in Philadelphia in the First Continental Congress. The delegates demanded the full rights of British people for those in the colonies. They also pledged to support one another in the future and agreed to meet the following year if Great Britain did not repeal the Intolerable Acts.

Relations between Great Britain and the colonies went from bad to worse. In 1775 British troops marched from Boston to seize guns and gunpowder that the colonists had stored nearby. At the towns of Lexington and Concord, the British were met by armed resistance and had to retreat to Boston.

Outbreaks of fighting continued, but neither

Paul Revere

Paul Revere is best known for the midnight ride he made to warn the minutemen before the battles at Lexington and Concord. Revere, however, was also a fine silversmith, well known enough to have his portrait painted by a prominent American artist several years before his famous ride.

The painter, John Singleton Copley, was self-taught and learned most of what he knew by studying engravings imported from Europe. (Like many early American artists, he eventually emigrated to England, where he lived the rest of his life.) Copley's portrait shows Revere seated at a table on which lie his engraving tools. The natural "everyday" quality of the setting contrasts with European portraits of the same period, which tend to emphasize the grandeur and dignity of their subjects.

Lovely engraved silver teapots such as this one were not only practical but an investment for their owners. In the early American colonies there were no banks to keep silver coins. Therefore the coins were often melted down and crafted into household objects. The teapots and serving trays were marked with the name or family crest of the owner and the initials of the maker, in this case the fine silversmith and patriot Paul Revere.

the colonists nor the British termed it a war at first. The British regarded the colonists as rebels. The colonists felt that they were merely resisting unjust acts of Parliament.

The Declaration of Independence

Meanwhile, in May 1775, delegates to a Second Continental Congress were meeting in Philadelphia. By this time the spirit of independence was strong. The delegates voted to declare their freedom from Great Britain. On July 4, 1776, they adopted the **Declaration of Independence,** which established the United States of America as an independent nation. Thomas Jefferson, its chief author, expressed American sentiments with nobility and grandeur, for the Declaration was a document for the entire world to read.

The Declaration of Independence shows the influence of such political philosophers as Locke and Rousseau (see Chapter 15). It states that all people are created equal and are given by their Creator certain "unalienable rights" that cannot be taken from them. Among these rights are "life, liberty, and the pursuit of happiness." This idea—that every human being has the right to equal opportunity and must be treated with equal justice—is the foundation of the democratic ideal. Although the ideal was not then stated so as to include women, the demand for equality created a new aim in politics.

The Declaration went on to say that all powers of government belong to the people. No government can exist without the consent of its citizens. Citizens create governments to protect their rights. If a government fails to protect the people's rights, or attempts to destroy them, the people have a further right "to alter or to abolish it" and to set up a new government that will safeguard their rights.

These were extreme ideas, even for those who had rejected the unlimited authority of monarchs. Such ideas were especially bold when stated by a group of small, weak colonies against one of the most powerful nations in the world.

The battle for independence

After the adoption of the Declaration of Independence, the fighting between the Americans and the British became truly a Revolutionary War. Each side had certain advantages and weaknesses as the war began. The Americans were fighting in defense of their own homes in territory they knew well. The British had to fight far from home, bringing with them most of their military supplies and equipment. Although the American troops could fire at marching lines of British soldiers, they could seldom successfully oppose the well-trained British forces in a large-scale battle.

Many people in Great Britain did not eagerly support the war. Some even sympathized with the Americans' complaints. Since Great Britain did not regularly maintain a large army, King George III had to hire soldiers. Many of these hired troops were foreign born. The Americans eventually received help from Great Britain's European enemies—France, Spain, and the Netherlands. The alliance between America and France, signed in 1778, was of particular importance.

The Americans had good leaders, particularly General George Washington, who commanded the Continental Army. In addition, military officers came from other nations to help the Americans. They included the Marquis de Lafayette of France, Casimir Pulaski and Thaddeus Kosciusko (kah·zee·US·koh) of Poland, and Baron von Steuben of Prussia.

British strength lay in the size and power of its army and navy. British troops were well trained, and the British fleet was the strongest in the world. It could land a British army anywhere on the American coast.

The British were helped by the lack of unity among the American states. The only organization attempting to unify the states was the Second Continental Congress. The states voluntarily sent representatives to the Congress, but they did not give them power to act. When the Congress wanted to take any action, the proposal had to be sent to the states for approval.

The Continental Congress had to ask the states for money because it had no power to tax. It borrowed money, and it also printed its own paper money. Since it had no sure way of paying its debts, its credit was poor.

The weaknesses of the American government made it difficult to build up a strong army. At first, American forces consisted mostly of state volunteers, poorly trained and undisciplined. The troops enlisted for only a few months at a time and then went home to carry on their ordinary duties. The writer Thomas Paine called them "sunshine patriots, summer soldiers."

Ending the war. As you have read, fighting broke out before independence was declared. Most of the war was fought between 1776 and 1781, with neither side winning a clear victory. Then, in 1781, the Americans won a decisive battle at Yorktown, Virginia. There the British general, Lord Cornwallis, surrendered his army to American and French forces. The British still had more troops in America than George Washington had in the Continental Army, but Great Britain was tired of the costly American war. It was at war also with France, the Netherlands, and Spain, and the fighting was going badly there, too.

In their eagerness to end the war, the British accepted many of the peace terms offered by Benjamin Franklin, the shrewd and persuasive chief American negotiator. Franklin was able to win terms that were very favorable to the Americans.

After two years of negotiation, the Treaty of Paris was signed in 1783. The Americans won not only the independence they wanted but also a territory much larger than the original 13 states (see map, this page). The country's boundaries stretched west to the Mississippi River, north to the Great Lakes, and south to Florida.

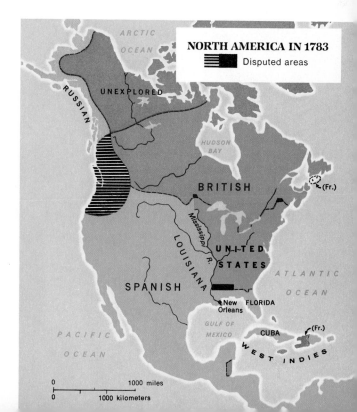

NORTH AMERICA IN 1783
Disputed areas

The American Revolution

The stages through which the American colonies moved toward independence left a vivid visual record. As early as 1754 Benjamin Franklin drew a cartoon (right) emphasizing the need for unity among the colonies. Like a snake, if divided they could not survive. An issue that soon united the colonies was the tax on tea. All tea was supposed to have the hated new tax stamp (above left).

The focus of the colonists' anger came to be the British troops, especially in Boston. They are shown landing there in 1768 (above right) in an engraving made by Paul Revere, one of the later heroes of the resistance to Great Britain. When fighting at last broke out, the Virginian George Washington emerged as the leader of the troops and early in the war won an important victory at Princeton (below).

JOIN, or DIE.

The Articles of Confederation

In 1781, eight months before the American victory at Yorktown, the American states ratified, or accepted, the **Articles of Confederation.** This document was a plan of government that had been adopted at the Second Continental Congress at Philadelphia in 1777. It provided for a stronger central government, creating a one-house Congress in which each state had a single vote. Congress was given the power to declare war, make peace, conduct foreign relations, and settle disputes between the states.

Congress under the Articles of Confederation did not have the power to tax. It had to ask the states for money. Congress was also not allowed to regulate trade with foreign countries or among the states.

The government under the Articles of Confederation lasted from 1781 to 1789, but it was not an effective government. There was a legislature with power to pass certain laws. However, there was no president, so the individual states had to enforce and administer all the laws. The only courts were state courts, which tried all cases.

The Constitution of the United States

Americans soon realized that the Articles of Confederation were inadequate. In 1787 delegates from 12 states (Rhode Island did not take part) met in Philadelphia to write a new plan of government, a new constitution.

The delegates who attended the Constitutional Convention in 1787 faced several problems. They wanted to create a central government strong enough to act on matters that concerned all of the states. At the same time they wanted to leave the states some freedom to act for themselves. To solve this problem, the authors of the Constitution decided to adopt the **federal system.** Powers would be divided between a central government and individual states. The central government alone was given power to declare war, make treaties, produce money, raise armies, and regulate trade with foreign countries. All powers not given to the central government or prohibited to the states belonged to the states and the people.

Another problem facing the framers of the Constitution involved the branches of the central government. The delegates made use of ideas stated by the French writer Montesquieu in *The Spirit of the Laws* (see Chapter 15). They created three branches—executive (the President), legislative (Congress), and judicial (the federal courts). Each branch was given certain powers and could act as a check on each of the others. James Madison, one of the most influential delegates to the Constitutional Convention, described the American system as a republic, where the government "derives all its power directly from the great body of people, and is administered by people holding their offices."

The new Constitution was ratified in 1788. In the following year, George Washington became the first president of the United States.

Effects of American independence

In addition to the immediate political effects, the American Revolution put into practice the ideas of John Locke and the French philosophers. These ideas had previously existed only on paper. The idea stated in the Declaration of Independence that all people have certain unalienable rights is the foundation of democracy. Another mighty idea behind the Revolution was that all the powers of government belong to the people. The American experience gave encouragement to people in other parts of the world who opposed autocracy and privileged classes.

It should be noted, however, that the democracy the Americans achieved in 1789 was not the one that is familiar to us today. The states restricted voting to adult, free males, who, as a rule, owned a certain amount of property. Thus, people without property usually could not vote. Women were completely excluded from voting, and the large black slave population of the South was given no political rights at all.

Many further liberties still had to be won, but what emerged from the Revolution was certainly a new kind of government and a new relationship among the citizens in America. This may not have been what most Americans who opposed Great Britain intended when the Revolution began. However, their common beliefs, the pressures of war, and the economic and political needs of the new nation created a country that inspired devoted loyalty. It also inspired others—especially the French—to seek for themselves the freedoms and equality that had been achieved in the United States.

CHECKUP

1. IDENTIFY: Stamp Act, Loyalists, Patriots, Intolerable Acts, George III, Lafayette, Pulaski, Kosciusko, Steuben, Cornwallis, Franklin.

2. How did mercantilism affect the English colonies in North America?

3. What were the results of the French and Indian War?

4. How did the Declaration of Independence show the influence of Locke and Rousseau?

5. List the strengths and weaknesses of each side in the Revolutionary War.

6. Describe the organization of government under the Articles of Confederation. Why was it ineffective?

2

The French Revolution affected all of Europe

In 1789 France was the largest and most powerful European nation. Thus, when the French Revolution began that year, all of Europe was astonished by what happened. The king lost his power to make laws and eventually was killed. The new rulers of France were chosen in a new way—through elections. These new rulers wrote a constitution and reformed many laws. Everything seemed so changed that people felt they were living in a new era. They began to refer to the period before 1789 as the Old Regime.

The Old Regime

How did the French Revolution happen? To answer that question, we must look first at the Old Regime. You will remember from earlier chapters that France was a monarchy in which the king's will was law. You will remember, too, that society was organized into three classes called Estates. There was great inequality among the three Estates. The First and Second Estates had the fewest people but the most wealth, power, and privilege.

The First Estate consisted of the clergy of the Roman Catholic Church and totaled less than 1 percent of the population. The Church still retained many of the privileges it had held during the Middle Ages. The clergy did not have to pay taxes and could be tried only in Church courts. The Church owned about a tenth of all French land and received enormous amounts of money from rents, taxes, and fees. Most of this wealth was concentrated in the hands of the higher clergy—archbishops, bishops, and abbots. Some of these people had become lazy, worldly, and neglectful of their spiritual duties.

The lower clergy, made up of the parish priests, were poorly paid and overworked. They did most of the work of the Church. In addition to religious guidance, they gave money and food to the poor and provided all education.

The Second Estate in France were the nobles, less than 2 percent of the population. Many of them had special privileges that had been granted in the Middle Ages. The nobles, too, did not have to pay the heaviest taxes, and they still collected feudal dues from the peasants. Nobles held the highest positions in the army and government. Although some were concerned for the welfare of France, as a class the nobility were thoughtless, irresponsible, and extravagant.

All the other people of France—approximately 97 percent—belonged to the Third Estate. This Estate itself was subdivided into three groups.

At the top was the bourgeoisie—the city-dwelling middle class—made up of merchants, manufacturers, and professional people such as doctors and lawyers. Many of them were people of wealth and education. Below the bourgeoisie were the laborers and artisans of the cities. At the bottom of the social scale, and poorest of all, were the peasants. Although most peasants were no longer serfs, most still owed feudal dues and services. They paid rent for the land they worked and the heaviest taxes and Church tithes. They worked long and hard, but they had no right to influence the laws that kept them under the control of landlords and the king.

Growing discontent throughout France

Beginning in the mid-1700's, discontent in France began to grow. There were several reasons for this discontent. The first had to do with the growth of the French population in the late 1700's. Families had more children to support, and they needed more food and money. During the same period prices began to rise. Clothing and food cost more than they had at the beginning of the 1700's.

Discontent was also spurred by changing economic conditions in France. In order to get more money, the nobles and clergy and some of the bourgeoisie who owned land raised the rents they charged peasants. They hired lawyers to find old feudal laws that would get them more dues from the peasants. They tried to sell things they had once given away. For example, instead of letting peasants pick up twigs and branches in the woods for use as fuel, the landlords sold them wood. Now peasants had to pay for firewood that once had been free.

In the cities, artisans found food prices rising higher and higher, but wages did not go up as quickly. The artisans and the peasants resented the rich, who collected their rents and who lived in big houses with servants and plenty to eat. The poor also blamed the king for allowing prices to get so high. They resented having to pay taxes to the king when the nobles and clergy did not. Sometimes the poor refused to pay higher prices and taxes. Their violent refusal to pay taxes caused many riots. The poor economic conditions also made the first two Estates even more determined to protect their most important privilege—freedom from taxation.

Although the bourgeoisie prospered during this time, they, too, were discontented. They wanted political power equal to their economic strength. Merchants and manufacturers resented the fact that they were rich but still had to pay taxes. They wanted their sons to have important positions in the Church and army and government. They also wanted to be included in the king's luxurious royal court at Versailles, but they were not admitted because they were not nobles. Since they were not part of the king's administration, the bourgeoisie—the bankers, merchants, and manufacturers—could not influence government policy.

The bourgeoisie wanted to influence government mainly because government interfered with their business. They had at first welcomed mercantilist ideas and practices. By the mid-1700's, however, these ideas were less popular. The bourgeoisie now disliked mercantilist regulations governing wages and prices. They resented the government's interference with a merchant's freedom to trade in foreign countries.

The discontent of the nobles and upper clergy had also simmered for a long time. These groups resented the fact that French kings since Henry IV had been getting more and more powerful. As the kings became more powerful, they gained control over more territory and larger armies. In turn, the nobles lost some of their influence over the government. Louis XIV had been a strong ruler. He arrested nobles who protested his actions, or he dismissed them from office.

Louis XV and Louis XVI were not strong rulers. During the reign of Louis XV (1715–1774), the nobles often protested the king's actions. Their protests grew even louder when, as you will see, a financial crisis erupted for Louis XVI.

Different grievances, similar ideas

The various groups in French society had different kinds of grievances, but they used the same ideas and the same words to express them. They all talked of "liberty" and "equality" as their natural right. For peasants and artisans, liberty and equality meant that all people had the right to eat and to have some reward for their labor. For the bourgeoisie, liberty and equality meant the liberty to trade without restrictions. It also meant the right to advance to the highest levels of society if talented enough. They called this "equality of opportunity." For the nobility, liberty and equality meant the liberty to enjoy their ancient privileges and to limit the authority of the king.

These ideas of liberty and equality came from the thinkers of the Enlightenment, such as Voltaire, Rousseau, and Montesquieu. They were also embodied in the American Declaration of Independence. Even though they meant different things to different people, these ideas of liberty unified France's various groups in a major challenge to the king's power in 1789.

The financial crisis

From the 1750's on, the French monarchy faced a severe financial crisis. The wars of Louis XIV had left a huge debt. The debt was increased by the

France on the eve of the Revolution

The nobles who dominated France in the late 1700's held beliefs that would one day bring them down in revolution. One was that the various classes of the Old Regime lived together in harmony and mutual acceptance of their lots. These classes were (top, left to right) the clergy, the nobles, the peasants, and the learned professions like lawyers.

The nobles idealized peasant life as being filled with contentment. They dressed up as happy peasants enjoying rustic peace (right). Actual life for the peasants was anything but idyllic, oppressed as they were by taxes and forced labor. Few of them would agree with the caption for the picture of the royal family (above), offering them the thanks of their "true subjects."

assistance the French gave to the United States during the American Revolutionary War. The extravagant royal household at Versailles also cost vast sums of money.

Even with heavy taxes, the amount of money available to the government was never enough. As you have read, the poorest part of the population was taxed most heavily, but there were limits to what it could pay. The main cause of France's financial problems was that the wealthiest people were free from having to pay taxes.

When taxes did not produce enough money to meet expenses, Louis XV borrowed more and more from the bankers. Warned that his actions endangered France, the king remarked, "It will survive for my time. After me, the deluge."

In 1774 Louis XVI came to the throne. Louis cared less for running the country than for hunting, but he was forced to face France's financial difficulties. He asked financial experts how to solve the problem. Whether they were nobles or bourgeoisie, they came up with the same advice— tax the first two Estates. Each time new taxes were proposed, however, the nobles protested and refused to cooperate. Sometimes they led riots that the king found hard to control. Louis was not even sure if the army, with its officers from the nobility, would be on his side. In 1787 the country's credit was exhausted, and bankers refused to lend the government more money. France was faced with financial disaster.

Reluctantly, Louis XVI sent out a call to the representatives of the Estates-General to meet at Versailles in May 1789. He hoped that by calling together the representatives of all the Estates, he could get approval for his plan to tax the wealthy.

The meeting of the Estates-General

The Estates-General met in an atmosphere of confusion and uncertainty. Besides the immediate financial crisis, there were many other problems. France was suffering from a business depression and from unemployment. The harvest of 1788 had been poor and, as a result, food prices were high. The meeting of the Estates-General created feelings of excitement and expectation among the people. They hoped the meeting would solve their problems and end all their difficulties.

The Estates-General had not met for almost 200 years. No one knew exactly what its powers and rules were. Many people felt that if it had power only to advise the king, and not to make and carry out laws, its meeting would be useless. As for the rules, there was conflict and argument over many questions. In the past the three Estates had met separately, and each Estate had cast one vote. This procedure had always allowed the clergy and nobles of the First and Second Estates to outvote the Third Estate.

Many representatives of the Third Estate were young lawyers. A few of them, like the Count de Mirabeau, were men of noble birth who had consented to represent the Third Estate. Almost all were acquainted with the ideas of Montesquieu and Voltaire. As the representatives of the majority of the people, they insisted on having a real voice in decisions, without being automatically outvoted by the other two Estates. The Third Estate had as many representatives as the other two Estates combined. Therefore, they wanted the Estates to meet together, with representatives voting as individuals.

The Estates-General assembled first in a combined meeting on May 5, 1789. The king greeted the delegates and asked their help in solving France's financial problems. Then he instructed them to follow the old custom, each Estate meeting and voting separately as one body. The representatives of the Third Estate refused. They claimed that the Estates-General represented the French people, not the three classes. Therefore, the representatives should meet together and vote as individuals.

When Louis XVI failed to take action, the Third Estate proclaimed itself a National Assembly. This declaration, made on June 17, 1789, has been called the first act of the French Revolution. The rebellious representatives then invited the members of the other two Estates to join them in working for the welfare of France. When the king had the representatives of the Third Estate locked out of their meeting place, they met at a nearby indoor tennis court. There, on June 20, they made a pledge called the Tennis-Court Oath. The representatives pledged that they would not adjourn until they had written a constitution for France and seen it adopted. Finally, the king gave in and ordered the three Estates to meet together.

The revolution spread through France

Now Louis XVI tried to do secretly what he had feared to do openly. He began to bring troops to Paris and to Versailles, where the representatives were meeting. Fearing that he planned to drive out the Estates-General by force, the people of Paris took action. On July 14, they stormed and captured the Bastille, the hated prison-fortress, in search of weapons. They planned to use the weapons to defend the National Assembly against the royal troops.

The actions of the artisans and shopkeepers of Paris on July 14 showed that the new government had widespread support. In France this event is still celebrated as Bastille Day—a national holiday similar to Independence Day in the United States.

The events in Paris were repeated throughout France. In July and August, the so-called "Great Fear" swept across the land. The peasants believed rumors that the nobles planned to send bandits into the countryside to round them up and kill them. Eager to take revenge because of old wrongs, the peasants attacked monasteries and the manor houses of the rich. They robbed and destroyed government offices, burning the documents that recorded rents, feudal dues, and other obligations. They killed some nobles and their agents, and some government officials, especially tax collectors. These actions showed how widespread was the hatred of the social system of the Old Regime.

CHECKUP

1. IDENTIFY: Old Regime, bourgeoisie, Estates-General, National Assembly, Tennis-Court Oath, Bastille Day.

2. Describe the social structure of France during the Old Regime.

3. Why did discontent grow in France in the mid-1700's?

4. How were the terms "liberty" and "equality" interpreted by the peasants? How were these terms interpreted by the bourgeoisie?

5. For what reason did Louis XVI call a meeting of the Estates-General? Why did representatives of the Third Estate insist that all three groups of the Estates-General meet and vote together?

3

After a period of turmoil, the French monarchy was overthrown

France was in great disorder after the storming of the Bastille and the outbreaks of violence throughout the country. With the support of the people, the National Assembly assumed power.

The end of the Old Regime

Many members of the National Assembly felt that the way to deal with revolutionary violence was to remove the oppression and injustice that produced it. In a little more than a month, they took several important steps in this direction.

Beginning August 4, 1789, the National Assembly, with the support of the nobles who had joined it, abolished the last remains of feudalism in France. Delegates canceled all feudal dues and services of the peasants and repealed the Church tithe, or tax. They also did away with the special privileges of French nobles and clergy and forced them to pay taxes.

All of these reforms were included in a decree known as the Law of the Fourth of August. It was followed on August 27, 1789, by the adoption of the **Declaration of the Rights of Man.** This document was strongly influenced by the English Bill of Rights, by the writings of Rousseau and other philosophers, and by the American Declaration of Independence.

The Declaration of the Rights of Man began by saying that men are born and remain equal before the law. The law must be the same for all. It went on to proclaim freedom of speech, of the press, and of religion. Men have a right to take part in their government and to resist oppression. All citizens have an equal right to hold public office. They have a right to personal liberty, which can be taken from them only by fair trial. The Declaration stated and defined the principles that became the slogan of the French Revolution—"liberty, equality, and fraternity."

These principles, however, did not include women. During the Revolution a group of women led by Olympe de Gouges (duh GOOZH), wrote a declaration of rights for women, but it was reject-

connections

Independence Days

Most modern nations celebrate a day in honor of their nation each year. For many, this takes the form of an Independence Day, marking the date when the nation became a distinct political unit.

The oldest such Independence Day is August 1st in Switzerland. It commemorates the day in 1291 when three Swiss cantons, or states, agreed to form a union. Switzerland has now grown to 21 cantons, and they all celebrate on August 1st.

After World War II, many colonies of European nations gained independence. Each year they hold festivals celebrating their freedom (center).

Even nations so ancient that they cannot record an independence date have established a national festive day. In England, for instance, there are fireworks on November 5th, to commemorate the day in 1605 on which a plot to blow up Parliament was uncovered and foiled.

A number of nations regard themselves as having been created by revolutions. The French observe Bastille Day every July 14th. It marks the day in 1789 on which a Paris mob stormed the dreaded royal prison, the Bastille (top left). The French people regard this event as the beginning of their freedom in modern times.

In the United States, Americans commemorate July 4th, the day in 1776 on which the Declaration of Independence was adopted (right). It is celebrated with parades, speeches, and fireworks (top right).

It was around the time of the American Revolution that the techniques for making fireworks were first applied to the making of rockets for warfare. One of the earliest uses for rockets was in the War of 1812 with Great Britain. Francis Scott Key wrote of "the rockets' red glare" that he had seen in the bombardment of Fort McHenry. This phrase became part of the American national anthem and is thus linked with the fireworks that honor Independence Day.

How do we know?

OFFICIAL DOCUMENTS When we try to understand a society and its actions, it is important that we read its official documents. These can be laws, the decisions of judges, treaties, and similar formal statements. Because they are official, the language is usually precise. Before we can understand a situation, or the aims of a particular group, therefore, we must make sure we understand what is said in these carefully prepared documents.

A case in point is the Declaration of the Rights of Man (see page 396). It was issued by the French National Assembly in 1789, the first year of the French Revolution. The Declaration laid out the basic aims of all the efforts to change France's government and society over the next few years. Violations of these rights had been a major cause of the revolution, and the Assembly wanted to make sure such violations would not happen again. Another purpose was to define universal standards of justice.

In the same year as the Declaration of the Rights of Man, ten amendments were added to the Constitution of the United States. After they were ratified in 1791, they came to be known as the Bill of Rights. It is interesting to compare the two sets of rights. What do they tell us about the issues that most concerned the French and Americans during their revolutions? Was their view of law, and its importance, similar or not? By studying documents like these and comparing them, we can learn a great deal about major movements, such as revolutions, and about the nations that launched them.

---

ed. The leaders of the Revolution did not believe that women should have legal rights or participate in politics. Although they believed in equality, they did not believe that women were the equals of men.

Although the National Assembly swept away the remains of feudalism in France, the Old Regime died hard. Many nobles fled to neighboring countries such as Great Britain, Italy, and Prussia. There they plotted continuously to return and to stop the revolutionary changes. They were known as *émigrés* (EM·ee·gray), French for "emigrants." The *émigrés* were a constant source of trouble for France in the years to come.

Some nobles remained at Versailles with the king. Their opposition to some of his policies had helped start the revolution. Now, however, the nobles sided with the king against the representatives of the Third Estate who were making major changes in the government. They urged him to use force to restore the old order. Louis XVI again called in troops to Versailles.

When this news reached the people, a crowd led by women marched from Paris to Versailles. They felt the king's actions were interfering with the revolution. They also blamed the king for food shortages and the high price of bread. The crowd stormed into the palace and forced the king and his family to return to Paris, away from the plotting and scheming royal advisers.

The National Assembly became more open during the fall of 1789. Meetings were held in a public hall, and spectators often interrupted the debates with shouts or rose to give their own opinions from the gallery. This kind of participation in government was far more open and democratic than the king's rule before 1789 had been.

Reforms in government

The abolition of feudalism and the issuing of the Declaration of the Rights of Man established the guiding principles of the French Revolution. The National Assembly then began to work out details. Between 1789 and 1791 the Assembly passed more than 2,000 laws aimed at correcting abuses and setting up a new government.

First the Assembly reformed the national administration of France. The old provinces were abolished and the country was divided instead into 83 equal districts called *départements*. All officials of local governments were to be elected.

The control of nobles and clergy over the peasants had already been abolished. Now the Assembly seized land from the Church and offered it for sale to the public. Most of this land was bought by the peasants who had been renting it. Thus, French peasants became the owners of the land they farmed. As a result, they gained an important influence in French affairs.

In 1790 the Assembly issued a document known as the Civil Constitution of the Clergy. This law stated that priests and bishops were to be elected by the voters of their parishes and dioceses. They were subject to the national government and had to follow its laws. Priests and bishops were to be paid by the government. The pope refused to allow the clergy to accept this arrangement, and the majority refused to do so. Some left the country, while others helped the remaining nobles stir up hatred against the Revolution.

The Constitution of 1791

The National Assembly finally completed writing a constitution for France in 1791. This constitution limited the authority of the king and set up separate executive, legislative, and judicial branches.

The powers of the king were greatly reduced. He could not proclaim laws, nor could he block laws passed by the legislature. The legislature, called the Legislative Assembly, consisted of one house, elected by male voters who had to be taxpayers. It was to begin meeting in October 1791. No members of the National Assembly were eligible for election to the Legislative Assembly. To hold office a man had to own considerable property. Women were not permitted to vote or run for office.

Despite the guarantees of equal rights and powers in the Declaration of the Rights of Man, most of the political power of France was given to those with wealth. The bourgeoisie, you will recall, had demanded political power equivalent to their economic strength. They received this power under the Constitution of 1791.

Louis XVI reluctantly consented to the limitations that the new constitution imposed on him. At the same time he encouraged the plotting of the *émigrés* with foreign governments. Such plots, he hoped, would result in the overthrow of the new government and a return to the Old Regime.

Some of the king's advisers urged him to flee and seek help directly from friendly nations. In June 1791 Louis, together with Queen Marie Antoinette and their young son, tried to escape from France to the Austrian Netherlands. He was disguised as an ordinary citizen, but the military escort for his coach aroused suspicion and he was recognized. The coach was stopped at the town of Varennes, near the northern border of France. Louis and his family were arrested and returned to Paris.

Despite Louis' flight to Varennes, the National Assembly decided to allow him to remain king if he would accept the revised constitution. His decision to do so revived his popularity. People felt that conditions would now be more settled and the revolutionary disturbances would be at an end.

The Legislative Assembly and war

The new government provided for by the Constitution of 1791 went into effect in September 1791, but it lasted less than a year. The revolutionaries had been more skillful in overthrowing the Old Regime than in creating a sound government to replace it. They had set up a weak executive and a powerful but inexperienced legislature elected by a minority of the population.

The Legislative Assembly was divided into three groups of people with differing attitudes toward the Revolution. One group believed that the Revolution had gone far enough. They considered the ideal form of government to be one in which the king had limited authority. They were the **conservatives**—that is, they did not want to change existing conditions. Another group wanted to get rid of the king and set up a republic. They were the **radicals,** and they wanted far-reaching changes. A third group, the **moderates,** had no extreme views. They sided with conservatives or radicals, depending on the situation.

The French Revolution and its aftermath

The images of the early years of the French Revolution are of masses of people. The crucial moment in June 1789, for example, came when the Third Estate separated itself from the Estates General and called itself the National Assembly. In a nearby tennis court, the group took an oath not to separate (above). Other groups formed in the following years. Women started patriotic clubs (left). When war broke out in 1792, an effort was made to rally the entire nation. The first mass army was conscripted, and everyone else with the necessary skills was recruited to make weapons (below). The old royal garden in Paris, the Tuileries, became a manufacturing center for weapons.

In the hall where the Legislative Assembly met, conservatives sat on the right, moderates in the center, and radicals on the left. Since that time, the terms *right* (conservative), *center* (moderate), and *left* (radical) are often used to designate different degrees of political opinion.

The Legislative Assembly was frequently deadlocked on domestic issues, but it united in facing a foreign threat brought by Emperor Leopold II of Austria and King Frederick William II of Prussia. In August 1791 they had proclaimed that European rulers should restore the monarchy in France to its full power. Each group in the Legislative Assembly hoped that a successful foreign war would increase its influence. Only a few farsighted people feared that war would lead to military dictatorship. There was little opposition when the Legislative Assembly forced Louis XVI to declare war on Austria in April 1792. Soon afterward an army of Austrian and Prussian troops invaded France.

The end of the monarchy

The invasion of France by Austrian and Prussian armies touched off mass uprisings in Paris. A group of radicals seized control of the city government and set up an organization called the Commune. The Commune menaced the lives of the royal family and threatened the Legislative Assembly with violence unless it abolished the monarchy. Members of the Commune argued that there was danger to the Revolution as long as the king remained. They also accurately accused Louis XVI of plotting with the Austrian and Prussian monarchs to overthrow the Constitution of 1791.

On August 10, 1792, the Legislative Assembly, by order of the Commune, voted to suspend the office of king. Troops marched on the royal palace, massacred many of the king's guards, and imprisoned Louis XVI and his family. France was declared a republic. The king no longer ruled, and his will was no longer the law. Instead, law was made by and for the people by elected representatives. In theory, the representatives could not dictate to the nation what it did not want. A date was set for the election of delegates to a National Convention to draw up another new constitution for France. Thus the brief constitutional monar-

chy ended amid great danger and confusion. In the midst of a foreign war, France faced a national election and a complete change of government.

CHECKUP

1. IDENTIFY: Declaration of the Rights of Man, Olympe de Gouges, *émigrés*, *départements*, flight to Varennes, Commune.

2. What was the Law of the Fourth of August?

3. List the most important accomplishments of the National Assembly.

4. Describe the organization of the government under the Constitution of 1791.

5. What three political groups made up the Legislative Assembly?

The French Republic faced disorder at home and war abroad

The delegates to the National Convention were elected by **universal manhood suffrage**—that is, every man could vote, regardless of whether he owned property. Although there were some 7 million qualified voters in France, only 10 percent cast their ballots.

France under the National Convention

The National Convention held its first meeting in September 1792. The delegates, like those in the Legislative Assembly, were divided into three main groups. This time, however, there were no supporters of the king. On the right sat the Girondists. They were so called because many of them came from the province of Gironde in southwestern France. On the left were the Jacobins, members of a radical, mostly middle-class political club of that name. Among the most powerful Jacobins were Georges Jacques Danton and Maximilien Robespierre (ROHBZ·pyair). Between the two groups was a large number of delegates who at first had no definite views. Later, they came to favor the Jacobins. The Convention also included some extreme radicals, who wanted reforms to benefit all the people, not just the middle class. Their most important leader was Jean Paul Marat, a doctor from Paris.

The National Convention governed France for three years. As soon as it met, it proclaimed the end of the monarchy and the beginning of a republic. Besides drawing up a new constitution, it had to assume many of the responsibilities of government. It had to suppress disorder and revolt at home, and fight a war against foreign invaders.

The National Convention tried Louis XVI on charges of plotting against the security of the nation. By a small majority vote, he was declared guilty and sentenced to death. On January 21, 1793, Louis was beheaded by the guillotine.

Exporting the Revolution

In September 1792 the National Convention heard encouraging news. The French army had inflicted defeats on the Austrian and Prussian forces and stopped the invasion. These French military victories were followed by a French invasion of the Austrian Netherlands and the capture of Brussels. Joyful over these victories, the National Convention declared that the French armies would liberate all the peoples of Europe from oppression.

The French decision to export the ideas of the Revolution by force of arms alarmed the monarchs of Europe. Great Britain, the Dutch Netherlands, Spain, and the kingdom of Sardinia joined Austria and Prussia in an alliance against France. This alliance came to be called the First Coalition. For a time the enemies of France were successful. French troops were driven out of the Austrian Netherlands, and France itself was again invaded.

In 1793 the National Convention took extreme steps to meet the dangers faced by France. It set up the Committee of Public Safety to direct the army in crushing foreign invaders. It also established a court called the Revolutionary Tribunal to try "enemies of the revolution."

The Committee of Public Safety met danger from the outside by adopting **conscription**—the draft. All men between 18 and 45 were liable for military service. The French army took on a new spirit. It was an army of loyal, patriotic young men. Its officers were men of all classes who proved their ability and daring. For the first time the talents and ability of an entire nation, and all the classes, were called upon to fight a war.

Despite the optimism of the army, France's troubles were far from over. War created shortages of food. Prices rose. Working people in the cities demanded that the government do something about food supplies. In the countryside the clergy had refused to take the oath of loyalty to the Revolution. Instead, they organized small armies of peasants to fight against the Revolution. They were joined by some nobles. In the western part of France known as the Vendée (vahn·DAY), the "Royal and Catholic army" fought against the regular French army. Their action was called **counter-revolution** because it was aimed counter to, or against, the revolution.

Jacobins, including Danton and Robespierre, controlled the Convention. Soon they arrested many Girondist delegates. Others fled to outlying districts, where they stirred up rebellion. Charlotte Corday, a young woman from Normandy influenced by Girondist propaganda, journeyed to Paris and assassinated Marat.

The Reign of Terror

To meet the danger of opposition and revolt within France, the Convention started a program to suppress all opposition. The **Reign of Terror,** as it was known, lasted from September 1793 to July 1794. According to one delegate: "What constitutes the Republic is the complete destruction of everything that is opposed to it."

The Revolutionary Tribunal conducted swift trials and handed down harsh sentences. Many people were arrested, tried, and executed on mere suspicion. The guillotine became the symbol of the times.

Queen Marie Antoinette was among the first to be executed. People of all classes suspected of disloyalty to the Revolution were guillotined by the hundreds. The Girondist leaders were also executed. Antoine Lavoisier, the famous chemist, was condemned because he had once been concerned with tax collection. The tribunal sent him to death with the words: "The Republic has no need of genius."

Danton and Robespierre also arrested the fol-

HISTORY THROUGH ART

"The Death of Marat"

Here we see the Jacobin leader Jean Paul Marat dying. Marat suffered from a painful skin disease and found relief by sitting in a warm bath. It was there that he was assassinated by Charlotte Corday. Convinced that Marat was destroying France, she determined to stab him as Brutus had stabbed the tyrant Caesar.

In the painting Marat holds a letter from Corday. Her knife lies on the floor. The drama of the scene is highlighted by the memorial inscription, "To Marat." This was not a conventional subject for a painting, but the artist, Jacques Louis David, succeeded in creating a moving and forceful work.

David was well known as a fervent Jacobin, who later became a loyal supporter of Napoleon. David's classic style reflects the revolutionary changes that took place in painting, just as they occurred in politics. The refined elegance of the French court disappeared and made way for the realistic concerns of the common people.

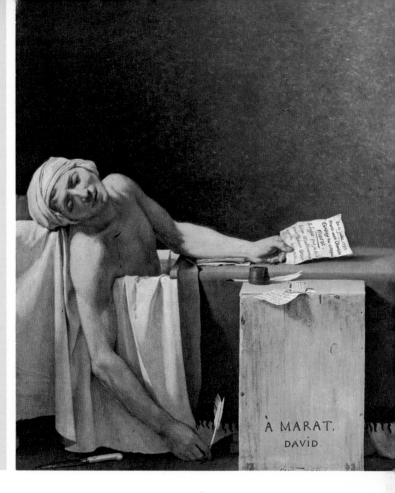

lowers of Marat, extreme radicals who wanted reform for the good of all the people. The Reign of Terror was not directed only against the nobility. Among those executed were as many bourgeois as nobles and clergy combined. Nearly three times as many peasants and laborers as people from other classes were executed.

In the spring of 1794, Danton felt that the Reign of Terror had accomplished its purpose and should be relaxed. Robespierre became even more fanatical and accused Danton of disloyalty to the Revolution. Danton and his followers were then executed. As he prepared to die, Danton is reported to have said, "Show my head to the people; they do not see the like every day."

For 100 days, Robespierre carried out a policy of suppression that aroused fear even among his supporters. He was convinced that only he could protect the Revolution from its enemies. Finally, the members of the National Convention called a halt. In July 1794 Robespierre himself was arrested and then guillotined. The Reign of Terror was ended. The moderates, or what remained of them, were again in control.

Work of the National Convention

In spite of the dangers and difficulties of the time, the National Convention brought about many reforms in France. For example, it began organizing and arranging French laws into a single system, or code. It provided for a national system of public education. It also abolished slavery in the French colonies.

In addition, the Convention did away with the law of **primogeniture,** under which only the oldest son could inherit his father's property. It also adopted the metric system of weights and measures. The metric system is used today in most parts of the world.

Meanwhile the citizen army continued to win victories. By 1795 the French had driven the invaders out and had conquered territory as far east as the Rhine River in Germany. Even more

Disorder reigned in France

The destruction of the old order in France was accompanied by violence. The first action was the destruction of the Bastille in July 1789. Three months later, mobs in Paris protested food shortages. One group marched to Versailles (left), carrying the three-colored hat that was the symbol of the revolutionaries. They also carried farm tools, to emphasize their hunger, and seals showing the scales of justice. The royal family was saved by troops, but in 1793 Louis XVI was executed. His head was displayed to the cheering crowd (below). In that same year the Jacobins began a reign of terror, killing many revolutionaries. A cartoon shows the Jacobins "purifying" their ranks like a cook (above).

important, the anti-French coalition had begun to break up. Spain, Prussia, and the Dutch Netherlands had withdrawn. Great Britain, Austria, and Sardinia were on the defensive. The French had paid a heavy price for victory. At home the spirit of militarism made it possible for the National Convention to use the army to crush opposition of any sort. In other countries the French army was so arrogant and harsh that it was hated by the people it supposedly "liberated."

In 1795 the National Convention drafted still another constitution for France. In October, just as it was to go into effect, there was an uprising in Paris. It was quickly suppressed, indicating that popular participation was not welcome in the new government.

The Directory

The new constitution written by the National Convention in 1795 again made France a republic. Only property owners were allowed to vote. Control of the government was back in the hands of the wealthy, as it had been during the period of the National Assembly. There was a legislature of two houses. The executive branch, which controlled the government, consisted of five men who were chosen by the legislature. These five men were called Directors. Therefore, the government created by the Constitution of 1795 was known as the Directory.

The Directory governed France for four years. It was unsatisfactory in many ways, and it pleased neither the radicals nor the conservatives. The government was made up of weak, corrupt, and selfish people. The Directors quarreled among themselves and were unable to agree on solutions to the problems of France. Prices rose out of control, but the Directors, unlike Jacobin leaders, made no effort to control them. They did not interfere with the activities of corrupt business leaders and speculators. As a result, the economic situation got worse. When crowds protested, the army was called in to put them down. A worker in Paris summed up his feelings this way: "Under Robespierre," he said, "blood was spilled and we had bread. Now blood is no longer spilled and we have no bread. Perhaps we must spill some blood in order to have bread."

The Directory soon became as unpopular as the Old Regime had been. It repeated history by going bankrupt, and it prepared the way for military dictatorship.

Napoleon Bonaparte

The Directory did encourage good leadership in the French army. The continuing war with Great Britain, Austria, and Sardinia provided opportunities for able military leaders. The years 1795–1799 saw the rapid rise of a relatively unknown general named Napoleon Bonaparte. As a young general he had suppressed the uprising in Paris that had tried to prevent the Directory from being established.

Napoleon Bonaparte was born in 1769 of Italian parents on the island of Corsica, a French possession in the Mediterranean. In his youth he attended military school in France and graduated as an artillery officer. He served in the revolutionary armies and became a general at the age of 24.

Napoleon was overwhelmingly ambitious, in addition to being vain and domineering. He was a superb organizer and administrator in both political and military affairs. Above all, he was a military genius who ranks among the great generals of all time. Because of the dominant role played by Napoleon beginning in 1796, the wars fought by France from this time until 1815 are generally known as the Napoleonic Wars.

Napoleon was especially skillful in the rapid movement of troops and in massing forces at critical points on the battlefield. These two techniques gave him superiority over the older, slower army tactics of his opponents.

Napoleon quickly showed his ability in Italy. The French army was small, weak, and poorly equipped. Within weeks, however, he had so organized and inspired it that he forced the Sardinians to make peace. Napoleon defeated the Austrians twice, and in 1797 they were forced to sign a humiliating peace treaty. France gained control of all of northern Italy, which had been under Austrian domination.

Napoleon became so popular in France that the Directors were worried that he might seize power. Napoleon, on the other hand, was seeking new conquests to keep his name before the French people. He proposed to weaken the British by cutting off their trade with the Middle East. The

Directory quickly agreed, since such a campaign would remove him from Paris.

Napoleon's campaign in the Middle East was a disaster. British forces destroyed the French fleet near Alexandria in Egypt and thus cut the French army off from home. Napoleon left his army to its fate and secretly returned to France. He concealed the true situation in Egypt and made exaggerated claims of victories.

Napoleon became the popular hero of the time. However, his reputation and popularity could not change the facts. France was in a truly dangerous situation. The British had organized a Second Coalition against France. This new anti-French alliance included Great Britain, Austria, and Russia. French armies were driven out of Italy, and French control over the other conquered states was slipping.

Napoleon's seizure of power

Many people in France believed that Napoleon was the only one who could win victory abroad and restore order at home. A plot was organized to overthrow the government and place Napoleon in power. In 1799 three of the Directors resigned and the other two were arrested. Troops with bayonets surrounded the meeting place of the legislature and forced most of the delegates to leave. Those that remained turned the government over to Napoleon and two of his fellow plotters.

This sort of seizure of power by force is called a **coup d'état** (koo day·TAH), meaning literally a "stroke of state." Napoleon himself said later: "I found the crown of France lying on the ground, and I picked it up with a sword."

CHECKUP

1. IDENTIFY: universal manhood suffrage, Danton, Robespierre, Marat, conscription, counter-revolution, Directory, coup d'état.

2. Describe the three main groups in the National Convention.

3. What was the Reign of Terror? What kinds of people were among its victims?

4. What were the accomplishments of the National Convention?

5. Explain the circumstances that made Napoleon's coup d'état possible.

Napoleon built an empire that spread across Europe

The coup d'état of 1799 made Napoleon dictator of France. The government he set up kept the form of a republic, but Napoleon was the real ruler. Under one title or another, and under several constitutions, he ruled France as a military dictator from 1799 until 1814. He had such great influence on France and the rest of Europe that this period is known as the **Napoleonic Era,** or the Age of Napoleon.

The people of France accepted Napoleon's dictatorship. Some wanted security after a long period of instability. Others were afraid to protest because they would be arrested by the police. Napoleon, in turn, did not try to abolish the results of the Revolution. The ideals of the Declaration of the Rights of Man remained. Serfdom and feudal privileges were not restored. The land the peasants now owned remained theirs. Napoleon did not want the old nobility to come back and challenge his power.

However, liberty meant only freedom of opportunity. It was not liberty from control, because Napoleon believed that the people should obey orders given by a leader.

Napoleon and the Consulate

Napoleon reorganized and centralized the administration of France. To begin with, he gave France its fourth government in ten years. Napoleon's government was designed to give him unlimited power. It was known as the Consulate because the executive branch was made up of three Consuls. Napoleon took the title of Consul from the chief executive of the Roman republic in an attempt to appeal to popular admiration for ancient Roman strength and virtues.

Real power was concentrated in the hands of Napoleon, who had the title First Consul. Napoleon commanded the army and navy, and had the right to appoint and dismiss all officials and to propose all new laws. The legislature was powerless. There were several assemblies, but none had any real authority.

Napoleon submitted the constitution of his new government to the people for a vote, a procedure known as a **plebiscite** (PLEB·ih·site). They were allowed only to vote yes or no and could not make any changes. The vote showed a vast majority in favor of the new constitution.

Napoleon is usually remembered as a military leader. However, his work as the head of government was more important, and much of it was more lasting. Under Napoleon's direction, scholars completed the revision and organization of all French law begun by the National Convention. This system, called the **Napoleonic Code,** was widely copied. Today it still forms the foundation of the laws of many governments in Europe and elsewhere.

Napoleon wanted a central, national financial institution. He therefore established the Bank of France. Although the bank was privately owned, it was closely supervised by the government. The government also set up a system of public education, as had been planned by the National Convention. It included elementary schools, high schools, universities, and technical schools. These were all supervised and directed by a central agency called the University of France.

The Civil Constitution of the Clergy of 1790 had begun a long quarrel between the Roman Catholic Church and the government of France. Napoleon ended the conflict by an agreement with the pope in 1801. This agreement gave the Catholic Church a favored position in France, but it did not abolish the religious toleration guaranteed by the Declaration of the Rights of Man.

Napoleon as emperor

Napoleon soon moved to increase his power even more and to make it permanent and hereditary. In 1804 the French people voted in favor of a constitution that declared France an empire. Napoleon Bonaparte was named Emperor Napoleon I.

As emperor, Napoleon continued to show his three great skills—as an organizer, as a diplomat, and as a military genius.

He reorganized the French army and improved military discipline and the method of selecting officers. Napoleon was able to create among his troops a tremendous sense of patriotism and loyalty to him.

Government of France 1774–1814	
1774	Louis XVI became king
1789	Third Estate, as National Assembly, assumed power
1791	Legislative Assembly, with Louis XVI as constitutional monarch, began rule
1792	Monarchy suspended National Convention began governing
1795	Directory took control
1799	Consulate established, with Napoleon as First Consul
1804	Napoleon crowned emperor
1814	Napoleon overthrown and Bourbon monarchy restored

Napoleon also engaged in some shrewd and skillful diplomacy. He was able to destroy the coalition of European powers against France. In 1799 he had convinced Russia to desert its allies, Great Britain and Austria, and make peace with France. By 1801 Austria was forced to ask France for peace. In 1802 a peace treaty was signed between Great Britain and France.

For a time it looked as though Napoleon would keep his promises to the French people—peace with military victory, firm and steady government, and economic prosperity. However, Napoleon soon began to train additional troops. It was widely believed that he planned to invade and conquer Great Britain.

War with the Third Coalition

By 1802 France had expanded far beyond its old boundaries. Throughout Europe, people wanted to throw off French control. The British knew that Napoleon's ambition threatened their commerce, their empire, and their control of the seas.

Great Britain declared war on France in 1803 and in 1805 organized the Third Coalition against Napoleon. Austria, Russia, and Sweden allied themselves with Great Britain. Spain was allied with France. Napoleon planned to strike at the British by defeating the British navy and then invading Great Britain.

Napoleon Bonaparte

Few people in European history have so completely dominated their age as did Napoleon. Even after his defeat at Waterloo, Napoleon was a symbol of glory for the French. A painting showing him amid the defeats of 1812 (above) still suggests his grandeur and nobility.

Whether adored or hated, Napoleon aroused passionate opinions. For many, he was the ideal leader—calm and rational—as he was shown during his early days of power (left). The artist captured Napoleon's famous gesture of his hand tucked into his jacket and, above all, his look of intelligence. Other artists were not so complimentary. A cartoonist showed Napoleon and an English statesman carving the world (below). The caption reads: "The great globe itself is too small to satisfy such...appetite."

However, in 1805 a British fleet led by Admiral Horatio Nelson defeated a combined French and Spanish fleet near Cape Trafalgar off the southern coast of Spain. Nelson was killed, but the French and Spanish fleets were almost completely destroyed. Napoleon was successful only in battles on land against Austria and Russia.

The Continental System

Napoleon believed that if the British lost their foreign trade and its profits, they would be willing to make peace on his terms. Therefore, he ordered a blockade of the British Isles. This blockade was called the **Continental System** because Napoleon held control over so much of the continent of Europe. Napoleon refused to allow British goods to be imported into any country under French control. He also tried to force other European countries to stop buying British products.

The British responded with a blockade of France. Ships of neutral countries were made to stop at British ports to get a license before trading with France or its allies. Napoleon, in turn, ordered the French navy to seize any neutral ship that obeyed the British order.

Neutral nations were thus placed in an awkward position. If they disregarded the British order, their ships might be captured by the British. If they obeyed the British, their ships would be seized by the French. The United States was especially hard hit, for it depended to a great extent on trade with both Great Britain and the continent of Europe. Both France and Great Britain stopped American ships, but British ships did the most damage. This conflict over trade was one cause of the War of 1812 between Great Britain and the United States.

Although the British blockade was hurting France, British leaders were not satisfied with the blockade alone. They wanted the complete military defeat of Napoleon, who continued to win battles against the European powers.

Once more Napoleon proved himself a great general. His strategy was to strike his enemies before they could unite effectively. In December 1805 Napoleon smashed the combined forces of Russia and Austria at Austerlitz, a town in the Austrian Empire north of Vienna. Shortly thereafter, the Third Coalition broke up.

The reorganization of Europe

By 1808 Napoleon completely dominated Europe. Austria and Prussia had been forced to sign humiliating peace treaties, and Russia allied itself with France. Napoleon ruled the Austrian and Dutch Netherlands and Spain. He also forced Denmark and the Papal States to ally with France. To stop the possibility of any Russian gains, Napoleon formed the territory that Prussia had taken from Poland into a Grand Duchy of Warsaw (see map, page 411). He gave this territory to his ally, the king of Saxony.

Various treaties since 1795 had given France the right to intervene in the hundreds of small German states. He organized the most important states into the Confederation of the Rhine, with himself as Protector. He abolished the Holy Roman Empire and forced its emperor to take the lesser title of emperor of Austria. All of the small states of northern Italy were unified into the kingdom of Italy and were made dependent on Napoleon. He placed many of his relatives on the thrones of the conquered countries.

The changes Napoleon made in Europe were not confined to enlarging his empire and reorganizing the territories he conquered. Wherever the French army went, the Napoleonic Code was put into effect, feudalism and serfdom were abolished, and the modernized methods of the French army were introduced.

Without intending it, the French also helped awaken in the people they conquered a spirit of **nationalism,** or love of nation. In France the events of the revolution and the stirring words of the Declaration of the Rights of Man had produced feelings of patriotism for the country as a whole, rather than for local regions. People thought of themselves as French, with a country and ideals worth fighting for. Now these same nationalistic feelings of loyalty and patriotism appeared among the conquered peoples—not, of course, for France but for their homelands.

At first the French were received as liberators, but they soon came to be regarded as foreign invaders. Taxes in the conquered countries increased steadily to pay the costs of war and occupation. Troops were housed in private homes. People in the conquered countries were tired of being forced to fight for Napoleon. In every country, people wanted to get rid of the French occupation forces and to regain control of their own national affairs.

CHECKUP

1. IDENTIFY: Consulate, plebiscite, Napoleonic Code, Nelson, Confederation of the Rhine, nationalism.

2. Why did the people of France accept Napoleon's dictatorship?

3. What were Napoleon's chief accomplishments as First Consul?

4. How did Napoleon attempt to control Great Britain's trade? How did the British react?

5. What changes did Napoleon's invasions spread?

European nations united to defeat Napoleon

In 1807–1808 Napoleon was master of Europe, but time was working on the side of his enemies. The armies of his opponents were getting stronger. The generals who opposed Napoleon had learned his methods of rapid movement and massing of troops. Other nations, especially Great Britain and Prussia, had learned how to train large bodies of troops. In addition, new feelings of nationalism strengthened Napoleon's enemies.

The Peninsular Campaign

To the south of France, on the Iberian Peninsula, lay Spain and Portugal. In 1807 Portugal refused to observe the Continental System because the nation's prosperity depended on trade with Great Britain. The French army therefore occupied Portugal and drove the king into exile.

Napoleon then decided to conquer Spain. After forcing the Spanish king to abdicate, Napoleon made his brother Joseph king of Spain. In 1808 the Spanish people rose in revolt. The British sent an army under Arthur Wellesley, the future Duke of Wellington, to help the Spanish and Portuguese drive out the French. In spite of everything Napoleon did, he could not suppress the Spanish uprising or drive out the British army.

The Peninsular Campaign, as this war was called, lasted six years (1808–1814). Napoleon continued to control the government of Spain, but the campaign was a drain on the French army at a time when it was needed elsewhere.

In 1814 the Spaniards, with British aid, captured Madrid and drove out the French king. They then proceeded to draw up a new constitution that provided for limited monarchy. The Spanish revolt and the new constitution showed the tremendous influence of the ideals of the French Revolution. It also showed the rising spirit of nationalism and opposition to Napoleon.

Catastrophe in Russia

Czar Alexander I of Russia viewed Napoleon's domination of Europe with alarm and distrust. The French Continental System broke up a long-established exchange of Russian grain and raw materials for British manufactured goods. Gradually, enforcement of the blockade was relaxed in Russia. In 1812 Alexander announced that trade with Great Britain would be renewed.

Inefficient as it was, the blockade was Napoleon's only way of striking at the British. For Russia, an ally, to ignore it openly was intolerable. Napoleon decided to invade Russia, and he exerted pressure on all parts of his empire to supply soldiers.

Napoleon's army totaled 600,000 soldiers when finally assembled. However, it was vastly different from the enthusiastic, loyal, and patriotic armies of the early French Empire. Fewer than half of the soldiers were French. The larger part of this "Grand Army" was made up of soldiers from Denmark, Germany, the Netherlands, the Balkan region, Italy, Switzerland, and Poland. They fought because they were forced to.

In May 1812 Napoleon began his march eastward toward Russia (see map, opposite). Instead of battling the French on the vast plains of western Russia, the Russian army retreated slowly, drawing Napoleon's army deeper into the country. As they retreated, the Russians burned everything that might be of value to the invaders.

In mid-September of 1812 the French army captured Moscow, but it was a hollow victory. The Russian winter was about to begin. The Russians had destroyed the city so that nothing would be

NAPOLEON'S EMPIRE IN 1810

- French Empire
- States controlled by Napoleon
- States allied with Napoleon
- Independent European states
- ✕ Battle sites

left for the French. So many buildings in Moscow were burned that there was not enough housing for the French troops. The supply line from France was long and in danger of being broken. Facing these horrible hardships, Napoleon decided to lead his army back to France.

Napoleon's retreat from Moscow was one of the greatest military disasters of all time. The Russian winter was exceptionally severe. In addition to the snow and bitter cold, the French troops had to pass back through the devastated countryside. The Russians attacked the retreating French without mercy. French discipline broke down, and

there were many desertions. When the army reached Prussia in December, it had lost four-fifths of its troops. The Russian army followed the French and invaded Napoleon's empire, and the Prussians joined in the attack.

Final defeat

Everywhere in Western Europe people were rising to throw off French rule and join the invading Russians. Napoleon abandoned his army and hurried to France to raise new forces to defend his empire, but he faced overwhelming odds. Prussia,

Austria, Great Britain, and Sweden joined Russia in a new alliance to invade France.

Napoleon tried his old strategy of striking before his enemies could unite, but this time he was too late. In October 1813 Napoleon's forces and the army of the new alliance met at Leipzig, in Saxony. The new French army was decisively defeated and Napoleon retreated into France. The allies captured Paris in March 1814 and forced Napoleon to abdicate.

Napoleon gave up all claims to the throne of France for himself and his family. He was granted a pension and allowed to retire to the small island of Elba off the west coast of Italy.

The victorious allies who had defeated Napoleon agreed that the boundaries of France should be the same as they had been in 1792. They restored the Bourbon monarchy to the throne in the person of Louis XVIII, brother of the executed Louis XVI.

The Hundred Days

Napoleon had no intention of spending the rest of his life on the island of Elba. There were many people in France who wanted him back, and he began at once to plot his return. He escaped from Elba and landed in France on March 1, 1815.

Napoleon had only a small group of troops with him at first. Gradually, however, resistance to Napoleon collapsed, and on March 20 he entered Paris in triumph. Then began the period that is called the Hundred Days. To avoid war, Napoleon announced that France gave up all claims to territories it had formerly conquered.

Napoleon hoped that disputes among his opponents over the division of territory would keep them from opposing his return, but he was mistaken. The combined armies of Prussia, Great Britain, and the Dutch Netherlands, under the command of the Duke of Wellington, began to move toward France. Napoleon once more assembled a French army to battle them.

On June 18, 1815, the allied and the French armies met at Waterloo in the Austrian Netherlands. The French were badly defeated. Again Napoleon abdicated, and again the Bourbon monarchy was restored.

Napoleon surrendered to the British, asking to be allowed to escape to England. The British were unwilling to take such a chance. Instead, they sent the defeated emperor to live under constant guard on the lonely, dismal island of St. Helena in the South Atlantic. There Napoleon died in 1821.

As the years passed, Napoleon's legend grew. People forgot the wars and failures and remembered only the glories and achievements. Napoleon was transformed from a vain and ambitious dictator into the "Little Corporal," the "Good Emperor," the "true patriot of the Revolution."

Effects of the revolution and Napoleon

In every sense of the word, the events in France from 1789 to 1815 constituted a revolution. French society changed permanently. The division of people into three Estates had ended. The privileged position of the nobility and clergy had been abolished. They no longer controlled the army, the Church, and the government. They no longer monopolized the ownership of land.

The ideals of liberty, equality, and fraternity were spread throughout Europe by Napoleon's armies and conquests. Within France and outside it, there grew up a revolutionary tradition.

Another consequence of the French conquests was the rise of nationalism as a major new political force. Nationalistic feelings gained strength and began to have wide influence.

In the early 1800's, as various countries reacted to conquest by the French, the rising spirit of nationalism spurred groups wishing to unify weak or fragmented nations. Nationalism helped the Spaniards rally in opposition to Napoleon. In Germany, where Napoleon combined many small states, there grew up a desire for national unity. The various groups in the Austrian Empire—Czechs, Hungarians, Slavs, Italians—craved independence and self-government.

CHECKUP

1. IDENTIFY: Peninsular Campaign, Duke of Wellington, Czar Alexander I, Grand Army, Louis XVIII, Hundred Days.

2. LOCATE: Leipzig, Elba, Waterloo.

3. Why did Napoleon declare war on Russia? How did his Russian campaign end?

4. What was the battle of Waterloo? What happened to Napoleon afterward?

CHAPTER REVIEW

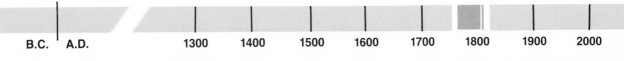

| B.C. | A.D. | 1300 | 1400 | 1500 | 1600 | 1700 | 1800 | 1900 | 2000 |

1754–1763	French and Indian War	1789	Beginning of French Revolution	1805	Battle of Trafalgar
1775–1783	Revolutionary War	1793	Execution of Louis XVI	1808–1814	Peninsular Campaign
1776	Declaration of Independence	1795–1799	France ruled by Directory	1812	Napoleon's invasion of Russia
1783	Treaty of Paris	1799	Napoleon's coup d'état	1814	Abdication of Napoleon
1788	Ratification of United States Constitution	1804	Napoleon crowned emperor	1815	Napoleon defeated at Waterloo

CHAPTER SUMMARY

The late 1700's and early 1800's were years of upheaval and revolution in the Western world. The first upheaval occurred in the British colonies in North America. After the French and Indian War, Great Britain enforced trade laws strictly and imposed new taxes on the colonies. Relations worsened steadily, and war broke out in 1775. The Second Continental Congress adopted the Declaration of Independence the next year. In 1781 the Americans won a decisive victory at Yorktown, Virginia. After two years of negotiations, a peace treaty was signed, and the American states were recognized as independent.

At first the American states were governed by the Articles of Confederation. The central government was weak, with most power remaining with the individual states. A new Constitution, ratified in 1788, established a federal system. Power was divided among three branches of the government.

In 1789 the French launched a revolution that was to affect all of Europe. Discontent had been growing in France since the mid-1700's. Louis XVI, facing a financial crisis, summoned a meeting of the Estates General in 1789. When he insisted on the old voting procedures, the Third Estate met separately and proclaimed itself a National Assembly.

The National Assembly issued the Declaration of the Rights of Man and wrote the Constitution of 1791, creating a limited monarchy. Invasion by Austrian and Prussian troops touched off riots that ended this government in less than a year.

The National Convention, which ruled France for three years, proclaimed a republic and executed the king. Threatened by new invasions, it drafted an army and suppressed opposition at home with the Reign of Terror.

France was later ruled by the Directory, which was inefficient and corrupt. In 1799 Napoleon Bonaparte took over the government in a coup d'état. Napoleon ruled France as a military dictator and extended French control over much of Europe.

By 1808 Napoleon dominated Europe. However, after several military defeats, he was forced to abdicate and was sent to exile in Elba in 1814. Napoleon soon escaped, only to be defeated again at Waterloo. Although the Bourbon monarchy was restored to France, Napoleon's conquests had spread revolutionary ideas and feelings of nationalism throughout Europe.

CHECKING WHAT YOU KNOW

1. Match each description at the left with the appropriate law at the right:

   a. Listed colonial products that could be sold only in England.

   b. Required special taxes for publications, contracts, and other documents.

   c. Set special taxes on many items imported into North America from non-British colonies.

   d. Closed the port of Boston and canceled the Massachusetts charter.

   1. Sugar Act
   2. Intolerable Acts
   3. Navigation Act
   4. Stamp Act

2. Match each quotation at the left with the person at the right who said it:

a. "Perhaps we must spill blood in order to have bread."

b. "I found the crown of France lying on the ground, and I picked it up with a sword."

c. "After me, the deluge."

d. "Show my head to the people; they do not see the like every day."

1. Danton
2. citizen under the Directory
3. Louis XV
4. Napoleon

3. Compare the organization of American government under the Articles of Confederation with its organization under the Constitution.

4. Describe the organization of the French government under each of the following:

a. the Legislative Assembly
b. the National Convention
c. the Directory
d. the Consulate

5. What were the lasting effects of the French Revolution? In what ways did Napoleon both fulfill and destroy its ideals?

PRACTICING YOUR SKILLS

1. **Understanding chronology.** In each of the following groups of events, place the items in chronological order:

a. capture of the Bastille
calling of the Estates-General
Tennis-Court Oath

b. Constitution of 1791
Declaration of the Rights of Man
Reign of Terror

c. flight to Varennes
Napoleon crowned emperor
Louis XIV becomes king

d. First Coalition formed
Continental System
Napoleon invades Russia

e. battle of Waterloo
Hundred Days
Peninsular Campaign

2. **Organizing information.** Prepare a chart of the American and French revolutions, listing in columns the political, economic, and social causes. Identify what you would consider to be the most significant causes of each. Be prepared to defend your choice

RELATING PAST TO PRESENT

1. Before the American Revolution, many colonists refused to buy British goods. What did the colonists hope to accomplish? How have similar actions been used in recent times? Give examples in which the United States or any other country has refused to trade with countries with which it disagrees.

2. Spain used guerrilla warfare against Napoleon's forces. How is guerrilla fighting conducted? Describe how guerrilla fighting was used in a modern war. Why is this type of warfare effective against modern armies?

INVESTIGATING FURTHER

1. Read *A Tale of Two Cities* by Charles Dickens. Describe how the French Revolution affected the lives of the main characters in the book.

2. The ideas of Locke and Rousseau greatly influenced political and social thought in the 1700's. Describe how their ideas applied to each of the following:

a. the Declaration of Independence
b. the United States Constitution
c. the Declaration of the Rights of Man

A suggested resource for your research is J. Bronowski and B. Mazlish, *Western Intellectual Tradition: From Leonardo to Hegel* (Harper & Row).

3. Working with other students, prepare a report on Napoleon Bonaparte. Each student can research one aspect of Napoleon's life. You may choose from the following:

a. Napoleon's rise to power
b. his domestic reforms
c. his military exploits
d. his defeat and exile
e. the aftermath of his rule

You may use encyclopedias or biographies of Napoleon in your research.

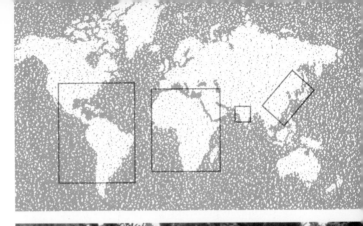

(1400–1840)

18

As Europe Expanded, Changes Occurred Throughout the World

As you have read in Chapters 14 through 17, the centuries from about 1500 to 1800 were a time of great cultural, political, economic, and social change in Europe. New ideas and attitudes flourished, and strong centralized governments replaced feudal societies in many European countries. Curious and adventurous European explorers traveled to the far corners of the world, trading and establishing colonies wherever they went.

China and Japan, the two major countries of East Asia, did not participate directly in any of these developments. The rulers of each country chose to ignore the outside world as much as possible. Instead of looking outward, they looked inward. Instead of encouraging change, they tried to keep their countries stable. Both China and Japan did change between 1500 and 1800, but the changes were not as rapid as those in Europe. China and Japan had been equal to Europe in 1500. In a few respects, they may have been more advanced. However, after 1500 they fell gradually behind.

The same fate overtook India, which more easily came under domination by Europeans. This pattern of domination was visible also on the continent of Africa. In Latin America, few native cultures survived after the Europeans claimed the land. However, a willingness grew among the

A stone lion guarding a Chinese temple

colonial settlers to resist the rule of the home country on many issues. Inspired by the French Revolution, a series of independence movements swept Latin America around 1800.

THE CHAPTER SECTIONS

1. China changed gradually under the Ming and Ch'ing dynasties

2. Japan prospered under the Tokugawa shogunate

3. Europeans influenced East Asia and India

4. European nations began to dominate Africa

5. The nations of Latin America gained their independence

China changed gradually under the Ming and Ch'ing dynasties

As you read in Chapter 8, Chu Yüan-chang overthrew the Yüan dynasty of the Mongols in China in 1368. At that time he established the Ming dynasty, which remained in power until 1644, when the Ch'ing dynasty was established in its place. The Ch'ing dynasty was to remain in power until 1911.

Under these two dynasties China enjoyed more than 400 years of peace. Except for the fighting that took place when the Ming dynasty was overthrown, there was very little rebellion or warfare from the late 1300's to about 1800. In Europe during these same centuries, warfare caused destruction, and it also caused change. In China, peace contributed to stability.

Ming policy toward the outside world

During the early Ming period, the Chinese were probably the most skillful sailors in the world. They built large, solid ships known as junks, which were sometimes over 400 feet (125 meters) long. Since the early 1100's the Chinese had used the compass, which they probably invented, in navigation. They also drew detailed charts of Asian sea routes. A Chinese fleet, financed by the emperor, sailed to India in 1407. Another fleet

crossed the Indian Ocean and reached Aden, at the southern tip of the Red Sea, in 1415.

These and other voyages occurred almost 100 years before Vasco da Gama sailed around Africa from Portugal to India. The Chinese clearly had the ability to become a great seafaring power, as both Portugal and England later did. What the Chinese lacked was the continued support of their emperors for overseas expansion.

As you read in Chapter 8, the naval expeditions of the early Ming period suddenly came to an end in the mid-1400's. The later Ming emperors— unlike Henry the Navigator in Portugal or Queen Elizabeth in England—were not interested in foreign trade or seapower. After 1430 they stopped financing naval expeditions, and for a time they outlawed overseas trade.

There were two reasons for the lack of interest in foreign trade and seapower on the part of the Ming emperors. One resulted from Confucian attitudes toward trade. Another stemmed from concern over the land frontier between China and central Asia.

Confucian attitudes toward trade

After having defeated the Mongol conquerors in 1368, the Ming emperors tried to rid China of all Mongol influences. They looked to the great ages of China's past for inspiration and tried to re-create the grandeur of the Han, T'ang, and Sung dynasties. As part of that effort, Confucianism— to which the Mongols had only paid lip service— was restored to its central place as the philosophy of the government.

According to Confucianism, society was divided into four different classes. First in importance were the scholar-officials, who governed the country for the emperor. Second were the peasants, who produced food and paid the taxes that supported the empire. Third were the artisans, who made useful objects. Fourth and last were the merchants, who were said to live off the labor of other people, making profits from selling things that the peasants and artisans had produced. Merchants were looked down upon as "parasites," and trade was regarded as a necessary evil, not as something desirable.

As followers of Confucius, the Ming emperors believed that peasants were more valuable to the

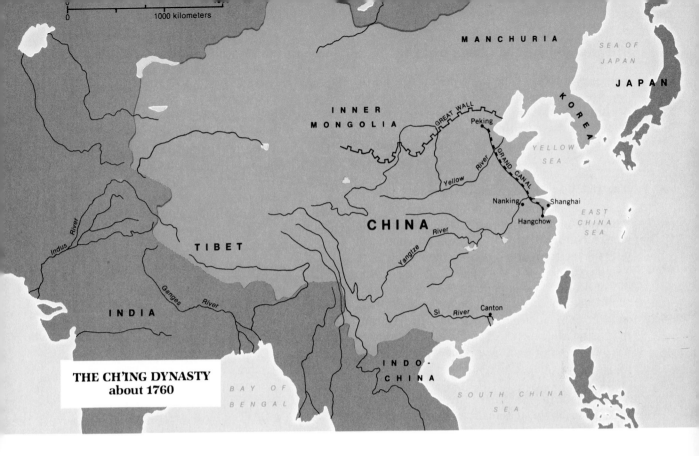

THE CH'ING DYNASTY
about 1760

empire than merchants and that agriculture was far more important than trade. They tried to regulate all trade within China Proper, keeping it to a minimum. Unlike European monarchs, they did not believe that any benefit could come to the country from foreign trade. They were willing to receive gifts, called tribute, from such foreign governments as Korea, Japan, and Tibet. In return they gave lavish gifts. However, the aim of these exchanges was not to increase China's wealth. Instead, the tribute system was designed to increase China's prestige and security.

The northern frontier

After their victory over the Mongols, the Ming emperors wanted to make sure that no central Asian people from the north ever again conquered China. Thus the long northern land frontier was of much greater concern to them than the sea.

To protect that frontier, they strengthened the Great Wall and built new observation towers. They encouraged Chinese soldiers to move with their families into the frontier zone, where they were offered free land in exchange for their defense of strategic mountain passes.

In 1421 the Ming imperial capital was moved from Nanking in central China to Peking in the north (see map, this page). From there, only 40 miles (64 kilometers) south of the Great Wall, the emperors tried to prevent the various nomadic tribes to the north from uniting into a powerful fighting force. Individual tribes that submitted to the Ming were allowed to send yearly tribute missions to Peking and exchange gifts. The chiefs of the nomadic tribes were given titles, honors, and money in return for their loyalty.

Defending the frontier required constant attention. It was also very costly. Every year the hundreds of nomads who came to Peking on tribute missions had to be entertained by the emperor and presented with lavish gifts. The Ming emperors did not have the financial resources to encourage overseas expeditions as well. One of the reasons they ended the overseas expeditions of the early 1400's was to save money for frontier defense.

The founding of the Ch'ing dynasty

Throughout most of the Ming period, the northern frontier remained secure. There were only occasional border raids by small bands of nomads, who sought greater riches than they could obtain by means of tribute relations with the emperor. The Chinese were always able to drive these raiders away.

In the early 1600's, however, a new and very serious threat emerged in Manchuria, to the northeast of China Proper. There, a chieftain named Nurhachi (NER·HAH·CHEE) succeeded in unifying the many tribes of nomadic Jurchen into a single people—the Manchus. In the 1630's one of Nurhachi's sons conquered Korea and Inner Mongolia. Another son captured Peking in 1644, with the help of a Chinese general. The Manchus then established the Ch'ing dynasty, which was to last until 1911. Once again, and despite all the efforts of the Ming, China had been conquered by "barbarians."

Even though the Ch'ing dynasty was non-Chinese in origin, it actually became one of the most "Chinese" dynasties. That is, the Ch'ing emperors mastered Chinese culture and used traditional Chinese techniques of government in their rule.

A good example is the Emperor K'ang-hsi (KAHNG·SHEE), who reigned from 1661 to 1722. He had inherited the throne of China when he was only seven years old, although he did not actually begin to rule until he was thirteen. For the next 50 years he served not only as a capable general of the Manchu army but also as a model Chinese emperor.

K'ang-hsi knew the Chinese classics well and sponsored many important literary projects. He presided over the examination system and appointed successful candidates to offices in the civil service. He also saw to it that efforts were made to control flooding on China's major rivers and that storehouses were established throughout the land to hold grain for use in case of famine. He urged officials and the common people to behave virtuously. In short, he ruled in accordance with the teachings of Confucius, just as the Ming emperors had done.

At the same time, K'ang-hsi and the other Ch'ing emperors tried to preserve distinctions between the Manchus—who were a minority in the empire—and the Chinese people. All Manchus had to study the Manchu language and Manchu cultural traditions. The Chinese people were not allowed to marry Manchus. No Chinese people were allowed to settle in northern Manchuria. This region was maintained as a tribal homeland for the Manchus. Finally, all Chinese men were required to wear their hair in a single braid, called a queue. The braid distinguished them from the Manchus and indicated their submission to Manchu rule.

The economy of the Ming and Ch'ing

The Ch'ing emperors, like the Ming emperors before them, believed that agriculture was the basis of China's wealth. They maintained traditional political institutions, and they supported traditional Chinese ideas and values. Both the Ming and Ch'ing emperors were uninterested in change. Nevertheless, change occurred. New patterns of commerce and trade began to appear.

You read in Chapter 8 about the growth of cities during the Sung dynasty. This trend continued during the Ming and Ch'ing dynasties and contributed to the growth of internal trade within China. In theory, merchants were looked down upon, but in practice they were needed to supply the urban population with food, textiles for clothing, and other essential goods.

Certain regions of the country began specializing in the production of certain goods. For example, Canton, in the south, became a center for the manufacture of woks—the shallow iron cooking pans that are still used in Chinese cooking today. The region near Shanghai, in central China, became a center for the weaving of cotton cloth.

Products such as these were transported by barges and junks along the rivers, canals, and coastal waters to Peking, the new and growing capital city, and to other large urban centers. Such goods as tea and silk were transported by caravan to central Asia, and even to Russia. Chinese ships sailed to Southeast Asia and India on trading missions, despite the government's disapproval of these voyages.

In the countryside, where most of China's people continued to live, more land was now farmed.

Such new crops as sweet potatoes, peanuts, and tobacco were introduced from the Americas. The sweet potato became known as "the poor man's food" in South China, because it thrived in soils that were unsuited to growing rice. It also provided more basic nutritional value than most other crops.

The growth of popular culture

With the growth of cities and the increasing wealth of urban merchants and artisans came the rise of popular culture, just as in Europe.

As early as the Yüan dynasty in the 1300's, novels and plays for city people had been written in the common, everyday language, rather than in literary language. During the Ming and Ch'ing periods, these popular writings increased in number. Old tales about bandits, corrupt officials, and beautiful women, which had once been recited by storytellers in the streets, were now printed in inexpensive books. New stories, realistically portraying the society and family life, were written by professional authors.

Scholarship also flourished during the Ming and Ch'ing periods. During the Ming dynasty, Chinese scholars wrote long and detailed histories of earlier dynasties and essays on Confucian ethics. During the Ch'ing dynasty, scholars became interested in philology—the history of words. And, as in Europe during the Renaissance, they applied intensive study to ancient writings to determine their exact meaning.

A few scholars, mostly Taoists, compiled encyclopedias of plants and animals. In 1579 a scholar completed a huge book describing almost 2,000 animal, vegetable, and mineral drugs then known to Chinese medicine. The book included information, for example, on how to inoculate people against smallpox. In contrast to Europe, however, pure science and the scientific method did not take hold in China.

City life contributed to the development of popular culture and scholarship, but it also contributed to a decline in the status of Chinese women. In rural China everyone, including women, had to work on the land so that families could survive. In the cities, however, women did not have such an important economic role. It became customary, especially among officials and wealthy merchants,

to think of women as useless playthings. One sign of this was the practice of footbinding.

When a girl was about five years old, her feet were bound tightly with strips of cloth. Gradually, over the course of several years, the arch of each foot would break. This created what the Chinese called a "lily foot," half normal in size and curved under instead of straight. Women with bound feet could hardly walk, a sign that their fathers or husbands were rich enough not to need their labor. This practice, which began among the upper classes in the Sung period, spread throughout Chinese society during later dynasties. It was not brought to an end until the 1900's.

Decline of the Ch'ing dynasty

You read in Chapter 3 about the concept of the dynastic cycle in China—the similar patterns of growth and decline of different dynasties. By about 1800 it was clear that the Ch'ing dynasty was entering the stage of dynastic decline, as had other dynasties before it.

After more than a century of peace, the soldiers of the Manchu army had lost much of their skill as warriors. They had grown used to peacetime life. Despite government policies to keep them separate from the Chinese people, they had developed closer ties to the Chinese and had become more and more like them in their behavior and values. Sensing that the Manchu army was weak, central Asian tribes began to threaten the frontier.

Another problem was the breakdown of government services for the people. During the Ming and Ch'ing dynasties, China's population had grown dramatically. There had been roughly 150 million Chinese in the late Ming period. By 1800 there were 300 million—twice as many. This growth in population had been brought about by peace and by increases in agricultural output. More crops were grown, making it possible to feed more people. However, increases in population were not matched by increases in the number or efficiency of government officials. There were only about 20,000 officials in the Ming period, or one for every 7,500 people. In 1800 there were still only 20,000 officials, one for every 15,000 people.

As in the past, these officials relied on powerful local families, the gentry, to make the political

Ming and Ch'ing China

When the Ming dynasty gained control in China, it tried to wipe out all Mongol influences on Chinese life. The Ming sought to enforce the teachings of Confucius—that people should live virtuously, seek learning and knowledge, and show reverence and respect for all, especially the family and its ancestors.

The Ch'ing dynasty changed little concerning these aims for Chinese society. Life among the upper classes was formal, polite, and graceful, as shown in the silk painting (above) celebrating a noble's return home. Family portraits (left) were prized possessions, honored and passed down through generations. Learning, too, was honored and passed on, like the chart (below) contained in a manual for acupuncture.

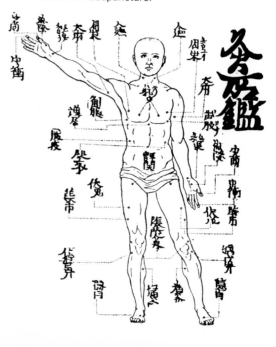

system work. The gentry were rural landlords who had passed the lower-level civil service examinations but had not yet received the higher degrees that qualified them for important posts. They collected taxes from the peasants and sent the revenue to the government. They also supported local schools and supervised road repairs and other public works projects. In return they received praise from the emperor. They were also permitted to keep a small portion of the taxes and other money they collected for themselves.

In normal times this system functioned very smoothly. A small number of government officials was able to administer a large country. However, in the late Ch'ing period, official corruption caused serious problems. High-ranking bureaucrats began to use their positions in the emperor's service to acquire great personal fortunes. They pressured local officials throughout China to give them money and expensive gifts.

Local officials, forced to pay bribes or lose their jobs, pressured the gentry for more tax revenues. The gentry in turn squeezed more taxes out of the peasants. Less and less of the money that was collected went to provide for flood control or orphanages or road repairs. Instead, the money ended up in the hands of high-ranking officials in the government.

Discontent and rebellion

In 1796 discontent over increased taxes and decreased services erupted in a great peasant rebellion. The revolt was not put down until 1804. Called the White Lotus Rebellion, it was led by members of the White Lotus Society, the same secret society that had risen up against the Mongols centuries earlier. Peace was restored only after eight years of effort and great expense. The emperor tried to eliminate official corruption, but he did not have the financial resources to increase the number of officials and reform government at the local level. Thus, the basic cause of the discontent remained, and uprisings and rebellions steadily increased in number.

The Ch'ing dynasty seemed to be following in the footsteps of all previous Chinese dynasties. It had gained the Mandate of Heaven in battle and achieved great heights over the next hundred years or so. Now it was being challenged by the

discontent of the people. If the pattern of past Chinese history had repeated itself, eventually a powerful rival to the Ch'ing emperor would have emerged, defeated the Ch'ing army in battle, and claimed the Mandate of Heaven for himself. A new and more vigorous dynasty would have been established.

That, however, was not to be. Just as the Ch'ing dynasty started to decline, a new element was introduced into Chinese life—the beginnings of European expansion into East Asia. Instead of repeating itself once more, the Chinese dynastic cycle—and the imperial government—came to an end after nearly a century of growing turmoil.

CHECKUP

1. IDENTIFY: tribute, Nurhachi, Manchus, queue, wok, "poor man's food," philology, White Lotus Rebellion.

2. What were the reasons for the decline in foreign trade and overseas explorations during the Ming dynasty?

3. What were the four classes of society, according to Confucianism? How did the Ming emperors reinforce this classification?

4. Give examples of the popular culture that developed in China during the Ming and Ch'ing dynasties.

5. Why did the population of China increase during the Ming and Ch'ing dynasties?

6. What were the reasons for the decline of the Ch'ing dynasty?

Japan prospered under the Tokugawa shogunate

Early Japan was influenced by the culture of China, its most powerful neighbor in Asia. However, until the late 1500's, Japan followed a course of political development that was more like that of Europe than of China.

As you read in Chapter 8, the ancient Japanese empire declined after 800. In its place came feudalism, similar to the system in medieval Europe.

From about 1460 to 1560 Japan experienced a period of complete, or "high," feudalism. There no longer was any central political authority. Emperors continued to reign in Heian (Kyoto), but they had long since ceased to rule the entire country. Instead, several hundred daimyo, or local feudal lords, controlled the land and people in their own domains.

In the late 1400's the Japanese daimyo began fighting among themselves for survival and supremacy. This also happened in Europe, as you will recall from your reading in Chapter 13. In France, England, and several other late feudal societies, these conflicts resulted in the establishment of strong central governments.

In Japan, however, the process did not go that far. Japan was isolated geographically. Unlike Europe, Japan did not have powerful religious or language differences among its people. The struggle among the daimyo resulted in a political system that was roughly halfway between feudalism and a centralized monarchy. This was the Tokugawa (toh·koo·GAH·wah) shogunate, which was established in 1603 and lasted until 1868.

Founding of the Tokugawa shogunate

In 1467, at about the same time as the Wars of the Roses in England, rival branches of the Ashikaga (ah·shee·KAH·gah) family in Japan became involved in a dispute over the naming of the next shogun. This conflict marked the beginning of one hundred years of almost constant warfare in Japan. Local daimyo, sensing the weakness of the Ashikaga, fought for control of the country. Three daimyo in turn emerged in the late 1500's as victors in this long struggle. They were able to establish themselves as overlords to the other daimyo, but not as absolute rulers of all Japan.

Oda Nobunaga. The first of these overlords was Oda Nobunaga (noh·boo·NAH·gah), who began his career as a minor daimyo. He succeeded, by means of conquest and alliances, in capturing Kyoto in 1568. Nobunaga ended the Ashikaga shogunate in 1573 and then began to establish his power in central Japan. Before he could defeat his remaining rivals, however, he was killed by one of his own vassals.

Toyotomi Hideyoshi. Nobunaga's position as overlord was taken over by one of his other vas-

sals, Toyotomi Hideyoshi (toh·yoh·TOH·mee hee·day·OH·shee). Born into a humble peasant family, Hideyoshi had risen to a high position in Nobunaga's army as a warrior and a general. In the 1580's Hideyoshi defeated several powerful daimyo in battle and won the submission of others by threats and diplomacy.

Rather than destroying the defeated daimyo, Hideyoshi made them pledge their loyalty to him and reduced the size of their territories so they could not threaten him again. He also carried out a "sword hunt" to disarm the peasants. In doing so, he put an end to the possibility of peasants rising to become warriors. Thereafter, only people born into warrior families were able to become warriors.

In 1592 Hideyoshi invaded Korea. He was ambitious to build a far-flung empire, but he also wanted to keep Japanese warriors busy with battles overseas while he increased his power at home. At first the Japanese invasion force was successful. However, the Korean navy sank Japanese ships carrying troop reinforcements, and a Chinese army pushed the invaders back to the coast of Korea. When Hideyoshi died in 1597, the Japanese withdrew to their homeland.

Tokugawa Ieyasu. Hideyoshi's position as overlord was taken over by his most powerful vassal, Tokugawa Ieyasu (ee·ay·YAH·soo), whose headquarters were in Yedo (modern Tokyo). When some of the other daimyo resisted Ieyasu, he mobilized his allies and defeated them in 1600. In 1603 he had the emperor name him shogun. The title of shogun was to be retained in the Tokugawa family for the next 250 years.

Like Hideyoshi before him, Ieyasu did not destroy his defeated rivals. Instead, he made them swear oaths of loyalty to him and his family. He allowed the daimyo, who then numbered about 250, to keep possession of their domains. However, he reserved for himself the right to expand or reduce the size of their territories in the future.

Each daimyo was almost an absolute ruler within his own domain. He collected taxes from the local peasants and used the revenue for his own support and the support of those in his service, particularly the samurai. The Tokugawa family had its own very large domain, which included about one-fourth of the land area of Japan. Thus, the Tokugawa did not rule the entire country

Japanese culture under the Tokugawas

The Tokugawa era, which began in the early 1600's, was a period of relative calm in Japanese history. As wars were eliminated, the samurai had to lay down their swords and find pursuits other than military ones. They turned to education and became the most educated class in society. Samurai soon made up the learned professions—scholarship, medicine, and law—and became Japan's cultural elite.

This cultural refinement was reflected in numerous pursuits. *No* drama grew in popularity, as educated audiences learned to appreciate its forms and traditions (above). Portrait painting (above right) became ornate and detailed, as did the creation of everyday objects such as a wine container (right).

directly, nor did they personally tax the entire population. A degree of political and economic decentralization was maintained.

Tokugawa power

As overlords, however, the Tokugawa did have considerable influence over how the lesser daimyo behaved. This influence was backed up by the Tokugawa wealth and military power. The less powerful daimyo could not build new castles within their domains or enter into alliances with other daimyo. The daimyo had to spend every other year in Yedo, the shogun's capital, and leave their families there when they went back to their own domains.

The expense of maintaining two grand residences—one in Yedo and the other in the provinces—and of traveling back and forth in elaborate processions between them was a drain on the resources of most daimyo. As such, it was financially difficult for them to engage in revolt. The threat that their families, especially their sons and heirs, would be executed if they did revolt was another factor that restrained the daimyo.

The Pax Tokugawa

The Tokugawa shogunate was established by means of warfare, but it brought Japan a long era of peace. For more than 250 years Japan, like China under the Ming and early Ch'ing dynasties, did not experience rebellion or other violent upheavals. This period may be referred to as the **Pax Tokugawa,** or Great Peace of the Tokugawa.

The hostage system and other controls over the daimyo were one cause of peace. Another was the disarming of the peasants, a policy that was begun by Hideyoshi and continued by the Tokugawa shoguns. Yet another important cause was the Tokugawa policy of isolation, adopted after a brief period during which overseas trade was permitted.

Foreign contacts. Even before the invasion of Korea under Hideyoshi, Japanese sailors and traders had gone overseas. In the early 1400's, during the Ashikaga shogunate, Japanese ships had sailed to Korea and China, seeking profitable trade. If refused, as they often were, the Japanese resorted to piracy, taking whatever they could get from the local inhabitants by force of arms.

These Japanese traders sailed mostly from ports in western Japan, closest to the Asian continent. The goods they brought back—whether paid for or stolen—contributed to the wealth of local daimyo in that part of the country.

In the mid-1500's these same daimyo found another source of wealth. This was by means of trade with the Portuguese ships that began appearing in Japanese waters in the mid-1500's. Portuguese traders introduced two things to Japan that later Tokugawa shoguns found undesirable. One was the musket, an early rifle that gave anyone who possessed it a clear advantage over an opponent armed only with a sword. The other was Christianity, which taught loyalty to a power greater than the Tokugawa shogun.

Closing the country. Fearing unrestricted foreign trade and the new foreign religion as possible sources of revolt against them, the Tokugawa "closed the country" in the late 1630's. No ocean-going ships could be built, and the Japanese were no longer allowed to go abroad. The Portuguese traders and the Catholic missionaries they brought with them—about whom you will learn more in the next section—were driven away. Only a small number of Dutch and Chinese merchants were allowed to live in Nagasaki, a port city on the island of Kyushu. The small amount of trade they conducted was controlled by the Tokugawa shoguns themselves.

Thus Japan, like China, turned inward and tried to ignore the outside world. As an island country, without any land frontiers across which people might slip unnoticed, Japan's isolation was even more complete than China's. Foreign contacts were almost completely eliminated.

Life and culture under the Tokugawa

The Tokugawa shoguns, like the emperors of China, did not believe in progress. They wanted to create a stable society instead. To achieve this goal, they borrowed a number of Confucian—that is, Chinese—ideas and institutions, which they learned about mostly from books.

To begin with, they adopted, with a few modifications, the Confucian view of social classes. Warriors were ranked first. They performed

Evening Squall at Ohashi

The emergence of popular culture in Tokugawa Japan was reflected in the subjects of woodblock prints. Recreational and theatrical scenes as well as commonplace activities such as fishing and farming were captured by the gifted artists and printmakers of the 1700's and 1800's.

In this woodblock print by Ando Hiroshige, working people are putting up umbrellas to protect themselves from the rain as they hurry over a wooden bridge. The artist shows a single moment caught in time. As we look at the picture, we can feel the suddenness of the storm and the sensation of the rain on our skin.

Prints such as this were the result of a collaboration of skilled artists and craftspeople. A publisher suggested the subject and directed the production of the print. The artist then made the first drawing, which the engraver cut into a series of woodblocks. Finally the printer chose the colors and applied one color to each block. Specially made paper would be pressed onto each of the blocks in succession, and the accumulation of color produced the total picture. Usually an edition of about 200 impressions was printed, to be sold in the publisher's shop.

The technique of printing by woodblock was first developed under the T'ang dynasty in China and was brought into Japan in the 700's A.D. In the late 1700's and early 1800's, as it became more popular, it reflected the tastes of a people emerging from a feudal society.

roughly the same role as scholar-officials in China. Warriors were followed by peasants, artisans, and merchants, in descending order of importance.

In Japan, membership in these classes was hereditary. Sons were required to follow the occupations of their fathers, and no one, male or female, was allowed to move freely about the country. If a person was born into an artisan family in the city of Osaka, he or she was considered a member of the artisan class for life and was expected to remain forever in Osaka.

Second, the Tokugawa shoguns encouraged education in the Confucian classics for members of the warrior class. Schools were established in every domain to prepare young warriors for their new, peacetime role as officials. No civil service examination system was established, however. In Japan, warriors became officials by birth alone. If they were born into low-ranking warrior families, they became low-ranking officials in their domains. If born into high-ranking families, they became high-ranking officials.

As a further means of achieving stability, all warriors were required to live in the castle town of their daimyo. Instead of living off the income of their own estates in the countryside, they now received yearly payments from their daimyo. The amount was determined by the warrior's rank. This policy deprived warriors of the opportunity to develop independent sources of wealth or power. Thus the chances that they could revolt against their lords were reduced.

Change in Tokugawa Japan

As in China, social, economic, and political change could not be prevented in Tokugawa Japan. Much of the change that occurred, slowly

425

but steadily, was similar to change in China. Cities grew in size and importance. Internal trade expanded, and different regions began to specialize in different crops and handicrafts. The growth of cities and the increasing wealth of merchants and artisans led to the rise of a popular culture. By the early 1700's new forms of literature, theater, and art had appeared and taken root. These new forms all catered to the tastes and life styles of ordinary city residents.

In at least one very important way change in Japan differed from change in China—and resembled the changes that had taken place in Europe.

As you recall from the previous section, the population grew steadily in Ming and Ch'ing China, reaching 300 million in 1800. This growth was brought about by peace and by the production of more food. When new lands were brought under cultivation and when more or better crops were grown, more people could be fed. In China, population growth followed and kept pace with improvements in agriculture. There was no surplus beyond what China needed to maintain its existing way of life.

In Tokugawa Japan, the population grew rapidly at first, for basically the same reasons as in China—peace and improvements in agriculture. After about 1750, however, population growth slowed down, while agriculture continued to improve. A surplus beyond what Japan needed to maintain its existing way of life was created. In England a similar surplus was used to finance the Industrial Revolution, about which you will read in the next chapter. No such revolution occurred in Tokugawa Japan, but the potential for it existed. Japan, like China, found itself behind the West in the 1800's. Unlike China, however, Japan was in a position to catch up fairly quickly. The surpluses that had been produced could be used to finance industrialization in Japan.

CHECKUP

1. IDENTIFY: Oda Nobunaga, Toyotomi Hideyoshi, Tokugawa Ieyasu, Pax Tokugawa.

2. How were the Tokugawa shoguns able to control the daimyo?

3. Why did the Tokugawa shoguns decide to "close the country"?

4. What Chinese ideas and institutions were adopted by the Tokugawa shoguns?

5. Why was Japan in a better position than China to finance industrialization?

Europeans influenced East Asia and India

By turning inward and abandoning overseas expansion, China and Japan had lost the chance to control the oceans of East Asia themselves. Eventually those oceans came to be dominated by European nations, as you read in Chapter 16. The presence of Europeans—first in trading ships and then in gunboats—confronted China and Japan with serious problems.

First to arrive were the Portuguese in the 1500's, followed by the Dutch. In the 1700's British ships sailed into East Asian waters, followed by French and American ships. China and Japan were able to fend off the Portuguese, but not the later, more powerful seafaring nations.

The Portuguese in China and Japan

The first Portuguese ships reached the southeastern coast of China about 1514 and reached Japan, farther to the east, in the mid-1500's. After long years of negotiation the Chinese, as you recall, allowed the Portuguese to establish a trading station at Macao. In Japan the Portuguese engaged in trade with some of the daimyo. In both countries, however, Portugal's commercial impact was less important than its religious impact.

The Jesuit missionaries who arrived on Portuguese ships enjoyed considerable success in China and Japan. In China they used their knowledge of advanced Western astronomy to gain admission to the emperor's circle. By helping to revise the Chinese calendar, they proved themselves useful to the emperor, whose duties still included predicting eclipses and the timing of the seasons. The emperor gave the Jesuit missionaries official positions in his palace, where they were able to make numerous converts to Christianity among high-ranking Chinese officials.

In Japan the Jesuits concentrated their efforts on converting the daimyo. When a daimyo was converted, the missionaries were able to build churches and seek converts throughout the domain that he controlled. By the early 1600's almost 500,000 Japanese had been converted to Christianity.

The success of the Jesuits caused concern among the Tokugawa shoguns. Fearing that Japanese Christians might revolt against their rule and receive help from Europe in doing so, the shoguns outlawed Christianity. The Portuguese traders and the missionaries were forced to leave Japan in the early 1600's. In China, about 100 years later, the Ch'ing emperors also turned against the Jesuits—who had become involved in palace politics—and began to suppress Christianity. In 1724 Christianity was denounced as a subversive, anti-Confucian sect.

By this time Portugal's position in Asia had been weakened by troubles at home and by competition from the Dutch. Portugal and the Roman Catholic Church had to retreat from China and Japan. The Dutch, whose interests centered on the spice trade in Southeast Asia, did not press actively for contacts with China. They were also willing to accept a strictly controlled trading relationship with the Tokugawa shogunate.

The British in China

In the early 1700's British ships began arriving frequently at Canton, China, where a British trading post had been established in 1699. The product they wanted most was tea, which the Dutch had introduced to Europe in the previous century. Great Britain was rapidly becoming "a nation of tea drinkers," and Chinese teas were thought to be the best in the world.

The new trade in Chinese teas was monopolized by the British East India Company. The company was willing to accept Chinese restrictions on its activities in order to get adequate supplies of tea. Its ships came only to Canton and traded only with a small number of officially licensed Chinese merchants. The Chinese merchants in turn paid large fees to the Chinese government. Only a few representatives of the East India Company were allowed to stay in Canton, in a special "foreign settlement" located outside the city walls. They could not bring their families with them, and they were subject to Chinese laws.

Crisis in Chinese-British relations

For a time, the Chinese were able to control the British in these and other ways. Contact between the British and the Chinese was kept at a minimum. In the late 1700's, however, two new developments led to a crisis in China's relations with Great Britain and other Western countries.

One of these developments was the result of the steady expansion of the tea trade in previous decades. The East India Company had paid for its purchases of Chinese tea by imports of raw cotton from India to China. Eventually, Chinese demand for raw cotton, used to supply the many weavers in central China, reached its upper limit. The British demand for tea, however, kept on increasing. The company had to find some new product to exchange for tea. That product was opium, a habit-forming narcotic.

Opium was produced in British India and exported to China in increasing quantities from the late 1700's onward. As opium addiction spread among the Chinese people, the government became alarmed. Addiction spread among soldiers and low-ranking officials, as well as among merchants and artisans. The government was also alarmed because so much of China's silver supply was being used to pay for the growing volume of opium imports.

The second development was the spread of free trade ideas in the West. Not all British traders worked for the East India Company. Those who tried to operate independently in Asia resented the monopolies enjoyed by the British company. So did American traders, who began sailing from New England to China in the 1780's.

The British government also became increasingly concerned about securing overseas markets for the products of British industry. It sent an official mission to Peking in 1793 to request that several more Chinese ports be opened to British ships. In 1834 the British government decided that the East India Company was not being aggressive enough in encouraging British exports. It therefore abolished the company's monopoly on trade with China. An official of the British government was sent to Canton to develop greater trade.

The British in Asia

The most remarkable British commander in Asia was Robert Clive (above), who dominated India in the mid-1700's. Clive's greatest victory was the battle of Plassey. With his Indian allies, he defeated a much larger force of French and other Indian troops. The Indians came to the battle led by richly decorated elephants and musicians (below right).

Asian culture captured the British imagination. Porcelain was made in China especially for the European market. A plate, for example, was decorated with a European couple in a garden (above right). The British were attracted to another Asian product, tea. A vase painting (below) shows tea leaves being prepared for the beverage that the British would make almost a national drink.

British demands

Unlike the representatives of the East India Company, officials of the British government would not accept restrictions on their behavior while in China. They demanded to be treated as the representatives of a nation equal to China in every respect. China, however, demanded that the tribute system be maintained. Only those who accepted China and the Chinese emperor as superior were allowed to petition the government for "favors." The British mission to Peking in 1793 had not succeeded in getting more ports opened. The official sent to Canton in 1834 was unable to work out a trade agreement between Great Britain and China.

In the mid-1830's the Chinese launched a campaign to eliminate the opium trade. The British demanded full and equal diplomatic relations as the price for their cooperation. Neither side would compromise. The result was the Opium War of 1839, which lasted for three years. You will read about this war in Chapter 23.

Europeans in India

In India the Europeans had less trouble establishing their influence than in China or Japan. The Portuguese had established trading posts in the 1500's. The Mogul emperors, the chief local power, were unable to dislodge the Portuguese. Nor could they resist the English, who in the 1600's began increasingly to replace the Portuguese as the chief European presence in India.

As you read in Chapter 16, England's trade with India was controlled by the East India Company, founded in 1600. The main purpose of the company was to obtain Indian products, such as cotton, silks, and spices, for trade.

The East India Company had footholds at Bombay, at Calcutta, and at Madras (see map, page 378–79). Its chief rivals were the French, who had established a trading company at Pondicherry. The English and French companies were interested in commercial profits, not in Indian colonies. They used armed guards or soldiers only to protect their property. There were just a few English and French citizens living in India.

Competition between the British and the French in India increased during the 1700's, when the Mogul Empire dissolved into hundreds of small states. Taking advantage of the chaos, each side made alliances with rival Indian states.

British-French rivalry in India came to a head during the Seven Years' War, which began in 1756 (see Chapter 15). The British trading post at Calcutta lay within the important Indian state of Bengal, whose ruler was allied with the French. Bengal troops captured Calcutta, imprisoned 146 British, and locked them up overnight in a small jail cell that has since been called the "Black Hole of Calcutta." By the next morning, 123 of the prisoners had died of suffocation.

The British East India Company, under its military leader Robert Clive, fought back. In a series of decisive victories in the 1750's and 1760's, the British took Pondicherry and crushed the French and their Indian allies.

Although the Treaty of Paris in 1763 restored Pondicherry to the French, most of India now lay open to the control or influence of Great Britain. Despite uprisings and wars in India, British control there was not seriously challenged again for nearly 200 years.

CHECKUP

1. IDENTIFY: Black Hole of Calcutta, Clive.

2. Why were the Jesuits successful at first in making converts to Christianity in China? Why were they later expelled?

3. How did the opium trade between British India and China begin?

4. What were the results of the Seven Years' War in India?

European nations began to dominate Africa

European nations also began to establish themselves in Africa. As in Asia, their main interest was trade. Trade was also an important feature of the African economy, and therefore most Africans welcomed the opportunity to barter with Europeans for new or scarce goods. Many Afri-

How do we know?

ORAL HISTORY From the earliest times, people have told stories about the past. Often lacking a written language, they have passed these stories from generation to generation. We call such tales "oral history" or the "oral tradition."

Some of the best examples of oral history come from Africa. Africans developed writing long after the Europeans did, and therefore their histories were kept alive by word of mouth. Every village had an old man called a "griot" who memorized long narratives about the local tribes and families. The "griot" trained younger men, who listened to the oral histories until they knew them well enough to become "griots" themselves. This required remarkable feats of memory. Sometimes the training took as much as 40 years.

These stories have been the chief means of keeping records in Africa since ancient times. American Indians used a similar system to preserve tribal histories. In recent years historians have begun to tap this extraordinary source of information. In some cases, it can help us understand a tribe's attitudes. The stories describe how land was obtained, how people were named, and how rules of behavior were established. They also deal with the nature of the gods, with death, and with the physical universe. Thus we can learn what a people believes and considers important.

Historians can also learn what actually happened in the past, by checking the stories against other kinds of information, such as traveler's accounts or archeological findings. They can trace families; they can obtain accounts of great battles; and they can discover why a city was abandoned or another one was built.

Oral history exists in almost every civilization, from the epics of ancient Sumer and Greece to the ballads of the Russian past. In recent years, thanks to the invention of the tape recorder, there have been systematic efforts to build up our store of oral history in many areas, from Presidents of the United States to the tellers of tales in Africa's villages.

---

cans also viewed the Europeans as possible allies in local political struggles.

At first the Europeans did not venture into the interior of Africa but remained on the coast. There, from ships or forts, they carried on their trade for African products, such as gum, grain, and gold.

One of the most important trade goods brought by the Europeans was iron, which was used to make hoes and other agricultural tools. Although iron was common in Africa, the European bars of iron were often cheaper and of better quality than the local variety. The Europeans also introduced new food crops, such as corn, which spread quickly through much of the African continent.

In the early stages of trade, Europeans and Africans shared relationships that benefited both.

Unfortunately, this positive relationship between Europeans and Africans did not last very long.

The Portuguese in Africa

Portuguese explorers, as you recall, had sailed along the African coast in their search for a new route to the East. A series of forts and small settlements along the African coast marked the gradual progress of the Portuguese on the route eastward. These forts and settlements served as strongholds from which passing ships could take on provisions. They were also the starting points of missionaries who were to convert Africans. The relationship that Portugal established with Africa set the pattern for other European nations that followed in Portugal's footsteps.

At first the Portuguese, largely under the influence of missionaries, were friendly with the Africans. In the Kongo kingdom the Portuguese treated the king as a legitimate ruler and "brother" king to the Portuguese ruler. In turn, the king of the Kongo welcomed the newcomers and accepted baptism. His advisers adopted European dress and manners. Envoys from the Kongo traveled to Europe, and the king corresponded with the pope. The cordial relations, however, soon collapsed because of the economic interests of Portuguese traders.

Portugal and the slave trade

On an island off the coast of West Africa, the Portuguese had set up plantations that required slaves to work the land. The Portuguese turned to the African mainland for slaves. As plantation agriculture spread to Brazil and the Caribbean islands, the demand for slaves increased. As a result, by the early 1500's the slave trade had become the main basis of European relations with Africa.

In the Kongo the effects of the slave trade were disastrous. Slave raids undermined the authority of the king, and slave traders, taking advantage of local rivalries, soon dominated politics. In the 1600's the authority of the Kongo king finally collapsed totally and was replaced by a number of small, independent chiefdoms.

A similar fate befell the neighboring kingdom of Ndonga, in what is today Angola. A Portuguese settlement was founded there in 1575. Slave raiding from this base weakened central authority in the kingdom. Civil wars broke out, and the kingdom was doomed.

Other nations and the slave trade

In the 1500's Portugal had dominated international commerce. However, in the 1600's, as you have read, the Netherlands emerged as the leading naval power. It founded a colony at Java, in the East Indies. In 1652 it set up a provisioning station in southern Africa, at the Cape of Good Hope, to supply meat and fresh vegetables to ships sailing to the East Indies from Europe. Unlike the Portuguese, the Dutch government never wanted to establish colonies in Africa. Despite official opposition, however, the small station at Cape Town

expanded and destroyed the native population of herders and hunters. After 1800 the British took over the Dutch colony at the Cape and from it developed the modern nation of South Africa.

In the 1700's Great Britain and France became the dominant naval powers of the world. At strategic points along the West African coast, they built forts from which to carry on the slave trade. Great Britain, with the largest merchant fleet in the world, took the lead in the slave trade. In 1713, following the War of the Spanish Succession, it had received a monopoly to transport slaves to the Americas. Although Great Britain was the biggest carrier of slaves, French, Dutch, and Spanish ships actively participated also.

The slave trade had a brutal and dehumanizing effect on all involved. In the 1500's about 2,000 slaves per year were shipped from Africa. At the height of the trade, in the 1780's, as many as 80,000 slaves per year were forcibly taken. It is estimated that a total of 11 million to 14 million Africans were enslaved. Possibly as many more died on the hard trip from the interior of the continent to the coast. This tragic loss meant that Africa's population did not increase between 1650 and 1800, when Europe's population was growing rapidly.

African slavery

Africans themselves practiced slavery, but it was very different from that of the Americas. African slavery included a wide range of relationships, from voluntary service to enforced captivity. In each case, however, the slave had a recognized place in the society, with rights as well as obligations. In addition, slave children were usually considered free, and slaves generally had the right to buy back their freedom. Africans treated slaves as people with a role in the society. Europeans, on the other hand, considered slaves as property to be bought or sold for the profit of their labor. Slaves had no place in the society.

Europeans often obtained the help of Africans in gathering and transporting slaves. Some African societies and individuals had joined in the slave trade willingly to obtain arms and other goods from Europe. In turn, neighboring groups either had to participate in the trade or be victimized by it. Slave raiding introduced a cycle of vio-

Varieties of slavery in Africa

The use of Africans as slaves began long ago. During the Middle Ages, Arab traders bought captives from African chiefs and sold them for a profit in the Middle East. At one of the Middle Eastern slave markets, a picture of the 1200's shows a merchant with his human wares, while the price is weighed out in a scale (above). In the 1700's the slave trade continued to begin in African villages (below). A French engraving shows a group of slaves at the start of a long journey that would take them, most probably, across the Atlantic.

The distaste for slavery was growing, however. Slavery had slowly been dying out in Europe, and in the 1770's it was abolished in Great Britain. Yet, despite petitions for freedom (right), emancipation in North and South America had to wait until the late 1800's.

lence from which it was difficult to escape. In these violent circumstances, some African groups grew more powerful, while others, victims of the trade, were weakened or destroyed. As the demand for slaves sputtered to a halt in the 1800's, many of these victimized societies were able to recover. Others, it is believed, disappeared entirely.

The European impact on Africa

Despite the slave trade, not all of the effects of European contact with Africa were negative. New crops, such as corn, peanuts, and manioc, were brought to Africa from the Americas and became important foods for Africans. In many cases, European religious ideas and symbols enriched African religious traditions. In central Africa, for example, the cross became an important folk symbol, and local churches combined Christian and African practices.

Contact with Europeans also led to the emergence of a new class of Africans, so-called merchant princes, who made fortunes from the slave trade. In many cases, these new leaders used their influence to obtain the respect of Europeans for local customs and to lessen European violence on local populations.

Thus the impact of Europe on Africa was enormous. Most significant was the slave trade, which affected both Africans and Europeans. Although Europeans continued to remain on the coast, the effects of the slave trade penetrated into the African interior. Only a few societies were able to escape its impact.

One of the most subtle effects of the slave trade was the gradual development by Europeans of certain mistaken ideas, or myths. Myths of white "racial superiority" and African "primitiveness" grew up as a justification for the slave trade. These myths would persist long after the slave trade ended in the 1800's.

CHECKUP

1. IDENTIFY: Kongo, Ndonga, merchant princes.

2. Why did Portuguese traders begin to acquire slaves from Africa?

3. How did the African slave trade affect the African kingdoms?

4. How were slaves treated differently by Africans than by Europeans?

5. What effects did European contact have on the African people?

The nations of Latin America gained their independence

You will remember from Chapter 16 that several European nations established colonies in southern North America, Central America, and South America. This region, from the northern border of Mexico southward to the tip of South America, and including the West Indies, is called Latin America. Most of it was settled by Spaniards and Portuguese, whose languages are derived from Latin. Even though the Latin American colonies were far away from Europe, they were controlled and strongly influenced by the home countries of Spain and Portugal for over 300 years.

By the early 1800's, European nations had been strongly affected by the French Revolution and the Napoleonic Wars. Some of the effects were also felt by their colonies in Latin America.

The land

Latin America is about 8 million square miles (20.7 million square kilometers) in area. Brazil alone is almost as large as the United States.

Vast rivers reach deep into the heart of South America. The Orinoco, the Amazon, and the Río de la Plata, with their tributaries, make up some of the world's most extensive river systems.

Latin America has many rugged and impressive mountains. The Andes Mountains extend along most of the western coast of South America. There is a great variety of climate: dry semi-desert areas in Mexico and along the west coast of South America; rain forests in Central America and northeastern South America; grassy plains, called pampas, in southeastern South America; and the llanos (LAH·nohs), flat, treeless plains in northern South America (see map, page 435).

The Americas were first inhabited by people who had migrated from Asia (see Chapter 11).

Latin America was the home of advanced civilizations—those of the Mayas, Aztecs, and Incas—and had a greater population than regions to the north.

Brazil was settled by the Portuguese, while almost all the rest of Latin America was colonized by the Spaniards. Eventually Spanish possessions in the Americas were divided into four parts, called viceroyalties because each was ruled by a viceroy (see inset map, page 439).

The economy

Colonial society in the Americas—in both the Spanish and Portuguese territories—was organized to provide as much income as possible for the rulers of the home country, for merchants engaged in overseas trade, and for the white colonists. The profit of the colonial system came mostly from the mining of silver and gold and the planting of sugar and other tropical products.

The basic economic unit of colonial Latin America was a self-sufficient farming estate that resembled a medieval manor. Many such estates were given as royal grants to court favorites. The owners were often absentee landlords—that is, they did not live on their estates. Overseers managed the estates and supervised the workers.

It was difficult to find enough workers for mines and farms because many Spaniards and Portuguese felt that physical labor was degrading. Europeans enslaved the native Indians, but forced labor and new diseases brought death to thousands of them. In the Peruvian mines, the Indian death rate was as high as 90 percent.

In the early 1500's, the first slaves from Africa arrived in the West Indies. Each year thereafter, thousands were captured in Africa and shipped to Latin America to work as slaves in mines and on farming estates.

The Spanish and Portuguese colonies seemed very wealthy to other Europeans. Mexico City, Lima, and other cities were large and had cathedrals, universities, and government palaces. The Spanish Empire was protected by immense fortresses at ports like San Juan in Puerto Rico. The Spaniards and Portuguese, fearing competition from the British and French, greatly improved the trade and administration of their Latin American colonies during the 1700's.

Colonial society

As in the home countries, society in the colonies was divided into social classes based on privilege. The highest ranks of society consisted of the royal bureaucrats, the owners of large estates, and the great merchants. There was an enormous social gap between them and the town workers, peasants, and slaves. The situation in Latin America was worse than in Europe because of racial discrimination. Colonial society was ruled by whites, while those at the bottom were native Americans and blacks, many of them still speaking different languages. There were laws, furthermore, that upheld racial distinctions.

In between there were people of mixed race—**mestizo,** who were of Indian and white backgrounds, and **mulatto,** who were of black and white ancestry. Mestizos and mulattoes were useful to the upper class because they were often town dwellers with special skills. For example, they were often able to read. However, mestizos and mulattoes had no special status in the colonial legal system. They were looked down upon by the whites, who feared their ambition.

Growing discontent

By the late 1700's there was increasing unrest in the Latin American colonies. It fed upon news and ideas from North America and Europe. For mestizos and mulattoes especially, the equality proclaimed by the American and French revolutions had great meaning.

Even the white upper class had reasons to look upon those revolutions with interest. Native-born whites—called **creoles**—found it difficult to rise to higher official jobs because persons born in Spain or Portugal were given preference.

Moreover, the mercantile system angered the creoles because it raised the prices of imported goods. British colonists had had the same complaint, but the Spanish and Portuguese colonists were worse off. Their home countries had little industry, and their merchants supplied the colonies with goods from Great Britain and France, after taking a further profit as go-betweens. Smuggling was therefore widespread. The Spanish colonies also resented having to pay taxes to finance Spain's wars.

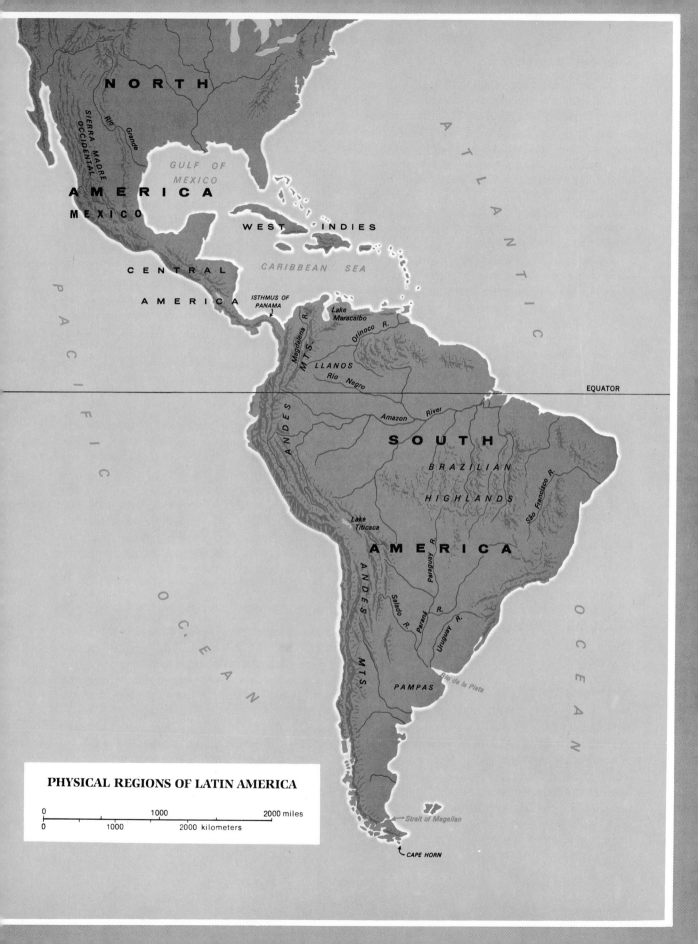

PHYSICAL REGIONS OF LATIN AMERICA

Haiti's slave revolution

By the early 1800's the situation in Spain's American colonies was ripe for revolution. There had been uprisings in several of the Spanish viceroyalties in the 1780's, but they were put down. The only successful revolt that began before 1800 took place on the island of Hispaniola, in the West Indies. The French owned the western part of the island and the Spanish the eastern part (see inset map, page 439).

In the western part of Hispaniola—Haiti—the French had set up a plantation colony to grow sugar and coffee. The plantations were worked by African slaves. When the French Revolution broke out, the free mulattoes and the black slaves of Haiti revolted, demanding the same rights as the white French settlers. Under the leadership of François Dominique Toussaint L'Ouverture (too·SAN loo·ver·TOOR), a black man who had been a slave, they won control of the island.

Napoleon sent an army to try to reestablish slavery and French authority. The French captured Toussaint, and he eventually died in prison. Later, the French were defeated by the rebel army and in 1803 gave up the island.

Haiti was proclaimed an independent nation in 1804. The eastern portion of Hispaniola—Santo Domingo—eventually was regained by Spain and did not become independent until 1821. Today this eastern portion is known as the Dominican Republic.

The Haitian revolution was the only large slave rebellion to succeed completely. It sent a shock wave all through the Americas, where slavery was still practiced everywhere. It was important to the United States, because it forced Napoleon to abandon his idea of a North American empire.

Mexico and Central America

As you have read, Napoleon conquered Spain in 1808 and made his brother king. In the following years the country was the scene of savage fighting in the Peninsular Campaign. Even after Napoleon's defeat at Waterloo, Spain was weakened by internal troubles. These circumstances provided the Spanish colonists with a golden opportunity, since Spain was not in a position to offer much resistance to independence movements.

One of the first important uprisings in Spanish territory was started in 1810 by Miguel Hidalgo, a Mexican priest. He advocated the independence of Mexico from Spain. Hidalgo was the leader of an enormous army of Indian peasants, who attacked creoles as well as Spanish-born whites.

After some early victories, Hidalgo was captured and executed, and his peasant army was dispersed in 1811. Another priest, José Morelos, assumed leadership. Morelos wanted land reform and the abolition of slavery. He was captured and shot in 1815.

In 1814 the Spanish king had been restored to his throne. He was very conservative and was looked upon favorably by the Mexican white upper class, which had been frightened by Hidalgo. When the king's power was taken away by a liberal army rebellion in 1820, the Mexican upper class feared that reforms would be applied in the colonies. Therefore, in 1821 they carried out an independence movement of their own. Its principal leader was a militia general named Agustín Iturbide (ee·toor·BEE·thay), who proclaimed himself emperor. He was soon overthrown, and in 1824 Mexico became a republic.

Central America, where there had also been revolts against Spanish authority, was briefly a part of Iturbide's Mexican empire. By 1823, however, representatives from Guatemala, El Salvador, Honduras, Nicaragua, and Costa Rica met to form the United Provinces of Central America. This union had a federal constitution, an elective president, and an assembly.

Spanish South America

Independence came quickly in the southernmost viceroyalty of La Plata. In 1810, as the Spanish government was falling to French troops, creole rebels seized control of the government in La Plata. In 1816 they declared the independence of the United Provinces of La Plata, later named Argentina. Meanwhile, Paraguay had already broken away and declared its own independence.

In the rest of South America, the struggle became a civil war and was long and bloody. Its leader was Simón Bolívar (boh·LEE·vahr). Bolívar led a revolt in his native city of Caracas in 1810. It was unsuccessful, as were further revolts in 1813 and 1815. Finally in 1819 he raised another army

Latin American society

As the people of Latin America struggled for independence, strong leaders emerged. José de San Martín, shown with his military aides (left), was a creole born in Argentina. He became famous for leading a rebel army in an extraordinary march across the Andes. San Martín liberated Peru, but then gave up his command to Simón Bolívar (above). Bolívar was also a creole, but he had been to Europe and was much influenced by the French Revolution. Like San Martín, he was revered as a warrior hero.

Yet independence did not bring freedom to all the people, or change the way in which the upper classes in Latin America lived. Well-to-do families continued the patterns set much earlier, such as the Brazilian family (below), leaving for church accompanied by slaves.

in what is now Venezuela, crossed the Andes, and defeated the Spanish at Boyacá (see map, opposite). Bolívar was made president, with almost absolute power, of a new nation called Great Colombia. It included the countries that are known today as Colombia, Venezuela, Ecuador, and Panama.

Despite Bolívar's success, the Spanish remained strongly entrenched in the viceroyalty of Peru. An Argentine general, José de San Martín, gathered an army and made a difficult crossing of the Andes into the region known as Chile. He joined forces with the Chileans and overcame Spanish resistance there in 1818.

From Chile, San Martín's forces sailed north to capture the city of Lima. They were met there by the army of Bolívar, to whom San Martín turned over leadership. After several years of hard fighting, the rest of Peru was cleared of forces loyal to Spain. By 1825 the northern territory of Upper Peru became a separate republic, named Bolivia in honor of Bolívar.

Brazil

When Napoleon's army invaded Portugal in 1808, King John VI fled to Brazil and set up his headquarters at Rio de Janeiro. Once there, he elevated Brazil to a realm equal to Portugal, under his crown, and opened its ports to foreign trade. Even after the overthrow of Napoleon, King John stayed in Brazil. In 1820 there was a revolt in Portugal, similar to Spain's, and John was persuaded to return. He left his son Pedro in charge of the Brazilian government.

The Brazilian creoles were angered when the Portuguese tried to turn Brazil back into a colony. They persuaded King Pedro to become ruler of an independent Brazil, and he agreed. Independence was declared in 1822, and a constitutional empire was proclaimed. Brazil and Argentina struggled over territory between them. After several invasions, local patriots in this territory succeeded in gaining independence in 1825, calling their new country Uruguay.

Thus, almost all of Latin America had become independent by 1825 (see map, opposite). Only in Cuba, Jamaica, Puerto Rico, the Guianas, British Honduras, and a few smaller islands of the Caribbean did colonial rule continue.

Latin American independence

The British had helped the Latin Americans gain their independence. They were eager to increase their trade with the region, which they imagined to be richer than it really was. Also, they saw Latin Americans as potential allies against continental Europe, which was growing more conservative. (You will read more about this in Chapter 20.) Therefore the British provided arms and ships and lent funds to the rebels.

The United States had been distracted by its war with Great Britain in 1812. It also had then been unwilling to anger Spain while trying to get that country to agree to give up Florida. Even after that was achieved in 1819, sympathy for the Latin American patriots was limited. Americans, however, saw the region as a vast new market and became alarmed, along with the British, when the Spanish tried to regain their colonies.

The Monroe Doctrine. In 1823 President James Monroe sent a message to Congress that came to be known as the **Monroe Doctrine.** It declared that the United States would not interfere in any of Europe's remaining colonies in the Western Hemisphere. However, it would oppose any attempt by European nations to reestablish lost colonies, to form new colonies, or to interfere with any of the American governments. The United States pledged at the same time not to intervene in Europe's affairs.

Although European leaders denounced the Monroe Doctrine, no nation of Europe tried to defy it or test it. The British, with their powerful navy, supported Latin American independence. This combination of both British and United States opposition discouraged European powers from meddling in Latin American affairs.

The Latin American governments had not been informed beforehand of the Monroe Doctrine and at the time did not attach great importance to it. The United States became the first country to grant them diplomatic recognition, and Great Britain helped them to obtain recognition from their former home countries.

New nations. Of the former Spanish and Portuguese territories, only Brazil managed to maintain national unity. Ecuador and Venezuela broke away from Great Colombia. The United Provinces of Central America crumbled into five sepa-

NEW NATIONS IN LATIN AMERICA
about 1825

LIBERATED TERRITORY

Formerly Spanish
Formerly Portuguese
Formerly French

× Battle site

0   1000 miles
0   1000 kilometers

UNITED STATES

MEXICO

GULF OF MEXICO

Mexico City

PACIFIC OCEAN

BAHAMAS (Br.)

WEST INDIES

CUBA (Sp.)

JAMAICA (Br.)

SANTO DOMINGO

PUERTO RICO (Sp.)

HAITI

BRITISH HONDURAS

GUATEMALA

HONDURAS

EL SALVADOR

NICARAGUA

COSTA RICA

PANAMA

UNITED PROVINCES OF CENTRAL AMERICA

CARIBBEAN SEA

TRINIDAD (Br.)

Caracas

Boyacá 1819 ×

VENEZUELA

COLOMBIA

Bogotá

GREAT COLOMBIA

GUIANAS

(Br.) (Du.) (Fr.)

ATLANTIC OCEAN

Quito

ECUADOR

BOLÍVAR

PERU

Lima

SAN MARTÍN

BOLIVIA

La Paz

Sucre

BRAZIL

PARAGUAY

Asunción

Rio de Janeiro

ARGENTINA

Mendoza

Santiago

Buenos Aires

URUGUAY

Montevideo

CHILE

PATAGONIA (UNEXPLORED)

Strait of Magellan

LATIN AMERICA ABOUT 1790

Spanish
Portuguese
French
British
Dutch

NEW SPAIN

Mexico City

CUBA (Br.)

HISPANIOLA (Br.)

WEST INDIES

PACIFIC OCEAN

ATLANTIC OCEAN

NEW GRANADA

Bogotá

GUIANAS (Br.)

BRAZIL

PERU

Lima

LA PLATA

Rio de Janeiro

Buenos Aires

rate countries, and Argentina threatened to break up. By 1840 there were 17 countries in Latin America.

Enormous distances and geographical barriers were partly responsible. Regional rivalries arose that were impossible to overcome. Also, British and American interests discouraged Latin American unity. If Latin America were united, it would be a threat to the economic interests of the United States and Great Britain.

In 1826 Simón Bolívar had called a congress of the Latin American nations at Panama to carry forward unification. Although the outcome was not a success, the idea of Latin American unity continued to be influential.

Internal problems

The benefits that the creole upper classes in Latin America had hoped for were realized by independence. They were able to sell more abroad than ever before, at higher prices, and they were able to buy manufactured goods more cheaply. However, they were rarely able to build lasting political institutions. Latin American governments succeeded each other as often by rebellion as by elections.

The problem in part was that the growth in trade, as fast as it was, was not enough to provide the revenues needed for strong central governments. Local interests therefore challenged central authority repeatedly and successfully. Another reason was that during colonial times the figure of the king had powerfully bonded together different interests within colonial society. The new republican institutions did not have a king or the almost mystical qualities of royalty. Brazil did have an emperor—Pedro I—and was by comparison untouched by these struggles.

Another great difficulty faced by the new nations of Latin America was social injustice. The creole upper classes were not very interested in eliminating the inequalities inherited from colonial society. Some within the upper-class groups felt that even the reforms that had been carried out had gone too far.

The creoles reluctantly abolished slavery in every country—in some not until the 1850's, and in Brazil not until 1888. For the most part, creoles sought to take over the positions of privilege.

They also battled to take over the communal lands that belonged to the Indian population, claiming that they were a cause of economic backwardness. The large landed estates continued to grow during the next hundred years, even though they were inefficient as well as unjust.

The position of the Roman Catholic Church also became a tremendous issue in the new nations. Since colonial times the Church had been an important force in Latin American society. Many clergymen had held high political office, and the government had given a great deal of financial support to the Church.

After Latin American countries gained independence, liberals proposed changes in the powers of the Church. They wanted the government to take over functions that the Church had had in colonial times—for example, the exclusive right to run schools and cemeteries. In some countries, liberals wanted the government to take over the Church's extensive landholdings. Conservatives, on the other hand, resented the loss of Church rights.

It is not surprising with all these conflicts that the first 50 or 60 years of independence were a time of great internal difficulties in many Latin American countries. However, in the latter part of the 1800's, trade and government tax revenues increased. After many of the controversies had been battled to a conclusion, Latin American countries achieved some stability and economic growth.

CHECKUP

1. IDENTIFY: mestizo, mulattoes, creole, Toussaint L' Ouverture, Hidalgo, Morelos, Iturbide, Bolívar, San Martín, John VI, Pedro I, Monroe Doctrine.

2. LOCATE: Lima, Haiti, Santo Domingo, Caracas, Boyacá, Great Colombia, Rio de Janeiro.

3. What was the significance of the revolution that took place in Haiti?

4. What were the goals of the revolutions that took place in Mexico and Central America? What were the results?

5. Why did unification of large regions in South America ultimately fail?

6. What were the economic and social problems in Latin America after independence?

CHAPTER REVIEW

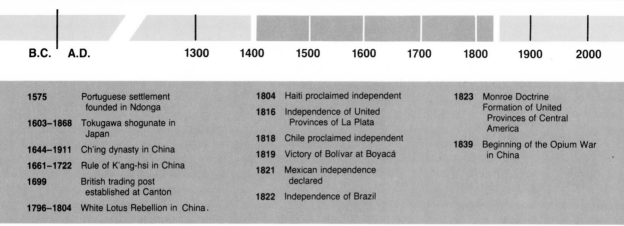

B.C.	A.D.		1300	1400	1500	1600	1700	1800	1900	2000

1575	Portuguese settlement founded in Ndonga	**1804**	Haiti proclaimed independent	**1823**	Monroe Doctrine Formation of United Provinces of Central America
1603–1868	Tokugawa shogunate in Japan	**1816**	Independence of United Provinces of La Plata		
		1818	Chile proclaimed independent	**1839**	Beginning of the Opium War in China
1644–1911	Ch'ing dynasty in China	**1819**	Victory of Bolívar at Boyacá		
1661–1722	Rule of K'ang-hsi in China	**1821**	Mexican independence declared		
1699	British trading post established at Canton				
1796–1804	White Lotus Rebellion in China.	**1822**	Independence of Brazil		

CHAPTER SUMMARY

The Ming emperors of China had little interest in foreign trade or seapower, and contacts with the outside world were kept to a minimum. In the 1600's China was conquered by the Manchus. They established the Ch'ing dynasty, which lasted until 1911. Under the Ming and Ch'ing, China enjoyed more than 400 years of peace.

During these years, the population grew rapidly, cities became larger, and trade within the country increased. By the early 1800's, however, the stability of China was declining. Discontent over increased taxes and decreased services led to a number of peasant rebellions.

In Japan, the Tokugawa shogunate was established after 100 years of almost constant warfare. A long period of peace and stable government followed. The Tokugawa shoguns limited contact with foreigners, and the country developed largely in isolation.

The impact of Europeans began to be felt increasingly in the 1700's. The Portuguese had been the first Europeans to reach China and Japan. Portuguese missionaries won many converts but were eventually expelled from both countries. The British established a trading relationship with China, but disagreements between the two countries led to the Opium War of 1839. In India, the British and the French were rivals. By the 1760's, however, the British had crushed the French and dominated India completely.

In Africa, the impact of the Europeans was even greater than in Asia. Trade, particularly of slaves, was the main feature of Europe's relations with Africa. The Europeans remained on the coast, but the effects of the slave trade reached into the interior. Millions of Africans were taken from their families, and in some cases entire kingdoms were destroyed.

Most of the colonies in Latin America had been controlled by Spain and Portugal for centuries. By the late 1700's, however, there was increasing discontent in Latin America. Haiti, a French colony, was the first to wage a successful revolt. The Spanish and Portuguese possessions soon followed suit. By 1825 nearly all of Latin America had become independent.

Great Britain and the United States supported Latin American independence. In 1823 the American president issued the Monroe Doctrine, opposing any attempt by European powers to regain former colonies.

CHECKING WHAT YOU KNOW

1. Match each item at the left with an Asian ruling family at the right. You may use a ruling family more than once.

   a. Closed off trade with the outside world except at Nagasaki.

   b. Overseas trade declined due to interest in maintaining northern frontiers.

   c. Required Chinese men to wear a queue.

   d. Moved the capital from Nanking to Peking.

   e. Encouraged education for members of warrior class.

   1. Ming dynasty
   2. Ch'ing dynasty
   3. Tokugawa shogunate

2. Match each leader at the left with the country at the right with which he is most closely associated:

a. Toussaint L'Ouverture
b. Simon Bolívar
c. Pedro I
d. Miguel Hidalgo
e. José de San Martín

1. Brazil
2. Mexico
3. Great Colombia
4. Peru
5. Haiti

3. What steps were taken by the Ming dynasty to protect China's northern frontier?

4. Why was the Pax Tokugawa successful?

5. What conditions favored revolutions in Latin America during the 1800's?

6. What was the Monroe Doctrine? Why was it issued?

PRACTICING YOUR SKILLS

1. Making comparisons. Compare the purpose of the Monroe Doctrine with the Tokugawa policy of "closing" Japan. In what ways were their goals similar? How did these policies affect European influence on Latin America and on Japan?

2. Making charts. Make a chart of the independence movements in Central and South America. Show leaders, dates of independence for each country, and the European nation that had claimed the colony or territory.

3. Analyzing information. Explain the results of European contact with each of the following: China, Japan, India, Africa. Which area most successfully resisted European influence? Why?

RELATING PAST TO PRESENT

1. Review the military problems of the Ming and Ch'ing dynasties along their land borders with central and northern Asia. Then use the *Readers' Guide to Periodical Literature* to find magazine articles that deal with the tensions between China and the Soviet Union in recent years. What are the reasons for these tensions?

2. You read on page 430 about the importance of oral history to various peoples. To get some idea of how oral history is collected today, ask several relatives or acquaintances who lived during the 1930's to recall their memories of the Depression. If possible, tape record these interviews. Are there any differences between the accounts? How would you explain them? What information can we get from oral history that we cannot get from other sources? How might you verify the accuracy of this information?

3. As you have read, Europeans transmitted their culture to the parts of the world that came under their domination. Choose an area of the world today that is experiencing the influence of Western ideas and culture. Describe some of these influences. What impact might they have on the traditional way of life in the area?

INVESTIGATING FURTHER

1. As you read on page 425, the art form of woodblock prints became popular in Japan during the Tokugawa period. Use books in your library to find the answers to the following questions: Why was this art form so popular? What was its subject matter? How did Japanese woodblock prints change in the 1800's? One source for your research might be Seiichiro Takahashi, *Traditional Woodblock Prints of Japan* (Weatherhill).

2. African tribes had long made slaves of their captives in war. However, the coming of Europeans brought great changes to the slave trade. Read Olaudah Equiano's account of his capture and sale in Philip D. Curtin, editor, *Africa Remembered* (University of Wisconsin Press). What were Equiano's reactions to the other Africans he met on his trip to the coast? What were his impressions of the Europeans?

3. Choose one of the following leaders of Latin American revolutions and find out more about his life: Simon Bolívar, José de San Martín, Miguel Hidalgo, Bernardo O'Higgins. Present your findings to the class.

UNIT REVIEW

1. Match each of the following people with the appropriate description from the list below:

   a. Leonardo da Vinci   i. Peter the
   b. Prince Henry   Great
   c. Bartholomeu Dias   j. Louis XVI
   d. Maria Theresa   k. Michelangelo
   e. Petrarch   l. Machiavelli
   f. Copernicus   m. Charles V
   g. Catherine the Great   n. Cromwell
   h. Henry VIII

   1. Built a new capital in Russia that would be a "window to Europe."
   2. Painted the "Mona Lisa."
   3. Concluded that the sun was the center of the universe.
   4. English king who broke with the Catholic Church.
   5. Hapsburg ruler protected by the Pragmatic Sanction.
   6. Sailed around the southern tip of Africa.
   7. Poet who is often called the founder of humanism.
   8. Led the revolt against Charles I in England.
   9. Russian ruler who gained the Sea of Azov and most of the Black Sea's northern shore.
   10. Started a navigators' school in Portugal.
   11. King who was executed during the French Revolution.
   12. Painted the murals on the ceiling of the Sistine Chapel.
   13. Italian Renaissance thinker who wrote about politics and government.
   14. Hapsburg who was king of Spain and emperor of the Holy Roman Empire.

2. In what ways did European art of the 1500's and 1600's reflect the new ideas and attitudes of the Renaissance?

3. How did the ideas of humanism and the Scientific Revolution change Europe?

4. What strengths and weaknesses did Austria and Prussia each have in their conflict for leadership among the German states?

5. How did each of the following rulers help to turn Prussia into a major power in Europe by the end of the 1700's: Frederick William, Frederick William I, Frederick the Great.

6. What developments in Europe made possible the explorations of the 1400's?

7. According to the theory of mercantilism, what benefits did European nations hope to get from colonial empires? How did the building of empires affect the people of the colonial areas?

8. List the powers that Parliament gained at the expense of the English monarch between 1603 and 1714.

9. How did each of the following contribute to the split between Great Britain and the American colonies:

   a. the French and Indian War
   b. the Stamp Act
   c. the Intolerable Acts

10. Describe the changes that occurred in China during the Ming and Ch'ing dynasties.

11. How did the Tokugawa shoguns achieve their goal of creating a stable society in Japan?

12. Compare the goals and achievements of the French Revolution to those of the Latin American revolutions.

13. Place each of the items listed below in one of the following categories:

    a. political change   c. religious change
    b. economic change   d. scientific change

    1. The sweet potato was introduced as an alternative to rice in China.
    2. The Council of Trent adopted many reforms.
    3. The barometer, microscope, and thermometer were invented.
    4. The 95 Theses were published, challenging the accepted authority of the time.
    5. The Spaniards established a system of viceroyalties in Latin America.
    6. Napoleon organized the Continental System.
    7. The National Convention declared France a republic.
    8. The use of the astrolabe revolutionized navigation.
    9. The Treaty of Utrecht settled the issue of the succession to the Spanish throne.

THE DEVELOPMENT OF INDUSTRIAL SOCIETY

Women in a factory packing room, showing the changing patterns of work during the Industrial Revolution

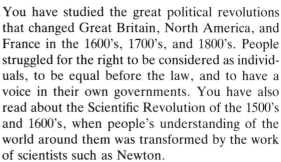

(1700–1900)

19

The Industrial Revolution Transformed the Modern World

You have studied the great political revolutions that changed Great Britain, North America, and France in the 1600's, 1700's, and 1800's. People struggled for the right to be considered as individuals, to be equal before the law, and to have a voice in their own governments. You have also read about the Scientific Revolution of the 1500's and 1600's, when people's understanding of the world around them was transformed by the work of scientists such as Newton.

Now we are going to look at a third kind of revolution, one that is neither political nor scientific. This revolution began in the 1800's, when many new machines were invented to do the work that people had done before. The changes brought about by these new inventions—this new technology—were so widespread, and affected manufacturing, or industry, so deeply, that they are referred to as the **Industrial Revolution.**

The Industrial Revolution brought a vast change in the way that goods were produced. For example, before the Industrial Revolution, cloth and tools had been made by hand, usually by skilled laborers working in their own homes or in small shops. Beginning about 1750, however, more and more goods were produced by machines. This development was possible largely because the usual source of power—animals, wind, and water—were harnessed more efficiently, and

New York City in the early 1900's

also because a new power source—steam—came into use.

The Industrial Revolution led to a large number of changes in the way people lived. Factories took the place of home workshops, and skilled artisans were replaced by factory workers. The number and the power of capitalists also grew because trade, transportation, and communications expanded, offering more opportunities and greater profits for those with money to invest. At the same time, trains replaced horse-drawn carts, and steamboats replaced sailboats. This meant that people could travel in a day to places it had taken their parents a week or more to reach. Cities grew as people moved to them looking for jobs in the new factories.

These developments took place first in Great Britain, then spread gradually to other countries. France, Germany, and the United States had a large number of industries by the late 1800's. Russia did not begin to develop major industries until after 1918, and countries like China and India are still becoming industrialized.

THE CHAPTER SECTIONS

1. The Industrial Revolution began in Great Britain

2. The factory system changed working and living conditions

3. Technology transformed transportation and communications

4. New methods and giant businesses produced an industrial economy

5. Industrialization altered population patterns and popular culture

6. Workers protested the effects of industrialization

1

The Industrial Revolution began in Great Britain

The Industrial Revolution began in Great Britain because of a combination of conditions that existed in that nation. What economists call the **factors of production**—that is, the basic resources necessary for industrialization—were available there. These factors were (1) land, (2) labor, (3) capital, (4) management, and (5) government.

Land, to the economist, includes all natural resources, of which Great Britain had a good supply. It had a great deal of coal and some iron ore. In addition, its excellent harbors aided trade, and its many rivers provided water power and inland transportation.

Great Britain also had a good labor supply. Workers were available chiefly because of changes in agriculture, about which you will read shortly.

Capital, too, was available in Great Britain. Many British people had grown wealthy from trade since the time of the Commercial Revolution (see Chapter 16). Thus they had surplus funds to invest in new businesses.

In addition, Great Britain had the people who bring together land, labor, and capital—that is, management, or those who manage businesses. In Great Britain it was not considered dishonorable for young people from the upper and middle classes to go into business. Many became managers, and a few people of the lower class now had some opportunity to rise in business.

Equally important was the fact that the British government tried to aid commercial interests. It passed laws that protected businesses and helped them expand.

In addition to all these factors of production, there was a large demand for the goods the British produced, because the British Isles and their colonies overseas were huge markets. There were also trade opportunities in many other parts of the world, which could be reached by the British navy and merchant fleet, the best in the world.

The agricultural revolution

The revolution in industry was preceded and made possible by a revolution in agriculture. It, too, began in Great Britain.

Beginning in the 1600's, English farmers began to fence off, or enclose, common lands (lands formerly used by the villagers jointly) into individual holdings. This **enclosure movement** continued into the 1700's. In this way scattered lands were combined to form larger holdings that were efficient for large-scale farming.

The enclosure movement had two chief results. (1) As large landowners added to their holdings, they forced small owners either to become tenant farmers or to give up farming and move into the cities. (2) Since land did not have to be farmed in common, agreement among numerous farmers was not necessary. Thus, it became easier for the individual farmer to experiment with different agricultural methods.

Among the first who experimented were the so-called gentlemen farmers. One of them was Jethro Tull, who lived in the early 1700's. He was bothered by the wasteful practice of scattering seeds by hand on top of the soil and over a wide area. He therefore invented what he called a seed drill, which enabled seeds to be planted in the soil in regular rows.

Experiments showed Tull that crops grew better if the weeds were removed and the soil between the rows of plants was broken up regularly. To do this work, he invented a cultivator that could be drawn by horses.

Viscount Charles Townshend, who was also an English gentleman farmer, found a way to avoid another wasteful practice. This was the system under which a certain amount of a farmer's fields remained unplanted each year. By repeated experiments, Townshend learned that soil fertility could be preserved by alternating crops of different kinds. This system, called **crop rotation,** has become a basic principle of modern farming.

Improvements in machinery made farm labor easier and increased production. For example, iron plows replaced wooden ones. An American blacksmith added a further improvement by inventing an iron plow in three parts so that a broken part could be replaced at low cost.

Some of the new agricultural techniques and machines were expensive, and farmers with small holdings could not afford them. The changes also meant that fewer farm laborers were needed. Thus, improvements in agriculture led to the movement of many farmers to the cities, where they created a large labor force.

The cotton textile industry

The cotton textile industry was the first industry in Great Britain to undergo mechanization—that is, the first to use automatic machinery that increased production. As you study the developments that took place, note how one invention led to others in a kind of chain reaction.

Cotton cloth had been imported into England since the late Middle Ages. It was both popular and expensive. In the 1600's business people began importing raw cotton and employing spinners and weavers to make it into cloth in Great Britain. This industry was an example of the domestic system—that is, men and women working in their homes (see Chapter 13). Although production increased, it was still not possible to produce enough cotton cloth to meet the demand for it.

New inventions. The first development came in the loom for weaving. A loom is set up with a series of vertical threads, called the warp. A shuttle, a device containing the thread running horizontally (the woof), is pushed back and forth across the loom. It is a slow process, and to speed it up a clockmaker named John Kay invented the flying shuttle in 1733. This was an invention that moved the woof thread more rapidly through the loom. Now the weavers could weave faster than the spinners could produce thread for them on their simple spinning wheels. The demand for more thread grew, and prizes were offered for a better spinning machine.

A poor English worker, James Hargreaves, won the prize in 1764 with a machine named the spinning "jenny." A single wheel, turned by hand, operated eight spindles by a series of belts. This machine could produce eight times as much thread as a single spinning wheel. Five years later, Richard Arkwright made further improvements with a machine called the water frame because it was driven by water power.

The flying shuttle and the jenny were small, hand operated, and relatively inexpensive. They could be used in workers' homes as part of the domestic system. The water frame, though, was large, costly, and operated by water power. Arkwright, therefore, opened a spinning mill and, within 10 years, employed several hundred workers. This was the beginning of the modern **factory system.**

Ten years later, Samuel Crompton combined the best features of the spinning jenny and the water frame in another machine, the spinning mule. Now there was plenty of thread of fine qual-

An age of industrialization

The late 1700's and the 1800's were a period of great inventiveness, and each invention seemed to spur another. The invention of the spinning jenny (below) and other spinning machines led to the production of more thread than weavers could handle. So larger and more powerful looms were invented. The invention of the steam engine spurred the development of the locomotive, and railroads (above) soon became a major new industry.

The many new machines required a strong metal for their construction. The Bessemer process (left) made possible the mass production of steel, giving rise to an industry rivaling railroads in size—the steel industry.

ity. However the weavers, even with the flying shuttle, fell far behind.

In 1785 an English minister, Edmund Cartwright, met the need for an even faster weaving process with a power loom in which the shuttle was automatically operated by water power. With this loom one person could weave as much cloth as 200 hand-loom operators. At about the same time, a method was invented to print colored patterns on cotton cloth.

With all these improvements, cotton cloth was now cheaper to produce and sell. As the price went down, the demand increased, and so did the need for more raw cotton. In 1701 England imported 1 million pounds (450,000 kilograms) of cotton. In 1802 it imported 60 million pounds (27 million kilograms).

Most of the imported raw cotton came from the southern United States. At first, cotton cultivation had not been profitable there because of the difficulty of removing the seeds to prepare the cotton for market. By hand, one person could clean only a pound (.45 kilograms) of cotton a day. Then, in 1793, Eli Whitney invented the cotton gin, a machine that could do the work of 50 people. Aided by Whitney's invention, the southern United States met the demands of the British textile manufacturers and became the cotton-producing center of the world.

Steam engines

The early machines of the Industrial Revolution were driven by water power. It was a great improvement over human, animal, and wind power, but it did have drawbacks. A factory had to be located beside a stream or river, preferably near a natural waterfall or a place where a dam could be built. This location might not be near transportation, raw materials, a labor supply, or markets. In addition, the flow of water was likely to vary with the seasons. A new source of power was needed, one that was continuous, dependable, and portable. All of these desirable features were found in steam.

The power contained in steam had been observed by people since ancient times. It was not until 1712, however, that Thomas Newcomen, an English engineer, produced the first successful steam engine. Newcomen engines were used to pump water from mines. They were more powerful and dependable than water wheels, but they were very crude machines, slow and expensive to operate.

In the 1760's James Watt, a Scottish instrument maker and engineer, studied the Newcomen engine. He invented several ways of improving it and in 1769 produced the modern steam engine. The Watt engine was quickly adapted for use in driving the new spinning and weaving machines. As a result of Watt's invention, steam replaced water as the major power source.

Iron and steel

As more and more machines were invented, there was a great demand for iron to make them. From early times iron had been produced in the British Isles, with wood or charcoal as the fuel used to separate the iron from its ore. Then it was discovered that coal worked even better. Thus, iron and coal became the two major raw materials of modern industry. Great Britain had an enormous advantage, because it had large amounts of these resources.

Many early steam engines blew up because the iron used to build them was too weak to withstand the high pressures of steam. A stronger, harder metal was needed. This was steel, which is iron with certain impurities removed. The existing process for making steel was slow and expensive, and the metal remained rare until the 1850's. Around that time an American, William Kelly, and an Englishman, Henry Bessemer, discovered a new way of making steel. The Bessemer process, as it was called, reduced the cost so much that steel became what it is today—the basic material of our industrial civilization.

Industrialization in other fields

Using steam engines and iron and steel, British manufacturers quickly introduced power-driven machinery in many industries. The production of shoes, clothing, ammunition, and furniture became mechanized, as did printing and paper making. Machines were used to cut and finish lumber, to process foods, and to make other machines.

Some new inventions and processes had important byproducts—that is, secondary products that result from manufacturing something else. These often developed into separate industries. For example, coke, which is a byproduct of coal, improved the smelting of iron. Then it was discovered that the gases released from the coal in making coke could be burned to give light.

During the 1830's gas was piped into London and burned in street lamps. By the 1850's gas was used for lighting streets and homes in hundreds of cities throughout the Western world.

Another new industry of the 1800's was the production of rubber. It was first used to make waterproof shoes and coats, but they became sticky in warm weather. In 1839, after years of experimenting, Charles Goodyear of the United States discovered a process of "curing" rubber to make it more elastic and usable. He mixed the raw rubber with sulfur and then heated it. His method, called vulcanizing, became the basis of the modern rubber industry.

Still another industry grew up after 1850, when people discovered how to use crude oil, or petroleum. During the 1850's people learned that it could be distilled to produce paraffin for candles, lubricating oil for machinery, and kerosene for lighting and heating.

Thus, starting from a few simple inventions to improve the production of textiles, a mighty economic revolution had grown. The inventions had multiplied with ever increasing speed, and basic changes in the social system as well as the economic system were bound to follow.

CHECKUP

1. IDENTIFY: factors of production, Tull, Townshend, domestic system, factory system, Newcomen, Watt, vulcanizing.

2. What was the Industrial Revolution? Why did it begin in Great Britain?

3. How did the enclosure movement lead to changes in agriculture?

4. What were the principal effects of the agricultural revolution?

5. List the contributions made to the cotton textile industry by Kay, Hargreaves, Arkwright, Crompton, Cartwright, and Whitney.

6. What is the Bessemer process? Why was it so important to the Industrial Revolution?

The factory system changed working and living conditions

For centuries goods of all kinds had been produced by skilled artisans at home or in small shops. The artisan had control over the training of apprentices, over the quality and price of goods, and over the pace of each workday. As you will read, the Industrial Revolution dramatically changed the way that goods were produced and the way that people lived their lives.

The effect of machines on work

The introduction of steam-powered machinery changed the way work was done. It made work easier to do. Instead of spending several years as an apprentice learning a trade, a person could learn to work a machine in a few days.

Employers now looked for people who could be taught a few simple tasks. They preferred to hire young men and women rather than older, skilled people. Young people did not expect high wages, and they were not set in older ways of working. In the early textile factories, most employees were children and young adults under the age of 30.

As more and more machines were introduced, older skilled workers often found themselves unemployed. Their abilities as weavers or spinners were no longer needed, and factories would not hire them for simpler work. To make up for their loss of income, many of these people did odd jobs in the cities or on nearby farms and sent their children to work in textile factories.

Factories brought together large numbers of people. Instead of working on a product from beginning to end, workers did only a small part of the entire job. Instead of working in a shop with a few others, dozens worked in the same room, under the direction of a shop supervisor.

The wage system

Under the domestic system a master had been both worker and employer. Under the factory system a few masters became factory owners, but most became workers. Instead of owning a shop or some tools, artisans were now hired by capitalists—the people who owned the machines and the factories. Factory owners paid their workers wages—an amount of money for the number of hours they spent at work or for the amount they produced.

Factory workers' wages were determined by several factors. First, employers wanted to produce goods as cheaply as possible. Thus, wages were set in relation to other costs of production.

Second, wages were low when there were many people available to compete for jobs. They were higher when there were fewer workers and many jobs to be filled.

Third, wages often depended on what people could earn at other kinds of work. For example, early employers in textile factories paid young women more than they would have earned as household servants. They did this to attract young women to work in the new factories.

Fourth, wages took into account the needs of a worker and his or her family. The wages of adult men were higher than those of adult women because men were thought to be the main support of the family. Women were thought to be adding "a little something" to a man's wage, even if in reality a woman was the only one earning money for her family.

Workers who earned wages depended entirely on their earnings. Under the domestic system artisans had owned their tools and the shops they worked in, and apprentices had eventually become masters. Now, most workers were employed by someone else throughout their lives, and for their work they received money.

Factory rules and regulations

Factory workers had many rules to follow. They had to arrive at work promptly, and they were allowed only a certain, set time for eating meals and taking breaks. They worked whether it was hot or cold, winter or summer, day or night. If they did not follow the rules and if they were absent from work, they were fined or their pay was cut.

In the early factories, workers spent 14 hours a day, 6 days a week, on the job. This was very different from work schedules under the domestic system or on farms. Instead of the work being adjusted to the seasons, factory workers had to adjust their lives to the demands of machines, and the machines never needed to rest. Some workers even complained that they were expected to become machines themselves.

Factories were uncomfortable places—noisy, dirty, and poorly ventilated. The air was hot and steamy in summer and cold and damp in winter. Sanitary facilities were primitive. Early machines had no safety devices and serious injuries were frequent. There was no accident insurance or any other form of compensation for injury.

One of the worst features of early industrialization was child labor. It was common for five-year-old children to be employed in cotton mills and mines. Conditions were particularly bad in coal mines, where women and children pulled carts through tunnels under roofs that were too low to allow a donkey to pass through.

Living conditions of workers

If life in the mines and factories was hard and monotonous, life in the workers' homes was not much better. Working people lived in cramped and crowded tenements, with as many as a dozen people to a room. As late as 1840, one out of every eight working-class families in Manchester lived in a cellar. Rooms were sparsely furnished, and many children shared the same bed. Food was poor; fresh meat and milk were rare. City workers usually ate bread, tea or coffee, potatoes, and a few other vegetables. Because of their poor diets, people developed diseases such as rickets—a bone disease caused by a vitamin deficiency.

Living conditions could change quite suddenly. The illness, death, or unemployment of a working father or mother could drive a family to the edge of starvation. A rise in the price of food or in rent could also make life very difficult.

The development of the middle class

The Industrial Revolution enlarged the middle class. This group consisted of many different kinds of people—bankers, manufacturers, merchants, lawyers, doctors, engineers, professors, and their families. Middle-class people owned property and could afford to hire servants, to eat well, and to enjoy some comfort.

Changing working and living conditions

Industrialization brought great economic advances, but for ordinary workers in the new industrial cities it also brought hardship. Previously, people had had to work hard on the land. Now instead of the open air of the village there were grimy streets, crowded houses, and airless factories. City dwellers suffered from the smoke of the factories, whose tall chimneys rivaled the old churches as city landmarks (bottom).

Inside the factories men and women had to work 12 hours or more. They tended machines that required intense concentration but offered no relief from boring, repeated activity. The workers usually had to remain standing all day (below). Even children worked long hours, often in filthy conditions (left).

The members of the middle class were literate and educated. The children of middle-class families went to school and were trained for good jobs. Often they inherited money and social position from their parents.

The life of the middle class contrasted sharply with that of the working class. The two groups lived apart—workers in crowded slums, middle-class people in larger houses in more spacious neighborhoods. The two groups dressed differently. Workers wore work shirts, while lawyers and merchants wore suits. Working-class women dressed in plain skirts and blouses, but the women of the middle class wore lace and frills. The widening gap between the two groups was immediately noticeable to anyone living in a city.

Industrialization affected women's lives

The changes brought by the Industrial Revolution affected women of different classes in different ways. In the past, beyond helping in the fields, women had made clothing at home, spun yarn, woven cloth, and prepared all meals. They manufactured goods for sale and assisted their husbands in craft shops or small family businesses. However, the Industrial Revolution moved most manufacturing into factories. Now people purchased food and clothing instead of producing them at home. As a result, important work that women had done at home was now performed elsewhere.

Working-class women. The first type of manufacturing to move into factories was textile production. The early mills hired women to tend machines that spun cotton into thread. Many women, both single and married, who had spun thread at home took jobs in the new factories. These women earned wages to help their families buy food and clothing and pay the rent.

The jobs for women in textile mills required little skill and paid low wages. They were defined as "women's jobs," and few men were hired to do them. The attitude that certain jobs were suitable only for women and others only for men was not new. For many centuries there had been ideas about what women should do and what men should do. Industrialization changed the location of work for working-class women, but it did not raise the status of their jobs.

Domestic service. While some working-class women took factory jobs, many others continued to work at a traditional job for women—domestic service. Young, single women had been hired as maids in other people's houses or businesses for centuries. After industrialization, more middle-class families could afford to hire servants. As a result, there were more jobs for servants.

Most often young women who lived in the country took jobs in the city as servants. As the number of farms declined during the Industrial Revolution, rural life in general offered few jobs. Daughters of farm families now took jobs in the city. For many country women, domestic service was a first step into city life. Becoming a servant did not require special skill. In addition, servants lived with the families for whom they worked. Thus, a girl moving from the country was guaranteed a place to live and food to eat. After living for a while in the city as a servant, she might take a job in a shop or factory.

Middle-class women. The Industrial Revolution brought new wealth and greater luxury to middle-class women, who could hire servants to cook, clean, and take care of their children. While their husbands left home to work each day, middle-class wives stayed home. The idea developed that women belonged at home, while men were fit for the world of work. According to some writers of the day, woman's nature was fit only for raising children and caring for the home. Earning money, even doing chores in the house, were considered corruptions of "true womanhood." Some women accepted and enjoyed this role, but others began to express a very different attitude.

Single middle-class women. One place the new attitude arose was Great Britain, where in the mid-1800's many middle-class women did not marry. Many came from families who could not support them for their entire lives. Therefore, they had to support themselves by going out to work. Some women whose families could support them felt that women should be allowed to work even if they did not need money, and this idea gradually gained acceptance.

During the late 1800's, more jobs became available for women. Public health care was developing, and there was a need for nurses and social workers. Florence Nightingale, an English nurse, made a major contribution to this increase in opportunities for women by developing training programs for nurses.

Demands also arose for improvements in education. College courses were opened to women, and special women's colleges were established. As public education spread in the 1870's and 1880's in France and Great Britain, there was a need for teachers. Women began to enter the field of teaching in large numbers. By the end of the 1800's, elementary school teaching was almost entirely a female profession.

CHECKUP

1. How did machines change the way work was done?

2. How were the wages of factory workers determined?

3. Describe working conditions in factories and mines.

4. What jobs did women do in the late 1800's? How did these jobs affect their lives?

3

Technology transformed transportation and communications

When the Industrial Revolution began, land transportation hardly differed from what it had been during the Middle Ages. Roads were little more than trails that were thick with dust in dry weather and deep with mud when it rained. For a passenger in a stagecoach, 50 miles (80 kilometers) was a day's uncomfortable journey. Packhorses and clumsy wagons were used to carry heavy goods.

Roads, canals, railroads, and steamboats

The changes of the Industrial Revolution made better transportation necessary. Raw materials had to be carried to factories and finished products to market without too much delay. A Scottish engineer, John McAdam, worked out a new way of building roads that improved travel conditions. First came a roadbed of large stones, then layers of carefully selected smaller stones. These roads were called macadam roads. They are still constructed, although modern road builders use asphalt to bind the smaller stones together.

Great Britain and other countries of Western Europe also had extensive networks of rivers that could be used as water highways. Some canals had been dug to connect them, but many more canals were constructed after engineers began using locks—gates that regulate the level and flow of water. The period from 1760 to 1850 was one of extensive canal building. Canals made possible a cheaper and slightly faster form of transportation than roads, but they soon met with competition from a new form of transportation.

Watt's steam engine offered many possibilities for new means of transportation. In 1814 George Stephenson, an English engineer, perfected a moving engine, or locomotive, that propelled itself by steam and ran on rails. In 1829 Stephenson's famous locomotive, the *Rocket,* pulled a line of cars from Liverpool to Manchester at a speed of 29 miles (46 kilometers) an hour. Networks of railroads were soon built throughout the Western world. Almost continuous improvements—steel rails, air brakes, more comfortable coaches, and special cars for different kinds of freight—made railroad transportation fast, safe, and cheap.

Many people tried adapting the steam engine to ships. Credit for doing this successfully is usually given to Robert Fulton, an American who established the first regular inland steamboat service. His boat, the *Clermont,* was launched on the Hudson River in 1807 and at once began regular trips between New York City and Albany. Steamboats soon appeared on many of the rivers and lakes of the world.

In 1838 the *Great Western,* a ship that operated by steam alone, crossed the Atlantic Ocean in 15 days, less than half the time it took a sailing ship. Regular steamboat traffic across the Atlantic was developed by Samuel Cunard of Great Britain, who founded the Cunard Line shipping company. Soon, ships were built of iron and steel instead of wood, and goods were moved more quickly and cheaply all over the world.

The communications revolution

Science played only a small role in the invention of textile machinery, the steam engine, the locomotive, and the steamship. These inventions were the work of amateur inventors and engineers, and did not come from the laboratory of the scientist. In communications, however, scientific and technical developments began to be linked more directly.

From early times, people had observed electricity and its connection with magnetism, but they had not put their knowledge to much practical use. For one thing, no one had found a way to provide a steady flow of electric current. Around the year 1800 an Italian, Alessandro Volta, was able to build the first battery, a device that provided a steady current of electricity. Soon afterward, André Ampère of France worked out principles governing the magnetic effect of an electric current.

The work of Volta and Ampère was put to practical use by Samuel Morse of the United States. He sent electricity over a wire, at the other end of which was a machine. When electricity was passed along the wire, the machine clicked. Morse worked out a system of dots and dashes—the Morse code—by which these clicks could be translated into letters of the alphabet. By 1844 Morse's invention—the telegraph—had become a practical instrument. Telegraph wires were soon stretched across continents, and ideas could then be transmitted at the speed of electricity.

People soon began experimenting to find a way to carry electricity under the sea by using cables— telegraph wires that were heavily insulated to protect them from water. Early in the 1850's Great Britain was connected with the European continent by a cable across the English Channel. However, the problem of spanning the great distance of the Atlantic Ocean presented enormous difficulties. It was not until 1866 that Cyrus Field and a group of Americans finally laid a cable across the Atlantic Ocean. Soon afterward, all the continents were joined by cables.

The spread of industry

The rapid changes in agriculture, industry, transportation, and communications did not have much effect on the European continent for several years. There were various reasons for the delay. Many European countries did not have raw materials or large, accessible markets in which to sell their products. Great Britain, in order to keep its monopoly on new methods, prohibited the export of machines. It also refused to allow skilled workers to leave the country. In addition, the wars of the French Revolution and the Napoleonic Era slowed the industrial development of Europe.

France did develop some industry, especially textiles, iron, and mining. The French government helped this development in two ways. It imposed high tariffs to keep out foreign manufactured goods, and it encouraged the building of railroads. However, in the 1800's France never became as completely industrialized as Great Britain. It continued to be largely an agricultural country, with its fertile farm land held mainly in small plots.

Industry grew slowly in the German states because they were not united. Thus there was no efficient central government to aid industrial growth. Although some factories were established in the middle 1800's, real industrialization had to await the unification of Germany in the 1870's. (You will read about Germany's unification in Chapter 22.)

In the United States, British inventions and methods were eagerly adopted. The United States had everything that was needed for industrial development—national unity and a vast country with rich natural resources. It also had a rapidly increasing population, inventive genius, and a willingness to adopt, to adapt, and to take chances.

Many canals and railroads were built in the United States during the 1800's, and industry moved west as transportation developed. The steel industry grew in Pittsburgh and the Great Lakes region, and farm machinery was manufactured in Chicago. By 1869 a railroad had been built connecting the east coast of the United States with the west coast. By 1870 the United States was second only to Great Britain as a manufacturing nation.

Along with the growth of American industry came significant changes in farming. You have already read about Whitney's cotton gin and how it enabled the southern states to supply raw material for the British textile industry. Another invention was a machine for harvesting grain, patented by Cyrus McCormick in 1834. The McCormick

Inventions and inventors

The stream of new inventions in the 1800's captured the imagination of people everywhere. An exhibition displaying the marvels of English inventors became one of the great events of the century. It was held in a huge glass pavilion that was built in 1851 in a London park (below and bottom right).

Inventors themselves became heroes. The American Thomas Edison, for example, worked for five straight days and nights to perfect his phonograph (left). He believed hard work was the key to success, and at the age of 70 he said there would be plenty of time to rest at 100. Perhaps the most sensational invention was the airplane. In 1909 Louis Blériot, the first person to fly across the English Channel, was greeted with a French flag raised over the white cliffs of Dover (bottom left).

reaper, drawn by horses, freed many farmers from the slow, backbreaking work of cutting grain with a sickle or a scythe. The invention of the reaper was followed by other devices, such as the mechanical thresher for separating the grains of wheat from their stalks and hulls. As transportation and communication improved, the spread of the Industrial Revolution could not be halted.

Developments after 1870

Beginning about 1870, the findings of pure science were increasingly applied to manufacturing. The result was a new wave of industrial growth. The application of science to industrial problems had particular impact in three directions: (1) additional inventions that provided rapid communications over long distances; (2) the development and use of new sources of power; and (3) the creation of new products and materials and the improvement of old ones.

Communications. An important development in the communications field occurred in the 1870's when Alexander Graham Bell sent the human voice over a long distance by means of an electrical circuit. Bell, an American, patented his telephone in 1876. Then, in 1895, an Italian inventor, Guglielmo Marconi, developed a way to send messages through space without wires.

Marconi's invention was based on the work of two earlier scientists, James Clerk Maxwell of Great Britain and Heinrich Hertz of Germany. Maxwell had made a mathematical study of electricity and magnetism. In 1864 he predicted the existence of invisible electromagnetic waves that travel through space with the speed of light. In the 1880's Hertz not only proved that such waves did exist, by transmitting and receiving them, but also measured their length and speed.

Marconi invented instruments for sending and receiving these radio waves, as they came to be called. His wireless telegraph soon proved itself valuable for ship-to-ship and ship-to-shore communication. In 1901 he sent the first wireless message across the Atlantic Ocean.

Electric power and light. As industry grew during the 1800's, manufacturers were always on the lookout for new and better sources of power. In the 1870's a tremendous new power source—electricity—was developed.

The scientific key to the problem was a discovery made by an English scientist, Michael Faraday, in 1831. From the work of Ampère and other scientists, Faraday knew that electricity could produce magnetism. He wanted to find out whether magnetism could produce electricity. He found that by moving a magnet through a coil of wire, he could produce an electric current in the wire.

Faraday had been interested chiefly in exploring the nature of electricity. Others took his discovery and used it to develop the dynamo, or electric generator. Driven by a steam engine or by water power, the dynamo transformed mechanical power into electrical energy. This in turn could be used to run machinery in factories.

English and American inventors kept trying to make use of another scientific discovery about electricity—that a current passing through certain kinds of wire caused the wire to glow. Here was a possible source of light for city streets, homes, and factories. Electric light bulbs were first produced in 1845, but they burned out in a very short time. In 1879 Thomas Edison, an American, made a bulb that glowed for two days before burning out. In a few years, after further improvements, lighting by electricity replaced gas light.

To make electricity practical, it had to be carried from the place where it was generated to the place where it would be used. After much work on the problem, Edison developed a successful central powerhouse and transmission system that was put into effect in 1882 in New York City, London, and Milan.

The electrical industry grew by leaps and bounds. Waterfalls, such as Niagara Falls, were tapped to run huge dynamos, whose hydroelectric power was sent long distances through wires. Tremendous dams were built in many countries to provide artificial sources of water power.

As electricity came to be produced and transmitted on a large scale in the late 1800's, electric motors replaced steam engines in factories. Where hydroelectric power was not available or was too expensive, steam engines turned the generators at central powerhouses.

The internal-combustion engine

The electric motor had one limitation—it had to be connected with its power supply. Therefore it was not very useful for moving vehicles. Then an engine was invented that could use a portable fuel supply of gasoline or oil. It was called the internal-combustion engine because the combustion, or burning, of fuel took place inside a closed cylinder. (In the steam engine, combustion takes place outside the cylinder.)

Automobiles. In the late 1800's several European inventors worked on engines that would use a portable fuel supply of oil or gasoline to propel individual vehicles. (The word *automobile* was first used for such self-propelled vehicles in 1876.) Pioneers in this field included Gottlieb Daimler and Karl Benz of Germany and Louis Renault of France. The first successful gasoline-driven automobile in the United States was built by Charles and Frank Duryea in 1893. Three years later the American inventor Henry Ford produced his first automobile.

Airplanes. Since the 1700's people had used balloons, which are lighter than air, to float above the earth. Beginning in the 1800's, inventors tried to devise a heavier-than-air machine that would actually fly. Many early airplanes were models and were not designed to carry people. The first people to succeed in flying an airplane in powered, sustained, controlled flight were Wilbur and Orville Wright of the United States. They achieved this flight at Kitty Hawk, North Carolina, in 1903. It lasted 12 seconds and covered 120 feet (37 meters).

The Wright brothers' achievement was another instance of the combination of science and technology. The Wrights succeeded where others had failed because they studied aerodynamics (the principles governing the movement of air around objects) and used the internal-combustion engine to drive their plane through the air. From this modest beginning, an important airplane industry developed.

CHECKUP

1. IDENTIFY: Faraday, Edison, Daimler, Renault, Duryea, Wright brothers, aerodynamics.

2. What were four important developments in transportation during the Industrial Revolution?

3. Why was the United States able to make such rapid progress in the development of its industry?

4. Describe the contributions of Bell and Marconi to the communications revolution. How did Marconi use the work of earlier scientists?

5. What developments made electricity a new source of power?

6. What is an internal-combustion engine? How was it first put to use?

New methods and giant businesses produced an industrial economy

Throughout the 1800's, inventions and new methods of production, distribution of goods, and sales were transforming industry. The rapid growth caused by these developments brought many changes to the factory system and to the organization of businesses. Some of these changes date back to the early Industrial Revolution. Others came about as science transformed industry from 1870 on.

The factory system also introduced a new phase in the development of capitalism. Most earlier capitalists were merchants who bought, sold, and exchanged goods. This early phase of capitalism is sometimes called **commercial capitalism.** However, the capitalists of the Industrial Revolution were more involved in producing and manufacturing goods themselves. Therefore the capitalism of this period is often referred to as **industrial capitalism.**

Division of labor

As we have seen, industrialization changed the way in which goods were produced. Instead of relying on a master and his apprentices, factory owners hired large numbers of unskilled laborers, divided the manufacturing process into a series of simple steps, and then assigned a step to each worker. This process was a form of **division of labor.** Because a large number of items could be produced in a given length of time, the cost of the items was lowered. The use of machinery aided the division of labor, since machines performed many of the steps.

Industrial giants and their methods

The remarkable American financiers and industrialists of the late 1800's and early 1900's transformed industry. In his factory (above) George Westinghouse used one of the first assembly lines, greatly increasing productivity. Andrew Carnegie (below left), a poor Scottish immigrant, became the dominant figure in the American steel industry. He then retired and devoted the last 20 years of his life to philanthropy. He used his huge fortune to endow libraries, foundations, and other institutions that promoted learning. Henry Ford (below right) brought motor cars within reach of most people, thus revolutionizing transportation. Ford, too, endowed a foundation for charitable work.

But people did not think kindly of these industrialists. The feeling grew that a few rich men were beginning to dominate the world. A cartoon (above left) showed the banker J. P. Morgan greedily holding the entire globe.

Interchangeable parts

The American inventor Eli Whitney used division of labor in making muskets in the early 1800's. In Whitney's factory, some people worked on musket barrels, others on trigger mechanisms, and still others on the wooden stocks or handles.

An essential part of Whitney's system was the use of interchangeable parts for his firearms. He designed machinery that could be operated by unskilled workers and yet turn out identical, interchangeable parts. It was this development that made division of labor possible in a product made of several parts that had to fit together. Whitney's system resulted in the speedy production of a large number of muskets that were inexpensive and could be easily repaired. If part of a musket broke, it could be replaced by a part that was identical.

Other manufacturers quickly realized the usefulness of interchangeable parts, and Whitney's principle was widely adopted. The increasing use of precision power tools after 1900 was of great importance in the making of interchangeable parts for complex products.

The assembly line

Division of labor and the system of interchangeable parts were two essential elements of **mass production.** Mass production is the system of manufacturing large numbers of items exactly alike.

A third element of this process was the assembly line. Until the late 1800's the actual assembling of separate parts into a final product was done at a central point and was a slow and inefficient process. Then manufacturers devised the assembly line. This made use of a conveyor belt that carried the unfinished products past each worker in turn. As each item passed, a worker performed a special task. This saved time and energy and increased the number of times per hour the task could be performed.

Henry Ford saw great potential in the mass-production system. By applying it to the making of automobiles, he founded one of the largest industries in the United States. In 1913 Ford assembly-line workers were producing automobiles at the rate of one every 93 minutes. The frame of the automobile was carried along on a conveyor belt from one worker to the next. Each made a small contribution to the finished product by adding one or more of the 5,000 interchangeable parts that made up the Ford Model T. Mass production lowered the price of automobiles and made them available to most American families.

American and European industrialists began to mass-produce clothing, furniture, and heavy machinery. Mass production usually lowered the cost of an item. Therefore, more and more people in the industrialized nations were able to buy more and more things and enjoy a higher standard of living.

The corporation

Mass-production methods could not be used by small companies having few workers. Nor could small companies afford to buy the machinery necessary for large-scale production. These things required great amounts of capital.

As the scale of business grew during the 1800's, the **corporation** became the dominant form of business organization. Corporations were similar to the joint-stock companies of the Commercial Revolution. Individuals bought shares of stock, elected directors to decide policies and hire managers, and received dividends according to the number of shares they owned.

In a joint-stock company, however, shareholders were responsible for the company's debts. If a company went bankrupt, someone who had invested only a few dollars might have to contribute thousands to pay off creditors. In a corporation, the shareholder's financial responsibility was limited to the amount invested. For this reason, corporations could attract greater numbers of investors.

In the late 1800's the size of corporations increased greatly both in the amounts of capital invested and in the size of the manufacturing establishment or group of enterprises. When the American financier J. P. Morgan and his associates formed the United States Steel Company in 1901, the new company had a capital investment of a billion dollars. This was only the first of many billion-dollar corporations. Banks and other financial institutions played an increasingly important role in forming and operating these large corporations.

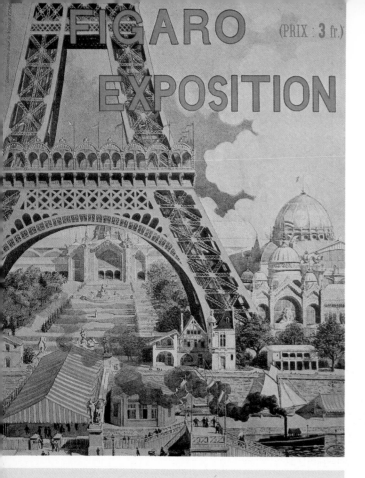

HISTORY THROUGH ART

Paris Exposition Poster

In 1889 the French held a spectacular exposition in Paris to celebrate the hundredth anniversary of the French Revolution. In its many buildings it featured examples of the tremendous industrial progress that had been made during the century. To celebrate the exposition, the French newspaper *Le Figaro* published a special supplement using this poster as its cover. In the foreground is the Seine River with the Eiffel Tower soaring behind. At the time the tower was the tallest structure in the world.

This was the first exposition where electricity was used in a major way, and at night the lower part of the tower and surrounding fountains were lit up, creating a spectacular show. Thousands of examples of advanced machinery, military aircraft, glass, and applied arts were exhibited. In the Gallery of Machines, under the arch of the tower, visitors stood on a high moving platform to view the wonderful inventions that had been developed during the Industrial Revolution. The exposition demonstrated to the world that the 1800's had indeed been technically dynamic.

Increasing the size of a corporation did not solve all its problems. If a number of corporations were producing the same products, competition became very keen. If they tried to sell their products by cutting prices, the smaller and less efficient businesses suffered. Often they had to sell out to larger firms.

As a result, although the size of individual corporations increased steadily, the number of individual corporations decreased. In 1927 almost half the wealth and income of corporations was owned by 200 companies.

Not only were there fewer corporations, but many that did survive were controlled by a single individual owning more than half the stock. In the United States, such people included John D. Rockefeller of Standard Oil and Andrew Carnegie of Carnegie Steel.

Monopolies

Even the giant corporations found that competition was not a blessing—at least, not to the owners. Competition that reduced selling prices also reduced profits. Therefore, corporations tried to avoid competition by getting together to create **monopolies.** A monopoly has complete control of a commodity, a service, or a market. In this way corporations could control competitive production and fix prices to ensure maximum profit to the stockholder. The consumer either had to pay these prices or go without the goods. Monopolies could also keep wages down, or force down the prices the corporations paid for raw materials and supplies.

By 1900 a number of giant corporations in Germany had combined to control entire industries. These combinations of corporations were known as **cartels.** For example, a cartel might own coal and iron mines, steel mills, and factories that used steel to build machines, thus controlling all parts of an industry.

Business cycles

As industrial production became more and more important, it influenced a country's entire economy. The Industrial Revolution brought with it alternating periods of prosperity and decline—a pattern known as the **business cycle.**

When one industry did well, other industries also prospered. If, for example, there was a great demand for machines, there would also be a demand for the coal and iron needed to make them. If, on the other hand, a large firm reduced its orders of iron and laid off workers, other companies would also be affected. The suppliers of iron might have to cut down production and also lay off workers. The workers then would have to find other jobs, because without wages they could not pay their rent or buy food. When there were more workers available than jobs, employers could reduce wages. The effects would go on spreading to other industries, until the entire economy was in a **depression**—the lowest point of a business cycle. Cycles of prosperity and depression, occurring every 25 years or so, became characteristic of industrial society in the 1800's and 1900's.

The lives of all the people in an industrialized country were affected by these economic developments, even if they did not work in factories. Events in one country also could affect the economy of another country. During the American Civil War, for example, cotton was not available to send to Great Britain. This set off a period of depression in the British textile industry.

Technology and progress

It is no wonder that people living in the late 1800's believed in progress. The world was changing more rapidly than it ever had before. More and more new machines had been invented during the 1800's. They were eventually improved and by 1900 were in use in most countries of Western Europe and the United States.

Railroad lines covered Great Britain, France, Germany, and the United States, enabling people to travel far from home. Manufactured goods could be shipped from New York to California or from the north to the south of France.

Discoveries by chemists led to new techniques for dyeing cloth, producing synthetic textiles, and making new types of fertilizers and paints. At the same time, the use of electricity also stimulated the development of new industries. The invention of the light bulb spurred the building of large dams to generate electrical power. Wires and lamps and, later, radios were manufactured as well. Technological advances thus led to new factories, jobs, and industries.

By the end of the 1800's many new inventions produced in great numbers became available to ordinary consumers. Bicycles became a means of transportation for some people, a leisure product for others. As you have read, automobiles arrived in the 1890's and were in wide use by 1910.

Typewriters, first invented for businesses and referred to as "mechanical pianos," were also purchased for private use. Telephones became a convenient form of communication, especially after long-distance lines were put into service in 1885. Vacuum cleaners slowly replaced brooms. Family life, as well as the world of business and manufacturing, was becoming industrialized.

The growing industries required many kinds of workers. They needed people not only to manufacture products but also to keep track of business arrangements, to type, and to file. Many industries also needed people to advertise and sell products. Large numbers of jobs were created in clerical and sales work. Since the work was clean and permitted people to dress nicely, it was referred to as "white-collar" work.

By 1900 most people thought of technology and progress as the same thing. Science seemed an endless source of new ideas and inventions. Machines seemed capable of constantly improving life. There seemed to be no end to the progress of industrialization. People thought that science and technology were capable of solving any of the problems that might be created by the Industrial Revolution. Whether their hopes were to be realized only the 1900's would tell.

CHECKUP

1. IDENTIFY: commercial capitalism, industrial capitalism, Ford, Morgan, Rockefeller, Carnegie, cartels, business cycle, white-collar jobs.

2. What is the chief advantage of mass production? What three elements are needed to make mass production possible?

3. What is the principal difference between a joint-stock company and a corporation? Why was this difference an advantage to the growth of industry?

4. Why did corporations combine into monopolies?

5. What were the new industries created by 1900?

463

5

Industrialization altered population patterns and popular culture

For about 150 years before 1750, the population of Europe had grown very little. When the Industrial Revolution began, Europe had 140 million people. By 1850, only a hundred years later, the population was 266 million. The rate of growth for most of the period was highest in Europe and the United States, the areas in which industrialization advanced most rapidly. The increase in population led to new ways of living and new ways of spending leisure time.

Reasons for population growth

There were two reasons that population grew. Fewer people died at an early age, and more children were born than in the past.

Decreasing death rates. In earlier times large numbers of people died, especially at an early age, from starvation and disease. It was common for children growing up to have only one living parent. And it was rare for children to know their grandparents, because the grandparents usually died before grandchildren were born.

After the Industrial Revolution fewer people starved, because changes in farming methods increased the food supply. Soil yielded more food than it had in the past, especially after 1750, when more and more people began to grow potatoes. Potatoes were easy to raise and were very nourishing. By 1830 potatoes were the main food that peasants ate.

In addition, new methods of transportation and better roads made it possible to send food to areas that needed it. In the past, if there was a poor harvest in an area, the people there simply ate less or starved. Now food could be sent from one area to another quickly and cheaply, and thus fewer people starved.

After the mid-1700's, people also had fewer diseases than in the past. This was due partly to better nutrition; people who have enough to eat are less likely to get sick. The drop in the death rates was also partly the result of a decline in certain diseases that had killed many people in the past.

Improvements in medicine benefited the population, as you will read in Chapter 21. As a result, epidemics of deadly diseases such as bubonic plague and cholera had disappeared from Europe by the 1830's. The reduction in starvation and disease, which enabled more people to live longer, was thus one of the main reasons for the growth of population.

Increasing birth rates. The second reason the population grew was that more children were born. After the Industrial Revolution people married at younger ages than they had in the past. They also began having children earlier because they needed the money that children could earn.

Before the 1700's in Europe men generally married when they were about 25 or 26 years old and women at about 23 or 24. They married only when they could support a family. If they were artisans, that meant they first had to learn a skill. If they were peasants, they had to wait until they inherited land. Men and women were expected to bring skills or money or land to a marriage.

As factories replaced artisan workshops, young people no longer had to spend long years learning a skilled trade. Jobs in factories made it possible for men and women to marry younger—in their late teens or early twenties. When men and women were both working, they could earn enough to support a household, so there was no reason to wait to marry.

Effects of population growth

The growth in population had many effects. More people had to be fed, so farmers sought more ways of improving their harvests. Growing population meant there were more people to work in industry as it expanded, and more people to buy the goods being produced in factories. Cities grew and new kinds of housing had to be constructed for the expanding population. As a result, there were more jobs, because construction workers were needed.

The population of industrializing countries was young, because people married at an early age and had many children. Most people in France, for example, were under the age of 40 in the early 1800's. Societies adapted to the interests of these young people. And the worries of young parents about jobs and families influenced politics, literature, and the arts.

Emigration. As population grew in industrialized countries, it also became more mobile. Large numbers of people moved across national boundaries, and across oceans, to foreign lands. The great movement was away from Europe to North and South America, Africa, Australia, and New Zealand.

Like so many other things, this movement to other lands, or **emigration,** speeded up after 1870. Between 1870 and 1900, more than 10 million people left Europe for the United States alone. Such a mass movement of people has no equal in human history.

Much of the emigration was from countries where economic conditions were poor, such as Ireland and Italy, or where there were oppressed minority groups, such as Jews, Armenians, and Slavs. The general trend of emigration was toward the more sparsely populated nations where industry was new and growing rapidly and where there was a demand for factory labor. Higher wages in the new country encouraged people to move, and steamships and trains made travel faster, safer, and cheaper than ever.

Malthus on population. In 1798 an English minister named Thomas R. Malthus wrote *An Essay on the Principle of Population As It Affects the Future Improvement of Society*. In this essay Malthus said that population was increasing so quickly that the food supply of the world would run out. He urged people, especially the poor, not to marry and have children at a young age.

Malthus believed that overpopulation caused poverty. His theory was much debated during the 1800's. People who disagreed with him said that high birthrates were the result, not the cause, of poverty. Debates about the reasons for population growth and its effects continue today.

The shift to the cities

As the population was increasing, changes in agriculture, industry, and transportation produced another striking result—the rapid growth of cities. The greatest spur to city growth was the factory system. The developing industries, located in or near cities, offered a chance for employment, which was declining on farms.

Many early factories were located in already established cities, which grew tremendously. The population of Manchester, England, for example, grew from 25,000 in 1772 to 455,000 in 1851. When factories were located in rural areas, cities grew up around them. City living became the way of life for increasing numbers of people.

Before the Industrial Revolution, the vast majority of people had lived in rural areas or in small villages. By 1900, however, in many nations more people lived in or near cities than in the country. In Great Britain about 10 percent of the people lived in cities in 1800. By 1921 that figure had grown to 80 percent. Similar changes took place in other countries. In 1800 not a single city in the Western world had a population of a million people. A hundred years later, there were 11 cities around the world with over a million inhabitants, including New York, London, Paris, Moscow, Berlin, Tokyo, and Shanghai.

Sanitation and public order

European and American cities in the 1800's were very different from cities today. Until very late in the century cities did not have sewers. People got their daily water supply from public fountains, because houses did not have running water inside them. The water in fountains came from polluted rivers, and no one knew how to purify it.

Because there were no public or private companies to collect garbage, it was dumped on the streets. In industrial cities, smoke from the factories added to the bad smells from sewage and garbage. It is no wonder that people thought of cities as evil-smelling places.

After the 1870's improvements began to appear. Closed public sewers were installed, and water was piped into houses. City governments passed laws requiring better heating and better construction of buildings. Street lights were installed, and roads were paved. Many of these improvements were possible because of new technology—for example, iron pipes, toilets, and water systems.

The governments of the growing cities also found they needed a new kind of police force. Streets had to be patrolled to prevent robberies. Crowds had to be guided safely, and the lives and property of city people had to be protected.

connections

Marriage Customs

From the earliest times, men and women have contracted marriages and created families in which children could be protected and nurtured. Through the ages there have been many different reasons for forming marriages, and many different ways of deciding who should marry whom. During most periods of history, parents decided who should marry whom, and when.

In medieval times (below) a marriage was looked upon as a way of joining two families together—for economic advantage, for example. Among royal families, in particular, marriages were frequently arranged for political reasons. Marriages could be arranged in childhood, infancy, and sometimes even before birth.

In many cultures marriage was accompanied by an exchange of money or gifts. Because many societies regarded the man as superior, the woman's family had to provide a gift or money, known as a dowry, to have the daughter married. In other cultures, the husband's family gave money to the bride's family.

The social and economic changes of the Industrial Revolution had numerous effects on the institution of marriage. As the Industrial Revolution spread, young people could earn a living in the new factories. Greater independence made it easier for young people themselves to decide whom to marry and not have to depend on their parents' choice.

The marriage ceremony itself has taken many different forms. Perhaps most familiar to Westerners is the traditional ceremony with the bride in white gown and the groom in formal clothes (above).

Many wedding traditions symbolize the union between the two partners. In ancient China the bridal couple drank from cups that were made from two halves of the same melon. At Japanese weddings (left), the couple drink wine together, exchanging cups nine times.

In 1829 Sir Robert Peel, a member of the British government, organized a permanent police force for London. This force was responsible for maintaining order and making sure people obeyed the law. The London police were nicknamed "bobbies" after Peel's first name, Robert, and they are still called that today. Other major cities soon followed London's lead and established police forces.

The development of suburbs. As cities grew and became more crowded, their boundaries expanded to include surrounding areas. In addition, people moved outside cities to new areas called suburbs—residential areas on the outskirts of cities. Suburbs first began to develop in the late 1800's. Families lived in the suburbs, where there was less crowding, noise, and dirt, but the working members journeyed each day to jobs in the city.

Railroad and bus lines made this travel possible. During the late 1800's, more and more cities established public transportation systems so that people could travel from home to work. At first the fares of trains and horse-drawn buses were too high for ordinary working people to afford. Only employers, managers, merchants, and professionals were able to pay the fares. They could therefore afford to live fairly long distances from work, in the new suburbs. Factory workers, on the other hand, had to live within walking distance of their jobs. By the end of the 1800's, however, lower fares made it possible for most city dwellers to take trolleys or horse-drawn buses to work.

Leisure and cultural activities

Many forms of entertainment that we are familiar with today first developed during the 1800's. Before the 1800's, of course, there were concerts and plays, and people played games and sports. As the populations in cities grew during the industrial age, these activities increased. Large audiences now paid to hear professional musicians or to watch professional athletes perform.

Sports. People had participated in athletic events for many centuries. The rich hunted and played a form of tennis. The poor organized informal games on the village common. In fact, the origins of football (known in the United States as soccer) have been traced to a game played by villagers using an inflated pig's bladder as a ball.

During the 1800's, however, many games began to be organized formally. In Great Britain, football was among the first games to change from an informal community activity to a professional spectator game.

Football clubs for working-class people were created in the 1850's. By then laws had been enacted granting factory workers Saturday afternoon and Sunday as rest days. Groups of players gathered each week to compete, and the rest of the community came to watch. By the 1860's rules of the game were formally written down, and in 1871 a national competition among football clubs was established.

Soon certain football clubs had reputations for their skill, and they attracted large crowds. Many people who did not play football themselves knew, nonetheless, what the rules of the game were. By the mid-1880's players were being hired as full-time athletes. Football had become a sport played by professionals and watched by paying spectators.

Concert halls, museums, and libraries. Before the 1800's most cultural activities were privately sponsored. Concerts were performed in the homes of the rich or as part of religious services. Paintings were commissioned by wealthy individuals who wanted to commemorate a family or personal event. Paintings and sculpture were also ordered as decoration by individual families and by religious organizations. For the most part art objects were displayed in private homes or in churches.

During the 1800's art and music became available to ordinary people. City governments built concert halls and opera houses, and theaters offering a wide variety of plays were opened in large and small towns. Music halls offered popular entertainment and vaudeville generally to working-class audiences, while middle-class people were more often attracted to classical drama.

Cities began to support symphony orchestras, bands, and choral groups. Performances were held in the large concert halls. Bands performed on Sunday afternoons in parks, where people picnicked, fished, or walked.

During the 1800's art moved from churches and private homes to public museums. The Louvre Museum in Paris had contained the art collections of the kings of France. Now, it became a public

Leisure activities

During the 1800's people of all classes began to find new ways to spend their leisure time. New sports, such as football, became popular among working people. The middle and upper classes were drawn to other sports, such as tennis (above). The growing cities offered many opportunities for recreation to their increasing populations. A large open space was preserved in New York City, for example, and laid out as Central Park. Here people could walk, play games, or go skating in the winter (below). City governments also built concert halls and libraries, offering music and literature to their residents. The Louvre in Paris became a public museum, and people in London flocked to see the wonders at the British Museum (left).

museum. Paintings were organized and displayed by historical period and by country. The museum received money from the French government, which wanted to educate its citizens in matters of art.

Great libraries were opened—for example, the Bibliothèque Nationale in Paris and the British Museum in London. They contained great collections of books and were open to public use in the 1840's. In some cities, too, lending libraries with small collections offered books to subscribers for a small fee.

Public parks and urban planning. Crowded cities had few places for outdoor recreation. When railroads were built, people often rode trains to the countryside. They could spend the day there, away from the congestion, noise, and dirt of city streets. Some people demanded, in addition, that city governments provide parks within cities for recreation.

In a number of cities, small areas were set aside as parks. At the end of the 1800's, playgrounds for children were built. Private lands were donated or purchased by city governments and given to the people as parks. Large areas within city limits—for example, the Bois du Bologne in Paris and Central Park in New York City—were set aside as parks and opened to the public.

At the end of the 1800's, amusement parks began to appear in some cities. To entertain the crowds who came to them, the amusement parks offered games and rides, circuslike shows, and food. A famous example of an amusement park was Coney Island, which opened in 1895 in Brooklyn, New York.

CHECKUP

1. IDENTIFY: Malthus, bobbies.

2. Give two reasons that population increased after the Industrial Revolution.

3. What were some of the effects of population growth during the Industrial Revolution?

4. What improvements in the city were made possible by new technology?

5. How did transportation help give rise to suburbs in the early 1800's?

6. What new forms of leisure activities developed in the 1800's?

6

Workers protested the effects of industrialization

As the Industrial Revolution progressed, the interests of employers and workers often conflicted. Employers needed workers who would come to work on time, do their jobs quickly and well, follow the rules of the factory, and accept relatively low wages.

Workers, on the other hand, needed wages high enough to support their families even in time of illness or high prices. They wanted some say about the hours they worked and the conditions in the factories and in the towns where they lived. Ideas about what was fair differed between workers and employers. The employers claimed that their factories and money were indispensable. Without these means of production, the workers would have no work and they would starve. The workers claimed that without their labor, factories would not run and goods would not be produced.

Machine breaking

Early in the Industrial Revolution some artisans protested the effects of machinery on their work. They organized groups and, late at night, entered the new factories, where they broke machines and set fire to the buildings.

In Great Britain the machine breakers left notes after they attacked, warning employers not to try to open their factories again. They said that the new machines were destroying the work and life of spinners and weavers and other artisans. The machine breakers believed they were an army avenging the fate of the artisans. They claimed they were led by a general named Ned Ludd. As a result, the machine breakers became known as Luddites. When similar actions occurred in France, machine breakers there were also referred to as Luddites.

Worker strikes

One way for workers to protest working conditions and low wages was to refuse, as a group, to work. A group of miners, for example, who felt

Thonet Rocker

In the 1840's Michael Thonet, an Austrian cabinetmaker, invented a process that revolutionized furniture making. His bentwood rocker, shown here, may look familiar. Ones like it are still sold in stores today. Thonet's patent consisted of bending solid wood by steaming it and then clamping a thin strip of steel along one side. This process eliminated complex jointing and carving. It meant that Thonet could hire local people, not expensive artisans, for his European factories. Men did the cutting and bending; women and children the sanding, polishing, and packing.

Thus, well before the Industrial Revolution affected the rest of the furniture industry, Thonet's chairs, hat stands, and other pieces were being factory produced and marketed to the new middle class. By the end of the 1800's, Thonet's company was making 4,000 pieces of furniture a day—over one million a year—a triumph in mass production.

they were being paid too little for their work would all refuse to enter the mines. When an entire group of workers refused to work, they were said to be on **strike.** Workers often made a list of their demands and told the employer they would not work until these demands were met. Employers sometimes agreed to give the strikers what they wanted. At other times, they fired all the strikers and hired new workers, or they just waited until the workers returned to work.

Hundreds of strikes took place in industrializing countries during the first half of the 1800's. The strikes were usually over two kinds of demands— higher wages for workers and more control over working conditions.

Strikes were usually local events. Workers in a particular mine or factory would refuse to work until their demands were met. But in some cases the strikes spread from one town to another. In the 1830's, for example, shoemakers in one town after another in France went out on strike demanding higher wages. There were also similar waves of strikes by tailors and carpenters during this period.

Sometimes strikes turned into larger protests.

They began as demands for higher wages, but they soon became protests against general working and living conditions of the working class. Leaders demanded a reorganization of society to end the differences between rich and poor, employers and workers.

These large-scale protest movements occurred in northern England in 1811 and 1812, in the silk-weaving city of Lyons, France, in 1831 and 1834, and in Silesia, in eastern Europe, in 1844. They ended with the governments sending in troops to arrest protesting workers.

The union movement in England

In order to strengthen their position, workers sought ways to organize together permanently. They felt their efforts would be more successful if they belonged to associations of workers. One of the functions of these associations would be to collect dues and use the money to pay workers when they were on strike. The associations could plan actions and coordinate the demands of different types of workers in the same factory. These associations came to be called **unions.**

Organizing unions was not easy. English law, for instance, regarded workers' associations as illegal. When workers tried to unite anyway, employers were successful in getting Parliament to pass laws against them. An act of 1800 stated that persons who combined with others to demand higher wages, shorter hours, or better working conditions could be sent to prison. Eventually, however, the workers began to make some progress. In 1825 Parliament passed a law that permitted laborers to meet in order to agree on wages and hours.

In the 1840's many English workers joined the Chartist movement for election reform, about which you will read in Chapter 20. When this movement failed, they worked harder to strengthen labor unions. The National Association for the Protection of Labor was formed in 1845, and it helped persuade Parliament to allow peaceful picketing. In the 1870's, Parliament passed laws legalizing strikes.

Unions in France and Germany

In France, the labor movement made slower progress. French trade unions were outlawed in 1791, but they began to emerge illegally in the 1820's. It was not until 1884 that they were legalized. In Germany, workers' associations came into existence in the 1840's. The movement grew so fast during the late 1800's that the government became alarmed. It banned all unions in 1878 with a law that remained in effect until 1890.

To get around laws forbidding unions, workers formed secret societies. They sometimes used legal organizations, such as burial societies, as "fronts" or covers for union activity.

Once workers had gained the legal rights to form unions and to strike, they had more power to deal with employers. Gradually, factory owners granted unions recognition—that is, they agreed that union representatives could speak and bargain for all the members. Union and management met to negotiate wages, hours, and working conditions. If the bargainers could agree, they wrote their agreements into a contract to last for a fixed period of time. This whole process of negotiation is called **collective bargaining.** However, collective bargaining became an accepted process only during the 1900's.

Reform laws

In response to workers' protests and to the appeals of reformers, governments passed laws to deal with working conditions.

The first attempts to improve working conditions by legislation were made in Great Britain, where industrialization was more widespread than elsewhere. The earliest laws dealt with the employment of women and children. The Factory Act of 1819 showed how far the movement had to go. It prohibited the employment of children under 9 years of age in cotton mills. Children between the ages of 9 and 18 were limited to 12 hours of work a day. In 1833 this law was applied to all textile factories, where children under 9 could no longer be employed. Children from the ages of 9 to 13 were limited to 9 hours daily, while those from ages 13 to 18 were permitted to work 12 hours a day.

Nine years later another law prohibited the employment in mines of all women and girls and of boys under ten years old. A great advance came in 1847 with the passage of the Ten Hours Act. This law established a ten-hour working day for women and children under the age of 18 in textile factories. Since it was not profitable to keep the factories running when the women and children were gone, the ten-hour workday became the rule for all textile workers.

Despite these reform laws, the conditions under which many workers labored continued to be harsh. Laws often were not strictly enforced, and they did not solve all of the workers' problems. For example, the factory reform laws did not deal at all with wages. Eventually, workers would be able to improve their working conditions by organizing more widely and by government legislation.

CHECKUP

1. IDENTIFY: Luddites, strike, collective bargaining, Factory Act of 1819, Ten Hours Act.

2. List three methods of protest that were used during the Industrial Revolution to demand changes in working conditions.

3. What were the two kinds of demands usually made by strikers?

4. Why were unions created?

CHAPTER REVIEW

early 1700's	Agricultural revolution	1819	Factory Act passed in Great Britain
1733	Invention of flying shuttle		
1769	Watt's steam engine	1834	McCormick's reaper patented
1785	Cartwright's power loom	1839	Goodyear's vulcanizing of rubber
1793	Development of cotton gin		
1807	Launching of Fulton's *Clermont*	1844	Morse's telegraph in wide use
1814	Stephenson's locomotive	1847	Ten Hours Act passed in Great Britain

1850's	Kelly and Bessemer steel processes
1866	First transatlantic cable
1876	Bell's telephone patented
1879	Electric light bulb developed by Edison
1901	First transatlantic wireless message transmitted by Marconi
1903	Wright brothers' flight

CHAPTER SUMMARY

The Industrial Revolution—the production of goods by machinery in factories—changed the world. It began in Great Britain because of that country's favorable balance of the factors of production. It was preceded by an agricultural revolution characterized by increased production and the movement of farm workers to the cities.

In the cotton textile industry, the first to be mechanized, each invention stimulated others. Basic to the Industrial Revolution was the replacement of water power by steam power. Almost as important was the development of better methods of making steel.

By gathering workers together in factories, the Industrial Revolution brought an end to the traditional practices of artisans. Workers became reliant on wages and no longer controlled the pace of their work. Living and working conditions were often poor. Low wages, long hours, child labor, and slum housing were among the worst features of industrialization. At the same time, as a result of the Industrial Revolution, the middle class grew and gained importance. Different working opportunities for women also became available.

Transportation improved with better roads, networks of canals and railroads, and the use of steam power in ships. New inventions, such as the telephone and the wireless telegraph, made rapid communication possible. The use of electricity became widespread, and the development of the internal-combustion engine made travel by automobiles and airplanes possible.

A series of innovations in business practices accompanied the Industrial Revolution. Mass production—based on the division of labor, interchangeable parts, and the assembly line—transformed several industries. Mass production permitted the growth of enormous corporations, which came to dominate the economies of the industrialized nations.

The technological developments of the Industrial Revolution had profound effects. The population of Western countries increased rapidly, and cities grew larger than ever before. Masses of people in the cities created a need for better sanitation and new methods of public safety. Sports and leisure activities also developed.

Workers began increasingly to protest harsh working conditions and low wages. The first labor unions were organized to seek improvements in working conditions. Although some governments passed reform laws, working conditions continued to be harsh in the last years of the 1800's.

CHECKING WHAT YOU KNOW

1. Match each item at the left with an inventor at the right.

   a. radio
   b. crop rotation
   c. flying shuttle
   d. telegraph
   e. reaper
   f. seed drill
   g. cotton gin
   h. efficient steel production
   i. modern steam engine

   1. McCormick
   2. Marconi
   3. Whitney
   4. Tull
   5. Watt
   6. Bessemer and Kelly
   7. Townshend
   8. Kay
   9. Morse

2. How did the Industrial Revolution change the relationship between workers and employers?

3. Why might each of the following be considered a result of advances in technology:
   a. establishment of corporations
   b. rapid increase in population
   c. growth of cities
   d. organization of unions

4. Describe how industrialization affected the lives of working-class and middle-class women.

PRACTICING YOUR SKILLS

1. **Making a time line.** Prepare a time line showing the important inventions mentioned in this chapter. Use books in your library to find at least four other inventions not mentioned in the chapter. You might use Gertrude Hartman, *Machines and the Men Who Made the World of Industry* (Macmillan). Add the items to your time line.

2. **Using readings.** During the early years of the Industrial Revolution, it was not uncommon for five-year-old children to work in dark coal mines or poorly ventilated textile mills for as much as fourteen hours a day. The lines below, from a poem by Elizabeth Barrett Browning, describe the life of working-class children.

   > For oh," say the children, "We are weary, and we cannot run or leap;
   >
   > . . . .
   >
   > For all day, we drag our burden tiring Through the coal-dark underground; Or all day, we drive the wheels of iron In the factories, round and round.

   How did Browning view working conditions in Great Britain? What evidence in the poem supports your answer? Based on information in this chapter, how were working conditions gradually improved?

3. **Analyzing information.** What were the advantages and disadvantages of each of the following: rapid transportation, large business companies, the factory system, large cities, and specialization of labor?

4. **Using pictures.** Turn to the picture essay on page 457. What technological developments are shown in these pictures? How did each of these advances contribute to future industrial growth and progress?

RELATING PAST TO PRESENT

1. Study the poster advertising the 1889 Technological Exposition on page 462. Then investigate some of the important technological achievements of the 1970's. Use this information to design a poster for a similar exposition in 1979. If desired, your poster may be presented in the form of a collage.

2. Make a list of the ten leisure or cultural activities that you most enjoy doing. Which of these activities developed in the 1800's? Which are the result of more recent technological advances? Use your answers to these questions to write an essay entitled "Entertainment—Yesterday and Today."

INVESTIGATING FURTHER

1. By the 1850's, iron and coal had become the two major raw materials of modern industry. Using an atlas, draw an outline map of the world showing the global distribution of these resources today. Which nations have the largest concentration of coal? of iron?

2. Read the chapter entitled "No Way Out" in *Hard Times* by Charles Dickens. As you read, consider the differences between the worker (or "hand") and the owner of the factory. How did Dickens portray industrial society in the 1800's? What aspects of that society did he seem to be criticizing?

3. Some people believe that the United States is entering a second industrial revolution—a time of computers, lasers, microelectronics, and space-age technology. Research current articles on new inventions and recent scientific discoveries in the *Readers' Guide to Periodical Literature*. Be prepared to present your findings in a general discussion of technology in the 1980's.

4. The factory system changed working and living conditions. Using books in your library, investigate the reasons why people left farms and rural areas to move to cities and to work in factories. How did working conditions in factories and mines compare with those on farms?

(1770–1914)

20

Governments Sought Order While New Political Ideas Gained Influence

You have been reading about the economic and social changes brought by the Industrial Revolution. While these changes were occurring, much of Europe was in turmoil as a result of the French Revolution and the Napoleonic Wars.

Europe in 1815 was vastly different from the way it had been in 1789. As a result of the long period of warfare, there was much damage and destruction of property. Ruling families had been driven from their thrones. States had been shuffled about and combined to suit Napoleon.

The period following 1815 was notable for the effort to restore and maintain political order. Above all else, governments sought stability. However, new and vital forces were emerging after 1815. Two forces in particular had wide influence—nationalism and liberalism.

As you have read, nationalism is a feeling of loyalty and patriotism toward one's nation. Several factors work together to develop the feeling of nationalism. Among them is the sense of shared experiences, dangers, and problems. The years of unrest under Napleon had nurtured feelings of nationalism throughout Europe.

Liberalism was a movement that extended the principles of the American and French revolutions. Its followers believed that people ought to be free to think and work as they please. They felt that laws should protect individual rights, and

A richly furnished Victorian parlor

they believed that the way to improve society was to change laws. When all people were represented in the government, they said, fair laws would be passed.

For most of the 1800's, European leaders did everything they could to hold back forces that might lead to upheaval, such as those which had erupted in the French Revolution. The conflict between those who wanted to restore the old ways and those who sought change can be regarded as a key to understanding much that happened in the 1800's.

THE CHAPTER SECTIONS

1. The great powers readjusted boundaries and suppressed revolts

2. Reformers sought political and economic change

3. Liberal theories affected Great Britain and its empire

4. The United States grew and experienced social change

5. France underwent revolutions and changes of government

1

The great powers readjusted boundaries and suppressed revolts

Napoleon was finally defeated in 1815, as you have read, and an important turning point was reached in European history. For more than 25 years, the most powerful political influence had been the French Revolution. Even though Napoleon did not always uphold the ideals of the revolution—liberty, equality, and fraternity—he did carry its influence throughout Europe.

As long as Napoleon ruled France, the governments of other nations had reason to fear that political unrest or rebellion might challenge their own authority. Once Napoleon was defeated, therefore, the major powers were determined to restore order and keep peace. Their policies in the years after 1815 were designed, above all else, to maintain stability and to suppress any danger of political upheaval.

The Congress of Vienna

To achieve stability, it was necessary to settle political and territorial questions arising from the Napoleonic Wars. The settling of these questions was in the hands of the Congress of Vienna, a conference held in the Austrian capital. It had been called in September 1814, while Napoleon was in exile on Elba. About 700 diplomats attended at one time or another. The Congress was interrupted in 1815 by Napoleon's return from exile. After his defeat at Waterloo, however, the Congress resumed its work.

Despite the presence of many notable figures, the real decisions at the Congress of Vienna were made by only a few. The four great powers that had done the most to defeat Napoleon were Great Britain, Austria, Russia, and Prussia. These countries were represented by outstanding leaders. They were Lord Castlereagh (KAS·ul·ray), foreign secretary of Great Britain; Prince Klemens von Metternich, chief minister of Austria and chairman of the conference; Czar Alexander I of Russia; and King Frederick William III of Prussia.

It is not usual in peace conferences for the losers to have much of a role. However, the representative of defeated France, Charles Maurice de Talleyrand, was soon playing an important part at the Congress of Vienna. He was a shrewd negotiator and a master at changing sides. Talleyrand had wielded great influence from the days of the Estates-General through the reign of Napoleon. At the Congress of Vienna he was the foreign minister of the Bourbon king, Louis XVIII.

Talleyrand urged that settlements should be based on the principle of **legitimacy.** This meant that all the former ruling families—that is, the legitimate rulers—should be restored to their thrones. As you have read, the Bourbon monarchy was restored in France. Bourbon rulers also returned to power in Spain and Italy.

Territorial settlements

The winning powers soon began quarreling over the division of spoils. The two most difficult problems concerned Poland and the German state of Saxony. From Prussia's Polish territory, Napoleon had created the Grand Duchy of Warsaw, which he gave to his faithful ally, the king of Sax-

EUROPE IN 1815
after the Congress of Vienna

——— Boundary of the German Confederation

ony. Russia now demanded all of this territory. Prussia agreed, provided that the king of Saxony be deposed and Saxony be given to Prussia.

This arrangement was opposed by both Great Britain and Austria. Great Britain did not want to see Russia become too strong. Austria feared that the addition of Saxony might make Prussia too powerful in German affairs. For a time, war seemed to threaten. Then, Talleyrand was admitted to the conference. He suggested a compromise that settled the argument. Prussia received part of Saxony; most of what had been the Grand Duchy

of Warsaw went to Russia, with a small portion going to Prussia (see map, this page).

The Dutch Netherlands, one of Napoleon's early conquests, received the Austrian Netherlands and became the single Kingdom of the Netherlands. To compensate for this loss, Austria was given the northern Italian states of Venetia and Lombardy. Austrian Hapsburgs were also placed at the head of the northern Italian states of Parma, Modena, and Tuscany.

In addition to gaining the largest share of the Grand Duchy of Warsaw, Russia had acquired

Finland as a result of war with Sweden. Since Sweden had fought Napoleon, it was compensated by receiving Norway, formerly a Danish possession. Denmark was thus punished for cooperating with Napoleon. Prussia, in addition to its share of Saxony and Poland, received an area along the lower Rhine River.

The reason for all this territorial reshuffling was to set up a ring of strong states around France so that it could not again threaten the peace of Europe. The feelings of the people involved were not considered when regions changed hands. Territories were parceled out as if they were uninhabited deserts.

Although Great Britain did not receive territory in continental Europe, it did gain possessions overseas. They included several of the French West Indies and the Mediterranean island of Malta. From the Danish the British gained Helgoland, an island in the North Sea. From the Dutch they took Cape Colony in Africa and what became British Guiana in South America.

France was stripped of its conquests, and its boundaries were fixed as they had been in 1792. In addition, it had to pay a large **indemnity**—compensation to other nations for damages it had inflicted on them. France also had to pay for forts that the victorious nations maintained on the French borders.

Reaction, absolutism, and nationalism

The first few years after the Napoleonic Era have been called a time of **reaction,** a time when those in authority wanted to return to the orderly conditions of an earlier period. **Reactionaries** are extremists who not only oppose change, but generally would like to turn the clock back to the time before certain changes occurred.

In Europe after 1815, reaction took the form of attempts by the victors to restore conditions to what they had been before the upsets and revolutions had taken place.

In Spain, Naples, and the states of northern Italy, the reinstated rulers abolished the constitutions that had been adopted during Napoleon's rule. They returned to **absolutism**—government under which the ruler has unlimited power—as if nothing had ever happened. Switzerland alone was allowed to retain its constitutional republican

government, but had to promise that it would remain neutral in European wars. This neutrality was guaranteed by the European powers.

One result of Napoleon's conquests had been the spread of new political ideas, which the reactionary powers considered dangerous and tried to stamp out. Another result was the rise of nationalism. In the early 1800's, as various countries had reacted to conquest by Napoleon, a desire for unity had developed in fragmented nations.

National feelings began to have such wide influence that they were accepted as a basic political ideal. Writers, artists, and politicians justified nationalism by stressing a people's shared history, common language, or cultural achievements.

The desire for unity caused concern among the major powers of the time, and they tried to hold it back. For a while they were successful, and the Congress of Vienna left nationalistic groups disappointed. Some Italians, for example, had hoped for a united Italy. This hope was not fulfilled. To make matters worse, many Italian states were placed under a hated foreign rule. The desire of the Polish people for national independence was also blocked. Nor was there self-government for national groups living in the Austrian Empire.

The German desire for national unity came closer to fulfillment. Napoleon had consolidated many of the German states into the 16-member Confederation of the Rhine. Now more states, including Prussia, were added to form the German Confederation, with 39 members. Austria dominated this Confederation, since the Confederation's assembly was always presided over by an Austrian delegate.

Alliances among the great powers

The four allies that had finally defeated Napoleon—Great Britain, Austria, Russia, and Prussia—agreed in 1815 to continue their alliance. This became known as the Quadruple Alliance. The chief purpose of the alliance was "to guarantee Europe from dangers by which she may still be menaced"—that is, revolutionary movements. Members of the alliance agreed to see that France carried out the terms of the peace treaty. They planned to hold periodic conferences to keep the major powers in agreement on matters that concerned them all.

Czar Alexander I of Russia doubted that peace could be maintained and revolutions prevented simply by alliances. He was a firm believer in absolute monarchy. However, he believed just as firmly that monarchs should be guided by Christian moral principles, with a strong sense of duty toward their subjects. Shortly before joining the Quadruple Alliance, he had urged that all rulers should pledge themselves to rule as Christian princes by signing an agreement called the Holy Alliance. It had been signed by all the rulers of Europe except the king of England, the Turkish sultan, and the pope, who refused to be instructed in Christian principles by the czar.

If the rulers who signed the Holy Alliance had lived up to its ideals, the history of the next 50 years might have been different. However, they had agreed to the Holy Alliance only to humor the czar and had little intention of following its principles. Castlereagh scoffingly called it "a piece of sublime mysticism and nonsense."

Out of the practical Quadruple Alliance grew what was called the Concert of Europe—a form of international government by concert, or agreement. It was aimed at maintaining peace and the status quo (a Latin phrase meaning roughly "the condition in which things exist"). In this case, of course, the status quo was the balance of power established by the Congress of Vienna.

The first of the periodic conferences provided for by the Quadruple Alliance was held in 1818. France, having fulfilled the terms of the peace settlements, was restored to the European family of nations and was admitted to the Quadruple Alliance to make it a Quintuple Alliance. Although these various alliances were relatively short-lived, the Concert of Europe lasted until 1848, and the principles on which it was based came into play again several times later in the 1800's. The political leaders at Vienna, although ignoring popular national and liberal movements, did give Europe something very valuable—peace and order. After the Vienna settlements, there was no major war among the great powers for almost 40 years.

The Age of Metternich

For 30 years after the Congress of Vienna, Prince Metternich, chief minister of Austria, influenced Europe so strongly that the period is sometimes known as the Age of Metternich. Metternich was a reactionary and believed that absolute monarchy was the only good government. He looked with fear and horror at liberalism, constitutions, and such ideals as freedom of speech, religion, and the press. He believed the best way to handle such ideas was to suppress them completely.

Metternich's aims were simple. He was determined to prevent war or revolution and to preserve absolutism. At home in Austria, he had little difficulty in achieving these aims. He set up an efficient system of secret police to spy on revolutionary organizations and individuals. Liberals were imprisoned, fined, or exiled.

Because Austria controlled the German Confederation, Metternich was able to persuade the rulers of most German states to adopt the same methods. Hapsburg rule in northern Italy made sure that no revolutionary movements would succeed there. In France the king, Louis XVIII, had to move cautiously in domestic affairs. He was quite willing, however, to join in suppressing revolutions elsewhere.

Reaction to Metternich

Liberals reacted strongly against Metternich's repressive system. They were angered at the outcome of the Congress of Vienna and at Metternich's actions to check liberalism. As a result, there were a number of uprisings in Europe. Metternich turned the Concert of Europe into an instrument for suppressing liberal ideas. Whenever there was a threat to the status quo, representatives of the five powers gathered to discuss ways of handling it. Austria, Russia, and Prussia went further. They agreed to act together to put down any attempt at revolution anywhere.

Great Britain could not agree to this last step. It opposed interfering where liberal popular movements were attempting to overthrow absolute rulers. Great Britain itself had a representative government. The British people (though not their rulers) sympathized with other peoples in their struggles for similar governments. More important, Great Britain was a trading nation. Meddling with other countries was not good for British commerce. Under the influence of George Canning, who became foreign secretary in 1822, Great Britain withdrew from the Quintuple Alliance.

The Age of Metternich

After the fall of Napoleon, the leading diplomats of Europe assembled at the Congress of Vienna (above) to redraw the map of Europe. The moving spirit behind the discussions was Prince Metternich (standing and pointing), the chief minister of Austria. Hating liberalism and disorder in government, Metternich used his position as chairman of the Congress to assure the strength of the traditional European regimes.

Metternich became a symbol of conservative government. He kept a tight rein over the Austrian Empire, but resentment grew steadily. In the late 1840's the anger of the people exploded in uprisings against repressive governments. An engraving (below) shows citizens looking at a poster promising the overthrow of Metternich.

In einem Monat wird
Fürst Metternich
gestürzt sein
Eslebe das constitutionelle
Oesterreich!

The Metternich system in operation

For a time the Metternich system operated successfully. When discontent flared up among German university students in 1819, Metternich called together the leaders of the larger states of the German Confederation at Carlsbad in Bohemia. At his insistence they adopted measures known as the Carlsbad Decrees. Students and faculty members of the universities were placed under strict watch. Newspapers and periodicals were rigidly censored. An organization was formed to search for secret revolutionary activities. There were to be no political reforms that conflicted with the principle of absolute monarchy.

In spite of repression, there were several underground movements that opposed the status quo. In 1820 a revolt in Spain forced King Ferdinand VII to restore the constitution he had abolished. The four continental members of the Quintuple Alliance were alarmed. Despite British protests, they sent a French army to Spain. In 1823 Ferdinand was restored to full power.

The Spanish revolt inspired other uprisings in 1820. In Naples, revolutionaries forced the ruler to grant a constitution. This revolt was soon put down by an Austrian army. In Portugal, too, the ruler was forced to accept a constitution. A few years later, however, he abolished it and assumed absolute power.

In 1821 nationalism upset the international order when the Greeks revolted against the harsh rule of the Ottoman Turks. Influenced by Metternich, European rulers refused Greek pleas for aid. However, many individuals came to the support of the Greeks, either as volunteers or by sending arms. One of these volunteers was Lord Byron, the British poet, who died in Greece in 1824.

Finally, the nations that had usually sided with Metternich—Russia, Great Britain, and France—brought pressure on the Ottoman sultan. By the Treaty of Adrianople in 1829, Greece became an independent state. The Serbs and Rumanians, to the north in the Balkan Peninsula, received some rights of self-government.

Greek independence was the first real failure of the Metternich system in Europe. It showed that the sense of nationalism encouraged by the French Revolution could not be suppressed forever.

CHECKUP

1. IDENTIFY: Castlereagh, Talleyrand, indemnity, reactionaries, Concert of Europe, Carlsbad Decrees, Treaty of Adrianople.

2. LOCATE: Saxony, Kingdom of the Netherlands, Venetia, Lombardy, Malta, Helgoland.

3. Give an example of the principle of legitimacy as it operated at the Congress of Vienna.

4. What was the Quadruple Alliance? the Holy Alliance? the Quintuple Alliance?

5. Why is the period after 1815 called the Age of Metternich? What were Metternich's aims?

Reformers sought political and economic change

Liberalism grew out of the Enlightenment, particularly the writings of people like Locke and Rousseau. It linked ideas about individual freedom not only to politics but economic affairs and the government's role in them. At the same time, liberalism offered a different vision of the future than did the governments that were primarily concerned with maintaining order.

Smith and Ricardo

The economic ideas of liberalism were expressed by Adam Smith, a Scot, in his book *The Wealth of Nations,* published in 1776. Smith believed there were certain natural laws that governed economic life. Any attempt to interfere with these natural economic laws was certain to bring disaster.

Smith reasoned that all business and economic activity is regulated by two natural laws—the law of supply and demand and the law of competition. In any business, prices—and therefore profits—will be fixed by the relationship of supply to demand. If an article is scarce and in great demand, people will pay a high price for it. Thus profits from its sales will rise. People with money will then invest it to produce more of the scarce article. Soon there will be a plentiful supply.

Now each manufacturer will face competition.

In order to get people to buy a product, the price must be reduced or the quality improved, or both. If too many manufacturers enter the same business, the price will go down so far that some manufacturers will not make enough money to cover their costs. Some may be forced out of business entirely. This will generally happen to the least efficient businesses—the ones that are so poorly organized and managed that their production costs are high. When such manufacturers have to quit, the supply of the article will decrease and the price will go up. Then the capable, efficient, and well-organized producers will make a reasonable profit.

Thus, Adam Smith wrote, every person should be free to do what he or she thinks best—to go into any business and to operate it for the greatest advantage. The result would be beneficial to everyone. Laborers would have jobs, investors and owners would make profits, and buyers would receive better goods at lower prices. Smith's system was one of complete **free enterprise.**

Another English writer, David Ricardo, applied these ideas to wages. In his book *Principles of Political Economy and Taxation,* published in 1817, Ricardo stated that wages were determined by supply and demand. When labor was plentiful, wages were low. When it was scarce, wages were high. As population grew, Ricardo wrote, there would be more and more workers and wages would inevitably go down. This idea became known as the "iron law of wages."

Smith and Ricardo said that governments should not interfere with the operations of business. If there was any interruption of supply, demand, and competition, the system would not work well. Laws and regulations, they believed, would interfere with these natural laws. This attitude was summed up in a French phrase **laissez faire** (les·ay FAIR), meaning "let do"—that is, leave things alone.

Growing interest in reform

As time went on, more and more people realized that things could not be left entirely alone. Reforms were urged by humanitarians—people who work to improve the conditions of others. Ministers preached against what they considered the un-Christian selfishness of business people.

Influential writers did much to make people aware of the terrible conditions in mines and factories. Novels by the great English writer Charles Dickens were especially important. *Dombey and Son* and *Hard Times* both attacked selfish business leaders. In *David Copperfield* Dickens described his own wretched boyhood experiences as a worker in a warehouse. Essayists and critics like Thomas Carlyle and John Ruskin denounced the materialism—the obsession with money and the neglect of spiritual values—of their times.

As you read in Chapter 19, many people began to feel that government interference was necessary to regulate hours of work and set minimal standards for wages and working conditions. They argued that these laws would not interfere with the natural workings of the economy.

Utilitarianism. In Great Britain, some reformers adopted the ideas associated with the writings of Jeremy Bentham. Bentham believed that the principle of utility, or usefulness, was the standard by which to measure a society and its laws. His theory was thus known as **utilitarianism.** Bentham felt that reform should be undertaken to ensure "the greatest good for the greatest number" of people. The greatest good was that which gave pleasure and avoided pain. Bentham felt that people needed education so that they would want things that were good for them.

Bentham and his followers advocated reform of prisons, education, and law. They felt that government ought to create the conditions for the realization of happiness by as many people as possible.

John Stuart Mill

The philosopher John Stuart Mill, although a believer in laissez faire, was critical of the economic injustices and inequalities of British society. He thought that the government should intervene to protect working children and improve housing and factory conditions. Mill's father had been associated with Bentham and had taught his son the principles of utilitarianism.

Mill believed that government should work for the well-being of all its citizens. He also wrote that governments must represent all citizens—that is, that everyone of a certain age should be allowed to vote. Governments would pass good laws, he said, only if the interests of all individuals and

Reformers and their ideas

The responses to the social problems caused by industrialization were almost as varied as the problems themselves. The English reformer Robert Owen wanted to create ideal communities separated from the rest of society. He founded one such community at New Harmony, Indiana, in the United States. Its 2,000 inhabitants were to reside in one huge building, which was designed (below) but never built. A German philosopher, Karl Marx (left), was even more radical. He predicted that the workers would one day take control of society and then all repressive governments would "wither away."

Such calls for change, combined with the inspiration of the French Revolution, brought people into the streets in frequent protest (bottom). They hoped to improve their living conditions through action, not theory.

groups were taken care of. Laws would be obeyed by people who felt they had a part in making them. Mill also believed that women as well as men should have the right to vote. "All human beings have the same interest in good government," he wrote in 1861. "The welfare of all is alike affected by it, and they have equal need of a voice in it to secure their share of its benefits."

In his most famous essay, "On Liberty," published in 1859, Mill insisted that freedom of thought was a key to progress. Unless people could debate ideas, important new outlooks would never be allowed to develop and people would not progress. Individual liberty was a basic human right, in Mill's view. Liberty to think as one pleased and express one's views was the most important part of individual liberty. Mill felt that governments should guarantee that liberty.

Political liberalism

The ideas of liberals greatly influenced politics during the 1800's. As you have read, liberals reacted strongly against the Metternich system of absolute rule. Their ideas were very much at odds with those of Metternich.

The ideas of liberalism were evident in the internal political conflicts of Great Britain, France, Italy, the United States, and Germany during the 1800's. Liberal ideas took many different forms in these countries, but certain key ideas were the same. These included (1) a belief in the importance of individual liberty, (2) a guarantee of individual rights by governments in the form of a constitution, (3) freedom of speech, assembly, and press, (4) religious freedom, (5) representative government, and (6) education.

Most liberals did not believe that all people should have the right to vote immediately. Instead, most felt that this right should be extended gradually, to those with enough education to vote intelligently.

Socialism and economic change

Many people were disturbed by the fact that the great wealth produced by the Industrial Revolution was so unevenly distributed. That is, a few people became enormously rich, while most remained poor. Some reformers became con-

vinced that laissez-faire capitalism was not the best economic system. They argued that laws could not do enough to remedy inequalities. They thought that a better distribution of wealth could be achieved only by changing the way in which the means of production were owned and operated. The means of production include everything used to produce and exchange goods—for example, land, mines, railroads, factories, stores, and banks. Like the liberals, these reformers cared less about keeping social order than achieving social justice.

Some reformers of the 1800's advocated a political and economic system called **socialism.** It was based on the belief that the means of production should be owned publicly, or socially, and should be operated for the welfare of all the people.

Under capitalism the means of production are owned by private citizens and operated by them for private profit. Socialists wanted to establish an economic system that would do away with the profit motive and competition. They believed that everyone had a right to share in the profits of industry.

Early socialists. The early socialists tried to work out detailed schemes for model communities and to persuade people to join in setting them up. You will remember that Thomas More described a model community in his *Utopia.* Thus these early socialists were sometimes called **utopian socialists.** They believed that people could live at peace with each other if they lived in small cooperative settlements, owning all the means of production in common and sharing the products.

Various utopian schemes were advocated in the early 1800's, many by French reformers such as Charles Fourier (foo·RYAY). In Great Britain the most influential utopian socialist was Robert Owen.

Owen, who lived from 1771 to 1858, left school as a boy and went to work. He was extremely successful in business, and he soon became manager of a cotton mill. Eventually he became both owner and manager of a large mill in New Lanark, Scotland, which employed over 1,500 people.

Owen believed that people were naturally good. If they lived in a good environment, they would cease to act selfishly. As a factory owner, he felt responsible for his workers and devoted much time and money to making their lives happier and more secure. He built good homes for them, paid them decent wages, and established a store where they could buy inexpensive food. He also set up schools for their children.

Owen believed, however, that workers should not be completely dependent on their employers. He encouraged them to form unions. He also established cooperative communities in both Great Britain and the United States. Owen's best-known settlement in the United States was at New Harmony, Indiana.

The theories of Karl Marx

Some thinkers were impatient with early socialism, which they felt was impractical. The most important of such critics was Karl Marx, who was born in Prussia in 1818. Marx was a journalist, whose radical political views made him unpopular in his own country. Forced to leave, he eventually settled in London, where he lived until his death in 1883.

In 1848, with a fellow German, Friedrich Engels, Marx published the *Communist Manifesto,* a pamphlet outlining his ideas. Marx believed that all the great changes in history came from changes in economic conditions.

Marx wrote that human history had moved through several stages. First there had been small communities or tribes in which people shared property and work. Then slavery arose. Some people owned all the property and owned people who were forced to work for them. Feudalism followed slavery, according to Marx. In that stage landowners controlled the lives of serfs, who depended on them for land and food. Capitalism emerged from feudalism and brought with it industrial development. Those who owned machinery and tools were the capitalists, who employed workers in their factories.

Marx stated that each stage of history involved inequality and therefore struggle between those who owned property and those who did not. In the capitalist stage, the struggle was between the owners, or capitalists, and the working class, or **proletariat** (proh·luh·TAIR·ee·ut).

Marx argued that all wealth is created by labor. Under capitalism, he said, labor receives only a small fraction of the wealth it creates. Most of the wealth goes to the owners in the form of profits.

As a result of this inequality, the capitalist system necessarily suffered from increasingly severe depressions, because working people lacked money to buy the products manufactured in the factories. He thought the time would soon come when capitalist society would be divided into a few capitalists and a vast mass of workers, or proletarians. The proletarians, gathered in cities, would suffer poverty and unemployment.

In these circumstances the proletarians in the most advanced and industrialized nations would unite, seize power by force in a revolution, and establish socialism. Since many people would not be ready to accept socialism, the workers would have to control the government. Marx referred to this phase as the "dictatorship of the proletariat." After a period of education, people would become experienced in working together cooperatively. Force would no longer be needed and the state would "wither away." It was this last stage, characterized by a truly classless society, that Marx called pure communism.

In Marx's time the terms *communism* and *socialism* were used in many different ways. For Marx and Engels, a communist was one who believed that people could live cooperatively without being forced to do so. Today, as you will read later, a communist is usually someone who belongs to a political party that seeks revolutionary change.

Marx believed that pure communism was the inevitable outcome of human history. Each person would contribute what he or she could and receive what he or she needed. Said Marx: "From each according to his abilities, to each according to his needs."

Marx called his variety of socialism "scientific socialism" because he thought he was describing objective laws of historical development—that is, laws that would work inevitably. Marx published many of his ideas in *Das Kapital* (German for "capital"), a book that analyzed capitalism in detail.

Socialism after Marx

Socialists began to form political parties to put their ideas into practice in the mid-1800's. Many of these parties were influenced by the ideas of Marx and Engels. Marxist, or radical, socialists generally believed that revolution was necessary to overthrow the capitalist system.

Another group of socialists, though influenced by Marx, believed that socialism could come gradually by education and through democratic forms of government. These moderate socialists believed that when enough people were educated about socialism, they would elect socialist representatives to their government. Then the government would take over the means of production peacefully. The owners would be paid for their property, and the government would then operate the means of production in the interest of all the people.

Marx believed that workers had to unite in order to fight capitalism successfully. In 1864 he helped found the International Workingmen's Association, called the First International. This organization came to an end in 1876. A Second International was formed in 1889, after Marx's death. It was torn by disagreements between moderate and radical socialists and survived as an international organization only into the early 1900's.

You will read in later chapters about socialist parties in various European countries. You will also read about Marxist ideas as they were put into practice in Russia and elsewhere during the 1900's.

CHECKUP

1. IDENTIFY: free enterprise, "iron law of wages," laissez faire, *Hard Times,* Bentham, Mill, means of production, Owen, Marx, Engels, *Communist Manifesto,* proletariat, First International.

2. According to Adam Smith, how did the law of supply and demand and the law of competition work? What conclusion did Smith draw from these laws?

3. Define utilitarianism. How was this theory applied to social reform?

4. What six points did most liberals support during the 1800's?

5. Describe the stages of history, according to Marx, that would lead to pure communism.

6. Explain what is meant by each of the following: utopian socialism, scientific socialism, Marxist socialism, moderate socialism.

3

Liberal theories affected Great Britain and its empire

Those who believed in liberal theories were often active in politics during the 1800's. In Great Britain, in parts of the British Empire, and in the United States, they were able to enact a number of reforms aimed at accomplishing liberal ideals. These reforms included extension of the right to vote to working men and to women and the abolition of slavery, which had denied the human rights of black people.

British reforms of the 1800's

In Great Britain a series of reform laws passed between 1832 and 1919 made the government more democratic.

Great Britain was one of the first European nations to do away with divine-right monarchy. The Glorious Revolution of 1688 had made Parliament the real ruler of the country. As you have read, the country became a limited constitutional monarchy with executive power vested in a cabinet led by the prime minister. The government, however, was not a complete democracy because not all the people had a chance to participate in it.

Voting restrictions. Theoretically the House of Commons represented the British people in the government. Members of Commons were elected by the voters of their districts. The right to vote, however, was severely restricted in several ways:

(1) Only property owners and a few other privileged people could vote.

(2) Catholics, Jews, and Dissenters (non-Anglican Protestants) could not hold political office.

(3) Voting in elections was done openly instead of by secret ballot. This system encouraged bribery and the influencing of voters.

(4) The boundaries of election districts, or boroughs, had not been changed since 1664. In some districts, called "rotten boroughs," the population had decreased or even disappeared, but the districts still sent members to the House of Com-

mons. On the other hand, some areas that had greatly increased in population, such as the industrial cities, had no representation in Parliament at all.

(5) In some boroughs the choice of a representative was completely controlled by the nobles, who were members of the House of Lords. These were called "pocket boroughs" because in each the noble had the representative "in his pocket." This meant that the representative would vote as he was told to by the noble.

(6) Only men who owned considerable property could be elected to the House of Commons. Representatives received no salary. Thus a man who was not a large landowner could not be elected, and a man without a large income could not afford to serve.

The Reform Bill of 1832. King George IV took a small step in the direction of reform near the end of his reign in 1829. He supported passage of the Catholic Emancipation Act. This law permitted Roman Catholics to be elected to Parliament if they recognized the Protestant monarch as the true ruler of Great Britain.

As time went on, the middle class and workers began to demand more extensive reforms. Several times the House of Commons passed bills to give more people the right to vote, and to reapportion, or divide, election districts more fairly. Each time the House of Lords refused to pass the bill. Finally the Whigs came to power in 1830. They forced King William IV to announce that he would create as many new lords as necessary to give the bill a majority in the House of Lords. To avoid this move, the lords grudgingly gave in and passed the bill in 1832.

The Reform Bill of 1832 took power in Commons away from the rotten boroughs and pocket boroughs and gave it to the new industrial cities. Property qualifications for voting were lowered. Now about one out of thirty Englishmen could vote. As a result, parliamentary power came more into the hands of the owners of factories and banks, the merchants, and the shipowners.

The Whig Party, which had forced the passage of the Reform Bill of 1832, had the support of the new voters. Since many voters favored even more liberal reforms, the party changed its name and became the Liberal Party. The Tory Party of the large landowners had opposed the reforms and

was reluctant to go any further. It became known as the Conservative Party.

Chartism. Beginning in the 1830's, a group known as the Workingman's Association petitioned Parliament to adopt reforms such as universal manhood suffrage and the secret ballot. These proposals were made in a document called "A People's Charter," and those who advocated them were known as Chartists. They advocated complete democracy for Great Britain.

Chartist conventions were held in 1839, 1842, and 1848. Although their proposals were relatively mild, the Chartists were denounced as people who threatened the very foundations of society. In 1848 the British authorities were worried that revolution might occur in Great Britain. Although the Chartists were unable to secure their goals and the movement declined, workers continued to press for voting rights. Leaders of both political parties came to realize that reforms might gain the support of new voters.

In 1867 a second Reform Bill was passed. It was more sweeping than the first, and almost doubled the number of those who could vote. By lowering property qualifications, the second Reform Bill extended the vote to most city industrial workers. Some groups were still left out—household servants, members of the armed forces, agricultural workers, and all women.

Disraeli and Gladstone

In 1837 King William IV died and was succeeded by his 18-year-old niece, Victoria. She reigned for more than 60 years, until 1901. This period was so outstanding in British history that it has become known as the Victorian Era.

Victoria gave her prime ministers a great deal of power. The period between 1866 and 1894 was dominated by two of her prime ministers. One was Benjamin Disraeli, a leader of the Conservative Party, who served twice as prime minister. He was witty, shrewd, and greatly interested in foreign affairs and the enlargement of the British Empire. The other was William Gladstone, the leader of the Liberal Party, who served as prime minister four times. Gladstone was most concerned with British domestic and financial matters. Under his leadership, additional reforms were attempted, and some were put into effect.

The Age of Victoria

The Victorian Era began when an 18-year-old princess was crowned Queen Victoria. Three years later she married her German cousin, Prince Albert, who became her chief adviser. Victoria and Albert handled many matters of state, including accepting the homage of Great Britain's colonial subjects (below). Their close-knit family life and high moral standards were much admired and imitated.

When Albert died, Victoria went into deep mourning, not appearing in public for the next three years. She dressed only in black for the rest of her long life (left). For the last 30 years of her reign, a major force in British politics was William Gladstone (above), shown here making his final speech to the House of Commons in 1894.

The Victorians and King Arthur

Waving farewell to the magical sword Excalibur, Sir Bedivere watches as the mysterious Lady of the Lake takes back the weapon that had served his beloved King Arthur for so many years.

This ancient legend of Arthur, the ideal king, and his Knights of the Round Table dates back to the 600's A.D. Stories about a good and powerful leader were spread by word of mouth throughout England, Wales, and France for centuries. Then, in the 1400's, the English writer Sir Thomas Malory adapted these tales and William Caxton, one of England's first printers, published them. Children and adults have loved them ever since.

King Arthur was a special favorite during the Victorian Era. This scene was drawn in 1893 by Aubrey Beardsley, who was only 21 when he was commissioned to illustrate the King Arthur stories. Beardsley established a personal form of art, blending the ornate curves of art nouveau (new art) with the feeling and pattern of Japanese prints. He quickly became the leading illustrator of his day, but his fame was very short. Beardsley died of tuberculosis when he was only 25. Although often imitated, his exquisite, flat black-and-white style has remained unique.

One area in which reform was attempted unsuccessfully was the "Irish Question." In 1801 Ireland and Great Britain had been joined by the Act of Union into the United Kingdom of Great Britain and Ireland. The Irish were poorly represented in the British Parliament, however, and the people—most of them Roman Catholics—resented having to pay taxes to help support the Anglican Church.

The Irish hated British rule, especially the absentee landlords who owned much of the land. Several times in the mid-1800's, famine swept Ireland when the potato crop failed. Many abandoned their homes and went to the United States. Those who remained wanted new land laws and home rule—that is, self-government. Gladstone tried unsuccessfully to get home-rule bills passed.

Other reform measures were more successful. The secret ballot was adopted in 1872. It meant that a man could vote privately, without being afraid that he might suffer because someone disapproved of his political views. This move also reduced bribery, which had been common.

In 1884 the Liberals took the lead in pushing through Parliament the third Reform Bill, which gave the vote to most agricultural workers. In the following year the Redistribution Bill divided Great Britain into electoral districts that were approximately equal in population.

British reforms of the early 1900's

During the late 1800's and early 1900's, the labor union movement grew stronger in Great Britain. Socialism, too, attracted many followers. In 1884 a group of intellectuals founded the Fabian Society, a socialist organization aimed at "reconstructing society in accordance with the highest moral possibilities." At first the Fabians worked through the established political parties. In 1906 they helped found a new organization, the British Labour Party.

In 1905 the Liberal Party came to power. Under Herbert Asquith, prime minister from 1908 to 1916, the Liberals adopted extensive social welfare legislation. Laws provided for child care, old-age pensions, better housing, and health and unemployment insurance. These changes meant that the government had to spend more money and that taxes had to be increased to raise it.

The budget of 1909 called for changes in taxation that increased the tax burden of the wealthy. Opposition to the budget was so strong in the House of Lords that the Liberals decided to deprive the lords of their power to block reforms. The Parliament Bill of 1911 took away many of the lords' powers. The lords were bitterly opposed and passed the act only after George V, who had become king in 1910, threatened to create enough new Liberal lords to pass it.

Women's voting rights. An even more far-reaching change soon followed. Since the late 1880's, women's groups in Great Britain had been demanding the right to vote. Led by energetic and outspoken women such as Christabel Pankhurst and her mother, Emmeline, they were known as **suffragettes**—women who wanted suffrage, or voting rights for all women. Suffragettes had petitioned Parliament and marched to achieve voting rights. Many had expected that women would receive the right to vote in 1910, when George V became king, but this was not the case.

The campaign intensified. Women were sent to jail for their efforts to draw attention to their cause. After many years, women with property won the right to vote in 1919. In 1928 another bill granted all British women the right to vote.

Creating the Canadian dominion

As social and political reforms were being instituted in Great Britain, other changes were taking place within its empire. Canada, Australia, and New Zealand were three of the most important colonies of the British Empire. They were areas where British settlers and their descendants ruled themselves in comparative independence. During the 1800's these colonies benefited from some of the same liberal policies that were being enacted in Great Britain.

The Durham Report. In 1838 the British government sent a new governor general, Lord Durham, to Canada. A leader of the Liberal Party, he had helped to write the Reform Bill of 1832. Then he was given broad powers to try to reform Canada's government.

In 1839 Lord Durham submitted a report to Parliament with a basic recommendation that was to guide all later British colonial policy. Lord Durham recommended that if Great Britain granted

Reforming the Parliamentary System	
1829	Catholic Emancipation Act permitted Roman Catholics to be elected to Parliament
1832	First Reform Bill redistributed seats in Parliament and lowered property qualifications for voting
1867	Second Reform Bill further lowered property qualifications, almost doubling electorate
1872	Secret ballot adopted
1884	Third Reform Bill gave vote to most farm workers
1885	Redistribution Bill divided Britain into approximately equal electoral districts
1911	Parliament Bill limited power of House of Lords
1928	Bill passed granting all British women the right to vote

self-government to colonies like Canada, it would keep them in the empire.

The Durham Report also recommended that the British government aid immigration to Canada, build a railroad to help unite and develop the country, reform the tax and court systems, and expand education. In 1840 the British Parliament passed laws to carry out the recommendations of the Durham Report. These laws are known as the Act of Union. This act joined Upper Canada (part of what is now Ontario) and Lower Canada (part of what is now Quebec). It created a parliament in which each region had equal representation. Between 1846 and 1848 the British enlarged the powers of the Canadian parliament and granted self-government to the people of Canada.

The British North America Act. The union of Upper and Lower Canada did not work well in every respect. Each region was suspicious of the other. Their equal strength in parliament resulted in many deadlocks. A way out came in 1864 when the eastern colonies of New Brunswick, Nova Scotia, and Prince Edward Island were considering a federal union. Delegates from Canada and the colonies met in the city of Quebec. They recommended a plan of federation, which the British Parliament approved as the British North America Act of 1867. It created the Dominion of Canada with the provinces of Ontario, Quebec, Nova Scotia, and New Brunswick.

By the terms of the British North America Act, each province kept its own legislature to deal with local affairs. The federal parliament, which dealt with national problems, met in Ontario at the Dominion capital, Ottawa. Dominion government was a parliamentary democracy with a cabinet based on the British model. The political parties in Canada—Liberals and Conservatives—were similar to those in Great Britain. The party in power appointed the premier, who had much the same influence as the British prime minister.

In 1869 Canada purchased a huge area of land from the Hudson's Bay Company—a private trading company in Canada. The province of Manitoba was created out of a segment of it. British Columbia and Prince Edward Island became provinces during the 1870's. The completion in

1885 of the Canadian Pacific Railway (see map, this page) opened western Canada to immigration. As a result, two more provinces—Alberta and Saskatchewan—joined the Dominion of Canada in 1905.

The Canadian provinces did not become completely independent through the British North America Act. Canada remained part of the British Empire. Canada recognized the British king or queen, whose representative, the governor general, had the power of veto. (This power, however, was rarely used.) The British government exerted a definite and strong influence over Canada's foreign relations.

Australia and New Zealand

Australia is a huge island, a continent in itself. Yet it remained unknown to the rest of the world for centuries. The European explorers who sailed

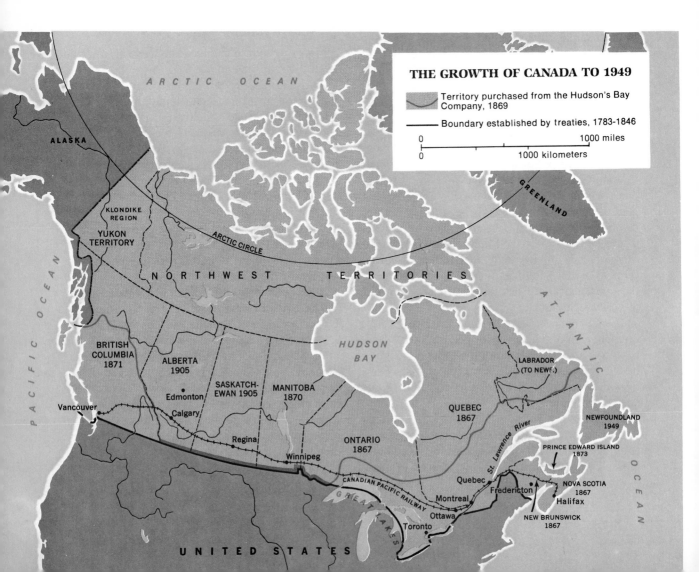

THE GROWTH OF CANADA TO 1949

Territory purchased from the Hudson's Bay Company, 1869

Boundary established by treaties, 1783-1846

0   1000 miles
0   1000 kilometers

ARCTIC OCEAN

ALASKA

KLONDIKE REGION

YUKON TERRITORY

ARCTIC CIRCLE

GREENLAND

NORTHWEST TERRITORIES

PACIFIC OCEAN

HUDSON BAY

ATLANTIC OCEAN

BRITISH COLUMBIA 1871

ALBERTA 1905

SASKATCHEWAN 1905

MANITOBA 1870

LABRADOR (TO NEWF.)

Edmonton

Calgary

Vancouver

Regina

Winnipeg

ONTARIO 1867

QUEBEC 1867

NEWFOUNDLAND 1949

CANADIAN PACIFIC RAILWAY

St. Lawrence River

PRINCE EDWARD ISLAND 1873

GREAT LAKES

Quebec

Montreal

Fredericton

NOVA SCOTIA 1867

Halifax

Ottawa

Toronto

NEW BRUNSWICK 1867

UNITED STATES

into the Pacific Ocean in the 1500's missed it entirely. The Dutch sighted the continent in the early 1600's and named it New Holland, but considered it too poor a land to colonize. Captain James Cook, an English sailor on a scientific expedition for the navy, sailed along the eastern shore of Australia in 1770. He named the region New South Wales because of its resemblance to southern Wales, and claimed it for Great Britain.

Before the American Revolution, Great Britain had sent many convicted prisoners to North America. After the loss of the 13 American colonies, the British decided to send prisoners to Australia. The first shiploads arrived in New South Wales in 1788, and soon the town of Sydney was founded on the southeast coast. Free settlers arrived shortly afterward. Land grants were made to them, and land was also available to prisoners who had served their time, gained their freedom, and wished to stay on in Australia.

Explorations by the British revealed that New South Wales was only part of a large continent. Much of it was desert but some of the land was fertile and could be developed. Sheep and cattle raising became important industries. In 1829 the British, alarmed by French explorations along the coasts, claimed the entire continent of Australia. By 1836 the colonies of Tasmania, Western Australia, and South Australia had been organized. The colony of Victoria was formed in 1851, and Queensland in 1859 (see map, this page.)

For many years, each Australian colony was independent and self-governing. It was not until the 1890's that the Australian colonies began seriously to consider uniting into a federal union as protection against European nations seeking to expand their territories. Finally, in 1901, the Commonwealth of Australia was created.

Like Australia, the islands of New Zealand, to the southeast, were sighted by the Dutch and later by Captain Cook. Early development there was carried on by private companies in the 1820's and 1830's. In 1840 British sovereignty was established through a treaty with the Maori (MAH·oh·ree) chieftains, who were the native rulers of the islands. A few years later the British Parliament gave New Zealand a constitution, and the islands became a self-governing colony.

Disputes over land brought the British settlers into conflict with the native inhabitants, and sev-

AUSTRALIA AND NEW ZEALAND: 1788–1911

eral Maori wars were fought in the 1840's and 1860's. In 1893 New Zealand became the first country in the world to adopt voting rights for women. In 1907 New Zealand joined the British Empire as a dominion.

CHECKUP

1. IDENTIFY: rotten borough, Liberal Party, Conservative Party, Chartists, Queen Victoria, Disraeli, Gladstone, home rule, Fabian Society, Pankhurst, suffragette, Durham Report.

2. LOCATE: Ontario, Quebec, New Brunswick, Nova Scotia, Prince Edward Island, Ottawa, Manitoba, British Columbia, Alberta, Saskatchewan, New South Wales, Sydney, Queensland, New Zealand.

3. List the ways in which the right to vote was restricted in Great Britain in the early 1800's.

4. What important reforms were made in Great Britain between 1832 and 1867?

5. Explain the terms of the British North America Act of 1867.

The United States grew and experienced social change

In 1788, when the Constitution of the United States was ratified, the new nation consisted of 13 states along the Atlantic coast and additional territories that stretched westward to the Mississippi River. Its population totaled about four million

491

people, most of whom lived in farming communities in the eastern part of the country. During the next hundred years, the territory of the United States grew to almost four times its original size, and its population increased to 60 million. By 1900 the United States was ready to take its place among the great nations of the world.

Territorial and political growth

You have read that many European powers in the 1500's and 1600's expanded overseas and set up colonies. The United States, in contrast, expanded overland, within the continent of North America. In governing the territories gained by expansion, the United States differed significantly from European governments. The new nation was determined to expand without acquiring any colonies, in the usual sense of the word.

The Northwest Territory. The land between the Appalachian Mountains, the Ohio and Mississippi rivers, and the Great Lakes was known as the Northwest Territory. This area had been turned over to the United States by those states that had originally claimed it at the time the Articles of Confederation were ratified in 1781. Once independence had been gained, hundreds of settlers pushed across the mountains into this land. In 1787 Congress passed the Northwest Ordinance to provide some form of government for them.

The Northwest Ordinance of 1787 guaranteed to the people who lived in territories rights equal to those who lived in the original 13 states. It provided that the Northwest Territory would be divided into states that were to be admitted into the Union on a basis of equality with existing states. The ordinance, therefore, ensured orderly expansion.

During the late 1700's and early 1800's, pioneers on horseback, in wagons, and on foot moved around and through the Appalachian Mountains. They settled on the land between the mountains and the Mississippi River. As a result, 10 new states joined the United States between 1791 and 1820.

Louisiana Purchase and Texas. In 1803 Napoleon sold the vast territory of Louisiana (which Spain had ceded to France in 1800) to the United States for $15 million. Extending westward from the Mississippi River roughly to the Rocky Mountains, the so-called Louisiana Purchase almost doubled the size of the United States. The United States also purchased Florida from Spain in 1819 (see map, opposite page).

In 1836 American settlers in Mexican territory to the south of the Louisiana Purchase declared themselves independent and set up the Republic of Texas. The United States annexed Texas by treaty in 1845, and war with Mexico resulted. The United States won the Mexican War and gained the Mexican Cession. This was a huge region that became the states of Utah, Nevada, California, and parts of Arizona, Colorado, New Mexico, and Wyoming. In 1846 Americans signed a treaty with Great Britain by which they gained the so-called Oregon Country. The states of Oregon, Washington, Idaho, and parts of Montana and Wyoming were created from this land.

Thus, by 1850, the relatively new nation stretched from coast to coast and from Mexico to Canada. With the Gadsden Purchase in 1853, additional territory was added to the southwest.

Most of the principles of the Northwest Ordinance were applied to all these lands. People settled in the new territories. When the population was large enough to justify it, the territories would be admitted to the nation as states.

In the early days of the country, some states had limited the right to vote to those white males who owned property. The new states farther west imposed no such property qualifications. In the eastern states property qualifications for male voters were gradually dropped.

During the presidency of Andrew Jackson in the early 1830's, many changes were made. Public education became more widespread. An increasing number of political offices became elective instead of appointive. Political candidates came to be chosen by party conventions rather than by small groups of legislators. Foreign visitors spoke of the "great democratic revolution" taking place in the United States.

The slavery question

Although the United States had a unified federal government, it was not free from **sectionalism**—a rivalry among the various sections of the country. During the early 1800's, three chief sections emerged—the Northeast, a region of growing cit-

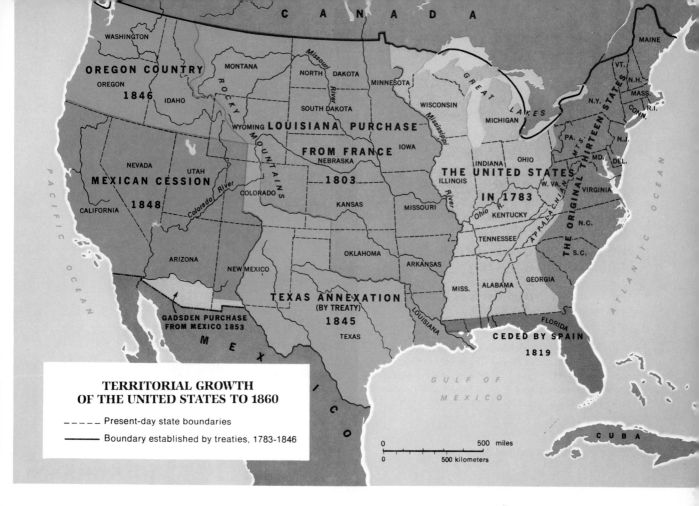

TERRITORIAL GROWTH
OF THE UNITED STATES TO 1860

– – – – – Present-day state boundaries

———— Boundary established by treaties, 1783-1846

ies and industry; the South, an area of many large farms, especially cotton plantations; and the West, a frontier region of small, independent farmers between the Appalachians and the Mississippi. The greatest single issue dividing these sections was that of slavery.

Black slavery had existed in the American colonies almost from the beginning. The Constitution accepted slavery, but left its regulation up to the states. In states where it existed, it could be abolished only by action of the state itself.

Slavery was not practiced in the Northeast and West, where it was not profitable. In the southern states the principal crops, cotton and tobacco, were thought to require slave labor. Therefore, slavery increased in the South, especially after the invention of the cotton gin made cotton a profitable crop.

Both cotton and tobacco were crops that exhausted the soil. Southerners needed new lands—the unsettled lands of the territories—to which they could move when their soil was exhausted. Thus the question arose: should slavery be permitted in the territories? Southerners argued that Congress did not have the power to prohibit slavery in the territories. Northerners and Westerners argued that it did. A growing number of people came to advocate **abolition**— the ending of slavery everywhere in the United States.

Secession and war

The slavery question led to bitter sectional quarrels throughout much of the 1800's. Southern states threatened to **secede**—that is, to withdraw from the Union. Each time compromises were arranged so that secession was avoided. Then in 1860 Abraham Lincoln, who led the newly formed Republican Party, was elected president. The Republicans had pledged to prevent the spread of slavery into the territories.

493

Westward expansion in the United States

The United States in the 1800's was a country teeming with new economic opportunities and new ideas. The old colonial ports, such as Charleston, South Carolina (above), engaged in worldwide trade and became increasingly prosperous.

New areas of the country were also beckoning. Huge empty tracts of fine farm land attracted streams of settlers, who were lured by advertisements for cheap land (below right). Hardy individuals could head even farther west, where a Gold Rush had begun. Thousands of prospectors (right) left the East in search of a quick fortune. In the rough-and-tumble frontier communities, new social attitudes took hold. It did not seem at all unusual, therefore, that women took part in elections in the Wyoming Territory in the 1880's (below).

MILLIONS OF ACRES

IOWA AND NEBRASKA LANDS

FOR SALE ON 10 YEARS CREDIT

BY THE

Burlington & Missouri River R.R. Co.

AT 6 PER CT. INTEREST AND LOW PRICES.

Only One-Seventh of Principal Due Annually, beginning Four Years after purchase
20 PER CENT. DEDUCTED FROM 10 YEARS PRICE, FOR CASH.

LAND EXPLORING TICKETS SOLD
and Cost allowed in First Interest paid, on Land bought in 30 days from date of ticket

Thus our Land Buyers GET A FREE PASS in the State where the Land bought is located.
These TERMS are BETTER at $5, than to pre-empt United States Land at $2.50 per Acre.
EXTRAORDINARY INDUCEMENTS on FREIGHT and PASSAGE are AFFORDED to PURCHASERS and THEIR FAMILIES.

Address GEO. S. HARRIS, LAND COMMISSIONER,
or T. H. LEAVITT, Ass't Land Comm'r, Burlington, Iowa.

Or apply to

Shortly after the results of the election were known, South Carolina seceded and was soon followed by other states. They formed the Confederate States of America, with Jefferson Davis as president. Eventually 11 southern states joined the Confederacy.

President Lincoln and Congress said that the Constitution did not give a state the right to secede. They declared that the Southerners had rebelled and it was the duty of the United States government to suppress the rebellion. Efforts to compromise proved useless. The Civil War began in 1861 and lasted four years.

As time went on, it became clear that the agricultural South lacked the industries and railroads necessary to supply its armies. By 1865 its troops were hungry and in rags, its land devastated by Northern troops. The Confederacy surrendered in April 1865. The Union was preserved.

Changes after the war

In January 1863 President Lincoln had issued the Emancipation Proclamation, freeing slaves in those parts of the country that were "still in rebellion against the United States." Later, three amendments to the Constitution freed all the slaves, gave them citizenship, and granted them the right to vote. Thus the principle of equality before the law was strengthened.

The Union was saved only at a tragic cost. The North and South together had lost nearly 600,000 people. Families had been torn apart as brother fought against brother. Nor did freedom solve the problems of the former black slaves. The war left deep scars on the nation that were to remain well into the 1900's.

However, the war paved the way for a number of reforms. Among those who had campaigned for the abolition of slavery were large numbers of women. Some of these abolitionists, such as the sisters Sarah Moore Grimké and Angelina Emily Grimké, had begun to speak out about the position of women. They insisted that equality be extended to all, women as well as men.

In 1848 a women's rights conference, organized by Elizabeth Cady Stanton and Lucretia Mott, was held in Seneca Falls, New York. The delegates drew up a list of demands, including suffrage for women.

In the 1890's and early 1900's, many women continued the campaign for the right to vote. It was finally granted in 1920, with the ratification of the Nineteenth Amendment to the Constitution.

Immigration. The period from 1865 to 1900 was one of phenomenal growth in the United States. One important factor in this growth was immigration. For many decades, many people had come to the United States from England and Scotland. In the middle 1800's a heavy wave of immigration came from two other regions—Ireland, which suffered severe potato famines, and Germany, where revolutions in 1848 caused many people to flee.

The late 1800's also saw increased immigration from southern and eastern Europe, especially Italy, Russia, and Austria-Hungary. The United States absorbed more immigrants than any other country in the world and became known as a "melting pot."

CHECKUP

1. IDENTIFY: sectionalism, abolition, secede, Emancipation Proclamation, Grimké sisters, Stanton, Mott, Nineteenth Amendment.

2. LOCATE: Louisiana Purchase, Mexican Cession, Oregon Country, Gadsden Purchase.

3. List the steps in the territorial expansion of the United States from 1787 to 1853.

4. In what ways did the United States become more democratic during the 1800's?

5. How did differences over slavery lead to the Civil War in the United States?

France underwent revolutions and changes of government

As you have read, the Bourbon monarch, King Louis XVIII, was restored to the throne of France following Napoleon's exile in 1814. Louis, who was glad to be king and did not want to upset things, continued many of the reforms established between 1789 and 1815. He retained the Bank of France, the state-supported schools, and the Napoleonic Code. He accepted a constitution that limited his power. This constitution set up a legislature to assist in governing the country, although only wealthy people could vote.

Charles X

When Louis XVIII died in 1824, he was succeeded by his brother, Charles X. Charles was an ardent believer in absolute monarchy. He abolished most of the liberal provisions of the weak constitution that his brother had accepted. In fact, he tried to restore many features of the Old Regime of the 1700's. Such moves were certain to cause trouble in France. In the years since 1789, the nation had learned too much about throwing off autocratic rule to accept these changes peacefully. In July 1830 a revolt broke out and spread throughout the country. Charles X was forced to abdicate. A revolt in the same year in the neighboring Netherlands led to the creation of a new independent country, Belgium.

Louis Philippe, the "Citizen King"

The leaders of the French revolt of 1830 were sure that they wanted to be rid of Charles X, but could not agree on the kind of government they wanted after he was gone. Those who favored a republic were not strong enough to win. Finally a compromise was reached. All groups agreed on the choice of another king. He was Louis Philippe, Duke of Orléans, who belonged to a branch of the Bourbon family but had a record of liberal beliefs.

Louis Philippe was in a delicate position. He was a king, but an elected king. He therefore called himself the "Citizen King."

The group that benefited most during the reign of Louis Philippe was the upper middle class. After the revolt of 1830, the right to vote was extended to include the 200,000 wealthiest citizens. Many of these were newly rich manufacturers. Under Louis Philippe, workers were forbidden to organize, and labor unions were outlawed. High tariffs were placed on imported goods. The tariffs benefited the owners of industries because foreign-made goods were kept out of France. However, the tariffs resulted in higher prices for domestic goods.

Louis Philippe's foreign policy also pleased the middle class. He began to build a new colonial empire, especially in North Africa. (You will read about this empire in Chapter 23.)

While the middle class generally favored Louis Philippe, he faced opposition from both monarchists and republicans. One group of monarchists wanted a direct descendant of Charles X to be king, while another group, the Bonapartists, wanted to revive the empire of Napoleon. At the other extreme from the monarchists were the republicans. They believed that France should become a republic and grant political rights and social changes to benefit all the people. Most French workers agreed. They disliked Louis Philippe's antilabor measures and the high prices that resulted from his tariff policy. Their discontent was increased between 1846 and 1848 by food shortages and widespread unemployment.

The revolutions of 1848

By 1848 there was sufficient opposition to the regime of Louis Philippe to spill over into violence. Trouble began over a matter that was important because it involved the principle of free speech. In February, opponents of the government organized meetings where they spoke out against official policy. Louis Philippe then issued a decree prohibiting the final meeting.

The publication of the decree led to riots in Paris. The disorders did not seem serious until the National Guard, summoned to restore order, joined the rioters. The disturbances grew until Louis Philippe was forced to abdicate and flee to England.

The people of Paris then set up a temporary government and proclaimed the Second French Republic in 1848. (The First Republic had lasted from 1792 until 1804, when Napoleon became emperor.) The most active group in the new government was the city working class. Many of its leaders believed in socialism. France at this time was suffering from an economic depression, and there was much unemployment. The socialist members of the government therefore established "national workshops" to give people work. It was the first appearance in modern times of the idea that the government has a responsibility to do something about unemployment.

The Second Republic, adopting universal manhood suffrage, held elections in April to choose a

National Assembly that would write a constitution for a permanent government. When the new National Assembly met in June, conservative members in the majority voted to stop the program of national workshops.

This action led to violent rioting in Paris. Fearing a widespread revolution, the Assembly allowed army officers to assume power. For three days Paris was a battlefield, but the army was too strong for the workers. The rebellion was crushed and its socialist leaders were imprisoned, exiled, or executed. Among those who fled France at this time was Karl Marx, the founder of modern socialism.

Louis Napoleon

The new constitution written by the National Assembly provided for a republican form of government, with a president elected by all the people. The president would serve a four-year term and would not be eligible for a second term. The National Assembly would be a single legislative body, consisting of representatives elected by universal manhood suffrage.

In December 1848 elections were held for the new government. The person who was elected president was not one of those who had helped to create the Second Republic. Instead, by an overwhelming vote, the people chose Louis Napoleon Bonaparte, the nephew of Napoleon.

It was soon clear that Louis Napoleon wanted to be more than a president. He began to work for the support of various groups in France. Like his uncle, he did everything he could to gain the backing of the army. To win support from French Catholics, he helped the pope to suppress an attempt by Italian patriots to set up a republic in Rome. He also repealed certain laws so that the Catholic Church could have more control of French education.

Louis Napoleon favored the middle class by encouraging the development of manufacturing and railroads. At the same time he tried to keep the favor of the workers by generous promises and by a program of public works that gave employment to many. To the peasants, who owned their land, he spoke of his devotion to the principle of private property. He also reminded them of the prosperity he had brought them through better

HISTORY THROUGH ART
"The Gleaners"

"This art offends me and disgusts me," said the French director of fine arts about the work of Jean-Francois Millet. Millet not only rejected the popular romanticized style of his day—the 1850's and 1860's—but also used peasants and workers as his subjects. Gleaners are the poorest peasants, who gather the leavings from a field after reaping; here they appear noble and dignified. That "The Gleaners" seems sentimental and idealized today is evidence of constantly changing tastes and values in art.

transportation and larger markets. He established a new bank that provided funds for agricultural improvements.

In addition to all this, Louis Napoleon was able to pose as a champion of democratic rights. In 1851 he issued a decree giving voting rights to all men who were of legal age. Meanwhile, however, he limited criticism of his actions through strict censorship and by driving his critics out of France.

Louis Napoleon now asked the French people to permit him to draft a new constitution for the Second French Republic. Most people thought of him as their champion and believed that he was defending law and order. The vote was almost twelve to one in his favor.

The Second French Empire

Under the new constitution, Louis Napoleon's term as president was extended to ten years. He was given greater power, but he was still not satisfied. He was determined to follow in the footsteps of his uncle, and Napoleon I had been an emperor.

In 1852 there was another vote on still another constitution. By cleverly handling the votes, Louis Napoleon gained the consent of the French people to allow him to drop the title of president and take the title Emperor Napoleon III. (He called himself the "third" Napoleon because Napoleon I had had a son. "Napoleon II" had never reigned and died in 1832.)

On the surface the Second French Empire looked like a democracy. There was a constitution and a legislature elected by universal manhood suffrage. In reality, however, France was under a new style of absolutism. The legislature could pass only those laws proposed by the emperor. The legislature had no power over spending. It could not question the emperor's ministers.

People suspected of opposing the government could be imprisoned or exiled without trial. Newspapers were strictly censored. A paper that criticized the emperor or his government was warned twice, then suppressed. There was no freedom of speech. Liberal professors in the universities were discharged. Organized opposition to the government of Louis Napoleon was almost impossible.

Problems in the Crimea and Mexico

In order to quiet discontent at home, Napoleon III tried to win glory abroad. His chance to do so came about through the weakening Ottoman Empire. (You will read more about the Ottoman Empire in Chapter 22.)

Because of earlier agreements, Russia claimed the right to protect all Orthodox Christians living under the rule of the Ottoman Turks. France was the protector of Roman Catholics. In the 1850's both Russia and France claimed jurisdiction over certain holy places in Palestine. Napoleon III took a firm stand against Russian demands and won an alliance with Great Britain, which feared Russian expansion toward the eastern Mediterranean.

The Ottoman Turks, backed by France and Great Britain, resisted Russian claims in the Palestine dispute. In 1853 the three allies went to war against Russia. War was not officially declared until March 1854, and full-scale fighting did not begin for another six months. It took place mostly in the Crimea, in southern Russia. This war is therefore known as the Crimean War.

After two years of fighting, with huge losses on both sides from battle and disease, Russia was defeated. As the nation that had most desired the Crimean War, France won glory but little else.

Napoleon III now turned to the building of the French colonial empire. In North Africa he took advantage of a native revolt to strengthen French rule over Algeria. In 1859 French engineers began the construction of the Suez Canal in Egypt. In Asia, Napoleon established French control over Cambodia, thus beginning a move into Indochina. He also tried unsuccessfully to intervene in Mexico. From 1863 until 1867, French troops protected the Archduke Maximilian, the brother of the emperor of Austria, who had become ruler of Mexico with Napoleon's help. The Mexicans hated Maximilian, and he was finally overthrown and executed in 1867.

After his unsuccessful interference in Mexico, Napoleon faced mounting opposition in France. Elections held in 1869 showed strong opposition by both liberals and conservatives.

The Franco-Prussian War

Napoleon III decided to try to regain the support of all groups in France by another bold and risky venture. Prussia at this time was working to unite all the German states under its leadership, as you will read in Chapter 22. By opposing this unification, Napoleon could gain the support of almost all French people because Prussia was universally disliked in France.

Napoleon really hoped that Prussia would back down and that war would not be necessary. However, Otto von Bismarck, the head of the Prussian government, had decided that war with France was necessary to achieve German unification. A clever series of maneuvers by Bismarck angered the French, and in July 1870 the French legislature declared war on Prussia.

French defeat. From the very start of the Franco-Prussian War, as it is called, there were disastrous French defeats. Although ill at the time, Napoleon III went to the front to take command of the army. At the battle of Sedan, he fell into the enemy's hands. The nephew of Napoleon I became a common prisoner of war.

France after 1830

The Second French Empire, ruled by Napoleon III, was marked by two major political events. The first, considered a triumph by the French, was the victory over the Russians in the Crimean War (below). It was a brutal war, in which the use of long-range artillery and an outbreak of epidemic disease caused enormous suffering.

The second event was a catastrophe, which brought Napoleon's rule, and the Second Empire, to an end. In August 1870 the Prussians invaded France, and Napoleon was captured on September 2. When the news reached Paris, a mob gathered and forced the declaration of a new republic. The event was commemorated in a poster showing the traditional figure of Liberty (right). She is urging Parisians to live free or die—free as republicans against an emperor and as French citizens against the Prussians.

Immediately after the capture of Napoleon III, the Legislative Assembly proclaimed the fall of the Second French Empire and the establishment of a Third Republic. The new government tried to defend the nation but was cut off when Paris was besieged by the Prussians. Paris finally fell in January 1871, and the war was over.

France under German domination

The Treaty of Frankfort dictated harsh terms to France. France had to give up its claims to the territories of Alsace and the eastern part of Lorraine. It also had to pay a huge indemnity (equivalent to about $1 billion) to Germany within three years. German troops were to occupy northern France until the money was paid. Bismarck thought that France would not be able to pay for many years, if ever. Thus German forces would be able to control France indefinitely.

Bismarck permitted the election of a National Assembly in February 1871 to decide whether France wanted to resume the war or was willing to sign the peace treaty. During the election campaign the republicans urged renewal of the war. The monarchists took the position that France was already defeated and should negotiate with the conquerers. About 70 percent of the elected delegates were monarchists—not because the French people were overwhelmingly in favor of monarchy but because they overwhelmingly wanted peace.

As in the days of the revolutions of 1848, the people of Paris were strongly republican. They had fought almost alone to defend the city against the Prussians and were angered by the terms of the peace treaty.

In March the socialists and radical republicans of Paris, supported by the National Guard, set up a municipal council to govern the city. It was called the Commune, like the Paris government established in 1792 during the French Revolution. The Communards, as members of the Commune were called, proposed a program to reform France. This included decentralization of the gov-

How do we know?

CITY PLANNING Historians learn a great deal about people from the way they design their cities and their buildings. For example, they know that in ancient times cities were clustered around holy places or easily fortified centers, such as the Acropolis in Athens. Roman cities, they have discovered, were designed in grids, to make military movements easier. In the Middle Ages a powerful castle or a great cathedral was usually the focus of a city.

The emphasis on religion and defense began to change with the Renaissance. In Italy, rich patrons supported architects and put huge sums into building magnificent buildings and palaces. An emphasis on order and splendor developed that continued for centuries. It is visible in the great palace that Louis XIV built at Versailles in the 1600's. It is noticeable, too, in the wide boulevards that the architect Georges Eugène Haussmann cut through Paris in the 1800's. These streets were designed to beautify a great capital, but they were also wide enough to create lines of fire if troops had to disperse rioting mobs.

Before long, however, Haussmann's boulevards became a symbol of elegance. In the late 1800's Paris was thought of as a center for artists and fashionable people. The boulevards came to be lined with expensive shops, indications of Paris's leadership in style and the creation of luxury goods. The trees, broad spaces, open vistas, and outdoor cafes conveyed an image of a sophisticated and relaxed city life, which was not quite what the planners had intended.

ernment, separation of church and state, and replacement of the army by a national guard.

Wide discontent among the Communards led them to start a violent and revolutionary uprising in Paris. Troops sent by the National Assembly entered Paris and fought several bitter and bloody battles with the Communards. Finally, in May, the forces of the Commune were defeated and its leaders were executed, imprisoned, or exiled. That same month the National Assembly approved the Treaty of Frankfort.

The members of the National Assembly agreed that the money owed to Germany should be paid as soon as possible. The government was able to borrow money to pay the sum that Bismarck had thought to be a crushing burden, and German soldiers left France in September 1873.

The Third Republic

Although the Third Republic of France was set up in 1870, after the fall of Napoleon III, quarreling factions in the National Assembly were unable to agree on a constitution until 1875. Finally the assembly passed a group of laws known as the Constitution of 1875, which made France officially a republic. It was, as one French leader said, "the form of government which divided France the least."

The president, who could not be a member of the legislature, was to be elected by it for a term of seven years. The cabinet had to approve the president's actions and was responsible for government policy. The constitution did not specifically provide for a premier, or prime minister, but the position soon became established. The Senate was to be elected by an indirect system, while members of the Chamber of Deputies were to be elected by universal manhood suffrage. Although Paris was the capital, the legislators feared Paris mobs and chose to meet at Versailles.

The Dreyfus case. The republic faced a number of problems during the 1880's, but the most serious danger to the Third Republic began in 1894. An attempt to betray French military secrets to Germany was uncovered. A Jewish officer, Captain Alfred Dreyfus, was accused, convicted, and sentenced to life imprisonment. Evidence soon came to light which indicated that Dreyfus had been falsely convicted. However, the French army would permit no criticism of its actions, and it was supported by monarchists, many Catholics, and anti-Semites—people who dislike Jews.

Although the real traitor was discovered, he was cleared by the army. Émile Zola, the famous French novelist, wrote an open letter, *"J'Accuse"* ("I Accuse"), in which he placed blame for this scandal on the army and its supporters. It was not until 1906 that Dreyfus's name was cleared.

The Dreyfus case led to a clash between the two major groups in France—those who had condemned Dreyfus and supported the army, and those who supported his cause.

Continuing difficulties

After the Dreyfus case, French republicans planned several reforms. Steps were taken to end the favored position of the Roman Catholic Church in France, a situation that had been established under Napoleon I in 1801. In 1905 Church and state were officially separated. France was to have complete religious freedom.

In the early 1900's France was disturbed internally by strikes and labor troubles. Political instability continued, largely because there were so many different political parties. They ranged from the monarchists on the far right to radical socialists on the far left. There were also a number of "splinter groups," smaller divisions within the important parties. No one party ever had complete control of the French government. It was necessary for parties to unite temporarily, or form **coalitions,** in order to get anything accomplished. When a coalition collapsed, a new effort would have to be made to establish a majority.

CHECKUP

1. IDENTIFY: Louis XVIII, Charles X, the "Citizen King," Second Republic, national workshops, Crimean War, Archduke Maximilian, Franco-Prussian War, Communards, Third Republic, Dreyfus.

2. Which class benefited most during the rule of Louis Philippe? What groups opposed Louis Philippe?

3. How did Louis Napoleon become emperor?

4. What were the results for France of the Franco-Prussian War?

5. Describe France's internal political problems in the late 1800's and early 1900's.

CHAPTER REVIEW

B.C.	A.D.	1650	1700	1750	1800	1850	1900	1950	2000

1776	Adam Smith's *The Wealth of Nations*	**1837–1901**	Reign of Queen Victoria in Great Britain	**1863**	President Lincoln's Emancipation Proclamation
1801	Ireland and Great Britain joined by Act of Union	**1848**	Karl Marx's *Communist Manifesto*	**1867**	Dominion of Canada created
1814–1815	Congress of Vienna		Revolutions and establishment of Second Republic in France	**1870–1871**	Franco-Prussian War
1814–1824	Reign of Louis XVIII			**1870**	Establishment of Third French Republic
1819	Carlsbad Decrees	**1852**	Second French Empire founded by Napoleon III	**1894–1906**	Dreyfus case in France
1821	Beginning of Greek revolt			**1901**	Creation of Commonwealth of Australia
1832	First Reform Bill in Great Britain	**1854–1856**	Crimean War		
		1861–1865	Civil War in the United States	**1907**	Dominion of New Zealand formed

CHAPTER SUMMARY

Nationalism played a small role at the Congress of Vienna. Diplomats met there to restore legitimate rulers to power and reshuffle territories in order to prevent further aggression by France. Reactionary leaders disappointed nationalist hopes for self-government in Italy, Poland, and Austria, although the German Confederation was a step toward unity.

Both the Quadruple Alliance and the Holy Alliance grew out of the Congress of Vienna. So did the Concert of Europe, which tried to maintain the status quo.

Metternich, who dominated Europe for years, worked to suppress liberal and nationalistic movements that threatened absolutism. He succeeded in Germany, Italy, and Spain, but failed in Greece.

After the fall of Napoleon, governments tried to establish order and repress dissent. At the same time, the industrializing countries were grappling with the problems created by a growing working class. To meet these problems, new political and social theories were put forward. Liberals such as John Stuart Mill believed that reforms were needed to give all citizens a voice in their own affairs and to protect them from injustice. Socialists like Karl Marx believed that a more fundamental transformation of politics and society was necessary. They wanted to give power to the working class and end all special privileges.

In Great Britain, its empire, and the United States, liberal ideas made considerable headway. Voting rights were broadened, and in the early 1900's women, too, gained the right to vote for the first time. Other reforms reduced the powers of aristocrats and the rich.

Liberalism had a more uncertain effect on France. Here a series of upheavals—in 1830, 1848, and 1871—made possible brief recurrences of the revolutionary spirit of the 1790's. Each time politics soon returned to more stable forms. The monarchy was eventually abolished, as was the position of emperor that Napoleon III created for himself. By the early 1900's France was a republic, governed by coalitions of parties that represented monarchist, liberal, and socialist beliefs.

CHECKING WHAT YOU KNOW

1. Match each idea at the left with a philosopher at the right.

   a. utilitarianism
   b. utopian socialism
   c. free enterprise
   d. individual liberty
   e. "iron law of wages"
   f. scientific socialism

   1. Smith
   2. Mill
   3. Ricardo
   4. Marx
   5. Bentham
   6. Owen

2. Briefly explain the meaning of the phrase "Age of Metternich." What forces in Europe helped bring that age to a close?

3. John Stuart Mill and Karl Marx both criticized the economic injustices that grew out of the Industrial Revolution. How did their solutions to such problems differ?

4. What were the aims of the Chartists? How did they contribute to the growth of democracy in Great Britain?

5. Louis Napoleon Bonaparte once said, "I believe that from time to time men are created . . . in whose hands the destinies of their countries are placed. I believe myself to be one of those men." How did Louis Napoleon attempt to fulfill this prophecy? Would you describe his actions as liberal or reactionary? Explain.

PRACTICING YOUR SKILLS

1. **Using maps.** Turn to the map on page 493. After 1783, how did the United States acquire most of its territory? Was the land in your state part of the United States at the start of the 1800's? If not, when was it acquired? How long did it take for the United States to expand its borders from the Mississippi River to the Pacific Ocean? Why might such rapid growth encourage the development of liberalism? of nationalism?

2. **Writing an editorial.** Write an editorial in support of one of the bills listed in the chart entitled "Reforming the Parliamentary System" on page 489. Keep in mind that an editorial should do more than express a point of view, or opinion, on an issue. It should also present arguments and facts that might sway the opinions of others.

RELATING PAST TO PRESENT

1. Before taking office, William Gladstone pledged, "My mission is to pacify Ireland." Review the events that prompted Gladstone to make this remark. Then investigate the situation in Ireland today. Which of the problems faced in the 1880's have lingered into the 1980's?

2. In the 1800's many people held different opinions about the role government should play in the economy. Writers such as Adam Smith believed that government should not interfere with the natural operation of business. Others thought that the Industrial Revolution had made government regulation a necessity. What recent items in the news prove that this debate continues in the present?

3. How did the spread of liberalism inspire the start of the women's suffrage movement in Great Britain and the United States? Even though women now have the vote, some people are still working to extend the rights of women. What are some of the reforms that women have called for during the last decade?

INVESTIGATING FURTHER

1. Use encyclopedias to learn more about the ministries of Benjamin Disraeli and William Gladstone. What types of programs did each support? How did these two officials influence the direction of Great Britain's domestic and foreign policy?

2. During the revolutions of 1848, the people of Paris set up a provisional government and proclaimed the Second French Republic. Prepare a report on the form that this republic was to take. One source you may use is the "Proclamations of the French Provisional Government, February–March, 1848" in Louis Snyder, *Fifty Major Documents of the Nineteenth Century* (Van Nostrand Reinhold).

3. Study a copy of the Emancipation Proclamation and the thirteenth, fourteenth, and fifteenth amendments to the United States Constitution. How did each of these documents help put the ideals of political liberalism into practice in the United States?

Science and Culture Were Revolutionized During the Industrial Age

You have read about how the Industrial Revolution changed the economy and society. It also had a profound effect on science, art, music, and literature. The ideas of scientists and artists reflected the impact of technology and the sense of progress that followed industrialization.

Scientists sought greater understanding in many areas. Scientific activity developed so rapidly that specialized branches of science appeared—for example, physics, biology, and chemistry. Some people began to apply scientific methods to the study of people, as individuals and in relation to one another. Thus the **social sciences**—those investigations dealing with people and society—made their appearance.

In literature and the arts there were those who glorified progress, science, and change. Other writers and artists, however, disagreed with this view. They looked to the past and insisted that no branch of science could ever describe the true, spiritual nature of human beings. In music, sculpture, and painting, styles underwent frequent and rapid change, also reflecting the impact of industrialization on people's lives.

In these years, compulsory education laws in many countries led to the creation of public schools. As more and more people were educated, a larger audience for intellectual and cultural activities began to develop.

Statue of a "Young Dancer" by Edgar Degas

1

Advances in physics and biology helped explain the nature of life

The **physical sciences** are those that deal with the inanimate, or nonliving, aspects of nature. They include astronomy, geology, physics, and chemistry. The most significant developments in the physical sciences during the 1800's and early 1900's centered on the atomic theory.

The atomic theory

According to modern atomic theory, all matter in the universe is made up of very small particles called atoms. The arrangement and structure of these atoms, and their chemical combinations, account for the different characteristics of the materials we find in the world.

The atomic theory, like many other scientific ideas, can be traced back to the Greek philosophers, such as Democritus, about whom you read in Chapter 4. For many centuries, however, atomism was merely one of several philosophical theories about physical reality. During the Scientific Revolution in the 1500's and 1600's, the atomic theory began to be an accepted part of science, although it could not yet be supported by experimental proof or mathematical demonstration.

John Dalton, an English chemist and schoolteacher, was the first scientist to obtain convincing experimental information about the atom. In 1803 he outlined a method for "weighing" atoms. After studying the ratios of elements in various gases, Dalton assigned an arbitrary weight of 1 to the lightest element, hydrogen. He then expressed the weights of other elements in relation to it.

During the 1800's many scientists explored the paths opened up by Dalton, and much was learned about the atom. In 1869 a Russian chemist, Dmitri Mendeleyev (men·duh·LAY·uf), produced the first workable classification of the elements. Mendeleyev's Periodic Table, somewhat modified today, is a familiar part of every chemistry textbook.

Although modern atomic theory had its origin in the study of chemistry, it soon became part of physics—the science of matter and energy. This began to occur when scientists studying heat and gases explained their findings with a new theory of atoms in motion.

In the 1800's some scientists began to think of heat as the result of the motion of a body's atomic particles. In a cold substance—ice, for example—the motion of the atoms is relatively slow. In a hot substance—such as hot water—the atoms move much more vigorously, bouncing into one another. If water is heated to its boiling point, the atoms move extremely fast and the water is turned into a gas—water vapor. With these discoveries, the atomic theory became a part of physics.

The structure of the atom

In 1895 a German physicist, Wilhelm K. Roentgen (RENT·gun), was passing electricity through a vacuum within a glass tube. He noticed that a fluorescent substance on a table nearby glowed brightly when the electric current was switched on in the tube. Roentgen immediately concluded that the tube was sending out a new form of ray. Soon he discovered that the rays penetrated many substances, including human skin and tissue, and would leave an impression on a photographic plate. Because he did not know what caused this powerful penetrating radiation, Roentgen named the rays X-rays. X-rays became an important tool in medicine, and they raised new questions about the material world.

An English physicist, J. J. Thomson, probed further into the nature of matter. In 1897 he discovered the electron, a tiny particle that had a negative electrical charge. He announced that an electron was more than a thousand times lighter than the smallest known atom, and he suggested that all atoms contained electrons. Therefore, subatomic particles (that is, particles inside atoms), rather than the atoms themselves, must be the true building blocks of all matter in the universe.

While the electron was being accepted reluctantly by most physicists, a French team of chemists, Pierre and Marie Curie, provided new evidence that atoms were not the simple, indivisible particles pictured by earlier scientists. The Curies experimented with uranium and radium. They found that the atoms of these elements were constantly disintegrating and releasing energy on their own. This process is called **radioactivity.** Elements that disintegrate and release this energy are called radioactive elements.

Thomson's electrons and the Curies' disintegrating atoms were combined in a new theory of the atom by Ernest Rutherford of Great Britain. Rutherford maintained that at the center of the atom was an extremely small and heavy nucleus, or core. Electrons whirled in circular orbits around this nucleus. When Rutherford bombarded the nucleus with heavy particles from radioactive elements, he found that it contained still smaller particles, which he called protons. Thus, the atom was no longer thought of as a solid piece of matter.

Rutherford's description of the atom was modified by scientists who followed him. He had thought in terms of two subatomic particles—electrons and protons. However, his successors discovered another, the neutron, and eventually more than 30 elementary atomic particles.

Planck and Einstein

In 1900 the German physicist Max Planck overturned the then common belief that energy was continuous and that it could be divided into any number of smaller units. Planck proved that energy could only be released in definite "packages," which he called *quanta* (the plural of *quantum,* the Latin word for "how much"). Planck's **quantum theory** formed the basis for a completely new approach to the study of matter and energy.

In 1905 an extraordinary young German scientist, Albert Einstein, published three papers that revolutionized physics. In one of them, he extended Planck's quantum theory to light. In a second paper, Einstein developed his equation $E=mc^2$. According to this equation, E (energy) is equal to m (mass) multiplied by c^2 (the speed of light times itself). This formula means that a small amount of mass can be transformed into a tremendous amount of energy.

In a third paper, Einstein examined some of the basic concepts and ideas of mechanics, the science of motion, and he developed the **special theory of relativity.** He concluded the following: (1) No particles of matter can move faster than the speed of light. (2) Motion can be measured only relative to some particular observer. Thus it does not make sense to speak of absolute motion, space, or time.

Einstein's theories overturned long-held ideas. Isaac Newton and the scientists who followed him had thought of the universe in terms of the three dimensions of length, breadth, and depth. They claimed that all particles of matter move toward one another because they possess a power of attraction called gravity. Einstein declared that all events occur not only in the three dimensions of space but also in a fourth dimension—time. This he called the space-time continuum. Gravity, he said, is not a property of matter, but a property of the space-time continuum.

Cell theory in biology

Scientists in the 1800's were as interested in explaining the nature of life as they were in the nature of nonliving matter. However, matter is extremely complex in the **biological sciences**—those dealing with living organisms.

Biologists had long been familiar with the idea of cells, the tiny units of living matter. Various scientists of the 1600's had seen what we now know to be plant and animal cells as they examined living matter under their microscopes. The cells of different species were of different shapes and sizes, but early observers did not draw any general conclusions about them.

In 1805 a German naturalist, Lorenz Oken, suggested a new theory of the nature of life. He claimed that all living organisms were made up of small living particles, and his ideas stimulated other biologists to investigate this theory. In 1831 Robert Brown, a British botanist, studied living

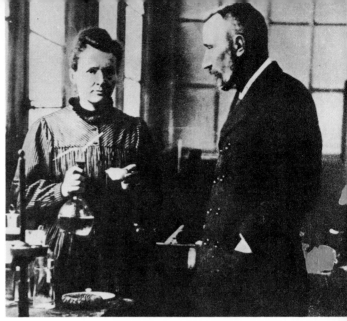

A golden age of science

Inquiry into the biological and physical sciences reached previously unparalleled heights during the Victorian Era. One of the most influential of the scientific investigators was Charles Darwin (left). His observations in the islands of the South Pacific led eventually to his theory that natural selection governed the biological world. The research of Marie and Pierre Curie (above) into the nature of matter led them to discover that some elements send out energy in the form of rays. Marie Curie won major awards for her experiments with radioactive elements, but she remained puzzled by the relationship of matter to energy. As the Victorian Era drew to a close, a brilliant physicist named Albert Einstein (below) proposed an equation that clarified this relationship, as part of his famous theory of relativity.

plant cells and noticed that each cell had a dark spot in the fluid portion between the walls. He called this spot the nucleus.

In the late 1830's, two German biologists, Matthias Schleiden and Theodor Schwann, announced a general cell theory, based on a close study of plants and animals. According to their theory, (1) all living material is composed of cells, and (2) the nucleus is important to the life of the cell.

The cell theory was expanded in 1858 with the work of the German scientist Rudolf Virchow. Virchow showed that the destruction or the change of cells by some outside force or agent was the cause of disease in living organisms. From his study of cells, Virchow also concluded that every new cell must come from some older cell and that only living matter can produce new living matter. Thus, by the latter 1800's, the cell was generally accepted as the basic unit of living matter.

Lamarck's theory of inheritance

The cell theory, however, could not explain why there is such a rich variety of plants and animals on the earth. Until the mid-1800's, most people explained the variety of living things by the concept of "special creation." They believed that all the different kinds of plants and animals had been created at one time.

One group of scientists, however, offered a different theory. They argued that the thousands of modern plants and animals evolved, or developed, from common ancestors of long ago. This kind of development is called **evolution.**

In science new theories often raise new questions. Those who believed in evolution now had to explain how plants and animals evolved. A French biologist, Jean Baptiste Lamarck, in the early 1800's suggested that living beings changed their form in response to their environment. A giraffe, for example, acquired a long neck because it always had to eat leaves high up in trees. Such changes were then passed on by inheritance to their descendants. Other characteristics gradually could disappear if they were not used at all.

Changes of this sort, going on from generation to generation for millions of years, could have produced present-day plants and animals out of the first bits of living matter.

Lamarck's theory did not become a part of modern biology because it was later disproved. However, it influenced other scientists, among them a British biologist named Charles Darwin.

Darwin's theory of evolution

Charles Darwin had spent 25 years studying plant and animal life. In 1859 he published his theory of evolution in a book called *On the Origin of Species by Means of Natural Selection.*

Darwin began with a well-known biological fact—no two creatures are exactly alike, and offspring are not exactly like their parents. Next, he brought in the ideas of Thomas Malthus. As you have read, Malthus believed that there were always more creatures born than could survive because of natural dangers, including the limited food supply. Therefore, Darwin said, in any generation some creatures will survive and some will perish. Those who survived would, in general, be those whose characteristics were best adapted to the existing environment. This idea is often called the "survival of the fittest." The strongest survivors would have offspring, and the process would be repeated. Thus, Darwin claimed, one could explain the evolution of all forms of life.

To illustrate the point with the giraffe: According to Darwin's theory, the ancestors of the giraffe may not have had long necks, but they gave birth to offspring that were not exactly like their parents. Some had necks slightly longer than their parents. Others had shorter necks. In an environment where leaves were found on tall trees, the offspring born with the longer necks had an advantage. They could eat leaves on higher branches. Therefore, Darwin believed that nature "selected" the longer-necked offspring. These offspring lived and gave birth to another set of offspring. The short-necked giraffes starved. Once again natural selection was repeated, and the longer-necked individuals survived.

Darwin's theory had a great impact on scientists. It set them gathering evidence to prove or disprove it—in the records of fossils as well as in the study of living organisms. It stirred up controversy because (1) it placed human beings in the animal kingdom, an idea many did not think was true, and (2) many people believed it contradicted the story of Creation in the Bible.

Genetics

Darwin left an important question unanswered: why were the offspring not like their parents? Unknown to Darwin, a monk in Austria, Gregor Mendel, had been gathering evidence on this question. Mendel was the founder of **genetics**— the study of the ways in which inborn characteristics of plants and animals are inherited by their descendants. He did much of his work in the 1860's and 1870's, although scientists did not know about it until later.

Mendel worked in a quiet monastery garden, where he bred pea plants. He took tall plants and short plants and mated them. The result was not medium-sized pea plants but all tall plants. Then Mendel fertilized these tall offspring with their own pollen and was surprised to find that they produced a mixed generation of short and tall plants. In some way, the characteristic of shortness had been hidden away in the tall plants.

From these experiments Mendel concluded that inborn characteristics were not necessarily blended or mixed together. Instead, he believed, they were all inherited as if they were separate particles. For example, tall plants could carry and pass on to the next generation the particles that would cause shortness.

Mendel never discovered the actual particles that were responsible for the inheritance of the inborn characteristics of his plants. It was another biologist, Walther Flemming of Germany, who observed threadlike bodies in cells that were dividing to form new cells. These bodies were later named chromosomes.

Biologists studying chromosomes soon learned that: (1) Each cell in a given organism has the same number of chromosomes. In humans, for example, each cell has 46 chromosomes. (2) When reproductive cells divide, the new cells contain half the usual number of chromosomes. In 1902 an American biologist, Walter S. Sutton, concluded that the chromosomes were the particles involved in Mendel's experiments with plants.

A human being, for example, has far more characteristics than there are chromosomes in a cell. Thus it soon became necessary to suppose that any given characteristic must be associated with a very small portion of a chromosome. In 1909 this small portion was named the gene.

CHECKUP

1. IDENTIFY: physical sciences, Mendeleyev, Roentgen, Pierre and Marie Curie, radioactivity, Planck, quantum theory, biological sciences, evolution, genetics, Flemming, chromosomes, gene.

2. What contributions to atomic theory were made by Dalton? Thomson? Rutherford?

3. Summarize the chief contributions to physics made by Albert Einstein.

4. How did the work of Oken, Brown, Schleiden, Schwann, and Virchow contribute to our knowledge of cells?

5. Explain how Lamarck's theory of evolution differed from that proposed by Darwin. What differences of opinion did Darwin's theory cause?

6. In what ways did Gregor Mendel's ideas build upon Darwin's theory?

Advances in medicine improved human life

The advances in science were accompanied by remarkable breakthroughs in medicine. Taken together with the changes brought about by industrialization, about which you read in Chapter 19, these advances spurred population growth. People lived longer, and year after year there were fewer deaths than births.

The fight against disease

Until the late 1800's, two out of every three children died while very young. Epidemics of diseases killed more people than did wars, famines, or natural disasters. Little was known about the causes of diseases. Scientists had seen bacteria under the microscope as early as the 1600's, but their connection with disease was not suspected.

One dreaded disease was smallpox, which swept through cities in periodic plagues. It was most common among children. There was a saying that mothers did not count their offspring until they had had smallpox and lived through it.

Edward Jenner. An English physician of the late 1700's, Edward Jenner, made a thorough investigation of smallpox in the hope of finding a way to prevent it. He learned that milkmaids who had once had cowpox (a mild disease similar to smallpox) did not get the dreaded disease even when there was an epidemic. After years of experimenting, Jenner developed the principle of inoculation, which had been known in India 1,300 years earlier. In 1796 Jenner made a vaccine from cowpox sores and scratched it into the skin of a boy's arm. The boy had a mild case of cowpox, but quickly recovered. When the boy was later exposed to smallpox, he did not contract it.

Louis Pasteur. Jenner had developed a method, inoculation against smallpox, but he did not know the scientific principle that made it work. This principle came to light in the late 1800's with the work of the French chemist Louis Pasteur. Until Pasteur's time, scientists believed that certain living things, including bacteria, came to life out of nonliving matter. This process was called spontaneous generation. Pasteur's experiments showed that bacteria reproduced like other living things and were carried from place to place in the air, on people's hands, and in other ways.

Pasteur learned that bacteria are responsible for many phenomena. For example, some cause fermentation, turning grape juice into wine or making milk sour. In the 1860's Pasteur developed a process of heating liquids to kill bacteria and prevent fermentation—a process that was named **pasteurization** in his honor. He also determined that some bacteria cause diseases in animals and humans. These harmful bacteria are often called germs or microbes.

During the 1870's Pasteur worked with the germ that caused anthrax, a disease often fatal to both animals and humans. He produced a vaccine containing weakened anthrax germs, injected animals with the vaccine, and prevented them from catching the disease. He determined that when weakened germs enter the body, the system builds up so-called antibodies to fight them. These antibodies remain and are strong enough to kill the more deadly germs if exposure occurs. Thus Pasteur showed why Jenner's smallpox inoculations had been effective.

Pasteur used this same technique in fighting rabies. This fatal disease was communicated to humans by dogs or other animals infected with a certain virus (a minute organism smaller than bacteria). In the 1880's Pasteur found a way of weakening the rabies virus. He injected a vaccine into a boy who had been bitten by a rabid dog, and the boy survived.

Pasteur thus made several great contributions to medical science. He showed that microscopic organisms are not spontaneously created. He proved that bacteria can be killed by heat, or pasteurization. He introduced what is called the germ theory of disease by showing that germs cause illness. He also uncovered the principle by which inoculation works.

The development of surgery

Down through the centuries, surgery had been a desperate measure, always painful and often fatal. Only operations that could be completed in a few minutes, such as tooth extractions and limb amputations, were attempted. Patients were forcibly held down, or their senses were dulled with liquor or opium.

In the 1840's it was discovered that ether and chloroform would cause unconsciousness or deaden sensation and thus eliminate pain. Such anesthetics not only relieved the patients' suffering but also made longer operations possible.

Even after anesthetics came into use, however, many patients survived the surgeon's knife only to die from infection soon afterward. Pasteur's discoveries about germs helped to resolve this dilemma. An English surgeon, Joseph Lister, studied Pasteur's work and developed antisepsis—the principle of killing germs that were the cause of infection. Lister used carbolic acid as an antiseptic; milder chemicals later came into use for this purpose. The use of antiseptics helped to reduce bacterial infection not only in surgery but also in childbirth and in the treatment of battle wounds. Hospitals were transformed from houses of death into houses of healing.

Other medical advances

A German physician, Robert Koch, made discoveries that reinforced those of Pasteur. In 1882 he isolated the germ that causes tuberculosis. He also identified the germ causing Asiatic cholera and developed sanitary measures, such as water filtration, to prevent disease.

How do we know?

LETTERS Ever since people could write, they have been communicating with one another through letters. Indeed, letters got that name because the communication is through written symbols and not through sounds or signals. A letter is often a vivid source of information, because it is such a personal form of expression.

Sometimes, a special occasion inspires a letter that is particularly revealing. In 1936 the founder of psychoanalysis, Sigmund Freud (left), celebrated his eightieth birthday. To his surprise, he received a letter of congratulations from a famous scientist whom he had never met. This letter, from the physicist Albert Einstein, suggests how broad scientists' interests are. In his letter to Freud, Einstein indicated how he reached conclusions about the truth of scientific work. He also described an aspect of science that is not normally appreciated—that there is a beauty to scientific discovery.

Dear Mr. Freud,

I am happy this generation has the opportunity to express its gratitude to you as one of its great teachers. You have undoubtedly not made it easy for a skeptical ordinary person to judge your work. Until recently I could appreciate only the power of your thought, and its enormous influence on our era. I could not form a definite opinion about the amount of truth it contains. Not long ago, however, I heard a few examples which in my view cannot be interpreted except by your theories. I was delighted to come across these examples, because it is always delightful when a great and beautiful idea turns out to fit reality.

Your
A. Einstein

The work of Pasteur, Lister, and Koch was the starting point of an international fight against disease. When the nature and role of germs and viruses were known, scientists could isolate the causes of many diseases and develop vaccines for inoculation.

Some epidemic diseases, including malaria and yellow fever, were traced to germs carried in the bodies of mosquitoes and transmitted by their bite. Thus the battle against disease was extended to the mosquitoes that carried it. Bubonic plague, found to be carried by rat fleas, was brought under control in Western countries through rat-extermination campaigns.

Sanitation became an important part of the fight against sickness. By 1900 such sanitary measures as garbage and sewage disposal, the purification of drinking water, and cleanliness in food preparation had considerably reduced the death rate from infectious diseases.

Many new drugs were tested and developed. Among them was insulin, which was introduced in the 1920's. It saved diabetics from certain death and enabled them to lead normal lives. Aspirin, made available in the 1890's, reduced pain and fever. Alexander Fleming of Great Britain discovered penicillin in 1928. The sulfonamides, or sulfa drugs, were developed in Germany in the 1930's. However, neither penicillin nor the sulfas came into wide use until the 1940's.

Improvements in diet and food storage

Another reason why more people lived longer after 1850 was that there was more food available, and more was known about the relation of food to

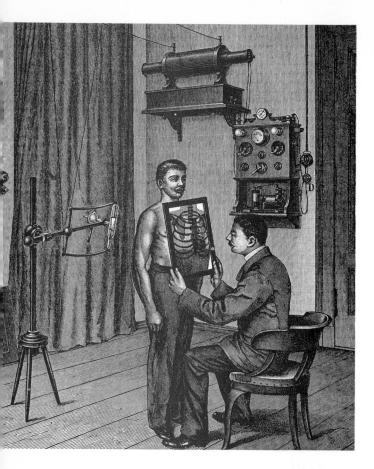

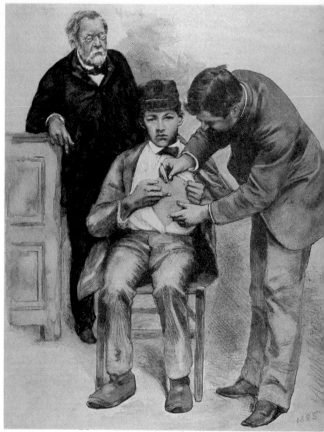

Medical advances

Inventions and discoveries transformed the practice of medicine in the 1800's. In all three major areas of medical work—prevention, diagnosis, and treatment—new methods led to important breakthroughs. The French scientist Louis Pasteur established the effectiveness of inoculations as a means of preventing disease. An injection administered by Pasteur's assistant—with Pasteur himself watching in the background—saved a young man who had been bitten by a rabid dog (above right).

Once a problem arose, the remarkable new technique of X-ray photography allowed a doctor to diagnose the problem inside the body (above). Then, thanks to the invention of anesthetics, a surgeon could remedy the problem by painlessly operating on the patient (right).

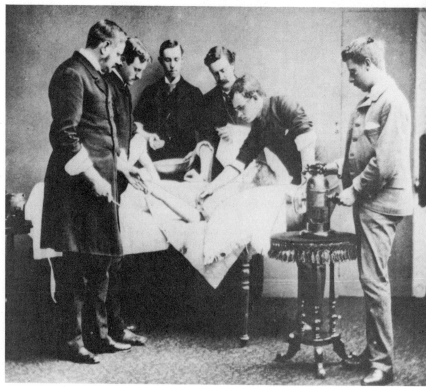

health. In the early 1900's biologists discovered the importance of vitamins and minerals in the diet. Diseases resulting from vitamin deficiencies, such as beriberi and rickets, were wiped out in advanced regions of the world.

Science and technology combined to produce better methods of preserving and transporting food. Pasteurization was one important step. So was refrigeration, which also retards the growth of bacteria. Refrigerators made their appearance in the late 1800's. They later became an indispensable feature of the home in many industrialized countries. Refrigerator cars on railroads began to be used around 1850 to transport meats, fruits, and vegetables. All these developments made a balanced diet available the year round.

CHECKUP

1. IDENTIFY: Jenner, inoculation, spontaneous generation, antibodies, Lister, antisepsis, Koch.

2. What were four great contributions made by Louis Pasteur?

3. What were some major medical advances that followed the work of Pasteur, Lister, and Koch?

4. Describe how the preservation of food was improved after 1850.

3

Interest in the social sciences grew during the late 1800's

The social sciences are those branches of knowledge that study people as members of society. The subjects with which they deal are economic development, political institutions, history, and relations among people. The idea of making the study of these subjects objective and factual—of treating them like sciences—was new in the 1800's.

Political science and economics

The study of politics dates back to the Greek philosophers Plato and Aristotle. It was the subject of such thinkers as Machiavelli, Locke, and Rousseau. In the 1800's, however, the study of politics became known as political science, and writers tried to study law and government in the scientific manner of physicists and biologists.

Another social science, economics, was already well developed in the work of Adam Smith, about whom you read in Chapter 20. However, not until the later 1800's did economists begin to imitate scientists and collect and arrange statistics in order to test their theories.

History

Like political science, the study of history dates back to the Greeks. History, too, underwent change in the 1800's. Influenced by nationalism, many scholars wrote histories detailing the accomplishments and glories of their native countries. Historical writing became based more and more on systematic study of original materials and the careful organization of facts. Historians began a massive search for evidence of the past in documents, diaries, letters, and other sources. New interpretations of history began to emerge.

Among the greatest historians of the 1800's were Leopold von Ranke of Germany, Thomas Macaulay of England, and Francis Parkman of the United States. Ranke made the study of original documents the central activity of historical research. He produced the basic outline of the political history of the 1500's and 1600's that we accept to this day. Macaulay wrote on the history of England, which he argued was a story of the rise of liberty and the defeat of oppressive government. Parkman wrote about the early years of American history and created a vivid portrayal of a new nation. Thus, in the 1800's historians established stricter methods for their work, emphasizing original sources. At the same time, they used their writings to strengthen national feeling.

Another way historians encouraged nationalism was by observing and including in their studies all the people in the society. Here a writer of the 1700's proved influential—the French philosopher Voltaire, who was noted for his attention to social and intellectual history. He influenced many historians to concentrate less on wars and great leaders and devote more time to the study of ordinary people and how they lived. Later historians, influenced by Darwin, also tried to see historical events in terms of evolution.

Anthropology

One social science that emerged in the 1800's was anthropology—the study of people and their cultures. You have already read about some of the dramatic discoveries in the field of archeology, which is a branch of anthropology. It was in the 1800's that scientists realized how old the earth was and how long humans had lived on it. They found prehistoric cave paintings, discovered Egyptian, Sumerian, and Assyrian remains, and excavated such cities as Troy and Mycenae.

Anthropologists also began to explore the continuity in the attitudes of human societies and in the way people relate to one another. An English anthropologist, E. B. Tylor, adopted the German term *kultur,* describing the set of beliefs and behaviors that a society shares. He studied this concept in his book *Primitive Culture* (1871). In it he looked at one particular subject, religion, as it evolved in all human cultures.

Another English anthropologist, James George Frazer, took this approach further in his book *The Golden Bough* (1890). Frazer compared the customs of different societies and tried to show links between magical beliefs, religion, and attitudes toward authority. This attempt to show similarities and differences among different societies has remained a major interest of anthropologists.

Sociology

Another social science that first appeared in the 1800's was sociology—the study of human relationships in society. This branch of the social sciences was much influenced by the work of the French philosopher Auguste Comte. Comte argued that the study of society should imitate the methods of the scientists, using objective facts and avoiding personal interpretations. In the 1800's sociologists were particularly interested in adopting the theories of the biological sciences.

Herbert Spencer, for example, was an early sociologist who believed that Darwin's theory of evolution could be used as the basis for studying human communities. As you have read, Darwin claimed that nature selected certain individuals—those most fit to survive—and permitted others to die. Spencer applied this theory of natural selection to society in his *Principles of Sociology,* pub-

lished between 1877 and 1896. In society, he said, there are superior people who are well adapted to it. In exercising their "natural rights," these people also contribute to the progress of civilization. At the same time, society will contain inferior types—the poor, the lazy, the ignorant, the criminal—who contribute nothing.

Spencer wrote that society, like the plant and animal worlds, had evolved from lower to higher forms through natural selection. If so-called inferior types were permitted to die out, then society would be made up exclusively of superior people. This application of Darwin's theory came to be known as **Social Darwinism.** It was rejected when sociologists found it impossible to divide human beings into the superior and the inferior.

Social scientists soon realized that they could not get quick results by borrowing theories from one science and applying them to another. Gradually, they came to believe that sociology could become a science not by borrowing theories but by using scientific methods—observing closely, gathering facts, and basing theories on these facts. This approach became increasingly important in sociological research.

Psychology

Psychology was another new science of the 1800's. It is the study of the human mind—how it works and how it affects behavior. Its origins can be traced back to Greek thinkers, and it was long considered a branch of philosophy because it was not experimental. Then, in the mid-1800's, a number of scientists determined to make psychology an experimental science like biology.

Pavlov. Darwin's theory of evolution had a strong impact on psychology. Among other things, it influenced psychologists to study animal behavior and to relate their findings to humans. The most famous of these early experimenters was a Russian biologist, Ivan Pavlov, who discovered the conditioned reflex in the 1890's. Psychologists had long known that certain behavior was automatic. A child does not have to be taught to pull its hand away from fire, but removes it automatically. In the same way, a dog does not have to be taught to salivate—water at the mouth—when eating food. This kind of involuntary response is called a reflex action.

connections

Science Fiction

Storytellers since the time of the ancient Greeks have enjoyed imagining that people are capable of breaking the normal laws of nature, gaining fantastic strength or powers. They have also invented amazing machines (top) and mythical figures with magical abilities.

Since the time of the Scientific Revolution, these fantasies have often taken a special form, inspired by the achievements of science. They are usually referred to as science fiction.

A favorite subject of science fiction has been travel in space. In fact, one of the earliest works of science fiction was written by Johann Kepler, who played a major part in the revolution in astronomy during the 1600's. He wrote a book called *The Dream,* in which he imagined his mother flying to the moon on a broomstick. This book created problems for his mother, for it was used as evidence that she was a witch. However, it is one of the most imaginative descriptions of life in space ever written.

Science fiction was particularly popular in the 1700's and 1800's. The French philosopher Voltaire imagined a visit to earth by an enormous native of the star Sirius. An English novelist, Mary Wollstonecraft Shelley, invented a medical student called Victor Frankenstein, who created a monster out of a corpse. In the late 1800's a French writer, Jules Verne, wrote a series of stories about incredible journeys—in a balloon, on a rocket (bottom), and even on a submarine. The English novelist H. G. Wells imagined a machine that could stop time, plants that ate people, and Martians who invaded Earth.

In more recent times, much of science fiction has dealt with outer space—in films as well as books. But the basic appeal has remained the same: fantastic people or creatures who can do things that normally are impossible. By showing us the impossible, science fiction tries to teach us something about the limits under which we live.

HISTORY THROUGH ART

"Anxiety" by Edvard Munch

"We should stop painting interiors with people reading and women knitting. We should create people who breathe and feel and suffer and love." So said Edvard Munch, a Norwegian artist of the late 1800's. Although he had been born in Oslo, Munch spent many of his creative years in Germany.

With his interest in people's deepest feelings—especially their undefined fears and tensions—Munch mirrored in art what many psychologists were investigating in science. "Anxiety" shows a ghostly procession of people with masklike faces, fear blotting out all their individuality. The painting could be said to echo Munch's statement: "I hear the scream in nature."

By experimenting with dogs, Pavlov proved that an animal could be conditioned, or taught, to have certain reflex actions. First he offered food to a dog. The dog salivated. Second, he rang a bell each time the food was presented to the dog. The animal salivated and also began associating the sound of the bell with food. Finally, he offered no food to the dog but rang the bell. The dog salivated when the bell was rung. It had been conditioned to salivate when it heard the bell. As a result of his research, Pavlov believed that all habits, even mental activity, are a series of connected conditioned reflexes.

Freud. Another explanation of human behavior was developed by the Austrian physician Sigmund Freud (FROID) in the early 1900's. Freud introduced the revolutionary concept of the unconscious—that is, the mental processes of which a person is unaware—as a determining factor in behavior.

Freud had hypnotized certain mentally disturbed patients. He had found that under hypnosis they could remember past experiences they could not otherwise recall. Freud believed that early experiences had led to their illness. He treated his patients by gradually bringing the disturbing memories, fears, and conflicts to the level of consciousness. To do this he studied their dreams and encouraged them to talk about whatever came to their minds. Then he interpreted their dreams and thoughts to show what lay beneath them in the unconscious mind.

It was Freud's belief that, unknowingly, troubled patients had forced unpleasant experiences into the unconscious. In order to cure such patients, it was necessary to make them conscious of these experiences again. This process of revealing and analyzing the unconscious is called **psychoanalysis.** Freud discussed his theory fully in a book titled *A General Introduction to Psychoanalysis,* published in 1920.

Details of Freud's theories were later challenged. However, much of his basic theory and method forms the foundation of psychiatry—the study and treatment of mental illness. In addition, his ideas had great influence on literature, art, and thought in the modern world.

CHECKUP

1. IDENTIFY: Ranke, Macaulay, Parkman, Tylor, Frazer, Comte, reflex action.

2. How did the study of politics, economics, and history change in the 1800's?

3. What is anthropology? What is sociology? Summarize Spencer's theory of Social Darwinism.

4. Describe Pavlov's experiments in conditioning. What were his findings?

5. How did Freud use psychoanalysis in treating mentally disturbed patients?

4

Literature, music, and art reflected the spirit of the times

Literature, music, and art reflected the social and economic developments during the industrial age. Even in their most personal statements, the artists' works provided a sense of the times and of the influences of scientific ideas and of rapid change.

The romantic movement

Many writers of the early 1800's belonged to what is known as the **romantic movement.** Their work appealed to sentiment and imagination and dealt with the romance of life—life as it used to be, or ought to be, rather than as it actually was. The romantic movement was partly a reaction to the Enlightenment, the movement in the 1700's that had emphasized reason and progress. Romantics glorified feeling, emotion, and instinct. They looked to nature and the golden past.

The romantic movement, or romanticism, was also a product of the revolutions of the 1700's and 1800's. Political revolution in France had overturned the old order of society and released the spirit of liberty and equality. So, too, romanticism overturned the formal patterns of literature in the 1700's and released a spirit of creativity, enthusiasm, and individuality.

In Great Britain the most famous romantics were a group of young, intense poets whose works were filled with emotion and a strong love for beauty and nature. Among them were William Wordsworth, Percy Bysshe Shelley, John Keats, Lord Byron, and Samuel Taylor Coleridge.

Many romantic writers glorified the past, especially the Middle Ages. The Scottish novelist Sir Walter Scott wrote about the days of knighthood in *Ivanhoe. The Hunchback of Notre Dame,* by the French author Victor Hugo, was also set in medieval times. Alexandre Dumas told the tale of *The Three Musketeers,* who roamed France in the days of Cardinal Richelieu.

Interest in the past was related to the growing nationalism of the times. Writers in many countries turned to folklore, songs, and the history of their own countries for their subject matter. Germany was not yet a unified nation in the early 1800's, but a national literature arose. The Grimm brothers collected the famous fairy tales that bear their name. Friedrich von Schiller wrote of liberty in *William Tell,* a drama about a Swiss hero. Johann Wolfgang von Goethe (GUHR·tuh), a master of the novel, poem, and drama, wrote during this period of rising national feeling. Most famous of his works is the drama *Faust,* the story of a man's bargain with the devil.

In the United States, writers in the early 1800's were also influenced by romanticism. James Fenimore Cooper wrote adventure stories that idealized the Indian and the frontier. Washington Irving produced romantic stories set in the Hudson River valley.

Romantic music

In music, as in literature, the 1800's began with a shift to romanticism. A major influence on this transition was the German composer Ludwig van Beethoven (BAY·toh·vun). Beethoven brought to music the same interests and aims as the British poets of his time brought to literature. His love of nature was expressed in a symphony (known as the Pastoral Symphony) devoted entirely to the atmosphere of the countryside. His call for liberty and freedom dominated the opera he wrote, *Fidelio,* and the final movement of his last symphony. Beethoven's music was designed to arouse emotion, for it was powerful and passionate. Like all the romantics, he praised human heroism and achievement and thought that people should express their feelings strongly.

The romantic movement led to a great outpouring of music, especially in Austria and Germany. Johannes Brahms wrote powerful symphonies and concertos that were classical in form but surged with rich, intensely emotional music. Franz Schubert, Robert Schumann, and Felix Mendelssohn brought to music the lyric quality of romantic poetry. Schubert and Schumann are especially remembered for their great songs, or lieder. Frédéric Chopin, (SHOH·pan), a Polish-born composer who lived in France, wrote graceful yet dynamic piano pieces. Franz Liszt of Hungary at times used native folk songs and dances in his compositions.

(continued on page 520)

The spirit of the times reflected in art

The 1800's opened with the romantic movement in the arts in full swing. Great artists were thought of as powerful geniuses. Some, like the Polish composer Frédéric Chopin (lower left), led anguished, tormented lives, and their work drew on deep human emotions. Some artists conveyed a fascination with the ancient and heroic myths of a nation's past. The German composer Richard Wagner drew on these myths in a series of operas known as *The Ring of the Nibelungs*. One of its heroines was a warrior goddess named Brünnehilde, who was thought to represent true German womanhood (left). There was also an interest in nature, lushly and emotionally painted, as in the boating scene by the French artist Jean-Baptiste Camille Corot (below).

Late in the 1800's, however, there was a reaction against romanticism. The French novelist Honoré de Balzac could still be portrayed heroically (right). But French artists began to experiment with showing what they considered the beauty of ordinary life. People at an outing in a park (below right) were an appropriate subject for Pierre Auguste Renoir. So too was a bedroom, simple but bathed in color, in this painting by Vincent Van Gogh (far right).

518

He also developed the tone poem, a symphonic piece based on a literary or philosophical theme, often taken from romantic literature.

In Russia, Peter Ilyich Tchaikovsky (chy·KAHF·skee) wrote symphonies, operas, ballet music, and orchestral works that are highly emotional and melodic. Often his works were built around stories, such as the fairy tale of *The Nutcracker,* the romance of *Romeo and Juliet,* and Napoleon's defeat at Moscow in the *1812 Overture.* He and other Russian composers, especially Modest Moussorgsky—known for his opera *Boris Godunov*—developed nationalistic music that made use of Russian folk themes. Strong national feeling was an essential part of the romantic movement in music as in literature.

The greatest Italian operatic composer of the 1800's was Giuseppe Verdi. His best known works, such as *Otello* and *Aïda,* contain some of the most beautiful and dramatic music ever written for the human voice. In keeping with the spirit of his age, the stories and themes of many of his early operas were highly nationalistic. They inspired a generation of Italians who were not yet politically united.

The greatest German operatic composer of the 1800's was Richard Wagner (VAHG·nur). He called his operas "music dramas," and in them he tried to unite singing, orchestral music, dancing, costumes, and scenery to create an overwhelming theatrical effect. Like his contemporaries, Wagner was an intense nationalist. He based many of his plots, including his four-part cycle, *The Ring of the Nibelungs,* on German myths.

Several composers of the late 1800's followed in the general tradition of romantic music. They are sometimes called post-romantics. Gustav Mahler of Austria, for example, used vast orchestras and choruses in his lengthy symphonies. Another trend, however, was to break away from older styles. Claude Debussy (duh·BYOO·see) of France developed unusual harmonies and rhythms in trying to create delicate impressions of clouds, sea, or moonlight.

Romantic painting and architecture

While Germans, Austrians, Russians, and Italians dominated the world of music in the 1800's, the French were the outstanding painters and sculptors. In the 1820's and 1830's, romantic painters, like romantic writers, used subjects from the past and depicted episodes bursting with action and drama. Such a painter was Eugène Delacroix (del·uh·KRWAH) of France. John Constable and J. M. W. Turner in Great Britain, both landscape painters, reflected the romantic interest in nature. Their work had color and vitality, partly because they often went outdoors to paint instead of working in their studios.

Romanticism in architecture expressed itself first in the so-called Gothic revival of the mid-1800's. This was an attempt to recreate a great period of the past. The British Houses of Parliament, American churches and college buildings, and other public structures were built in the Gothic style.

The rise of realism

The rich imagination and flowery style of the romantics produced a literature and art usually remote from the lives of most people. In the mid-1800's writers and artists began to abandon this approach and turn to the realities of everyday life—that is, to **realism.** One of the most important realists was Gustave Flaubert (floh·BAIR) of France. His novel *Madame Bovary* described with extraordinary attention to detail the life of an ordinary woman. In Great Britain, Mary Ann Evans wrote realistic novels under the name George Eliot. In *Middlemarch* she focused on country life of the Victorian period.

Often the realists made social and economic conditions their theme. The Russian Leo Tolstoy, in his monumental novel *War and Peace* (published in 1868–69), showed war not as a romantic adventure but as a vast confusion of misery and death. The Norwegian dramatist Henrik Ibsen brought human problems into the theater. His play *A Doll's House* (1879) advocated the equality of husband and wife in marriage.

In the United States, realism took the form of **regionalism**—the portrayal of everyday life in different parts of the huge country. Outstanding in regional fiction were Mark Twain's novels *Tom Sawyer* (1876) and *Huckleberry Finn* (1884), with their earthy and humorous depiction of life along the Mississippi River.

Toward the end of the 1800's, a number of writers called **naturalists** carried realism even further. They wrote of the ugly and sordid in life, carefully screening emotion and opinion from their writings. The French novelist Émile Zola was a leader in this approach. He wrote as if he were a scientist objectively studying and carefully recording all human activities. Though people objected to his frankness, his exposure of shocking conditions helped bring reform. Another realist was the English novelist Charles Dickens, who often wrote about the poor people of London.

In painting, the kind of realism that portrayed people and everyday life in the industrial age characterized the works of the French artists Gustave Courbet (Koor·BEH) and Honoré Daumier (doh·MYAY). Another kind of realism was attempted by a group of French painters who are known as **impressionists.** Impressionist painting flourished during the 1860's and 1870's. The aim of impressionist painters was to give vivid impressions of people and places as they might appear in a brief glance. To do this, the impressionists studied light and color. They experimented with small patches of different colors placed side by side to create shimmering effects. Claude Monet (moh·NEH) and Pierre Auguste Renoir (ruh·NWAHR) were leading impressionist painters.

Experiments in art forms

In painting and sculpture, romanticism and realism were brief movements, followed quickly by experimentation that was intensely individualistic. There was less nationalism in art than in literature or music, and more "art for art's sake." Like writers and musicians, painters and sculptors often rebelled against the materialism and mechanization of an industrial world.

In the late 1800's, experimentation became more popular in painting. Form, color, and emotion became more important than subject matter. Realism was left to the newly invented camera, and painting became individualistic.

Paul Cézanne's landscapes and still lifes emphasized the forms and shapes of the objects he painted. He was beginning to move beyond surface appearances to explore the abstract qualities of color and design in a painting. This shift away from showing recognizable, real scenes was to be very influential.

Also influential was Paul Gauguin (goh·GAN). Gauguin, who left Europe to live in Tahiti, stressed color and simple, flat design in his paintings. Henri Matisse painted many decorative scenes of southern France. He was also ready to emphasize design at the expense of realism. The Dutch painter Vincent van Gogh (van GOH) expressed intense emotions. He used thick blobs of pure color, swirling brush strokes, and distorted perspectives that rejected any attempt to show realism. Edgar Degas, Henri de Toulouse-Lautrec, and Édouard Manet each painted scenes of Parisian life in his own style.

The French sculptor Auguste Rodin (roh·DAN) also broke with tradition. Some of his statues included unworked portions of the marble from which they were carved, giving his work a deliberately unfinished quality. Rodin rejected the traditional demands that art should show people, objects, and scenes as they appeared in real life. The growing interest in abstract forms marked the end of the emotional strivings of romanticism. It pointed the way toward the new artistic interests of the 1900's.

CHECKUP

1. IDENTIFY: Shelley, *William Tell,* Goethe, Beethoven, Tolstoy, Twain, Monet, van Gogh.

2. Briefly explain the romantic movement of the early 1800's. Give three examples of romanticism in literature, music, art, and architecture.

3. Define realism. How did Tolstoy and Ibsen use the ideas of realism in their literature?

4. What was the aim of the impressionist painters? How was it accomplished?

Education developed into an important institution

In 1800 illiteracy was widespread, even in those countries of the world that were becoming industrialized. In European countries schools were private. The majority of schools were run by religious groups. Only the wealthy or people of the middle class could afford to educate their chil-

As the years went by, many things encouraged the development of free public education—that is, schooling free of charge for all, regardless of class. Schools were easier to establish in larger towns and cities. Industrialists wanted literate workers as well as more engineers, scientists, and skilled technicians. Others wanted government schools in order to develop patriotic citizens. Military leaders wanted educated soldiers for their armies. As more people gained the right to vote, they voted for more education. They believed that education would improve their children's chances for a better life.

After 1870, governments in Western Europe and the United States began to pass laws making some form of education universal and compulsory. In a number of countries only elementary education was offered by the government. In other countries public education was available through high school. In the United States public schools were expanded to include kindergarten for young children and state universities for advanced study. Many new subjects, especially the sciences, were added to the curriculum, and vocational and technical training were introduced. Special training was required for teachers.

In Europe, school systems were established and controlled by the central government. In the United States, where local governments were stronger, the states established schools and set standards. Local school districts administered schools and levied taxes to support them.

For the most part, children of the lower classes attended school only as long as it was required. Then they went to work to earn money for their families. Middle-class children, however, went to secondary school and often to college.

dren, although there were some charity schools. Most children did not go to school, or went for only a few years.

Growth of public education

The American and French revolutions, with their ideas of liberty, equality, and representative government, made it seem important that all citizens be educated. In France and the United States, steps were taken to establish a public-school system in the years following the revolutions. Many people opposed the idea, however. They feared that education would encourage revolutionary ideas and would make people less willing to do farm and factory work. They also believed that it would be costly and thus increase their taxes.

Education for women

During the 1800's there was a great deal of debate about whether or not women should be educated. Some people argued that most education was unsuitable or unnecessary for women. Others insisted that education was important because it made women better wives and mothers. Still others said that women should have equal opportunity in every area, including education.

Toward the end of the 1800's, when many countries passed laws guaranteeing education for all, elementary education for women was included. Opportunities for secondary education were more limited. In the United States, as in Great Britain and France, high schools for girls had different courses than did schools for boys. Girls' schools emphasized foreign languages, literature, history, and home economics. Boys, on the other hand, were taught sciences, mathematics, and philosophy as well as classics, history, and literature.

There were many people who objected to different courses for boys and girls. For example, Emily Davies, an Englishwoman, urged her government to improve women's education sufficiently to allow women to go on to the universities. She said in 1865: "We are not encumbered [burdened] by theories about equality and inequality of mental power in the sexes. All we claim is that the intelligence of women, be it great or small, shall have full and free development. And we claim it not especially in the interests of women, but as essential to the growth of the human race."

Few colleges admitted women as students during the 1800's. Therefore, those who believed women should receive university educations opened colleges for women. In the United States, Mary Lyon founded the Mount Holyoke Female Seminary in 1837. This school later became the present Mount Holyoke College. In Great Britain, Girton College was opened in 1874 and Newnham College in 1875. Both were in Cambridge, although they were only unofficially recognized as part of Cambridge University. It was not until 1921 that women were officially granted Cambridge University degrees.

The effects of education

The spread of education had many results. People became more informed about issues and took an interest in government activities. Since more people could read, newspapers, magazines, and books were published in massive quantities.

Newspapers became especially important. Before 1800, newspapers were not widely read. They were more like pamphlets than what we think of today as newspapers. During the 1800's, however, newspapers expanded their coverage to include politics, foreign affairs, and art and science. To attract readers the editors ran weekly stories by famous authors such as Zola and Dickens. Cartoons commenting on the politics of the day were also included.

Newspapers often advocated a particular political position. They supported the policies of one government figure or another, or they supported the opposition. In France, for example, there were republican newspapers and monarchist newspapers as well as Catholic newspapers.

As more and more people bought newspapers, the prices were lowered. Editors also used advertising as a way of increasing income. In addition, new technology, such as the linotype, which set type by machine instead of by hand, and the electric-powered rotary press improved printing processes. The invention of the telegraph made it possible to transmit the news quickly.

As newspapers grew, so did the number of jobs for journalists and editors. In the past, writing was something that people did in addition to their other work. It was not a fulltime profession. In the 1800's, however, the profession of journalist became an accepted and respected occupation.

Public debate

The spread of literacy and the appearance of newspapers made it possible for people to read and think about issues of the day. Many topics were debated in newspapers and magazines. Politicians could reach larger and larger audiences. Increasingly, more and more people were getting the same information, even if they did not all have the same opinions. People became more aware of events around them. They tried to influence those events by writing about their ideas, by organizing groups and political parties, and by voting, or—in the case of women—by demanding the right to vote. As people became more educated and informed, they began to have more say in the events that affected their lives.

CHECKUP

1. List some of the reasons for the growth of public education.

2. What were some of the arguments for and against the education of women? What colleges were opened for women in the 1800's?

3. Describe the effects of the spread of education.

CHAPTER REVIEW

1796	Jenner's first smallpox inoculation	1860's	Pasteurization developed	1895	Roentgen's discovery of X-rays
early 1800's	Romantic movement in literature, art, and music	1860's–1870's	Impressionism in painting	1897	Discovery of electron by Thomson
1803	Dalton's theory of relative atomic weights	1869	Mendeleyev's Periodic Table of elements	1900	Planck's quantum theory
mid-1800's	Realism in literature and art	1882	Isolation of tuberculosis germ by Koch	1905	Einstein's special theory of relativity
1859	Darwin's *Origin of Species*	1890's	Pavlov's discovery of conditioned reflex	1920	Freud's *General Introduction to Psychoanalysis*

CHAPTER SUMMARY

The 1800's were a time of remarkable advances and changes in the world of ideas. Science developed rapidly during this period. In the physical sciences, the atomic theory became the basic way of understanding matter. The brilliant work of Einstein revolutionized the study of energy and matter. Progress was also made in the biological sciences. Knowledge of the cell, the basic unit of living matter, increased. The theory of evolution proposed by Darwin had an enormous impact. And the new science of genetics, founded by Mendel, answered many questions about biological inheritance.

Advances in medicine were made by the discoveries of Jenner, Pasteur, Lister, and Koch. New drugs and medical techniques, such as surgery with anesthesia, were developed. Researchers discovered the importance of a balanced diet and how to make enough food available to more people.

Those who studied the behavior of people in societies began to use scientific methods. Their investigations came to be known as social sciences and included new techniques for understanding history, politics, and economics. New social sciences included anthropology, sociology, and psychology. An important contributor to the field of psychology was Freud. He introduced the idea of the unconscious and developed a treatment that was known as psychoanalysis.

The arts reflected the social and economic changes of the industrial age. In the early 1800's writers, musicians, and artists were swept by the romantic movement, emphasizing emotion, nature, and nationalism. In the late 1800's romanticism gradually gave way to realism. In painting and sculpture, romanticism and realism were followed by an intensely individualistic period.

Compulsory education won gradual acceptance in Western Europe and the United States in the late 1800's. More and more people learned to read and write. Thus they could participate in the cultural activities of the time. This new audience made possible the publication of books, magazines, and newspapers that reflected a wide range of opinions and ideas.

CHECKING WHAT YOU KNOW

1. Match each individual at the left with an idea or accomplishment at the right.

   a. Pasteur
   b. Einstein
   c. Pavlov
   d. Mendeleyev
   e. Mendel
   f. Jenner
   g. Ranke
   h. the Curies
   i. Darwin
   j. Freud

   1. Periodic Table
   2. theory of evolution
   3. introduced the idea of the unconscious
   4. discovered radioactivity of uranium and radium
   5. historical research based on original documents
   6. germ theory of disease
   7. study of genetics
   8. $E = mc^2$
   9. discovery of conditioned reflexes
   10. smallpox inoculation

2. Match each author or composer at the left with a literary or musical work at the right.

   a. Wagner
   b. Tolstoy
   c. Flaubert
   d. Eliot
   e. Verdi
   f. Twain
   g. Beethoven
   h. Ibsen
   i. Tchaikovsky

   1. *Madame Bovary*
   2. *Middlemarch*
   3. *A Doll's House*
   4. *Tom Sawyer*
   5. *Fidelio*
   6. *The Ring of the Nibelungs*
   7. *The Nutcracker*
   8. *War and Peace*
   9. *Aïda*

3. How did advances in the physical and biological sciences affect the development of other branches of knowledge?

4. Why might each of the following be considered a response to industrialization:
   a. romanticism
   b. realism
   c. compulsory education

PRACTICING YOUR SKILLS

1. **Studying original documents.** During the 1800's social scientists began to make original documents the focus of historical inquiry. Turn to the letter on page 511. What insight does this letter give you into the personality of Albert Einstein? What does it tell you about Sigmund Freud? Based on this letter, what conclusions might you draw about the acceptance of Freud's theories during the 1930's?

2. **Using pictures.** Turn to the picture essay on pages 518–19. Which pictures show the influence of romanticism? of realism? Which pictures illustrate artistic experimentation and a movement toward abstract forms?

RELATING PAST TO PRESENT

1. To investigate medical progress during the 1900's, interview a physician, nurse, pharmacist, or public health official in your community. How have advances made during the 1800's been improved upon in the present? What has been the most significant medical breakthrough in recent years? Record the responses to such questions for use in a general discussion of medical technology in the 1980's.

2. Newspapers and magazines became very popular during the late 1800's. What newspapers and magazines can you find on the newsstands in your town or city? Select several of these and research the year in which they were first published. Did any originate in the 1800's? If so, ask your librarian about the availability of early issues. Notice the type of articles and advertisements that ran when the magazine or newspaper first appeared. How do they compare with those printed today?

INVESTIGATING FURTHER

1. Use encyclopedias or books in your library to learn more about one of the scientists or physicians discussed in this chapter. Be prepared to present your findings to the class.

2. If your school or local library lends records, you might borrow a recording such as Beethoven's *Pastoral Symphony* or Tchaikovsky's *1812 Overture*. As you listen to the music, note the techniques or styles that illustrate the influence of romanticism.

3. Using books on the history of art, research two political paintings by Honoré Daumier. You might use Helen Gardner, *Art Through the Ages* (Harcourt Brace Jovanovich) or H. W. Janson, *History of Art* (Prentice-Hall) as sources. What is the subject of each painting? What techniques did Daumier use to influence public opinion? Why might a painting sometimes have a greater impact than a written commentary?

4. Writers in the early 1800's sought to appeal to the emotions and sentiments of their readers. They turned to nature and the past for inspiration, and their stories were often filled with adventure, romance, and personal heroics. Read one of the following novels, and explain how it reflected the romantic movement: Sir Walter Scott, *Ivanhoe* (Pocket Books); Rafael Sabatini, *Scaramouche* (Houghton Mifflin); Baroness Emmuska Orczy, *The Scarlet Pimpernel* (Macmillan).

(1786–1914)

Unification of New Nations Added to Rising Tensions in Europe

In the mid-1800's, relations among the major nations of Europe were much the same as they had been about a hundred years before. The dominant powers were Great Britain, France, and Prussia in the west, and Austria and Russia in the east.

A major force was at work that eventually would change these longstanding relationships. That force was nationalism, which made people who were linked by ties of history, language, culture, and territory seek to unite in national states. In Italy and Germany, in particular, there was a feeling that political organization had lagged behind the rest of Europe. Although the people in each region had many bonds to one another, they remained divided among many small states. As nationalistic feelings grew stronger, this situation could not continue.

At the same time, political methods and ideas in Europe were changing in the mid-1800's. In the early part of the century, those who wanted to improve conditions had done so with noble aims for reforming society. Few of them had much practical experience in the world of politics, however. They thought that their causes would win wide support simply because they represented right and justice.

Political life in the later 1800's was dominated by people of a different kind. These were not ide-

Parade honoring Victor Emmanuel II of Italy

alists but realists. They believed in facing life as it was, not as it should be. Revolutionaries found that idealism was not enough to solve the difficult problems of changing a political system and governing a nation. Such leaders strove to chart practical courses for the future. They learned to balance groups against one another. Politics became a matter not of idealism but of compromise.

During the second half of the 1800's, therefore, political life in Europe changed significantly. The pattern of relationships among states was altered as both the Italians and Germans united to form large and powerful nations. In eastern Europe, nationalism became an increasingly significant political influence. After more than a century of relative stability, the international situation was becoming more and more complex.

THE CHAPTER SECTIONS

1. After years of struggle, Italy became a unified nation

2. Prussia created a unified and powerful German Empire

3. Industrialization and socialism created opposition to Bismarck

4. In spite of some reforms, Russia remained a rigid autocracy

5. Austria-Hungary's interest focused on the Balkans

1

After years of struggle, Italy became a unified nation

The conquests of Napoleon I had given the Italian peninsula something resembling unity for a few years. Italians, inspired by liberal and national ideals, had overthrown many rulers of the Italian states. However, after the Congress of Vienna in 1815, Italy was again divided. Lombardy and Venetia were annexed by Austria. The rest of Italy was divided into several large and small states (see map, page 528). Most of them were dominated by Austria, and most were ruled by reactionaries who tried to wipe out any advances made during Napoleon's time.

Early movements for unification

Italian nationalism became a strong force in the early 1800's. Many thinkers and writers tried to revive interest in Italy's traditions. This nationalistic movement, whose goals were liberation and unification, became known as the **Risorgimento** (ree·sor·jee·MEN·toh)—Italian for "resurgence." Because nationalists could not support their cause openly, they formed secret societies. An early group of this sort was the Carbonari. One of its most famous members, who had great influence on later Italian history, was Giuseppe Mazzini.

Mazzini, born in 1805, had a vision of a united Italy, and to this goal he devoted his entire life. Mazzini was imprisoned and then exiled for his part in an unsuccessful uprising against Sardinia in 1830. In 1831 he called for all Italian patriots to join a new movement, called Young Italy, to spread the ideals of the Risorgimento among the Italian people. Mazzini referred to Young Italy as "a brotherhood of Italians who believe in Progress and Duty."

In 1848 there were liberal and nationalistic rebellions in several of the Italian states. Sardinia, the Kingdom of the Two Sicilies, and Tuscany were forced to grant constitutions to their subjects, and Austrian rule was overthrown in Lombardy and Venetia. Revolutionaries seized Rome in 1849 and set up a republic that was governed by Mazzini himself and two other leaders. All but one of these revolutionary movements soon failed. The former rulers were returned to power, and the constitutions were revoked. Mazzini had to flee the country once more. Only in Sardinia was the revolt successful. Sardinia remained independent, with its own constitution.

Despite the failure of the revolts of 1848 and 1849, Italian patriots continued their efforts. They now agreed on their principal aim—a united Italy. However, they could not agree on how to achieve unity or the ideal form of government after unification had succeeded.

Many Italians, especially the Catholic clergy, wanted a federation of Italian states headed by the pope. Liberals, however, wanted an Italian republic. They opposed federation, partly because the papacy had turned against liberalism after 1849. Still others wanted a constitutional monarchy under the king of Sardinia.

Cavour in Sardinia

The kingdom of Sardinia included not only the island of Sardinia but also the mainland regions of Savoy, Piedmont, and Nice (see map, this page). It was the only state in northern Italy not dominated by Austria. The constitution of Sardinia provided for a parliament, whose elected representatives had considerable influence in the government. The Sardinian king, Victor Emmanuel II, was sympathetic to liberal aims.

However, it was not the king of Sardinia but his chief minister, Count Camillo Benso di Cavour, who actually led the nation. Born in 1810, Cavour was an aristocrat, well educated and widely traveled. He edited a nationalist newspaper in 1847, took part in the revolutions of 1848, and in 1852 became premier of Sardinia.

Cavour disliked absolutism and admired the British system of parliamentary government. He wanted Italy to be both united and industrialized. Cavour hoped to make Sardinia strong and liberal so that it could become a leader among the forces of nationalism in Italy.

Cavour reorganized and strengthened the army. He helped to establish banks, factories, and railroads, encouraged shipbuilding, and negotiated treaties with other countries to increase trade. Under the slogan "a free church in a free state," he tried to reduce the influence of the Roman Catholic Church in politics. The politically powerful Jesuit order was expelled from the country.

Napoleon III and war with Austria

Since Austrian control of part of northern Italy was the greatest obstacle to Italian unity, Cavour searched for allies against Austria. You will remember that Napoleon III had become unpopular with the French people and was seeking ways to gain glory outside of France. Cavour proposed to him an alliance of France and Sardinia against Austria. Napoleon was reluctant at first to take this step, fearing that it would antagonize the pope and the French Catholics. However, he hoped that with Austria driven out of Italy, France could dominate a weak confederation of Italian states. Cavour, on the other hand, believed that with Austria out of Italy, the other Italian states would join Sardinia and make a strong alliance against both France and Austria.

Cavour and Napoleon made a secret agreement in 1858. Napoleon agreed that if Austria declared war on Sardinia, France would send troops to help drive the Austrians out of Lombardy and Venetia. In return for this help, Cavour promised to give the regions of Nice and Savoy to France.

In 1859 Cavour began to make preparations for war. Fearing that Cavour planned to attack Austria, the Austrian emperor demanded that the military buildup in Sardinia be stopped in three days. Cavour rejected Austria's attempt to interfere in the affairs of Sardinia. Austria declared war.

At first the war went according to Cavour's plans. The combined Sardinian-French forces quickly drove the Austrians out of Lombardy and marched on into Venetia. Patriots in Tuscany, Modena, and Parma overthrew their Austrian rulers and asked to be annexed to Sardinia.

This was more than Napoleon III had planned on. He did not want a strong, united Italy any more than he wanted a united Germany. He was afraid that if the war lasted a long time, Prussia, for its own ends, might help Austria. Napoleon did not want to get involved in a war against both Austria and Prussia. In July 1859, only three

UNIFICATION OF ITALY • 1858-1870

- Kingdom of Sardinia before 1859
- From Austria to Sardinia in 1859
- Added to Sardinia in 1860 to form the Kingdom of Italy
- Added to Italy in 1866
- Added to Italy in 1870

months after the war began, Napoleon broke the agreement with Cavour by signing a secret armistice with Austria. According to its terms, Sardinia received Lombardy, but Austria kept Venetia. Austrian rulers were restored to Tuscany, Modena, and Parma.

This was a severe setback for Cavour and the Italian nationalists. Napoleon III had delivered only half of his side of the bargain—control of Lombardy to Sardinia. However, he insisted on receiving his full price—Nice and Savoy. Fearing to lose the partial victory, King Victor Emmanuel II agreed to the French terms.

The Italian people refused to give up their goals. Popular feeling ran far ahead of governmental caution. Rebellions in Parma, Modena, and Tuscany again expelled the Austrian rulers and set up popular temporary governments. The people of Romagna, a province in the Papal States, also revolted. When elections were held in all these areas, the votes were overwhelmingly in favor of joining Sardinia.

Napoleon III was completely opposed to any such arrangement. For a time there was a chance of war between France and Sardinia in which the Italians would try to regain Nice and Savoy. Then, in 1860, Cavour made another agreement. France was to keep Nice and Savoy. In return, Sardinia was to be allowed to annex Parma, Modena, Tuscany, and Romagna. Although it was difficult for Italians to give up Nice and Savoy, they thus took a long step toward Italian unity.

Garibaldi's Red Shirts

The lower half of the Italian Peninsula, together with the large island of Sicily, made up what was called the Kingdom of the Two Sicilies. It was ruled by a harsh Bourbon king, Francis II. Earlier revolts there had been unsuccessful, but it now became the target of the Italian nationalists. Giuseppe Garibaldi, a man with a long history of devotion to Italian freedom, led the way.

Garibaldi was born in Nice in 1807. As a youth, he joined Mazzini's Young Italy movement and in 1834 had to flee for his life. He lived for several years in Latin America. Returning to Italy, he fought in the revolutions of 1848. Forced to flee again, he lived in the United States for several years, returning once more to Italy in 1854.

The Unification of Italy

1848	Sardinia granted a constitution
1852	Cavour became premier of Sardinia
1859	Lombardy ceded to Sardinia
1860	Sardinia lost Nice and Savoy, gained Parma, Modena, Tuscany, and Romagna
	Garibaldi took Sicily and Naples
1861	Kingdom of Italy proclaimed
1866	Italy gained Venetia
1870	Rome became capital of united Italy

With financial assistance secretly furnished by Cavour, Garibaldi recruited an army of 1,100 soldiers. They were called Red Shirts because of the uniform they wore into battle. In the spring of 1860, Garibaldi and his Red Shirts invaded the island of Sicily, where they were welcomed by the people. Crossing to the Italian mainland, Garibaldi and his force seized Naples, the capital city, and drove Francis II and his forces north to the border of the Papal States.

Garibaldi now planned to continue his march northward and capture Rome and then Venetia. Cavour was afraid that France or Austria might enter the conflict and that Garibaldi might try to set up a republic. An army was sent south to stop Garibaldi's advance, and most of the territory of the Papal States was annexed to Sardinia. Cavour left the city of Rome under the control of the pope.

In the fall of 1860, Garibaldi and Cavour met in Naples. Garibaldi was reluctant to abandon his plan for conquest of the entire Italian peninsula. However, Cavour persuaded him to agree to the establishment of the kingdom of Italy, with Victor Emmanuel II of Sardinia as its ruler.

Final unification

In 1860 elections were held everywhere in Italy except in Venetia and Rome. The people voted overwhelmingly for national unity under the king of Sardinia. Representatives met at a parliament in the city of Turin in February 1861. They con-

The unification of Italy

The creation of a united Italian kingdom was largely the work of two people, Camillo Benso di Cavour and Giuseppe Garibaldi. Cavour (below) was a master diplomat. He gained recognition from foreign rulers for Italian claims to independence. Garibaldi, a dramatic military leader, was a man of action rather than negotiation. When it seemed that the southern part of Italy might not gain independence, he led a band of 1,100 soldiers in an invasion of Sicily and Naples (bottom). Garibaldi's successful expedition became a national legend, and the kingdom of Italy was established. Thus it was appropriate that a cartoonist show Garibaldi putting a boot, the shape of the map of Italy, on the leg of the new king, Victor Emmanuel II (right).

firmed Victor Emmanuel II as king of Italy "by grace of God and the will of the nation." Cavour died four months later.

The new kingdom included every part of Italy except Venetia, which still belonged to Austria, and the western part of the Papal States around the city of Rome, which was ruled by the pope (see map, page 528). European governments now had only two choices—to recognize the new state or to fight it. Most embarrassed of all was Napoleon III. He did not make war on the new country, but he sent French troops to Rome to prevent the Italian nationalists from seizing it.

The unification of Italy was not complete in 1861, but the end was in sight. Italy was able to gain Venetia in the Seven Weeks' War of 1866, about which you will read in the next section. When the Franco-Prussian War broke out in 1870, Napoleon III had to recall his troops from Rome. The Italians entered the city, and the citizens of Rome voted overwhelmingly for union with Italy. That same year, Rome was proclaimed the capital of the kingdom of Italy.

The pope protested bitterly. He shut himself up in the Vatican palace, saying he would remain "the prisoner of the Vatican" until the Papal States were restored to him. They never were, and relations between the papacy and the Italian government remained troubled for many years.

Problems of united Italy

Although Italy was politically united, many problems remained. Few Italians were experienced in self-government, and scandals were common. The various regions of the country remained divided by their own traditions and independence. There was tension between the north, which became industrialized, and the agricultural south. In Sicily, local leaders organized a secret society known as the Mafia. The society formed a kind of state within the state, which the central government was powerless to control.

The leaders of Italy admired the military strength of Germany and hoped to follow a similar course in their own country. Within a few years, Italy had the third largest navy and the third largest merchant marine in the world.

Italy's buildup of military and naval strength was achieved by taxing its people heavily. This led to unrest, and there were peasant uprisings, particularly in Sicily, in the 1890's. Looking for victories to build the country's prestige, Italy engaged in colonial ventures in Africa, about which you will read in Chapter 23. A brief war against the Ottoman Empire in 1911 cost a great deal of money and brought Italy little in return. There were strikes and riots all through Italy during the next several years in protest against taxes and governmental inefficiency. Unification had been achieved, but stability was difficult to maintain.

CHECKUP

1. IDENTIFY: Risorgimento, Carbonari, Young Italy, Victor Emmanuel II, Cavour, Francis II, Garibaldi, Red Shirts.

2. LOCATE: Lombardy, Venetia, Sardinia, Kingdom of the Two Sicilies, Tuscany, Rome, Savoy, Piedmont, Nice, Modena, Parma, Romagna, Papal States, Turin.

3. Who was Mazzini and what was his place in Italian history?

4. Trace the steps toward Italian unification as they occurred in the following years: 1848–49, 1852, 1858, 1859, 1860, 1866, and 1870.

5. Describe the problems that Italy faced following its unification in 1870.

Prussia created a unified and powerful German Empire

You have read in Chapter 15 how Prussia was built up into a strong and prosperous state during the 1700's as a result of rule by Frederick William I and his son Frederick the Great. Their reigns extended from 1713 to 1786.

The beginnings of German unity

A new situation was created when Napoleon I dominated Prussia from 1806 until 1812. He seized Prussian lands, formed new states from them, and gave them to his relatives and allies. He also imposed restrictions on Prussia. The Prussian army was limited in size. The country had to pay to France a large sum of money, support an occupation army within its territory, and contribute soldiers to the French armies.

These restrictions eventually helped Prussia because they led to a revival of patriotism. Prussians wanted to get rid of the French and to regain the greatness and power they had enjoyed under Frederick the Great. They demanded reforms that would rebuild the nation.

Napoleon's territorial changes in Germany also worked in Prussia's favor. Austria had been Prussia's strongest rival. An Austrian Hapsburg had held the position of Holy Roman Emperor since the 1400's, thus giving Austria a vague claim over the German states. Napoleon abolished the Holy Roman Empire and weakened Austria's power over the German states. He also reorganized and consolidated many German states into the Confederation of the Rhine, which Prussia found easier to influence.

Prussia played a major part in the final struggle against Napoleon. Prussian armies fought at Waterloo, and Prussia earned the right to be one of the four great powers represented at the Congress of Vienna. It also was a member of the Quadruple Alliance.

In 1815 the Congress of Vienna, as you read in Chapter 20, turned Napoleon's Confederation of the Rhine into the German Confederation, with additional members that included Prussia. The Congress gave Prussia much important territory, including two thirds of Saxony and an area along the lower Rhine River. Prussian lands now stretched almost unbroken from Russia to the Rhine and beyond (see map, page 476). The government was well organized and efficient, with a strong economy. The population included some Poles and other Slavs, but the overwhelming majority of the people were German.

Yet Germany as a whole was by no means united. Apart from Prussia, it contained dozens of states. Some of these were quite small, such as the tiny principality of Waldeck. At the opposite extreme were the vast territories of the Hohenzollerns and such large states as Hanover, Saxony, Bavaria, and Württemberg.

Almost every one of these German states insisted on maintaining its own laws, coinage, army, and tariffs. Elaborate palaces were built to imitate the splendors of Versailles. Each ruler had absolute power. The chief aim of the ruler—often the only aim—was to preserve the realm exactly as it had always been.

Religious differences were also a barrier to German unification. Prussia and northern Germany were Protestant. The southern German states were Catholic.

The Zollverein

The first major step toward German unity after the Congress of Vienna came in the economic field. The movement of goods from one German state to another was extremely difficult because of the tariffs that each state placed on goods coming in from the outside. There were even tariffs on items shipped from one Prussian possession to another. The tariffs, of course, increased the prices of goods and reduced the amount that was sold.

The drive for freer movement of goods was begun by the **Junkers** (YOONG·kurs)—the aristocratic landowners of Prussia—who wanted to sell their farm products. In 1818 they persuaded the king of Prussia to abolish all tariffs within his territories. Beginning the next year, Prussia made treaties with other German states, thus setting up a customs union called the **Zollverein** (TSAWL·fer·ine). By 1844 it included almost all the German states except Austria.

The Zollverein benefited its members by making prices lower and more uniform. It also led to the spread of industrialization in the German states by providing a wide, free market for German goods and by offering tariff protection against foreign competition. Uniform systems of weights, measures, and currency were adopted. More goods were produced and bought, and business leaders became strong supporters of German unification.

The establishment of the Zollverein had no immediate political effects, and each of the various states in the German Confederation continued to act independently. However, by making their economies dependent on each other, the Zollverein paved the way for later political union.

Prussia was the leader of the movement for a customs union. As the strongest industrial state, it more and more became the economic and political

"Two Men Looking at the Moon"

Many artists were filled with the nationalistic spirit that flooded Europe during and after the Napoleonic Era. Caspar David Friedrich, who painted the work at right, was a patriotic German. He admired German art of the Middle Ages and deliberately included in his paintings some of its common motifs. Among these were gnarled and twisted trees, like the one here. This brooding nighttime scene, with its air of melancholy, is typical of the romantic movement. Romanticism emphasized the past and thus was especially appealing to Germans, who, in the early 1800's, were taking a new interest in their national traditions and customs.

leader. Austria, which was not a member of the Zollverein, was increasingly considered to be outside "the real Germany."

In the years after the Congress of Vienna, there were strong nationalistic and democratic movements within the states of the German Confederation. In 1848 the uprising in France touched off demands for liberal reforms throughout Germany. Agitation was intense for a while, and elections were held for representatives to a National Assembly which would try to unify Germany. Eventually, however, the demands of liberals for representative government were defeated. German unification was to be accomplished by the policies of a king and his powerful prime minister.

Bismarck and Prussian strength

William I became king of Prussia in 1861. In 1862 he called upon Otto von Bismarck, a conservative Junker politician, to head the Prussian cabinet. Bismarck accepted.

Bismarck was opposed to democracy and the idea of a parliament. He also believed strongly that Prussia was destined to lead the German people to unity. He was willing to help this destiny come about by using trickery, bribery, or military force. Bismarck had great contempt for idealists. He regarded them as mere talkers, not people of action. He once said of German policy that it could not be carried out by "speeches, shooting-matches, and songs, but only through blood and iron."

For years, Bismarck was the real ruler of Prussia. He had the thorough cooperation of the king and the generals in charge of the army. They agreed with Bismarck that it was necessary to reorganize the Prussian army and strengthen it even more. First, however, an increase in taxes was needed.

The Prussian parliament refused to approve the money for a military expansion program. Bismarck simply dismissed the parliament and collected the taxes without parliamentary authorization. In so doing, he paid no attention to the protests of the liberals. His plan was to stop the criticism with military victories.

Bismarck and his generals proceeded to make the Prussian army a great war machine. Prussian military strategists tried to plan for every possible situation that their army might encounter in the field.

Unification through war

Bismarck had to overcome two major obstacles to increase the power and size of Prussia. First, he had to drive Austria out of its position of leadership in the German Confederation. Second, he had to overcome Austria's influence over the south German states, which he considered the major opponents to Prussian leadership. He did this in three wars—the Danish War, the Seven Weeks' War, and the Franco-Prussian War.

The Danish War. On the border between Denmark and Germany lay two small states—the duchies of Schleswig and Holstein (see map, page 536). The population of Holstein, which had been part of the German Confederation since 1815, was entirely German. Schleswig's population was a mixture of Germans and Danes. The duchies were ruled by the Danish king under a constitution which provided that they were separate from Denmark. In 1863 King Christian IX came to the Danish throne. At the insistence of many Danes, he proclaimed a new constitution that tried to annex Schleswig to Denmark.

Both Prussia and Austria protested against the new Danish constitution. Acting together, they demanded that it be revoked. When Denmark refused, Prussia and Austria declared war against Denmark. In 1864, after three months of fighting, Denmark was defeated.

The peace treaty gave the two duchies to Prussia and Austria jointly. Austria demanded that the two duchies form a single state within the German Confederation. Prussia opposed this settlement. After bitter quarreling, it was decided that Prussia should administer Schleswig, and Austria should administer Holstein.

The Seven Weeks' War. Now Bismarck moved to drive Austria out of the German Confederation. He prepared the way by a series of skillful diplomatic actions. First, he persuaded Napoleon III of France to remain neutral if war developed between Prussia and Austria. In return for French neutrality, France demanded certain territory held by the southern German states. Bismarck persuaded Napoleon III to put these demands in writing, but Bismarck's vague promises to Napoleon III were never written down.

Bismarck's next step was to form an alliance with the new nation of Italy. In return for fighting against Austria, Italy was to receive the Austrian territory of Venetia. Then, by various complicated moves, Bismarck provoked Austria into declaring war on Prussia in 1866.

Austria had as allies several German states, including Bavaria, Saxony, and Hanover. However, it had not counted on the superb training and preparation of the Prussian army. In fact, Prussia's conduct of the war came as a surprise to the whole world. Prussian forces moved by train wherever railroad tracks were available and used the telegraph to keep in communication. Prussia defeated Austria in only seven weeks.

The Treaty of Prague ended the so-called Seven Weeks' War in the summer of 1866. The German Confederation was dissolved, and Austria surrendered its rule of Holstein to Prussia. The Italians gained Venetia.

In north Germany the duchies of Schleswig and Holstein, the states of Hanover, Hesse-Cassel, and Nassau, and the free city of Frankfort were all added to Prussia. Now Prussia included a large part of the land and population of Germany (see map, page 536). The remaining states north of the Main River were allowed for a time to remain independent. In 1867 they were united with Prussia into a North German Confederation. Each state had self-government, but the king of Prussia was hereditary president of the Confederation. As the largest state, with the most powerful industry and army, and with the greatest number of representatives, Prussia dominated the legislature of the new Confederation.

Only the three southern states of Bavaria, Baden, and Württemberg and the southern part of Hesse-Darmstadt remained outside Prussia's influence. If they could be persuaded to join Prussia, German unity would be complete. Catholic and Austrian influence was strong there. It would take some great outside danger to persuade the states to unite willingly.

The Franco-Prussian War. You have read in Chapter 20 that Bismarck provoked war with France in 1870. When France declared war on Prussia, Bismarck showed the leaders of the south German states the 1865 document in which Napoleon III had demanded their territory for France. He persuaded them that their greatest danger was from France, not Prussia. He thus converted the states from rivals into allies against France and secured their help in winning a Prussian victory.

The Franco-Prussian War was short but decisive. No outside nation made any move to help France. The Prussian army was superbly trained and equipped and ably led. Within a few months the French were totally defeated.

Bismarck had been lenient with Austria when it was conquered because many of its people were Germans and he did not want them as enemies. He had no such feeling about France. As you have read, France was occupied by German troops, lost Alsace and part of Lorraine, and had to pay a huge sum of money to Germany.

Formation of the German Empire

For Germany the peace was not as important as an event that took place before the treaty was signed. On January 18, 1871, representatives of the allied German states met in the Hall of Mirrors of the palace of Versailles near Paris. There they issued an official proclamation declaring the formation of the German Empire, which included all of the German states except Austria (see map, page 536). The capital of the empire was to be Berlin, capital of Prussia.

King William I of Prussia was proclaimed German emperor. Bismarck became the chancellor—or chief minister—of the German Empire. Because of his policy of "blood and iron," he was often called the "Iron Chancellor."

Much as he disliked constitutions, Bismarck accepted one that united the 25 German states in a federal form of government. Each state had its own ruler as well as the right to handle its own domestic matters, including public health, education, law enforcement, and local taxation.

The federal government was given control of all common matters, such as national defense, foreign affairs, tariffs, and commerce. At the head of the German government was the emperor, called the **Kaiser** (KY·zur), who was also king of Prussia. He was not, as Bismarck would have liked, an absolute monarch, but he did have tremendous power. He could appoint the chancellor, and he commanded the army and navy and controlled

The Unification of Germany
1815 German Confederation formed
1862 Bismarck became prime minister of Prussia
1864 After Danish War, Schleswig turned over to Prussian administration
1866 Prussian victory in Seven Weeks' War resulted in dissolution of German Confederation and Prussian annexation of several north German states
1867 North German Confederation established
1870 Southern German states joined Prussia in Franco-Prussian War
1871 All German states (except Austria) united to form German Empire

foreign policy. The emperor could declare a defensive war on his own, and he could order an offensive war with the agreement of the upper house of the legislature.

The legislative branch of the government was composed of two houses. The Bundesrat (BOON·dus·raht), a federal council, was the upper house. It had 58 members, who were appointed by the rulers of the various states. The emperor appointed 17 of the members. Since 14 votes could block a change in the constitution, the emperor could thus defeat any amendment that he opposed.

The Reichstag (RYKS·tahk), or legislative assembly, was the lower house of the German legislature. Its nearly 400 members were elected by universal manhood suffrage. The Bundesrat drew up all the bills for consideration by the Reichstag and could veto its actions. The Bundesrat and the emperor acting together could dismiss the Reichstag. Thus, there was little chance that the Reichstag would pass any liberal democratic laws that the Bundesrat or emperor might oppose.

The German constitution strongly favored Prussia. The king of Prussia had become emperor of Germany. Prussia had the greatest number of delegates in the Bundesrat. As the most populous state, it also had the largest number of delegates in the Reichstag. Power in Prussia was in the hands of the king and the Junkers. Thus, with

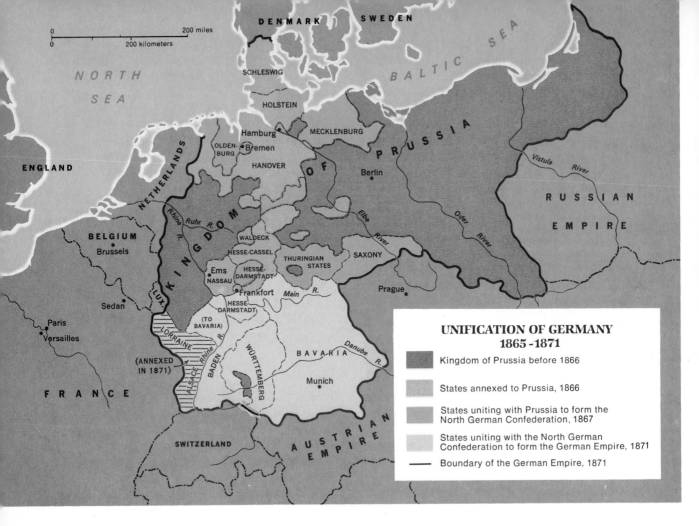

UNIFICATION OF GERMANY 1865-1871

Kingdom of Prussia before 1866

States annexed to Prussia, 1866

States uniting with Prussia to form the North German Confederation, 1867

States uniting with the North German Confederation to form the German Empire, 1871

— Boundary of the German Empire, 1871

Prussia in control, there was little chance that the German Empire would adopt any democratic measures.

CHECKUP

1. IDENTIFY: Junkers, William I, Treaty of Prague, Iron Chancellor, Kaiser, Bundesrat, Reichstag.

2. LOCATE: Saxony, Hanover, Bavaria, Württemberg, Schleswig, Holstein, Hesse-Cassel, Nassau, Frankfort, Main River, Baden, Berlin.

3. What was the Zollverein? What purpose did it serve?

4. Prussia fought three wars to unite Germany. Name them and list what territory was acquired by each.

5. How did Bismarck persuade the south German states to accept Prussian leadership in Germany?

6. Name the powers held by the emperor of the new German Empire.

3

Industrialization and socialism created opposition to Bismarck

Because Bismarck could not at first get the absolute monarchy he wanted, he tried to achieve it in other ways. However, in the years after the formation of the German Empire, he had to accept many compromises to make the political system work. Even though the constitution did not give the people much voice in their own affairs, their demands had to be taken into account.

Opposition to Bismarck

In spite of rigid control by the aristocratic Prussians, the new German federal government soon ran into difficult problems. Dissatisfied groups formed political parties that opposed Bismarck's policies. Some wanted the government to be more liberal and democratic and to enact social reforms. Others feared Bismarck's military policy and the ever-growing army and navy.

Deputies from the south German states, especially from Bavaria, resented the interference of the federal government in what they considered to be their local affairs. They thought their own state governments should deal with such matters.

Relations with the Roman Catholic Church presented special problems for Bismarck. The long-standing claim of the pope to administer Church property seemed like foreign interference in German domestic affairs. Bismarck came to feel that the Catholic Church was a threat to the German Empire. The fact that the south German states were Catholic made this feeling stronger. In 1872 diplomatic relations between the government and the papacy were broken off. Then there began what was called the *Kulturkampf*—German for "war of civilization." This was a bitter struggle between the Roman Catholic Church and the German government.

Germany passed strict laws to control the Catholic clergy and Catholic schools. The Jesuits were expelled. All the Catholic clergy had to be Germans, educated in German schools. Any member of the clergy who opposed these measures was imprisoned or banished. This religious policy stirred up a great deal of opposition. A Catholic party was formed to oppose the *Kulturkampf* and to work for other changes. Many non-Catholic liberals also joined the opposition. By 1880 Bismarck began to modify the *Kulturkampf* because he needed the support of the Catholic party. In addition, he thought that the menace from Catholicism was no longer real. Diplomatic relations were reestablished with the papacy, and the laws against Catholics were repealed. By 1887 the *Kulturkampf* was ended.

Industrial development under Bismarck

The Zollverein, as you have read, had aided industrialization beginning in 1819. Political unification after 1871 helped it further. The victory over France in the Franco-Prussian War had brought with it the rich iron mines of the Lorraine region as well as a billion dollars in gold for capital.

The German government owned the railroads and managed them in order to promote industrial development. A system of canals provided cheaper, though slower, transportation. Germany was rich in natural resources. North of Lorraine were the great coal deposits of the Ruhr Valley. A huge steel industry developed in this area because of the availability of iron and coal.

The fact that industrialization came later in Germany than in Great Britain and France proved to be an advantage. German industries could use the best methods and most improved machinery developed elsewhere. German scientists worked out further changes and improvements.

Under Bismarck's leadership, the government helped industry in many ways. All money and banking laws became uniform throughout the empire. Postal and telegraph services—the means of communications by which so much business is conducted—were centralized. The government encouraged German industrialists to form cartels, a type of business organization about which you read in Chapter 19. In addition, a high-tariff policy was adopted to protect German industries from foreign competition.

With all of these influences at work, Germany rapidly became an industrial nation. It exported manufactured goods and imported food and raw materials. By 1900 it was threatening the positions of leading producers of steel and machinery, such as Great Britain and the United States. Germany was also rivaling these nations for leadership in world trade.

Agriculture did not decline in Germany as industry increased. Through the application of scientific methods and the use of fertilizers, even the poor soil of northern Germany was made productive. Like its manufactured goods, German farm goods were protected by tariffs.

Berlin increasingly became the center of the new empire. Connected with all parts of Germany by rail and canal, it grew into a major commercial city with a rapidly expanding population.

Socialism in Germany

With the growth of German industry, cities increased greatly in population, and a class of factory workers appeared. German laborers, like those in other nations, wanted decent working

The power of a united Germany

An astonishingly easy victory over France in 1870 paved the way for German unification. Only a few days after crossing the French border, German troops were at the Loire River, hundreds of miles away (below). The ruler of the new German Empire was William I, but the main architect of his military victories was his chief minister, Otto von Bismarck. A French cartoon shows Bismarck as the bloodthirsty ogre that many Europeans feared he had become (right).

Along with Germany's military power went economic power. Its industrial output rapidly came to rival Great Britain's, and in such areas as iron production (bottom), Germany soon became a model for other nations.

conditions. Some people believed that the cartels led to lower wages for workers and higher prices for consumers. Many thought that these various problems needed government action. They wanted the government to pass laws to benefit workers and regulate industry.

Socialist reformers went even further, advocating government ownership of all major industries. German socialists banded together in 1869 to form the Social Democratic Party. The party grew quickly, with most of its members coming from the ranks of the city workers. In 1871 it was able to elect two members to the Reichstag. By 1877 that representation had increased to twelve.

Even if the Social Democrats had had a much greater representation, they could have done very little. The Reichstag was powerless to pass any laws that the Bundesrat opposed. Since the Bundesrat represented the hereditary rulers, there was little chance that it would propose or pass the laws that the socialists wanted. The Reichstag, however, made a good public forum in which socialist members could express their grievances and complaints.

Bismarck's antisocialist campaign

By 1877 the Social Democrats were receiving half a million votes. Every gain in socialist voting strength—and every demand for reform— alarmed Bismarck. The chancellor decided to use all of his power to fight the socialists. His opportunity came in 1878, when there were two attempts to assassinate the emperor. Neither of the would-be assassins had any connection with socialism, and Bismarck knew this. However, he took advantage of the public excitement to accuse the Social Democrats of plotting the attempts. The emperor and the Bundesrat dissolved the Reichstag and called for new elections. There followed a widespread campaign against socialists and their ideas.

The election did not change the strength of the Social Democrats in the Reichstag. Bismarck, however, was able to push through laws aimed at repressing the socialists. The new laws made it unlawful to spread socialist ideas through newspapers, books, or pamphlets. Socialists were forbidden to hold public meetings.

Despite such restrictive laws, the socialists continued their efforts. By 1884 Social Democratic representation in the Reichstag had increased to 24 despite the restrictions. As he did in the *Kulturkampf*, Bismarck had to examine his tactics and see how to achieve what he wanted against growing opposition.

Since repression had failed, the Iron Chancellor was forced to try something else. He decided to grant many of the reforms the socialists had proposed. If the government granted reforms, Bismarck believed, people would have less reason to join the socialists, and the party would therefore lose strength.

Bismarck's new policy was called "stealing the socialists' thunder." He said that he wanted to pass laws that would help workers so that the Social Democrats "will sound their bird call in vain." Beginning in 1883, he put through several far-reaching reforms. First came insurance against sickness, then insurance against accidents—both paid for by employers. Other laws limited hours and provided for certain holidays from work. The final step was a law that provided for payments to workers when they were physically disabled or too old to work.

Germany thus adopted a pioneering program of government-directed social reforms. The reforms did not wipe out socialism in Germany, but they did remove many of the workers' grievances. This program of social legislation was later copied in many other industrial nations.

Bismarck's foreign policy

Bismarck's foreign policy was based largely on German military strength. He once declared: "We Germans fear God, but nothing else in the world." The military draft was adopted throughout Germany. The army constantly increased in size and used the most modern weapons and equipment. Professional soldiers held important positions in nonmilitary branches of the government as well as in the army. However, after unification the country pursued a policy of peace rather than war.

Bismarck's greatest worry was that some day Germany might have to fight a war on the eastern and western fronts at the same time. Therefore, he did not want France (on the west) and Russia (on the east) to become allies. He worked to keep strong the friendship between Germany and Russia. Bismarck considered Austria a natural ally, even though Prussia had displaced Austria as the leader of Germany.

Prussia had helped Italy gain Venetia in 1866, an action that brought Germany the friendship of Italy. Bismarck strengthened this friendly relationship, and Germany and Italy became allies. In 1882 Bismarck succeeded in forming an alliance—formally called the Triple Alliance—made up of Germany, Austria, and Italy.

The resignation of Bismarck

Emperor William I died in 1888. His son reigned only a few months before he died, and was succeeded in turn by his son, William II. The young monarch and the old chancellor soon disagreed violently. William II felt that Bismarck was too powerful. Bismarck believed that the young emperor was taking away the powers the chancellor had used wisely for years. He also feared that William was too rash and undisciplined to use his considerable authority with wisdom.

For a long time Bismarck had thought himself indispensable to Germany. However, in 1890 William forced him to resign, which he did with a great deal of bitterness. Although he and William II were later reconciled personally, Bismarck did not serve Germany again.

With Bismarck gone, William II set out to build up Germany's colonial empire. He increased the size and strength of the German army and began to build up the German navy. This move brought Germany into conflict with Great Britain, which was the world's strongest naval power. New agreements with neighboring nations were signed, and by the early 1900's Germany was stronger than ever before.

CHECKUP

1. IDENTIFY: *Kulturkampf,* Social Democratic Party, Triple Alliance, William II.

2. What were three problems faced by the German Empire in the 1870's and 1880's?

3. What were the major factors in the rapid industrial development of Germany?

4. Describe the chief social reforms adopted under Bismarck. Why did he favor these reforms?

In spite of some reforms, Russia remained a rigid autocracy

By the mid-1800's, Russia had the largest territory and population of any European nation. Yet it was a weak nation. Industrial development, which so strengthened the West, lagged in Russia. Most of the country's extensive natural resources were undeveloped. Despite its size, Russia was mostly landlocked. Either its ports were frozen with ice for much of the year, or the exits were controlled by other countries. This situation led to continuous Russian efforts to win access to the Mediterranean, past Constantinople and the Dardanelles. These efforts led to conflicts with the Ottoman Empire, which controlled the Dardanelles.

Russia had another problem. It was by no means a unified nation like Great Britain or France. The huge Russian Empire included a great variety of peoples and national groups. Most people in the European part of Russia belonged to one of three related groups: (1) the Great Russians, in central and northern Russia, (2) the Ukrainians, in the south, and (3) the White Russians, in the west. They all belonged to the Orthodox Church. Scattered throughout the empire were smaller racial, national, and religious groups speaking many languages. Many of them, such as the Poles and Finns, had been conquered by the Russians and did not like Russian rule.

Russian domestic and foreign policies

The liberal movement that influenced other European nations so strongly in the 1800's made little progress in Russia. The czar was an **autocrat**—that is, he held absolute power over the huge Russian Empire. The domestic program of the czars was designed to keep Russia an autocracy. However, political developments in Western Europe were bound to have some effect.

Western influence had been felt in Russia since the time of Peter the Great. Improved transportation and communication made this influence stronger still. Nationalistic ideas appealed to the Russian minorities, especially to the strongly

Fabergé Egg

This unusual piece of art is an enameled gold egg containing a completely accurate model of the Gatchina Palace near St. Petersburg. Only five inches (13 centimeters) high, it includes the tiny flag flying from the palace tower. It is decorated with precious pearls and diamonds. This egg was probably given to the mother of Czar Nicholas II on Easter morning, 1902. It was customary for the Russian royal family to exchange eggs like this one every Easter. An egg symbolized the resurrection of Jesus as well as the ancient concepts of fertility and the rebirth in spring.

The Gatchina egg was created in the St. Petersburg jewelry firm of Carl Fabergé. Founded in 1842, this company employed the finest jewelers and goldsmiths in all of Europe. They also designed magnificent boxes, clocks, tableware, and jewelry. It was the series of eggs, however, that made Fabergé's reputation. Most of the eggs were signed by Michael Perchin, one of the few native Russians employed by Fabergé.

The House of Fabergé was closed in 1918 by officials of the new government. In order to raise money, they sold all but ten of the eggs. Today, many of these priceless eggs are housed in private collections and museums.

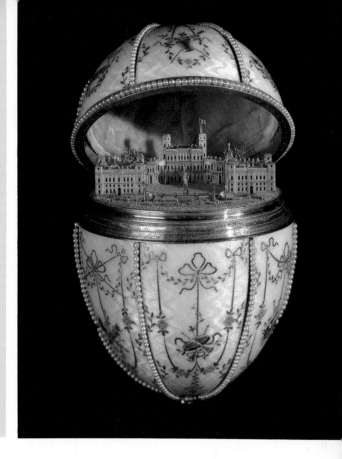

patriotic Poles and Finns. Liberalism, by the early 1800's, began to attract some of the educated members of the Russian aristocracy.

Faced with problems caused by restless nationalities and liberal ideas, the czars used harsh measures. There was strict censorship of speech and press, enforced by secret police, the army, and government officials. The czars rejected all demands for a constitution. In the 1830's Czar Nicholas I began a program of "Russification." Non-Russian peoples in the empire were forced to use the Russian language, accept the Orthodox religion, and adopt Russian customs.

The foreign policy of the Russian rulers had two goals. (1) In the Balkans they backed what was called **Pan-Slavism**—the union of all Slavic peoples under Russian leadership. (2) Elsewhere the Russian rulers followed the program of expansion that was begun under the first czars—eastward into Asia and southward toward the Ottoman Empire. Russian expansion received a setback with its defeat in the Crimean War, when it lost both territory and privileges.

Alexander II and reforms

Alexander II became czar in 1855. Although basically conservative and autocratic, he was easily influenced by public opinion. At this time liberal reformers were advocating freedom for all serfs. Serfdom and feudalism had not taken the same forms in Russia as they had in the rest of Europe. Even though serfs were not able to move freely from the land, they still retained a few civil rights such as being able to sue in court. In spite of this protection, millions of peasants were bound to the land. They could not leave unless so ordered by government officials or permitted to do so by the nobles who owned the land.

Toward the middle of the 1800's, liberal reformers began to receive some support in their campaign against serfdom from a new group of people—the middle-class industrialists. As industries were established, factory owners began to urge that the serfs be freed. The industrialists did not believe in liberal ideas. They simply needed workers for their factories.

541

Alexander II appointed committees to study the problem of the serfs. In 1861 he issued an Emancipation Edict that freed all the serfs. The terms of the edict also provided that the government would buy part of the land owned by the nobles and sell small tracts to the serfs.

Emancipation did not improve conditions very much for the serfs. The land was sold to them in small plots and at high prices. Peasants could not afford enough land to allow them to earn the payments for the land, pay the taxes, and still make a living. Therefore they had to rent additional land from landlords. Rents were high. Some peasants, unable to buy or rent land, moved to the towns and cities, where they provided a source of cheap labor for the factories.

Alexander II attempted other liberal reforms. Beginning in 1864, each province of European Russia was allowed to have an assembly of nobles and of delegates elected by townspeople and peasants. These assemblies decided on local taxes and controlled public health, schools, relief for the poor, and some public works.

Alexander also reformed the courts. Civil and criminal cases, which formerly were tried in secret by administrative officials, were now tried by juries in open courts. However, political offenders accused of plotting against the government were still tried in secret.

Alexander's policies did not please everyone. Those who were extremely conservative opposed them and tried to convince the czar that such actions endangered the position and privileges of the ruler and the nobles. Liberals considered Alexander's reforms as only modest first steps and pointed out the need for further changes. Radicals were even more critical.

Radicals and government reaction

Radical political activity in Russia was carried on by several groups. The Nihilists (NY·ih·lists) were active in the 1860's. They wanted to abolish the whole political and social structure and build a completely new Russia. They rebelled against the traditions of family, school, and society. Nothing of the old values and standards, they felt, was worth keeping. (Their name comes from the Latin word *nihil*, meaning "nothing.")

Another group, the Populists, urged their fol-lowers to live among peasants as teachers and doctors. Some believed that all the large estates of the nobles should be seized and the land divided among the peasants. The government arrested many Populists. Many Russian radicals then turned to violent action, joining a movement known as the People's Will. They favored the use of terrorism—bombings and assassinations of high officials—to force the government to grant their demands.

Radical activity frightened Alexander II, and in the late 1860's he turned to repressive measures. Gradually, however, he became convinced that reforms were necessary. Yet in 1881 he was assassinated by a terrorist.

The assassination of Alexander II put a definite end to liberal reforms and led to another intensive campaign of repression. Under Alexander III and his successor, Nicholas II, all means were used to stamp out liberalism—censorship, control of the church and of education, spies and informers, and imprisonment and exile. "Russification" was intensified. Jews were severely persecuted and frequently murdered in massacres called **pogroms** (poh·GRUMS). Finns, Poles, and other minorities were oppressed under the slogan "One Czar, One Church, One Language."

These harsh actions met with much opposition. The development of industry in Russia had produced a class of city workers who wanted the right to form unions and to strike. Middle-class industrialists wanted a voice in the government. Liberals and radicals were more determined than ever to gain reforms.

The attempts of the Russian government to suppress all of these varied aims produced an explosive situation. Terrorism increased. Socialists, who in 1898 had founded the Social Democratic Labor Party in imitation of the German Social Democratic Party, grew increasingly radical in their demands.

The Revolution of 1905

In 1904 and 1905, Russia fought a war with Japan in East Asia. You will read about the Russo-Japanese War in Chapter 26. To the surprise of the world, the Russians were badly defeated by the Japanese. Russia's defeat revealed that its government was corrupt and inefficient as well as

Russia at the turn of the century

At the turn of the century, Russia was a nation of poverty and repression. Most Russian manufactured goods were produced with primitive tools and outdated methods (below). The Russian economy was still overwhelmingly agricultural. Much of the grain produced was sold for low prices in depressed world markets, leaving the peasants poor and hungry (right).

Sometimes the suffering of the poor led them to desperate attempts at revolution, as it did in 1905. The poorly armed revolutionists were no match for the czar's well-equipped troops (above). The soldiers simply aimed their guns at the protesting crowds and fired, ending the rebellion.

autocratic, reactionary, and oppressive. The defeat in turn provided the spark for all the discontented groups in the country.

The result was the Revolution of 1905. Workers struck and held demonstrations. Merchants closed their stores, and industrialists shut down their factories. Lawyers refused to plead cases, and servants deserted their employers. Czar Nicholas II faced a crisis. Reforms had to be granted or the government would be overthrown.

The czar issued a decree called the October Manifesto. It guaranteed individual liberties and provided for the election, by limited suffrage, of a parliament called the Duma. No law was to be valid without the approval of the Duma. These measures ended the strikes and the revolution.

The treaty that ended the Russo-Japanese War was signed in 1905. After the war the czar's government was in a better position to deal with its critics at home. Two sessions of the Duma were dismissed because members insisted that the czar's ministers be responsible to the Duma. Then the qualifications for voting were changed so that only large landowners could vote. The result was a more conservative Duma, and one more cooperative with the czar.

The revolutionary movement of 1905 failed to achieve more widespread results for three chief reasons. (1) The army remained loyal to the czar and thus would not overthrow the regime. (2) The French, bound to Russia by a military alliance, lent money to support the government. (3) The revolutionary groups were divided in their goals. Moderates were frightened by radical demands. Radicals disagreed among themselves. Workers lost heart and deserted their leaders.

The Russian government learned very little from the Revolution of 1905. Revolutionary leaders were hunted down and imprisoned, exiled, or executed. All the repressive measures were used as before, and the government tried to remain just about what it had been—an autocracy.

CHECKUP

1. IDENTIFY: "Russification," Pan-Slavism, Emancipation Edict, Nihilists, Populists, People's Will, Social Democratic Labor Party, October Manifesto, Duma.

2. What were the most important aims of Russian foreign policy?

3. What two groups favored the abolition of serfdom in Russia? Did emancipation improve the condition of the serfs? Why or why not?

4. List the liberal reforms that Alexander II accomplished in Russia.

5. Why did the Revolution of 1905 fail to achieve its goals?

Austria-Hungary's interest focused on the Balkans

"When France sneezes, all Europe catches cold," a European leader said in 1848. He was describing how uprisings in France had set off revolts in almost every other European nation. The Austrian Empire was no exception.

In Vienna there were clashes between demonstrators and the army. Emperor Ferdinand ordered Metternich, his chief minister, to resign. Metternich fled the country. Later in 1848 Ferdinand himself abdicated, and the throne went to Francis Joseph I, who was only 18 years old.

In Hungary, too, there were uprisings. The people of this region—one of the largest parts of the Austrian Empire—were discontented. Most of them were Magyars—descendants of the nomadic warrior group that had migrated to Hungary from Russia and Rumania in the 900's. The Magyars spoke a language unlike other European languages and maintained a distinctive culture. There was a strong nationalist movement aimed at making the Magyars dominant in Hungary and freeing the region from Austrian domination.

The Hungarian patriot Louis Kossuth led the revolt in 1848. For a time it looked as though Hungary would gain its independence. However, the revolutionaries were soon defeated by Austria and Russia. Czar Nicholas I offered his help because he was afraid that the revolt might spread to Russian Poland. Kossuth fled the country.

Formation of the Dual Monarchy

For almost 20 years, Austria managed to keep liberalism and nationalism from becoming major issues. However, after Austria's defeat by Prussia in 1866, Hungarian demands for freedom became more insistent. Austria tried to solve this problem in 1867 by forming the **Dual Monarchy**—also called Austria-Hungary—in which the Hungarians shared power with the Austrians.

The Dual Monarchy had a common monarch, Francis Joseph I, whose title was Emperor of Austria and King of Hungary. There were three joint ministries—war, finance, and foreign affairs. Austria and Hungary each had its own parliament. The Austrian parliament met at Vienna, and the Hungarian at Budapest. Each could deal with all matters except those that concerned war, finance, and foreign affairs.

From an economic standpoint, the Dual Monarchy was a practical arrangement. The various parts of the empire fitted together into one economic unit. Hungary was chiefly agricultural, furnishing raw materials and food. Austria was strongly industrial, producing manufactured goods. Each furnished a market for the other.

There were, however, many problems. Austria, because of its manufacturing interests, wanted high protective tariffs. Hungary, as a farming region, favored low tariffs and freer trade.

The formation of the Dual Monarchy did not solve the problem of nationalities. The Austrian Germans and the Hungarian Magyars dominated the population in what were almost separate national states. There were national minorities in both Austria and Hungary—the Czechs, Serbs, Croats, Rumanians, Poles, and Italians. These people benefited very little from the Dual Monarchy and continued to agitate for self-government.

There were also problems in the common army over command and language. The Austrians spoke German. The Hungarians spoke Magyar, which had been declared the official language of Hungary and was now known as Hungarian. There were also soldiers who spoke the various Slavic languages.

You have read how Bismarck, to strengthen Prussia and form a united Germany, declared war on Austria in 1866. Defeat in the Seven Weeks' War forced Austria out of positions of power in Germany and Italy. To compensate for this, the Dual Monarchy tried to gain influence and territory in the Balkans, a region to the southeast controlled chiefly by the Ottoman Empire.

The Ottoman Empire

The Ottoman Turks controlled a vast empire. By the late 1600's, it included the North African coast, Egypt, western Asia, southern Russia, the Balkan Peninsula, and Hungary (see map, page 349). Then Ottoman power gradually declined. By 1700 the Austrians had regained Hungary. From that time on, the Ottoman Turks were on the defensive.

The Ottoman government was completely autocratic. The sultan was a commander in chief, controlling both governmental and religious affairs. Early sultans had been responsible rulers. Later sultans turned to the pleasures of palace life and left government affairs to lesser officials.

Government officials were administrators as well as military commanders, for the army and the government were one and the same. Power rivalries, favoritism, bribery, and corruption existed everywhere.

Government in the provinces was poor. Governors—called pashas or beys—gave little consideration to the welfare of their subjects. Their chief responsibility was to collect revenue and recruit soldiers for the central government. Pashas received and held on to their offices by bribery. They had the taxes collected and paid themselves well from the revenues.

Economic and social weaknesses. Turkish rulers did little to improve agriculture, maintain irrigation, or build roads, hospitals, and schools. The tax system discouraged both agriculture and industry, and production declined. Most peasants planted only enough land to produce a crop that they could harvest quickly and hide from the tax collector. The Ottoman Turks were not regarded favorably by their subject peoples. Many of the people of the empire were Christians or Jews. In strictly religious matters the Turks granted toleration to non-Muslims under their own religious leaders. However, if Jews or Christians were rebellious or plotted with enemy powers, the Turks slaughtered them unmercifully.

Discontent in the Balkans

In the early 1800's, discontent in the Balkan area of the Ottoman Empire was increased by the rise of nationalism. The Balkan region was the home

DECLINE OF THE OTTOMAN EMPIRE IN EUROPE • 1683-1913

Territory lost by the Ottoman Empire, 1683-1913

The Ottoman Empire in 1913

New boundaries of 1913, after the Balkan Wars

of many peoples—Serbs, Bulgarians, Rumanians, and Greeks (see map, this page).

The Turks tried to suppress nationalistic movements. During the 1820's, as you have read, the Greeks and Serbs revolted. Aided by outside powers, Greece gained independence in 1829, and Serbia achieved some self-rule. Encouraged by these successes and by the evident weakness of the Turks, Serbia and Greece tried to gain more territory. Rumanians and Bulgarians also wanted self-rule.

Foreign countries intervened for their own ends in the struggles between the Turks and these nationalist groups. Russia supported Balkan nationalists for several reasons. The Russians were Slavs, like the Bulgarians and Serbs in the Balkans. The Russians were Orthodox Christians, as were many of the discontented Balkan groups. More important was the fact that if the Ottoman Empire collapsed, Russia might be able to gain

control of the water route from the Black Sea to the Mediterranean.

The Russian attempt to gain influence in the eastern Mediterranean caused the British to give their support to the crumbling Ottoman Empire. Great Britain did not want the Russians in the Mediterranean, where they might challenge British sea power.

It was a curious alignment of nations. The Russian government was autocratic, but it promoted the freedom and independence of the Balkan peoples. Democratic Great Britain supported the autocratic Turks in suppressing freedom.

The Congress of Berlin

In 1875 revolts broke out in several Turkish provinces in the Balkans. Two years later, Russia decided to support the rebels and declared war on the Ottoman Empire. The Turks were defeated and forced to sign the Treaty of San Stefano in 1878. The treaty granted independence to Rumania, Montenegro, and Serbia. It also created an enlarged Bulgaria, which Russian troops were to occupy for some years. The new boundaries of Bulgaria extended far enough south to give Russia a seaport on the Aegean Sea, in the eastern Mediterranean.

Other European powers were alarmed by the sudden increase of Russian influence in the Balkans. Before the Treaty of San Stefano could go into effect, a group of nations, led by Great Britain and Austria, forced the Russians to consent to an international conference at Berlin to rewrite the treaty.

All the major European powers met at the Congress of Berlin in 1878. It approved several terms. Serbia, Montenegro, and Rumania were to retain their independence. Bulgaria was to have self-government, but its area was reduced in size and kept within the Ottoman Empire. This provision removed Russia's access to the Aegean Sea. Austria was to govern Bosnia and Herzegovina, but was not permitted to annex them.

The British were given the right to occupy and administer the island of Cyprus, long held by the Turks. The Turkish sultan still officially ruled the island, but Great Britain actually took it over. The use of Cyprus as a naval base increased Great Britain's power in the eastern Mediterranean and was a move to keep Russia out of this region.

Other nations continued to reduce both the size and the power of the Ottoman Empire. France, Great Britain, and Italy seized parts of its African territory, as you will read in Chapter 23. In 1908 Bulgaria became completely independent. In the same year, Austria broke the agreement of the Congress of Berlin by annexing Bosnia and Herzegovina outright. In 1912 Italy seized several islands in the southeastern Aegean Sea, including Rhodes. The island of Crete was the scene of revolts in 1896 and 1905, which resulted in a degree of self-government and, finally, annexation by Greece in 1913.

The Balkan Wars

In 1912 and 1913, two wars fought in the Balkans resulted in the further alteration of boundaries and increased international tensions. Turkish mis-

rule and the desire to liberate fellow nationals within the Ottoman Empire brought Bulgaria, Serbia, Greece, and Montenego into an alliance known as the Balkan League. These countries wanted to take and divide among themselves the Balkan territories of the Ottoman Empire. In 1912 the Balkan League declared war on the Turks and quickly defeated them. The Balkan allies, however, could not agree on the partition of the Turkish territories in the Balkans, and hostilities broke out again in 1913. This time, Serbia, Greece, Montenegro, Rumania, and the Ottoman Empire fought against and defeated Bulgaria.

As a result of the first war, Serbia gained a seaport on the Adriatic Sea, and Albania became independent. Bulgaria claimed considerable territory in the central Balkans and along the Aegean Sea. As a result of the second war, however, Austria forced Serbia to give the Adriatic seaport to Albania. Bulgaria suffered humiliating territorial losses to Serbia and Greece and was left with only a small outlet on the Aegean.

By the end of 1913, the territory of the Ottoman Empire in Europe had shrunk dramatically. It included only the city of Constantinople and a small region that gave it control of the vital water route from the Black Sea to the Mediterranean (see map, opposite page).

Everywhere in Europe, therefore, aggression and expansion marked the behavior of nations both new and old in the early 1900's. Tension and hostility were rising to dangerous levels. They were made worse by rivalries overseas that were the result of a new force—imperialism. You will read about this in the next chapter.

CHECKUP

1. IDENTIFY: Magyars, Kossuth, Francis Joseph I, pashas, Treaty of San Stefano, Balkan League.

2. LOCATE: Rumania, Budapest, Serbia, Montenegro, Bulgaria, Bosnia, Herzegovina, Cyprus, Rhodes.

3. When was the Dual Monarchy formed? What were its strengths and weaknesses?

4. Explain how each of the following factors contributed to the decline of the Ottoman Empire: (a) its system of government, both central and local; (b) its economy; (c) its rule of other peoples.

5. How was the Ottoman Empire reduced in size between 1878 and 1913?

CHAPTER REVIEW

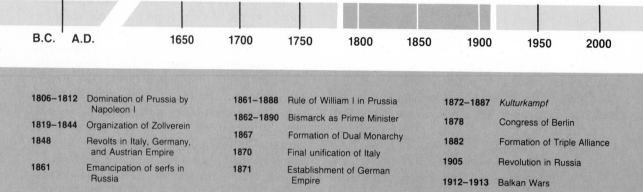

B.C.	A.D.	1650	1700	1750	1800	1850	1900	1950	2000

1806–1812	Domination of Prussia by Napoleon I	**1861–1888**	Rule of William I in Prussia	**1872–1887**	*Kulturkampf*
1819–1844	Organization of Zollverein	**1862–1890**	Bismarck as Prime Minister	**1878**	Congress of Berlin
1848	Revolts in Italy, Germany, and Austrian Empire	**1867**	Formation of Dual Monarchy	**1882**	Formation of Triple Alliance
1861	Emancipation of serfs in Russia	**1870**	Final unification of Italy	**1905**	Revolution in Russia
		1871	Establishment of German Empire	**1912–1913**	Balkan Wars

CHAPTER SUMMARY

Major new forces entered the European scene with the formation of a united Italy and a united Germany. Due to the efforts of Mazzini, Garibaldi, and Cavour, Italy was unified by 1870. A kingdom was established, with Rome as its capital.

The leader of unification in Germany was the kingdom of Prussia. An economic union, the Zollverein of the early 1800's, and an attempt to create a nationwide elected assembly in 1848 were steps toward German unity. However, the final unification was mainly the work of a determined Prussian government leader, Otto von Bismarck.

In both cases, but especially that of Germany, the new unity was accompanied by aggressive behavior. The Italians militarized rapidly, until their navy was the third largest in the world. The Germans went further. Bismarck had used three victorious wars—the Danish War, the Seven Weeks' War, and the Franco-Prussian War—to crush rivals and strengthen German national feeling. After the unification in 1871, he continued to build up German military strength and to act as a powerful force in Europe. Bismarck clashed with the new emperor, William II, and was forced to resign in 1890. However, Germany remained both prosperous and aggressive.

The older nations also experienced changes. In Russia the czar maintained autocratic control over the country, despite such reforms as the freeing of the serfs. He, too, built up military strength and pursued a vigorous foreign policy as a means of strengthening national feeling. The same was true of Austria-Hungary, the new Dual Monarchy created in southeastern Europe. Holding its various nationalities together was a major problem of the Dual Monarchy.

In the declining Ottoman Empire, corruption was widespread and government was inefficient. Discontent in its Balkan territories led to interference by European nations. Russia's defeat of the Turks and resulting gains alarmed other European powers, who met at the Congress of Berlin to revise the Treaty of San Stefano. Two Balkan Wars followed. Each juggled boundaries further and created international tensions that would eventually lead to a greater show of hostility.

CHECKING WHAT YOU KNOW

1. Match each leader at the left with a country at the right. You may use a country more than once.

   a. Bismarck   1. Russia
   b. William I   2. Italy
   c. Nicholas I   3. Austria-Hungary
   d. Francis Joseph I   4. German Empire
   e. Mazzini
   f. Alexander II
   g. Garibaldi
   h. William II
   i. Cavour
   j. Nicholas II

2. What contributions did each of the following make to Italian unification:

   a. Garibaldi
   b. Mazzini
   c. Cavour
   d. Victor Emmanuel II

3. Otto von Bismarck once remarked, "Politics is the art of the possible, the art of the attainable." How did Bismarck's actions in the *Kulturkampf* and in the antisocialist campaign prove his belief in this statement?

4. Why did the liberal movement make little progress in Russia during the 1800's? How did Russian radicals attempt to bring about change?

5. Why might each of the following events be considered a response to the rise of nationalism:
   a. unification of Italy and Germany
   b. start of the "Russification" program
   c. establishment of the Dual Monarchy
   d. decline of the Ottoman Empire

PRACTICING YOUR SKILLS

1. **Using charts.** Study the two charts on pages 529 and 535 showing the key events in the unification of Italy and Germany. What similarities and differences do you see between the two unification processes? Based on the information in these charts, what generalizations can you make about the way in which these two nations came into existence?

2. **Analyzing information.** You read in Chapter 15 about the rivalry between Prussia and Austria to dominate central Europe. To study the outcome of this struggle, compare the two maps on pages 347 and 536. How did the balance of power change during the period from 1721 to 1871? Using the information in this chapter and in Chapter 15, briefly explain how Prussia came to rule the German Empire.

RELATING PAST TO PRESENT

1. The Zollverein was a major step toward German unity. Who belonged to this customs union? How did the various member states benefit from economic cooperation? Using American history or civics books, find out about the rules regulating trade among the states in this nation. Can the states impose or collect tariffs? Can the federal government grant special trade concessions to any one state or region? What evidence of trade among the states can you find in your home?

2. Review the objectives of Russia's foreign policy during the 1800's. Then clip newspaper and magazine articles that illustrate foreign-policy objectives of the Soviet Union today. Compare the objectives of the 1800's with those of the present day. What seem to be the similarities and differences?

INVESTIGATING FURTHER

1. Read Garibaldi's "Proclamation to the Italians" and Bismarck's "iron and blood" speech in Louis Snyder, *Fifty Major Documents of the Nineteenth Century* (Van Nostrand Reinhold). Why might each of these documents be considered an expression of nationalism? Which is more idealistic? Explain.

2. Garibaldi and his comparatively small army succeeded in conquering the Kingdom of the Two Sicilies, which later became part of a united Italy. Prepare a report on Garibaldi's exploits in Sicily. One source for your report is "Garibaldi and His Thousand Redshirts Win Palermo" in Louis Snyder and Richard Morris, *A Treasury of Great Reporting* (Pocket Books).

3. Russia had a larger territory and population than any European nation, but it lagged behind Great Britain and the United States in industrial development. Use books in your library to research the reasons for this lag.

CHAPTER

23

(1798–1914)

Imperialist Powers Competed in Many Areas of the World

Beginning in the late 1400's and continuing into the 1700's, European nations extended their power to far parts of the world. As you have read, explorers, traders, and missionaries traveled to distant places they had not known before.

The earliest travelers were followed by settlers and government officials, who established colonies in many places for the benefit and glory of European nations. An important factor in these early ventures was mercantilism, which held that colonies added considerably to a nation's wealth.

In the late 1700's, European interest in empire building declined. Great Britain and France lost colonies in North America. A French economist wrote that colonies, once they matured, were like ripened fruits dropping from the tree. In addition, the French Revolution and Napoleonic Wars kept attention focused on European affairs for many years. Further, during the early 1800's, much capital that had formerly been invested in colonies was used instead to finance the industrialization of Europe.

Political movements in Europe also diminished the interest in empires. The drive toward democratic governments, attempts to gain national unity, labor and land reforms—all these movements occupied time and attention.

The diminished interest in empire building showed in several ways in the early 1800's. In accordance with the principles of laissez-faire eco-

A teacher in a Japanese public school

nomics, trade with colonies was opened to the ships of all nations, not just to those of the home country. Rarely did European nations attempt to annex new colonies. Great Britain, having learned a bitter lesson in the American Revolution, granted a large degree of self-government to Canada and other territories.

Beginning about 1870, the situation changed. During the next 40 years, many nations became involved in a new kind of empire building called **imperialism**—the practice of establishing colonies in order to control raw materials and markets. Imperialism differed from the colonization of the 1500's and 1600's mainly because the colonies established after 1870 were both more heavily populated and more thoroughly dominated. By the end of this period, European nations, the United States, and Japan had brought most of the world under their control.

This chapter tells that story and shows how imperial rivalries became an important cause of World War I. This chapter also tells how imperialism engulfed almost all of the continent of Africa as well as Asia and Latin America.

THE CHAPTER SECTIONS

1. Several different forces stimulated imperialism

2. Imperialism transformed the continent of Africa

3. The British secured firm control over India

4. Japan became a powerful force in East Asia

5. Foreign influence over Southeast Asia and the Pacific increased

6. The United States intervened in Latin America

1

Several different forces stimulated imperialism

Imperialism arose out of a complex mixture of political, economic, and social forces. Historians do not agree on which ones were most important. Whether or not the reasons for seeking colonies were good ones, many people believed them. They acted on their beliefs by trying to create new empires or enlarge older ones.

Desire for self-sufficiency

After 1850 the Industrial Revolution picked up speed as new sources of power, new machinery, and new industries were developed. Increased industrial production spurred the demand for traditional raw materials such as iron and coal. There was also now a need for new raw materials such as manganese and tungsten to make steel alloys, copper for the electrical industry, and rubber for a variety of uses. Industrialization also brought rising standards of living in Europe and the United States and increased demands for such tropical products as coffee, tea, and spices.

None of the industrialized nations produced all of these products. Nevertheless, no industrial nation wanted to be dependent on another for its raw materials. In the thinking of the late 1800's and early 1900's, there was an ever-present possibility of war. Thus it seemed necessary for an industrial nation to control the sources of its raw materials in order not to be at the mercy of an enemy.

Need for new markets

After 1870 new technology made it possible to turn out goods in enormous quantities. Indeed, goods now had to be produced in large quantities to make production profitable. Only when the new and expensive machinery was used to full capacity could it pay for itself and make profits for its owners.

People in Europe and the United States, even with their rising standards of living, could not buy all the things being produced. Industrialists began to look for new markets in regions that were not industrialized, especially in Asia, Africa, and Latin America.

It was believed that people in these areas would buy manufactured goods if they knew about them and could get them. It was even argued that the customs of these people might be changed to create new markets. Articles were written telling how busy European and American factories would be, and how much profit they would earn, if only the people of central Africa could be persuaded to wear shirts and ties.

Many people argued that industrialized nations should control their new markets abroad, just as they controlled the sources of their raw materials. Industrialists wanted their governments to guarantee them exclusive rights to sell in these markets, just as they were demanding protective tariffs to assure their exclusive markets at home.

Investing surplus capital

The Industrial Revolution produced large profits and created immense fortunes for owners of industry. Wealth increased tremendously, and it became concentrated in the hands of relatively few people.

Wealthy people looked for places to invest their money profitably. Undeveloped regions promised large profits, though with many risks. Companies sent out prospectors to find minerals that could be mined profitably. Banks lent money to local rulers in undeveloped areas to build railroads, establish plantations, and open mines.

The special risks of investment abroad often brought demands for protection. Foreign-owned mines, plantations, and factories were sometimes attacked and damaged by natives. Those who had invested money demanded that their governments protect their investments. In response to these demands, governments put pressure on native rulers or sent troops. Thus, economic imperialism often led to political imperialism—the establishment of a colony.

Outlets for population

Industrialization was accompanied, as you read in Chapter 19, by a rapid growth of population. Industrial development created many jobs, but in Europe there was not enough work to employ all the new job seekers. As a result, people left Europe in great numbers for the more thinly settled regions of the United States, Latin America, Africa, and Australia.

Nationalists regretted seeing people leave because the emigrants often became naturalized citizens of the countries where they settled. Ties with the former homeland weakened and finally disappeared. How much better, the nationalists thought, if emigrants could go to colonies. There they would still be loyal subjects under the political control of the home country.

Many new colonies were unsuited for settle-ment by Europeans or were already heavily populated. However, these considerations did not trouble the patriots.

Nationalism

Nationalism, a strong force throughout the 1800's, was particularly powerful in the period from 1870 to 1914, as you read in Chapter 22. Nationalists now argued that colonies added to the strength and prestige of the nation. For one thing, armies were growing larger, and colonies came to be considered a source of troops for the military. Gurkhas and Pathans, the fighters of Nepal and Afghanistan, joined Australians and New Zealanders to build up British armies. The Senegalese, from West Africa, fought for the French.

Imperialism appealed to people's desire for national glory and prestige. Germany and Italy did not become unified nations until the late 1800's. Now each felt that it had to build up a colonial empire in order to compete with longtime colonial powers such as Great Britain, France, and the Netherlands. However, it is interesting to note that the British, who already had a large empire, entered the imperialistic race for colonies as enthusiastically as the Germans or Italians. National "honor" would not allow them to watch territorial prizes go to rival nations.

Missionary motives

The urge to spread the Christian religion, as you have read, was influential in the colonial expansion of the 1500's and 1600's. Roman Catholic missionaries had carried on their work since that time, and they increased their activities in the period of imperialism. There were also an increasing number of Protestant missionaries.

Missionaries did other important work. Education became a regular missionary activity. Trained people went out from Europe and America as medical missionaries. Knowledge of medicine, hygiene, and sanitation spread with Christianity.

The "white man's burden"

Closely related to the missionary motive was the idea that the people of advanced Western nations had a duty to transmit Western ideas and tech-

Motives for imperialism

Imperialism in the late 1800's developed as a result of a number of overlapping motives. On the one hand, rival nations attempted to control as much of the world and its resources as possible. Under the leadership of Cecil Rhodes, for example, a band of territories running the length of Africa came into British hands. A cartoon (right) compared him to one of the seven wonders of the ancient world, a gigantic statue known as the Colossus.

The imperialists also saw themselves as having a mission to "civilize" the natives. Amidst much hardship, dedicated missionaries brought the gospel to people such as the Africans (above). And educators, like the American teacher at a school in the Philippines (below), were in some ways as important as the navy in carrying Western ideals to new parts of the world.

niques to more "backward" people. People were considered "backward" if their religion or their culture was different from that of the West.

The British poet Rudyard Kipling wrote a poem that urged members of his race to "take up the white man's burden." He meant the obligation of carrying Western civilization to those he considered less fortunate. The French spoke of their "civilizing mission." The people of each industrial nation considered its civilization and culture to be the highest, and therefore the one most suited to be taken to the "backward" peoples of the earth.

Opponents of imperialism claimed that the only burden the white man wanted to take up was the burden of colonial wealth, which he wanted to carry back home as fast as possible. Such opponents, however, were a minority with little influence in their countries.

The nature of imperialism

You have now read about the major forces that stimulated imperialism. The consequences of imperialism were to affect the world for years to come.

Were the new colonies worth what they cost? Imperialism created bitter rivalries among the imperial powers and hatred among the colonized. Rivalries led to the building of larger armies and navies. Colonial rivalries were an underlying cause of World War I, as you will read in Chapter 24. Much of the suspicion and hatred among nations today stems from imperialism.

Some terms used in connection with imperialism need explanation. Originally a **colony** was a settlement established by citizens of a country in another region. Ancient Greek colonies and British colonies in North America were like this. During the imperialistic era, however, a colony came to be an area in which a foreign nation gained total control over a given region and its native population. A colony was gained by settlement or conquest, and was annexed, becoming a part of the empire.

In a **protectorate,** the native ruler kept his title, but officials of the foreign power actually controlled the region. The "protecting" power kept out other foreign nations. In a **condominium,** two nations ruled a region as partners. A **concession**

was the grant of economic rights and privileges in a given area. Concessions were given to foreign merchants or capitalists who wanted to trade, to build railroads, or to develop mineral deposits and other natural resources. Concessions held exclusively by one foreign power were called monopoly concessions. A **sphere of influence** was a region where one nation had special, sometimes exclusive, economic and political privileges that were recognized by other nations.

CHECKUP

1. IDENTIFY: imperialism, "white man's burden," colony, protectorate, condominium, concession, sphere of influence.

2. Why did European interest in colonies decline between the late 1700's and the late 1800's?

3. Describe four motives behind imperialism that were related to the Industrial Revolution.

4. List and explain three other reasons for seeking colonies.

Imperialism transformed the continent of Africa

The imperialism that began in North Africa in the early 1800's overwhelmed the entire African continent by the latter part of the century. Despite the many causes of imperialism, its effects on Africa were relatively uniform throughout the continent. The consequences of imperialism are still evident in Africa today.

The pattern of imperialism

Imperialism in Africa often followed a common pattern. European explorers, traders, and missionaries, using African guides and following trails pioneered by Africans, would push into the interior. They were sometimes driven by a desire for profits or an interest in bringing Christianity to Africa. Inevitably they would call upon a European government to support their commercial or missionary activities.

Taking advantage of rivalries and divisions within African society, the Europeans often found local allies to help them. If there was resistance—and African resistance was widespread and fierce—European soldiers with modern, automatic weapons arrived to restore order.

In this way almost all of Africa was divided up among European nations in the last quarter of the 1800's. European law and administration, business, and culture penetrated the interior of Africa more gradually, profoundly changing African institutions and African society.

Thus, the peoples of Africa, less advanced technologically than the Europeans, were politically dominated by them. Labor and land were exploited and traditional African customs and beliefs were transformed.

The French intervene in North Africa

North Africa, as you have read, knew many conquerors, including the Romans, the Byzantines, and the Arabs. In the 1800's most of the region was part of the Ottoman Empire, although Turkish control in many areas was weak.

For a long time, expert Muslim seafarers, called the Barbary pirates, operated off the coast of North Africa. The term *Barbary* means "of the Berbers." The Berbers were a people of North Africa who were converted to Islam during the 600's. Four Muslim states—Morocco, Algiers, Tunis, and Tripoli—made up the so-called Barbary States. (These countries are now called Morocco, Algeria, Tunisia, and Libya.) The swift sailing ships of the Barbary pirates had taken a heavy toll of Mediterranean shipping, including, during the early 1800's, some American ships.

The operations of the Barbary pirates gave France an excuse to intervene in North Africa. The French needed to expand their empire to compensate for the loss of French prestige after the defeat of Napoleon in 1815.

The French complained about the Barbary pirates to the Algerian ruler and received what they considered an insulting reply. In 1830 a French force occupied Algeria, arrested the ruler, and settled down to stay. For more than 40 years, the French had to fight against almost continuous local rebellions and violence. Economically, the struggle was worth the price. Algeria was a rich land, and many French people and other Europeans moved in, taking over the best land and running the businesses. Algeria became an exporter of farm products, wine, and meat, playing an important part in French economic life.

Seizure of Tunisia. East of Algeria lies Tunisia, a small country with a long history. Its capital, Tunis, grew up near Carthage, the rival of ancient Rome. A poor and backward country, Tunisia was part of the Ottoman Empire. Its Turkish ruler, the bey of Tunis, was a lavish spender and carefree about finances. He borrowed heavily from European bankers, until they refused further loans. The French government, seeing a chance to gain influence, lent him money.

When the French loan was due, the bey raised taxes, which were already heavy. This caused a rebellion against him. A commission of the bey's creditors was established to restore order and reorganize Tunisia's finances. The commission, formed in 1869, included representatives of the British, French, and Italian governments.

All three of these nations wanted Tunisia. Italy, in the process of being united and eager for colonies, had encouraged many Italians to emigrate to Tunisia. In a complicated series of negotiations, France and Great Britain reached an agreement, which was announced in 1878 at the Congress of Berlin. The French were to have a free hand in Tunisia, and the British could occupy the island of Cyprus. Italy—new, poor, and inexperienced at the diplomatic game—had nothing to trade and was ignored.

In 1881 Tunisia was made a French protectorate. The bey remained ruler in name, but the real ruler was the senior French official in Tunis. French rule brought certain improvements to Tunisia—public order, roads, schools, industries, and sound finances. However, religious differences, local pride, and a rising spirit of nationalism inspired many Tunisians to keep working for independence.

Rivalry over Morocco. After acquiring Algeria and Tunisia, France felt it needed Morocco in order to protect its interests in North Africa. Morocco's strategic location and riches made it a tempting prize for imperialists. However, so many European countries wanted the country that each one was afraid to take it because doing so might touch off an explosion.

By the early 1900's, France was willing to take the necessary risks. As a result, France and

Carved and Painted African Mask

Comfortable in their prejudices, Europeans of the imperialist era regarded most African art as "primitive" and "barbaric." Missionaries, especially, scorned it since much of it was associated with African religious rituals. (The mask above, made by a tribe in the western Sudan, was probably worn by a dancer in rites to ensure crop fertility.) For this very reason, however, much African art survived; missionaries often confiscated objects as trophies after converting their African owners to Christianity.

Germany became entangled in a bitter dispute over Morocco. A compromise was reached in 1911, when Germany let France have a free hand in Morocco in exchange for territory in West Africa. The small northern strip of Spanish Morocco was acquired by Spain, and the city of Tangier was placed under international control. The rest of rich Morocco, like Tunisia, became a French protectorate.

The British in Egypt

Egypt had been part of the Ottoman Empire for centuries. By the mid-1800's, when the empire was crumbling, the Turkish viceroys in Egypt, called khedives (kuh·DEEVZ), had become almost entirely independent. They still paid some tribute to the Ottoman sultan, but they were absolute rulers in Egypt.

In 1854 a French company headed by Ferdinand de Lesseps gained a concession to build a canal through the Isthmus of Suez. Almost half the stock of the company was bought by the Egyptian government. Individual French citizens bought most of the rest. The canal was completed in 1869 (see map, page 559).

Within a short time the Egyptian government fell into financial difficulties. Ismail Pasha, the khedive, had very expensive habits and little concern with financial management. Between 1869 and 1879, he increased the foreign debt of his government by more than 20 times. Finally, foreign banks refused to lend him more money.

Ismail's solution to his financial problem was to sell Egypt's stock in the Suez Canal. This was an opportunity for the British. They were very eager to control the canal because it was a vital link in the trade route between Great Britain and India, Australia, and New Zealand. In 1875 the British government bought the Egyptian stock and became the largest single stockholder, thus gaining virtual control of the canal.

In 1882 the British and French sent a combined fleet toward Alexandria to settle an Egyptian rebellion. The French withdrew and the British proceeded alone. They bombarded Alexandria, landed troops, and soon occupied the entire country. There they remained, claiming that they had to safeguard the Suez Canal, their main route to India. The Egyptian government remained outwardly independent, but real control was in British hands.

British rule brought certain benefits to Egypt. Finances were put on a sounder basis. In 1902 the building of a storage dam at Aswan and an extensive irrigation system placed more land under cultivation. Courts became less corrupt. Forced labor and degrading forms of physical punishment were abolished. These improvements, however, reached only a few people.

Egyptian aristocrats disliked British rule even though they benefited from it. The longer the British remained, the stronger grew nationalist feeling against them, and the more the British feared to pull out and risk losing control of the Suez Canal.

The Italians in Libya

Tripoli, a region lying to the west of Egypt, was mostly desert. Like Tunisia, it belonged to the Ottoman Empire, but Turkish control was weak. The region had almost no economic value, but Italy wanted a colony in North Africa.

First, Italy secured guarantees of neutrality from several European powers. Then, in 1911, Italy declared war on the Ottoman Empire. The Turks showed surprisingly strong resistance but finally fell.

Italy took Tripoli as a colony and renamed it Libya. It was a profitless victory. Except for a narrow strip along the coast, the land was barren. The population was small, but the people violently opposed Italian rule. As a result, Italy had the expense of keeping the country pacified for many years.

The competition for West Africa

West Africa had been a major center of the slave trade. First the Portuguese and the Dutch, and later the British and the French, had established trading posts along the coast. When most European countries abolished the slave trade in the early 1800's, these former slaving centers turned increasingly to other types of commerce. They traded in palm oil, hides and feathers, ivory, rubber, and other natural products. With the end of the slave trade, more systematic development of the interior also began to take place.

By pushing into the interior, European countries sought to link their coastal possessions. In the "bulge" of western Africa, the French pushed inland and took possession of the ancient city of Timbuktu. They also increased the number of commercial settlements in the coastal areas of French Guinea, the Ivory Coast, and Dahomey. By 1900 France had claimed a vast area called French West Africa (see map, page 559). The French seaports provided outlets for the products of this region.

The British competed with the French throughout West Africa. They too sought to connect their coastal settlements and expand into the interior. They were particularly interested in the Gold Coast (modern Ghana). From their coastal bases there, the British made a major thrust inland, coming up against the powerful African kingdom of Ashanti. By 1901, however, Great Britain had annexed all the territory of Ashanti and made the Gold Coast a colony.

The British were also expanding in Nigeria, a territory to the east of the Gold Coast that took its name from the Niger, one of the great rivers of Africa. Control of the Niger River assured control of a huge region rich in resources. In 1861 the British annexed the port city of Lagos and then pushed steadily inland. They were opposed in their push inland by African merchants who competed with British traders, and in northern Nigeria by African Muslim states. British military forces crushed all African resistance. Eventually, Nigeria was made a protectorate.

Germany also joined in the competition. To gain a firm foothold in Africa, Germany cleverly played British and French rivalries against each other. On the south shore of West Africa, Germany claimed Togo and, farther to the southeast, the Cameroons. However, these two protectorates, thinly populated and with few natural resources to offer, were really the "leftovers" after Great Britain and France had already made their choices.

In the scramble for West African territory, Spain acquired two colonies: a narrow strip along the northwest coast called Río de Oro, and Río Muni, just south of the Cameroons. Spain also held the Canary Islands in the Atlantic and the island of Fernando Po off the coast of the Cameroons. Portugal held two territories—Portuguese

Guinea, south of Senegal on the "bulge," and Angola, the oldest colony in Africa.

By the early 1900's European nations had claimed all of West Africa except Liberia. Settled by freed slaves from the United States, Liberia had become a republic in 1847. The British trained the Liberian army and served as its officers. A board of "foreign experts" controlled Liberian finances and forced the country to grant extensive concessions and accept heavy loans.

Although Liberia was economically and militarily weak, it was able to maintain its status as an independent nation. It no doubt would have become the protectorate of an ambitious European power if not for its special relationship to the United States. American diplomatic pressure discouraged European attempts to take over the small republic.

The competition for central Africa

The rapid expansion of European influence in West Africa was paralleled by events in central and East Africa. In the vast area drained by the Zaïre (Congo) River, King Leopold II of Belgium, acting as a private citizen, carved out a personal empire of 900,000 square miles (2.3 million square kilometers). Employing the journalist and explorer Henry Stanley, Leopold established a claim to the Congo region.

Leopold's rule of the Congo is an example of the worst aspects of imperialism. His only interest was in extracting as much wealth as possible from the colony. Forming a corporation, he sold concessions to speculators who shared his interest in a fast profit. Their exploitation of the Congo's supply of natural rubber became an international scandal. Whole regions were set aside as monopolies, and Africans were ruthlessly uprooted from their homes and forced to collect rubber. Large areas of rubber trees and vines were carelessly destroyed without any replanting for the future. Finally, as a result of international criticism of conditions there, falling world rubber prices, and dwindling rubber supplies in the Congo, Leopold transferred his private colony to the Belgian government in 1908.

North of Leopold's Congo, the French explorer Pierre de Brazza founded the city of Brazzaville on the lower Zaïre (Congo) River in 1880. The founding of this city laid the basis for French claims to an area known as the French Congo. The French extended their claims to the northeast, gaining control of a large region north of the Congo and adjoining French West Africa. Combined with the French Congo, this region formed French Equatorial Africa (see map, opposite).

Europeans in East Africa

On the east coast of Africa, Portugal strengthened and extended its control over Mozambique. To the north of Mozambique, Great Britain and Germany competed for territorial domination. Slave raiding had taken place in the 1700's and 1800's in East Africa. These slave raids disrupted political relations among African peoples and made penetration of the interior easier. At the same time, the efforts of missionaries to end the slave trade focused public attention on the area and helped to justify European intervention.

Although the British had first explored the area east of Lake Tanganyika, it was the Germans who officially claimed the region. They established a protectorate over the area in 1885.

The German declaration of a protectorate disturbed Great Britain and France, both of whom had territorial ambitions in East Africa. All three nations, however, were willing to settle their differences by negotiation. As a result, France claimed the large island of Madagascar in the Indian Ocean. Great Britain received the coastal strip north of German East Africa, and Germany was permitted to keep its protectorate. This settlement, however, ignored the claims of the Sultan of Zanzibar, whom the coastal people recognized as their ruler.

Pushing inland from their coastal strip, the British created the protectorate of British East Africa in what is modern Kenya. An additional territorial adjustment occurred when Germany received the strategically important island of Helgoland in the North Sea. In exchange, Germany recognized Great Britain's claims to Uganda, a rich territory north of German East Africa and west of British East Africa, and to the island of Zanzibar (see map, opposite).

Italy, a late entry in the competition for colonies, gained some territories in East Africa. These were two strips of desert, one in Somaliland on

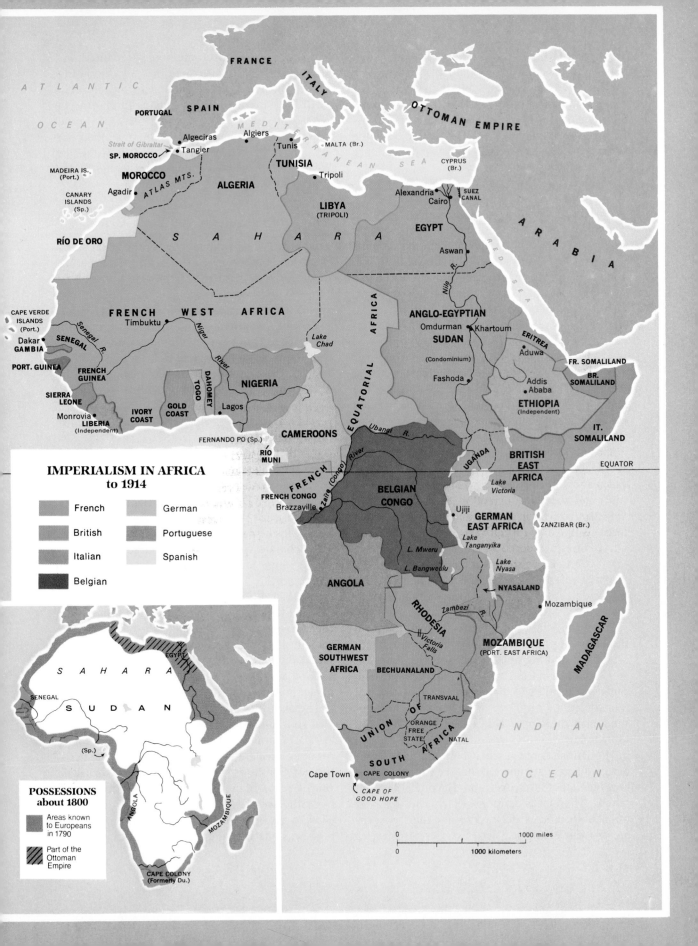

FRANCE

SPAIN

PORTUGAL

ITALY

OTTOMAN EMPIRE

ATLANTIC

OCEAN

Algeciras
Tangier
SP. MOROCCO

Algiers

Tunis

MEDITERRANEAN SEA

MALTA (Br.)

CYPRUS (Br.)

MADEIRA IS. (Port.)

MOROCCO

Agadir

ATLAS MTS.

TUNISIA

Tripoli

CANARY ISLANDS (Sp.)

ALGERIA

LIBYA (TRIPOLI)

EGYPT

Alexandria
Cairo

SUEZ CANAL

ARABIA

RÍO DE ORO

S A H A R A

Aswan

RED SEA

Nile R.

CAPE VERDE ISLANDS (Port.)

FRENCH WEST AFRICA

Timbuktu

Senegal R.

Niger River

Lake Chad

EQUATORIAL AFRICA

ANGLO-EGYPTIAN SUDAN

Omdurman Khartoum

(Condominium)

ERITREA

Aduwa

FR. SOMALILAND

Dakar
GAMBIA

SENEGAL

PORT. GUINEA

FRENCH GUINEA

DAHOMEY

TOGO

NIGERIA

Lagos

Fashoda

Addis Ababa

BR. SOMALILAND

SIERRA LEONE

IVORY COAST

GOLD COAST

ETHIOPIA (Independent)

IT. SOMALILAND

Monrovia
LIBERIA (Independent)

FERNANDO PO (Sp.)

CAMEROONS

RÍO MUNI

FRENCH

French Congo River

Ubangi R.

UGANDA

BRITISH EAST AFRICA

EQUATOR

IMPERIALISM IN AFRICA
to 1914

FRENCH CONGO
Brazzaville

Zaire (Congo) River

BELGIAN CONGO

Lake Victoria

Ujiji

GERMAN EAST AFRICA

ZANZIBAR (Br.)

	French		German
	British		Portuguese
	Italian		Spanish
	Belgian		

Lake Tanganyika

L. Mweru

L. Bangweulu

Lake Nyasa

ANGOLA

NYASALAND

Mozambique

RHODESIA

Zambezi R.

MOZAMBIQUE (PORT. EAST AFRICA)

MADAGASCAR

GERMAN SOUTHWEST AFRICA

Victoria Falls

BECHUANALAND

INDIAN

TRANSVAAL

UNION OF

ORANGE FREE STATE

AFRICA

NATAL

OCEAN

SOUTH

Cape Town
CAPE COLONY

CAPE OF GOOD HOPE

POSSESSIONS
about 1800

S A H A R A

EGYPT

SENEGAL

S U D A N

(Sp.)

ANGOLA

MOZAMBIQUE

	Areas known to Europeans in 1790
	Part of the Ottoman Empire

CAPE COLONY
(Formerly Du.)

0 — 1000 miles

0 — 1000 kilometers

the Indian Ocean, and the other, known as Eritrea, on the Red Sea. In an attempt to push into the interior from the coast, Italy invaded Ethiopia, which was ruled by a native emperor. To the amazement of the world, the Ethiopian army, trained and equipped by the French, defeated the Italian army at Aduwa in 1896. The independence of Ethiopia was thus preserved.

Anglo-Egyptian Sudan

The Sudan is a vast geographic region of savannas south of the Sahara, stretching from the Atlantic Ocean to the Nile Valley and beyond. In the imperialistic era, the term *Sudan* also referred to a specific eastern part of this region south of Egypt. It was inhabited by Arabs and various native tribes. Egypt claimed the Sudan, having conquered it in the early 1800's.

After Great Britain established control over Egypt in 1882, the Sudan became important to the British. The upper Nile River flows through the Sudan (see map, page 559). Control of the region would afford a chance to build dams for irrigation and to control the flow of water in the lower Nile. France also wanted the Sudan, both because of its possessions farther west and because it already had a toehold on the Red Sea (French Somaliland) and wanted to extend its territory inland.

In the 1880's the British and Egyptians sent a force to put down a native revolt in the Sudan. Great Britain ordered another military force in the 1890's to move southward along the Nile from Egypt. Under General Herbert Kitchener, these troops defeated a Sudanese army at Omdurman, then moved farther south.

Meanwhile the French sent an expedition from the French Congo, under Major J. B. Marchand. Marchand and his small force of Senegalese soldiers made a daring two-year journey through some 3,000 miles (5,000 kilometers) of tropical rain forest. In July 1898 Marchand reached Fashoda, on the Upper Nile River, and raised the French flag.

The British force reached Fashoda in September, and Kitchener insisted that the French flag be lowered and the British and Egyptian flags be raised. There was tension, which was relieved when both officers decided to ask their governments for instructions.

Since neither government really wanted war, they negotiated a settlement of the Fashoda Incident. The French were willing to recognize the British as masters of the Sudan. In return, the French received the northern part of French Equatorial Africa and recognition of all their possessions in French West Africa. Great Britain and Egypt established a condominium in the Sudan, known as the Anglo-Egyptian Sudan.

The competition for southern Africa

Southern Africa contained several coastal settlements established by Europeans in the great age of exploration that began in the late 1400's. As in the rest of Africa, movement into the interior speeded up in the 1800's.

European settlement in South Africa began in 1652, when Dutch settlers founded Cape Town as a resupplying station for ships sailing to the East Indies. The Dutch settlement grew into a profitable colony called Cape Colony. During the Napoleonic Wars of the early 1800's, the British seized Cape Colony, which then became a British possession.

As British administration became established, many people left the colony and moved to the north and east. These people were **Boers** (BOHRZ)—descendants of the original Dutch settlers, who had their own language, known as Afrikaans. In the new territories the Boers carved out three colonies—Natal, on the southeast coast, the Orange Free State to the west, and the Transvaal to the north.

In 1845 Great Britain annexed Natal, but allowed the economically weak Boer republics of the Orange Free State and the Transvaal to remain independent. The naval supremacy of Great Britain and the agricultural wealth of Cape Colony and Natal ensured the region's predominance in southern Africa.

The discovery of vast gold reserves in the Transvaal soon intensified the competition in southern Africa. Germany, hoping to find rich mineral reserves, declared a protectorate over the territory of Southwest Africa in 1884. In the same year, Great Britain began moving into the interior from the south, greatly increasing its holdings. Closely associated with these territorial acquisitions was one individual, Cecil Rhodes.

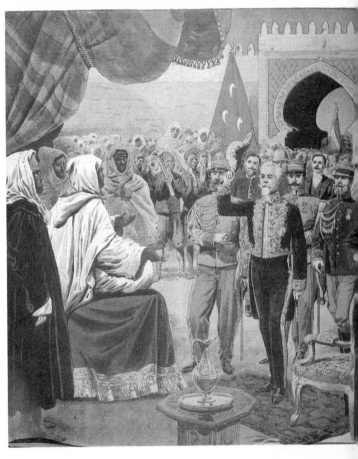

Imperialism in Africa

European imperialism in Africa in the late 1800's had several faces. One was the face of compassion and generosity. Europeans believed they were bringing the benefits of civilization to primitive people, as when the French ambassador appeared at the court of the sultan of Morocco (right). Another face of imperialism was its heroism. Pictures of British soldiers dying nobly for their country (below) stirred strong feelings of national pride in the British.

Imperialism also had a greedy face. Europeans wanted to exploit their colonies and keep all rivals away. The cartoon (above) shows this side of imperialism. John Bull, a character representing Great Britain, takes control of "Hotel Egypt" and warns other nations that there is no room for them.

Rhodes and his influence. Rhodes arrived in Cape Colony in 1870, a sickly young man who hoped the climate would improve his health. Moving to the diamond fields in northern Cape Colony, he soon demonstrated a talent for business and a genius for organization. Within ten years he had gained a complete monopoly of South African diamond production.

Rhodes had a vision of a vast British empire within Africa, with a corridor of land reaching from Cape Colony to Cairo. He hoped his business would build all the railroads and obtain a monopoly over all mineral development. However, the division of Africa among the European powers prevented Rhodes' Cape-to-Cairo dream from becoming a reality. Nonetheless, the Transvaal gold discoveries gave him a chance to increase his wealth as well as British prestige.

Rhodes pushed for the British acquisition of Bechuanaland. He later organized the colonization of a huge territory north of Bechuanaland and the Transvaal. This territory was named Rhodesia after him. In 1890 Rhodes sent several hundred adventurers out in search of gold in Rhodesia. He staked his reputation and much of his fortune on this hope. When little gold was found, it became essential for Rhodes to make up his losses by increasing production and profits in the Transvaal mines.

Before he could do so, however, he had to overcome several obstacles. Gold had brought prosperity to the Boer government of the Transvaal, but the increased revenues were used to support Boer agriculture rather than the mining industry. Moreover, the Transvaal government regulations made mining extremely costly. Rhodes and others with financial interests in South Africa opposed such restrictions on the development of the gold fields. They therefore decided to overthrow the Boer republics.

In 1895 a colleague of Rhodes tried to topple the Transvaal government. The attempt failed, but Great Britain's apparent support of the attempt made relations between the Boers and the British openly hostile. In 1899 war broke out. After three years of costly fighting, the British defeated the Boers and imposed a settlement that favored mining interests.

To ensure Boer support of the peace, the British allowed the Boers to continue using the Afrikaans language in their schools and courts. They also provided funds for Boers, but not for Africans, to rebuild their destroyed farms. In 1910 a federal constitution united the Cape Colony, Natal, the Transvaal, and the Orange Free State into the Union of South Africa, a British dominion. The constitution made it virtually impossible for nonwhites to be given voting rights. The settlement of the South African War, or the Boer War, thus laid the basis for the later development of a system of complete racial segregation.

Costs and gains of imperialism

Imperialism was a harsh experience for all of Africa. However, the costs and the benefits resulting from European expansion were unevenly distributed across the continent.

The Europeans built roads and railroads. These means of transportation were used mostly to connect areas of European settlement with the coast. They also served to make African produce available for the world market. The Europeans built cities, but crowded and unsanitary slums inevitably appeared around them. Europeans introduced medicines to prolong life, but almost everywhere reduced the land available to Africans for crop cultivation. Thus they contributed to malnutrition among the African people.

Despite the hardships, some individuals and groups in African society did benefit. In West Africa, profits realized by Africans from the rubber trade helped to finance the cultivation of cocoa plants. The spread of cocoa farming, in turn, brought prosperity and raised living standards. In Uganda, British support of cotton cultivation gave rise to a large class of wealthy peasant producers. Even in South Africa, the gold discoveries introduced a brief period of prosperity for African farmers, who planted more food crops for market.

The abolition of slavery allowed many Africans to return to their homelands. The introduction of Western laws and courts often were a benefit to the unprotected members of society, especially women. Missionary and government schools introduced Africans to the foreign culture to which they would now have to adapt themselves. From the experience would come a new group of African leaders in the 1900's.

1. IDENTIFY: Barbary pirates, Ashanti, Leopold II, Stanley, de Brazza, Fashoda Incident, Boers, Afrikaans, Rhodes.

2. LOCATE: Suez Canal, Timbuktu, French Guinea, Gold Coast, Liberia, Zaïre (Congo) River, French Equatorial Africa, Angola, Mozambique, Lake Tanganyika, Madagascar, British East Africa, Ethiopia, Anglo-Egyptian Sudan, Cape Colony, Natal, Orange Free State, Transvaal.

3. Why did the Europeans want territorial possessions in the interior of Africa?

4. What were the reasons for British and Boer competition? What were the results of the South African, or Boer, War?

5. What were some of the costs and benefits of imperialism in Africa?

3

The British secured firm control over India

The strong forces of imperialism that swept outward from Europe in the 1800's brought important and fateful changes to India. In that vast subcontinent, however, with its ancient civilization and huge population, the changes were not abrupt as they were in so many parts of Africa. Rather, they were intensifications of European influence that had been present in India for centuries.

Europeans in India

You read in Chapter 16 how India was important to European traders during the age of exploration. After the decline of the Portuguese Empire in the 1600's, England and France formed trading companies that established bases in India.

Early in the 1700's the Mogul Empire began to disintegrate. Many different factions vied for power. Great Britain and France each tried to gain control in India. As you read in Chapter 18, this rivalry resulted in the Seven Years' War (1756–1763), in which the British were victorious. Following the war, most of India, with the exception of a few French and Portuguese trading posts, fell under the control or influence of the British East India Company.

Expansion of British authority

After the Seven Years' War, the British government became uneasy at the thought of a commercial company controlling the lives of millions of Indian people. In the 1770's it assumed the right to appoint the company's highest official, the governor general. For all practical purposes, however, the company was free to earn profits and to use its officials and troops as it chose.

For a long time the British East India Company had been dealing with what was left of the Mogul Empire, employing many Indians in company positions. In the late 1780's the British government named Lord Cornwallis to be governor general of India, an appointment that would have long-lasting effects.

One of Cornwallis' first actions was to clean up widespread corruption among company employees. For this purpose he created a civil service of company officials who were forbidden to have any part in the company's commercial activities. Believing that the Indian employees were responsible for some of the corruption, Cornwallis ordered that Indians be excluded from all important company positions. Indian resentment over this discrimination lasted for years.

Several strong Indian states engaged in constant jealous rivalries and even warfare. The British took advantage of such warfare until they won control of these regions. Religious hatred between Hindus and Muslims, as well as the caste system, prevented Indians from uniting against the foreigners. The British usually did not need to employ any of their own troops. Instead, when actual fighting was necessary, they made use of native troops, called **sepoys** (SEE·poys), who were trained and led by British officers.

As time went on, the British were drawn deeper into Indian political rivalries. During the early 1800's the British East India Company extended its power into more and more areas.

Until about 1830, the British made no attempt to impose their way of life on India. In the 1830's, however, English became the language of instruction in Indian schools, and pupils studied Western literature, history, and science.

The British also enforced several social reforms. Slavery and the killing of infant girls were prohibited. The ritual suicide known as suttee was declared illegal. Suttee was a practice of high-caste Indian families in which a widow threw herself on her husband's funeral pyre. Thuggee, a religious cult that required its members to commit ritual murder and robbery, was suppressed. (It is from this cult that we get our word *thug*.)

By 1857 the British East India Company ruled about three fifths of the subcontinent directly. It ruled most of the rest indirectly through its control over native princes. Great Britain also controlled the island of Ceylon, which it had seized during the Napoleonic Wars.

The Indian Mutiny

India in the mid-1800's presented the strange spectacle of a huge land, with millions of people and an ancient civilization, controlled by a foreign commercial corporation. British population in India had grown rapidly and by this time included British wives and families. Many of the British officials copied the autocratic habits of the Indian rulers they had replaced.

Indians resented the rule of the British as well as the increasing tendency to impose Western ways of life upon India. The sepoys were particularly dissatisfied because they had been forced to fight for the British in numerous campaigns in faraway Afghanistan and Burma. Then, in 1857 they mutinied.

The immediate cause of the Indian Mutiny, or Sepoy Rebellion, involved a new kind of rifle that the British East India Company issued in 1857. The cartridges for this rifle had been greased to make the bullets slide more easily through the barrel. In order to load his rifle, the sepoy had to bite off part of the cartridge. According to rumors, the cartridges were greased with the fat of cows and pigs. To Hindus the cow is sacred. Muslims are forbidden to eat pork. India's forces included both Hindus and Muslims. Thus, biting the cartridge would violate the religious customs of both groups.

Agitators were able to whip up existing resentments by claiming that the company had purposely tried to insult the two religions. With help from the Indian people, the sepoy troops staged a widespread and violent mutiny against their British masters.

The Indian Mutiny almost drove the British out of India, but the rebellion was finally suppressed by troops sent from Great Britain. In 1858 the British Parliament dissolved the British East India Company and transferred the rule of India to the British government. In 1877 Queen Victoria was proclaimed Empress of India.

British imperialism in India

Although India was ruled directly by the British government after 1858, conditions did not change much. British India made up about three fifths of the subcontinent (see map, page 566). The rest consisted of over 550 states, headed by native princes. The British government, through its viceroy, controlled their right to make treaties and declare war, either with foreign countries or with one another. Great Britain also regulated their internal affairs when it seemed necessary.

To control both British and native India, the British government used the old Roman method of "divide and rule." It granted favors to those princes who cooperated with British rule and dealt harshly with those who did not. It treated Hindus and Muslims equally, but did little to ease religious hatred between them.

The British were interested chiefly in profitable trade in India. To get it, they maintained public order by ending the many local wars and massacres. They set up efficient governmental administration and guarded against foreign invasions. They built roads, bridges, railroads, factories, hospitals,and schools. They tried to improve agricultural methods, health, and sanitation.

Naturally, many of these improvements helped the Indians, but other effects of British rule were harmful. The Indian handicraft industry almost disappeared. British cotton mills made cloth so cheaply that it could be transported to India and sold for less than the product of Indian hand weavers. Local artisans had to search for work in the cities or earn a miserable living from farming small plots of land.

During the late 1800's and early 1900's, British rule in India had created a situation where the peoples of two alien cultures lived side by side with almost no contact. The British had imposed

The British in India

India under British rule was a mixture of pomp, ceremony, and exploitation. There were many grand and colorful occasions, such as the receptions given by the British East India Company (above). The Indians themselves were part of the pageantry. Soldiers from the Sikh tribes, in their traditional turbans, turned out to honor the visiting Prince of Wales (right). These able warriors were much in demand for the British army.

There was another side to British rule, however. The British were a privileged group, set apart from the native population. They thought of the Indians as uncultured and primitive. As cartoonists pointed out, the British were sustained by dozens of servants and enjoyed the luxury of being waited on (below).

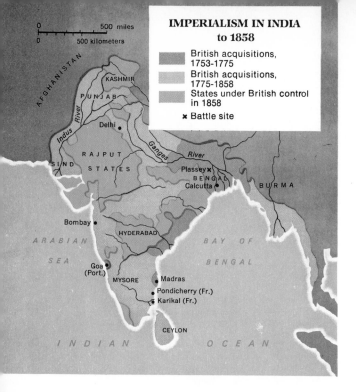

IMPERIALISM IN INDIA
to 1858

British acquisitions,
1753-1775
British acquisitions,
1775-1858
States under British control
in 1858
✕ Battle site

belonged to the highest caste) were educated. Indian merchants might have some simple schooling in reading, writing, and mathematics. All women and men of the lower castes were uneducated. During the 1800's the British East India Company, the British government, missionaries, and private individuals started schools and colleges in India. They educated only a small percentage of the people, but, among other things, they taught them about nationalism and the liberal ideals of democracy. Indian scholars could, and did, condemn British imperialism by using quotations from British writers. Many Indians also came to learn about and believe in the ideas of socialism.

A movement for Indian self-rule began in the late 1800's. Not all Indian nationalists agreed on the same approach. Some, especially those who had been educated in British schools and universities, wanted to advance toward independence gradually and by democratic methods. They also wanted to keep certain aspects of Western culture and industry that they thought could benefit India. This moderate approach was advocated by the Indian National Congress, a political party founded in 1885. Others wanted to break all ties with Great Britain and to sweep away all Western influence. They wished to revolt not only against Western culture but also against Islam.

The views of this second group alarmed Indian Muslims. They were a minority in the land, and British rule protected them from discrimination and violence. They feared that if British rule were removed, their future might be in danger. The Muslims were therefore much less enthusiastic about driving out the British than were the Hindus. In 1906 they formed the Muslim League to protect their interests. The independence movement in India gathered strength very slowly, and the British kept the country under a tight rein.

themselves above Indian society as a superior race, a sort of super-caste. The British formed exclusive circles, open to any European but closed to any Indian, no matter how distinguished. Posted everywhere—in railway carriages and waiting rooms and even on park benches—were signs reading "for Europeans only." For generations all Indians were insulted, humiliated, degraded, and subjected to contemptuous treatment by the British.

The rise of Indian nationalism

Although the British did not mingle socially with the Indians, Western civilization had a powerful impact on India. For one thing, it led to a serious conflict of values.

Both Hinduism and Islam stressed age-old customs and respect for tradition. Western culture, on the other hand, emphasized material progress and political change. British discrimination against Indians injured their pride in their ancient civilization. Indians, especially educated Indians, regarded Europeans as materialists and money-grubbers who cared little for the higher values of mind, soul, and spirit.

British education had a profound effect on India. In earlier days, only Brahmans (who

CHECKUP

1. IDENTIFY: Lord Cornwallis, sepoys, thuggee, Indian National Congress, Muslim League.

2. What important decision was made by Lord Cornwallis?

3. What were the causes of the Indian Mutiny?

4. List the beneficial and harmful effects of British rule in India.

4

Japan became a powerful force in East Asia

As the surge of imperialism swept across Africa and India in the late 1800's, it was bound to reach East Asia. One part of East Asia, however, did not succumb to Western imperialism—Japan. Japan, indeed, became a competitor of the Western powers in the acquisition of colonies and special privileges in the region.

The end of Japanese isolation

Earlier chapters told how Japan, after nearly a century of contact with Portuguese traders and missionaries, expelled all foreigners in the 1630's. Japan, ruled by shoguns of the Tokugawa family, then retreated into isolation. To help maintain Japanese isolation, the government refused to give shelter to ships of other nations during storms. Shipwrecked sailors were treated harshly. Such treatment of American whaling and merchant ships finally brought Japanese isolation to an end.

In 1853 United States President Millard Fillmore sent a naval force to Japan under Commodore Matthew Perry. Perry had orders to negotiate a commercial treaty that would open Japanese ports to American trade as well as guarantee the safety of American sailors. He presented a letter from President Fillmore, urging the treaty, and said he would return for an answer the following year.

In Japan there was controversy over the decision. Some powerful leaders favored military resistance and continued isolation. Others believed that Japan could not hold out, and their views prevailed. The shogun reluctantly agreed to negotiate when Perry returned in 1854.

The negotiations were accompanied by colorful ceremonies, symbolic of the two contrasting cultures. The Japanese gave the Americans beautiful silk, lacquer ware, and other articles exquisitely made by hand. The Americans presented the Japanese with guns, a telegraph set, and a model railroad train on which dignified Japanese officials took rides with their loose robes flying.

The negotiations led to the Treaty of Kanagawa in 1854, a turning point in Japanese history. Two Japanese ports were opened to Americans, both for shelter and trade. Such ports were known as treaty ports. The treaty also provided for better treatment of shipwrecked sailors. Within two years Japan signed similar treaties with Great Britain, Russia, France, and the Netherlands. They opened several Japanese seaports where representatives of foreign nations had the right to live, trade, purchase naval supplies, and establish **consulates**—diplomatic offices headed by consuls. Consulates protect a nation's citizens and business interests in a foreign country.

At first, conservative Japanese isolationists held out successfully against any real contacts with the outsiders. Foreign consuls were ignored, and contacts with foreign traders were kept to a minimum. Nevertheless, in 1858 another treaty was signed in which the Japanese and the United States governments agreed to exchange diplomatic representatives. Now more American consuls were admitted and more treaty ports were opened. Tariff regulations were written. Foreigners living in Japan were given the right to observe their own religious ceremonies. Similar treaties with other nations soon followed.

The decision to modernize

The end of isolation brought Japan face to face with a great question. Should Japan resist Western influence, by force if necessary? Or should the nation try to become strong in the only way the imperial powers would respect—by Westernizing and industrializing?

The decision was not made without a struggle. In the 1860's a civil war broke out between rival factions of the warrior class. On one side were those who wanted to maintain the existing political system. On the other were those who wanted to overthrow the Tokugawa shogunate and restore the Japanese emperor, long neglected in Kyoto, to power. The pro-emperor forces won out in 1868. The last Tokugawa shogun resigned and turned his extensive domain over to the emperor. The daimyo soon followed suit. The emperor, a boy of 15, took the name Meiji (MAY·JEE), meaning "enlightened rule," for his reign. It lasted until 1912 and is called the Meiji Era.

The Influence of Japanese Art

Though she wears a kimono and is studying Japanese woodblock prints, this figure is not an Oriental woman. Rather she is a model used by the American painter James McNeill Whistler (1834–1903). Many years later he would paint a picture of his mother in a similar pose, but with more restrained colors.

Like many artists of the time, Whistler went to Paris to study. There he discovered the enchantments of Oriental art, particularly Japanese prints, which were increasingly popular in Europe at the time. Though his paintings reflected the influence of Europe, he eventually adapted the use of both Oriental subjects and techniques.

Whistler was a leader of the new attitude of "art for art's sake." A flamboyant figure for his time, Whistler sued an art critic in 1878 who criticized him for "flinging a pot of paint in the public's face." Although Whistler won the libel suit, the court costs forced him into bankruptcy.

The Meiji Restoration

Real power in the new imperial government was exercised not by the emperor, but by samurai from several domains in western Japan. These samurai had grown impatient under the strict, hereditary system of the Tokugawa period, in which only birth, not ability, counted. They persuaded the emperor that Japan must take the road toward modernization. Even though they themselves were members of Japan's traditional ruling class, they advocated and carried out radical changes in Japan. The Meiji Restoration, as the change from the Tokugawa shogunate to imperial government is called, was really a social, political, and economic revolution. It corresponded in its scope to the revolutions in the Western nations during the 1700's.

The old system of social classes was abolished, and all Japanese became free to choose whatever occupations they wished. Universal compulsory education was established, and soon illiteracy was eliminated almost entirely. The draft was estab-

lished for all Japanese men. For almost 300 years Japanese commoners had been denied the right even to own swords. Only samurai, as members of the warrior class, had been allowed to bear arms. Now this distinction was removed, and a new, highly centralized and modernized military system was created.

A centralized government was established to replace the political system of the Tokugawa period. Domains came under the control of officials in Tokyo, as Yedo was renamed when it became the new imperial capital. The central government imposed taxes on the Japanese people as a whole, and it established laws that applied to the entire population.

During the 1880's a constitution was written by an appointed commission. It was accepted by the emperor and proclaimed in 1889. One aim of the constitution was to impress Western governments with Japan's progress. Another was to provide a limited voice in national affairs for the Japanese people.

The leaders of the Meiji government were monarchists who did not believe in democracy. However, they knew from their study of Western history that political absolutism led to popular discontent. The new constitution gave supreme power to the emperor. At the same time, it established a two-house national assembly, called the Diet, one part of which was elected. Only those Japanese who owned a substantial amount of property were given the right to vote at first, and the powers of the elected house of the Diet were very limited.

Nevertheless, most Japanese were satisfied with the new constitution and with the Diet, at least for the time being. The government did not have to deal with the problems of political instability that afflicted so many developing nations. Instead it could concentrate its energies and its resources on promoting industrialization.

The Meiji government and industrialization

To the leaders of the Meiji government, one of Japan's most pressing needs was for industrialization and economic development. Unless the country could catch up with the Western nations in technology and wealth, it would never be safe from foreign domination.

Fortunately, Japan was in a position to catch up fairly rapidly. As you read in Chapter 18, its traditional economy based on agriculture had created surpluses that could be used to finance industrialization. The government invited foreign experts to Japan to help modernize transportation and communications. The government also established several model factories, using machinery purchased from Western countries. A new commercial code was enacted to encourage private investment in industrial enterprises.

By 1900 Japan had acquired the foundations of an industrial economy. Japanese cities were linked by railroads, the telegraph, and the telephone. Banks existed throughout the country. Light manufacturing, especially of textiles, was well developed, and Japan had begun exporting machine-made cotton cloth to other countries. The money that these exports earned helped to pay for imports of industrial raw materials such as iron and petroleum, which Japan lacked. These raw materials were then used in steel production

and shipbuilding, two heavy industries that began to develop in the 1890's. Japan's economy still was smaller and weaker than the economies of the Western nations, but the gap was narrowing. In fact, Japan was the first country in Asia to industrialize.

A sense of security, however, was lacking. Japan's leaders continued to feel threatened by imperialist expansion in Asia. As you will learn later, that was the basic reason why the Japanese embarked on a course of imperialist expansion themselves. Before dealing with that subject, it is necessary to describe developments in China, which was to be one of the main targets of Japanese imperialism.

The Opium War in China

As you read in Chapter 18, the Ch'ing dynasty had begun to decline by 1800. At roughly the same time, the British began to demand more extensive trading privileges in China and equal diplomatic relations with the Chinese government.

Since the 1700's, British merchants at Canton had developed a profitable trade by bringing in opium from India and selling it throughout southern China. The trade caused severe physical and moral damage among the Chinese and began to drain China's silver supply, which was used to pay for the opium. Chinese authorities demanded that opium sales be stopped and that all opium cargoes be turned over to them.

When the Chinese tried to suppress the opium traffic in South China and insisted on maintaining the traditional tribute system, what has become known as the Opium War broke out. It lasted from 1839 to 1842.

During the Opium War, Chinese army and naval forces were no match against the better-armed and better-trained British. A small British naval force, which included iron-hulled steamships, moved up the coast from Canton, defeating Chinese resistance with relative ease. In 1842 the British secured control of an important region near Nanking. At that point the Ch'ing officials agreed to negotiate on British terms.

In the treaty of 1842 that ended the Opium War, China was compelled to give the island of Hong Kong to the British and to open the cities of Amoy and Shanghai to foreign trade. These ports, together with Canton, were the first Chinese treaty ports (see map, this page). No tariff of more than five percent could be charged on British goods. A further provision stated that British subjects in these ports were to be governed by British, not Chinese, laws and were to be tried in British courts. This exemption of foreigners from the laws of the nation where they live or do business is called **extraterritoriality.**

Great Britain could not hold its privileged trade monopoly in China for long. France and other Western powers, including the United States, soon demanded and received similar trade treaties with similar provisions of extraterritoriality. These trade treaties were not negotiated with China. Instead, China was forced to sign them. Among the Chinese they came to be called "unequal treaties."

IMPERIALISM IN EAST ASIA TO 1914

British
French
German
Portuguese
Dutch
Russian
Japanese
United States

Major Chinese treaty ports after 1842 underlined

Rebellion and its aftermath

The intrusion of the Western powers into China was made easier by an event that occurred in China itself. In the mid-1800's southern and central China were torn by a rebellion that threatened to overthrow the Ch'ing. The leader was a southern Chinese influenced by Christian teachings. He claimed to be the younger brother of Jesus, charged with the mission of establishing a new dynasty—the Taiping (ty·PING), or "Great Peace." His ideas attracted many followers among the Chinese.

When the government tried to suppress the Taiping movement, it turned into a political rebellion. It lasted from 1850 to 1864 and caused great destruction in southern China and the Yangtze Valley. With the aid of some regional armies and foreign adventurers, the Ch'ing suppressed the rebels.

Both the Ch'ing dynasty and the country were weakened by the Taiping Rebellion. To raise money, the government established a system of internal tariffs. These tariffs hurt trade without providing much help to the central treasury because tariff collectors stole most of the money. The treasury was further weakened when foreigners took over the collection of foreign customs duties in Chinese ports.

During the Taiping Rebellion the Ch'ing were unable to protect foreign citizens as Western governments had demanded. In 1856 war with Great Britain again broke out, and British forces, with French aid, again defeated the Chinese.

The Chinese were forced to sign another "unequal treaty," which opened additional treaty ports on the coast and along the Yangtze River. The Chinese had to allow the British to open an embassy in the Ch'ing capital, Peking. Soon there were also embassies of the other foreign powers at Peking. The Chinese government pledged to protect Christian missionaries and their converts. Great Britain took possession of a small section of the Chinese mainland opposite Hong Kong.

In separate treaties, Russia gained even more than trade privileges and extraterritoriality. It received territory north of the Amur River and east of the Ussuri River, bordering on the Sea of Japan. In the southern part of this newly gained territory, the Russians founded the port of Vladivostok and established a naval base there (see map, opposite page.)

The Sino-Japanese War

Japan, as you have read, had embarked on a course of modernization after the Meiji Restoration of 1868. In the 1890's Japan also became an imperialist power.

The territory that most interested Japan was the nearby peninsula of Korea, long a dependency of China. Korean authorities had to refer all matters involving foreign relations to the Chinese emperors. No foreigners were allowed in the country. However, Russia, France, and the United States were all interested in gaining trade privileges there. Fearing that a Western-controlled Korea might threaten its safety, Japan began to demand privileges in the Korean peninsula.

Japan maintained that Korea was independent, while China still claimed Korea as a dependency. Out of this confusion, Japan secured a treaty that opened some Korean ports to Japanese trade. China then allowed the Koreans to make similar treaties with six Western nations.

In 1894 a rebellion broke out in Korea. Both Japan and China sent armed forces to put it down. It was an explosive situation, and it exploded. In the short war that followed—the Sino-Japanese War—China was defeated by Japan. (*Sino* is a combining word form meaning "Chinese.")

In addition to trade privileges, the Japanese wanted territory. By the Treaty of Shimonoseki in 1895, China was forced to recognize the complete independence of Korea. China also had to give to Japan the island of Formosa and the nearby islands, the Pescadores. In another provision, China gave Japan the strategic Liaotung Peninsula on the southern coast of Manchuria. At the tip of the Liaotung Peninsula, which juts into the Yellow Sea, was the excellent harbor of Port Arthur (see map, opposite). Finally, China also had to pay a sum equivalent to $150 million to Japan.

Russia and the East Asian mainland

The Western powers were displeased with the Treaty of Shimonoseki, especially Russia. It did not want a strong power in Korea close to the Russian naval base at Vladivostok. In addition, Rus-

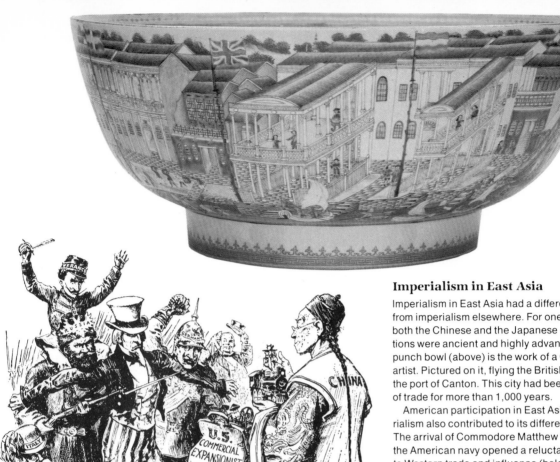

Imperialism in East Asia

Imperialism in East Asia had a different flavor from imperialism elsewhere. For one thing, both the Chinese and the Japanese civilizations were ancient and highly advanced. The punch bowl (above) is the work of a Chinese artist. Pictured on it, flying the British flag, is the port of Canton. This city had been a center of trade for more than 1,000 years.

American participation in East Asian imperialism also contributed to its different flavor. The arrival of Commodore Matthew Perry and the American navy opened a reluctant Japan to Western trade and influence (below). In China, the United States sought to restrain the ambitions of the other imperialist powers (left) and thus to protect its own interests.

sia had plans of its own for Manchuria, including the Liaotung Peninsula.

In 1891 the Russians had begun a gigantic project—the building of a railroad from western Russia across Asia to Vladivostok. If this Trans-Siberian railroad had to follow along the Amur River, it would be 350 miles (560 kilometers) longer than if it could cut straight across Manchuria to Vladivostok. The Manchurian route also presented fewer engineering difficulties across rivers and mountains. Russia also hoped to link its Trans-Siberian railroad to the Liaotung Peninsula by a line from Harbin, in central Manchuria, to Port Arthur, at the tip of the peninsula.

With these plans afoot, Russia was more than willing to help China keep Japan off the Asian mainland. France, which had recently concluded an alliance with Russia, was also willing to help. Germany, eager to get on better terms with Russia and perhaps to weaken the alliance between France and Russia, also offered its services. In a joint note, Russia, France, and Germany advised the Japanese government to withdraw from the Liaotung Peninsula.

The Japanese were furious, but they were not ready to face such powerful forces. They gave the Liaotung Peninsula back to China in return for money. France and Russia gave China further aid—a loan to help pay the sum to Japan.

The price of European aid

There was a catch, of course, in all of this aid to China. China had to pledge that no foreign power would receive any special rights in Chinese financial affairs unless France and Russia received them, too. Great Britain and Germany quickly made similar loans with similar provisions.

Beginning in 1896, there were still more demands on China. France demanded and received special trading privileges and the right to develop mineral resources in southern China. It also received a 99-year lease to the territory of Kwangchowan and the right to build a railroad linking southern China with the French protectorate in Indochina.

Germany was given a 99-year lease to the port of Tsingtao (CHING·DOW) and surrounding territory on the south shore of the Shantung Peninsula, which juts into the Yellow Sea. Germany also received mining rights and permission to build a railway in Shantung.

Great Britain would not be left out. It negotiated for more trading privileges in the Yangtze Valley and the right to build a naval base at Weihaiwei, on the north shore of the Shantung Peninsula. This base was to balance the German base at Tsingtao.

Russia demanded and received the right to lease a tax-free right of way for its railroad across Manchuria—to be called the Chinese Eastern Railway. It also received permission to police the Manchurian route and certain other extraterritorial privileges. In effect, northern Manchuria would be under Russian economic and military domination. In a further and secret treaty, Russia and China formed an alliance for mutual aid in case either should become involved in war with Japan.

When the Germans and British seized their bases in the Shantung Peninsula, Russia demanded entry to the Yellow Sea, too. The Russians forced China to lease to them the southern part of the Liaotung Peninsula, including the important base at Port Arthur. Russia also was given the right to build a branch of the Chinese Eastern Railway from Harbin to Port Arthur.

These territorial privileges greatly angered the Japanese. They had been forced by the Western powers to give up the spoils of their victory and now had to watch those spoils being divided up. Both China and Japan were to recall these humiliations over the next 50 years when they created newly powerful positions in East Asia.

CHECKUP

1. IDENTIFY: Commodore Perry, Treaty of Kanagawa, consulate, extraterritoriality, "unequal treaties," Taiping Rebellion, Treaty of Shimonoseki, Trans-Siberian railroad.

2. In what sense can the Meiji Restoration be considered a revolution? What were its results?

3. What foundations of an industrial economy had Japan acquired by 1900?

4. List the main provisions of the treaty that ended the Opium War.

5. Describe the causes and results of the Sino-Japanese War.

Foreign influence over Southeast Asia and the Pacific increased

The tide of imperialism did not stop in China. It affected Southeast Asia and the islands of the Pacific as well.

East of India and south of China lies a large peninsula that thrusts southward from the mainland of Asia (see map, page 570). This peninsula, along with some islands in the Indian Ocean and Pacific Ocean, is known as **Southeast Asia.** The region consists of the present-day countries of Burma, Thailand, Laos, Cambodia, Vietnam, Malaysia, Singapore, and Indonesia. The Philippine Islands are sometimes considered part of Southeast Asia.

Southeast Asia was strongly influenced by India, especially the religious teachings of Hinduism and Buddhism. Several powerful empires flourished there at various times.

Imperialism in Southeast Asia

You have read how, in the late 1400's and early 1500's, the East Indies were the target of European traders. They were searching for the spices so highly prized in Europe at that time. In the seaports of these islands and the nearby mainland, Portuguese and Dutch merchants enjoyed a rich and active trade until the early 1800's. However, they largely ignored the inland areas.

In the 1800's and early 1900's, imperialism came to Southeast Asia as it did to nearby India and China. In addition to spices, the area became an important source for the world's tea and coffee, and later for such valuable products as tin and oil. For the imperialists, there were rich prizes to be won in Southeast Asia.

British successes. The kingdom of Burma, on the eastern border of India, was of interest to the British imperial power in India. Several wars involving the British and Burmese were fought in the 1800's. By 1886 all of Burma came under British control and was administered as part of British India.

At the tip of the Malay Peninsula is the island of Singapore. The British moved onto this island,

then uninhabited, in the late 1700's. Throughout the 1800's they gradually pushed their influence northward to include large parts of the peninsula up to the southern borders of Siam (today known as Thailand). They also created a city at Singapore, which became an important naval base in the British Empire and one of the world's busiest seaports.

Great Britain also gained control of two other island regions. One was the northern part of the island of Borneo, which became a British protectorate in the 1880's. The other was the southeastern portion of New Guinea.

French gains. The eastern part of the mainland of Southeast Asia contained several small, weak nations that were under Chinese influence and that paid annual tribute to the government of China. Beginning in the late 1700's, French merchants gained trading rights at seaports on the South China Sea. Gradually, French influence expanded. In the latter 1800's French imperialists forced China to give up its influence in the area, and the French became the dominant power in what became known as French Indochina.

Siam. The kingdom of Siam was better organized and ruled than were other parts of Southeast Asia. The British on the Malay Peninsula and the French in Indochina nibbled at the borders of Siam. To maintain their independence, Siamese rulers skillfully maneuvered British interests against French interests. The British and French finally decided that an independent Siam was a useful **buffer state** between their possessions. A buffer state, located between two hostile powers, is a small country that often lessens the possibility of conflict between them.

The Dutch East Indies. As you read earlier, the Dutch East India Company, formed in 1602 to exploit the island possessions of the Netherlands, was highly successful for a long time. By the late 1700's, however, it had become corrupt and inefficient. In 1798 the Netherlands revoked the company's charter and made the Dutch East Indies (also called the Netherlands East Indies) a royal colony.

The Dutch East India Company had used a system of forced labor in the East Indies. The Dutch government somewhat improved working conditions for the natives. By the late 1800's several native revolts led the government of the Netherlands to make basic reforms in the administration of its richest imperial possession.

Interest in the Pacific islands

Only a few of the islands and island groups in the Pacific were economically attractive to the imperialist powers. These few areas had large native populations that could be taught to want and buy manufactured goods. Some of the areas had fertile soil that could be taken over and made into rich plantations. Other islands had minerals to be exploited. Imperialism in most of the Pacific islands, however, was based on another motive—the need for coaling stations and naval bases.

In the days of sailing ships, captains might stop at almost any populated island in the Pacific to buy meat, vegetables, and fruit, and to get fresh water. As sailing ships gave way to steamships in the late 1800's, dependable coaling stations, where ships could refuel, became an urgent necessity. A steamship did not have to wait for favorable winds, but it did need to refill its coal bunkers. Thus, with the coming of steam power, coal freighters fanned out over the Pacific to replenish coal supplies at coaling stations.

Naval bases also became a necessity. On sailing ships, the ship's carpenter and crew could repair almost anything that broke down or wore out. The power machinery of a steamship, on the other hand, was heavy and complicated. It could be repaired or replaced only by massive equipment and trained workers at special naval bases.

Since the imperialist powers were rivals in the Pacific, as elsewhere, none was willing to trust the other for its coal supplies and naval repairs. Each of the powers, therefore, sought out its own Pacific islands.

European powers in the Pacific

You have read how the English explorer Captain Cook rediscovered Australia and New Zealand in the late 1700's. He and other explorers, from France and the Netherlands, also sailed to many of the smaller Pacific islands. Missionaries went out to Christianize and educate the natives, and some small settlements were made.

connections

Sunken Ships

Ships have been an important form of transportation since the earliest times. Unfortunately, as long as there have been ships, there have been shipwrecks. One expert estimates that 40,000 ships had sunk in the Mediterranean even before the birth of Christ.

Since early times, too, people have tried to recover sunken ships and the objects that went down with them. As early as the 200's B.C., the Greeks were diving for sunken treasure. In the 1500's Indians on the coast of Florida dived for coins and gold from Spanish shipwrecks.

Treasure is not the only object of underwater exploration. Archeologists, too, are interested in recovering sunken ships and the objects they carried (right). One of the first expeditions recovered artifacts

from a ship that sank off the coast of Turkey around 1200 B.C.

Sunken ships are seldom found intact. Sometimes, however, the hulls have been buried in the sand and preserved. The sunken Roman ships from the naval battle of Actium, fought in 21 B.C., have been found intact. More complete ships are being raised to the surface as special equipment is developed for the work.

Because fresh water preserves better than salt, many sunken ships in lakes are still in prime condition. Two warships that sank in Lake Ontario in 1812 are still intact with their guns on deck.

The French were among the first actually to annex territory. They claimed the Marquesas Islands and established a protectorate over Tahiti and the other Society Islands in the 1840's. Shortly afterward they took over New Caledonia and used it as a colony for prisoners. However, in the Pacific, as in Africa and much of Asia, the heyday of imperialism did not begin until the 1870's. In 1876, only about half of the Pacific islands were owned by Western powers. By 1900, nearly all of the islands were controlled by imperialist nations (see map, this page).

During the imperialistic era, Great Britain took the Fiji Islands, established a protectorate over the Gilbert Islands and some of the Solomons, and annexed the Cook Islands to New Zealand. With France, it took possession of the New Hebrides Islands in 1896. These islands became a condominium in 1906.

Germany acquired some of the Solomons in the 1880's, but later transferred all but two to Great Britain. The Germans also established a protectorate over the Marshall Islands. In 1899 they bought the Caroline Islands and the Mariana Islands (except for Guam) from Spain.

The Samoan Islands

The most serious rivalry over territory in the Pacific area involved the Samoan Islands. Here the United States played a major role. American interests in Samoa had been developing for a number of years. In 1878 Americans gained the right to use the harbor city of Pago Pago (PAHNG·oh PAHNG·oh) on the island of Tutuila as a trading post, coaling station, and naval base. Great Britain and Germany secured similar rights in other parts of the Samoan Islands.

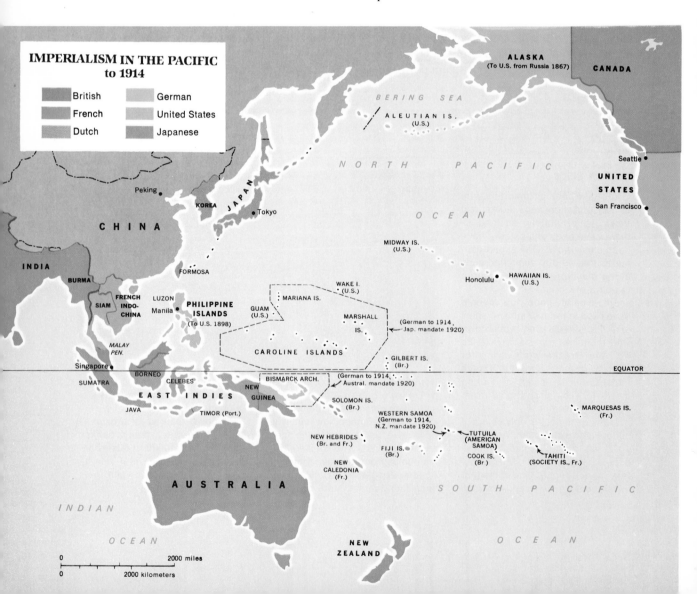

IMPERIALISM IN THE PACIFIC
to 1914

British   German
French   United States
Dutch   Japanese

For a number of years, rivalry among the three foreign nations for control of the Samoan Islands was so intense that they almost went to war. To prevent further trouble, the three nations set up a system of joint control in 1889, but it did not work.

In 1899 a solution was worked out by treaty. Great Britain, preoccupied with the South African War, withdrew its interests. The United States established firm control over Tutuila and six other small islands whose combined area was only about 75 square miles (195 square kilometers). These possessions became known as American Samoa. Germany gained control of all the other islands in the Samoan group, eventually called Western Samoa. Since the major value of American Samoa lay in the naval base at Pago Pago, the area was placed under the control of the United States Navy.

The Hawaiian Islands

Far more important to the United States than its Samoan possessions were the Hawaiian Islands (see map, opposite page). This group of islands had fertile soil, good rainfall, and a mild climate. Foreign traders and missionaries, including Americans, had begun settling there in the 1820's, but interfered little with the government and economy of the natives. After 1865, however, business people from the United States and other foreign nations began to develop sugar cane and pineapple plantations on the islands.

The native rulers of the Hawaiian Islands resented foreign influence and announced that they intended to bring an end to it. American planters then asked the United States representative in the islands to call for a force of American marines. Native troops, ill-prepared to match this show of force, refused to fight. By 1893 the foreign business leaders, supported by American marines, were in control of the islands.

American planters then asked the United States government to annex the Hawaiian Islands. At first there was a loud outcry in the United States against the use of American military force on behalf of business interests far outside the nation's borders. However, the American planters kept up their pressure and were successful in 1898, when the United States annexed the islands. Unlike

imperialist nations elsewhere, however, the United States made the Hawaiian Islands a territory. This meant that they were legally entitled, in due time, to become a state of the federal Union.

The Philippines, Guam, and Wake Island

Since the 1500's and 1600's, the Philippine Islands and Guam in the western Pacific Ocean had been parts of Spain's far-flung empire. In 1898 the United States declared war on Spain, as you will read in the next section. Most of the fighting took place in Cuba and Puerto Rico, but the first United States military action against Spain took place in the Pacific.

When war was declared, United States naval forces in the western Pacific moved quickly into the harbor of Manila, capital of the Philippine Islands. They destroyed a small Spanish fleet stationed there. Within a few months, American land forces, supported by native revolutionaries, defeated the Spanish forces in Manila. With the collapse of Spanish power at Manila, the entire Philippine Islands came under the control of the United States. At about this time, American forces also occupied Guam, a small, Spanish-held island east of the Philippines (see map, page 576).

Under the treaty of 1898 that settled the war between the United States and Spain, the United States retained control of Guam and the Philippine Islands. Although Guam was small and weak, it quickly became an important American naval base.

The Philippine Islands presented the United States with a more complex problem. The combined area of the more than 7,000 islands was about 115,000 square miles (298,000 square kilometers). Most of the islands were very small, uninhabited specks in the ocean, but a few, including Luzon with the capital of Manila, were large and heavily populated.

Some Filipinos welcomed the Americans and even fought with them against the Spaniards. Most of the native population, however, had suffered under Spanish rule for centuries and saw little advantage in changing one foreign master for another. Under a leader named Emilio Aguinaldo (ah·gee·NAHL·doh), Filipino natives fought thousands of American troops for three years, hoping

Imperialism in the Pacific

In the late 1800's and early 1900's, American imperialism was directed mainly at territories in the Pacific, such as the Philippine Islands. During the Spanish-American War of 1898, battles over these islands depended mainly on naval superiority. The victory of the American fleet in Manila Bay was a key factor in the conquest of the Philippines (bottom). Equally important was a native uprising against the Spaniards. Emilio Aguinaldo (right), who led the revolt, thought the uprising would lead to independence for the Philippines. When Americans took over after the war, Aguinaldo led another revolt, this time against the new rulers. After three years of fierce fighting, the American forces were finally victorious. The United States now held a dominant position in the Pacific, strengthened by the annexation of Hawaii, with its splendid harbor at Honolulu (below).

for independence. The Filipinos were finally defeated in 1902.

The United States government and many of its citizens were uneasy over the role of the United States as an imperialist power in the far Pacific. Accordingly, government for the Philippine Islands was created. The governor and an executive council were United States citizens, but there was a legislative assembly elected by the Filipinos. The islands were promised their independence when the United States was satisfied that they could govern themselves and resist the domination of other foreign powers. In the meantime the United States helped the Filipinos to build schools and roads, improve health and sanitation, and develop foreign trade.

Besides acquiring the Philippine Islands and Guam, the United States also took possession of Wake Island in the central Pacific. Thus the United States acquired another link in a chain of island possessions running from its west coast across the vast distances of the Pacific Ocean all the way to East Asia.

CHECKUP

1. IDENTIFY: buffer state, Aguinaldo.

2. Using the map on page 576, list the possessions in Southeast Asia of various world powers by 1914.

3. Why was Siam a useful buffer state?

4. Why were the Pacific islands important possessions?

5. Explain briefly how the United States gained the following: (a) American Samoa, (b) Hawaii, (c) the Philippines.

6

The United States intervened in Latin America

Imperialism in Latin America was different from that in the Pacific. Although the Latin American countries were weak, they could not be turned into colonies again. This had been proved earlier in the century. Mexico had survived an occupation by French forces who were trying to set up a puppet emperor (see Chapter 20). Spain had also tried to recolonize the Dominican Republic but was unsuccessful.

Nevertheless the countries of Latin America were subjected to economic interference as they increasingly became a field for investment from Europe and the United States.

New opportunities for trade

As the pace of the Industrial Revolution increased in Europe and the United States, more agricultural products and raw materials were bought from Latin American countries. Americans, for example, acquired a taste for bananas, which they bought in Central America, and for coffee, which came mostly from Brazil. They bought sugar made from sugar cane grown in Cuba, and they smoked cigars that were made from Cuban tobacco.

The British bought large quantities of the wool needed in their factories, as well as wheat, beef, and mutton from Argentina and Uruguay. Chile mined nitrates from natural deposits in its northern deserts and sold them to the industrial countries to make fertilizers and explosives. Brazil exported natural rubber from its vast Amazon forests.

To bring these goods to the port cities of Latin America, railroads were built. The ports were improved to enable the newly perfected steamships to be loaded. All these developments brought prosperity to those countries of Latin America that had the opportunity to engage in this trade. Argentina, especially, benefited greatly from all these developments. Other Latin American countries, such as Bolivia and Paraguay, hardly participated in this trade at all. Within each country, nearly all the benefits of the trade were concentrated in the capital cities and the ports.

A few of the Latin American countries—most notably Argentina, Brazil, Uruguay, and later Cuba—attracted a large number of immigrants from Europe, similar to the wave that came to the United States. In Latin American countries with the greatest export trade, industries also began to be developed. Factories such as sugar mills were built to process the export goods. Other new factories were built to produce consumer goods for

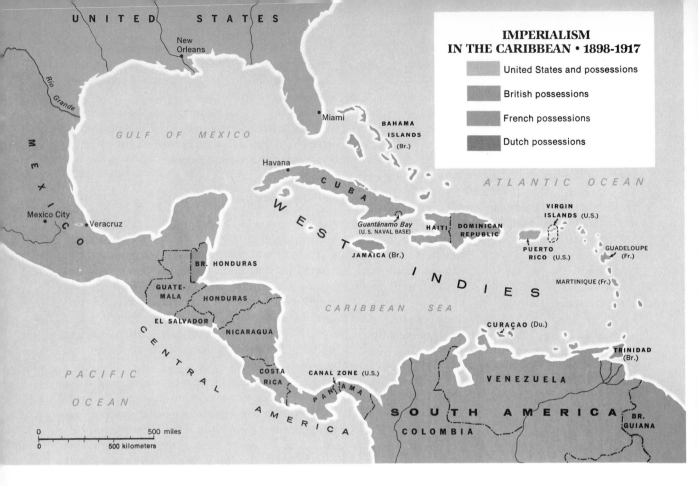

IMPERIALISM
IN THE CARIBBEAN • 1898-1917

United States and possessions

British possessions

French possessions

Dutch possessions

local markets—textile mills, flour mills, and metal-working shops.

The central governments now had more tax revenues. As a result, foreign banks were willing to lend funds to them on a large scale for public improvements. Some of this money was spent on strengthening their armies and navies, which made it easier for the central governments to suppress internal rebellions. Some money was spent on installing electricity and streetcars in the capital cities. Some money was wasted by being distributed to politicians in power.

Economic imperialism

Many of the new railroads, ranches, plantations, and mines in Latin America were foreign-owned. Foreign investments received many special favors from the governments—for example, monopoly privileges, free land, and exemption from taxes. These favors were granted by the central governments in the hope that the foreigners would develop the economy by establishing new businesses

there. However, the profits from these businesses and the interest payments from the loans were sent out of the region and back to the foreign bankers and investors.

As you have read, many Latin American governments borrowed money from foreign banks. Often the government that had borrowed the money was overthrown in a revolution, and the new government would refuse to pay its debts.

Loans that were not repaid frequently led to intervention by the foreign powers. European leaders would persuade their governments to bring pressure to get payments. Sometimes warships were sent and troops were landed to compel payment. A typical method was to take over the collection of the customs—the principal tax—and hold back enough money to pay the debts.

American intervention

As the United States became an industrial power, it began to challenge Great Britain, its main rival for dominance of the Western Hemisphere. In the early 1800's the Americans had not made an issue of the Monroe Doctrine in any region farther away than Central America when the offender was Great Britain. For example, the British had occupied the Falkland Islands, near the tip of South America, in 1837. Although Argentina protested, the United States did not support the Argentinians.

In 1895, however, the United States did intervene in a dispute between Great Britain and Venezuela. Early in the 1800's, Great Britain had acquired British Guiana (gee·AHN·uh), on the northern coast of South America (see map, opposite page). On a number of occasions, Great Britain had tried to push the boundary of British Guiana westward into territory that was also claimed by Venezuela.

Venezuela then asked the United States for support in its demand that the border dispute be submitted to **arbitration**—to a settlement of the dispute by a party agreed upon by all sides. When Great Britain refused, President Grover Cleveland insisted. Finally, Great Britain, which was overcommitted in the South African War, gave in and the dispute with Venezuela was settled. The United States had championed the cause of a weak Latin American nation against powerful European interests. Yet the United States had its own motives for helping Venezuela. The gold that was thought to be in the region was now more accessible to American investors.

Trouble with Spain

In 1898 the United States became even more deeply involved in Latin American affairs. Its involvement grew out of disputes with Spain.

The main cause of tension between Spain and the United States was Cuba (see map, opposite), a Spanish colony in the West Indies. For many years the Cubans had been discontented with Spanish rule. There were several rebellions, which the Spanish government suppressed with great difficulty. United States citizens and corporations had invested money in Cuba, especially in railroads and in sugar plantations and mills. When another rebellion broke out in 1895, this property was endangered.

Concern for American-owned property was only one reason for the tense relations. Many Americans felt sympathetic toward Cuba's desire for independence and indignant over Spanish treatment of the Cuban rebels. These sentiments were stirred up by anti-Spanish speeches and writings by Cubans who had settled in the United States. It was also fueled by sensational stories in American newspapers telling of Spanish atrocities in Cuba.

More anger arose in 1898 when an American battleship, the *Maine,* blew up in Havana harbor. The *Maine* had been sent to Cuba to protect American citizens and their property. No one knew the cause of the explosion, but many in the United States assumed that the Spaniards were to blame. American newspapers played on this assumption. The result was a rising popular demand in the United States for a declaration of war on Spain.

The Spanish-American War

Spain showed some willingness to come to terms with the United States over Cuba. President McKinley and his cabinet did not want war. However, American leaders felt unable to resist the rising popular demand for aggressive measures. War was declared in April 1898.

Congress declared that it was fighting only for the independence of Cuba and had no intention of taking the island for itself. This statement was adopted at the insistence of members who opposed rising American imperialism.

The leaders of the Cuban independence movement had not wanted United States intervention, which they feared as much as Spanish rule. They judged themselves able to win the war on their own. Cubans saw American intervention as a victory that was being taken away from them at the last moment.

The Spanish-American War has been called "brief, glorious, and inexpensive." Fighting took place in Cuba and Puerto Rico and also, as you have read, in Spanish possessions in the Pacific—the Philippine Islands and Guam. After being defeated in all of these places and on the sea, Spain was unable to continue fighting and asked for peace. A treaty was signed in December 1898.

The United States did not invite the Cubans to the peace conference. Instead it dealt only with

Imperialism in Latin America

The United States presence in Latin America in the late 1800's and early 1900's took many forms. The most visible example was the construction of the Panama Canal under the supervision of American engineers (right).

Latin America was also a source of important products. Bananas, shipped by rail from such countries as Costa Rica (below), were one of the products that provided American companies with enormous profits. It was thought essential, therefore, that the stability of these nations be maintained. The chief example of direct intervention by the United States was the expulsion of Spain from Cuba in the Spanish-American War of 1898. Theodore Roosevelt rose to fame during the war as the leader of the "Rough Riders" (above).

Spain. By the terms of the peace treaty, Spain surrendered its claim to Cuba. It also ceded Puerto Rico and the Pacific islands of Guam and the Philippines to the United States.

The United States recognized Cuba's independence. However, Cuba was not turned over to its own leaders, but to a provisional military government. The United States permitted a Cuban assembly to draw up a constitution. However, the United States insisted that the Cuban constitution include the so-called Platt Amendment. This amendment gave the United States the right to intervene in Cuba whenever it thought orderly government was endangered. The United States also insisted on four naval bases in Cuba, but later accepted one at Guantánamo Bay.

Thus Cuba was lowered to the status of a protectorate of the United States. Many of the heroes of the independence movement resigned in anger and despair, leaving the government to politicians more favorable to the wishes of the United States.

The United States' pledge of independence for Cuba did not apply to the other areas it had won from Spain. It kept control of Puerto Rico, Guam, and the Philippine Islands, for which Spain was paid $20 million. The government in Puerto Rico was similar to that of the Philippines. It consisted of an appointed governor and executive council who were United States citizens and a legislative assembly elected by the local people.

The Panama Canal

In addition to governing its new and far-flung possessions, the United States was also obliged to defend them. The major problem of defense came to light during the Spanish-American War.

Before the war the American battleship *Oregon* had been stationed on the Pacific coast of the United States. When war became likely, this battleship was needed to strengthen American forces in the Caribbean Sea. It had to go at high speed all the way around the South American continent, a distance of over 11,000 miles (17,600 kilometers). The United States realized that it would either have to build two complete navies to protect its empire or find some easier and quicker way to move warships between the Atlantic and Pacific oceans.

A canal across the Isthmus of Panama had long been considered. In the late 1800's, the United States government began negotiating for permission and a right of way to build a canal. It asked Colombia for a lease to a strip of land across the isthmus in Panama, at that time a province of Colombia (see map, page 580).

After a treaty had been negotiated, the Colombian senate adjourned without ratifying it. There was indignation in the United States. President Theodore Roosevelt thought that Colombia was trying to bargain for more money.

There was also indignation in the province of Panama. The people of the province were eager to have the canal built there because it promised them great benefits. When negotiations seemed to break down, certain business leaders, including American residents there, began a revolution to gain independence from Colombia.

American warships stationed at Panama prevented Colombian troops from moving in to suppress the revolt, and the revolution succeeded. The United States then quickly recognized the independence of Panama. In 1903 a treaty between the two governments was drawn up and speedily ratified. The treaty gave the United States all the rights necessary to build a canal across Panama.

The Panama Canal, one of the world's greatest engineering projects, was opened in 1914. It shortened the sea route from New York to San Francisco by over 5,000 miles (8,000 kilometers), and the sea route from New York to the new territory of Hawaii by 4,400 miles (7,100 kilometers). Fleets in the Atlantic and Pacific could now be quickly shifted when necessary. The canal was open to the merchant ships of all nations upon payment of toll charges. The toll was well worth the cost. The shortened route lowered the operating cost of a ship many times more than the toll it paid to use the canal.

The Panama Canal had an important effect on the countries in Central and South America bordering on the Caribbean Sea. Formerly this region had been a sleepy backwater of the world, a dead end of commerce. The canal made it an important trading area of the world.

The Roosevelt Corollary. Long before the Panama Canal was completed, the United States recognized that a strong European power with a foothold in the Caribbean region could threaten the canal or the sea lanes leading to it. Therefore the United States adopted a new policy toward Latin America.

In 1904 President Roosevelt's annual message to Congress included a section on Latin America. Roosevelt said that if any situation threatened the independence of any country in the Western Hemisphere, the United States would act as an "international police power" to prevent a foreign country from stepping in. This statement became known as the Roosevelt Corollary to the Monroe Doctrine (about which you read in Chapter 18). It was regarded as a natural consequence of the earlier policy, and it would be called into use several times over the next years.

Further American expansion

The United States continued to expand in the Caribbean. It occupied and set up military governments in Nicaragua from 1912 to 1933, Haiti from 1915 to 1934, and the Dominican Republic from 1916 to 1924. Cuba was also subjected to an occupation government again from 1906 to 1909, and United States marines were stationed there from 1917 to 1922.

The United States intervened in these countries for several reasons. It feared that these governments were falling into anarchy or into the hands of leaders who would refuse to pay the debts owed to foreign banks. European nations might have used this failure to receive payments on their debts as a pretext to intervene in the Caribbean area.

During the early 1900's, as world tensions were increasing, the economies of the Caribbean nations were on the verge of collapse. In this crisis, the United States decided to purchase three of the Virgin Islands from Denmark in 1917. At the same time Puerto Ricans were granted United States citizenship and a little more self-government in order to guarantee their loyalty in dangerous times.

Mexico's revolution

The greatest upheaval in Latin America during the age of imperialism was the Mexican revolution. For 34 years Mexico had been dominated by one dictator, Porfirio Díaz. He had permitted many of the country's natural resources to be developed by foreign companies and much of its land to be taken away from poor peasants. In 1910 the country presented an appearance of stability and prosperity, but in that year Díaz's regime suddenly collapsed.

A rebellion against the aging dictator put Francisco Madero in power in 1911. He was assassinated in 1913 and Victoriano Huerta (WAIR·tah), one of Díaz's former generals, seized the government. Then a rebellion against Huerta began and deepened to intensive warfare among various factions. The war went on for ten years and cost perhaps a million lives. Underlying these struggles were widespread demands for rights to the land. These demands were voiced by the peasant leader Emiliano Zapata.

Americans had billions of dollars invested in Mexico and were troubled by the violence and unrest. President Woodrow Wilson refused to recognize Huerta's government and tried to force his overthrow. In 1914, after the arrest of some American soldiers, marines were sent to occupy Veracruz. Two years later, United States troops were sent into Mexico to try to capture Pancho Villa (VEE·yah), a revolutionary leader who had raided a New Mexican border town, killing several Americans. Bad feeling between the two countries mounted, and for a time there was a threat of war. Only when American troops withdrew in 1917 did tensions ease.

CHECKUP

1. IDENTIFY: arbitration, *Maine*, Platt Amendment, Roosevelt Corollary, Díaz, Huerta, Zapata, Villa.

2. LOCATE: Cuba, British Guiana, Puerto Rico, Panama Canal, Nicaragua, Haiti, Dominican Republic, Virgin Islands.

3. Give examples of economic imperialism in Latin America.

4. Explain how the United States exerted its influence (a) in Venezuela's dispute with Great Britain, and (b) in Cuba.

5. What were the results of the Spanish-American War?

6. Why was the United States interested in building a Panama Canal? What were the results?

CHAPTER REVIEW

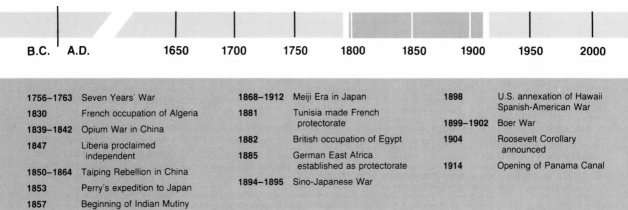

B.C.	A.D.	1650	1700	1750	1800	1850	1900	1950	2000

1756–1763	Seven Years' War	1868–1912	Meiji Era in Japan
1830	French occupation of Algeria	1881	Tunisia made French protectorate
1839–1842	Opium War in China	1882	British occupation of Egypt
1847	Liberia proclaimed independent	1885	German East Africa established as protectorate
1850–1864	Taiping Rebellion in China	1894–1895	Sino-Japanese War
1853	Perry's expedition to Japan		
1857	Beginning of Indian Mutiny		

1898	U.S. annexation of Hawaii Spanish-American War
1899–1902	Boer War
1904	Roosevelt Corollary announced
1914	Opening of Panama Canal

CHAPTER SUMMARY

In the late 1800's European nations became involved in a new kind of empire building—imperialism. It arose from a need for self-sufficiency, new markets, and places to invest surplus capital and settle excess population.

European nations divided up almost all of Africa in the late 1800's. Communications and transportation improved, slavery was abolished, and some Africans profited from the many economic investments. For the most part, however, Africa was mercilessly exploited, and tensions developed that would lead to further struggles later in the 1900's.

In India, British-French rivalry was resolved by the British victory in the Seven Years' War. After 1763 the British East India Company controlled most of the country. When Indian discontent culminated in the Indian Mutiny, the British government assumed direct control of India.

Japan, isolated until the 1800's, came under Western influence when the United States and European powers forced the opening of several treaty ports. After a civil war, the emperor was restored to power in 1868. The Japanese then began a remarkably quick and successful process of industrialization.

Like Japan, China had been isolated for centuries. Chinese isolation, however, was ended by a conflict—the Opium War—and a series of humiliating treaties and settlements. Western powers first gained trading privileges and, after the Taiping Rebellion, actual territories.

Imperialism was also a strong force in Southeast Asia and the Pacific. By the late 1800's, the kingdom of Siam was the only area of Southeast Asia that remained free. The Pacific Islands became valuable as coaling stations and naval bases. France, Great Britain, Germany, and the United States all established claims in the Pacific.

The Latin American countries were weak and vulnerable to economic imperialism. The United States sought to extend its influence and to protect Latin America from powerful European interests. The easy American victory in the Spanish-American War dramatized the growing strength of the United States. In the early 1900's, the United States became increasingly involved in Latin American affairs, often invoking the Roosevelt Corollary to the Monroe Doctrine.

CHECKING WHAT YOU KNOW

1. Match each African colony at the left with an imperialist nation at the right. You may use a nation more than once.

   a. Libya
   b. Togo
   c. Algeria
   d. Gold Coast
   e. Río de Oro
   f. Sudan
   g. Angola
   h. Mozambique
   i. Equatorial Africa

   1. France
   2. Italy
   3. Portugal
   4. Great Britain
   5. Germany
   6. Spain

2. What is the difference between economic imperialism and political imperialism? Why did one often lead to the other during the late 1800's?

3. How did European imperialism encourage the growth of nationalism in other parts of the world?

4. How were each of the following nations able to preserve their independence:
   a. Liberia
   b. Ethiopia
   c. Japan
   d. Siam

5. In what ways did the colonial policy of the United States differ from that of other nations? In what ways was it similar?

6. What were the positive and negative effects of imperialism in Africa and in India?

PRACTICING YOUR SKILLS

1. **Analyzing information.** Read the lines below from the Rudyard Kipling poem "The White Man's Burden," and answer the questions that follow.

   > Take up the white man's burden—
   >   Send forth the best ye breed—
   > Go bind your sons to exile
   >   To serve your captives' need;
   > To wait in heavy harness,
   >   On fluttered folk and wild—
   > Your new-caught, sullen peoples,
   >   Half-devil and half-child.

   What does Kipling mean by the phrase "white man's burden"? How does he characterize the people who must be "served"? Based on what you have learned about early African, Asian, and Indian civilizations, what arguments might you use to prove Kipling wrong?

2. **Using maps.** Turn to the map of Africa on page 814. How many independent nations exist in present-day Africa? How does this number compare with the number shown on the map on page 559? Which imperialist power gave up the most territory? the least?

RELATING PAST TO PRESENT

1. Using a world atlas, prepare a map showing the distribution of natural resources in Africa. Compare this map with the map on page 559. What resources did each imperialist nation stand to gain through its possession of African colonies? Which of these resources are most important to industrial nations today?

2. Review the reasons why the United States government decided to build a canal across the Isthmus of Panama. Then investigate the debate surrounding the 1978 decision to turn ownership of the canal over to Panama by the year 2000. Why did some members of the United States Senate support such a treaty with Panama? Why did others oppose it? What rights does the United States retain in this region?

INVESTIGATING FURTHER

1. Prepare a report describing how Indians reacted to British rule. The following selections are possible sources: "The Sepoy Rebellion" and "The Growth of National Feeling in India" in Sydney Eisen and Maurice Filler, *The Human Adventure,* Volume 2 (Harcourt Brace Jovanovich); Donald Johnson and Jean Johnson, *Through Indian Eyes* (Holt, Rinehart and Winston).

2. Japanese artists recorded their first impressions of Commodore Matthew Perry and his warships in a number of vivid woodblock prints and water-color paintings. One such picture is found on page 572. Locate other examples of these pictures in a history of Japanese art or in back issues of *American Heritage* magazine. Based on evidence in these pictures, what conclusions can you draw about the way in which people of different cultures sometimes view each other? What details in the paintings or prints support your answer?

3. Imperialism arose out of a complex mixture of political, economic, and social forces. One of these was the missionary motive. Using books in your library, prepare a report on missionary activities in colonial areas. What benefits did missionaries bring to the areas in which they worked?

UNIT REVIEW

1. Match each individual at the left with the correct movement or idea at the right.

   a. Mazzini
   b. Bismarck
   c. Spencer
   d. Smith
   e. Marx
   f. Daumier
   g. Beethoven
   h. Pankhurst
   i. Mill
   j. Monet
   k. Einstein
   l. Metternich
   m. Kipling
   n. Freud

   1. romanticism in music
   2. psychoanalysis
   3. liberalism
   4. relativity
   5. absolutism
   6. impressionism
   7. Risorgimento
   8. "white man's burden"
   9. pure communism
   10. *Kulturkampf*
   11. realism in art
   12. Social Darwinism
   13. laissez faire
   14. women's suffrage

2. How did the agricultural revolution help to create a large labor force? Why was this necessary for the development of an industrial economy?

3. What effect did the Industrial Revolution have on each of the following:
   a. living conditions
   b. women's lives
   c. family size
   d. use of leisure time

4. During the 1800's liberalism emerged as a vital force in Europe. What were some of the political ideas associated with liberalism? In what nations did liberalism make the greatest progress? the least? Explain.

5. Metternich once commented, "When France sneezes, all Europe catches cold." What do you think he meant by this remark? In light of the actions taken by Napoleon III, would you agree or disagree with Metternich? Why or why not?

6. Identify the major accomplishments of each of the following scientists:
   a. John Dalton
   b. Marie Curie
   c. Albert Einstein
   d. Charles Darwin
   e. Edward Jenner
   f. Louis Pasteur
   g. Joseph Lister
   h. Sigmund Freud

7. What conditions encouraged the growth of nationalism in Europe? How did the spirit of nationalism affect the development of each of the following countries:
   a. Italy
   b. Germany
   c. Austria-Hungary
   d. Russia

8. Both Bismarck and Cavour used a series of local wars to help unify their respective countries. List the various wars that took place between 1848 and 1871. How did each of these wars contribute to the unification of Italy and of Germany?

9. How did the Industrial Revolution and the rise of nationalism rekindle the desire for colonies? What other factors promoted the renewed interest in empire building?

10. How did the imperialism of the late 1800's differ from the colonization of the 1500's and 1600's?

11. Why did Japan decide to embark on a program of rapid industrialization and aggressive expansion in the late 1800's? What regions of the world became targets of Japanese imperialism? With what European nations did Japan come into conflict?

WORLD WAR IN THE TWENTIETH CENTURY

The United States fleet under attack at Pearl Harbor, Hawaii, on December 7, 1941

(1899–1920)

24

World War I Drastically Altered the Course of History

In the early 1900's many people believed that the world was on the verge of a long era of prosperity and peace. They thought that scientific and industrial progress would create a better life than anyone had ever known. They believed that widespread education would prepare people to govern themselves with wisdom and moderation.

During the late 1800's efforts were made to further cooperation among nations. The Red Cross was established to provide care for the victims of disaster, whether in peace or wartime. The invention of devices such as the radio and telegraph made communication among the peoples of the world easier. A further symbol of international cooperation was the revival of the Olympic games, which had not been held since ancient times.

Philanthropists—those interested in the welfare of the human race—gave of their time and money to bring nations closer together. Alfred Nobel, the Swedish inventor of dynamite, contributed part of his large fortune to set up the Nobel Prizes. One of these awards was to be given annually to outstanding contributors to the cause of peace. Andrew Carnegie, an American financier, built a Palace of Peace at The Hague, in the Netherlands, for international conferences.

Efforts were also made to try to limit armaments. Representatives of several nations met at The Hague, in 1899 and again in 1907, for disarmament talks. Even as nations met to discuss

The assassination at Sarajevo

peace, however, they prepared for war. Although they cooperated in some fields, they continued to fear and distrust one another. In 1910 an Englishman wrote a book "proving" that war was impossible. It was clear, he said, that the winners would suffer as much as the losers. As if in answer, a book published by a German the following year stated that war was not only a "biological necessity," but that Germany must strike the first blow.

Whether or not it was a "biological necessity," war did break out three years later. The Englishman was right, too. By the time the war was over, most of the victors had indeed suffered as much as those who had been defeated.

The war that began in the summer of 1914 was different from any previous war. It involved nations all over the world and was fought on battlefields from the plains of central France to Africa and the Middle East. It also involved industrial technology, especially the mass production of armaments. The war dragged on for more than four years, causing incredible property damage and taking the lives of more soldiers than any previous war.

The people of the time rightly called it the Great War. Because the world has experienced another global conflict more recently, we know it as World War I.

THE CHAPTER SECTIONS

1. Conflicting national interests set the stage for war

2. The nations of the world fought a new kind of war

3. After defeating the Central Powers, the Allies drafted peace terms

4. The peace treaties created a "new Europe"

Conflicting national interests set the stage for war

Some historians have referred to the years before 1914 as a period of "international anarchy." They meant that each nation in Europe pursued policies without regard for the wishes or interests of its neighbors.

Since 1815, when the Congress of Vienna met after the Napoleonic Wars, relations among European powers had been more or less harmonious. Beginning in the late 1800's, however, cooperation among nations was made difficult by the growth of intense rivalries. As you have read, these rivalries developed both within Europe as new nations were formed and overseas as a result of imperialism.

As rivalries intensified in the early 1900's, the great powers built up their military strength and formed secret alliances to protect themselves. Soon they were plunging toward war, pressed forward by four factors: nationalism, imperialism, militarism, and the system of alliances.

Nationalism and imperialism

Nationalism has been defined as the strong feeling of belonging among a group of people bound by the ties of a common culture, a common history, and common problems. As you have seen, after the French Revolution and the Napoleonic Wars, national groups tried to unite under governments controlled by their own people.

This desire to unite all the people of a nation under a single government, however, had explosive possibilities in a Europe where many nationalities mingled. The tension in the Balkans in eastern Europe was just such a situation. You will read shortly about how events in the Balkans helped kindle World War I.

In the early 1900's the imperialist nations came to the brink of war several times as they scrambled to partition Africa among themselves. Germany and France, for example, narrowly avoided war over their rival claims to Morocco on two occasions between 1905 and 1911. Each incident was settled by makeshift compromises that usually left one or more of the participants dissatisfied.

In East Asia, the rival ambitions of Russia and Japan had already produced a war, but it was limited to the two nations. (You will read about this war in Chapter 26.) Imperialistic rivalries in China continued to be dangerous to the peace.

The declining Ottoman Empire threatened to be the source of still further conflicts among imperialist nations. Its weakness offered temptations to Great Britain, Russia, France, Austria, and Italy, each eager for a share of the spoils.

Militarism

The thinking of many European leaders before World War I was dominated by **militarism**—the glorification of armed strength. These leaders believed that international problems could best be solved by the use of force. The nation that was militarily strong usually got what it wanted, as Prussia had proved in its wars with Denmark, Austria, and France. The weaker nations lost out, as Italy had learned on several occasions in its imperialistic ventures in Africa.

Most European nations in the late 1800's began to build reserve armies of men who were drafted, given military training, and then returned to civilian life. These soldiers, using arms and equipment stored at convenient places throughout the country, could be called into service at any time. If a nation mobilized by ordering its reserves into active service, other nations would begin to mobilize for their own protection. It was a process that once begun was hard to stop.

As the international situation became increasingly tense, each European nation felt it necessary to keep its armed forces stronger than those of any potential enemy. Thus an armaments race began. Armies increased in size, and large sums were spent for new weapons and for the fortification of national boundaries. In the 1890's Germany began to build a large and modern navy to rival that of Great Britain. Germany's example was followed by France, the United States, Japan, and Italy. This prompted Great Britain to increase its navy still more.

The system of alliances

During the late 1800's the balance of power in Europe was changed by the unification of Germany and of Italy. Germany, especially, created an entirely new situation. Instead of a group of relatively weak states divided into rival groups, there appeared the German Empire under the leadership of Prussia. Its policy, as you have read, was shaped by Otto von Bismarck.

The Triple Alliance. Bismarck's primary goal in foreign policy was to keep France isolated and without allies. In doing so, one of his aims was to prevent France from trying to retrieve the regions of Alsace and Lorraine from Germany. In order to achieve this goal, Bismarck formed the Triple Alliance with Austria-Hungary and Italy. Bismarck considered Italy a weak link in the Triple Alliance. However, the forging of the alliance did isolate France.

Bismarck also tried to maintain friendly relations with Great Britain and Russia. Great Britain was much more interested in overseas expansion than in events on the continent of Europe. Bismarck was perfectly willing to let Great Britain control the seas and have a free hand in gaining new colonies as long as it kept out of Europe's affairs. At this time he was not interested in gaining colonies but in making Germany the strongest land power in Europe.

The formation of the Triple Alliance completely upset the balance of power in Europe. France became uneasy and began to seek allies. For a while, Bismarck's skillful diplomacy kept France isolated.

In 1888 Emperor William II came to the throne of Germany and, as you have read, soon dismissed Bismarck. William II reversed Bismarck's policies toward Great Britain and Russia. He entered the race for colonies with full force, demanding that Germany be given its "place in the sun." He also began a great naval buildup.

The Triple Entente. France's opportunity to gain allies came soon. Russia needed foreign money and sought a loan. The French hurried to lend the money and to take other steps to win Russia's friendship. In 1894 France and Russia formed an alliance ending their isolation. As a result, Bismarck's great fear of facing potential enemies on two sides became a reality.

The rapid growth of the German navy troubled the British. They tried to reach agreement with Germany to stop the naval race, but all efforts failed. Germany also began to interfere with some of Great Britain's imperial schemes. The goods of the rapidly expanding German industries created competition for the British in world markets.

Great Britain, too, began to look for allies. In 1904 the British and French were able to reach an agreement over how to control Morocco and Egypt. It was an **entente**—a friendly understanding or agreement between nations—rather than an alliance. Still, in order to counterbalance the Triple Alliance, there had to be an agreement between Great Britain and Russia as well. However, they were rivals in the Middle East, and so it was difficult for them to get together. With French help an understanding was finally reached in 1907. The resulting alignment was called the Triple Entente. Both France and Russia also had secret understandings with Italy, which meant that the Italians had a foot in both camps.

Dangers of the alliance system. By 1907 the powers of Europe faced each other in two potentially conflicting systems of alliances. These were the Triple Alliance—Germany, Austria-Hungary, and Italy—and the Triple Entente—Great Britain, France, and Russia (see map, this page).

As far as hopes for world peace were concerned, the alliance system was dangerous because it divided Europe into two armed camps. Should hostilities develop between any two rival powers, all six nations would become involved in the fighting, whether or not the original dispute concerned all of them. A minor quarrel could have serious consequences, as events in 1914 would prove.

The Balkan powder keg

The Balkans had long been a region of conflicts. This region was well named the "powder keg of Europe." Slavic nationalists in Serbia, which had become independent in 1878, hoped to make their country the center of a large Slavic state. It would include territories still under Ottoman rule as well as areas under Austrian control, including the provinces of Bosnia and Herzegovina. Landlocked Serbia hoped to obtain these two provinces because of their Slavic population and as a step toward obtaining an outlet on the Adriatic Sea.

The decision of the Congress of Berlin to make the two provinces protectorates of Austria was a severe disappointment to the Serbs. Austria's annexation of Bosnia and Herzegovina in 1908 infuriated them. Serbian nationalists distributed anti-Austrian propaganda to influence public opinion, and the rivalry between Serbs and Austrians became bitter and intense.

Russia supported Serbia's nationalistic goals, in the hope of assuming leadership of a Slavic league. Great Britain, however, opposed Pan-Slavism, the nationalist movement that pressed for the political and cultural unity of all Slavs. The

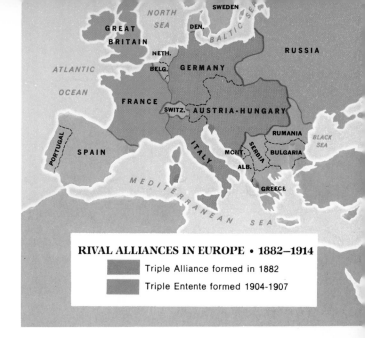

RIVAL ALLIANCES IN EUROPE • 1882–1914
- Triple Alliance formed in 1882
- Triple Entente formed 1904-1907

British distrusted Russian influence in the Balkans. They also feared for the safety of the Suez Canal—the main route to India and the most important British possession of that day.

Germany, a new source of friction. These rivalries made the Balkans an area of hatred and antagonisms. Then still another factor was introduced that made the situation even more explosive. The young, arrogant, and reckless Emperor William II of Germany began to push German ambitions in the Balkans. To strengthen the Triple Alliance and make up for the weakness of Italy, Germany sought new allies. It began negotiating to bring the Ottoman Empire into the Triple Alliance and thereby extend German influence in the Balkans.

Germany also planned to build a railroad from Berlin through the Balkans to Constantinople and on to Baghdad, near the Persian Gulf. This plan aroused many fears. The British regarded the proposed railroad as a threat to their Mediterranean-Red Sea "lifeline" to India. They feared that such a railroad would provide a better route to India than the British sea route through the Suez Canal. The Russians also were afraid. They feared that Germany would become a strong protector of the Ottoman Empire. This would decrease Russia's chances of gaining Constantinople and the Dardanelles and the Bosporus.

Germany secured the first concessions to construct the Berlin-to-Baghdad railroad in 1902. The

Preparations for a new kind of war

Europe slid into a World War in an extraordinary atmosphere of light-heartedness and confidence. Emperor William II of Germany and King George V of Great Britain (above right), were first cousins, grandsons of Queen Victoria. They met often in family reunions while their nations were becoming bitter rivals. At sea, especially, their nations maintained an expensive and furious competition. In 1906 the British launched the first battleship completely outfitted with heavy guns (above left). The Germans then responded with an all-out naval arms race. The stakes were high—control of the seas, of trade, and of territory. When, at last, war broke out, the soldiers left for the front in high spirits (right). Those who waved them on could hardly have guessed how quickly the confidence and joy would fade.

railroad was built in sections and was still in the early stages of construction in 1914.

Germany's actions in the Balkans complicated an already confused situation. The chief result was something Bismarck had carefully avoided—the strengthening of ties between Great Britain and Russia. Both countries were determined to resist German expansion in the Balkans. On the other hand, Austria feared Pan-Slavism and gained Germany as an ally in its opposition to Slavic nationalism.

Assassination at Sarajevo

The spark that touched off the explosion of the Balkan "powder keg" and led to war came on June 28, 1914. On that day the heir to the Austrian throne, Archduke Francis Ferdinand, and his wife were visiting Sarajevo (sah·rah·YEH·voh), the capital of Bosnia and Herzegovina, on a mission of good will. As the two drove through the streets in an open automobile, a young man rushed forward and fired a revolver, killing both the archduke and his wife.

The assassin was a member of one of the many secret societies of Serbian nationalists opposed to the Austrians. The incident brought to a head the long struggle between Serbia and Austria. The Austrian government was determined that the troublesome Serbs should be punished. But before Austria acted, it made sure of German support in case the Russians should try to protect the Slavs in Serbia. Germany promised to back Austria in anything Austria did. The Austrians then presented an **ultimatum** to the Serbian government. An ultimatum puts forth the final terms offered for a settlement. If the ultimatum is rejected, negotiations are ended.

War between Austria and Serbia

In its ultimatum, Austria demanded that the Serbian government officially condemn all anti-Austrian propaganda and suppress anti-Austrian publications and societies. Austria also wanted Serbia to eliminate all anti-Austrian books and teachers from Serbian schools, and dismiss any officials who had promoted anti-Austrian propaganda. In addition, it demanded that Austrian judges be allowed to conduct the trial of those accused of the crime at Sarajevo. All of these terms had to be accepted within 48 hours or Austria would declare war.

The reply of the Serbian government was mild and conciliating. Serbia accepted all the terms except the last two, but expressed willingness to submit the entire dispute to an international court recently created at The Hague. However, not counting on Austria to be reasonable, the Serbian government also ordered mobilization of all troops. In spite of the Serbian reply, Austria declared war on Serbia on July 28, after the time limit on the ultimatum had elapsed.

Mobilization of Europe

All attempts to get Austria to continue negotiations were in vain, especially as Germany continued to support Austria. Russia prepared to defend Serbia by mobilizing troops along the Russian-Austrian border. Expecting Germany to join Austria, Russia also sent troops to the German border. Germany immediately demanded that Russia cancel mobilization within 12 hours or face war.

Russia did not submit to this ultimatum. Germany declared war on Russia on August 1, 1914. Convinced that France was prepared to side with Russia and hoping to gain a military advantage by swift action, Germany declared war on France two days later. Germany also took steps that would bring Great Britain into the war.

The entry of Great Britain

The neutrality of Belgium had been guaranteed by the great powers in 1839, shortly after Belgian independence. Under the terms of this guarantee, Belgium agreed to stay out of any European war and not to help any of the **belligerents,** or warring nations. The other powers agreed not to attack it. However, Belgium's location was of great importance to Germany's military plans. It lies on the flat European coastal plain and has borders on both France and Germany (see map, page 597).

As soon as the German government had declared war on France, it sent an ultimatum to Belgium, demanding that German troops be permitted to cross Belgian territory. The British protested, insisting that the guarantee of neutrality be observed. The German foreign minister replied that surely Great Britain would not fight a war over "a scrap of paper." The Germans marched into Belgium on August 4, 1914, and Great Britain declared war on Germany later that day.

Other participants

Japan declared war later in August, siding with Great Britain in accordance with the terms of the Anglo-Japanese alliance of 1902, about which you will read in Chapter 26. Japan captured the German base of Tsingtao, China, and then the entire Shantung Peninsula.

Within six weeks after the assassination at Sarajevo, all the nations of the Triple Alliance and the Triple Entente were at war except Italy. The Italian government took the position that the Austrians and Germans were the aggressors. Therefore the Triple Alliance, a defensive treaty, did not require Italy to help them.

Italy remained neutral for nine months, during which time each side bargained desperately for its aid. Finally, secret treaties were drawn up among Great Britain, France, Russia, and Italy. These treaties divided the spoils of war in case of victory over Germany and Austria. In May 1915 Italy entered the war against its former allies, Germany and Austria.

In the meantime, Germany had been negotiating to win other allies. In November 1914 the Ottoman Empire had plunged into the war on the side of Germany and Austria. The Turks were not a strong military power, but they occupied a strategic position. Control of Constantinople and the Dardanelles bottled up Russia's Black Sea fleet. Furthermore, Russia lacked the industry to allow it to fight a modern war for very long without help from its allies. The Turks' decision made it impossible for such help to reach Russia through the Mediterranean and Black seas. Germany also made tempting offers to Bulgaria, and in October 1915 that nation entered the war on Germany's side.

CHECKUP

1. IDENTIFY: Nobel, Carnegie, militarism, entente, "powder keg of Europe," ultimatum, belligerents.

2. What was the Triple Alliance? What was the Triple Entente?

3. Describe the chief aims in the Balkans of the following nations: Serbia, Russia, Great Britain, and Germany.

4. What event can be said to have "lit the fuse" in 1914?

5. How did Belgium play a strategic role in the outbreak of World War I?

The nations of the world fought a new kind of war

The nations that went to war in the summer of 1914 thought that the conflict would be brief and decisive. Each side expected to win a quick victory. They were wrong. The fighting dragged on for four years. During that time it became clear that this was a war unlike any in history.

The opposing sides

Germany, Austria-Hungary, Bulgaria, and the Ottoman Empire became known as the Central Powers. Notice on the map on the opposite page that they formed an almost solid block of territory from the North Sea to the Persian Gulf. Their closeness to one another geographically was one advantage, and there were others. Germany was superbly prepared, and its army was excellently organized and trained. It was equipped with superior weapons and fought in enemy territory rather than on its own soil. In addition, its lines of communication with its allies were far better than those of its enemies.

Great Britain, France, Russia, and their partners in the war became known as the Allied Powers, or the Allies. Although they did not have the geographic advantages of the Central Powers, they had more soldiers and a greater industrial potential. They also controlled the seas. Therefore, they could obtain food and raw materials more easily and could blockade and attempt to starve the Central Powers.

As a result of diplomatic maneuvers, Greece and Rumania joined the Allies in 1916. Eventually there were 32 countries on the Allied side.

Innovations in warfare

World War I was a new kind of war, an industrialized war. Weapons were produced with the same efficient methods of mass production that industrialists had applied to other products. All the industries of the warring powers were organized to aid in the war effort.

One of the most important weapons of World War I was the machine gun. Largely because of its effectiveness, land armies often found any advance difficult and costly. To protect themselves from the machine gun's raking fire and from artillery bombardments, armies dug extensive systems of trenches. There they might live for weeks or even months.

Both sides used weapons that had never been widely used before. In 1916 the British introduced the tank, an armored vehicle mounted with guns.

Tanks enabled troops to break through enemy lines. Another new weapon was the airplane, only recently invented. Airplanes in the early 1900's were neither very maneuverable nor very fast. They were used primarily for observing troop movements and for dropping explosives.

Germany was the first nation to make extensive use of submarines. Its U-boats, as these undersea boats were called, did serious damage to Allied shipping. The Germans were also the first to use poison gas, which the Allies later employed.

Most European wars before this time had been fought by professional soldiers who worked simply for their pay and rations. World War I, on the contrary, was fought by armies of drafted citizens. Those who could not fight worked at home to help the war effort. Many women participated in the war effort by working in factories. To stir the patriotism of the people, governments made wide

WORLD WAR I IN EUROPE • 1914-1918

- Central Powers
- Allied Powers
- Neutral nations
- × Battle sites

use of propaganda. Newspapers and popular magazines portrayed the enemy as brutal and subhuman, while national aims and achievements were praised.

The war from 1914 to 1916

The German attack on France, launched through Belgium in August 1914, nearly succeeded. By September, German troops reached the Marne River, near Paris (see map, opposite). However, the French stood fast. French reserve troops were moved out from Paris by every means of transportation available, even city taxicabs. The French army counterattacked, the Germans were forced to withdraw, and Paris was saved.

The battle of the Marne, which lasted eight days, changed the entire nature of the war. Germany's hope of swift victory was ended, and the two sides settled in for a long fight. Both armies dug long lines of trenches on the so-called western front that stretched from the Swiss border through Germany, France, and Belgium to the shores of the North Sea.

On the eastern front the Russians completed mobilization much more quickly than the Germans had expected. One Russian army moved westward toward Budapest, the capital of Hungary. Another moved through East Prussia, threatening the important Baltic seaport of Danzig.

In late August a German force met this second Russian army in a fierce battle at Tannenberg, in East Prussia (see map, page 597). The Russians were driven back after suffering a humiliating defeat. Soon afterward the Germans launched an offensive in the east and drove the Russians completely out of Germany and eastward into Russian Poland.

The Gallipoli campaign. It was clear that Russia's greatest weakness was lack of equipment. In 1915 Great Britain and France decided on a daring venture to try to get aid to Russia. They would attempt to force their way through the Dardanelles and capture Constantinople.

It was thought at first that battleship bombardment of the fortifications of the Straits would result in the surrender of Constantinople. After five days of bombardment, troops were landed on the Gallipoli Peninsula to try to establish a foothold on the beach. The Turks, supervised by German officers, resisted stubbornly. After eight months of fighting, the Allied attempt was abandoned. The Gallipoli campaign cost the Allies a total of 145,000 men killed and wounded.

Naval warfare. Since the British had been unable to achieve quick victory on land, they decided to blockade the North Sea to keep merchant ships from reaching Germany. Originally the blockade was meant to keep raw materials for war equipment from the Germans. Gradually, however, the blockade became an attempt to starve the Germans and ruin their economy.

Germany also set up a naval blockade. Employing its fleet of submarines, Germany tried to force Great Britain to surrender by sinking the ships bringing food and munitions to the British. In May 1915, without warning, a German submarine sank the British passenger liner *Lusitania* off the coast of Ireland. Of the 1,200 lives lost, more than 100 were American. Woodrow Wilson, the American President, sharply warned Germany that another such incident would not be tolerated. For the next two years Germany used submarine warfare only sparingly. It did not wish to provoke the neutral Americans into entering the war on the side of the Allies.

In May 1916 the only large naval battle of the war was fought off the coast of Jutland, in the North Sea. Neither side could claim total victory, but the German navy retired into the Baltic Sea, where it remained until the end of the war.

The war of stalemate

By 1916 the war had reached a stalemate. No naval battles were expected while the German fleet remained in the Baltic Sea. On land there was also a deadlock. Each side learned that it could not break through the other's line of trenches. A small area of land on the western front changed hands over and over, costing each side thousands of lives. The conflict had become a war of attrition—a slow wearing-down process in which one side tries to outlast the other.

The most famous example of such warfare occurred at Verdun, in northeastern France (see map, opposite). The Germans attacked Verdun in February 1916. They did not expect to capture the town, but they thought the French would defend it. In this way Germany hoped to use the Verdun offensive to bleed the French army to death. However, after six months of fighting, the Germans gave up. At Verdun, Germany had lost 330,000 soldiers to France's 350,000.

The role of the United States

When World War I began in 1914, the United States immediately declared its neutrality. Many Americans followed the course of the war with interest, favoring one side or the other. However, almost everyone felt that the war was a European affair in which the United States should not become involved.

Trade with the belligerents. Nevertheless, the war soon affected the United States in many ways. As the strongest industrialized neutral nation, the United States became a supplier of food, raw materials, and munitions. The United States government insisted on the right of American citizens and business firms to trade with either side without interference. However, if an American ship were carrying **contraband**—war materials supplied by a neutral to a belligerent nation—the goods might be seized. The United States also insisted on the right of its citizens to travel in safety on ships of any nation, neutral or belligerent.

Because the United States was a neutral nation, its government could not lend money to either side. Yet no effort was made to stop banks, corporations, or private citizens from buying bonds of foreign governments or selling goods on credit.

At the beginning of the war, American investors and businesspeople were dealing with both sides. However, as the British blockade of Germany tightened, American trade became more and more one-sided. Soon the United States was trading only with the Allies, who were paying for most of the goods with money borrowed from American interests.

American entry into the war. British propaganda was far more successful in impressing Americans than was Germany's. Graphic stories of German atrocities—brutal crimes of war, often committed against defenseless civilians—stirred up American feelings. Many of these stories were untrue, but since the United States depended largely upon British sources for war news, they were widely believed.

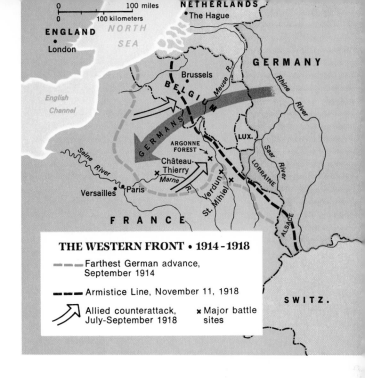

THE WESTERN FRONT • 1914-1918

- - - Farthest German advance, September 1914

▬▬▬ Armistice Line, November 11, 1918

Allied counterattack, July-September 1918   ✕ Major battle sites

Early in 1917 the issue of American involvement was settled. In January the German foreign minister, Alfred Zimmermann, sent a secret telegram to the German ambassador in Mexico. It instructed him to attempt to draw Mexico into the war on Germany's side. In exchange, Germany promised Mexico the return of some parts of the southwestern United States that had been lost by Mexico in 1848. The British intercepted the telegram, decoded it, and sent it on to Washington. Publication of the Zimmermann telegram in American newspapers enraged the public.

At the same time, Germany was faced with extreme food and munitions shortages. Hoping to bring the war to a conclusion before all hope of victory was gone, Germany decided to resume unrestricted submarine warfare. German submarines had orders to attack any naval vessel, enemy or neutral, found in a "war zone." As a result, sinkings of American ships became frequent.

Meanwhile, in March 1917 the autocratic czarist government of Russia was overthrown by a revolution whose leaders promised to establish a constitutional government. (You will read about this revolution in Chapter 25.) It was expected that Russia would have to withdraw from the war. One important result of the revolution was that, after the fall of the czar's government, all the major

(continued on page 602)

599

BOOTE HERAUS!

Fighting a World War

World War I changed the lives of ordinary people in the West enormously. It introduced more powerful weapons of destruction than the world had ever seen. Airplanes, which had only recently been invented, became the source of heroic legends. Fitted with machine guns and bombs, they were able to attack enemy planes and ground troops from above the battlefield (above left). German submarines, or U-boats (left), made it possible to launch surprise attacks on vital shipping from under the water. And more powerful artillery could bombard an unseen target from miles away, reducing a French town to rubble (below right) or a forest to a pile of sticks.

Hand-to-hand combat continued more traditional methods of warfare. Troops on both sides lived in foul, damp trenches (above, far right) for weeks, sometimes even months. Every now and again the soldiers would go "over the top" to try to capture the enemy's trenches.

With so many men in the military services, women had to take on additional roles. Posters urged them to be "the woman behind the man behind the gun" (above, near right). In France, women aided the military effort by working in munitions factories (above).

Joan of Arc Saved France

Haskell Coffin

W.S.S.
WAR SAVINGS STAMPS
ISSUED BY THE
UNITED STATES
GOVERNMENT

WOMEN OF AMERICA
SAVE YOUR COUNTRY
Buy WAR SAVINGS STAMPS
UNITED STATES TREASURY DEPARTMENT

Allied powers were now democracies. Americans would more readily accept a war in which the lines were drawn between democratic and nondemocratic countries.

On April 2, 1917, President Woodrow Wilson appeared before Congress to ask for a declaration of war. He said that "the world must be made safe for democracy." On April 6, Congress voted, by an overwhelming majority, to declare war on Germany and enter the war on the side of the Allies.

It was not until the spring and summer of 1918 that troops of the newly drafted and trained American army arrived in Europe in large numbers. Meanwhile, the hard-pressed Allied troops had to hold on. American entry into the war, however, gave the Allies a needed morale boost.

CHECKUP

1. IDENTIFY: U-boats, *Lusitania,* war of attrition, contraband, Zimmermann.

2. LOCATE: Marne River, Tannenberg, Gallipoli Peninsula, Jutland, Verdun.

3. Name the principal Central Powers and Allied Powers. What advantages did each side have?

4. What were some important new weapons and military techniques introduced in World War I?

5. How was the United States as a neutral power affected by World War I? What factors led to its entry into the war?

3

After defeating the Central Powers, the Allies drafted peace terms

President Wilson's statement of America's aim in entering the war—to make the world "safe for democracy"—was lofty and idealistic. Late in 1917, however, a serious blow hurt the Allies' morale. In November there was a second Russian revolution in which the Communist Party seized control. In March 1918, in the Russian town of Brest-Litovsk, the new Russian leaders signed a separate peace treaty with Germany. Meanwhile they published the terms of the secret treaties signed by the Allies when Italy entered the war.

The revelation that their governments were fighting for bits of land made the war seem shoddy to many people on the Allied side.

The Fourteen Points

The British Prime Minister, David Lloyd George, tried to undo the bad impression left by these revelations. He stated more idealistic aims in a speech to Parliament. However, it was President Wilson who best expressed what many people thought the Allied aims should be. In a speech to Congress in January 1918 Wilson announced his **Fourteen Points.** There were six points of a general nature (points 1–5 and 14) and eight points that dealt with specific countries and regions, such as Russia, Belgium, Alsace and Lorraine, and the Balkans.

The six general proposals may be summarized as follows:

(1) No secret treaties. All treaties should be openly negotiated and all made public.

(2) Freedom of the seas for all nations, in peace and war.

(3) Removal of all economic barriers or tariffs; equal opportunity for trade among nations.

(4) Reduction of national armaments "to the lowest point consistent with domestic safety."

(5) Fair adjustment of all colonial claims. The interests of the people of a region were to be considered equally with those of the nation claiming title to the territory.

(14) "A general association of nations," which would guarantee political independence and protection to large and small states alike.

The Fourteen Points caught the imagination of people everywhere and raised the morale of Allied troops. Copies dropped behind the German lines made the German people more willing to surrender. Some historians feel, however, that Wilson made one serious mistake. He did not use his influence during the war, when it was greatest, to get the Allies to agree definitely to the Fourteen Points.

Defeat of the Central Powers

The collapse of the Russians allowed the Germans to withdraw troops from the eastern front. This enabled the Germans to concentrate their efforts on a huge offensive in the west during the spring and summer of 1918. It was their last desperate gamble to break through the Allied lines, capture Paris, and end the war before the Americans could turn the tide.

The German offensive of 1918 lasted until mid-July. It failed by a very narrow margin. In May the Germans reached the Marne River, only 37 miles (59 kilometers) from Paris. By this time, however, more than 250,000 Americans were landing in France every month.

Under a newly organized joint command, headed by the French general Ferdinand Foch (FOHSH), the Allied forces stopped the Germans in June at Château-Thierry (shah·TOH·tyeh·REE).

In July the Allies began to counterattack. A final Allied push in September at St. Mihiel (SAN mee·YEL) and in the Argonne Forest proved successful (see map, page 599). The German armies were forced back to the borders of Germany.

At the same time, things were going badly for the Central Powers in the Middle East and the Balkans. Bulgaria, seeing little hope for victory or for aid from its allies, surrendered first, in September. The Turks soon followed, asking for peace. By November a revolution in Austria-Hungary brought the old empire to an end. Austria and Hungary formed separate governments.

In Germany, the government of William II, the Kaiser, also fell as a result of the war. Woodrow

connections

Codes and Ciphers

Codes are secret ways of communicating, and they have been used for thousands of years. The ancient Egyptians flew code flags on their ships, and in medieval Europe the Beggars Association marked houses with signs meaning "food" or "vicious dog." Anyone knowing the key to a code, whether flags, signs, or smoke signals, can understand the message.

Most often we think of codes as involving secret messages, danger, and spying activities in wartime (right). The most common way to devise codes for secret messages is by the use of ciphers. A cipher is a letter, number, or symbol that replaces the normal alphabet in a coded message. Since the Japanese and the Chinese languages do not use alphabets, they cannot create ciphers. But all other languages have found this the best method of sending secret, coded messages.

By the time of World War I, coded communication had become so important that the British decided to create a special department of cryptanalysts or cryptographers. These were people who studied ways of solving codes and ciphers. The department operated in the Office of Naval Intelligence and helped the war effort significantly. For example, the British captured the keys to two German codes: the book of naval codes and the official diplomatic cipher system. This enabled them to read a number of vital secret messages and also helped them to figure out how other German codes worked.

In modern times, computers have become the main tools for cryptographers. Although they are now much more complicated, codes and ciphers remain an essential form of communication.

Wilson had said that he would deal only with a government that truly represented the German people. Many Germans, wishing to end the war, looked upon the Kaiser as an obstacle to peace. On November 9, the Kaiser was forced to abdicate. A republic was proclaimed, and two days later the war ended.

On November 11, 1918, the chancellor of the new German Republic signed an **armistice**—an agreement to stop fighting until a treaty could be drawn up. According to the terms of the armistice, Germany had to cancel the humiliating peace treaty it had forced the Russians to sign. It had to surrender all its submarines and a large part of its surface fleet. In addition, it had to release all war prisoners and turn over munitions that might make additional fighting possible.

Costs of the war

The costs of World War I stagger the imagination. Each of the belligerent nations suffered enormous and lasting effects. Reliable estimates indicate that over 8 million people lost their lives in battle. Many more were wounded, and millions were crippled for life.

Militarily, Russia was the most severely hit, losing more than 2 million people. Germany lost almost that many, and France and its colonies lost nearly 1½ million. Austria-Hungary counted 1¼ million dead after the war, and Great Britain almost 1 million. American lives lost numbered 115,000.

For the first time in history, the loss of life among the civilian population was almost as great as that among the armed forces. Naval blockades, artillery and aerial bombardments, famine, disease, and political violence all took their toll. The destruction of property was appalling. One historian has estimated that the total cost to all the warring powers was $400 billion.

The effects of the war on attitudes and ideas were no less far-reaching. These effects will be examined in Chapter 25.

The peace conference at Paris

After the armistice in November 1918, the Allies faced the task of arranging peace terms. President Wilson had written and spoken of a peace conference in which both sides would be represented and which would write a treaty fair to all. However, the war had caused much bitterness and had been costly in terms both of human lives and of property. The Allies had won the war, and in spite of Wilson's protests, it was the Allies alone who wrote the terms of peace.

Delegates of the victorious nations met in Paris in January 1919. Almost all of the Allied Powers sent representatives. Russia, which was now in the midst of a civil war, was the only Allied Power not invited.

The defeated powers were not represented at Paris. The victors decided to work out the terms among themselves. They agreed to call in representatives of the defeated powers only to accept the terms of the treaties.

The Allies decided that a separate treaty should be written for each of the defeated Central Powers. Since Austria and Hungary now had separate governments, five different treaties were to be drawn up. Technically, the work of writing the treaties was done by the representatives of all the victorious nations. In fact, however, the work had been done in advance, behind the scenes, by the representatives of the four most powerful Allies—Great Britain, France, the United States, and Italy. The leaders of the Big Four, as they were called, were Prime Minister David Lloyd George of Great Britain; Premier Georges Clemenceau (klem·un·SOH) of France; President Woodrow Wilson of the United States; and Premier Vittorio Orlando of Italy.

Problems facing the peacemakers

By 1919 the political situation in much of Europe was confused. Three great empires—Germany, Austria-Hungary, and Russia—were no longer hereditary monarchies, but republics. A fourth empire, that of the Ottoman Turks, was tottering. Nationalist groups pressed their claims in many areas of Europe—Russia, Germany, Austria, Hungary, and the Ottoman Empire. Each group wanted independence, self-government, and unity within the borders of a single nation. Nationalism was strong in colonial possessions, too.

Territorial claims. The victorious nations had many territorial demands that were difficult to reconcile. France wanted, above all, security from

Duchamp and the Dadaists

World War I raged violently for four years and when it ended, more than 10 million civilians and $8\frac{1}{2}$ million soldiers had lost their lives. Such devastation did not go unnoticed in the art world. Artists expressed their anger and bitterness over the war by producing anti-art, works that mocked the values of a society that could have supported the war. This school of art was called Dada. Some critics refer to Dadaistic works as non-art.

Marcel Duchamp's painted glass is an example of Dada art. Its seemingly meaningless design served to criticize the war-mad world. Even its title is Dadaistic, or nonsensical: "To be looked at (from the other side of the glass) with one eye close to, for almost an hour." When this piece and others by Duchamp were accidentally cracked, the artist seemed not to care. He said the fracture lines actually enhanced his initial design. Perhaps Duchamp, like other Dadaists, felt the war had cracked the world beyond repair.

German attack in the future. It insisted on the return of the regions of Alsace and Lorraine, which had been guaranteed in the Fourteen Points. In addition, it demanded that the French boundary be extended to the Rhine River so that France would gain the Rhineland. This was the territory on the west bank of the Rhine that had formerly belonged to Germany. France also demanded the valley of the Saar River, which had valuable deposits of coal.

Italy claimed the Tyrol region and the city of Trieste in accordance with the secret treaties it had made in 1915. It also claimed Fiume, although this city had not been promised in the secret treaties. Lloyd George, Wilson, and Clemenceau were willing to give in on the Tyrol region. However, Wilson steadfastly opposed giving Fiume to Italy. The controversy over this point became so bitter that Orlando left the conference and went home in disgust. The Big Four then became the Big Three.

Great Britain and Belgium also made demands. Great Britain wanted all of Germany's African colonies. It also insisted that the German navy be destroyed and that Germany be prohibited from building warships. Belgium requested two small portions of German territory along its borders.

During the war, Japan had occupied the German-held Marshall, Caroline, and Mariana islands as well as Tsingtao and most of the Shantung Peninsula. It now demanded permanent ownership of all these regions. Japan also asked that the powers recognize its "special position" in China. This meant, in effect, that in any further seizure of Chinese territory, Japan was to have the first choice and largest share. There was a bitter fight over the Japanese demands. Japan threatened to follow Italy's example and withdraw from the conference. To keep Japan at the conference, Wilson gave in on the Shantung Peninsula.

Reparations and peacekeeping. In the west the war had been fought mainly in France and Belgium. The destruction it caused brought up the problem of **reparations**—payment for war damages. Who should pay for restoring the land? Did war damages include damage to property only? Or should reparations also include pensions to wounded veterans, widows, and orphans?

Finally, there was the problem of a world organization to maintain peace. A League of Nations was the last of Wilson's Fourteen Points. While it had widespread appeal, many European political leaders were quite skeptical about its chances for success.

The peace: justice or vengeance?

Very early in the conference, two conflicting viewpoints appeared. The British, French, and Italian governments had appeared to support the Fourteen Points. Yet they had never really given up the aims stated in the secret treaties—to divide the territories taken from the Central Powers among themselves after the war. Thus, the idea of a "peace of justice" came to be represented by the Fourteen Points, whereas the idea of a "peace of vengeance" was represented by the terms of the secret treaties.

Wilson believed that it was essential to write a "peace of justice." Unless all countries, including the defeated powers, were treated justly, the treaties would only stir up new hatred and desire for revenge. In time, he thought, these would surely lead to another war.

Many people disagreed. The war had left bitterness, hatred, and a longing for revenge. Among the victors there was a strong feeling that the defeated must be taught a lesson. Only by harsh treatment, they reasoned, could Germany and Austria be taught the penalty for starting a war. Some went further and argued that Germany should be divided up and disarmed completely. This feeling was especially strong in France and Belgium.

CHECKUP

1. IDENTIFY: Lloyd George, Foch, armistice, Big Four, Clemenceau, Orlando, reparations.

2. LOCATE: Brest-Litovsk, Château-Thierry, St. Mihiel, Saar River, Tyrol, Trieste, Fiume.

3. What were the six general proposals of Wilson's Fourteen Points? What effect did the Fourteen Points have?

4. Describe the territorial demands made after World War I by the following nations: France, Italy, Great Britain, Belgium, Japan.

5. Why did Wilson believe in a "peace of justice"? Why did others oppose this belief?

The peace treaties created a "new Europe"

As you have read, separate treaties were made with each of the Central Powers at the Paris peace conference. The most famous was the Versailles Treaty with Germany.

The Versailles Treaty

In May 1919 representatives of the new German Republic were called in, presented with a peace treaty, and told to sign it. The Germans complained bitterly that the treaty did not follow the Fourteen Points. They objected especially to two features: (1) The treaty made Germany admit that it alone was guilty of starting the war and therefore must pay reparations. (2) Since the total amount of reparations had not been agreed upon by the victors, Germany was being asked to sign a "blank check." In spite of their protest, the Germans had no choice but to sign. This they did on June 28 in the famous palace built by Louis XIV at Versailles, near Paris.

Under the Versailles Treaty, Germany agreed to pay $5 billion in reparations within two years and to pay an unnamed sum later. In 1921 the Allies set the total bill at $33 billion. The Treaty also provided for the formation of the League of Nations and for numerous territorial adjustments.

Germany lost considerable territory along its northern, western, and eastern borders (see map, opposite). These losses included Alsace and Lorraine, which were returned to France. Germany agreed not to fortify the Rhineland, which was to be occupied by Allied troops for an unspecified period of time. The Saar Valley was to be administered by the League of Nations for 15 years. During that time all of the coal mined in the area was to go to France in partial payment of reparations. At the end of 15 years, the people of the region were to vote on whether to continue under the League, to become part of France, or to rejoin Germany.

A large area was given back to the restored nation of Poland. This region, called the Polish

Corridor, cut East Prussia off from the rest of Germany and gave Poland an outlet to the Baltic Sea. Danzig, on the northern coast of the Corridor, became a free city, administered by the League of Nations.

In addition, Germany lost all of its overseas colonies in Asia, Africa, and the Pacific. They were divided among Japan, Great Britain, Australia, and New Zealand, who were to supervise them on behalf of the League of Nations.

Germany had to abolish conscription and was forbidden to maintain a reserve army. The manufacture of heavy artillery, tanks, military airplanes, and poison gas was forbidden. There were to be no battleships larger than 10,000 tons and no submarines at all. Thus the treaty makers tried to make sure that Germany would be a peace-keeping nation. However, although the provisions regarding Germany were strict, the means of enforcing them were not.

Austria-Hungary

As you have read, the Dual Monarchy split in two as the war was ending. Separate treaties, therefore, were arranged with Austria in September 1919 and with Hungary in June 1920.

Austria was recognized as an independent republic. It lost the southern Tyrol and the city of Trieste to Italy. The new Austrian nation had 6 million people, 2 million of whom lived in its capital, Vienna. It was said that Austria became "a capital without a country." It could not grow enough food for its people, nor supply its indus-

607

tries with adequate raw materials. Austria rapidly sank into a state of financial crisis and poverty.

Hungary lost a great deal of territory. It became landlocked, and although it remained primarily an agricultural nation, it could produce barely enough food to feed its citizens.

Two new nations were created out of the old Dual Monarchy. One was Czechoslovakia, in central Europe. It included the Slavic peoples called Czechs, Slovaks, and Ruthenians. The other was Yugoslavia, in the western Balkans (see map, page 607). It united the old kingdoms of Serbia and Montenegro, the former provinces of Bosnia and Herzegovina, and part of the Adriatic coast.

Bulgaria and the Ottoman Empire

Like the other Central Powers, Bulgaria was penalized by the victors. According to the terms of the peace treaty, signed in 1919, it was reduced in size and lost its outlet to the Aegean Sea, which went to Greece. The Ottoman Empire, however, paid an even higher price for being on the losing side. The treaty, signed in 1920, resulted in a great loss of territory. Constantinople and the Dardanelles and Bosporus, however, remained in Turkish hands, but were to be unfortified and controlled by an international commission.

Several new nations—Palestine, Trans-Jordan, and Syria (including Lebanon)—were eventually created out of former Turkish territory along the eastern Mediterranean Sea (see map, page 607). Turkish territory still farther east became the country of Iraq. None of these countries, however, was independent. Palestine, Trans-Jordan, and Iraq were administered by Great Britain under the supervision of the League of Nations. Syria and Lebanon were to be administered by France. In Arabia, the kingdom of Hejaz was recognized as independent.

New problems after the war

By altering political boundaries and territories, the peace settlements also created some serious problems. Four new nations—Finland, Estonia, Latvia, and Lithuania—were formed along the Baltic Sea, in what was previously Russian territory. In 1918 they had declared their independence from Russia, and their sovereignty was recognized by the victorious powers at the end of the war. Much of the territory of the new Poland also came from Russia. In addition, Russia lost the province of Bessarabia, in the southwest, to Rumania.

In fact, Russia, a former Allied Power, actually lost more territory than Germany did. There were two reasons for this: (1) Russia had withdrawn from the war late in 1917 and signed a separate treaty with Germany in the spring of 1918. (2) The Western European powers feared that the Russian Revolution, in which the Communists were victorious, would spread westward. It was therefore decided to isolate Russia from Western Europe by creating a ring of buffer states around Russia's western boundaries. Such harsh treatment of a former Allied Power seemed bound to cause trouble.

Another problem grew out of the attempt by the treaty makers to unite members of each European nationality under their own government. This did not always succeed. For example, there were 250,000 German-speaking Austrians in the Tyrol, which was partly under Italian rule. There were Germans in Danzig and the Polish Corridor. There were also 3 million former Austrian subjects—a German-speaking group called Sudeten Germans—in Czechoslovakia.

These national minorities—people living under governments controlled by foreign nationalities—presented a problem. Therefore, all five treaties contained clauses in which each government pledged to treat fairly any such group within its borders. Each minority group was guaranteed certain rights, to be protected by the League of Nations.

The League of Nations

In helping to draft the peace settlements, President Wilson had made several compromises with the ideals he had stated in his Fourteen Points. He realized that the treaties failed in many respects to provide a "peace of justice." He consoled himself, however, with the thought that the new League of Nations would be able to remedy the injustices inflicted by various treaties.

While the treaty settlements were being worked out, a special commission, including Wilson,

Making the peace

The ending of the terrible "Great War" of 1914-1918 brought feelings of immense relief and hope. The final peace treaty was signed in France in the magnificent Hall of Mirrors at the palace at Versailles. Statesmen and politicians gathered for the ceremony around the three central leaders of the victorious Allies (above). At the center of the table were President Woodrow Wilson of the United States, Premier Georges Clemenceau of France (with the bushy mustache), and British Prime Minister David Lloyd George.

The destruction in Europe had been devastating, as shown by the symbolic drawing of Wilson and Uncle Sam standing in the ruins of the cathedral of Reims (above left). But the joy of returning home to peace was overwhelming. The ships that brought cheerful American soldiers back to the United States were crammed to overflowing (left).

wrote the covenant, or constitution, of the League of Nations. This covenant was adopted by the Paris conference and was included as part of the Versailles Treaty.

Organization. According to the covenant, the League of Nations had two main aims: (1) to promote international cooperation, and (2) to maintain peace by the peaceful settlement of disputes and by a reduction of armaments. The League was to include all independent sovereign nations. It was to function through three main agencies: an Assembly, a Council, and a Secretariat. The League was to work closely with a related but independent body, the Permanent Court of International Justice, or World Court, located in The Hague.

The Assembly was to be a sort of lower house. It was to be composed of representatives of all member nations. Regardless of size, each nation was to have one vote. The Council, an upper house, was to be composed of nine member nations (later increased to fifteen). Its five permanent members were to be Great Britain, France, Italy, Japan, and the United States. The additional seats on the Council were to be filled by rotation from among the smaller nations. The Secretariat, a staff composed of expert advisers and clerical workers, was to manage the routine business of the League.

Peacekeeping measures. The League of Nations provided a way to deal with the many problems created by imperialism in so-called "backward" regions of the world. Until the people of an area were considered ready for independence, the League took the area in trust—that is, took over responsibility for it. The League assigned the area as a **mandate** to be administered by the government of an advanced nation. The administering nation was pledged to prepare the people for independent self-government. It was also required to make annual reports to the League concerning its progress.

The members of the League of Nations accepted an obligation not to resort to war. They promised to submit any disputes to arbitration. Arbitration could be carried on by the World Court, or by special boards or commissions set up for a particular case.

The covenant also provided that if a member nation broke its pledge to submit to arbitration, or

went to war, the League could impose penalties on it. Possible penalties included breaking diplomatic relations, imposing economic sanctions—the refusal to trade with the offending member nation—or blockades. The use of military force was considered a last resort.

Although the League of Nations had been Wilson's idea, the United States never became a member of the organization. Because the covenant was a part of the Versailles Treaty, its adoption depended on ratification of the treaty by the United States Senate. Some senators disapproved of the League itself, while others wanted changes in the peace settlement. Because of this opposition, and Wilson's unwillingness to make any compromises, the treaty—and thus the League of Nations—failed to win Senate approval. Since the Versailles Treaty was never ratified, the United States technically remained at war with the Central Powers until 1921, when it signed separate treaties with them.

Thus the League of Nations began without the membership and support of the United States, by then the most powerful nation in the world. President Wilson prophetically stated that if the United States did not join, a war would be fought again.

The new organization held its first meeting at Geneva in November 1920. Forty-two member nations were represented. Germany was not allowed to join the League until 1926, and Russia did not become a member until 1934. By 1935 there were 62 members.

CHECKUP

1. LOCATE: Polish Corridor, Danzig, Vienna, Czechoslovakia, Yugoslavia, Finland, Estonia, Latvia, Lithuania, Bessarabia.

2. Summarize the provisions of the Versailles Treaty concerning (a) reparations, (b) Germany's colonies, and (c) German military power.

3. Name six nations that lost territory and six nations that gained territory as a result of the peace treaties. What new nations were created in Europe?

4. How did the peace settlements create problems with regard to Russia and national minorities?

5. What were the aims of the League of Nations? its main agencies? What provisions did it make for peace-keeping?

CHAPTER REVIEW

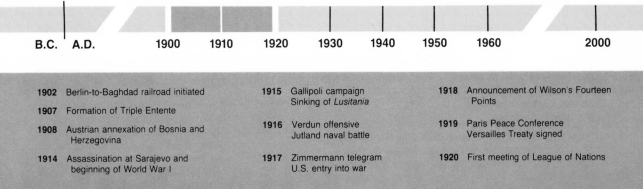

| B.C. | A.D. | 1900 | 1910 | 1920 | 1930 | 1940 | 1950 | 1960 | 2000 |

1902 Berlin-to-Baghdad railroad initiated

1907 Formation of Triple Entente

1908 Austrian annexation of Bosnia and Herzegovina

1914 Assassination at Sarajevo and beginning of World War I

1915 Gallipoli campaign
Sinking of *Lusitania*

1916 Verdun offensive
Jutland naval battle

1917 Zimmermann telegram
U.S. entry into war

1918 Announcement of Wilson's Fourteen Points

1919 Paris Peace Conference
Versailles Treaty signed

1920 First meeting of League of Nations

CHAPTER SUMMARY

The suspicions of one another among European nations intensified in the early 1900's. This was a result of strong national feelings, the spread of imperialism, growing militarist buildups, and a system of rival alliances. In 1914, when trouble erupted in the particularly unstable region of the Balkans, the tensions exploded. The major powers turned to fighting to resolve their differences. Within a few months almost all the nations of Europe, plus Japan, were at war.

Everyone expected the conflict to be over quickly, with a few battles deciding the outcome. Instead, the struggle dragged on for four years, as the two sides faced each other from lines of trenches. Even new military inventions—the machine gun, the tank, the submarine, the airplane, and poison gas—did not bring the war to a quick end.

The turning point seemed to come with the entry of the United States into the war. In 1917 Germany, the main combatant for the Central Powers, was running short of munitions and food. In early 1918, following the Russian Revolution, a peace agreement was made between Russia and Germany. As a result, Russia, one of the main Allied Powers, was out of the war. The Americans provided the fresh troops and new resources that helped to defeat the Central Powers.

Although the war ended in 1918, the problems it caused continued to plague governments for years. There had been huge losses of life and property, and many problems remained unresolved. New national groups demanded recognition, especially in eastern Europe. The victors wanted to punish the losers. There was unrest in Germany, Russia, and the former Austro-Hungarian and Ottoman territories.

To try to stabilize the situation, the Allies attempted new political arrangements. Woodrow Wilson's "Fourteen Points" offered idealistic goals that might have created a more peaceful and lasting framework among nations after the war. At the peace negotiations at Versailles, however, many of these goals were forgotten as the Allies sought to collect reparations for their wartime losses and to gain additional territory.

Only one of Wilson's major aims was realized. In 1920, 42 nations founded the League of Nations. This was an attempt to establish an international organization that would help keep the peace and settle disputes among countries. However, the United States did not join, and the League's efforts were thus crippled from the start. The 1920's were to witness new tensions and uncertainties in Europe and in other parts of the world.

CHECKING WHAT YOU KNOW

1. Match each term at the left with a definition at the right.

   a. entente
   b. contraband
   c. militarism
   d. belligerent
   e. mandate
   f. reparations
   g. armistice
   h. ultimatum

   1. territory being prepared for independence
   2. payment for war damages
   3. friendly agreement between nations
   4. final terms offered for a settlement
   5. agreement to stop a war
   6. war materials supplied by a neutral to a belligerent nation
   7. glorification of armed strength
   8. warring nation

2. What was the immediate cause of World War I? What were four underlying causes?

3. President Wilson believed World War I would be the "war to end all wars." What ideals in the Fourteen Points worked toward this goal? What obstacles blocked Wilson's efforts to carry out his plan?

4. How did peace negotiations readjust the balance of power in the world? Did these changes correct the causes of World War I or ignore them? Explain.

PRACTICING YOUR SKILLS

1. **Using maps.** Study the map on page 607. Which of the Central Powers lost the most territory as a result of World War I? the least? Which Allied Power lost territory? Based on evidence in this map, what new problems might have been created by changing the political boundaries of Europe?

2. **Using pictures.** As you learned in this chapter, governments used propaganda to encourage citizens to support the war effort. Turn to the poster on page 601. What techniques or symbols used might arouse a sense of patriotism? To what other emotions does this poster seem to appeal?

3. **Analyzing information.** In assessing World War I, Prime Minister Lloyd George once commented that ". . . no one at the head of affairs quite meant war. It was something into which they glided, or rather staggered and stumbled." Do you agree with this interpretation of the war? What evidence in the chapter supports your answer?

RELATING PAST TO PRESENT

1. Review the following causes of World War I: militarism, imperialism, international alliances, and nationalism. Which of these forces are still present in the world? Clip newspaper or magazine articles that support your answer.

2. Before World War I, the Balkan region was known as the "powder keg" of Europe. Why was it given this name? Are there any similar trouble spots in the world today? If so, what actions might be taken to keep them defused? What can be done to prevent another Balkan situation from occurring?

3. In 1899 and again in 1907, several nations participated in disarmament conferences held at The Hague. Using the *Readers' Guide to Periodical Literature*, locate articles about recent armament talks between the United States and the Soviet Union. Are any of the obstacles to disarmament the same as those faced in the late 1800's and early 1900's? Are any unique to the present? Explain.

INVESTIGATING FURTHER

1. While troops bogged down in the muddy trenches of Europe, other battles were taking place in the skies. Write a short report on developments in air warfare at this time. Also investigate the pilots who flew these missions, such as Baron von Richthofen (the "Red Baron"), Eddie Rickenbacker, or members of the Lafayette Escadrille. One source for your report is Quentin Reynolds, *They Fought for the Sky: The Dramatic Story of the First War in the Air* (Holt, Rinehart and Winston).

2. In 1915 women from 12 countries took part in the International Conference of Women held at The Hague. The delegate from the United States was Emily Green Balch, a college professor and prominent leader in the women's movement for peace. Using encyclopedias and books in your library, prepare a report on Balch and the meeting she attended.

3. Read one of the following novels, and present a book report to the class: Ernest Hemingway, *A Farewell to Arms* (Scribner); Erich Maria Remarque, *All Quiet on the Western Front* (Fawcett); Willa Cather, *One of Ours* (Random House). Note the author's point of view on war. How does it compare with the idealism expressed by President Wilson at the start of World War I?

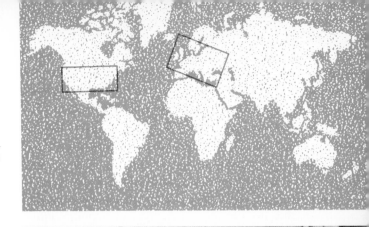

CHAPTER

25

(1917–1936)

The Western Nations Faced Many Tensions After World War I

World War I, according to Woodrow Wilson, was fought to make the world "safe for democracy." In 1919 it seemed as if this aim had been achieved. The Western democracies had won the war. The new nations created at the Paris peace conference each established democratic governments. Older nations that underwent governmental change during this period also announced democratic goals.

It soon seemed, however, that many of the new governments had been set up more in imitation of Western governmental systems than out of any deep devotion to democratic principles. Most of the people who administered them had no experience in democratic government. Social and economic troubles multiplied, and serious signs of weakness began to appear.

Even the older and more experienced democracies felt the strain of the postwar years. Although Great Britain, France, and the United States remained democracies, important changes occurred in these nations as well. Democracy came under severe pressure in Europe, particularly when economic difficulties arose in the 1920's and 1930's. In the United States, the leading Western democracy, the government used new powers and policies to overcome the problems caused by the spreading economic crisis.

In some nations, the postwar situation led to impatience with the democratic process itself as a means of solving problems. The result was a will-

A farmer in the 1930's facing hard times

ingness to accept totalitarian regimes—highly centralized governments that allowed no opposition and held total control. These governments seemed to offer an escape from the instability and uncertainty of the period.

Politics was not the only aspect of life reflecting a sense of uneasiness after the war. In literature and the arts there was a reaction against traditional forms. Writers and painters, dismayed by World War I and its aftermath, sought to disturb and unsettle their audiences. In popular culture people were drawn to escapism and sensational exploits. Tragically, the 1920's and 1930's would prove to be only the prelude to a new and even more devastating World War.

THE CHAPTER SECTIONS

1. The Russian Revolution ended the czarist regime

2. The 1920's witnessed political tensions in much of Europe

3. Fascist dictatorships were established in Italy and Germany

4. A worldwide depression began in the United States

5. Ideas and the arts reflected the uneasiness of the postwar era

1

The Russian Revolution ended the czarist regime

Russia, which had been torn by revolutionary disturbances throughout the 1800's, faced continuing problems in the early 1900's. The Revolution of 1905, about which you read in Chapter 22, had brought about changes that were more apparent than real. The elected legislative body, the Duma, had little power. The czar remained an almost absolute ruler. The Russian people were denied the democratic rights and civil liberties that they had been promised. Citizens who sought further reforms joined secret societies, which often expressed their members' frustration in violence.

There were also grave economic problems.

Russia was far behind Western European countries in its industrial development and agricultural methods. For example, in 1914 only 1½ percent of Russia's people were industrial workers, compared with 40 percent of Great Britain's population. For their part, the peasants in Russia were unhappy with the results of their emancipation. Debts, taxes, and rents kept the Russian peasants in poverty.

Russia in World War I

World War I exposed Russia's weaknesses. There were not enough railroads or good roads. Russian industry could not adequately equip or supply the army. When the Ottoman Empire entered the war on the side of the Central Powers, Russia was cut off from outside supplies.

Nevertheless, for over three years, Russian troops held back more than half the troops of the Central Powers. During this period, over 2 million Russians were killed, 5 million were wounded or crippled, and more than 2 million were taken prisoner by the enemy. If the Russians had not fought so well, the Allies might have lost the war.

By the spring of 1917, the Russians were weary of hardships and disheartened by the appalling casualties they had suffered. They had lost all faith in their government and Czar Nicholas II. Strikes and street demonstrations broke out in Petrograd, as St. Petersburg had been called since 1914. The czar ordered them put down by force. When the Duma demanded reforms in the government, Nicholas ordered the Duma dissolved.

In the past the government had always been able to use the army against disturbances such as those in Petrograd. Now, however, the soldiers joined the rioters. The Duma, encouraged by the army's disobedience, refused the czar's order to disband.

On March 15, 1917, unable to control his subjects or his army, Nicholas II abdicated. He and his family were executed the following year. The 300-year-old Romanov dynasty had ended.

The Bolsheviks

A liberal provisional government was set up to rule Russia until a constitutional assembly could be elected to decide upon a permanent system of government. While the provisional government tried to restore order, a rival force was working for change in Russia. It was known as the Petrograd Soviet of Workers' and Soldiers' Deputies. (*Soviet* is the Russian word for council.)

The Petrograd Soviet had been quickly organized when disorders began in Russia. It was modeled on similar organizations that had participated in the Revolution of 1905. The Petrograd Soviet was composed chiefly of moderate socialists, called Mensheviks. It also contained a small number of radical socialists, known as Bolsheviks. Most of the prominent Bolsheviks lived outside of Russia, having been exiled in 1905.

Other soviets similar to the one in Petrograd were soon established throughout Russia. They won much support, for their program was more attractive than that of the provisional government. They called for immediate peace, land reforms, and the turning over of factories to the workers.

Lenin. The leader of the Bolsheviks was N. Lenin. He was born Vladimir Ilyich Ulyanov, but assumed the name N. Lenin as a young man.

Lenin was intelligent and forceful. He came from the ranks of the lower nobility and had studied law. After his older brother had been executed by the czarist police as a revolutionary, Lenin became a revolutionary himself.

On April 16, 1917, Lenin returned to Russia from exile in Switzerland. His first act was to insist that all governing power be turned over to the soviets.

Lenin was a radical socialist, but he favored a modified Marxism, partly because of the conditions that existed in Russia. Lenin believed that in Russia the forces of history might not move in the direction Marx had predicted, since there was little industry and only a small working class. Therefore, he advocated the use of a small group of devoted Marxists. This group would train the workers to become a revolutionary force. Lenin's adaptation of Marxism formed the basis of what we now know as Russian communism. His slogan, "Land, Peace, and Bread," reached the heart of the masses.

On November 7, 1917, the Bolsheviks overthrew the provisional government and seized control of Russia. This revolution is often called the second Russian revolution (the first having been in March), or the Bolshevik Revolution. The following spring, in 1918, the Bolsheviks renamed themselves the Communist Party.

Civil war

As you have read, the communists signed separate peace treaties with each of the Central Powers in the spring of 1918 at Brest-Litovsk. Russia was anxious to make peace on any terms, since its army was exhausted from three years of bitter fighting. The treaties were harsh toward Russia, and it lost a sizable amount of territory.

The new regime then turned its attention to internal problems. The communists faced much opposition within Russia. It came not only from former aristocrats and other reactionaries, but also from middle-class liberals and the Mensheviks. In scattered groups, under various leaders, they tried to overthrow the communists in a civil war.

The communists had adopted red, the symbolic color of European revolutionary socialism, as their color. They were therefore called the "Reds." Those who opposed the communists were called the "Whites."

The civil war, which began in early 1918, lasted almost three years, adding to the devastation begun by World War I. The Red Army—as the forces of the new government were called—and the several White armies fought many battles and left an appalling trail of destruction.

The Allies had been angered by the separate treaties that the new Russian government had signed. They also feared that if the communists gained control of Russia, the revolution would spread. Therefore the Allies aided the White forces with arms and money. Several nations, including the United States, even sent small forces of troops to help overthrow the communist government. The Allies helped prolong the civil war, but they could not change the result. By 1921 the communists had completely defeated the White forces.

Russia under Lenin

As soon as the communists had seized power in 1917, they began to reorganize Russia's system of government. The capital was moved from Petro-

The Russian Revolution

The early years of the Russian Revolution aroused tremendous enthusiasm among the Russian people. Their leader, Lenin, could inspire thousands of listeners with his speeches (above). Lenin's stated goal was to improve the life of ordinary people and then see Russia's example change the world. In a propaganda poster (right), crowds watch as the revolutionary banner is hoisted over Russia, to cast its shadow over the entire world.

The revolution inspired workers to new efforts. Coal miners were urged on by Aleksey Stakhanov (below), a worker who was famous for increasing productivity. Now, the workers were told, they were working for themselves, not for the capitalist mine owners.

grad to Moscow. A cabinet, the Council of People's Commissars, was hastily formed. It was headed by Lenin. A National Congress was also established. This huge body was made up of over a thousand representatives from the soviets. Officially, the National Congress, the legislative body of the nation, had supreme authority. Real power, however, rested with the People's Commissars.

In 1922 the communist leaders gave Russia a new name, the Union of Soviet Socialist Republics (U.S.S.R.). This change indicated that power had been transferred to the soviets. After 1922 it became appropriate to speak of the Soviet Union and the Soviet people. The term Russia, however, continued to be used by many people to refer to the Soviet government.

The guiding economic system of the U.S.S.R. was to be socialism. Politically, the country was to be divided into separate republics, which were to be joined in a federal union. Eventually there were 16 of these republics in the U.S.S.R.

Between 1918 and 1921, Soviet leaders had followed a policy known as War Communism. All the Russian industries were **nationalized**—put under government control or ownership. However, social and economic measures were not based on a long-range plan. After the end of the civil war, the communist leaders had to develop a program to build their "new society" in Russia.

The New Economic Policy. In the spring of 1921 Lenin decided that it was necessary to take "one step backward" before Russia could take "two steps forward." Departing from strict Marxist theory, he announced what was called the New Economic Policy (NEP).

This system allowed some free enterprise, but only in order to stimulate the Soviet economy. The NEP permitted individuals to buy, sell, and trade farm products. The major industries—oil, mining, steel, and the railroads—remained under government ownership and management. Smaller businesses and home industries could be privately owned and operated for profit. Foreign capital was welcomed for the development of government-controlled industries, and investors were promised a high rate of return.

While Lenin attempted to build up Soviet industries, agriculture remained a problem. During the revolution, farm lands had been seized from the wealthy landlords and divided among the peasants. The government tried to persuade the peasants to form **collective farms**—the pooling of land into large farms where people can work together as a group. Thus they could share the scarce modern farm machinery. However, the great majority of peasants held on to their small strips of land and to the old ways of farming.

A power struggle

Lenin died in 1924, and there followed a struggle for power among the high officials of the Communist Party. The main contenders were Leon Trotsky and Joseph Stalin. Trotsky was a talented party organizer who had played an important role in the Bolshevik Revolution. He had almost single-handedly created the Red Army that defended the communists in the civil war. Stalin was secretary general of the Communist Party.

One issue in the dispute between Trotsky and Stalin concerned the future of the revolution. Trotsky followed the strict Marxist belief that the revolution, to be successful, had to take place all over the world. Stalin, however, broke with accepted doctrine and advocated "socialism in one country"—the U.S.S.R. After socialism had been successful there, said Stalin, the revolution would spread to the rest of the world.

The struggle between the two factions was bitter, savage, and merciless. By 1928, as a result of a series of betrayals and assassinations, Stalin was securely in power. Trotsky went into exile. He was later murdered in Mexico, probably on Stalin's orders.

In 1928 Stalin announced the end of the NEP and the return to a completely controlled economy such as Russia had experienced under War Communism. The economic controls from 1918 to 1921 had been emergency measures. Now Stalin's goal was to make the planned economy a permanent feature in the Soviet Union.

The Five-Year Plans

A master plan for economic growth, the first Five-Year Plan, was published in 1928. It set industrial, agricultural, and social goals for the next five years. There were also plans for expanding the educational system and for building more hospitals and housing.

The resources of backward, agricultural Russia were stretched to the breaking point to enable the country to become a modern, industrialized society. Heavy industries were vastly expanded at the expense of consumer goods—those products, such as food and clothing, that satisfy human needs.

The planners hoped that collective farming with modern machinery would produce enough food for the Soviet people, with a surplus for export. Money from these exports would help pay for the expansion of industry. Therefore the future of the Soviet Union as an industrial nation depended on a rapid increase in farm production. All farms were to be merged into collectives. Peasants had to join or suffer severe consequences. Hundreds of thousands of the wealthier peasants were executed, imprisoned, or sent into exile when they attempted to withhold their lands from this collective movement.

The first Five-Year Plan was successful in most industries. About 70 percent of the productive farm land was collectivized. A second Five-Year Plan was begun in 1933. It was even more comprehensive than the first. Again the program called for production increases in heavy industries. As a reward for the hard work and sacrifices of the people, the production of consumer goods, such as food and clothing, was also increased.

Stalin's dictatorship

As time went on, Soviet leaders admitted that many years would have to pass before the classless society of pure communism could be attained. For the time being, Soviets would be rewarded according to their work, not according to their needs. Thus, although the Soviet Union was considered by most people to be a communist country, Stalin and other leaders described it as a socialist dictatorship of the proletariat.

A police state. The czars had used secret police and spies to maintain their absolute rule. Now Stalin used similar tactics. Under Stalin, the Soviets were still ruled by fear. People had to conform, to agree, to express no opinion at all, or to express only the "party line," the policy of the Communist Party.

The Soviets had disestablished the Orthodox Church and seized its property. Religious worship was ridiculed, and children were taught atheism. Artists, writers, and musicians were ordered to produce "socialist realism" in the service of the state. Their works were subject to rigid control and censorship.

Government under Stalin. In 1936 Stalin proclaimed a new constitution for the Soviet Union. The "Stalin Constitution," as it was called, preserved the essential framework that had existed in Russia under Lenin. The parliamentary body was to be called the Supreme Soviet. It was to meet twice every year. While in recess, its authority was assumed by the Presidium, a small committee elected by the Supreme Soviet. Executive and administrative authority was given to the Council of People's Commissars, later renamed the Council of Ministers.

On paper the Soviet government appeared to be representative, democratic, and parliamentary. In reality, however, most power lay in the hands of the Politburo (Political Bureau) of the Communist Party. As head of the party, Stalin controlled the Politburo. In other words, he was a dictator, with virtually complete authority over his people.

The Soviet Union's totalitarian dictatorship under Stalin gradually grew harsher. In 1934, following the assassination of a high party official, Stalin began a purge of party members disloyal to him. Through public trials, intimidation, and brutality, he began to rid the party of all members who would not submit to his will. It has been estimated that by 1938, nearly 8 million persons had been arrested. Arrest was usually followed by deportation, imprisonment in forced labor camps, or execution.

The Comintern

Soviet foreign policy during the 1920's and 1930's was contradictory. On the one hand, the new communist government wanted to be accepted by the established nations of the world. On the other hand, it supported the Third, or Communist, International (often called the Comintern). This was an organization that Lenin had founded in 1919 to help spread the revolution throughout the world. The Comintern continued to agitate for the overthrow of the governments of the capitalist democracies.

There were communist parties in many countries outside Russia. The Comintern worked through them to arouse workers and urge rebellion. Such open calls for revolution caused fear, suspicion, and hostility in the outside world.

CHECKUP

1. IDENTIFY: Petrograd Soviet, Mensheviks, Bolsheviks, Lenin, "Reds," War Communism, collective farms, Trotsky, Presidium, Politburo, Comintern.

2. What were the causes of the revolution in Russia in March 1917?

3. Describe the New Economic Policy of Russia.

4. What was the main political difference between Trotsky and Stalin?

5. What economic policies did Stalin initiate? What were the consequences for those who resisted Stalin's policies?

The 1920's witnessed political tensions in much of Europe

The older and more experienced European democracies, such as France and Great Britain, experienced strain in the postwar years. One problem, resulting from demobilization of the armed forces, was widespread unemployment and intense competition for jobs. Another was overproduction by farms and factories. Production had expanded to fill wartime needs and now too much was available and unused.

An attempted solution was for governments to play a more active role in economic matters. Before World War I, many people had felt that governments should not interfere with business. However, wartime needs had led several nations to adopt a **planned economy**—governmental regulation and direction of national resources to fill a definite goal. Since the system had worked well in wartime, why not use it to solve peacetime economic problems?

In the new European nations, such as Poland, different sorts of problems arose. Many of these countries had set up governments more in imitation of Western systems than from any deep devotion to democratic principles. Most of the people

who administered them had no experience in democratic government. Therefore, social and economic troubles multiplied, and serious signs of weakness began to appear.

France's postwar difficulties

During the four years of World War I, northern France had been a battleground. At war's end, cities lay in ruins, farmhouses had been destroyed, and the land itself was scarred with trenches and shell holes. Wharves needed replacing. Railroads and roads were worn out. Most tragic of all, a large percentage of the young men of France had been killed during the war.

Thus France emerged from World War I victorious but unstable. It still owed money that it had borrowed from its citizens and from the United States during and after the war. Inflation took its toll, too. The burden fell mostly on industrial workers and the lower middle class, those least able to pay.

The expenses of the French government continued to be high for several reasons. The number of civil servants increased during and after the war. The government had to repair war-damaged areas and pay interest on its heavy debt. Most important, perhaps, was military security.

The Maginot Line. Twice in less than 50 years, France had been invaded by Germans. To prevent this from happening again, the French army was rebuilt. A series of steel and concrete fortifications nearly 200 miles (320 kilometers) long was constructed along the frontiers of Germany and Luxembourg. This fortification was named the Maginot (MAZH·ih·noh) Line, after the person who had planned it.

Enormous sums of money were spent on the construction of the Maginot Line. Since trench warfare had been the basic feature of World War I, the French planned to make their defenses so strong that the country could never again be invaded by land from the east.

International affairs. The French government went through many upheavals during the 1920's and 1930's. There were a great number of political parties in France, causing difficulties in its parliamentary government. According to the French electoral system, party seats in the National Assembly were based on the percentage of the

"The City" by Fernand Léger

During World War I, many soldiers suffered as a result of severe attacks of poison gas. One of these was the French artist Fernand Léger. Before he joined the army, Léger's paintings had glorified machines and technology. While recovering in a hospital, he realized that individuals, not things, were more important. When he began painting again, Léger included people in his canvases. In this painting of city life, human figures descend the staircases, walk on the streets, and appear in the posters.

Léger was a Cubist painter, part of an art movement that started in Paris about 1907. Cubists believed objects could best be shown by breaking them down into their basic geometric forms, just as machines were made by assembling many parts. In theory, a Cubist painter stepped into the picture and then walked around the subject, trying to show all sides at once. Thus the artist could expand what the human eye could see.

total national vote each party had won in the general election. Thus many political parties could be represented in the parliament. As a result, no one party held a majority of seats. Therefore, in order to agree upon or accomplish anything, a coalition had to be formed. These coalitions rarely held together for long, resulting in a constant turnover in leadership.

France, therefore, seemed an unreliable ally. Not only was it weak financially, but its shifting government made a consistent foreign policy impossible.

In July 1922 Germany had informed the Allies that it could not continue to pay reparations on schedule. Over British objections, France, assisted by Belgium, marched troops into the Ruhr Valley in January 1923. The Ruhr Valley was the source of most of Germany's coal and iron. France intended to occupy the area and operate the steel mills there until it collected the money Germany owed. The German workers refused to cooperate, and the attempt ended in failure. The troops were soon withdrawn.

In 1925 the political situation in Europe seemed to be improving. In that year, representatives of Great Britain, France, Germany, Belgium, Italy, Czechoslovakia, and Poland met at Locarno, Switzerland. There they signed a number of treaties known together as the Locarno Pact. The delegates to the conference pledged their countries to the peaceful settlement of all future disputes. The existing Franco-German boundaries were guaranteed. France signed mutual assistance treaties with both Poland and Czechoslovakia. Germany was invited to join the League of Nations.

However, France's protective alliances began to show serious weaknesses. By the mid-1930's, Belgium canceled its defensive alliance with France and declared itself neutral in any future war. France's prewar ally, Russia, was now under a communist government. France and Russia formed an alliance, but it was a shaky one. France's wartime ally, Italy, was now under a militarist dictatorship and resumed its old opposition to France. France, in keeping with its aim of encircling Germany, made postwar alliances with Yugoslavia and Rumania as well as with Poland and Czechoslovakia. However, these relatively weak nations, although they shared France's mistrust of Germany, were undependable allies.

Political unrest in France

In early 1934 a scandal in the government touched off riots in Paris. Rioters demanded an end to the republican form of government. They called for a military dictatorship to "discipline" the country and reunite the opposing parties.

The trade unions responded to this threat from the right by calling a **general strike**—the refusal of workers in various industries to continue working until their demands are met. Shortly thereafter the parties of the left organized a coalition government. The name this coalition took was the Popular Front. Its leader, Léon Blum, a socialist, was elected premier in 1936. United for the moment against the threat of a coup d'état, Blum's government carried out many reforms.

The Popular Front first persuaded the leaders of industry to grant an immediate pay raise to all workers. A 40-hour week was established, and workers were to be given vacations with pay. The government promised its protection to labor-union organizers and set up a system for the arbitration of labor disputes. The Bank of France was put under public control and the armaments industry was partially nationalized.

Prices soon rose so high that the increase in wages was of little help. In addition, industrialists proved less than cooperative in carrying out their part of the bargain. Blum's ministry lasted only about a year. For this brief period, however, France had a government with the power and determination to act.

After the fall of the Popular Front, the French working classes were hard hit. The 40-hour week was abolished in 1938. The workers protested by organizing general sit-down strikes during which they stayed at their jobs but refused to work. Severe antilabor legislation followed.

France remained a democracy, but the French people were bitterly divided. They were also fearful of German military power, which was reviving at an alarming rate.

Great Britain after World War I

Great Britain, like France, faced grave economic difficulties after World War I. There was a huge war debt, owed both to people at home and to the United States. Taxes were extremely heavy.

British industry and trade suffered. The coal mines, on which industry depended, were beginning to give out. Factories were run down. Machinery was worn out or inefficient compared with newer American or Japanese machines. During the war the United States and Japan had taken over many of the British world markets. These markets were hard to regain.

In addition, several new nations adopted a policy of **economic nationalism**. That is, they tried to improve their own economic well-being through protective tariffs and similar restrictions, without consideration for other countries. This policy, too, damaged British trade. Yet Great Britain had to sell abroad to pay for needed imports of food and raw materials.

Labor troubles. By 1921, about 2 million workers were out of work and had to be supported by the government. Labor unions fought hard to keep the high wages and full employment of the war years. Industrialists fought just as hard to resist the unions' demands.

In 1926 the coal miners went on strike and their action led to a general strike. Soon almost half of Great Britain's 6 million unionized workers had left their jobs. The government declared a state of emergency and sent soldiers and sailors to replace the striking workers. The general strike failed and the miners returned to work. The Trades Disputes and Trade Unions Act of 1927 imposed controls on unions and declared general strikes illegal.

Discontented workers found a spokesman in Ramsay MacDonald, leader of the Labour Party. The Labour Party was growing in strength. Meanwhile, the Liberal Party declined rapidly because it could not attract working-class members. MacDonald formed a coalition with the Liberal Party and was elected prime minister in 1924 and again in 1929. His government was able to bring about moderate reforms, such as the extension of unemployment benefits and old-age insurance. Thus, Great Britain was able to avoid the social unrest that toppled democratic institutions elsewhere in Europe during the postwar years.

Ireland. In the 1920's Great Britain faced a major problem in a country it had ruled for centuries. During the 1800's Great Britain had given Ireland a degree of self-government, but it was not enough to satisfy most Irish. They wanted complete independence.

PHOTOGRAPHY   Ever since the invention of the camera, photographs have provided important information for historians. Photographs give a sense of how places looked at a particular time—a city street, for example, before old buildings were torn down. They also provide an insight into people's feelings at a particular time. The joy at the end of World War II, for instance, was captured forever by photographers. And the picture reproduced here (left), one of the most famous ever taken, brings to life the early 1900's in America.

The title of the photograph is "The Steerage," and it was taken by an American, Alfred Stieglitz, in 1907. What does it tell us? First, we have to know that when this picture was taken the flow of immigrants from Europe into the United States was at its height. Many people eventually returned to their homelands. Stieglitz captured the atmosphere aboard the transatlantic ships. He documented the crowding, the different types of people, the youthfulness of the travelers, and even the need to hang up the wash on shipboard.

The subject of migration was a favorite one for photographers, and their pictures help recreate the atmosphere of the times better than any other source. The impact made by the thousands of immigrants who crowded into New York is vividly captured by this photograph of Ellis Island (below left), taken in the early 1920's. The island, in New York Harbor, served as the main clearinghouse for immigrants. Here their health and credentials were checked before they entered the United States. But the size of the flow of people, made tangible by pictures like these, led to a reaction, and the immigration laws of the 1920's severely restricted the migration. It was again a photograph that most dramatically captured the change in policy—a picture of a deserted Ellis Island (below), a stark indication of America's changing attitude toward the rest of the world.

During World War I, when Great Britain was busy elsewhere, Irish nationalists rose up in the Easter Rebellion of 1916. The British put down the rebellion, but fighting broke out again in 1918. For years the Irish Republican Army fought British troops in a violent and bitter struggle.

In 1921 the British gave in and signed a treaty. The following year, southern Ireland became the Irish Free State, a self-governing dominion with loose ties to the mother country. Six counties in northern Ireland chose to remain in the United Kingdom, with representatives in the British Parliament. This region became known as Northern Ireland.

In 1937 the Irish Free State adopted a new constitution and the name Eire (AIR·uh). Eamon De Valera was elected its first prime minister. (In 1949 Eire became completely independent, calling itself the Republic of Ireland.)

The division of the island was religious as well as political. The Republic of Ireland was Roman Catholic. Northern Ireland was mostly Protestant. The split continues to trouble relations between Great Britain and Ireland today.

Eastern Europe

While the countries of western Europe were attempting to recover economically, the new nations of eastern Europe were just beginning to create their own economies. However, they lagged far behind the western democracies in industrial development. For centuries, the economy of the region had focused on landed manors, and serfdom existed in some areas until the mid-1800's. At the time of World War I, the economy was still mainly agricultural. Most of the land was owned by a few wealthy aristocrats.

In some of the new countries, the large estates were broken up and given to the peasants. This happened successfully in Czechoslovakia, Rumania, Bulgaria, and the Baltic countries (Estonia, Latvia, and Lithuania). Yet most of the peasants were too poor to buy the necessary equipment, fertilizer, and seeds to make their farms productive. In addition, their farms were usually too small to be operated efficiently.

Most of the new eastern European countries tried to industrialize. They turned to economic nationalism to protect their industries. As a result, trade among them was difficult. Goods produced by the new industries could not be sold to neighboring countries at a reasonable profit. The push toward economic development created a period of instability in the new nations of eastern Europe. Finland, Czechoslovakia, and the Baltic countries managed to sustain democratic regimes, but few other nations in eastern Europe succeeded in doing so. Three examples will help illustrate what happened.

Austria. The Austria created after the war was a small country. Many Austrians wanted *Anschluss* (union) with Germany, but the peace treaties forbade it. Austria's economic weakness and a constant struggle between socialists and conservatives weakened the democratic system. In 1922 a reactionary Catholic priest became chancellor of Austria. The country became less democratic, and the Catholic Church began to take control of the Austrian government.

Hungary. The new country of Hungary was declared a republic in November 1918. In the following year, Béla Kun, a Hungarian communist who had participated in the revolution in Russia, overthrew the republic. Kun tried to establish a communist system modeled on Russia's new government. He planned to break up the large estates and distribute land to the peasants. However, Kun was bitterly opposed by the aristocrats who owned the land.

A counterrevolution of aristocrats and army officers seized power and attempted to restore the Hapsburg monarchy. Although the new government declared Hungary to be a monarchy, the Allies would not permit the Hapsburgs to return to power. By 1920 Hungary was ruled by Admiral Nicholas Horthy, a reactionary representative of the military class. Within two years, Hungary had gone from a democracy to a military dictatorship. Under Admiral Horthy's rule, landlocked Hungary was called "a kingdom without a king ruled by an admiral without a fleet."

Poland. Soon after the war a constitutional assembly met in Poland. It adopted a democratic constitution closely modeled on that of the Third French Republic (see Chapter 20). However, bitter opposition from both the right and the left prevented the new government from operating effectively. In 1926 Poland followed the example of Hungary and turned to military dictatorship. Dictator Marshal Jozef Pilsudski (peel·SOOT·skee), like Admiral Horthy in Hungary, represented the aristocracy and the military.

CHECKUP

1. IDENTIFY: planned economy, Maginot Line, Locarno Pact, Popular Front, Blum, economic nationalism, MacDonald, Easter Rebellion, De Valera, Kun, Horthy, Pilsudski.

2. What internal problems did France experience after World War I?

3. What economic problems did the British face in the period after World War I?

4. Define *Anschluss*. What prevented Austria from achieving *Anschluss?*

5. How did eastern European countries try to improve their economies after World War I?

3

Fascist dictatorships were established in Italy and Germany

The war and its aftermath took their toll in Italy and Germany as elsewhere. There was heavy loss of life, a crushing burden of debt, unemployment, and inflation. In Italy, labor troubles included many violent strikes. The Italian government, a constitutional monarchy, seemed helpless to meet the pressing needs of the situation.

The rise of fascism in Italy

One person who did offer a positive plan was Benito Mussolini. The son of a blacksmith, he had been a socialist as a young man and had edited a socialist newspaper. His ideas had brought him a term in jail and a period in exile. During World War I, his views changed. He became an extreme nationalist and was expelled from the Italian Socialist Party. After Italy joined the Allies, he enlisted in the army and was wounded in battle.

When Mussolini returned from the war, he began to organize his own political party. He called it the Fascist Party and called its doctrine **fascism.** The words *fascist* and *fascism* come from the Latin word *fasces*. In ancient Rome the *fasces* was a bundle of rods bound tightly around an ax. It symbolized governmental authority. The various groups of the nation, Mussolini said, should be bound together like the rods of the fasces. He defined fascism as "the dictatorship of the state over many classes cooperating."

Fascism, like communism, relies on dictatorial rule and a totalitarian regime, in which rigid control is maintained by the government through force and censorship. The state is supreme, and individuals are completely subordinate to it. However, there are important differences. Communism, which is based on a socialist economy, seeks international revolution. It appeals to workers and promises a classless society. Fascism, on the other hand, is extremely nationalistic, appeals to the middle class, and promises to preserve existing social classes. Each system is violently opposed to the other.

Mussolini gained power

Mussolini found his first followers among demobilized soldiers and discontented nationalists. Gradually, the fascists attracted wealthy landowners and businesspeople, especially large manufacturers who were attracted by the anticommunist program. These new supporters gave the fascists much financial assistance. Professionals also joined. There was strong support too among the lower middle classes, who had been severely hurt by inflation, and among the unemployed.

Realizing the appeal of strong anticommunism, Mussolini emphasized that part of his program. Fascism began to stand for the protection of private property and of the middle class. Mussolini promised to prevent a proletarian revolution. At the same time, he offered the industrial working class full employment and social security. He stressed national prestige. Italy would gain all its war aims, and there would be a return to the glories of the Roman Empire.

The Fascist Party began a violent campaign against its opponents, especially socialists and communists. Rowdy groups broke up strikes and political meetings and drove properly elected socialist officials from office. The fascists adopted a black shirt as their uniform and thus were called Black Shirts.

624

In October 1922 Black Shirt groups from all over Italy began to converge on Rome. They claimed that they were coming to defend Italy against a communist revolution. Liberal members of the Italian parliament insisted that the king declare martial law. When he refused, the cabinet resigned. Conservative advisers persuaded the king to appoint Mussolini as the premier and ask him to head a coalition government.

Mussolini had often criticized democracy as a weak and ineffective form of government. Once in office, he began to destroy democracy in Italy and set up a dictatorship. Fascists were appointed to all official positions both in the central government and in the provinces. A new election law was passed. It provided that the party receiving the most votes would automatically gain two-thirds of the seats in the Chamber of Deputies, the lower house of parliament. The fascists won the election in 1924. Once they had their majority in the Chamber of Deputies, they voted "decree powers" to Mussolini—that is, his decrees would have the force of law. He took the title *il Duce* (DOO·chay), Italian for "the leader."

Italy as a police state

Now all the trappings of a dictatorship began to appear. Opposition parties were wiped out. Freedom of speech, press, and assembly were suspended, as was trial by jury. Labor unions were reorganized under the control of the government, and strikes were outlawed. Uniformed and secret police spied on everyone.

Mussolini became commander in chief of the army, navy, and air force, and head of the police. Although he allowed the king to reign as a figurehead, real power was concentrated in the hands of the Grand Council of the Fascist Party. At its head was Mussolini.

The corporate state. Mussolini worked out a complicated plan for governing Italy. Arguing that geographic representation in a parliament was outmoded in a modern industrial society, he introduced in its place representation by occupation or profession. The principal economic activities, such as agriculture, transportation, manufacturing, and commerce, were formed into syndicates that were like corporations. Thus Italy was called a corporate state.

By the 1930's there were 22 of these syndicates in Italy. In each syndicate, representatives of management, labor, and the government met to establish wages, prices, and working conditions. Labor unions and capitalists alike were subjected to the will of Mussolini's government. Private property was left in the hands of its owners, and profits were allowed. All parts of the society were forced to cooperate with one another for the welfare of the nation.

At the top of the entire system was the fascist dictator, Mussolini. The army and navy were greatly strengthened and armaments increased. This system achieved a double purpose. It added to the military strength of Italy and helped to reduce unemployment. War was advertised as a glorious, patriotic adventure.

Germany's postwar difficulties

As with Italy, difficulties in postwar Germany gave rise to political change during the years following World War I. In November 1918 Germany was declared a republic. The following year, an assembly met in the city of Weimar (VY·mahr) and drafted a constitution that made Germany a federal republic, known as the Weimar Republic.

Germany's new government had a president and a two-house parliament. The president and members of parliament were elected by universal suffrage. In the upper house, the Reichsrat (RYKS·raht), the 17 states of the federal republic were represented. In the lower house, the Reichstag, political parties were represented directly according to the number of votes they received. A prime minister, called the chancellor, was appointed by the president.

The Weimar Republic was not popular with the German people. Many felt that it had been created to satisfy Woodrow Wilson's demand that a new German government be elected by the people. Moreover, the Weimar representatives had signed the humiliating Versailles Treaty.

Many of the difficulties of the Weimar Republic reflected the economic, social, and political problems that affected all of Europe after the war. Unemployment was high. Inflation reached fantastic proportions. In 1913 a German mark was worth about 25 cents. In 1923 it took 1 trillion marks to equal 25 cents.

Fascist dictators in power

Fascist dictators of the 1920's and 1930's glorified military authority. Neither Adolf Hitler nor Benito Mussolini (below) had risen past the rank of corporal in World War I. Yet they now dressed in impressive uniforms and made themselves the center of attention in grand military parades.

Hitler and Mussolini also encouraged military training in their countries beginning at an early age. Sons of the Wolf (above) were Mussolini's youngest military trainees. They ranged in age from six to eight years old. Their counterparts in Germany were members of the Hitler Youth. These fascists sometimes made great bonfires (right) of books that contradicted what they believed to be the noble and worthy aims of fascism.

The Nazis and Hitler

One of the many political parties formed in Germany after World War I was the German Workers' Party. In 1920 the party, attempting to broaden its appeal, changed its name to the National Socialist German Workers' Party, or Nazi Party. The party was not, as its name might indicate, a working-class group. Rather, it was extremely nationalistic and violently anticommunist. Promising to protect Germany from communism, it in time attracted the support of wealthy business leaders and landowners.

One of the first Nazi recruits was an ex-soldier named Adolf Hitler. Hitler was born in Austria in 1889, the son of a minor government official. As a young man, he had gone to Vienna, where he was unsuccessful as an artist and worked for a while at various odd jobs. In Vienna, a city in which many Jews had risen to respected positions, Hitler became resentful and violently anti-Semitic.

Hitler served in the German army in World War I. He later moved to the city of Munich, where he joined the Nazi Party. In 1923 Hitler took part in a Nazi uprising in Munich. It failed and he was sentenced to prison. While there, he wrote *Mein Kampf (My Struggle)*, a rambling, hate-filled book that expressed the spirit of the Nazi movement. After his release from prison, Hitler became the leader of the Nazis.

Hitler was a hypnotic orator. In the confused situation of the postwar years, his emotional speeches attracted enthusiastic listeners. The frustration, self-pity, and hatred he expressed reflected the feelings of many other Germans.

Hitler's program sought to appeal to almost every element in the German population. He promised solutions to all problems and new power for Germany. In addition, he spoke of a new racial doctrine. According to this doctrine, the Germans, as "Aryans" (an incorrect use of the word), were the "master race." All other people were inferior.

Hitler's rise to power

Throughout the 1920's, Nazi strength was low. Then came the Great Depression, about which you will read in the next section. The hardships it brought led to a great increase in Nazi strength.

In the election of 1930, many middle-class voters turned to the Nazis. These voters had experienced economic hardships and had seen their savings destroyed. Many of them were afraid of a communist revolution. Two years later the Nazis won 230 seats in the Reichstag. They were the largest single party there, but did not have enough votes to form a government by themselves.

In January 1933, when it appeared that no other party could successfully form a government, the president of the republic, Paul von Hindenburg, appointed Hitler chancellor.

The Nazis still lacked a majority. Hitler used the Nazis' private army—called Storm Troopers, or Brown Shirts—to intimidate the parliament. Hitler was granted emergency powers to deal with an alleged communist revolt. He used these powers to make himself a dictator.

The Nazi program in action

Once in power, Hitler, who often modeled his fascist policies on Mussolini's, took the title *der Führer* (FYOOR·ur), German for "the leader." He began to turn Germany into a fascist police state. Opposition parties and labor unions were ordered to disband. The Gestapo, a secret-police force, was given much power. Opposition newspapers were suppressed, and the government controlled all radio stations.

Liberals, socialists, and communists were thrown into large prisons called concentration camps. Members of the so-called "inferior races" were subjected to increasingly severe persecutions. This policy was applied with special harshness to the Jews. They were deprived of many of their rights, publicly humiliated, and even murdered by Storm Troopers. Jews were forced to live in segregated areas and to wear yellow stars of David, the six-pointed star that is a symbol of Judaism. This policy was later carried to a monstrous extreme, as you will read in Chapter 27.

The Third Reich. Like Mussolini, Hitler promised to restore the glories of his country's past. He called his regime the Third Reich. *Reich* is the German word for "empire." (The first empire in Germany had been the Holy Roman Empire, and the second was the German Empire of the Hohenzollerns.) Hitler promised the Germans that the Third Reich would last a thousand years.

Germany's racial superiority, Hitler claimed, justified taking land from the Slavs of eastern Europe to expand Germany's borders. Such expansion would necessitate a large, well-equipped army. Germany had been secretly rearming since the 1920's. Now it began to defy openly the disarmament provisions of the Versailles Treaty.

According to the Versailles Treaty, the Rhineland, Germany's territory on the French side of the Rhine River, was to be left unfortified. In the spring of 1936 Hitler's army marched into the Rhineland. France sent a note of protest; however, the other European powers did nothing.

Encouraged by his unexpected success in the Rhineland, Hitler sought an alliance with Mussolini in order to have support for future aggressive moves. In the fall of 1936 the two dictators formed an alliance, called the Rome-Berlin Axis.

CHECKUP

1. IDENTIFY: fascism, Black Shirts, *il Duce,* corporate state, *Mein Kampf,* Storm Troopers, Gestapo, *der Führer,* Third Reich, Rome-Berlin Axis.

2. Explain Mussolini's ideas of fascism. List the various groups of people in Italy who supported him.

3. Why was the Weimar Republic unpopular with the German people?

4. Describe the main features of Hitler's program.

5. What economic problems in Italy and Germany contributed to the rise of fascism and Nazism?

A worldwide depression began in the United States

Like France and Great Britain, the United States had fought on the victorious Allied side in the war. Unlike them, however, it had fought for less than a year. It had been separated from the battlefields by the Atlantic Ocean, and there had been no devastation of American land. At the end of the war, the United States was much stronger economically than it had been in 1914. Both industry and agriculture had expanded tremendously, and there was an economic boom, a sudden increase in prosperity.

Postwar prosperity

The United States emerged from the war as the apparent successor to Great Britain as a world leader. It had tipped the balance in favor of an Allied victory and had taken a strong role in drawing up the peace settlement. The most dramatic indication of America's new position, however, was financial.

In 1914 the United States had owed about $4 billion to foreign governments and businesses. In 1919 conditions were reversed. Foreign governments owed the American government about $10 billion. Much more was owed to individuals who had bought foreign bonds.

However, the refusal of the United States to join the League of Nations indicated that it did not want the responsibility of world leadership. Americans seemed to want to sit back and enjoy their new-found prosperity and avoid entanglement in European affairs.

The Roaring Twenties

This was an era in American history often referred to as the "Roaring Twenties" because of the fast pace of life and sometimes frantic pursuit of pleasure. Some attributed the atmosphere to the effect on innocent Americans of European attitudes they had encountered during World War I. However, there were other causes.

During the 1920's, many changes affected peoples' lives. Automobiles became a popular means of transportation. Commercial airlines began carrying mail (passenger service did not begin until the 1930's). Telephones were installed in millions of homes, and movies became a favorite form of entertainment. This was the era when jazz became popular, when new fast dances like the Charleston gained acceptance, and when movie stars became public idols. Charles Lindbergh gained fame overnight for piloting an airplane alone across the Atlantic Ocean.

It was not only a time of enormous confidence but also a time of revolt against traditional morality and standards. One sign of change was more freedom for women. They won the vote and went out to work in greater numbers than ever before. Another sign of changing morality was widespread evasion of prohibition—the law forbidding the manufacture, sale, and transportation of alcoholic beverages. Smuggling and bootlegging—the illegal manufacture and sale of liquor—made prohibition ineffective.

America and the world economy

In the mid-1920's, it seemed to many people as if the world economy had completely recovered from the war. Agricultural and industrial production soared, and profits were enormous.

There were flaws in the economic system, however. For one thing, the wages paid to laborers did not keep pace with the increase in productivity. In other words, there was not enough money in the hands of consumers to buy everything that was produced. Profits were either reinvested in new machinery and additional factories or paid out to wealthy stockholders. Increased use of labor-saving machinery not only stimulated production but also reduced employment.

The agricultural economy was not healthy either. Farmers had greatly increased production during the war to help feed the Allies. Now that market was gone. The use of modern machinery and methods led to serious overproduction of food, and prices fell. This was especially true in the wheat market, where production far outstripped consumption in the 1920's.

Another flaw in the system was economic nationalism. A healthy world market demanded a free flow of goods from one country to another. Now, however, there were tariffs, set up to protect expanding industries from foreign competition. Home markets could not consume all that was being produced, and high tariffs made it difficult for foreign buyers to absorb the surplus.

During the 1920's the United States raised its tariffs to the highest level in its history. It insisted upon American dollars in exchange for goods sold abroad. High tariffs now made it hard for European countries to sell goods in America. If they could not sell goods *to* the United States, there was no way for them to acquire dollars to purchase goods *from* the United States. American banks and business people were willing to lend money to Europeans so that they could buy American goods. Yet this practice merely created more indebtedness, and European nations already had heavy war debts.

Speculation, panic, and crash

Millions of Americans were speculating in the stock market—that is, making risky investments in stocks in the hope of quick, high profits. Prices of stocks sold through the New York Stock Exchange rose to high levels, and many investors did make large profits. The trouble was that much of the money invested in the stock market had also been borrowed. Frequently the only security the borrowers had to offer to the lender was money that they expected to make in the future. Everyone expected the prices of stocks to rise indefinitely.

In October 1929 a wave of panic swept the investors in the New York Stock Exchange. Within a few hours the stock market collapsed completely. No one was willing to buy stocks while the prices were declining. As a result, most of the stocks on the exchange became virtually worthless. Vast fortunes were swept away. Hundreds of American banks, factories, mining companies, and business firms went bankrupt.

The collapse of the New York stock market was the beginning of a worldwide depression, called the **Great Depression.** Some of the most reliable European banks were forced to close their doors. By 1932 there were more than 30 million workers unemployed and hungry in countries all around the world. Germany stopped paying reparations. The Allied nations ceased debt payments to the United States.

The strange thing about poverty during the Depression was that it occurred in the midst of plenty. The prices of goods fell very low, but goods could not be sold because people simply did not have the money to buy them. Manufactured products piled up in warehouses and farm crops rotted. Some countries tried to force prices higher by destroying surpluses. Canada burned part of its wheat crop. Brazil dumped coffee into the sea. European exports and imports declined over 60 percent in three years, and United States trade abroad went down 68 percent.

Responses to the Depression

The United States responded to the Depression by resuming the policy of economic nationalism. It raised tariffs even higher than before and cut off

American loans to Europe. Germany and Austria wanted to establish a customs union to aid their economies. However, several European nations opposed the project and it was forbidden by the World Court. In every case, it appeared, the immediate response to the Depression made recovery more difficult.

In 1933 an International Monetary and Economic Conference met in London, but it failed to promote greater financial cooperation among the industrial nations. Most of these countries had already decided upon economic nationalism as the proper answer to the Depression.

Great Britain tried to induce full employment and stimulate production by making low-interest loans to its industries. Besides raising its tariffs against foreign goods, Great Britain tried to find a solution for Depression problems. In 1931 Great Britain formed within its empire a system for economic cooperation. You will learn more about this system in Chapter 26. In 1932, at a conference in Ottawa, Canada, Great Britain devised a system of "imperial preferences." Through this system the dominions and possessions within the British Empire agreed to apply low tariffs to one another's products. In a period of international economic uncertainty, they were attempting to become economically self-sufficient.

France, which was less industrialized than Great Britain, was less hard hit by the Depression. However, French trade declined, unemployment increased, and industrial production dropped sharply. The uncertainty of the Depression years caused even greater political instability in France than the troubles following the war had created. In 1933 alone there were four changes of government.

Elsewhere in the world the Depression caused unrest and violence. In Germany, as you have read, it helped destroy the Weimar Republic. Representative governments survived the shock of severe depression only where democratic traditions were strong.

The New Deal

The United States had lagged behind most other industrial nations in social legislation. There was no unemployment insurance and little in the way of government relief programs. When the Depression came, American workers had to rely on their savings, if any, and on charity provided by private organizations. People stood in breadlines to receive a bowl of soup or a plate of stew. Some earned money by selling apples in the streets.

Under President Herbert Hoover, the federal government tried to remedy conditions, but the measures adopted were not far-reaching. Hoover believed that prosperity was "just around the corner."

Elections brought a new President, Franklin D. Roosevelt, to office in 1933. He immediately embarked upon a program of relief and reform that was called the **New Deal.** The government made grants of money to the states for direct relief—food, shelter, and clothing for the needy. It began a program of public works to provide employment.

Roosevelt's emergency relief program was followed by a sweeping reform of America's economic system. Banks and stock exchanges were put under strict regulation. A Social Security Act, passed in 1935, provided for unemployment and old-age benefits. A 40-hour week and minimum wage levels were established. The federal government had previously remained neutral or sided with the industrialists in labor disputes. Now it guaranteed workers the right to establish unions.

The federal government also tried to relieve the desperate situation of farmers by paying them to take land out of production and to plant crops that would revitalize the soil. Later the government adopted a program of buying and storing surplus farm crops. This program helped prevent the prices of farm goods from plunging.

Another federal program of far-reaching economic and social significance was the Tennessee Valley Authority. The TVA, as it was called, was established in the valley of the Tennessee River and its tributaries. There the government built a series of multipurpose dams, intended to generate cheap electricity, help prevent floods and soil erosion, and improve navigation.

The Roosevelt administration also tried to revive world trade. The Trade Agreements Act, passed in 1934, allowed the President to make special agreements with foreign countries. If a foreign nation lowered its tariff rates on some American products, the President was empowered to

The Depression in the United States

For millions of Americans, the effects of the Depression were shattering. There was misery not just for individuals but for large groups of the population. Enormous numbers of people lost their jobs, and unemployment lines (top) included people of all races and backgrounds.

The affection and respect aroused by President Franklin D. Roosevelt (left) helped give people a renewed confidence. The image of the paralyzed Roosevelt, courageously campaigning from the back of a railroad car, was inspiring to many. As President, Roosevelt battled with the nation's problems as he had with his physical handicap. The New Deal programs he launched helped turn the country around. Major public works projects, such as the building of dams (above), provided employment for thousands.

lower American tariff rates on some of that country's products. With measures such as this, United States foreign trade began to recover.

Under the New Deal the United States government was more deeply involved than ever before in the welfare of the individual citizen. It attempted in many ways to restore prosperity. However, the causes of the Depression were too deeply rooted to be cured completely even by such an ambitious program as the New Deal. The hardships caused by the Depression were not fully overcome until the United States once more mobilized for war in the late 1930's.

CHECKUP

1. IDENTIFY: boom, "Roaring Twenties," prohibition, speculating, Hoover, Social Security Act, Tennessee Valley Authority, Trade Agreements Act.

2. Why was the United States considered a world leader after World War I?

3. How did American economic policies during the 1920's and 1930's affect economic conditions in Europe?

4. What conditions helped to bring about the Great Depression?

5. What measures did Great Britain take to cope with the Depression?

6. What was the New Deal? Give specific examples of its measures.

Ideas and the arts reflected the uneasiness of the postwar era

World War I caused profound uneasiness in both Europe and America. Everything seemed unsettled. All traditional values seemed under attack. A journalist writing in 1938 offered an impression of these times: "Spiritually and morally, civilization collapsed on August 1, 1914—the civilization . . . which with all its shortcomings did give more satisfaction to more people than any other yet evolved. Young people cannot realize how the world has been coarsened and barbarized since 1914. They may feel the loss of security . . . , but they cannot appreciate how much else has been lost." The work of the leading thinkers, writers,

and artists of the time only heightened this sense of disquiet and uncertainty.

The effects of new scientific ideas

Scientists, who since the 1600's had been the chief source of the belief that human beings could solve any problem, had begun to suggest something else in the early 1900's. The ideas of Freud in psychology, for example, implied to some that people could no longer be quite so confident about the powers of rational thought.

Freudian psychology. You have read about Sigmund Freud's theories of the unconscious. He said that human behavior was governed by the unconscious mind. It was Freud's belief that people were unaware of the mental processes of the unconscious. Freud had begun writing in the early 1900's, but it was not until after World War I that his ideas about the unconscious and irrationality gained popularity. If one believed that people could not rationally control their actions, then much that seemed bewildering could be explained. These ideas seemed to help people understand why the dreadful devastation had taken place; why things had not come out as they had hoped; and why the uneasiness was continuing.

Einsteinian physics. You have read about the theory of relativity that made Albert Einstein famous. In this theory he had argued that even such seemingly absolute and definite concepts as space, motion, and time had to be seen as relative—dependent on one another. This had given comfort to those who were denying that any standard, whether of morality or artistic taste, was absolute. They were arguing that attitudes depended on the individual—that they were relative to each person. They claimed that Einsteinian physics supported their view.

Certainty in basic scientific measurements no longer seemed possible. As a result, science was no longer seen as a provider of sure knowledge. This change unsettled the assumption that there would be constant progress in unlocking the secrets of nature. It also added to the sense of unease, to the feeling that confidence about the future was no longer possible. The scientists intensified, rather than relieved, the uncertainty and the doubts about traditional attitudes that marked the postwar world.

Charlie Chaplin in "Modern Times"

Mechanization created feelings of uneasiness in many people. Among them was the brilliant comedian Charlie Chaplin. Characterizing the human spirit in its loneliness and humor, he used the new invention, the movie, as the vehicle for his satire. One of his most famous films was "Modern Times," which was released in 1936. The movie depicts him, in his usual role as a gentle tramp, at work in a huge factory. Here he is shown tightening bolts on an endless assembly line. In pursuit of one neglected bolt, he knocks other workers over, upsets the entire factory routine, and ends as a captive of the machinery.

New directions in literature

The major writings of World War I and afterward revealed a dissatisfaction not only with the times but with the way books and poems had been written in the past. It was a time of experimentation with forms. Writers, influenced by Freud, began to probe unconscious motivations.

Novels. The French novelist Marcel Proust, for example, suggested that reason and thinking delude people. The only reality is sensation, what is felt through the senses. Proust, in great detail, brought tastes, touches, and smells vividly to life. His main work, *Remembrance of Things Past,* is a multi-volume novel. The first part appeared in 1913, but most of it was published after World War I. In the 1920's his work became famous and widely read.

Thomas Mann, Proust's German contemporary, used as his themes the constant presence of death amidst life, and the alienation of the writer from society. There is a constant atmosphere of decay and sadness in his novels, a reflection of the 1920's and 1930's. It is most notable in *The Magic Mountain* (1927). This book is set in a hospital and deals symbolically with the moral sickness of Europe.

In Germany one of the most influential writers of this period was a Czech, Franz Kafka.

Although he died in 1924, many of his books were not published until after his death. Kafka used a technique known as **surrealism**—an attempt to portray and interpret life as if it took place in a dream. In *The Trial* (1925) the main character is being tried in a menacing atmosphere for a crime he knows nothing about. In *The Castle* (1926) a man is supposed to see someone in a castle, but despite going down endless corridors and seeing lots of people, he can never reach his goal. Kafka's writings had a great influence on the work of many later writers.

A writer at this time who caused a great stir was an Irishman, James Joyce. In his masterpiece, *Ulysses* (1922), he tries to convey everything that happens to a man, and everything the man thinks, both consciously and unconsciously, in a single day. This sometimes bewildering book uses a technique called "stream of consciousness." Influenced by psychoanalysis, the technique demands that everything that comes into a character's mind be set down. The result is difficult to follow because it lacks normal punctuation, and seems to jump about just like one's own thoughts.

Ulysses was a revolutionary work, breaking away from many of the traditions of the novel. It revealed both the dissatisfaction with the past and the restlessness of the people of that time.

(continued on page 636)

Dramatic changes in the arts

In the years following World War I the arts underwent profound and dramatic changes. In Paris, Pablo Picasso and Georges Braque continued their development of cubism, with its interaction of planes and shapes. Picasso used cubist techniques to paint his portrait of the writer Gertrude Stein (left). Braque accented the flatness of a painting's canvas with imaginative two-dimensional designs (right).

Architecture was also becoming more abstract. Frank Lloyd Wright used asymmetrical shapes to create his buildings. In "Falling Water," a residence in Bear Run, Pennsylvania (lower far right), Wright fitted the house into its natural surroundings.

Americans were taking the lead in revolutionizing still other art forms. Ernest Hemingway (upper far right) wrote novels that had a new and powerful simplicity. And jazz, the distinctly American form of music, reached great heights. King Oliver (above, second from right) and Louis Armstrong (next to him) were among its pioneers.

634

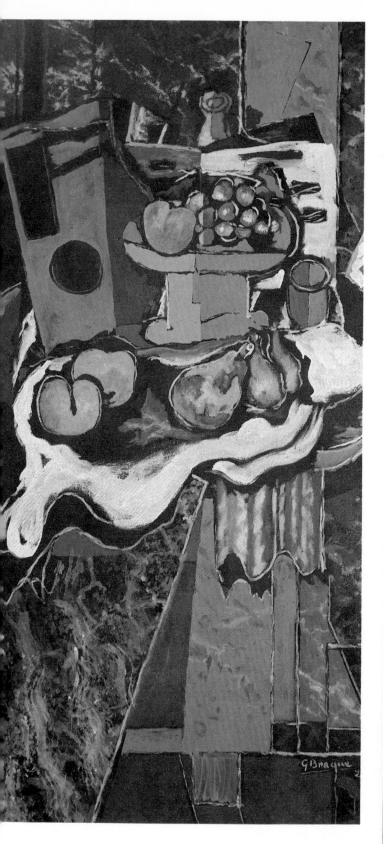

Similar effects can be found in much of the literature of the 1920's and 1930's. One of the most popular books of the age was *The Decline of the West,* by Oswald Spengler, a German. Spengler predicted that European civilization would disintegrate and said that World War I was only the first step in the process.

Equally pessimistic was the best known American writer of the period, Ernest Hemingway. Hemingway wrote in clear, simple prose. His aim—especially in *A Farewell to Arms* (1929)—was to express the disillusionment about human behavior that was so common in the years after World War I.

Poetry. In poetry, the combination of a break with old forms and deep pessimism was best expressed by T. S. Eliot, an American poet who spent most of his life in England. Most of the poets of this period abandoned the traditional patterns of rhymes and regular meters. Instead, they wrote without rhymes, in lines of varying lengths and stresses. They also experimented with punctuation and even the physical appearance of their poems. In Eliot's most famous poem, *The Waste Land* (1922), he gave a despairing description of a world without faith, incapable of restoring its spiritual and moral values.

New directions in music and painting

Musicians and painters rejected earlier forms and styles with the same determination as did the writers of this period. Some of their breakthroughs began before World War I, but it was not until the unsettled postwar world that these new forms took hold.

Music. One of the pioneers of the new directions in music was Igor Stravinsky. Born in Russia, he lived most of his life in western Europe and the United States. Stravinsky's *The Rite of Spring* (1913) caused a minor riot at its first performance because it broke so completely with traditional methods of composition. Different instruments played in different keys at the same time, making a total effect that was disturbing to the ear.

Three Austrians, Arnold Schoenberg and his students Alban Berg and Anton von Webern, were even more revolutionary. They wrote what is called atonal music. In Schoenberg's atonal com-

positions, he discarded the conventional eight-tone musical scale completely and used a twelve-tone scale. Schoenberg and his followers abandoned such traditional forms as the sonata, the symphony, and the concerto. They wrote pieces for unusual collections of instruments, such as Webern's Quartet for Violin, Clarinet, Saxophone, and Piano. Melodies were not developed in the expected way, and the music often sounded strange and unfamiliar.

Painting. The same rejection of traditional expectations was seen in painting. The standards of beauty and the recognizable portrayal of nature, taken for granted since the Renaissance, were overturned by the artists of the early 1900's.

The first pioneers were a Spaniard, Pablo Picasso, and a French artist, Georges Braque, who worked in Paris. They created a new style called **cubism** that emphasized forms, shapes, and design. Using shapes such as cones, cylinders, spheres, flat planes, and especially cubes, they showed the structure of the object they painted, but not its surface appearance. In fact, they often depicted the object from several different perspectives at the same time. Thus one would see half of a face in profile and the other half from the front.

Picasso justified the severe distortions of reality by saying that "nature and art, being two different things, cannot be the same thing. Through art we express our concept of what nature is not." Like the composers of the time, he knew that his work disturbed those who saw it, but that was part of his purpose. He was protesting the easy acceptance of old forms.

Other painters turned away from traditional art in various ways. Surrealistic painters attempted to symbolize the unconscious. Their works featured perfectly painted objects that did not seem to relate to one another. A Spanish surrealist, Salvador Dali, painted *The Persistence of Memory* (1931). This painting depicts a dreamlike landscape with what look like liquid clocks draped over a tree branch and the edge of a shelf. Other artists, notably the Russian Wassily Kandinsky and the Dutch Piet Mondrian, reduced painting to pure abstract design.

Like the writers of the age, the musicians and the painters were breaking dramatically with the past. They were creating disturbing works that reflected the pessimism and doubts of the late 1920's and the 1930's.

Popular culture

Novelists like Franz Kafka and musicians like Arnold Schoenberg appealed only to a small audience. Their works were difficult to understand. Many people found escape from the troubled times in new forms of entertainment.

Popular music. One favorite diversion was listening to phonograph records and music. More and more households had radios in the 1920's and 1930's, and music aimed at a mass audience filled the air waves. This was the era of the so-called "Big Bands." These bands played dance music and catchy melodies written by composers like Irving Berlin and Cole Porter. The musical, a play with songs and dances, became a major attraction in the theater.

The most innovative popular musicians played a distinctive form of music known as jazz. Jazz was born in the southern United States in the late 1800's. Performed primarily by black musicians, it developed particularly in New Orleans. Using African as well as American music as inspiration, it emphasized individual experimentation. One of its major forms, the blues, concentrated on sad, pessimistic themes. The work of the jazz musicians was thus not that different from the writing and painting of the day—experimental and rejecting the past.

Films. The chief entertainment for popular audiences of the 1920's and 1930's was another new art form, the film. Invented around the year 1900, motion pictures swept through Europe and America. Thousands of movie houses were opened in the 1920's and 1930's. The first public showings were in the 1910's, and by the 1920's there were millions of moviegoers.

Films, too, reflected the pessimism of the times. Although the earliest movies were often simple dramas or hilarious comedies, they also carried disturbing messages. The greatest film director in America, D. W. Griffith, and his equivalent in Russia, Sergei Eisenstein, both made powerful films about human intolerance and cruelty. Most movies, however, offered viewers an escape from a difficult world.

Architecture

Architecture also underwent great change during the postwar years. New technical advances, such as the use of structural steel, made a remarkable transformation possible.

The American Louis Sullivan was a leader in the new architecture. Not only did he help to develop the skyscraper, but he also developed a style called **functionalism.** This form of architecture was based on the principle that a building should be designed for its specific use, rather than according to popular styles.

His pupil, Frank Lloyd Wright, adopted Sullivan's ideas and added his own. One of Wright's major theories was that buildings should be related to their environment. In the Middle West his prairie houses, as they were called, were low buildings with long horizontal lines. In the 1920's Wright went to Tokyo, where he built the Imperial Hotel. Adapting it to its location, he floated it on a cushion of mud instead of anchoring it rigidly to rock. Because of this adaptive construction, it was the only large structure in Tokyo to survive the severe earthquake that occurred in 1923.

European architects also developed a new style of architecture. Influenced by Sullivan and Wright, a group including the Frenchman Le Corbusier and the German Walter Gropius developed a functional architecture called the **international style.** This style was plain and severe, using uninterrupted expanses of steel and glass.

The new art forms all showed radical change during the postwar period—a break as dramatic as the one between medieval and Renaissance styles. It was as if nothing could be the same again after World War I, whether music, books, paintings, or buildings.

CHECKUP

1. IDENTIFY: Proust, Mann, Kafka, surrealism, Hemingway, *The Waste Land*, Stravinsky, Picasso, Braque, cubism, functionalism, Wright, international style.

2. Why was popular culture often escapist during the 1930's?

3. The 1920's and 1930's witnessed much experimentation in art forms. Give an example of this experimentation in each of the following categories: literature, music, painting, film, and architecture.

CHAPTER REVIEW

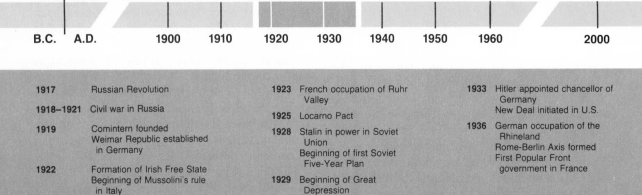

| B.C. | A.D. | | 1900 | 1910 | 1920 | 1930 | 1940 | 1950 | 1960 | | 2000 |

1917	Russian Revolution
1918–1921	Civil war in Russia
1919	Comintern founded
	Weimar Republic established in Germany
1922	Formation of Irish Free State
	Beginning of Mussolini's rule in Italy

1923	French occupation of Ruhr Valley
1925	Locarno Pact
1928	Stalin in power in Soviet Union
	Beginning of first Soviet Five-Year Plan
1929	Beginning of Great Depression

1933	Hitler appointed chancellor of Germany
	New Deal initiated in U.S.
1936	German occupation of the Rhineland
	Rome-Berlin Axis formed
	First Popular Front government in France

CHAPTER SUMMARY

The period following World War I was a time of major stresses and uncertainties. European nations and the United States adjusted to the new situation that emerged from the war. The most dramatic upheaval took place in Russia, where a revolution toppled the 300-year-long rule of the Romanov dynasty and abolished the monarchy. In its place the Russians created a government following the principles of Marx and communism. However, when its first leader, Lenin, died, his successor, Stalin, maintained his control only by a brutal crushing of his opponents.

Elsewhere in Europe, instability was widespread. Both the British and the French maintained their democratic traditions despite labor unrest and the problems of unemployment caused by the Great Depression of the 1930's. In eastern Europe, a number of the new nations abandoned democracy for rule by dictators.

In Italy and Germany there was dissatisfaction with the weakness and hesitations of democratic governments. This led to an extreme form of dictatorship, fascism. Mussolini in Italy and Hitler in Germany established totalitarian regimes that were as repressive as Stalin's. Both Mussolini and Hitler had expansionist foreign ambitions that undermined Europe's stability even further.

In the United States, following victory in World War I, there was the realization that Americans were now the richest people in the world. A sense of optimism and the influence of European contact brought about rapid change. The pace of life quickened, and the decade was appropriately called the Roaring Twenties.

The bubble burst with the stock market crash and the beginning of the Great Depression in 1929. However, President Roosevelt's policies of recovery, known as the New Deal, gradually eased the widespread economic hardship.

The new outlook and the uncertainties of the period were reflected by the science, literature, music, and art of the time. Traditional forms were overturned by such pioneers as Joyce and Picasso. Their work had disturbing implications. Even new popular art forms, films and jazz, had pessimistic overtones. The Western world had entered an unsettled and less optimistic era.

CHECKING WHAT YOU KNOW

1. Match each leader at the left with a country at the right. You may use a country more than once.

   a. Horthy
   b. Mussolini
   c. Lenin
   d. Roosevelt
   e. De Valera
   f. Stalin
   g. Hitler
   h. Pilsudski
   i. Blum
   j. MacDonald
   k. Hoover
   l. Kun
   m. Hindenburg

   1. France
   2. Poland
   3. Germany
   4. Hungary
   5. Great Britain
   6. United States
   7. Italy
   8. Soviet Union
   9. Ireland

2. Compare War Communism with the New Economic Policy. How did each program attempt to stimulate the Soviet economy?

3. Why did demobilization put economic pressures on the nations of Europe? Why were Great Britain and France better able to deal with these problems than the new nations of eastern Europe?

4. What are the similarities and differences between fascism and communism?

5. How did each of the following contribute to the rise of Nazism in Germany:
   a. creation of the Weimar Republic
   b. signing of the Versailles Treaty
   c. high unemployment and soaring inflation

6. How did the economic situation in the United States compare with the situation in Europe during the postwar years? What brought these boom years to an end?

7. How was the disillusionment of the postwar era reflected in the arts? in popular culture?

PRACTICING YOUR SKILLS

1. **Using primary sources.** Read the following excerpt from Adolf Hitler's *Mein Kampf.* Then answer the questions that follow.

   If the National Socialist movement really wants to be consecrated [honored] by history with a great mission for our nation, . . . it must find the courage to gather our people and their strength for an advance along the road that will lead this people from its present restricted living space to new land and soil. . . .

   The National Socialist movement must strive to eliminate the disproportion between our population and our area. . . . And in this it must remain aware that we, as guardians of the highest humanity on this earth, are bound by the highest obligation.

   Based on this passage, what can you conclude about Hitler's foreign policy goals? How does Hitler appeal to the German sense of nationalism? Using what you have learned about the Versailles Treaty, why might many Germans have been swayed by Hitler's words?

2. **Studying photographs.** Turn to the photograph at the top of page 631. What mood did the photographer capture? What evidence supports your answer? Using the information in this photograph, what general statements can you make about the effects of the Depression? How do these statements compare with what you read in this chapter? Did the photograph give you any additional insight into the Depression? Explain.

RELATING PAST TO PRESENT

1. What did the leaders of the 1917 Russian Revolution hope to accomplish? Based on what you know about conditions in the Soviet Union today, which of these goals have been achieved? Which have not?

2. List the programs instituted by President Roosevelt during the New Deal. Which of these programs are still in existence? Choose one of these, and find out why this program continued long past the Depression. What is its main purpose? Do any groups of people think the program should be discontinued? If so, why?

INVESTIGATING FURTHER

1. Using encyclopedias and books in your library, prepare a brief biographical sketch of Benito Mussolini, from his youth to the time he became a dictator. Then write a similar biographical sketch of Adolf Hitler. Compare and contrast Hitler's career with Mussolini's.

2. Consult the *Statistical Abstract of the United States,* and prepare a graph of unemployment in the United States from 1920 to 1940. When did unemployment start to rise? When did it reach its highest point? In that year, approximately how many Americans were out of work? Based on the evidence in your graph, what conclusions can you draw about the impact of the New Deal?

3. Prepare a report on the response of the United States and European nations to the Great Depression, explaining why the policy of economic nationalism created more problems than it solved. Based on your research, what conclusions can you draw about economic nationalism as a policy for nations to follow?

(1900–1936)

26

New Political Forces Stirred in Africa, Asia, and Latin America

As you have read, Europe and the United States faced many problems after World War I. In other parts of the world, the aftermath of the war was not as painful. Most of Asia and Africa had not advanced economically enough to feel the worst effects of the Depression. People's main concern in these areas was with political change.

In the countries that formed the British Empire, political developments were of central importance. India started on the path toward independence, and in other areas of the empire new relationships were created with Great Britain. The major independent countries of the Middle East—Turkey and Persia—also began rapid political transformations, and new political forces were stirring throughout Africa.

The great civilizations of China and Japan went through profound changes. In China the rule of emperors had been abolished, and a long and difficult process of creating new political structures began. Neighboring Japan set its course for economic growth and foreign expansion, which led to growing importance for the military.

Totalitarian regimes were on the rise in Latin America. Its countries were concerned mainly with economic and social change, and with their shifting relationship toward their powerful neighbor, the United States. Many of their governments, like others in the 1920's and 1930's, found that strong central power seemed to be the best answer to their problems.

Mao Tse-tung leading the Long March

The British Empire adjusted to the postwar era

Although the British Empire was larger as a result of the peace treaty agreements, it had many weaknesses. From all parts of the British Empire came demands from colonial people for more freedom, for self-government, or for complete independence.

Independence for Egypt

As you read in Chapter 23, Egypt was technically under Turkish rule but had been controlled by the British since 1882. In 1914, when the Ottoman Empire joined the Central Powers, Great Britain declared Egypt independent and set it up as a protectorate. In 1922 this protectorate was formally ended. Great Britain continued to exert influence through the Egyptian king, however, because of its interests in the Suez Canal.

During the 1920's and early 1930's, a strong independence movement grew in Egypt. In 1936 the British and Egyptian governments reached an agreement. In the previous year Italy had invaded Egypt's neighbor, Ethiopia. The British needed Egyptian support to prevent further Italian aggression. Thus they agreed to help Egypt become a member of the League of Nations. The two nations pledged to help one another in time of war. Egypt agreed that Great Britain should hold military control of the Suez Canal for 20 years. With this agreement, Egypt became completely independent.

The Palestine issue

In the peace settlements after World War I, Great Britain had received as mandates Trans-Jordan, Iraq, and Palestine. These lands were all formerly part of the Ottoman Empire.

The spirit of nationalism had made Arabs discontented under the Ottoman Empire. They were equally unhappy under British control. In Trans-Jordan, which was recognized as independent by the League of Nations in 1923, the British kept control through army advisers. In Iraq, discontent led to many uprisings. By 1930 the British recognized the kingdom of Iraq as an independent nation. However, Great Britain kept some rights there, especially concessions in the country's rich oil fields.

Palestine was important to the British because of its strategic location and because a vital oil pipeline from Iraq ended at the Palestinian port of Haifa. The British were in a difficult position in Palestine, however. In 1917, during the war, the Jewish chemist Chaim Weizmann had turned over to the British government a formula for making an important ingredient of high explosives. Weizmann was a leader in **Zionism,** a movement to resettle Jews in Palestine. The British diplomat Arthur Balfour was grateful to Weizmann and eager to secure Jewish support for the Allies. Balfour told Zionist leaders that the British would "view with favor" the creation of a Jewish "national home" in Palestine. This Balfour Declaration, as it came to be called, would not threaten the civil and religious rights of non-Jews, the majority in Palestine.

The British had also promised to aid the formation of an independent Arab state that might include parts of Palestine. Therefore the Balfour Declaration had to be cautiously worded because the British wanted Arab support against the Turks.

With the British holding mandates in the Middle East after the war, both Jews and Arabs wanted Great Britain to fulfill the promises it had made. Existing tensions between Arabs and Jews intensified. Heated disputes arose over places of worship claimed by both groups.

During the 1930's many Jews fled to Palestine to avoid being persecuted by the Nazis. The British, however, strictly controlled the number of Jews allowed to immigrate to Palestine. Although this policy was bitterly resented by Jewish groups, it was not modified in spite of increasing Nazi persecution of Jews in Europe. Thus the Middle East remained an area of unrest and problems for the British.

Independence movements in India

As the largest British colony, India posed even greater difficulties. India had entered World War I on the side of the Allies. It had contributed important support in both troops and money. In return, Great Britain had promised India a greater degree of self-government.

Any settlement for India had to satisfy many conflicting groups. British conservatives opposed giving up this important part of the British Empire. Indian princes, many of whom were almost absolute rulers in their domains, also favored the existing state of affairs. Many groups in India were hostile to one another. There was bad feeling between Hindus and Muslims, and wide gulfs between upper-caste and lower-caste Hindus. Indian nationalists demanded complete self-government.

The chief advocate of Indian nationalism was Mohandas Gandhi, who in 1920 became leader of the Indian National Congress—India's most important political party. He was not only a political leader but was also revered as a spiritual force. The Indians called him Mahatma, meaning "saintly one."

Gandhi wanted complete self-government for India. He also urged Indians to give up Western ways and to strengthen their ancient culture and religion. Gandhi was opposed to all use of force and violence. He developed an approach—based partly on the New Testament and Hindu scriptures—called "nonviolent noncooperation." This technique was a form of **passive resistance,** or **civil disobedience.** It called for the peaceful refusal of citizens to cooperate with their government in order to win concessions from it.

Among other things, Gandhi's program included refusal to buy British goods or to pay taxes. He and many of his followers were often put in prison. The British broke up many of his political gatherings with force and the suppression of civil liberties.

In 1935, after many conferences and investigations, Great Britain granted India a new constitution with more self-government. However, India did not gain dominion status. The British viceroy still controlled India's national defense and foreign affairs, as well as many areas of domestic affairs. Discontent among the many Indian groups continued.

The Statute of Westminster

Even in those parts of the British Empire that already had almost complete self-government, there were demands for greater independence. In Canada, Australia, New Zealand, and the Union of South Africa, Great Britain still appointed a governor general. This official had a veto power over laws, although it was rarely used. Great Britain also controlled the foreign policy of these areas.

After World War I these dominions demanded complete self-government. The British showed a genius for accommodation, adjustment, and acceptance of the political realities of life. They gave in without a struggle.

In 1931 an act of the British Parliament, called the Statute of Westminster, recognized Canada, Australia, New Zealand, and South Africa as completely independent. They were to be considered equal partners with Great Britain in a very loose organization called the British Commonwealth of Nations. Members of the Commonwealth were considered self-governing. The British Parliament had no power to make laws for them or interfere in their affairs. However, each member agreed to declare its loyalty to the British monarch and to recognize its cultural ties with Great Britain.

Over the years, several British colonies became independent and joined the Commonwealth. Membership was made attractive by favorable trade arrangements with Great Britain. It was a time when major nations were faced with the Great Depression and needed increased trade to stimulate their economies. As you have read, British trade abroad had been hurt by economic nationalism. Thus, the Commonwealth's economic arrangement worked remarkably well for both Great Britain and the regions that had formerly been British colonies.

Politically, however, Great Britain's vast empire was burdensome. In the Middle East and India, especially, the empire became more a source of problems than of support.

CHECKUP

1. IDENTIFY: Weizmann, Zionism, passive resistance, Statute of Westminster.

2. How did Egypt achieve its independence from Great Britain?

3. Why was Palestine important to the British? What was the Balfour Declaration, and why was it issued?

4. What was Gandhi's major objective? What means did he use to achieve it?

5. What is the British Commonwealth of Nations? What are the obligations of its members?

2

Varied political forms developed in Turkey, Persia, and Africa

Outside influences, particularly from the West, continued to play a major role in the independent countries of Turkey and Persia and throughout Africa after the war. As a result, new political forces began to stir in these areas. Developments varied from place to place, but all reflected the impact of the feelings of nationalism that were sweeping the world.

Turkey under Mustafa Kemal

You have read about the harsh peace treaty that was forced upon the Ottoman Empire after World War I. For some time a group of nationalists, called the Young Turks, had been trying to reform the inefficient and corrupt Turkish government. Discontent over the terms of the treaty brought Turkish unrest to a head. The result was a revolution in 1922 led by an able and energetic leader, Mustafa Kemal. The revolutionists demanded that the postwar treaty be canceled and a new one written. Wishing to avoid further unrest, the European powers agreed.

By the new treaty, written in 1923, the Turks regained eastern Thrace, Smyrna, and full control of Constantinople (now Istanbul). The Dardanelles and the Bosporus were still to be left unfortified and were to be administered by a commission of the League of Nations. They were to be open to the ships of all nations in peacetime and to neutral ships in wartime.

The revolution led by Mustafa Kemal put an end to the Ottoman Empire and established the Republic of Turkey. The capital was moved from Constantinople to Angora (now Ankara) in Asia Minor (see map, page 607). The government was to be a Western-style parliamentary democracy, headed by a strong executive. Kemal became the first president.

Kemal wanted Turkey to become a progressive nation, modeled on the industrialized powers of the West. He ordered his subjects to adopt Western clothing. The fez, the traditional hat of Turkish men, was prohibited. He insisted that all Turks adopt family surnames, like Europeans. He himself took the Muslim name Atatürk, meaning "father of the Turks." Women received the right to vote, and polygamy—having more than one wife—was abolished.

The position of caliph, or head of the Muslim faith, held by the Ottoman Sultan was abolished. For the first time the Muslim religion was separated from political affairs, and there was an attempt to lessen its influence over the people.

There were more changes to be made. Turkey adopted the Western calendar, the metric system of weights and measures, and the Roman alphabet. This last change made it possible for many more people to learn to read and write because the Roman alphabet was easier than Arabic script. Atatürk also began a program of economic development. The government paid subsidies to farmers and aided new industries.

Modernizing Persia

The ancient country of Persia also underwent change after World War I. Before the war it had been divided into British and Russian spheres of influence, with a zone in the center where both were allowed to have concessions. After the war the country was torn by civil wars and the conflicting ambitions of the British and Russians.

New forces in India and the Middle East

A spirit of nationalism and the desire for independence began to stir in Asia and the Middle East in the early 1900's. These forces in time affected the political control there. As the Ottoman Empire crumbled, Great Britain took over many of its possessions in the Middle East, including Palestine (right). Arabs disliked British rule, especially because the British allowed Jewish settlers into Palestine. Even T.E. Lawrence (below), a British soldier and adventurer who worked unsuccessfully for Arab independence, could do little to hold down the growing hostility.

The British also faced unrest in their largest colony, India. A new form of resistance grew under the leadership of Mohandas Gandhi. As a young man Gandhi had gone to live in South Africa, where he practiced as an attorney (bottom right, seated at center). After his return to India, he stirred a new spirit of nationalism among the Indian people by peaceful resistance.

In 1925 an army officer, Reza Khan, deposed the ruling shah and assumed power as Reza Shah Pahlavi. In his foreign policy he was anti-Russian. Domestically he followed a policy much like that of Kemal Atatürk. He introduced Western industries and customs into Persia. In 1935 the name of the country officially became Iran.

Although there was a limited, constitutional monarchy, much power remained in the hands of the large landowners. Reza Shah suppressed political parties and strictly controlled the press and education.

Africa after World War I

For Africa, the years after World War I were a period of political and cultural agitation. Throughout the continent, Africans organized to protest against colonial rule.

There were many reasons for the increased political activity after World War I. The war itself had been a broadening experience for Africans. Military service took many individuals away from their homes. It forced them for the first time to look beyond their immediate kin and village for friendship and protection. When ex-soldiers returned home, they often became the local leaders of anticolonial protest.

The education provided by missionaries and by the government was also an important influence. Churches and schools taught the Western ideals of equality and self-improvement. Yet the colonial governments denied Africans the opportunity for self-determination and economic advancement. More and more Africans personally experienced this contradiction between Western teachings and the actual nature of colonialism. Racism and political repression radically changed the thinking of many Africans. It awakened in them a desire for reform and national independence.

New political pressures. Despite the efforts of colonial governments to close off avenues of protest, Africans found many opportunities to organize. They did so, for instance, in the former German colony of Tanganyika, administered by Great Britain as a League of Nations mandate. Here Africans who filled the lower ranks of the civil service, mainly teachers and tax collectors, formed a civil servants association. It effectively overcame tribal and language barriers and became a focus of anticolonial protest. In a similar way, trade unions emerged among Nigerian and South African railroad and dock workers. These became important forums for the expression of African grievances.

As new associations were formed, colonial governments reacted by strengthening the authority of chiefs who cooperated with colonial rule. They were rewarded with pensions and positions of local power—as judges, for example. At the same time, colonial authorities did institute some reforms, particularly against the harsher types of forced labor. Yet neither cooperative chiefs nor limited reforms were enough to reverse the rising wave of opposition to colonialism.

By the 1930's Africans increasingly spoke of independence rather than reform. Young men like Jomo Kenyatta in Kenya and Nnamdi Azikiwe (ah·ZEEK·way) in Nigeria had become leaders of large groups that were no longer willing to tolerate colonial rule.

By the end of the 1930's, there existed a small but important movement dedicated to ending colonialism.

CHECKUP

1. IDENTIFY: Young Turks, fez, caliph, Reza Shah Pahlavi, Kenyatta, Azikiwe.

2. What changes and reforms were made in Turkey by Kemal Atatürk?

3. Give two reasons for increased African protest against colonialism after World War I.

4. How did colonial governments in Africa deal with protest movements?

3

China struggled to become a modern nation

Many historians feel that in order to understand the changes that occurred in China in the 1920's, it is necessary to go back to events around 1900. Up to that time the imperialist powers had operated mainly along the Chinese coast and up the Yangtze River. Then they began to carve the interior of China into spheres of influence.

The United States watched this new development with some concern. It did not want its merchants to be excluded from Chinese trade. In 1899, therefore, the American government appealed to the powers interested in China. It asked these powers to recognize what it called the **Open Door Policy.** According to this policy, no nation would claim exclusive trading rights, and all nations would have equal rights to trade anywhere in China. The interested nations agreed, but in practice, they continued as before. No nation wanted to be exposed before the world as the only one to refuse, but none really intended to observe the Open Door Policy.

The Boxer Rebellion

By 1900 the fate of China seemed to be sealed. The Chinese had been unable to forestall the numerous grants of special privileges to foreign powers. Foreign traders and missionaries were active in the interior. Foreign governments held long-term leases on Chinese territory.

In 1898 the aging Ch'ing dowager empress (widow of an earlier ruler) forced her nephew, the emperor, to give up the throne so she could rule. The Chinese scholar-officials were increasingly criticizing the Ch'ing dynasty. In order to divert their attention, the empress did everything she could to stir up hatred for foreigners, especially the missionaries.

Within a year there were widespread attacks on foreigners in every part of China. The attacks were led by members of a patriotic society called the "Righteous Fists." In English they became known as "Boxers." Foreigners who could do so fled to the protection of their embassies at Peking. There they were besieged by an army of angry Chinese.

Despite their rivalries, the imperialist nations were determined to protect their common interests. Acting jointly, Great Britain, France, Germany, Russia, Japan, and the United States sent a combined army to China. They rescued the embassies and put down the rebellion in 1901. Then they imposed heavy penalties, including payment of a large indemnity. In addition, foreign powers were given the right to maintain troops at Peking and along the Chinese Eastern Railway to the coast (see map, page 570).

This move completed the domination of China by foreign powers. Had it not been for China's neighbors, Russia and Japan, the other imperialist powers might have divided China then and there. However, they realized that, because of location, Russia and Japan would benefit most from the actual breakup of China. As it was, Russia had taken advantage of the Boxer Rebellion by moving 100,000 troops to Manchuria.

Eventually, as you will see, Japan and Russia went to war, partly because of their interest in China. The Japanese were victorious, and they signed a secret agreement with Russia, dividing Manchuria into two spheres of influence. The northern half went to Russia, the southern half to Japan.

Overthrow of the Ch'ing dynasty

Anti-imperialist sentiment grew among the Chinese people, especially among the young and well-educated. Instead of attacking foreigners, as the Boxers had done, they advocated the reform of China itself. Many of the leaders of this movement had studied in Western Europe or the United States. One of these leaders was Sun Yat-sen. He had lived most of his life in the United States, attended school in Hawaii, and studied medicine in Hong Kong. Sun Yat-sen was the founder of the **Kuomintang** (KWOH·MIN·TANG), or Nationalist People's Party.

Influenced by Western ideas, reformers now wanted constitutional government, with freedoms guaranteed by a bill of rights. They also wanted industrialization, so that China could defend itself economically against the imperialist powers. In their view, the only way to protect China from foreign domination was to make China a modern nation.

The Ch'ing rulers tried to carry out reforms, but their reforms were too few and came too late. Many Chinese called for a complete break with "Old China." Arguing that the Ch'ing dynasty was both corrupt and of foreign origin, they called for its overthrow.

In 1911 rebellion spread throughout southern China. In a last desperate gesture, the Ch'ing declared the establishment of a constitutional monarchy. Their opponents, however, would accept nothing but the creation of a republic.

Forming the Chinese republic

In February 1912 the last Ch'ing emperor, a young child, was forced to abdicate. The Kuomintang then proclaimed China a republic. It was based on what Sun Yat-sen called "The Three Principles of the People": people's government, people's rights, and people's livelihood. Briefly expanded, these principles were: (1) political unification and the ending of foreign influence; (2) a gradual change to democratic government, with full personal liberties and rights for all Chinese people; and (3) economic improvements, including land reform and industrialization.

It turned out to be easier to proclaim revolutionary change than to accomplish it. At first the Republic of China existed mainly on paper. The Kuomintang controlled only a small region around Canton, in southern China. The rest of the country was divided among the leaders of regional armies. These leaders, known as warlords, had acquired power during the last years of the Ch'ing dynasty. They were reluctant to give up that power. Some of them hoped to defeat their rivals and start a new imperial dynasty.

The Nationalists, as members of the Kuomintang were called, asked for help from foreign powers. They sought to defeat the warlords and establish the Republic of China as a strong central government. The only country that offered help was Russia. In the early 1920's the communist government in Russia sent technical and political advisers to help reorganize the Kuomintang and build up a modern Chinese army.

Sun Yat-sen died in 1925. Leadership of the Nationalists was taken over by a young general, Chiang Kai-shek (CHYAHNG KY·SHEK), who had studied for a time in Moscow. The Nationalist army grew in strength. In 1926 it moved against the warlords of the north and seized Hankow. Two years later the Nationalists occupied Peking, which they renamed Peiping.

Although the Kuomintang was expanding the area under its control, disagreements began to divide its membership. A left wing of the party, composed of socialists and communists, wanted to put more power into the hands of workers and peasants. A conservative right wing opposed radical change, especially land reform. Chiang Kai-shek became leader of this right wing.

HISTORY THROUGH ART

Chinese painting

For many centuries, Chinese painters saw only works of art created within their own country. With the formation of the Chinese republic in 1912, painters began to study in Japan and Europe, bringing back new ideas and art forms.

Ch'i Huang (1863–1957), one of China's most famous poets and painters, lived through both of these periods. As a young man, he worked in the fields by day and learned to paint by night. By the age of 30, he was a professional artist, had acquired a classical education, and had founded a poetry society.

To Chinese painters as well as calligraphers, the mastery of brushstrokes was very important. They wanted to be quick enough to paint or write their impressions while they were still fresh in their minds. The blending of calligraphy and art, of poetry and painting, was accomplished most elegantly by Ch'i Huang. This painting, done in 1935, was strongly influenced by Japanese art. It illustrates the artist's respect for learning and how he pursued knowledge by candlelight at night. The inscription reads: "Returning home one night, I find mice perusing the pages of a book. Why are you awake when everyone else is sleeping?"

In 1927, before the northern offensive was completed, Chiang expelled the left-wing members of his party. Many were captured and executed. All Russian advisers were sent home. Chiang then set up a Nationalist government in Nanking.

Chiang Kai-shek's regime

Chiang's regime was a one-party government with Chiang as virtual dictator. He and his followers wanted a strong China with an efficient government, but not a democratic one. They tried to promote economic development, but at the same time they wanted to preserve as much of China's traditional political system as possible.

Lack of capital hindered attempts to industrialize. Much government revenue was spent on maintaining the army. The control of many of China's natural resources by foreign powers also held back economic development.

By 1937 the area of China under Nationalist control had made progress despite many obstacles. The Nationalists had begun a program of building roads and of repairing, rebuilding, and extending railroads. They improved finances and reformed the educational system.

However, because the Nationalists needed the backing of landowners and merchants, they failed to deal with two crucial problems. No changes were made in the oppressive, age-old system of land ownership or in the method of collecting taxes in the countryside. In short, nothing was done to eliminate the causes of suffering and discontent among Chinese peasants.

The growth of Chinese communism

In July 1921 a small group of Chinese intellectuals met in Shanghai and founded the Chinese Communist Party. Inspired by the example of the Russian revolution and by the ideologies of Marx and Lenin, the founders of Chinese communism hoped to free their country from foreign domination and economic backwardness. They set about building strong party organizations and labor unions in the cities of China. They also cooperated with the Kuomintang in efforts to defeat the many regional warlords within China.

At first, when their own movement was weak and in need of as much help as it could get, the Nationalists welcomed communist support. As the Communist Party grew stronger, however, conservative Nationalists became alarmed. The Kuomintang expelled all communists from the Nationalist People's Party in 1927. In the early 1930's Chiang Kai-shek carried out five large-scale military campaigns to "exterminate" communists once and for all.

The Long March. Those communists who escaped capture and execution fled first to Kiangsi province, in southeastern China. There they set up their own government. It was modeled after the Russian communist regime and was called the Chinese Soviet Republic. After repeated attacks by Nationalist forces, this group finally was forced to evacuate Kiangsi in 1934.

In a famous "Long March" lasting almost two years, about 100,000 communists made their way on foot to northern Shensi province. They traveled across 18 mountain ranges and 24 rivers, a distance of over 5,000 miles (8,000 kilometers). Many did not survive the journey. Those who did established their new headquarters in the isolated mountain town of Yenan. Their leader was Mao Tse-tung.

Mao Tse-tung. Born in the countryside of Hunan province, Mao had long argued that Chinese peasants, not the urban proletariat, could provide the best basis for a communist revolution in China. Now, far from the major cities of China, where almost all factories and factory workers were located, he had a chance to put his ideas into practice.

Mao and his followers carried out land and tax reforms in the region they controlled. They met with peasants and listened to their problems. They explained China's difficulties and urged the peasants to support the revolution.

At first the peasants of Shensi did not trust the communists. They were suspicious of all outsiders because the only outsiders they had ever known before were tax collectors and absentee landlords. However, when they found that the communists did try to solve their problems, they rallied to the communist cause. Many volunteered to serve in the communist army, called the Red Army. Others provided the communists with useful information about the location of Nationalist troops.

Because they had the support of the local peasant population, the communists were able to

Struggles in China

Centuries of imperial rule in China were brought to an end in 1912, when the Republic of China was proclaimed. Its provisional president was Sun Yat-sen, who addressed the republic's first representative assembly (above). He had been educated in Hawaii and had traveled widely in the West. His wife (shown with him, right), was an influential figure in China for more than 50 years.

In his drive to unify and modernize China, Sun Yat-sen received support in the form of money, arms, and advisers from Russia. After Sun-Yat-sen's death in 1925, his successor, Chiang Kai-shek, split with the Chinese communists and fought with them for control of the Chinese mainland. The communists, under their young leader Mao Tse-tung (below), consolidated their strength on the Long March to Yenan in northwestern China.

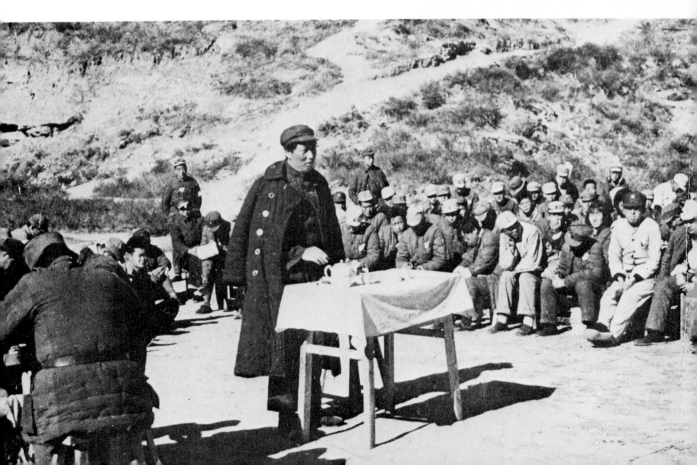

rebuild their strength and resist the efforts of the Nationalists to destroy them. As you will read in Chapter 29, they were eventually able to take the offensive.

CHECKUP

1. IDENTIFY: Open Door Policy, Kuomintang, warlords, Mao Tse-tung, "Long March."

2. What was the Boxer Rebellion? What were its results?

3. Describe Sun Yat-sen's three goals for the Chinese republic.

4. What obstacles did the Nationalists meet in trying to industrialize China?

5. How was Mao Tse-tung able to involve the peasants in the communist revolution?

Japan underwent change and increased its military strength

Japan had begun to modernize in the late 1800's. It now had to deal with the problems that earlier economic, social, and political reforms had created. Its efforts were complicated by its expansion on the Asian continent.

Territorial conflicts

As you read in Chapter 23, Japan modernized its army and navy under the Meiji Restoration. It was not long before the Japanese showed the world how much they had learned.

A region that had long interested Japan was Korea, a dependency of China. You will remember that when a rebellion broke out there in 1894, both China and Japan sent troops. These forces clashed with each other, bringing on the Sino-Japanese War. Japan defeated China early in 1895. The terms of the peace treaty provided independence for Korea. It gave Taiwan and the Pescadores to Japan as colonies.

China was the indirect cause of another Japanese conflict, this one with Russia. After the Boxer Rebellion, when most foreign powers withdrew their troops, the Russians lingered on in Manchuria. Despite several protests by the Japanese government, the Russians were slow to depart. The Japanese, who looked on Manchuria as a future sphere of influence, prepared to force them out.

In 1902 Japan signed an alliance with Great Britain. Each agreed that the other had the right to defend its special interests in China, Manchuria, and Korea against any third power. Each of the two powers agreed to remain neutral if the other became involved in a war with a single power. They would aid each other, however, if a third power joined the conflict. The alliance was aimed at Russia, although neither country openly admitted it.

The Anglo-Japanese alliance meant great prestige for Japan. It no longer stood alone but now had the support of the most powerful nation in the world. The Japanese placed increased pressure on Russia to withdraw its troops from Manchuria. The Russians agreed to negotiate, but they were in no hurry.

The Russo-Japanese War

Early in 1904, without any declaration of war, the Japanese attacked the Russian naval force at Port Arthur and sank a number of ships. The Russians later sent part of their Baltic fleet all the way around Africa to Asia. It, too, was defeated by the Japanese navy. The Japanese army marched northward through Korea to Manchuria. Another force landed on the Liaotung Peninsula and forced its way inland.

Japan had the advantage over Russia in the fighting. Its supply lines were shorter, its military better prepared, and its people more united in support of the war effort. However, the Japanese army suffered many casualties, and there was a danger that the Japanese economy would collapse. Theodore Roosevelt, President of the United States, acted as mediator in bringing about peace negotiations. In 1905 a treaty ending the Russo-Japanese War was signed at Portsmouth, New Hampshire.

The Treaty of Portsmouth. In the Treaty of Portsmouth, Russia turned over to Japan its lease on the Liaotung Peninsula, including Port Arthur, and control of the southern branch of the Chinese Eastern Railway (see map, page 570). Russia agreed to withdraw all troops from Manchuria, except for railway guards. Instead of paying an indemnity, Russia turned over to Japan the southern half of the Russian island of Sakhalin, north of Japan. Russia also gave the Japanese special fishing rights along the Siberian coast.

In a later, secret agreement, Japan promised not to interfere with Russia's ambitions in Outer Mongolia, and Russia promised not to interfere with Japan's interest in Korea. When Japan proclaimed the annexation of Korea (renaming it Chosen) in 1910, there were no protests from other imperialist powers. In 1912 Outer Mongolia, aided by Russia, declared its independence.

Problems of modernization

Japan had become a constitutional monarchy with a strong centralized government in a relatively short time. It had laid the foundations of an industrial economy. Its victories over China and Russia established it as a military power to be reckoned with. Yet all of these achievements caused new problems for the island nation.

As in Europe, industrialization and scientific development produced a sudden increase in Japan's population. Cities grew rapidly. Every inch of suitable land was farmed. Even so, the food supply did not increase as rapidly as the population. There were more people than the land would support and more people than there were jobs. Therefore, Japanese people began to emigrate to Korea, Taiwan, Hawaii, and other islands of the Pacific. Thousands moved to the United States.

In time, the United States, Canada, and Australia passed laws restricting immigration. The United States completely prohibited the immigration of Japanese, as well as Chinese, while still permitting the immigration of Europeans. As proud people, both Japanese and Chinese resented this discrimination.

Japanese industrial development created another problem. Japan lacked almost all of the raw materials needed in modern industry, so it had to import them. The only way for a nation to pay for its imports is by exporting, or selling its own goods abroad. Since Japan needed imported food as well as industrial raw materials, it had to export or face economic collapse.

In exporting goods Japan met with restriction, just as it did in its "export" of people. Many countries passed tariff laws to protect their home markets against Japanese competition. They argued that Japanese manufactured goods cost less than their own manufactured goods because Japanese labor was cheaper. This was true. Although wages had risen in Japan, they were still lower than in the West.

Social tensions in the 1920's

During the Meiji era, Japan's leaders had been able to count on social and political stability. The Japanese people did not demand greater rights or benefits than their leaders were willing to give them. In the 1920's, however, this was no longer the case. As a result of economic development, universal education, and new ideas from the West, many Japanese began to protest that the status quo was unfair and unjust. Change had benefited the nation. Now they wanted change that would benefit the people.

Industrial workers organized labor unions and went out on strike for higher wages and better working conditions. Tenant farmers organized unions, too, and demanded lower agricultural rents.

Urban intellectuals and university students were inspired by the victory of the Western democracies over Germany in World War I. They argued that democracy was the wave of the future. They organized a movement to press for universal manhood suffrage, which they saw as a first step in promoting democracy within Japan. Others became interested in socialism and communism. They protested against Japanese imperialism and tried to organize workers and tenant farmers into a revolutionary political movement.

Many young Japanese also began to question the traditional values of their society. They were taught in school that they must obey and respect their parents, especially their fathers. Whether in choosing a job or choosing a husband or wife, they were supposed to accept their parents' choice. In military training, young soldiers and sailors were taught to follow orders without question or hesitation. They were told that it was an honor to die in battle for the emperor.

Few young Japanese could or did reject these

651

Increased Japanese military power

The first industrialized nation outside the West, Japan soon began to put its economic and technical skills to increasingly militaristic uses. Emperor Hirohito, an expert horseman, rode to military inspections in full uniform (right). During the 1930's Japan's expansionist aims grew bolder, and its armies began strenuous training. Under the Japanese flag showing the rising sun, soldiers mastered mountainous areas as well as flat and beach terrains (above). The heart of Japan's strength was its navy, which posed a direct challenge to the United States in the Pacific (below). As the 1930's drew to a close, the competition between the two nations intensified. It appeared that open conflict was not far away.

values openly. In their personal lives, however, they tried to escape, at least temporarily, and experience greater freedom. They listened to jazz and played baseball. City girls cut their hair short, like "flappers" in the United States, and refused to wear the traditional female dress, a long kimono. Whenever a new translation of a Western novel appeared, the bookstores were jammed. Young Japanese writers wrote about the loneliness and frustration of individuals in Japanese society. These works, too, enjoyed great popularity.

Growing influence of the military

By the 1920's only two of the original leaders of the Meiji Restoration remained alive. The second generation of political leaders were not as united or as successful as the first. They were able to deal with only some of the demands of the people. For example, a universal manhood suffrage law was passed in 1925. Yet the political leaders could not agree on what to do about other demands. Nor were they able to solve Japan's economic problems. In this atmosphere the influence of the Japanese military grew steadily stronger.

The constitution of 1889 had granted special powers to the military. Top-ranking officers recommended to the emperor who should serve as minister of war and minister of the navy in the government. Civilians could not hold these posts. If the ministers of war and of the navy disapproved of a government policy, they could resign and force all the other ministers to resign. Civilian authorities had almost no control over the armed forces.

Until the late 1920's military leaders generally cooperated with civilians in government. Then, however, they began to assert their special powers to influence government policy. Like army officers around the world, those in Japan had studied World War I closely. They saw it as a new kind of war. Victory depended on total mobilization, not just of fighting men, but of the entire spiritual and material resources of a people. Believing that any future war would be of the same kind, they were concerned about discontent within Japan. This discontent was a sign of weakness and a threat to the nation's security in the event of war.

The economic problems Japan faced in the late 1920's also influenced military leaders to take a more active role in government. Officers in the army and navy believed that Western nations would never treat Japan as an equal. The restrictions imposed on Japanese immigration and exports were proof of that. They concluded, therefore, that the government's policy of cooperation with the Western powers was unproductive. Japan should pursue a more independent course, especially in Asia.

Acting on these conclusions, military leaders began to insist on greater attention to traditional Japanese values. They also insisted on a larger army and a stronger navy. They advocated a Japanese "Monroe Doctrine." It would allow Japan to control East Asia just as the United States controlled the Western Hemisphere. In particular, they saw Manchuria as a region for future expansion. In time, the growing influence of the Japanese military had far-reaching consequences, as you will read in Chapter 27.

CHECKUP

1. IDENTIFY: Anglo-Japanese alliance, Treaty of Portsmouth, "Monroe Doctrine for Asia."

2. What caused the Russo-Japanese War? What did Japan gain as a result of its victory?

3. What problems did modernization bring to Japan?

4. How did the Japanese constitution favor the military? In what ways did the military leaders assert their power in the late 1920's?

Latin America was shaken by the world economic crisis

At the end of the war in Europe, Latin America appeared headed for prosperity. However, the region would soon suffer from the effects of the worldwide economic crisis of the 1930's.

Economic developments

In the 1920's Mexico became a leading exporter of oil. Oil was also discovered in Venezuela, Peru, Bolivia, and Colombia. Petroleum resources were at first entirely owned by foreign companies,

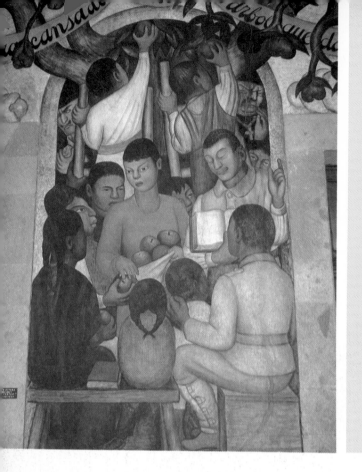

Rivera's "Fruits of Labor"

After World War I, life in Mexico changed dramatically. Cities grew, factories were built, people began working for wages, trade unions developed, and strikes occurred. This new way of life was recorded by one of Mexico's greatest artists, Diego Rivera. As a youth, Rivera had studied in Spain and then went to Paris. There, after World War I, he painted with the Cubists and later traveled through Europe. Rivera returned to Mexico in 1921, and the need for social reform in his country changed the direction of his work.

As a member of the art movement known as Social Realism, Rivera produced many paintings that dealt with current problems. The Mexican government liked Rivera's art and commissioned him to paint murals for many schools and government buildings. Above is a detail from his mural "Fruits of Labor" in which he honors working people and their children. Done for the Ministry of Education in Mexico City, this impressive wall painting took Rivera and a crew of assistants from 1923 to 1929 to complete.

mainly American and British. Other resources were mined in much larger quantities than before the war. These included copper in Chile and Peru, tin in Bolivia, and bauxite in Guiana.

In addition, there was a great expansion in electric power generation, also financed mainly by foreign countries. Petroleum and hydroelectric power enabled Latin American countries to increase their industrialization. During the 1920's the larger countries began to produce cement, iron, steel, and machinery and started to assemble automobiles and to refine petroleum.

Changes in society

The growth of cities, which had begun during the late 1800's, continued after World War I. Mexico City, Rio de Janeiro, São Paulo, and Buenos Aires all had a million or more inhabitants by 1935. These cities and others, like Caracas, Lima, Santiago, and Montevideo, extended their trolley car lines, sewer and water systems, and electric lines, and had many consumer-goods factories.

Many more people in Latin American countries worked for wages after the war. Among the wage earners were factory, office, and transportation workers, as well as paid laborers on farms and sugar plantations. Many women and children were paid laborers. This represented a major change in Latin America. Previously, most of the labor force in the region had consisted of peasants working for shares of the crop.

Trade unions became more important, trying to win benefits for their members. During World War I and for a year or two afterward, several countries had experienced waves of strikes. These were put down violently by the police and the army. Although the unions gained temporarily in the 1920's and 1930's, they had great difficulty in surviving. Most of the governments declared strikes and unions illegal.

The middle class began to grow as new jobs opened up in government service, commerce, and industry. Sons of the middle class obtained most of the places in the new military academies, which gave them access to additional power. Changes in university programs created opportunities for middle-class youth in engineering, business, and public administration.

Political changes

Because of social changes in the 1920's, political life in the more economically advanced Latin American countries began to resemble that in Europe and the United States. In Chile, Argentina, Peru, and Brazil, political parties backed by the middle class began to emerge. In Uruguay and Colombia traditional parties were restructured. In Mexico, by 1917, a single party arose out of the revolution. It brought together all of its supporters, including labor unions, peasants, and civil servants. In Uruguay, reformers led by President José Batlle y Ordóñez put through a broad reform program. It included free elections, social security, and nationalization of railroads and public utilities.

Nevertheless, these governments were still not very democratic. Voting was restricted to literate males, who usually accounted for less than one fourth of all adults—in some countries less than 10 percent. Elections were often dishonest. In rural areas they were manipulated by large landowners, who controlled how their tenants voted. In the most economically backward and socially divided countries, such as Bolivia, forcible overthrow remained the more usual way of changing governments.

The effects of the Depression

The economic weakness of Europe during these years created severe problems for Latin America. Europe's demand for the region's products faltered. Europe was less able than before to supply Latin America with capital. The United States began to act as a trading and financial partner on a larger scale, but its own economy had also slowed down.

In the late 1920's prices for Latin America's major agricultural products, such as sugar and coffee, began to fall. Chile suffered a crippling economic blow. During the war German scientists had perfected a process for making synthetic nitrates, used in fertilizers and explosives. This ruined the market for Chile's major export.

The Depression in the United States and elsewhere caused the prices of Latin America's exports to fall even further. Many Latin American nations found it impossible to continue importing any but the most essential goods. Some had to stop payments on their foreign debt. Unemployment was widespread, causing political unrest.

The economic nationalism practiced by Europe and the United States struck hardest at Latin America. For example, the trade system within the British Commonwealth made it much more difficult for Argentina to sell its wheat and beef in the British market.

Authoritarian regimes

Economic crisis led to political crisis. Most of the governments of Latin America were overthrown in the 1930's. In several cases this brought to an end constitutional systems that had worked for 30 or 40 years. The few exceptions included Uruguay, which experienced only a minor crisis between 1933 and 1935, and Mexico, which had gone through a revolution from 1911 to 1917.

Most of the new governments were no longer controlled by the planters or exporters, whose fortunes had been destroyed during the Depression. Instead, the new governments were strongly influenced or controlled by the military. In the Caribbean countries that had been occupied by the United States, American forces had reorganized and trained local armies. The result was that the military became the best equipped to take power. In Nicaragua, General Anastasio Somoza seized power in 1936 and assassinated the guerilla leader Augustino Sandino. In the Dominican Republic, General Rafael Trujillo (troo·HEE·yoh) began a 31-year dictatorship in 1930.

The military officers believed the upper-class landowners and exporters were corrupt. Military leaders accused them of having conducted dishonest elections and of allowing foreigners to take over national resources. Military leaders were also frightened by the increasing numbers of city workers and their labor unions. Many of the military leaders simply abolished unions and jailed leaders and strikers. Sometimes the military reacted even more violently. In El Salvador the army massacred thousands of striking peasants thought to have been influenced by communists.

Some of the new leaders admired European styles of authoritarianism, such as fascism. Thus, they did not simply declare unions illegal, as the limited democratic governments had done before 1930. The new rulers saw that they could control unions by selectively recognizing and giving favors only to those that were loyal to the military.

At the same time, the governments under such rulers gained popularity by responding to some of the needs of the masses of ordinary people. The governments passed or enforced for the first time laws giving workers certain benefits, such as paid vacations and accident compensation. Through these concessions, the governments hoped to undercut the potential appeal of communism among the workers.

Relations with the United States

In its relations with Latin America, the administration of President Franklin D. Roosevelt tried to undo the ill will and suspicion created by the earlier American policy of intervention. Roosevelt fostered a program, begun in the 1920's, called the **Good Neighbor Policy.** This policy stressed mutual cooperation and noninterference in Latin American affairs.

In 1933 the United States joined with other American nations in an agreement called the Montevideo Pact. The pact declared, "No state has the right to intervene in the internal or external affairs of another state." As proof of its intentions, the United States then withdrew American troops that had occupied Haiti since 1915. It also surrendered its right to interfere in the affairs of Panama.

The Roosevelt administration was embarrassed by a situation in Cuba. There a dictator was overthrown in 1933 just after Roosevelt came into office. The new government took over the American-owned electric and telephone companies. To put pressure on the new government, the United States refused to grant it diplomatic recognition. The Cubans now feared the United States would intervene again, which was its right under the Platt Amendment (see page 583).

When an army general, Fulgencio Batista, decided to overthrow the reformers, the United States ambassador encouraged him. Once in power, the United States gave Batista economic aid. In order to strengthen Batista's regime, the United States signed a treaty with Cuba, canceling the Platt Amendment.

Economic nationalism

The Latin American governments created during the Depression followed a policy of economic nationalism. They reacted to declining markets for their exports by encouraging industry. In this way, they tried to be more self-sufficient.

Foreign nations responded in a number of ways to this new Latin American initiative. On the whole, the United States and Great Britain tried to discourage these efforts for fear of competition. The German government under Hitler cleverly promoted exports of its own machinery to equip Latin American factories. It hoped to undercut the financial and political influence of the United States and Great Britain.

The most significant act of economic nationalism occurred in Mexico in 1938. American and British-owned oil companies operating there became involved in a wage dispute with their workers. The foreign-owned oil companies refused to accept the decision of the supreme court of Mexico. As a result, President Lázaro Cárdenas nationalized the oil industry and formed a government-owned oil company.

The United States had renounced intervention. However, it now applied various indirect pressures to force the Mexican government to pay the oil companies what they claimed their holdings were worth. Finally a compromise was reached. The threat of war in Europe was growing, and the United States felt that it would need the cooperation of Mexico.

CHECKUP

1. IDENTIFY: Batlle y Ordóñez, Somoza, Sandino, Trujillo, Good Neighbor Policy, Montevideo Pact, Batista, Cárdenas.

2. How did Latin American society change in the period after World War I?

3. What economic problems did Latin America experience in the postwar period? What political effects did these difficulties have?

4. What steps did the United States take toward nonintervention in Latin America?

CHAPTER REVIEW

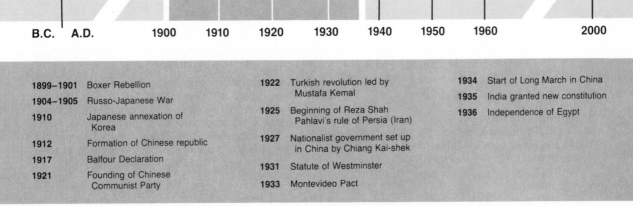

B.C.	A.D.	1900	1910	1920	1930	1940	1950	1960	2000

1899–1901 Boxer Rebellion	**1922** Turkish revolution led by Mustafa Kemal	**1934** Start of Long March in China
1904–1905 Russo-Japanese War		**1935** India granted new constitution
1910 Japanese annexation of Korea	**1925** Beginning of Reza Shah Pahlavi's rule of Persia (Iran)	**1936** Independence of Egypt
1912 Formation of Chinese republic	**1927** Nationalist government set up in China by Chiang Kai-shek	
1917 Balfour Declaration	**1931** Statute of Westminster	
1921 Founding of Chinese Communist Party	**1933** Montevideo Pact	

CHAPTER SUMMARY

In territories controlled by Great Britain, major political changes took place during the 1920's and 1930's. Egypt became completely independent. Trans-Jordan and Iraq gained limited self-government while Palestine's future remained in doubt. In India the first steps were taken toward independence. In the rest of the British Empire, new relationships were forged with the formation of the British Commonwealth of Nations.

Political and social reforms were also attempted in Turkey and in Persia. Africa witnessed the stirrings of activity that were to lead to major transformations in the years ahead.

The Chinese began a long and difficult process of adjusting to the modern world. Revolution brought imperial rule to an end, but the Kuomintang had trouble establishing its power in the republic. Their rivals, the communists, gathered strength because of their appeal to the peasants.

Dramatic change took place in Japan, which defeated China and then Russia at the turn of the century. The Japanese also faced economic and social pressures after World War I. The military, always potentially strong, began to assert its power in the late 1920's.

Developments in Latin America reflected the worldwide economic crisis. The 1920's and 1930's were also a time of rapid social change, and in a number of countries governments became more authoritarian. Relations with the United States improved as a result of the Good Neighbor Policy, but economic nationalism led to a certain degree of tension.

CHECKING WHAT YOU KNOW

1. Match each leader at the left with a country at the right.

   a. Anastasio Somoza
   b. Kemal Atatürk
   c. Chiang Kai-shek
   d. Mohandas Gandhi
   e. Chaim Weizmann
   f. Fulgencio Batista
   g. Reza Shah Pahlavi

   1. Palestine
   2. China
   3. India
   4. Iran
   5. Turkey
   6. Cuba
   7. Nicaragua

2. Match each idea or event at the left with a country or region at the right.

   a. Monroe Doctrine for Asia
   b. Long March
   c. Balfour Declaration
   d. Statute of Westminster
   e. Montevideo Pact

   1. Latin America
   2. Japan
   3. Canada, Australia, New Zealand, South Africa
   4. Palestine
   5. China

3. Compare the British reaction to demands for Indian independence with the reaction to similar demands from Canada, Australia, New Zealand, and the Union of South Africa.

4. How did Sun Yat-sen hope to bring democracy to China? What obstacles prevented him from succeeding?

5. What changes did the Nationalists begin in China? What problems did they fail to solve?

6. What economic and social problems did Japan face as a result of its rapid modernization and industrialization?

7. Why did President Roosevelt support a continuation of the Good Neighbor Policy? How did his programs change the meaning of American foreign policy as stated in the Monroe Doctrine?

PRACTICING YOUR SKILLS

1. **Interpreting evidence.** The lines below are from a poem entitled "Reproach" by Muhammad Iqbal, an Indian poet and nationalist. Read these lines, and answer the questions that follow.

> Your fate, poor hapless India, there's no telling—
> Always the brightest jewel in someone's crown;
>
> . . . .
>
> Mortgaged to the alien, soul and body too,
> Alas—the dweller vanished with the dwelling—,
> Enslaved to Britain you have kissed the rod:
> It is not Britain I reproach, but you.

How does Iqbal view India's fate? Whom does he blame for this situation? Why? What actions do you think Iqbal might want the Indian people to take? Explain.

2. **Classifying information.** Make a list of the major changes that took place in Latin America during the 1920's and 1930's. Then prepare a chart in which you classify each of the items on your list under one of the following headings: economic, social, or political.

RELATING PAST TO PRESENT

1. Use a historical atlas to find a map of the Middle East in the 1930's. What nations existed as mandates or protectorates? What nations were independent? How does this map compare with a map of the Middle East today? What nations hold the land that once made up Palestine?

2. What issue caused a strain in relations between the United States and Mexico in the 1930's? Does this issue still cause difficulties between these two nations? Explain.

3. Review the information in this chapter on the importance of the military in Japan, Persia (Iran), and Latin America. Choose one of these areas. Use newspapers and magazines to determine what role the military plays in these areas today. Is the military stronger or weaker than in the 1920's and 1930's?

INVESTIGATING FURTHER

1. As you read in this chapter, Mohandas Gandhi advocated the use of passive resistance to achieve his goals. One of his concerns was improving life for the "Untouchables," those in the lowest caste in India. Read "Gandhi's 'Fast Unto Death' " in Sydney Eisen and Maurice Filler, *The Human Adventure,* Volume 2 (Harcourt Brace Jovanovich). Why did Gandhi begin this fast? What was its effect?

2. Prepare a report on the rise of nationalism in Turkey. Your report should focus on the efforts of the Young Turks and the role of Mustafa Kemal. Some sources for your report include the following: Desmond Stewart, *Turkey* (Time-Life Books); and "The Transformation of Turkey" in Sydney Eisen and Maurice Filler, *The Human Adventure,* Volume 2 (Harcourt Brace Jovanovich).

3. Empress Ts'u Hsi held power in China from 1861 until her death in 1908. Using encyclopedias and books in your library, prepare a brief report on the life of this leader. In your report note reasons why her policies might have helped to bring about the end of the Ch'ing dynasty.

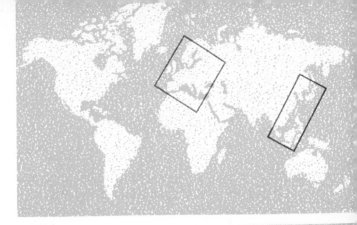

CHAPTER

27

Local Aggressions Brought About World War II

By the 1930's the nations of the world were once more divided into opposing camps. One group included the nations that were generally satisfied with the World War I peace settlement. The other group consisted of dissatisfied nations that wanted change. With each passing year, international relations grew more strained.

The League of Nations tried valiantly to preserve the peace. However, it suffered from two serious weaknesses. First, its membership was incomplete. The United States never joined, and the Soviet Union was not admitted until 1934. The absence of these major world powers proved a handicap to the League's effectiveness.

Another, more basic weakness was that the League could not make laws for its members, but could only recommend actions. The League had no means of enforcing its recommendations. Whether they were carried out depended on whether the member nations wanted to do so.

Because of the political weakness of the League, the major powers began to hold diplomatic conferences outside the world organization. The first of these meetings was held in 1921 and 1922 in Washington, D.C. Nine of the powers interested in East Asia (excluding the Soviet Union, which was not invited) attended this Washington Naval Conference.

Several treaties resulted from this conference. The Five-Power Treaty, for example, provided for a ten-year "naval holiday," during which no

Surrender aboard the **Missouri***, August 1945*

warships would be built. The participating nations also signed a Nine-Power Treaty, agreeing to take no further territory from China and to maintain the Open Door Policy.

The most optimistic of the postwar diplomatic conferences was held in 1928 at Paris. The American secretary of state, Frank B. Kellogg, and the French foreign minister, Aristide Briand, drafted a treaty condemning war. Eventually, more than 60 nations signed the Kellog-Briand Pact. War was thus made "illegal," but no one had yet found a way to make war impossible.

THE CHAPTER SECTIONS

1. Local conflicts threatened world peace

2. Hitler's aggressions brought on World War II

3. The Axis made significant gains in the early years of the war

4. Russia and the United States entered the war

5. Allied victories over Germany and Japan ended the war·

Local conflicts threatened world peace

As a result of the series of conferences and diplomatic settlements, peace was preserved throughout the 1920's. In the 1930's, however, it became clear that such makeshift arrangements would no longer be effective.

Japanese aggression in Asia

You have read how the military gained increasing power in Japan beginning in the late 1920's. In 1930 Japan's liberal prime minister, Yuko Hamaguchi, was fatally shot. Political disorder followed, and within two years the government of Japan was controlled by the militarists.

Attack on Manchuria. In September 1931 there was a mysterious explosion near Mukden, Manchuria, which damaged a Japanese-controlled railroad. Without warning and without the consent of China, Japanese troops occupied Mukden. The Republic of China appealed to the League of

Nations for help. The Japanese delegate to the League stated that the occupation of Mukden was purely a local matter and warned the League not to interfere. This incident sparked a conflict between Japan and China that was to continue, off and on, until 1945.

The League of Nations sent an investigating commission, headed by Lord Lytton of Great Britain, to Manchuria. At the same time, Japan continued its conquest. In 1932 it declared Manchuria to be an independent nation, under the name Manchukuo (MAN·CHOO·KWOH).

The Lytton Commission advised the League not to recognize Manchukuo's independence and recommended that the region be restored to China. When the League voted on this recommendation, only Japan voted against it. As a result of its diplomatic defeat, Japan withdrew from the League of Nations. Some historians regard Japan's successful aggression against China as the actual beginning of World War II.

The League was unable to stop Japan's ambitions. The major nations were willing to join in condemning aggression, but they did not press for further action. Japanese aggression, unchecked, started a chain reaction that led to the collapse of peace in the West as well as in the East.

War in China. Japan pressed further demands on China. It announced its intention to extend its influence to China Proper and not merely to outlying regions. In July 1937 Japanese and Chinese troops clashed near Peiping, the former imperial capital. Japanese armies captured Peiping and at once began to move southward. China resisted the invasion of Japanese troops, but its armies were inferior to those of Japan.

By 1939 the Japanese occupied about a fourth of China (see map, opposite), including all its seaports, the Yangtze Valley as far as Hankow, and many cities in the interior. Still the Chinese refused to give up. The war was an enormous strain on both countries. By 1939 Japan had lost nearly half a million troops in China and spent $10 billion. Chinese losses were uncountable.

Italy's defeat of Ethiopia

As you have read in Chapter 25, Mussolini and the Fascist Party had risen to power in Italy in the 1920's. Mussolini sought to solve his country's economic problems by overseas expansion. The object of his ambitions was Ethiopia, one of the few independent nations in Africa.

A border incident provided the pretext for aggression. In December 1934 an Italian border patrol in Italian Somaliland clashed with an Ethiopian border patrol. Mussolini at once sent Italian forces from Eritrea and Italian Somaliland to invade Ethiopia to "restore order."

Ethiopia was poorly prepared to resist such an invasion and asked the League of Nations for protection. The League made only a mild effort to bring the dispute to arbitration. In October 1935 Mussolini waged an all-out campaign to conquer and colonize Ethiopia.

The League then declared Italy an aggressor and applied economic sanctions—stoppage of trade and other economic relations with an offending nation. The sanctions were sweeping enough, but observance was half-hearted. In a long war, Italy might have been weakened and

forced to give in to the demands of the League. However, the Ethiopian army was not equipped to make it a long war. The Italians entered the Ethiopian capital, Addis Ababa, in the spring of 1936. Mussolini declared Ethiopia a part of the Italian Empire and proclaimed the Italian king, Victor Emmanuel III, emperor of Ethiopia.

By this time it was apparent that the League of Nations was ineffective. During the summer of 1936, it called off the sanctions on Italy. In 1937 Italy withdrew from the League. Thereafter the institution was not respected. Its inability to prevent aggression, despite almost universal disapproval of Italy's actions, caused deep concern. Meanwhile Japan and Italy had learned that the democracies were apparently unwilling to go to war to prevent aggression unless their own territory was threatened.

The Rome-Berlin Axis, which you have read about, was formed in the same year that Italy took Ethiopia. Shortly afterward, Japan and Germany

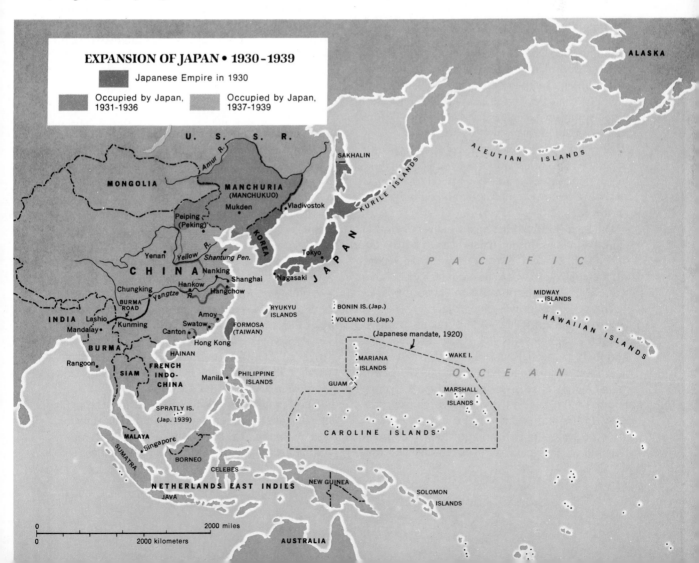

EXPANSION OF JAPAN • 1930-1939

- Japanese Empire in 1930
- Occupied by Japan, 1931-1936
- Occupied by Japan, 1937-1939

pledged to work together to prevent the spread of Russian communism. They signed an agreement called the Anti-Comintern Treaty. It was soon endorsed by Italy.

Civil war in Spain

Spain had lagged far behind the rest of Western Europe during the 1800's. It was a poor country. Much of the land was barren, and there were few mineral resources. There was some industry, but the economy was mainly agricultural. Much of the land was owned in large estates by the nobility. The Catholic Church, the established church, was wealthy and powerful. It controlled the educational system.

By the early 1900's, the government of Spain was a constitutional monarchy. The king's power was limited by an elected parliament called the Cortes. Politically, the country was unstable. Throughout the early 1900's, the nation was troubled by violent strikes, political assassinations, military plots, and separatist movements in the provinces. There were several radical parties, including socialists, communists, and anarchists.

In the period after World War I, the disordered conditions in Spain grew worse. In 1923 General Miguel Primo de Rivera led a revolt and established a military dictatorship. The king, Alfonso XIII, remained as a figurehead, but Primo de Rivera was the actual ruler. Primo de Rivera depended upon the support of the army. He lost this support by 1930 and was forced to resign. In 1931 King Alfonso abdicated and Spain became a republic.

The Spanish Republic. Spain's new government planned many reforms. There was to be freedom of religion. Church and state were to be separated, and education was to be secular. By 1934 there were to be free elections by universal suffrage.

The government was given much control over industry and property. Land taken from the Church and nobles was given to landless peasants. Members of the clergy were barred from teaching in schools and were no longer paid by the government. Workers received many benefits—shorter hours, better wages, the right to organize, and a voice in the management of business.

These sweeping reforms antagonized conservatives in both Spain and its colonies abroad.

Shortly after the establishment of the republic, conservatives organized a fascist party called the Falange (FAY·lanj). The Falange was determined to preserve the power of the army, landowners, and the Church, regardless of whom the voters might elect to office.

Nationalists versus Loyalists. In February 1936 a Popular Front government was elected. The Spanish Popular Front, like the Popular Front in France, represented a coalition of left-wing working-class parties united in their opposition to fascism. Prominent rightists were jailed, and the Falange responded with acts of terrorism. In July a conservative leader was assassinated. His murder was followed by army uprisings, led by Falangists, in Spanish Morocco, the Canary Islands, and Spain itself. This began a bitter civil war that was to last for almost three years.

The Falangist rebels, led by General Francisco Franco, called themselves Nationalists. Those who supported the republic were known as Loyalists, or Republicans. By the end of 1936, the Nationalists held most of the north and west of Spain. The Loyalists held the east and southeast, most of the northern coastline, and the capital city of Madrid.

Foreign aid to Spain

The Spanish Civil War soon became a small European war. Germany and Italy saw a fascist Spain as a link in their chain around France and as a threat to Great Britain. They helped the Nationalists with fully equipped military units.

The Soviet Union was sympathetic to the republican government. It helped the Loyalists by sending planes, technicians, and military advisers. This aid, however, was not nearly as extensive as that given to Franco by his fascist allies.

Volunteers from France, Great Britain, the United States, and other nations also went to the aid of the Spanish Republic. These anti-fascist volunteers became known as the International Brigade. The International Brigade, however, numbered only about 40,000 while Italy alone sent more than 50,000 trained troops.

The Spanish Civil War brought into the open the struggle between fascism and socialism that was seething in Europe in the 1930's. It also was a testing ground for new weapons and tactics.

Threats to the peace

Local conflicts in the 1930's were grim preludes to World War II. The first serious breakdown of international order was the Italian invasion of Ethiopia in 1935. Haile Selassie (below), the emperor of Ethiopia, appeared before the League of Nations and appealed for help. The League supported his cause but was unable to stop the aggression.

In the following year, 1936, civil war broke out in Spain. Anti-fascist resistance was brave, but the fascists received reinforcements and supplies from Germany and Italy. Despite emotional calls for help throughout the West (left), the forces of fascism won in the end. In East Asia, the Japanese invaded China in 1937 (below left). Once again, aggressive forces were successfully on the march.

France and Great Britain were afraid that the Spanish Civil War might spread to the rest of Europe and involve them. In September 1936, at the suggestion of the French government, a Nonintervention Committee was established, representing 27 nations. All agreed to a policy of nonintervention in Spain, with a blockade to stop the flow of volunteers and supplies. The blockade stopped most aid to the Loyalists, but not German and Italian aid to Franco. To Hitler and Mussolini this was one more proof that Great Britain and France would do nothing to stop aggression unless it involved their own territory.

Spain under Franco

By the spring of 1938, the Nationalist forces in Spain had grown strong enough for a large-scale offensive. The weakened Loyalist troops were defeated in March 1939, when the Nationalists captured Barcelona and Madrid.

Franco then set up a fascist government modeled on Mussolini's dictatorship in Italy. Franco became head of the state with unlimited power. He was responsible, as one decree said, "only to God and history." He assumed a title—*el Caudillo* (cow·DEE·yoh)—Spanish for "the leader." His political party, the Falange, was the only one permitted. Its National Council, chosen by Franco, "advised" him on legislation.

The economic organization of Spain resembled that of fascist Italy, with syndicates, or corporations, organized according to occupations and economic activities. Free elections and most civil rights were abolished. Under Franco's regime, the old ruling groups—the army, landowners, and the Roman Catholic Church—continued to hold positions of power. Yet, although Spain had become a fascist dictatorship, Franco did not join the Rome-Berlin Axis.

CHECKUP

1. IDENTIFY: Kellogg-Briand Pact, Hamaguchi, Lytton Commission, Anti-Comintern Treaty, Cortes, Falange, Franco, International Brigade.

2. LOCATE: Mukden, Manchukuo, Peiping, Hankow.

3. How did the League of Nations respond to the Japanese takeover of Manchuria and to Italy's invasion of Ethiopia?

4. How did the Nationalists and the Loyalists in Spain differ politically?

5. What policy did Great Britain and France adopt toward the Spanish Civil War? How did Germany and Italy view this policy?

Hitler's aggressions brought on World War II

As Germany grew increasingly stronger, Hitler's foreign policy became more aggressive. In 1933 he had taken Germany out of the League of Nations and announced his intention to rearm. In 1936, as you have read, Germany marched troops into the Rhineland. Soon afterward Hitler and Mussolini formed the Rome-Berlin Axis. Hitler became convinced that he could do as he pleased, and for a time he seemed right. The democratic nations had done very little to halt the spread of fascism in Ethiopia and Spain.

Annexing Austria

A Nazi party had been formed in Austria in the late 1920's. By the early 1930's, the Austrian government had become extremely conservative and a near-dictatorship. It did little to resist Nazi inroads. By 1938 threats from both Hitler and Mussolini forced the Austrian government to include Nazi members in the cabinet.

When the Austrian chancellor offered to take a vote of the Austrian people on the question of *Anschluss* (union) with Germany, Hitler refused to permit it. The chancellor resigned, and a German army marched into Austria unopposed. In March 1938 Hitler proclaimed Austria a part of the Third Reich. The League of Nations took no action. Great Britain and France sent protests to Hitler, which he disregarded. Once again, no stronger steps were taken. The democracies seemed to prefer inaction to the danger of war.

The addition of Austria enlarged Germany's population, territory, and resources. It also increased Hitler's influence in Europe. Strategically, Germany had now penetrated the heart of central Europe and reached a common border

HISTORY THROUGH ART

"Guernica" by Pablo Picasso

Although he lived in France, Pablo Picasso had been born in Spain and was keenly sympathetic to the Loyalist cause during the Spanish Civil War. This painting expressed his outrage over the bombing of the town of Guernica, which had no strategic value. Using only blacks, grays, and whites, Picasso evoked anguish and horror with his distorted figures writhing in agony under a stark electric light. The painting was on tour in New York City in 1939, when World War II began. Picasso suggested that it stay in the United States until "the re-establishment of public liberties" in Spain. "Guernica" was returned to Spain in 1981 and was placed in the Prado Museum in Madrid.

with its ally, Italy. A glance at the map on page 666 will show what the annexation of Austria did to Czechoslovakia, which Hitler had announced as the next step in his program of expansion. Germany now almost completely encircled the Czech republic. Nazi propaganda, however, claimed that Czechoslovakia had become "a dagger aimed at the heart of Germany."

Czechoslovakia and the Sudeten crisis

Around the western rim of Czechoslovakia, in a region known as the Sudetenland, lived more than 3 million Germans. This territory had been included in Czechoslovakia after World War I. It is separated from Germany and Austria by a chain of mountains, which gave the new state a natural and defensible frontier. Czechoslovakia had fortified these mountains heavily. Now they were a defensive line second in Europe only to France's Maginot Line.

The Czech government made efforts to protect the rights of the Sudeten Germans. Still, many of them wanted to be united with Germany. With the victory of Nazism in Germany, a Nazi party grew among the Sudeten Germans. After 1935 the Nazis had more votes in the Czech parliament than any other party. However, the Nazis still did not comprise a majority.

After the annexation of Austria, the Sudeten Nazis demanded a completely self-governing Sudetenland. Hitler took up their demand, ranting against the Czech "oppression" of Germans. Many fictitious stories of discriminations and atrocities against the Sudetens were spread by Nazi propagandists. Riots broke out, and in September 1938, the situation became so critical that the Czech government placed the country under military law. The Sudeten Nazi leader fled to Germany.

Hitler announced that the German army would invade the Sudetenland to protect Germany's "Sudetenland brothers." He also claimed that the Sudetenland would be annexed to Germany. Without its heavily fortified mountain region, Czechoslovakia would be defenseless against

665

Germany. When Germany sent troops to the frontier, the world waited tensely to see what action Czechoslovakia's allies would take.

The Czechs had defensive alliances with both France and the Soviet Union. The Soviet alliance provided that the Soviet Union would aid the Czechs only on condition that France did. France turned to Great Britain for support. Great Britain, however, urged France to be patient and advised the Czechs to make every possible concession to avoid war. The result was increased independence for the Sudetens.

Hitler was still not satisfied and began to increase Germany's military preparations. On September 22, 1938, Hitler demanded that the Sudetenland be returned to Germany. If it were not, he said, he would invade it and take it by force.

Appeasement at Munich

As tensions mounted in Europe, Hitler unexpectedly suggested a conference. It would be attended by himself, Mussolini, British Prime Minister Neville Chamberlain, and Edouard Daladier, the premier of France. The conference would begin on September 29 in Munich, and the participants would try to settle the Czech problem peaceably.

**AGGRESSIONS LEADING TO WORLD WAR II
1935-1939**

Axis Powers

Axis-controlled lands,
September 1, 1939

Conspicuously absent from the meeting were: (1) the Soviet Union, which was, with France, pledged to defend Czechoslovakia, and (2) a representative of Czechoslovakia itself. The Soviet Union was not invited because Hitler wanted to isolate it from the West.

At Munich, Chamberlain and Daladier were eager to avoid war at any cost. They accepted Hitler's demand that the Sudetenland be annexed to Germany. The policy they followed—attempting to preserve peace by yielding to the demands of the aggressor—is known as **appeasement.** Since 1938 the name Munich, where the conference took place, has become symbolic of appeasement and surrender.

Soon after the Munich conference, France announced that it would not honor its alliance with Czechoslovakia or come to its aid. Germany began to occupy the Sudetenland. The small country of Czechoslovakia, deserted by its allies, was now left defenseless. Yet another step had been taken toward the rule of force and chaos in international affairs.

Hitler, in speaking of the Sudetenland, said, "This is the last territorial claim I shall make in Europe." Poland and Hungary, however, soon seized Czechoslovakian territories along their borders, claiming that these lands were inhabited by Poles and Hungarians.

In March 1939 Hitler sent his troops throughout the Czech area of Czechoslovakia and made it a German protectorate. He then declared the remainder of the country an independent state called Slovakia, but soon seized that too.

Czechoslovakia had been the last democracy in central Europe, and the most prosperous of the nations formed after World War I. Yet, within a period of six months, this independent republic was wiped completely from the map of Europe. As a result, the League of Nations was compelled to cross another name from its list of members. The League's helplessness could now no longer be remedied. In the meantime, the political situation in Europe was heading rapidly toward anarchy.

Memel and Albania

While Hitler was in the process of annexing Czechoslovakia, he was also making moves toward Lithuania. Hitler's quarrel with Lithuania involved the former East Prussian seaport city of Memel (see map, opposite). Germany had surrendered Memel to the Allies in the Versailles Treaty. In 1923 the city had been taken by Lithuania. After studying the matter, the League of Nations recommended, with Lithuania's approval, that Memel should be recognized as part of Lithuania. Memel, however, would be given considerable self-government.

After Hitler came to power, a Nazi party sprang up among the Germans in Memel. They demanded that the city be annexed by Germany. Hitler echoed these demands. The Lithuanian government responded by taking oppressive measures against the Memel Nazis. In 1935, however, the predominantly German population of Memel elected a Nazi majority to the city government.

After Germany and Hungary had taken what was left of Czechoslovakia, Hitler increased his demands on Lithuania. In March 1939 the pressure became too great and Lithuania ceded Memel and adjacent territory to Germany.

Still another area lost its independence in the spring of 1939. Mussolini, once a model for other dictators, had by now become the imitator of Hitler. In April 1939 he invaded Albania, on the east coast of the Adriatic Sea (see map, opposite). The Italians took the country in a few days. Consequently the king of Italy, who had recently become emperor of Ethiopia, gained an additional title—king of Albania.

Preparations for war

By the summer of 1939, British and French leaders could no longer maintain illusions about the peaceful intentions of the fascist dictators. They therefore began to prepare for war. In France the premier was given special powers to speed wartime preparations. In Great Britain, Neville Chamberlain rushed through Parliament a huge armaments program and a draft law. France already had a defensive alliance with Poland. Great Britain announced that it, too, would help Poland if Germany attacked it.

France also had a nonaggression treaty with the Soviet Union. Now Great Britain and France approached the Soviet Union, suggesting a mutual alliance against Germany. Stalin, however, was suspicious of the Western democracies. Until this time, the Soviet Union had been excluded from all major decisions in Europe and the rest of the world. The Soviet leaders were fearful that the Western powers would welcome a chance to turn Hitler loose on them.

The Soviets insisted that any mutual assistance pact they signed with Great Britain and France had to guarantee the independence of Poland, Finland, and the Baltic countries of Estonia, Latvia, and Lithuania. The Soviets also wanted a military alliance with all these countries to ensure instant response in the event of a German attack. This suggestion brought instant protests from the nations involved. All but Lithuania had common borders with the Soviet Union. A common military agreement would mean that, in case of a German attack, Soviet armies would have the right to move into their countries to meet the Germans. The negotiations dragged on, resulting in a stalemate.

The Hitler-Stalin Pact

At the same time that Stalin was negotiating with Great Britain and France, he was carrying on secret negotiations with the German foreign minister. In August 1939 the Western democracies received a tremendous shock. Hitler proudly announced that Germany and the Soviet Union had signed a nonaggression treaty. The announcement was soon confirmed in Moscow.

The reasons for such an agreement between openly declared enemies were not immediately apparent. However, many historians believe that neither side expected the treaty to be a lasting one. Hitler and Stalin may simply have been playing for time. Hitler wanted to assure himself of Soviet neutrality while he dealt with France and Great Britain. Stalin apparently hoped that Hitler would find himself bogged down in the West. This would give the Soviet Union adequate time to prepare for its eventual encounter with Germany.

Publicly, the Hitler-Stalin Pact pledged that Germany and the Soviet Union would never attack each other. Each would remain neutral if the other were involved in war. Secretly, however, the two dictators agreed to divide eastern Europe into spheres of influence. Germany was to take western Poland. The Soviet Union was to have a free hand in the Baltic countries, in eastern

Poland, and in the province of Bessarabia, which it had lost to Rumania in 1918.

There was little doubt of the meaning of the pact. The Western nations had lost a possible ally in the east, and Germany had a pledge of the Soviet Union's neutrality. It was a tremendous military advantage, which Hitler was quick to use.

Danzig and the Polish Corridor

The crisis that finally touched off World War II began in Poland. Hitler's dispute with Poland involved the Polish Corridor. This was the strip of territory cut through Germany to allow Poland to reach the seaport of Danzig (see map, page 666). Danzig, a free city protected by the League of Nations, was a port for both Germany and Poland.

Danzig had its own elected two-house legislature. The executive was a commissioner appointed by the League. Since Danzig had a large German population, Hitler claimed that the city had been "torn from the fatherland." He attacked the commissioner as a foreigner.

A strong Nazi party developed in Danzig, encouraged by propaganda and financial help from Berlin. By 1937 it had won control of the city government. It took actions and issued demands that made relations with Poland increasingly difficult. The League commissioner was powerless to do anything.

After he secured Austria and Czechoslovakia, Hitler stepped up his campaign against Poland. The Nazis demanded the return of Danzig to the fatherland. A propaganda campaign claimed that the Poles were mistreating the Germans in the Polish Corridor. Within a week after signing the nonaggression pact with the Soviet Union, Hitler demanded a "German solution" to the Polish question: Danzig must be returned to Germany, and the Germans must be allowed to occupy a strip through the Corridor.

On the morning of September 1, 1939, Hitler declared that Danzig was annexed to the Reich. At the same time, without warning, his air force made a massive attack on Poland. Nazi troops, led by tank columns, struck across the border. Two days later, two of the Allied Powers, Great Britain and France, decided that they would not tolerate further Nazi aggression. They kept their

Hitler's aggressions

Despite mounting aggressions by the fascists in the 1930's, there were some in the West who were reluctant to fight force with force. They hoped that by appeasing Hitler, they might avoid another war in Europe and keep Germany as protection against Soviet communism. The most famous of those favoring appeasement was Prime Minister Neville Chamberlain of Great Britain (below). Chamberlain believed that granting the Sudetenland to Hitler would mean "peace in our time." In 1939 German forces moved into Czechoslovakia (below right).

The next year Hitler won appeasement in another form when he and Stalin (right) signed a nonaggression pact. Stalin promised not to prevent Hitler from moving into Poland, if the Soviet Union could take a piece of the country as well.

promises to Poland and declared war on Germany. Within 48 hours the unannounced attack on Poland became the beginning of World War II.

CHECKUP

1. IDENTIFY: Chamberlain, Daladier, appeasement.

2. LOCATE: Sudetenland, Munich, Memel, Albania, Danzig.

3. How did Hitler's annexation of Austria benefit Germany?

4. Describe the steps by which Hitler took over Czechoslovakia.

5. How did France and Great Britain prepare for war in the summer of 1939?

6. What was the Hitler-Stalin Pact? What may have been Hitler's and Stalin's reasons for signing it?

7. What incident marked the start of World War II?

3

The Axis made significant gains in the early years of the war

Hitler's invasion of Poland set the example for a new kind of warfare. The German attack was called a **blitzkrieg**—German for "lightning war." Dive bombers screamed down, dropping explosives on cities below. Panzer units—tanks and armored trucks—advanced swiftly. It was a devastating war of rapid movement, and the Poles surrendered to Hitler on September 27.

The "phony" war

While Germany was attacking Poland, France moved its army up to the Maginot Line, the chain of fortifications guarding France's eastern frontier (see map, opposite). British forces crossed the English Channel and landed on the northern coast of France. The British navy blockaded Germany's ports. The Germans massed troops behind the Siegfried Line, the system of fortifications they had built in the Rhineland. German submarines had begun to sink merchant ships—both enemy and neutral—but there was little action on the western front. Although mobilization and arms production escalated, newspapers began to speak of the "phony" war in Western Europe. Many people still hoped that an all-out war could be avoided.

As the Germans marched into Poland, the Soviet army massed on the Soviet-Polish border. Then, in accordance with the secret provisions of the Hitler-Stalin Pact, the Soviets moved into eastern Poland. As a result, Poland disappeared from the map of Europe. The Soviets then took control of the Baltic countries of Estonia, Latvia, and Lithuania.

On November 30, 1939, the Soviet Union attacked Finland. The Finns appealed to the League of Nations, which expelled the Soviet Union for its aggression against a member nation. The Finns fought bravely for three months, but their resistance crumbled in March 1940.

Scandinavia and the Low Countries

On April 9, 1940, the "phony" war ended with a sudden German invasion of Denmark and Norway. Hitler had prepared the way in these Scandinavian countries by sending Germans there as workers. These Germans were to secure the services of native **collaborators,** people who were willing to assist their country's enemies. In a single day, German troops seized several of Norway's strategic North Sea ports. Both Denmark and Norway were under German control by the end of April.

The reasons for Hitler's invasion of these countries soon became clear. By seizing them, Germany secured an outlet to the Atlantic. Thus, Hitler made certain that his country would not be bottled up in the Baltic Sea as had happened in World War I. The long Scandinavian coastline gave Germany excellent bases for submarines. There were also many good sites for airfields. Thus, shipping to France and Great Britain was put in grave danger.

The British soon realized that Hitler posed an immediate threat to their safety. Neville Chamberlain, who symbolized the policy of appeasement, was forced to resign as prime minister in May 1940. He was succeeded by Winston Churchill, a statesman who had attacked appeasement. Churchill had been one of the few prominent politicians in the 1930's to warn against the Nazi menace in Europe.

Hitler, meanwhile, continued to attack. He intended to take as much territory as possible before his opponents could mount an offensive against him. On May 10, 1940, German armored units invaded the Low Countries—the Netherlands, Belgium, and Luxembourg. Luxembourg fell in one day, the Netherlands in five. When the Dutch city of Rotterdam resisted the German army, Hitler ordered his air force to attack it. Even while a surrender was being negotiated, Nazi bombers leveled the heart of the city. Belgium also surrendered at the end of May.

Hitler's forces were now in a position to outflank France's Maginot Line. The German panzers drove westward, toward the English Channel. British, Belgian, and French troops at Dunkirk, a seaport in northern France, were cut off from the major French force to the south. Outnumbered and with no room to maneuver, the encircled Allied troops could only surrender or withdraw. They chose to withdraw.

Evacuation of Dunkirk. At this point, the British air force was able to gain momentary control of the air to defend the trapped forces at Dunkirk from bombing attacks. Every available ship and boat in England, including fishing craft and

WORLD WAR II IN EUROPE AND NORTH AFRICA 1939-1945

- Chief Axis Powers
- Maximum area of Axis control
- → Allied advances
- ✕ Battle of the Bulge
- Maginot Line
- ▲▲▲▲▲ Siegfried Line
- ─·─·─ Boundaries of September 1, 1939
- Neutral or non-belligerent nations <u>underlined</u>

rowboats, was ordered to Dunkirk. Between May 27 and June 4, some 340,000 men were safely transported across the channel to England.

The evacuation of Dunkirk was a military defeat for the Allies. However, the success of the astounding rescue operation helped raise British morale considerably. On June 4, Prime Minister Churchill addressed one of his most stirring speeches to the British people. "We shall defend our island," he said, "whatever the cost may be. We shall fight on the beaches, we shall fight on the landing grounds, . . . we shall fight in the hills; we shall never surrender."

The fall of France

After the evacuation of Dunkirk the French were left to fight alone on the European continent. The Maginot Line was useless. Having overrun Belgium, the Germans were in a position to attack France from the north, where few fortifications had been built.

Germany began its offensive against France early in June 1940. The French fought a desperate, losing battle. Their army was not trained or equipped for the new kind of war. Northern France was a scene of utter confusion. Civilians, carrying whatever goods they could save, blocked roads and attempted to flee southward. German planes bombed and machine-gunned the fleeing refugees, causing panic and disorder.

Mussolini, taking advantage of France's weakness, declared war on France and Great Britain on June 10, and Italian forces invaded southern France. On June 14 the Germans entered Paris, and French armed resistance collapsed. Rather than surrender, the French cabinet resigned.

There were, however, some French leaders who were willing to surrender. The aged Marshal Henri Pétain (pay·TAN), a hero of World War I, formed a government and assumed dictatorial powers. Late in June the Pétain government signed an armistice with Hitler and Mussolini.

The armistice terms were severe. German troops were to occupy northern France, including Paris, and a strip of territory along the Atlantic coast southward to Spain. The costs of the occupation were to be paid by France. The French navy was to be disarmed and kept in French ports. Pétain's government moved to the city of Vichy (vee·SHEE), in the south. Thus France was divided into Occupied France, administered by the Germans, and Vichy France, which collaborated with the Germans (see map, page 671). The Vichy government also controlled most French possessions in North Africa and the Middle East. This government became another symbol of appeasement and surrender to fascism.

The French resistance. Some of the French who wanted to continue to fight against Germany escaped to Africa or to England. Under the leadership of General Charles de Gaulle (duh·GOHL), they formed the Free French government, with headquarters in London.

Within France itself there grew up an underground movement, the resistance. Its members worked secretly to oppose the German occupation forces. Similar resistance movements developed in most of the countries that were occupied by Germany. Their members, known as **partisans,** engaged in sabotage. They blew up bridges, wrecked trains, and cut telephone and telegraph lines. When discovered by the Germans, the partisans were usually tortured and executed. Nevertheless, the underground fighters continued their work with great courage.

The Battle of Britain

After the fall of France, French generals predicted that Great Britain would "have her neck wrung like a chicken's in three weeks." Hitler began scattered bombing raids on Great Britain, which gradually increased in intensity.

Great Britain was poorly prepared for war. Hitler appealed to "reason and common sense" in Great Britain. He offered to negotiate a peace settlement, but he was rebuffed by Churchill. Germany stepped up the air attacks on Great Britain, striking centers of civilian population as well as railroad and industrial targets. The period of the heaviest attacks, from August through November 1940, is known as the Battle of Britain.

German bombers blasted British cities with explosives and fire bombs. London was bombed continually during September and October. In November the city of Coventry was burned almost to the ground. The German aim was to lower morale and destroy the people's will to fight, but

World War II in Europe

World War II began disastrously for the Allies. There was fierce fighting as Nazi tanks rolled through Europe (below). One of the saddest moments was the evacuation of the last British soldiers from the continent of Europe in 1940. A flotilla of small ships heroically rescued the troops from the beaches of Dunkirk, in France (bottom).

As the Germans bombed Britain, Prime Minister Winston Churchill inspected the damage and offered comfort, even while the attacks continued (left). Often his only protection was a pile of sandbags, but Churchill's smile and determination set an example for everyone. Finally, with the help of American troops, the Allies were able to cross the English Channel again and push on to victory over the Axis.

the British doggedly dug out of the ruins and fought on. Essential to their resistance was the defense by fighter planes of the Royal Air Force.

British planes, though fewer, were better in quality than the German planes. They were piloted by daring and skillful fliers. British planes also had the advantage of radar, a new tracking device that had been developed recently. During the summer and fall of 1940, the British shot down a great number of German planes. The British air force challenged German control of the air and prevented German invasion across the channel. Of these British fighter pilots, Churchill said, "Never in the field of human conflict was so much owed by so many to so few."

The Germans continued night bombing raids for almost two years. At the same time British bombers made increasingly heavy raids on German cities. By the middle of 1941, air warfare had reached a stalemate. However, because of Germany's blockade of British shipping from European ports, there was a chance that Great Britain could be starved out. This might have happened, had it not been for the United States.

United States involvement

The Neutrality Act of 1937 expressed the determination of the United States to remain neutral in future wars. This legislation forbade Americans to sell war equipment to belligerent nations.

When war in Europe broke out in 1939, opinion in the United States was divided. Many people felt that Nazi Germany was a threat not only to Europe but to civilization itself. Others believed that Europe's wars were no affair of the United States. These **isolationists,** as they were called, had been powerful since the end of World War I when they had kept the United States out of the League of Nations. Now, however, their power faded as the fear of a Nazi conquest of the world increased.

As the war progressed, the United States gradually found itself becoming more involved. In 1939 a revised Neutrality Act allowed the sale of munitions to belligerent nations, but only on a cash-and-carry basis. In spite of German submarine attacks, the British still controlled the sea routes between the United States and Great Britain. Thus, in effect, this law permitted the sale of arms only to Great Britain.

After the disaster at Dunkirk and the fall of France, Americans' sympathies for the British increased. In September 1940 President Roosevelt, by executive agreement, transferred 50 old American naval destroyers to Great Britain. In exchange Great Britain gave the United States long-term leases on British naval and air bases in Newfoundland, the British West Indies, and British Guiana. In that same month, Congress passed the first national draft law ever adopted by the United States during peacetime.

Early in 1941 Churchill appealed to the United States: "Give us the tools, and we will finish the job." In March, Congress passed the Lend-Lease Act, authorizing the President to supply war materials to Great Britain on credit. Now the direction of America's involvement was clear.

The Atlantic Charter

Because they wanted to avoid the secret-treaty incidents of World War I, Roosevelt and Churchill decided to announce the war aims of the democracies. In August 1941 they met on board a British battleship off the coast of Newfoundland and drew up a statement that became known as the Atlantic Charter.

Among its provisions were these: (1) Neither nation sought territorial gains. (2) No territorial changes were to be made without the consent of the people concerned. (3) All people were to have the right to choose their form of government. (4) All nations were to have equal rights to trade and to raw materials. (5) Nations were to cooperate on economic matters to ensure everyone a decent standard of living. (6) People everywhere were to have the right to security and freedom from want and fear. (7) Freedom of the seas was to be guaranteed. (8) All nations were to end the arms race.

By the fall of 1941, the United States Navy was waging an undeclared war on German submarines. The nation had moved far away from its neutrality of 1937. The only remaining restrictions prohibited American merchant ships from being armed or entering war zones. In November 1941 Congress abolished these restrictions. The United States, as a nonbelligerent ally, was now giving the British "all aid short of war."

1. IDENTIFY: blitzkrieg, panzer units, collaborators, Churchill, Pétain, de Gaulle, partisans, Battle of Britain, isolationists, Lend-Lease Act, Atlantic Charter.

2. LOCATE: Siegfried Line, Rotterdam, Dunkirk, Occupied France, Vichy France, Coventry.

3. What was the "phony" war? What advantages did Germany gain by seizing Norway and Denmark?

4. Why was the Maginot Line useless in June 1940? What were the "three Frances" after the French were defeated?

5. Describe the involvement of the United States in World War II, from the Neutrality Act of 1937 to giving Great Britain "all aid short of war."

The Soviet Union and the United States entered the war

By the fall of 1940, Germany held almost all of Western Europe. It controlled the Atlantic coastline from the tip of Norway to Spain, and its submarines were allowed to use Spanish ports. Spain did not join the fighting, but neither was it neutral. Franco called his country a "nonneutral nonbelligerent." Germany and Italy—now called the Axis Powers—also controlled much of the western Mediterranean coastline, an important advantage to their side.

Great Britain still held Gibraltar, on the southern coast of Spain; the islands of Malta and Cyprus, in the Mediterranean; and Alexandria, in Egypt. British troops were stationed in Palestine and in Egypt, protecting the Suez Canal.

In September the Japanese government joined the Rome-Berlin Axis as an ally of Hitler and Mussolini. This move strained Hitler's "master race" doctrine, with its contempt for non-Caucasians. However, Hitler announced that the Japanese were "yellow Aryans."

Eastern Europe and the Mediterranean

Mussolini hoped to build a Mediterranean empire for Italy. In the fall of 1940, he sent his troops into British Somaliland, Egypt, and Greece. The Greeks routed the invading Italian army. The British stopped the advance into Egypt. In their counterattack, the British took Tobruk, a port city of Libya (see map, page 671). The Italian invasion of British Somaliland also failed, and a counterattack by the British drove the Italians out of Ethiopia as well.

Not until Hitler turned his attention to the Balkans did Axis fortunes in the east improve. Germany seized Rumania, which it needed for the rich oil fields there. In March 1941 German pressure on Bulgaria resulted in the occupation of that country by German troops. By November Rumania, Bulgaria, and Hungary had allied themselves with Germany.

In April 1941 Hitler invaded Yugoslavia, after failing to persuade its government to allow German troops to march through the country to Greece. In less than two weeks, Yugoslav resistance was crushed.

Next came Greece. Despite stubborn resistance by the Greeks, aided by British and other Allied troops, the German panzers prevailed. The British withdrew to the island of Crete. Now the Germans used a new technique. German troops parachuted into Crete, and by the end of May the British were forced to abandon the island and flee to Egypt. Thus Germany controlled the entire Balkan Peninsula except the city of Istanbul and the Dardanelles and the Bosporus (see map, page 671). In June, Germany and Turkey signed a treaty assuring Turkish neutrality.

The German victories in Greece and Crete enabled Hitler to launch the next move in his giant strategy—a huge pincers movement against the Suez Canal. One part of the Axis force was to come by way of North Africa, the other through Syria, Iraq, Trans-Jordan, and Palestine. The rich oil fields of the Middle East would also give Hitler a considerable advantage in the war. Vital war equipment such as airplanes, tanks, and trucks needed fuel to operate.

Hitler hoped that political pressure would force Turkey to allow German troops to pass through its territory. This tactic failed, however, and Turkey remained neutral. The British and Free French held Iraq and, in July 1941, drove the Vichy French out of Syria. One month later, Allied forces also occupied Iran.

(continued on page 678)

Civilian life during World War II

World War II, the war that involved the greatest number of people in human history, affected all life deeply, civilian as well as military. In the United States, posters urged civilians "to do their part" to aid the war effort (left). This often meant working night shifts in war factories, a disruption of normal family life. Limited supplies of food, clothing, gasoline, and other goods were sold to civilians through the use of ration coupons (top far right).

Such hardships could not compare with the dislocations suffered by civilians in the midst of the actual fighting. Jews in Europe, made to wear yellow Stars of David to identify themselves, were forced by the Nazis to sort weapons in slave labor conditions (above right). As the war progressed, Jews were systematically killed in concentration camps. The Allied soldiers who liberated these camps were sickened by the sights they found (above).

When the fighting finally subsided, the survivors wandered through devastated cities such as Nuremberg (right), looking for family members among the thousands who lay dead or dying.

"THE GIRL HE LEFT BEHIND" IS STILL BEHIND HIM
She's a WOW
WOMAN ORDNANCE WORKER

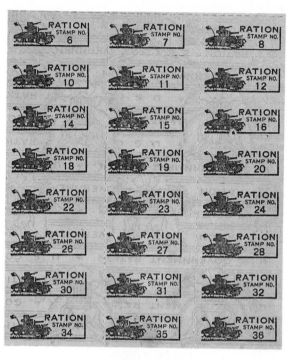

Meanwhile the Germans had moved forces across the Mediterranean to North Africa. Throughout 1941, Italian and German troops led by General Erwin Rommel—known as the "Desert Fox"— fought the British in Libya. In the summer of 1942, Rommel's forces drove the British out of Libya and back into Egypt. At El Alamein, only 70 miles (112 kilometers) from Alexandria (see map, page 671), the German offensive began to run down for lack of supplies. The British made a stand, and Rommel remained stalled at El Alamein.

Germany's attack on the Soviet Union

The Soviets regarded the German victories in the Balkans with alarm and anger. They considered the Balkans, especially Rumania and Bulgaria, within their sphere of influence.

A Soviet-German conference took place in Berlin in November 1940. The Soviets demanded that Bulgaria, Istanbul, and the Dardanelles and the Bosporus be included in their sphere of influence. Hitler suggested instead that Germany should have all of Europe, and that the Soviet Union should establish a sphere in Asia that would provide an outlet to the Indian Ocean. These suggestions, of course, were totally unacceptable to Stalin.

On June 22, 1941, the war entered a new phase. Without a declaration of war, German armies invaded the Soviet Union. The Germans were soon aided by Hungarians, Italians, Rumanians, and Finns. (Finland had allied itself with Germany.) Franco sent a division of troops from Spain. Hitler had opened a new front in the east, 2,000 miles (3,200 kilometers) long. Churchill declared that, although he did not admire communism, any nation that fought the Nazis was an ally and should receive help. The United States also declared its willingness to provide aid to the Soviets.

As in World War I, getting aid to the Soviet Union was extremely difficult. The sea route was across the Mediterranean and through the Straits and the Black Sea. Ships had to risk submarine and air attacks from Italy and the Balkans. The route through the Baltic Sea was impossible. There were two Soviet ports, Murmansk and Archangel, in the Arctic. Convoys to them had to pass the long, Axis-held coast of Norway under constant plane and submarine attack. A new route, therefore, was developed from the Persian Gulf across Iran by train and truck to the southern part of the Soviet Union (see map, page 671). It became a lifeline for supplies from Great Britain and the United States.

The Soviet defense

The initial force of the Nazi armies was tremendous. Everywhere the Soviet armies were driven back. Within a very short time, Moscow and Leningrad (as Petrograd had been called since 1924) were under siege. There, however, the attack bogged down.

The Soviets used the same tactics against Hitler that their ancestors had used against Napoleon. The retreating armies and civilians carried away what they could and destroyed everything else. Thus the territory gained by the Germans was more a hindrance than a help. Many Soviet soldiers remained behind, hiding out in swamps and forests and making guerrilla attacks on railroads, bridges and trains.

Hitler had expected the Soviets to surrender after a short campaign. The Soviet stand at Leningrad and Moscow wrecked his timetable. When the short Soviet autumn came, Hitler faced the same decision Napoleon had had to make: should he retreat or should he stand? Hitler chose to stand.

Soon the Germans had to face a new enemy—a bitterly cold winter. The Soviets chose the winter for a counterattack, especially to relieve pressure on Moscow. For the first time in World War II, the Germans had to retreat.

Nevertheless, the year 1941 ended with the Germans deep in Soviet territory. In the spring of 1942 they struck southward, aiming to cut the supply line from Iran. One German spearhead drove toward the city of Stalingrad. Another drove toward the Caucasus, the oil-producing region of the Soviet Union (see map, page 671).

The southern German army drove deep into the Caucasus toward the Caspian Sea. Fighting fiercely, the Soviets stopped the Germans before they reached their goal, the port of Baku. North of the Caucasus, however, the Soviets were forced back until they reached Stalingrad.

"New Order" and "Final Solution"

The invasion of the Soviet Union was part of Hitler's master plan for the creation of a "New Order" for Europe. Europe was to be organized into a single political and economic system. It would be ruled from Berlin and dominated by the "Aryan race." According to this plan, the Soviet Union would supply Germany with food and raw materials. An official economic plan issued by the German government stated: "There is no doubt that . . . many millions of people will be starved to death if we take out of the country the things we need." Causing the Soviets to starve did not concern Hitler. Soviets were Slavs and, according to Nazi ideology, "racially inferior."

Another aspect of Hitler's plan for a "New Order" went into effect as the Germans continued their offensives. In 1941 Hitler ordered the annihilation of the entire Jewish population of Europe. The Nazis referred to this program as the "Final Solution" of the "Jewish problem." This unbelievably barbaric goal was possible in Hitler's Germany because so many people had accepted as fact Nazi theories about the racial superiority of the "Aryans."

Jews by the hundreds of thousands from Germany and from countries occupied by the Germans were transported to eastern Germany and Poland. There they were herded together in concentration camps. Among the most infamous were Dachau and Buchenwald in Germany, and Treblinka and Auschwitz in Poland. Some inmates were used as slave laborers. Most, however, were murdered by poison gas, or shot, sometimes hundreds at a time. In some Western European countries, especially Denmark, efforts were made to protect native Jews from the Nazis. In the east, however, a long tradition of anti-Semitism made the Nazi program easier and more devastating.

The Final Solution was helped by the confusion of the wartime situation, but it did not further the German war effort. In fact, it actually damaged it. Jewish workers were removed from the labor force by the extermination policy. Soldiers, railroads, and vital equipment were committed to the program, and the expense was great. It is estimated that, by the time the Nazi government fell, its leaders had murdered 6 million European Jews.

This systematic destruction of European Jews by the Nazis is referred to as the **Holocaust.** Nearly as many non-Jews—mainly Slavs, gypsies, and partisans—were also murdered.

Japanese aggressions in the Pacific

A major source of assistance in the struggle against the Axis Powers came in December 1941, when the United States joined the war. The United States was drawn into the conflict because of events in the Pacific area.

You have read about Japanese militarism and aggression in the 1930's. Early in 1939, with the situation in Europe growing increasingly tense, Japan saw a long-awaited chance to extend its control over East Asia. Japan's first move was to take the island of Hainan and some small islands off the coast of French Indochina (see map, page 661). Thus Japan cut the British route from Hong Kong to Singapore. Neither France nor Great Britain was able to stop this move.

After the fall of the Netherlands and France, Japan made further aggressive moves in East Asia. The Japanese government declared the Netherlands East Indies to be under Japanese "protective custody." Japanese pressure forced the Vichy government to allow French Indochina to become a Japanese protectorate.

In September 1940, as you have read, Japan formed an alliance with Hitler and Mussolini. The United States met these Japanese moves in three ways: protests against violations of the Nine-Power Treaty, aid to Chiang Kai-shek, and an embargo on the sale of oil and scrap iron to Japan. Japan became even more intent on removing any rivals who might jeopardize its badly needed oil reserves in the Netherlands East Indies. Now only the American-held Philippines and the Hawaiian Islands threatened Japanese supremacy in East Asia. The United States, meanwhile, had already moved a large part of its Pacific fleet to Hawaii.

During 1941 relations between the United States and Japan grew steadily worse. Japan and the Soviet Union signed a five-year nonaggression treaty. An even more militaristic government came to power in Japan under Premier Hideki Tojo. Late in 1941 the Japanese government sent special representatives to Washington, D.C., to confer.

American entry into the war

On December 7, 1941, while Tojo's representatives were in Washington, the Japanese launched a surprise attack on the American naval base at Pearl Harbor, Hawaii. Their aim was to strike such a severe blow that the United States would not rival the Japanese in the Pacific. Several American ships were sunk; others were badly damaged. American dead totaled over 2,300.

On December 8, 1941, Congress declared war on Japan, as did the British Parliament. Three days later, Germany and Italy declared war on the United States, and Congress replied with its own declaration of war. The United States became a full-fledged belligerent in World War II.

The Japanese were quick to take advantage of American unpreparedness. On the same day as the attack on Pearl Harbor, Japan began aerial attacks on the Philippines. Soon afterward the Japanese landed on Luzon. Within a month, they had captured the American island outposts of Guam and Wake. In less than three months, the mainland areas of Burma, Thailand, and Malaya, including the mighty British fortress of Singapore, had been added to Japan's conquests (see map, opposite).

The Japanese went on to conquer a vast island empire: most of the Netherlands East Indies, the Philippines, and the Gilbert Islands. Australia remained as the last stronghold of resistance in the southwest Pacific. However, it could be supplied only over a long route from Hawaii. Japanese landings on New Guinea and the Solomon Islands threatened even this supply line.

CHECKUP

1. IDENTIFY: "yellow Aryans," Rommel, "New Order," Auschwitz, Holocaust, Tojo.

2. LOCATE: Tobruk, El Alamein, Murmansk, Archangel, Stalingrad, Hainan, Pearl Harbor, Guam, Wake, Gilbert Islands, Solomon Islands.

3. What gains did the Germans make in southeastern Europe in 1941?

4. What was Hitler's strategy concerning the Suez Canal? How well did it succeed?

5. By what route did Great Britain and the United States get help to the Soviet Union?

6. Describe Hitler's "Final Solution."

Allied victories over Germany and Japan ended the war

Representatives of 26 nations met in Washington, D.C., in January 1942 to unite in the common purpose of defeating the Axis. Chief among these Allies were Great Britain, the Soviet Union, and the United States. Other nations in Europe, Asia, and the Americas contributed what they could to the Allies. Each nation pledged to use all its resources to defeat the Axis, not to sign a separate peace, and to abide by the provisions of the Atlantic Charter.

Important offensives

The German summer offensive of 1942 had pushed the Soviets back to Stalingrad (see map, page 671). There a tremendous battle, the most spectacular of the war, was fought for six months. The Germans penetrated the city, suffering terrible losses. The Soviets did not retreat but defended the city street by street and house by house.

In November 1942 the Soviets began a counterattack, encircling the German troops in Stalingrad. Although Hitler ordered his trapped forces to fight to the death, what was left of his army in the city surrendered in January 1943. The heroic and successful defense of Stalingrad was a crucial turning point in the war. The Germans never completely recovered from this defeat.

North Africa. The Allies also made progress in North Africa. Late in the summer of 1942, Allied reinforcements were rushed to El Alamein, where British troops were under German attack. In a decisive battle in October, troops under British General Bernard Montgomery routed Rommel's force. The Germans were pushed westward across Libya into Tunisia.

In November 1942 American and British forces under American General Dwight Eisenhower landed in Morocco and Algeria. They pushed eastward into Tunisia as Montgomery's army moved westward. Rommel's army was thus trapped between the two. The campaign was hard-fought, but by the middle of May 1943, the

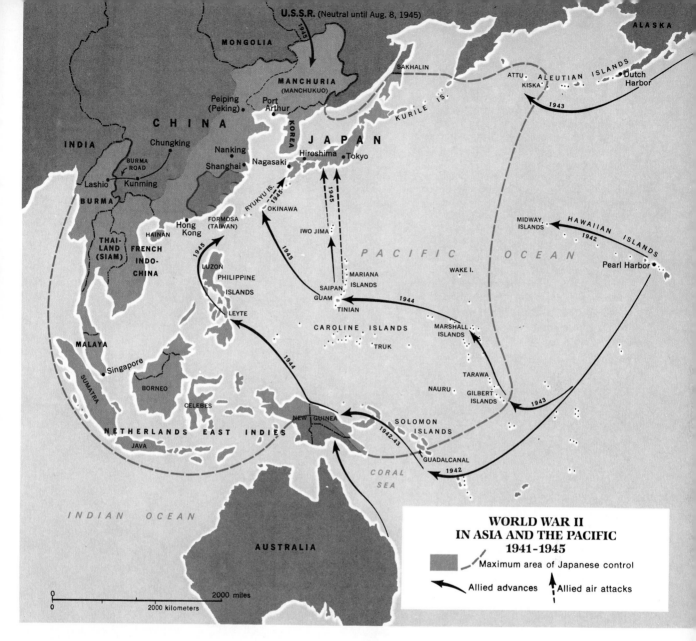

**WORLD WAR II
IN ASIA AND THE PACIFIC
1941-1945**

Maximum area of Japanese control

Allied advances ↑ Allied air attacks

Axis Powers in North Africa were forced to surrender to the Allies.

As a result, the Allies gained a stronghold in North Africa. Italy's African empire disappeared and the French colonies in Africa passed to the Free French. The Suez Canal was controlled by the Allies, and the Mediterranean was made more secure for Allied naval operations.

The invasion of Italy

Throughout 1942 Stalin had made constant demands that the British and Americans open a second front in Europe to relieve the German pressure on the Soviet Union. The Allies argued that they were not ready. An attack before they were fully prepared would be dangerous. Stalin suspected that the Allies hoped that Germany and the Soviet Union would destroy each other.

When North Africa was secured by the Allies, Stalin renewed his demands for a landing in Europe. Churchill insisted upon an attack on what he called the "soft underbelly of the Axis"— through Italy and the Balkans. In July 1943 Allied armies from North Africa landed on the strategic island of Sicily. Resistance was strong, but the

War in Asia

Until its last days, the war in the Pacific was decided primarily at sea. Control of territory—in many cases, islands of great strategic value—depended on control of the seas. In the early years of the war, the outnumbered American forces were overwhelmed. Often the wounded had to be treated aboard evacuation planes (bottom right). Gradually, however, the tide turned. As the Americans fought to take such islands as Okinawa (below) and Kwajalein (bottom left), casualties were high. But mastery of the seas was regained, and the territory was conquered.

To force the Japanese to surrender, President Harry Truman ordered an atomic bomb to be dropped on the city of Hiroshima (right). The devastation caused by the bomb was horrible, but at the time it seemed the only way to bring the war to a rapid conclusion.

island was taken in little more than a month. Then the Italian mainland was bombed in preparation for a landing.

In Italy, Mussolini was forced to resign, and Marshal Pietro Badoglio (bah·DOH·lyo) became premier. His first act was to dissolve the Fascist Party. When the Allied army landed on the southwestern Italian mainland in September 1943, the Italians surrendered unconditionally. They then declared war on Germany.

German troops in Italy, however, continued to resist the Allied advance with skill and determination. The Allied advance up the peninsula was slow. Mussolini retreated with the Germans, a virtual prisoner.

Sea and air attacks

Meanwhile, the Battle of the Atlantic was being won. This conflict between German and Allied ships had begun in the spring of 1940. An enormous number of Allied ships were sunk by German submarines. Yet by the fall of 1943, convoys of troop and supply ships from the United States were well protected by destroyers and other escort ships. Planes based both on land and on aircraft carriers also protected the convoys. New scientific devices, such as sonar, were perfected to locate submarines.

Allied air attacks against Germany and the occupied countries rose steadily in intensity. At first the Allies, operating from bases in the British Isles, concentrated on strategic sites. Later they began to bomb civilian areas as well. Almost every German city was bombed. Some, like Hamburg, were almost wiped out.

The war in the Pacific

The Japanese advance in the Pacific received its first setback in May 1942. A Japanese fleet thrusting toward Australia was defeated by American and Australian air and naval forces in the five-day battle of the Coral Sea. Soon afterward a larger Japanese fleet, pushing eastward to try to capture the Midway Islands, northwest of Hawaii, was met by an American fleet (see map, page 681). In the crucial naval battle of Midway, fought from June 3 to June 6 by ships and by carrier-based planes, the Japanese were defeated. With these two victories, the United States Navy began to turn the tide in the Pacific.

Early in August 1942, to protect the Australian supply line, American marines landed on the Solomon Islands, seizing the airfield on Guadalcanal. This was the first invasion of Japanese-held territory. Four times in the next three months the Japanese launched savage attacks on the American forces. All were repulsed, with terrible losses on both sides.

In 1943 the Allied nations took the offensive in the Pacific. Sea, air, and land forces of the United States were aided by forces from Australia and New Zealand. They waged a long series of battles to drive the Japanese entirely out of the Solomon Islands. In the central Pacific, Tarawa—one of the Gilbert Islands—was captured after a savage fight.

The Allies adopted a strategy called "island hopping." Certain Japanese-held islands were captured, while others were bypassed and left helpless for lack of supplies.

During 1944 the Americans cleared the Japanese from the Marshall Islands, New Guinea, and the Marianas. Saipan and Tinian, in the Marianas, became bases for long-range bombing attacks on Japan. In October 1944 an American army under General Douglas MacArthur landed at Leyte (LAY·tee) in the central Philippines. Shortly after the landing, the Japanese fleet suffered a crushing defeat in a great air and sea fight, the battle of Leyte Gulf. After six months of heavy fighting, the Philippine Islands were recovered.

Victory in Europe

As the Allies were fighting their way through Italy in late 1943, plans were being made for another, larger invasion of Europe. The landing was to be made on the beaches of the narrow, heavily wooded French peninsula of Normandy (see map, page 671). These were the same beaches from which William the Conqueror had invaded England in 1066.

The long-awaited landing came on June 6, 1944, D-Day as it was called by the military. Soldiers and material were transferred across the English Channel in one of the most daring invasion operations in military history. Within a month, more than a million troops had landed in France. The

Germans had expected a landing in France, but the exact location of the assault had successfully been kept secret. German forces were rushed to Normandy to meet the Allied invasion, but were outnumbered.

After heavy fighting, Allied troops broke out of Normandy and moved into northern France. At the same time, Allied forces landed on the Mediterranean coast of France and fought their way northward. On August 25, 1944, Allied troops entered Paris. By September they faced the strongly fortified Siegfried Line along Germany's western frontier.

The drive from the east. In June 1944 the Soviets began a major drive against Germany from the east. By the end of 1944, the Red Army had taken Finland, Estonia, Lithuania, Latvia, Rumania, Bulgaria, and Albania. The British aided in driving the Germans from Greece. Yugoslavia had earlier been liberated with the help of resistance fighters under Marshal Tito. By far the heaviest Soviet fighting, however, was in Poland. By July 1944 Soviet troops were approaching Warsaw.

The drive from the west. The Americans pierced the "unconquerable" Siegfried Line in October after five weeks of fighting. The Allies took port cities in France and Belgium, easing the problem of supplying the Allied forces. The Allies cleared Alsace and Lorraine of German troops and prepared to continue the attack.

The Germans had strength for one desperate counterattack. Just before Christmas in 1944, they drove a 50-mile (80-kilometer) wedge into Allied lines in Belgium. After a costly ten-day battle—the Battle of the Bulge—the Allies turned back the German drive. Finally, in early spring 1945, German defenses collapsed.

At the end of April, the German army in Italy surrendered unconditionally. Italian guerrillas pursued and captured Mussolini. The ex-dictator was shot and his body displayed in public, hanging upside down, before jeering crowds.

The Soviet and American armies made their first contact at Torgau, in eastern Germany, on April 25, 1945. It was agreed that the Soviets should take Berlin. On April 30, as the Soviets neared Berlin, Hitler committed suicide. Two days later the Soviets captured the battered and devastated city. Within a week the German high command surrendered unconditionally. May 8, 1945, was V-E Day—the day of victory in Europe.

Attacks on Japan

Though the war had ended in Europe, it continued in the Pacific. The main islands of Japan could now be reached by long-range bombers from Saipan. Systematic raids on Japanese industrial cities began early in 1945. However, the Allies needed still closer islands as fighter bases and emergency landing fields.

The first move was into a group of islands about 750 miles (1,200 kilometers) directly south of Tokyo. American marines landed on the small volcanic island of Iwo Jima (see map, page 681). They captured the island after a month of the bitterest fighting of the war. Okinawa, largest of the Ryukyu Islands, was taken after more desperate fighting. Japanese resistance became stronger as their home islands were approached. At Okinawa, nearly 250 ships were damaged by suicide attacks of Japanese pilots who crashed their planes, loaded with explosives, into the ships. These suicide attacks were called kamikaze attacks, after the "Divine Wind" that had saved Japan from Chinese-Mongol attack in 1281.

Despite such bitter resistance, the Allies continued the intensive bombing of Japan. Japanese ports were effectively blockaded by the Allies, and the Japanese navy was immobilized. Nevertheless, the Japanese government still refused to surrender.

Yalta and Potsdam

Roosevelt and Churchill had long hoped to persuade the Soviets to enter the war in the Pacific. Before the defeat of Germany, the Soviet Union had been completely occupied in defending itself. Moreover, it considered the war against Japan the business of the United States.

In February 1945, Roosevelt and Churchill met with Stalin at Yalta, in the Soviet Union. The Big Three, as these Allied leaders were called, agreed that Germany should be temporarily divided and occupied by troops of the victorious powers, including France. The liberated areas of Europe were to have democratically elected govern-

How do we know?

WHO IS THIS WILSON?

POLITICAL CARTOONS Political cartoons can use a picture to express a point of view more easily and vividly than hundreds of words. Because they are simple, cartoons are often sharper and more extreme than written comments. They must make their point at once, and they provide little room for shadings of opinions. For these very reasons, however, cartoons are an excellent source of information for historians.

What cartoons reveal, quickly and dramatically, is the attitude of a period toward its political leaders and important events. After World War I, the enthusiasm of Europeans for Woodrow Wilson was best caught by a cartoon (left). The people of Paris had a new hero in Wilson. An old one, Napoleon, looked unhappily at all the cheering below from his perch atop his monument. This cartoon made a point not only about Wilson but also about how heroes can fade.

Franklin D. Roosevelt's decision to help the Allies in World War II before the United States had officially entered the war inspired a different technique of cartooning (below). Instead of a portrait, we see only a hand, giving out destroyers. The caption, using the phrase "advice and consent" (which marks Senate approval of Presidential decisions), showed that Roosevelt was being criticized for acting on his own.

In each of these cases, a powerful image was created that enables historians to understand the feelings of the time more directly than they could by reading many pages of comment and description.

I, WITHOUT ADVICE AND CONSENT OF THE SENATE.

ments. The Soviet Union was to enter the war against Japan. As compensation, it was to receive several Japanese territories.

Another conference began July 17, 1945, at Potsdam, near Berlin. Roosevelt had died in April. The Big Three were now Harry Truman, Winston Churchill, and Joseph Stalin. Before the conference ended August 2, another change in the Big Three took place with the defeat of Churchill's Conservative Party by Clement Attlee's Labour Party. Attlee, who was already at the conference, became prime minister and took Churchill's place at the conference.

Most important, however, was the fact that the United States had produced a workable atomic bomb. Scientists from many nations—including refugees from fascism, such as Enrico Fermi of Italy—had worked to harness the enormous energy released by splitting atoms. They had succeeded in creating the most destructive weapon known up to that time. With this weapon in the American arsenal, it would not be necessary for the Allies to invade Japan. At the Potsdam Conference, the Big Three decided to issue an ultimatum to Japan, demanding unconditional surrender. They also made various decisions on peace settlements in Europe, as you will read in Chapter 28.

Defeat of the Japanese

The Japanese government refused to surrender. Therefore on August 6, 1945, a single American bomber dropped an atomic bomb on the Japanese city of Hiroshima. The bomb exploded with a force equal to 20,000 tons of TNT. Some 80,000 persons were killed, and more than half of Hiroshima was destroyed. Two days later, the Soviet Union declared war on Japan. Soviet armies swept into Manchuria, where they met little resistance. On August 9 an American plane dropped a second and even more powerful atomic bomb on the city of Nagasaki.

On August 14 the Japanese surrendered unconditionally, asking only that the emperor be allowed to keep his throne. The Allies agreed on condition that he accept the orders of the Supreme Allied Commander in the Pacific, General Douglas MacArthur. On September 2, 1945 (known as V-J Day), the official Japanese surrender documents were signed aboard the American battleship *Missouri* in Tokyo Bay.

Costs of the war

World War II, to a much greater extent than World War I, was a war of movement and of machines. Military casualties were enormous. Battle losses of the Soviet Union have been estimated at 7 million lives, although an accurate count has never been made. Germany lost 2¼ million people in battle. Japan's total loss—civilian and military—was nearly 2 million. Great Britain, France, and the United States each lost hundreds of thousands in battle. Six million Jews died in German concentration camps and gas chambers. Millions of civilians were uprooted by the war or killed or injured by bombs. A total of 45 million people died in the war.

As the war progressed, weapons and tactics became more devastating. More shocking, perhaps, is the fact that people grew more accustomed to this increased destructiveness. At the beginning of the war, the German bombing of Rotterdam and of British cities caused a wave of horrified protest throughout the world. Attacks from the air on helpless civilians were considered the height of needless and savage brutality.

By 1943, however, Allied air attacks on Axis civilian centers were accepted simply as part of modern warfare. The destruction of Hamburg and the atomic bombings of Hiroshima and Nagasaki did not immediately bring any great public protest. By 1945 the killing of thousands of civilians had come to be accepted as a normal practice of war.

CHECKUP

1. IDENTIFY: Montgomery, Eisenhower, Badoglio, "island hopping," MacArthur, D-Day, Tito, Battle of the Bulge, V-E Day, kamikaze attacks, Truman, Attlee, V-J Day.

2. LOCATE: Coral Sea, Midway Islands, Guadalcanal, Tarawa, Saipan, Tinian, Iwo Jima, Okinawa, Hiroshima, Nagasaki.

3. Why did Stalin want a second front? Describe the circumstances under which it was launched.

4. What were the fates of Mussolini and Hitler?

5. List the chief decisions that were made at Yalta and Potsdam.

6. What action did the United States take against Japan to end the war?

CHAPTER REVIEW

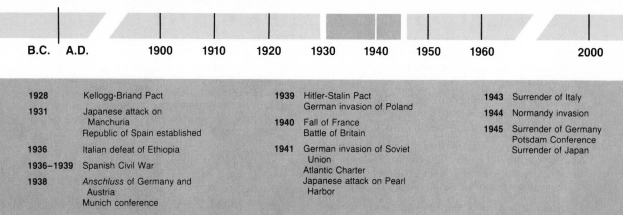

B.C.	A.D.	1900	1910	1920	1930	1940	1950	1960	2000

1928	Kellogg-Briand Pact	**1939**	Hitler-Stalin Pact
1931	Japanese attack on Manchuria		German invasion of Poland
	Republic of Spain established	**1940**	Fall of France
1936	Italian defeat of Ethiopia		Battle of Britain
1936–1939	Spanish Civil War	**1941**	German invasion of Soviet Union
1938	*Anschluss* of Germany and Austria		Atlantic Charter
	Munich conference		Japanese attack on Pearl Harbor

1943	Surrender of Italy
1944	Normandy invasion
1945	Surrender of Germany
	Potsdam Conference
	Surrender of Japan

CHAPTER SUMMARY

In the 1930's a series of aggressions by the Japanese and the fascists brought about World War II. At first the democracies were reluctant to resist them, preferring a policy of appeasement. The Japanese made gains in Manchuria and China. Italy captured Ethiopia, fascists took over Spain following the civil war, and the Germans took over Austria and Czechoslovakia. The League of Nations proved incapable of halting these advances.

Only when Hitler invaded Poland in September 1939 did his principal opponents, Great Britain and France, decide at last to stand firm. They were at a severe disadvantage, because their obvious ally, the Soviet Union, had signed a pact with Germany. Nevertheless, Great Britain and France declared war on Germany in 1939.

By the fall of 1940 the Axis Powers had conquered most of Scandinavia, defeated France, and forced British troops off the continent of Europe. They had also formed an alliance with Japan. During the next year, their success in battle reached its highest level and then began to decline.

Despite some isolationist opposition, the United States began to send supplies to Great Britain in 1940. During this same year, Great Britain's air force turned back German air attacks and prevented an invasion of England.

In 1941, after considerable successes in the Balkans, Germany suddenly attacked the Soviet Union. In that same year the Japanese attacked the American fleet at Pearl Harbor, in Hawaii. This assault brought the United States into the war.

Within Germany, a vicious policy of exterminating all the Jews of Europe was put into effect. In addition to its barbarity, the Holocaust diverted essential efforts away from the front line. The Soviets counterattacked, and the German army was engaged in heavy fighting on the eastern front.

In 1943 the Allies invaded Sicily from North Africa. At the same time, an offensive to drive the Japanese out of the Pacific islands was begun. The following year the Allies invaded France. Finally, in 1945, they conquered Germany. Following the atom bombing of Hiroshima and Nagasaki, Japan was forced to surrender.

The cost of the war, in suffering and death, was worse by far than that of any war in history. There was hope that the aims proclaimed in the Atlantic Charter of 1941—including an end to wars, and self-determination and decent living conditions for all people—might now be realized.

CHECKING WHAT YOU KNOW

1. Match each item at the left with a definition at the right.

a. appeasement
b. Holocaust
c. blitzkrieg
d. partisans
e. isolationists
f. collaborators

1. members of resistance movements
2. those who oppose involvement in affairs of other nations
3. systematic destruction of Jews by the Nazis
4. people who cooperate with their country's enemies
5. lightning war
6. attempt to preserve peace by giving in to aggressor's demands

2. Many historians regard the Japanese conquest of Manchuria as the start of World War II. Why? At what point do you think war became inevitable? Explain.

3. In certain respects, the Spanish Civil War was a preview of the global war to come. Why? What role did Spain play once World War II started?

4. Which nations participated in the conference at Munich? What did each of these nations hope to achieve? How did the decisions reached at Munich affect the future of Czechoslovakia?

5. List the major events that took place in the war during 1942. Why might this year be considered a turning point in the war?

6. Which was probably more difficult to wage— the war in Europe or the war in the Pacific? Explain.

7. What new weapons and war tactics were employed during World War II?

PRACTICING YOUR SKILLS

1. **Interpreting maps.** Turn to the map on page 671. What nations did the Axis Powers hold at the height of their power? What nations remained neutral or nonaligned? Based on information in this map, why might Churchill have considered Italy the "soft underbelly of the Axis"?

2. **Understanding political cartoons.** Turn to the political cartoon from World War II on page 685. How does the cartoonist view the decision to send United States destroyers to Great Britain? What symbols or words support your answer? How would you draw a cartoon expressing an opposite point of view?

RELATING PAST TO PRESENT

1. "The next war," declared Albert Einstein after the bombing of Japan, "will be fought with stones." What might he have meant by this comment? What efforts are being made today to limit the production and sale of nuclear weapons? What nations are participating in these efforts?

2. Prior to American entry into the war, President Roosevelt called the United States the "arsenal of democracy." Based on what you read in this chapter, what did he mean by this statement? Does the United States still play this role in world affairs? Why or why not? If possible, clip current newspaper or magazine articles that illustrate your answer.

3. Review the failure of the League of Nations to end Italian aggression in Ethiopia during the 1930's. Then find information on Soviet intervention in Afghanistan and Poland during the 1980's. What actions did the United Nations take? Were any of the problems faced by the United Nations similar to those experienced by the League? Explain.

INVESTIGATING FURTHER

1. Review the information on codes in the Connections feature on page 603. Then use books in your library to investigate the use of codes during World War II. If possible, locate information on an American code that completely baffled Japanese military experts—the Navaho language.

2. Prepare a report on one of the following books about the Holocaust: Anne Frank, *Diary of a Young Girl* (Doubleday); John Hersey, *The Wall* (Pocket Books); Ilse Koehn, *Mischling, Second Degree* (Greenwillow); Arnost Lustig, *Night and Hope* (Avon); Elie Wiesel, *Night* (Avon). In your report, note whether the story is fiction or nonfiction. Also briefly discuss the background of the author. Then describe the way in which each of the central characters responded to Nazi persecution.

3. Interview a friend or relative who remembers the war years. Ask this person to explain the meaning of the following words or phrases: victory garden, ration books, blackouts, dog tags, Rosie the Riveter, war bonds, C-rations, black market. Try to discover other World War II terms that might be added to the list. Be prepared to present your findings to the class.

UNIT REVIEW

1. Match each item at the left with a description at the right.

   a. Kellogg-Briand Pact
   b. Balfour Declaration
   c. Hitler-Stalin Pact
   d. Atlantic Charter
   e. Zimmermann telegram
   f. Fourteen Points
   g. Yalta Conference
   h. *Mein Kampf*
   i. Treaty of Portsmouth
   j. Versailles Treaty

   1. Called for "peace with justice."
   2. Stated principles underlying Nazi movement.
   3. Settled Russo-Japanese War.
   4. Levied heavy reparations on Germany.
   5. Outlawed war.
   6. Announced war aims of the democracies.
   7. Pledged Soviet Union's neutrality.
   8. Temporarily divided Germany.
   9. Favored creation of Jewish "national home."
   10. Invited Mexico to join the Central Powers.

2. Match each event at the left with the correct time period at the right. You may use a time period more than once.

   a. overthrow of czarist regime
   b. the Long March
   c. D-Day
   d. armistice ending World War I
   e. Italian invasion of Ethiopia
   f. attack on Pearl Harbor
   g. conference at Munich
   h. collapse of New York stock market
   i. Japanese conquest of Manchuria
   j. assassination of Archduke Francis Ferdinand
   k. Russo-Japanese War
   l. Nazi invasion of Poland
   m. Spanish Civil War
   n. atomic bombing of Hiroshima and Nagasaki

   1. before 1914
   2. 1914–1920
   3. 1921–1930
   4. 1931–1940
   5. 1941–1945

3. How did World War I help bring about a boom period in the United States? What conditions brought this boom period to an end?

4. Choose two of the following and discuss how they reflected the uncertainties of the period following World War I:
   a. literature
   b. music
   c. painting
   d. architecture
   e. film

5. How did Sun Yat-sen, Chiang Kai-shek, and Mao Tse-tung differ in their future plans for China? Include the following topics in your answer:
   a. the role of the people
   b. foreign interference in China
   c. economic reforms
   d. constitutional government
   e. the need for modernization

6. What were the foreign policy objectives of Italy, Germany, and Japan in the 1930's? Why were these nations able to gain their objectives?

7. Compare the causes of World War I with the causes of World War II. Why might the Versailles Treaty be considered a cause of World War II?

8. Compare the principles expressed in the Atlantic Charter with those in the Fourteen Points. How did each of these documents seek to establish "peace with justice"?

9. How did the United States aid the Allies before December 1941? Why did the United States move away from its position as a neutral nation?

10. How did the bombings of Hiroshima and Nagasaki change the nature of warfare? What other developments grew out of World War II?

11. President Truman once declared, "Men make history and not the other way around." Discuss the meaning of Truman's remark, using three of the following leaders as examples:
    a. Woodrow Wilson
    b. Sun Yat-sen
    c. Mustafa Kemal
    d. Mohandas Gandhi
    e. Winston Churchill
    f. Franklin Roosevelt

THE MODERN WORLD SINCE 1945

Old and new, East and West, meeting in Hong Kong harbor

(1945 to the Present)

28

The Superpowers Became Rivals As Europe Recovered from the War

After every major war in history the combatants have hoped that a way could be found to establish a peace that would last for generations. World War II was no exception. Events of the 1930's and 1940's had proved that once a major war broke out, it was impossible for a great power to remain neutral. After World War II, the only hope for lasting peace seemed to be some sort of collective security through an international organization with authority to act in case of disputes among nations.

Plans for such an organization had been discussed throughout the war by the Allied leaders. They hoped that this institution would be stronger and more effective than the League of Nations. The new organization, known as the United Nations, held its first meetings in 1945. Yet despite this attempt at international cooperation, discord among the victorious powers began to develop.

The United States and the Soviet Union emerged as the two strongest nations in the postwar world. Relations between the two had never been friendly, but they had united to defeat their common enemy, Germany. After the war, the antagonisms between these two great powers revived.

A split soon developed among the former Allies. On one side were the democratic and other

French General Charles de Gaulle

noncommunist countries, led by the United States, Great Britain, and France. These countries were called the West, or the free world. On the other side were the communist nations, led by the Soviet Union. The communist alliance, or bloc, was known as the East, or the communist world.

Mutual suspicion and hostility between communist and Western nations led to the so-called **Cold War.** This conflict was waged by political and economic means rather than with weapons. The Cold War would shape and color almost all events in Europe and throughout the world for many years. It would particularly overshadow the early efforts in Europe toward recovery from the devastation of World War II.

THE CHAPTER SECTIONS

1. The United Nations was created to give a voice to all nations

2. The victors attempted to settle Europe's political problems

3. The Cold War influenced events throughout Europe

4. Cooperative ventures aided the economic recovery of Western Europe

1

The United Nations was created to give a voice to all nations

Like the League of Nations, the United Nations (UN) was organized by the victorious powers after a world war. However, because both the United States and the Soviet Union were members from the beginning, the UN reflected the true power structure of the world more accurately than had the League.

The founding of the UN

Plans for an international organization were discussed throughout World War II by the Allied leaders. Beginning in August 1944, representatives of Great Britain, the Soviet Union, China, and the United States met to draft a provisional charter for an organization to be known as the "United Nations." President Roosevelt had first used the term "united nations" in referring to the countries allied against the Axis powers.

As you have read, the leaders of the three major powers met at Yalta in February 1945. There Roosevelt, Churchill, and Stalin discussed the proposed charter and agreed on voting procedures to be followed in the United Nations. They set the time and place for the first General Assembly, at which the final Charter of the organization would be drawn up.

In April 1945 the General Assembly, made up of representatives from 51 nations, met in San Francisco. After two months it agreed to a final version of the Charter, which was then submitted to the governments of those nations for ratification. By October 1945 the required number of nations had ratified the Charter and the United Nations was established.

In ratifying the Charter, member nations agreed to the following purposes of the United Nations: (1) to maintain peace and security; (2) to promote equal rights and the self-determination of peoples; (3) to develop international cooperation; and (4) to encourage respect for human rights and fundamental freedoms without regard to race, sex, language, or religion.

The United Nations is composed of six main bodies—the General Assembly, the Security Council, the International Court of Justice, the Trusteeship Council, the Secretariat, and the Economic and Social Council. The UN is also linked with several related boards, commissions, and specialized agencies.

The General Assembly

The General Assembly is made up of representatives of all the member nations. Each nation is entitled to five delegates, five alternates, and as many advisers as necessary.

The Assembly is responsible for drawing up the UN budget and assessing each member nation's share of the cost. It elects the temporary members of the Security Council and the members of the Economic and Social Council. Acting with the Security Council, the General Assembly elects the Secretary-General and the judges of the International Court of Justice. It receives and considers the reports of the various agencies of the United Nations. The Assembly may consider and discuss any problem that relates to world peace unless that problem is already being considered by the Security Council.

When a matter is brought to a vote in the General Assembly, each member nation has one vote. On procedural matters, those involving comparatively routine details, a simple majority vote is needed. On substantive, or important, matters, a two-thirds vote is required. Nations may also abstain—choose not to vote.

The Security Council

The Security Council is made up of representatives of 15 member nations. Five of them, usually called the Big Five, are permanent members: the United States, Great Britain, the Soviet Union, France, and China. Ten are temporary members. They are elected for two-year terms by the General Assembly and cannot be reelected immediately. Each member nation on the Council has a representative who is allowed one vote.

Settling disputes. The Security Council is chiefly responsible for maintaining peace, settling disputes among nations, and preventing or resisting aggression. When the Council is considering a dispute, it may ask questions of the parties involved, or with their consent, send UN representatives to investigate.

After the dispute has been discussed, the Council usually urges the nations involved to meet and work out their own solution. Sometimes it appoints mediators to aid the negotiations. The Council may suggest some kind of compromise, or it may send the case to the International Court of Justice in The Hague for a decision. Only when these peaceful measures have failed, and the Council believes that a threat to peace still remains, can it use force.

The Council can order United Nations members to break diplomatic relations with an offending nation. It can also call for economic sanctions against the offender. Finally, it can ask the members to provide the military force necessary to stop armed aggression.

Veto power. The voting procedures used in the Security Council have an important impact on the total effectiveness of the UN system. On procedural matters, decisions are made by the affirmative votes of any nine Council members. On substantive matters, however, an affirmative majority must include the votes of the five permanent members. Thus any one of the Big Five can prevent the Council from taking an important action by using the veto power—the power to vote against a measure.

The veto was included in the Charter at the insistence of both the United States and the Soviet Union. In the first 20 years of the Council's operation, the United States and its allies formed a majority among UN member nations. During these years the Soviet Union used the veto power more than a hundred times. The other Big Five members cast only eight vetoes during the same period. After 1965, however, the United States and its Western allies lost the UN majority they had previously enjoyed. Since then, the United States has used the veto frequently.

The International Court of Justice

The International Court of Justice (also called the World Court) is made up of 15 judges elected by the Security Council and General Assembly, each for terms of 9 years. They are elected, not as representatives of governments, but as individuals who are legal and judicial experts.

The power of the Court is limited in three ways. (1) It hears cases involving only governments or UN agencies. (2) It accepts those cases involving only legal disputes between nations. In 1979, for example, the Court was asked to decide a case concerning the Iranian seizure and detainment of American hostages. (3) The Court can consider a case only if all the parties are willing to accept its power. In 1985, for example, the United States said it would submit to the authority of the World Court in only certain cases.

These restrictions, along with the unwillingness of nations to allow certain cases to be tried, limit its usefulness.

The Trusteeship Council

The Trusteeship Council was established to oversee the former League of Nations colonies and trust territories that had not achieved independence at the end of World War II.

Efforts at peacekeeping

Maintaining peace among nations after World War II was the primary aim of the United Nations. The Security Council was called into session (above) whenever there was a threat of conflict between nations. If other methods failed to settle the dispute, the Secretary General, Dag Hammarskjöld, could send troops, supplied by member nations, into troubled areas to restore order (right). Nevertheless, the United States and the Soviet Union sometimes negotiated directly to resolve their differences. American President Jimmy Carter and Soviet leader Leonid Brezhnev signed the SALT II agreement in 1979 (below) in an attempt to slow the arms race.

It might be said that the purpose of the Trusteeship Council was to work itself out of existence by helping its trust territories to become independent. Eleven trust territories were placed under the trusteeship system in 1945. In 1986 only the Trust Territory of the Pacific Islands remained. It is administered by the United States and consists of about 2,100 islands, including the Marshall and Caroline chains and the Federated States of Micronesia.

The Secretariat

The Secretariat consists of clerical and administrative workers, technical experts, and advisers. All are permanent employees of the United Nations. The Secretariat is headed by the Secretary-General, who is nominated by the Security Council and elected by the General Assembly for a term of five years. The Secretary-General has many responsibilities. They include acting as mediator in the settlement of international disputes, attending all Security Council and General Assembly meetings, and carrying out tasks assigned by UN agencies. The Secretary-General also reports annually to the General Assembly on the progress of the United Nations.

The Economic and Social Council

The Economic and Social Council was created to improve world economic and social conditions. It has 54 member-nations, each elected by the General Assembly to a three-year term.

The Council may recommend action on such topics as population, transportation, communication, human rights, the status of women, and the narcotics traffic. Any follow-through on these recommendations, however, depends on the good will and self-interest of member nations, as well as on public support. The actual work of the Council is carried out by specialized agencies.

Specialized agencies

The UN is associated with a number of specialized agencies. Each of these specialized agencies handles a single problem or a related set of problems. Every agency has its own charter, organization, membership, and budget.

The work of the specialized agencies is supervised and coordinated by the Technical Assistance Board, whose main aim is to help nations help themselves. It gives assistance only when aid is requested by a government and works chiefly in the developing countries.

The Technical Assistance Board, for instance, greatly aided India in the 1950's. For centuries, India has had problems supplying its people with food. Less than half the land of the subcontinent is cultivated. One area of rich soil, at the base of the Himalayas, was a rain forest that swarmed with malarial mosquitoes. At the request of the Indian government, Technical Assistance Board officials agreed to a combined project there.

The World Health Organization (WHO) supplied a Greek expert on malaria and a British public-health nurse. The Food and Agriculture Organization (FAO) sent in experts to work with Indian agricultural specialists. Supplies and equipment for this project were provided by the United Nations Children's Fund (UNICEF), which carried on a mother-and-child health program. The Indian government used tractors and bulldozers to clear the rain forest. As soon as part of the land was cleared, people began moving in from other parts of India. The malaria rate was reduced considerably, and a whole new region in India was made productive.

One of the most important specialized agencies in the 1980's is the United Nations Development Programme (UNDP). It was founded to assist developing countries in the effective use of their human and economic resources.

The International Bank for Reconstruction and Development, often called the World Bank, is another of the specialized agencies. It was established to help finance the rebuilding of devastated areas and to help developing regions.

Another agency, the International Atomic Energy Agency (IAEA), works directly with the General Assembly and the Security Council to promote peaceful uses of atomic energy.

Increased membership

The founders of the United Nations hoped that all countries would eventually become members. Therefore, a way for them to be admitted was provided. Recommendation of a new member is made by the Security Council, where it is subject to a veto. Admission is by a two-thirds vote of the General Assembly. By 1986 the UN had a membership of 159 nations.

Most of the new members were nations of Asia and Africa. In 1945 Asian and African members numbered only 13, but by 1986 they made up more than half the total UN membership.

By the mid-1980's, the balance of power in the UN had also shifted significantly. Previously the United States and its allies could almost always get the two-thirds vote needed to pass a resolution in the General Assembly. Now many nations vote in regional blocs or in accordance with their own self-interest.

Armaments control

The Charter of the United Nations stated a need to relieve the world's people of the crushing economic burden of armaments. It directed the Security Council to make plans for the regulation and reduction of armaments. A Disarmament Commission was established.

During the early 1950's, the United States and the Soviet Union developed nuclear weapons. The group of so-called "nuclear powers"—the United States, the U.S.S.R., and Great Britain—increased to five nations with the addition of France and China in the 1960's. In 1974 India became the sixth nuclear power in the world. By 1986 at least seven other nations were developing the capability to produce nuclear weapons.

Some limited progress towards arms control, however, has been made:

(1) The United States, Great Britain, and the Soviet Union agreed to stop testing nuclear weapons everywhere except underground (August 1963). Neither France nor China, however, signed this agreement.

(2) Under the Nuclear Nonproliferation Treaty (NPT), nations without nuclear weapons agreed not to produce or receive them (May 1968). The nuclear powers agreed to share with other nations the peaceful benefits of nuclear research and to work toward arms control. Only a few nations, however, signed the NPT. Even among those who did, some continued to develop nuclear weapons.

(3) In the Strategic Arms Limitation Talks (SALT), the United States and the U.S.S.R. agreed to limit their antiballistic missile (ABM) sites (SALT I, May 1972). The progress of SALT in the 1970's reflected an era of good Soviet-American relations. The SALT II agreement of 1979, for example, limited the number of missiles each side could have. Relations between the two nations deteriorated later that year, however, when the Soviet Union invaded Afghanistan. The United States Senate never ratified SALT II.

CHECKUP

1. IDENTIFY: Secretary-General, Big Five, WHO, FAO, UNICEF, UNDP, World Bank, IAEA, SALT.

2. List the four purposes of the United Nations.

3. Name the six major bodies of the United Nations and describe the major functions of each.

4. How has increased membership in the UN affected voting in the General Assembly?

5. Describe the progress made toward arms limitation between 1963 and the mid-1980's.

The victors attempted to settle Europe's political problems

At the Yalta Conference in 1945, Churchill, Roosevelt, and Stalin had agreed that both Germany and Austria were to be divided into four zones. The United States, the Soviet Union, Great Britain, and France would be responsible for the administration of one zone in each country. The two capitals, Berlin and Vienna, were also to be divided into four zones, to be administered separately by the four Allies. Supervision of the occupied regions was to be in the hands of an Allied Control Council, composed of military leaders of the occupying armies. Decisions of this council had to be unanimous.

At the Potsdam Conference, later in 1945, Stalin, Attlee, and Truman agreed that the peace treaties should be written by a Council of Foreign Ministers. The ministers would represent the

Soviet Union, Great Britain, the United States, France, and China. All decisions that were made by the Council had to be satisfactory to all its members.

Problems of peacemaking

When the war in Europe was over, occupation zones were set up (see map, opposite), and the Allied Control Council and Council of Foreign Ministers began their work. Such arrangements were practical as long as the Allies remained on friendly terms. As the postwar hostility grew, however, unanimous decisions by the councils became more and more difficult to reach.

The governments of the United States, the Soviet Union, and Great Britain had survived the test of war. Elsewhere, however, changes had to be made. In Italy a plebiscite—a direct vote by the people on a national issue—was held in June 1946. As a result, the monarchy was abolished and a republican form of government was set up. In France, after the Allied liberation in August 1944, a provisional government headed by General Charles de Gaulle ran the country until 1946. Late that year, a Fourth French Republic was proclaimed.

Much of the rest of Europe faced major changes. As you have read, Germany's eastern European allies were occupied and ruled by Soviet armies. National governments had to be restored in Poland and Czechoslovakia. The monarchy in Greece was tottering. The future of both Germany and Austria seemed uncertain.

Postwar treaties

Early in 1947, after months of debate and disagreement, the Council of Foreign Ministers reached agreement on a treaty with Italy. The defeated nation renounced all claims to countries that it had invaded during the war. Italy also ceded the Dodecanese Islands in the Aegean Sea to Greece, and small areas along its western boundary to France (see map, opposite).

The city of Trieste, on the Adriatic coast, caused an especially difficult problem. Trieste had a mixed population of Italians and Yugoslavs. The 1947 treaty established a Free Territory of Trieste as an independent, neutral area, guaranteed by the Security Council of the United Nations. This settlement proved unsatisfactory to Marshal Tito, the communist leader of Yugoslavia.

In October 1954 a new agreement was reached, dividing the Free Territory of Trieste. Italy received the city of Trieste and pledged to maintain a free port. Yugoslavia received an adjacent area. Each side promised to respect the rights of national minorities in its territory.

The Council of Foreign Ministers also drew up treaties with Rumania, Hungary, Bulgaria, and Finland. The terms of these treaties were similar. The defeated countries had to return territory they had taken, and their prewar boundaries were changed. They had to pay reparations to nations that their armies had invaded. Their armed forces were reduced in size.

The four-way occupation of Austria continued for years without any agreements on peace terms. It was not until 1955, ten years after the war ended, that a treaty with Austria was finally negotiated and signed.

Austria had been occupied, first by the Germans, then by the Allies, for a total of 17 years. The treaty of May 1955 made it once more a "sovereign, independent, and democratic state." The treaty forbade political or economic union between Austria and Germany in "any form whatsoever." Austrian boundaries were defined as those that had existed on January 1, 1938.

German settlements

It had taken ten years to reach an agreement over Austria. No final agreement was reached on Germany.

Look at the map on the opposite page and notice the division of Germany into four zones of occupation. Notice that Berlin is in the eastern, or Soviet, zone. The city itself was divided into four occupation sectors. Supplies for the city had to pass through Soviet-held territory.

At the end of the war Germany was a devastated country, with its territory greatly reduced in size. At the Potsdam Conference in 1945 the Allies had agreed that Poland's western boundary should be fixed temporarily at the line of the Oder and Neisse rivers. Thus, part of prewar Germany was included in Poland. Stalin tried to have the Oder-Neisse line accepted as permanent. However, the British and Americans insisted that the final decision be made at the peace conference. This transfer of territory to Poland stripped Germany of a large farming area that had formerly produced a fourth of its food supply. Poland also took part of East Prussia, and the Soviet Union took the rest.

The postwar population of Germany was constantly increased by an influx of Germans who had formerly lived outside the boundaries of prewar Germany. Czechoslovakia, for example, insisted that those Sudeten Germans who had supported Hitler's invasion of Czechoslovakia must leave the country. The Soviets adopted the same policy toward Germans in East Prussia and in the Soviet-controlled Baltic countries. Poland followed suit, expelling Germans from the area of prewar Poland as well as from the territory taken from Germany after the war.

These moves were not surprising in view of prewar troubles with German minorities. However, the burden of housing, feeding, and employing these refugees in shrunken postwar Germany created a serious problem.

German industry

The immediate problem of keeping Germany peaceful was easily solved. The Allied Control Council moved swiftly to disband all German land, air, and sea forces. The German General Staff, with all its military schools and institutions, was abolished. German industry was forbidden to manufacture big guns, tanks, or airplanes—even private or commercial planes. The plan was to make sure that Germany could not rearm. All industrial plants and equipment that could be used for war production were to be dismantled.

This plan proved difficult to enforce. There was, first of all, the complex question of what constituted a war industry. A factory that manufactures tractors, for example, may easily be converted to the production of tanks. A steel plant may turn out armor plate as well as steel beams.

There was an even more basic problem. In the Soviet zone, industrial plants were dismantled and shipped east to replace Soviet factories destroyed during the war. The Soviets changed their policy, however, as they came to realize that this would

**TERRITORIAL CHANGES IN EUROPE
1945–1948**

■ Territorial changes after World War II

■ Soviet occupation zones

□ Occupation zones of Western powers

-·-·- International boundaries after World War II

result in vast unemployment. They allowed the factories to remain, but took as reparations part of the goods produced.

In the Western zones a similar economic problem arose. An agricultural Germany, with only light industries, could not support the German population. There seemed to be only two alternatives for the nations occupying Germany—either allow Germany to industrialize fully, or face the prospect of having to feed and support the German population indefinitely.

The British and Americans gradually moved toward a more lenient treatment of Germany and its industries. This policy was violently opposed by

699

World War II, so devastating for people in Europe and elsewhere, also had among its casualties many great works of art. Numerous old and beautiful churches were damaged or destroyed. It was with great joy, then, that Europeans hailed the construction of this new place of worship. Built between 1951 and 1955 by the great architect Le Corbusier, the chapel stands proudly in the green fields of Ronchamp, in France.

Called Notre Dame du Haut, this was one of Le Corbusier's most famous works. The idea for its dramatic roof line came to the architect when he saw a large crab shell on a beach in Long Island, New York. The chapel, which almost resembles sculpture, was one of the first buildings completed by the architect after the war. It is unique both in design and overall effect.

Le Corbusier also developed the modular, or unit, system of design. In it all the architectural elements are alike, though not identical. They can be individually arranged, yet are well suited to mass production.

the French, who had good reason to fear the neighboring industrial power of Germany.

The Allied Control Council, therefore, found it increasingly difficult to reach unanimous decisions regarding German industry. Meetings of the Council of Foreign Ministers were unproductive. In 1948 the Council adjourned indefinitely.

War trials and denazification

The military occupation of Germany revealed to the world the full extent of the horrors of German concentration camps. As you have read, the Nazi policy of extermination led to the death of millions of people. More than 6 million of the estimated 10 million Jews living in Europe had been killed by the Nazis during the Holocaust. Many had died of disease and starvation in concentration camps. Many others had been shot, hanged, or suffocated in gas chambers. Some were subjected to horrible tortures, serving as subjects for so-called "scientific" experimentation on the human body. The Nazi victims also included almost 6 million non-Jewish Europeans—Poles, Czechs, Russians, Yugoslavs, Dutch, French, and Gypsies.

In 1945 and 1946 a special international court met at Nuremberg, Germany, to try the captured Nazi leaders who had taken part in these murders. Hitler was dead, and some of his highest officers had escaped to Spain and Latin America. However, many of the top Nazi leaders had been captured.

The court tried 22 of the principal Nazi leaders. The charges were "conspiracy to wage aggressive war," "crimes against the peace," and "crimes against humanity" in the extermination camps, the slave-labor camps, and in the conquered countries. Twelve were sentenced to death, seven to life imprisonment, and three were acquitted. At the same time, the court declared the Nazi Party a criminal organization.

Trials of other war criminals continued for many years in postwar Germany. Hundreds of ex-Nazis were prosecuted, including high-ranking officers, camp guards, minor officials, and doctors who had taken part in "medical experiments." They were convicted of murder, the use of slave labor, and violation of the laws of war concerning the treatment of war prisoners and civilians.

The Allies also pursued a policy of removing former Nazis from positions of authority in government, industry, and education. They set up denazification courts, before which suspected Nazis had to appear and try to clear themselves. Difficulties soon developed, however. The German economy had broken down almost completely. Its rebuilding required technically skilled leaders, many of whom had been Nazis. In addition, there was no agreement as to what degree of connection with the Nazi Party justified purging in the four occupation zones. By 1948 the denazification courts had almost ceased to function.

CHECKUP

1. IDENTIFY: Allied Control Council, Council of Foreign Ministers, de Gaulle, Nuremberg trials, denazification courts.

2. LOCATE: Berlin, Dodecanese Islands, Trieste, Oder-Neisse line, East Prussia.

3. What postwar settlement was made between Italy and Yugoslavia?

4. Describe the main terms of the Austrian peace treaty.

5. What problems arose after the Allied Control Council limited German industry?

3

The Cold War influenced events throughout Europe

Difficulties over the writing of the treaties and over the government of occupied Germany grew increasingly severe during the early postwar years. Many persons in the West feared that communist nations, led by the Soviet Union, were planning to take over all of Europe.

The United States was the strongest major power and the sole possessor of atomic weapons at that time. The rest of the Western powers were exhausted. France and Italy had to reorganize their economies and governments. Great Britain had spent almost all its strength in the long fight. Thus it appeared that if communist expansion was to be stopped, the United States would have to take the lead.

Soviet advances

As you have read, the Soviets fought their way toward Germany at the end of World War II. The Soviet army had liberated and occupied Poland and Germany's eastern allies—Rumania, Bulgaria, and Hungary. The Soviets set up communist-controlled governments in these countries. In Albania and Yugoslavia, governments were established by local communists who had led native resistance groups during the war.

The Allies had promised the people of these Eastern European countries free elections. Local communists, however, eliminated all opposition, and elections were rigged in their favor. By 1947 these nations had become communist dictatorships. They came to be known as Soviet **satellites** because, like planets circling the sun, they were dependent upon the Soviet Union. In matters of both domestic policy and foreign policy, the satellite countries were subordinate to the Soviet Union. In 1946 Winston Churchill noted, "an iron curtain has descended across the Continent." Hence these nations were often referred to as **iron-curtain countries.**

The Soviet Union soon made known its intentions to foster communism throughout Europe. In 1947 a Soviet-sponsored agency, the Communist Information Bureau (Cominform), began to publish propaganda about the supposed unity of European communist parties. This campaign continued until the dissolution of Cominform in 1956.

The Truman Doctrine

Early in 1947 the United States emerged as leader of the West against Soviet expansion. When the British government announced that it could no longer defend the eastern Mediterranean region, the Western powers feared that Greece, Turkey, and the Middle East—with its rich oil resources—might fall to communism.

The United States decided to take action. In March 1947 President Truman, speaking before Congress, announced what came to be called the

Truman Doctrine. The United States, Truman said, considered the continued spread of communism a menace to democracy. The United States would not try to stamp out communism where it already existed, or in any country that freely chose communism. It would, however, use its money, materials, technical knowledge, and influence to help countries threatened by communism if they asked for help. This policy is often referred to as **containment** because it aimed to "contain," or restrict, the spread of communism.

Truman further declared that the United States would "support free peoples who are resisting attempted subjugation by armed minorities or by outside pressures." He asked Congress to appropriate $400 million to help defend Greece and Turkey from communist aggression. After a United Nations investigating committee reported that neighboring communist countries were helping the Greek rebels, the United States Congress granted this request. With American financial and technical aid, the Greek government put down the rebellion. Thus the policy of containment scored an important victory.

The Marshall Plan

The United Nations Relief and Rehabilitation Administration (UNRRA) was formed in November 1943 to provide emergency aid for the war-torn countries of Europe and Asia. Nations that had escaped invasion were asked to contribute one percent of their national income for 1943 to the relief project. The largest contributions were made by the United States, Great Britain, and Canada.

Yet by 1947 Europe's most pressing need was still more economic aid. To be effective, the aid would require a coordinated effort on a continent-wide scale. European nations would have to help themselves but would also need outside help.

In 1947 United States Secretary of State George C. Marshall suggested a new policy that formed the basis for legislation adopted the following year by Congress. The European Recovery Program, often called the Marshall Plan, stipulated that the United States was prepared to give the needed aid to Europe on certain terms. The European countries were to: (1) confer and determine their needs on a continental basis; (2) show what resources they could put into a common pool for economic rebuilding; (3) stabilize their currencies; and (4) try to remove trade barriers so that goods could flow freely throughout the continent. It was hoped that this plan would minimize the influence communism might have on war-damaged nations.

Eventually, 17 European nations participated in the European Recovery Program. Congress appropriated about $13 billion to carry out the program for its first four years. Thus the benefits of the American economy were shared with war-ravaged Europe. The American offer of aid was extended also to the Soviet Union and its satellites, but was rejected.

The Cold War in central Europe

Prewar Czechoslovakia had been the most democratic of all the central European countries. The postwar government was democratic, too, although it included many communist officials.

In February 1948 national elections in Czechoslovakia showed a decline in the communist vote. A few weeks later, shortly after the death (some thought murder) of the Czech foreign minister, the communists held a new election. The voters were offered a single list of communist-approved candidates. The communists wrote a new constitution, which the president of Czechoslovakia refused to sign. In June he resigned and was succeeded by a communist, who approved the revised constitution. Thus Czechoslovakia became a full-fledged member of the Soviet-dominated communist bloc of Eastern Europe.

Only one break appeared in the iron curtain that divided East and West. During the spring of 1948, there was a disagreement between Stalin and Marshal Tito of Yugoslavia. Tito objected to Soviet domination, announcing that Yugoslavia would follow an independent course. By June 1948 the split became definite, and Yugoslavia was expelled from the Cominform.

The division of Germany

By 1948 joint government in Germany by the four former Allies was becoming impossible. The country was in great economic difficulty. The three Western occupying powers began discussions aimed at uniting their zones. In response, in June 1948 the Soviets blockaded all land and

EUROPEAN ALLIANCES 1980's

European members of NATO
(Iceland also a member)

Neutral
nations

Communist nations (all except Yugoslavia and Albania
bound by Warsaw Pact)

water traffic into Berlin from the west. They refused to allow trucks, barges, and trains to pass the checkpoints at the borders. Thus the people of West Berlin were threatened with starvation.

The Western nations acted swiftly during the Berlin blockade. The United States and Great Britain organized an airlift to supply West Berlin. The 2 million inhabitants of the Western sectors of the city received daily supplies of food and coal by plane. The airlift operated so efficiently that raw materials were soon being supplied to West Berlin factories. The Soviet Union lifted its blockade of the city in May 1949.

Meanwhile the Western occupying powers announced that if no peace treaty with Germany were written, they would allow the Germans in their zones to write a constitution and set up a democratic government. A constitutional assembly was held, and on May 23, 1949, the Federal Republic of Germany was proclaimed. However, the Federal Republic, known as West Germany, was still under the control of the Western occupation authorities. The Western powers also unified their sectors of Berlin and permitted democratic elections of a municipal government.

In October 1949 a provisional communist government, the German Democratic Republic, was established in the Soviet zone of Germany. This region became known as East Germany (see map, this page).

The Berlin Wall

After 1948, Berlin remained a major trouble spot in the East-West struggle. With American aid, West Berlin made an astonishing recovery from the devastation of war. In East Berlin, however, recovery was slow. People in East Berlin, discontented with the totalitarian communist rule there, were constantly fleeing to West Berlin. Political refugees also streamed into West Berlin from East Germany and other satellite countries.

In 1961, the East German government tried to stop the flow of refugees to the West by building walls and fences along the boundary between the Allied and Soviet sectors of Berlin. Crossing points were guarded at all times. East and West Berliners could move through them only with authorization. The flow of refugees was greatly reduced. East German guards shot at anyone trying to escape to West Berlin. The concrete portion of the Berlin Wall, which was topped by barbed wire, became a symbol of world tensions.

Political alliances

With the takeover of satellite nations in Eastern Europe, many people feared a Soviet push to the west. Indeed, Churchill later said that it was only fear of American atomic bombs that had prevented the Soviet Union from overrunning Western Europe. Increasingly the Western Nations felt a need to deter any Soviet drive.

NATO. In April 1949 a mutual defense pact provided for creation of the North Atlantic Treaty Organization (NATO). The North Atlantic Treaty was signed by 12 nations: the United States, Great Britain, France, Italy, Portugal, Norway, Denmark, Iceland, Canada, Belgium, the Netherlands, and Luxembourg. Greece and Turkey joined NATO in 1952, West Germany in 1955, and Spain in 1982 (see map, page 703). The signers agreed that in the event of an attack on one member nation, all members would take united action against the aggressor.

As a mutual-defense pact, the North Atlantic Treaty did not provide for a standing army. Two events were instrumental, however, in strengthening the alliance. One was the explosion of the first Soviet atomic bomb in the fall of 1949. The second event was the communist invasion of South Korea in 1950 (see Chapter 29).

In 1954 the NATO members drew up a detailed plan of defense, under which each nation was to contribute to an ever-ready NATO force of about 750,000 troops. The plan also called for extensive commitments of ships and aircraft.

Not all the goals set in 1954 were reached. Consequently, NATO members came to rely increasingly on American nuclear weapons rather than on the proposed ground troops.

The Warsaw Pact. The Soviet response to a strengthened NATO was immediate. In May 1955, in Warsaw, Poland, the Soviet government held a meeting of representatives of the European communist bloc—the Soviet Union, Poland, East Germany, Czechoslovakia, Hungary, Rumania, Bulgaria, and Albania (see map, page 703). Yugoslavia was the only European communist country that did not take part.

These nations adopted a 20-year agreement called the Warsaw Pact. Under the pact the nations pledged, in the event of war, to furnish about 1.5 million troops. Added to the already vast human resources of the Soviet Union, the Warsaw Pact provided the communist bloc with a potentially formidable force.

The Third World. An important influence on the postwar period was a rapid increase in the number of independent nations of the world. The breakup of European empires in Asia and Africa triggered a widespread decolonization process affecting more than 1.5 billion people between 1945 and 1985. As these newly freed peoples began to form their own governments and develop their own economies, they faced difficult economic, political, and social problems. As early as 1955 they began to meet together to discuss their common goals and concerns.

The new, developing nations neither allied themselves with the West nor with the communist-bloc countries. They were more interested in meeting their own economic needs than in the political differences separating the industrialized, developed nations. Eventually the nonaligned nations came to be known collectively as the **Third World.** By the mid-1980's the nonaligned group had grown from a handful of participants to more than 100 independent nations. Developing nations were now vocal participants in international affairs, and they were demanding more influence in the world's economic system.

Relations with the Soviet Union

The death in 1953 of Joseph Stalin, the Soviet dictator, created a power struggle within the Soviet government. Eventually, Nikita Khrushchev (kroosh·CHAWF) emerged as both Communist Party leader and Soviet premier.

Soviet foreign policy under Khrushchev seemed less threatening than it had been under Stalin. The Cold War, however, continued for many years. By the late 1960's and early 1970's both the United States and the U.S.S.R. had come to feel that their interests could be better served by negotiations. Thus the Cold War gradually gave way to an era of improved Soviet-American relations known as **détente** (day·TAHNT), a French word meaning "an easing of strain." By 1979 détente had ended, however, because neither nation was willing to abandon its basic beliefs.

Summit conferences. After Stalin's death, many people in the West hoped that the world's major leaders could meet face to face and reach general agreement on various issues. These meetings, begun in the 1950's, were called "summit conferences" because they involved the highest officials of the participating countries in face-to-face discussions.

Summit meetings, which have occurred at irregular intervals during the last 30 years, have rarely produced substantive results. The May 1960 summit meeting between Premier Khrushchev and President Eisenhower, for example, ended quickly when it was revealed that an American spy plane had been shot down over the Soviet Union. The plane had been photographing Soviet military operations. Neither was the 1963 meeting between Khrushchev and President Kennedy a success. Still, most Americans felt that it was important to keep lines of communication open with the Soviets.

Khrushchev's successor, Leonid Brezhnev (BREHZH·nehf), met with presidents Nixon and Carter in the 1970's. But no summit meetings were held during President Reagan's first term, a reflection of increased tensions between the superpowers. Summit meetings were finally resumed in late 1985, when Reagan met with a new Soviet leader, Mikhail Gorbachev (gawr·baht·CHAWF).

The Helsinki Agreement. In 1975, representatives of 35 nations including the United States and the Soviet Union met in Helsinki, Finland, to take part in the Conference on Security and Cooperation in Europe. The delegates at Helsinki agreed to encourage the process of détente, to fully support the United Nations in settling international disputes, and to cooperate on humanitarian and cultural matters. By the mid-1980's it was clear that the Helsinki Agreement had fallen short of its goals, particularly in the promotion of basic human rights. A decade after Helsinki, the Soviet Union continued to repress internal dissent, and the United States continued to respond by denouncing Soviet behavior.

Satellite upheavals

During the early postwar years, the communist bloc seemed a solid, firmly knit group of nations, united by common beliefs, policies, and goals. However, the satellites had once been independent nations, some with longstanding antagonisms toward the Soviet Union.

Yugoslavia's growing independence from the Soviet Union after 1948 aroused envy among the satellites. "Titoism," named after the independent leader of Yugoslavia, became a kind of goal for some people in the satellite countries. In 1953 a revolt by East German workers had to be put down by Soviet tanks and troops. In 1956 Poland threatened revolt and gained a small amount of independence in domestic policy-making.

In 1956 Hungary revolted against Soviet domination. For a time the rebels controlled all of western Hungary. Soviet troops were at first withdrawn, but they later returned and bloodily suppressed the revolt. No help for the rebels came from the Western powers.

In 1968 Czechoslovakia under Alexander Dubcek (DOOB·chek), began a program of reforms, promising civil liberties, democratic political reforms, and a more independent political system. Within six months, Warsaw Pact troops, chiefly from the Soviet Union, invaded Czechoslovakia. They seized the reform leaders and replaced them with pro-Soviet people.

An unprecedented series of events began in Poland in 1980, catching the Soviet Union off guard.

Europe after the war

The hopes for peace after World War II quickly faded as tensions rose between East and West. The city of Berlin, divided at the Brandenburg Gate (below right), symbolized the hostilities between the two sides. To strengthen the West, the United States started the Marshall Plan in the late 1940's to help Europe to economic recovery. In 1950 the program was broadened to include all areas of the world opposed to the communists. As the slogan on the jeep put it, the aid was to provide "strength for the free world" (right).

In the communist bloc, the Soviet Union was determined to maintain control over its satellites in Eastern Europe. When the people of Czechoslovakia tried to rise up against the Soviets in 1968, their banners of hope and freedom soon vanished in the face of Soviet tanks (below).

Polish shipbuilders under the leadership of Lech Walesa (vah·WEHN·sah), an electrician, forced the government to recognize some of their demands, including the rights to strike and to form unions. By 1981 the independent trade union Solidarity had almost 10 million members. Late in 1981 the Polish government, fearful of Soviet intervention, imposed martial law in Poland. The government arrested Walesa and other union leaders. The government lifted martial law in December 1982. The situation in Poland, however, remained tense.

These satellite upheavals pointed to several changes that seemed to be taking place between the Soviet Union and its satellites. First, many people in the satellites seemed less willing to accept continued Soviet domination. Second, the troops from satellite countries, promised in the Warsaw Pact, might prove of little help to the Soviet Union in the event of war.

Weakening alliances

During the late 1950's, many NATO members became discontented with the organization for several reasons. (1) The alliance had grown increasingly dependent for its defense on nuclear weapons, which could be used only when the President of the United States gave permission. This meant, in effect, that the United States controlled the defense of Europe. (2) Because of the growing strength of Western Europe, and problems of the Soviet Union in its own sphere, Western leaders felt that the Soviets would not risk a military push in Europe. Thus the West no longer considered the NATO force a military necessity. (3) With the development of long-range missiles, however, Europeans feared that the Soviet Union could conquer Europe and threaten to destroy cities in the United States. In this case, they thought, the United States might not risk its own destruction in order to defend Western Europe from Soviet domination.

The chief challenge to NATO came from the President of France, Charles de Gaulle. Wishing to take a more independent course, he partially withdrew French troops from NATO in 1966 and asked the United States to give up its NATO bases in France. De Gaulle's successors supported the Western alliance. They acted independent-ly from NATO, however, in dealing with the Soviet bloc.

Other nations reevaluated their own roles in NATO. In 1974, for example, in response to the Turkish invasion of Cyprus, Greece withdrew its armed forces from NATO. Although Greece eventually rejoined the organization, other disagreements thwarted NATO unity.

In the 1980's NATO members continued to reevaluate the purposes of the alliance. The placement of United States cruise missiles in Europe touched off protests throughout the continent. Also, many NATO members sought greater independence in their foreign policy.

Similar challenges arose within the Warsaw Pact, NATO's rival. In 1969 the Warsaw Pact nations approved the idea of reducing conflicts with NATO through the creation of a collective security system for all Europe. Disunity among the nations of the Warsaw Pact, however, interfered with the establishment of any cooperative efforts with NATO. Albania, an original member of the Warsaw Pact, had been expelled for refusing to cooperate with other members. Rumania increasingly urged that the satellite nations be allowed greater independence.

Outside the Warsaw Pact a major split occurred between the Soviet Union and China, where a communist government had taken control in 1949. This development, as you will see, had important implications for international relations in the 1970's and 1980's.

CHECKUP

1. IDENTIFY: satellites, iron curtain, Cominform, containment, Third World, Khrushchev, détente, Brezhnev, Helsinki Agreement, Solidarity

2. What was the purpose of the Truman Doctrine?

3. Describe the basic features of the Marshall Plan.

4. Briefly describe the East-West struggle over the city of Berlin.

5. Describe the functions of NATO and the Warsaw Pact. Why were they formed?

6. What events have occurred in the Soviet satellites to indicate resistance to Soviet domination?

7. What challenges arose within NATO and the Warsaw Pact?

4

Cooperative ventures aided the economic recovery of Western Europe

One of the most outstanding characteristics of postwar Europe was its economic recovery. In a comparatively short time, the rubble of bombed cities was cleared away, industries returned to full production, and roads, rail lines, and bridges were rebuilt. In West Germany the rate of recovery was so rapid that many people referred to it as the "German miracle."

There were also important political changes, particularly in the older, more established democracies like Great Britain and France. These nations no longer wielded as much power as they had in earlier times. Yet their role in shaping opinion and in influencing younger nations was still important.

Germany: "One Nation, Two States"

Throughout the postwar period, Germany remained divided—or, as the Germans preferred to say, "One Nation, Two States." National unification remained a lingering idea and for years remained the chief postwar problem. The question of free access to West Berlin, which was entirely surrounded by East Germany, continued to be a disturbing issue.

In the 1960's East Germany began to make impressive economic progress. Within a decade it was highly industrialized, becoming one of the most technologically advanced members of the communist bloc. In the late 1970's, however, East Germany's economy faltered. Resources and labor were scarce. Moreover, the nation faced a severe foreign debt in the 1980's.

The challenges facing West Germany were more of a political than an economic nature. Relations with the Soviet Union posed a difficult foreign policy problem. Nevertheless, under the leadership of Chancellor Willy Brandt, who came to power in 1969, West Germany became more flexible in its relations with the Soviet Union and with East Germany. This controversial approach, known as **Ostpolitik** (policy toward the East) resulted in a 1972 agreement by which West Germany formally recognized the existence of East Germany.

In 1973 Leonid Brezhnev became the first Soviet leader to visit West Germany. He agreed to a ten-year period of economic cooperation between the two countries. The agreement provided for the exchange of raw materials, skills, and manufactured goods.

During the postwar years, the West German government successfully provided housing and jobs for refugees from East Germany and other Eastern European nations. The labor of these refugees contributed to West Germany's rapidly growing economy. The German automobile industry, for example, made impressive advances and became a strong competitor of the American industry. The West German currency, the mark, became one of the most stable in the world. Technological innovation, a commitment to quality, and the absence of strikes and other labor troubles made German industry flourish.

By the mid-1980's West Germany was the richest and most influential nation in Western Europe. The worldwide recession of the early 1980's, however, had its effects on West Germany. For the first time in many years West Germans were faced with unemployment and increasing inflation. Many of them also objected to NATO's installation of nuclear missiles on West German soil.

Great Britain after the war

You have read how, in 1945, Winston Churchill and the Conservative Party were defeated and Clement Attlee, head of the Labour Party, became prime minister of Great Britain.

The Labour Party was a moderate socialist party whose leaders made many changes in the British economic and social systems. Railroads, utilities, coal mines, and the Bank of England were nationalized. Many welfare measures were passed, including one extending free education to the age of 16. Another welfare measure provided free medical care for everyone. Great Britain became a **welfare state**—that is, one in which the government undertakes primary responsibility for the social welfare of its citizens. This form of social and political organization has had wide appeal in Western Europe.

Recovery in Europe

The speed of Europe's economic recovery after World War II, aided by the Marshall Plan, was remarkable. Industries that had been converted to the war effort resumed full operation. The Dutch port of Rotterdam, devastated during the war, became a major shipping center (below). German industry also quickly resumed its prewar efficiency. German cars, in particular, became a common sight throughout the world (right).

As industrial output rose and commerce expanded, Europeans became more prosperous. Many goods became more available to consumers. In supermarkets like this one in France (below right), people could now purchase a variety of attractively packaged products. This gave the average citizen a sense of participation in the economic recovery.

Great Britain faced many severe economic problems after the war. Its industrial equipment was outdated and inefficient. Many workers had been killed in the war. In addition, the country had lost, and continued to lose, scientists and managers. Many migrated to Canada, Australia, and the United States.

Valuable colonies and possessions were lost, and the cost of the nation's remaining overseas commitments was a heavy burden. In 1960 Cyprus became independent from Great Britain. By the 1970's Great Britain was prepared to abandon all its remaining bases east of the Suez Canal. British problems in Northern Ireland also continued.

Despite its many problems, Great Britain began to experience favorable economic development in the 1950's. The government reduced unemployment, stabilized its currency, improved housing conditions, and raised the general standard of living.

Limited economic freedom and incentives helped bring a decline in these favorable trends. Great Britain's industrial productivity fell to one of the lowest levels in the industrialized world. Some of its main industries, such as auto manufacturing, experienced hard times. Racial problems arose because of the growing immigration into Great Britain of blacks from Commonwealth countries. Competition for jobs also caused problems, and in the early 1970's this immigration was halted.

The discovery of huge oil deposits in the North Sea raised British hopes for economic revival. Yet the country's economy was still lagging in the mid-1980's. The Conservative prime minister, Margaret Thatcher, carried out controversial economic policies that were designed to reduce inflation. The staggering price increases that came with inflation caused more unemployment. Despite its record of political stability, Great Britain's economic future looked uncertain.

The Fifth French Republic

Postwar France also faced severe problems. In spite of Marshall Plan aid, economic recovery was slow. The French Empire was crumbling in Southeast Asia and in North Africa, where, as you will read later, there were bitter and costly struggles. Among France's many bickering political parties, none was able to form a lasting coalition to run a stable government.

Finally, in 1958, the French legislature, under pressure from army leaders, authorized General Charles de Gaulle to write a new constitution and to rule by decree until the new constitution was ratified. Thus, the Fourth French Republic ended without a struggle.

The new constitution, approved by French voters in October 1958, created the Fifth French Republic. Much power was concentrated in the hands of the president. The president appointed the prime minister and could dissolve the legislature and assume dictatorial powers in a national emergency. Through the prime minister, the president could enact laws unless a majority of the National Assembly opposed them.

The first president of the Fifth Republic was General de Gaulle. He ended France's colonial warfare and established stability at home. This stability was attained, however, at a high cost to the French taxpayer.

In foreign policy, de Gaulle was a staunch nationalist. He believed that Europe could prosper only under a system of national states. De Gaulle opposed British and American influence in Europe and believed that Germany must be kept weak. He hoped to maintain cordial relations with the Soviet Union and Poland as a check on possible German aggression.

In the late 1960's political conditions within France became unstable. Violent riots shook the nation in 1968. Militant students demanded reforms in the educational system, and strikes for higher wages and better working conditions spread rapidly throughout industrial areas. To meet the crisis, de Gaulle dissolved the National Assembly and called for a general election.

Departure of de Gaulle. To win a favorable vote, de Gaulle acknowledged the need for social improvements in France. When reelected, he approved a 15 percent increase in workers' wages. This concession strained the finances of the nation without increasing industrial production. The result was rising prices that cut deeply into the workers' recent wage increases. De Gaulle's popularity declined. In April 1969 his proposals for reform were defeated in a direct vote by the French people. The 79-year-old president then resigned.

De Gaulle's successors, Georges Pompidou (PAHM·pih·doo) and Valery Giscard d'Estaing (zhee·SKAHR des·TANG), maintained France's independent position in international affairs. They kept close ties with former French colonies in Africa, sending troops to quell any unrest. They improved relations with the Soviet Union and individual communist-bloc countries. Giscard established good relations with China.

With the election of François Mitterand (MEE·tehr·ahn) in 1981, the Fifth Republic received its first socialist president. The government rapidly nationalized many major corporations and banks. In the 1986 legislative elections, voters gave the conservatives a majority. Clearly Mitterand's socialist policies were in disfavor.

European economic cooperation

In the early 1950's the French proposed that the six nations producing most of Western Europe's steel and coal unite all their facilities and production. The European Coal and Steel Community (ECSC) was formed in 1952 by France, West Germany, Italy, and the Benelux countries (Belgium, the Netherlands, and Luxembourg). A central authority was established to regulate production and prices, and members agreed not to charge each other tariffs on coal or steel. A remarkable feature was that the ECSC was free of national control.

The Common Market

In 1957 the same six nations took another important step toward economic union by establishing the European Economic Community (EEC)—usually called the Common Market. The treaty provided that tariffs and import quotas among the six member nations would gradually be abolished. A common tariff would be placed on goods coming into the Common Market from nonmember nations. A European Investment Bank was established with capital contributed by the member governments. The bank's purposes were to finance projects beyond the means of individual nations and to invest in developing industries in poor areas of member nations.

At the same time, the six nations also created the Atomic Energy Community (Euratom). Each of the members agreed to share information on the peaceful uses of atomic energy.

In the 1960's Greece, Turkey, and many of the newly independent African nations became associate members of the European Economic Community. As associate members they did not have the right to vote but were entitled to other privileges and could eventually join as full-fledged members.

The Common Market made steady progress toward European economic unity in the 1960's. In 1967 it adopted a five-year plan to provide greater price and wage stability and more uniform tax levels among member countries. Also in 1967 the EEC merged with the European Coal and Steel Community and the Atomic Energy Community. The three communities set up a single European commission with headquarters in Belgium. This was a step toward greater economic unity.

The founding members of the Common Market had also dreamed of political unity for Europe. But many unsolved issues stood in the way. The political issue of whether Great Britain should join the EEC, for example, was debated for almost 15 years. Supporters of Great Britain's entry argued that British influence in European affairs would decline and Great Britain would suffer economically if it remained outside the Common Market. Opponents argued that Great Britain's entry might damage economically the nations of the British Commonwealth from whom Britain traditionally had imported most of its agricultural products.

After lengthy disagreements and negotiations Great Britain finally became a member of the EEC in 1973. Ireland and Denmark also joined that year. Greece became a full member of the Common Market in 1981. By 1986 when Spain and Portugal entered the organization, the original membership of the EEC had doubled.

Effects of the Common Market

The members of the European Economic Community were able to reduce internal tariffs easily. By the mid-1960's tariffs on industrial goods moving from one member country to another had been reduced to 30 percent of their starting level. Early in 1965 the European commission approved a plan to eliminate all industrial tariffs by mid-1967 instead of the originally planned date of 1970.

Agreements on a common agricultural policy were more difficult to reach. An accord signed in 1966, after five years of hard bargaining, resulted in higher farm prices and a rise in food costs for consumers. It was hoped, however, that the common policy would eventually lead to increased and more efficient production.

During the first seven years of the EEC, trade among the member nations increased 66 percent. Trade with nonmembers increased 50 percent. During that same period, world trade as a whole increased only 46 percent. The figures for industrial production are almost as striking. In the Common Market region, industrial production increased 38 percent. In the United States, it increased only 23 percent, while in Great Britain it increased just 18 percent.

By 1986, the members of the European Economic Community were predicting that they would acieve full economic integration by 1992. Certainly, the EEC had made great headway toward setting common practices in taxation, credit, and social security. The members of the community had also introduced a European Monetary System, hoping that Europeans would eventually share one currency.

In the political area, however, unity still seemed an elusive goal. Even so, an important achievement of the European Economic Community during its first three decades was the creation of Europe's first international political structures, including a European Parliament and a Council of Ministers.

The communist response. In 1949 several communist nations joined to form their own common market, the Council for Mutual Economic Assistance (Comecon). Its members were the Soviet Union, Poland, East Germany, Czechoslovakia, Hungary, Rumania, Bulgaria, Albania, and Mongolia. (Albania was excluded in 1961.) Over the years, China, North Vietnam, North Korea, and Yugoslavia sometimes attended Comecon meetings as observers.

The main purpose of Comecon was to coordinate industrial development and trade within the Soviet bloc. The organization tried to integrate the economies of its members and to expand trade with the capitalist countries.

Comecon was far less successful than its counterpart, the EEC, chiefly because it lacked trading flexibility. Trade was conducted on a nation-to-nation and balanced basis. Bulgaria, for example, would sign an agreement with Poland, providing for an exchange of a certain amount of Bulgarian products for products of about the same value received from Poland. No money would change hands in the trade. Deliveries from one country would be checked off against deliveries from the other.

Comecon members found this system cumbersome and unsatisfactory. Some also objected to plans under which they were to supply raw materials while other members—especially the Soviet Union—did the manufacturing.

Effects on the United States. Europe had always been an important customer for American manufactured products and foodstuffs. Alarm at the possibility of losing this market to the EEC produced two kinds of action in the United States. First, many American corporations hurried to build factories or to buy shares in corporations located in the Common Market countries. In this way they could participate indirectly in the EEC. Second, the United States Congress passed a new Trade Expansion Act. This law gave the President power to cut American tariffs in bargaining with other countries for tariff cuts on American goods.

CHECKUP

1. IDENTIFY: Brandt, welfare state, Pompidou, Giscard d'Estaing, Mitterrand, ECSC, Benelux countries, Euratom, Trade Expansion Act.

2. What improvements were made in relations between the Soviet Union and West Germany in 1973?

3. What changes did the Labour Party bring about in Great Britain?

4. What problems did Great Britain begin to experience in the 1960's?

5. What were the provisions of the constitution that created the Fifth French Republic?

6. Describe French foreign policy under de Gaulle and his successors.

7. What were the purposes of the Common Market and Comecon? Why was Comecon less successful than the Common Market?

CHAPTER REVIEW

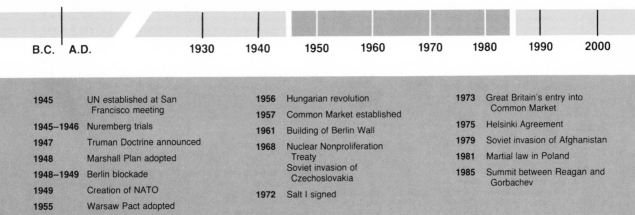

| B.C. | A.D. | | 1930 | 1940 | 1950 | 1960 | 1970 | 1980 | 1990 | 2000 |

1945	UN established at San Francisco meeting	1956	Hungarian revolution	1973	Great Britain's entry into Common Market
1945–1946	Nuremberg trials	1957	Common Market established	1975	Helsinki Agreement
1947	Truman Doctrine announced	1961	Building of Berlin Wall	1979	Soviet invasion of Afghanistan
1948	Marshall Plan adopted	1968	Nuclear Nonproliferation Treaty	1981	Martial law in Poland
1948–1949	Berlin blockade		Soviet invasion of Czechoslovakia	1985	Summit between Reagan and Gorbachev
1949	Creation of NATO	1972	Salt I signed		
1955	Warsaw Pact adopted				

CHAPTER SUMMARY

Following World War II, the United Nations was established to help the world's nations maintain peace. The UN also took on humanitarian functions in such areas as human rights and world health. By 1986 it had 159 members.

Despite the establishment of the UN, conflicts among nations continued, especially between the Soviet Union and the United States. The antagonisms of the Cold War made peace settlements difficult. Germany was divided into four zones and occupied. Many Nazi leaders were tried, convicted, and sentenced. The flow of refugees into Germany created problems, as did the question of German industry.

The creation of satellite nations and establishment of the Cominform revealed Soviet plans to spread communism throughout the world. The United States, the strongest Western nation, tried to contain communism through the Truman Doctrine and the Marshall Plan. When the Soviets blockaded Berlin in 1948, a Western airlift supplied the city. Soon afterward, Germany was divided into West and East Germany. In 1961 the Soviets built the Berlin Wall to stop the flow of refugees from East Berlin.

The Soviet threat in Europe resulted in the formation of NATO, originally a mutual defense pact but later maintaining a joint army. The Soviet Union responded with the Warsaw Pact. Satellite rebellions, especially in Hungary, Czechoslovakia, and Poland, indicated opposition to Soviet domination. As the two sides in the Cold War moved toward détente in the 1970's, NATO and the Warsaw Pact began to weaken.

Europe was able to recover from World War II in a relatively short time. Germany remained divided into two states, but both prospered. West Germany became a major influence in the West. Great Britain faced difficult economic conditions. Political stability continued, however, helped by the creation of a welfare state. In France, a contrasting situation developed—economic prosperity, despite the political uncertainties of the 1940's and 1950's. A major source of the growing wealth of Western Europe was the European Economic community, which included twelve nations by 1986. The communist equivalent, Comecon, had only limited success.

CHECKING WHAT YOU KNOW

1. Match each part of the UN at the left with its description at the right.

   a. General Assembly
   b. Security Council
   c. Trusteeship Council
   d. Economic and Social Council
   e. Secretariat
   f. International Court of Justice

   1. Administers dependent territories.
   2. Deals with such subjects as population and human rights.
   3. Settles disputes involving international law.
   4. Headed by the Secretary-General.
   5. Draws up UN budget and assesses each nation's share.
   6. Maintains peace, prevents or resists international aggression.

2. Match each leader at the left with a country at the right.

   1. Brandt   a. United States
   2. Brezhnev b. Great Britain
   3. de Gaulle c. Yugoslavia
   4. Attlee   d. France
   5. Truman   e. West Germany
   6. Tito   f. Soviet Union

3. How are decisions made in the Security Council? in the General Assembly? In which body does the United States have more power? Explain.

4. What developments in the occupation of Eastern Europe and Germany increased tensions between the Soviet Union and the Western nations?

5. Define the term "Cold War." Why did the Cold War develop? How did it gradually give way to détente?

6. What was the containment policy? How were the Marshall Plan and the Truman Doctrine designed to carry out this policy?

7. What alliance systems were set up in Europe by the Western nations and by the communist bloc after 1945? What was the purpose of each?

8. What were the effects of the Common Market in Europe? in the United States?

PRACTICING YOUR SKILLS

1. **Interpreting primary sources.** At the Nuremberg trials, former Nazi leaders pleaded innocent, claiming that as soldiers they were bound to obey the orders of their superiors. Read the selection below, from the judges' response, and answer the questions that follow.

   > Hitler could not make aggressive war by himself. He had to have the cooperation of statesmen, military leaders, diplomats, and businessmen. When they, with knowledge of his aims, gave him their cooperation, they made themselves parties to the plan. . . . That they were assigned their tasks by a dictator does not absolve them from responsibility for their acts.

   Why did the judges refuse to accept an innocent plea? Do you agree with the last sentence in this selection? Why or why not?

2. **Using maps.** Turn to the map on page 703. Which European nations belong to NATO? to the Warsaw Pact? Which nations have remained neutral? How has the system of alliances changed since World War II? What factors account for this realignment?

RELATING PAST TO PRESENT

1. The policies of containment and economic aid were used after World War II to stem the spread of communism. Does the United States still try to prevent the spread of communism? What methods does it use today?

2. In the 1950's several satellite nations tried to free themselves from Soviet control. Are there any instances today of satellite nations in Eastern Europe trying to lessen Soviet control? Explain.

3. In the postwar years the term "superpower" crept into common usage. At first only two nations fit this description—the United States and the Soviet Union. What, if any, present-day nations might be added to this list? What standards determine if a nation is a superpower?

INVESTIGATING FURTHER

1. After Franklin Roosevelt's death his widow, Eleanor Roosevelt, became the United States delegate to the United Nations. Using the *Dictionary of American Biography* or the most recent edition of *Notable American Women,* research Eleanor Roosevelt's diplomatic career. Be prepared to present your findings to the class.

2. The position of Secretary-General of the United Nations has been a demanding and sometimes controversial job. Use encyclopedias and books in your library to find out more about each of the following Secretaries-General: Trygvie Lie, Dag Hammarskjöld, U Thant, Kurt Waldheim, and Javier Pérez de Cuéllar. What were the accomplishments of each?

3. Use resource materials in your library to research the satellite upheavals discussed in the chapter (Yugoslavia, 1945–48; Hungary, 1956; Czechoslovakia, 1968; Poland, 1980–present). Why did each nation try to free itself from Soviet control? Evaluate to what extent each of these nations was successful in its objectives.

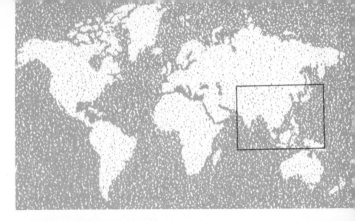

29

(1945 to the Present)

Asian Nations Struggled to Gain Political Stability and Economic Strength

Until World War II, the Western powers had regarded Asia as a vast area for them to control and exploit. Despite the achievements of their cultures, Asian countries had not been able to resist European colonial and imperial expansion. As a result, Asia had been dominated by outsiders for centuries and had had only a minor influence on the West. After World War II, however, the relationship changed significantly.

The movements for self-rule in eastern Asia that had begun decades earlier came to fulfillment in the postwar period. Between 1947 and 1962, the vast colonial empires of Great Britain, France, and the Netherlands fell apart and were replaced by native governments. Few of these transitions to independence were accomplished peaceably. Even in Asian countries that were already independent, great political change occurred. For example, after many years of internal struggle, a communist government came to power in China in 1949.

As independence came to Asia, events there began to have significant consequences in other parts of the world. After World War II, eastern Asia became a battleground for armed conflict arising from the Cold War. Korea and Vietnam became the focus of serious confrontations between communist and Western nations. Many people—Asian, American, and European—died

Superexpress speeding past Mount Fuji

in these wars. There were also violent tensions among the Asian nations themselves.

Despite these tensions, there were many important signs of Asia's potential impact on world economics, politics, and culture. A vivid example of the region's new influence could be seen in Japan. In the years after 1900, it had become a world power. Even though the Japanese were defeated in World War II, the nation's economic strength rose to new heights in the next decades. Its economic influence extended far beyond Asia.

Other areas of Asia strived to follow Japan's example. It became apparent that Asia was assuming an active instead of a passive role in world affairs.

THE CHAPTER SECTIONS

1. Communists took control in China and created a new society

2. Japan became an economic giant in the postwar world

3. India, Pakistan, and Bangladesh became independent nations

4. The countries of Southeast Asia achieved independence

5. Conflict in Vietnam affected other countries in Southeast Asia

6. Asian nations sought security and economic growth

1

Communists took control in China and created a new society

During World War II, Nationalist and communist Chinese had agreed to halt their civil war and form a united front against their common enemy, the Japanese. Before the war ended, however, their alliance had broken down. In the fighting that followed, the communists soon gained the upper hand. With support from China's peasants, the communists were able to increase their military strength and expand the territory under their direct control.

The Nationalists were weakened by extensive desertion, and many of their armies were captured. In 1949 Chiang Kai-shek and his supporters fled to the island of Taiwan and established a government there (see map, opposite). On the Chinese mainland the communists, led by Mao Tse-tung, established the People's Republic of China. Less than 40 years after the creation of a republic, China had experienced a second revolution. The United States had tried to prevent the defeat of the Nationalists by sending them military equipment and advisers. It refused to recognize the new communist government on the mainland.

The Chinese economy

Like the Nationalists before them, the communists wanted to create a modern, industrialized nation. They also wanted to create a classless society in which people worked for common goals, not for their own private gain.

The first step the communists took was political. Communist Party members were elected or appointed to all key posts in government and in the armed forces. Executive power rested with a committee of the Political Bureau of the Communist Party, a group of seven headed by Mao Tse-tung. Under this committee, a pyramid of bureaus controlled every phase of Chinese life.

China had been devastated by more than 30 years of fighting. The people were miserably poor and had suffered periodic epidemics and famines. Farms lay destroyed, and industry and transportation had almost ceased to function.

Under communism, China had recovered enough by 1953 to be ready for its first Five-Year Plan for economic growth. The Soviet Union offered help in the form of loans, but most of the capital came from China itself. Land reform was carried out. Some land was given to peasants, who later formed collective farms. Some land was operated as state farms.

Despite droughts, floods, peasant opposition, and poor planning, the first Five-Year Plan showed gains in agricultural and industrial production. In 1958 a second Five-Year Plan, the **Great Leap Forward,** was announced. It aimed to speed up economic development drastically.

In some places, huge rural communes were established in which men, women, and children lived in separate barracks. The men and women worked in the fields under strict supervision. They were also expected to develop local industries. Three successive crop failures, poor planning, and peasant resentment about communal living conditions led to abandonment of this plan in 1960.

The communes were modified and kept as administrative units. Families now lived in their own homes in China's many small villages. Men and women still worked in the large fields of the communes, but each family also had a small plot of land where it could raise some of its own produce. Many communes also developed successful small industries. During the early 1960's, under these modified communal arrangements, agriculture recovered and became successful.

To promote industrialization, the government purchased modern machinery and even complete factories, first from the Soviet Union and then from the countries of Western Europe. Between 1952 and 1975, industrial production expanded rapidly, averaging increases of 11 percent per

EAST ASIA · 1980'S

0   500 miles

0   500 kilometers

year. Meanwhile the Chinese demonstrated their technological progress by exploding their first nuclear device in 1964. By 1982 China had become the world's largest producer of coal, second largest producer of cement, third largest producer of steel, and sixth largest producer of petroleum.

Since the late 1970's China has liberalized its economic policies. The latest Five-Year Plan (1986–1990) focuses less on industrial growth and more on economic reforms, particularly in the banking and agricultural sectors. The Chinese government now accepts foreign loans and foreign investment. It also encourages a degree of free enterprise. One result of the new trend in Chinese economic policy is reflected in a rising standard of livng for the Chinese people. Per capita income, for example, increased more than 14 percent between 1982 and 1983.

China's leaders

Since 1949 officials of the Chinese Communist Party have remained in agreement about the two goals of their revolution: (1) economic development, and (2) the creation of a classless society. They have often disagreed, however, about the way to achieve these goals. One group believed that economic development had to come first. If necessary, wage incentives should be used to increase production. The other group believed that both goals should be pursued at the same time. If there was a conflict between these goals, priority should be given to social, not economic, change. This group also believed wage incentives were dangerous, because they created inequality and rivalry among workers.

In the 1950's and 1960's Liu Shao-chi (LYOO SHOU·CHEE) was the leading advocate of the first point of view. Mao Tse-Tung was the leading advocate of the second point of view. In the early 1960's Liu and his supporters successfully put their economic development policies into effect. In opposition to these policies, Mao launched the Great Cultural Revolution in 1966. This was a violent attempt to rid China of traditional ideas and customs. During this period, many people were purged, or expelled, from the government. Liu was denounced.

During the Cultural Revolution, Mao followed a policy that was a compromise between revolutionary ideals and the need for economic growth. Upon Mao's death in 1976, Liu's supporters won the major governmental posts. The new government denounced Mao and proceeded on a path of economic development.

Among the new leaders was Deng Xiaoping (DUNG SHOU·PING), who had been exiled during the Cultural Revolution. In the late 1970's, Deng played a major role in determining China's new priority—economic modernization. By 1985 Deng was the most important leader in China.

Foreign relations

In the early 1950's the Soviet Union and the People's Republic of China were allies, united by political ideology and common economic interests. They soon disagreed, however, over the interpretation of Marxism and over foreign policy.

Soviet leaders believed that world communism could be achieved through scientific and economic successes. They believed that peaceful coexistence with the West was possible. War was not inevitable, because nuclear weapons made victory impossible. In the economic realm, Soviet leaders felt that each communist country should produce only those things it could produce best. The Soviet leaders also felt that the communist nations should integrate their production under the direction of the most prominent communist country—the Soviet Union.

Chinese leaders, on the other hand, claimed that power came from revolutions. Communists must support "national wars of liberation." In the long run peaceful coexistence was impossible. The Soviets, said the Chinese, had abandoned true Marxism. The Chinese held that each communist country should develop its own economy, and that no one country should dominate. They argued that the Soviet model of economic development stressed heavy industry, which was not suitable for China with its large agricultural population. The Chinese, proud of their hard-won independence, did not want to yield to the wishes of any foreign country, not even the Soviet Union.

At first this Chinese-Soviet struggle was confined to bitter public speeches and to competition

China under Mao

Under Mao Tse-tung's rule, China was a mixture of traditional and revolutionary ways. The clothes people wore, from schoolchildren (above) to old people, were identical, and a picture of Mao could be seen everywhere. The constant sameness and the reminder of authority were used to instill discipline. Yet the old coexisted with the new. While some people went to work in factories or steel mills (below), others continued to work the fields as they had for centuries. Wearing their traditional hats, women still tended the crops by hand (left). Sometimes old cultural forms took on new meanings. Acrobats, for example, had been part of Chinese culture from ancient times, but now their feats were presented as the achievements of a revolutionary nation (below).

for leadership among other communist countries and the developing nations. During the 1960's, the Chinese-Soviet border was the scene of many skirmishes. A number of clashes occurred in Sinkiang, the province in which Chinese nuclear facilities were located. Both sides stationed troops along their common border. New Soviet settlements grew up along the Siberian borders of China.

Mao Tse-tung decided China's foreign policies by deciding who was the main enemy. He then built a united front to resist that enemy. For 20 years no one questioned his decision that the main enemy was the United States. China's main fear was United States military power in Indochina, Japan, the Philippines, and Taiwan.

As Chinese-Soviet relations worsened, China grew more willing to come to terms with the United States. In 1972 after much diplomatic maneuvering, both open and secret, President Nixon visited China. The two nations soon began to permit the exchange of news representatives, business leaders, and private citizens. Finally in 1979, the United States gave full diplomatic recognition to the People's Republic of China. At the same time, the United States withdrew its recognition of the Nationalist government on Taiwan.

The Nationalists in Taiwan

In 1949, as you have read, the Chinese Nationalists established themselves on the island of Taiwan, about 100 miles (160 kilometers) from the Chinese mainland. Their government, called the Republic of China, appeared to be democratic. In reality, however, all power was exercised by the Kuomintang through Chiang Kai-shek. The Taiwanese people, who had inhabited the island before the Nationalists arrived, were excluded from the government.

The Republic of China, also called Nationalist China, occupied China's permanent seat on the United Nations Security Council until 1971. In that year the UN admitted the People's Republic and expelled the Nationalists. The Nationalists, however, had already withdrawn from the organization.

The United States had given aid to Chiang Kai-shek for many years and had kept troops and a fleet based on Taiwan. Under the terms of the 1972 agreements between the United States and the People's Republic, however, the United States promised to withdraw its troops from Taiwan "as soon as tension in the area was reduced."

The Taiwanese government was dismayed by the renewal of diplomatic ties between the United States and the People's Republic. The United States, however, maintained its commercial, if not its military and diplomatic, relations with Taiwan. Indeed, the United States continued to sell armaments to Taiwan in the 1980's. This action remains a controversial issue with the People's Republic.

The Korean War

You have read about the tension between the People's Republic of China and the United States. Contributing to the tension were events that took place in Korea after World War II.

By agreement, at the end of World War II the Soviet Union occupied northern Korea and the United States occupied southern Korea. The dividing line was the 38th parallel of latitude.

Each occupying power organized the government in its zone. A United Nations commission was sent to supervise elections for a government that would rule the entire Korean peninsula. However, the Soviets would not allow the commission into their zone. In 1948 elections held in the south resulted in the creation of the Republic of Korea, known as South Korea, with Syngman Rhee as president. Its capital was Seoul (SOUL). At the same time a Democratic People's Republic, known as North Korea, was created in the north. Its president was Kim Il Sung. The United Nations recognized South Korea as the legal government, while communist countries recognized only North Korea.

In June 1950 the North Korean army invaded South Korea. The United Nations Security Council, meeting in emergency session, declared North Korea an aggressor. It called on UN members to furnish troops and supplies to resist the aggression.

The UN army, composed mainly of American troops, was commanded by General Douglas MacArthur. In the war that followed, which took on a see-saw pattern, the UN allowed its forces to cross into North Korea. It ordered them, however, to stop south of the Yalu River, the border between North Korea and China. As UN troops neared the Yalu, Chinese forces joined those of North Korea, driving the UN forces south of the 38th parallel.

A controversy then arose over MacArthur's desire to bomb China's supply bases in Manchuria and to blockade the coast of China. President Truman and the UN General Assembly opposed these actions. They feared that the Soviet Union would come to China's assistance, and a third world war might result. When General MacArthur continued to urge reprisals against China, Truman removed him from his post.

Under MacArthur's successor, General Matthew Ridgeway, UN forces fought their way slowly up the Korean peninsula. In July 1951 armistice negotiations were started.

The armistice. After two years of negotiations, an armistice was signed in July 1953 at Panmunjom. It fixed the boundary line between the two Koreas near the 38th parallel. A demilitarized zone of 1.25 miles (2 kilometers) was established on either side of the boundary. The armistice also provided for a peace conference to be held within three months. The conference never took place, however, and no peace treaty was every signed. Thus the Korean War came to an inconclusive end, with the Korean peninsula still divided.

South Korea in the 1980's

In 1986 Korea remained divided. Each half of divided Korea sought reunification with the other, but only on its own terms.

South Korea is a small country, only slightly larger than Indiana. Despite its small size, the country was not unified. Various antagonisms existed—between provinces that fought one another in the past, between Buddhists and Christians, and between farmers and city residents.

Despite their differences, South Koreans were united by fear of North Korea. After 1953 South Korea's leaders used the threat of invasion from the north to increase government power and curb criticism of their policies. Although it was established as a democracy in 1948, South Korea became more and more a dictatorship.

President Syngman Rhee became increasingly autocratic in the late 1950's. He resigned in 1960,

and for a brief time a more democratic government prevailed. Then in 1961 about 250 army officers staged a coup. Their leader was General Park Chung Hee.

For the next 18 years, Park ruled with an iron fist. He had a new constitution drafted. It reduced the power of the legislature and guaranteed his reelection as president every six years. He imposed strict controls on the press and created a powerful secret police force, the Korean Central Intelligence Agency (K.C.I.A.), to suppress political opposition. Hundreds of dissident political leaders, students, members of the clergy, writers, and labor organizers were arrested.

President Park also used his power to promote economic development. South Korea's economy, which had grown slowly during the 1950's and 1960's, began to grow very rapidly. Steel mills and textile factories were established. Exports increased dramatically. Because wages were kept relatively low and labor unions were closely controlled, Korean manufactured goods were priced to compete successfully in world markets.

In 1979 President Park was assassinated by the chief of the K.C.I.A. For a while it appeared that democratic government might be restored under a new civilian government. Then the military resumed control, claiming that it would keep the nation prepared for a possible invasion from the north. Many advocates of democracy were arrested. The United States, which kept troops in South Korea to defend that country, objected to these dictatorial policies. Martial law, however, was still in effect in 1986.

CHECKUP

1. IDENTIFY: Great Leap Forward, Liu Shao-chi, Deng Xiaoping, Syng-man Rhee, Kim Il Sung, Ridgeway, Park, K.C.I.A.

2. LOCATE: 38th parallel, South Korea, Seoul, North Korea, Yalu River.

3. What were the two goals of the communist revolution in China? What disagreements arose over these goals?

4. What was the aim of the Great Cultural Revolution in China? What happened after the Great Cultural Revolution ended?

5. Over which issues did the Chinese and Soviets disagree? How did they differ in their goals for economic development?

2

Japan became an economic giant in the postwar world

After World War II, Japan lost all the territory gained during its earlier period of expansion. Its large and growing population was now confined to the home islands. The country still needed to import food and raw materials. Most of the industries that had produced export goods to pay for these imports had been damaged or destroyed during the war.

The occupation of Japan

After its defeat, Japan was occupied by American troops under General Douglas MacArthur, who became the country's virtual ruler. The first aim of the occupation was demilitarization. It was planned that the war industries that remained should be taken as reparations and divided among the countries Japan had invaded.

Taking factories for reparations created the same difficulties in Japan as in Germany. Unless the victors wished to support them indefinitely, the Japanese had to be allowed to provide for themselves. To do so, the Japanese needed to keep their factories, so that they could be converted to peacetime industries. The United States, therefore, insisted that the payment of reparations be postponed indefinitely.

The occupation's second aim was to create a peaceful and democratic government. Under MacArthur's supervision, the Japanese adopted a new constitution in 1947. This so-called "MacArthur constitution" revived the parliament, or Diet, which was to be elected by universal suffrage. Executive power rested with a prime minister and a cabinet responsible to the Diet. War was prohibited, and armed forces were limited to those needed for police purposes. The emperor remained, but he had little power and was no longer considered divine.

In 1951 Japan and 48 other nations signed the World War II peace treaty. Japan formally renounced its claims to occupied lands. The Japanese pledged to settle all disputes peacefully and to pay reparations for war damages. The contin-ued presence of American troops was assured by two American-Japanese treaties. One was a mutual-defense alliance. The second treaty allowed American forces to use bases in Japan until the nation was able to defend itself.

Postwar developments

Before World War II Japan had been the most industrialized of the Asian nations. Although the destruction of many factories and loss of its Asian possessions hurt Japan's economy, its postwar recovery was rapid and impressive.

Agricultural output increased dramatically. Before the war many Japanese had farmed land owned by others and paid rent in cash or in a share of crops. The land reform program carried out during the American occupation virtually eliminated this practice. Loans were available to small farmers who wanted to improve their land by irrigation or buy small tractors.

In the postwar years Japan also developed large and efficient industries that made products of high quality. Before the war Japanese goods had been known for low prices and poor quality. Postwar products—photographic, optical, electronic, and automotive—could compete with any in the world, in quality as well as price.

Japan entered the 1980's as Asia's leading industrial power. Surpassing all other nations in shipbuilding and electronics manufacturing, Japan had become the world's third-ranking industrial nation. The country's economic leaders faced a growing problem in finding markets for a rapidly expanding volume of production. Nevertheless, Japan continued to enjoy general prosperity. As much of the rural population moved to the cities, Japan became a truly urbanized and industrialized society.

For many years the United States had been Japan's best customer and principal supplier of raw materials and agricultural products. More American exports were bought by Japan than Japanese imports were purchased by the United States. Thus the trade balance favored the United States for many years.

Beginning in the late 1960's, the balance of trade swung heavily in favor of Japan. In response, the United States increased pressure to limit Japanese exports to the United States.

It also advocated the abolition of controls restricting the number of American imports into Japan. By the mid-1980's the issue of the trade imbalance between the two countries had become critical.

Social change. Postwar prosperity did not benefit everyone in Japan equally, but it did begin to affect a large part of the population. Two far-reaching social changes occurred after the war. (1) Women received greater legal, political, and social freedom. (2) The authority of the family, traditionally the center of all Japanese life, declined. Consequently, Japanese youths were freed from much of the parental supervision of earlier days.

Industrial growth did not lead to an automatic increase in the standard of living for most Japanese. In the mid-1980's, most families lived in crowded apartments, often without central heating or other modern conveniences. Land for houses was scarce and expensive, and environmental pollution was a serious concern. Many Japanese wanted the government to pay more attention to the quality of life and less attention to further industrial development.

Political life and foreign relations

The Cold War led to a reversal of Japan's international position. As you have read, under American occupation Japanese armed forces and military production were limited. The Japanese were also required to make a constitutional promise to renounce war. The communist victory in China and the stalemate in Korea changed American policy toward Japan. It now seemed necessary to the United States that Japan be able to defend itself and aid the West in case of war in Asia. Japan was therefore urged to increase its armed forces.

The Japanese were not eager to rearm. Many of them feared a return of the military governments of prewar days. They preferred to spend their money building peacetime industries, expanding exports, and raising living standards. In response to continued pressure from the United States, however, Japan did begin to develop a small self-defense force.

Japanese political life continued to reflect disagreements over the nation's domestic and for-

HISTORY THROUGH ART
Japanese Ceremonial Gate

Although Japan today is a leading modern nation, traditional customs are still very much in evidence. Here we see a ceremonial gate, or torii, that has been carefully preserved. Standing in the waters of the Inland Sea, southwest of Hiroshima, the torii greets visitors to the sacred Shinto shrine of Itsukushima. Records of the shrine go back to the year 811, when it was dedicated to the three daughters of the Shinto god Susano. At one time it also enshrined the Japanese god who protected fishermen. In the 1300's the shrine was carefully restored, at great cost, by a samurai ruler and his family.

Today the buildings form a unique architectural complex extending into the sea. The shrine itself is made up of several structures joined together by covered pathways and bridges. One of these buildings, a five-story pagoda built in 1407, contains beautiful treasures of the past. An impressive hall was added by Toyotomi Hideyoshi (see page 422) in the 1600's, and in 1875 this huge torii was completed.

Once each year a favorite Japanese tradition is re-created in front of the torii. On the seventeenth day of the sixth month of the lunar calendar, a colorful water festival takes place, reproducing some of the customs of ancient times through music and dance.

723

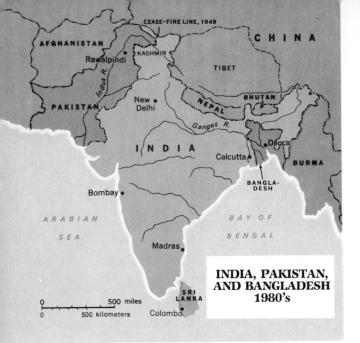

INDIA, PAKISTAN, AND BANGLADESH 1980's

over trade and defense policies. Many Americans were alarmed at the growing trade deficit with Japan, which reached almost 50 million dollars in 1985. At the same time, many Japanese felt that the time had come for Japan to pursue a more independent course in international affairs.

CHECKUP

1. IDENTIFY: demilitarization, "MacArthur constitution."

2. What difficulties would have arisen if Japanese war industries had been taken as reparations?

3. What social changes occurred in postwar Japan?

4. How did the Cold War change Japan's international position?

5. Briefly describe Japanese-American relations between 1970 and the present.

eign policies. The conservative Liberal Democratic Party controlled the Diet, but socialist and other left-wing parties voiced strong criticism of the government. They severely criticized the signing of the mutual-defense pact with the United States, which was renewed in 1970. Government critics denounced the presence of American bases on Japanese soil. They also protested the visits of American nuclear-powered vessels to Japanese ports.

Relations with the United States continued to be friendly, however. In 1968 the United States returned the Bonin and Volcano islands, including Iwo Jima, to Japan. By 1972 Okinawa had also been returned to Japan. Although the United States removed its nuclear weapons from Okinawa, it retained military bases on the island for the security of both nations.

United States-Japanese relations were shaken during the Nixon administration. When President Nixon reestablished relations with the People's Republic of China in 1978, the Japanese were dismayed because they had not been informed beforehand. The Japanese also resented the new economic pressures put upon them by the United States and other nations.

Japan had been a faithful ally of the United States since its defeat in World War II. By the mid-1980's, however, the United States-Japanese relationship was complicated by disagreements

3

India, Pakistan, and Bangladesh became independent nations

As you read in Chapter 26, a movement for independence from Great Britain developed in India after World War I. Strong demands by Indian nationalists for immediate independence continued during World War II. The British Labour Party government, elected in 1945, finally agreed that India would gain its independence no later than 1948.

In 1947, after negotiations, a plan for partitioning India along religious lines was agreed upon. Two widely separated areas in the northwest and northeast of India, inhabited mostly by Muslims, became independent Pakistan. The rest of the Indian subcontinent was designated as India (see map, this page).

In contrast to the people of Pakistan, India's population was overwhelmingly Hindu. It also included Muslims, Sikhs, Jains (JINES), Parsees, Christians, and Jews. States ruled by princes, with the exception of Kashmir in the north, were quickly absorbed into either India or Pakistan. Both India and Pakistan became part of the British Commonwealth of Nations.

India's government and leaders

In 1950, after completing its new constitution, India became a federal republic with an elected president and parliament. The president was the official head of state, but the prime minister and cabinet, chosen by the parliament, wielded the executive power.

Jawaharlal Nehru (NAY·roo), the first prime minister, served from 1950 until his death in 1964. A wealthy Brahman, Nehru was educated at Cambridge University in England. Under Gandhi's influence, he had devoted himself entirely to the independence movement.

As prime minister, Nehru favored the West's emphasis on scientific modernization. His main goals were: (1) unity of India, overcoming the dividing forces of religion, language, caste, and regional interests; (2) a government free of religious interference; (3) economic planning, in a socialist but noncommunist pattern; (4) a democratic government; and (5) nonalignment in foreign affairs. After Nehru's death, his policies were carried forward by his daughter, Indira Gandhi, who became prime minister in 1966.

The controversial Indira Gandhi dominated Indian politics for nearly two decades. She continued as prime minister following the elections of 1967 and 1971, although charges of fraud during the 1971 election were later brought against her. In 1975 she was convicted of some of these charges, and opposition political leaders called for her resignation. Gandhi's government then declared a constitutional state of emergency, giving her power to arrest opposition leaders on the grounds that they threatened internal security.

Gandhi's harsh policies during the two-year emergency turned many Indians against her. She then fell from power in the elections of 1977. In 1980 Gandhi returned as prime minister. She continued to govern India until her assassination by Sikh extremists in 1984. Her son, Rajiv Gandhi, succeeded her.

Social and economic problems

Despite efforts toward unity, religious riots and social discrimination continued after independence. The language problem was especially difficult. India had 15 major languages, 55 minor languages, and several dialects. English was widely spoken. The constitution of 1950 made English the official language for 15 years. Thereafter, Hindi, spoken by 40 percent of the people, was to become official. When the time came for the change, riots forced the government to adopt English as an alternate language.

Under Nehru, India developed a **mixed economy,** in which some industries were privately owned and some were owned by the government. The government used a series of Five-Year Plans to chart the nation's economic development.

In the mid-1980's, India was self-sufficient in agricultural production and exported crops to other countries in Southwest Asia. The country also experienced growth in its production of textiles and steel. In addition, India exported steel products such as bicycles to other Asian nations.

Despite some progress, India continued to face economic problems, many of which stemmed from its ever-growing population. India had 15 percent of the world's population on 2 percent of the world's land area. A population of 350 million in 1947 had increased to over 760 million by the mid-1980's.

Government attempts to encourage smaller families met resistance because Indians traditionally took pride in large families. Most rural Indians felt that large numbers of children represented low-cost labor in the fields.

Millions of Indians lived on the verge of starvation, and annual per capita income averaged about $260. Nearly 19 million people were unemployed. Thousands in the cities were homeless and slept in the streets.

Foreign relations

Partition left India and Pakistan with a difficult problem in the northern state of Kashmir (see map, opposite). India claimed Kashmir because the ruling prince, a Hindu, chose to join India. Pakistan claimed Kashmir because 85 percent of its people were Muslim. Border fighting was uneasily settled in 1949 by a United Nations cease-fire line. At this point India was in control of two thirds of Kashmir. Pakistan controlled one third. India promised to hold an election in Kashmir to determine the political wishes of the

India and Pakistan

Partition of the Indian subcontinent in 1947 was followed by more than 25 years of conflict between Hindus and Muslims. More than one million people died in these clashes, and millions of refugees (bottom) fled from Pakistan into India, seeking safety. The substantial number of Muslims who remained in India (right) created the largest religious minority in that Hindu nation.

Heavy military spending hurt the economies of both countries. Under the rule of Ayub Khan, Pakistan began an economic development program and constructed a new national capital at Islamabad (below right). And in India, a more authoritarian government, led by Indira Gandhi (below), tried drastic measures to promote economic advance.

population. That election never took place.

In 1957 India officially annexed its part of Kashmir. Pakistan protested, and a border war erupted again in 1965. In 1966 the prime ministers of the two countries agreed to withdraw their troops behind the cease-fire line and to negotiate a settlement later. Twenty years later, Kashmir was still in dispute between India and Pakistan.

In world affairs India tried to cultivate friendship with both the communist bloc and the West. It also held a leadership role in the nonaligned movement. Relations with China, cordial at first, became strained in 1959 when the Chinese moved into Tibet to put down a revolt. India had been a long-time supporter of the Dalai Lama (dah·LY LAH·muh), Tibet's major religious and political leader. During this conflict the Dalai Lama and some of his followers fled to India.

In 1960 discovery of a Chinese-built military base and a strategic road in territory claimed by India caused border skirmishes. The Indian and Chinese governments were unable to come to any agreement on the location of their common boundary. In 1962 the Chinese invaded northeastern India, winning easy victories and making their way to the Indus-Ganges plain. There they declared a cease-fire and withdrew.

India's conflicts with both Pakistan and China forced its government to spend heavily on military forces instead of financing economic development.

Pakistan

Until 1971 Pakistan was composed of two widely separated parts. West Pakistan included the Indus River valley, site of India's earliest civilization. East Pakistan was in the Ganges Delta. With only 15 percent of the land area, East Pakistan had over half of the population. Between the two parts of the country lay a wedge of Indian territory 1,000 miles (1,600 kilometers) wide.

With nearly 100 million people, Pakistan in 1947 was the world's most populous Muslim state. The population continued to increase rapidly. Economic development was hindered by a lack of natural resources and by Pakistan's peculiar geographic separation. Like India, Pakistan was troubled by poverty, illiteracy, and differences in language and culture. Conflicts with

India over Kashmir caused the government to spend large sums for defense, which further drained Pakistan's economy.

At first a dominion of the British Commonwealth, Pakistan became a parliamentary republic in 1956. Soon, however, the government turned to military leaders. General Ayub Khan, the first of these, tried to eliminate political corruption and improve education. In 1965 Ayub Khan had himself elected president of a "guided democracy," but opposition to his rule grew. There were demands for economic reforms, direct elections, democratic government, and greater autonomy for East Pakistan.

Bangladesh

In 1969 corruption and scandal forced Ayub Khan to resign. An election was held in December 1970, and East Pakistan won many seats in the national assembly. When the central government, fearful of being outvoted, refused to convene the assembly, strong protest arose in East Pakistan. The new president sent troops to arrest the leaders of the opposition. The arrests turned into a massacre and then into a civil war in which one million people were killed. About 10 million fled from East Pakistan to India. The powerful government army met strong resistance, as India come to the aid of the rebels in East Pakistan. Government troops soon surrendered, and a cease-fire was arranged. As a result of this conflict, East Pakistan became the new nation of Bangladesh.

In 1973 India, Pakistan, and Bangladesh signed a peace settlement. They agreed to an exchange of prisoners of war and the repatriation of people who chose to live either in Pakistan or in Bangladesh. Pakistan pledged to recognize the independence of Bangladesh (see map, page 724).

In the early 1980's, Bangladesh was very densely populated. Located in the delta of the Ganges River, it often experienced devastating floods. It had a jute industry and some agriculture, but little else.

The government of Bangladesh had difficulty solving its economic problems and healing the scars of the war with Pakistan. After 1975 Bangladesh underwent a series of military coups by young army officers. Pakistan, too, after a brief period of parliamentary government in the early 1970's, returned to military rule. The military leaders of each nation promised political and economic reforms. Both Bangladesh and Pakistan, however, remained under martial law in the mid-1980's.

CHECKUP

1. IDENTIFY: Nehru, Indira Gandhi, mixed economy, Dalai Lama, Ayub Khan.

2. LOCATE: Pakistan, Kashmir, Tibet, Bangladesh.

3. What were Nehru's main goals for India?

4. List the major social and economic problems of India.

5. How did the partitioning of India cause problems between India and Pakistan?

The countries of Southeast Asia achieved independence

Southeast Asia consists of nine countries: the Philippines, Indonesia, Malaysia, Singapore, Vietnam, Kampuchea (Cambodia), Laos, Burma, and Thailand (see map, page 717). With the exception of Thailand, all were at one time colonies. After World War II these countries gained independence. Some did so peacefully, others by means of war. Then each began the long and difficult process of political and economic development, which continues today.

The Philippines

As you recall from Chapter 23, Spain ceded the Philippines to the United States in 1898. Many Filipinos resisted American rule. In 1905 the United States crushed this resistance but promised to eventually grant the Filipinos their independence.

In 1934 the United States Congress passed an act granting independence to the Philippines. Independence was delayed by World War II and by Japanese occupation of the islands. On July 4, 1946, an independent Republic of the Philippines was proclaimed.

The United States kept military bases in the Philippines under long-term leases. It contributed large sums of money to repair war damage and rebuild the Philippine economy. Philippine foreign policy was strongly pro-Western.

In the 1970's peace in the Philippines was threatened by guerilla warfare and by a revolt of Muslims, who represented 5 percent of the population. To deal with the internal disorder, President Ferdinand Marcos declared martial law, or rule by the military. He extended his power by arresting hundreds of political opponents. In 1973 Marcos proclaimed himself premier, as well as president, of the Philippines.

Marcos described his government as "constitutional authoritarianism" and promised to "make democracy real." He ended martial law in 1981 and released hundreds of political prisoners, but made little progress toward democracy. Meanwhile, economic conditions in the Philippines worsened.

The assassination of opposition leader Benigno Aquino (ah·KEE·noh) in 1983 sparked widespread rioting against the Marcos regime. In early 1986 Corazon Aquino, widow of Benigno Aquino, ran against Marcos in a nationwide election. After accusations of election fraud, Marcos was forced to give up the presidency to Aquino.

Indonesia

The Dutch East Indies had been administered by the Netherlands since the 1600's. This group of some 3,000 islands includes Sumatra and Java. The Dutch also controlled parts of Borneo and New Guinea.

During World War II the Dutch East Indies were occupied by the Japanese. After the war, Achmed Sukarno led a nationalist independence movement against the Dutch return. Following bitter fighting, the United Nations intervened to secure a cease-fire. In 1949 the Netherlands granted independence to the islands. They became the Republic of Indonesia, with Sukarno as the first president.

Indonesia faced problems similar to those of many other newly independent countries. It had few trained civil servants or competent business administrators, a high rate of illiteracy, and several small political parties. Political power was concentrated on the heavily populated island of Java, where the capital, Jakarta, is located.

Sukarno governed Indonesia for 15 years. In the early 1960's he had himself proclaimed "President for Life." Thereafter the country's problems multiplied. The economy slowed almost to a standstill. Wild and reckless government spending brought the nation close to bankruptcy.

In 1966 General Suharto launched a coup and took over the central government. As president, he emphasized a tightened economy and more control over government spending. With Western aid he began rebuilding the country. In the 1983 elections Suharto ran unopposed for office and was reelected to a fourth five-year term. The United States, however, was worried by reports of alleged human rights abuses in Indonesia.

Possessing substantial oil reserves, Indonesia benefited from the increase in petroleum prices after 1973. The state-owned oil company used its revenues to promote industrial development. Owing to poor management and corruption, however, the company went bankrupt in 1976. A large share of government oil revenue had to be used to pay off debts to foreign investors in the company's projects. As a result, the pace of industrial development in Indonesia slowed in the 1980's.

Malaysia and Singapore

In 1963 Malaya, Singapore, and British (northern) Borneo, which had all become independent from Great Britain, united to form the Federation of Malaysia. The new nation faced difficult problems. Externally, the Philippines claimed part of northern Borneo. At the same time, Sukarno accused the newly formed Federation of being a pretext for the British to maintain colonialism and "encircle" Indonesia.

Internally, the Federation was threatened by a clash of cultures. In the nation as a whole there were more Malays than Chinese, with a small percentage of other ethnic groups. Singapore, however, had a large majority of Chinese. Most Malays were uneducated farmers. The Chinese were mainly city dwellers, technically trained and experienced in commerce. Malays controlled the Federation government. The Chinese controlled most of the business and the wealth.

Fearing that the Chinese might increase their political influence, the Malays forced Singapore to secede from the Federation in 1965. Then, in 1969, serious riots broke out in Malaysia. Malay mobs threatened to eliminate the Chinese and Indians from any part of political life and drive them out of the country. The Chinese retaliated by raising the prices of goods and by refusing loans to farmers. The Malays could not run the economy by themselves. The important rubber industry was badly affected and Malaysia's continued survival was threatened.

Following these riots, the government began to promote rural development as a means of raising the living standard of Malays. It also increased educational opportunities for Malays and required that the Malay language be used in government schools and universities. Thus the government hoped to eliminate the educational and economic differences between Malays and other ethnic groups by raising the status of the Malay majority. Some progress was made, but the situation remained tense.

The Republic of Singapore. Consisting of one major island and 54 small islands, Singapore is smaller than 240 square miles (620 square kilometers) in area. Only one political party was represented in its parliament. The government imposed controls on labor unions, political activity, and news reporting.

Singapore prospered as an independent country after it seceded from the Federation of Malaysia. A program of industrial development, emphasizing petroleum refining, textiles, and electronics, was begun. By the mid-1980's, Singapore's per capita income was $6,500, the highest in Southeast Asia. The country's free enterprise economic policies helped bring prosperity to many, though not all, of its 2½ million people.

Burma

Since before World War II, British-held Burma had been important as the starting point of the Burma Road, over which supplies moved to China. Japanese armies invaded Burma in 1942 and held it until the war's end. After the war the Burmese did not want the British back, nor did the British try to return. In 1948 Burma was declared an independent republic.

The new nation faced difficulties such as the lack of a strong central government, a scarcity of trained civil servants, tribal and political fighting, and communist attempts to seize the country. The first premier, U Nu, headed a coalition government that restored order. Reforms were made in land distribution, agriculture, education, and public health.

Democratic government did not last long, however. The coalition that had brought order broke up into bickering groups. In 1962 the army took over the government. It proceeded to suppress uprisings, cut living costs, and eliminate political corruption.

Burma tried to remain neutral in its relations with the world's powers. The government accepted help from the United States, the Soviet Union, China, and Japan, but refused to take sides in the East-West conflict. In 1974 a new constitution proclaimed Burma a socialist democratic republic. The country remained neutral and sought what it called "the Burmese Way" to socialism. Like the Philippines, Indonesia, Malaysia, and Singapore, Burma tried to develop its own distinct national policies in the 1980's.

CHECKUP

1. IDENTIFY: Marcos, Sukarno, Suharto, U Nu.

2. LOCATE: Philippines, Indonesia, Malaysia, Singapore, Sumatra, Java, Jakarta.

3. Describe the Filipino government under Marcos.

4. Why did Singapore secede from the Federation of Malaysia?

5. What were the difficulties Burma faced as a new nation?

Conflict in Vietnam affected other countries in Southeast Asia

As you have read, after World War II most of the countries of Southeast Asia attained their independence with little or no violence. However, independence for Vietnam, Laos, and Cambodia resulted in years of conflict.

The French in Indochina

In the early 1900's the French became the dominant power in French Indochina, the eastern part of Southeast Asia. In 1945, however, the Japanese expelled the French and set up three independent kingdoms—Laos, Cambodia, and Vietnam (see map, page 717). When the French tried to return after the war, the League for the Independence of Vietnam (the Viet Minh) resisted them. The League was led by a long-time communist, Ho Chi Minh. At first Ho and the French agreed that Vietnam should be a free nation, associated with France but not completely independent. This arrangement led to conflict, and in 1946 war broke out between the French and the Viet Minh.

Ho Chi Minh and his followers set up a government in the north. The French set up an emperor in the south. The northern Democratic Republic of Vietnam was recognized and supported by the communist bloc. South Vietnam was recognized and supported by France, Great Britain, and the United States.

The French fought a long and costly war against Viet Minh forces, which were aided by China. The French received military supplies from the United States. In May 1954 the Viet Minh crushed a French army at Dienbienphu (dyen·byen·FOO), and France agreed to negotiate.

The Geneva Agreements. During the next months, delegates from North and South Vietnam, Cambodia, Laos, China, France, Great Britain, the United States, and the Soviet Union met at Geneva, Switzerland. They tried to work out arrangements for the future of Indochina. According to the Geneva Agreements, Laos was to remain independent. All foreign troops were to withdraw, but a communist-dominated group, the Pathet Lao, was left in control of two northern provinces in Laos. Cambodia was recognized as independent and was not divided. Neither Laos nor Cambodia could make foreign alliances.

Vietnam was divided into two zones at the 17th parallel (see map, page 717), with Ho Chi Minh in control of the north. There was to be an election in 1956 that would choose a government to unite the country.

South Vietnam and the United States were the only nations that refused to sign the Geneva Agreements. The South Vietnamese opposed any

How do we know?

JOURNALISM Newspapers began appearing regularly in the 1600's. Since then they have been a vital source for historians. In the earliest newspapers, developments in the Thirty Years' War (1618–1648) were major items. English newspapers reported Protestant victories; other newspapers reported when their side was winning.

In recent years television has enlarged the role of journalism. In the late 1960's journalism shaped as well as reflected the change in American public opinion about the Vietnam War. When reporters visited the front lines, they sent back dispatches suggesting that this was a war America could not win. These reports, together with televised scenes of the fighting, helped turn Americans against the war.

On February 24, 1968, at the end of a week in which 545 Americans had been killed and some 1,600 wounded, a *New York Times* editorial said: "The only sound policy is to move from the battlefield to the negotiating table with fullest speed." After one of the most important television journalists, Walter Cronkite, visited Vietnam and returned opposed to the war, President Johnson was reported to have said, "If I've lost Cronkite, I've lost Middle America"—that is, most Americans.

Thus, by following contemporary journalism we can find out not only the facts about a particular period but also its mood. Because newspapers and television reports are read and watched by so many people, they reflect a wide range of opinion. They are essential for an understanding of popular attitudes at various times.

continued partition of the country. The United States felt that the terms represented a surrender to the communist bloc.

War in Vietnam

The Geneva Agreements of 1954 meant a victory for Ho Chi Minh. Most of the industry and minerals of the region were in North Vietnam. It had enough good land to grow food and to be almost self-sufficient. With Chinese and Soviet help, the North Vietnamese rebuilt and expanded their industry.

In contrast, South Vietnam was in chaos. A newly formed government faced a shattered economy, many refugees from the north, and a disorganized army. In addition, there was fighting among political and religious factions, several of which had private armies.

The head of the new South Vietnamese government was Ngo Dinh Diem (NOH DIN ZIM). He dis-

armed the private armies and restored order. With American help he reorganized and strengthened the army. He outlawed the Communist Party, tried to suppress all other opposition, and showed little interest in reform. He refused to hold elections.

In 1959 war broke out again in South Vietnam, waged by guerrillas called the Viet Cong. Many of the guerrillas were Vietnamese from the north who wanted to "liberate" the south and unite Vietnam. Others were southern peasants who sided with Ho Chi Minh's communist government. They were taken north, trained in guerrilla warfare, and then returned to the south. The Viet Cong were fierce fighters, skilled in sudden attacks, ambushes, and terrorism. By persuasion and terror, they won either active support or passive acceptance from the peasants.

Ngo Dinh Diem responded to both internal dissatisfaction and the Viet Cong danger with harsher repression. In November 1963 Diem was assassinated in a military coup. During the next three years, nine different military groups ruled South Vietnam.

American involvement

United States involvement in the Vietnam War began almost unnoticed. It grew slowly, without a declaration of war by Congress or much information given to the American people.

President Eisenhower sent military and economic aid. President Kennedy continued this policy, and also sent American advisers to the South Vietnamese government and army. As the guerrilla war increased in intensity, so did American commitments. American advisers soon went into battle with the South Vietnamese troops.

American troop strength began to reach significant size in the mid-1960's under President Lyndon Johnson. American soldiers went openly into battle. Different reasons were given for the American presence: that the spread of communism must be halted; that if South Vietnam fell, other nations of Southeast Asia would fall; that the North Vietnamese were aggressors in South Vietnam.

In 1965 President Johnson ordered air attacks on North Vietnam, and the country was subjected to heavy bombing. Opposition grew in the United States to American participation in the war. (You will read more about this in Chapter 31.)

In January 1968 the North Vietnamese and the Viet Cong mounted a major offensive. They overturned many village governments and threatened several South Vietnamese cities, including Saigon, the capital (see map, page 717).

In March, President Johnson announced a limited halt to the bombing of North Vietnam. Then an agreement was made with North Vietnam to begin negotiating. A peace conference was held in Paris, but it soon became deadlocked.

In 1968 Richard Nixon was elected President. The number of American troops involved in the Vietnam War reached a high of 543,400 in April 1969. Nixon soon announced a limited withdrawal of American troops. The Paris peace talks however, remained deadlocked. In 1970 President Nixon announced an invasion of Cambodia. He resumed the bombing of North Vietnam in 1972.

Ending the war

In 1973 the major parties in the Vietnam War agreed on a cease-fire. The United States withdrew its remaining troops. Americans who had been prisoners of war in North Vietnam came home. The United States air force withdrew only to Thailand, however, and the American fleet remained along the coast. American bombing in Cambodia continued until it was outlawed by Congress. In April 1975 North Vietnamese troops entered Saigon. Within hours the South Vietnamese government surrendered, and the long war finally came to an end.

The Vietnam War caused widespread devastation throughout the Indochinese peninsula. When the war ended in 1975, over 1,300,000 Vietnamese people had been killed. More than 47,000 Americans had died in combat. The neighboring countries of Cambodia and Laos also suffered death and destruction. The efforts of these three countries to recover and rebuild were complicated by long-standing rivalries among them.

A reunited Vietnam

After the war North Vietnamese officials began administering all of South Vietnam. In July 1976 the two Vietnams were united into one country, the Socialist Republic of Vietnam. Hanoi, in the north, became the capital.

Even before unification, the North Vietnamese had been working to reform the politics, economy, and society of the south. People were required to exchange their South Vietnamese money for a new national currency. Any amount above a certain limit had to be deposited in state-controlled banks. Many goods were rationed, and controls were imposed on private enterprise in Vietnam.

All schools in the south were closed while textbooks were revised and teachers retrained by North Vietnamese advisers. After 1976, when these educational reforms were completed, only the children of workers and small farmers were allowed to attend universities. All students had to spend part of every school year working on farms or doing other manual labor of some kind.

The Hanoi government had planned to use the

agricultural and commercial wealth of the south to repair war damage and promote industrial development. Unfortunately, bad weather from 1976 to 1978 ruined many crops. Food shortages caused widespread suffering. Instead of importing machinery for new factories, the government had to import rice and other grains.

The flight of the South Vietnamese. After the fall of Saigon in 1975, more than 6 million South Vietnamese fled their country as refugees. Some fled because food was scarce. Many business people left because the new economic controls threatened their way of life. Many young people who disliked the state-controlled educational system also left.

Usually these refugees had to pay bribes to government officials to get out of the country safely. Then they faced a dangerous voyage to Malaysia, Thailand, or some other Southeast Asian country. Many of these "boat people," as the refugees were called, died at sea. Those who survived spent long months in refugee camps before obtaining permission to resettle permanently. Several hundred thousand of these "boat people" were admitted to the United States.

Relations with China. During the Vietnam War, North Vietnam had received aid from both China and the Soviet Union. Once the war ended, however, relations between China and the new Vietnamese government broke down. One reason was economic. The controls on private enterprise in Vietnam had hurt the country's small shopkeepers, many of whom were of Chinese ancestry. Over 200,000 of them fled to China, causing problems for the Chinese government.

A more basic reason for the breakdown in relations was political. Throughout their history the Vietnamese had been afraid of Chinese influence and of the political absorption of their country by China. During the war the Vietnamese had needed Chinese aid. As soon as the war ended, the Vietnamese wanted to end their dependence on China and reduce Chinese influence within Vietnam.

In 1978 Vietnam signed a 25-year treaty of friendship and cooperation with the Soviet Union, China's rival. The treaty guaranteed Vietnam all the aid it needed. Relations between China and Vietnam worsened. Tension mounted along the border between the two countries, and shooting incidents continued to occur in the 1980's. Chinese criticism of the Vietnamese government increased. China also increased aid to Kampuchea (Cambodia), Vietnam's neighbor to the southwest.

Cambodia

Cambodia had acquired independence from France in 1953. Under the leadership of Prince Norodom Sihanouk, it tried to remain neutral during the Vietnam War. Neutrality proved difficult, however. North Vietnamese and Vietcong troops continually fled into Cambodia to escape South Vietnamese and American troops. In March 1970 Sihanouk was overthrown by Lon Nol. Lon Nol promised to take a firmer stand against the Vietnamese who were using Cambodia as a refuge. Sihanouk established a government in exile in Peking.

In April 1970, presumably with Lon Nol's consent, American and South Vietnamese troops crossed into Cambodia in pursuit of North Vietnamese and Viet Cong forces. The North Vietnamese retreated farther into Cambodia. They encouraged a small number of procommunist Cambodians to oppose Lon Nol's government. With North Vietnamese aid these Cambodians, known as the Khmer Rouge, grew more and more powerful. In 1975 they captured the Cambodian capital, Phnom Penh, and established a new communist regime under the leadership of Pol Pot.

Under the Pol Pot government, all the cities of Cambodia were evacuated. Their residents were sent into the countryside to create new agricultural villages. Lacking experience and tools, and without food to tide them over until the first harvest, many people died of starvation. At the same time, almost all government officials, army officers, teachers, and intellectuals were systematically and brutally executed. More than a million people were murdered or died from starvation between 1975 and 1979. Thousands fled to makeshift refugee camps in the neighboring country of Thailand.

The centuries-old rivalry between Cambodia and Vietnam continued after 1975. Territorial disputes and border incidents indicated the tension between the two countries. Finally Vietnam decided to take decisive action. In December 1978 Vietnamese troops invaded Cambodia.

Conflict in Vietnam

Guerrilla warfare characterized the many years of fighting in Vietnam. Ho Chi Minh, the communist leader of North Vietnam (below), organized the guerrilla movement known as the Viet Cong. Small groups of guerrilla fighters hid in the terrain and launched quick hit-and-run campaigns. For the American troops, the effort to search out an enemy in the jungles (right) proved all but impossible.

The United States finally withdrew its troops in 1973. Two years later the capital of South Vietnam, Saigon, fell to the North Vietnamese, and the war ended. In a mass exodus, thousands of South Vietnamese fled, often in small and unsafe boats (below right).

By February, Vietnam was fighting a two-front war—in Cambodia and along its northern border with China. China had invaded Vietnam with 100,000 troops. The fighting lasted only 17 days. China captured several towns across the border and then began to withdraw. The Chinese did not achieve their major aims—getting the Vietnamese to withdraw from Cambodia and restoring Sihanouk to power. By the end of the conflict, the Vietnamese had overthrown Pol Pot and established a pro-Vietnamese government in Phnom Penh. Cambodia was renamed the People's Republic of Kampuchea (kam·poo·CHEE·uh).

In the 1980's Vietnam periodically raided refugee camps on Kampuchea's border with Thailand. Vietnamese troops also remained in Phnom Penh.

Laos

The landlocked country of Laos became a French colony in the late 1890's. During World War II an independence movement developed, led by relatives of the Laotian king. When France resumed control over Laos at the end of the war, the independence movement continued.

France reestablished the Laotian monarchy in 1949 but did not give Laos total independence until 1954. In the meantime, civil war had broken out among communist, neutralist, and conservative factions. This unrest continued for more than 20 years.

Laos also became increasingly involved in the Vietnam War. North Vietnamese forces moved supplies down the mountain valleys of eastern Laos into Cambodia and South Vietnam. The United States retaliated with heavy bombing of the supply route.

In 1975 the Laotian monarchy was abolished, and a communist regime was established.

The new Laotian government tried to steer a nonaligned course in the complicated politics of Asian communism. It received aid from both the Soviet Union and China. It also avoided taking sides in the growing dispute between Cambodia and Vietnam. Ultimately that proved impossible. The Laotian government needed Vietnam's help to control anticommunist forces in the northern part of Laos. In 1979 it confirmed that 30,000 Vietnamese troops were stationed in Laos. Vietnam had used Laos as a staging area for its invasion of Cambodia.

The Laotian government demanded that China remove its advisers and roadbuilding crews from northern Laos. The Chinese ignored the demand, however. Relations between China and Laos, like those between China and Vietnam, remained tense in the 1980's.

Thailand

Thailand, formerly called Siam, had never been a European colony. In World War II it was occupied by Japan. Under Japanese pressure, Thailand declared war on Great Britain and the United States and became a Japanese ally. Later it renounced the alliance and was the first former Axis ally admitted to the United Nations.

The strains of the war and postwar years brought many changes in Thailand's government. In 1958 the army took control, establishing a military dictatorship. The new Thai government was strongly pro-Western, and received military and economic aid from the United States. During the Vietnam War the United States bombed other parts of Southeast Asia from bases in Thailand. Thai troops fought in Cambodia on the Allied side. When United States forces were withdrawn from Vietnam, some of the troops and aircraft went to bases in Thailand.

Communist victories in Vietnam, Cambodia, and Laos in 1975 forced Thailand to reconsider its policies. It persuaded the United States to remove its troops and aircraft from Thailand. The government established diplomatic relations with China and sought accommodation with the Soviet Union and Vietnam. In 1979 it signed an agreement with Laos pledging to make the Mekong River, the border between the two countries, a "river of peace and friendship."

The Vietnamese invasion of Cambodia caused problems for Thailand's new diplomacy. Vietnam accused Thailand of aiding the Pol Pot regime and of cooperating with China against Vietnam. The influx of refugees from Cambodia added to Thailand's difficulties. Hundreds of thousands of people, including many "boat people" from Vietnam, had already sought refuge in Thailand. Announcing that its camps were filled and its economy too weak to stand the strain, Thailand closed the

Cambodian border. As you have read, Vietnamese troops continued however, to violate that border in the 1980's.

CHECKUP

1. IDENTIFY: Viet Minh, Ho Chi Minh, Ngo Dinh Diem, Viet Cong, "boat people," Sihanouk, Lon Nol, Khmer Rouge, Pol Pot.

2. LOCATE: Laos, Cambodia, Dienbienphu, 17th parallel, Saigon, Thailand, Hanoi.

3. What were the provisions of the Geneva Agreements? Why were these agreements a victory for Ho Chi Minh?

4. Describe the changes that occurred in Vietnam after the war.

5. How did Pol Pot's regime affect Cambodia?

6. What problems did Thailand experience in the late 1970's and early 1980's?

6

Asian nations sought security and economic growth

Asia is a region of great diversity. Asian nations differ as significantly from one another as Asian peoples. A closer look, however, will reveal the common experiences of Asian nations, as well as the impact of Asia on the West.

Political development

Most of the countries of Asia had been colonies in the past. After World War II, most of the newly independent nations established representative governments and attempted to build democratic societies. With the passage of time, however, democracy faded in most of Asia. As you have read, revolutions established communist regimes in China and, later, in Vietnam, Cambodia, and Laos. Elsewhere—in the Philippines, and in India during the "emergency" of 1975–1977—civil rights were restricted, political opposition was silenced, and authoritarian rule emerged.

Authoritarianism in Asia. There were three reasons for the trend toward authoritarianism in Asia. The first was a result of the ethnic and cultural diversity within Asian nations. In India, Malaysia, and the Philippines, there were age-old antagonisms among groups with different heritages or religions. From time to time these disputes erupted into violence and threatened to tear these new nations apart. To maintain domestic peace, government leaders relied heavily on their military and police forces. These forces, in turn, argued that strict controls were necessary. In some cases, the military forces themselves took over the government when civilian leaders seemed reluctant to impose controls.

The second reason for the trend toward authoritarianism was that most Asian nations have felt threatened by their neighbors. For example, India feared invasion from both Pakistan and China. Because of the communist movements in the Indochinese peninsula, leaders of the Philippines, Indonesia, and Thailand feared the spread of revolutionary ideas to their own countries. As a result, they cracked down on leftist groups and granted sweeping powers to the military to combat the slightest signs of communist influence. Even communist countries, who feared the anticommunist policies of the free world, were also afraid of one another. For all these countries, fear led to a desire for a strong central government and national unity. Debate and dissent, therefore, could not be tolerated.

The third reason was economic. Many Asian leaders perceived democratic government as wasteful and inefficient. It did not lead quickly enough to policies and programs permitting industrialization. Therefore, the desire for rapid economic development contributed to the emergence of authoritarian regimes. To understand how this happened, we need to examine the issue of economic development in Asia.

Economic development

In the mid-1980's, roughly 2.8 billion people lived in Asia, more than half the total population of the world. A significant number lived in poverty and suffered its consequences—malnutrition, illiteracy, and short life spans.

To help create more prosperous and stable societies, most Asian governments began encouraging industrialization in the 1950's. Their approaches

Ikat Cloth

During the last 30 years, in an effort to reduce the tremendous poverty in their countries, Asian governments began to encourage industrialization and economic growth. Many started exporting both manufactured items and handcrafted goods to other areas of the world.

The woven cloth shown here, from Java, was made by an ancient method of dyeing and weaving known as ikat. This technique, more than 1,000 years old, is particularly common in Indonesia and Japan. The process involves winding the yarn over a frame and then tying the strands at certain points. When the yarn is dyed, the places where the strands are tied together do not absorb color, thus creating the pattern. After the yarn is dyed, it is woven on a loom. The entire process of producing the ikat cloth—from growing the cotton to dyeing the cloth to designing and executing the weaving—is done completely by women.

Decorated textiles such as these have been an important part of Indonesian culture for centuries. Ikat cloths were used to wrap around newborn babies, given as wedding gifts between families, worn as ceremonial costumes, and used as wrappings for the bodies of the dead. Because of the long time needed to produce them and the high quality of the weaving, the cloths became a symbol of wealth.

varied. Some used capitalist means, encouraging private enterprise. Others used socialist means, with the central government taking charge of the economy. Still others pursued a middle course, combining government planning with private enterprise. Whatever the method, the results were similar. With a few exceptions—such as Japan, Singapore, and Taiwan, which encouraged private enterprise—economic development proceeded very slowly, if at all.

The basic reason for the slow pace of economic development was that most Asian countries had little wealth to begin with. Industrialization required large investments of money in machinery, factories, and distribution networks. The later a country began industrialization, the greater the investment required to compete successfully with other, more advanced countries.

In order to get the investment funds they needed, Asian countries depended on loans and on the sale abroad of their natural resources: tea, spices, timber, rubber, and copper and other min-

erals. Throughout most of the 1950's and 1960's, however, the prices of these items in world markets were relatively low. A country had to sell a large quantity of cocoa, teakwood, or tin to earn the foreign exchange it needed to import industrial technology. When periodic recessions slowed economic growth in the West, there was less demand for the goods of developing nations.

Economic development was also slow because factory workers and managers lacked the experience to produce goods efficiently. Vocational schools and training programs had to be established. Moreover, nationwide school systems had to be set up to wipe out illiteracy. It took time for these programs to take effect.

Cooperating for development. In the 1970's Asian countries began to find means of dealing with these and other problems. They joined together, for example, to demand higher prices for their exports and greater economic aid from the advanced industrial countries. International meetings were held periodically under the super-

737

vision of the United Nations. In these talks the less developed countries, in Latin America and Africa as well as Asia, began to win concessions providing them with more investment funds.

Another form of international cooperation was the Association of Southeast Asian Nations, known as ASEAN. Organized in 1967 by Indonesia, Malaysia, the Philippines, Singapore, and Thailand, ASEAN's original aim was to fight communism. Beginning in 1976, however, the member nations began to consider cooperation in economic policy. Whether this cooperation, modeled after that of the European Economic Community, would succeed would take a number of years to determine.

Probably the most widespread response to the problems of industrialization was greater government control. To spur economic growth, many leaders of Asian countries established powerful central agencies. Some leaders nationalized certain key industries—petroleum in Indonesia, for example. By this action, they hoped to ensure that profits would be reinvested in the country's development, rather than pocketed by individuals or foreign companies. In addition, they passed laws prohibiting strikes by factory workers to prevent interruptions in production. These and other authoritarian measures led in some cases to higher rates of economic growth, but at the expense of individual rights and freedoms.

Asia's influence on the Western world

Two hundred years ago it took months to sail from the West to Asia. In 1986, people could fly from the West to the remotest part of Asia in less than 24 hours. Modern technology brought East and West closer together. Yet to many Westerners, Asia still seemed far away.

As in the past, however, Asia continued to influence the West. Judo and other ancient Chinese and Japanese martial arts were popular in the West. Oriental carpets from India adorned many homes. More modern Asian influences were found in manufacturing. Having "exported" the industrial revolution to Asia, the West began to import many Asian manufactured goods. Radios, cameras, video equipment, and automobiles manufactured in the East became familiar around the world. Economic competition

from Asia, however, caused problems for Western business.

At the same time, this competition made Westerners curious. In the 1970's and 1980's, researchers traveled to Japan, Asia's most successful industrial economy, to study the factories there. They wanted to know what made Japanese goods so competitive in world markets. Some researchers thought it was the cooperative relationship between management and workers. Japanese workers felt they had a stake in the factory's future and worked to produce goods efficiently.

Western economists also noted the availability of business development loans at low interest rates. This enabled Japanese industrial managers to buy new and improved machinery. Economic researchers urged Westerners to learn from these and other Japanese business practices.

Asian thought also influenced Westerners. During the 1800's and early 1900's, the West "exported" many ideas to Asia. Books about politics and philosophy, as well as masterpieces of Western literature, were translated into Asian languages. After World War II, however, Asian ideas began attracting attention in the West and other regions of the world. You read earlier about Mahatma Gandhi, for example, the spiritual leader of the independence movement in India. His ideas about nonviolent resistance had a powerful impact on the civil rights movement in the United States in the 1960's.

In the late 1800's the English writer Rudyard Kipling wrote, "East is East, and West is West, and never the twain shall meet." He meant that cultural differences were so great that the peoples of Asia and the West could never understand each other. For a long time his observation seemed correct. Since the early 1970's, however, the situation has improved. If peaceful relations can be maintained among Asian nations and between Asia and the West, people in each region will learn more about one another.

CHECKUP

1. List three reasons for the development of authoritarian governments in Asia.

2. What problems have Asian nations faced in bringing about industrial development?

3. Give examples of Asia's influence on the West.

CHAPTER REVIEW

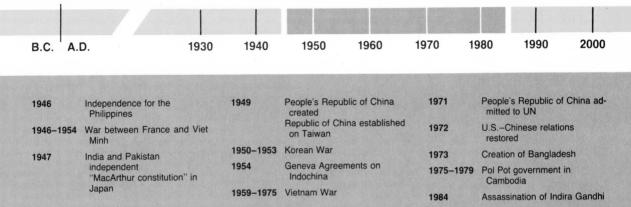

B.C.	A.D.	1930	1940	1950	1960	1970	1980	1990	2000

1946	Independence for the Philippines	**1949**	People's Republic of China created
1946–1954	War between France and Viet Minh		Republic of China established on Taiwan
1947	India and Pakistan independent "MacArthur constitution" in Japan	**1950–1953**	Korean War
		1954	Geneva Agreements on Indochina
		1959–1975	Vietnam War

1971	People's Republic of China admitted to UN
1972	U.S.–Chinese relations restored
1973	Creation of Bangladesh
1975–1979	Pol Pot government in Cambodia
1984	Assassination of Indira Gandhi

CHAPTER SUMMARY

The period following World War II was a time of conflict and tension for many Asian nations. The victory of Mao Tse-tung in 1949 brought the communists to power in China. The Chinese Nationalists, led by Chiang Kai-shek, fled to the island of Taiwan. The government they established there remained closely allied with the United States. The communist government on the mainland attempted to create a classless society. China shifted away from the Soviet Union and in the 1970's established diplomatic relations with the United States.

Korea was divided after World War II. When communist North Korea invaded South Korea in 1950, it was repulsed by UN forces and an armistice was eventually signed.

Japan achieved extraordinary economic success in the postwar period and became the most advanced industrial nation in Asia. Japanese society also changed, as the rights of women gained recognition and the family lost its dominant role in daily life. Japan remained closely tied to the United States in foreign policy.

India, under Nehru, adopted a mixed economy but could make few gains because of its constantly growing population. Foreign affairs were complicated by conflicts with Pakistan and China. Pakistan faced similar domestic problems. In addition, Pakistan was separated into two parts. After civil war, East Pakistan became Bangladesh.

In the Philippines, Indonesia, Malaysia, Singapore, and Burma, economic development was fostered by strong central governments. Despite social problems, these nations began a slow and gradual process of industrialization.

In Southeast Asia, France was defeated in a long war with the communist-led Viet Minh. The Geneva Agreements divided Vietnam, but war broke out a few years later. The United States became heavily involved in the fighting. North Vietnam conquered South Vietnam and united the nation in the early 1970's. Vietnam then dominated its neighbors, Cambodia and Laos. It also had considerable influence on Thailand. All of these nations struggled with the problems caused by war.

The difficulties of economic development led many Asian nations to rely on strong central government. On the other hand the Asian nations attempted to promote greater international cooperation. Despite Asia's problems, other areas of the world became increasingly interested in Asian culture and ideas.

CHECKING WHAT YOU KNOW

1. Match each leader at the left with a country at the right.

a. Mao Tse-tung	1. Indonesia
b. Park Chung Hee	2. Philippines
c. Marcos	3. India
d. Indira Gandhi	4. South Vietnam
e. U Nu	5. China
f. Sukarno	6. North Vietnam
g. Sihanouk	7. South Korea
h. Diem	8. Pakistan
i. Ho Chi Minh	9. Tibet
j. Dalai Lama	10. Cambodia
k. Ayub Khan	11. Burma

2. What political and economic changes did the communists bring about in China?

3. How did President Truman and General MacArthur disagree over the conduct of the Korean War? Why did Truman replace MacArthur as commander of the UN forces?

4. Explain how Japan became the third largest industrial nation in the world. What problems and benefits accompanied this rapid growth?

5. What economic problems did India face after achieving independence? How did it attempt to solve these problems?

6. What were the causes of the Vietnam War? How did the United States become involved?

7. List reasons for past hostilities between the following countries:
   a. the Soviet Union and China
   b. India and Pakistan
   c. Pakistan and Bangladesh
   d. Vietnam and China
   e. Singapore and the Federation of Malaysia

PRACTICING YOUR SKILLS

1. **Using maps.** Turn to the map of Asia on page 717. How many miles separate Taiwan and the People's Republic of China? How many kilometers? Why is Japan in a strategic location for defense of American interests in the Pacific? Based on your knowledge of current events, what Asian nations might be most concerned with protecting their borders today? Explain.

2. **Making comparisons.** Compare the Korean War with the war in Vietnam. How did the two wars differ in terms of causes and results? How were they similar? What roles did the United States and the People's Republic of China play in each of these wars?

3. **Using historical documents.** Below is the preamble to the Indian constitution. Read this selection and answer the questions that follow.

   We, the people of India, having solemnly resolved to constitute India into a sovereign democratic republic and to secure to all its citizens: *justice*—social, economic, and political; *liberty* of thought, expression, belief, faith and worship; *equality* of status and of opportunity; and to promote . . . *fraternity* assuring the dignity of the individual and the unity of the nation . . . do hereby adopt, enact, and give to ourselves this Constitution.

   What type of government does the constitution promise to the Indian people? What ideals does it swear to uphold? How do these ideals compare with those stated in the preamble to the United States Constitution?

RELATING PAST TO PRESENT

1. On a sheet of paper, list evidence that your community has contact with the nations of Asia. For example, observe the cars on a busy street. How many of them are Japanese? Can you buy a shirt made of Indian cotton or a book of Chinese or Japanese poetry? Based on this information, write a short essay discussing Asia's influence on the Western world.

2. Use the *Readers' Guide to Periodical Literature* to find articles on China today. Then prepare a report on how the communists have changed traditional Chinese society, what economic problems still exist in China, and what life in China is like.

INVESTIGATING FURTHER

1. Use books in your library to gather information on the Vietnam War. One source for your research is Frances Fitzgerald, *Fire in the Lake* (Little, Brown). Use the information you have found to answer the following questions:
   a. What were the goals of Ho Chi Minh between 1945 and 1954?
   b. Why did the Viet Cong receive the support of the peasants?
   c. How did American involvement end? What was the final outcome of the war?

2. One way to gain insight into a culture is to read its literature. Present a short report to the class on one of the following Japanese novels: Yukio Mishima, *Sound of Waves* (Knopf), and *Spring Snow* (Knopf); Junichiro Tanizaki, *Some Prefer Nettles* (Knopf).

3. Chiang Ching—the wife of Mao Tse-tung—acted as director of cultural activities during the Cultural Revolution. Prepare a short oral report on Chiang's role in shaping China's new "revolutionary art." Also investigate her trial, after Mao's death, by the communist leaders she once helped depose. The *Readers' Guide to Periodical Literature* will help you find articles.

4. Unlike most other Asian nations, Japan, Singapore, and Taiwan experienced rapid economic growth after 1945. Using reference materials in your library, gather information on the economic policies that made such development possible.

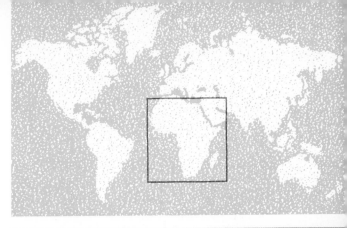

(1945 to the Present)

30

The Nations of Africa and the Middle East Became Independent

One of the most important long-term consequences of World War II was the destruction of the empires of the European nations. More than 1.5 billion people won independence in the four decades after World War II. During these years, the number of nations in the world tripled, mainly as a result of the dissolving of the old European empires. Most of the new nations were located in Africa and the Middle East.

The advance toward independence by 1.5 billion people was impressive. Yet the newly independent nations faced many problems in their first years of freedom. The issues they faced were political, economic, social, and cultural.

Politics in the new nations usually revolved around one central question: Could the government win the authority it needed to rule? Representative government, which had developed gradually over many centuries among Western nations, was relatively new to the former colonial areas. In many cases, political experience and qualified leaders were lacking. Old loyalties to ethnic groups or ruling families complicated the formation of political parties.

The principal economic and social issues had to do with the well-being of the people. The level of education in most of the new nations was low. In some parts of Africa, for example, scarcely 3 percent of the people could read and write. The supply of physicians, teachers, and skilled workers was inadequate.

A busy harbor in modern Ghana

As colonies, many of the new nations had been integrated into the economic systems of the imperialist nations. After gaining independence, they often lacked the proper balance of industry and agriculture necessary for successful economic growth.

In addition to political, economic, and social development, the new nations sought a cultural identity. Every nation needs a feeling of self-respect, a sense that its beliefs and intellectual and artistic achievements are important. In Africa and the Middle East, this search for self-identity took many forms—religious, racial, and political.

THE CHAPTER SECTIONS

1. African nations achieved independence after 1945

2. The new African nations faced various problems

3. The nations of the Middle East secured their independence

4. Wars, oil, and revolution transformed the Middle East

5. A struggle between old and new ways developed in the Middle East

African nations achieved independence after 1945

The postwar years were momentous ones for the African nations south of the Sahara. In 1914 only Liberia and Ethiopia had been fully independent. After World War II, independence came rapidly. In a relatively short span of time, from 1946 to 1980, all the African colonies except Namibia (Southwest Africa) achieved independence.

African nationalism

Although nationalism became a popular force in the postwar world, its roots went back many years. In the British colonies of West Africa, the families of African merchants, along with chiefs from the interior, formed an elite, or select, group. These Africans were involved in trade and other business relationships with Europeans. Many received an education in Great Britain. Some were missionaries, spreading Christianity in Africa. Others were employed in the lower ranks of the civil service in Africa.

The members of this elite group were influential representatives of the African point of view. They petitioned the British government in London for constitutional reform. In addition, they started newspapers and organized political associations. They accepted the European point of view, however, that it would be many years before Africans were ready for independence.

These early nationalists were in a difficult position. As members of a privileged group, they were separated from their own people and in fact did not seek broad popular support. At the same time, because of their African heritage, they were excluded from European society. Nonetheless, the reforms for which they fought helped pave the way for the nationalism of the postwar era.

As you have read, Great Britain and France had been weakened by World War II. Neither nation had the economic strength or the political backing to maintain its immense prewar empire. Gradually their overseas possessions broke away. India, as you have read, became independent in 1947. This success, as well as Gandhi's policy of nonviolent resistance, was a model and inspiration to the colonial world.

In Africa, a new generation of nationalists gained power after World War II. They were less patient and more determined to obtain equality in the world community. Leaders such as Kwame Nkrumah (en·KROO·mah) in the Gold Coast, Jomo Kenyatta in Kenya, and Nnamdi Azikiwe in Nigeria typified this new generation. Unlike earlier leaders, they appealed to the whole population and demanded immediate independence.

The march to independence

The struggle for national independence in Africa took many forms. Some colonies followed a constitutional process, with popular elections and a peaceful transfer of power. Others, such as Angola, Mozambique, and Zimbabwe (formerly Rhodesia), suffered lengthy wars of national liberation. In each case the specific form of the independence effort depended on the particular experience of imperialism in that part of Africa. The following examples demonstrate the various roads to independence.

Ghana gained independence. The first sub-Saharan colony to achieve independence was in West Africa. In 1957 the British Gold Coast colony became the independent nation of Ghana (see map, page 744). This name was chosen by its leader Kwame Nkrumah to commemorate the ancient African kingdom of Ghana.

Nkrumah had been educated in the United States where he was president of the African Students Association. He returned to the Gold Coast colony in 1946. The United Gold Coast Convention, a political organization of the Westernized elite, invited him to be party secretary. From this post, Nkrumah began to build up a national following based on the slogan "Self-government now." In 1948 he started a newspaper that criticized the British administration and called for civil disobedience.

In 1949 Nkrumah started his own Convention People's Party (CPP). It became the first political party in Africa supported by a large part of the population. The CPP's activities forced the British government to make concessions, and in 1951 it agreed to a national election in the Gold Coast colony. Nkrumah's party won a huge victory, and he formed a government with limited powers under British direction. Nkrumah continued to pressure the British for complete independence. It was finally granted in 1957.

Rebellion in Kenya. National parties, inspired by Nkrumah's success, began to appear in other British colonies around the same time. Often, however, they had to face problems very different from Ghana's. For example, in Kenya in East Africa (see map, page 744), white settlers held large tracts of fertile land in the central highlands. Africans were prohibited from owning land in this area. Following World War II the African population grew rapidly and land shortage became a critical issue. The exclusion of Africans from the highlands became a source of tension. The Kikuyu, Kenya's largest ethnic group, considered this area to be an ancestral homeland.

In the early 1950's the question of land ownership exploded into violence that lasted for several years and took thousands of lives. The British finally succeeded in suppressing the terrorist

movement the Kikuyu formed, known as the Mau Mau. Jomo Kenyatta, a leader of the Kikuyu people, was arrested and jailed until 1961. However, the British were unable to suppress the demand for independence.

Kenyatta emerged as the natural leader of the Kenyan independence movement. His popular leadership helped overcome ethnic rivalries and brought about a shared sense of Kenyan nationalism. In 1963 Kenya became independent, and Kenyatta served as president from 1964 until his death in 1978.

By the mid-1960's all the former British colonies except Southern Rhodesia had become independent nations.

The French colonies

Developments in the French-controlled territories of Africa reflected a different political experience. During World War II, France's African colonies had contributed to the Free French forces led by General de Gaulle. Following the Allied victory, the French sought to improve political conditions in French Africa through a system of political federation. Africans elected representatives who then sat in the French Assembly in Paris and served in the French government. Although this system provided many Africans with political experience, it fell short of real independence. African economic and political interests were still subordinate to those of France.

Political parties with broad-based popular support, such as Nkrumah's CPP in Ghana, began to emerge in French Africa. Led by Africans educated in France, such as Léopold Senghor of Senegal, Félix Houphouët-Boigny (oof·WAY-BWAH·nyee) of the Ivory Coast, and Sékou Touré (too·RAY) of Guinea, these parties began to demand complete independence.

In 1958 Charles de Gaulle, the French President, offered the African colonies a choice. They could remain within the French community, subject to French control of their foreign affairs, but otherwise independent. Or they could sever ties to France and become totally independent. Only Guinea chose complete independence.

Those nations that chose to remain within a French-style commonwealth received aid from the French government and from private investors.

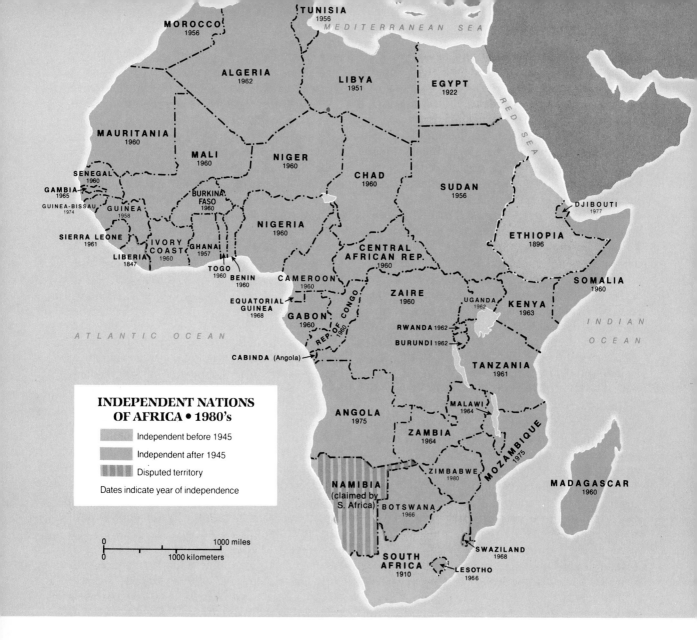

INDEPENDENT NATIONS
OF AFRICA • 1980's

Independent before 1945
Independent after 1945
Disputed territory

Dates indicate year of independence

0	1000 miles
0	1000 kilometers

TUNISIA 1956
MEDITERRANEAN SEA
MOROCCO 1956
ALGERIA 1962
LIBYA 1951
EGYPT 1922
RED SEA
MAURITANIA 1960
MALI 1960
NIGER 1960
CHAD 1960
SUDAN 1956
DJIBOUTI 1977
SENEGAL 1960
GAMBIA 1965
GUINEA-BISSAU 1974
BURKINA FASO 1960
GUINEA 1958
NIGERIA 1960
ETHIOPIA 1896
SIERRA LEONE 1961
IVORY COAST 1960
GHANA 1957
CENTRAL AFRICAN REP. 1960
SOMALIA 1960
LIBERIA 1847
TOGO 1960
BENIN 1960
CAMEROON 1960
ZAIRE 1960
UGANDA 1962
KENYA 1963
EQUATORIAL GUINEA 1968
GABON 1960
REP. OF CONGO 1960
RWANDA 1962
BURUNDI 1962
INDIAN OCEAN
ATLANTIC OCEAN
CABINDA (Angola)
TANZANIA 1961
ANGOLA 1975
MALAWI 1964
ZAMBIA 1964
MOZAMBIQUE 1975
MADAGASCAR 1960
NAMIBIA (claimed by S. Africa)
ZIMBABWE 1980
BOTSWANA 1966
SWAZILAND 1968
SOUTH AFRICA 1910
LESOTHO 1966

Guinea, on the other hand, was politically and economically isolated. Although they were later granted full independence, the French-speaking nations of Africa continued to coordinate their economic and foreign policies with France.

The Belgian Congo

Zaïre, formerly the Belgian Congo, experienced one of the most difficult transitions to independence. Because of the colony's great wealth from its timber and mineral resources, Belgium was reluctant to grant independence. The Belgian colonial administration was noted for its harshness and provided few opportunities for Africans to develop their skills in government.

A strong independence movement sprang up in the Congo after World War II. In the 1950's nationalists demanded the right to choose their own government. Finally, when nationalist leaders were arrested and rioting broke out, the Belgians were forced to give in. General elections were held in 1960, and the nationalist leader, Patrice Lumumba, was elected premier. His rival, Joseph Kasavubu, became president.

The Congo became independent as the Democratic Republic of the Congo in June 1960. However, it still faced serious problems. In July, Congolese soldiers mutinied against their Belgian officers. A period of bloodshed followed during which many people lost their lives.

The turmoil increased and threatened Belgian interests in the mining province of Katanga (see map, opposite). The Belgian government supported the secession of Katanga under a local leader, Moise Tshombe (SHOM·bay).

The Congo moved rapidly toward complete anarchy. Lumumba was taken prisoner by Tshombe forces in Katanga. There he was murdered following an alleged escape.

The UN Security Council called on Belgium to withdraw its troops from Katanga. It also authorized a UN force to restore order in the Congo. This force, composed mainly of troops from other African nations, was sent into the Congo in the summer of 1960. By the beginning of 1963, Tshombe's army was defeated and he went into exile.

Continuing difficulties. When UN troops were withdrawn from the Congo in mid-1964, revolts by small groups, often armed only with hoes, knives, and stones, broke out in several provinces. Kasavubu invited Tshombe to return from exile and become premier in a "government of national reconciliation." When the Congolese army was unable to put down the revolts, Tshombe took the drastic step of hiring white mercenary troops. Most of the nations of independent Africa condemned this decision. In 1965 Tshombe was removed from office by President Kasavubu. Kasavubu himself was then overthrown in a military coup led by Joseph Mobutu, an army general. Mobutu later took the African name Mobutu Sese Seko (SAY·say SAY·koh).

Leadership of the Congo was not clearly established for several years. In 1970 Mobutu was elected president of what became, in the following year, the Republic of Zaïre. Zaïre began gradually to recover from the political chaos and civil wars of the 1960's.

The Portuguese colonies

The pattern of constitutional development that unfolded in much of Africa was blocked in the Portuguese colonies and in Rhodesia. The Portu-guese colonies were the oldest in Africa and among the last to be liberated. African leaders in Angola, Portuguese Guinea, and Mozambique organized "liberation armies" to fight for freedom. The wars they waged were long and cost many lives. They were able to gain control of much of the countryside. However, they were unable to dislodge the Portuguese from the major urban centers.

This bloody stalemate continued until 1974, when the military staged a coup in Portugal and announced that Portugal would withdraw from Africa. Within months of the announcement, Portuguese Guinea, Mozambique, and Angola became independent. Only Southern Rhodesia, South Africa, and the trust territory of Namibia remained under minority rule.

Rhodesia

Developments in the British colony of Rhodesia represented an unusual example of both guerrilla warfare and constitutional change. Rhodesia had a large white population that controlled colonial politics. As in their other colonies, the British supported a policy that would gradually allow the African population to gain the right to vote. This would eventually lead to rule by the African majority. Within the colony, however, the white government, led by Ian Smith, refused to allow its privileged position to be jeopardized.

In 1965 the colony declared its independence. Great Britain and the rest of the world, except for South Africa, refused to recognize the independence of Rhodesia. The Smith government was isolated internationally. Yet it refused to meet with African leaders or initiate needed reforms. Consequently, as happened in the neighboring Portuguese colonies, a war of national liberation began. Little success was achieved in the early years of fighting. However, when Angola and Mozambique became independent in 1975, the liberation forces gained a military advantage. They now had countries friendly to their cause in southern Africa.

Under the leadership of Robert Mugabe (moo·GAH·bee) and Joshua Nkomo (en·KOH·moh), the African forces intensified their attacks and succeeded in disrupting the economy of Rhodesia. As the war became increasingly unpopular among the white population, Smith was forced to seek a solution. An arrangement was worked out with moderate African leaders to form a new government under African leadership. It would guarantee to continue the privileged economic and social status of the whites.

In 1978 Bishop Abel Muzorewa (moo·zuh·RAY·wah) became the new prime minister. However, his new government, which included Ian Smith, did not receive international recognition. The guerrilla war continued. In 1979 the Muzorewa-Smith government was finally forced to accept a cease-fire and agree to hold free elections. The elections were to be open to all parties, including the liberation leaders. The cease-fire and elections were to be supervised by the British government. The elections were held in the fall of 1979. Robert Mugabe, considered the most radical of the candidates, won an absolute majority.

The new African nation, named Zimbabwe, came into existence in April 1980. The needs of the nation, battered by years of civil war, were clear, and the government turned its energies to economic recovery. The advance of independence had now reached the borders of the nation of South Africa.

South Africa

South Africa's experience differed from that of any other African nation. It gained independence from Great Britain in 1910, as a white-ruled nation with dominion status. It was linked to Great Britain in foreign affairs, but was free to rule itself internally as it saw fit. Relying on its resources of gold, diamonds, and cheap labor, South Africa experienced an industrial revolution in the early 1900's. Although industrialization was based on their labor, blacks were almost totally excluded from the benefits of South Africa's economic success.

Before World War II, English-speaking whites had dominated the government. By custom, non-whites were kept out of better jobs and were segregated socially. In 1948 the Afrikaans-speaking whites, descendants of the original Dutch settlers, came to power in South Africa. They passed a series of laws designed to ensure that these customs would not change. This policy, based on the principle of racial separation, became known as

apartheid (uh·PART·hyt), the Afrikaans word for apartness. Apartheid was the official policy of the South African government after 1948.

Out of a population of some 32.5 million in 1986, whites numbered only about 5.8 million. The non-white population included about 1 million Asians, 3 million "coloreds"—people of mixed heritage—and 22.7 million blacks. Many whites, who were in the minority, were alarmed by the rapidly growing black population. The whites used apartheid laws to guarantee their privileged position.

The effects of apartheid. The apartheid system controlled every aspect of life in South Africa. Hundreds of laws concerning jobs, education, social relations, and intellectual pursuits governed the lives of nonwhites. The government forced most nonwhites to live in restricted areas, which were located in or near cities or in rural areas. No nonwhite could vote or run for office until 1984. In that year a new constitution went into effect, granting coloreds and Asians the right to be represented in the previously all-white Parliament. Blacks, however, were still denied any political participation.

South Africa also extended apartheid to Namibia (Southwest Africa), which it had acquired as a mandate from the League of Nations after World War I. Although the United Nations voted in 1966 to end South Africa's control of Namibia, South Africa ignored the ruling. South Africa's harsh policies led to an increasingly militant nationalist movement in Namibia.

Within its own territory, South Africa attempted to form separate "tribal states," known as "homelands" or "bantustans," for Africans. The homelands had no economic resources of their own and were completely dependent on the South African government.

Although many Western nations condemned apartheid, they continued to invest large sums of money in South Africa. South Africa had rich mineral resources, and it had cheap labor to mine them. Also some African countries were economically dependent on South Africa. They had no choice but to trade with it.

In 1976, the South African police brutally crushed a peaceful demonstration by black schoolchildren at Soweto, a township near Johannesburg. After the Soweto incident, which triggered massive uprisings around the country, many people in South Africa were no longer willing to wait peacefully for change. Thousands of South Africans have since died in civil unrest.

In July 1985 the South African government, faced with the prospect of urban guerilla warfare, substantially increased its own military and police powers by declaring a state of emergency. As a result the political situation in South Africa also became an international crisis.

CHECKUP

1. IDENTIFY: Kenyatta, CPP, Mau Mau, Touré, Kasavubu, Mobutu, Smith, Mugabe, Bantustans.

2. LOCATE: Zimbabwe, Ghana, Kenya, Zaïre, Katanga, South Africa.

3. What problems did the Belgian Congo experience after achieving independence?

4. How did France deal with its African colonies that wished to be independent?

5. Why was independence so difficult to achieve in Rhodesia?

6. Describe the South African policy of apartheid.

2

The new African nations faced various problems

Having achieved independence, the nations of Africa still faced many serious problems. Each new nation had to create a sense of national unity among peoples often divided by differences of language and culture. Many of them had to overcome economic underdevelopment. Finally, a sense of pride in Africa's history and its cultural achievements had to be restored.

National unity

The most pressing need for each of the new African nations was developing a sense of national identity among its citizens. This proved to be a difficult task. The boundaries of the new nations were often artificial, having been drawn by the imperialist powers in the 1800's for their own convenience. In some cases, people of similar racial or cultural backgrounds were separated. In other cases, peoples of different heritages were grouped together.

In addition, colonial administrations had encouraged regional and ethnic differences. In this way they had hoped to discourage the development of national political parties. Ethnic rivalries continued after independence. On occasion they led to civil war, as happened in Nigeria.

Nigeria's civil war

The former British colony of Nigeria gained independence in 1960. The new constitution created a federation of four regions, each of which retained a large degree of local independence. Strong ethnic and regional differences existed in Nigeria, and the government hoped that this loose plan would prevent warfare among the various tribes. The plan, however, did not work.

In 1966 the military took over the government, but it could not overcome the tensions created by ethnic and regional distrust. In 1967 the Eastern Region, home of the Ibo-speaking people, seceded from the federation and declared itself the independent Republic of Biafra.

The country plunged into civil war. Throughout the fighting, Nigerian officials maintained that the war with Biafra was a purely domestic problem. They regarded any aid to the Biafrans as interference in Nigeria's internal affairs. For this reason most African nations refused to recognize Biafra. After 4 years of war and the deaths of about 2 million Biafrans from starvation and disease, Biafra surrendered.

Gradually the Nigerian government restored stability at home and regained a position of leadership in Africa. Nigeria became a respected voice for African interests in the United Nations. Ethnicity and regionalism, however, remained sensitive issues in Nigeria.

A democratically elected government returned to Nigeria in 1970. At the same time, the country's oil wealth provided Nigerians with the opportunity to escape the poverty that threatened most other African nations. It also appeared that Nigeria might be the first African nation other than South Africa to achieve a high degree of industrialization.

African independence

The desire for independence swept Africa after World War II. In Kenya, for example, Jomo Kenyatta led a long and bloody rebellion against British rule. Kenyatta was jailed, but the rebellion continued until at last he was freed to go to London to negotiate Kenyan independence. On his return, Kenyatta told a cheering crowd (above), "I have the British lion by the tail." In 1964 Kenya became a republic, with Kenyatta as its first president.

Once independence was won, Kenya and the other new nations in Africa had to develop their economies to support their growing populations. This meant building new industries and making use of existing resources. A fertilizer factory in Senegal (right) and a dam in Ghana (below) were two of the thousands of economic projects undertaken by modern African nations.

In the 1980's, however, the reduction in the international demand for oil caused Nigeria's oil revenues to fall. Nigeria's economy suddenly faltered. In late 1983 military officers overthrew the civilian government and boldly introduced new economic measures. As of 1986, however, the Nigerian economy had not recovered.

Angola and the Horn of Africa

Superpower rivalry complicated the efforts of new African nations to achieve national unity. The problems of the new nations, which included the need for financial and technical assistance, created opportunities for the United States and the Soviet Union to establish their influence in Africa.

When civil war broke out in Angola after independence in 1975, the United States and the Soviet Union rushed arms and support to the rival factions. A Marxist faction that was aided by Soviet and Cuban troops finally came to power. Cuban troops remained in Angola to ensure the continuation of the regime.

Although the Angolan government continued in the mid-1980's to rely on Cuban troops, it actively sought Western investment in the country. As Angola's actions indicate, the nations of modern Africa often are more concerned with economic aid and development than with political ideologies.

Soviet-American rivalries were even more complex in the Horn of Africa, a strategic area that includes Ethiopia and Somalia (see map, page 744). The Horn overlooks the Red Sea as well as the Indian Ocean sea lanes to the oil-rich Persian Gulf. It is also an area of relative instability, characterized by frequent border disputes and local independence movements.

When Haile Selassie, the Ethiopian emperor, was overthrown in 1974, a socialist regime came to power. To support the socialist governments in Ethiopia and in nearby Somalia, the Soviet Union provided military aid and advisers. Cuban and East German troops were stationed in Ethiopia. In exchange, Somalia and Ethiopia granted the Soviets rights to local air and naval bases.

Although the Soviet Union gained a temporary advantage, it had provided arms to two traditionally hostile neighbors. When Somalia invaded Ethiopia in 1977, the Soviets sided with Ethiopia. Somalia then expelled all Soviet diplomats and advisers. It also granted the United States rights to a navy base in exchange for military assistance. This topsy-turvy situation again seemingly demonstrated that African nations preferred practical assistance to ideological commitments. This was even more true by the 1980's, when a devastating famine threatened millions of Africans with starvation.

Economic difficulties

In addition to political challenges, the new African nations faced economic uncertainty. As colonies, they had been part of the economic system of imperialism. In most cases, upon receiving their independence, they lacked the balance between agriculture and industry that was required for economic growth. Many of them depended on a single crop or mineral resource for most of their income. These products, such as cocoa in Ghana, copper in Zambia and Zaïre, or cotton in the Sudan, were subject to large price swings in world markets.

Overcoming dependence on a single resource continued to be one of the greatest challenges facing the nations of Africa in the mid-1980's. Nations with few resources were unable to escape the cycle of poverty. Zaïre, for example, borrowed heavily from international banks to finance its economic expansion. It became the largest debtor nation in sub-Saharan Africa. Most of its people lived in rural poverty.

Tanzania tried a different approach, based on a traditional African social system. It organized local, cooperative villages, known as "ujamaa" (family) villages, to increase productivity and improve standards of living. Unfortunately, most of these villages failed and economic conditions worsened. Tanzania was a vivid reminder of the economic problems that African nations still had to overcome.

Revival of African culture

Despite the economic and political disappointments that followed independence, the people of Africa made great strides in one very important area. They experienced a rebirth of cultural self-confidence.

During the colonial era, many Africans lost faith in their own culture as they adopted European attitudes toward Africa. African art and music were considered primitive and crude. Magnificent constructions like Great Zimbabwe, about which you read in Chapter 11, or exquisite artifacts like the bronze masks of Benin, were wrongly attributed to foreign influences. They were thought to be works of ancient Greeks or other people who had been shipwrecked on Africa's shores and had wandered into the interior. The literature of Africa—a treasury of oral traditions, including myths, proverbs, and folk tales—was largely unknown to Europeans. Seeing the attitudes of Europeans, most Africans themselves turned away from their history and their cultural heritage.

Not all Africans, however, followed the European example. In East Africa, Swahili poetry and tales continued to be studied as they had been for hundreds of years. The traditions of Swahili were kept alive in the Islamic mosque schools of coastal towns. The written records of this Bantu language go back to the 1600's. The language itself has continued to evolve. James Mbotela's novel, *Uhuru wa Watumwa (Freedom for the Slaves)* (1934), helped give Swahili the modern form from which it continued to grow. Many plays and novels were written in Swahili, the national language of Tanzania and Kenya.

In West Africa, a new literary tradition developed, using the colonial languages of English and French. Many African authors, especially those from French-speaking areas, first achieved international recognition through works of protest against colonial oppression. In a very intense and personal style, the poems of Léopold Senghor, who later became president of independent Senegal, described the hardships of colonialism. Senghor's works, and the novels of Camara Laye of the Cameroons, proudly pointed to the deep, spiritual traditions of Africa and its sense of social community.

Varieties of African expression. These African writers created a new artistic tradition carried on and enlarged by the succeeding generation of Africans. This younger group of authors reflected on the experience of independent Africa. The result was a remarkable and varied artistic outpouring. Similar achievements were made in re-

awakening an interest in African music. In addition, a film industry was begun.

In South Africa, themes protesting racial oppression continued to be important. *The Rhythm of Violence,* a play by Lewis Nkosi, and *Down Second Avenue,* an autobiographical novel by Ezekiel Mphalele, were major cultural contributions. They revealed in a very vivid style the difficulty and bitterness of life in South Africa for the black majority.

The creativity of Africa's contemporary literature, music, and films was also seen in sculpture. At workshops in Nigeria, Zimbabwe, and elsewhere, African artists employed age-old techniques to give shape to wood and copper. Others were more clearly influenced by Western art. Throughout Africa, this willingness to mix African and outside influences gave an unusual vitality to the arts. More and more Westerners began to appreciate the achievements of African art. At the same time, Africans themselves found a new pride in their ancient heritage and in Africa's unique contribution to world culture.

CHECKUP

1. IDENTIFY: Biafra, Selassie, "ujamaa" villages.

2. What were the causes and results of the civil war in Nigeria?

3. How did the Soviet Union and the United States become politically involved in Angola, Ethiopia, and Somalia?

4. Explain why dependence on one crop can result in an unstable economy. How did Zaïre and Tanzania try to improve their economies?

5. List some examples of contemporary African cultural achievements.

3

The nations of the Middle East secured their independence

The Middle East, as it is usually defined today, contains the nations of Iran, Israel, Turkey, and the entire Arab world (see map, opposite). One can think of the Middle East as the southwestern corner of Asia, plus the northern part of Africa.

During the years from 1945 to 1962, the nations of the Middle East made great advances in securing independence. Many gained their independence from Western imperial rule. Others, such as Egypt and Iran, were officially independent but were dominated by outsiders. They too achieved greater freedom from foreign influence during this period. They also sought to increase their power within the Middle East.

Iran

At the end of World War II, Great Britain and the Soviet Union still occupied Iran. The young ruler, Shah Muhammad Reza Pahlavi, was powerless. Iranian leaders wanted to free their country from both Soviet and British influence. With United States support, Iran was able to stop efforts by the Soviet Union to gain greater control over the country.

In the early 1950's, Iran acted to reduce British influence. The popular Iranian prime minister, Muhammad Mussadegh (MOO·sah·daig), nationalized the British-owned Anglo-Iranian Oil Company in 1951. Mussadegh also led a nationalist struggle against Iranian conservatives who supported the Shah and the monarchy.

The struggle within Iran between Mussadegh and the Shah reached a showdown in 1953. For a brief time the Shah had to flee Iran. He returned in triumph after the military, supported by the United States, overthrew Mussadegh.

Thereafter, the Shah worked to establish his power and to impose rapid modernization upon his country. He relied on close ties with the United States and on his army. By the early 1960's the Shah appeared to be firmly in control.

Turkey

Turkey faced Soviet pressure after World War II and turned to the West for support. After 1947 Turkey relied increasingly on military and economic aid from the United States, and in 1952 became a full member of NATO.

At the same time Turkey moved toward democratic rule. In late 1945 the successor to Kemal Atatürk announced the end of one-party government. The more authoritarian aspects of Atatürk's government were abolished. Free elections were held in May 1950, and the opposition party under Prime Minister Adnan Menderes came to power.

In the late 1950's the Menderes government lost

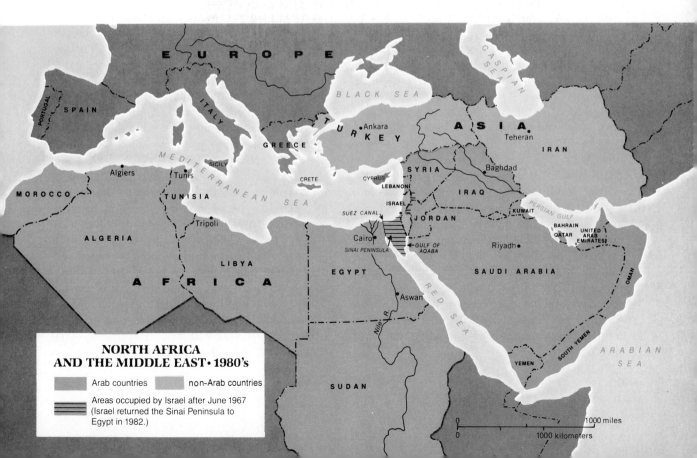

NORTH AFRICA AND THE MIDDLE EAST · 1980's

Arab countries   non-Arab countries

Areas occupied by Israel after June 1967 (Israel returned the Sinai Peninsula to Egypt in 1982.)

popularity and began to impose restrictions on its opposition. The Turkish army intervened in 1960, fearing Menderes would eventually destroy some of the reforms Atatürk had instituted. Menderes and many others were arrested, and the former prime minister was later executed. Although the army restored civilian government, the precedent of military intervention in Turkish politics had been established.

Egypt

After 1945 Egyptians were concerned with two foreign issues, both involving Great Britain. The Egyptians wanted to remove the British military base at Suez. They also wanted to eliminate British control over Sudan and to unite that country with Egypt.

The Egyptian ruler, King Farouk, had lost favor with ordinary Egyptians, most of whom lived in extreme poverty and resented the king's extravance. In addition, Egyptians were impatient with the government's delay in implementing economic reforms. Egypt was therefore ripe for revolution, and in July 1952 a group of young military officers overthrew the government of King Farouk.

After a power struggle, Gamal Abdel Nasser emerged as Egypt's new leader. From 1954 until his death in 1970, Nasser enjoyed almost complete control in Egypt. He took care, however, to observe the formalities of democratic rule.

Nasser and his fellow officers represented Egyptians of modest means in revolt against corrupt rulers. The former ruling class has been allied, both commercially and politically, with Great Britain and the West. Hence Nasser's revolution also was characterized as a revolt against the West.

The Nasser government emphasized land reform, industrialization, greater governmental control over the economy, and the expansion of education. By 1954 Great Britain had agreed to evacuate the Suez base and to allow free elections in Sudan. Sudan, however, chose independence rather than union with Egypt.

Nasser still feared Western influence in the Middle East. He launched Egypt on an assertive foreign policy aimed at dominating the Arab world.

Israel and the Arabs

After the Holocaust, about which you read in Chapter 27, the Zionists became more determined to have Palestine as a Jewish homeland. Palestinian Arabs continued to resist what they saw as an invasion of their homeland. Neighboring Arabs supported the Palestinians.

Great Britain, which held the mandate for Palestine following World War I, was never able to obtain an agreement between Zionists and Palestinians. After World War II, Great Britain referred the problem to the United Nations. In November 1947 the United Nations voted to partition Palestine into separate Jewish and Arab states with Jerusalem as an international city. When the last British troops left Palestine in May 1948, Zionist leaders proclaimed the creation of the Republic of Israel. Chaim Weizmann became its first president and David Ben-Gurion its first prime minister.

The Palestinians were angered by the establishment of a Jewish nation on land they claimed. War broke out as soon as British troops withdrew from the area. Armies from neighboring Arab countries moved against Israel.

Although outnumbered by the Arabs, the determined Israelis triumphed. When the war ended in early 1949, Israel had won more territory than it had been allotted in the UN partition plan. The Arab nations accepted a cease-fire, but UN-sponsored efforts to negotiate permanent peace failed. Moreover, some 750,000 Palestinians had been uprooted by the conflict and were living as refugees in neighboring Arab lands. Attempts to work out either the return or resettlement of these Palestinian refugees also failed.

In the three years from 1949 to 1952, Israel absorbed nearly 600,000 immigrants, many of them from Arab lands. These arrivals almost doubled the Jewish population of the new country. Impressive social and economic programs were also advanced. Collective farms (the best-known form of which is called the **kibbutz**) proved successful in turning former desert areas into productive land. However, an armed truce existed between Israel and its neighbors.

Among the Arab nations, only one emerged from the 1948 war with territorial gains. What remained of the proposed Palestinian state was absorbed into Trans-Jordan in 1949. (Trans-Jordan then changed its name to Jordan.) This was bitterly opposed by other Arabs, including many Palestinians.

Algeria

Most of the Middle East had gained independence after limited violence. In Algeria, however, independence came only after a long, brutal war that lasted from 1954 to 1962.

Algeria was not just a colony but had been legally absorbed into France. In addition, Algeria contained about one million French citizens. Many were from families that had lived in French Algeria for several generations. Some families had been there since France had taken over the country in 1830.

There were also French settlers in the neighboring countries of Morocco and Tunisia, but not so many. Moreover, these countries were French protectorates, not part of France. France finally gave in to persistent Moroccan and Tunisian nationalist movements, granting independence to both countries in 1956.

In Algeria, however, the French were determined to keep control. An Algerian group called the National Liberation Front (FLN, the initials for its name in French) had launched a guerrilla war in 1954. France kept sending in more troops, but the determined FLN could not be crushed. Although bottled up by the strong French army, the FLN won increasing support from all classes of Algerians.

In 1958, as you have read, General de Gaulle became head of the French government. The French in Algeria thought he would push the war there to a successful finish for France. They were disappointed. Slowly de Gaulle prepared the French to accept Algerian independence.

Talks between French and Algerian representatives began in 1961, but the negotiations were long and difficult. Finally, in 1962, the two sides reached a settlement. Algerian independence was achieved in July 1962.

The Middle East in world politics

Soon after the end of World War II, Soviet pressures on Iran, Greece, and Turkey provoked an

HISTORY THROUGH ART

Windows in Jerusalem

At the beginning of World War II, there were nearly 16 million Jews scattered throughout the world. Then, during the Nazi terrorism that engulfed Europe, as many as 6 million Jews lost their lives. In 1948, when the state of Israel was proclaimed, many Jews went to live there, to join earlier settlers in developing the land.

During the early years when Israel experienced tremendous growth, the Israelis constructed houses, schools, and other facilities for the growing population. One of these was a hospital in the capital, Jerusalem. This brilliantly colored stained-glass window from the hospital's chapel, or synagogue, is called "The Tribe of Joseph." It is one of a series of 12 windows, each devoted to one of Jacob's 12 sons, the founders of the tribes of ancient Israel.

The windows were designed by Marc Chagall, a Russian Jewish artist who fled to France in the 1920's in search of freedom. There are no figures of human beings in any of these windows because, by Jewish law, images of people are not permitted to appear in synagogues. The artist cleverly used symbols and abstractions of animals, birds, plants, and fish to tell the stories of the Old Testament. An intensely devout man, Chagall conveyed his love for his faith as well as his sense of history in these beautiful windows.

American-led Western response. American resistance to Soviet efforts in the Middle East, formalized in the Truman Doctrine (see Chapter 28), proved successful in the late 1940's and early 1950's. In general, the West was eager to maintain a strong presence in the Middle East through economic agreements and military bases.

The Soviet Union challenged Western influence in the area by entering into an arms deal with Egypt in 1955. Nasser was willing to accept Soviet arms because he feared continued Western domination more than the possibility of Soviet control. He also had ambitions for Egypt to play a larger role in the Middle East.

The United States and its allies responded to the Soviet-Egyptian arms deal by offering to help finance a major developmental project—a dam at Aswan, on the Nile River. The dam would irrigate new lands for an expansion of agriculture and also produce hydroelectric power. It was hoped this would keep Egypt from slipping farther into the sphere of Soviet influence. When Nasser later displeased the West, the Aswan Dam offer was abruptly withdrawn. Nasser retaliated by nationalizing the Suez Canal in July 1956.

The Suez crisis

Egyptian nationalization of the Suez Canal posed many problems, including a possible threat to Europe's oil supply. The industrialized nations of the West depended heavily on oil shipped from oil fields in the Middle East through the canal. In addition, as more Soviet arms poured into Egypt, the West feared increased Soviet influence in the Middle East.

The Egyptian moves were especially alarming to Israel. Relations between Israel and the neighboring Arab nations, especially Egypt, had been most unfriendly. Egypt had refused to allow Israeli ships or ships of other countries with cargoes bound for Israel to pass through the Suez Canal.

Egypt's seizure of the canal in 1956 brought tensions to a head. Israel, in a lightning invasion, seized the Gaza Strip—an Egyptian-administered coastal district adjoining Israel's southern border. The Israelis then defeated the Egyptians in the Sinai Peninsula and advanced toward the canal.

Great Britain and France, in secret agreement with Israel, sent an ultimatum to Egypt. The ultimatum demanded a cease-fire and insisted on temporary British-French occupation of the canal. When Egypt refused, Great Britain and France seized the Mediterranean end of the canal, driving back the Egyptian army. Both sides sank ships in the canal to block it.

The matter was brought before the United Nations. The General Assembly demanded a cease-fire and withdrawal of the invading forces. It also authorized UN forces to patrol the cease-fire line. Great Britain and France, facing pressure from hostile world opinion, withdrew their troops. The Israelis tried to gain Egypt's agreement to their use of the canal, but failed. Then they too withdrew.

In the short war over the Suez Canal, Israel had crippled Nasser's growing military power. Arab fear and distrust of Israel intensified. A negotiated Arab-Israeli peace became even more remote.

Aftermath of the Suez crisis

The years 1956 to 1958 brought Soviet influence in the Middle East and Egypt's influence among the Arab nations to a peak. American efforts to rally Middle Eastern nations against further Soviet moves in the Middle East failed. The Soviet Union then agreed to help build the Aswan Dam and also began to develop close ties with other Middle Eastern nations.

Nasser's influence in the Middle East grew to such an extent that an Egyptian-led Arab unity movement, pan-Arabism, appeared possible. In 1958 Egypt and Syria merged to form the United Arab Republic, partly to coordinate efforts against Israel. Later that year the pro-Western monarchy in Iraq, the strongest Arab opponent to Nasser's leadership, was overthrown by a military coup. This strengthened Nasser even further.

After 1958, however, Nasser's pan-Arabism policies achieved no more gains. Syria broke away from the United Arab Republic in 1961. In addition, Israel remained strong, despite its isolation from its Arab neighbors.

International politics now settled into a fragile balance. The Middle East was no longer solidly in the Western camp, but the Soviet Union had no major diplomatic triumphs after the 1950's.

Indeed, by the end of 1962 no outside power dominated the Middle East. Nor was any power from within the Middle East likely to do so. It was apparent that the prospects for stability and peace were not bright.

CHECKUP

1. IDENTIFY: Mussadegh, Menderes, Farouk, Nasser, Weizmann, Ben-Gurion, kibbutz, FLN, Aswan Dam, pan-Arabism.

2. What changes did Nasser's government bring to Egypt?

3. Why was Algerian independence difficult for the French to accept?

4. What factors led to the Suez crisis of 1956? How was it resolved?

Wars, oil, and revolution transformed the Middle East

During the years after 1962, the struggle against colonialism was no longer an issue in the Middle East. Most of the countries had achieved independence. The remaining British dependencies in the Persian Gulf area gained their independence without conflict in the early 1970's. Great power rivalries in the Middle East continued, however, especially between the Soviet Union and the United States. Yet these rivalries were not as intense as they had been in the years between 1945 and 1962. The major issues during the next decades concerned adjustments within the Middle East itself.

The Arab-Israeli confrontation

After the breakup of the union between Egypt and Syria in 1961, Nasser became more cautious about pan-Arabism. Yet Egypt's president did not want to forfeit his country's leadership role in the Arab world. He therefore faced a difficult choice when, in late 1966, tension rose along Israel's border with Syria and Jordan. He could support his Arab neighbors at the risk of war with a militarily strong Israel. Or he could hold back at the risk of losing his standing as leader of the Arab world. Nasser decided to act.

In May 1967 Nasser demanded the withdrawal of UN troops who had been policing the border between Egypt and Israel since the end of the Suez crisis in 1956. Nasser also announced the closing of the Gulf of Aqaba to block Israel's direct sea route to Africa and Asia (see map, page 751).

The Six-Day War. Seeing the danger of delay, Israel entered into a lightning war on June 5, 1967. In six days of fighting, Israel captured the Sinai Peninsula and the Gaza Strip from Egypt, seized the Golan Heights from Syria, and took from Jordan the entire west bank of the Jordan River. The so-called "West Bank," part of the original Palestine mandate, had remained in Arab hands after the Arab-Israeli war of 1948. Israel also captured the Jordanian section of Jerusalem. Israel then annexed Jerusalem, despite a UN ruling making it an international city.

The Six-Day War, as it came to be called, radically changed Middle Eastern politics. Israel's military superiority over its neighbors was confirmed, but peace remained elusive. The displaced Palestinians no longer expected help from Arab governments to restore them to what had been Palestine. They now relied more on their own guerrilla organization, the Palestine Liberation Organization (PLO).

The United States and the Soviet Union, realizing that they might be drawn into an Arab-Israeli war, became interested in arranging a permanent peace settlement in the area. Egypt, Jordan, and Syria wished to regain lost territory. All parties involved had reason to seek a compromise settlement after 1967. However, mutual suspicions and fears doomed many efforts to work out a peace over the next six years.

Egypt under Sadat

Nasser died in September 1970 and was succeeded by Anwar al-Sadat. Egypt and Syria secretly planned a war against Israel that began on October 6, 1973. This war lasted until the end of October. Although the Arabs fought hard, Israeli troops pushed them back and crossed the Suez Canal to occupy Egyptian land. However, the Israelis suffered severe losses.

Tensions in the Middle East

The history of the Middle East after World War II was dominated by war. In 1967 the Israelis struck a decisive blow against the Arabs by capturing control of Jerusalem (below), a city sacred to both Muslims and Jews. Golda Meir (above), a vigorous leader and negotiator, was Israeli prime minister when war began once again in 1973. Following this war, there were many efforts to achieve a lasting peace in the Middle East. President Anwar Sadat of Egypt (far right) made a bold and dramatic journey to Israel in 1977 in an effort to promote peace between the two nations. This was an aim that his successor, Hosni Mubarak (saluting, right), continued to support.

A complicating factor in the Middle East throughout the 1970's was the growing importance of oil. Because the industrial nations depended on oil from the Middle East, Arab oil ministers (below right) exerted great influence in international affairs.

As had been true after the Six-Day War, all sides had reason to seek a compromise settlement. The United States Secretary of State, Henry Kissinger, began an intensive campaign of **shuttle diplomacy**—moving back and forth from Israel to Egypt to Syria to try to reach agreement. He eventually achieved two settlements between Israel and Egypt and one between Israel and Syria. Thereafter, the peace initiative ran out of steam. In November 1977, however, Sadat surprised the world. He went to Israel to speak in person to the Israeli Parliament and to Israeli prime minister Menachem Begin. This was the first time that an Arab leader dealt directly with Israel.

Sadat's action opened a new path of negotiations between Egypt and Israel. Sadat and Begin were supported and encouraged by the United States. Many more months of delicate negotiations were required, aided by the direct intervention of President Jimmy Carter. In September 1978 Carter invited the two leaders to the Presidential retreat at Camp David, in Maryland. After meetings and negotiations there, Sadat and Begin were able to agree upon the framework for a peace settlement. This "Camp David agreement" was followed by a peace treaty that was signed by Israel and Egypt in March 1979.

Sadat's actions divided the Arab world. His opponents claimed he had sold out the Palestinians to regain Egyptian territory. His supporters argued that he had started a process that could lead to peace for all, including the Palestinians. Most Israelis supported the peace with Egypt, but resisted the idea of a process that might lead to a Palestinian state.

Egypt and Israel had achieved a great breakthrough. There was doubt, however, whether it would lead to an eventual agreement between the Israelis and the Palestinians—and thus end the Arab-Israeli confrontation. The assassination of Sadat in October 1981 further darkened the hopes for peace.

Oil and world energy needs

The Middle East and the West have dealt with each other over oil since 1901. In that year the Shah of Iran (then Persia), granted a concession to a British prospector. Seven years later oil was discovered.

Other foreign companies, mainly British and American, later obtained oil concessions from Middle Eastern countries. A few companies found no oil and lost their investments. Others spent many years and much money before succeeding. Even with modern technology, oil exploration remained a risky business. Most companies, however, eventually discovered huge oil fields, for the Middle East has vast oil reserves.

Until the years after World War II, the foreign oil companies had little trouble dealing with Middle Eastern governments. These governments were usually weak and poor. Many were still under direct or indirect Western domination. In addition, there was no world shortage of oil. The Middle Eastern countries had little bargaining strength.

With the rising tide of nationalism following World War II, many of the oil-producing countries began to demand more of the profits. Often the companies were willing to grant these demands. In Iran, however, the Anglo-Iranian Oil Company and the government were unable to reach agreement. As a result, the oil industry in Iran was nationalized, as you have read. This was a political victory for Iran, but the economic terms it received were less favorable. Oil was still plentiful on the world market. For this reason Iran had little economic bargaining power. Neither did the other Middle Eastern oil producers.

The formation of OPEC

A decade later the situation in the oil industry began to change. In 1960 the Latin American nation of Venezuela and the oil-producing nations in the Middle East organized the Organization of Petroleum Exporting Countries (OPEC). OPEC was to be the bargaining agent between the oil companies and oil-consuming industrial nations.

Some successes were achieved by OPEC in the 1960's. Its important advances, however, began in the 1970's. The world oil shortage was by then apparent to everyone. During the war with Israel in October 1973, the Arab members of OPEC used their oil as an economic weapon. They proposed to cut back production as a means of pressuring Israel and its Western supporters. Their oil embargo caused world oil prices to skyrocket. The production cutbacks were later eased, but it became clear that OPEC had the economic power to fix oil prices.

This power, however, eventually created difficulties as well as benefits for the oil-producing nations of the Middle East. The increases in oil revenues led to rapid and unpredictable social change. Furthermore, the international oil surplus of the early and mid-1980's caused many OPEC nations to go into debt.

The Iranian revolution

Throughout the 1960's the Iranian government carried out ambitious modernization programs. These included land distribution to the peasants, a campaign against illiteracy, increased industrialization, and women's liberation. These efforts continued into the 1970's.

Iran's increasing oil revenues, combined with political changes in surrounding nations, gave Shah Mohammed Reza Pahlavi an opportunity to play a major role in the Middle East. In 1968 Great Britain announced plans to withdraw from the Persian Gulf and to grant independence to Qatar, Bahrain, Oman, and the Trucial Sheikdoms (later called the United Arab Emirates). All of these former British colonies were independent nations by 1971 (see map, page 751). Iran thereafter was the major military power in the Persian Gulf area.

Ties between the Shah and the United States were especially close during this period. In addition, since the mid-1960's Iran had enjoyed good relations with the Soviet Union. As a result, the Shah's regime appeared strong and stable in the late 1970's. Many Iranians, however, opposed the Shah. Some of these discontented persons were extreme leftists seeking to establish a communist state. Others were traditionalists eager to rid the country of Western influences and create a government ruled by religious leaders.

The rapid pace of modernization in Iran had created problems. These increased when the boom oil years after 1973 were followed by an economic slump. Millions had left the countryside for Iran's cities. These uprooted masses were ready to accept the call for revolution.

The Shah failed to win loyalty even from those Iranians who had directly benefited from the modernization programs. Thousands of young Iranians had been sent abroad at government expense for higher education. Yet most of them feared and detested the Shah's rule. They felt it was symbolized by the Savak, the hated secret police who were believed responsible for many atrocities. Moreover, the Shah tried to keep all power in his hands. As a result, not even his own ministers developed strong loyalty to him.

Riots and mass demonstrations throughout 1978 set the stage for revolution. By this time the 76-year-old religious leader Ayatollah Khomeini (hoh·MAY·nee) had become the revolution's leader. Banished from Iran since 1964, Khomeini directed the fight from exile in France.

Downfall of the Shah. The Shah made concessions, but they came too late. Finally, in January 1979, he left the country, appointing a prime minister to preside over a gradual transition of power. However, Khomeini insisted that the monarchy be replaced by an Islamic republic, run according to religious principles.

Khomeini returned to Iran in February 1979. Support for the government quickly faded. Leadership within the army was divided, and by mid-February Khomeini's revolution had triumphed. Iranians overwhelmingly voted to establish an Islamic republic and elected a president in January 1980. Real power, however, remained with Khomeini.

On November 4, 1979, Iranian militants captured the American Embassy in Teheran and seized more than 50 American hostages. The militants were protesting the American decision to let the ailing Shah enter the United States for medical treatment. They demanded that the Shah be returned to Iran to stand trial. The Shah left the United States in December 1979. He died in Egypt in July 1980.

Although Iran had become one of the most influential nations in the Middle East, it was widely condemned around the world for taking the American hostages. The Iranian economy was in disarray. Even the release of the hostages in 1981 did not ease the problems facing the nation. In the meantime, Iraq had launched an attack against Iran in September 1980 because of a dispute involving a waterway that divides the two countries. That border war was still raging more than five years later, with both sides suffering heavy casualties.

1. IDENTIFY: PLO, Sadat, Kissinger, shuttle diplomacy, Begin, Camp David agreement, Savak, Khomeini.

2. LOCATE: Gulf of Aqaba, Qatar, Bahrain, Oman, United Arab Emirates, Teheran.

3. Describe the efforts to attain peace in the Middle East after the Arab-Israeli war of October 1973.

4. How has OPEC demonstrated its power in world affairs?

5. What factors led to the Iranian revolution of 1979? Why did Iranian militants seize American hostages in 1979?

A struggle between old and new ways developed in the Middle East

After 1945 the Middle East changed as rapidly as any area in the world. The political and economic transformation of the region brought about great social change as well. This brought about a clash between old and new that still continues.

People and politics

The Middle East is a vast territory, twice the size of the United States. In the mid-1980's, nearly 270 million people lived in the region, and over 90 percent were Muslims. Population densities varied widely. Saudi Arabia, for example, more than three times the size of Texas, had only 10.8 million inhabitants. This amounted to 12.9 persons per square mile. Egypt's Nile Valley, by contrast, averaged almost 3,000 persons per square mile. (A square mile equals 2.59 square kilometers.)

The countries of the Middle East varied in size and importance. Qatar, the size of Delaware, had only some 276,000 inhabitants in 1984. Turkey, larger than Texas, had about 50 million inhabitants. In fact, just two countries, Egypt and Turkey, contained one third of the total population of the entire Middle East.

It was not just the size of their populations that made some of the Middle Eastern countries important. The four Persian Gulf states of Kuwait, Qatar, Bahrain, and the United Arab Emirates, for example, contained less than one percent of the Middle East's population. However, they possessed enormous oil wealth, and thus had considerable influence.

For centuries, three major languages—Arabic, Persian, and Turkish—were used throughout the region. After the creation of the state of Israel, Hebrew also became an important language in the Middle East.

Until modern times the Middle East was not so politically divided. The Ottoman Empire, which lasted until after World War I, controlled most of the Middle East for some 400 years. Only Morocco in the west and Iran in the east escaped Ottoman rule.

The political breakup of the region into separate countries began with Western imperialism. The Middle East, as you have read, was colonized by four different European powers. Great Britain and France divided up most of the area between them. Italy ruled Libya, and Spain controlled part of Morocco. Turkey, Iran, and most of the Arabian peninsula were never directly colonized. However, they were subjected to persistent economic and military pressures from Europe.

After World War II there were a number of attempts to create a new political unity in the Middle East. The creation of the Arab League in 1945 was the most important. Egypt, Saudi Arabia, Yemen, Syria, Lebanon, Trans-Jordan, and Iraq formed the League to promote economic and cultural ties among the member nations. Fourteen other Arab nations joined the League after 1945. Nevertheless, in the mid-1980's the Arab nations remained politically divided, especially on foreign policy.

Unequal distribution of resources

Great differences also exist in the distribution of natural resources in the region. As you have read, most of the oil-rich Middle Eastern countries are thinly populated. Only Iran, Iraq, and Algeria have both large populations and large oil resources. By contrast, most heavily populated areas such as Turkey, Egypt, Sudan, and Morocco have little oil.

Egypt's great agricultural wealth does not meet the needs of its enormous population. Sudan can-

Social changes in the Middle East

Startling contrasts are apparent in the modern Middle East. Extraordinary oil wealth has poured into the tiny Persian Gulf sheikdoms, enabling them to build splendid new apartment houses. Yet most of the people continue to live as before, selling Oriental rugs and other handcrafted goods (top far right). In Teheran, the Iranian capital, well-stocked modern shopping centers have been built (bottom far right). Yet the traditional religion of Islam is still a powerful force in Iran. The crowds that greeted the spiritual leader Ayatollah Khomeini in 1980 showed the religious emotion that gave him enormous political power (right). In Israel, rich grapefruit orchards (above) and large flocks of sheep (below) present the striking contrast of thriving agriculture in an arid land.

not exploit its agricultural potential because of limited transportation facilities. Other countries, such as Morocco, have a good mix of agricultural and mineral resources. For the entire Middle East, however, only oil is a source of imposing wealth.

Thus, the unequal distribution of natural resources and of population produces difficult economic conditions. The national wealth (what economists call the gross national product, or GNP) in Kuwait, Qatar, and the United Arab Emirates is significantly higher than in the United States. In 1984 the GNP in the United States was more than $15,000 per person per year. In those three tiny Persian Gulf states the average GNP per person was more than $25,000. At the other end of the scale, the GNP per person was less than $1,000 in Egypt, Sudan, and Yemen.

Cities and population growth

Cities have existed in the Middle East since the dawn of history. Damascus is believed to be the world's oldest continuously occupied city. In 1945 the Middle East already had a significant proportion of its population living in cities. The increase since then has been dramatic.

The population of Cairo, Egypt, was less than 2 million in 1945. It was at least 7 million in 1985. Teheran, the capital of Iran, expanded tenfold in the same period, from 500,000 to 5 million. Baghdad, in Iraq, with a population in 1945 of about 440,000, had over 3 million inhabitants 40 years later.

In the mid-1980's, nearly half of Lebanon's total population lived in the capital city of Beirut. Israel, often thought of as a land of agricultural pioneers, had a population that was 90 percent urban.

Traditional Middle Eastern cities had narrow, winding streets, bazaars—market streets with rows of tiny shops—and city walls with handsome gates. Although much of this older style remained, urban growth in recent years took the form of high-rise buildings and wide streets for automobiles.

Before modern times most city dwellers lived in one- or two-story houses hidden behind window-less walls. The few outside windows were heavily shuttered with ornate patterns of metal or wood.

761

Rooms of such city homes opened on an interior patio. All this assured greater family privacy. In the mid-1980's, more and more people lived in apartment buildings. Also, as industrialization intensified, increasing numbers of people worked in factories and offices.

Much of the growth of Middle Eastern cities was due to migration from the countryside. Much also stemmed from high population growth rates. This population increase was caused both by declining death rates and high birth rates. The result was a very young population. For example, about one half of Iran's population in 1985 was under the age of 15, while two thirds was under the age of 30.

Education and women's status

The large percentage of young people in the population increased the need for schools and teachers. Middle Eastern countries made great progress in schooling after 1945. At that time probably fewer than 15 percent of the primary-school-age children were actually in school. In 1980, despite the vast population increase, the average was closer to 65 percent. Several countries, such as Israel, Lebanon, and Tunisia, had almost all primary-school-age children in school.

The years since 1945 also brought significant expansion in secondary and higher education. Turkey, for example, had over 240,000 students in colleges and universities in the mid-1980's. The figure for Egypt was more than 500,000.

The students spent their time on subjects similar to those studied in the West. Many of them trained to become government officials. With the coming of industrialization, there was also a growing need for people with technical skills. Many became mechanics, electricians, and business managers.

Women, too, achieved gains. Only a fraction of the female population received schooling before 1945. After that time the percentage of females in school increased even more rapidly than that of males. Each year more women finished school and took jobs in factories, offices, and in such professions as medicine. A few women entered politics. In general, Middle Eastern societies continued to be male dominated, but improvements in women's status after 1945 were striking.

Religious nationalism

Many Muslims in the Middle East reacted to the rapid changes of the times by turning to Islamic fundamentalism. This was an attempt to revive the stability and values of the past, and was a form of religious nationalism. It was a way for Muslim nations to reject Western influences.

Followers of Islamic fundamentalism differed on leadership and policy, but they agreed in rejecting foreign influences. They wanted to return to traditional Muslim ways. They wished to create religious nations that would apply Islamic law strictly. They opposed such modern trends as women's emancipation.

Ayatollah Khomeini, leader of the Iranian revolution against the Shah, was the best-known spokesman of Islamic fundamentalism. Colonel Muammar al-Qaddafi (kah·DAH·fee), who overthrew the Libyan monarchy in 1969, claimed as well to represent traditional Islamic political values. The religious conservatives of Saudi Arabia were also Muslim fundamentalists, but they opposed both Khomeini and Qaddafi. In the 1970's and 1980's, Muslim and Christian factions in Lebanon engaged in bloody guerilla warfare. The Lebanese civil war killed thousands of people and destroyed the nation's economy.

Many young people in these countries were impatient with traditional ways. They rejected outside political influence, but they sought education and were eager to modernize their societies. There was often tension between them and the religious nationalists.

Thus, after 1945 the nations of the Middle East became more industrialized, more urbanized, and better educated. However, the struggle between continuity and change, between old and new, seemed destined to continue.

CHECKUP

1. IDENTIFY: Arab League, bazaars, Qaddafi.

2. LOCATE: Kuwait, Yemen, Lebanon, Damascus, Baghdad, Beirut.

3. What changes in education were made in the Middle East after 1945? What gains did women in the Middle East achieve?

4. Define Islamic fundamentalism. Give two examples in the Middle East.

CHAPTER REVIEW

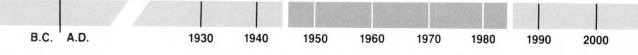

| B.C. | A.D. | | 1930 | 1940 | 1950 | 1960 | 1970 | 1980 | 1990 | 2000 |

1945	Arab League formed	1960	UN intervention in Congo OPEC organized	1975–present	Fighting in Lebanon
1948	Republic of Israel proclaimed	1962	Algerian independence achieved	1979	Israeli-Egyptian peace treaty Iranian revolution
1948–1949	First Arab-Israeli war	1967	Arab-Israeli Six-Day War	1980–present	Iran-Iraq war
1952	Egyptian monarchy overthrown	1967–1970	Civil war in Nigeria	1981	Assassination of Sadat
1956	Suez crisis	1973	Fourth Arab-Israeli war	1985–present	State of emergency in South Africa
1957	Independence for Ghana				

CHAPTER SUMMARY

Independence came rapidly to the African nations after World War II. Most African nations achieved independence peacefully, but a few resorted to war and violence. Only South Africa resisted any efforts to give the black majority of the population a real voice in their own government.

Africa's new nations faced a number of difficulties. There was often hostility among the groups within a country. This led to a bitter civil war in Nigeria. In Angola the superpowers intervened, as they did in the conflict between Ethiopia and Somalia in the Horn of Africa. Africans also faced economic difficulties and, in the early years of independence, a sense of inferiority about their culture. However, African cultural achievements gradually gained wide recognition and admiration.

Many nations in the Middle East also gained independence after 1945. In addition, nations that were already officially independent were able to reduce foreign influences. A revolution in Iran resulted in the overthrow of the Shah and the establishment of an Islamic republic.

A continuing problem in the Middle East was the relationship between Israel and its Arab neighbors. Four Arab-Israeli wars were fought between 1948 and 1973. An offer of peace by Egypt led to the signing of a peace treaty in 1979, but the other Arab nations rejected the pact.

The nations of the Middle East varied enormously in size, population, and wealth. A number of them gained considerable power as a result of the rise in oil prices in the 1970's. The rapid changes of the period after World War II led to upheaval and a revival of Islamic fundamentalism. The region faced continuing uncertainties and tension in the mid-1980's.

CHECKING WHAT YOU KNOW

1. Match each leader at the left with a country at the right. You may use a country more than once.

   a. Mugabe
   b. Nkrumah
   c. Weizmann
   d. Sadat
   e. Qaddafi
   f. Kenyatta
   g. Nasser
   h. Khomeini
   i. Touré
   j. Begin
   k. Azikiwe
   l. Senghor

   1. Egypt
   2. Libya
   3. Zimbabwe
   4. Israel
   5. Nigeria
   6. Ghana
   7. Senegal
   8. Guinea
   9. Iran
   10. Kenya

2. How did nationalists after 1945 differ from earlier African leaders? How did each of the following contribute to the rise of nationalism in Africa:

   a. Nkrumah
   b. Kenyatta
   c. Mugabe

3. Which African nations achieved independence with relatively little opposition? Which did not? What reasons might account for these different experiences?

4. How did economic problems and ethnic rivalries threaten the stability of many newly independent African nations?

5. What were the causes of the Arab-Israeli war of 1948–1949? What were the results?

6. What changes occurred in the nations of the Middle East in the years after 1945?

PRACTICING YOUR SKILLS

1. **Using maps.** Turn to the map on page 751. Which Middle Eastern nations are considered Arab states? Which are not? Which Arab nations share borders with Israel? In which of these nations does Israel hold disputed territory? Based on evidence in this map, why might use of the Suez Canal be especially important to Israeli security?

2. **Interpreting readings.** The lines below are from a poem, "Dawn in the Heart of Africa," by Patrice Lumumba. Read these lines carefully and answer the questions that follow.

> The dawn is here, my brother! Dawn! Look in our faces,
> A new morning breaks in our old Africa.
> Ours alone will now be the land, the water, mighty rivers
> Poor Africa surrendered for a thousand years.
>
> ....
>
> The moment when you break the chains, the heavy fetters,
> The evil, cruel times will go never to come again.
> A free and gallant Congo will arise from black soil,
> A free and gallant Congo—black blossom from black seed!

What did Lumumba mean by the phrase "the dawn is here"? To what "evil, cruel times" was he referring? Why might this poem appeal to an emerging sense of African nationalism?

RELATING PAST TO PRESENT

1. In the mid-1980's the situation in the Middle East remained unsettled. In some cases, affairs changed on almost a weekly basis. Using the *Readers' Guide to Periodical Literature,* locate recent articles on events in one of the following nations: Egypt, Israel, Saudi Arabia, Iran, Iraq, Syria, Jordan, or Lebanon. How have conditions changed since the printing of this book? How have the United States and the Soviet Union responded to these changing conditions?

2. Examine the pictures of African art on pages 221, 222, 373, and 556. Then find examples of present African art in sources such as *National Geographic* or general histories of Africa. Based on evidence in these pictures, support or challenge the following statement: "Modern African art reflects a pride in the cultural achievements of earlier African civilizations."

INVESTIGATING FURTHER

1. Prepare a report on the policy of apartheid practiced in the Republic of South Africa. You may consult the *Readers' Guide to Periodical Literature* for articles on this topic. Include in your report answers to the following questions:
   a. What is the origin and racial makeup of the population in the Republic of South Africa?
   b. How does the government defend apartheid?
   c. By what means does the government enforce apartheid?
   d. How do other African nations react to this racial policy? How does the rest of the world react?

2. The novels of Chinua Achebe give Westerners a glimpse into Nigerian society and a changing Africa. Read one of these novels and prepare an oral report on the effects of modernization and the struggle to save or adapt old ways. Possible titles include *Man of the People* (Doubleday), *No Longer at Ease* (Fawcett), and *Things Fall Apart* (Fawcett).

3. Prepare a report on the capture of the American Embassy in Teheran and the seizure of more than 50 American hostages by Iranian militants on November 4, 1979. In your report describe the effects of the incident on the Iranians, the hostages, the United States, and the world.

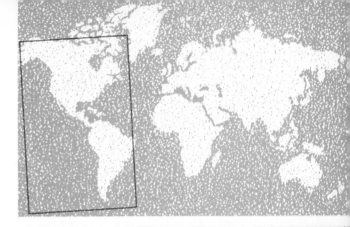

31

(1945 to the Present)

The Western Hemisphere Played an Important Role in World Affairs

One of the most remarkable developments in the modern world has been the growing importance of the Western Hemisphere. The two continents in this region, North America and South America, were sparsely populated and barely known by the rest of the world as recently as the early 1700's. Yet two hundred years later they played a decisive part in two world wars and became the center of enormous political and economic power.

During the years after 1945, the full extent of this power became apparent. The United States became one of the two superpowers, the home of the United Nations, and the most potent economic force in the world. Although the United States often overshadowed its neighbors—Canada to the north, Latin America to the south—the importance of the other nations of the Western Hemisphere also increased after 1945.

The impact of the nations of the Western Hemisphere was partly a result of their wealth. It was also due to the enormous size of their populations and their political and intellectual achievements. These nations, however, were not without problems. The United States faced the natural difficulties of a country made up of many different ethnic, racial, religious, and cultural groups. In Canada, French-speaking and English-speaking citizens had wide political differences. In Latin America, enormous wealth

Workers on a construction site

existed side-by-side with extreme poverty. The Latin American nations also inherited a tradition of unstable and often authoritarian governments.

Nevertheless, the accomplishments of this region of the world in the years after World War II were remarkable. Millions would have starved without the food that the Western Hemisphere, especially the United States, produced. Medical and technological advances were equally extraordinary. Few areas of the world remained unaffected by what happened in the Americas.

THE CHAPTER SECTIONS

1. The United States entered a new era after 1945

2. Canada became a vital area of the modern world

3. Political conflicts occurred in many Latin American nations

4. Latin America experienced dramatic changes

The United States entered a new era after 1945

Despite a flourishing economy and a powerful role in world affairs, the United States faced a number of problems in the postwar years. These included internal conflicts, political problems, and a gradual realization that economic growth is not unlimited. The commitment to a position of great influence, however, remained strong.

Presidential leadership

Between the end of World War II and the mid-1980's, the United States had eight Presidents (see chart, opposite page). Although half of these presidents were Democrats and half were Republicans, their policies had much in common. In foreign affairs, in social concerns, and in the growth of governmental activities, these presidents followed similar paths. Some of the problems that arose were especially significant in specific periods, and we will look at these individually. However, the outlines of national policy during these 40 years can be traced.

The challenge of foreign affairs

For most of the postwar period, the consistent aim of foreign policy was to resist the ambitions of communist nations throughout the world. Harry S Truman, for example, successfully blocked a communist attempt to take over the government of Greece. Truman also implemented the Marshall Plan, which helped European nations recover from World War II. During his administration the United States took part in the Berlin airlift and helped form NATO. Both of these decisive actions attempted to contain Soviet aggression in Europe. In Asia, the United States sent troops to South Korea in a police action to stop the Soviets and the Chinese from taking over the country.

Truman's successor, Dwight D. Eisenhower, brought the Korean War to an end and created the Southeast Asia Treaty Organization (SEATO) in an attempt to halt further communist advances in that region. He also announced the Eisenhower Doctrine, which provided military aid to anti-communist countries in the Middle East. During the administrations of John F. Kennedy and Lyndon B. Johnson, the war in Vietnam was the major focus of foreign policy. Under Ronald Reagan, United States troops helped bring down a Marxist government in Grenada, an island nation in the Caribbean Sea.

All of these undertakings were part of the Cold War between Western and communist nations. The United States, however, had other concerns during this period. It provided economic assistance to developing countries in Latin America, Asia, and Africa. It also made major efforts to reduce tensions in troubled regions. Eisenhower intervened to end the 1956 war in the Middle East. Carter negotiated the Camp David agreements between Israel and Egypt. He also ended United States control of the Panama Canal. Reagan's diplomacy was partially responsible for a peaceful transition from dictatorship to democracy in the Philippines.

Very often, conflicts in some remote part of the world were viewed as additional chapters in the Cold War. Nevertheless, for a brief period during the 1970's, tensions between East and West were temporarily reduced. As we will see, however, this situation did not last long.

Domestic concerns

At home, the consistent aims of the presidents were to resolve social and political problems and to maintain a flourishing economy. Following the example of the New Deal, presidents created new programs to address social problems. The most important social programs were the work of Kennedy and Johnson. Kennedy introduced a broad program of domestic reforms, especially legislation to reduce social inequalities. Tragically, he was assassinated in November 1963 before Congress had passed much of his legislation.

Vice President Johnson succeeded Kennedy and aimed to create what he called the Great Society. His program included much of Kennedy's domestic reform legislation, along with important new proposals to strengthen Americans' civil rights. Much of the legislation was passed, but the costs of the Vietnam War and the economic problems of the 1970's drew attention to the growing size of the federal government. In the early 1980's, Ronald Reagan began an effort to reduce the government's social programs sharply.

The economy

After World War II the American economy reached new peaks of productivity, with huge new industries and much construction. Nevertheless, during the 1940's and 1950's, there were several **recessions**—periods of temporary business slowdown and increased unemployment. The 1960's had no recession, but toward the end of the decade prices began to rise at a faster rate than people's incomes. As a result, the dollar began to buy fewer and fewer things. This economic situation is known as **inflation.**

The 1970's began with a recession. The country slowly recovered but was left with high unemployment and continuing inflation. The Nixon administration tried many solutions. Most of them tended toward **protectionism**—using government means to reduce imports. It persuaded foreign trading partners "voluntarily" to hold down their sales of steel and textiles to the United States. At this time, however, most major nations were making some moves toward dismantling trade barriers. Many economists believed that Nixon's protectionism was self-defeating.

Presidents of the United States 1945–1980's		
Harry S Truman	Democrat	1945-1953
Dwight D. Eisenhower	Republican	1953-1961
John F. Kennedy	Democrat	1961-1963
Lyndon B. Johnson	Democrat	1963-1969
Richard M. Nixon	Republican	1969-1974
Gerald Ford	Republican	1974-1977
Jimmy Carter	Democrat	1977-1981
Ronald Reagan	Republican	1981-

An indication of the declining confidence in the American economy was the loss in value of the dollar against foreign currencies. In countries where inflation was low, like Switzerland, West Germany, and Japan, the currency remained strong. American currency, in contrast, was growing weaker and weaker. As a result, the American dollar was worth less against these foreign currencies. For example, in 1970 one dollar was worth three German marks, but in 1980 it was worth only two marks. At the same time, because of inflation, the American dollar bought less and less at home. For example, many items that had cost one dollar in 1970 cost two dollars in 1980. These two processes, taken together, had a dramatic effect on imports and exports.

The economic problems were made worse in the 1970's by steep increases in the cost of importing oil. The United States imported a large portion of its oil from nations belonging to the Organization of Petroleum Exporting Countries (OPEC). In 1973, as you have read, OPEC briefly cut off supplies in protest of American support of Israel during the war in the Middle East. Then OPEC raised its prices to four times their previous level. Gasoline shortages occurred, economic problems increased, and the dollar fell further against foreign currencies. In 1979 a new recession began, more severe than that of the early 1970's.

Interest rates—the cost of borrowing money—rose sharply in the early 1980's, and unemployment increased markedly. President Reagan enlarged the government's deficit with heavy mil-

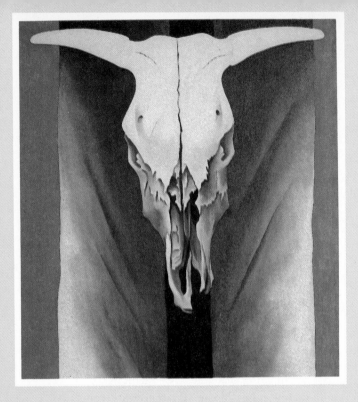

HISTORY THROUGH ART

Georgia O'Keeffe

This stark and powerful skull set against a blue sky was painted by an American artist, Georgia O'Keeffe. O'Keeffe lived in New York with her husband, the photographer Alfred Stieglitz (see page 622). Each summer she traveled to the desert in the Southwest. She wrote, "I brought home the bleached bones as my symbols of the desert. To me they are as beautiful as anything I know."

O'Keeffe's confident American style made a clear statement that American artists were no longer dependent on European training and influence. She, like millions of other Americans, was excited about the endless variety of the country. She commented about her work, "As I painted along on my cow's skull I thought to myself, I'll make it an American painting. They will not think it great with the red stripes down the sides—Red, White, and Blue—but they will notice it."

Today the painting hangs in the Metropolitan Museum in New York—for all the world to notice.

itary spending. He hoped that a tax reduction, especially for businesses, would stimulate economic recovery. By 1986, however, the United States was running a total deficit of almost $1.8 trillion. This tremendous federal debt was a major public-policy issue of the mid-1980's.

Political problems

Many of the American successes of the postwar world were long-term. However, many of the defeats and setbacks were immediately apparent and discouraging. Some Americans did not understand why the United States had allowed the Soviet Union to spread its sphere of influence over Eastern Europe and other parts of the world. A number of people tried to explain these setbacks by a "conspiracy theory." They believed that Soviet gains had occurred because certain people in the government were "soft on communism."

Senator Joseph McCarthy of Wisconsin was the most dramatic spokesman for the "conspiracy theory." Between 1950 and 1954 he questioned the loyalty of many government officials and built up a large following. In the process, the reputations of many Americans were badly damaged.

In 1954 a Senate committee investigated McCarthy's conduct and found his charges groundless. The Senate then censured him for "conduct unbecoming to a Senator," and his influence collapsed.

Civil rights

Black Americans freed from slavery during the Civil War had been officially granted their rights as citizens but, in fact, still lived under many restrictions. In many regions, in both North and South, black people were prevented from voting and from obtaining decent education, jobs, and housing. Dissatisfaction grew, especially after World War II. Organizations like the Urban League and the National Association for the Advancement of Colored People (NAACP) worked to find employment and to secure civil rights for black Americans. They did this by means of legal action and **lobbying**—trying to get legislators to vote for or against a measure.

A turning point in the black civil rights movement came in 1954. In the case of *Brown v. Board of Education of Topeka*, the United States Supreme Court unanimously declared that state laws requiring black children to attend separate schools were unconstitutional. States having such laws were ordered to integrate their schools "with all deliberate speed."

This important decision encouraged the growing civil rights movement. The most prominent leader of that movement was Dr. Martin Luther King, Jr., a minister who advocated the use of nonviolent methods—boycotts, marches, and sit-ins—to bring about change. In the 1960's blacks held mass protests against discrimination on public transportation and in hotels and restaurants. Many of these protests were peaceful, but some resulted in violence. From 1964 to 1967, more than 100 people died in 329 riots across the nation.

The assassination of Dr. King in 1968 was a severe blow to the civil rights movement. His death sparked another wave of violence in cities such as Chicago and Washington, D.C.

In the 1960's Congress passed several civil-rights and voting-rights acts guaranteeing political equality for blacks and other minorities. Economic equality, however, continued to be an elusive goal for blacks in the 1970's and 1980's.

In the mid-1980's the unemployment rate for blacks was much higher than for whites. Black families, especially those headed by females, were three times more likely to be impoverished than white families. Clearly, the basic issue of equal rights for all Americans had not yet been resolved.

Antiwar protest

Another social issue of major concern in the 1960's and 1970's was the continued involvement of American troops in Vietnam. Many supporters of the civil rights movement were also involved in the antiwar movement. Most antiwar protesters were college students who expressed their discontent by staging demonstrations on university campuses. The protesters stressed that United States involvement in Vietnam was causing needless loss of life and served no real American interest.

Antiwar protests sometimes ended in violence. At the Democratic Party Convention of 1968, which was held in Chicago, the proceedings were interrupted by a confrontation between antiwar protesters and the police. Far more serious was an incident that occurred on May 4, 1970, at Kent State University in Ohio. Four students died when the Ohio National Guard attempted to break up an antiwar rally.

After the Kent State incident, antiwar protests reached an all-time high. They did not completely end until President Nixon began to withdraw American troops from Vietnam, almost three years later.

Watergate

Nixon's administration ended in a scandal over the misuse of presidential power. During the 1972 presidential campaign burglars had broken into Democratic headquarters in the Watergate office building in Washington, D.C. The burglars had tried to photograph documents and install listening devices.

In 1973 a Washington newspaper charged that this episode was the work of President Nixon's reelection campaign officials. The Senate set up a special committee to investigate the charges. The committee heard evidence that members of the White House staff had secretly used illegal funds to cover up the Watergate burglary. Finally it became clear that Nixon himself was implicated in the coverup. Impeachment proceedings began in the House of Representatives in 1974, but Nixon resigned from office before a vote was taken. The new president, Gerald Ford, pardoned Nixon for his wrongdoing.

Concern over nuclear power

In the 1970's and 1980's the issue of nuclear power aroused many protests in the United States. Much concern surrounded the buildup of nuclear weapons, as well as the spread of nuclear power stations. These power stations, which generated electricity with nuclear reactors, were thought to be unsafe. This concern was intensified in 1979, when an accident at the power station at Three Mile Island, in Pennsylvania, released radioactivity into the air. Some protesters against nuclear power advocated the use of alternative sources of energy, such as solar power or wind power.

Although these dissenters won few major victories, their concerns did affect American society. In particular, Americans became more aware of environmental and energy problems.

(*continued on page 772*)

The United States in transition

In an unusual occurrence, four Americans who served as president appeared together in November 1961 (center right, from left to right: John F. Kennedy, Lyndon B. Johnson, Dwight D. Eisenhower, and Harry S Truman). They and the Presidents who succeeded them had to deal with a variety of domestic and foreign issues during their years in office.

The late 1900's were years of change in the United States. Many Americans organized to seek reform in their society. Demands for civil rights for black Americans often took the form of peaceful marches, led by Dr. Martin Luther King, Jr. (opposite bottom). Women began to seek and get many jobs once held only by men (top right). The war in Vietnam and the use of nuclear power were other issues of concern, evoking wide disagreement among Americans (opposite top, left and right).

While dealing with these issues at home, the United States sought to maintain its strong leadership in world affairs. In 1978 President Jimmy Carter helped arrange the Camp David peace agreement between Israel and Egypt (bottom).

Changes in foreign policy

New policies in foreign affairs developed during the 1970's. In 1972, as you have read, President Nixon visited the People's Republic of China. His visit resulted in an improvement in relations between the United States and China.

Nixon also made an effort to keep on good terms with the Soviets. In May 1972 he became the first American president to visit the Soviet Union. At that time the two nations signed an arms control treaty and several agreements relating to environmental, health, and technological cooperation. The improvement in United States-Soviet relations was known as détente. It was continued by Presidents Ford and Carter through much of the 1970's.

In the late 1970's, however, strains began to show in the relationship between the two nations. The Soviets opposed American peacemaking efforts in the Middle East. The United States resented Soviet-Cuban intervention in Africa, primarily in the Angolan and Ethiopian civil wars.

In 1979, international terrorism became for the first time a major problem for United States foreign policy. The Carter administration appeared unable to secure the release of more than 50 Americans who had been taken hostage by Iranian militants. In the meantime, the Soviet Union invaded Afghanistan to boost the shaky communist government there. The United States retaliated against the Soviets by cutting trade ties and refusing to attend the 1980 Olympic Games in Moscow.

By the 1980's détente had come to an end. President Reagan, who accused the Soviets of worldwide aggression, increased United States defense spending. His administration gave financial assistance to anticommunist governments, regardless of their civil-rights records. The United States also blamed the Soviets for the imposition of martial law and for the continuing unrest in Central America.

By the mid-1980's the United States-Soviet relationship had deteriorated to such an extent that many people talked of a new Cold War. Finally, in an effort to remedy this situation, President Reagan and Soviet leader Mikhail Gorbachev held a summit meeting in Geneva in November 1985. Although the two leaders made little, if any, progress on substantive issues, people around the world were relieved that the leaders of the two superpowers were talking again.

1. IDENTIFY: SEATO, Great Society, recession, inflation, protectionism, McCarthy, NAACP, lobbying, King, Kent State University, Watergate.

2. Describe the foreign policy concerns of the Presidents after 1945.

3. What was the "conspiracy theory" and why did it develop?

4. What organizations, events, and legislation helped the civil rights movement to progress?

5. What issues caused political dissent during the 1960's and 1970's?

Canada became a vital area of the modern world

Canada was relatively isolated for many years before World War I, but was brought actively into world affairs by the two world wars. After World War II, Canada became a vigorous supporter of the United Nations and an important member of NATO. It loaned almost $4 billion to other countries after World War II and welcomed thousands of refugees from Europe.

Economic growth

Canada experienced considerable economic development after World War II. Much of the country remained basically agricultural. Production of crops such as wheat, barley, flax, and feed grains provided a surplus for export. During the 1960's and 1970's, world shortages brought large purchases by China and the Soviet Union. Most of the surplus disappeared.

Canada's industries also grew after World War II. The large Canadian forest areas provided many wood products. The wood pulp and paper industries expanded, with most of the paper sold to the United States. Development of electric power and improvement of transportation stimulated the mining of iron, coal, and uranium, and greater production of oil and gas. Aircraft, electrical, textile, and automobile industries developed in the provinces of Quebec and Ontario. Much of the capital for this industrial development was furnished by the United States.

Relations with the United States

For more than a century Canada has had a close relationship with the United States. During and after World War II this relationship was strengthened, especially in military and economic affairs.

Canadian national defense relied heavily on the United States. Together the two nations built a line of radar installations across the Arctic, called the Distant Early Warning (DEW) Line, to furnish early warnings against air attacks. They also established the North American Air Defense Command.

In 1959 close economic cooperation between Canada and the United States produced the St. Lawrence Seaway, a 2,400-mile (3,840-kilometer) waterway linking the Great Lakes and the Atlantic Ocean. The Seaway enables oceangoing ships to reach every port on the Great Lakes. Another important cooperative venture was the development of the Columbia River basin. This project doubled the water-storage capacity of the Pacific Northwest.

In the mid-1980's the United States bought more than two thirds of Canada's exports. Meanwhile, Canada was the largest importer of American goods. Yet the economic relationship between the two nations was sometimes difficult. Canadians were uneasy because many of their industries were owned or controlled by Americans, either as branches of American corporations or through large stock holdings. Canadians were also concerned because American industries near the Canadian border were emitting hazardous pollution into the atmosphere. The two countries had further disagreements about coastal fishing rights in the Pacific Northwest.

Separatism

Canada has, from early modern times, been the home of two different ethnic groups—Canadians of French descent and Canadians of British descent. In the province of Quebec, where French is the primary language, English- and French-speaking Canadians have lived side by side. Yet the French Canadians have remained essentially separate because of differences in language, religion, and traditions.

During the 1960's a French-Canadian separatist movement began to gather strength in Quebec. In 1968 Pierre Trudeau, a French Canadian, became prime minister of Canada. Trudeau supported bilingual programs and limited independence for the provinces. He did not approve, however, of separatism, or complete independence, for Quebec.

Quebec politics were being reshaped by three forces: urbanization, modernization, and secularization—the decreased role of religion in political and public affairs. As the society urbanized, the need for jobs became more pressing. Even moderate French-Canadians complained of job discrimination in government and industry. The ambitious French-speaking middle class demanded a greater share of economic and political control in Quebec. Meanwhile, French-Canadians looked to the state, not to the church, to help preserve French culture.

In 1976 the moderate Quebec Party gained control of the Quebec provincial government. The party proposed a language bill to make French the official language in public offices and schools. The bill was opposed by English-speaking Canadians. The Quebec Party then put the separatism issue to a vote by holding a referendum in 1980. By a 60-percent majority, the people of Quebec voted not to seek independence from Canada.

Yet it was clear that a restructuring of the relationship among the Canadian provinces and their people was necessary. This was especially so because some of the western provinces, which were rich in oil, wanted a greater share of governmental revenues.

In 1980, after a brief period out of office, Trudeau was reelected prime minister. He secured a new constitution that ended Canada's formal allegiance to Great Britain. The people of Quebec, however, felt that the constitution gave the provinces too few rights. They refused to sign the constitutional accord.

In the mid-1980's Canada had a conservative prime minister, Brian Mulroney. Mulroney was confronted with the continuing issue of separatism for Quebec and with severe unemployment, the highest since the depression of the 1930's.

3

Political conflicts occurred in many Latin American nations

Political developments in Latin America were more turbulent than those in the United States or Canada. Most Latin American countries experienced considerable conflict and change in the decades following World War II. The region's influence in world affairs was growing.

The Organization of American States

During and just after World War II, the nations of the Western Hemisphere entered into several mutual defense pacts. Inter-American cooperation went a step further in 1948, when delegates from 21 Western Hemisphere countries met at Bogotá, Colombia, and founded the Organization of American States (OAS). By 1986 the OAS had 31 members. Each member nation was represented on a policy-making council. The OAS met regularly at five-year intervals and also in special sessions from time to time. Each member nation agreed to consult the OAS before taking action against another member.

The founding of the OAS represented a continuation of the Good Neighbor Policy, through which the United States sought cooperation with its southern neighbors. This ideal, however, was not always achieved in the postwar era.

United States involvement

In the early 1950's the United States became heavily involved in Latin American politics. In Guatemala in 1954, for example, the United States intervened to help overthrow a leftist government. The Guatemalan government had passed a land-reform law permitting it to take over and redistribute unused land. Much of this land was owned by an American fruit-exporting company.

John Foster Dulles, the United States Secretary of State, was convinced that the Guatemalan government was controlled by communists. He was instrumental in gathering United States support for an opposition rebel group in Guatamala. The rebel group, with the assistance of American arms, was able to overthrow the Guatamalan president. The United Nations and the Organization of American States harshly criticized the United States for its role in the overthrow.

The United States became even more involved in Latin America in the 1960's, particularly in Cuba. (see pages 775-79). By the 1980's, the United States was also playing a complex and controversial role in the internal affairs of Nicaragua and El Salvador. President Reagan believed that the leftist leaders of Nicaragua, the Sandinistas, were trying to topple the government of El Salvador. Reagan wanted to send United States military assistance to anti-Sandinista rebels in Nicaragua. In the mid-1980's, the related issues of Nicaragua and El Salvador aroused heated debate in the United States.

Argentina

In Argentina, General Juan Perón came to power in the 1940's. Perón claimed to be a defender against foreign interference and a supporter of the labor movement. Perón was elected president by a huge majority in 1946. He depended greatly on the advice and assistance of his wife, Eva, a former film and radio star. Eva Perón had a keen understanding of the political uses of the mass media. The Peróns were able both to win the support of the people and to create an authoritarian regime that suppressed all political opposition.

During World War II, Argentina had profited from selling beef and wheat to the Allies. The Peróns used these profits to nationalize British-owned railways and utilities. The Perón regime reduced the cost of living for city dwellers. Other attempted reforms, however, did not improve the economy. The upper-class landowners did not want to cooperate with the Peróns. By the early 1950's, the Argentine economy was in trouble.

When Eva Perón died in 1952, her husband's popularity suffered. Finally the army overthrew him in 1955. A series of dictatorships followed, and Argentina remained politically divided for the next 18 years.

In 1972 Perón returned from exile, ran for the presidency, and was elected. His wife, Isabel Perón, was elected vice president. When Juan Perón died, his widow became the first woman to be president in the Americas.

Political and economic conditions in Argentina continued to deteriorate in the 1970's. Isabel Perón was overthrown in 1976. The military regime that succeeded her led the country into a costly war with Great Britain over the Falkland Islands in 1982. Human rights abuses were common in Argentina. Between 1976 and 1983, thousands of Argentinians either disappeared or were jailed and tortured to death for political reasons.

The Cuban Revolution

In 1959 a revolution in Cuba overthrew Fulgencio Batista, the dictator who had come to power in 1934. The revolution was led by Fidel Castro, who had fought a three-year guerrilla campaign. The Cuban Revolution was the greatest political upheaval Latin Americans had experienced since the Mexican Revolution of 1910.

Castro's revolutionary government immediately executed several hundred of Batista's officers and soldiers. The executions provoked worldwide criticism of the new leader.

Under Castro's openly communist regime, land reform was proclaimed. The government took over large holdings. Payment to the owners was determined according to values declared on the tax rolls. These values were much less than the land's real worth. American companies, which owned about 40 percent of the sugarlands in Cuba, were opposed to this measure.

The Castro regime caused major political disagreements in Cuba between the lower and upper classes. The lower class, which made up the majority of the population, supported Castro because his policies guaranteed jobs. Before the revolution, unemployment had exceeded 20 percent, and most workers had frequently been unemployed. Castro's government also showed a strong commitment to racial equality in a country where blacks and mulattoes accounted for more than 25 percent of the population. Improvements in welfare, education, and medical care also benefited the lower class.

On the other hand, many of these reforms angered the upper class. The government took over businesses and buildings. Employees ran newspapers that previously had been privately owned. People who had been associated with the Batista dictatorship fled the island. They were followed by increasing numbers of business leaders, land owners, professionals, and technicians. An armed revolt broke out against the Castro government, but it was unsuccessful.

The Bay of Pigs. In 1961 the Cuban government ordered the two American-owned oil refineries on the island to process fuel supplied by the Soviet Union. When the refineries refused, Cuba intervened in their operations. The United States responded by refusing to import sugar from Cuba. Left without a customer for its main product, Cuba offered to supply sugar to the Soviet Union in exchange for arms.

The United States government believed that the relationship between Castro and the Soviets was a threat to American national security. President John Kennedy, elected in 1960, continued President Eisenhower's policy of providing secret assistance to anti-Castro rebels. Accordingly, in 1961 Kennedy approved a landing in Cuba of rebels who had been secretly trained and equipped in the United States. The invasion, which took place at the Bay of Pigs, on Cuba's south shore, was a failure.

The Cuban missile crisis. Fidel Castro was convinced that the United States would attempt another invasion of Cuba. In 1962 American intelligence services learned that the Soviet Union was sending nuclear missiles to Cuba and building missile sites there. After a tense confrontation, Soviet leaders agreed to dismantle the bases and remove the missiles. The United States agreed not to invade Cuba.

Political developments in Latin America

Latin American countries were often dominated by leaders who inspired fierce popular loyalty. In many cases, these leaders first became well known as military officers. In Argentina, for example, a general, Juan Perón, was elected president in 1946. With the help of his wife, Eva, he established a strong dictatorship (above).

Another route to power was through revolution. In Cuba, Fidel Castro led an armed uprising and took over the government. Castro became an influential figure throughout Latin America. When a revolutionary government was elected in Chile, Castro came to speak to students, who greeted him warmly (below). Within a few years, however, the Chilean army overthrew this government. The president's palace was bombed, and tanks roamed the streets of Santiago, the capital (right).

The United States persuaded the Organization of American States to expel Cuba and to join in an economic boycott. Cuba began a long period of political and economic isolation from other hemispheric nations. Yet the Cuban missile crisis marked a turning point in the political affairs of a number of developing nations. During the next two decades revolutionaries in other countries, including Nicaragua, Angola, and Ethiopia, looked to Cuba, as well as to the Soviet Union, for military assistance.

The United States takes action

Cuba was not the only troubled nation in Latin America in the 1960's. Many countries experienced a shift toward the left. Many Latin American nations were disrupted by a series of coups and assassinations.

In the Dominican Republic, for example, the dictator Rafael Trujillo was assassinated in 1961. He was succeeded by Juan Bosch, the first democratically-elected president in that country in 38 years. Bosch was overthrown by the military in 1965. His followers, some of whom were communists, started an uprising to return him to power. For the first time in many years, the United States intervened openly in Latin America. President Johnson sent 400 marines to support the Dominican Republic's military regime.

The political events in the Dominican Republic made a lasting impression on leaders in other Latin American countries. They feared that the United States would not hesitate to intervene against governments whose policies it did not like.

The Alliance for Progress. United States involvement in Latin America was not always of a military nature. In 1961 President Kennedy announced a ten-year program aimed at improving the quality of life in Latin American nations. The "Alliance for Progress" focused on housing, education, sanitation, public services, and tax and land reforms. The United States and 20 Latin American countries participated in the program. The United States alone contributed about $10 billion to the Alliance in the 1960's.

Despite the large amount of financial assistance provided through the Alliance for Progress, most of the program's initial goals were never met. Much of the money fell into the hands of corrupt leaders and never reached the poor people for whom it was intended. By the early 1970's the Alliance for Progress came to an end, mainly because of funding cuts.

Brazil

Political unrest continued to grow throughout Latin America. It was often accompanied by economic chaos, as the example of Brazil illustrates. Brazil's president in the early 1960's was João Goulart (GOO·lahr), who was supported by a growing labor movement. Goulart's policies shifted income to the lower class. Wealthy Brazilians and foreign companies converted their profits into American dollars and deposited them in banks outside the country.

In 1964 the army overthrew Goulart and tried to save the economy. The military government forced wages down by setting a low minimum wage and by pressuring the labor unions. These policies shifted income to business owners. To encourage productivity, the government also made low-cost loans available to businesses. Foreign corporations were urged to reinvest in Brazil.

The economy grew so fast that it was widely hailed as the "Brazilian Miracle." The gains from this miracle, however, went mostly to the rich. In fact, most of the population was somewhat poorer than before, even though more family members took jobs and worked longer hours. In order to maintain its economic program, the government had to control elections, forbid strikes, and censor television and newspapers. The government also went heavily into debt. By the mid-1980's Brazil had a total foreign debt of $100 billion, the highest in the world.

Guerrilla warfare

The failure of reforms and the loss of democratic rights encouraged the development of guerrilla movements in Latin America. In many countries revolutionaries took up arms in remote rural areas, imitating Castro's campaign in Cuba. The most famous guerrilla leader was Ernesto "Che" Guevera, an Argentinian who had fought under Castro. Guevera led revolutionary groups throughout Latin America until his death in 1967 at the hands of the Bolivian army.

Guerrilla movements continued to operate in the 1970's and 1980's. As you know, the activities of such groups in El Salvador and Nicaragua were of direct concern to the United States.

Chile's elected revolutionaries

Chile was another Latin American country undergoing important governmental changes in the 1970's and 1980's. In Chile an alliance of the socialist and communist parties resulted in the election of Salvador Allende (ah·YEN·day) in 1970. With Allende as president, a Marxist government had come to power through peaceful means. Allende's administration quickly nationalized all American-owned copper mines. The companies were dissatisfied with the amount of compensation they received.

The Allende government then implemented an across-the-board wage increase, which raised incomes for people in the lower class. For a time the demand for goods increased, producing a business boom. The upper class, however, became fearful of the changes taking place and stopped investing in the economy.

The government became hard-pressed for funds. Foreign banks were reluctant to make loans to the government. Allende's treasury therefore printed more money to meet its needs. By 1972 inflation was creating hardships for all segments of the population. As the economy worsened, unrest and disillusionment spread.

Rebellion against Allende. In September 1973 a military rebellion broke out. Allende was killed and the army took power. The military government swiftly eliminated all forms of opposition. About 8,000 persons were executed, and thousands fled into exile. Many people believed that the United States had been involved in the overthrow and had provided funds for the anti-Allende forces. Widespread violence continued in Chile in the mid-1980's. The military regime showed no signs of liberalizing its policies.

Puerto Rico

Puerto Rico had been administered since 1898 from Washington, D.C. (see chapter 23). In the early 1930's Puerto Ricans under the leadership of Luis Muñoz Marín (mah·REEN) began to lobby for increased autonomy from the United States. In the 1940's, under pressure from Marín and the United Nations, the United States permitted Puerto Rico to draft a new constitution.

Puerto Rico's new status as a commonwealth was approved by Puerto Rican voters and the United States Congress in 1952. As a commonwealth, Puerto Rico was permitted certain tax advantages. As a result, the Puerto Rican economy developed very quickly over the next two decades. This growth depended on capital from the United States and on access to American markets.

Puerto Rico, however, had no real autonomy. During the 1970's economic growth began to slow down. Many Puerto Ricans, went to the United States to find jobs. In the 1980's many Puerto Ricans were demanding a new political status—either independence, statehood, or autonomy as a commonwealth.

Mexico

During the early years of the postwar period, Mexico appeared to be one of the most stable countries in Latin America. Its revolutionary party remained in control, functioning smoothly under a presidential system of government. Occasional political dissent was swiftly contained by the government.

Mexico faced economic problems, however, caused by inflation and a negative trade balance. To remedy these difficulties, the government in 1976 lowered the value of the currency and cut back its spending. Despite intensive governmental efforts, agricultural production failed to improve. The Mexican population was growing faster than the number of jobs. As a result, tens of thousands of Mexicans slipped illegally into the United States each year to look for jobs. The issue of illegal immigrants troubled United States-Mexican relations in the 1980's. President Reagan attempted to reduce the tension by easing restrictions on immigration to the United States.

Mexico's future seemed promising with the discovery of huge oil reserves in the 1970's. By the mid-1980's, however, Mexico was affected by the worldwide slump in oil prices. The nation was also heavily in debt, and its economy was further damaged when a tremendous earthquake ravaged Mexico City in late 1985. The government was faced with rebuilding the shattered capital and providing for the 50,000 persons left homeless by the earthquake.

Continuing political change

In the late 1970's and early 1980's many Latin American nations showed signs of entering a more democratic period. The United States encouraged this trend. Under the administration of Jimmy Carter, military regimes in Latin America were no longer guaranteed support.

In addition, the United States negotiated a new treaty to gradually turn over control of the Panama Canal to Panama by the year 2000. This had been the desire of the Panamanians since the original 1903 treaty (see page 583). These new policies were taken as a sign of more open dealing by the United States.

On the other hand, Latin America nations were suspicious of American intentions regarding Nicaragua. In that country Sandinista revolutionaries had overthrown Anastasio Somoza, Jr., a dictator who had been backed by the United States for 30 years. The United States then attempted to influence the overthrow of the Sandinista government.

Meanwhile all over Latin America dictatorships were giving way to democratically elected governments. In January 1986 Guatemalans voted for their leaders for the first time in 15 years. The following month, in Haiti, the 30-year-old dynasty of the Duvalier family came to an end. Only the nations of Surinam, Guyana, Chile, and Paraguay still had authoritarian governments in early 1986.

CHECKUP

1. IDENTIFY: OAS, Sandinistas, Juan Perón, Eva Perón, Isabel Perón, Castro, Bay of Pigs, Cuban missile crisis, Alliance for Progress, Guevara, Allende, Somoza, Duvalier.

2. How was the United States politically involved in Guatemala in the 1950's? in El Salvador and Nicaragua in the 1980's?

3. What were the results of the Cuban Revolution?

4. What was the "Brazilian Miracle"? How was it achieved?

4

Latin America experienced dramatic changes

The countries of Latin America underwent enormous changes after World War II. Once relatively unimportant in world affairs and economically backward, Latin America became a focus of world attention. Its growing population, the discovery of vast petroleum deposits and other resources, and its rapid industrialization increased its importance to the rest of the world.

Since achieving independence in the early 1800's, most Latin American societies had followed traditional social and economic patterns. After 1945, however, Latin America seemed to be not merely catching up with the industrialized world, but creating its own patterns.

Rapid population growth

The most important change in Latin America after World War II was the sudden surge in population. In 1940 the total population of Latin America was about 126 million. By 1984 it was estimated at 398 million.

The cause of this surge in population was a decline in the death rate. Public measures, such as insecticide sprays against malaria-carrying mosquitoes, were initiated. These sprays reduced the number of deaths from malaria each year. Most significant was the decline in the death rate of children and infants. More children survived their first years of life and went on to adulthood and to have children of their own.

Rapid population growth had enormous consequences for Latin America. Birthrates were highest in rural regions. Land was unequally divided, and in some areas was in short supply. More and more people had no land at all or too little to support a family. Therefore they moved to the cities.

The growth of cities

Cities exercised a powerful attraction of their own. Most of the available social services, schools, and popular entertainments were concentrated there. The populations of cities grew twice as fast as the general population rate. In 1940, approximately 16 million Latin Americans lived in various cities of more than 100,000 inhabitants. By 1980, about 150 million were living in cities of that size.

City and national governments had to deal with complex administrative problems. The new city dwellers, for example, required transportation, a water supply, and sewage removal. Sewer lines, water mains, and electric lines had to be built. Large investments had to be made in road building, public buses, and even subway systems. The heavy machinery and other equipment for all of these building projects was not available in most Latin American countries. It had to be imported, creating a financial burden on the economy.

Many other problems arose in connection with the growth of cities. Most cities had a severe shortage of housing. The governments, with so many other new expenses, could not afford to build public housing for the expanded city population. Most of the rural migrants received wages too low to afford any housing. They therefore "squatted" on steep hillsides, tidal flats, and even garbage dumps that were publicly owned. In the poorest cities of Latin America, as many as half the inhabitants became squatters.

The expanded urban population also required a reliable food supply. Up until the 1940's commercial agriculture had been designed to supply overseas markets. The supply of food for the cities came from small farmers who sold off their surpluses when they had any to spare. With the growth of cities, however, many Latin American countries needed to import food.

New political forces

Most of the constitutions of Latin American countries allowed only literate persons to vote. As they moved to the cities, people were more likely to gain some schooling or learn to read. Thus, the lower class, able to read and therefore to vote, suddenly acquired political importance.

The votes of rural workers had always been controlled by the large landowners, through the bonds of loyalty or fear. These pressures did not exist in the cities. Now, for the first time, politicians had to appeal to a large mass of people to gain votes.

Women had gained the right to vote in a few Latin American countries in the 1930's. However, it was not until the mid-1950's that women were given the right to vote throughout the region. Thus their votes also increased the electorate.

Labor also became a force of political power in postwar Latin America. As employment in factories increased, labor organizing spread and the union movement grew stronger. Governments sensed a danger in allowing unions to grow on their own. Therefore, government leaders followed the policy, begun in the 1930's, of attempting to control the unions. The unions continued to gain strength, however, especially through political parties that represented their interests.

Another active political force was religion. More than 90 percent of Latin Americans were Catholics. In the past, the Catholic Church had represented conservative ideas in Latin American society and in politics. At the same time, the Church's concern for the poor and uneducated was an important tradition in many countries. Now the Church's leaders began to take stands on the political issues of welfare and human rights.

The Church's stand on such issues placed it in opposition to government and military leaders and to members of the upper and middle classes. These dominant elements of Latin American society thought of the growing urban class as a danger. They resisted social reforms and the labor movement as threats to order and the existing political system.

Problems of economic development

During World War II, Latin America had provided vast quantities of raw materials and food to the Allies. After the war Latin American nations found it difficult to stabilize their economies. They continued to supply a few unfinished goods to the industrialized countries. However, demand for their agricultural products and raw materials was not growing fast enough. Meanwhile the list of goods that Latin America needed to import was growing longer.

Most political leaders in Latin America believed economic development was the key to resolving the region's problems. Economic development would provide jobs for the increased population. Industrialization would lessen the

Social change in Latin America

In contemporary Latin America, powerful contrasts exist between tradition and change, between rapid economic development and grinding poverty. The traditional force of Catholicism remains powerful throughout Central and South America. When Pope John Paul II visited there in 1979, he was greeted with an enormous outpouring of emotion (left). Yet the most modern influences are also evident. The nation of Brazil built an entirely new capital city, Brasilia (bottom), in the center of its vast interior lands. Its gleaming buildings display the most modern architecture and planning. There are, however, large sections of the continent's population on whom modernization has had little effect. Raised in poverty, these children in the slums of Santiago, Chile (below), are untouched by the rapid changes taking place around them.

country's dependence on foreign sources for vital manufactured goods and would provide consumer goods for everyone. In every country, the drive for economic development became a major government project.

Foreign corporations and manufacturers were invited to establish businesses in Latin America. It was believed their investments and technology would help to get factories started. Since foreign participation would bring in machinery and capital, it seemed to be the cheapest and most rapid way to promote economic development.

The relations between the foreign-owned businesses, known as **multinational corporations,** and their host countries soon became a major political issue. Latin Americans began to resent the foreign ownership of important factories. In addition, the foreign-owned companies were relatively independent of government control. However, they were able to influence governments through political contributions. Attempts by the governments to control the flow of profits out of the country were generally futile.

Industrialization to reduce imports

Between 1956 and 1960, Brazil's president became a leading supporter of a new economic policy known as **import substitution.** This came to be one of the few political programs on which most Latin Americans could agree. Under import substitution, the list of goods that a country imported would be examined to find those items that could be produced inside the country. The government would then grant various kinds of favors to encourage manufacturers to produce these items. Tariffs or quotas would be set to discourage or prevent importation of similar goods. This would give the native industries a chance to develop.

Import substitution worked fairly well in the largest countries—Brazil, Mexico, and Argentina. Their markets and resources were big enough to accomplish the task. By the early 1960's these countries were able to produce steel, heavy machinery, automobiles, pharmaceuticals, and many other consumer goods. This represented 20 percent of the national output of all goods and services. Some other countries of Latin America, such as Venezuela, Chile, Colombia, Peru, and

Uruguay, experienced lesser but significant rates of development.

By the mid-1980's all the easier substitutions of imports had been made. Many other problems could not be resolved quickly. Refrigerators and washing machines and other expensive consumer products could be bought only by the wealthy. Meanwhile many people could barely afford to buy enough food, or "luxuries" such as toothbrushes and shoes. Many of the new factories producing these products were therefore running at half capacity due to lack of demand for their output.

Recent economic developments

In the postwar years, Latin American countries attempted new forms of economic association. Their aim was to lessen dependence on industrialized countries and to cooperate in areas of production, tariffs, and trade. The Andean Pact, begun in 1969, had some success in meeting these goals. It restricted foreign investment and encouraged both lower tariffs and economic cooperation within Latin America.

Latin American influence also grew in other parts of the world. Trade with other decolonized nations in Africa and Asia increased. The countries of Latin America took leading roles in political and economic world forums. They expressed positions that were no longer aligned with the United States, but were closer to the countries of Africa and Asia.

During the mid-1980's Latin Americans still felt hindered by their dependence on the more developed countries. Yet at the same time they were closing the gap between themselves and the industrialized world.

CHECKUP

1. IDENTIFY: multinational corporations, import substitution, Andean Pact.

2. What problems arose as a result of the growth of Latin American cities?

3. Briefly describe three new political forces that emerged in Latin America in the postwar years.

4. Why were foreign corporations encouraged to establish businesses in Latin America? Why did their participation become a political issue?

CHAPTER REVIEW

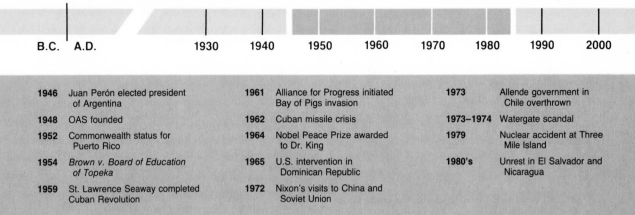

| B.C. | A.D. | 1930 | 1940 | 1950 | 1960 | 1970 | 1980 | 1990 | 2000 |

1946	Juan Perón elected president of Argentina
1948	OAS founded
1952	Commonwealth status for Puerto Rico
1954	*Brown v. Board of Education of Topeka*
1959	St. Lawrence Seaway completed Cuban Revolution
1961	Alliance for Progress initiated Bay of Pigs invasion
1962	Cuban missile crisis
1964	Nobel Peace Prize awarded to Dr. King
1965	U.S. intervention in Dominican Republic
1972	Nixon's visits to China and Soviet Union
1973	Allende government in Chile overthrown
1973–1974	Watergate scandal
1979	Nuclear accident at Three Mile Island
1980's	Unrest in El Salvador and Nicaragua

CHAPTER SUMMARY

In the years after World War II there was a continuity of policies by the Presidents of the United States. The main aim in foreign policy was to resist the spread of communism. During the 1970's efforts were made to reduce tensions between the United States and the Soviet Union and replace them with détente. In the 1980's, however, renewed communist activity outside the Soviet Union again became a major concern.

The American economy reached new peaks of productivity, but poverty, recessions, inflation, and the government's deficit were serious problems. In the early 1950's Senator McCarthy won many followers, but was quickly discredited. The Supreme Court's school desegregation decision led to increased demands for civil rights. Americans also expressed their concern over American involvement in Vietnam and the use of nuclear energy. The Watergate scandal over the misuse of Presidential power resulted in President Nixon's resignation.

Canada enjoyed a manufacturing and mining boom after 1945. The Canadians feared being too economically dependent on the United States. The trade balance with the United States was a major concern, but a strong separatist movement among French Canadians was even more serious.

Many countries in Latin America were controlled by dictators or the military. In Cuba, Castro set up a communist regime. Soviet aid to Cuba brought a grave Soviet–United States confrontation in 1962. In 1965 the United States became openly involved in Latin American affairs when President Johnson sent marines to the Dominican Republic. Allende, elected president of Chile, worked to establish a Marxist state but was overthrown by military forces.

The rapid increase in population and growth of the cities changed traditional Latin American society. The lower classes in the cities, women, and labor all emerged as new political forces. The role of foreign-owned corporations in Latin America became a major political issue. Attempts to reduce imports and efforts at economic cooperation were among the steps taken to reduce Latin America's dependence on more developed countries.

CHECKING WHAT YOU KNOW

1. Match each leader at the left with a country at the right. You may use a country more than once but use each country at least once.

   a. Allende   1. Brazil
   b. Castro   2. Canada
   c. Goulart   3. Chile
   d. Perón   4. Dominican Republic
   e. Trudeau   5. Cuba
   f. Batista   6. Nicaragua
   g. Trujillo   7. Argentina
   h. Somoza

2. What economic problems did the United States face in the 1970's? What policies sought to reduce these problems? How successful were they?

3. What was the Watergate scandal? What were the results of Watergate?

783

4. What ties do the United States and Canada have in economic and military affairs?

5. What were the causes of the population increase in Latin America? What were the consequences of this rapid population growth?

6. Why did Latin American nations feel that economic development was necessary? What efforts did they make to achieve it?

PRACTICING YOUR SKILLS

1. **Drawing a graph.** The following figures show the declining buying power of the dollar since the start of World War II.

Year	Value of the dollar
1939	$1.00
1942	.85
1952	.52
1962	.46
1972	.33
1982	.15

On a sheet of paper, present this information in a bar graph and think of an appropriate title for your graph. How much has the dollar declined in your own lifetime? Using what you have learned in this chapter, what factors might account for such a drop?

2. **Using maps.** Turn to the map of North America on page 812. How many miles separate Cuba from the United States? How many kilometers? What effect might the presence of a communist government in Cuba have on United States policy toward Latin America?

3. **Analyzing quotations.** Read the following quotation from President Reagan's 1980 inaugural address, and answer the questions that follow.

. . . government is not the solution to our problems; government is the problem. . . . It's not my intention to do away with government. It is rather to make it work—work with us, not over us. . . .

Based on this quote, does Reagan think government has assumed too much or too little power? Explain. Using your knowledge of current events, how did Reagan seek to redefine the role of the federal government?

RELATING PAST TO PRESENT

1. World Wars I and II united Canada and the United States against a common enemy. Cooperation between the two nations continued after 1945. Using information in the textbook and recent articles in the news, identify some of the ways in which Canada and the United States work together today. What actions might be taken to strengthen our ties with Canada?

2. As you read in this chapter, political affairs in many Central American countries were unsettled after 1945. Choose one of the Central American countries and use the *Readers' Guide to Periodical Literature* to find articles on recent developments there. How have changes in Central America affected American foreign policy?

INVESTIGATING FURTHER

1. Conflict between English- and French-speaking Canadians has occasionally been tense. Prepare a report on the background of the differences between the two cultural groups in Canada. Also report on recent moods and moves for separatism. Consult the *Readers' Guide to Periodical Literature* for articles on these topics.

2. Although the Brazilian economy grew rapidly in the 1960's and 1970's, many Brazilians still lived in poverty in large slums at the edges of cities. Find out about living conditions in the slums. You might read Carolina de Jesus, *Child of the Dark* (New American Library). Why don't the people of the slums trust the government? How is Carolina different from most people in the slums?

3. Select a country in Latin America and prepare a report on the positive and negative effects of foreign-owned corporations there. You may use the *Readers' Guide to Periodical Literature* to locate articles on this topic.

CHAPTER

(1945 to the Present)

32

The Modern World Faced the Challenge of Rapid Change

The years following 1945 were marked by vast changes in the way people lived and in their attitudes toward the world around them. The shocks of World War II, with its millions of casualties, remained. The threat of total destruction by nuclear weapons hung over everyone. No one escaped this fear because the world was much more closely united. A hydrogen bomb could kill millions, and a war of hydrogen bombs would destroy most of the world's population.

The world was more united, also, because communications had become so much faster. Since the early 1900's, telephone and radio had allowed voices to travel instantly around the globe. After 1945 pictures could move just as quickly, thanks to television. People could see what was happening thousands of miles away, at the moment it was happening. Television coverage of the Vietnam War shaped public opinion in the United States and eventually helped turn Americans against the war. People the world over were thrilled when they watched the first human being walk on the moon. The Olympic Games became truly a world event, as families sat at home and cheered the participants. When the space shuttle *Challenger* exploded shortly after liftoff on January 28, 1986, millions of horrified viewers were watching on television.

Thus, developments in one country could have effects far away. Attitudes and behavior could be shaped across great distances. When describing

Launching of the space shuttle Columbia

785

social change and new attitudes in the years after 1945, one could speak, for the first time in history, of worldwide shifts. Many developments were, of course, limited to certain countries, or took different forms in different countries. Nevertheless, it was possible to see general trends.

THE CHAPTER SECTIONS

1. Technological change affected ideas and behavior

2. The arts and literature followed new directions

3. Patterns of living took new forms

Technological change affected ideas and behavior

Dramatic advances in technology affected all the nations of the world. Industrialized societies felt the effects most directly. Developing nations in the Third World also were changed by the inventions and new devices that spread throughout the world.

It would be impossible to list all the discoveries and applications of new ideas that affected the way people thought or lived after 1945. However, a look at some of the most spectacular will indicate the range and importance of the advances that took place in only about 40 years.

Air travel

Improvements in air travel transformed communications among people. Passenger airliners became both larger and faster. In the 1970's the so-called jumbo jet became a common means of transportation. These giant airplanes could carry over 350 passengers in full comfort. A jumbo jet could carry more cargo in one year than could all the airliners in the world in 1939.

The jumbo jet could also fly much farther and faster. A journey by air from London to New York in 1945 took at least 15 hours. This trip included a stop because the plane could not fly more than 2,000 miles (3,200 kilometers) without refueling. In 1986 a regular jet airliner could complete the trip in less than six hours. The *Con-*

corde, an airliner developed by the British and the French, cut the trip to three hours.

The ease of movement enabled millions of people to fly distances that few would have imagined in the 1940's. In 1986 Chicago's O'Hare Airport, the busiest in the world, served almost 80 million passengers.

Space exploration

Engineers had experimented with rockets, which could fly at enormous speeds, in the 1930's and 1940's. Finally, in 1957, Soviet engineers developed one that could fly fast enough to break out of the earth's gravitational pull. The Soviet rocket placed a small artificial satellite, called *Sputnik,* into orbit around the earth. In 1959 the Soviets crashed a rocket into the moon. In 1961 they built one with enough power to put a person in orbit around the earth. The United States responded with its own huge program for space exploration. In 1969 this effort succeeded in transporting two American astronauts to the moon.

The main results of space exploration in the 1970's came from unmanned spacecraft. Orbiting satellites transmitted television, telephone, and radio signals around the earth, vastly improving communication. Orbiting cameras transformed weather forecasting. The American *Voyager* spacecraft provided important new information about the makeup of other planets.

A new phase of space exploration began with the launch of the first space shuttle, *Columbia,* in 1981. By 1986 reusable shuttles, which contained elements of both the traditional space capsule and the airplane, had completed two dozen successful missions. Early that year, however, the explosion of the shuttle *Challenger* and the loss of its crew temporarily halted the human exploration of space.

Miniaturization

Rockets can lift only limited weights. Therefore, to be sent into space, equipment had to be made as light and as compact as possible. An important consequence of space exploration was the invention of ways of making machines, especially electrical equipment, smaller. This process is called miniaturization.

The most useful device in the process of miniaturization is the transistor. This tiny electronic device, invented in 1948, can do the work that previously had to be done by a much larger vacuum tube. Entire electronic circuits, consisting of transistors, can fit into smaller spaces and use less electricity than a single vacuum tube.

Miniaturization made possible dozens of new products. Portable radios, pocket calculators, digital watches, compact tape recorders, and automatic cameras were developed. These, in turn, affected the lives and leisure activities of people throughout the world.

Computers

The most remarkable product of miniaturization was the modern computer. In the 1600's, the French scientist Blaise Pascal had invented a machine that could perform arithmetical calculations. The idea intrigued scientists and engineers for the next 300 years. However, the necessary machinery was too large and cumbersome to have many applications.

It was not until the 1950's that machines capable of storing and processing information quickly and compactly were developed. These computers rapidly made an impact on society and were improved from year to year. They not only operated ever more quickly, but they required a smaller and smaller amount of space to store gigantic amounts of information.

By the mid-1980's computers performed many varied functions. They guided the flights of spacecraft and recorded every airline reservation in the world. They drew maps, kept accounts, and printed newspapers. Computers also played games with children, controlled the flow of fuel to a car's engine and solved complex mathematical questions. Problems in every field could be tackled that would have been considered impossible 40 years earlier.

Lasers

In 1960 a device called a laser was invented. It could store energy and release it all at once in an intense beam of light. This beam remained

connections

Postal Service

This block of stamps was issued by the U.S. Postal Service when the space shuttle *Columbia* made its first flight in May 1981. The four large stamps in the center show various phases of the mission. Around the center are stamps showing the first moon landing in 1969, *Pioneer* surveying the planets, and *Skylab* studying the sun. On the lower right is the space telescope that was launched in 1985.

Although letters have been stamped only since 1847, there has been mail service in the United States since 1639. Stage coaches, the Pony Express, and trains carried mail during various times in our history. Today most mail is sent by airplane.

In Europe carrier service goes back to the Roman Empire. The magnificent Roman roads were used to get messages from the

provinces to the capital. The English postal service has been operating since the 1600's, when it took over the routes of the royal mail.

Over 2,000 years earlier the Greek historian Herodotus described the Persian mail service of Cyrus the Great, saying, "There is no mortal thing faster than these messengers." Marco Polo encountered a series of postal stations in China around 1300 A.D. At the same time the Aztecs in Mexico had relay stations and runners to carry the news between villages.

Mail has been getting through for a long time. Perhaps in the next century it will travel to the moon.

straight, narrow, and very concentrated, even after it had traveled millions of miles. Its uses were extraordinarily varied—a perfect example of the combination of scientific discovery and engineering applications. Lasers were used in surgery to weld damaged tissue in the eye, to burn away skin growths, and to repair decayed parts of teeth. They were used to measure distances. A mirror placed on the moon by the Americans who landed there allowed scientists to calculate the distance to the moon more accurately than ever before.

Lasers helped engineers make tunnels and pipelines straight. They enabled manufacturers to cut precisely into hard substances, such as diamonds. Lasers also transmitted radio, television, and telephone signals. They made it possible to show three-dimensional pictures on a television or film screen. Thus one invention had effects in dozens of activities.

Genetic research

In 1962 the Nobel Prize in medicine, the most honored scientific award in the world, was given to an American and two British scientists. What they had discovered, in the 1950's, was the structure of DNA (deoxyribonucleic acid), an essential component of genes. As you read in Chapter 21, genes are the small units of chromosomes that convey characteristics, such as color of hair and eyes, from parent to child. By understanding DNA, one can understand how a gene is structured—what scientists call the "genetic code."

By unraveling the genetic code, the experimenters with DNA came closer to explaining how different life forms are created. This breakthrough made possible new research into viruses, bacteria, human cells, and diseases such as cancer. Scientists found it possible to reproduce life forms in the laboratory. Major advances in treating illness were anticipated.

The atom

Just as biologists were able to probe inside the cell, physical scientists became more knowledgeable about the smallest of nature's building blocks, the atom. With ever more powerful instruments, tiny particles within the atom could now be examined. As a result of these studies, it became possible to use the enormous energy released when the structure of the atom is altered.

Atomic energy was used to build more powerful bombs. It was also used to develop efficient generators that produce electricity. Even peaceful uses, however, had their dangers. Whenever atomic energy is tapped, dangerous radiation, known as radioactivity, is released. When carefully controlled, radioactivity can have medical uses—for example, in the treatment of cancer. However, it can also alter genes and kill life forms. Thus the advances in understanding the atom offered both benefits and dangers.

Plastics

The first synthetic substances—substances that do not occur in nature—were developed by chemists in laboratories in the 1800's. A few of these substances began to have wide applications. For example, celluloid was used to make movie films, and bakelite was used for electrical equipment. It was not until after 1945, however, that these substances, called plastics, began to appear in every area of life. By the mid-1960's, for example, there was more synthetic rubber than natural rubber in the world.

Plastics became an essential part of daily existence. They were used to equip and furnish kitchens. They changed the way buildings were constructed and affected the manufacture of objects from toys to cars. They completely altered the appearance as well as the manufacture of most of the things people use every day, from toothbrushes to telephones. Synthetic fibers were woven into easy-care fabrics for clothing, upholstery, and many other uses.

Many plastics were made from oil products. The production of plastics, therefore, depended on the unpredictable nature of international oil prices. Nevertheless, plastics continued to be essential to modern life in the 1980's.

Antibiotics

As you have read, Alexander Fleming discovered penicillin in 1928. Penicillin stopped the growth of disease-carrying bacteria. Thus it could help cure illnesses caused by these bacteria. In the years

Technology and its applications

In the years after 1945 machines and technology revolutionized almost every activity on earth. In the fertile Kashmir valley in India, women still planted rice by hand as they had done for countless generations (below). However, improved seed and fertilizer greatly increased food production.

Engineers and scientists changed the nature of hundreds of research and manufacturing tasks. The level of water under the ground—known as the water table—could be measured constantly by an electronic "map" (bottom right). Surgery could be performed with the ray of light produced by a laser (right). And as space exploration continued, the rockets had to be prepared for flight in dust-free "super clean" laboratories (bottom left).

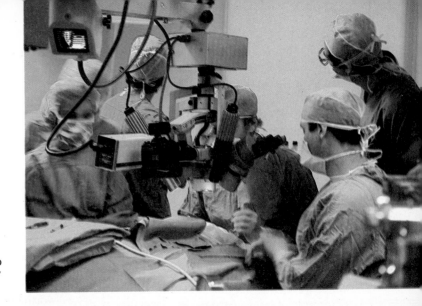

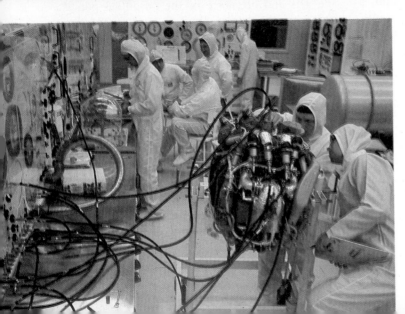

after Fleming's discovery, other substances were discovered to have similar effects. Streptomycin, which was discovered in 1944, attacked bacteria that could resist penicillin. All of these substances are called **antibiotics,** and after 1945 they transformed the fight against disease. They cured certain illnesses, such as tuberculosis, that previously could not be treated, and they made surgery safer from infections. Antibiotics were also used to improve the health of animals that are used for food. Although some bacteria came to resist antibiotics, these substances became essential in reducing sicknesses and providing more food.

The "Green Revolution"

As a result of intensive research, scientists in the 1960's discovered ways of producing seeds that yielded much more rice and wheat than ever before. The new seeds were also improved by the use of better fertilizers and by advances in the techniques of irrigation.

The ability to feed large numbers of people became increasingly critical as the world's population grew, reaching almost 5 billion by 1986. Unfortunately, most of the fastest-growing countries were also the poorest and the least able to feed themselves. In the 1980's, for example, Ethiopia was unable to cope with the long period of drought and famine that plagued the country, and millions of people starved to death.

Other developments since 1945

These are only ten of the most spectacular developments that have taken place since 1945. The list does not mention the conquest of polio, a crippling disease that killed or permanently disabled many children. It does not touch on the development of personal computers, video-cassette recorders, and compact discs.

Many other breakthroughs have occurred. Human organs, including the heart, have been successfully transplanted. An artificial heart has also been developed. The invention of xerography, or electrostatic copying, has made office work easier and has streamlined the dissemination of information. New technologies may soon make it possible to fly from Washington, D.C., to Tokyo, Japan, in two hours.

Commercial applications

Some of the inventions or discoveries mentioned here took place before 1945. What was so remarkable in the period since then was their widespread application. Entire new industries, such as television manufacturing, sprang up. Millions of people were employed in new kinds of jobs.

Devices such as telephones, radios, refrigerators, and cameras had been known before 1945. However, only after 1945 were they manufactured cheaply enough to be bought by millions of people. These products are more common in the industrialized nations, but they have also had an enormous impact on Third World countries. Technological advances have transformed the world since 1945.

CHECKUP

1. IDENTIFY: jumbo jet, *Sputnik, Concorde, Columbia, Challenger,* transistors, lasers, DNA, antibiotics, Green Revolution, xerography.

2. Define miniaturization. Give examples of new products made possible by miniaturization.

3. List three technological advances that have taken place since 1945. Explain the importance of each.

4. How can technology be both a benefit and a burden?

The arts and literature followed new directions

Two characteristics were particularly noticeable in the arts and literature of the post-1945 period. One was the commitment to experimentation, which had been visible throughout the 1900's. The other was the enormous popular interest in artistic and intellectual developments.

Painting and sculpture

In the years after 1945, the liveliest center of new ideas and styles in painting was New York. During this period the dominant style of painting was **abstract expressionism.**

The leading abstract expressionist was an American, Jackson Pollock. Pollock felt that the form, colors, and shapes of a painting were its most important features. A painting did not have to show recognizable objects; therefore it was abstract. At the same time, it had to reflect the nature of the artist who was expressing feelings or ideas in paint. Pollock chose to express himself by laying a canvas on the floor and randomly dripping different colors of paint onto its surface. When the paint dried, his painting was finished.

Other abstract expressionists used different techniques. Mark Rothko, also an American, created large areas of rich colors. They blurred into one another, creating a dazzling effect.

In the 1950's, painters moved away from abstract expressionism to experiment in other ways. It was no longer possible to speak of one dominant style. In Great Britain and the United States, a number of artists returned to showing reality, but of a special kind. Developing a style called **Pop Art,** these artists painted popular objects, such as soup cans, pictures from comic books, or flags.

An interest in experimentation could also be seen in the sculpture of the period. The American sculptor Louise Nevelson, for example, created monumental designs out of "found" objects, such as wooden boxes.

New styles of painting arose in the 1960's. One group concentrated on **Op Art**—the use of optical effects. These artists rejected reality as the subject of paintings, instead using brilliant colors and shapes. They, too, were only one small group. Another group, the "hard-edge" school, produced bright stripes and slabs of color with well-defined edges.

In the 1970's and 1980's a return to realism in paintings of scenes, objects, and people took place. Experiments continued, however, and all styles seemed acceptable in the art world.

Architecture

The same search for new ideas and techniques dominated architecture, as it had since the invention of the skyscraper in the early 1900's. Materials changed almost from year to year.

One of the new characteristics of architecture was the use of rough-cast concrete. This mixture contained pebbles and created a grainy, rough finish. A pioneer in the use of this technique was the French architect Le Corbusier, one of the most influential architects of the century. Between 1946 and 1952, Le Corbusier built an enormous apartment complex in Marseille, France, using rough-cast concrete.

The opposite effect, smoothness and polish, also interested architects. They created this smoother finish mainly by the use of huge walls of glass. Le Corbusier himself took this approach when he designed the headquarters of the United Nations in New York City. One of its buildings has two enormous walls of glass, with narrow walls of solid concrete at either end. The Lever House in New York, completed in 1952, set the pattern for a wave of skyscrapers sheathed in glass and supported on the inside by steel and reinforced concrete.

Architects also experimented with new ways of building houses. Some were cast in concrete in standard units and then shipped to the site. Others made use of new plastic materials.

There were also experiments with shapes. Notable among these unusual buildings was the group of concrete shells that make up the Sydney Opera House in Australia. The narrowing cone of the Guggenheim Museum in New York City, designed by the American architect Frank Lloyd Wright, is another building of unconventional shape. Amid all these new ideas and techniques, no single form or method of building dominated architecture in the years after 1945.

Music and dance

Experimentation was equally apparent in the world of music. The use of instruments, rhythm, harmony, and melody was new and constantly changing. Some composers, however, did write traditional types of music. The British composer Benjamin Britten, for example, wrote operas. The Russian composer Dimitri Shostakovich wrote symphonies divided into four distinct movements, which had been the form since the late 1700's.

After 1945 new kinds of sound entered the world of serious music. Experiments with computers revealed that they could produce sounds. Innovative composers wrote pieces for special machines known as synthesizers or for combinations of traditional instruments and machines.

Sydney Opera House

Like a ship with its sails set for the future, the Opera House dominates the harbor in Sydney, Australia. Built out on a peninsula, the building is a series of concrete shells that house a center for the performing arts.

Geographically an Asian country, Australia has an English heritage strongly influenced by its isolation from Europe. Australia has also taken in many European refugees who have helped to make its culture more international.

Thus, when the Australian government decided to build a center to celebrate the arts, it sponsored a worldwide competition to choose its architect. Joern Utzon, a Dane, was the winner. His building rests on a high platform, and the shells rise more than 200 feet (60 meters) above ground level. It contains four theaters, each acoustically perfect for the type of performance held. There is a concert hall, an opera theater, a drama theater, and a chamber music and film hall. Completed in 1973, the Sydney Opera House is today considered one of the modern world's outstanding buildings.

Composers also began to write music that gave performers a major role in determining how a piece would sound. The composer might provide a few notes and some instructions. Then the performer could decide the order, the length, and the mood of a composition. The pioneer of these methods was an American composer, John Cage.

The determination to break new ground, to leave the past behind, was also obvious in popular music. During the 1950's a form was created in the United States known as rock-and-roll. It had a heavy, accented beat and a simple, repetitive melody. A number of different styles, with such names as folk rock, hard rock, punk rock, and disco, soon developed. Another form of popular music, country and western music, usually consisted of simple and sentimental ballads. Black musicians developed such styles as soul music and rhythm and blues.

These musical forms spread rapidly throughout the world, especially among teenagers. A new song quickly became as familiar to the young in Indonesia as in Indiana. The most successful performers, such as the British singing group the Beatles, became world famous.

The world of dance headed in new directions after 1945. Ballet was especially influenced by artists who had left Russia after its revolution. The greatest of these was George Balanchine. He continued in the United States the traditions that had made Russia a remarkable center of ballet in the 1800's and 1900's. Balanchine was joined in the 1960's and 1970's by young ballet stars who came from the Soviet Union to make their careers in the West.

Ballet after 1945 was much influenced by the freer and looser forms of modern dance. The most influential teacher of modern dance was the American Martha Graham. She collaborated with ballet dancers in trying to combine the two forms. More modern music was used to accompany the dancers, forcing performances to change. As in all the performing arts, the tendency was to leave uniformity behind, to experiment, and to allow more individual expression.

Film

Traditional subjects—adventure stories, comedies, and social dramas—dominated most filmmaking after 1945. Spectacular productions, costing millions of dollars, continued to appear. In other films, however, there were efforts to break free of traditional restrictions. A group of Italian directors produced shattering attacks on social and political injustice in the 1940's and 1950's. French filmmakers known as the "New Wave" created experimental movies in the 1950's and 1960's. They rejected traditional story-telling techniques and created instead a mysterious and powerful atmosphere in their films. The Japanese director Akira Kurosawa produced films that used violence and psychological insight to create startling new effects.

In the American film industry, a number of directors turned their attention to ordinary people in the cities and to changing patterns in family life. Technical mastery was particularly evident in American films. Nevertheless, it was apparent by the 1980's that filmmaking had become a major art form all around the world.

Drama

In the theater, too, important new techniques developed. In East Germany the company founded by the playwright Bertolt Brecht put on plays with an emphasis on their artificiality. The members of the audience were not to be drawn in but were to be reminded that they were watching a play. In Great Britain traditional forms of Asian drama influenced theatrical productions. There was also greater emphasis on the actors' spontaneous reactions. Performers were encouraged to improvise, and thus to create something new each night.

Perhaps the most powerful new vision was that of the playwrights of the so-called Theater of the Absurd. Its leaders were Samuel Beckett and Eugène Ionesco, an Irishman and a Rumanian who both lived in France.

Beckett's most famous play, *Waiting for Godot* (1956), is a long, apparently aimless dialogue between two tramps. It portrays a bleak world, in which human beings have great difficulty in communicating with one another. There is no real plot and no attempt to bring out the character of the two figures. Bewilderment and absurdity run throughout Beckett's works. These qualities are apparent also in the plays of Ionesco, such as *Rhinoceros* and *The Bald Soprano*.

More realistic but no less biting attacks on modern society were apparent in the works of other playwrights of this period. The most notable were the English playwright John Osborne and the American Arthur Miller. Miller's powerful dramas explored human weaknesses and the tensions in families. Another American, Tennessee Williams, looked at similar themes in a particular setting—the society of the American South.

Social analysis and comment even entered the boisterous world of American musical theater. To some, the most remarkable musical of the post-1945 period was *West Side Story*. It recounted the struggles between rival gangs of New York teenagers. Leonard Bernstein, the noted composer and conductor, wrote the score.

Poetry and novels

The aim of these playwrights was to take a stand against the comfortable assumptions of an ever more complicated world. Its most prosperous citizens and their values were the target of another group of writers, the so-called Beat Generation. These poets and novelists, living mainly in San Francisco and New York, began writing in the 1950's. They attacked the commercialism they saw in America. They thought that writing should be completely spontaneous, and they rejected the traditional forms of the novel and the poem.

Protest was a major theme of the leading writers of the postwar years. The most powerful black American writers were Ralph Ellison and James Baldwin. Each explored, with dismay and anger, the life of a black person in the United States. The Nigerian novelist, Chinua Achebe, examined the effects of colonial rule on his native land. The leading German novelists, Günter Grass and Heinrich Böll, explored Hitler's impact on Germany. Boris Pasternak and Alexander Solzhenitsyn wrote works that were savage descriptions of the repressions of the Soviet system.

The theme of escape from an increasingly hostile and confusing world was particularly notice-

(continued on page 796)

The arts and leisure

In the second half of the 1900's people around the world enjoyed many of the same forms of leisure and cultural activities. Popular music and sports, for example, became international favorites, linking people in every land. In the 1960's a British singing group, the Beatles (below left), attracted huge crowds wherever they went. Soccer became universally popular (below right), with more people watching the World Cup competition than any other sports event.

Popular interest in the arts also increased during this period. The French artist Henri Matisse used the bright colors and simple forms (center right) that are characteristic of African and Oriental art. The American sculptor Alexander Calder created monumental sculptures that adorn cities in the United States and abroad (above left). The work of the American painter Jackson Pollock, done by dripping paint in random patterns (above), also became world famous. Even classical ballet (top far left) gained new popularity and appealed to audiences everywhere. Its leading dancers gained international reputations.

795

able in post-World War II literature. Writers like the American Kurt Vonnegut, Jr., created fantasies about imaginary worlds. They used these fantasies to suggest alternatives to what they saw as the brutality and uncaring behavior of the times.

Prominent Latin American writers chose a similar approach. Octavio Paz, a Mexican poet, contrasted the savagery and the civilized grace of his country's history in surrealistic, dreamlike poems. The Colombian Gabriel García Márquez and the Mexican Carlos Castaneda wrote mystical novels that move puzzlingly through time. Castaneda implied that there are profound levels of wisdom that ordinary people cannot achieve.

Not all writers and poets emphasized protest or disturbing uncertainties. Some, like the American poet Wallace Stevens, enjoyed the traditional poetic function of celebrating nature. Many of his poems, for example, try to capture the lushness of the tropics. Stevens and another American poet, Marianne Moore, gained recognition mainly after 1945. Moore urged poets to be genuine, useful, and to write about topics ordinary people could understand. Attacking snobbery, she cited business documents and school books as acceptable subjects for her poetry. She liked to quote from magazines in her poems and wrote one poem to celebrate her favorite baseball team, the Brooklyn Dodgers.

The variety of the interests and the styles of poets and novelists was astonishing. There had never been so many books, stories, and poems published before and in so many countries throughout the world.

The audience for the arts

The excitement of postwar artistic and literary activity had enormous appeal, particularly in the United States. Between 1950 and 1980, Americans spent more than half a billion dollars to construct new space for museums and art centers. The number of Americans who paid to go to museums, concerts, operas, ballets, or theaters each year was larger than the number of those who paid to attend sporting events. In the late 1970's an exhibition of treasures from the tomb of the Egyptian pharaoh Tutankhamen drew almost 7 million people to museums in six American cities.

In the early 1980's, more than 91,000 books were published annually in the United States, representing more than $8.5 billion in sales. Other major book-producing countries were the U.S.S.R., with more than 83,000 titles published annually; West Germany, about 57,000 titles; and Great Britain, about 43,000 titles.

There were three major reasons for such staggering figures. First, all over the world, more people were completing the equivalent of a high school education, and more were going to college. Second, people had more time for leisure activities, particularly in industrialized countries. Third, television exposed more people to more kinds of cultural activities. Music, dramatizations of books, plays, and movies were made available to people at home. Many of them sought out similar entertainment elsewhere. Thus, education, extra leisure time, and new awareness combined to give the arts and literature greater support than they had ever enjoyed before.

CHECKUP

1. IDENTIFY: abstract expressionism, Pop Art, Nevelson, Britten, the Beatles, Balanchine, Graham, Kurosawa, Beat Generation, Baldwin, Castaneda, Stevens, Moore.

2. Describe changes since 1945 in architectural styles and building materials.

3. What new kinds of sounds were heard in the music of the postwar period?

4. How did film and theater reflect new techniques and themes? Give examples.

5. List three authors of different nationalities who wrote works that protested conditions in their native countries.

3

Patterns of living took new forms

As the pace and opportunities of life speeded up in industrialized nations, the way people spent their lives changed. There was less change in Third World countries, but the differences were narrowing.

Life styles

One feature of life after 1945 that set it apart from earlier periods was the speed with which things happened. Once it would have taken months for someone to recover from an illness. In the 1980's new medicines made cures possible in a few days. A worker might live many miles away from a job and still expect to get there from home in less than an hour. No one had to wait for a sports result. The game itself could be watched, live, in the comfort of one's home. And if one wanted a quick meal, from Finland to the Philippines, one could go to a so-called fast-food restaurant. There a hot meal was served in less than a minute.

An important result of these changes, especially in industrialized countries, was a greater amount of leisure time for the individual. With the leisure there sometimes came a restlessness and uncertainty about the best way to spend one's time. The use of drugs, the number of crimes committed, and the rate of divorce all increased markedly. However, additional leisure time also made possible new interests and opportunities.

Popular music, for example, gained worldwide appeal. People listened to the latest songs, played them on guitars and other popular instruments, and danced to them. Thus they expressed themselves through music in new ways. And the rapidly growing interest in sports was not just for spectators. As people found more time for themselves, they could also play more often the games that had become so popular since the late 1800's: soccer, baseball, tennis, basketball.

Leisure time increased in industrialized countries because the working year became shorter as machines took over more work. Families took holiday trips for granted, especially as travel became cheaper and easier. Even in nonindustrialized nations, television and movies brought news and entertainment to the most remote villages. As a result, attitudes and behavior changed rapidly, but it was far from clear what the long-term consequences would be.

The search for stability

Amid rapid changes, people looked for ways to create anchors of stability. One way was to renew their commitment to religion.

In the nonindustrialized countries a major response to modernization was a return to traditional beliefs. For example, the 1970's saw a strengthening of Islam in the Middle East. In many cases it was accompanied by a rejection of non-Muslim ideas and developments.

In Western countries, Christian revivalism had an impact, perhaps for similar reasons. The religious renewal among Christians took a number of different forms. In 1962 Pope John XXIII, then head of the Catholic Church, called a special council to the Vatican, the papal palace in Rome. The effects of the council, which came to be known as Vatican II, were wide reaching. The council modernized the Roman Catholic religious service. It also condemned anti-Semitism and called for reconciliation among all Christian churches.

This ecumenical movement, which sought unity among Christians, made some progress after the 1960's. The appeal of individual religions, and the sense of unity among those of the same faith, reflected one way that people tried to come to terms with rapid change in the modern world.

Social concerns

Another feature of the world after 1945 was the heightened sense of social concern. In earlier ages, it was of little interest to one nation whether the rights and freedoms of the people in another nation were being abused. One country might help a revolution in another, but the oppression of citizens was usually considered to be an internal problem.

Harsh conditions became more widely noted after 1945. The Red Cross, founded in 1863, had long been devoted to relief work after disasters, especially war. Now the United Nations established agencies to deal with refugees, hungry children, and medical care. In addition, new organizations were formed. Amnesty International tried to help political prisoners and mistreated prisoners all over the world. Oxfam devoted itself to relieving famine. After the civil war in Nigeria in the 1960's and the destruction of Cambodia in the 1970's, Oxfam and other organizations fed millions of starving people.

Repressive governments were also pressured to ease conditions for their citizens. The Soviet

Union, for instance, was urged to give its citizens certain rights—such as the right to emigrate. As a result of these efforts, thousands of Jews, many of whom had been severely treated, were permitted to leave the Soviet Union. Similar pressures were applied to harsh governments in Africa and the Middle East. For example, South Africa was expelled from the United Nations because of its policy of apartheid.

In Latin America the criticism was less consistent. There, however, the Catholic Church became the main force for social change. Priests were often the main critics of governments and the most important activists seeking reforms and helping the distressed.

Some concerns went beyond the policies of specific governments. The continuing growth of the world's population, especially in poorer countries, caused worries about food. The problem was made more difficult by the growing awareness that the world's resources were limited. Oil and such vital metals as copper and chrome appeared likely to become more and more scarce.

Perhaps the most crucial resource that was endangered was the environment itself. As industries grew, and as developing countries struggled to create their own industries, the air, the oceans, and the earth became polluted by industrial waste products. New international organizations arose to tackle these problems. They did not find it easy to get countries to cooperate with one another. However, they were able to make some progress. Nuclear tests in the atmosphere were prohibited, and regulations were set up for the protection of the seas.

Understanding human behavior

To absorb the many changes of this period, people had to understand them better. One means of doing so was through the increased information gained from the studies of social and individual behavior.

The social sciences—history, political science, economics, anthropology, psychology, and sociology—enjoyed a golden age after 1945. They employed many more researchers than ever before. And their work was revolutionized by the computer, which enabled them to study large amounts of information efficiently. The result was an expanded search for answers and a new understanding of such matters as population growth, voting behavior, the effects of living in suburbs, the appeal of religious beliefs, and the ways in which family members interact.

Such understanding will undoubtedly continue to advance into the 1990's and beyond. With greater understanding may come better means of dealing with the world's social, political, and economic problems.

The lessons of history

The search for answers and the attempt to understand oneself brings us back to the question with which this book began: Why does anyone bother to study history? Some, and perhaps all, of the answers that others have come up with may have occurred to you by now. You may have enjoyed a story here or there and been pleased when justice or right seemed to win out. You may have come to realize how and why certain kinds of change take place. Or you may have become better able to understand something that you do or believe, or something that you see in the world around you.

To the extent that you have learned this last lesson, you yourself have acted as a historian. You have not just read history; you have discovered why it is important. More than any of the specific facts or ideas that you may have read about for the first time, this insight will have been an essential addition to your education. It will have taught you a new way of thinking. In the end the most vital reason for studying history is that it teaches us how to think about, and thus how to understand, people, events, ideas, particular ages, and ourselves.

CHECKUP

1. IDENTIFY: Vatican II, Red Cross, Amnesty International, Oxfam.

2. How did increased leisure time affect life styles in the postwar period?

3. Give examples of religious revivalism in the 1960's and 1970's.

4. What progress was made in each of the following areas of social concern: health, human rights, the environment?

CHAPTER REVIEW

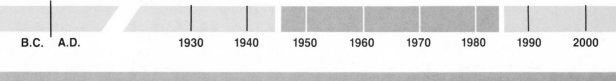

B.C.	A.D.	1930	1940	1950	1960	1970	1980	1990	2000

1944	Discovery of streptomycin	1960's	Green Revolution
1948	Invention of transistor	1962	Vatican II
1950's	Discovery of DNA	1969	First American moon landing
1957	Launching of *Sputnik* by Soviet Union	1970's	Jumbo jets introduced
1960	Invention of laser	1981	First mission of space shuttle *Columbia*

1982	First artificial heart transplant
1985	United States space telescope launched
1986	*Challenger* explosion

CHAPTER SUMMARY

Ten major technological advances indicated the degree of changes in ideas and behavior that took place in the years after 1945. The ten were air travel, space exploration, miniaturization, computers, lasers, knowledge of heredity and genes, understanding of the atom, plastics, antibiotics, and the Green Revolution. They transformed communications, the understanding of the universe, the processing of information, the products people used every day, economic activities, medicine, and food production.

The arts and literature continued the experimentation that had marked their development in the 1900's. New forms of painting, notably abstract expressionism, Pop Art, and Op Art, transformed the aims and the styles of art. New materials and shapes were created in architecture. Musicians experimented with new kinds of sounds, both in serious compositions and in popular forms. New styles of creativity were also evident in dance and filmmaking. Drama moved in new directions as traditional plays were transformed by the Theater of the Absurd. Writers all over the world expressed new ideas of protest and escape.

All of these cultural activities enjoyed large and growing audiences. People went to museums, attended concerts and plays, and bought books in larger numbers than ever before. Better education and increased leisure created more viewers, listeners, and readers than had existed in any previous period.

The effects of all these changes on the life styles of ordinary people can be summed up by the word speed. Events happened more quickly, and people expected rapid developments. People sought stability amid this rapid change. There was a renewed commitment to religious beliefs. There were concerns, too, about political repression and the dwindling of the world's resources.

Hoping to explain the changes of the period, social scientists sought to understand social and individual behavior more fully. A number of efforts were under way in the late 1900's to make rapid change easier for societies to manage in the future.

CHECKING WHAT YOU KNOW

1. Match each technological advance at the left with an invention or discovery at the right.

   a. increased information storage
   b. miniaturization
   c. Green Revolution
   d. genetic research
   e. space exploration
   f. production of synthetic substances
   g. use of antibiotics
   h. faster air travel
   i. improved eye surgery

   1. transistor
   2. DNA
   3. streptomycin
   4. jumbo jet
   5. laser
   6. plastics
   7. computer
   8. *Columbia*
   9. high-yielding seeds

2. Choose one of the following and discuss the major trends after 1945:

   a. painting and sculpture
   b. architecture
   c. music and dance
   d. drama and film
   e. poetry and novels

   How did changes in the arts reflect changes in society as a whole?

3. What are some of the benefits of atomic power? What are some of the dangers?

4. Give evidence to indicate that more people participate in cultural activities today than ever before. What are some of the reasons for this increased participation?

5. How did life styles change during the late 1900's? What factors account for these changes? How did many people come to terms with the new pace of life?

6. What are some of the many reasons that people study history? How can a knowledge of the past help one understand the present?

PRACTICING YOUR SKILLS

1. **Interpreting pictures.** Turn to the pictures on page 789. What technological advances does each photograph illustrate? What new industries have developed as a result of these discoveries? How have such changes affected your own life?

2. **Analyzing a point of view.** In 1970 Alvin Toffler wrote a book about the effect of rapid change, about people facing the future too soon. Read the passage below from Toffler's *Future Shock*, and answer the questions that follow.

   The high velocity [rapid rate] of change can be traced to many factors. Population growth, urbanization, the shifting proportions of young and old—all play their part. Yet technological advance is clearly a critical node [force] in that network of causes; indeed, it may be the node [force] that activates the entire net.

   According to Toffler, what factors bring about rapid change? Which of these factors is most important? Based on what you learned in this chapter and on your knowledge of current events, do you agree? Why or why not?

RELATING PAST TO PRESENT

1. Compare the picture essay on pages 794–95 of this chapter with one of the following picture essays from earlier periods: pages 302–03, pages 518–19, or pages 634–35. What forms of artistic expression are shown in each essay?

What noticeable changes in style have taken place between the two periods? What factors might explain these changes? How could the evidence in these essays be used to prove the expression that "the arts reflect the times"?

2. Using a tape recorder, prepare a program of popular music of the 1980's. Then prepare a similar tape for a previous decade. Possible sources of recordings include friends, relatives, and your school or local library. What do the tapes reveal about each period? How have popular tastes changed? What, if any, new instruments are used today? How might musical recordings contribute to an understanding of history?

INVESTIGATING FURTHER

1. Read Aldous Huxley, *Brave New World* (Harper & Row) or George Orwell, *Nineteen Eighty-four* (New American Library). Then prepare a book report in which you consider the author's vision of the future. What events or changes did Huxley or Orwell fear might take place in the late 1900's? Have any of these predictions come true? Explain. Using information in this chapter and your knowledge of world affairs, how do you think the world will look in the year 2020?

2. Use the *Readers' Guide to Periodical Literature* to find articles on the *Voyager* spacecraft. What planets did this satellite explore? What new moons of other planets were discovered? What other new information about the planets did *Voyager* provide? You might also want to investigate what space exploration programs the United States plans for the future.

3. The space era began in 1957 with the launching of the Soviet satellite *Sputnik.* Using reference materials in your library, prepare a report on why the United States has emerged as the world leader in space exploration. Based on your research, what are some reasons for the success of the United States space program?

4. Technological advances have had an impact not only in industrialized societies but also in the nations of the Third World. Select one area of scientific or technological progress, and prepare a report on how advances in this area have changed life in the developing nations of Asia, Africa, and Latin America.

UNIT REVIEW

1. Match each leader at the left with a description at the right.
   - a. Ho Chi Minh
   - b. Indira Gandhi
   - c. Sadat
   - d. Mao Tse-tung
   - e. Castro
   - f. Nkrumah
   - g. Khomeini
   - h. MacArthur
   - i. Sukarno
   - j. Pol Pot
   - k. Juan Perón

   1. Authoritarian leader of Argentina.
   2. Commanded UN army in Korea.
   3. Leader of Cuban revolution.
   4. Became president of Egypt in 1970.
   5. Led Iranian revolution against the Shah.
   6. Directed communist forces in Vietnam.
   7. Led independence movement in Ghana.
   8. Began the Cultural Revolution in China.
   9. First president of Indonesia.
   10. Became prime minister of India in 1966.
   11. Instituted a reign of terror in Cambodia.

2. Match each person at the left with an art form at the right. You may use an art form more than once.
   - a. Pollock
   - b. the Beatles
   - c. Nevelson
   - d. Graham
   - e. Beckett
   - f. Ellison
   - g. Le Corbusier
   - h. Pasternak
   - i. Balanchine
   - j. Kurosawa
   - k. Bernstein
   - l. Baldwin
   - m. Ionesco
   - n. Shostakovich

   1. architecture
   2. dance
   3. painting
   4. music
   5. literature
   6. drama
   7. film
   8. sculpture

3. What major problems faced the Allied Powers after their victory in World War II? How did they try to solve them?

4. Discuss three major areas of disagreement between the United States and the Soviet Union after 1945. Which was most threatening to world peace? Why?

5. What common problems faced many Asian nations after gaining independence? Why did democracy have relatively little success as a solution?

6. How did the Vietnam War affect political and economic conditions in other parts of Southeast Asia?

7. What obstacles stood in the way of national unity in many newly independent African nations? Give examples of how African leaders attempted to overcome these problems.

8. How did the United Nations attempt to resolve each of the following crises:
   - a. civil war in the Congo
   - b. South African intervention in Namibia
   - c. Egyptian seizure of the Suez Canal

9. Give recent evidence of both cooperation and friction among the nations of the Western Hemisphere. What steps were taken to further improve relations in the Americas?

10. Why were politics and economic development so closely linked in Latin America? Compare efforts toward economic development in Cuba with those in Brazil.

11. Describe five technological and scientific advances that took place after 1945. Explain the importance of each.

REFERENCE
SECTION

	EUROPE	MIDDLE EAST	AFRICA	ASIA	AMERICAS
4,000,000 YEARS AGO			OLD STONE AGE		
			Earliest humanlike creatures		
			Humanlike creatures using tools	Peking people	
				Java people	
70,000- 40,000 YEARS AGO	Neanderthal people				Migrations across Bering Strait
	Cro-Magnon people				
	←		MIDDLE STONE AGE		→
6,000 YEARS AGO	←		NEW STONE AGE		→

	ITALY	GREECE	TIGRIS-EUPHRATES VALLEY	WESTERN FERTILE CRESCENT	ASIA MINOR
4000 B.C.			Copper in use		
		Neolithic culture on Crete and Aegean Islands	Bronze in use		
			Sumerians		
					Hittite migration into region
		Minoan civilization	**HAMMURABI'S** code		
		Mycenaean civilization	Hittite invasion		Hittite Empire
		Dorian invasion		Hebrews in Canaan	Destruction of Troy
1000 B.C.	Latins	Age of Kings	Assyrians	Phoenicians	
	Etruscans	**HOMER**	Chaldeans	**SOLOMON**	
	Latins conquer Etruscans	Control by nobles	**ZOROASTER**	Israel conquered by Assyrians	Rule by Persia
		Age of Tyrants	Persians	Judah conquered by Chaldeans	
500 B.C.	Roman Republic established	Golden Age			
		Persian Wars			
		Age of **PERICLES**			
400 B.C.		Peloponnesian War			
		XERXES			
		Conquest by **PHILIP OF MACEDON**			
		EMPIRE OF ALEXANDER THE GREAT			
300 B.C.		HELLENISTIC AGE ————————			
	Punic Wars				
200 B.C.					
		Conquest by Rome			Western portion conquered by Rome
100 B.C.	Civil war				
	JULIUS CAESAR				
0	**AUGUSTUS**			**BIRTH OF CHRIST**	

Chronology of Historical Events

By coordinating the dates, along the sides, with the areas, across the top, you can see what was happening in various parts of the world at the same time—for example, that the Latins came into Italy during the Greek Age of Kings. For ease of reading, certain features are highlighted. Major historical periods and events that affected many places over a span of time, such as the NEW STONE AGE or the HELLENISTIC AGE, appear in red. All names of persons appear in boldface type, such as MENES or JULIUS CAESAR.

EGYPT	AFRICA	INDIA	CHINA	THE AMERICAS	
					4000 B.C.
Copper in use					
Egypt united under MENES					
Old Kingdom		Indus Valley civilization			
Middle Kingdom			Hsia dynasty		
Hyksos rule Empire		Aryan invasion			
AKHENATON		Vedic Age	Shang dynasty	Olmec culture	
		Epic Age	Chou dynasty	Chavin culture	1000 B.C.
Assyrian domination	Nok culture		CONFUCIUS		
Persian domination		GAUTAMA BUDDHA	LAO-TZU		500 B.C.
		Rule of Nine Nandas			400 B.C.
		ALEXANDER'S invasion		Mayas	300 B.C.
		Maurya Empire ASOKA			
	Height of Kush kingdom				
			Ch'in dynasty		
			Great Wall		200 B.C.
		Greco-Bactrian Empire	Han dynasty WU TI		
					100 B.C.
Conquest by Rome					
					0

803

THE ROMAN EMPIRE

0

Julian Emperors **PAUL'S** journeys

Britain added to
Roman Empire

PAX ROMANA

100

Good Emperors

GALEN

Roman Empire at height

200

← Civil wars →

EASTERN ROMAN EMPIRE (BYZANTINES)

300

DIOCLETIAN

CONSTANTINE

Constantinople made capital

Battle of Adrianople

GERMANIC INVASIONS

Christianity made official religion

400

Sack of Rome by Visigoths

ST. PATRICK
in Ireland

Huns defeated at Châlons

ENGLAND	FRANCE	GERMAN STATES	ITALY	

500

Saxon kingdoms | Merovingians | | | **JUSTINIAN'S** code

600

POPE GREGORY I

Lombard invasions

ST. AUGUSTINE

700

Muslim invasion stopped by
CHARLES MARTEL

CHARLEMAGNE

Wessex dominant

800

Carolingians
Treaty of Verdun | **LOUIS THE GERMAN** | | **CYRIL** and **METHODIUS**

INVASIONS BY VIKINGS, SLAVS, MAGYARS, AND MUSLIMS

900

HOLY ROMAN EMPIRE

OTTO I

Capetians

1000

Danish rule
EDWARD THE CONFESSOR

HENRY III
HENRY IV

East/West split of Church

Norman conquest

THE CRUSADES

Investiture struggle with **POPE GREGORY VII**

Seljuk Turk invasions

1100

HENRY I | **ABELARD** | Concordat of Worms

HENRY II
RICHARD I | **PHILIP AUGUSTUS** | **FREDERICK BARBAROSSA** | Victory of Lombard League

1200

RUSSIA	AFRICA AND MIDDLE EAST	INDIA	CHINA	JAPAN	THE AMERICAS	
		Kushan empire				0
	Destruction of Second Temple					
			Invention of paper			100
Slav settlements			Six Dynasties			200
	Axum kingdom	Gupta rule Ajanta paintings *Panchatantra*	Hun invasion in north			300
	Vandal invasions in North Africa			Japanese adoption of Chinese writing		400
		Hun invasions		Buddhism introduced from China		500
			Sui dynasty			
		HARSHA				600
	MUHAMMAD'S Hegira	Rajputs in north Chalukya dynasty in Deccan	T'ang dynasty	First ambassadors to China		
	Muslim expansion from Spain to India	Muslim conquest of Indus Valley	Height of Buddhism **LI PO** **TU FU**	Law code modeled after that of China		700
Viking invasions Kievan state	Karanga state			Fujiwara control	Catastrophe strikes Maya civilization	800
			Diamond Sutra			
	RHAZES Height of Ghana kingdom					900
Official conversion to Christianity			Sung dynasty			
				The Tale of Genji		1000
YAROSLAV THE WISE	**AVICENNA** Islam imposed on western Sudan Rise of Turks	Beginning of Muslim invasions in north				
			Invention of gun powder		Toltecs in central Mexico	1100
			Chin dynasty in north	Zen Buddhism Minamoto control Shogunate established		
						1200

Year	ENGLAND	FRANCE	GERMAN STATES	ITALY	IBERIAN PENINSULA	RUSSIA	OTHER EUROPEAN STATES
1200	JOHN Magna Carta		FREDERICK II	INNOCENT III / ST. FRANCIS OF ASSISI			
1250						Mongol rule of Russia	
	SIMON DE MONTFORT vs. HENRY III			ST. THOMAS AQUINAS / DANTE			
1300	Growth of royal courts	PHILIP IV / Estates General	Hanseatic League	BONIFACE VIII / Babylonian Captivity		Rise of Moscow / IVAN I	
	Beginning of Hundred Years' War						

BEGINNING OF RENAISSANCE

Year	ENGLAND	FRANCE	GERMAN STATES	ITALY	IBERIAN PENINSULA	RUSSIA	OTHER EUROPEAN STATES
1350	CHAUCER			PETRARCH / Great Schism			
	WYCLIFFE						
1400				Council of Constance	PRINCE HENRY launches Portuguese voyages		HUSS / VAN EYCKS
		JOAN OF ARC					
1450	Wars of the Roses		GUTENBERG'S printing press	LEONARDO MICHELANGELO RAPHAEL TITIAN	Marriage of FERDINAND and ISABELLA	IVAN III	ERASMUS
	HENRY VII / Tudors	LOUIS XI	DURER	MACHIAVELLI		Mongols overthrown	
1500	HENRY VIII / Anglican Church created		LUTHER'S 95 Theses / Diet of Worms		CHARLES I (V) / MAGELLAN'S voyage		CALVIN'S Institutes
				Council of Trent	Jesuit order founded	IVAN IV (THE TERRIBLE)	COPERNICUS
1550	ELIZABETH I		Peace of Augsburg		PHILIP II		BRUEGEL
	Defeat of Armada / SHAKESPEARE	HENRY IV / Edict of Nantes			Portugal annexed by Spain	Cossack expansion eastward	Dutch revolt against Spain
1600	Stuarts	RICHELIEU	KEPLER				Dutch E. India Company organized

THIRTY YEARS' WAR

Year	ENGLAND	FRANCE	GERMAN STATES	ITALY	IBERIAN PENINSULA	RUSSIA	OTHER EUROPEAN STATES
	English Revolution	LOUIS XIV	Peace of Westphalia	GALILEO			
1650	CROMWELL / Restoration					PETER I (THE GREAT)	
	Glorious Revolution	Edict of Nantes revoked					

BEGINNING OF ENLIGHTENMENT

1700

WAR OF SPANISH SUCCESSION

Year	ENGLAND	FRANCE	GERMAN STATES	ITALY	IBERIAN PENINSULA	RUSSIA	OTHER EUROPEAN STATES
	GEORGE I					St. Petersburg built	
		MONTESQUIEU	MARIA THERESA				
1750							

BEGINNING OF INDUSTRIAL REVOLUTION

Year	ENGLAND	FRANCE	GERMAN STATES	ITALY	IBERIAN PENINSULA	RUSSIA	OTHER EUROPEAN STATES
	WATT'S steam engine	ROUSSEAU / LOUIS XVI	FREDERICK THE GREAT			CATHERINE THE GREAT	Partitions of Poland
		French Revolution					
1800							

BYZANTINE EMPIRE	AFRICA	INDIA	CHINA	JAPAN	OTHER EASTERN AREAS	THE AMERICAS	
Crusaders capture Constantinople	Rise of Mali kingdom	Delhi sultans rule in north	Mongol invasions		Mongol Empire **GENGHIS KHAN**	Toltecs defeated by Aztecs	1200
Byzantines regain Constantinople							1250
Empire reorganized			**KUBLAI KHAN** Yüan dynasty **POLOS'** visit	Mongols repulsed by "Divine Wind"			
Ottoman Turks in Asia Minor	**MANSA MUSA** Timbuktu center of learning	Delhi sultans conquer Deccan					1300
				Ashikaga control		Aztecs dominant in central Mexico	
							1350
			Ming dynasty				
	Benin kingdom	**TAMERLANE'S** invasion Mongol rule				Inca empire expanding in South America	1400
			Foreign contacts ended				1450
OTTOMAN EMPIRE	Songhai kingdom	Delhi sultans regain control		Beginning of "high" feudalism			
	DIAS' voyage around Cape of Good Hope	**DA GAMA'S** voyage				**COLUMBUS** reaches America	1500
SULAYMAN I		Mogul Empire begun by Babur	Portuguese in Macao		Portuguese in E. Indies	**CORTÉS** **PIZARRO** **CARTIER**	
				Portuguese traders and missionaries			1550
		AKBAR					
	Portuguese settlement founded in Ndonga			**NOBUNAGA**			
		English in Madras, Bombay, Calcutta		Tokugawa shogunate Pax Tokugawa Isolation begun	Dutch in E. Indies	Jamestown Quebec Plymouth	1600
		SHAH JAHAN Taj Mahal	Ch'ing dynasty				
	Dutch establish Cape Colony		**K'ANG-HSI**			Louisiana claimed for France	1650
		French in Pondicherry	Boundary treaty with Russia				
	British monopoly of slave trade						1700
		French defeated Rule by British E. India Company			Australia, New Zealand discovered by **COOK**, settled by British	French and Indian War American Revolution	1750
			White Lotus Rebellion				1800

807

	ENGLAND	FRANCE	GERMAN STATES	ITALY	RUSSIA	OTHER EUROPEAN STATES
1800			◄────────── N A P O L E O N I C W A R S ──────────►			
		NAPOLEON in power	Confederation of the Rhine		NAPOLEON'S invasion repulsed	
			CONGRESS OF VIENNA			
		Bourbons restored	German Confederation		Holy Alliance	
			Carlsbad Decrees			Revolt in Spain
1820	Factory Act		Zollverein			Greek revolt
	Development of railroads			Uprisings in Sardinia	NICHOLAS I "Russification"	
	Reform Bill of 1832	Revolution overthrows CHARLES X		Young Italy movement		Belgian independence
	VICTORIA	LOUIS PHILIPPE				
	Chartists					
1840						
		Second Republic	Communist Manifesto	Widespread revolts		
	BESSEMER steel process	NAPOLEON III				
		Second Empire	METTERNICH ousted from Austria	War against Austria	Crimean War	
					ALEXANDER II	
1860	DARWIN'S Origin of Species				Emancipation of serfs	
		Impressionists	BISMARCK in power	Unification and independence of Italy		
	Second Reform Bill	PASTEUR				
		Franco-Prussian War	GERMAN EMPIRE	Dual Monarchy of AUSTRIA-HUNGARY	TOLSTOY	
	Suez Canal acquired	Third Republic		VERDI	MENDELEYEV'S Periodic Table	
			Congress of Berlin	MENDEL		Rumania, Montenegro, Serbia recognized as independent
1880	Third Reform Bill		◄────────── Triple Alliance ──────────►		ALEXANDER III	
					Trans-Siberian railroad	
		DREYFUS case			NICHOLAS II	
			X-ray discovered by ROENTGEN	MARCONI'S wireless		
	THOMSON	CURIES				
1900	Labour Party	Cubism	EINSTEIN	Bosnia, Herzegovina annexed	War with Ottomans	War with Japan Revolution of 1905
	Triple Entente				Triple Entente	Balkan Wars
			◄────────── W O R L D W A R I ──────────►			
			GERMANY	AUSTRIA	Bolshevik Revolution under LENIN	Czechoslovakia, Yugoslavia formed
1920	Irish Free State	French occupation of Ruhr Valley	Weimar Republic	FREUD	NEP	
				Fascist march on Rome	STALIN in power	Locarno Pact
	Statute of Westminster	Popular Front	HITLER to power	MUSSOLINI		Spanish Civil War
			Anschluss with Austria			
1940			◄────────── W O R L D W A R I I ──────────►			
	CHURCHILL	Fourth Republic	Nuremberg trials	Republic created		Soviet satellites in eastern Europe
					Cominform	Hungarian revolt
	NATO formed					
		Fifth Republic	East and West Germanies established	Treaty with Allies; Austria reunified	Warsaw Pact	
		DE GAULLE			Sputnik I	
1960					Break with China	
			Berlin Wall			Czechoslovak revolt
					East-West détente	Helsinki Agreement
			◄────────── Common Market ──────────►		Beginning of SALT agreements	
1980						Strikes in Poland
1990						

AFRICA	MIDDLE EAST	INDIA	CHINA	JAPAN	OTHER EASTERN AREAS	NORTH AMERICA	LATIN AMERICA	
								1800
					Dutch E. Indies made royal colony	Louisiana Purchase	Haiti independent	
							HIDALGO	
							Spanish colonies win independence	
								1820
							Mexico independent	
	French in Algeria					MONROE DOCTRINE		
			Opium War			Durham Report		
						MORSE'S telegraph		**1840**
Liberia independent			Taiping Rebellion		French take Marquesas, Tahiti	Mexican War		
				Arrival of **PERRY**				
		Sepoy Rebellion	War with Britain					
								1860
	Suez Canal completed			Tokugawa shogunate ended		American Civil War	French in Mexico	
				Meiji Era		Dominion of Canada	**MAXIMILIAN**	
				Modernization	Seizure of Pacific Islands and Southeast Asian countries by France, Britain, Germany, U.S.	**EDISON**		
								1880
Seizure of African lands by Britain, France, Belgium, Germany, Italy		Indian National Congress		Meiji constitution				
Boer War			Sino-Japanese War					
					← Spanish-American War →			
								1900
	Moroccan crisis	Muslim League	Boxer Rebellion / Chinese Republic	Russo-Japanese War	Commonwealth of Australia Dominion of New Zealand	**WRIGHT BROTHERS** **ROOSEVELT** Corollary	Panama revolution	
			WORLD WAR I					
	Balfour Declaration	Passive resistance under **GANDHI**		Korea annexed			Panama Canal opened	
								1920
	ATATÜRK Persia ruled by **REZA SHAH**		**SUN YAT-SEN** **CHIANG KAI-SHEK** Long March	Invasion of Manchuria		Stock market crash; Great Depression		
Italy defeats Ethiopia	Egyptian independence		Japanese invasion			**ROOSEVELT'S** New Deal		
			WORLD WAR II					
								1940
	Arab League	Independence for India and Pakistan	Civil War	First atomic bomb, Hiroshima	Korean War	**TRUMAN** Doctrine		
	Republic of Israel proclaimed		Communists gain control of China			**MARSHALL** Plan	OAS	
	Suez crisis		**MAO TSE-TUNG**		French defeated in Indochina	*Brown vs. Topeka*	**CASTRO'S** revolution in Cuba	
UN intervention in Congo		Chinese invasion				St. Lawrence Seaway		
								1960
	OPEC established				U.S. intervention in Vietnam	**MARTIN LUTHER KING, JR.**		
Civil war in Nigeria	Six-Day War	Border war with Pakistan	Great Cultural Revolution		ASEAN	First moon landing by U.S.	Alliance for Progress	
	Civil War in Lebanon	**INDIRA GANDHI**	China in UN; Taiwan out	Great industrial power	Vietnam reunified	Watergate scandals	Overthrow of Marxists in Chile	
Angola independent	Egyptian-Israeli peace treaty	Independence for Bangladesh			Soviet invasion of Afghanistan			
								1980
	U.S. hostages released from Iran				*Columbia* space shuttle			
								1990

809

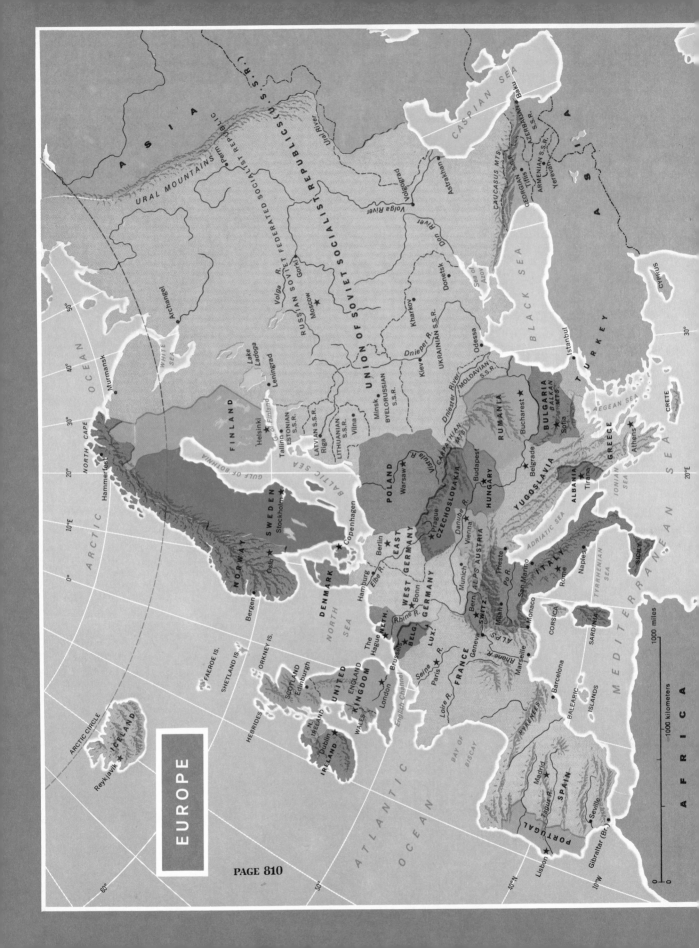

EUROPE

PAGE 810

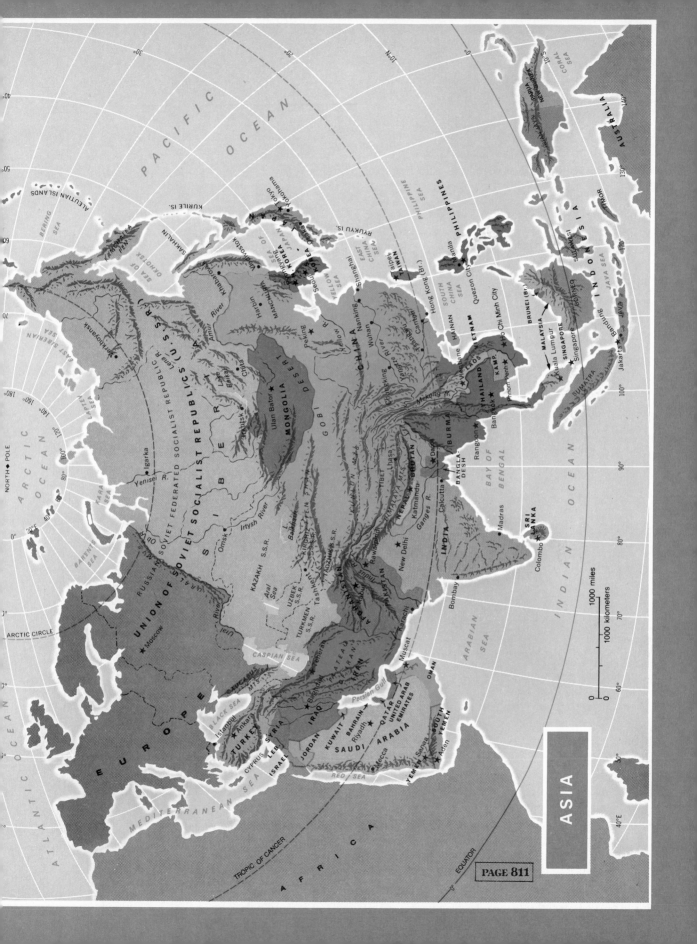

NORTH AMERICA

SOUTH AMERICA

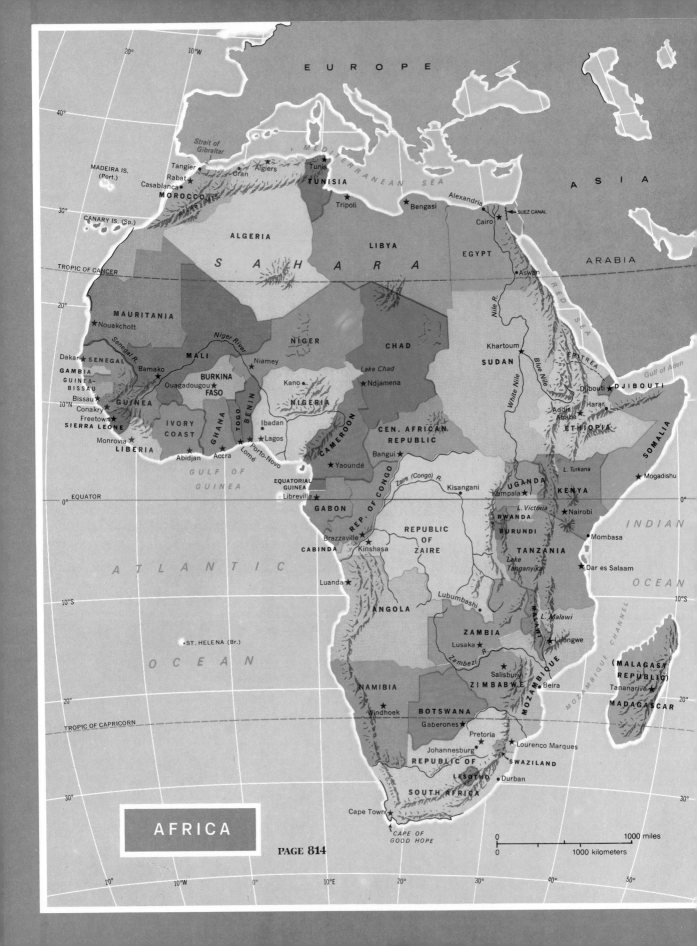

AFRICA

PAGE 814

GLOSSARY

This glossary defines many of the terms you need to understand as you study World History. Phonetic respellings have been included for many of the terms. The page number in parentheses after each definition refers to the page on which the term is introduced in the textbook. You may find it useful to turn to the page listed to read more about the term. Many of the terms appear in boldface type when they are first introduced and discussed in the textbook.

A

abolition the ending of slavery (page 493)

absolutism form of government under which the ruler has unlimited, or absolute, power (page 477)

abstract expressionism style of painting developed after 1945 that did not show recognizable objects but emphasized the artist's self-expression (page 790)

acropolis (uh·CROP·uh·lis) hill on which the public buildings of a city-state in ancient Greece were located (page 69)

adobe (uh·DOH·bee) sun-dried brick used by the Pueblo Indians to build communal houses (page 231)

agriculture cultivation of the soil in order to raise crops and livestock for food (page 9)

alliance close relationship between two or more nations for a common purpose or mutual advantage (page 95)

alphabet the system of letters representing sounds that was the final stage in the development of writing (page 12)

anarchy (AN·ahr·kee) the absence of any form of government (page 134)

ancestor worship reverence for the elders and forebears of a family (page 60)

animism the belief that spirits inhabit all natural objects, including animals, trees, and people (page 48)

anthropology (an·thruh·PAHL·uh·jee) the study of people and their cultures (page 514)

apartheid (uh·PART·hyt) South African policy of strict racial separation to guarantee the privileged position of the white minority (page 746)

appeasement policy of yielding to the demands of an aggressor in the hope of preserving peace (page 667)

apprentice during the Middle Ages, a boy legally bound for several years to a master worker from whom he learned a craft (page 276)

arbitration settlement of a dispute by a party agreed upon by all sides (page 581)

archeology (ar·kee·AHL·uh·jee) the study of ancient peoples through examination of the physical remains of past cultures (page 153)

archon (AHR·kahn) one of nine elected rulers who appointed all officials and made all laws in ancient Athens (page 78)

aristocracy (ar·is·TAH·krah·see) form of government that is headed by a privileged ruling class (page 73)

armistice (AR·muh·stis) agreement among nations to stop fighting until a treaty can be drawn up (page 604)

artifacts objects, such as tools or weapons, made by human skill (page 5)

artisan a worker skilled in a particular craft (page 11)

assembly line system in many factories by which a conveyor belt carries unfinished products past workers, each of whom performs a specialized task as the item passes (page 461)

astrolabe (AS·troh·layb) instrument used to calculate a ship's latitude (page 361)

Atman in Hinduism, the soul or essence of an individual person (page 140)

attrition slow wearing-down process in which each side in a war tries to outlast the other (page 598)

autocracy (aw·TAH·krah·see) form of government in which one person holds absolute power (page 540)

autocrat (AWT·oh·krat) ruler who holds absolute power (page 540)

B

balance of power principle of maintaining an equilibrium in international politics. Rival nations or groups of nations maintain approximately equal strength so that peace is preserved. (page 346)

balance of trade relationship between the amount of goods a nation sells in foreign countries and the amount of goods that nation buys from foreign countries (page 365)

Bantustans tribal states set aside for black Africans in South Africa (page 746)

barter the exchange of one item for another without the use of money (page 51)

belligerents warring nations (page 595)

blitzkrieg German for ''lightning war''; warfare characterized by sudden, destructive attacks (page 670)

blockade the shutting off of an enemy port or region to prevent goods from coming in or going out (page 409)

bourgeoisie (boor·zhwah·ZEE) term used to describe the city-dwelling middle class; from the French word for town (page 392)

boyars the local nobility in Kievan Russia (page 193)

Brahman in Hinduism, the basic divine essence filling everything in the world (page 140); also, a member of the Hindu caste of priests, scholars, and wise men (page 151)

Buddhism (BOOD·iz·um) religion and philosophy founded by Gautama Buddha in the 500's B.C. (page 143)

buffer state small state located between two hostile powers that lessens the possibility of conflict between the powers (page 574)

bureaucrats (BYOO·ruh·crats) name for government officials, from the French word *bureau,* or desk (page 341)

bushido (BOO·she·doh) code of honor of Japanese samurai (page 180)

business cycle economic pattern of alternating periods of prosperity and decline (page 462)

C

Cabinet group of advisers, most of them heads of government departments, who meet with the head of a government (page 340)

calendar a system for charting and recording the passage of time (page 12)

caliph (KAY·lif) title meaning ''successor to the prophet'' given to Muhammad's successors (page 202)

caliphate (kal·ih·FATE) one of the three divisions of the Muslim Empire, each ruled by a caliph (page 204)

capital wealth earned, saved, and invested in order to produce profits (page 271)

capitalism economic system in which the means of production are privately owned and operated to produce profits (page 271)

caravans groups of people banding together for safety while journeying through dangerous or hostile regions (page 24)

cartel combination of corporations that controls an entire industry (page 462)

caste system form of social organization in India in which society was divided into distinct, hereditary classes. Each class had its own fixed social position and rules about eating, marriage, labor, and worship. (page 140)

censors officials in the Roman republic who registered people according to their wealth for taxes and membership in the Assembly (page 110)

charter of liberties written statement of the rights granted to townspeople by their feudal lord (page 275)

chinampas (chih·NAHM·pahs) floating artificial islands on which the Aztecs farmed (page 229)

chivalry (SHIV·al·ree) the code of conduct for knights during the Middle Ages (page 248)

Christianity religion based on the teachings of Jesus Christ. Christianity was founded in Palestine in the first century A.D. (page 127)

city-state an independent town or city and the surrounding land controlled by it (page 28)

civil disobedience technique whereby citizens peacefully refuse to cooperate with their government in order to win concessions from it (page 642)

civil rights the political, social, and economic rights guaranteed by law to a nation's citizens (page 768)

civil service system that administers the government on a day-to-day basis; members are usually appointed on the basis of competitive examinations (page 152)

civilization an advanced society with complex technical skills, highly developed group living, division of labor, and advanced intellectual achievements (page 5)

coalition temporary alliance between two or more political parties in a legislature (page 501)

Cold War conflict between communist and non-communist nations after World War II that was waged by political and economic means rather than with weapons (page 693)

collaborators people who aid their country's enemies (page 670)

collective bargaining process of negotiation between union and management over wages, hours, and working conditions (page 471)

collective farms land pooled into large farms where people work together as a group (page 617)

colonus (koh·LOH·nuhs) an agricultural worker in ancient Rome who received a small plot of land. In exchange, the worker had to remain on the land for a certain period and pay the owner of the land with crops. (page 122)

colony during the age of imperialism, an area in which a foreign nation gained total control (page 554)

commercial capitalism early phase of capitalism in which capital was used mainly to buy, sell, and exchange goods (page 459)

Commercial Revolution name given to the great changes that occurred in the European economy from 1500 to about 1750 (page 362)

common law law based on judges' decisions rather than on a code of statutes (page 257)

communism economic and political system based on public ownership of the means of production. Communism seeks the overthrow of capitalism by violent revolution. (page 484)

concentration camps large prisons in which millions of people died or were murdered by the Nazis before and during World War II (page 627)

concession the granting of economic rights and privileges in a given area (page 554)

condominium a region ruled by two nations as partners (page 554)

conscription the drafting of citizens into military service (page 402)

conservatives those who do not want to change existing conditions (page 399)

constitution a document outlining the fundamental laws and principles that govern a nation (page 336)

constitutional monarchy see **limited constitutional monarchy**

consulates diplomatic offices that protect a nation's interests in a foreign country. These diplomatic offices are headed by officials known as consuls. (page 567)

consuls officials of the Roman republic who ran the government and were the army commanders (page 109)

containment United States policy, adopted in the late 1940's, that aimed to "contain," or restrict, the spread of communism (page 702)

contraband war materials supplied by a neutral nation to a belligerent (page 599)

corporation form of business organization that raises money by selling shares. Shareholders' financial responsibility is limited to the amount they have invested. (page 461)

Counter-Reformation revival effort begun by the Catholic Church in the 1530's to counteract the spread of Protestantism (page 307)

counter-revolution actions aimed counter to, or against, a revolution (page 402)

coup d'état (koo day·TAH) quick seizure of power by force (page 406)

craft guilds see **guilds**

creole (CREE·ohl) white person of European ancestry born in colonial Latin America (page 434)

crop rotation system of alternating different kinds of crops in order to preserve the fertility of the soil (page 448)

Crusades (croo·SAYDS) series of military expeditions launched by Christians in the Middle Ages to regain the Holy Land from the Muslims (page 265)

culture the sum total of the basic activities that humans perform; also, the way of life of a specific group of people (page 9)

cuneiform (kyoo·NEE·uh·form) the wedge-shaped writing of the ancient Sumerians (page 29)

curia group of counselors who advise the pope (page 250)

czar (ZAHR) the Russian word for Caesar; title of the former emperors of Russia. The title of the Russian empress was **czarina.** (page 349)

D

daimyo (DY·myoh) samurai with the highest status in feudal Japan (page 180)

democracy government in which all citizens take part (page 76)

depression the lowest point in the business cycle. It is characterized by decreased production, unemployment, and falling wages. (page 463)

détente (day·TAHNT) era of improved Soviet-American relations after World War II; from the French word meaning an easing of strain (page 705)

dictator a ruler with absolute power. In ancient Rome a dictator, chosen only when Rome was in danger, could hold absolute power for a period of six months. (page 110)

division of labor division of a manufacturing process into a series of simple steps, with a step assigned to each worker (page 459)

domain manor land that a feudal lord kept for himself (page 245)

domestic system method of production in which work is done in the workers' homes rather than in a shop or factory (page 274)

domesticate to tame wild animals for use by humans (page 8)

Duma before the Russian Revolution, the representative body that advised the Russian ruler (page 544)

dynasty family of rulers in which the right to rule is passed from one generation to the next (page 18)

E

economic nationalism policy of attempting to improve a nation's economic well-being through protective tariffs and similar restrictions (page 621)

economic sanction penalty imposed by a nation or group of nations that involves such measures as the refusal to trade with an offending nation (page 610)

emigration the movement of people out of their country to settle in another land (page 465)

émigré (EM·ee·gray) noble who fled France during the French Revolution (page 398)

empire form of government that unites different territories and peoples under one ruler (page 20)

enclosure movement in England, the fencing off of common lands, formerly held by villagers jointly, into individual holdings. This practice began in the 1600's and continued until the 1700's. (page 447)

Enlightenment philosophical movement in Europe during the 1700's that was characterized by the scientific attitude, rationalism, and belief in natural law (page 321)

entente (ahn·TAHNT) a friendly understanding or agreement between nations (page 592)

ephors (EEF·ors) officials in ancient Sparta who were the real rulers of the city-state (page 77)

epics long poems describing heroes and great events (page 71)

equites (EK·wih·teez) class of business people in ancient Rome who had great wealth but little political power (page 115)

Estates the three social classes in France before the French Revolution (page 284)

Estates-General the representative assembly of France, established in 1302. It was made up of three groups—the First Estate (the clergy), the Second Estate (the nobles), and the Third Estate (the common people). (page 284)

ethical monotheism (MAHN·uh·thee·iz·um) the Jewish form of monotheism, or belief in one God, that emphasizes proper conduct (page 41)

excommunication the act of completely cutting off an individual from the Church (page 250)

executive branch branch of government that administers the laws (page 346)

extraterritoriality exemption of foreigners from the laws of the nation where they live or do business (page 570)

F

factors of production the basic resources necessary for industrialization—land, labor, capital, management, and government (page 447)

factory building in which workers and machines are brought together to produce goods (page 448)

factory system production of goods in a factory, rather than in workers' homes (page 448)

fascism (FASH·iz·um) dictatorial, totalitarian system of government in which the state is supreme and individuals are subordinate to it (page 624)

federal system system in which powers are divided between a central government and individual states (page 391)

Fertile Crescent crescent-shaped area of fertile land extending from the eastern end of the Mediterranean Sea to the Persian Gulf (page 26)

feudalism (FYOOD·al·iz·um) political system based on small, independent local governments (pages 178, 244)

fief (FEEF) the grant of land from a lord to a vassal (page 244)

free enterprise economic system in which individuals are free to go into any business and operate it for their greatest advantage (page 481)

fresco painting made on wet plaster (page 68)

functionalism style of architecture based on the principle that a building should be designed for its specific use (page 637)

G

general strike collective refusal of workers in various industries to continue working until their demands are met (page 621)

geocentric theory (gee·oh·SEN·trik) theory stated by Ptolemy in the 100's A.D. that the earth was the center of the universe (page 317)

Glorious Revolution the forced abdication of James II and the accession to the English throne of William and Mary, who had been chosen by Parliament, in 1688 (page 338)

Good Neighbor Policy United States program begun in the 1920's to foster improved relations with the nations of Latin America (page 656)

Gothic style of architecture in medieval Europe that was characterized by height and delicacy of appearance, flying buttresses, pointed arches, and tall, pointed spires (page 282)

Great Cultural Revolution campaign launched by Mao Tse-tung in 1966 to rid the Chinese people of their attachment to traditional ideas and customs (page 718)

Great Leap Forward unsuccessful attempt, begun in China in 1958, to speed up economic development drastically (page 716)

guerrilla warfare (guh·RIL·uh) military technique that uses raids by small bands of soldiers, called **guerrillas,** to keep the enemy off balance (page 326)

guilds associations of merchants or artisans in the Middle Ages. **Merchant guilds** (page 275) were associations of the traders in a town, guaranteeing them exclusive rights to trade and setting quality standards. **Craft guilds** (page 276) consisted of workers in a particular craft and regulated wages, hours, working conditions, and prices.

H

hegira (hih·JY·ruh) flight of Muhammad and his followers from Mecca to Medina in 622 A.D. (page 201)

heliocentric theory (hee·lee·oh·SEN·trik) theory put forth by Copernicus in the 1500's that the sun was the center of the universe (page 317)

helot (HEL·ut) a serf in ancient Sparta (page 77)

heresy (HEH·ruh·see) the denial of the basic principles of the Christian religion or the preaching of unauthorized doctrines (page 252)

hieroglyphics (hy·ur·uh·GLIF·iks) the system of writing used by the Egyptians in which pictures or symbols represent words or sounds (page 18)

Hinduism (HIN·doo·iz·um) major religion of India that slowly developed from interpretations of the Vedas, the books of sacred knowledge (page 140)

history the period of time after people began to keep written records (page 5)

Holocaust the systematic destruction of Jews by the Nazis before and during World War II (page 679)

hubris (HYOO·bris) in Greek tragedy, an arrogant recklessness or disregard for moral laws (page 88)

humanism intellectual movement based on a renewed interest in classical learning that began in Europe about the mid-1300's (page 297)

I

Ice Age four periods in the last 1.5 million years when much of the earth was covered with ice (page 6)

icons (EYE·kahns) small religious pictures set up in churches or homes, or carried on journeys as aids to devotion (page 187)

ideogram a step in the development of written language, in which a picture sign represents an idea (page 12)

imam (ih·MAHM) to Shiite Muslims, a direct descendant of Muhammad who serves as intermediary between Allah and believers (page 204)

immigration the movement of people into a new country in order to settle there (page 495)

imperialism the practice of establishing colonies in order to control raw materials and markets (page 551)

import substitution policy under which the government encourages the manufacture of items that would otherwise be imported (page 782)

impressionism style of painting that flourished during the 1860's and 1870's and aimed to capture the impression of a subject as it might appear in a brief glance (page 521)

indemnity compensation given by one nation to another for war damages (pages 112, 477)

indulgence a pardon given to sinners by the Church in return for repentance. Indulgences were originally granted as rewards for pious deeds. (page 301)

industrial capitalism period of capitalism in which capital was used chiefly for producing and manufacturing goods (page 459)

Industrial Revolution name given to the widespread social and economic changes that occurred after machines and factories replaced labor by hand. The Industrial Revolution began in Great Britain in the late 1700's and gradually spread to other countries. (page 446)

inflation economic situation characterized by a rise in the general level of prices (page 767)

Inquisition during the Middle Ages, the attempt by the Church to seek out and eliminate heresy (page 252)

interchangeable parts the parts of a manufactured product, standardized so that the product can be quickly and cheaply produced in large numbers (page 461)

interdict the punishment of an entire region by the Church through such means as the denial of sacraments (page 251)

iron curtain term, first used in 1946 by Prime Minister Winston Churchill of Great Britain, referring to the barriers that were imposed by the Soviet Union to isolate Eastern Europe from the West (page 701)

irrigation the use of artificial means, such as canals and ditches, to bring water to farm land (page 11)

Islam religion founded in Arabia by the prophet Muhammad in the 600's A.D. (page 200)

Islamic fundamentalism a form of religious nationalism in some Muslim nations that rejects foreign influences and seeks to return to traditional Muslim ways (page 762)

isolationists people who oppose their country's involvement in international affairs (page 674)

J

Janissaries (JAN·ih·ser·eez) highly disciplined slave bodyguards of the Turkish sultans (page 207)

joint-stock company business organization that raises money by selling shares in the company to investors (page 363)

journeyman skilled worker during the Middle Ages who had completed his apprenticeship and worked for a master for daily wages (page 276)

Judaism the Jewish religion, the monotheistic religion that arose among the ancient Hebrews (page 41)

judicial branch branch of government that interprets and applies the laws (page 346)

Junkers (YOONG·kurs) aristocratic landowners in Prussia (page 532)

K

Kaiser (KY·zur) title of the ruler of the German Empire (page 535)

Kami Japanese gods, believed to be especially helpful in promoting fertility in families and crops (page 176)

kibbutz (kih·BOOTS) farm in Israel on which property is collectively owned and planning and work are done communally (page 752)

kingdom a government or country headed by a king or queen; also known as a monarchy (page 18)

knight in the Middle Ages, a noble who, after special training, was raised to honorable military rank in an elaborate religious ceremony (page 248)

L

laissez faire (les·ay FAIR) economic theory advocating freedom from government interference for business. The term comes from the French phrase meaning ''let do''—that is, leave things alone. (page 481)

lay investiture the granting of authority to a member of the clergy by a king or noble during the Middle Ages (page 252)

legion military unit of ancient Rome, consisting of about 4,500 to 6,000 soldiers (page 110)

legislative branch branch of government that makes the laws (page 346)

legitimacy after the Napoleonic Wars, the principle that former ruling families should be restored to their thrones (page 475)

liberalism political and economic movement in Europe in the 1800's that had as its aim the protection of individual rights and freedoms (page 474)

limited constitutional monarchy form of government with a king or queen whose powers are less than absolute and are defined in a written constitution (page 341)

linguist a scholar who studies languages (page 216)

llanos (LAH·nohs) flat, treeless plains in northern South America (page 433)

lobbying organized attempts to persuade legislators to vote for or against a measure (page 768)

M

Magna Carta document signed in 1215 that limited the power of the English king and guaranteed certain rights to ordinary citizens (page 255)

mandate area taken in trust by the League of Nations after World War I, to be administered by a League member (page 610)

manor a large, self-sufficient feudal estate that included a village (page 245)

martial law temporary rule by the military (page 728)

mass production system of manufacturing large numbers of items that are exactly alike and that have interchangeable parts (page 461)

means of production everything used to produce and exchange goods (page 483)

medieval (mee·dee·EE·vuhl) having to do with the Middle Ages (page 234)

mercantilism economic theory that emphasized increasing a nation's wealth by creating a favorable balance of trade. According to mercantilist theory, colonies were valued as sources of gold, silver, and raw materials, and as markets for the manufactured products of the home country. (page 363)

mercenaries professional soldiers who are paid to serve in a foreign army (page 32)

merchant guilds see **guilds**

mestizo (mehs·TEE·zoh) person in colonial Latin America who was of part Indian and part white ancestry (page 434)

metics (MET·iks) alien inhabitants of ancient Athens who were free but not citizens (page 78)

Middle Ages period between ancient times and the modern period, generally considered to have lasted from about 500 to 1500 A.D. (page 234)

migration the movement of groups of people from place to place (page 27)

militarism the glorification of armed strength and the belief that international problems can best be solved by using force (page 592)

millets (MIL·its) communities of religious minorities in the Ottoman Empire (page 207)

mixed economy economy in which some industries are privately owned and some are owned by the government (page 725)

monarchy a government headed by a king or queen (page 18)

monism (MOH·niz·um) the Hindu belief that God and humans are one and indivisible (page 141)

monopoly complete control of a commodity, a service, or a market (page 462)

monotheism (MAHN·uh·thee·iz·um) belief in one God (page 20)

monsoon a seasonal wind that often brings heavy rainfall (page 46)

mosaics (moh·ZAY·iks) pictures formed by inlaid pieces of stone, glass, or enamel (page 187)

mosque (MOSK) Muslim place of worship (page 202)

mulatto (muh·LAHT·oh) in colonial Latin America, a person who was of part black and part white ancestry (page 434)

mullah man learned in Islamic faith and law (page 202)

multinational corporation large business firm that is based in one country but operates in other countries as well (page 782)

Muslims followers of the religion of Islam (page 200)

mystery plays medieval religious dramas on Biblical subjects (page 278)

myths traditional stories about the deeds of gods, goddesses, and heroes (page 73)

N

nationalism feeling of patriotism and loyalty to one's country (page 409)

nationalize to bring industries, lands, or resources under government control or ownership (page 617)

naturalists name given to a group of writers in the late 1800's who depicted the ugly and sordid in life, screening emotion and opinion from their writing (page 521)

nirvana in Hinduism and Buddhism, the state of perfect peace, in which the soul is freed from having to be born again (page 143)

nomads people who wander from place to place in search of food (page 8)

O

oasis a place in the desert where irrigation or an underground spring provides enough moisture to make the ground fertile (page 17)

Op Art style of painting developed in the 1960's that rejected reality as the subject of its painting and instead used brilliant colors and shapes to create optical effects (page 791)

Open Door Policy policy put forth by the United States government in 1899 proposing equal trading rights for all nations in China (page 646)

oral traditions poems, songs, or stories passed by word of mouth from one generation to the next (page 219)

P

pampas grassy plains in southeastern South America (page 433)

Pan-Slavism movement seeking the political and cultural union of all Slavic peoples (page 541)

papyrus (puh·PY·rus) a reedy plant growing in marshes near the Nile River that the Egyptians used to make paper (page 18)

Parliament the representative assembly of Great Britain. It is made up of the House of Commons, representing the common people, and the House of Lords, representing the nobility and clergy. (page 257)

partisans members of resistance movements during World War II who engaged in sabotage against the Germans (page 672)

pashas provincial governors of the Ottoman Empire (page 545)

passive resistance see **civil disobedience**

patricians (puh·TRISH·unz) the aristocratic class in ancient Rome (page 108)

Pax Romana the ''Roman peace,'' a time of unity, peace, and stability in the Roman Empire that lasted from 27 B.C. to 180 A.D. (page 121)

Pax Tokugawa (toh·koo·GAH·wah) period of peace in Japan under the Tokugawa shogunate, beginning about 1603 and lasting approximately 250 years (page 424)

pharaoh (FAIR·oh)   title of the rulers of ancient Egypt who were religious as well as political leaders (page 18)

philosophy   inquiry into the basic questions of reality and human existence (page 85)

phonogram   a step in the development of written language, in which a picture sign represents a sound, usually a syllable (page 12)

pictogram   a step in the development of written language, in which a picture sign is used to represent an object (page 12)

planned economy   governmental regulation and direction of the resources of a nation (page 619)

plebeians (pluh·BEE·uhns)   the common people of ancient Rome, including all those who were not patricians (page 108)

plebiscite (PLEB·ih·site)   procedure by which a government proposal is submitted to the people for a direct vote (page 407)

pogroms (poh·GRUMS)   violent persecutions and massacres of Jews, particularly those in Russia in the 1800's (page 542)

polis (POH·lis)   the Greek word for city-state (page 69)

polytheism (PAHL·ee·thee·iz·um)   belief in many gods (page 20)

Pop Art   style of art developed in the 1950's that took popular objects, such as comic books and soup cans, as its subjects (page 791)

pope   the spiritual leader of the Roman Catholic Church (page 250)

popular government   government in which the people rule themselves (page 76)

popular sovereignty (SAHV·ren·tee)   the free choice of the people in choosing and controlling a government (page 347)

praetors (PREE·tors)   judges in the Roman republic who created much of the law by their decisions in court cases (page 109)

predestination   doctrine preached in the 1500's by John Calvin that God had already chosen who was to be saved and who was to be damned (page 307)

prehistoric age   the period of time prior to the keeping of written records (page 4)

prime minister   in Great Britain, the chief member of the Cabinet and the real head of the government (page 341)

primogeniture (pry·muh·JEN·ih·cher)   system under which only the oldest son can inherit the father's property (page 403)

proconsuls   governors of the ancient Roman provinces (page 115)

proletariat (proh·luh TAIR·ee·ut)   the working class (page 484)

prophet   term used by the ancient Hebrews to describe a great religious and moral thinker (page 41)

protectionism   economic policy of using government means to reduce imports, thus protecting domestic industries from foreign competition (page 767)

protectorate   a region controlled by a foreign power, although the native ruler continues to head the government (page 554)

Protestant   a member of any of the Christian religions that developed during the Reformation (page 305)

publicans   officials who collected the taxes in ancient Rome (page 115)

pyramids   huge stone structures that were built as tombs for the Egyptian pharaohs (page 24)

Q

queue (KYOO)   hair braid that all Chinese men were required to wear during the Ch'ing dynasty to indicate their submission to Manchu rule (page 418)

quipu (KEE·poo)   knotted string used by the Incas to keep records and to assist the memory (page 231)

R

rabbi   in Judaism, a scholar learned in the scriptures and commentaries on religious law (page 127)

radicals   those who seek extreme, far-reaching changes in existing conditions (page 399)

rajah   minor king or prince in India (page 139)

rationalism   the belief that truth can be arrived at solely by reason (page 321)

reactionary   person who not only opposes change but seeks to restore the conditions that existed before change occurred (page 477)

realism   beginning in the mid-1800's, a movement in literature and art that attempted to represent everyday life with truth and accuracy (page 520)

recession period characterized by temporary business slowdown and increased unemployment (page 767)

Reformation religious revolution that began in the early 1500's and split the Church in Western Europe (page 297)

regionalism in the art and literature of the United States, the portrayal of everyday life in various regions of the country (page 520)

reincarnation (ree·in·karh·NAY·shun) belief of Hinduism and Buddhism that the soul does not die with the body but enters the body of another being and thus lives second, third, and more lives (page 141)

Renaissance (REN·uh·sahns) philosophical and artistic movement that began in Italy around 1350 and was characterized by a revival of interest in the classical learning of Greece and Rome; also the period during which the movement flourished (page 297)

reparations payment for war damages (page 605)

republic form of government in which those entitled to vote choose representatives to run the government (page 108)

Restoration name given to the reign of Charles II, which restored the monarchy to England (page 337)

revolution violent attempt to change the structure of a country, government, and society (page 331); also, a total or far-reaching change in people's lives (page 9)

Risorgimento (ree·sor·jee·MEN·toh) name given to the nationalist movement in Italy during the 1800's (page 527)

Roman Catholic Church Christian church headed by the pope in Rome (page 186)

Romance languages languages that are derived from Latin—Italian, French, Spanish, Portuguese, and Rumanian (page 126)

Romanesque (roh·muhn·ESK) style of architecture dominant in Europe from about 1000 to 1200, characterized by round arches, domes, thick walls, few windows, and dark interiors (page 282)

romanticism movement in the arts in the 1800's that appealed to sentiment and imagination, depicting life in an idealized form rather than as it was (page 517)

S

sacraments rites of the Christian Church at which participants receive the grace of God (page 129)

samurai (SAM·oo·ry) warrior landlords who ruled local areas of feudal Japan (page 178)

Sanskrit language spoken by the Aryans who invaded India about 1500 B.C. (page 48)

satellites communist countries of Eastern Europe that are subordinate to the Soviet Union in matters of both domestic and foreign policy (page 701); also, objects placed in orbit around the earth, moon, or other heavenly body (page 786)

satires literary works that make fun of ideas and people (page 88)

savanna area of relatively dry grasslands (page 216)

scholasticism medieval philosophy that attempted to reconcile faith and reason (page 279)

Scientific Revolution name given to the new way of thinking, which relied on questioning and experimentation, that developed in Europe in the 1500's and 1600's (page 317)

sea dogs English sea captains of the 1500's who were both traders and pirates (page 375)

sectionalism rivalry among the various sections of a country, such as that among the Northeast, the South, and the West in the United States during the 1800's (page 492)

separatism movement advocating the complete separation of one group or section from another, such as the movement calling for independence of Quebec from Canada (page 773)

sepoys (SEE·poys) native troops in British India, who were trained and led by British officers (page 563)

seppuku (SEP·POO·KOO) ceremonial suicide, the honorable way for Japanese samurai to avoid torture, execution, or defeat in battle (page 180)

serfs rural laborers, or peasants, who were not allowed to move away from the land on which they worked (page 76)

shogun after 1192, the chief military officer of the Japanese emperor who actually controlled the government (page 178)

shuttle diplomacy process in which a negotiator moves back and forth between countries to try to arrange a peace agreement (page 757)

silt the fertile soil left behind when a flooding river recedes (page 17)

simony (SY·muh·nee) the buying and selling of Church positions during the Middle Ages (page 252)

Slavs a people with the same basic language who gradually spread over central, eastern, and southeastern Europe (page 184)

socialism political and economic system under which the means of production are owned publicly and operated for the welfare of all (page 483)

sphere of influence a region in which one nation has special economic and political privileges (page 554)

status quo the existing conditions at any given time (page 478)

steppes vast grassy, treeless plains of southeastern Europe and Asia (page 190)

Stone Age early period of human development during which artifacts were made of stone (page 5)

strike means of protest in which workers refuse to work until their demands have been met (page 470)

stupa (STOO·pah) hemisphere-shaped structure built to hold relics of Buddha (page 146)

stylus pointed stick used in cuneiform writing (page 29)

subsistence agriculture the raising of crops entirely for local consumption (page 196)

suffrage the right to vote (page 489)

suffragettes women who fought for voting rights for all women (page 489)

sultan title of the ruler of the Ottoman Empire (page 207)

superpower a nation possessing military and economic power far greater than those of most other nations. The United States and the Soviet Union emerged as superpowers after World War II. (page 692)

suttee suicide of a widow on her husband's funeral pyre, a common practice in ancient India (page 146)

T

taiga (TY·gah) forest zone of the Soviet Union, with abundant rainfall, cold temperatures, and short growing seasons (page 192)

tax farming system of tax collecting in ancient Rome whereby tax collectors agreed to pay a fixed amount to the Roman treasury, keeping for themselves whatever they collected in excess of this amount (page 115)

tepees cone-shaped tents, made of buffalo hide, of the Plains tribes of North America (page 231)

Third World developing nations, mostly in Africa and Asia, that are not aligned with either the free world or the communist world (page 704)

tithe during the Middle Ages, a Church tax collected from all Christians, equal to a tenth of their income (page 251)

totalitarian government type of government in which every aspect of the individual's life is controlled by the state (page 78)

totem pole post with wooden carvings of people and beasts, made by the tribes of the northwest coast of North America to symbolize tribal history (page 231)

treaty ports special ports in Japan, China, and Korea that, unlike other ports in these countries, were open to foreign trade in the 1800's and early 1900's (page 567)

tribunes officials in the Roman republic who represented the plebeians (page 109)

tribute money or gifts paid regularly by one government or group to another to acknowledge submission or in return for protection from invasion (pages 167, 417)

troubadour (TROO·bah·dor) traveling singers during the Middle Ages who wrote poems of love and chivalry and sang them in nobles' courts (page 278)

tyrant a leader in ancient Greece who seized power by force rather than by inheriting it (page 73)

U

ujamaa villages local cooperative villages in Tanzania organized in an attempt to increase standards of living (page 749)

ultimatum the final offer of terms for a settlement (page 595)

union association of workers joined together to promote their common interests (page 470)

universal manhood suffrage the right of all adult males to vote (page 401)

usury (YOO·zhur·ee)   in medieval times, the charging of interest for the loan of money; today the term means the charging of unfair rates of interest for the loan of money (page 269)

utilitarianism   theory that the principle of utility, or usefulness, is the standard by which a society and its laws should be measured (page 481)

utopian socialism   type of socialism that advocated forming small cooperative communities whose inhabitants would own the means of production and share the goods produced (page 483)

V

vassal   person granted land by a feudal lord in return for services (page 244)

veche   town meeting of all heads of household in Kievan Russian (page 193)

vernacular language   the everyday speech of a particular locality (page 278)

veto   the power of one branch of government to refuse to approve an act of another (page 109)

viceroys   representatives of the monarch who ruled the Spanish colonies in the Americas (page 374)

W

welfare state   country in which the government assumes primary responsibility for the welfare of its citizens (page 708)

Z

ziggurat   a Sumerian temple built in layers, each layer smaller than the one below (page 29)

Zionism (ZY·uhn·iz·um)   movement that sought to resettle Jews in Palestine (page 641)

Zollverein (TSAWL·fer·ine)   customs union set up among most of the German states in the 1800's (page 532)

Zoroastrianism (zoh·roh·AS·tree·uhn·iz·um)   Persian religion concerned with the struggle between good and evil (page 37)

INDEX

Anglican Church (Church of England), 306, 307, *m310*; English Revolution and, 331, 334, 336

Anglo-Egyptian Sudan, *m559*, 560

Anglo-Iranian Oil Company, 751, 757

Anglo-Saxon Chronicle, 243

Anglo-Saxons, *m184*, 241, 243

Angola, 742, *m744*, *m814*; as Portuguese colony, 369, *m371*, *m379*, 558, *m559*; becomes independent, 745; civil war in (1975), 749, 772

Angora, *m607*, 643, *m751*; battle at, 211, *m211*. *See also* Ankara.

animism, 48, 60, 110, 176

Anjou, *m254*, 255, *m284*, 285

Ankara, *m607*, 643, *m751*, *m811*

Anne, queen of England, 337–40

Anschluss, **623,** 664–65

anthropology, 5, 6, 514

antibiotics, 788–**90**

Anti-Comintern Treaty, 662

Antigonus, Macedonian dynasty, 99

Antioch, *m97*, 99, 100, *m133*; Christianity in, 129, *m129*, *m249*; in eastern Roman Empire, *m185*; Crusades in, 265, *m265*, *m267*, *c268*; in medieval trade, *m272*

Antiochus IV, Seleucid king, 100

Antoninus Pius, Roman emperor, *c118*, 120

Antony, Marc, 118

Anyang, 57, *m57*

apartheid, **746,** 798

Apennine Mountains, 107, *m108*

Aphrodite, Greek goddess, 73

Apollo, Greek god, 73, 76, 146

Apostles, 127

Appalachian Mountains, 385, 386, *m386*, *m387*, 492, *m493*

appeasement, **667,** *p669*

apprentice system, 276

Aqaba, Gulf of, *m751*, 755

aqueducts, *p124*, 125

Aquinas, Thomas, 279

Aquino, Benigno, 728

Aquino, Corazon, 728

Aquitaine, 253, *m254*, 255, 283, *m284*

Arab League, 759

Arabia: ancient empires in, *m31*, *m32*, *m33*, *m36*; Roman Empire in, *m120*; Muslim Empire in, 201–04, *m202*; in medieval trade, *m272*; in World War I, *m597*. *See also* Saudi Arabia.

Arabic language, 759

Arabs: Muslim Empire and, 201–08; Seljuk Turks and, 264; science of, 279; printing by, 298; slave trade of, *p432*; in Palestine, after World War I, 641, *p644*; in wars with Israel, 752–53, 755, *p756*; Pan-Arabism among, 754

Aragón, 285, *m285*, 329

arbitration, **581**

Archangel, *m350*, *m671*, 678, *m810*

archeology, *p153*, 219, 224, 514, 575

Archimedes, 103, 148

architecture: Egyptian, 24; Sumerian, 29; Babylonian, 33; of ancient Greece, *p66*, *p75*, 83, 84; in Roman Empire, *p124*,

125; of Gupta India, 146; of Byzantine Empire, 187; of Russian Orthodox Church, 197; of Mogul Empire, *p210*, 212; of early American civilizations, *p215*, 231; medieval, 246–48, 279–82, *p280–81*; Renaissance, *p303*; of czarist Russia, *p352*; romantic movement in, 520; after World War I, *p634–35*, 637; after World War II, 791, *m792*

archons, in ancient Athens, **78**

Argentina, 581, 655, *m813*; early history of, 224; becomes independent, 436, *m439*, 440; after World War II, 774–75, *p776*, 782

Argonne Forest, battle at, *m599*, 603

Aristarchus of Samos, 103

aristocracies, **73,** 87

Aristophanes, 88

Aristotle, 78, 87, 88, 99, 279, 317, 513

Arizona, 492, *m493*

Arkwright, Richard, 448

Armada, Spanish, 326, *p328*, 331, 376

Armenia, 27, *m27*, *m120*, *m202*, 203

armies: of ancient Sparta, 77–78; Macedonian, 96, 99; Roman, 110, *p114*, 116, 121–22, 134; Carthaginian, 112–13, *m117*; Persian, 143; of Chandragupta, 144; of Mongols, 171–72, 209–11; of feudal Japan, 180; of Byzantine Empire, 185; of Harsha, 208; of medieval England, 255, 283; of Crusades, 265, *m265*, 267, *m267*; guerrilla warfare, 326, *p734*, 777; in English Civil War, 334–36; French, under Louis XIV, 344; of czarist Russia, 351, *p543*; Austrian, under Maria Theresa, *p355*; Prussian, 356; in American Revolution, *p390*, 398; of revolutionary France, *p400*, 402–05; French, under Napoleon, 405–12; of Bolívar and San Martín, 437–38; Red Shirts, in Italy, 529; Prussian, under Bismarck, 533–35; German, under Bismarck, *p538*, 539; of Austria-Hungary, 545; imperialism and, 552; in British-controlled India, 563, 564, *p565*; before World War I, militarism and, 592; in World War I, 596–603, *p600*, 614; German, after World War I, 607; Red Army, in Russia, 615, 617; German, before World War II, 628, *p669*; Chinese, 647, 648; Japanese, before World War II, *p652*, 653; in Latin American politics, 655, 775, *p776*, 777, 778; in World War II, 668–72, *p673*, 675, 678, 680–84, *p682*; in NATO and Warsaw Pact, 704; UN, in Korean War, 720–21; of post-World War II Japan, 723; in Vietnam War, 731–33, *p734*; in post-World War II Africa, 745, 749; in Turkish politics, 752; French, in Algeria, 753; in Suez crisis (1956), 754; Israeli, 755

armistices: after World War I, 604; after Korean War, 721

Armstrong, Louis, *p634–35*

art(s): of early humans, *p4*, *p7*, 8, *p9*; of ancient Egypt, *p2–3*, 24, *p25*; Sumerian, *p28*, *p34–35*; of India, *p50*, *p140*,

p145, 146, *p147*, *p210*; Chinese, *p55*, 58, *p157*, 167, *p168*, *p170*; of Crete and Mycenae, *p70*; of ancient Greece, *p81*, 83–84, *p84*; Hellenistic, *p102*; Etruscan, *p109*; of ancient Rome, *p111*; of early Christians, *p130*; Japanese, *p179*, *p425*; of Byzantine Empire, *p186*, 187, *p188*; Russian, 193–94, *p195*, *p196*, *p541*; Islamic, *p203*, *p205*, 206; African, *p221*, *p222*, *p556*, 750; of early American civilizations, *p226*, *p228*, *p230*; medieval, *p236*, *p250*, *p276*, 279–82; Renaissance, 299–301, *p300*, *p302–03*, *p320*; of Rembrandt, 329, *p330*; of Vermeer, *p380*; during Industrial Revolution, *p462*, 467–69; of Beardsley, *p488*; of Munch, *p516*; in 1800's, *p518–19*; romantic movement in, 520, *p533*; realism and impressionism in, 521; after World War I, *p605*, *p620*, *p634–35*, 636–37, *p654*; photography, *p622*; political cartoons, *p768*; after World War II, *p768*, 790–96, *p792*, *p794–95*. *See also* architecture; painting; sculpture.

Arthur, legendary English king, 278, *p488*

Articles of Confederation, 391

artifacts, 5

Aryabhata, 148

Aryans, *m46*, 48–52, 139, 140

Ashanti, 557

Ashikaga family, 178, 180, 422

Asia, *m811*; early humans in, 5, 6, 10, *m10*, 44; early Indian civilization in, 45–48, *m46*; Aryan civilization of, 48–52; early Chinese civilization in, 52–60, *m53*, *m57*; Alexander's empire in, *m97*, 99; trade with Roman Empire, 122; Hinduism in, 140–41; Buddhism in, 141–43, *m142*, 166–67, 176–80; Maurya Empire in, 144, *m144*; Gupta civilization in, 145–48, *m146*; Mongol conquests in, *m172*; migration to Africa from, 219; migration to Americas from, 224; medieval trade of, 269, 271, *m272–73*, 361; Ottoman Empire in, *m349*; European exploration and, 366, 369–72, *m370*; European colonies in, about 1700, *m378*; Dutch colonies in, 380; French colonies in, 381; Ch'ing Empire in, *m417*; European trade with, 426–29; British in, *p428*; imperialism in, 563–75, *p572*, *m566*, *m570*, *m576*, 591; Japanese aggressions in 1930's in, 660, *m661*; World War II in, 679–80, *m681*, *p682*, 683–86; after World War II, 715–16, 728–38, *p734*; in 1980's, *m717*, *m751*. *See also* names of individual countries.

Asia Minor, *m751*, *m811*; Christianity in, *m249*; early human settlements in, 10, *m10*; Persian Empire in, 36, *m36*; Phoenicians in, 37–39, *m39*; ancient Greek settlements in, *m68*, *m77*; Mycenaean civilization in, 69, *m69*; Persian Wars in, 92, 93, *m93*; in Peloponnesian War, 96; under Alexander, *m97*, 99; Roman Empire in, 116, *m117*, 118, *m120*, *m133*; spread of Christianity in, *m129*; eastern

Beat Generation, 793
Beatles, 792, *p794–95*
Bechuanaland, *m559*, 562
Becket, Thomas à, 255, *p258*
Beckett, Samuel, 793
Bedouin, 201
Beethoven, Ludwig van, 517
Begin, Menachem, 757, *p770–71*
Beirut, 761
Belgian Congo, 558, *m559*, 744–45
Belgium, 327, *m810*; creation of, 496; in 1871, *m536*; Congo under, 558, *m559*, 744–45; before World War I, *m593*; in World War I, 595–96, *m597*, 598, *m599*; after World War I, 605, 606, *m607*; and France, 620; before World War II, *m666*; in World War II, 671, *m671*, 672, 684; after World War II, *m699*; in NATO, *m703*, 704; in Common Market, 711
Belgrade, *m546*, *m671*, *m699*, *m703*, *m810*
Belize, *m812*
Bell, Alexander Graham, 458
Benares, 59
Benedict, saint, 251
Benelux countries, 711
Bengal, 429, *m566*
Ben-Gurion, David, 752
Benin, *m217*, *p222*, 223, *m744*, 750, *m814*
Bentham, Jeremy, 481
Benz, Karl, 459
Berbers, *m202*, 203, 223, 555
Berg, Alban, 636
Bering Strait, 224, *m225*
Berlin, Irving, 637
Berlin, *m343*, *m347*, *m353*, *m411*, *m476*, *m597*, *m607*, *m666*, *m703*, *m810*; in War of Austrian Succession, 357; as capital of German Empire, 535, *m536*, 537; Congress of, 547, 555, 593; in World War II, *m671*, 678, 684; post-World War II division of, 697, 698, *m699*, *p706*; airlift to, 703, 766; wall built in, 704
Bernstein, Leonard, 793
Bessarabia, *m607*, 608, *m666*, 668
Bessemer, Henry, 450
Bessemer process, *p449*, 450
Bethlehem, 127, *m129*
Bhagavad-Gita, 139
Bhutan, *m724*, *m811*
Biafra, 747
Bible, 40; exodus of Hebrews in, 39; Dead Sea scrolls, *p40*; Old Testament of, 41; New Testament of, 40, 127, 128; Charlemagne's, *p238*; Lindisfarne Gospel, *p250*; Luther and, 304, 305; printed by Gutenberg, *p308*; King James Version, 332
Bill of Rights, English, 338, 340, *c340*, 341, 396
biological sciences, 506
biology, 319, 320, 506–09, 788
Bismarck, Otto von, *p538*, 545, 592, 595; Franco-Prussian War and, 498–501; unification of Germany under, 533–35, *c535*; opposition to, 536–40

Black Death, 277. *See also* bubonic plague.
Black Hole of Calcutta, 429
Black Sea; and ancient Greek colonies, *m68*, 73, 92; and growth of Russia, 190, 191, *m191*, 349, *m350*; and medieval trade, 269, *m272–73*; and Ottoman Empire, *m349*, *m546*
black Shirts, 624–25
blacks: in South Africa, 562, 746; civil rights for, in U.S., 768–69, *p770–71*; in Cuba, 775; in U.S., music of, 792; literature of, 793
Bleriot, Louis, *p457*
blitzkrieg, 670
Blum, Léon, 621
Boer War, 562
Boers, 560, 562
Bogotá, *m439*, 774
Bohemia, *m286*; Calvinism in, *m310*; under Hapsburgs, *m327*, *m343*, *m347*; Thirty Years' War in, 342; in 1815, *m476*
Bolívar, Simón, 436–40, *p437*, *m439*
Bolivia, *m813*; early cultures in, 225, 229; becomes independent, 438, *m439*; oil in, 653; after World War II, 774, 777
Böll, Heinrich, 793
Bologna, University of, 279
Bolshevik Revolution. *See* Russian Revolution.
Bolsheviks, 615, *p616*
Bombay, 376, *m378*, 429, *m566*, *m724*, *m811*
Bonaparte, Joseph, ruler of Spain, 410
Bonaparte, Louis Napoleon. *See* Napoleon III.
Bonaparte, Napoleon. *See* Napoleon Bonaparte.
Boniface, saint, *m249*, 251
Boniface VIII, pope, 287–89
Bonin Islands, *m661*, 724
Book of the Dead, *p21*, 26
books: sacred, 40; Lindisfarne Gospel, *p250*; printing of, 298–99, 301, *p308*; autobiographies, *p305*; publishing of, in 1970's, 796. *See also* printing.
Borneo, *m370*, *m378*, *m717*, 728, 729, *m811*; Buddhism and Hinduism in, *m142*; British and Dutch in, *m570*, 574, *m576*, *m661*; in World War II, *m681*
Bosch, Juan, 777
Bosnia, *m546*, 547, 593, 595, *m597*, 608
Bosporus, *m350*, 353; in World War I, *m597*; after World War I, *m607*, 608; in World War II, *m671*, 675, 678
Boston, *m386*, 387, *p390*, *m812*
Botswana, *m744*
Botticelli, Sandro, 299
Bourbon family, 329, *c407*, 412, 475, 495, 529
bourgeoisie, French, 392, 393, 399
Boxer Rebellion, 646
Boyacá, 438, *m439*
Boyle, Robert, 320
Brahma, Indian god, *p140*, 141
Brahmans, 51, 139, 140, 143, 145, 566
Brahms, Johannes, 517

Brandenburg, *m286*, *m327*; after Peace of Westphalia, 342, *m343*; Treaty of Utrecht and, 346
Brandenburg Gate, in Berlin, *p706*
Brandenburg-Prussia, *m343*, 354–56
Brandt, Willy, 708
Braque, Georges, *p635*, 636
Brasilia, *p781*, *m813*
Brazil, 433, 779, *m813*; early history of, 224; as Portuguese colony, 368, *m371*, 372, *m379*, 434; slavery in, *p437*; becomes independent, 438, *m439*, 440; in 1920's, 655; after World War II, 777, *p781*, 782
Brazza, Pierre de, 558
Brazzaville, 558, *m559*, *m814*
Brecht, Bertolt, 793
Bremen, 269–71, *m273*, *m536*
Brest-Litovsk, *m597*
Brest-Litovsk, Treaty of (1918), 602, 615
Brezhnev, Leonid, *p695*, 705, 708
Briand, Aristide, 660
Britain: under Roman Empire, 118, *m120*, 122, 240–41; spread of Christianity in, *m129*; barbarian invasions of, 133, *m133*; Saxon kingdoms in, 241, *m241*. *See also* British Empire; England; Great Britain; United Kingdom.
British Columbia, 490, *m490*
British Commonwealth of Nations, 642, 655, 711, 724
British East Africa, 558, *m559*
British East India Company, 427, 429, 563–66. *See also* English East India Company.
British Empire: Canada in, 489–90, *m490*, 773; Australia and New Zealand in, 490–91, *m491*; African colonies of, 556–58, *m559*; India in, 563–66, *m566*, 724; in Southeast Asia and Pacific, 574, 576, *m576*; in Caribbean and Latin America, *m580*; in Middle East, after World War I, *m607*, 608; tariffs within, 630; changes in, 640–43, *p644*; after World War II, 709, 729, 742, 743, 745–46. *See also* Britain; England; Great Britain; United Kingdom.
British Guiana, *m439*, 477, *m580*, 581, 674
British Museum, *p468*
British North America Act, 489–90
British Somaliland, *m559*, 675
British West Indies, 674
Brittany, *m254*, 255, *m284*, 285
Britten, Benjamin, 791
bronze, 11, *p55*, *p56*, 58
Brown, Robert, 506–08
Brown Shirts, 627
Brown v. Board of Education of Topeka, 768–69
Bruegel, Pieter, 301, *p313*
Bruges, 269, *m272*, *m273*, 277
Brunei, *m717*, *m811*
Brussels, 402, *m411*, *m536*, *m599*, *m810*
Brutus, Marcus, 117, 118
bubonic plague, 277, 511
Buchenwald, 679

Budapest, 545, *m546*, *m607*, *m699*, *m703*, *m810*; in World War I, *m597*, 598; in World War II, *m671*

Buddha, 138, 141–43, 146, *p147*

Buddhism, 141–43, *m142*; Asoka's conversion to, 144; under Guptas, 145; art of, *p145*; in southern India, 150; in T'ang China, 166–67; in Japan, 176–80

Buenos Aires, *m439*, 654, *m813*

Bulgaria, *m810*; Ottoman Empire and, *m546*, 547; before World War I, *m593*; in World War I, 596, *m597*, 603; after World War I, *m607*, 608, 623; before World War II, *m666*; in World War II, *m671*, 675, 678, 684; after World War II, 698, *m699*, 701; in Warsaw Pact, *m703*, 704; in Comecon, 712

Bulgarians, *m249*, 546

Burgundians, *m133*, 134, *m184*, 235

Burgundy, *m254*, *m284*, 285

Burma, *m661*, *m717*, *m724*, *m811*; Buddhism and Hinduism in, *m142*, 143; under Great Britain, *m566*, *m570*, 574, *m576*; in World War II, 680, *m681*; after World War II, 729–30

Burma Road, *m661*, *m681*, 729

Burundi, *m744*, *m814*

bushido, 180

business cycles, 462–63

businesses: corporations, 461–62; monopolies, 462; in Latin America, foreign-owned, 580, 656; multinational, 782

Byron, Lord, 480, 517

Byzantine Church, and the Byzantine Empire, 183, 186; and the Kievan states, 193–97, *p195*, *p196*

Byzantine Empire, *m172*, 183–90, *p183*, *p188*, *m202*, 211, *m240*; under Justinian, *m185*; Copts in, *p186*; Crusades and, 264–68, *m265*, *m267*; in medieval trade, *m272*

Byzantium, 132, *m133*, 183. *See also* Constantinople.

cabinet, 340

Cabot, John, *m371*, 375

Cabral, Pedro Alvares, 368, *m370–71*

cadastres, *p364*

Cádiz, 38

Caesar, Julius, 116–18, 126, 305

Cage, John, 792

Cairo, *m559*, *m751*, 761, *m814*; in Muslim Empire, *m202*, 204; in medieval trade, *m272*; in World War II, *m671*

Calais, battle at, 283, *m284*

Calcutta, 376, *m378*, 429, *m566*, *m724*, *m811*

Calder, Alexander, *p794–95*

calendar: development of, 12; of ancient Egypt, 24; Sumerian, 29; Chinese, 58, 158, 426; Greek, 73; Roman, 117

California, 492, *m493*

Caligula, Roman emperor, 118, *c118*

caliph, 202

caliphates, 204

calligraphy, 60

Calvin, John, 307, *p308*, 310, 314

Calvinism, 307, *m310*, 326–29

Cambodia, *m717*, *m811*; Buddhism and Hinduism in, *m142*, 143; France and, 499; after World War II, 730, 797; in Vietnam War, 732, 733; invaded by Vietnam, 735

Cambridge University, 523

Cameroon, 217, 557, *m559*, *m744*, *m814*

Camp David agreements, 757, 766, *p770–71*

Canaan, *m27*, 39, *m39*, 40, *m69*. *See also* Palestine.

Canaanites, 40

Canada, *m490*, *m812*; early cultures in, 224, 231; exploration of, *m371*; French exploration and colonies in, 380–81, *m386*; as British dominion, 489–90, *m576*; Statute of Westminster and, 642; in NATO, 704; after World War II, 765, 772–74

Canadian Pacific Railway, 490, *m490*

canals, in early civilizations, 11; in ancient Egypt, 17, 25; in Tigris-Euphrates Valley, 27; during Industrial Revolution, 455

Canary Islands, *m371*, *m379*, 557, *m559*, *m814*

Canning, George, 478

cannons, invention of, 362

Canossa, *m249*, 259

Canterbury, *m241*, 243, *m249*, 255, *m310*

Canterbury Tales, 278, *p280–81*

Canton, *m166*, *m167*, *m172*, *m175*, *m370*, *m378*, *m417*, *m811*; trade through, 167, *m273*, 418, 427, 570, *m570*, *p572*; in Opium War, 569; Kuomintang control over, 647; under Japan, *m661*

Canute, Danish king, 243

Cape Colony, 477, *m559*, 560, 562

Cape of Good Hope, *m217*, 366, *m371*, *m559*, *m814*; Dutch colony in, *m379*, 380

Cape Town, 431, *m559*, 560, 746–47, *m814*

Capet, Hugh, 253

Capetians, 253–54, 283

capitalism: in Middle Ages, 271–74; commercial, 459; socialism and, 483–85

capitalists, 452

Caracalla, Roman emperor, 123

Caracas, 436, *m439*, 654, *m813*

Carbonari, 527

Cárdenas, Lázaro, 656

Caribbean Sea, *m435*, *m439*, *m812*; exploration of, *m371*; European colonies in, about 1700, *m379*; imperialism in, *m580*; U.S. interventions in, 584. *See also* Latin America.

Carlsbad, *m476*, 480

Carlsbad Decrees, 480

Carlyle, Thomas, 481

Carnegie, Andrew, *p460*, 462, 590

Caroline Islands, 576, *m576*, 605, *m661*, *m681*, 696

Carolingians, 237, 253

Carpathian Mountains, 190, *m191*, *m810*

Carroll, Lewis, *p522*

cartels, 462, 537, 539

Carter, Jimmy, *p695*, *c767*, 769; foreign policy of, 705, 772, 779; Camp David agreements and, 757, 766, *p770–71*

Carthage, 38, *m68*, *m108*, *m113*; and Rome, 112–13, *m117*, *m120*; in Byzantine Empire, *m185*

Cartier, Jacques, *m371*, *p377*, 380

cartography, 361, *p364*

Cartwright, Edmund, 450

Caspian Sea, and Hittites, 31, *m32*; and early Russia, 190, *m191*; and Ottoman Empire, *m349*

Cassius, Gaius, 117, 118

Castaneda, Carlos, 796

caste system, 140, 141, 143, 145, 208, 211, 566

Castile-León, 285, *m285*

Castlereagh, Lord, 475, 478

castles, 246–48, *p247*

Castro, Fidel, *p734*, 775, *p776*, 777

Catherine II (the Great), czarina of Russia, *m350*, 351–53, *p352*

Catholic Church. *See* Roman Catholic Church.

Catholic Emancipation Act (1829), 486, *c489*

Catholic Reformation, 307–11

Caucasus, *m671*, 678

Caucasus Mountains, 190, *m191*, *m810*, *m811*

Cavour, Camillo Benso di, 528–29, *p530*

Caxton, William, *p488*

Celebes, *m370*, *m378*, *m570*, *m576*, *m661*, *m681*, *m717*

cell theory, 508, 509

Celts, 240, 241

censors, in Rome, 110, 115

Central African Republic, *m744*, *m814*

Central America, *m812*; early cultures in, 225–31, *m225*; Spanish colonies in, *m371*, 374, *m379*; geography of, 433, *m435*; independence won by nations of, 436, *m439*; imperialism in, *m580*. *See also* Latin America.

Central America, United Provinces of, 436–40, *m439*

Central Park, in New York City, *p468*

Central Powers, in World War I, 596, *m597*, 602–04, 606

Ceylon, 46, *m46*, *m209*, *m212*, *m273*; Buddhism and Hinduism in, *m142*; as Portuguese colony, *m370*, 372; as Dutch colony, *m378*, 380; under Great Britain, 564, *m566*. *See also* Sri Lanka.

Cézanne, Paul, 521

Chad, *m744*, *m814*

Chaeronea, battle at, 97, *m97*

Chaldeans, 33, *m33*, 36, *c38*, 41

Challenger, space shuttle, 785, 786

Châlons, battle at, *m133*, 134

Chalukya dynasty, 209

Chamberlain, Neville, 666, 667, *p669*, 670

Champagne, *m254*, 271, *m272*

Champlain, Samuel de, 381

Chan-Chan, 229
Chandragupta I, Gupta ruler, 145
Chandragupta II, Gupta ruler, 145
Chandragupta Maurya, 144
Changamire, African kingdom, 221
Changan, 152, m154, 156, 165, m166
Chao K'uang-yin, Sung ruler, 167
Chaplin, Charlie, p633
Charlemagne, 237–39, m237, p238, 257, 259
Charles I, king of England, 332–36, p339, c340
Charles II, king of England, 336, 337, 340, 385
Charles VII, king of France, 284
Charles X, king of France, 496
Charles IV, Holy Roman Emperor, 286
Charles V, Holy Roman Emperor, 325–26, p328, 354
Charles I, king of Spain. See Charles V, Holy Roman Emperor.
Charles the Bald, Frankish king, 239, m239
Charles the Bold, duke of Burgundy, 284
Charles Martel, Frankish ruler, 236
Charleston, m386, p494
Chartist movement, 471, 486
Chartres, m249; cathedral at, 282
Château-Thierry, battle at, m599, 603
Chaucer, Geoffrey, 278, p280–81
Chavin, 225, m225
chemistry, 320–21, 505–06, 788
Chiang Kai-shek, 647, 648, 679, 716, 720
Chibcha, 229
Chicago, 769, 786, m812
Chichén Itźa, m225, p226, 227
child labor, 452, p453, 471
Chile, m813; early cultures in, 224, 229; as Spanish colony, m379; becomes independent, 438, m439; in 1920's, 655; under Allende, p776, 778
Chimu, m225, 229
Chin dynasty, 167, m167, 172, c173
Ch'in dynasty, 151–52, c151, m152, 156, p157
China, m811; early human settlements in, 10, m10, 11, 44; geography of, 52–54, m53; dynastic cycle of, 54–55; under Shang dynasty, 55–60, p55, p56, m57, 369; Confucius in, 138; under Sui and T'ang dynasties, p138, 165, m166, p170; Buddhism in, m142, 143, 166–167; under Chou dynasty, 150–51, m151; under Ch'in dynasty, 151–52, m152, p157; dynasties of, c151, c173, under Han dynasty, 152–54, m154; ancient, philosophy and culture of, 155–58; under Sung dynasty, 167–71, m167; under Ming dynasty, p168, 173–75, m175, p415, 416–17, p420; conquered by Mongols, 171–73, m172, p174; Japan influenced by, 176, 178; trade between African kingdoms and, 220; in medieval trade, m272–73; printing in, 298; trade between Portugal and, 369; in age of exploration, m370, m378; and Russian boundary treaty, 381; under Ch'ing dy-

nasty, m417, 418–21, p420; Portugal and, 426–27; Great Britain and, 427–29, p428; Opium War in, 569–70; European imperialism in, 570–71, m570, p572, 573, m576, 645–46; Japanese claims in, post-World War I, 605; growth of communism in, p640, 648–50, p649; becomes republic, 647–48; Japanese aggression against, 660, m661, p663; in World War II, m681; in UN, 693, 694; nuclear weapons of, 697; splits with Soviet Union, 707; as People's Republic, 716–20, m717, p719, 724, 772; in Korean War, 720–21; India and, m724, 727; Vietnam and, 733, 735
Chinese Communist Party, 648
Chinese Eastern Railway, m570, 573, 646, 650
Chinese Soviet Republic, 648
Ch'ing dynasty, 54, 173, 416, m417, 418–21, p420, 427, 569, 571, 646–47
chivalry, 248
Chopin, Frédéric, 517, p518–19
Chou dynasty, 60, 150–51, m151, c151, 155, p157
Christ. See Jesus Christ.
Christian IX, king of Denmark, 534
Christianity: rise of, 127–31, m129, p130, 135; Constantine's conversion to, 132; Orthodox Church, 183, 185–87; Copts, p186; Byzantine Church, 183, 186, 191, 193–97, p195, p196; Islam and, 204; Frankish conversions to, 235; in England and Ireland, 241–43; in Middle Ages, 248–53, m249, 257–60, p280, 287–90; Crusades and, 264–68, m265, p266, m267, c268; banking and, 274; Renaissance and, 298, 299; Protestant Reformation, 301–06, p308; Calvinism and Counter-Reformation, 307–11; spread of Protestantism m310; in Russia, 348; exploration and colonization and, 365, 369–72; in Japan and China, 424, 426–27; in Africa, 430–33; Crimean War and, 499; imperialism and, 552; after World War II, 797
chromosomes, 509, 788
Chu Yüan-chang, Ming ruler, 173–75, 416
Chucuito, 229
Church of England. See Anglican Church.
Churchill, Winston, 686, 701, 704, 708; in World War II, 670–74, p673, 678; at Yalta, 684, 693, 697
Cicero, 125
ciphers, 603
Circus Maximus, in Rome, 123
Cisalpine Gaul, 108, m108, m113, 116, 117, m117, m120
cities: of early civilizations, 11; of ancient India, 47–48, p49; built by Alexander, 99, 100, p101; in Roman Empire, 115, 121, 135; of Sung China, 170; in medieval period, 274–82; of Ming and Ch'ing China, 418, 419; Latin American, 434, 654, 779–80; p781; growth of, dur-

ing Industrial Revolution, 465, p468; planning of, p500; in modern Middle East, 761–62
city-states, 28–29; Phoenician, 37–38; of Sparta, 76–78; of Athens, 78–82; of ancient Greece, 69, 71, 73, 76, 92; Delian League of, 95; Aryan, 139; in China, 151, 155; in Russia, under Mongols, 196, 197; African, 220–21; of medieval Italy, 260, 269
civil disobedience, 642, 743
civil rights, 768–69, p770–71
civil service, in China, 152, 158, 167–69
Civil War, in U.S., 495
civilizations, 5; beginnings of, 9–13; Egyptian, 16–26, m18, m20, p25; Sumerian, m27, 28–30; Babylonian, 30–31, m31; Hittite, 31–32, m32; development in India of, m46, 47–48; Chinese, 54–60; Greek, 66–68, m68; Muslim, 204–08; early African, 216–23, m217; early American, 224–31, m225
class structure: of ancient Egypt, 19, 24; Sumerian, 29; Babylonian, 31; Aryan, 51; in ancient Sparta, 76, 77; in ancient Athens, 78, 79, c79; in Hellenistic empire, 100; in Roman republic, 108; in Roman empire, 115; of caste system, 140, 141, 208, 211; in Sung China, 169–71; in Kievan Russia, 193; in Russia, under Mongols, 196; in feudal Europe, 244–48, p247; in medieval towns, 276–77; in Renaissance Europe, p315; in Tudor England, 332; in pre-Revolutionary France, 392–93, p394; in Ming China, 416, p420; in Tokugawa Japan, 424–25; African slaves in, 431–33; in colonial Latin America, 434; in Latin American nations, 440; Industrial Revolution and changes in, 452–54; Marx on, 484; in Russia, under the czars, 542; in British-controlled India, 566; in Japan, during the period of the Meiji Restoration, 568.
Claudius, Roman emperor, 118, c118, 126
Cleisthenes, 78, 79, c79, 139
Clemenceau, Georges, 604, 605, p609
Cleopatra, Egyptian ruler, 117, 118
Clermont, 264, m265, c268
Cleveland, Grover, 581
Clive, Robert, p428, 429
Clovis, king of the Franks, 235
coal, 450, 451
Cochin, m378, 380
Code of Great Ming, 175
Code of Hammurabi, 30, p34–35
Colbert, Jean Baptiste, 344, 346
Cold War, 693, 701–07, 766
Coleridge, Samuel Taylor, p174, 517
collaborators, 670
collective bargaining, 471
collective farms, 617, 618; in Israel, 752, p760–61
colleges. See universities and colleges.
collegia, Roman, 131
Colombia, m580, m813; early cultures in, 229; as Great Colombia, 438, m439;

Panama Canal and, 583; oil in, 653; in 1920's, 655

colonies: Assyrian, 32; Phoenician, 38; of Athens, 80; of ancient Greece, 73, *m77*, 92, 107, 108; mercantilism and, 365; of Portugal and Spain, 368–75, *m370–71*; English, 376–78; European, about 1700, *m378–79*; Dutch, 380; French, 381; in North America, 385–89, *m386, m387*; Latin American, 433, 434; Latin American, independence won by, 436–40, *m439*; and imperialism, 551–54; in Africa, 554–62, *m559*; in India, British, 563–66, *m566*; in East Asia, *m570*, 573; in Southeast Asia and Pacific, 574–79, *m576*; in Caribbean and Latin America, *m580*, 581; after World War I, 605, 607, 645; UN Trusteeship Council and, 694–96; Southeast Asian, after World War II, 728–30, 735; African, after World War II, 741–46, *p748*, 753

colonus, Roman, **122**

Colorado, 492, *m493*

Colosseum, in Rome, 72, 123

Columbia, space shuttle, *p785*, 786

Columbia River, 773

Columbus, Christopher, 192, 207, 366, *p367, m371*

Comecon (Council for Mutual Economic Assistance), 712

Cominform (Communist Information Bureau), 701, 702

Comintern, 618–19

commerce. *See* trade.

commercial capitalism, **459**

Commercial Revolution, **362**

Committee of Public Safety, in France, 402

Commodus, Roman emperor, 131

common law, **257**

Common Market (European Economic Community), 711–12

Commonwealth, in England, 336

Communards, 500–01

communications: during Industrial Revolution, 455–58; television for, 785; satellites for, 786

communism: Marx on, 484; Russian Revolution and, 615; in China, 648–50, *p649*, 716–20; after World War II, 693, 701, *m703*; Cold War and, 702; in Eastern European nations, 705–07; in Southeast Asia, 730–36, 738; U.S. foreign policy and, 766, 772, 774; McCarthy and, 768; in Cuba, 775, *p776*

Communist Information Bureau (Cominform), 701, 702

Communist Manifesto, 484

Communist Party: in China, 648, 716, 718; in France, 707; in Italy, 707; in South Vietnam, 731; in U.S.S.R., 602, 613, 615, 617, 618, 705

compass, invention of, *p318*, 361, 416

computers, 787, *p789*

Comte, Auguste, 514

concentration camps, 627, *p676–77*, 679, 686, 700

Concert of Europe, 478

concessions, 554

Concord, 387

Concorde, jet airliner, 786

Concordat of Worms, 259

condominium, 554

Coney Island, 469

Confederate States of America, 495

Confederation of the Rhine, 409, *m411*, 477, 532

Confucianism, 155, 156, 158, 416, 424

Confucius (K'ung Fu-tse), 138, 155, 158, *p420*

Congo, Democratic Republic of, 744–45. *See also* Belgian Congo; Zaïre.

Congo, Republic of, *m744, m814*

Congo (Zaïre) River, 216, *m217*, 558, *m559, m814*

Congress of Berlin, 547, 555, 593

Congress Party, in India, 725

Congress of Vienna, 475–78, *m476*, *p479*, 527, 532

Conrad III, Holy Roman Emperor, 267, *c268*

conscription: in revolutionary France, *p400*, 402; in German Empire, 539; during World War II, 674

Conservative Party (Tory Party), in Great Britain, 486, 686, 708, 709

conservatives, 399

Constable, John, 520

Constance, *m249, m286*, 290

Constantine, Roman emperor, 128, 132

Constantinople, 132, *m133*, 135, *m172*, *m191*; Christianity in, 129, *m129, m249*; as capital of Byzantine Empire, 183, 185–90, *m185, p188–89*, 211, *m240*, 264; Kievan states and, 191–93; Muslim Empire and, *m202*, 203; as capital of Ottoman Empire, 207, 208, *m211, m286, m327*, *m343, m347, m349, m350, m411, m476*, *m546*, 547; and Crusades, 265, *m265*, 267–68, *m267, c268*; in medieval trade, 269, *m272*; in World War I, 596, *m597*, 598; after World War I, *m607*, 608; control of, returned to Turkey, 643. *See also* Istanbul.

constitution: defined, **336**; British, 341; of U.S., 391, 398, 495; of France, 399, 405, 497–99, 501, 709; Metternich system and, 478, 480; of Germany, 535; of Japan, 568–69, 653, 722; Cuban, Platt Amendment to, 583, 656; of U.S.S.R., 618; of Czechoslovakia, 702; of West Germany, 703; of Canada (1982), 773

Constitutional Convention, in U.S., 391

constitutional monarchy, **341**

Consulate, in France, 406, *c407*

consulates, **567**

consuls, in Rome, 109

containment policy, **702**

Continental Congress, in U.S.: First, 387; Second, 388, 389, 391

Continental System, 409, 410

Convention People's Party, in Ghana, 743

Cook, James, 491, 575

Cook Islands, 576, *m576*

Cooper, James Fenimore, 517

Copernicus, Nicholas, 317–20

Copley, John Singleton, *p388*

copper, 11

Copts, *p186*

Coral Sea, *m681*, 683, *m811*

Corday, Charlotte, *p403*

Cordova, *m185, m202*, 204, 207, *m272*

Corinth, *m77, m93*, 95, *m97, m129*

Cornwallis, Lord, 389, 563

Coronado, Francisco Vásquez de, *m371*, 374

Corot, Jean-Baptiste Camille, *p518–19*

corporate state, **625**

corporations, **461**–62; multinational, 782

Corsica, *m810*; under Carthage, 112, *m113*; under Rome, *m117, m120*; Christianity in, *m129, m249*; barbarian invasions of, *m133*; in Roman Empire, *m185*; Muslims in, 239, *m240*; Catholicism in, *m310*; under France, *m411, m476*; in World War II, *m671*; after World War II, *m703*

Cortés, Hernando, *m371*, 374, *p377*

Cossacks, 349, 381

Costa Rica, 436, *m439, m580, p582*, *m812*

cotton, *p19*, 448–50

Council of Constance, 290

Council of Elders, in ancient Sparta, 77

Council of Foreign Ministers, after World War II, 697–98, 700

Council for Mutual Economic Assistance (Comecon), 712

Counter-Reformation, 307–16

coup d'état, **406**

Courbet, Gustave, 521

courts: in Athens, 78, 79; of Roman republic, 108; of Roman Empire, 121; records of, *p256*; of England, under Charles I, 334; Revolutionary Tribunal, in France, 402–03; in czarist Russia, 542; for war crimes, 700–01; International Court of Justice, 694. *See also* law(s).

Coventry, *m671*, 672

craft guilds, **276**

Cranach, Lucas, *p328*

Crassus, Marcus Licinius, 116, 117

Crécy, battle at, 283, *m284*

creoles, **434**

Crete, 67–69, *m68, m69, m77, m810*; art of, *p70*; under Roman Empire, *m120*, *m133*; Christianity in, *m129, m249*; in Ottoman Empire, *m349, m476*; annexed by Greece, *m546*, 547; in World War II, *m671*, 675; after World War II, *m703*

Crimea, *m349, m350*, 353, *m476, m546*

Crimean War, *p498*, 499, 541

Cro-Magnon people, 8, *p9, m10*

Crompton, Samuel, 448

Cromwell, Oliver, 334, 336, *p339*

Cromwell, Richard, 336

Cronkite, Walter, *p731*

crop rotation, 448

Crusades, 190, 207, 264–68, *m265, p266*, *m267, c268*, 269, 361

833

cryptography, 603
Cuba, m580, m812; as Spanish colony, m371, 372, m379, m387, m389, 438, m439; Spanish-American War and, 577, 581–83, p582; U.S. interventions in, 584; under Batista, 656; Castro revolution, p734, 775–77, p776; post-World War II Africa and, 749, 772
cubism, p620, p634–35, 636
culture, 9, 10; of ancient Egypt, 22–26, p25; Babylonian, 31; Phoenician, 38–39; of ancient China, 54–55, 57–60, 155–58; of ancient Greece, 83–88, 91, 100–03; of Roman Empire, 123–26; of Gupta India, 146–48; Japanese, Zen and, 180; of Byzantine Empire, 186–87; of Russia, under Mongols, 196; early American, 225–27; in medieval towns, 277–82, p280; of Renaissance and Reformation, 311–16; in Ming and Ch'ing China, 419; in Tokugawa Japan, p423; during Industrial Revolution, 464–69, p468, 517–21; anthropological study of, 514; after World War I, 633–37, p635; of present-day Africa, 749–50; arts and leisure after World War II, 790–96, p794–95
Cunard, Samuel, ·455
cuneiform, 29, p34–35
Curie, Marie, 506, p507
Curie, Pierre, 506, p507
currency. See money.
Cuzco, m225, 229
Cybele, 128
Cynics, 101
Cyprus, m811; under Roman Empire, m120, m133; Christianity in, m129, m249; in Ottoman Empire, m349; under Great Britain, m546, 547, 555, m559, m607; in World War II, m671, 675; after World War II, m703; becomes independent, 709
Cyril, Byzantine missionary, 186–87, m249
Cyrillic alphabet, 187, 348
Cyrus, Persian king, 33, 36, 41, 787
Czar, 349
Czechoslovakia, m810; after World War I, m607, 608, 623; Locarno Pact and, 620; Sudeten crisis in, 665–66; invaded by Germany, m666, 667; in World War II, m671; after World War II, 699, m699, 702; in Warsaw Pact, m703, 704; invaded by Soviet Union, 705, p706; in Comecon, 712

da Vinci, Leonardo, 300, p302–03, p318, p320
Dachau, 679
Dada, school of art, p605
Dahomey, 557, m559
Daimler, Gottlieb, 459
Daladier, Edouard, 666, 667
Dalai Lama, 727
Dali, Salvador, 636
Dalton, John, 505

Damascus, m129, 761; in Muslim Empire, m202; Tamerlane in, 211, m211; Crusades and, m265, 267, m267; in medieval trade, m272–73
dance, 792, p794–95
Danes, 239, 243. See also Vikings.
Danish War, 534, c535
Dante Alighieri, 278, p280–81
Danton, Georges Jacques, 401–03
Danube River, 133, m133, m353, m597, m810
Danzig: in medieval trade, m272–73; in partitions of Poland, m353; in World War I, m597, 598; after World War I, 607, m607, 608; annexed by Germany, m666, 668
Dardanelles, m350, 353, m476, m546; Ottoman control over, 540; in World War I, 596, m597, 598; after World War I, m607, 608; in World War II, m671, 675, 678
Darius the Great, Persian king, 36, 92, m93, p94, p98, 143
Darwin, Charles, p507, 508, 509, 513
Daumier, Honoré, 521
David, Hebrew king, 40, 44, 126
David, Jacques Louis, p403
Davies, Emily, 523
Davis, Jefferson, 495
D-Day, 683
de Gaulle, Charles, 672, p692, 698, 707, 710, 743, 753
de Gouges, Olympe, 396–98
De Soto, Hernando, m371, 374
De Valera, Eamon, 623
Dead Sea, 39, m39
Debussy, Claude, 520
Deccan, 45–46, m46, m144, m146, 148, 150; Muslims in, 209, m209; under Mogul Empire, 212, m212
Declaration of Independence, p384, 388, 393, 396, p397, 406
Declaration of the Rights of Man, 396, 398, 409
Degas, Edgar, p504, 521
Delacroix, Eugène, 520
Delhi, m212, m566; under Muslims, 209, m209; captured by Tamerlane, p210, 211, m211
Delhi sultans, 209
Delian League, 95
Della Robbia, p302–03
Delos, m93, 95
Delphi, p66, m77, m93; oracle of Apollo at, 73, 76
democracy, 76; in Athens, 78, 79, c79, 96; Socrates on, 85; after World War I, 613, 619
Democratic Party, U.S., 769
Democritus, 87, 505
Demosthenes, 96
denazification, 700–01
Deng Xiaoping, 718
Denmark, m810; in medieval trade, m272–73; Protestantism in, m310; in Thirty Years' War, 342; allied with Napoleon, 409, m411; Congress of

Vienna and, m476, 477; in war with Prussia and Austria, 534; Virgin Islands sold to U.S. by, 584; in World War I, m597; in World War II, 670, m671, 679; in NATO, m703, 704; in Common Market, 711
depressions, 463
Descartes, René, 319, 329
détente, 705, 766, 772
DEW Line. See Distant Early Warning Line.
Diamond Sutra, 169
Dias, Bartholomeu, 366, m371
Díaz, Porfirio, 584
Dickens, Charles, 481, 521, 523
dictators, in ancient Rome, 110
Diderot, Denis, 348
Diem, Ngo Dinh, 731–32
Dienbienphu, m717, 730
Diocletian, Roman emperor, 132
Diogenes, 101
Dionysus, Greek god, 73, 88
Directory, in France, 405, m407
disarmament: pre-World War I talks on, 590; UN and, 697
Disraeli, Benjamin, 486
Distant Early Warning (DEW) Line, 773
Divine Comedy, 278, p280–81
divorce, 206, 306
DNA (deoxyribonucleic acid), 788
Dnieper River, 190, 191, m191, m350, m353, m810
Dniester River, 190, m191, m350, m353, m810
Dodecanese Islands, m607, 698, m699
Domesday (Doomsday) Book, 254
domestic system, 274, 448, 451
Dominic, saint, 252
Dominican Republic, 579, m580, m812; becomes independent, 436, m439; U.S. interventions in, 584, 777; under Trujillo, 655
Dominicans, 252
Don River, 190, m191, m350, m810
Dorians, 69, 76
Draco, 78, 79, c79
draft. See conscription.
Drake, Sir Francis, m370–71, 375, 376
drama. See theater.
Dreyfus, Alfred, 501
Dual Monarchy. See Austria-Hungary.
Dubchek, Alexander, 705
Duchamp, Marcel, p605
Dulles, John Foster, 774
Duma, in Russia, 193
Dumas, Alexandre, 517
Dunkirk, 671–72, m671, p673
Dupleix, Joseph François, 381
Dürer, Albrecht, 301, p302–03
Durham, Lord, 489
Durham Report, 489
Duryea, Charles, 459
Duryea, Frank, 459
Dutch East India Company, 363, 379, 574
Dutch East Indies, 574–75, m661; in World War II, 679, 680, m681; becomes independent, 728

Estonia: after World War I, *m607*, 608, 623; before World War II, *m666*, 668; in World War II, 670, *m671*, 684; after World War II, *m699, m703, m810*

ethical monotheism, 41, 138

Ethiopia, 742, *m744, m814*; in age of imperialism, *m559*, 560; invaded by Italy, 641, 660–61, *p663, m666*; in World War II, 675; revolution in, 749

Etruria, 107, *m108*

Etruscans, 107, 108, *m108, p109*, 112, 125

Euclid, 103

Euphrates River: and early civilizations, 10, *m10*, 11, 16; and Sumerian civilization, 27–30, *m27*; and Babylonian civilization, 30–31, *m31*; and Hittite civilization, 31–32, *m32*; in Muslim Empire, *m202*

Eurasia, 190

Euripides, 88

Europe, *m810*; early humans in, 6, 8, *m10*; Roman Empire in, *m210*; Latin language used in, 126; spread of Christianity in, *m129*, 248–53, *m249*; barbarian tribes of, 132–34, *m133*; Mongols in, 172, *m172*; Germanic kingdoms of, *m184*; eastern Roman Empire in, *m185*; Muslim Empire in, *m202*; Charlemagne's empire in, 237–39, *m237*; invasions of (800–1000 A.D.), 239–40, *m240*; and Treaty of Verdun, *m239*; feudalism in, 244–48; medieval trade of, 269–71, *p270, m272–73*; development of nations in, 282–87, *m286*; Renaissance in, 297–301, *p300*; spread of Protestantism in, 301–11, *m310*; after Peace of Westphalia, 342–43, *m343*; after Treaty of Utrecht, 346, *m347*; Ottoman Empire in, *m349*; growth of Russia in, *m350*; partitions of Poland and, 353, *m353*; exploration by, 361–68, *p367, m370–71*; empires of, about 1700, *m378–79*; Napoleonic Wars and empire in, 405–12, *m411*; trade between Asia and, 426–29; trade between Africa and, 429–33; Monroe Doctrine and, 438; Congress of Vienna and, 475–78, *m476, p479*; immigration to U.S. from, 495; decline of Ottoman Empire in, *m546*, 547; imperialist policies of, 551–54; imperialism in Africa by, 554–62, *m559, p561*; East Asian colonies of, *m570*; Pacific colonies of, *m576*; imperialism in Latin America and Caribbean by, *m580*; before World War I, 592–93, *m593, p594*; World War I in, 595–604, *m597, m599, p600*; after World War I, 604–10, *m607, p609*; in 1920's, 619–24; rise of fascism in, 624–28; German aggression in, 664–68, *m666*; World War II in, 668–86, *m671, p673*; after World War II, 697–701, *m699, p706*; Cold War in, 701–07, *m703*; post–World War II economy of, 708–12, *p710*. See also names of individual countries.

European Coal and Steel Community (ECSC), 711

European Economic Community (Common Market), 711–12

European Investment Bank, 711

European Recovery Program (Marshall Plan), 702, *p706*, 709, *p710*, 766

evolution, theories of, **508**

excommunication, 250–51

exploration, *p367*; reasons for, 361–65; by Portugal and Spain, 365–68, *m370–71, p373*; by England, 375, 376; of Americas, *p377*; by France, 380; by China, 416; of space, *p785*, 786, *p787*

exports. *See* trade.

extraterritoriality, 570

Ezana, Axumite king, 220

Ezekiel, Hebrew prophet, 138

Fabergé, Carl, *p541*

Fabian Society, 488

factories, *p444–45*, 448, 451–52, *p453*; assembly lines and mass production in, *p460*, 461; growth of cities and, 465; Luddites and, 469; reform laws on, 471

Factory Act (1819), 471

factory system, 448, 451–52, 459

fairs, medieval, 271, *m272*

Faith, saint, *p236*

Falange, 662, 664

Falkland Islands, 581, *m813*

family: in early civilizations, 12–13; Chinese, 60, 158; in ancient Athens, 82; Roman, 110; in Gupta India, 146; in Islamic society, 204–06; in feudal Europe, 246, *p247*, 248; effect of industrialization upon, 464; marriage customs and, *p466*; in Japan after World War II, 723; in India after World War II, 725

Faraday, Michael, 458

farming. *See* agriculture.

Farouk, Egyptian king, 752

fascism, *p626*; in Italy, **624–25**; in Germany, 627–28; Latin American dictatorships and, 656; in Spain, 662, *p663*, 664

Fascist Party, in Italy, 624, 625, 660, 683

Fashoda, *m559*, 560

Faust, 517

federal system, 391

Ferdinand, king of Aragón, 285, 366

Ferdinand, Austrian emperor, 544

Ferdinand I, Holy Roman Emperor, 326

Ferdinand VII, king of Spain, 480

Fermi, Enrico, 686

Fernando Po, 557, *m559*

Fertile Crescent: 26–27, *m27, p34, c38*, 44; early empires in, 30–33, 36–37; Phoenicians and Hebrews in, 37–41; Greek civilization and, 67, 68

feudalism: in Japan, **178**–80, *p179*, 421–22; in Europe, **244**–48; in France, 253–54, 396, 398; in England, 254–57; Crusades and, 267, 268; development of nations and, 282, 283; in Russia, 541

fief, 244

Field, Cyrus, 456

Fiji Islands, 576, *m576*

Fillmore, Millard, 567

Finland, *m810*; Russia and, *m350*; in 1810, *m411*; Congress of Vienna and, *m476*, 477; after World War I, *m607*, 608, 623; before World War II, 668; in World War II, 670, *m671*, 678, 684; after World War II, 698, *m699, m703*

Finland, Gulf of, *m350*, 351

First Coalition, 402

First International (International Working-men's Association), 485

Fiume, *m597*, 605, *m607*

Five-Power Treaty, 659

Five-Year Plans: in Soviet Union, 617–18; in China, 716; in India, 725

Flanders: in medieval France, *m254*; in medieval trade, 269, 271, *m272, m273*; Hundred Years' War and, 283, *m284*; Renaissance in, 301

Flaubert, Gustave, 520

Fleming, Alexander, 511, 788

Flemming, Walther, 509

Florence: in medieval trade, *m272*; Renaissance in, 297, 299, *p320*; baptistery in, *p302–03*; money of, 363

Florida: Spanish explorers in, 372, 374, *p377*; as Spanish colony, *m379, m386, m387, m389*, 438; sold to U.S. by Spain, 492, *m493*

Foch, Ferdinand, 603

Food and Agriculture Organization (FAO), 696

football (soccer), 467, *p468, p794–95*

Ford, Gerald R., 766, *c767*, 769, 772

Ford, Henry, 459, *p460*, 461

Formosa, *m570*, 571, *m576*, 650, *m661, m681. See also* Taiwan.

Forum, in Rome, 109

Fourier, Charles, 483

Fourteen Points, 602, 605, 606, 608

France, *m810*; early humans in, 8; under Franks, 235–37, *m239*; invasions of, 240, *m240*; Christianity in, *m249*; medieval, 253–54, *m254*; English territories in, 255; Crusades and, 265, *m265*, 267; medieval trade of, 271, *m272*; development of nation of, 283–85, *m284*; in Hundred Years' War, *p288*; Great Schism and, 289–90; Huguenots in, 307, *m310*; under Henry IV, 329; under Louis XIII and Richelieu, 329–31; and Thirty Years' War, 342–43; *m343*; under Louis XIV, 343–44, *p345*, 346, *m347*; and the Enlightenment, 346–48; exploration by, 362, *m371*; colonies of, *m379*, 380–81, 385–86, *m386, m387, m389, m439*; American Revolution and, 389; Revolution in, 392–405, *p394, p400, p404, c407*; under Napoleon, 405–12, *p408, m411*, 475, 531–32; trade between India and, 429; slave trade of, 431; Haitian slave revolt against, 436; Industrial Revolution in, 456; labor unions in, 471; Congress of Vienna and, *m476*, 477; in Quintuple Alliance, 478; Louisiana sold to U.S. by, 492, *m493*; under Louis XVIII, 495–96; revolutions of 1848 in, 496–97; under Napoleon III, 397–500, *p499*, 528–31; under German domination, 500–01; in Franco-Prussian War, 534–35, *p538*; imperialism of, 552; African colonies of, 555–58, *m559*, 560, 743–44; Indochina under, *m570*, 574, *m576*; China and, 573; Pacific colonies of, 576, *m576*; Caribbean possessions of, *m580*; in Triple Entente, 592–93, *m593*; in World War I, 595, 596, *m597*, 598, 599, *m599*, 603; after World War I, 604–06, *m607*, 619–21, *p635*; Great Depression in, 630; Spanish Civil War and, 664; pre–World War II alliances of, 666–68; before World War II, *m666*; in World War II, 668–72, *m671*, *p673*, 675, 679, 681–86; after World War II, *p692*, 693, 698, *m699*, 700, 709–11, *p710*; in UN, 694; nuclear weapons in, 697; in NATO, *m703*, 704, 707; driven from Indochina, 730, *p734*, 735; Algeria wins independence from, 753; in Suez crisis, 754. *See also* Gaul.

Francis II, king of Sicily, 529
Francis of Assisi, saint, 252
Francis Ferdinand, Austrian archduke, *p590*, 595
Francis Joseph I, emperor of Austria, 544, 545
Franciscans, 252
Franco, Francisco, 662, 664, 675, 678
Franco-Prussian War, 498–500, *p499*, 531, 534–35, *c535*, 537, *p538*
Frankfort, *m272*, 534, *m536*
Frankfort, Treaty of, 500, 501
Franklin, Benjamin, 389, *p390*
Franks, *m133*, 134, *m184*, *m185*, 235–37; Muslims and, *m202*, 203; under Charlemagne, 237–39, *m237*
Frazer, James George, 514
Frederick II, Holy Roman Emperor, 260
Frederick I, king of Prussia, 356
Frederick II (the Great), king of Prussia, *p355*, 356–57
Frederick Barbarossa, Holy Roman Emperor, 259–60, 267
Frederick William, of Brandenburg, 356
Frederick William I, king of Prussia, 356
Frederick William II, king of Prussia, 401
Frederick William III, king of Prussia, 475
free enterprise, 481
Free French, in World War II, 672, 675, 681, 743
French Congo, 558, *m559*
French East India Company, 381
French Equatorial Africa, 558, *m559*, 560
French Guiana, *m439*, 557, *m559*, 743, *m813*
French and Indian War, 357, 386
French Indochina. *See* Indochina.
French language, 126, 278, 344; in Quebec, 773
French Revolution, 392–401, *p400*, *p404*; Napoleon and, 406
French Somaliland, *m559*, 560
French West Africa, 557, 558, *m559*, 560

frescoes, 68
Freud, Sigmund, *p511*, 516, 632, 633
Freudianism, 614, 632
Friedrich, Caspar David, *p533*
Fuggers, banking family, 325, 363
Fujiwara family, 178
Fulton, Robert, 455
functionalism, in architecture, **637**

Gabon, 217, *m744*, *m814*
Gadsden Purchase, 492, *m493*
Galen, 125, 148, 206, 279, 317, 319
Galileo Galilei, 319, 320
Gallipoli campaign, *m597*, 598
Gama, Vasco da, 466, *m370–71*
Gambia, *m559*, *m744*, *m814*
Gandhara, *p145*
Gandhi, Indira, 725, *p726*
Gandhi, Mohandas, 642, *p644*, 725, 738, 742
Gandhi, Rajiv, 725
Ganges River, 45, *m46*, 139, *m724*, *m811*; Muslim conquest of, *m209*; Mogul Empire and, *m218*
Gao, *m217*, 223
García Márquez, Gabriel, 796
gardens, *p177*
Garibaldi, Giuseppe, 529, *c529*, *p530*
Gascony, 253, *m254*, 255, 283, *m284*
Gaugamela, battle at, *m97*, 99
Gauguin, Paul, 521
Gaul, 108, *m113*; under Rome, 116–17, *m117*, *m120*, 121, 122; spread of Christianity in, *m129*; barbarian invasions of, *m133*, 134; under Franks, 235
Gauls, 108, *m108*
Gautama Buddha. *See* Buddha.
Gaza Strip, 754, 755
General Assembly (UN), 693–94, 697
general strikes, 621
genetics, 509, 788
Geneva, 307, *m310*, 610, *m703*, 730
Geneva Agreements, 730, 731
Genghis Khan, 171, 172, *p195*
Genoa, 265, *m265*, 269, *m272*, *m371*, *m528*
geocentric theory, 317
geometry: Egyptian, 25; Sumerian, 29; of Pythagoras, 87; of Euclid, 103; in Gupta India, 148
George I, king of England, 340
George II, king of England, 340
George III, king of England, 389
George IV, king of England, 486
George V, king of England, 489, *p594*
germ theory, 510
German Confederation, *m476*, 477–80, 532–34, *c535*
German Democratic Republic. *See* East Germany.
German East Africa, 558, *m559*
German Southwest Africa, 556, *m559*, 560
Germanic tribes, 116, *m120*, 132–34, *m133*, 184, *m184*, 235; Tacitus on, 125; Britain conquered by, 241, *m241*

Germany, *m810*; Christianity in, *m249*; medieval, 257–60; Hanseatic League in, 269–71, *m273*; as Holy Roman Empire, 285–87; Protestantism in, 301–07, *m310*; Thirty Years' War in, 342; Ottoman Empire and, *m349*; Prussia and, 354–57; Napoleon and, 409, *m411*; Industrial Revolution in, 456; labor unions in, 471; Congress of Vienna and, 476, *m476*, 477; as German Confederation, 478, 480; immigration to U.S. from, 495; France under domination of, 500–01; unification of, 531–36, *c535*, *m536*; under Bismarck, 536–40, *p538*; and imperialism, *m570*, 556–58, *m559*, 560, 573, 576, *m576*, 577; in Triple Alliance, 592, 593, *m593*; preparations for World War I in, *p594*; in World War I, 595–603, *m597*, *m599*; after World War I, 604–07, *m607*; invaded by France, 620; under Weimar Republic, 625, 630; rise of Hitler, *p626*; 627–28; Anti-Comintern Treaty and, 661–62; Spanish Civil War and, 662, *p663*, 664; aggressions leading to World War II, 664–68, *m666*, *p669*; in World War II, 668–79, *m671*, *p676–77*, 680–86; division of, 697–700, *m699*, 702–03; war crimes trials in, 700–01; post–World War II economy of, 708, *p710*. *See also* East Germany; West Germany.
Germany, Federal Republic of. *See* West Germany.
Gestapo, 627
Ghana, *m217*, 223, *p741*, 743, *p748*, 749, *m814*
Ghent, 269, *m272*, 277
Gibraltar (Jabal-al-Tarik), *m202*, 203, *m411*, *m810*; obtained by Britain from Spain, 346, *m347*; in World War II, *m671*, 675
Gilbert Islands, 576, *m576*, 680, *m681*, 683
Giotto, 299, *p300*
Girondists, in France, 401, 402
Giscard d'Estaing, Valéry, 711
Giza, 24
gladiators, 123, *p124*
Gladstone, William, 486, *p487*, 488
Glorious Revolution, in England, **338,** *c340*, 485
Goa, 369, *m370*, *m378*, *m566*
Gobi Desert, *m53*, 54, *m811*
Goethe, Johann Wolfgang von, 517
Golan Heights, 755
gold: from Central Africa, 221; in early American civilizations, 225, 229; of Spanish colonies, 363, 374, 375; mercantilism and, 365; in South Africa, 560, 562
Gold Coast, 557, *m559*, 743
Golden Age of Greece, 66, 83–84, 87, 88, 91, 93, 139
Golden Horde, 172, *m172*, 173, 194, 211, *m211*, 381
Good Emperors, in Rome, 118–20, *c118*, 125, 128, 131

Good Neighbor Policy, 656, 774
Goodyear, Charles, 451
Gorbachev, Mikhail, 705, 772
Gothic architecture, *p280–81,* 282
Gothic revival, 520
Goths, *m133*
Goulart, João, 777
government: beginnings of, 9, 12; of ancient Egypt, 18–19; of Sumerian city-states, 28–29; Assyrian, 32; of Persian Empire, 36; of ancient Hebrews, 40; of Aryans, 51; of ancient China, 54; of Shang China, 57; in ancient Greece, 73, 76; of Sparta, 77; of Athens, 78–79, *c79;* Plato on, 85–87; of Romans, 108–10, 115, 121, 132, 134, 135; of early China, 151, 152, 158, 167–69; of feudal Japan, 178; of Byzantine Empire, 184–85; in early Russia, 193, 196; in Muslim Empire, 204; in Charlemagne's empire, 237; of Saxon England, 241; in feudal Europe, 244–46; of Roman Catholic Church, 248–51; of Capetian France, 253–54; of medieval England, 255–57, 282–83; in medieval towns, 275; Spanish, under Philip II, 326; of Dutch Netherlands, 329; English Revolution and, 331–36; of English constitutional monarchy, 337–41, *c340;* Montesquieu on, 346–47; Russian, under Peter the Great, 351; exploration and, 362; of Spanish colonies, 374, 375; of English colonies, 376–78; of Dutch colonies, 380; of early U.S., 391; of revolutionary France, 396–405, *c407;* under Napoleon, 406–07; in Ch'ing China, 419–21; liberal philosophy on, 481–83; of Canada, 490; of French Third Republic, 501; of German Empire, 535; in Meiji Japan, 568–69; Russian, after Revolution, 615–17, 618; French, after World War I, 619–20; in fascist Italy, 625; in British dominions, after World War I, 642; of Japan, in 1920's, 653; in Latin America, in 1920's and 1930's, 655–56
Gracchus, Gaius, 116
Gracchus, Tiberius, 116
Graham, Martha, 792
Granada, 285, *m285*
Grand Canal, in China, 165, *m166, m167, m172,* 173, *m175, m417*
Grand Duchy of Warsaw, 409, *m411,* 475, 476
Granicus, battle at, *m97,* 99
Grass, Günter, 793
Great Britain: formation of, 340; as limited constitutional monarchy, 341; Treaty of Utrecht and, 346, *m347;* Prussia and, 357; American colonies and Revolutionary War, 385–89, *m386, m387, m389, m390, p397;* in Napoleonic Wars, 405–10, 412; trade between Asia and, 427–29, *p428;* slave trade of, 431; Latin America and, 438, *m439,* 440, 581, 656; Industrial Revolution in, 447–51, 456, 465; Luddites in, 469; labor unions in,

471; Congress of Vienna and, 475–77, *m476;* in Concert of Europe, 478; liberal reforms in, 485–89, *c489;* under Victoria, *p487;* Canada and, 489–90, 773; Australia and New Zealand and, 490–91; Oregon Country ceded to U.S. by, 492; in Crimean War, 499; Ottoman Empire and, 546; Cyprus given to, *m546,* 547, 555; imperialism of, 552, *p553, p561;* African colonies of, 556–62, *m559,* 742, 743, 745–46, *p748;* East Asian colonies of, *m570;* India under, 563–66, *p565, m566,* 724; China and, 569–73; Southeast Asian and Pacific colonies of, 574, 576, *m576,* 729; in Triple Entente, 592–93, *m593;* preparations for World War I in, *p594;* in World War I, 595–96, *m597,* 598–602; after World War I, 604–06, 608, 621–23; Locarno Pact and, 620; Depression in, 630; empire of, after World War I, 640–43, *p644;* Spanish Civil War and, 664; Sudeten crisis and, 666; before World War II, *m666,* 667–68, *p669;* in World War II, 668–86, *m671, p673;* in UN, 693, 694; after World War II, 698, 708–09; in NATO, *m703,* 704, 707; in Common Market, 711; and Middle East, after World War II, 752, 754, 755, 757, 758. *See also* Britain; British Empire; England.
Great Colombia, 438, *m439*
Great Cultural Revolution, in China, **718**
Great Depression, 613, *p613,* 629–32, *p631,* 655
Great Khan, Empire of the, 172, *m172*
Great Leap Forward, in China, **716**
Great Pyramid, at Giza, 24
Great Schism, 289–90
Great Serpent Mount, in U.S., 231
Great Society, in U.S., 767
Great Wall of China, 151, 152, *m152, m154, p157, m166, m167, m172, m175,* 417, *m417*
Great Zimbabwe, *m217,* 221, 223, 750
Greece, *m810;* Persian invasion of, 36; geography of, 67; early civilization of, 66–69, *m69;* religion in, 71–73, *p75;* government of, 73, 76; Sparta in, 76–78; Athens in, 78–82, 139; art of, *p81,* 83–84, *p84;* philosophy and literature of, 85–88; Hellenistic culture of, 91, 100–03; in Persian Wars, 92–93, *m93, p94,* 143; Peloponnesian War in, 95–96; conquered by Macedonia, 96–97; under Alexander, *m97,* 99, *p102;* end of Hellenistic Age in, 106; Italian colonies of, 107, 108, *m108;* under Rome, 113, *m113,* 117, *m117, m120;* Roman culture and, 125; Christianity in, *m129;* Visigoths in, *m133;* in eastern Roman Empire, *m185;* Crusades and, *m265,* 268; in Ottoman Empire, *m349, m476;* wins independence from Ottomans, 480, 546, *m546;* in Balkan League, 547; in World War I, 596, *m597;* after World War I, *m607,* 608; in

World War II, *m671,* 675, 684; after World War II, 698, *m699,* 702, *m751,* 753–54; in NATO, *m703,* 704; in Common Market, 711
Greek language, 100, 125
Green Revolution, *p789,* 790
Greenland, *m371, m379, m812*
Gregory I, pope, 241, 250, 257
Gregory VII, pope, *p258,* 259
Griffith, D.W., 637
Grigorios Theologos, saint, *p196*
Grimké, Angelina Emily, 495
Grimké, Sarah Moore, 495
Grimm, Jacob and Wilhelm, 517
Gropius, Walter, 637
gross national product (GNP), 761
Guadalcanal, *m681,* 683
Guadeloupe, *m379,* 381, *m580*
Guam, *m576,* 579, *m661;* Spanish-American War in, 577, 581, 583; in World War II, 680, *m681*
Guantánamo Bay, *m580,* 583
Guatemala, 436, *m439, m580,* 774, 779, *m812*
guerrilla warfare, 326, *p734,* 777
Guevara, Ernesto "Che," 777
Guggenheim Museum, New York City, 791
Guianas, *m379,* 438, *m439,* 477, *m580,* 581
guilds, 275–**76;** in ancient Rome, *p124;* universities and, 278, 279
Guinea, 743, 744, *m744,* 745, *m814*
Guinea-Bissau, *m744, m814*
gunpowder, 169, 268, 283, 362
Guptas, 145–48, *m146, p147,* 208
Gutenberg, Johann, 298, *p308*
Guyana, *m813*

Habeas Corpus Act, 337, *c340*
Hades, 71, 73
Hadrian, Roman emperor, *p106, c118, p119,* 120, 127
Hadrian's Wall, in Britain, *m120,* 122, *m133*
Hague, The, *m597, m599, m810;* Palace of Peace at, 590; World Court in, 595, 610, 694
Haifa, 641
Haile Selassie, emperor of Ethiopia, *p663,* 749
Hainan, *m570, m661,* 679, *m681, m717, m811*
Haiti, *m439, m580,* 779, *m812;* slave revolt in, 436; U.S. interventions in, 584, 656
Hamaguchi, Yuko, 660
Hamburg, *m546, m810;* in Hanseatic League, 269–71, *m272, m273;* in World War II, 683, 686
Hammarskjöld, Dag, *p695*
Hammurabi, Babylonian ruler, 30, *m31, p34–35,* 41
Han dynasty, *c151,* 152–54, *m154,* 156–58, *p157,* 166, 169
Han River, 152, *m154*

Hancock, John, 387

Hangchow, *m166*, 167, *m167*, 170, *m172*, *m175*, *m273*, *m417*, *m570*, *m661*

Hanging Gardens of Babylon, 33

Hankow, *m570*, 647, 660, *m661*

Hannibal, 112–13, *m117*

Hanoi, *m717*, 732, *m811*

Hanover, *m347*, 354, 532, 534, *m536*

Hanover dynasty, 340

Hanseatic League, 269–71, *m273*

Hapsburg family, *m327;* early growth of, 286–87, 354–57; Spain under, 325–27, *p328*; Thirty Years' War and, 342, *m343*; Treaty of Utrecht and, 346, *m347*; Congress of Vienna and, 476; Italy under, 478

Harappa, *m46*, 47–48

Harbin, *m570*, 573, *m811*

Hargreaves, James, 448

Harold, Saxon king, *p242*, 243

Harsha, 208

Harvey, William, 319

Hastings, 243, *m254*

Haussmann, Georges Eugène, *p500*

Havana, *m580*, 581, *m812*

Hawaiian Islands, *m576*, *m812*; annexed by U.S., 577, *p578*; in World War II, *p588–89*, 679, 680, *m681*, *p682*

Hawkins, Sir John, 375

health. *See* medicine.

Hebrew language, 759

Hebrews. *See* Jews.

Hector, legendary Trojan prince, 71

hegira, **201**

Heian (Kyoto), *m176*, 178, 369, *m370*, 422

Hejaz, *m607*, 608

Helen, legendary queen of Greece, 71

Helgoland, *m476*, m477, 558

heliocentric theory, **317**

Hellas, 76

Hellen, legendary Greek hero, 76

Hellenes, 76

Hellenistic Age, 97, 100–03, *p102*, 106. *See also* Age of Alexander.

Hellenistic culture, **91,** 100–03

helots, **77,** 95

Helsinki, 705, *m810*

Helsinki Agreement, 705

Hemingway, Ernest, *p635*, 636

Henry I, king of England, 254–55

Henry II, king of England, 255, *p258*

Henry III, king of England, 257

Henry VII, king of England, 283

Henry VIII, king of England, 301, 306, 331, 332, *p333*

Henry IV, king of France, 329, 330

Henry III, Holy Roman Emperor, 259

Henry IV, Holy Roman Emperor, 259

Henry the Navigator, prince of Portugal, 366, *p367*

Hera, Greek goddess, 73, *p74–75*, 112

Hercules, legendary Greek hero, *p74–75*

heresy, **252**

Hero, Greek scientist, 103

Herod the Great, king of Palestine, 126

Herodotus, 17, *p86*, 87, 92, 143, 787

Hertz, Heinrich, 458

Herzegovina, *m546*, 547, 593, 595, *m597*, 608

Hesse-Cassel, 534, *m536*

Hesse-Darmstadt, 534, *m536*

Hidalgo, Miguel, 436

Hideyoshi, Toyotomi, 422, 424

hierarchy, Church, **248**–50

hieroglyphics, 18, *p23*, *p34–35*

High Renaissance, 299–300

Himalayas, 45, *m46*

Hinayana Buddhism, 143

Hindenburg, Paul von, 627

Hindi language, 725

Hindu Kush, mountains, 45, *m46*

Hinduism, 139–41, *p140*, *m142*; Buddha and, 143; of Guptas, 145; in southern India, 150; Islam and, 211; in British-controlled India, 563–66; in independent India, 724

Hipparchus of Rhodes, 103

Hippocrates, 87, 148

Hirohito, emperor of Japan, *p652*

Hiroshige, Ando, *p425*

Hiroshima, *m681*, *p682*, 686

Hispaniola, *m371*, *m379*, 436, *m439*

history: Greek study of, 86, 87; studied in Roman Empire, 125; oral traditions of, 219, 430; Marx on, 484; as social science, 513

Hitler, Adolf: rise of, *p626*, 627–28; aggression by, 664–68, *p669*; in World War II, 670–72, 675–80; death of, 684

Hitler-Stalin Pact, 668, *p669*

Hittites, 31–32, *m32*, *p34–35*, 37, *c38*

Ho Chi Minh, 730, 731, *p734*

Hobbes, Thomas, 338

Hohenzollern family, 346, 354–56, 532

Hokkaido, 175, *m176*

Holbein, Hans, the Younger, 301, *p333*

Holland. *See* Netherlands.

Holocaust, **679,** 700, 752

Holstein, 534, *m536*

Holy Alliance, 478

Holy Roman Empire, 259–60, 285–87, *m286*; Crusades and, *m265*, 267; in medieval trade, *m272–73*; medieval France and, *m254*, *m284*; Lutheranism and, 304–06; under Hapsburgs, 325–26, *m327*, 354; in Thirty Years' War, 331, 342; after Peace of Westphalia, *m343*; abolished by Napoleon, 409, 532

Homer, 69, 71, 82, 125

Honduras, 436, *m439*, *m580*, *m812*

Hong Kong, *m661*, *p690–91*, *m717*, *m811*; under Great Britain, 569, *m570*; in World War II, 679, *m681*

Honolulu, *m576*, *p578*, *m812*

Honshu, 175, *m176*

Hooke, Robert, 320

Hoover, Herbert, 630

Horace, 125

Horn of Africa, 748

Horthy, Nicholas, 623, 624

Houphouët-Boigny, Félix, 743

House of Commons, 257, 283, 332, *p339*, 340, 486

House of Lords, 257, 283, 332, *p333*, 340, 486, 489

housing: in ancient Athens, 80–82; in Middle East, 761–62; in Latin American cities, 780. *See also* architecture.

Hsia dynasty, 55, 57

Hsien-Yang, 151, *m152*

Hsüan-tsang, Chinese traveler, 208

Hubertusburg, Peace of, 357

Hudson, Henry, *m371*, 376

Hudson Bay, 346, *m371*, 376, *m379*, *m490*, *m812*

Hudson's Bay Company, 490, *m490*

Huerta, Victoriano, 584

Hugh Capet, king of France, 253

Hugo, Victor, 517

Huguenots, 307, *m310*, 329, 330, 344

humanism, **297**–99, 301, *p303*

Hundred Days, 412, 475

Hundred Years' War, 283–84, *m284*, *p288*

Hungary, *m350*, *m810*; Mongols in, *m172*, 194; Magyars in, 239; in medieval trade, *m272–73*; about 1500, *m286*; Calvinism in, 307, *m310*; in Austro-Hungarian Empire, 343; in 1648, *m343*; under Hapsburgs, *m347*, 354; Ottoman Empire and, 349, *m349*; partitions of Poland and, *m353*; revolution of 1848 in, 544; formation of Dual Monarchy, 545; in World War I, 595, 596, *m597*, 603; after World War I, 604, 607, *m607*, 608, 623; before World War II, *m666*, 667; in World War II, *m671*, 675, 678; after World War II, 698, *m699*, 701; in Warsaw Pact, *m703*, 704; revolution in, 705; in Comecon, 712

Huns, 132–34, *m133*; in India, 144, 148, 208; in China, 154, *m154*, 171

Huss, John, 290

Hwang Ho. *See* Yellow River.

hydrogen bomb, 785. *See also* nuclear weapons.

Hyksos, 20, *m20*, 39

Iberian peninsula, *m68*, 106, 285

Ibn Battuta, 220

Ibos, 747

Ibsen, Henrik, 520

Ice Age, 5–6

Iceland, *m371*, *m379*, *m671*, 704, *m810*, *m812*

icons, **187,** 193–94, *p196*

Idaho, 492, *m493*

ideograms, **12**

Île-de-France, 253

Iliad, 71, 82, 83, 125

Ilkhan Empire, *m172*, 173

illuminated manuscripts, *p250*, **252**

Illyria, *m113*, *m117*

immigration: to U.S., in late 1800's and early 1900's, 495, *p622*; to Latin America, 579; of Jews to Palestine, 641–42; of Japanese, 651; to Great Britain, 709; of Mexicans to U.S., 778

Latin America after World War I, 654; in modern Japan, 738

labor unions, 470–71; European, after World War I, 621; New Deal and, 630; in Africa, 645; in Latin America, 654–56, 780; in Poland, 707

Labour Party, in Great Britain, 488, 621, 686, 708, 724

Laconia, 76, *m77*

Ladoga, Lake, 190, *m191*

Lafayette, Marquis de, 389

Lagos, 557, *m559*

laissez faire, 481, 550–51

Lamarck, Jean Baptiste, 508

Lamu, *m217,* 220

Lancaster family, 283

language: written, 12; hieroglyphics for, 18; cuneiform for, 29; Semitic, 30; alphabet for, 38–39; of early Indian civilization, 47–48, *p50,* 51; Chinese, 58–60, 176, 178; Etruscan, 107; Latin, 125–26, 277–78; Russian, Cyrillic alphabet for, 187, 348; Urdu, 211; of early Africa, 216–20; Quechua, 231; English, 243; codes for, 603; in India, 725; Swahili, 750; used in Middle East, 759; conflicts in Canada over, 765, 773. *See also* writing.

Laos, *m717,* 730, 732, 735, *m811*

Lao-tzu, .156

lasers, 787–88

Latin America: geography of, 433–34, *m435;* gains independence, 436–40, *m439;* society in, *p437, p781;* and imperialism, 579–84, *m580, p582;* after World War I, 640, 653–56; after World War II, 765–66, 774–82, *p776,* 798; literature of, 796

Latin language, 125–26, 277–78, 298

Latins, 107, 108, *m108*

Latium, 107, 108, *m108*

Latvia: after World War I, *m607,* 608, 623; before World War II, *m666,* 668; in World War II, 670, *m671,* 684; after World War II, *m699, m703, m810*

Lavoisier, Antoine, 320–21, 402

law: Babylonian, 30; Hittite, 31, *p34;* Jewish, 41; of Athens, 78, 79, *c79;* Roman, 108–09, 121; in Ch'in China, 151; Legalism and, 155–56; Code of Great Ming, 175; of early Japan, 178; in Byzantine Empire, 187; in the Kievan states, 191, 193; Indian, under Rajputs, 208; in feudal Europe, 244–45; canon, 252; in medieval England, 255, 257; of Napoleonic Code, 407, 409; labor and reform, 471; martial, 728

Lawrence, T.E., *p644*

lay investiture, 252, 259

Laye, Camara, 750

Le Corbusier, 637, *p791*

League of Nations: formation and organization of, 610; weaknesses of, 659; and Japanese aggression in Manchuria, 660; and Italian invasion of Ethiopia, 661, *p663;* and German annexation of Austria, 664; and Czechoslovakia, 667; and

Danzig, 668; expels Soviet Union, 670; isolationists and, 674; United Nations and, 692, 693; UN Trusteeship Council and former mandates of, 694–96

Lebanon, *m751, m811;* after World War I, 608; in Arab League, 759; education in, 762; civil war in, 764

Lebanon Mountains, 38, *m39*

Leeuwenhoek, Anton van, 320

Legalism, 155–56

Léger, Fernand, *p620*

Legislative Assembly, in France, 399–401, *c407*

Leibniz, Gottfried Wilhelm von, 320

Leipzig, *m272;* battle at, *m411,* 412

leisure. *See* recreation.

Lend-Lease Act, 674

Lenin, N. (Vladimir Ilyich Ulyanov), 615, *p616,* 617, 648

Leningrad, *m699, m703, m810;* in World War II, *m671,* 678. *See also* Petrograd; St. Petersburg.

Leo III, pope, *p238*

Leo X, pope, 301

Leonidas, king of Sparta, 92

Leopold II, emperor of Austria, 401

Leopold II, king of Belgium, 558

Leopold I, Holy Roman Emperor, 342

Lepanto, battle at, 326

Lepidus, Roman general, 118

Lesotho, *m744, m814*

Lesseps, Ferdinand de, 556

letters of credit, 274

Lever House, in New York City, 791

Leviathan, 338

Lexington, 387

Leyte, *m681,* 683

Li Po, Chinese poet, 165

Liaotung Peninsula, *m570,* 571, 572, 650

Liberal Democratic Party, in Japan, 724

Liberal Party (Whig Party), in Great Britain, 486–89, 621

liberalism, 474–75, 480–83; Metternich and, 478; in Great Britain, 485–89, *c489;* in Russia, 541, 542

Liberia, 558, *m559,* 742, *m744, m814*

libraries, 469

Libya, *m744, m751,* 762, *m814;* ruled by Italy, 557, *m559,* 759; in World War I, *m597;* in World War II, *m671,* 675, 678, 680

Lima, *m379,* 434, 438, *m439,* 654, *m813*

Lincoln, Abraham, 493, 495

Lindbergh, Charles, 628

Lindisfarne Gospels, *p250*

linotype, 523

Lisbon, *m272–73, m379, m411, m476, m810*

Lister, Joseph, 510, 511

Liszt, Franz, 517, 520

literature: Hebrew, 41; Aryan, 50, 51; of ancient Greece, 71, 88; of Roman Empire, 125; of early India, 139, 146; fairy tales, *p149;* Chinese, 165, 419; of early Japan, 178; of the Kievan states, 193; medieval, 278, *p280;* during Renaissance, 298–99; of Industrial Revolution, 481, 504; sci-

ence fiction, *p515;* romantic movement in, 517; realism in, 520–21; after World War I, 633–36; African, 750; after World War II, 793–96

Lithuania: in medieval trade, *m272–73;* about 1500, *m286;* after World War I, *m607,* 608, 623; before World War II, *m666,* 667, 668; in World War II, 670, *m671,* 684; after World War II, *m699, m703, m810*

Liu Pang, Han ruler, 152, 155

Liu Shao-chi, Chinese leader, 718

Li Yüan, T'ang ruler, 165

llanos, 433, *m435, m813*

Lloyd George, David, 602, 604, 605, *p609*

lobbying, 768

Locarno Pact, 620

Locke, John, 338, 346, 388, 391, 480, 513

Loire River, *p538*

Lombard League, 260

Lombards, *m133,* 184, *m184, m185, m202, m237,* 250

Lombardy, 260, 476, *m476,* 527–29, *m528*

Lon Nol, Cambodian leader, 733

London, *m241, m286, p294–95, m810;* in medieval trade, *m272–73;* population in Middle Ages, 277; during Tudor period, *p333;* formation of police force, 467; in World War I, *m597, m599;* International Monetary and Economic Conference in, 630; in World War II, *m671,* 672

Long March, in China, *p640,* 648

Long Parliament, 334

Lorraine, *m347;* and Germany, 500, 535, *m536,* 537, 592; in World War I, *m599;* returned to France, 605, 606, *m607;* in World War II, 684

Los Angeles, *p72,* 769, *m812*

Lothair, Frankish king, 239, *m239,* 284

Louis VII, king of France, 267, *c268*

Louis IX, king of France, 173

Louis XI, king of France, 284–85

Louis XIII, king of France, 329–30, *p345*

Louis XIV, king of France, 344, *p345,* 346, 351, 381, 393, 500

Louis XV, king of France, 346, 393, 395

Louis XVI, king of France, 393–402, *p404, c407*

Louis XVIII, king of France, 412, 475, 478, 495–96

Louis the German, Frankish king, 239, *m239*

Louis Napoleon. *See* Napoleon III.

Louis Philippe, king of France, 496

Louis the Pious, Frankish king, 239

Louisiana: as French colony, *m379,* 381, *m386, m387, m389;* sold to U.S., 492, *m493*

Louisiana Purchase, 492, *m493*

Louvois, François, 344, 346

Louvre Museum, in Paris, 467–69, *p468*

Loyalists, in American Revolution, 387

Loyalists, in Spanish Civil War, 662, 664, *p665*

Loyola, Ignatius, saint, 309

Lübeck, 269–71, *m273*

merchant guilds, 275–76
Mercia, 241, *m241*
Meroë, *m217*, 220
Meroveg, 235
Merovingians, 235
Mesolithic Age, 8
Mesopotamia, *m27*, 28, 30; conquered by Alexander, *m97*, 99; in Roman Empire, *m120*; in Muslim Empire, *m202*, 203
Messina, Strait of, 112, *m113*, *m117*
mestizos, **434**
metals: in development of civilizations, 10–11; in European coins, 362, 363, 369. *See also* gold; silver.
Methodius, Byzantine missionary, 186–87, *m249*
metics, **78**, 80
metric system, 403
Metternich, Prince Klemens von, 475, 478–80, *p479*, 483, 544
Mexican Cession, 492, *m493*
Mexican War, 492
Mexico, *m580*, *m812*; early cultures in, 225–29, *m225*, *p226*; in age of exploration, *m370–71*; in Spanish Empire, 372, 374, *m379*; geography of, 433, *m435*; becomes independent, 436, *m439*; war with U.S., 492; French intervention in, 499; revolution of 1910 in, 584; World War I and, 599; oil in, 635, 656; art of, *p654*; after World War I, 655; after World War II, 778–79, *p781*, 782
Mexico City, *m371*, *m379*, 434, *m439*, *m580*, 654, 778, *m812*
Michelangelo Buonarroti, 300, *p302–03*, *p320*
microscopes, 320
Middle Ages, **234**–35; and feudalism, 244–45; and manorial system, 245–46, *p246*; and life of the nobility, 246–48; the Church during, 248–53; and Crusades, 264–68, *c268*; revival of trade during, 269–74, *p270*, *m272–73*; growth of towns during, 274–77; culture during, 277–82, *p280*; development of nations in, 282–87, *m286*
middle class, 452–54, 496
Middle East, *m751;* Egyptian civilization in, 17–26, *m18*, *m20;* Sumerian civilization in, 27–30, *m27;* Babylonian civilization in, 30–31, *m31;* Hittite civilization in, 31–32, *m32;* Assyrians in, 32–33, *m32;* Chaldean Empire in, *m33;* Persian Empire in, 33, 36–37, *m36;* Phoenicians in, 37–39, *m39;* ancient Hebrews in, 39–41; under Alexander, *m97*, 99, 100; spread of Christianity in, *m129*, *m249;* Muslim Empire in, 201–04, *m202;* Crusades to, 264–68, *m265*, *m266*, *m267*, *c268;* medieval trade of, 269, 271, *m272–73;* Ottoman Empire in, *m349;* Napoleon in, 405–06; slavery in, *p432;* World War I in, 603; after World War I, *m607*, 641–42, *p644;* World War II in, *m671*, 675; after World War II, 750–62, *p756*, *p760–61*, *p770–71. See also* Asia Minor.

Middle Kingdom, in Egypt, 19–20
Middle Stone Age, 8
Midway Island, *m576*, *m661*, *m681*, 683
migration, **27**
Milan, *m129*, 132, *m133*, 260, *m343;* under Hapsburgs, *m327*, 346, *m347*, 354; and unification of Italy, *m528*
militarism: in Sparta, 77–78; in feudal Japan, 178–80; in feudal Europe, 245; as cause of World War I, 592, *p594;* fascism and, *p626;* Japanese, before World War II, *p652*, 653, 660, 679
Mill, John Stuart, 481–83
Miller, Arthur, 793
Millet, Jean-François, *p497*
Minamoto family, 178
Ming dynasty, 173–75, *c173*, *m175*, 369, *p415*, 416–19, *p420;* porcelain of, *p168*, *p428*
miniaturization, **786**–87
Minoan civilization, 67–69
Minorca, 346, *m347*
Minos, king of Crete, 68
Mirabeau, Count de, 395
Mississippi River, *m812;* De Soto's discovery of, 374; French control of, *m379*, 381, *m386*, *m387*, *m389;* growth of U.S. and, 492, *m493*
Missouri, battleship, *p659*, 686
Mithras, 128
Mitterrand, François, 711
mixed economies, **725**
Mobutu, Joseph (Mobutu Sese Seko), 745
Moctezuma, Aztec ruler, 374
Modena, 476, *m476*, 528, *m528*, 529, *c529*
Mogadishu, *m217*, 220
Mogul Empire, *p210*, 211–12, *m212*, 376, 429, 563
Mohawks, 231
Mohenjo-Daro, *p44*, *m46*, 47–48
Moluccas (Spice Islands), *m273*, 369, *m370*, *m378*, 380
monarchy, **18**; constitutional, in England, 337–41, *c340*, 485; in France, abolition of, 401, 402
monasticism, 251
Mondrian, Piet, 636
Monet, Claude, 521
money, *p369;* in ancient Sparta, 77; in Roman Empire, 122; in China, 151, 152; in medieval fairs, 271; development of banking and, 274; standardization of, 362–63
Mongolia, 52, *m53*, 171, *m661*, *m717*, *m811;* Buddhism in, *m142;* in World War II, *m681;* in Comecon, 712
Mongols, *m172;* in Asia, 171–73, *p174*, 176, 183–84, 348, 416, *p420;* in the Kievan states, 194–97; Ottoman Turks and, 207, 211; in India, 209–12, *m211*
monism, **141**
monks, 251–52
monopolies, **462**
monotheism, **20**, 41, 138, 141
Monroe, James, 438

Monroe Doctrine, **438**, 581; Roosevelt Corollary to, 584
monsoon, **46**–47
Montana, 492, *m493*
Monte Alban, 225
Monte Cassino, *m249*, 251, *m671*
Montenegro, *m546*, 547, *m593*, *m597*, 608
Montesquieu, Baron de, 346–47, 391, 393, 395
Montevideo, *m439*, 654, *m813*
Montevideo Pact, 656
Montfort, Simon de, 257
Montgomery, Bernard, 680
Montreal, *m371*, *m379*, 380, *m386*, *m490*, *m812*
Moore, Marianne, 796
Moors, 203, 285, *m285*, 375
More, Thomas, *p296*, 299, 301, *p333*, 483
Morelos, José, 436
Morgan, J.P., *p460*, 461
Morocco, *m744*, *m751*, *m814*; Barbary pirates in, 555; and European imperialism, 555–56, *m559*, *p561*, 591, 592, 759; in World War I, *m597*; in World War II, *m671*, 680; becomes independent, 753; economy of, 761
Morse, Samuel, 456
Mosaic law, 41
mosaics, 187
Moscow, *m191*, 196, 772, *m810*; rise of, 197; princes of, 348, *m350*; and Napoleon, 410–11, *m411*; becomes capital of Russia, 617; in World War II, *m671*, 678
Moses, Hebrew leader, 39–41
motion pictures, *p633*, 637, 793
Mott, Lucretia, 495
Mound Builders, *m225*, 231
Moussorgsky, Modest, 520
Mozambique, 742, *m744*, *m814*; as Portuguese colony, 369, *m371*, *m379*, 558, *m559*; becomes independent, 745
Mphalele, Ezekiel, 750
Mubarak, Hosni, *p756*
Mugabe, Robert, 745, 746
Muhammad, 200–04, *p205*
Muhammad of Ghor, 209
Muhammad Reza Shah Pahlavi, shah of Iran, 751, 758
Mukden, 660, *m661*
multinational corporations, **782**
mummification, *p23*, 26
Munch, Edvard, *p516*
Munich, *m536*, 627, 666–67, *m666*, *m671*, *m810*
Muñoz Marín, Luis, 778
Murasaki Shikubu, Lady, 178
Murmansk, *m350*, *m671*, 678, *m810*
museums, 467–69, *p468*, 796
music, *p218;* of early Africa, 219; romantic movement in, 517–20; after World War I, *p634–35*, 636, 637; after World War II, 791–92, *p794–95*, 797
Muslim League, in India, 566
Muslims: Muhammad and Islam, 200–02; invasions and conquests, *m202*, 202–03,

236, 237, 239, *m240*, 259; culture, 204, *p205*, 206–07; in India, *m209*, 209, *p210*, 210–12; Crusades against, 264–68, *m265*, *p266*, *m267*, *c268*; and medieval trade, *m272–73*; in Spain, 285, *m285*; in British-controlled India, 563–66; in Turkey, 643; and partition of India, 724, *p726*; in Pakistan, 727; in modern Middle East, 759, 762. *See also* Islam.

Mussadegh, Muhammad, 751

Mussolini, Benito, 624–25, *p626*; Hitler and, 627, 628; and invasion of Ethiopia, 660–61; and Spanish Civil War, 664; at Munich conference, 666; and invasion of Albania, 667; in World War II, 672, 675, 679, 683; death of, 684

Mustafa Kemal. *See* Atatürk, Kemal.

Muzorewa, Abel, 746

Mwene Mutapa, 221

Mycenae, 69, *m69*, *p70*, 514

Mycenaeans, 69, *m69*, *p70*, 71

Myron, 83

Nagasaki, *m176*, *m378*, 380, 424, *m681*; atomic bombing of, 686

Nalanda, *m146*, 148

Namibia (Southwest Africa), 742, *m744*, 745, 746, *m814*

Nanak, 212

Nanking, 175, *m175*, 417, *m417*, *m570*, 648, *m661*, *m717*, *m811*

Nantes, *m310*, *m343*

Nantes, Edict of. *See* Edict of Nantes.

Napata, *m217*, 220

Naples, city, *m411*, *m476*, 477, 480, *m810*; and unification of Italy, *m528*, 529, *p530*

Naples, Kingdom of, *m286*, *m327*, *m343*, 346, *m347*, 354

Napoleon I (Bonaparte), 405, *c407*; seizure of power, 406; as First Consul, 406–07; as emperor, 407, *p408*, 409–11; defeat, 411–12; effects of, 412; Haitian slave revolt and, 436; Louisiana sold to U.S. by, 492; Prussia dominated by, 531–32

Napoleon III (Louis Napoleon Bonaparte), 497–500, *p499*; unification of Italy and, 528–31; Bismarck and, 534–35

Napoleonic Code, 407, 409

Napoleonic Era, 406

Napoleonic Wars, 405–12, 475, 560, 564

Nara, *m176*, 178

Nassau, 534, *m536*

Nasser, Gamal Abdel, 752, 754, 755

Natal, *m559*, 560, 562

National Assembly, in France, 395–99, *p400*, *c407*, 496–97, 500, 501

National Association for the Advancement of Colored People (NAACP), 768

National Association for the Protection of Labor, in Great Britain, 471

National Convention, in France, 401–05, *c407*

National Liberation Front, in Algeria, 753

nationalism: during Napoleonic Era, **409,** 412; growth of, in 1800's, 474, 477, 526; Metternich system and, 480; romantic movement and, 517, 520; in Italy, 527; in Germany, 533; in czarist Russia, 540–41; in Hungary, 544–45; in Balkans, 545–46; and imperialism, 552; in Egypt, 557; in India, 566, 642; as cause of World War I, 591, 593, 595; after World War I, 604; fascism and, 624; in the Middle East, 641, 643, *p644*; in Southeast Asia, 728; in Africa, 742

Nationalists, Chinese, 646–50, 716, 720. *See also* Kuomintang.

Nationalists, in Spain, 662, 664

NATO. *See* North Atlantic Treaty Organization.

natural gas, 451

naturalism, in literature, **521**

Naturalism, philosophy, 155

Navarre, 285, *m285*

navies: of Byzantine Empire, 185; of Crusades, 265, *m265*; of Spanish Armada, 326, *p328*, 331, 376; British, 389, 409, 569; German, in 1890's, 540; coaling stations and bases for, 575; U.S., in Spanish-American War, *p578*; Panama Canal and, 583; before World War I, 592, *p594*; in World War I, 598, *p600*, 604; in Russo-Japanese War, 650; Japanese, before World War II, *p652*; Washington Naval Conference on, 659–60; in World War II, 670, 672, *p673*, 674, 678, 680, *p682*, 683

navigation: instruments for, 361, *p363*; Portuguese, 366; Chinese, 416

Navigation Act, 336, 385

Nazareth, 127, *m129*

Nazca, *p228*

Nazis: rise of, in Germany, 627–28; in Austria, 664; in Czechoslovakia, 665; in Memel, 667; in Danzig, 668; and extermination of Jews, 679, 700; denazification and, 701

Ndonga, *m217*, 431

Neanderthal people, 6–8, *m10*

Nebraska, *m493*, *p494*

Nebuchadnezzar, Chaldean ruler, 33

Nefertiti, Egyptian queen, *p21*

Nehru, Jawaharlal, 725

Nelson, Horatio, 409

Neolithic Age, 8–10, 18, *p56*, 107

Nepal, *m724*, *m811*

Nero, Roman emperor, 118, *c118*, 128

Nerva, Roman emperor, 118–20, *c118*

Netherlands, *m810*; as Burgundian possession, 284, *m284*; in Holy Roman Empire, *m286*; Calvinism in, 307, *m310*; independence, 326–29, 342, *m343*; in war with England, 337; in age of exploration, 362, *m370–71*, 378–80, *m378–79*; art of, *p330*, *p380*, 427; Congress of Vienna and, 476, *m476*; Australia and New Zealand discovered by, 491; and imperialism, 552, *m570*,

574–75, *m576*; in World War I, *m597*, *m599*; in World War II, 671, *m671*; in NATO, *m703*, 704; in Common Market, 711

Netherlands (Dutch) East Indies, 574–75, *m661*; in World War II, 679, 680, *m681*; becomes independent, 728

Neutrality Acts, 674

Nevada, 492, *m493*

Nevelson, Louise, 791

New Amsterdam, 337, *m379*, 380, *m386*

New Brunswick, 489, 490, *m490*

New Caledonia, 576, *m576*

New Deal, 630–32, *p631*

New Delhi, *m724*

New Economic Policy (NEP), 617

New England, 334, 375, *m386*

New France, 385, *m386*

New Guinea: in age of exploration, *m370–71*, *m378*; and imperialism, *m570*, 574, *m576*; in World War II, 680, *m681*, 683

New Harmony, *p482*, 484

New Hebrides Islands, 576, *m576*

New Holland, *m370*, *m378*, 491

New Kingdom, in Egypt, 20–22

New Mexico, 492, *m493*

New Orleans, *m379*, *m386*, *m389*, *m580*, 637, *m812*

New South Wales, 491, *m491*

New Stone Age, 8–9

New Testament, *p40*, 128

New York City, 337, *m379*, 380, *m386*, *p446*, *p468*, 769, 790, 791, 793

New York Stock Exchange, 629

New Zealand, 491, *m491*, *m576*, 642, 683

Newcomen, Thomas, 450

Newfoundland, 346, *m371*, 375, *m379*, *m386*, *m490*, 674, *m812*

newspapers, 523, 731

Newton, Isaac, 319–21, 347, 506

Nicaragua, *m580*, *m812*; in United Provinces of Central America, 436, *m439*; U.S. intervention in, 584; under Somoza, 655; revolution in, 779

Nice, *m347*, 528, *m528*, 529

Nicholas I, czar of Russia, 541, 544

Nicholas II, czar of Russia, 542, 544, 614

Nicomedia, 132, *m133*

Niger, *m744*, *m814*

Niger River, 216, *m217*, 557, *m559*, *m814*

Nigeria, *m744*, *m814*; early history of, 217, 221, 223; and imperialism, 557, *m559*; civil war in, 747–49, 797

Nightingale, Florence, 454–55

Nihilists, 542

Nile River, *m751*, *m814*; and early civilizations, 10, *m10*, 11; and ancient Egypt, 16–22, *m18*, *m20*; in Muslim Empire, *m202*; and medieval trade, *m272–73*; and early African civilizations, 217, *m217*, 219–20; and imperialism, *m559*, 560

Nilotic languages, 217

Nine Nandas, in India, 143

Nine-Power Treaty, 659–60, 679

Nineveh, *m32*, 32

Panmunjom, 721

Pan-Slavism, 541, 595

papacy: in Church hierarchy, 250; in Middle Ages, 257–60, *p258*; Babylonian Captivity, *p288*, 289; Great Schism, 289–90; Reformation and, 301–04; Counter-Reformation and, 309; unification of Italy and, 527, 531; and *Kulturkampf* in Germany, 537. *See also* Roman Catholic Church.

papal line of demarcation, 366, 368, *m370–71*

Papal States, *m239*, 252, *m286*, *m327*, *m343*, *m347*; creation of, 236; and Holy Roman Empire, 259, 260; expansion of, 287; and Napoleon, 409; and unification of Italy, *m528*, 529, 531

paper, 18, 156

Papua New Guinea, *m717*, *m811*

papyrus, 18, *p21*

Paraguay, 436, *m439*, 779, *m813*

Paris, legendary Trojan prince, 71

Paris: in Charlemagne's empire, *m237*, *m239*; and growth of France, 253, *m254*, *m284*; in medieval trade, *m272–73*; population of, in 1300's, 277; Notre Dame cathedral in, *p280–81*, 282; during French Revolution, 396, 398, 401, *p404*, 405; during Napoleonic Era, *m411*, 412; 1889 exposition in, *p462*; Louvre Museum in, 467–69, *p468*; during revolutions of 1848, 496, 497; and Franco-Prussian War, *p499*, 500–01; and city planning, *p500*; in World War I, *m597*, 598, *m599*, 603; peace conference at, 604, 613; post-World War I culture in, *p635*; in World War II, *m671*, 672, 684; Vietnam peace conference in, 732

Paris, Treaty of (1763), 386, 429

Paris, Treaty of (1783), 389

Paris, University of, 279, *p280–81*

Park Chung Hee, 721

Parkman, Francis, 513

parks, *p177*, *p468*, 469

Parliament: early development of, 257; and Hundred Years' War, 283; English Revolution and, 331–36; parties in, 337; in English constitutional monarchy, 338–41, *c340*; reforms in voting for, 485–89, *c489*

Parliament Bill, 489, *c489*

Parma, 476, *m476*, 528, *m528*, 529, *c529*

Parthenon, in Athens, *p81*, 83, 84

partisans, in World War II, **672**

Pascal, Blaise, 319, 787

Pasha, Ismail, 556

passive resistance, 642

Pasternak, Boris, 793

Pasteur, Louis, 510, 511, *p512*

pasteurization, 510, 513

Patagonia, *m439*, *m813*

Pataliputra, 144, *m144*

Pate, *m217*, 220

Pathet Lao, 730

patriarchs, 129

patricians, in Rome, 108–10

Patrick, saint, 241, 251

Paul, saint, 127–28, *m129*

Paul III, pope, 309

Pavlov, Ivan, 514–16

Pax Romana, 121, 122

Pax Sinica, 152

Pax Tokugawa, 424

Paz, Octavio, 796

Peace of Augsburg, 306, 326, 342

Pearl Harbor, *p588–89*, 680, *m681*, *p682*

Pechenegs, *m191*, 194

Pedro I, emperor of Brazil, 438, 440

Peel, Robert, 467

Peking (Peiping), *m576*, *m717*, *m811*; as Chin capital, 167, *m167*; in Mongol Empire, 172, *m172*; as Yüan capital, 173; in medieval trade, *m272–73*; and Ming dynasty, 175, *m175*, 417; and Ch'ing dynasty, *m417*, 418; as treaty port, *m570*, 571; and Boxer Rebellion, 646; under Nationalists, 647; captured by Japan (1937), 660, *m661*; in World War II, *m681*

Peking people, 6, *m10*

Peloponnesian War, 87, 95–96

Peloponnesus, 69, 76, *m77*, *m93*, 95

penicillin, 511, 788

Peninsular Campaign, 410, 436

Pennsylvania, *m386*, *m493*

People's Will, in Russia, 542

Pepin II, Frankish ruler, 235–36

Pepin III, Frankish ruler, 236–37

Perchin, Michael, *p541*

Pergamum, *p72*, *m77*, *p102*

Pericles, *p81*, 95, 96

Perón, Eva, 774, 775, *p776*

Perón, Isabel, 775

Perón, Juan, 774–75, *p776*

Perry, Matthew, 567, *p572*

Persepolis, *p34–35*

Persia: early history and culture, 36–37, *p34*, *m36*; in Persian Wars, 92–93, *m93*, *p94*; in Peloponnesian War, 96; and Alexander the Great, *m97*, 99; Indian conquests of, 143; in Muslim Empire, *m202*, 203, 204; in medieval trade, *m272–73*; in Ottoman Empire, *m349*; after World War I, *m607*, 643–45. *See also* Iran.

Persian Gulf, *m751*, *m811*; and early Fertile Crescent, 26, 27, *m27*; in medieval trade, *m272–73*; in World War I, *m597*; in World War II, *m671*, 678

Persian language, 759

Persian Wars, 92–93, *m93*, *p94*

Persians, 22, 33, 36–37, *c38*, 184

Peru, *m813*; cotton in, *p19*; early cultures in, 224–29, *p226*, *p228*; as Spanish colony, *m371*, 374, *m379*; becomes independent, *p437*, 438, *m439*; oil in, 653; in 1920's, 655

Pescadores Islands, *m570*, 571, 650, *m717*

Pétain, Henri, 672

Peter, saint, 250

Peter I (the Great), czar of Russia, 349–51, *m350*, *p352*

Petition of Right, 332, *c340*, 341

Petra, 275

Petrarch, Francesco, 298

Petrograd, *m597*, *m607*, 614, 615, 617. *See also* Leningrad; St. Petersburg.

petroleum (oil), 451; in Latin America, 653, 654, 656, 778–79; in World War II, 675, 679; discovered in North Sea, 709; in Indonesia, 729, 738; in Nigeria, 749; Suez crisis and, 754; in Middle East, *p756*, 759, 761; formation of OPEC and, 757–58; in U.S. economy, 767; plastics made of, 788

pharaoh, 18

Phidias, 83, *p84*

Philadelphia, *m386*, 387, 388, 391, *m812*

Philip IV (the Fair), king of France, 173, 254, 284, 287, 289, *p288–89*

Philip II, king of Spain, 326, *p328*, 375–76

Philip V, king of Spain, 346

Philip Augustus, king of France, 253, 255, *m265*, 267

Philip of Macedon, 96–97, 99

Philippine Islands, *p553*; in age of exploration, 368, *m370–71*, 373, *m378–79*; and U.S., *m570*, *m576*, 577–79, *p578*, 581, 583; in World War II, 679, 680, *m681*, 683; independence, *m717*, 728

Philistines, 37, *m39*, 40

philosophy: ancient Greek, 85–87; Hellenistic Age, 101–03; in ancient China, 155–56; during Middle Ages, 279; during Renaissance, 297–99; during Enlightenment, 321, 346–48; of Hobbes and Locke, 338; of liberalism, 474–75, 480–83

Phnom Penh, 733

Phoenicia, 37–39, *m68*, *m69*, *m120*

Phoenicians, 17, 37–39, *c38*, *m39*, 44, 69

phonograph, *p457*, 637

phonograms, 12

photography, *p622*

physical sciences, 505

physics: Hellenistic, 103; during Scientific Revolution, 317–21; during 1800's and early 1900's, 505–06, *p507*, 632; nuclear, 788

Picasso, Pablo, *p634–35*, 636, *p665*

pictograms, 12

Picts, 133, *m133*

Piedmont, *m347*, 528, *m528*

Pilsudski, Jozef, 624

Piraeus, *m77*, 78

Pisa, 265, *m265*, 269, *m272*

Pisistratus, 78, 79, *c79*, 139

Pizarro, Francisco, *m371*, 374

Plains Indians, *m225*, 231

Planck, Max, 506

planned economy, 619

Plassey, *p428*, *m566*

plastics, 788

Plataea, battle at, 93, *m93*, 143

Plato, 85–87, 513

Platt Amendment, 583, 656

plebeians, 108–10

plebiscite, 407, 698

Pliny the Elder, 150

Plutarch, 125
Pluto, Greek god, 73
Plymouth, 376, m379, m386
Po River, 108, m108, 113, m113, m117, m810
poetry: of Vedas, 50, 139; of Roman Empire, 125; of T'ang China, 165; romantic movement in, 517; after World War I, 636; of Africa, 750; after World War II, 793–96. *See also* literature.
pogroms, **542**
Poitiers, m237; battle at, 283, m284
Pol Pot, 733, 735
Poland, m810; Mongols in, m172, 194; in medieval trade, m272–73; Calvinism in, 307, m310; Ottoman Empire and, m349; Russia and, m350, 351; partitions of, 353, m353, 357; after Congress of Vienna, 475–77, m476; in World War I, m597, 598; after World War I, 606–08, m607, 623–24; and Locarno Pact, 620; German aggression in, m666, 668, 670; in World War II, m671, 684; after World War II, 698–99, m699, 701; in Warsaw Pact, m703, 704; crisis in, 705–07, 772; in Comecon, 712
police, 465–67
Polish Corridor, 606–08, m607, m666, 668
political cartoons, p685
political science, 513
Pollock, Jackson, 790–91, p794–95
pollution, 798
Polo, Marco, 170, m172, 173, 361, p367, 787
polytheism, **20**
Pompey, Gnaeus, 116, 117
Pompidou, Georges, 711
Ponce de Léon, Juan, m371, 372, p377
Pondicherry, m378, 381, 429, m566
Pontius Pilate, 127
Pop Art, **791**
Pope, Alexander, 320
popes. *See* papacy.
Popular Front, in France, 621
Popular Front, in Spain, 662
popular government, **76**
popular sovereignty, **347**
population: of early civilizations, 11; of Greek city-states, 69; of China, 151, 156, 419; of medieval towns, 277; exploration and, 365; of Spanish colonies, 374; of Japan, 426, 651; growth of, during Industrial Revolution, 464–65, 509; of U.S., 491–92; and imperialism, 552; of India, 725; of Asia, in 1970's, 736; of modern Middle East, 759–62; of Latin America, 779–80
Populists, in Russia, 542
porcelain, 156, 167, p168, p428
Port Arthur, m570, 571, 573, 650, m681
Porter, Cole, 637
Portsmouth, m386, 650
Portsmouth, Treaty of, 650–51
Portugal, m810; in medieval trade, m272–73; Catholicism in, m310; Spanish rule of, 326, 329; exploration by, 362,

365–68, p367, m370–71, p373; overseas empire of, 368–72, m378–79, 379, 380, 424, 426–27, 429, 430–31; Napoleon and, 410, m411; and Brazil, 434, 438, m439; revolt in early 1800's, 480; and imperialism, 557–58, m559, m570, 745; in World War I, m597; in World War II, m671; in NATO, m703, 704
Portuguese Guinea, 558, m559, 745
Poseidon, Greek god, 73
postal services, p787
Potsdam Conference, 686, 697–98
pottery: of Shang China, 58; of ancient Greece, 83
power. *See* energy.
Praetorian Guard, 121
praetors, 109–10
Pragmatic Sanction, **354**, 357
Prague, m249, m286, m607, m699, m703, m810
Prague, Treaty of, 534
Pravda Russkaia, 193
Praxiteles, 83
prehistoric age, 4, 5, p7, 13
Presbyterian Church, m310, 334, 336
Prester John, legendary African king, 366
Priestley, Joseph, 320, 321
Primo de Rivera, Miguel, 662
primogeniture, **403**
Prince, The, 298
Prince Edward Island, 489, 490, m490
Princeton, p390
printing: in early China, 169; in Renaissance Europe, 298–99, 301, p308, p318; Reformation and, 314; of newspapers, 523; of books, in 1970's, 796
proconsuls, 115
prohibition, in U.S., 628–29
proletariat, **484**
prophets, Jewish, 41
protectionism, **767**
protectorate, **554**
Protectorate (Cromwell's), 336
Protestantism, m310; Reformation, 301–06, p308; Calvinism, 307; and Counter-Reformation, 307–11; in Netherlands, under Philip II, 326; in France, 329, 330, 344, 365; in England, 331–36
Proust, Marcel, 633
Provence, m284, 285
Prussia: after Peace of Westphalia, m343; and Treaty of Utrecht, 346, m347; and partitions of Poland, 353, m353; and rise of Hohenzollerns, 354, 356; under Frederick the Great, p355, 356–57; during French Revolution, 401, 402; Napoleon and, 409, 411–12, m411; Congress of Vienna and, 475–77, m476; joins Quadruple Alliance, 478; in Franco-Prussian War, p498, 499–500, p538; and unification of Germany, 531–36, c535, m536
psychiatry, 516
psychoanalysis, **516**, 633
psychology, 514–16, 614, 632
Ptolemy, astronomer, 125, 279, 317, 319, 361
Ptolemy, Egyptian rulers, 99, 117

Pueblos, m225, p230, 231
Puerto Rico, m812; in age of exploration, m370–71, 372, m378–79; as Spanish colony, 438, m439; and Spanish-American War, 577, 581, 583; under U.S., m580, 584, 778
Pulaski, Casimir, 389
Punic Wars, 112–13
Puritans, 331–34, 365
Pylos, 69, m69
pyramids: in Egypt, 19, 24; in Americas, 225, p226, 227
Pythagoras, 87

Qaddafi, Muammar al-, 762
Qatar, m751, 758, 759, 761, m811
Quadruple Alliance, 477, 478
quantum theory, **506**
Quebec, city, m371, m379, 381, m386, 489, m490, m812
Quebec, province, 490, m490, 773
Quebec Liberation Front, 773
Quebec Party, 773
Quechua language, 231
Queensland, 491, m491
Quetzalcoatl, Indian god, p226, p228, 229
Quintuple Alliance, 478, 480
Quito, m439, m813

Rabban Sauma, 173
radicals, 399; in czarist Russia, 542, 544
radio, 458, 637
radioactivity, **506**, 788
railroads: early, p449, 455; in U.S., 456; in Canada, 490, m490; Trans-Siberian, m570, 573; Berlin-to-Baghdad, 593–95
rajahs, 139, 145
Rajputs, 208, m209, 211, m212, m566
Raleigh, Sir Walter, 375
Rama, Indian god, 139
Ramayana, 139–40, 146, 148
Rameses II, Egyptian pharaoh, p16, 22
Rameses III, Egyptian pharaoh, 37
Rangoon, m661, m717, m811
Ranke, Leopold von, 513
Raphael, 300, p320
rationalism, **321**
Ravenna, p130
Rawalpindi, m724, m811
reactionaries, **477**
Reagan, Ronald, 697, 767–69, c767, 772, 778
realism, in literature and art, **520**–21
recession, **767**
recreation (leisure): in Roman Empire, 123, p124; in Renaissance, 312, p315; and games, p313; during Industrial Revolution, 467–69, p468; after World War II, p794–95, 797
Red Army, in China, 648
Red Army, in U.S.S.R., 615, 617, 684
Red Cross, 590, 797
Red Sea, m18, m20, 24, 269, m272–73, m751, m811, m814
Red Shirts, in Italy, 529

848

Redistribution Bill, 488, *c490*
Reform Bill of 1832, 486
Reform Bill (second) of 1867, 486
Reform Bill (third) of 1884, 513
reform laws, 471
reform movements, 481
Reformation, 297, 301, 304–07, *m310,* 311–12
Regina, *m490, m812*
regionalism, in literature, **520**
Reign of Terror, 402–03
Reims, cathedral of, *p280–81,* 282, *p609*
relativity, Einstein's theories of, 506, *p507*
religion: in early civilizations, 6, 13; in ancient Egypt, 20–22, *p21,* 25–26; of Sumerians, 28–30; Babylonians, 31; of Persians, 37; of Phoenicians, 38; of Indus Valley civilization, 48; Aryan, 50–51; of Shang China, 60; of ancient Greeks, 71–73, *p75,* 76, 84; in ancient Rome, 110–12; of early American civilizations, *p226,* 227–29; and exploration, 365, 369–73; and imperialism, 552, *p553. See also* Buddhism; Christianity; Hinduism; Islam; Judaism; Shinto.
Rembrandt van Rijn, 329, *p330*
Renaissance, 297; literature and art of, 297–301, *p300, p302–03, p320;* society and culture, 311–16, *p315;* and science, 316–21, *p318*
Renault, Louis, 459
Renoir, Pierre Auguste, *p518–19,* 521
reparations and indemnities: after Congress of Vienna, 477; after Franco-Prussian War, 500, 501; after World War I, 605, 606; after World War II, 698, 699, 722
Republic, 85–87
republic, 108
Republican Party, in U.S., 493
Republicans, in Spain, 662
resistance movements, in World War II, 672, 684
Restoration, in England, **337**
Revere, Paul, *p388, p390*
Revolutionary War, American, *p384,* 388–89, *p390, p397*
revolutions of 1848: in France, 496–97; in Germany, 533; in Italy, 527; in Austria, 544
Reza Shah Pahlavi, 645
Rhapta, 220
Rhazes, 206–07
Rhee, Syngman, 720, 721
Rhine River, *m597, m599,* 605, *m607, m666, m810*
Rhineland, 605, 606, 628, 664, *m666*
Rhodes, *m68, m77,* 100, *m120,* 125, *m546,* 547
Rhodes, Cecil, *p553,* 560, 562
Rhodesia (Zimbabwe), *m559,* 562, 743, 745–46
Ricardo, David, 481
Richard I (the Lion-Hearted), king of England, 255, *m265,* 267
Richelieu, Cardinal, 330–31, 342, 343, *p345*

Ridgeway, Matthew, 721
Rio Grande, 231, *m435, m580, m812*
Rio de Janeiro, 72, 438, *m439,* 654, *m813*
Río Muni, 557, *m559*
Río de la Plata, 433, *m435*
Río de Oro, 557, *m559*
Risorgimento, 527
Rivera, Diego, *p654*
roads: Assyrian, 32; Persian, 36, *m36;* Roman, 122; toll, *p275;* during Industrial Revolution, 455
Roaring Twenties, 628–29
Robespierre, Maximilien, 401–03
rock-and-roll music, 792
Rockefeller, John D., 462
Rocky Mountains, 492, *m493*
Rodin, Auguste, 521
Roentgen, Wilhelm K., 505
Roland, legendary hero, *p238,* 278
Romagna, *m528,* 529, *c529*
Roman alphabet, 125–26, 643
Roman Catholic Church: earliest organization, 129, 130; Latin language and, 126; and Eastern Orthodox Church, 186; organization in Middle Ages, 248–53; and medieval life, 263–64, 279, *p280,* 282; and Crusades, 264–68, *m265, p266, m267, c268;* problems of, 289–90; and Protestant Reformation, 301–06, *p308;* Counter-Reformation in, 307–11; Galileo and, 319; in Ireland, 334; in England, 337, 486, *c489;* in France, 392, 399, 407, 497, 501; in Japan and China, 424, 426–27; in Latin America, 440, 780, *p781,* 798; in Ottoman Empire, 499; unification of Italy and, 528; in Germany, 537; and imperialism, 552; in Spain, 662, 664; and Vatican II, 797. *See also* papacy.
Roman Empire: founding of, 118; early emperors, 118, *p119,* 120; greatest extent, *m120;* life and culture during Pax Romana, 121–23, *p124,* 125–26; in 200's and 300's A.D., 131–32; barbarian invasions of, 132–34, *m133;* final collapse of, 134. *See also* Byzantine Empire; Roman republic.
Roman republic: founding of, 108–09; government and culture, 109–10, *p111,* 112; Punic Wars and expansion, 112–13, *m113,* 115; civil war and overthrow of republic, 116–18. *See also* Roman Empire.
Romance languages, 126
Romanesque architecture, 282
Romanov dynasty, 349, 614
romantic movement, in literature and art, **517**–20, *p518, p533*
Rome: founding of, 108; and spread of Christianity, *m129;* captured by Visigoths, 133, *m133;* and Papal States, 236, *m239, m286, m327, m343, m347;* and Crusades, *m265;* and medieval trade, *m272–73;* under Napoleon, *m411;* and unification of Italy, *m528,* 529, *c529,* 531; in World War II, *m671*

Rome-Berlin Axis, 628, 661, 664, 675, 679
Rommel, Erwin, 678, 680
Romulus and Remus, 125
Romulus Augustulus, Roman emperor, 134
Roosevelt, Franklin D., 656, 674, *p685,* 686; New Deal programs of, 630, *p631;* at Yalta, 684, 693, 697
Roosevelt, Theodore, *p582,* 583, 584, 650
Roosevelt Corollary, 584
Rothko, Mark, 791
Rotterdam, 671, *m671,* 686, *p710*
Rough Riders, *p582*
Rousseau, Jean Jacques, 347, 348, 388, 393, 396, 400, 513
Royal Air Force, 674
Royal Highway, in ancient Persia, 36, *m36*
rubber, 451, 558
Rubicon River, 108, *m108,* 112, *m113*
Ruhr Valley, *m597,* 620
Rumania, *m810;* becomes independent, *m546,* 547; in World War I, 596, *m597;* after World War I, *m607,* 608, 623, 668; alliance with France, 620; in World War II, *m671,* 675, 678, 684; after World War II, 698, *m699,* 701; in Warsaw Pact, *m703,* 704, 707; in Comecon, 712
Rump Parliament, 336
Rurik, legendary Viking king, 191
Ruskin, John, 481
Rus, 183, 194
Russia: origins in Byzantine Empire, 183; emergence as an independent state, 197; Christianity in, *m249;* in medieval trade, 269, 271, *m272–73;* and use of Cyrillic alphabet, 348; growth of, under Peter and Catherine, 349–51, *m350,* 352; partitions of Poland and, 353, *m353;* and War of Austrian Succession, 357; eastward expansion of, *m378–79,* 381; in Napoleonic Wars, 409–11, *m411;* Congress of Vienna and, 475–77, *m476;* in Quadruple Alliance, 477–78; in Crimean War, *p498,* 499; in late 1800's, 540–42, *p543;* Russo-Japanese War, 542, 650–51; Revolution of 1905 in, 542–44; and Congress of Berlin, 546–47; imperialism in China, 571, 573, 646, 650; in Triple Entente, 592–93, *m593;* in World War I, 595, 596, *m597,* 598, 599, 602; after World War I, *m607,* 608; Revolution of 1917, 613–15, *p616;* civil war in 615. *See* Union of Soviet Socialist Republics *for history after 1921.*
Russian Orthodox Church, 193, 196–97, 348, 540
Russian Revolution (1917), 613–15, *p616,* 648; World War I and, *m597,* 599, 602, 608
Russo-Japanese War, 542, 544, 646, 650–51
Rutherford, Ernest, 506
Rwanda, *m744, m814*
Ryukyu Islands, *m661, m681,* 684, *m717, m811*

Silk Route, in Asia, 152, *m154, m166, m272–73*

silver: in early American civilizations, 225, 229; of Spanish colonies, 363, 374, 375; mercantilism and, 365; Japanese, 369; as money, *p369*

Simon bar Kokba, 127

Sinai, Mount, 40

Sinai Peninsula, exodus of Jews across, 39–40; Israel-Egyptian fighting over, 754, 755

Singapore, *m661, m717, m811*; under Great Britain, *m570,* 574, *m576*; in World War II, 679, 680, *m681*; as republic, 729; in ASEAN, 738

Sinkiang, 52, *m53,* 720

Sino-Japanese War, 571, 650

Sistine Chapel, 300, *p303*

Sita, legendary Indian heroine, 139

Siva, Indian god, *p140,* 141

Six-Day War, 755

Six Dynasties, in China, *c151,* 154

slave trade, 431–33, *p432,* 557, 558; and Great Britain, 346; and Portugal, 366

slavery: in Assyrian Empire, 32, 33, 41; of ancient Hebrews, 39–40; in ancient Greece, 73, 78, 79, 82, 100, 103; Roman, 115, 116, 123, 134; in Muslim empire, 202, *p432*; in Africa, 220, 431–33, *p432*; in Saxon England, 241; in Latin America, 372, 434, *p437,* 440; in English colonies, 378; abolished in French colonies, 403; in U.S., 492–95; abolished in India, 564

Slavs, 184, *m185,* 187; in early Russia, 190, 191; invasions of Europe by, 239, *m240*; Pan-Slavism and, 541; in Balkans, 546, 593, 595; and Hitler, 679

Slovakia, 667

smallpox, 374, 509–10

Smith, Adam, 480–81, 513

Smith, Ian, 745–46

Smyrna, *m607,* 643

soccer (football), 467, *p794–95*

social classes. *See* class structure.

Social Contract, The, 347

Social Darwinism, 514

social sciences, 504, 513–16, 798

Social Security Act, 630

socialism: Utopian, 483–84; Marx and, 484–85; in Great Britain, 488; in France, 496, 497; in Germany, 537–39; Russian Revolution and, 615; in U.S.S.R., 617; in Ethiopia and Somalia, 749; in Chile, 778

socialist realism, 618

Society Islands, 576, *m576*

sociology, 514

Socrates, 85, 88

Sofia, *m546, m671, m703, m810*

Solidarity, Polish labor union, 707

Solomon, Hebrew king, 40

Solomon Islands, 576, *m576, m661,* 680, *m681,* 683

Solon, 78, 79, *c79*

Solzhenitsyn, Alexander, 793

Somalia, *m744,* 749, *m814*

Somaliland, 558–60, *m559,* 661

Somoza, Anastasio, 655

Somoza, Anastasio, Jr., 779

Songhai, *m127,* 223

Sophists, 82, 85

Sophocles, 88

South Africa, *m744,* 746–47, *m814*; imperialist competition for, *m559,* 560–62; Statute of Westminster and, 642; black literature of, 750; expelled from UN, 798

South America, *m813*; early migrations to, 224; early cultures in, *m225*; Incas in, 229–31; exploration of, 368, *m372–73*; Spanish colonies in, 372–74; European colonies in, about 1700, *m379*; geography of, 433–34, *m435*; independence won by nations of, 436–40, *m439*; imperialism in, 579–84, *m580. See also* Latin America.

South Carolina, *m386, m493,* 495

South China Sea, *m417, m570, m717, m811*

South Korea (Republic of Korea), 704, *m717,* 720, 721, *m811*

South Vietnam, 730–32, *p734*

South Yemen, *m751, m811*

Southeast Asia: imperialism in, 574–75, *m576*; after World War II, *m717,* 728–36, *p734*; economy of, 738. *See also* Asia.

Southeast Asia Treaty Organization (SEATO), 766

Southwest Africa. *See* Namibia.

Soviet Union. *See* Union of Soviet Socialist Republics.

Soweto, 746

space exploration, *p785,* 786, *p787*

Spain, *m286, m349, m751, m810*; Carthaginian territory in, 112, 113, *m113*; under Roman Empire, 117, *m117, m120,* 121, 122; Christianity in, *m129, m249*; barbarian invasions of, *m133,* 134; Muslims in, *m202,* 203, 204, 206, 207, *m240*; Charlemagne and, 237, *m237*; medieval France and, *m254*; Crusades and, *m265*; in medieval trade, 271, *m272*; development of nation of, 285, *m285*; Catholicism in, *m310*; under Hapsburgs, 325–29, *m327, p328, m343*; Armada of, *p328,* 331, 376; War of Spanish Succession and, 346; in 1721, *m347*; exploration by, 362, 365–68, *m370–71*; colonies of, 368–75, *m378–79, m386, m387, m389,* 434; under Napoleon, 410, *m411*; slave trade of, 431; revolts of Latin American colonies of, 436–38, *m439*; Congress of Vienna and, 475, *m476,* 477; 1820 revolt in, 480; imperialism in Africa, 556, 557, *m559*; in Spanish-American War, 577, *p578,* 581–83, *p582,* 728; Civil War in, 662–64, *p663, p665, m666*; in World War II, *m671,* 675, 678; after World War II, *m703*

Spanish-American War, 577, *p578,* 581–83, *p582,* 728

Spanish Civil War, 662–64, *p663, p665, m666*

Spanish Morocco, 556, *m559*

Spanish Netherlands, 327, *m343,* 346, 354

Sparta, *m68,* 69; history and government of, 76–78, *m77, m97*; in Persian Wars, 92, *m93*; in Peloponnesian War, 95–96

Spencer, Herbert, 514

Spengler, Oswald, 636

spheres of influence, 554

Spice Islands (Moluccas), *m273,* 369, *m370, m378,* 380

spices, *p192,* 361

sports, 467, *p468, p794–95,* 797. *See also* Olympic Games.

Sputnik, 786

Sri Lanka (Ceylon), 704, *m724, m811. See also* Ceylon.

stadiums, 72, *p124*

Stakhanov, Aleksey, *p616*

Stalin, Joseph, 617–18, 667, 702, 705; Hitler-Stalin Pact, 668, *p669*; in World War II, 678, 681; at Yalta, 684, 693, 697; at Potsdam, 686, 698

Stalingrad, *m671,* 678, 680

Stamp Act, 387

Stanley, Henry, 558

Stanton, Elizabeth Cady, 495

Star Chamber, Court of, 334

Statute of Westminster, 642

steam engines, 103, *p449,* 450

steel: Bessemer process, *p449,* 450; Carnegie and, *p460*; in People's Republic of China, *p719. See also* iron.

Stein, Gertrude, *p634–35*

Stephenson, George, 455

Stevens, Wallace, 796

Stieglitz, Alfred, *p622*

stock market crash, 629

Stockholm, *m272–73, m810*

Stoics, 101

Stone Age, 5, *p7*

Storm Troopers, 627

Strategic Arm Limitation Talks (SALT), *p695,* 697

Stravinsky, Igor, 636

streptomycin, 790

strikes, 469–70; general, 621; in Poland, 705–07. *See also* labor unions.

Stuart, 332–34

stupa, 146, *p147*

stylus, 29

submarines: in World War I, 597–99, *m597, p600,* 604; in World War II, 670, 674, 675, 683

suburbs, 467

Sudan, *m217, m744,* 749, *m751, m814*; under Great Britain and Egypt, *m559,* 560; after World War II, 752; economy of, 759–61

Sudetenland, 665–67, *m666*

Suez Canal, 499, 556, *m559,* 593, *m597, m607,* 641, *m814*; in World War II, *m671,* 675, 681; after World War II, *m751,* 752; crisis over, 754; in Arab-Israeli wars, 735

Suez, Isthmus of, 18, *m18,* 20, *m20, m39*
suffrage. *See* voting.
suffragettes, 489
Sugar Act, 387
Suharto, General, 729
Sui dynasty, 165, *c173*
Sukarno, Achmed, 728, 729
Sulayman I, Ottoman sultan, 349
Sulla, Lucius Cornelius, 116
Sullivan, Louis, 637
Sully, Duke of, 329, 330, 344
Sumatra, *m370–71, m378,* 380, *m717,* 728, *m811;* Buddhism and Hinduism in, *m142;* under Dutch, *m570, m576, m661;* in World War II, *m681*
Sumer, *m27,* 28, *p28,* 39
Sumerian civilization, 28–31, *m27, p28, p34–35, c38*
Summa Theologica, 279
summit conferences, 705
Sun Yat-sen, 646, 647, *p649*
Sung dynasty, 167–73, *m167, c173*
Sunni Ali, 223
Sunnis, 203–04
supply and demand, law of, 480
surgery, 510, *p789*
Surinam, *m813*
surrealism, in painting, **633,** 636
Susa, 36, *m36*
Susruta, 148
suttee, 146, 564
Sutton, Walter S., 509
Swahili language, 220, 750
Swaziland, *m744, m814*
Sweden, *m350, m810;* in medieval trade, *m272–73;* about 1500, *m286;* Protestantism in, *m310;* in Thirty Years' War, 342, *m343;* in war with Russia, 351; in 1810, *m411;* Congress of Vienna and, *m476,* 477; in World War II, *m671;* post–World War II, *m703*
Switzerland, 285, *m810;* as Swiss Confederation, *m284, m286, m327;* Calvinism in, *m310;* after Peace of Westphalia, 342, *m343;* under Napoleon, *m411;* Congress of Vienna and, *m476,* 477; in World War II, *m671;* after World War II, *m699, m703*
Sydney, 491, *m491, p792*
Sydney Opera House, in Australia, 791, *p792*
Syracuse, *m68,* 96
Syria, *m39, m751, m811;* under Hittites, 32, *m32;* under Alexander, *m97,* 99; under Roman Empire, 118, *m120, m133;* Christianity in, *m129, m249;* in Muslim Empire, *m202,* 203, 204; in medieval trade, 269, *m272;* after World War I, *m607,* 608; in World War II, *m671,* 675; in United Arab Republic, 754; in wars with Israel, 755, 757; in Arab League, 759

Tacitus, 125
Tahiti, 576, *m576*

Taiping Rebellion, 571
Taiwan, 716, *m717,* 720, *m811. See also* Formosa.
Taj Mahal, *p210,* 212
Tale of Genji, 178
Talleyrand, Charles Maurice de, 475, 476
Tamerlane, 209–11, *p210, m211*
Tanganyika, 645
Tanganyika, Lake, *m271, m559, m814*
T'ang dynasty, *p138,* 165–69, *m166, p170, c173*
Tangier, *m202, m272,* 556, *m559, m814*
Tannenberg, battle at, *m597,* 598
Tanzania, *m744,* 749, *m814*
Taoism, 156, 166
tapestries, medieval, *p276*
Tarawa, *m681,* 683
tariffs: Zollverein and, 532; in German Empire, 537; in China, 570, 571; economic nationalism and, 621, 623; during Depression, 629–30; in Common Market, 711–12; import substitution and, 782
Tarik, 203
Tarquins, 107
Tasmania, 491, *m491*
taxes: in Roman Empire, 115, 121, 122, 131, 135; in China, 151, 152, 156, 169, 421; in Russia, 196, 351; in England, 256, 257, 283, 332, 334; on Roman Catholic Church, 287; in France, 329, 344, 346, 392–96; on British colonies in America, 386–87, *p390;* in Prussia, under Bismarck, 533
Taxila, 143, *m144,* 148
Tchaikovsky, Peter Ilyich, 520
tea, 427, *p428*
Technical Assistance Board (UN), 696
technology: of prehistoric peoples, *p7;* of early civilizations, 10–11; of ancient Egypt, 18; Sumerian, 29; of early China, 150–51; Renaissance, *p318;* exploration and, 361–62, *p363;* of Industrial Revolution, 455–59, 463, *p449, p457;* twentieth century, 786–90, *p789. See also* science.
Teheran, *m671, m751,* 758, *p760–61,* 761, *m811*
telegraph, 456, 523
telescopes, 319
television, 785, *p794–95*
Tell el Amarna, *m20,* 22
Ten Commandments, 40, 41
Ten Hours Act, 471
Tennessee Valley Authority (TVA), 630
Tenniel, John, *p522*
tennis, *p468*
Tennis-Court Oath, 395, *p400*
Tenochtitlán, *m225, p228,* 229, *m371,* 374
Teotihuacán, 225
Tetzel, Johann, 301, 304
Texas, 492, *m493*
textile industry, 448–50, *p449*
Thailand, *m717,* 735–36, *m811;* in World War II, 680, *m681;* and Vietnam War, 732; Cambodian refugees in, 733; in ASEAN, 738. *See also* Siam.

Thatcher, Margaret, 709
theater, 335; in ancient Greece, 88; in Roman Empire, 123; in Gupta India, 146; Japanese, *p179,* 180, *p423;* medieval, 278; of Shakespeare, 299, *p335;* after World War II, 793
Thebes, in Egypt, 20, *m20,* 22, *m32, m217*
Thebes, in Greece, *m77, m93,* 96
Themistocles, 86, 92
Theodora, Byzantine empress, *p188–89*
Theodosius, Roman emperor, 128, 132
Thermopylae, battle at, 92, *m93*
Third Coalition, against France, 407, 409
Third Estate, 284, 392, 395, *p400, c407*
Third French Republic, 500–01
Third International (Comintern), 618–19
Third Reich, 627–28, 664
Third World, 704, 790, 796
Thirty Years' War, 331, 342, *m343,* 354, 356
Thomson, J.J., 505, 506
Thonet Rocker, *p470*
Thrace, 92, *m93, m97, m607,* 643
Three Mile Island, nuclear reactor at, 769, *p770–71*
Thucydides, 87, 96
thuggee, 564
Tiahuanaco, 225
Tiber River, 108, *m108*
Tiberius, Roman emperor, 118, *c118*
Tibet, 52, *m53, m273, m417, m717, m724, m811;* Buddhism in, *m142*
Tigris-Euphrates Valley: early civilizations in, 10, *m10,* 11, 16; Sumerian civilization in, 27–30, *m27;* Babylonian civilization in, 30–31, *m31;* Hittite civilization in, 31–32, *m32;* Assyrians in, 32–33, *m32;* in Muslim Empire, *m202;* Tamerlane in, *m211*
Timbuktu, *m217,* 223, 557, *m559*
Tinian, *m681,* 683
Tiryns, 69, *m69*
tithes, 251
Titian, 300
Tito, Marshal, 684, 698, 702
Titoism, 705
Tlinglits, *p230*
Tobago (Trinidad and), *m813*
Tobruk, *m671,* 675
Togo, 557, *m559, m744, m814*
Tojo, Hideki, 679
Tokugawa shogunate, 422–27, *p423, p425,* 567, 568
Tokyo (Yedo), *m176, m570, m576, m661, m717, m811;* under Tokugawa, 422, 424; as imperial capital, 568; Imperial Hotel in 637; in World War II, *m681*
Toledo, *m202,* 207, *m272, m286*
Toleration, Act of, 338
Tolstoy, Leo, 520
Toltecs, *m225,* 227–29
tombs: pyramids as, 19, 24; of ancient Egyptians, *p21;* Etruscan, *p109;* of Han China, *p157;* Taj Mahal as, *p210,* 212; of Mound Builders, 231
Torah, 40

Tordesillas, Treaty of, 366, *m370–71*
Torgau, *m671*, 684
Toronto, *m490*, *m812*
totalitarianism, 78, 614
Toul, *m327*, *m343*
Toulouse-Lautrec, Henri de, 521
Tours, *m202*, 203, 236, *m237*
Toussaint L'Ouverture, 436
Tower of London, *p333*
towns. See cities.
Townshend, Charles, 448
trade: in early civilizations, 11–12; of ancient Egypt, 22–24; Sumerian, 29; Babylonian, 31; Phoenician, 38, 39; of early Indian civilization, 47; of ancient Greeks, 80; in Hellenistic period, 100; in Roman Empire, 115, 122, 135; in early China, 152–54, 167, 175; of Byzantine Empire, 185; of Vikings, 190, *m191*; of Kievan Russia, 192–94; of Muslim Empire, 204; of early African kingdoms, 220–23; in Middle Ages, 269–76, *p270*, *m272–73*, 361; of Dutch Netherlands, 327; of England under Cromwell, 336; of France, under Louis XIV, 344, 346; mercantilism and, 363–65; exploration and, 366; of Spanish Empire, 374–75; of English colonies, 376–78; of Dutch colonies, 379, 380; between Great Britain and American colonies, 385, 387; Confucian attitude towards, 416–17; of European nations with Asia, 426–29; of Ming and Ch'ing China, 418; of Tokugawa Japan, 424; between Europe and Africa, 429–33; of colonial Latin America, 434; imperialism and, 551–52, 567, 570, 579–80, *p582*; during World War I, 599; during Depression, 629; New Deal programs and, 630–32; in British Commonwealth, 642; in East Asia, 646, 651; of Common Market, 711–12; in East Asia after World War II, 722–23, 737; import substitution and, 782
Trade Agreements Act, 630–32
Trade Expansion Act, 712
Trades Disputes and Trade Unions Act, 621
Trafalgar, battle at, 409, *m411*
Trajan, Roman emperor, *c118*, 120, 127, 135
Transalpine Gaul, 108, *m113*, 117, *m117*
transistors, 787
Trans-Jordan, *m607*, 608, 641, *m671*, 675, 753, 759. See also Jordan.
transportation: in Roman Empire, 122; during Industrial Revolution, *p449*, 455; public, 467; Panama Canal for, 583; modern, *p715*
Trans-Siberian railroad, *m570*, 573
Transvaal, *m559*, 560, 562
treaty ports, 570, *m570*
Treblinka, 679
trench warfare, World War I, 597, 598, *p600–01*
Trent, Council of, *p308*, 309
tribunes, in Roman republic, 109, 110

Trieste, *m597*, 605, 607, *m607*, *m810*; after World War II, 698, *m699*, *m703*
Trinidad, *m439*, *m580*
Trinidad and Tobago, *m813*
Triple Alliance, 540, 592, 593, *m593*, 596
Triple Entente, 592–93, *m593*, 596
Tripoli, *m202*, 555, *m751*, *m814*; Crusades in, 265, *m265*, *m267*; in medieval trade, *m272–73*; under Italy, 557, *m559*
triumvirate, 116–17
Trojan War, 71
Trotsky, Leon, 617
troubadours, 278
Troy, 37, 69, *m69*, 71, 83, 88, 125; excavation of, 514
Truce of God, 245
Trudeau, Pierre Elliott, 773
Trujillo, Rafael, 655, 777
Truman, Harry S., 697, *c767*, *p770–71*; in World War II, 686; foreign policy of, 701–02, 766; in Korean War, 721
Truman Doctrine, 701–02, 754
Trust Territory of the Pacific Islands, 696
Trusteeship Council (UN), 694–96
Tshombe, Moise, 745
Tsingtao, *m570*, 575, 595, 605
Tsinling Range, 52, *m53*
Tu Fu, Chinese poet, 165
Tudors, 283, 331–32, *p333*
Tuileries, in Paris, *p177*, *p400*
Tula, *m225*, 227
Tull, Jethro, 448
Tunis, *m272*, 555, *m559*, *m671*, *m751*, *m814*
Tunisia, *m744*, *m751*, *m814*; French seizure of, 555, *m559*; in World War I, *m597*; in World War II, *m671*, 680; becomes independent, 753; education in, 762
Tupamaros, 777
Turin, *m528*, 529
Turkey, *m751*, 759, *m810*, *m811*; after World War I, *m607*, 608; under Kemal, 643; in World War II, 675; after World War II, 751–54; Truman Doctrine and, 702; in NATO, *m703*, 704; Common Market and, 711; higher education in, 762. See also Ottoman Empire.
Turkish language, 759
Turks, 165, *m166*, 200; Seljuk, *m172*, 187–90, *m191*, 264; Ottoman, 207–08, 211, 325, 349–50, 353, 354; Crusades against, 265–68, *m265*, *m267*. See also Ottoman Empire.
Turner, J.M.W., 520
Tuscany, 476, *m476*, 527, 528, *m528*, 529, *c529*
Tutankhamen, Egyptian pharaoh, *p21*, 22, *p25*, 26; treasures from tomb of, 796
Tutuila, 576, *m576*, 577
Twain, Mark, 520
Twelve Tables, 109, 110, 121
Tylor, E.B., 514
typewriters, 463
tyrants, 73, 76

Tyre, 37–38, *m39*, *m272*
Tyrol, *m597*, 605, 607, *m607*, 608

U-2 incident, 705
Uganda, 217, *m744*, *m814*; under Britain, 558, *m559*, 562
ultimatum, 595
Umar, 202
UN. See United Nations.
UNDP. See United Nations Development Programme.
UNICEF. See United Nations Children's Fund.
Union of South Africa, *m559*, 562. See also South Africa.
Union of Soviet Socialist Republics (U.S.S.R.), *m810*, *m811*; in 1923, *m607*; under Lenin, 615–17; under Stalin, 617–19; China and, 647, 718–20; admitted to League of Nations, 659; Spanish Civil War and, 662; Sudeten crisis and, 666–67; Hitler-Stalin Pact and, 668, *p669*; in World War II, 670, *m671*, 678–81, *m681*, 684–86; after World War II, 692, 698, 699, *m699*, 701; in UN, 693, 694; disarmament attempts and, *p695*, 697; post-World War II Germany and, 702–03; in Warsaw Pact, *m703*, 704; after Stalin, 705–07; and Czechoslovakia, 705, *p706*; Western European nations and, 708–11; in Comecon, 712; Vietnam and, 733; post-World War II Africa and, 749; post-World War II Middle East and, 751, 753–55, 758; post-World War II U.S. and, 766, 768, 772; Cuba and, 775; ballet in, 792; emigration from, 797–98. See also Russia; Russian Revolution.
unions. See labor unions.
United Arab Emirates, *m751*, 758, 759, 761, *m811*
United Arab Republic, 754
United Kingdom, *m810*; Act of Union of, 488; Northern Ireland in, 623. See also Great Britain.
United Nations (UN), 692, *p695*, 797; founding of and organization of, 693–97; Korean War and, 720–21; Kashmir crisis and, 725–27; Dutch East Indies and, 728; Thailand admitted to, 735; international development and, 738; Congo crisis and, 745; Namibia and, 746; creation of Israel and, 752; in Middle East, 754, 755; New York headquarters of, 791; South Africa expelled from, 798
United Nations Children's Fund (UNICEF), 696
United Nations Development Programme (UNDP), 696
United Provinces of Central America, 436–40, *m439*
United States, *m812*; Revolutionary War of, *p384*, 389, *p390*, *p397*; independence declared by, 388; in 1783, *m389*; early government of, 391; in War of

ACKNOWLEDGMENTS: Positions are shown in abbreviated form as follows; t-top, c-center, b-bottom, l-left, r-right.

Key: Bettmann-The Bettmann Archive; Culver-Culver Pictures, Inc; DPI-Design Photographers International; EPA-Editorial Photocolor Archives; FPG-Freelance Photographers Guild; Granger-The Granger Collection; PR-Photo Researchers; UPI-United Press International; WW-Wide World Photos.

Cover: EPA/Scala; Title page, EPA/Scala; v, From the collection of David H. H. Felix, Philadelphia; xvii, Robert Rattner.

Unit I: 2-3, Metropolitan Museum of Art; 4, Waugh/Peter Arnold; 7tl, Dr. E. R. Degginger, FPSA; tr, HBJ Photo; c, © George Holton/PR; b, Jean McMann/DPI; 9, Dia France; 13, Dr. E. R. Degginger, FPSA; 16, Robert Rattner; 19, © Luis Villota; 21tl, © Francis G. Mayer/PR; tr, EPA/Scala; c, EPA/Scala; b, EPA/Scala; 23tl, © George Holton/PR; cl, Courtesy, HBJ Library; cr, Robert Rattner; b, EPA/Scala; 25, Photo F. L. Kenett, © George Rainbird, Ltd; 28, John Freeman, Trustees of the British Museum; 34tr, Courtesy of the Trustees of the British Museum; bl, EPA; br, Hirmer Verlag München; 35tl, EPA; tr, Anne Heimann; b, EPA/Scala; 40, Granger; 44, Borromeo/EPA; 49t, © Paolo Koch/PR; bl, Borromeo/EPA; br, EPA/Scala; 50, EPA/Scala; 55, Cultural Relics Bureau, Beijing, Courtesy Metropolitan Museum of Art; 56tl, Hoyt Collection, Courtesy Museum of Fine Arts, Boston; tr, Courtesy of the Smithsonian Institution, Freer Gallery of Art, Washington, D.C.; b, © Belzeaux/Rapho-PR; 59l, Musée Guimet, Cliche des Musées Nationaux, Paris; r, Bettmann.

Unit II: 64-65, Courtesy, Rizzoli, Milano; 66, Eberhard E. Otto/Alpha; 70tl, Gerald Clyde/FPG; tr, EPA; b, EPA/Scala; 72t, G. A. Mowat/Taurus; c, © Tom McHugh/PR; b, McNee Photo Communication; 74tr, EPA/Scala; bl, Photo, Don Renner; br, EPA/Scala; 75tl, Eberhard E. Otto/FPG; br, EPA/Scala; 81tl, Antikenmuseum, Staatlicher Museum Preussischer Kulturbesitz, West Berlin; tr, cr; Courtesy, Museum of Fine Arts, Boston. Frances Bartlett Fund; bl, EPA/Scala; br, Courtesy of the Trustees of the British Museum; 84, EPA/Scala; 86t, Bettmann; b, The Metropolitan Museum of Art, Rogers Fund, 1906; 91, The Metropolitan Museum of Art, Gift of Alexander Smith Cochran, 1913; 94tl, EPA; tr, EPA/Scala; b, EPA/Scala; 98tl, © The Greek Ministry of Culture and Science; tr, Granger; bl, © The Greek Ministry of Culture and Science/Professor Manolis Andronikos; br, © Robert Emmett Bright/PR; 101, New York Public Library, Map Room; 102tr, © Niepce/Rapho-PR; bl, Fred J. Maroon/PR; br, EPA/Scala; 106, © Robert Emmett Bright/Rapho/PR; 109, Metropolitan Museum of Art, Purchase 1940, John Pulitzer Bequest; 111tl, EPA/Scala; tr, Courtesy, HBJ Library; bl, EPA/Scala; 114 all, EPA/Scala; 119tl, © Robert Emmett Bright/PR; bl, EPA/Scala; r, EPA; 123, Thomas Hollyman/PR; 124t, © Ned Haines/Rapho-PR; c, EPA; b, SEF/EPA; 130tr, SEF/EPA; cr, EPA/Scala; b, © Bernard G. Silberstein/Alpha; 138, The Metropolitan Museum of Art, Rogers Fund, 1919; 140, The Cleveland Museum of Art, Purchase from the J.H. Wade Fund; 145, Photo: Constantino Astuti, Il Museo Nazionale D'Arte Orientale, Roma; 147t, Granger; l, Eliot Elisofon; b, © Paolo Koch/PR; 149t, Courtesy, Harcourt Brace Jovanovich, Inc., for the illustration by Enrico Arno reproduced from *The Tiger's Whisker and Other Tales and Legends From Asia and The Pacific,* © 1959 by Harold Courlander; b, Illustration by Tony Sarg, *Pinocchio,* © 1940, 1967 by Platt & Munk, publishers; 153 both, © An Keren/Pacific Press Service-PR; 157t, Collection of William Rockhill Nelson Gallery of Art, Kansas City, Missouri; bl, Photo O.E. Nelson, Dr. P. Singer Collection; br, © Paolo Koch/PR.

Unit III: 162-163, EPA; 164, The Metropolitan Museum of Art, Fletcher Fund, 1940; 168tl, Granger; tr, Granger; b, © Belzeaux/Rapho-PR; 170, Granger; 174t, Granger; r, Granger; b, Bettmann; 177t, Mary E. Browning/DPI; b, © Dick Davis/PR; 179tl, © Bradley Smith/PR; tr, FPG; b, Sekai Bunka; 183, EPA/Scala; 186, Borromeo/EPA; 188tl, Granger; b, Granger; 188-189t, Granger; 189tr, Alpha; b, EPA/Scala; 192, © Luis Villota; 195tr, Granger; bl, © George Holton/PR; br, Granger; 196, EPA; 200, Walter S. Clark; 203, The Metropolitan Museum of Art, Bequest of Joseph V. McMullen, Photo by Otto Nelson; 205tl, Granger; tr, Metropolitan Museum of Art, Harris Brisbane Dick Fund, 1959; b, The New York Public Library, The Spencer Collection; 206, Bettman; 210tr, EPA/Scala; bl, Cooke/PR; br, Granger; 215, George Schwartz/Alpha; 218tr, Photoworld/FPG; bl, Metropolitan Museum of Art, The Michael C. Rockefeller Memorial Collection, Gift of Nelson A. Rockefeller, 1972; br, Dennis Hallinan/FPG; 221, DeAntonis, Rome, Trustees of The British Museum; 222tl, Granger; tr, Granger; bl, © Diane Rawson/PR; br, Granger; 226tl, Granger; tr, EPA; b, © George Holton/PR; 228tl, Museum of the American Indian, New York City; tr, © George Holton/PR; br, Granger; 230tl, Museum of the American Indian, New York City; tr, EPA; bl, © George Holton/PR; br, Courtesy of The American Museum of Natural History; 234, The Pierpont Morgan Library; 236, Giraudon; 238tl, Granger; tr, FPG; bl, Granger; cr, Bettmann; 242t, Bettmann; c, Granger; b, Granger; 247tl, Granger; tr, Granger; bl, Bettmann; 250, Bettmann; 256, Granger; 258tl, Kunsthistorisches Museum, Vienna; tr, EPA; cl, Granger; br, Granger; 263, Granger; 266t, Granger; c, Joel Braun; b, Bettmann; 270tl, Bettmann; tr, EPA/Scala; br, Granger; 275, Bettmann; 276, Josse/EPA; 280bl, Granger; r, Rothwell/FPG; 281tl, Bettmann; tr, Bettmann; b, HBJ Photo; 288tl, Granger; tr, Granger; 288-289b, Granger; 289tr, Bibliotheque Nationale.

Unit IV: 294-295, Metropolitan Museum of Art, Bequest of Mrs. Annie C. Kane; 296, Granger; 300, EPA/Scala; 302-303 all, EPA/Scala; 305, EPA/Scala; 308bl, Mansell Collection; br, Granger; 313t, EPA; b, HBJ Photo; 315tl, Courtesy, HBJ Library; tr, From the collection of Barone Gabriele Chiaramonte Bordonaro, transparency from GREAT AGES OF MAN–*The Reformation,* photograph by David Lees © 1966 Time Inc., Time-Life Books, publisher; b, EPA/Scala; 318tl, EPA; tr, Granger; bl, Bettmann; br, New York Public Library; 320, EPA/Scala; 324, Granger; 328tl, Granger; tr, EPA; b, Mariners Museum, Newport News; 330, Metropolitan Museum of Art; 333tl, Bettmann; tr, Photoworld/FPG; b, Bettmann; 335t, G. Tomsich/PR; b, Bettmann; 339tl, Bettmann; tr, Bettmann; b, Granger; 345tl, Granger; tr, Brown Brothers; b, Granger; 352, Dr. Barbara Wolfson; bl, Granger; br, Granger; 355l, Bettmann; r, Brown Brothers; 360, Louvre, Paris; 363, David H. H. Felix, Philadelphia; 364tl, EPA; b, EPA/Scala; 367tl, Bettmann; tr, Mansell Collection; bl, Courtesy, HBJ Library; 369, Granger; 373t, Sekai Bunka; r, Granger; 377tl, Foto Biblioteca Vaticana; bl, Biblioteca Epostolica Vaticana; br, The Huntington Library; 380, Metropolitan Museum of Art, Gift of Henry G. Marquand, 1889; 384, National Geographic Photographer George F. Mobley, Courtesy U.S. Capitol Historical Society; 388, Gift of Joseph W., William B. and Edward H. R. Revere, Courtesy Museum of Fine Arts, Boston; 390, Courtesy, HBJ Library; 390tr, Bettmann; cr, Library of Congress; b, New York State Historical Association, Cooperstown; 394t, Bettmann; cl, EPA; br, EPA/Scala; 397tl, R.J. Segalat, Biblioteque Nationale; tr, John H. Anderson/DPI; cr, Leonard Wolfe/PR; br, Mimi Forsyth/Monkmeyer; 398, SEF/EPA; 400t, Bettmann; c, Granger; b, Granger; 403, Musée Royaux des Beaux Arts, Brussels; 404tl, Photoworld/FPG; tr, Bettmann; b, Bettmann; 408t, Bettmann; bl,

EPA/Scala; br, Mansell Collection; 415, R. Peter Henschel/FPG; 420t, Metropolitan Museum of Art, Gift of the Dillon Fund, 1973; bl, Metropolitan Museum of Art, Anonymous Gift, 1942; br, Bettmann; 423tl, Sekai Bunka; tr, Sekai Bunka; br, Metropolitan Museum of Art, Purchase, Gift of Mrs. Russell Sage, by exchange, 1980; 425, © Sotheby Parke-Bernet/EPA; 428tl, Granger; tr, Metropolitan Museum of Art, Purchase, The Lucille and Robert H. Gries Charity Fund, 1970; bl, SEF/EPA; br, Brown Brothers; 430, Marc and Evelyne Bernheim/Woodfin Camp and Associates; 432tl, Granger; tr, New York Public Library, Picture Collection; b, Granger; 437tl, Bettmann; tr, EPA; b, Granger.

Unit V: 444-445, Culver; 446, Bettmann; 449t, Joseph Martin, EPA/Scala; bl, Bettmann; br, Bettmann; 453tl, Brown Brothers; tr, Barfoot, *The Progress of Cotton: #6, Spinning*, Yale University Art Gallery, Mabel Brady Garvan Collection; b, Sheffield City Museum; 457tl, Bettmann; c, Granger; bl, Bettmann; br, Culver; 460tl, Bettmann; tr, Bettmann; bl, Bettmann; br, Brown Brothers; 462, EPA/Scala; 466tl, Bettmann; tr, Photoworld/FPG; bl, Information Center, Consulate General of Japan; 468t, Bettmann; b, Courtesy of the Trustees of The British Museum; br, Brown Brothers; 470, Gebruder Thonet, *Rocking Chair*, 1860. Collection, Museum of Modern Art, New York, Gift of Cafe Nicholson; 474, The Brooklyn Museum; 479 both, Bettmann; 482t, Bettmann; c, Library of Congress; b, The Phillips Collection, Washington, D.C.; 487tl, Bettmann; tr, Bettmann; b, Granger; 488, Illustration from *Morte D'Arthur*, 1909 edition, Courtesy Sobel Collection; 494tl, Library of Congress; tr, Bettmann; bl, Bettmann; 497, Louvre, Paris; 499t, EPA/Scala; b, Bettmann; 500, Granger; 504, Metropolitan Museum of Art, Bequest of Mrs. H. O. Havemeyer, 1929, The H. O. Havemeyer Collection; 507tl, Brown Brothers; tr, Brown Brothers; b, Bettmann; 511, Bettmann; 512tl, Bettmann; tr, Bettmann; br, Gernsheim Collection, Humanities Research Center, University of Texas at Austin; 515t, Bettmann; b, Culver; 516, Munch-Museet, Oslo; 518tl, Culver; bl, EPA/Scala; br, Metropolitan Museum of Art, Bequest of Benjamin Altman, 1913; 519tl, EPA/Scala; tr, EPA/Scala; b, EPA/Scala; 522, Courtesy, HBJ Library; 526, SEF/EPA; 530 all, Bettmann; 533, Staatliche Kunstsammlunger Dresden-Germaldegalerie Neue Meister; 538tr, Bettmann; c, Bettmann; b, Historical Picture Service, Chicago; 541, Walters Art Gallery, Photo: Forbes Collection; 543 all, Brown Brothers; 550, Information Center, Consulate General of Japan; 553tl, Methodist Missions; tr, Courtesy, HBJ Library; b, Brown Brothers; 556, Eliot Elisofon; 561 all, Bettmann; 565t, National Army Museum, London; c, Brown Brothers; b, Culver; 568, Courtesy of Smithsonian Institution, Freer Gallery of Art, Washington, D.C.; 572t, Metropolitan Museum of Art, Winfield Foundation Gift, 1958, The Helena Woolworth McCann Collection; c, Courtesy, HBJ Library; b, Library of Congress; 575, Jim Beck/PR; 578tr, Culver; c, Brown Brothers; b, Bettmann; 582t, Bettmann; bl, Brown Brothers; br, Brown Brothers.

Unit VI: 588-589, WW; 590, Bettmann; 594tl, Radio Times Hulton Picture Library; tr, WW; b, U.S. Signal Corps; 600tl, Culver; tr, Photoworld/FPG; b, Granger; 601tl, Granger; tr, Imperial War Museum; b, U.S. Signal Corps; 603, National Archives; 605, Marcel Duchamps, *To be Looked At (From the Other Side of the Glass) with One Eye, Close to, for Almost an Hour*, 1918, Collection, Museum of Modern Art, New York, Katherine S. Dreier Bequest; 609tl, Library of Congress; tr, Imperial War Museum; b, Courtesy, HBJ Library; 613, Library of Congress; 616tl, Bettmann; tr, Granger; b, WW; 620, Philadelphia Museum of Art, The A. E. Gallatin Collection; 622tl, Philadelphia Museum of Art Collection; bl, Granger; r, Rhoda Galyn; 626t, WW; bl, WW; br, Cornell Capa/Magnum; 63lt, FSA Photo; bl, Photoworld/FPG; br, Department of the Interior; 633, Film Library, Museum of Modern Art, New York; 634t, Bettmann; b, Metropolitan Museum of Art, Bequest of Gertrude Stein, 1946; 635l, EPA; tr, © 1937 Time Inc; br, EPA; 640, Barbara Horan; 644tr, Brown Brothers; bl, WW; br, WW; 647, Courtesy Museum of Fine Arts, Boston, Gift of Madame Fan Tchum-pi; 649tl, Bettmann; tr, Bettmann; b, Culver; 652 all, Photoworld/FPG; 654, Dr. E. R. Degginger, FPSA; 659, U.S. Army; 663tl, Courtesy, HBJ Library; bl, UPI; br, WW; 665, © SPADEM, Paris/VAGA, New York 1982; 669tr, FDR Library; bl, Photoworld/FPG; br, WW; 673tl, Photoworld/FPG; tr, U.S. Signal Corps; b, Imperial War Museum; 676t, WW; bl, FDR Library; 677tl, Photoworld/FPG; tr, Culver; b, UPI; 682tr, U.S. Army; c, U.S. Navy; bl, U.S. Army; br, U.S. Navy; 685tl, Library of Congress; b, Courtesy, HBJ Library.

Unit VII: 690-691, Rothwell/Alpha; 692, UPI; 695t, WW; c, WW; b, UPI; 700, E. Streichan/Shostal Associates; 706 all, WW; 709tr, WW; bl, © Farrell Grehan/PR; br, D. Berretty/PR; 715, © Dr. Georg Gerster/PR; 719tl, © George Holton/PR; tr, © Jerry Cooke/PR; bl, © George Holton/PR; br, © George Holton/PR; 723, © George Holton/PR; 726tr, Namajh/Taurus; cl, UPI; cr, © Paolo Koch/PR; br, UPI; 731, CBS Photo; 734tr, FPG; bl, WW; br, Alpha; 737, Cooper Hewitt Museum; 741, HBJ Photo; 748t, WW; cr, Pamela Johnson Meyer/PR; b, HBJ Photo; 753, EPA; 756tl, United Nations; tr, UPI; bl, WW; br, UPI; 760tl, Larousse/PR; tr, UPI; b, © Thomas Hopker/Woodfin Camp and Associates; 76lt, G. R. Richardson/Taurus; b, © Gerry Cranham/Rapho-PR; 765, William R. Wright/Taurus; 768, Metropolitan Museum of Art, The Alfred Stieglitz Collection, 1949; 770tl, © Katrina Thomas/PR; tr, UPI; b, WW; 771tr, © Bruce Roberts/PR; cr, UPI; b, WW; 776ty, WW; tr, UPI; b, UPI; 781tl, UPI; c, UNESCO; b, © Serraillier/Rapho-PR; 785, UPI; 787, U.S. Postal Service; 789tr, © Laimute E. Druskis/Taurus; c, © George Holton/PR; bl, © Farrell Grehan/PR; br, © Joe Munroe/PR; 792, © A. B. Joyce/PR; 794tl, Martha Swope; tr, © Robert Clark/PR; b, UPI; 795t, Metropolitan Museum of Art, George A. Hearn Fund, 1957; cr, Henri Matisse, *The Burial of Pierrot*, 1947, Museum of Modern Art, New York; br, Focus on Sports.

A 6
B 7
C 8
D 9
E 0
F 1
G 2
H 3
I 4
J 5